sendmail

sendmail

Second Edition

Bryan Costales
with Eric Allman

O'REILLY

Cambridge • Köln • Paris • Sebastopol • Tokyo

sendmail, Second Edition
by Bryan Costales with Eric Allman

Editor: Tim O'Reilly

Update Editor: Gigi Estabrook

Production Editor: John Files

Printing History:

November 1993:	First Edition.
February 1994:	Minor corrections.
September 1994:	Minor corrections.
January 1997:	Second Edition.
November 1997:	Minor corrections.

ISBN: 1-56592-222-0   [4/98]

Table of Contents

Preface

The primary reason for this book, the second edition of *sendmail*, is the release of version 8.8 of the *sendmail* program. V8.8 *sendmail* differs so significantly from earlier versions that a complete rewrite was called for.

Also, since the publication of the first edition, feedback from around the world made it clear that a number of improvements could be made. Some readers felt, for example, that the original offered too little in the way of real-world help, and that it lacked an annotated, major configuration file. Other readers offered suggestions of ways to make the book clearer. Some of these were minor but others, like the treatment of options, required extensive rewriting. One of the most noticeable changes between this edition and the original is the addition of section numbers and their attendant cross referencing.

Preface

King Gordias of Phrygia once created a knot so tangled that no one could undo it. The Gordian Knot stayed just that, or so the story says, until Alexander the Great came along and took a different approach to untying knots. It would be nice if the knot that is *sendmail* could be undone with one quick stroke of fresh insight, but, alas, it cannot. Instead, a more mundane approach must be taken, so in this book we untie it the hard way, one strand at a time.

But, you may ask, "Why the effort? Doesn't *sendmail* predate the dawn of computing time? Isn't it time to replace it with something new, something better, something modern?" Not so. Age has brought *sendmail* maturity and reliability. The *sendmail* program has withstood the test of time because it is more than just a program, it is a philosophy: a general-purpose, internetwork mail-routing facility with the flexibility and configurability to solve the mail-routing needs of all sites large or small, complex or simple.

These strengths of *sendmail* are also its weaknesses. Configurability has bred complexity. The *sendmail* program is difficult to configure and even more difficult to understand. Its configuration file, for example, can be positively frightening. But don't despair. With this book in hand, you should be able to configure *sendmail* to meet any need and bring the days of the *sendmail* guru to an end.

History

The *sendmail* program was originally written by Eric Allman while he was a student and staff member at the University of California at Berkeley. At the time, one campus machine (*Ingres*) was connected to the ARPAnet, and was home to the INGRES project where Eric was working. Another machine (*Ernie CoVax*) was home to the Berkeley UNIX project and had recently started using UUCP. These machines (as well as several others on campus) were connected by a low-cost network built by Eric Schmidt, called BerkNet. Software existed to move mail within ARPAnet, within UUCP, and within BerkNet, but none yet existed to move mail between these three networks.

A sudden increase in protocol types, coupled with the anticipation of an explosion in the number of networks, motivated Eric to write *delivermail*—the precursor to *sendmail*. The *delivermail* program was shipped in 1979 with 4.0 and 4.1 BSD UNIX. Unfortunately, *delivermail* was not flexible enough to handle the changes in mail routing requirements that actually occurred. Perhaps its greatest weakness was that its configuration was compiled-in.

In 1980, ARPAnet began converting from NCP (Network Control Protocol) to TCP (Transmission Control Protocol). This change increased the number of possible hosts from 256 to over one billion. Another change converted from a "flat" host-name space (like MIT-XX) into a hierarchical name space (like XX.MIT.EDU). Prior to these changes, mail was transported using the *ftp* protocol (File Transfer Protocol). Afterward, a new protocol was developed for transporting mail called SMTP (Simple Mail Transfer Protocol). These developments were not instantaneous. Some networks continued to run NCP years after most others switched to TCP. SMTP itself underwent many revisions before finally settling into its present form.

Responding to these and other changes, Eric evolved *delivermail* into *sendmail*. To ensure that messages transferred between networks would obey the conventions required by those networks, Eric took a "liberal" approach—modifying address information to conform, rather than rejecting it. At the time, for example, UUCP mail often had no headers at all, so *sendmail* had to create them from scratch.

The first *sendmail* program was shipped with 4.1c BSD (the first version of Berkeley UNIX to include TCP/IP). From that first release to the present,[*] Eric has continued to enhance *sendmail*, first at UC Berkeley, then at Britton Lee, then back at UC Berkeley, and now with InReference Inc. The current version of *sendmail* is 8.x (or V8 for short). V8 is a major rewrite that includes many bug fixes and significant enhancements.

But Eric wasn't the only one working on *sendmail*. In 1987, Lennart Lovstrand of the University of Linköping, Sweden, developed the IDA enhancements to BSD *sendmail* Version 5. IDA (which stands for "Institutionen för Datavetenskap") injected a number of improvements into *sendmail* (such as support for *dbm* files and separate rewriting of headers and envelopes) and fixed a number of bugs. As the '90s approached, two offspring of IDA appeared.

Neil Rickert (Northern Illinois University) and Paul Pomes (The University of Illinois) took over maintenance of IDA *sendmail*. With contributions from around the world, their version (UIUC IDA) represents a continuation of the work begun by Lennart Lovstrand. Neil focused on fixing and enhancing the configuration files into their current *m4*-based form. Paul maintained the code, continually adding enhancements and fixing bugs. In general, their version was large, ambitious, and highly portable. It succeeded in solving many complex mail routing problems.

A variation on IDA *sendmail* was also developed by Paul Vixie (while at Digital Equipment Corporation). Called KJS (for King James *sendmail*), it was a more conservative outgrowth of Lennart Lovstrand's last IDA release. The focus of KJS was on code improvement rather than changes to configuration files.

In addition to these major offshoots, many vendors have modified *sendmail* to suit their particular needs. Sun Microsystems made many modifications and enhancements to *sendmail*, including support for *nis* and *nisplus* maps. Hewlett Packard also contributed many fine enhancements including 8BITMIME support.

This explosion of *sendmail* versions has led to a great deal of confusion. Solutions to problems that work for one version of *sendmail* fail miserably with others. Beyond this, configuration files are not portable, and some features cannot be shared.

In 1994, Eric began work on V8.7 *sendmail*. The first major departure from tradition in years, V8.7 introduces multicharacter option and macro names, new interactive commands to use with –bt mode, and fixes many of the problems and limitations of earlier releases. But, more important, V8.7 has officially adopted most of the good features from IDA, KJS, Sun, and HP's *sendmail*, and kept abreast of the latest standards from the Internet Engineering Task Force. In 1996, Eric

---

[*] With one long gap between 1982 and 1990.

began work on V8.8 *sendmail*. This release continued the trend begun with V8.7, adding many requested new features and options, and tightening security. Since V8.8 is now the official release of *sendmail*, it is the one solely documented in this book.

Eric Allman Speaks

I have to admit that I'm surprised by how well *sendmail* has succeeded. It's not because of a large marketing organization or a deep-pockets budget. I think there are three reasons.

First, *sendmail* took the approach that it should try to accept, clean up, and deliver even very "crufty" messages instead of rejecting them because they didn't meet some protocol. I felt this was important because I was trying to gateway UUCP to the ARPAnet. At the time, the ARPAnet was small, UUCP was anarchy (some say it still is), and UNIX mail programs generally didn't even understand headers. It was harder to do, but after all, the goal was to communicate, not to be pedantic.

Second, I limited myself to the routing function—I wouldn't write user agents or delivery back-ends. This was a departure from the dominant thought of the time, where routing logic, local delivery, and often the network code was incorporated directly into the user agents. But it did let people incorporate their new networks quickly.

Third, the *sendmail* configuration file was flexible enough to adapt to a rapidly changing world: The 1980s saw the proliferation of new protocols, networks, and user agents.

And, of course, it didn't hurt that it was free, available at the right time, and did what needed to be done.

Configuring *sendmail* is complex because the world is complex. It is dynamic because the world is dynamic. Someday *sendmail*, like X11, will die—but I'm not holding my breath. In the meantime, perhaps this book will help.

When I started reviewing Bryan's manuscript, I had been avoiding any major work on *sendmail*. But then I started reading about various petty bugs and annoyances that all seemed easy to fix. So I started making small fixes, then larger ones; then I went through RFC1123 to bring the specs up-to-date, cleaned up a bunch of eight-bit problems, and added ESMTP. It would be fair to say that the book and *sendmail* Version 8 fed on each other—each has improved the presence of the other.

The Future

The explosive growth of the Internet, coupled with the universal acceptance of email as a desirable form of communication, guarantee that *sendmail* will continue to evolve and improve for years to come. Well before the release of V8.8, Eric was already thinking about V8.9. To glimpse some of what is in store, look at the file KNOWNBUGS distributed with the source. Note that some of the problems listed are thorny in the extreme and difficult to solve.

Also, percolating constantly in the back of Eric's brain is something he calls "Son of Sendmail" (or *sos*), a complete rewrite of *sendmail* from the ground up targeted for the far future. Those of you who have followed the evolution of the source may have noticed that functions are constantly being redesigned to make a future, massive rewrite easier and more modular.

Organization

We've divided this book into four parts, each addressing a particular aspect of *sendmail* as a whole.

Part I — A Tutorial

Part One is a tutorial than can serve as either a hands-on, step-by-step introduction to *sendmail* for the beginner or a succinct review for the more experienced user. Chapters 1 through 4 form an overview of email in general, and discuss the roles, behavior, and parts of *sendmail*. Chapters 5 through 15 examine the configuration file in detail. In them, we develop a mini-configuration file, suitable for use on some client workstations. Chapters 16 and 17 conclude the tutorial, tying up loose ends and transitioning into more complex configuration files.

Part II — Installation

Part Two covers compilation and installation of *sendmail*. Chapter 18 shows how to compile and install *sendmail* from the source. Chapter 19 shows how to create a configuration file with the *m4*(1) configuration technique. Chapter 20 concludes by illustrating the *checkcompat()* routine.

Part III — Administration

Part Three covers general administration of *sendmail* for more experienced users. Chapter 21 covers DNS in general and MX records specifically. Chapter 22 shows how to protect your site from intrusion. Chapters 23 through 26 round out the picture with details about the queue, aliases, mailing lists, logging, and statistics.

Part IV — Reference

Part Four is the nitty-gritty—a reference section that provides more detail about *sendmail* than you may ever need. Each chapter is dedicated to a specific aspect of *sendmail* or its configuration file. Chapter 31, for example, details defined macros, and includes an alphabetized reference. Chapter 37 shows all the debugging switches.

Audience and Assumptions

This book is primarily intended for system administrators who have been granted the dubious honor of administering email. But not all UNIX systems are managed by administrators. Many are managed by programmers, network engineers, and even by inexperienced users. It is our hope that this book satisfies all of you, no matter what your level of experience.

The true beginner should begin with Part 1, skipping ahead as needed.

The beginning system administrator should probably start with the tutorial in Part 1, then read Part 3 for help in understanding how to administer *sendmail*. Note that Parts 2 and 4 will reveal answers to many nagging questions that seem to be otherwise unanswered.

The experienced system administrator who wants to install and manage V8 *sendmail* should read Parts 2 and 3 first to gain the needed background. Then read Part 4.

UNIX gurus and *sendmail* specialists should find Part 4 to be of value (even Eric keeps a copy on his desk). In it, every arcane detail of *sendmail* is listed alphabetically. There is, for example, a single chapter dedicated to options, with every option listed and explained.

No matter what your level of expertise, the sheer size of this book forces us to assume that you are familiar with the day-to-day system workings of UNIX. If not, you must learn UNIX elsewhere.

UNIX and sendmail Versions

For the most part, we illustrate *sendmail* under BSD UNIX and its variants (such as SunOS 4.x). Where AT&T System V (SysV) differs (such as Sun's Solaris 2.x), we illustrate those differences.

Our primary focus throughout this book is on version 8.8 *sendmail*. For completeness, and where necessary, we also discuss V8.7 and earlier (such as BSD's version 5,[*] IDA, early Sun, Ultrix, and NeXT).

Conventions Used in This Handbook

The following typographic conventions are used in this book:

Italic
is used for names, including pathnames, filenames, program and command names, usernames, hostnames, machine names, and mailing-list names, as well as for mail addresses. It is also used to emphasize new terms and concepts when they are introduced.

`Constant Width`
is used in examples to show the contents of files or the output from commands. This includes examples from the configuration file or other files such as message files, shell scripts, or C language program source. Constant-width text is quoted only when necessary to show enclosed space; for example, the five-character "`From `" header.

Single characters, symbolic expressions, and command-line switches are always shown in constant-width font. For instance, the `o` option illustrates a single character, the rule `$-` illustrates a symbolic expression, and `-d` illustrates a command-line switch.

`Constant Bold`
is used in examples to show commands or some other text that is to be typed literally by the user. For example, the phrase **`cat/etc/sendmail.pid`** means the user should type "cat/etc/sendmail.pid" exactly as it appears in the text or example.

`Constant Italic`
is used in examples to show variables for which a context-specific substitution should be or will be made. In the string `$num`, for example, *num* will be a user-assigned integer. In the output `error: num`, for example, *num* will be a variable value printed by a program (usually *sendmail*).

---

[*] The versions jump from 5 to 8 because the managers of the BSD 4.4 UNIX distribution wanted all software to be released as version 8. Prior to that decision, the new BSD *sendmail* was designated Version 6. V6 survived only the alpha and beta releases before being bumped to V8.

%   indicates a user shell.

indicates a *root* shell.

Additional Sources of Information

The source for the *sendmail* program comes with two documents by Eric Allman that are required reading. *Sendmail—An Internetwork Mail Router* provides an overview of *sendmail*, including its underlying theory. *Sendmail Installation and Operations Guide* provides installation instructions and a succinct description of the configuration file. Many vendors also provide online manuals which may reveal vendor-specific customizations not documented in this book. Also, if you have the source, see the files *RELEASE_NOTES*, *src/READ_ME*, and *cf/README*.

The RFCs

A complete understanding of *sendmail* is not possible without at least some exposure to Request for Comments (RFC) issued by the Internet Engineering Task Force (IETF) at the Network Information Center (NIC). These numbered documents define (among other things) the protocols and operational requirements of the Internet. RFCs are available via anonymous FTP. See the Bibliography for information about how to retrieve individual RFCs.

RFC821

> When *sendmail* transports mail from one machine to another over a TCP/IP network, it does so using a protocol called the *Simple Mail Transfer Protocol*, or SMTP for short. SMTP is documented in RFC821.

RFC822

> The division of mail messages into a header and a body, as well as the syntax and order of header lines are all defined in RFC822, titled *Standard for the Format of ARPA Internet Text Messages*. It also describes the syntax of addresses.

RFC819

> RFC819 is entitled *Domain Naming Convention for Internet User Applications* and describes the hierarchical form of host naming used today. This document defines the form a hostname must take.

RFC976

> RFC976 is entitled *UUCP Mail Interchange Format Standard* and describes the format of mail messages transported between machines using UUCP.

RFC1123

> RFC1123 is an extension to RFC821 and RFC822. It makes several amendments to the original documents and cleans up some previously ambiguous information.

RFC1521 and RFC1522

> RFC1521 introduces and describes the standards for Multipurpose Internet Mail Extensions (MIME). MIME provides ways to embed non-text data (such as images, sounds, and movies) inside ordinary email messages.

RFC1651, RFC1652, and RFC1653

> RFC1651 describes a general extension mechanism for SMTP, called ESMTP. RFC1652 describes an extension for transport of 8-bit data, called the 8BIT-MIME extension. RFC1653 describes an extension for message size declaration (see §34.8.22).

RFC1891, RFC1892, RFC1893, and RFC1894

> RFC1891, *SMTP Service Extension for Delivery Status Notifications* (DSN), describes the ESMTP RCPT command's NOTIFY, RET, and ORCPT extensions. It also describes the ESMTP MAIL command's ENVID extension. RFC1892, *The Multipart/Report Content Type for the Reporting of Mail System Administrative Messages*, describes the `Content-Type:` header requirements for DSN. It also describes the order and requirements for *multipart/report* MIME parts of a mail status report's mail message. RFC1893, *Enhanced Mail System Status Codes*, describes the meaning of the DSN status number fields. RFC1894, *An Extensible Message Format for Delivery Status Notifications*, describes the machine readable part's header-style keywords, for the machine readable part of the DSN return message described in RFC1892.

Other Books, Other Problems

Two topics that are only touched upon in this book are The Domain Name System (DNS) and TCP/IP network communications. At a typical site, a significant number of problems with mail turn out to be problems with one of these other areas, rather than with *sendmail*.

The Domain Name System is well documented in the book *DNS and BIND, Second Edition* by Paul Albitz and Cricket Liu (O'Reilly & Associates, Inc., 1997).

The protocols used to communicate over the Internet are well documented in the book *TCP/IP Network Administration* by Craig Hunt (O'Reilly & Associates, Inc., 1992).

Finally, many mail problems can only be solved by the system administrator. The *sendmail* program runs as *root* and can only be installed and managed by *root*.

The art of functioning effectively as *root* is superbly covered in the *UNIX System Administration Handbook* by Evi Nemeth, Garth Snyder, Scott Seebass, and Trent R. Hein (Prentice Hall, 2nd edition 1995).

Acknowledgments

First and foremost, I must thank George Jansen, who literally spent months turning my first horrendous, stream of consciousness prose into a form suitable for publication. He is truly the unsung hero of this work, and an editor extraordinaire.

Jon Forrest and Evi Nemeth both beat the tutorial chapters to death. Their feedback was extremely valuable in helping to trim and focus those chapters into a more useful form. Never let it be said that too many cooks spoil the broth—in this case they helped flavor it toward perfection.

Cricket Liu kindly reviewd the DNS chapter, where he found a few errors that somehow slipped by all the others. Bruce Mah and Sean Brennan were guinea pigs for the first and second editions respectively. They set up and ran *sendmail* based on early drafts and thereby uncovered omissions and mistakes that required correction. Gavin Cameron bravely applied the *checkcompat()* examples to real-world situations, thereby helping to debug that code for me. And John Funk kindly allowed alpha versions of *sendmail* to run in production mode at Mercury Mail.

Needless to say, this book would not have been possible at all if Eric Allman had not written *sendmail* in the first place. Every draft has passed through his hands, and he has spent many hours ensuring technical correctness, providing valuable insight, and suggesting interesting solutions to *sendmail* problems.

Neil Rickert, too, saw every draft of the 1st edition. But, alas, circumstances beyond his control forced him to bow out from the 2nd edition.

For this 2nd edition, Cricket Liu kindly reviewed Chapter 21, *DNS and sendmail*, and found several errors that slipped by everyone else.

Thanks and praise must go to Tim O'Reilly for agreeing to do this book in the first place. His experience has shaped this book into the form it has today. He was aware of the "big picture" throughout and kept his fingers on the pulse of the reader. Without his advice, a book this complex and massive would have been impossible.

Additional thanks must go to Lenny Muellner for tuning *troff* macros to satisfy the needs of this somewhat unique manuscript, and to Edie Freedman for gracefully accepting my unhappiness with so many cover designs except the current one, which I consider perfect.

The production folks at O'Reilly & Associates did a yeoman's job of achieving an outstanding finished book. So a special thank you to John Files for managing the project, Barbara Willette for copy editing, Nancy Kotary for help with final production, Kismet McDonough-Chan for her help in each phase of the production, Chris Reilley for the figures, Mary Anne Weeks Mayo for helping with quality control, Curt Degenhart, Madeleine Newell, and Ellie Fountain Maden for making the edits, Seth Maislin for doing the index, and Danny Marcus for proofreading.

Finally, thanks to a list of folks, each of whom helped in small but notable ways: Keith Johnson; Paul Pomes; Frederick Avolio; John Halleck; John Beck; Brad Knowles; Andrew Chang; Shau-Ping Lo; Nelson Morgan; Julene and Jake Bair; William Carter; all the folks at the International Computer Science Institute; John Funk, Dan Casson, and others at Mercury Mail; to many of those who sent interesting questions to the *sendmail-questions@sendmail.org* mailing list; and to all the postings to the *comp.mail.sendmail* news group.

I

A Tutorial

The first part of this book is a tutorial intended mainly for those with a limited understanding of *sendmail*. Its aim is to provide the novice with a general introduction to V8 *sendmail*.

Chapter 1, Introduction
Covers mail transfer agents and mail user agents, explains why *sendmail* is so complex, gives an overview of *sendmail*, and describes the differences between the header, body, and envelope of a mail message.

Chapter 2, Have a V8
Shows where and how to get the source for V8 *sendmail* and how to compile and test a working binary.

Chapter 3, The Roles of sendmail
Shows how *sendmail* processes aliases, queues messages for later transmission, does local and remote delivery, and runs in the background listening for incoming mail.

Chapter 4, How to Run sendmail
Illustrates use of the −b (become), −v (verbose), and −d (debugging) command-line switches.

Chapter 5, The sendmail.cf File
Provides a quick overview of all the commands found in the *sendmail.cf* file.

Chapter 6, The Mail Hub and Delivery Agents
Describes the hub approach and shows how M (delivery agent) commands can be used to forward mail to a central hub machine.

Chapter 7, Macros
Shows how text can be automatically propagated throughout the configuration file.

Chapter 8, Addresses and Rules
Describes a fictional network, then uses addresses in that network to illustrate rules and rule sets.

Chapter 9, Rule Set 0
Shows how rules in rule set 0 can select delivery agents and handle errors.

Chapter 10, Rule Set 3
Explains rule set 3, the first to rewrite all addresses.

Chapter 11, Rule Sets 1 and S=
Develops an S= rule set to make all mail appear as though it comes from the hub machine.

Chapter 12, Class
Shows how multiple values can be referenced with a single expression in the LHS of rules.

Chapter 13, Setting Options
Explains how options "tune" *sendmail* and offers a few suggestions.

Chapter 14, Headers, Precedence, and Trust
Completes the *client.cf* file by adding H, P, and T commands.

Chapter 15, Install and Test the client.cf File
Shows how to install the *client.cf* file as your working configuration file.

Chapter 16, The null.mc File and m4
Shows how *m4* can be used to produce a *client.cf* file called *nullclient*.

Chapter 17, The Hub's Complex Rules
Concludes with a tour of a hub's major *sendmail.cf* file.

1

Introduction

Imagine yourself with pen and paper, writing a letter to a friend far away. You finish the letter and sign it, reflect on what you've written, then tuck the letter into an envelope. You put your friend's address on the front, your return address in the left-hand corner, and a stamp in the right-hand corner, and the letter is ready for mailing. Electronic mail (email for short) is prepared in much the same way, but a computer is used instead of pen and paper.

The post office transports real letters in real envelopes, whereas *sendmail* transports electronic letters in electronic envelopes. If your friend (the recipient) is in the same neighborhood (on the same machine), only a single post office (*sendmail* running locally) is involved. If your friend is distant, the mail message will be forwarded from the local post office (*sendmail* running locally) to a distant one (*sendmail* running remotely) for delivery. Although *sendmail* is similar to a post office in many ways, it is superior in others:

- Delivery typically takes seconds rather than days.

- Address changes (forwarding) take effect immediately, and mail can be forwarded anywhere in the world.

- Host addresses are looked up dynamically. Therefore, machines can be moved or renamed, and email delivery will still succeed.

- Mail can be delivered through programs that access other networks (such as UUCP and BITNET). This would be like the post office using United Parcel Service to deliver an overnight letter.

This analogy between a post office and *sendmail* will break down as we explore *sendmail* in more detail. But the analogy serves a role in this introductory material, so we will continue to use it to illuminate a few of *sendmail*'s more obscure points.

1.1 MUA Versus MTA

A mail user agent (MUA) is any of the many programs that users run to read, reply to, compose, and dispose of email. Examples of an MUA include the original UNIX mail program (*/bin/mail*); the Berkeley *Mail* program; its System V equivalent (*mailx*); free software programs such as *mush*, *elm*, and *mh*; and commercial programs such as *Zmail*. Many MUAs may exist on a single machine. MUAs sometimes perform limited mail transport, but this is usually a very complex task for which they are not suited. We won't be covering MUAs in this book.

A mail transfer agent (MTA) is a highly specialized program that delivers mail and transports it between machines, like the post office. Usually, there is only one MTA on a machine. The *sendmail* program is an MTA. Others include *MMDF*, *Smail 3.x*, and *Zmailer*, but we'll cover only *sendmail* in this book.

1.2 Why Is sendmail So Complex?

In its simplest role, that of transporting mail from a user on one machine to another user on the same machine, *sendmail* is almost trivial. All vendors supply a *sendmail* (and configuration file) that will accomplish this. But as your needs increase, the job of *sendmail* becomes progressively more complicated, and its configuration file becomes more complex. On hosts that are connected to the Internet, for example, *sendmail* should use the Domain Name System (DNS) to translate hostnames into network addresses. Machines with UUCP connections, on the other hand, need to have *sendmail* run the *uux* program.

The *sendmail* program needs to transport mail between a wide variety of machines. Consequently, its configuration file is designed to be very flexible. This concept allows a single binary to be distributed to many machines, where the configuration file can be customized to suit particular needs. This configurability contributes to making *sendmail* complex.

Consider, for example, when mail needs to be delivered to a particular user. The *sendmail* program decides on the appropriate delivery method based on its configuration file. One such decision process might include the following steps:

- If the recipient receives mail on the same machine as the sender, deliver the mail using the */bin/mail* program.

- If the recipient's machine is connected to the sending machine using UUCP, use *uux* to send the mail message.

- If the recipient's machine is on the Internet, the sending machine transports the mail over the Internet.

• Otherwise, the mail message may need to be transported over another network (such as BITNET) or possibly rejected.

1.3   Three Important Parts

The *sendmail* program is actually composed of several parts, including programs, files, directories, and the services it provides. Its foundation is a *configuration file* that defines the location and behavior of these other parts and contains rules for rewriting addresses. A *queue directory* holds mail until it can be delivered. An *aliases file* allows alternative names for users and creation of mailing lists.

1.3.1   The Configuration File

The configuration file contains all the information *sendmail* needs to do its job. Within it you provide information, such as file locations, permissions, and modes of operation.

Rewriting rules and rule sets also appear in the configuration file. They transform a mail address into another form that may be required for delivery. They are perhaps the single most confusing aspect of the configuration file. Because the configuration file is designed to be fast for *sendmail* to read and parse, rules can look cryptic to humans:

```
R$+@$+          $:$1<@$2>       focus on domain
R$+<$+@$+>      $1$2<@$3>       move gaze right
```

But what appears to be complex is really just succinct. The R at the beginning of each line, for example, labels a *rewrite* rule. And the $+ expressions mean to match one or more parts of an address. With experience, such expressions (and indeed the configuration file as a whole) soon become meaningful.

1.3.2   The Queue

Not all mail messages can be delivered immediately. When delivery is delayed, *sendmail* must be able to save it for later transmission. The *sendmail* queue is a directory that holds mail until it can be delivered. A mail message may be queued:

• When the destination machine is unreachable or down. The mail message will be delivered when the destination machine returns to service.

• When a mail message has many recipients. Some mail messages may be successfully delivered, and others may not. Those that fail are queued for later delivery.

• When a mail message is expensive. Expensive mail (such as mail sent over a long-distance phone line) can be queued for delivery when rates are lower.

- When safety is of concern. The *sendmail* program can be configured to queue all mail messages, thus minimizing the risk of loss should the machine crash.

1.3.3 Aliases and Mailing Lists

Aliases allow mail that is sent to one address to be redirected to another address. They also allow mail to be appended to files or piped through programs, and they form the basis of mailing lists. The heart of aliasing is the *aliases*(5) file (often stored in database format for swifter lookups). Aliasing is also available to the individual user via a file called *.forward* in the user's home directory.

1.4 Run sendmail by Hand

Most users do not run *sendmail* directly. Instead, they use one of many mail user agents (MUAs) to compose a mail message. Those programs invisibly pass the mail message to *sendmail*, creating the appearance of instantaneous transmission. The *sendmail* program then takes care of delivery in its own seemingly mysterious fashion.

Although most users don't run *sendmail* directly, it is perfectly legal to do so. You, like many system managers, may need to do so to track down and solve mail problems.

Here's a demonstration of one way to run *sendmail* by hand. First create a file named *sendstuff* with the following contents:

```
This is a one line message.
```

Second, mail this file to yourself with the following command line, where *you* is your login name:

```
% /usr/lib/sendmail you <sendstuff
```

Here, you run *sendmail* directly by specifying its full pathname.[*] When you run *sendmail*, any command-line arguments that do not begin with a – character are considered to be the names of the people to whom you are sending the mail message.

The <sendstuff sequence causes the contents of the file that you have created (*sendstuff*) to be redirected into the *sendmail* program. The *sendmail* program treats everything it reads from its standard input (up to the end of the file) as the mail message to transmit.

---

[*] That path may be different on your system. If so, substitute the correct pathname in all the examples that follow. For example, try looking for *sendmail* in */usr/sbin* or */usr/ucblib*.

Now view the mail message that you just sent. How you do this will vary. Many users just type *mail* to view their mail. Others use the *mh*(1) package and type *inc* to receive and *show* to view their mail. No matter how you normally view your mail, save the mail message that you just received to a file. It will look something like this:

```
From you@Here.US.EDU  Fri Dec 13 08:11:44 1996
Received: (from you@localhost) by Here.US.EDU (8.8.4/8.8.4)
        id AA04599 for you; Fri, 13 Dec 96 08:11:44 -0700
Date: Fri, 13 Dec 96 08:11:43
From: you@Here.US.EDU (Your Full Name)
Message-Id: <9631121611.AA02124@Here.US.EDU>
To: you                                        ← may be Apparently-To:

This is a one line message.
```

The first thing to note is that this file begins with seven lines of text that were not in your original message. Those lines were added by *sendmail* and your local delivery program and are called the *header*.

The last line of the file is the original line from your *sendstuff* file. It is separated from the header by one blank line. The body of a mail message comes after the header and consists of everything that follows the first blank line (see Figure 1-1).

Ordinarily, when you send mail with your MUA, the MUA adds a header and feeds both the header and the body to *sendmail*. This time, however, you ran *sendmail* directly and supplied only a body; the header was added by *sendmail*.

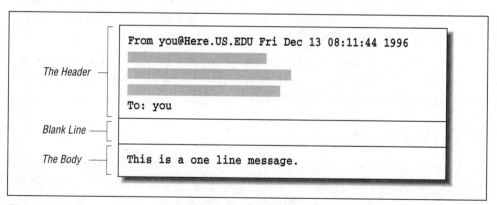

Figure 1–1: Every mail message is composed of a header and a body

1.5 The Header

Let's examine the header in more detail.

```
From you@Here.US.EDU  Fri Dec 13 08:11:44 1996
Received: (from you@localhost) by Here.US.EDU (8.8.4/8.8.4)
        id AA04599 for you; Fri, 13 Dec 96 08:11:44 -0700
Date: Fri, 13 Dec 96 08:11:43
From: you@Here.US.EDU (Your Full Name)
Message-Id: <9631121611.AA02124@Here.US.EDU>
To: you                                    ← may be something else (see §34.8.43)
```

Notice that most header lines start with a word followed by a colon. Each word tells what kind of information the rest of the line contains. There are many types of header lines that can appear in a mail message. Some are mandatory, some are optional, and some may appear many times. Those that appeared in the message that you mailed to yourself were all mandatory. That's why *sendmail* added them to your message. The line starting with the five characters "`From `" (the fifth character is a space) is added by some programs (such as */bin/mail*) but not by others (such as *mh*).

A `Received:` line is added each time a machine receives the mail message. (If there are too many such lines, the mail message will *bounce* and be returned to the sender as failed mail.) The indented line is a continuation of the line above, the `Received:` line. The `Date:` line gives the date and time when the message was originally sent. The `From:` line lists the email address and the full name of the sender. The `Message-ID:` line is like a serial number in that it is guaranteed to uniquely identify the mail message. And the `To:`* line shows a list of one or more recipients. (Multiple recipients would be separated with commas.)

A complete list of all header lines that are of importance to *sendmail* is presented in Chapter 35, *Headers*. The important concept here is that the header precedes, and is separate from, the body in all mail messages.

1.6 The Body

The body of a mail message consists of everything following the first blank line to the end of the file. When you sent your *sendstuff* file, it contained only a body. Now edit the file *sendstuff* and add a small header.

```
Subject: a test            ← add
                           ← add
This is a one line message.
```

---

* Depending on how the `NoRecipientAction` option was set, this could be an `Apparently-To:` header, a `Bcc:` header, or even a `To:` header followed by an "`undisclosed-recipients:;`" (see §34.8.43).

The Subject: header line is an optional one. The *sendmail* program passes it through as is. Here, the Subject: line is followed by a blank line and then the message text, forming a header and a body. Note that a blank line must be truly blank. If you put space or tab characters in it, thus forming an "empty-looking" line, the header *will not* be separated from the body as intended.

Send this file to yourself again, running *sendmail* by hand as you did before:

```
% /usr/lib/sendmail you <sendstuff
```

Notice that our Subject: header line was carried through without change:

```
From you@Here.US.EDU  Fri Dec 13 08:11:44 1996
Return-Path: you@Here.US.EDU
Received: (from you@localhost) by Here.US.EDU (8.8.4/8.8.4)
        id AA04599 for you; Fri, 31 Dec 96 08:11:44 -0700
Date: Fri, 13 Dec 96 08:11:43
From: you@Here.US.EDU (Your Full Name)
Message-Id: <9631121611.AA02124@Here.US.EDU>
Subject: a test                              ← note
To: you

This is a one line message.
```

1.7 The Envelope

To handle delivery to diverse recipients, the *sendmail* program uses the concept of an *envelope*. This envelope is analogous to the physical envelopes that are used for post office mail. Imagine that you want to send two copies of a document: one to your friend in the office next to yours and one to a friend across the country:

```
To: friend1, friend2@remote
```

After you photocopy the document, you stuff each copy into a separate envelope. You hand one envelope to a clerk, who carries it next door and hands it to friend1 in the next office. This is like delivery on your local machine. The clerk drops the other copy in the slot at the corner mailbox, and the post office forwards that envelope across the country to friend2@remote. This is like *sendmail* transporting a mail message to a remote machine.

To illustrate what an envelope is, consider one way in which *sendmail* might run */bin/mail*, a program that performs local delivery:

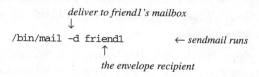

Here *sendmail* runs */bin/mail* with a **−d**, which tells */bin/mail* to append the mail message to friend1's mailbox.

Information that describes the sender or recipient, but is not part of the message header, is considered envelope information. The two may or may not contain the same information (a point we'll gloss over for now). In the case of */bin/mail*, the email message showed two recipients in its header:

```
To: friend1, friend2@remote        ← the header
```

But the envelope information that is given to */bin/mail* showed only one (the one appropriate to local delivery):

```
-d friend1                  ← specifies the envelope
```

Now consider the envelope of a message transported over the network. When sending network mail, *sendmail* must give the remote site a list of sender and recipients *separate from and before* it sends the mail message (header and body). Figure 1-2 shows this in a greatly simplified conversation between the local *sendmail* and the remote machine's *sendmail*.

The local *sendmail* tells the remote machine's *sendmail* that there is mail from you (the **sender**) and for **friend2@remote**. It conveys this sender and recipient information *separate from and before* it transmits the mail message that contains the header. Because this information is conveyed separately from the message header, it is called the envelope.

There is only one recipient listed in the envelope, whereas two were listed in the message header:

```
To: friend1, friend2@remote
```

The remote machine does not need to know about the local user, **friend1**, so that bit of recipient information is excluded from the envelope.

A given mail message can be sent by using many different envelopes (like the two here), but the header will be common to them all.

1.8 Things to Try

- Some files contain lines that begin with the five characters "**From** " (the fifth character is a space). What happens to such lines when the files containing them are delivered to a local mailbox? What UNIX utilities are available to aid in sending such a file with those lines intact?

- In the file *sendstuff*, we created a one-line header that began with **Subject:**. What would be the effect of making that header all lowercase? What does

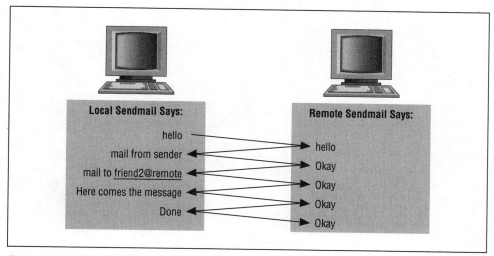

Figure 1-2: A simplified conversation

RFC822 have to say about this? (See "Additional Sources of Information" in the Preface.)

- How does *sendmail* behave when it is given a message that contains only a header? Does it add a blank line to create an empty body?

- If your MUA supports a **-v** (verbose) command-line switch, try to send mail to someone at a remote machine using that switch. You should be able to observe the actual conversation between your local *sendmail* and a remote machine's *sendmail*.

- If you can, send mail addressed both to yourself on the local machine and to yourself on a remote machine. Compare and contrast the header part of each.

- If you are at all fuzzy about the concept of envelope, review §1.7 now. We will refer to envelopes often throughout this tutorial.

- Leap ahead to Chapter 35 for additional information about specific headers.

2

Have a V8

To make the examples on your screen match those in this book, we have elected to use V8 *sendmail* for the rest of this tutorial. If you are already running the latest release of V8 *sendmail*, you may skip this chapter.[*] Otherwise, you will need to get and compile V8. In this chapter we show you how to do just that. But don't worry. We don't intend to show you how to do a full installation. All you need is a runnable *sendmail* binary, and compiling one is generally pretty easy.

2.1 Get the Source

V8 *sendmail* is officially available via anonymous FTP from:

```
ftp://ftp.sendmail.org/ucb/sendmail/
```

Its distribution consists of two forms of *tar*(1) files, one compacted with *compress*(1) and the other with *gzip*(1):

```
sendmail.*.tar.Z      ← compressed source tar
sendmail.*.tar.gz     ← gzipped source tar
```

The * in each of the above represents the current version number, such as 8.x.y, where x denotes a major release and y denotes a minor release. Get only one of these two files; they contain identical copies of the distribution. The `.gz` form is smaller and quicker to transfer with FTP.

---

[*] You may still have to get the latest release and compare it to your system version to find out whether you really have the latest release.

After you get the source distribution, you next need to unpack it. Assuming the current version is 8.8.4, you unpack it with one of these commands:

```
% zcat sendmail.8.8.4.tar.Z | tar xf -
% gzcat sendmail.8.8.4.tar.gz | tar xf -
```

Once successfully unpacked, you'll find a new subdirectory in the current directory. It has the same name as the source distribution, but with the `.tar.Z` or `.tar.gz` suffix removed and the first dot in the name turned into a hyphen:

```
% ls
sendmail.8.8.4.tar.gz    sendmail-8.8.4
```

Here, *sendmail-8.8.4* is the directory that contains the source and documentation for *sendmail.* Change into that directory and look at its contents:

```
% cd sendmail-8.8.4
% ls
FAQ              RELEASE_NOTES    mail.local       rmail
KNOWNBUGS        cf               mailstats        smrsh
Makefile         contrib          makemap          src
READ_ME          doc              praliases        test
```

2.2 Read the Documents

Read the documentation that comes with *sendmail.* The more important introductory documents to read are:

```
READ_ME            ← A description of what is where and how to compile
RELEASE_NOTES      ← A history of how sendmail reached this point
FAQ                ← A compendium of frequently asked questions
doc/op/op.ps       ← The Operations Guide in PostScript
```

The *READ_ME* file contains information about all the other parts of the distribution. It describes how to format the manual pages, explains which RFCs are important, and anticipates some problems you may encounter when building.

The *RELEASE_NOTES* file describes the history of *sendmail* in far more detail than you may ever need. The first part of this file lists important late-breaking news about the program. New features will be listed here, and critical bug fixes will be described.

The *FAQ* (Frequently Asked Questions) file is a copy of the one that is distributed in the Usenet newsgroup *comp.mail.sendmail.* Many people have already asked the very same questions you probably have percolating in your head. This document tries to anticipate the most common of those questions and to provide answers to them.

The *doc/op/op.ps* file is written by Eric Allman and is entitled *SENDMAIL Installation and Operations Guide.* It is the final and authoritative word on all matters relating to *sendmail*. It is dense reading, and not suited for the beginner, but well worth perusing in this early stage of learning *sendmail*. Unlike the first three files (which are directly readable text), *op.ps* is PostScript.[*]

2.3   *What's What in src*

When we describe building *sendmail*, we will refer to the source directory by the name *src*. That directory is the same as the **src** directory that is shown when you list the distribution directory:

```
% cd sendmail-8.8.4
% ls
FAQ             RELEASE_NOTES   mail.local      rmail
KNOWNBUGS       cf              mailstats       smrsh
Makefile        contrib         makemap         src        ← note
READ_ME         doc             praliases       test
```

Change into the *src* directory and look at what is there:

```
% cd src
% ls
Makefile        collect.c       mailq.0         pathnames.h     stats.c
Makefiles       conf.c          mailq.1         queue.c         sysexits.c
READ_ME         conf.h          mailstats.h     readcf.c        sysexits.h
TRACEFLAGS      convtime.c      main.c          recipient.c     trace.c
alias.c         daemon.c        makesendmail    savemail.c      udb.c
aliases         deliver.c       map.c           sendmail.0      useful.h
aliases.0       domain.c        mci.c           sendmail.8      usersmtp.c
aliases.5       envelope.c      mime.c          sendmail.h      util.c
arpadate.c      err.c           newaliases.0    sendmail.hf     version.c
cdefs.h         headers.c       newaliases.1    srvrsmtp.c
clock.c         macro.c         parseaddr.c     stab.c
```

The files whose names end in *.0* are pre-formatted manual pages. The files whose names end in *.1*, *.5*, and *.8* are unformatted. The method to format them for printing is described in *../READ_ME*.[†]

The files whose names end in *.c* and *.h* are the actual source. The *makesendmail* file is a shell script that makes building easy, and the *READ_ME* file contains the latest information about building. You should read the latter now. Pay special attention to the section titled *OPERATING SYSTEM AND COMPILE QUIRKS*. No matter what your operating system, this section probably contains information that is important to you.

---

[*] The source for the PostScript is in *op.me* and requires the latest *tmac.e* macros to format.

[†] Note that the *READ_ME* here in the *src* directory is different from the one in the parent directory (*../READ_ME*), even though they both have the same name.

2.4 Preliminaries

Now that you have the distribution and have changed into the *src* directory, you will find a script called *makesendmail*. For nearly all systems, all you have to do is run that script to build *sendmail*. To determine whether your system is supported, run the *makesendmail* script now, with the **-m** command-line switch:

```
% ./makesendmail -m
Configuration: os=SunOS, rel=4.1.4, rbase=4, arch=sun4, sfx=
Will run in virgin obj.SunOS.4.1.4.sun4 using Makefile.SunOS
%
```

Here, *makesendmail* indicates that it knows how to build a *sendmail* for SunOS 4.1.4. It will use the *Makefile* called *Makefile.SunOS*. If it is unable to determine a *Makefile*, it will print a message like this and exit:

```
Cannot determine how to support arch.os.rel
```

Here, *arch* is the generic type of machine, such as *sun4* or *9000/720*. The *os* is the operating system type, such as SunOS or HP-UX. And the *rel* is the version of the operating system, such as A or 4.1.3. If your system is not supported, you are going to have to do a port (ugh!). Read the *READ_ME* file, and skip ahead to Chapter 18, *Compile and Install sendmail*.

Fortunately *makesendmail* succeeded in this example, and, because we are running on a Sun system with SunOS 4.1.4, *makesendmail* selected *Makefile.SunOS* as the *Makefile* that we will be using. Had we been running on something else, for example, say an SGI machine, it might have selected a different *Makefile*, such as *Makefile.IRIX*. All the *Makefile* files are located under *src* in a subdirectory called *Makefiles*. That subdirectory should look something like this:

Makefile.386BSD	Makefile.ISC	Makefile.Solaris
Makefile.A-UX	Makefile.KSR	Makefile.SunOS
Makefile.AIX	Makefile.LUNA	Makefile.SunOS.4.0
Makefile.Altos	Makefile.Linux	Makefile.SunOS.5.1
Makefile.BSD-OS	Makefile.Mach386	Makefile.SunOS.5.2
Makefile.BSD43	Makefile.NCR3000	Makefile.SunOS.5.3
Makefile.CLIX	Makefile.NEWS-OS.4.x	Makefile.SunOS.5.4
Makefile.CSOS	Makefile.NEWS-OS.6.x	Makefile.SunOS.5.5
Makefile.ConvexOS	Makefile.NEXTSTEP	Makefile.Titan
Makefile.Dell	Makefile.NeXT	Makefile.ULTRIX
Makefile.DomainOS	Makefile.NetBSD	Makefile.UMAX
Makefile.Dynix	Makefile.NonStop-UX	Makefile.UNICOS
Makefile.EWS-UX_V	Makefile.OSF1	Makefile.UNIX_SV.4.x.i386
Makefile.FreeBSD	Makefile.PTX	Makefile.UX4800
Makefile.HP-UX	Makefile.Paragon	Makefile.UXPDS
Makefile.HP-UX.10.x	Makefile.RISCos	Makefile.Utah
Makefile.IRIX	Makefile.SCO	Makefile.dgux
Makefile.IRIX.5.x	Makefile.SCO.3.2v4.2	Makefile.dist
Makefile.IRIX64	Makefile.SVR4	Makefile.uts.systemV

Since we have thus far been successful, you can now go ahead and run *make-sendmail* for real. Be prepared to interrupt it with a control-C, because we will need to tune your *Makefile* after it has been copied:

```
% ./makesendmail
Configuration: os=SunOS, rel=4.1.4, rbase=4, arch=sun4, sfx=
Creating obj.SunOS.4.1.4.sun4 using Makefile.SunOS
Making dependencies in obj.SunOS.4.1.4.sun4
Making in obj.SunOS.4.1.4.sun4
cc -I. -O -I/usr/sww/include -DNDBM -DNEWDB -DNIS   -target sun4 -c  alias.c
^C
```

The *makesendmail* script first creates a directory in which you will eventually build *sendmail*. It then (invisibly) creates links inside that directory to all the source files and to an appropriate *Makefile*. Finally, it starts to build *sendmail*. You interrupt the build with a control-C just after the first compiler line of output. From this point forward we will work inside that new directory, so *cd* into it:

```
% cd obj.SunOS.4.1.4.sun4
```

As distributed, your newly created *Makefile* is not writable. But we may need to modify it, so we need to make it writable:

```
% chmod u+w Makefile
```

There are three important reasons to modify your default *Makefile*. If you don't have the Berkeley *db*(3) library, you need to remove *db* support from your *Makefile*. If you are not connected to the Internet and are not running a *named*(8) name server, you need to eliminate DNS support from your *Makefile*. Finally, you need to read the comments inside your *Makefile* and make any changes suggested there.

2.4.1 Eliminate or Keep db Support?

If you have not installed the Berkeley *db(8)* library package, or do not know whether you have, you need to remove support for that package from your *Makefile*. Edit your *Makefile* and look for the line that begins with the word DBMDEF:

```
DBMDEF= -DNDBM -DNEWDB -DNIS                    ← this line
                  ↑
        delete this from the line
```

Delete the string -DNEWDB from the DBMDEF line to form the following:

```
DBMDEF= -DNDBM -DNIS                            ← after delete
```

Next search for the line that begins with LIBS:

```
LIBS=    -ldb -ldbm -lresolv              ← this line (exact text may vary)
         ↑
    delete this from the line
```

Delete the string –ldb from the LIBS= line to form the following:

```
LIBS=    -ldbm -lresolv                   ← after delete
```

This completes the removal of Berkeley *db*(3) support from your *Makefile*.

If your site does support the Berkeley *db(3)* library package, you may still need to massage your *Makefile*. To include this support inside *sendmail*, you need to specify the correct include files and library path. Search for the line that begins with INCDIRS:

```
INCDIRS=-I/usr/sww/include                ← this line

# loader options
LDOPTS= -Bstatic

# library directories
LIBDIRS=-L/usr/sww/lib                    ← and this line
```

You need to change both lines to contain the correct paths where you installed the Berkeley *db*(3) library. If you aren't sure about any of this information, you should eliminate support instead.

```
INCDIRS=-I/usr/local/include/db           ← new

# loader options
LDOPTS= -Bstatic

# library directories
LIBDIRS=-L/usr/local/lib                  ← new
```

As shown in the two preceding examples, we installed the Berkeley *db*(3) include files in */usr/local/include/db* and the library in */usr/local/lib*.

2.4.2 Eliminate DNS Support

If you are on a machine that does not support DNS (such as a home workstation that connects to the outside world exclusively via UUCP), you will need to exclude DNS support from *sendmail*. One way to tell whether your machine supports DNS is to run the *nslookup*(8) program. It may not be in your path, so if it is not found when you try to run it, you have to find it. Try looking in */usr/etc* or */usr/sbin*. If *nslookup*(8) hangs when you run it, your system probably does not support DNS. If it doesn't hang, its output will look like this. Just type Control-D to exit:

```
% /usr/etc/nslookup
Default Server: localhost
Address:  127.0.0.1

> ^D
```

If your system lacks DNS support, you must then redefine the value of
NAMED_BIND as 0 in *Makefile*. One way to do that is to edit your *Makefile* and
search for the line beginning with the string ENVDEF:

```
ENVDEF=
```

Append to that line the following string, which turns off DNS support inside *send-mail*:

```
ENVDEF= -DNAMED_BIND=0
        ↑
        append this
```

2.4.3 Other Massaging in Makefile

Independent of support for *db*(3) and DNS, your operating system may impose its
own requirements. To discover whether it does and what they might be, edit your
Makefile, and look through it for operating-system-specific comments. A sampling
of the many such comments might look like this:

```
# you can use -O3 on AIX 3.2.4 or greater ONLY!          ← Makefile.AIX
# use DGUX_5_4_2 for versions prior to 5.4.3.            ← Makefile.DGUX
#  delete -144bsd if you are not running BIND 4.9.x      ← Makefile.SunOS.5.5
# define SPT_TYPE=SPT_NONE if you are using NEWS-OS 6.0.1  ← Makefile.NEWS-OS.6.x
```

No matter which *Makefile* is yours, all customizing should be done before this line:

```
##################  end of user configuration flags  ####################
```

Unless you are an expert at compiling *Makefiles*, avoid changing anything after this
line. You risk "breaking" your *Makefile* and ruining your ability to build.

2.5 Build

You are now ready to build a runnable version of *sendmail*. To do so, just run the
following command while in the *src/obj . . .* directory:

```
% make
```

This results in several screens full of output, so you should do this in a scrollable
window or something similar, such as *emacs*(1) or *script*(1).

```
cc -I. -O -I/usr/sww/include -DNDBM -DNEWDB -DNIS   -target sun4 -c  alias.c
cc -I. -O -I/usr/sww/include -DNDBM -DNEWDB -DNIS   -target sun4 -c  arpadate.c
cc -I. -O -I/usr/sww/include -DNDBM -DNEWDB -DNIS   -target sun4 -c  clock.c
. . . and so on.
```

Although we hope that everything will go smoothly, various things can go wrong at this point. For example, if you forgot to undefine NEWDB you, might get this:

```
map.c: 46: Can't find include file db.h
*** Error code 2
make: Fatal error: Command failed for target `map.o'
```

If so, go back to §2.4.1, and remove **-DNEWDB** from the *Makefile*. Other problems are covered in Chapter 18. If all goes well, you should end up with output looking like this:

```
... many lines here.
cc -I. -O -I/usr/sww/include/db -DNDBM  -DNEWDB -DNIS  -target sun4 -c  version.c
cc -o sendmail -Bstatic alias.o arpadate.o clock.o collect.o conf.o convtime.o daemon.
o  deliver.o domain.o envelope.o err.o headers.o macro.o main.o  map.o mci.o mime.o pa
rseaddr.o queue.o readcf.o recipient.o  savemail.o srvrsmtp.o stab.o stats.o sysexits.
o  trace.o udb.o usersmtp.o util.o version.o  -L/usr/sww/lib -ldb -ldbm -lresolv
%
```

The result of all this is a brand-new executable *sendmail* file in the current (*src/obj...*) directory. You can now copy that new *sendmail* to any convenient location—perhaps one where you will continue this tutorial. Your home directory is one possibility:

```
% cp sendmail $HOME
```

Or you can put a symbolic link to it in *../src*:

```
% ln -s sendmail ../src
```

Or you can leave it in the *src/obj...* directory. It really doesn't matter where you put *sendmail* for this tutorial. We will always refer to it as *./sendmail* to keep the examples uniform.

2.6 Test It

Just to make sure that *sendmail* built correctly, test it with the following arguments:

```
% ./sendmail -d0.1 -bt < /dev/null
Version 8.8.4
Compiled with:   LOG MATCHGECOS NETINET NETUNIX NEWDB USERDB XDEBUG
SYSTEM IDENTITY (after readcf):
              (short domain name) $w = here.us.edu
          (canonical domain name) $j = $w
               (subdomain name) $m = us.edu
                  (node name) $k = here
```

Pay no attention to the $ variables for now. They will be clarified a few chapters later. For now, just observe that *sendmail* ran, printed its version (and some other identifying information), and exited without error.

If, instead of running, *sendmail* hangs, you will have to go back to §2.4.2 and redefine NAMED_BIND. If your site has never run *sendmail* before, you will get a complaint like this:

```
/etc/sendmail.cf: line 0: cannot open: No such file or directory
```

This shows that *sendmail* ran but couldn't find its configuration file. If your site is new to *sendmail*, you won't be able to run the examples to follow. But don't worry, we'll be creating a configuration file of our own soon enough.

Another problem that might happen on a machine running an old (pre-V8) version of *sendmail* is the following:

```
/etc/sendmail.cf: line 273: replacement $3 out of bounds
/etc/sendmail.cf: line 297: replacement $3 out of bounds
```

If this happens, you will still be able to run *sendmail* to follow along in early examples. Just bear in mind that you will be seeing these errors until we start designing our own configuration file.

2.7 *Things to Try*

- If you have C language programming experience, look at the *conf.c* file. Observe how *sendmail* initializes its default values and how it accommodates many operating systems. Read the code in the *checkcompat()* function.

- Look in the *contrib* directory. Determine whether any of the contributed software or documents are of value to you or your site.

- For a historical understanding of the philosophy behind *sendmail*, read the document *doc/usenix/usenix.ps*. If you have access to the Internet, get and read the RFCs mentioned in the Preface.

3

The Roles of sendmail

The *sendmail* program plays a variety of roles, all critical to the proper flow of electronic mail. It listens to the network for incoming mail, transports mail messages to other machines, and hands local mail to a local program for local delivery. It can append mail to files and can pipe mail through other programs. It can queue mail for later delivery and understands the aliasing of one recipient name to another.

3.1 Role in the Filesystem

The *sendmail* program's role (position) in the local file system hierarchy can be viewed as an inverted tree (see Figure 3-1). When *sendmail* is run, it first reads the */etc/sendmail.cf* configuration file. Among the many items contained in that file are the locations of all the other files and directories that *sendmail* needs.

Files and directories listed in *sendmail.cf* are usually specified as full pathnames for security (such as */var/spool/mqueue* rather than *mqueue*). As the first step in our tour of those files, run the following command to gather a list of them:[*]

```
% grep =/ /etc/sendmail.cf
```

The output produced by the *grep*(1) command may look something like the following:[†]

```
O AliasFile=/etc/aliases
#O ErrorHeader=/etc/sendmail.oE
O HelpFile=/usr/lib/sendmail.hf
```

---

[*] If you are not currently running V8.7 or above *sendmail*, you will have to grep for "/[^0-9].*/" instead. If you're not running *sendmail* at all, you won't be able to do this, so for now just read along instead.

[†] Lines that begin with F or K may also appear. If so, ignore them for now.

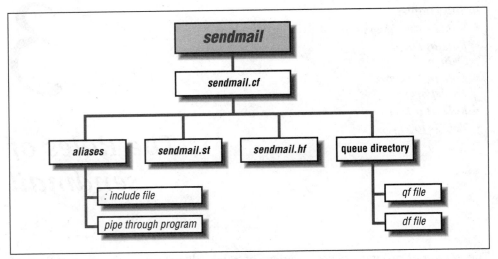

Figure 3-1: The sendmail.cf file leads to everything else

```
O QueueDirectory=/var/spool/mqueue
O StatusFile=/etc/sendmail.st
#O UserDatabaseSpec=/etc/userdb
#O ServiceSwitchFile=/etc/service.switch
#O HostsFile=/etc/hosts
#O SafeFileEnvironment=/arch
Mlocal,         P=/bin/mail, F=lsDFMAw5:/|@rmn, S=10/30, R=20/40,
Mprog,          P=/bin/sh, F=lsDFMoeu, S=10/30, R=20/40, D=$z:/,
```

Notice that some lines begin with an O character, some with an M, and others with a #. The O marks a line as a configuration option. The word following the O is the name of the option. The options in the above output show the location of the files that *sendmail* uses. `AliasFile`, for example, defines the location of the *aliases*(5) database. The lines that begin with M define *delivery agents*. The lines that begin with a # are comments.

First we will examine the files in the O option lines. Then we will discuss local delivery and the files in the M delivery agent lines.

3.1.1 The Aliases File

Aliasing is the process of converting one recipient name into another. One use is to convert a generic name (such as *root*) into a real username. Another is to convert one name into a list of many names (for mailing lists).

Take a few moments to examine your *aliases* file. Its location is determined by the `AliasFile` option in your *sendmail.cf* file. For example,

```
O AliasFile=/etc/aliases
```

Compare what you find in your *aliases* file to the brief example of an *aliases* file listed below:

```
# Mandatory aliases.
postmaster: root
MAILER-DAEMON: postmaster

# The five forms of aliases
John_Adams:     adamj
xpres:          ford,carter,bush
oldlist:        :include: /usr/local/oldguys
nobody:         /dev/null
ftphelp:        |/usr/local/bin/sendhelp
```

Your *aliases* file is probably far more complex, but even so, note that the example shows all the possible forms of aliases.

Lines that begin with **#** are comments. Empty lines are ignored. As the first comment indicates, there are two aliases that are mandatory in every *aliases* file. Both are the simplest form of alias: a name and what to change that name into. The name on the left of the : is changed into the name on the right. Names are not case-sensitive. For example, `POSTMASTER`, `Postmaster`, and `postmaster` are all the same.[*]

For every envelope that lists a local user as a recipient, *sendmail* looks up that recipient's name in the *aliases* file. (A local user is any address that would normally be delivered on the local machine. That is, *postmaster* is local, whereas *postmaster@remote* may not be.) When *sendmail* matches the recipient to one of the names on the left of the *aliases* file, it replaces that recipient name with the text to the right of the : character. For example, the recipient `postmaster` becomes the recipient `root`.

After a name is substituted, the new name is then looked up, and the process is repeated until no more matches are found. The name `MAILER-DAEMON` is first changed to `postmaster`. Then `postmaster` is looked up again and changed to `root`. Since there is no entry for `root` in the *aliases* file, the mail message is delivered into *root*'s mailbox.

---

[*] According to RFC822, all usernames *are* case-sensitive except postmaster. But *sendmail*, when processing its aliases file, views all names as case-insensitive.

Every *aliases* file must have an alias for **postmaster** that will expand to the name of a real user.* Mail about mail problems is always sent to **postmaster** both by mail-related programs and by users who are having trouble sending mail.

When mail is bounced (returned because it could not be delivered), it is always sent from **MAILER-DAEMON**. That alias is needed because users may reply to bounced mail. Without it, replies to bounced mail would themselves bounce.

The five types of lines in an *aliases* file areas are as follows:

```
John_Adams:     adamj
xpres:          ford,carter,reagan,bush
oldlist:        :include: /usr/local/oldguys
nobody:         /dev/null
ftphelp:        |/usr/local/bin/sendhelp
```

You have already seen the first (it was the form used to convert **postmaster** to **root**). In the above example, mail sent to **John_Adams** is delivered to the user whose login name is **adamj**.

The **xpres:** line shows how one name can be expanded into a list of many names. Each of those new names becomes a new name for further alias processing. If a name can't be further expanded, a copy of the mail message is delivered to it.

The **oldlist:** line shows how a mailing list can be read from a file. The expression **:include:** tells *sendmail* to read a specific file and to use the names in that file as the list of recipients.

The **nobody:** line shows how a name can be aliased to a file. The mail message is appended to the file. The */dev/null* file listed here is a special one. That file is an empty hole into which the mail message simply vanishes.

The **ftphelp:** line shows how a name can be replaced by the name of a program. The | character causes *sendmail* to pipe the mail message through the program whose full pathname follows (in this case, we specified the full pathname as */usr/local/bin/sendhelp*).

The *aliases* file can become very complex. It can be used to solve many special mail problems. The *aliases* file is covered in greater detail in Chapter 24, *Aliases*.

---

* The name **postmaster** is required by RFC822 and RFC1648, so resist the temptation to redefine it as **postperson** or **sysop**.

3.1.2 The Queue Directory

A mail message can be temporarily undeliverable for a wide variety of reasons, such as when a remote machine is down or has a temporary disk problem. To ensure that such messages are eventually delivered, *sendmail* stores them in its queue directory until they can be delivered successfully.

The `QueueDirectory` option in your configuration file tells *sendmail* where to find its queue directory:

```
O QueueDirectory=/var/spool/mqueue
```

The location of that directory must be a full pathname. Its exact location varies from vendor to vendor, but you can always find it by looking for the `QueueDirectory` option in your configuration file.

If you have permission, take a look at the queue directory. It may be empty if there is no mail waiting to be sent. If it is not empty, it will contain files like these:

```
dfQAA07038 dfMAA08000 qfQAA07038 qfMAA08000
```

When a mail message is queued, it is split into two parts, each part being saved in a separate file. The header information is saved in a file whose name begins with the characters `qf`. The body of the mail message is saved in a file whose name begins with the characters `df`.

The example above shows two queued mail messages. One is identified by the unique string `QAA07038` and the other by `MAA08000`.

The internals of the queue files and the processing of those files are covered in Chapter 23, *The Queue*.

3.2 Role in Local Delivery

Another role of the *sendmail* program is to deliver mail messages to local users. A local user has a mailbox on the local file system. Delivering local mail is done by appending a message to the user's mailbox, by feeding the mail message to a program, or by appending the message to a file other than the user's mailbox.

In general, *sendmail* does not put mail messages directly into files. You saw the exception in the *aliases* file, in which you could specifically tell *sendmail* to append mail to a file. This is the exception, not the rule. Usually, *sendmail* calls other programs to perform delivery. Those other programs are called delivery agents.

In your *sendmail.cf* file you found two lines that defined local delivery agents, the ones that *sendmail* used to deliver mail to the local file system:

```
Mlocal,     P=/bin/mail, F=lsDFMAw5:/|@rmn, S=10, R=20/40,
Mprog,      P=/bin/sh, F=lsDFMeu, S=10, R=20/40, D=$z:/,
```

The */bin/mail* program is used to append mail to the user's mailbox. The */bin/sh* program is used to run other programs that handle delivery.

3.2.1 Delivery to a Mailbox

The configuration file line that begins with **Mlocal** defines how mail is appended to a user's mailbox file. That program is usually */bin/mail* but can easily be a program such as *deliver*(1) or *mail.local*(8).

Under UNIX a user's mailbox is a single file that contains a series of mail messages. The usual UNIX convention (but not the only possibility) is that each message in a mailbox begins with the five characters "**From** " (the fifth is a blank space) and ends with a blank line.

The *sendmail* program neither knows nor cares what a user's mailbox looks like. All it cares about is the name of the program that it must run to add mail messages to that mailbox. In the example that program is */bin/mail*. The **M** configuration lines that define delivery agents are introduced in Chapter 6, *The Mail Hub and Delivery Agents*, and covered in detail in Chapter 30, *Delivery Agents*.

3.2.2 Delivery Through a Program

Mail addresses that begin with a | character are the names of programs to run. You saw one such address in the example *aliases* file:

```
ftphelp:        "|/usr/local/bin/sendhelp"
```

Here, mail sent to the address **ftphelp** is transformed via an alias into the new address **|/usr/local/bin/sendhelp**. The | character at the start of this new address tells *sendmail* that this is a program to run rather than a file to append to. The intention here is that the program will receive the mail and do something useful with it.

The *sendmail* program doesn't run mail delivery programs directly. Instead, it runs a shell and tells that shell to run the program. The name of the shell is listed in the configuration file in a line[*] that begins with **Mprog**:

---

[*] In actuality, delivery agent definitions often span multiple lines. You'll see this in Chapter 6.

```
Mprog,      P=/bin/sh, F=lsDFMeu, S=10, R=20/40, D=$z:/,
```

In this example the shell is the */bin/sh*(1). Other programs can appear in this line such as */bin/ksh*(1), the Korn Shell, or *smrsh*(1), the *sendmail* restricted shell that is supplied with the source distribution.

3.3 Role in Network Transport

Another role of *sendmail* is that of transporting mail to other machines. A message is transported when *sendmail* determines that the recipient is not local. The following lines from a typical configuration file define delivery agents for transporting mail to other machines:

```
Msmtp,      P=[IPC], F=mDFMuX, S=11/31, R=21, E=\r\n, L=990,
Muucp,      P=/usr/bin/uux, F=DFMhuUd, S=12, R=22/42, M=10000000,
```

The actual lines in your file may differ. The name **smtp** in the above example may appear in your file as **ether** or **ddn** or something else. The name **uucp** may appear as **suucp** or **uucp-dom**. There may be more such lines than we've shown here. The important point for now is that some delivery agents deal with local delivery, while others deal with delivery over a network.

3.3.1 TCP/IP

The *sendmail* program has the *internal* ability to transport mail over only one kind of network, one that uses TCP/IP; the following line instructs *sendmail* to do this:

```
Msmtp,      P=[IPC], F=mDFMuX, S=11/31, R=21, E=\r\n, L=990,
```

The [IPC] may appear as [TCP]. The two are equivalent.

When *sendmail* transports mail on a TCP/IP network, it first sends the envelope-sender hostname to the other site. If the other site accepts the sender's hostname as legal, the local *sendmail* then sends the envelope-recipient list. The other site accepts or rejects each recipient one by one. If any recipients are accepted, the local *sendmail* sends the message (header and body together).

3.3.2 UUCP

The line in the configuration file that tells *sendmail* how to transport over UUCP looks like this:

```
Muucp,      P=/usr/bin/uux, F=DFMhuUd, S=12, R=22/42, M=10000000,
```

This line tells *sendmail* to send UUCP network mail by running the */bin/uux* (*UNIX to UNIX eXecute*) program.

3.3.3 Other Protocols

There are many other kinds of network protocols that *sendmail* can use to transport email. Some of them may have shown up when you ran *grep* earlier. Other common possibilities might look like one of these:

```
Mfax,     P=/usr/local/lib/fax/mailfax, F=DFMhu, S=14, R=24, M=100000,
Mmail11,  P=/usr/etc/mail11, F=nsFx, S=15, R=25, A=mail11 $g $x $h $u
Mmac,     P=/usr/bin/macmail, F=CDFMmpsu, R=16, S=16, A=macmail -t $u
```

The `Mfax` line defines one of the many possible ways to send a FAX using *sendmail*. FAX transports images of documents over telephone lines. In the configuration line above, the */usr/lib/fax/mailfax* program is run, and a mail message is fed to it for conversion to and transmission as a FAX image.

The `Mmail11` line defines a way of using the *mail11*(1) program to transport email over a DECnet network, used mostly by Digital Equipment Corporation (DEC) machines.

The `Mmac` line defines a way to transport mail to Macintosh machines that are connected together on an AppleTalk network.

In all of these examples, note that *sendmail* sends email over other networks by running programs that are tailored specifically for that use. Remember that the only network that *sendmail* can use directly is a TCP/IP-based network.[*]

3.4 Role as a Daemon

Just as *sendmail* can transport mail messages over a TCP/IP-based network, it can also receive mail that is sent to it over the network. To do this, it must be run in *daemon* mode. A daemon is a program that runs in the background independent of terminal control.

As a daemon, *sendmail* is run once, usually when your machine is booted. Whenever an email message is sent to your machine, the sending machine talks to the *sendmail* daemon that is listening on your machine.

To see how your system runs *sendmail* in daemon mode, run one of the following commands:

```
% grep sendmail /etc/rc*          ← BSD-based systems
% grep sendmail /etc/init.d/*     ← SysV-based systems
% grep sendmail /etc/*rc          ← HP-UX systems (prior to 10.0)
```

---

* Actually, we're fudging for simplicity. V8 *sendmail* can also send messages over an ISO network.

One typical example of what you will find is

```
/etc/rc.local:if [ -f /usr/lib/sendmail -a -f /etc/sendmail.cf ]; then
/etc/rc.local:   /usr/lib/sendmail -bd -q1h; echo -n ' sendmail'
```

The second line above shows that *sendmail* is run at boot time with a command line of

```
/usr/lib/sendmail -bd -q1h
```

The **-bd** command-line switch tells *sendmail* to run in daemon mode. The **-q1h** command-line switch tells *sendmail* to wake up once per hour and process the queue. Command-line switches are introduced in Chapter 5, *The sendmail.cf File*, and covered in detail in Chapter 36, *The Command Line*.

3.5 Things to Try

* When your machine boots, it executes the commands in one or more Bourne shell scripts. Examine the script that runs the *sendmail* program in daemon mode. Write a small Bourne shell script that checks for the existence of the *echo*(1) program and then executes that program. Model it around the way *sendmail* is run.

* For each program that is mentioned in your configuration file's **M** lines (like */bin/mail* and */bin/uux*), read the appropriate online manual page. Examine the possible command-line arguments to determine how envelope information is passed. Compare what you discover to the **A=** part of each corresponding **M** line.

* Locate all the files mentioned in **O** lines in your configuration file. For any that exist, what kind of file is it: data or text? If it is text, read it. What purpose do you suppose it has?

4

How to Run
sendmail

One way to run *sendmail* is to provide it with the name of a recipient as the only command-line argument. For example, the following sends a mail message to george:[*]

    % /usr/lib/sendmail george

Multiple recipients can also be given. For example, the following sends a mail message to george, truman, and teddy:

    % /usr/lib/sendmail george,truman,teddy

The *sendmail* program accepts two different kinds of command-line arguments. Arguments that *do not* begin with a – character (such as george) are assumed to be recipients. Arguments that *do* begin with a – character are taken as switches that determine the behavior of *sendmail*. In this chapter we will cover only a few of these switch-style command-line arguments (see Table 4-1). The complete list of command-line switches, along with an explanation of each, is presented in the reference part of this book (Chapter 36, *The Command Line*).

Table 4–1: Some Command-Line Switches

Flag	Description
–b	Set operating mode
–v	Run in verbose mode
–d	Run in debugging mode

---

[*] For now, you can do this only with the system-supplied *sendmail.* It requires a configuration file that we have not yet written for our freshly compiled version.

4.1 Become a Mode (-b)

The *sendmail* program can function in a number of different ways depending on which form of –b argument you use. One form, for example, causes *sendmail* to display the contents of the queue. Another causes *sendmail* to rebuild the *aliases* database. A complete list of the –b command-line mode-setting switches is shown in Table 4-2. We will cover only a few in this chapter and will present the others as this tutorial proceeds.

Table 4–2: Forms of the –b Command-Line Switch

Form	Description
–ba	Use ARPAnet (Grey Book) protocols
–bD	Run as a daemon, but don't fork
–bd	Run as a daemon
–bH	Purge persistent host status
–bh	Print persistent host status
–bi	Rebuild alias database
–bm	Be a mail sender
–bp	Print the queue
–bs	Run SMTP on standard input
–bt	Test mode: resolve addresses only
–bv	Verify: don't collect or deliver
–bz	Freeze the configuration file (obsolete)

The effects of some of the options in Table 4-2 can also be achieved by running the *sendmail* executable using different names. Those names and a description of their results are shown in Table 4-3. Each name can be a hard link with, a symbolic link to, or a copy of *sendmail*.

Table 4–3: Other Names for sendmail

Name	Form	Description
hoststat	–bh	Print persistent host status
mailq	–bp	Display the queue
newaliases	–bi	Initialize alias database
purgestat	–bH	Purge persistent host status
smtpd	–bd	Run as a daemon

4.1.1 Daemon Mode (-bd)

The *sendmail* program can run as a daemon in the background, listening for incoming mail from other machines. The *sendmail* program reads its configuration file only once, when it first starts as a daemon. It then continues to run forever, never reading the configuration file again. As a consequence, it will never see any changes to that configuration file.

When you change something in the *sendmail.cf* configuration file, you *always* need to kill and restart the *sendmail* daemon. But before you can kill the daemon, you need to know how to correctly restart it. This information is in the */etc/sendmail.pid* file or one of your system *rc* files.

On a Berkeley UNIX-based system, for example, the daemon is usually started like this:

```
/usr/lib/sendmail -bd -q1h
```

The **-bd** command-line switch specifies daemon mode. The **-q** switch tells *sendmail* how often to look in its queue to process pending mail. The **-q1h** switch says to process the queue at one (1) hour (h) intervals.

The actual command to start the *sendmail* daemon on your system may be different from what we've shown. If you manage many different brands of systems, you'll need to know how to start the daemon on all of them.

4.1.1.1 Kill and restart, beginning with V8.7

Killing and restarting the *sendmail* daemon became easier beginning with V8.7. A single command[*] will kill and restart the daemon:

```
% kill -HUP `head -1 /etc/sendmail.pid`
```

This single command has the same effect as the two commands shown for V8.6 below.

4.1.1.2 Kill and restart, with V8.6

Before you can start the *sendmail* daemon, you need to make sure there is not a daemon running already. Beginning with V8.6, the *pid* of the currently running daemon is found in the first line of the */etc/sendmail.pid* file. The processes of killing the daemon looks like this:

```
% kill `head -1 /etc/sendmail.pid`
```

---

[*] Provided that the daemon was originally started with a full pathname.

After killing the currently running daemon, you can start a new daemon with the following simple command:

```
% `tail -1 /etc/sendmail.pid`
```

4.1.1.3 Kill and restart, old versions

Under old versions of *sendmail* you need to use the *ps*(1) program to find the *pid* of the daemon. How you run *ps* is different on BSD UNIX and System V UNIX. For BSD UNIX the command that you use and the output that it produces resemble the following:

```
% ps ax | grep sendmail | grep -v grep
  99    ?  IW    0:07 /usr/lib/sendmail -bd -q1h
% kill 99
```

Here the leftmost number printed by *ps* (the 99) was used to kill the daemon.

For System V-based systems you use different arguments for the *ps* command, and its output differs:

```
% ps -ae | grep sendmail
  99 ?          0:01 sendmail
% kill 99
```

Under old versions of *sendmail* you must look in your system *rc* files for the way to restart *sendmail*. We showed how to find this information in Chapter 3, *The Roles of sendmail* (see §3.4).

4.1.1.4 If you forget to kill the daemon

If you forget to kill the daemon before starting a new one, you may see a stream of messages similar to the following, one printed every 5 seconds (probably to your console window):

```
getrequests: cannot bind: Address already in use
getrequests: cannot bind: Address already in use
getrequests: cannot bind: Address already in use
getrequests: cannot bind: Address already in use
getrequests: cannot bind: Address already in use
getrequests: cannot bind: Address already in use
getrequests: cannot bind: Address already in use
getrequests: cannot bind: Address already in use
getrequests: cannot bind: Address already in use
getrequests: cannot bind: Address already in use
getrequests: cannot bind: Address already in use
opendaemonsocket: server SMTP socket wedged: exiting
```

This shows that the attempt to run a second daemon failed.*

4.1.2 Show Queue Mode (-bp)

The *sendmail* program can also display the contents of its queue directory. It can do this in two ways: by running as a program named *mailq* or by being run as *sendmail* with the **-bp** command-line switch. Whichever way you run it, the contents of the queue directory are printed. If the queue is empty, *sendmail* prints the following:

```
      Mail queue is empty
```

If, on the other hand, there is mail waiting in the queue, the output is far more verbose, possibly containing lines similar to these:

```
                    Mail Queue (1 requests)
--Q-ID--- --Size-- ----Q-Time------ -----------Sender/Recipient-----------
GAA29775*      702 Thu Mar 12 16:51 <you@here.us.edu>
               Deferred: Host fbi.dc.gov is down
                          <george@fbi.dc.gov>
```

Here, the output produced with the **-bp** switch shows that there is only one mail message in the queue. If there were more, each entry would look pretty much the same as this. Each message results in at least two lines of output.

The first line shows details about the message and the sender. The GAA29775 identifies this message in the queue. The * shows that this message is locked and currently being processed. The 702 is the size of the message body in bytes (the size of the df file as mentioned in §3.1.2). The date shows when this message was originally queued. The address shown is the name of the sender.

A second line may appear giving a reason for failure (if there was one). A message may be queued intentionally or because it couldn't be delivered.

The third and possibly subsequent lines show the addresses of the recipients.

The output produced by the **-bp** switch is more fully covered in Chapter 23, *The Queue.*

4.1.3 Rebuild Aliases Mode (-bi)

Because *sendmail* may have to search through thousands of names in the *aliases* file, a version of the file is stored in a separate *dbm*(3) or *db*(3) database format file. The use of a database significantly improves lookup speed.

---

* Note that some multicast-capable versions of UNIX allow multiple *sendmail* daemons to run simultaneously. This is a known bug in the SO_REUSEADDR *ioctl*(2) call for TCP under multicasting. Contact your vendor for a fix.

Although *sendmail* can automatically update the database whenever the *aliases* file is changed, there will be times when you will want to rebuild it yourself. You do this either by running *sendmail* using the command *newaliases* or with the **-bi** command-line switch. The following two commands do the same thing:

```
% newaliases
% /usr/lib/sendmail -bi
```

There will be a delay while *sendmail* rebuilds the *aliases* database; then a summary of what it did is printed:

```
/etc/aliases: 859 aliases, longest 615 bytes, 28096 bytes total
```

This line shows that the database was successfully rebuilt. Beginning with V8.6 *sendmail*, multiple alias files became possible, so each line (and there might be many) begins with the name of an alias file. The information then displayed is the number of aliases processed, the size of the biggest entry to the right of the : in the *aliases* file, and the total number of bytes entered into the database. Any mistakes in an alias file will also be printed here.

The *aliases* file and how to manipulate it are covered in Chapter 24, *Aliases*.

4.1.4 Verify Mode (-bv)

A handy tool for checking aliases is the **-bv** command-line switch. It causes *sendmail* to recursively look up an alias and report the ultimate real name that it found.

To illustrate, consider the following *aliases* file:

```
animals:       farmanimals,wildanimals
bill-eats:     redmeat
birds:         farmbirds,wildbirds
bob-eats:      seafood,whitemeat
farmanimals:   pig,cow
farmbirds:     chicken,turkey
fish:          cod,tuna
redmeat:       animals
seafood:       fish,shellfish
shellfish:     crab,lobster
ted-eats:      bob-eats,bill-eats
whitemeat:     birds
wildanimals:   deer,boar
wildbirds:     quail
```

Although you can figure out what the name **ted-eats** ultimately expands to, it is far easier to have *sendmail* do it for you. By using *sendmail*, you have the added advantage of being assured accuracy, which is especially important in large and complex *aliases* files.

In addition to expanding aliases, the **-bv** switch performs another important function. It verifies whether or not the expanded aliases are in fact deliverable. Consider the following one-line *aliases* file:

```
root:        fred,larry
```

Assume that the user **fred** is the system administrator and has an account on the local machine. The user **larry**, however, has left, and his account has been removed. You can run *sendmail* with the **-bv** switch to find out whether both names are valid:

```
% /usr/lib/sendmail -bv root
```

This tells *sendmail* to verify the name **root** from the *aliases* file. Since **larry** (one of **root**'s aliases) doesn't exist, the output produced looks like this:

```
larry... User unknown
fred... deliverable: mailer local, user fred
```

4.2 Verbose (-v)

The **-v** command-line switch tells *sendmail* to run in *verbose* mode. In that mode, *sendmail* prints a blow-by-blow[*] description of all the steps it takes in delivering a mail message. To watch *sendmail* run in verbose mode, send mail to yourself as you did in §1.4, but this time add a **-v** switch:

```
% /usr/lib/sendmail -v you < sendstuff
```

The output produced shows that *sendmail* delivers your mail locally:

```
you... Connecting to local...
you... Sent
```

When *sendmail* forwards mail to another machine over a TCP/IP network, it communicates with that other machine using a protocol called SMTP (Simple Mail Transfer Protocol). To see what SMTP looks like, run *sendmail* again, but this time, instead of using *you* as the recipient, give *sendmail* your address on another machine.

```
% /usr/lib/sendmail -v you@remote.domain < sendstuff
```

The output produced by this command line will look similar to the following:

```
you@remote.domain... Connecting to remote.domain via smtp...
220-remote.Domain Sendmail 8.6.12/8.5 ready at Fri, 13 Dec 1996 06:36:12 -0800
220 ESMTP spoken here
>>> EHLO here.us.edu
```

---

[*] Verbose mode is actually far more powerful than we've shown here.

```
250-remote.domain Hello here.us.edu, pleased to meet you
250-EXPN
250-SIZE
250 HELP
>>> MAIL From:<you@here.us.edu>
250 <you@here.us.edu>... Sender ok
>>> RCPT To:<you@remote.domain>
250 <you@remote.domain>... Recipient ok
>>> DATA
354 Enter mail, end with "." on a line by itself
>>> .
250 GAA20115 Message accepted for delivery
you@remote.domain... Sent (GAA20115 Message accepted for delivery)
Closing connection to remote.domain
>>> QUIT
221 remote.domain closing connection
```

The lines that begin with numbers and the lines that begin with >>> characters constitute a record of the SMTP conversation. We'll discuss those shortly. The other lines are *sendmail* on your local machine telling you what it is trying to do and what it has successfully done:

```
you@remote.domain... Connecting to remote.domain via smtp...
...
you@remote.domain... Sent (GAA20115 Message accepted for delivery)
Closing connection to remote.domain
```

The first line shows to whom the mail is addressed and that the machine remote.domain is on the network. The last two lines show that the mail message was successfully sent.

In the SMTP conversation your local machine displays what it is saying to the remote host by preceding each line with >>> characters. The messages (replies) from the remote machine are displayed with leading numbers. We now explain that conversation.

```
220-remote.Domain Sendmail 8.6.12/8.5 ready at Fri, 13 Dec 1996 06:36:12 -0800
220 ESMTP spoken here
```

Once your *sendmail* has connected to the remote machine, your *sendmail* waits for the other machine to initiate the conversation. The other machine says that it is ready by sending the number 220, a dash (to say that it has more to say), and its fully qualified hostname (the only required information). If the other machine is running *sendmail*, it also says the program name *sendmail* and the version. It also states that it is ready and gives its idea of the local date and time.

The second line also starts with a 220, but that 220 is not followed by a dash. A dash means that more lines will follow, and the absence of a dash means that this is the last line. The "ESMTP spoken here" means that the remote site understands the Extended SMTP protocol. If the other machine were running V8.7 or later *sendmail*, the ESMTP would precede `Sendmail` in the first line, and there would be no second line.

If *sendmail* waits too long for a connection without receiving this initial message, it prints "Connection timed out" and queues the mail message for later delivery.

Next the local *sendmail* sends (the >>>) the word `EHLO`, for Extended Hello, and its own hostname:

```
>>> EHLO here.us.edu
250-remote.domain Hello here.us.edu, pleased to meet you
250-EXPN
250-SIZE
250 HELP
```

The `E` of the `EHLO` says that the local *sendmail* speaks ESMTP too. The remote machine replies with 250 and the acknowledgment that your hostname is acceptable, then lists the ESMTP services that it supports.

One problem that could occur is your machine sending a short hostname ("here") in the `EHLO` message. This would cause an error because the remote machine wouldn't find `here` in its domain `remote.domain`. This is one reason why it is important for your *sendmail* to always use your machine's fully qualified hostname. A fully qualified name is one that begins with the host's name, followed by a dot, then the entire DNS domain.

If all has gone well so far, the local machine sends the name of the sender of the mail message:

```
>>> MAIL From:<you@here.us.edu>
250 <you@here.us.edu>... Sender ok
```

Here, that sender address was accepted by the remote machine.

Next the local machine sends the name of the recipient:

```
>>> RCPT To:<you@remote.domain>
250 <you@remote.domain>... Recipient ok
```

If the user `you` were not known on the remote machine, it would reply with an error of "User unknown." Here, the recipient is `ok`. Note that `ok` does not necessarily mean that the address is good. It can still be bounced later. The `ok` means only that the address is acceptable.

After the envelope information has been sent, your *sendmail* attempts to send the mail message (header and body combined).

```
>>> DATA
354 Enter mail, end with "." on a line by itself
>>> .
```

DATA tells the remote host to "get ready." The remote machine says to send the message, and the local machine does so. (The message is not printed as it is sent.) A dot on a line by itself is used to mark the end of a mail message. This is a convention of the SMTP protocol. Because mail messages may contain lines that begin with dots as a valid part of the message, *sendmail* doubles any dots at the beginning of lines before they are sent.[*] For example, consider when the following text is sent through the mail:

```
My results matched yours at first:
126.71
126.72
...
126.79
But then the numbers suddenly jumped high, looking like
noise saturated the line.
```

To prevent any of these lines from being wrongly interpreted as the end of the mail message, *sendmail* inserts an extra dot at the beginning of any line that begins with a dot, so the actual text transferred is

```
My results matched yours at first:
126.71
126.72
....                                          ← note extra dot
126.79
But then the numbers suddenly jumped high, looking like
noise saturated the line.
```

The SMTP-server program running at the receiving end (for example, another *sendmail*) strips those extra dots when it receives the message.

The remote *sendmail* shows the queue identification number that it assigned to the mail it accepted:

```
250 GAA20115 Message accepted for delivery
>>> QUIT
221 remote.domain closing connection
```

The local *sendmail* sends QUIT to say it is all done. The remote machine acknowledges by closing the connection.

Note that the –v (verbose) switch for *sendmail* is most useful with mail sent to remote machines. It allows you to watch SMTP conversations as they occur and can help in tracking down why a mail message fails to reach its destination.

---

[*] This is called the "hidden dot algorithm" and is documented in RFC821.

4.3 Debugging (-d)

The *sendmail* program can also produce *debugging* output. The *sendmail* program is placed in debugging mode by using the –d command-line switch. That switch produces far more information than –v. To see for yourself, enter the following command line, but substitute your own login name in place of the *you*:

```
% /usr/lib/sendmail -d you < /dev/null
```

This command line produces a great deal of output. We won't explain this output, because it is explained in Chapter 37, *Debugging with –d*. For now just remember that the *sendmail* program's debugging output can produce a great deal of information.

In addition to producing lots of debugging information, the –d switch can be modified to display specific debugging information. By adding a numeric argument to the –d switch, output can be limited to one specific aspect of the *sendmail* program's behavior.

Type in this command line, but change *you* to your own login name.

```
% /usr/lib/sendmail -d40 you < /dev/null
```

Here, the –d40 is the debugging switch with a category of 40. That category limits *sendmail*'s program output to information about the queue. The following output shows you some information about how your mail message was queued. A detailed explanation of this output is covered in §37.5.138.

```
>>>>> queueing GAA14008 (new id) queueall=1 >>>>>
queueing 95688=you:
        mailer 4 (local), host `'
        user `you', ruser `<null>'
        next=0, alias 95460, uid 0, gid 0
        flags=6008<QPRIMARY,QPINGONFAILURE,QPINGONDELAY>
        owner=(none), home="/home/you", fullname="Your FullName"
        orcpt="(none)", statmta=(none), rstatus=(none)
<<<<< done queueing GAA14008 <<<<<
```

In addition to a category, a *level* may also be specified. The level adjusts the amount of output produced. A low level produces little output; a high level produces greater and more complex output. The string following the –d has the form

```
category.level
```

For example, enter the following command line:

```
% /usr/lib/sendmail -d0.1 -bp
```

The –d0 instructs *sendmail* to produce general debugging information. The level .1 limits *sendmail* to its minimal output. That level could have been omitted, because a level `.1` is the default. Recall that **-bp** causes *sendmail* to print the contents of its queue. The output produced looks something like the following:

```
Version 8.8.4
 Compiled with: LOG NAMED_BIND NDBM NETINET NETUNIX NIS SCANF
                XDEBUG

============ SYSTEM IDENTITY (after readcf) ============
      (short domain name) $w = here
  (canonical domain name) $j = here.us.edu
         (subdomain name) $m = us.edu
             (node name) $k = here
========================================================

Mail queue is empty
```

Here, the **-d0.1** switch causes *sendmail* to print its version, some information about how it was compiled, and how it interpreted your host (domain) name. Now run the same command line again, but change the level from `.1` to `.11`:

% /usr/lib/sendmail -d0.11 -bp

The increase in the level causes *sendmail* to print more information:

```
Version 8.8.4
  Compiled with: LOG NAMED_BIND NDBM NETINET NETUNIX NIS SCANF
                 XDEBUG
     OS Defines: HASFLOCK HASGETUSERSHELL HASINITGROUPS HASLSTAT
                 HASSETREUID HASSETSID HASSETVBUF HASUNAME IDENTPROTO
                 IP_SRCROUTE
    Config file: /etc/sendmail.cf
       Pid file: /etc/sendmail.pid
 canonical name: here.us.edu
  UUCP nodename: here
         a.k.a.: [123.45.67.89]

============ SYSTEM IDENTITY (after readcf) ============
      (short domain name) $w = here
  (canonical domain name) $j = here.us.edu
         (subdomain name) $m = us.edu
             (node name) $k = here
========================================================

Mail queue is empty
```

4.4 *Things to Try*

- If you have access to two machines, kill the *sendmail* daemon on one, then send mail to that machine from the other using the **-v** (verbose) switch. What does this tell you about why it is important to always restart the daemon after you have killed it? How can you tell that a remote *sendmail* daemon has died?

- Using the –v switch, send mail to yourself. In the message body, include nothing but lines that begin with dots. Does the message get through intact?

- Begin forming the habit of routinely running *mailq* several times per day. Start to learn the many reasons that mail is queued rather than sent.

- Write a shell script that runs *sendmail* with the –bv (verify) switch to determine whether every alias in the *aliases*(5) file is good and print those that aren't. Be sure to filter the output so that good addresses (those marked as deliverable) are not printed.

- Read the online manuals for all the MUAs on your system, such as that for */usr/ucb/Mail*. For which MUAs is it possible to indirectly run *sendmail* in verbose mode? That is, which will pass a –v command-line switch through to *sendmail?*

5

The sendmail.cf File

The lines of text in a *sendmail.cf* file have been described by some as resembling modem noise and by others as resembling Mr. Dithers swearing in the comic strip *Blondie*.

```
R$+@$=W        ← sendmail.cf file
{$/{{.+        ← modem noise
!@#!@@!        ← Mr. Dithers swearing
```

Constructs like the following can certainly be intimidating to the newcomer:

```
R$+@$=W        $@$1@$H        user@thishost -> user@hub
R$=W!$+        $@$2@$H        thishost!user -> user@hub
R@$=W:$+       $@@$H:$2       @thishost:something
R$+%$=W        $@$>3$1@$2     user%thishost
```

But think back to your early days of C programming. Did you feel any more comfortable with an expression like this?

```
#define getc(p)   (--(p)->_cnt>=0? ((int)*(p)->_ptr++):_filbuf(p))
```

Like any new language, learning the language that is used in the *sendmail.cf* file requires time and practice. In the chapters that follow, we introduce that language, but first we present an overview of the *sendmail.cf* file.

5.1 Overview

The *sendmail.cf* file is read and parsed by *sendmail* every time *sendmail* starts. It contains information that is necessary for *sendmail* to run. It lists the locations of important files and specifies the default permissions for those files. It contains options that modify *sendmail*'s behavior. Most important, it contains rules and rule sets for rewriting addresses.

The *sendmail.cf* configuration file is line-oriented. A configuration command, composed of a single letter, begins each line:

```
V7                      ← good
  V7                    ← bad, does not begin a line
V7 Fw/etc/mxhosts       ← bad, two commands on one line
Fw/etc/mxhosts          ← good
```

Each configuration command is followed by parameters that are specific to it. For example, the V command is followed by a number, whereas the F command is followed by the letter w, then the full pathname of a file. The complete list of configuration commands[*] is shown in Table 5-1.

Table 5–1: The sendmail.cf File's Configuration Commands

Command	Description
V	Define configuration file version (beginning with V8.6)
M	Define a mail delivery agent
D	Define a macro
R	Define a rewriting rule
S	Declare a rule-set start
C	Define a class macro
F	Define a class macro from a file or a pipe
O	Define an option
H	Define a header
P	Define delivery priorities
T	Declare trusted users (ignored in V8.1, back in V8.7)
K	Declare a keyed database (beginning with V8.1)
E	Define an environment variable (beginning with V8.7)
L	Include extended load average support (contributed software, not covered)

Some commands, such as V should appear only once in your *sendmail.cf* file. Others, such as R, may appear often.

Blank lines and lines that begin with the # character are considered comments and are ignored. A line that begins with either a tab or a space character is a continuation of the preceding line:

```
# a comment
V7
        /Berkeley   ← continuation of V line above
  ↑
  tab
```

---

[*] Note that other versions of *sendmail*, such as Sun or IDA, may have more, fewer, or different commands. We don't document those other versions in this book.

Note that anything other than a command, a blank line, a space, a tab, or a # character causes an error. If the *sendmail* program finds such a character, it prints the following warning, ignores that line, and continues to read the configuration file:

```
sendmail.cf: line 15: unknown control line "v6"
```

Here, *sendmail* found a line in its *sendmail.cf* file that began with the letter **v**. Since a lowercase **v** is not a legal command, *sendmail* printed a warning. The line number in the warning is that of the line in the *sendmail.cf* file that began with the illegal character.

An example of each kind of command is illustrated in the following sections. They are actual commands that you will see described throughout this tutorial. Don't be concerned if you don't understand the details at this time. All that is now mysterious will eventually become clear.

5.2   The Minimal File

The smallest possible configuration file contains absolutely nothing. Create an empty configuration file by copying */dev/null* to it:

```
% cp /dev/null client.cf
```

This is the configuration file that we will continue to develop throughout this tutorial. We call it *client.cf* to avoid the possibility of overwriting the system *sendmail.cf* file.

Now run *sendmail* to test the validity of this new file:

```
% ./sendmail -Cclient.cf -bt < /dev/null
%
```

The **–C** command line switch tells *sendmail* to use your (empty) configuration file in place of the system configuration file. The **–bt** switch tells *sendmail* to run in rule-testing mode (which we will use frequently in the chapters to follow). Notice that *sendmail* reads your empty configuration file, runs, and exits without complaint. Also notice that you can now begin to run the version of *sendmail* that you compiled in Chapter 2, *Have a V8*. You couldn't run it before because you lacked a configuration file, but now you have one (although it contains nothing useful).

5.2.1   Version

To prevent older versions of *sendmail* from breaking when reading new style *sendmail.cf* files, a **V** (for *version*) command was introduced beginning with V8.1. The form for the version command looks like this:

```
V7
```

Edit the *client.cf* file and add this single line. The V must begin the line. The version number that follows must be 7 to enable all the new features of V8.8 *sendmail.cf.* The number 7 indicates that the syntax of the *sendmail.cf* file has undergone seven major changes over the years, the seventh being the current and most recent. The meaning of each version is detailed in §27.5.

5.2.2 Comments

Comments can help other people to understand your configuration file. They can also remind you about something you might have done months ago. They slow down *sendmail* by only the tiniest amount, so don't be afraid to use them. As was mentioned earlier, when the # character begins a line in the *sendmail.cf* file, that entire line is treated as a comment and ignored. For example, the entire following line is ignored by the *sendmail* program:

```
# This is a comment
```

Besides beginning a line, comments can also follow commands.* That is,

```
V7                      # this is another comment
```

Add some comments to your *client.cf* file. It should look something like this:

```
# This is a comment
V7          # this is another comment
```

The *sendmail* program will still read this file without complaint:

```
% ./sendmail -Cclient.cf -bt < /dev/null
%
```

5.3 A Quick Tour

The other commands in a configuration file tend to be more complex than the version command you just saw (so complex, in fact, that whole chapters are dedicated to most of them). Here, we present a quick tour of each command —just enough to give you the flavor of a configuration file but in small enough bites to be easily digested.

5.3.1 Mail Delivery Agents

Recall that the *sendmail* program does not generally deliver mail itself. Instead, it calls other programs to perform that delivery. The M command defines a mail

---

* Before V8 *sendmail*, comments could follow *only* three commands: S (rule set), P (priority), and R (rewriting rule).

delivery agent (a program that delivers the mail). For example, as was previously shown:

```
Mlocal,    P=/bin/mail, F=lsDFMAw5:/|@rmn, S=10, R=20/40,
```

This tells *sendmail* that `local` mail is to be delivered by using the */bin/mail* program. The other parameters in this line are introduced in Chapter 6, *The Mail Hub and Delivery Agents*, and detailed in Chapter 30, *Delivery Agents*.

5.3.2 Macros

The ability to define a value once and then use it in many places makes maintaining your *sendmail.cf* file easier. The D *sendmail.cf* command defines a macro. A macro's name is either a single letter or curly-brace-enclosed multiple characters. It has text as a value. Once defined, that text can be referenced symbolically elsewhere:

```
DRmail.us.edu              ← a single letter
D{REMOTE}mail.us.edu       ← multiple characters (beginning with V8.7)
```

Here, R and {REMOTE} are macro names that have the string `mail.us.edu` as their values. Those values are accessed elsewhere in the *sendmail.cf* file with expressions such as $R and ${REMOTE}. Macros are introduced in Chapter 7, *Macros*, and detailed in Chapter 31, *Defined Macros*.

5.3.3 Rules

At the heart of the *sendmail.cf* file are sequences of rules that rewrite (transform) mail addresses from one form to another. This is necessary chiefly because addresses must conform to many differing standards. The R command is used to define a rewriting rule:

```
R$-      $@ $1 @ $R     user -> user @ remote
```

Mail addresses are compared to the rule on the left ($-). If they match that rule, they are rewritten on the basis of the rule on the right ($@ $1 $@ $R). The text at the far right is a comment (that doesn't require a leading #).

Use of multicharacter macros and # comments can make rules appear a bit less cryptic:

```
R$-                      # If a plain user name
       $@ $1 @ ${REMOTE}    #    append "@" remote host
```

The details of rules like this are more fully explained beginning in Chapter 8, *Addresses and Rules*, and detailed in Chapter 28, *Rules*.

5.3.4 Rule Sets

Because rewriting may require several steps, rules are organized into sets, which can be thought of as subroutines. The S command begins a rule set:

```
S3
```

This particular S command begins rule set 3. Beginning with V8.7 *sendmail,* rule sets can be given symbolic names as well as numbers:

```
SHubset
```

This particular S command begins a rule set named **Hubset**.[*] Named rule sets are automatically assigned numbers by *sendmail.*

All the R commands (rules) that follow an S command belong to that rule set. A rule set ends when another S command appears to define another rule set. Rule sets are introduced in Chapter 8 and detailed in Chapter 29, *Rule Sets.*

5.3.5 Class Macros

There are times when the single text value of a D command (macro definition) is not sufficient. Often, you will want to define a macro to have multiple values and view those values as elements in an array. The C command defines a class macro. A class macro is like an array in that it can hold many items. The name of a class is either a single letter or, beginning with V8.7, a curly-brace-enclosed multicharacter name:

```
CW localhost fontserver            ← a single letter
C{MY_NAMES} localhost fontserver   ← multiple characters (beginning with V8.7)
```

Here, each contains two items: **localhost** and **fontserver**. The value of a class macro is accessed with an expression such as $=W or $={MY_NAMES}. Class macros are introduced in Chapter 12, *Class,* and detailed in Chapter 32, *Class Macros.*

5.3.6 File Class Macros

To make administration easier, it is often convenient to store long or volatile lists of values in a file. The F *sendmail.cf* command defines a file class macro. It is just like the C command above, except that the array values are taken from a file:

```
FW/etc/mynames
F{MY_NAMES}/etc/mynames            ← multiple characters (beginning with V8.7)
```

Here, the file class macros W and {MY_NAMES} obtain their values from the file

---

[*] This is an actual symbolic name that we will use when developing the *client.cf* file (specifically in Chapter 11, *Rule Sets 1 and S=*).

/etc/mynames.

The file class macro can also take its list of values from the output of a program. That form looks like this:

```
FM|/bin/shownames
F{MY_NAMES}|/bin/shownames        ← multiple characters (beginning with V8.7)
```

Here, *sendmail* runs the program `/bin/shownames`. The output of that program is appended to the class macro. File class macros are introduced in Chapter 12, *Class*, and detailed in Chapter 32, *Class Macros*.

5.3.7 Options

Options tell the *sendmail* program many useful and necessary things. They specify the location of key files, set timeouts, and define how *sendmail* will act and how it will dispose of errors. They can be used to tune *sendmail* to meet your particular needs.

The O command is used to set *sendmail* options. An example of the option command looks like this:

```
OQ/var/spool/mqueue
O QueueDirectory= /var/spool/mqueue      ← beginning with V8.7
```

Here, Q option (beginning with V8.7 called `QueueDirectory`) defines the name of the directory in which mail will be queued as */var/spool/mqueue*. Options are introduced in Chapter 13, *Setting Options*, and detailed in Chapter 34, *Options*.

5.3.8 Headers

Mail messages are composed of two parts: a header followed (after a blank line) by the body. The body may contain virtually anything.[*] The header, on the other hand, contains lines of information that must strictly conform to certain standards. The H command is used to specify which mail headers to include in a mail message and how each will look:

```
HReceived: $?sfrom $s $.by $j ($v/$Z)$?r with $r$. id $i$?u for $u$.; $b
```

This particular H command tells *sendmail* that a `Received:` header line must be added to the header of every mail message. Headers are introduced in Chapter 14, *Headers, Precedence, and Trust*, and detailed in Chapter 35, *Headers*.

---

[*] With the advent of MIME (Multipurpose Internet Mail Extensions), the message body can now be composed of many minimessages, each with its own MIME header and sub-body.

5.3.9 *Priority*

Not all mail has the same priority. Mass mailings (to a mailing list, for example) should be transmitted after mail to individual users. The P command sets the beginning priority for a mail message. That priority is used to determine a message's order when the mail queue is processed.

```
Pjunk= -100
```

This particular P command tells *sendmail* that mail with a **Precedence:** header line of junk should be processed last. Priority commands are introduced in Chapter 14 and detailed in Chapter 35.

5.3.10 *Trusted Users*

For some software (such as UUCP) to function correctly, it must be able to tell *sendmail* whom a mail message is from. This is necessary when that software runs as a different user identity (*uid*) than that specified in the **From:** line in the message header. The T *sendmail.cf* command[*] lists those users that are *trusted* to override the **From:** address in a mail message. All other users have a warning included in the mail message header.

```
Troot daemon uucp
```

This particular T *sendmail.cf* command says that there are three users who are to be considered trusted. They are *root* (who is a god under UNIX), *daemon* (*sendmail* usually runs as the pseudo-user *daemon*), and *uucp* (necessary for UUCP software to work properly). Trusted users are introduced in Chapter 14 and detailed in Chapter 22, *Security*.

5.3.11 *Keyed Databases*

Certain information, such as a list of UUCP hosts, is better maintained outside of the *sendmail.cf* file. External databases (called *keyed* databases) provide faster access to such information. Keyed databases were introduced with V8.6 and come in several forms, the nature and location of which are declared with the K configuration command:

```
Kuucp hash /etc/mail/uucphosts
```

This particular K command declares a database with the symbolic name uucp, with the type hash, located in */etc/mail/uucphosts*. The K command is detailed and the types of databases are explained, in Chapter 33, *Database Macros*.

---

[*] The T command was ignored from versions V8.1 through V8.6 and restored under V8.7. With V8.7 it is actually implemented as the class $=t.

5.3.12 Environment variables

The *sendmail* program is ultraparanoid about security. One way to circumvent security with *suid* programs like *sendmail* is by running them with bogus environmental variables. To prevent such an end run, V8 *sendmail* erases all its environment variables when it starts. It then presets the values for a small set of variables (such as TZ and SYSTYPE). This small, safe environment is then passed to its delivery agents. Beginning with V8.7 *sendmail*, sites that wish to augment this list may do so with the E configuration command.

```
EPOSTGRESHOME=/home/postgres
```

Here, the environment variable POSTGRESHOME is assigned the value */home/postgres*. This allows programs to use the *postgres*(1) database to access information. The E command is detailed in Chapter 22.

5.4 Things to Try

- Examine the *sendmail.cf* file on your system. Although you don't yet know what any of it does, you should be delightfully surprised to discover that you already know what most of the configuration commands are generally meant to do.

- Determine how your site is organized. Is it arranged to be convenient for users or for the administrator? Are the two necessarily exclusive?

- If you are running a vendor-supplied V8 *sendmail*, the V configuration command may modify how *sendmail* behaves. That is, there may be vendor-specific text following the version number (such as /sun). If so, read your online documentation to find what has been modified.

6

The Mail Hub and Delivery Agents

Instead of having each individual workstation in a network handle its own mail, it can be advantageous to have a powerful central machine that handles all mail. Such a machine is called a *mail hub* and is analogous to the way Federal Express originally handled package delivery. In the old days, when you sent a package via Federal Express from, say, San Francisco to Paris, or even from San Francisco to Los Angeles, that package was first sent to Memphis, Tennessee (see Figure 6-1). The Memphis location was the Federal Express hub. All packages, no matter what their origin or destination, were sent to the hub first and then were transported outward from there.

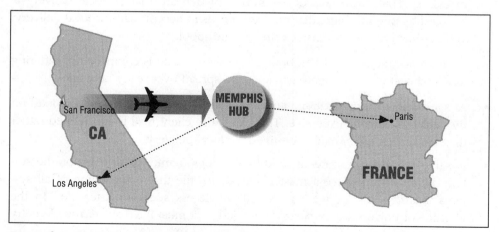

Figure 6–1: The Federal Express hub approach

The advantage to this approach is that the Memphis hub was the only Federal Express office that needed the special knowledge of how to deliver packages anywhere in the world.[*] Local offices needed to know only how to deliver to the hub.

In a similar way, your workstations can be thought of as the outlying offices (client machines) and your central mail-handling machine as the hub. For mail, the hub performs the following functions for the entire site:

- All incoming mail is sent to the hub, meaning that no mail is sent directly to a client machine. This hub approach has several advantages. No client needs to run a *sendmail* daemon to listen for mail. No client's name needs to be known to the outside world, thus insulating client machines for easier security.

- Rather than having each client send its mail directly to the outside world, all outgoing mail from clients is sent to the hub, and the hub then forwards that mail to its ultimate destination. The advantages are that clients do not need to be continually aware of changes in the Internet; deferred mail queues on the hub, not on the client machine, making management simpler; and a single, simple *sendmail.cf* file may be shared by, or distributed to, all the clients.

- All outgoing mail is modified so that it appears to have originated on the hub. The alternative is to have *reply* mail returned directly to each client. The advantages of the hub approach are that all mail appears to come from a single, giant machine (making replying to mail easier).

- All mail to local users is delivered to, and spooled on, the hub. The alternative is to have one or more separate mail spool directories on separate client machines. The advantages of the hub approach are that all local delivery is handled by one machine, that no client needs to accept mail for local delivery, and that management is easier with a single spool.

There are disadvantages to the hub approach when a site is composed of differing machine architectures and when machines are spread over many networks:

- At sites where there is a huge amount of mail constantly flowing, the load on the hub can become excessive. This can cause client mail to be queued rather than sent, even when mail is destined for local delivery.

- For the hub to work, it needs to know the login names of all users on the system. Either it must have a master */etc/passwd* file that is the union of all systems' *passwd* files, or it must use NIS to access such a master file.[†] In the absence of universal user *passwd* knowledge, it must have an *aliases* file entry for every local user.

---

[*] Federal Express now has several regional hubs.

[†] See *Managing NFS and NIS* by Hal Stern (O'Reilly & Associates, 1992).

- Because all mail passes through the hub, rather than being sent to the recipient directly, there are unavoidable delays. Those delays are negligible at small sites (a couple of hundred or so users) but can become significant at sites with a huge number of users.

- If a client machine has direct UUCP connections or is connected to multiple networks, a more complex configuration file is needed.

6.1 The client.cf File

The purpose of this tutorial is to develop a small *sendmail.cf* file for the clients of a hub scheme. As we did in the previous chapter, we will call our file *client.cf*.*
We will be developing it in pieces and examining those pieces individually in the chapters that follow. In this chapter we will begin the process of developing a *client.cf* file from scratch. It will perform only two tasks:

- It will instruct *sendmail* to send all mail to another machine that serves as a mail hub. (Recall that in the hub design, no workstation receives mail, and all mail from clients is sent first to the hub and from there to the outside world.)

- It will make all outgoing mail appear as though it originally came from that hub. (Thus, replies to mail will be delivered to the hub, not to the client.)

In this chapter we tackle the first task: how to get mail from the client machine to the hub.

6.2 Define a Mail Delivery Agent

Other than forwarding mail messages over a TCP/IP network, *sendmail* does not handle mail delivery itself. Instead, it runs other programs that perform delivery (see Figure 6-2). The programs it runs are called *delivery agents*. Information about which agent performs which kind of delivery is defined in the *sendmail.cf* file.

The first item to put in your *client.cf* file is a definition of the program (delivery agent) that forwards mail to the hub machine. That definition provides *sendmail* with the information it needs to deliver mail using that delivery agent. Initially, *sendmail* needs to include only the name and location of that program. Therefore, in its preliminary form, the definition for the mail delivery program looks like this:

```
# This is a comment
V7      # this is another comment
```

---

* The *client.cf* file is a teaching tool. Although it can be used to send mail when it is finished, alternatives presented in Chapter 16, *The null.mc File and m4* are generally more useful. Consequently, we never show the completed *client.cf* file.

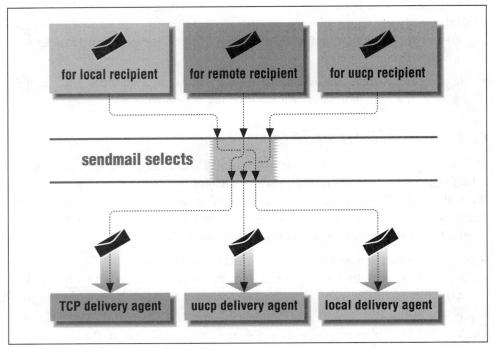

Figure 6–2: The nature of the recipient determines the delivery agent

```
# Delivery agent definition to forward mail to hub          ← new
Mhub, P=[IPC], A=IPC $h                                     ← new
```

This is a minimal (and still useless) configuration file. Go ahead and add these new lines to *client.cf*. The second line is a configuration command that defines a delivery agent. It contains three parts, each separated from the others by commas: a symbolic name and two equates.

Mhub

> The M that begins the line defines a mail delivery agent. The hub immediately following is the symbolic name for the delivery agent. This symbolic name will be referenced by other parts of the configuration file when you write them.

P=[IPC]

> The P= equate stands for Path. This says that the full pathname of the program that is used to handle the delivery is called [IPC]. ([IPC] is a special name used internally by *sendmail* to represent its *internal ability* to communicate over TCP/IP networks. It stands for interprocessor communications). For other mail delivery agent definitions the name following the = would be the full pathname of a program, such as */bin/mail*.

```
A=IPC $h
```

The A= equate stands for Argument vector (list). It is used to specify the command-line arguments that will be given to the P= program when it is run. The zeroth argument is the name of the program (here IPC without brackets). The rest of the arguments, of which there is only one here, the $h, are the actual command-line arguments. The $h is a macro that contains the recipient's hostname. We'll describe macros in the next chapter. The A= equate is traditionally the last item in a delivery agent definition.

6.2.1 Testing the client.cf File

Run *sendmail* with this command line:

```
% /usr/lib/sendmail -oQ/tmp -Cclient.cf -bp
```

Note that you need to include –oQ/tmp in the command line to prevent *sendmail* from trying to change to the *mqueue* directory (which probably doesn't exist under the current directory). If you leave out the –oQ/tmp switch, *sendmail* exits with this confusing error:

```
cannot chdir((null)): Bad file number
```

The –Cclient.cf switch tells *sendmail* to use the file *client.cf* in the current directory as its configuration file, rather than the system */etc/sendmail.cf* file. The –bp switch tells *sendmail* to print the contents of the queue. The above command line should produce output like the following:

```
No local mailer defined
```

The lack of a local mailer is not important yet.* The *sendmail* program prints it and stops but otherwise found no errors in our *client.cf* file.

6.3 The local Delivery Agent

When you ran *sendmail*, it complained that the local delivery agent definition was missing. To keep *sendmail* happy, this definition will now be added to the *client.cf* file. As it happens, it is already in your system *sendmail.cf* file (if you have one), and you can copy it by typing the following command:

```
% grep "^Mlocal" /etc/sendmail.cf >> client.cf
```

---

* A local delivery agent is not required in rule-testing mode (–bt) but is required for all other modes.

Note that the ^M above is actually two characters ^ and M, not a CTRL-M. Now load the *client.cf* file into your editor. It will look something like this:*

```
# This is a comment
V7        # this is another comment
# Delivery agent definition to forward mail to hub
Mhub, P=[IPC], A=IPC $h
Mlocal, P=/bin/mail, F=lsDFMAw5://|@rmn, S=10, R=20/40, A=mail -d $u
```

Right off the bat, you'll notice three new equates† that are a bit more complicated than our original hub equates. This new M configuration command declares a symbolic name, such as hub. Here, that name is local—the name that *sendmail* complained was missing. Although the local definition is important and heavily used in a full-fledged *sendmail.cf* file, the *client.cf* file uses it only to keep *sendmail* from complaining.

The new delivery agent definition is composed of six parts (each separated from the others by commas), a symbolic name and six equates. The F=, S=, and R= equates are new. You've seen the M, P=, and A= before in the hub definition.

M All mail delivery agent definitions begin with the M configuration-file command. Like all configuration commands, that M must begin a line:

```
Mhub,    P=[IPC], A=IPC $h
Mlocal, P=/bin/mail, F=lsDFMAw5://|@rmn, S=10, R=20/40, A=mail -d $u
↑
```
define a delivery agent

The symbolic name for each delivery agent follows the M, with no intervening space. The symbolic names here are hub and local. The delivery agent called hub forwards mail to the central hub machine. The local delivery agent delivers mail to users on the local machine.

P= The P= equate (for Path) specifies the full pathname of mail delivery programs:

```
Mhub,    P=[IPC], A=IPC $h
Mlocal, P=/bin/mail, F=lsDFMAw5://|@rmn, S=10, R=20/40, A=mail -d $u
         ↑
```
full pathname of program

Your program names may differ, but in general, the program for local places a mail message into the local user's mail spool file.

A= The A= equate (for Argument vector) specifies the command-line arguments to be supplied to each mail delivery program.

---

* If any of the equates shown here are missing, you need to type them in by hand.

† You may also find a T= equate. We describe it later in this chapter.

```
Mhub,    P=[IPC], A=IPC $h
Mlocal, P=/bin/mail, F=lsDFMAw5:/|@rmn, S=10, R=20/40, A=mail -d $u
                                                                 ↑
```
command line (argv)

Notice that `local` uses the `$u` macro, whereas `hub` uses the `$h` macro. The `$u` macro contains the name of the recipient (such as *bob*). The `$h` macro contains the name of a host (such as *here.us.edu*). Macros are explained in the next chapter. By convention the `A=` equate is usually last.

Three parts in the new `local` definition were not used in the `hub` definition. They are:

F= The `F=` equate (for Flags) specifies certain flags that tell *sendmail* more about the delivery agent. Each flag is a single character, and each is Boolean—either set (if it is present) or not (if it is absent).

```
Mhub,    P=[IPC], A=IPC $h
Mlocal, P=/bin/mail, F=lsDFMAw5:/|@rmn, S=10, R=20/40, A=mail -d $u
                     ↑
```
flags for delivery agent

There are many flags to choose from. They are all described in Chapter 30, *Delivery Agents*, but we will cover a few of them later in this chapter.

S= The `S=` equate (for Sender) specifies which rule set to use in rewriting the sender's address:

```
Mhub,    P=[IPC], A=IPC $h
Mlocal, P=/bin/mail, F=lsDFMAw5:/|@rmn, S=10, R=20/40, A=mail -d $u
                                        ↑
```
sender rule set

Addresses need to be rewritten because different delivery agents require addresses to be in different forms. For example, the `[IPC]` agent requires the form *user@host.domain*, while the `uucp` agent (if you had need for one) requires the form *host!user*. Here, the `S=` says that addresses should be rewritten by using rule set 10. We will cover rule sets later, in Chapter 8, *Addresses and Rules*.

R= The `R=` equate (for Recipient) specifies which rule set to use in rewriting the recipient's address:

```
Mhub,    P=[IPC], A=IPC $h
Mlocal, P=/bin/mail, F=lsDFMAw5:/|@rmn, S=10, R=20/40, A=mail -d $u
                                               ↑
```
recipient rule set

Again, those addresses need to be rewritten because different delivery agents require different forms of addresses. Here, the `R=` says to use rule set 20 in rewriting an envelope address and rule set 40 in rewriting a header address.

In addition to the three new equates, and beginning with V8.7 *sendmail*, you may discover another new equate in the `local` delivery agent definition:

T= Not shown in our examples is the `T=` equate (for Type), which lists three fields of information about the delivery agent. You will find this equate in configuration files beginning with V8.7 *sendmail*.

> Mlocal, ..., **T=DNS/RFC822/X-Unix**

First is the type of MTA used (here **DNS** because *sendmail* is using DNS to lookup addresses); then a slash followed by the type of addressing used (here **RFC822**, but it could also be, for example, **X.400**); and last a slash followed by the type of error messages produced (here **X-Unix** which says that the program */bin/mail* will produce UNIX errors). The **T=** equate is used to support Delivery Status Notification (DSN) as described in RFC1891, RFC1892, RFC1893, and RFC1894.

6.3.1 Skipping Rule Sets

Because we won't be covering rule sets for a while, and to simplify things for now, edit the *client.cf* file once again and change the **S=** and **R=** equates in the new `local` definition:

```
# Mailer to forward all mail to the hub machine
Mhub,    P=[IPC], A=IPC $h
Mlocal, P=/bin/mail, F=lsDFMAw5:/|@rmn, S=0, R=0, A=mail -d $u
                                        ↑    ↑
                                       new  new
```

Both equates are changed to zero because there are no rule sets yet. When an **S=** or an **R=** equate in a delivery agent definition is zero or missing, *sendmail* skips the delivery-agent-specific part of rule-set processing.

6.3.2 Adding Comments

Comments are an important part of every configuration file. They remind you of what you are trying to do now and what you have done in the past. Edit the *client.cf* file now. Remove two old comments and add a new one:

```
                                        ← removed comment
V7                                      ← removed comment
# Delivery agent definition to forward mail to hub
Mhub,    P=[IPC], A=IPC $h
# Sendmail requires this, but we won't use it.    ← added comment
Mlocal, P=/bin/mail, F=lsDFMAw5:/|@rmn, S=0, R=0, A=mail -d $u
```

We threw away the earlier comments because they were only for demonstration purposes.

6.3.3 Testing the New Delivery Agent Definitions

This time, run *sendmail* differently than you did last time:

```
% /usr/lib/sendmail -d0.15 -Cclient.cf -bt </dev/null
```

The –d0.15 debugging switch tells *sendmail* (among other things) to show you how it interpreted your delivery agent definitions. The –bt causes *sendmail* to run in rule-testing mode so that the delivery agents will be displayed. Running the above command line produces output like the following (but with long lines unattractively wrapped at the right-hand margin):

```
←assorted other information here and above
mailer 0 (prog): P=/bin/sh S=0/0 R=0/0 M=0 U=0:0 F=Dlos L=0 E=\n T=DNS/RFC822/X-U
nix A=sh -c $u
mailer 1 (*file*): P=[FILE] S=0/0 R=0/0 M=0 U=0:0 F=DEFMPlosu L=0 E=\n T=DNS/RFC8
22/X-Unix A=FILE
mailer 2 (*include*): P=/dev/null S=0/0 R=0/0 M=0 U=0:0 F=su L=0 E=\n T=<undefine
d>/<undefined>/<undefined> A=INCLUDE
mailer 3 (hub): P=[IPC] S=0/0 R=0/0 M=0 U=0:0 F= L=0 E=\n T=<undefined>/<undefine
d>/<undefined> A=IPC $h
mailer 4 (local): P=/bin/mail S=0/0 R=0/0 M=0 U=0:0 F=/5:@ADFMlmnrsw| L=0 E=\n T=
<undefined>/<undefined>/<undefined> A=mail -d $u
```

This output, in addition to verifying that *sendmail* properly interpreted the *client.cf* file, reveals four equates you haven't seen before: M=, U=, L=, and E=. We won't explain them here, because you don't need them for the *client.cf* file. They are explained in detail in Chapter 30.

In the preceding output, also note that there are several equates that were not included in the original **Mhub** delivery agent definition. The **hub** definition included only the P= and A= equates:

```
Mhub,    P=[IPC], A=IPC $h
```

When *sendmail* saw this definition, it did not find specifications for any of the equates other than A= and P=. Rather than complaining, it gave E= the value of the newline character (\n), T= three instances of <undefined>, and the other equates each a value of zero:

```
mailer 3 (hub): P=[IPC] S=0/0 R=0/0 M=0 U=0:0 F= L=0 E=\n T=<undefined>/<undefine
d>/<undefined> A=IPC $h
```

Note that when the F= equate has a zero value, it is displayed as an empty list of flags.

6.4 Add the Missing Parts to Mhub

The final step in creating the hub mail delivery agent definition is to fill in its missing F=, S=, R=, and T= equates.

Edit the *client.cf* file again and add the new parts shown below to the Mhub definition:

```
# Delivery agent definition to forward mail to hub
Mhub,    P=[IPC], S=0, R=0, F=mDFMuXa, T=DNS/RFC822/SMTP, A=IPC $h
                  ↑    ↑    ↑           ↑
                  new  new  new         new
```

Here, the S= and R= equates are given a value of zero. The S= equate specifies the sender-rewriting rule set. The R= equate specifies the recipient-rewriting rule set. Because there are no rule sets yet, these equates are set to zero. You will be giving them real rule-set numbers when we begin to cover rule sets in Chapter 8.

The T= is the same as the T= in local except that instead of expecting UNIX errors, we will expect SMTP errors because we will be speaking SMTP to the hub. More about this later.

The flags listed in the F=mDFMuXa equate of the hub definition are typical of those generally used in [IPC] delivery agent definitions. You may want to change these depending on your needs. All the available flags are listed in Chapter 30. The ones we selected are summarized in Table 6-1.

Table 6-1: The hub Delivery Agent's F= Flags

Flag	Description
m	This agent can deliver to more than one user at a time.
D	Include a Date: in the header (if one is not present).
F	Include a From: in the header (if one is not present).
M	Include a Message-ID: in the header (if one is not present).
u	Preserve the case of the recipient name.
X	Pass lone dots on a line by doubling them.
a	Run extended SMTP protocol

The mailer delivery agent definitions are now roughed out. Remember that the symbolic name (hub or local) is the only part of these definitions that will be referenced in later rule sets. Also notice that the last equate of each definition, the A= command-line equate, ends with a macro ($h or $u). We cover macros in the next chapter.

6.5 *Things to Try*

- Create a mail delivery agent definition that has no symbolic name or one that has what you suspect is an illegal name. What happens when you run *send-mail* with the −d0.15 command-line argument?

- Define two different mail delivery agents that have the same symbolic name. Does *sendmail* catch the error, or does it replace the first with the second?

- Make a typo in one of the equates. For example, instead of S=6, enter s=6. What happens?

- The P= equate is used to state the full pathname of the program that delivers the mail message. Since the parts are separated from each other by commas, is it possible to include a comma in that pathname? If so, how? Use −d0.15 to test your proposals.

- What happens if the program shown in the P= equate does not exist or if that program is not executable? Is this detected by *sendmail* when the *sendmail.cf* file is read?

- The A= equate specifies the command-line arguments that are given to the P= program when it is run. Can you include commas in those command-line arguments?

- When a line in the *sendmail.cf* file begins with a space or tab character, it is joined (appended) to the line above it. Try splitting delivery agents over multiple lines for readability using this mechanism. Test the result with the −d0.15 debugging switch (review §6.2.1).

```
Mhub,              # Delivery agent definition to forward mail to hub
    P=[IPC],       #  use SMTP over the network
    S=0,           #  no sender rewriting
    R=0,           #  no recipient rewriting
    F=m,           #  flag: deliver to more than one user at a time
    F=D,           #  flag: include Date: in the header
    F=F,           #  flag: include From: in the header
    F=M,           #  flag: include Message-ID: in the header
    F=u,           #  flag: preserve the case of the recipient name
    F=X,           #  flag: pass lone dots on a line by doubling
    F=a,           #  flag: run extended SMTP protocol
    T=DNS/RFC822/SMTP,
    A=IPC $h
```

- Gather all of the lines in your system's current *sendmail.cf* file that define mail delivery agents. In each of the lines printed, you will see one field that declares the full path of a mail delivery program. For each of those P= fields, locate and read the online manual page for the program specified. Do the arguments in the A= field make sense to you?

In this chapter:
- *Overview*
- *Defining Macros*
- *Predefined Macros*
- *Things to Try*

7

Macros

One of the major strengths of the *sendmail.cf* file is that it allows text to be referenced symbolically. This is very similar to how variables in the Bourne and C shells are used:

```
REMOTE=mailhost          ← Bourne shell
set REMOTE=mailhost      ← C shell
D{REMOTE}mailhost        ← sendmail.cf file
```

The statements above all cause a variable with the name **REMOTE** to be assigned the value `mailhost`.

The expression for using (referencing) the value stored in **REMOTE** is similar for all three:

```
$REMOTE                  ← Bourne shell
$REMOTE                  ← C shell
${REMOTE}                ← sendmail.cf file
```

That is, all of the above expressions yield the value stored in **REMOTE**, in this case the text `mailhost`. Once you define the value of **REMOTE** as `mailhost`, you can use the expression `${REMOTE}` anywhere you need to use the text `mailhost`.

7.1 Overview

Macros can greatly simplify your work. They allow you to represent text symbolically and to define it in one central place. Changes in that text are automatically propagated to the rest of the file. For example, consider the following definition in your *sendmail.cf* file:

```
D{REMOTE}mailhost
```

If you use the expression ${REMOTE} anywhere in that file, a single change to the definition of D{REMOTE}mailhost changes the value of ${REMOTE} throughout the entire file.

Here is the format for defining macros:

    DXtext

The letter D must begin the line. The D is immediately followed by the name of the macro, here X, with no intervening space. The name is then followed (again with no intervening space) by the text (value) for the macro's definition. The value is all the text up to the end of the line.[*]

Macros may have single-character names or multicharacter names. Multicharacter names *must* always be enclosed in curly braces. Single-character names *may* be enclosed in curly braces if you desire. Prior to V8.7 you could use single characters only without curly braces.

    DRmailhost   ← *single-character name (prior to V8.7)*
    D{R}mailhost   ← *same beginning with V8.7*
    D{REMOTE}mailhost   ← *multicharacter name (beginning with V8.7)*

Except for header and delivery agent configuration commands,[†] macros, in general, are expanded (the text replaces the symbol) when the configuration file is read. Consequently, you must define them *before* you use them:

    D{ROLE}son
    S${ROLE}   ← *use the text value "son"*
    D{ROLE}mother
    S${ROLE}   ← *use the text value "mother"*

Here, ROLE was first given the value son. When the first S command is processed, *sendmail* replaces the expression ${ROLE} with its current value to form

    Sson

Then ROLE is redefined and given a different value, that of mother. The second S command is processed, and its ${ROLE} is replaced with the new value:

    Smother

Please note that this is very bad style. In general, each macro should be defined only once to avoid confusion.

---

[*] Trailing whitespace is automatically stripped in V8.7 but not in earlier versions. Leading whitespace is not, so the D, name, and text must be right smack against each other.

[†] And configuration commands for which macros make no sense and are ignored.

7.2 *Defining Macros*

In the previous chapter you roughed out delivery agent definitions for the hub and local delivery agents. Notice that the last part of each, the A= command-line part, ended with a macro:

```
V7
# Delivery agent definition to forward mail to hub
Mhub,   P=[IPC], S=0, R=0, F=mDFMuXa, T=DNS/RFC822/SMTP, A=IPC $h
# Sendmail requires this, but we won't use it.
Mlocal, P=/bin/mail, F=lsDFMAw5:/|@rmn, S=0, R=0, A=mail -d $u
                                                             ↑
                                                          macros
```

There are two kinds of macros: those that you define and those that *sendmail* defines. Macros that begin with uppercase letters, such as R and {REMOTE}, are ones that you optionally define. Those that begin with a lowercase letter, such as h and u, are ones that *sendmail* either defines or requires you to define.

You have already seen an example of an uppercase macro:

```
D{REMOTE}mailhost
```

This gives the macro named {REMOTE} the value mailhost.

Somewhere on your network, there may be a machine whose alias is *mailhost* or something similar, such as *mailrelay*. This is the alias of the machine that serves your site's mail hub. If no such alias exists, you must use an actual machine name (such as *mail.us.edu*). Now edit *client.cf*, and add your first macro, {REMOTE}:

```
V7  .
# Defined macros                                        ← new
D{REMOTE}mailhost          # The name of the mail hub    ← new
                                                         ← new
# Delivery agent definition to forward mail to hub
Mhub,   P=[IPC], S=0, R=0, F=mDFMuXa, T=DNS/RFC822/SMTP, A=IPC $h
# Sendmail requires this, but we won't use it.
Mlocal, P=/bin/mail, F=lsDFMAw5:/|@rmn, S=0, R=0, A=mail -d $u
```

Here, three new lines have been added to the *client.cf* file. The first is a comment, and the third is a blank line to visually separate macro definitions from delivery agent definitions. The second line is the new macro definition. As the comment says, this {REMOTE} macro will contain as its value the name of the host to which all mail will be forwarded.

Take a moment to test this new version of the *client.cf* file:

```
% ./sendmail -Cclient.cf -bt </dev/null
```

The *sendmail* program reads and parses the *client.cf* file. There are no errors in the *client.cf* file, so *sendmail* prints no error messages.

7.3 Predefined Macros

The *sendmail* program internally defines many macros for you. You have already seen u (which contains the recipient's username) and h (which contains the recipient's hostname) in our delivery agent definitions. They are given values by *sendmail* instead of being given values with D macro definitions in your configuration file. A short list of some of the more common predefined macros is shown in Table 7-1.

Table 7-1: Some Predefined Macros

Macro	Description
n	Identity of the error message sender
v	Version of the currently running *sendmail*
w	The short hostname
j	The canonical hostname
m	The domain name
k	The UUCP node name
b	Date in RFC1123 format
_	Identification information
opMode	Current operating mode (beginning with V8.7)

To watch the processing of all the macro definitions, run *sendmail* once again. This time, add a –d35.9 debugging switch, which tells *sendmail* to print each macro as it is defined:

```
% ./sendmail -d35.9 -Cclient.cf -bt < /dev/null
```

The output that is produced is surprisingly long, considering the small size of the *client.cf* file:

```
define(* as $*)
define(+ as $+)
define(- as $-)
define(= as $=)
define(~ as $~)
define(# as $#)
define(@ as $@)
define(: as $:)
define(> as $>)
define(? as $?)
define(| as $|)
define(. as $.)
define([ as $[)
define(] as $])
define(( as $()
define() as $))
define(& as $&)
define(0 as $0)
```

```
define(1 as $1)
define(2 as $2)
define(3 as $3)
define(4 as $4)
define(5 as $5)
define(6 as $6)
define(7 as $7)
define(8 as $8)
define(9 as $9)
define(n as MAILER-DAEMON)                          ← note
define(v as 8.8.4)                                  ← note
define(w as here.us.edu)                            ← note
define(j as here.us.edu)                            ← note
define(m as us.edu)                                 ← note
define(k as here)                                   ← note
define(b as Fri, 13 Dec 1996 07:11:47 -0700 (PDT)) ← note
define(_ as you@localhost)                          ← note
define(opMode as t)                                 ← note
redefine(w as here)                                 ← note
define(REMOTE as mailhost)                          ← note
```

This output will differ from version to version. For example, 1, o, and e were macros prior to V8.7 but, beginning with V8.7, are now options. The first 27 lines of this output show *sendmail* reserving macro names that will be used as operators. (Operators are introduced in the next chapter.) The last 11 definitions are the only ones we are interested in for now. The first 10 of those are internally defined by *sendmail* for your use. The last definition is caused by *sendmail* processing the D{REMOTE}mailhost line in the *client.cf* file.

This output demonstrates another concept. Some internal macros are defined before the configuration file is read, so you can change them from inside your *client.cf* file. To change w, for example, you might place the following into your configuration file:

```
Dwmyhost.my.domain
```

Doing this would then cause the text myhost.my.domain to replace the text here.us.edu as the value of the macro named w.

Note that in the preceding output there were no definitions for the h and u macros used in the delivery agent definitions. These macros, although internally defined, are not actually given values until mail is sent. You cannot change their values from within your configuration file, because they are not defined until after the configuration file is read.

Finally, note that proper defaults are set only by V8 *sendmail*. All older versions require you to manually provide defaults for the e, 1, n, o, and q macros in your *client.cf* file.

7.3.1 The hostname

The name of your local machine is composed of two parts. The host part is the machine name and never contains a dot (such as *here*). The domain part is composed of at least two parts separated from each other by dots (such as *us.edu*). The *fully qualified* name of your local machine is made by specifying the host part, then a dot, and finally the domain part (e.g., *here.us.edu*). The machine's name needs to be fully qualified to uniquely identify it worldwide.

The name of the local machine also needs to be *canonical* (official and fully qualified). A machine can have multiple names (such as *mailhost* or *printserver*), of which only one is official. The official name for the local machine can be found by issuing the *hostname*(1) command:

```
% hostname
here.us.edu
```

The official name, when fully qualified with a domain, is the *canonical* name of the machine. Any other names are aliases.[*]

To see how *sendmail* interprets your local hostname, enter the following command, which uses the -d0.1 debugging switch:

```
% ./sendmail -Cclient.cf -d0.1 -bt </dev/null
Version 8.8.4
 Compiled with: LOG NAMED_BIND NDBM NETINET NETUNIX NIS SCANF XDEBUG

============ SYSTEM IDENTITY (after readcf) ============
      (short domain name) $w = here
  (canonical domain name) $j = here.us.edu
        (subdomain name) $m = us.edu
             (node name) $k = here

========================================================
```

Many things can go wrong here. For example, if you're not on the Internet, you may not have assigned your machine a domain name yet. Or you may be running NIS and have listed only the short name in the *hosts.byname* map. The important thing to observe in the above output is that *sendmail* correctly found your short and canonical names:

```
      (short domain name) $w = here          ← short hostname
  (canonical domain name) $j = here.us.edu   ← fully qualified canonical name
        (subdomain name) $m = us.edu         ← domain
```

If any are wrong, you need to fix the system problem that led to the error. At the system level, investigate:

---

[*] We are fudging for simplicity. The canonical name is the name associated with the DNS A record. If a machine has multiple network interfaces (and therefore multiple A records), it can have multiple canonical names.

- The */etc/hosts* file. You may have wrongly listed only short names in it. Prior to V8.7, a fully qualified name had to be listed first. Beginning with V8.7, a fully qualified name can appear anywhere in a line.

- The *nis* maps. Make sure hostnames are looked up with DNS by specifying the –b in */var/yp/Makefile*.

- The *nsswitch.conf* or *svc.conf* files. Make sure the method used to look up hosts is correctly specified.

If you can't find or don't have permission to fix things at the system level, you can fix them in your *client.cf* file. Suppose, for example, that the canonical name showed up as the short-hostname:

```
(canonical domain name) $j = here          ← wrong
```

To fix this, you would need to redefine the j macro with a D command in the *client.cf* file:

```
Dj$w.$m                # The local official domain name
```

This defines the canonical (fully qualified official) name to be the same as the local hostname ($w) with a dot and the domain name ($m) appended. Rerunning *sendmail* as above would now display the correct information:

```
(canonical domain name) $j = here.us.edu     ← correct
```

In a similar manner you can fix $w and $m if either of them is wrong. But here we should stress that *sendmail* goes to great lengths to get this information right.

7.4 *Things to Try*

- Macro names that begin with uppercase letters are for your use. Names that begin with lowercase letters are reserved for *sendmail*'s use. Twenty-seven special characters are also reserved by *sendmail* for use as operators. What happens if you try to define a macro whose name is another character, such as a tab or an underscore?

- What happens if you try to define a macro whose name is an operator?

- Using the –d35.9 command-line switch, determine what happens if you define two macros, each with the same name.

- Any *sendmail.cf* command may be continued and extended by beginning the next line with a tab or a space. Using the –d35.9 command-line switch, determine the effect of continuing a macro definition. For example,

```
D{FOO}something
tab    somethingmore
```

- The text value of a macro must immediately follow the name of that macro, with no intervening space. Can the text value contain arbitrary spaces or tabs?

- Using *grep*(1), find all the D commands in your site's actual *sendmail.cf* file. If you find any that begin with a lowercase letter and that you haven't seen before, try looking them up in Chapter 31, *Defined Macros*.

8

Addresses and Rules

Before delving into the inner workings of rules, we need to create a fictional network to provide a common ground for discussing mail addresses.

8.1 A Fictional Network

Consider the network shown in Figure 8-1. It consists of three sites (the clouds) that are interconnected by high-speed networks (the solid lines). Each site is a DNS *domain* composed of many individual computers. Each domain is set up differently, as we will show, but from the user's point of view, the process of sending mail from a machine in one domain to a machine in another is the same in all cases.

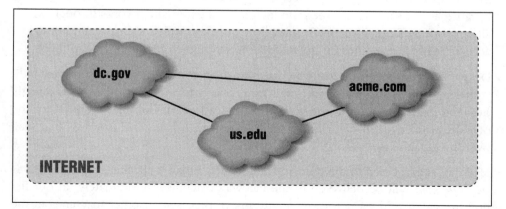

Figure 8-1: Domains in our fictional network

A domain name is interpreted right to left. The *com* in *.acme.com*, for example, means that *acme* is a part of the top-level domain *com* (for *commercial*). There are many commercial sites in the *com* top-level domain, but only one *acme* among them. Similarly, *edu* is the top-level domain for educational institutions (such as colleges and universities), and *gov* is the top-level domain for government organizations.

A domain can consist of many machines. Each machine inside a domain has a *fully qualified domain name* that consists of a hostname, a dot, and then its domain name. For example, *sec.acme.com* is a fully qualified domain name because it consists of the hostname *sec*, a dot, then the domain name *acme.com*.

Host and domain names are case-insensitive. That is, *sec.acme.com* may be expressed in any of the following ways:

```
sec.acme.com          ← good
SEC.Acme.COM          ← also good
sEc.aCmE.cOm          ← ugly, but also good
```

8.1.1 The dc.gov Domain

Figure 8-2 shows the *dc.gov* domain from the inside. It is composed of three machines (although in the real world it might be composed of many more). These three machines are connected together on a private network for security (the solid lines). Only one machine, *fbi.dc.gov*, has a connection to the outside world. Mail from the outside world always goes to *fbi.dc.gov* first; from there it is forwarded to the appropriate machine on the internal network. For example, the user *george* eventually receives his mail on his own machine (*wash.dc.gov*), even though that mail is first handled by *fbi.dc.gov*. The *fbi.dc.gov* machine is called a *gateway* because it forms a gate between the internal and external networks through which all network traffic (such as mail) must flow. It is also called a *forwarder*, because it accepts mail for machines on the internal network, then forwards mail to them.

Despite the presence of a gateway, users in *.dc.gov* still receive mail on their individual machines. Inside *.dc.gov*, mail from one machine to another goes directly over the internal network. The gateway is not involved. But mail destined for the outside world must always first go to the gateway, which then forwards that mail over the outside network.

Mail that is addressed to the domain (*dc.gov* rather than a specific machine such as *wash.dc.gov*) will be delivered to the gateway machine. Unfortunately, in our fiction the gateway does not know about any of the users at other machines in the domain. As a consequence, mail to a user at the domain (*user@dc.gov*) will bounce.

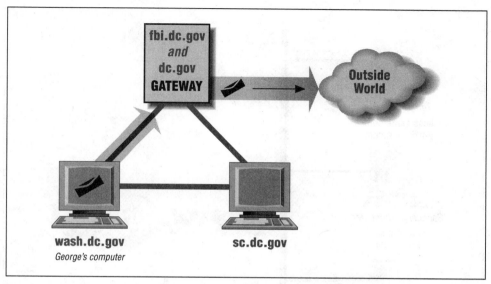

Figure 8–2: The dc.gov domain is accessible only through fbi.dc.gov

8.1.2 The acme.com Domain

Figure 8-3 shows the *.acme.com* domain. It is different from *.dc.gov* because all machines are connected directly to the outside world and to one another. All machines can directly receive mail from the outside world. For example, the user *tim* receives and reads his mail on the machine *boss.acme.com*, but unlike the previous network, there is no gateway.

Like *fbi.dc.gov*, the machine *sec.acme.com* will receive all mail addressed to the domain *acme.com*. But unlike the gateway *fbi.dc.gov*, *sec.acme.com* knows about all the users in its domain.[*] So mail to *tim@acme.com* will be correctly forwarded to *tim* at *boss.acme.com*.

8.1.3 The us.edu Domain

Figure 8-4 shows a third way to set up a domain. In this domain, all mail (both inside and outside) is delivered to the machine *mail.us.edu*. Unlike the previous two examples, no mail is ever delivered to the other machines. Instead, it is delivered into the master spool directory on *mail.us.edu*. The other machines then network *mount* that directory so that users can read their mail from any machine.

---

[*] It runs *nis* (formerly Yellow Pages) and can mount the home directories of all users.

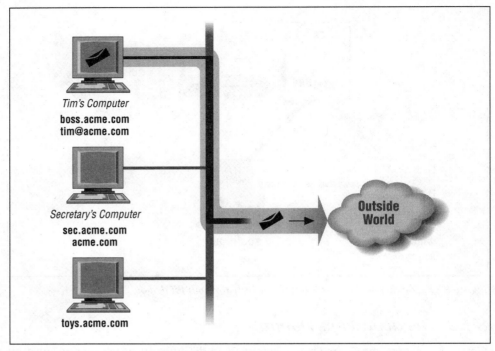

Figure 8–3: All machines in acme.com connect to the outside world

Under this system, mail addresses need to contain only the name of the local recipient, an @, and the name of the domain (such as *user@us.edu*). This arrangement eliminates the need for users elsewhere in the world to know any specific machine's name.

All three forms of domains have their advantages and disadvantages. We don't favor any one above another. In this and the chapters to follow, we consider our machine to be in the *us.edu* domain. We selected it only because it allows the simplest *sendmail* configuration file to be used.

8.1.4 UUCP and Host Paths

In addition to our fictional network, consider two hosts that are connected to *acme.com* using dial-up lines (see Figure 8-5). Under UUCP, one needs to know exactly how hosts are connected in order to send mail to any one of them. To get from *sec.acme.com* to *sonya*, for example, the mail needs to go through *lady* first.

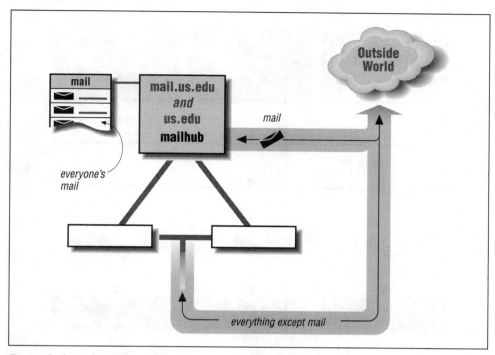

Figure 8–4: Only mail.us.edu receives mail in the domain us.edu

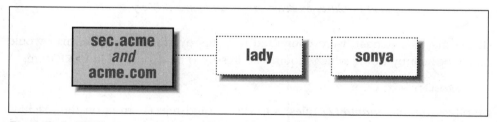

Figure 8–5: UUCP connections to sec.acme.com

8.2 Why Rules?

Rules in a *sendmail.cf* file are used to rewrite (modify) mail addresses, to detect errors in addressing, and to select mail delivery agents. Addresses need to be rewritten because they can be specified in many ways, yet are required to be in particular forms by delivery agents. To illustrate, consider Figure 8-6, and the address

```
friend@uuhost
```

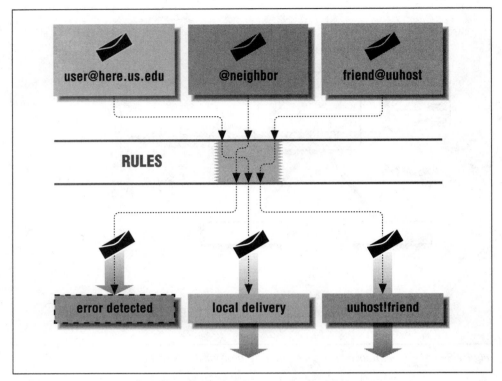

Figure 8–6: Rules modify addresses, detect errors, and select delivery agents

If the machine uuhost were connected to yours over a dial-up line, mail would likely be sent by UUCP, which requires addresses to be expressed in UUCP form:

    uuhost!friend

Another role of *sendmail.cf* rules is to detect (and reject) errors on the machine from which the mail originated. This prevents them from propagating over the network. Mail to an address without a username is one such error:

    @neighbor

It is better to detect this kind of error as early as possible, rather than having the host neighbor reject it.

Delivery agents are the means used by *sendmail* to actually transmit or deliver mail messages. Rules examine the address of each envelope recipient and select the appropriate delivery agent. For example,

    root@here.us.edu

Here, rules detect that **here.us.edu** is the name of the local machine and then select the **local** delivery agent to perform final delivery to the user *root*'s system mailbox.

In the previous two chapters you were introduced to delivery agent and macro definitions. In this chapter we will begin our coverage of rule sets: the way those rule sets process addresses.

8.3 Rule Sets

Sequences of rules are grouped together into rule sets. Each set is similar to a subroutine. A rule set is declared with the **S** command, which must begin a line in *sendmail.cf*. For example:

    S0

This begins the declaration of the rules that form rule set number 0. Rule sets are numbered starting from 0.[*] Sets 0 through 5[†] are internally defined by *sendmail* to have very specific purposes, as shown in Table 8-1. We'll expand on them throughout the rest of the tutorial. Rule-set definitions may appear in any order in the configuration file. For example, rule set **S5** may be defined first, followed by **S2** and then **S7**. The rule sets are gathered when the *sendmail.cf* file is read and are then sorted internally by *sendmail*.

Table 8–1: The Purposes of Rule Sets

Rule Set	Purpose
0	Resolve a mail delivery agent
1	Process sender address
2	Process recipient address
3	Preprocess all addresses
4	Postprocess all addresses
5	Rewrite unaliased local users

The *client.cf* file contains no rule-set definitions yet. To observe the effect of nonexistent rules, rerun *sendmail* on that file:

    % ./sendmail -Cclient.cf -bt
    ADDRESS TEST MODE (ruleset 3 NOT automatically invoked)
    Enter <ruleset> <address>
    >

---

[*] Beginning with V8.7, rule sets may have symbolic names too. We show this in Chapter 11, *Rule Sets 1 and S=*.

[†] Other rule sets may be used by future versions of *sendmail*, so avoid using rule sets 6 through 9.

The −bt command-line switch causes *sendmail* to run in address-testing mode. In this mode, *sendmail* waits for you to type a rule set and an address.[*] It then shows you how the rule set *rewrites* the address. At the > prompt, you can now enter an address by specifying a rule-set number, then a space, and then a mail address:

```
> 0 gw@wash.dc.gov
rewrite: ruleset  0   input: gw @ wash . dc . gov
rewrite: ruleset  0 returns: gw @ wash . dc . gov
>
```

The rule set specified is 0, but you can specify any number.

The **rewrite:** word that begins each line of address-testing mode output is there simply to distinguish rewriting lines when they are mixed with other kinds of debugging output. The **input** means that *sendmail* placed the address into the workspace (more about this soon). The **returns** shows the result after the rule set has rewritten that address on the basis of its rules.

The address that is fed to *sendmail*, gw@wash.dc.gov, is first split into parts (tokens) based on two sets of separating characters. Both are defined internally. One can be changed in your configuration file;[†] the other cannot:

```
.:@[]              ← you can change these
()<>,;\"\r\n       ← you cannot change these
```

The two sets are combined into one, and the result is used to separate the various parts of email addresses. The address *gw@wash.dc.gov* is divided into seven tokens because the @ and dot are both in the list of separation characters.

```
rewrite: ruleset  0   input: gw @ wash . dc . gov
rewrite: ruleset  0 returns: gw @ wash . dc . gov
```

The **input:** line shows seven tokens passed to rule set 0. The **returns:** line shows, since there is no rule set 0, that the undefined (empty) rule set returns those tokens unchanged.

If a rule set is undefined, the result is the same as if it were defined but had no rules associated with it. It is like a C language subroutine that contains nothing but a *return* statement. It does nothing and produces no errors.

---

[*] V8.7's rule-testing mode can do much more (see §38.1).

[†] Prior to V8.7, the o macro was used in the configuration file to define different or more characters. Beginning with V8.7, the OperatorChars option is used instead.

8.4 Rules

Each rule set may contain zero or more individual rules. Rules begin with the R configuration command, and each rule is composed of three parts:

```
S0
Rlhs        rhs          comment
```

The first line, the S0, declares the start of rule set 0. All the lines following the S line and beginning with R belong to that rule set. A new rule set begins when another S line with a different number appears.[*]

Each R line is a separate rule in the series of rules that form a rule set. In the *send-mail.cf* files of major mail-handling sites, a given rule set can have a huge number of rules. But our hypothetical rule set 0 will have only one rule and hence only one line that begins with an R:

```
S0
Rlhs        rhs          optional comment
    ↑            ↑
   tab          tab
```

Each rule has three distinct parts, each divided from the others by one or more tab characters. You can use space characters inside each part, but you *must* use tabs to separate the parts.

The leftmost part of the rule is called the LHS, for *left-hand side*. The middle part is called the RHS, for *right-hand side*. These form the rule. A comment may optionally follow the RHS and (if present) must be separated from the RHS by one or more tab characters.

The LHS and RHS form an *if-then* pair. If the LHS evaluates to true, the RHS is evaluated. If the LHS evaluates to false, *sendmail* skips to the next rule in the rule set (if there is one):

```
    if true →         do this
      ↓                 ↓
    Rlhs              rhs
      ↓
    otherwise, go to next rule
```

---

[*] If another S line appears with the same number, *sendmail* will print a warning. Prior to V8.7, the second definition wiped out the first. Beginning with V8.7, the second rule set's rules are appended to the rules of the first.

8.5 The Workspace

Whether the LHS test is true or false is determined by making comparisons. When an address is processed by a rule set for rewriting, *sendmail* first tokenizes it, then stores those tokens internally in a buffer called the *workspace*:

```
"gw" "@" "wash" "." "gov"   ← in the workspace
```

When the LHS of a rule is evaluated, it too is tokenized; then those tokens are compared to the tokens in the workspace. If both the workspace and the LHS contain exactly the same tokens, a match is found, and the result of the LHS comparison is true. Now, for illustration, create a demo rule by temporarily adding the following two lines to the end of the *client.cf* file:

```
S0
Rleft.side      new.stuff
```

Don't forget that the LHS is separated from the RHS by tab characters. Now run *sendmail* in rule-testing mode, just as you did before:

```
% ./sendmail  -Cclient.cf -bt
ADDRESS TEST MODE (ruleset 3 NOT automatically invoked)
Enter <ruleset> <address>
>
```

In rule-testing mode you can view rules with the =S command[*] (see §38.4.1). Try it now:

```
> =S 0
Rleft . side           new . stuff
>
```

This shows that *sendmail* found only one rule for rule set 0, the one we created.

Now enter rule set 0 and a typical email address at the prompt:

```
> 0 gw@wash.dc.gov
rewrite: ruleset  0   input: gw @ wash . dc . gov
rewrite: ruleset  0 returns: gw @ wash . dc . gov
>
```

The address was not rewritten by the rule because the workspace and the LHS did not exactly match:

```
gw@wash.dc.gov                    ← the workspace
       ↑
    don't match
       ↓
Rleft.side      new.stuff         ← the rule
```

---

[*] One of several brand-new –bt commands introduced with V8.7 *sendmail*.

Now, at the prompt, enter the exact text that appears in the LHS of the demo rule:

```
> 0 left.side
rewrite: ruleset  0   input: left . side
rewrite: ruleset  0 returns: new . stuff
```

An amazing thing has happened. The rule has actually rewritten an address. The address `left.side` was given to rule set 0 and rewritten by the rule in that rule set to become the address `new.stuff`. This transformation is possible because the workspace and the LHS exactly match each other, so the result of the LHS comparison is true:

```
left.side          ← the workspace
    ↑
    exact match, so: "true"
    ↓
Rleft.side      new.stuff
  ↑               ↑
  if true,      then do this
```

Before leaving this demo rule set, perform one final experiment. Enter the uppercase text `LEFT.SIDE`:

```
> 0 LEFT.SIDE
rewrite: ruleset  0   input: LEFT . SIDE
rewrite: ruleset  0 returns: new . stuff
>
```

Notice that the workspace and the LHS are still considered to match, even though they now differ by case. This illustrates that all comparisons between the workspace and the LHS of rules are done in a case-insensitive manner. This property enables rules to be written without the need to distinguish between uppercase and lowercase letters.

8.6 The Flow of Addresses Through Rules

When rule sets contain many rules, addresses flow from the first rule that is declared through the last (top down). To illustrate, remove the demo rule that you added to the *client.cf* file, and replace it with three new demo rules:

```
Rleft.side     new.stuff          ← remove
Rx     y                          ← new
Rz     x                          ← new
Rx     w                          ← new
```

Remember that the LHS of each rule must be separated from the RHS by one or more tab characters.

Before you test these new rules, consider what they do. The first rule rewrites any **x** in the workspace into a **y**. The second rule rewrites any **z** in the workspace into an **x**. The last rule rewrites any **x** that it finds in the workspace into a **w**.

Now run *sendmail* in rule-testing mode once again:

```
% ./sendmail -Cclient.cf -bt
ADDRESS TEST MODE (ruleset 3 NOT automatically invoked)
Enter <ruleset> <address>
>
```

Enter rule set 0 and the letter **x**:

```
> 0 x
rewrite: ruleset  0   input: x
rewrite: ruleset  0 returns: y
```

This shows that any **x** in the workspace is rewritten by the first rule to become a **y**. The new workspace is carried down to the second rule, where it fails, then to the third rule, where it also fails:

```
x               ← the original workspace
↑
exact match, so: "true"
↓
Rx      y       ← first rule rewrites
y               ←   the workspace to be this
↑
does not match, so skip
↓
Rz      x       ← second rule
y               ←   the workspace is still this
↑
does not match, so skip
↓
Rx      w       ← third rule
y               ←   the workspace is still this
```

The important point here is that each rule matches its LHS to the *current* contents of the workspace. Preceding rules may have modified that workspace. The third rule, for example, tries to match an **x** but fails because the first rule changed our **x** into a **y**.

Now enter rule set 0 and the letter **z**:

```
> 0 z
rewrite: ruleset  0   input: z
rewrite: ruleset  0 returns: w
```

Notice that any z in the workspace is rewritten to be a **w**. Look at the flow of the z through the rules to see why this happened:

```
z                ← the original workspace
↑
does not match, so skip
↓
Rx      y        ← first rule
z                ←   the workspace remains this
↑
exact match, so ...
↓
Rz      x        ← second rule rewrites
x                ←   the workspace to be this
↑
exact match, so ...
↓
Rx      w        ← third rule rewrites
w                ←   the workspace to be this
```

In this instance the first rule does nothing. The second rule matches the z and changes the workspace into an **x**. The third rule sees the rewritten workspace. It changes the **x** (the current contents of the workspace) into a **w**.

Now feed one more letter into *sendmail* in rule-testing mode. This time, enter anything other than an **x** or **z**:

```
> 0 b
rewrite: ruleset  0    input: b
rewrite: ruleset  0 returns: b
```

Here, the workspace remains unchanged because b does not match the left-hand side in any of the three rules. If the LHS of a rule fails to match the workspace, that rule is skipped, and the workspace remains unchanged.

8.7 *Wildcard Operators*

Rules would be pretty useless if they always had to match the workspace exactly. Fortunately, that is not the case. In addition to literal text, you can also use wildcard operators that allow the LHS of rules to match arbitrary text in the workspace. To illustrate, consider this rule:

```
R$+     rhs is here
↑
lhs
```

This LHS begins with the first character following the R. The LHS in this example is

```
$+
```

This is a wildcard operator. The truth of this if statement is determined by a process called *pattern matching*. The LHS $+ (a single token) is a pattern that means "match one or more tokens." The address that is being evaluated is tokenized and placed into the workspace, and then the workspace is compared to that pattern:

```
gw@wash.dc.gov
    ↓
    tokenized into
    ↓
gw @ wash . dc . gov   ← in the workspace
```

When matching the workspace to an LHS pattern, *sendmail* scans the workspace from left to right. Each token in the workspace is compared to the wildcard operator (the $+) in the LHS pattern. If the tokens all match the pattern, the if part of the if-then pair is true.

The $+ wildcard operator simply matches any *one or more* tokens:

```
workspace        pattern
gw               $+       ← match one token ("one")
@                         ← and optionally more ("or more")
wash                      ↓

.
dc
.
gov
```

As you can see, if there are any tokens in the address at all (the workspace is not empty), the LHS rule $+ evaluates to true.

8.7.1 Other Text in the LHS

A rule of $+ (match one or more tokens) is not sufficient to handle all possible addresses (especially bad addresses):

```
gw@wash.dc.gov      ← $+ should match and does
@wash.dc.gov        ← $+ matches an incomplete address
```

To make matching in the LHS more effective, *sendmail* allows other text to appear in the pattern. To make sure that the address in the workspace contains a user part, the @ character, and a host part, the following LHS pattern can be used:

```
$+@$+
```

Just like the address in the workspace, this pattern is tokenized before it is compared for a match. Wildcard operators (like $+) count as one token, and @ is a token because it is a separator character:

```
.:@[]           ← you can change these
()<>,;\"\r\n     ← you cannot change these
```

The pattern of $+@$+ is separated into three tokens:

```
$+ @ $+
```

Text in the pattern must match text in the workspace *exactly* (token for token) if
there is to be a match. A good address in the workspace (one containing a user
part and a host part) will match our new LHS ($+@$+):

```
workspace        pattern
gw               $+         ← match one or more
@                @          ← match exactly
wash             $+         ← match one
.                           ↓  or more
dc
.
gov
```

Here, the flow of matching begins with the first $+, which matches one token (of
the one or more) in the workspace. The @ matches the identical token in the
workspace. At this point, the $+@ part of the pattern has been satisfied. All that
remains is for the final $+ to match its one or more of all the remaining tokens in
the workspace, which it does.

A bad address in the workspace, on the other hand, will not match the pattern.
Consider an address, for example, that lacks a user part:

```
@wash.dc.gov                       ← in the workspace

workspace        pattern
@                $+         ← match one
wash                        ←  or more
.
dc
.
gov
                 @         ← match exactly (fails!)
                 $+
```

Here, the first $+ incorrectly matches the @ in the workspace. Since there is no
other @ in the workspace to be matched by the @ in the pattern, the first $+
matches the entire workspace. Because there is nothing left in the workspace, the
attempt to match the @ fails. When any part of a pattern fails to match the
workspace, the entire LHS fails (the if part of the if-then is false).

8.7.2 *Minimal Matching*

One small bit of confusion may yet remain. When a wildcard operator such as $+
is used to match the workspace, *sendmail* always does a *minimal match*. That is,

it matches only what it needs to for the next part of the rule to work. Consider the following:

```
R$+@$+
```

In this LHS the first $+ matches everything in the workspace up to the first @ character. For example, consider the following workspace:

```
a@b@c
```

In the above, $+@ causes the $+ to match only the characters up to the first @ character, the a. This is the minimum that needs to be matched, and so it is the maximum that will be matched.

8.7.3 *More Play with LHS Matching*

Take a moment to replace the previous demo rules with the following three new demo rules in the *client.cf* file:

```
S0
R@          one
R@$+        two
R$+@$+      three
```

Again, these three rules are for demonstration purposes only (you'll see how to declare a real one soon enough). We've given each temporary RHS a number to see whether it is selected. Now run *sendmail* in rule-testing mode:

```
% ./sendmail -Cclient.cf -bt
ADDRESS TEST MODE (ruleset 3 NOT automatically invoked)
Enter <ruleset> <address>
```

Now print the rules to remind yourself what they are:

```
> =S 0
R@          one
R@ $+       two
R$+ @ $+              three
```

We'll test those rules with an assortment of test addresses. The first address to try is a lone @:

```
> 0 @
rewrite: ruleset  0   input: @
rewrite: ruleset  0 returns: one
```

The @ causes the first temporary RHS to be selected because the rule is

```
R@          one
```

The LHS here (the pattern to match) contains the lone @. That pattern matches the tokenized workspace @ exactly, so the RHS for that rule rewrites the workspace to contain **one**. Since **one** does not contain an @ character, neither the second nor third rules match, so the entire rule set returns **one**.

Next enter an address that just contains a host and domain part but not a user part:

```
> 0 @your.domain
rewrite: ruleset  0   input: @ your . domain
rewrite: ruleset  0 returns: two
```

The first thing to notice is what was *not* printed! The workspace does not match the pattern of the first rule. But instead of returning an error, the workspace is carried down *as is* to the next rule—where it does match:

```
@your.domain does not match, so ...
    ↓
R@       one
    ↓
try the next rule
    ↓
R@$+     two
```

Now enter an address that fails to match the first two rules but successfully matches the third:

```
> 0 you@your.domain
rewrite: ruleset  0   input: you @ your . domain
rewrite: ruleset  0 returns: three
```

The flow for this address is

```
your@your.domain does not match, so ...
    ↓
R@       one
    ↓
try the next rule, which also does not match, so ...
    ↓
R@$+     two
    ↓
try the next rule, which does match.
    ↓
R$+@$+   three
```

Try other addresses such as your login name or UUCP addresses such as *you@host.uucp* and *host!you*. Can you predict what will happen with weird addresses like *@@* or *a@b@c*?

When you are done experimenting, exit rule-testing mode and delete the four temporary lines that you added for this demonstration.

8.8 Things to Try

- Try feeding *sendmail* an extremely long address in rule-testing mode, something like `a.a.a . . .` with 100 `a` and dot characters. What does this tell you about the limit on the size of the workspace? Is this a limit of tokens or of characters?

- Look through your system *sendmail.cf* file for all lines that declare rule sets (S lines). Are there any that have no rules (R lines) associated with them? Do the comments near them explain clearly why no rules are present?

- What happens if you use spaces rather than tabs to separate the LHS from the RHS of rules? Is the error message clear? What happens if the RHS is separated from the comment with spaces instead of tabs? How does this illustrate the importance of testing all new rules with rule-testing mode?

- Minimum matching is one of the most misunderstood aspects of rules. If you are still the tiniest bit confused about this topic, review §8.7.2 and possibly leap ahead to §28.5.1.

9

Rule Set 0

The function of rule set 0 is to decide which mail delivery agent will handle delivery for a particular recipient address. Figure 9-1 shows how rule set 0 relates to the other rule sets.

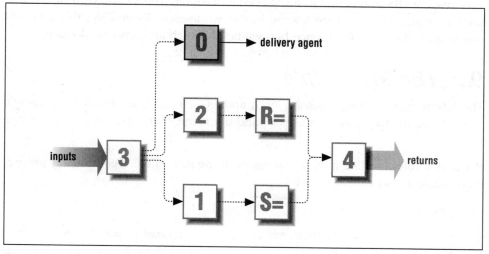

Figure 9–1: The flow of addresses for rule set 0

Rule set 0 is called once for each recipient of a mail message. Rule set 0 determines a *triple* for each address. The triple is composed of three parts: the symbolic name of the mail delivery agent, the name of the user to whom the mail is addressed, and the name of the host to which the mail will be sent. We'll expand on these soon and cover the other rule sets in later chapters.

9.1 Introducing Rule Set 0

Recall that one goal of the *client.cf* file is to cause *sendmail* to forward all mail to
a central hub machine for processing. To lay the groundwork for this, we designed
the hub delivery agent in Chapter 6, *The Mail Hub and Delivery Agents*, and
declared it like this:

```
# Delivery agent definition to forward mail to hub
Mhub,    P=[IPC], S=0, R=0, F=mDFMuXa, T=DNS/RFC822/SMTP, A=IPC $h
```

As this goal implies, we don't want to design any fancy rules for rewriting the
recipient's address, we simply want to send it to the hub as is.

The rule set that we show below does just that. It may look complicated, but recall
that its one rule is basically just an if-then statement:

```
S0
R$+      $#hub $@${REMOTE} $:$1         forward to hub
```

The first line (the S0) declares the start of rule set 0. The R line in this example is
the first of many possible rules that will form rule set 0.

You saw the LHS of this rule in the preceding chapter. The $+ wildcard operator is
used to match *one or more* tokens in the workspace. Essentially, this LHS will
match anything in the workspace but will fail to match an empty workspace.

9.2 The RHS Triple

The job of rule set 0 is to resolve each address into a triple: the delivery agent's
symbolic name, the name of the host, and the name of the user in that order (see
Figure 9-2).

Recall that rules are like if-then statements. If the rule in the LHS evaluates to true,
then *sendmail* evaluates the RHS:

```
if true→           do this
  ↓                  ↓
R$+                $#hub $@${REMOTE} $:$1           forward to hub
  ↓
otherwise go to next rule
```

This RHS resolves all three parts of the triple. To accomplish this, the text of the
RHS is *transformed* and then copied into the workspace:

$#hub	→ copied as is (delivery agent part)
$@${REMOTE}	→ defined macro is expanded (host part)
$:$1	→ positional macro is expanded (user part)

We examine these parts in order, showing how each is transformed and copied
into the workspace. The transformation operators are shown in Table 9-1.

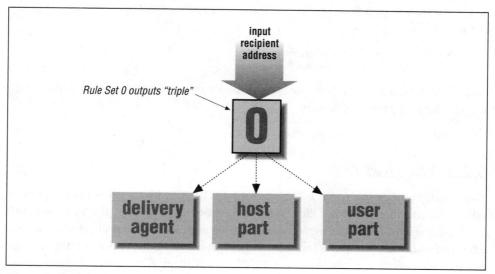

Figure 9–2: Rule set 0 resolves a triple

Table 9–1: Rule Set 0 RHS Transformation Operators

Operator	Description
$#	The mail delivery agent
$@	The host
$:	The user

9.2.1 The Delivery Agent ($#)

The first part of the triple is the name of the delivery agent. The RHS $# transformation operator tells *sendmail* that the text following (up to but not including the next operator, ignoring spaces) is the symbolic name of the delivery agent to use.

The symbolic name **hub** was defined in the *client.cf* file as

```
# Delivery agent definition to forward mail to hub
Mhub,    P=[IPC], S=0, R=0, F=mDFMuXa, T=DNS/RFC822/SMTP, A=IPC $h
```

When the RHS is copied into the workspace, any transformation operators such as $# are copied as is and become new tokens:

```
$#       ← the workspace thus far
```

When text, such as hub, is copied into the workspace, it is tokenized by using the separation characters:[*]

```
.:@[]            ← you can change these
()<>,;\"\r\n     ← you cannot change these
```

Since our symbolic name hub contains none of those characters, it is copied as a single token into the workspace:

```
$# hub       ← the workspace thus far
```

9.2.2 The Host ($@)

The second part of the triple is the hostname. The RHS $@ transformation operator tells *sendmail* that the text following (up to, but not including, the next operator and ignoring spaces) is the name of the host to which the mail will be sent. Whenever *sendmail* encounters ${*name*} in the RHS, it uses the value of the named macro. You previously defined ${REMOTE} to contain the name of the host to which all mail will be sent:

```
D{REMOTE}mailhost              # The name of the mail hub
```

The second part of the triple is now copied to the workspace. The name of the host is in ${REMOTE}. Combined, they look like this:

```
$@${REMOTE}
```

$@ is copied as is. ${REMOTE} is expanded (its value taken), and then that value is broken into tokens and copied into the workspace. If the value of the ${REMOTE} macro is mailhost, the workspace will look like this:

```
$# hub $@ mailhost    ← the workspace thus far
```

9.2.3 The User ($:)

The third part of the triple is the username. The RHS $: transformation operator tells *sendmail* that the following text (up to, but not including, the next operator and ignoring spaces) is the user to whom mail is being sent. Here, the username is determined by the $1, which is called a "positional operator":

```
$:$1
```

When *sendmail* sees a positional operator, a $ followed by a single digit in the RHS, it counts up the number of wildcard operators in the LHS. In this example the LHS has only one wildcard operator, $+, so $1 refers to that operator. If there were more than one wildcard operator in the LHS, for example,

---

[*] As a result, the symbolic name of the mail delivery agent cannot contain any separation characters.

```
$+.$+
 ↑  ↑
$1 $2
```

then $1 would refer to the first $+ and $2 to the second $+.

A *$digit* tells *sendmail* to copy whatever tokens the corresponding LHS wildcard operator matched. If the original workspace had contained

  boss @ acme   ← *in the original workspace*

then the lone $+ (match one or more) LHS wildcard operator would match the entire workspace (all of its tokens).

All of the original workspace's tokens are then copied. The workspace contains

  $# hub $@ mailhost $: boss @ acme

After *sendmail* has completed writing the workspace, the workspace (the triple) is returned.

9.3 Testing Rule Set 0

To see that what we describe is actually what happens, take a moment to add rule set 0 to the end of your *client.cf* file:

```
S0 # select delivery agent                              ← new
R$+      $#hub $@${REMOTE} $:$1        forward to hub    ← new
```

Now run *sendmail* in rule-testing mode and give it the address boss@acme:

```
% ./sendmail -Cclient.cf -bt
ADDRESS TEST MODE (ruleset 3 NOT automatically invoked)
Enter <ruleset> <address>
> 0 boss@acme
rewrite: ruleset  0   input: boss @ acme
rewrite: ruleset  0 returns: $# hub $@ mailhost $: boss @ acme
```

The change to the workspace caused by rule set 0 is exactly as predicted:

  $# hub $@ mailhost $: boss @ acme

Components from the workspace triple are used by *sendmail* to define macros used by delivery agents. For example, the text after $@ is copied into the h macro. Similarly, the username appearing after $: is copied into the u macro:

```
                                                    from $@  in rule set 0
                                                          ↓
Mhub,    P=[IPC], S=0, R=0, F=mDFMuXa, T=DNS/RFC822/SMTP, A=IPC $h
Mlocal,  P=/bin/mail, F=lsDFMAw5:/|@rmn, S=0, R=0, A=mail -d $u
                                                                 ↑
                                                    from $:  in rule set 0
```

Rule set 0 is different from the other rule sets in several important ways. We'll begin explaining the other rule sets in the next chapter. For now, just be aware that there are a few exceptions to rules in *sendmail*:

- Rule set 0 is one of the few rule sets that may use $# to return the symbolic name of a delivery agent.[*] If any other rule set returns a $#, the $# can cause unpredictable errors.

- $@ and $: in rule set 0, when following $#, have different meanings than they do in all the other rule sets. They are even different from the way they are in rule set 0 itself when they don't follow $#. We'll expand on this concept in the next chapter.

9.4 The error Delivery Agent

Although all mail, under the hub scheme, should be passed to the hub for processing, certain errors should still be handled locally. By recognizing these errors locally, the user is advised of mistakes immediately, rather than having to wait for mail to bounce.

When we discussed delivery agents, we showed you that *sendmail* requires the `local` delivery agent. Because *sendmail* requires it, you had to define it yourself (to keep *sendmail* from complaining):

```
Mlocal, P=/bin/mail, F=lsDFMAw5:/|@rmn, S=0, R=0, A=mail -d $u
```

Inside *sendmail*, a specially defined delivery agent exists. Called **error**, that delivery agent is one that you can't define yourself.

The **error** delivery agent is the internal mechanism that *sendmail* uses to process errors. When that delivery agent is selected, it causes *sendmail* to print the offending address, then the username part of the triple (the $: part) as an error message.

For example, recall the earlier experiment with three demo rules:

```
S0
R@        one
R@$+      two
R$+@$+    three
```

When this rule set was given an address of *@host* (note the missing user part), the RHS rewrote the workspace to be **two**.[†] We use a similar technique to select *sendmail*'s built-in error handling delivery agent **error**.

---

* Rule set 5 can also return a $#.

† We are fudging here for the sake of a simple example. In reality a leading @ is legal for route addresses (see the `DontPruneRoutes` option in §34.8.20, how route addresses are handled in rules in §29.4.3, and the F=d delivery agent flag in §30.8.16).

Add the following new line to the *client.cf* file's rule set 0. Don't forget that the
LHS, RHS, and comment must be separated from each other by tab characters, not
spaces. But note that the RHS may contain space characters (not tabs) for clarity.

```
S0 # select delivery agent
R@$+      $#error $: Missing user name                          ← new
R$+       $#hub $@${REMOTE} $:$1              forward to hub
```

Run *sendmail* again, this time to see which addresses are caught locally as errors
and which are passed onward to the central hub.

```
% ./sendmail -Cclient.cf -bt
ADDRESS TEST MODE (ruleset 3 NOT automatically invoked)
Enter <ruleset> <address>
> 0 @acme
rewrite: ruleset  0    input: @ acme
rewrite: ruleset  0 returns: $# error $: Missing user name
```

Here, you are supplying an address that lacks a username. As expected, the
`error` delivery agent is selected. If someone attempted to send mail to this
address, they would get the error

```
@acme... Missing user name
```

Now feed *sendmail* a legal address:

```
> 0 boss@acme
rewrite: ruleset  0    input: boss @ acme
rewrite: ruleset  0 returns: $# hub $@ mailhost $: boss @ acme
```

This legal address, one with both a user and host part, bypasses the error-handling
rule and will be accepted for delivery via the `hub` delivery agent.

Take some time to experiment. Give *sendmail* an assortment of addresses and try
to predict which will produce errors and which will not.

9.5 *Things to Try*

- Devise an error-handling rule that will detect an address that contains a username and an `@` character but no host part.

- Is it possible to have text in the LHS that is literally `$+`, rather than an operator
  with the same characters?

- The *client.cf* file uses `$#error` to handle errors in rule set 0. Examine your
  site's *sendmail.cf* file to see if it is legal to use `$#error` in other rule sets.

10

Rule Set 3

The job of rule sets 1 through 4 is to change recipient and sender addresses in both the header and the envelope[*] into a form appropriate for a given delivery agent. Each kind of address takes a different path through the rule sets. The possibilities (which can be confusing) are illustrated in Figure 10-1.

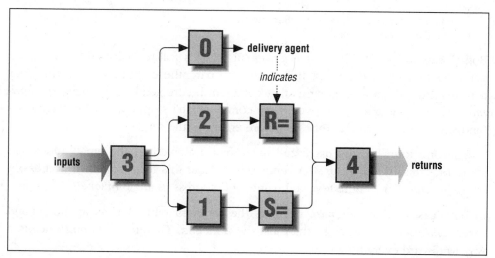

Figure 10-1: The flow of addresses through rule sets

The sender's address on the envelope, for example, is first rewritten by rule set 3, then by rule set 1, then by the rule set specified by the S= equate in the delivery agent definition, and finally by rule set 4.

---

[*] Headers and envelopes were introduced in Chapter 1, *Introduction*.

All addresses are first processed by rule set 3. All sender addresses flow through rule set 3 and then 1. All recipient addresses flow through 3 and then 2. Each then flows through the rule set that is specified by the S= or R= equate for the delivery agent that will handle the message. Each is then postprocessed by rule set 4. But because the role of rule set 0 is to select a delivery agent (and therefore the appropriate S= and R= equates), rule set 0 needs to process an address before it can go through rule set 1 or 2.

In the previous few chapters you began to learn about rules sets in general and rule set 0 specifically. However, before the recipient address can be processed by rule set 0, it must first be processed by rule set 3. All addresses are preprocessed by rule set 3.

10.1 Why Preprocess?

To understand why a preprocessing rule set (rule set 3) is needed, we need to briefly examine how users specify addresses. One common way to send mail is by using the reply feature of your mail-reading program (MUA). That feature looks at the From: line in the mail message's header and uses the text that follows as the address for the reply. That text can take one of two forms:

```
From: address (Full Name and other comments)
From: Full Name <address>
```

Both forms are legal. The first is an email address followed by arbitrary text in parentheses, usually the user's full name. The parentheses form a comment. Your mail reading program often strips that comment before sending the mail, so *sendmail* sees only **address**. But even if the comment isn't stripped, *sendmail* removes (and saves) the text in parentheses before entering rule set 3.

The second form has the user's full name first, followed by the email address in angle brackets. When your MUA sends email using this form of return address, it hands *sendmail* the entire text: full name, and address in angle brackets.

In both cases, what *sendmail* needs is the **address** part. But, as in the second case, *sendmail* can get more than just the **address**. Therefore *sendmail* needs a way to discard everything else:

```
Full Name <address>
```
↓

needs to be transformed into

↓
```
address
```

The *sendmail* program handles this initial transformation by preprocessing addresses using rule set 3.

10.2 Rule Set 3

In its initial form, rule set 3 looks like this:

```
S3 # preprocessing for all rule sets
R$* < $* > $*    $2              basic RFC822 parsing
```

As with rule set 0, the definition of rule set 3 begins with the S configuration command. The S character must begin a line, and the 3 must follow with no intervening nonspace characters.

The only rule in rule set 3 is composed of three parts, each separated from the others by one or more tab characters:

```
R$* < $* > $*    $2              basic RFC822 parsing
  ↑          ↑ ↑       ↑              ↑
 LHS        tabs RHS  tabs        comment
```

Note that we will now separate the tokens in the LHS with *spaces* (not tabs) to make the LHS easier to understand. Spaces always separate tokens, yet are never themselves tokens.

10.2.1 The LHS

The wildcard operator in this LHS, the $*, is different from the $+ wildcard operator that you saw in rule set 0. Recall that the $+ wildcard operator matches one or more tokens in the workspace. To review, consider the LHS rule:

```
$+ @ $+
```

This LHS easily matches an address like *you@here.us.edu* in the workspace:

workspace	LHS	
you	$+	← *match one or more*
@	@	← *match exactly*
here	$+	← *match one*
.		↓ *or more*
us		
.		
edu		

This same LHS, however, does not match an address like *@here.us.edu*:

workspace	LHS	
@	$+	← *match one*
here		↓ *or more*
.		
us		
.		
edu		
	@	← *match exactly, fails!*
	$+	

Because the $+ wildcard operator needs to match one or more tokens, it fails when there is nothing in front of the @.

The $* wildcard operator is just like the $+ wildcard operator, except that it *will* match nothing (zero tokens). If the LHS had used $* instead of $+, an address like *@here.us.edu* would be matched:

workspace	*LHS*	
	$*	← *match zero or more (matches zero)*
@	@	← *match exactly*
here	$*	← *match zero*
.		↓ *or more*
us		
.		
edu		

The LHS in rule set 3 matches anything or nothing, provided that there is a pair of angle brackets in the workspace somewhere:

```
R$* < $* > $*     $2              basic RFC822 parsing
```

For example, consider an address that might be given to *sendmail* by your MUA:

```
Your Fullname <you@here.us.edu>
```

This address is tokenized and placed into the workspace. That workspace is then compared to the LHS:

workspace	*LHS*	
Your	$*	← *match zero*
Fullname		↓ *or more*
<	<	← *match exactly*
you	$*	← *match zero*
@		↓ *or more*
here		
.		
us		
.		
edu		
>	>	← *match exactly*
	$*	← *match zero or more*

10.2.2 The RHS

Recall that the objective of rule set 3 is to strip everything but the address part (the text between the angle brackets). That stripping is accomplished by rewriting the workspace using the $2 positional operator in the RHS:

```
R$* < $* > $*     $2              basic RFC822 parsing
                  ↑
          strip all but the address
```

Remember, when a $digit appears in the RHS, that digit is used as a count into the wildcard operators of the LHS.

```
$* < $* > $*
↑   ↑   ↑
$1  $2  $3
```

$1 refers to the first $*, $2 refers to the second, and $3 to the third. Comparing this ordering of operators to the test address, you see

```
workspace       LHS                             RHS
Your            $*      ← match zero             $1
Fullname                ↓   or more
<               <       ← match exactly
you             $*      ← match zero             $2
@                       ↓   or more
here
.
us
.
edu
>               >       ← match exactly
                $*      ← match zero or more     $3
```

This illustrates that the middle (second) $* matches the *you@here.us.edu* part of the workspace. When the RHS rewrites the workspace, it does so by copying the tokens matched by the second wildcard operator (specified in the RHS with the $2 positional operator).

10.2.3   Test Rule Set 3

Take a few moments to experiment. Observe the transformation of a user-specified address into one that *sendmail* can use. Add the following new rule set 3 to the rule sets in the *client.cf* file:

```
S3 # preprocessing for all rule sets                             ← new
R$* < $* > $*          $2              basic RFC822 parsing      ← new
```

Now run *sendmail* again. Up to now, you have been testing rule set 0, so you have specified a 0 following the > prompt. Instead, you will now specify a 3 because you are testing rule set 3:

```
% ./sendmail -Cclient.cf -bt
ADDRESS TEST MODE (ruleset 3 NOT automatically invoked)
Enter <ruleset> <address>
> 3 Your Fullname <you@here>
rewrite: ruleset  3   input: Your Fullname < you @ here >
rewrite: ruleset  3 returns: you @ here
```

As expected, the new rule causes everything except the "good" email address, the address between the angle brackets, to be thrown away.

Before we improve rule set 3, take a few moments to experiment. Experiment by putting the `fullname` last. Try omitting the email address between the angle brackets. Try nesting angle brackets in an address, like `<a<b>c>`.

As a closing note, recall that *sendmail* does the minimum matching possible when comparing operators to the workspace. Although `$*`, for example, can match zero or more, it prefers to match zero if possible and, if not, to match the fewest tokens possible. A LHS of `$*@$+`, for example, will match as shown in Table 10-1.

Table 10–1: What $ in $*@$+ Matches for Different Addresses*

Address	$* matches	@	$+
a.b.c@d.e	a.b.c	@	d.e
a@b@c	a	@	b@c
@b@c		@	b@c

Expecting operators to match more than they do can cause you to misunderstand the effect of rules.

10.3 Missing Addresses

The current, and only, rule in rule set 3 accepts anything or nothing (the `$*`) between the angle brackets:

```
    R$* < $* > $*        $2                    basic RFC822 parsing
```

But "nothing" can be a legal address. The expression `<>` is a legal sender address that is used when sending bounced mail to prevent further bouncing. To catch such addresses, a new rule needs to be written preceding the first. That new rule looks like this:

```
    R$* <> $*        $n                    handle <> error address
```

Here, the LHS matches any address that has nothing between the angle brackets. Observe how this new LHS catches such an address:

workspace	LHS	
	$*	← *match zero or more*
<	<	← *match exactly*
>	>	← *match exactly*
	$*	← *match zero or more*

When such an empty address is matched by the LHS of the new rule, the workspace is rewritten by the RHS of that rule to contain only the single macro $n. Recall from Chapter 7, *Macros*, that $n was defined to be the name of the user from whom all bounced mail is sent:

```
define(n as MAILER-DAEMON)
```

To observe the effect of this new rule in action, add it to the *client.cf* file. This new rule should precede the existing rule in rule set 3:

```
S3 # preprocessing for all rule sets
R$* <> $*            $n                   handle <> error address   ← new
R$* < $* > $*        $2                   basic RFC822 parsing
```

Now run *sendmail* in rule-testing mode once again:

```
% ./sendmail -Cclient.cf -bt
ADDRESS TEST MODE (ruleset 3 NOT automatically invoked)
Enter <ruleset> <address>
> 3,0 Your Fullname <you@here>
rewrite: ruleset 3   input: Your Fullname < you @ here >
rewrite: ruleset 3 returns: you @ here
rewrite: ruleset 0   input: you @ here
rewrite: ruleset 0 returns: $# hub $@ mailhost $: you @ here
```

Here, two rule sets (3 and 0) are specified instead of one as you have been doing all along. Rule set 3 is called first, and it throws away everything but the address between the angle brackets. The rewritten workspace is then given to rule set 0, which selects the **hub** delivery agent. This is as it should be, with a good address being forwarded to the mail hub. Note that there must be no space on either side of the comma.

But now give *sendmail* an empty address, with nothing in the angle brackets:

```
> 3,0 <>
rewrite: ruleset 3   input: < >
rewrite: ruleset 3 returns: MAILER-DAEMON
rewrite: ruleset 0   input: MAILER-DAEMON
rewrite: ruleset 0 returns: $# hub $@ mailhost $: MAILER-DAEMON
```

As you may expect, the empty address is caught by the new rule in rule set 3 and converted (in the workspace) to the value of **$n**. Rule set 0 then arranges to forward the message to the hub for delivery to user **MAILER-DAEMON**.

10.4 Nested Angle Brackets

Another kind of address that can cause problems is one containing nested angle brackets. These occur because of bugs in MUAs.[*] For example, consider the following address:

```
<a<b>c>
```

---

[*] Also because RFC733 misspecified angle bracket use.

Run sendmail in rule-testing mode, using the current *client.cf* file and give the nested address shown above to rule set 3:

```
> 3 <a<b>c>
rewrite: ruleset  3   input: < a < b > c >
rewrite: ruleset  3 returns: a < b
```

Clearly, this is wrong. The correct address should have been b, the address inside the innermost of the nested angle brackets. The rule that caused the mistake is this one:

```
R$* < $* > $*        $2                     basic RFC822 parsing
```

And here is why:

workspace	LHS	
	$*	← *match zero or more*
<	<	← *match exactly*
a	$*	← *match zero*
<		↓ *or more*
b		
>	>	← *match exactly*
c	$*	← *match zero*
>		↓ *or more*

Because the workspace is scanned left to right, the second < is not seen as anything special. That is, there is no concept in this rule of innermost and outermost angle brackets pairs.

To handle nested angle brackets, another rule needs to be designed.[*] That new rule looks like this:

```
R$* < $* < $* > $* > $*    $2<$3>$4        de-nest brackets
```

This new rule matches any address in the workspace that contains nested brackets. Using the count of LHS operators, the RHS strips away the outermost layer:

```
R$* < $* < $* > $* > $*    $2<$3>$4        de-nest brackets
     ↑     ↑     ↑     ↑     ↑
    $1    $2    $3    $4    $5
```

To test this new rule, add it to the *client.cf* file:

```
S3 # preprocessing for all rule sets
R$* <> $*            $n                handle <> error address
R$* < $* < $* > $* > $*    $2<$3>$4    de-nest brackets         ← new
R$* < $* > $*        $2                basic RFC822 parsing
```

---

[*] In Chapter 29, *Rule Sets*, we show a rule that de-nests a nearly unlimited number of angle brackets.

Run *sendmail* again to test this new rule:

```
> 3 <a<b>c>
rewrite: ruleset  3   input: < a < b > c >
rewrite: ruleset  3 returns: b
```

As predicted, the second rule de-nested, thus allowing the third rule to isolate the address part.

Using what you have learned so far, predict how *sendmail* will handle this address:

```
<<<a>>>
```

Feed it to *sendmail* in rule-testing mode to see whether you are correct. Remember that *sendmail* performs minimum matching.

As a general motto when designing your own rule sets, be liberal in what you accept (including addresses such as <<<*a*>>>), but conservative in what you create (never send out such ugly addresses).[*]

10.5 *Details of Rule Flow*

To better see what is happening inside each rule, rerun *sendmail* with a –d21.12 debugging command-line switch:

```
% ./sendmail -Cclient.cf -d21.12 -bt
```

The –d21.12 switch tells *sendmail* to print each rule as it is processed. Run *sendmail* again with this new switch. This time, when you feed in a nested address, you get considerably more output:

```
> 3 <a<b>c>
rewrite: ruleset  3   input: < a < b > c >
-----trying rule: $* < > $*
----- rule fails
-----trying rule: $* < $* < $* > $* > $*
-----rule matches: $2 < $3 > $4
rewritten as: a < b > c
-----trying rule: $* < $* < $* > $* > $*
----- rule fails
-----trying rule: $* < $* > $*
-----rule matches: $2
rewritten as: b
-----trying rule: $* < $* > $*
----- rule fails
rewrite: ruleset  3 returns: b
```

---

[*] Paraphrased from *The Robustness Principle*, RFC793, TCP specification. Jon Postel, Ed.

This output may appear complicated, but it is really fairly straightforward. The first two lines and last line are what you have been seeing all along (when you *didn't* use the –d21.12 switch):

```
> 3 <a<b>c>
rewrite: ruleset  3   input: < a < b > c >
rewrite: ruleset  3 returns: b
```

Everything in between those lines is new output caused by the –d21.12 switch. That new output shows each rule in rule set 3 being called and processed in turn. The first rule looks for empty angle brackets:

```
R$* <> $*              $n                      handle <> error address
```

The workspace (tokenized from the input of <a<b>c>) is compared to the LHS of this rule:

```
-----trying rule: $* < > $*
----- rule fails
```

The LHS doesn't match (the rule fails) because the angle brackets of the workspace are not empty. Consequently, the RHS of the first rule is not called, and the workspace is unchanged.

The second rule is the de-nesting one:

```
R$* < $* < $* > $* > $*      $2<$3>$4           de-nest brackets
```

The workspace (still <a<b>c>) is compared to the LHS of this rule.

```
-----trying rule: $* < $* < $* > $* > $*
```

The LHS matches the workspace, so the workspace is rewritten on the basis of the RHS of that rule, and the extra angle brackets are stripped away:

```
-----rule matches: $2 < $3 > $4
rewritten as: a < b > c
```

The new workspace is then compared to the LHS of the same rule *once again*— that is, to the rule that just did the rewriting. If it were to match again, it would be rewritten again. This property (which in error can continue forever) can be useful in solving many configuration problems. We'll cover this property more fully in the next chapter.

So the rewritten workspace is compared once again to the second rule. The workspace (having been rewritten by the second rule) now contains

```
a < b > c
```

This time the comparison fails:

```
-----trying rule: $* < $* < $* > $* > $*
----- rule fails
```

The last of the three rules then gets a crack at the workspace. That rule is

```
R$* < $* > $*        $2                    basic RFC822 parsing
```

That workspace is still

```
a  <  b  >  c
```

The workspace is once again matched, so it is rewritten again on the basis of the RHS of the third rule:

```
-----trying rule: $* < $* > $*
-----rule matches: $2
rewritten as: b
```

After the third rule rewrites the workspace, it again tries to match that rewritten workspace and fails:

```
-----trying rule: $* < $* > $*
----- rule fails
```

As you can see, the −d21.12 debugging switch can be very useful. It shows you exactly what each rule is trying to do. It shows you each rewrite of the workspace, and it shows you the order in which rules are being applied. (Note that in real rule sets, this output can easily span many screens.)

10.6 Things to Try

- Design a rule whose LHS always matches anything in the workspace and whose RHS always rewrites so as to leave the workspace unchanged. What happens when you test this rule?

- Design a rule whose LHS will match *name* in the workspace but will not match *name@host*. Is this possible with just $+ and $*?

- What happens if you arrange rules in a different order? Try reversing the first two rules in our rule set 3.

11

Rule Sets 1 and S=

Recall that the *client.cf* file that we have been developing has two purposes: to forward all mail to a central mail hub for processing and to make all mail appear as though it originated from the hub. The first purpose was fulfilled by the creation of a rule set 0 that always selects the hub delivery agent. In this chapter we begin the process of fulfilling the second purpose, by designing rule sets 1 and S=.

But first, to review, recall also that the recipient's address is first processed by rule set 3 and then by rule set 0. Rule set 3 finds an address among other text and cleans up the address by removing nested angle brackets. After that, rule set 0 selects a delivery agent on the basis of the recipient's address. If the address is bad, rule set 0 selects the error delivery agent. For a valid address, rule set 0 selects the hub delivery agent. Once the delivery agent is selected, the processing of other addresses, such as the sender's address, may proceed.

11.1 Flow of the Sender's Address

When *sendmail* begins processing a mail message for delivery, it first looks for the envelope[*] recipients. Each recipient address that is found is first processed by rule set 3, and then by rule set 0, which selects a delivery agent.

After appropriate delivery agents have been selected for all recipients, *sendmail* processes the sender's address. There is usually only a single sender[†] for any given mail message. The sender's address (or addresses) may appear in the envelope or in a From: header line, or it may be derived from the *uid* of the process that ran *sendmail.*

---

[*] See Chapter 1, *Introduction,* for a review of the concepts of header versus envelope.

[†] The envelope sender and the header sender are not necessarily the same.

As shown in Figure 11-1, the address is processed by rule set 3 first and then by rule set 1. Then, for each recipient in the list of recipients, each sender's address is custom processed by the rule set specified in the recipient delivery agent's S= equate. This custom processing is necessary because different delivery agents may want the sender's address to have a different appearance. One example is the difference between a domain-based delivery agent (needing an address such as *gw@wash.dc.gov*) and a UUCP-based delivery agent (needing a routing path such as *fbi!wash!gw*).

We will examine the custom S= processing first, then discuss why a generic rule set 1 is not needed in the *client.cf* file.

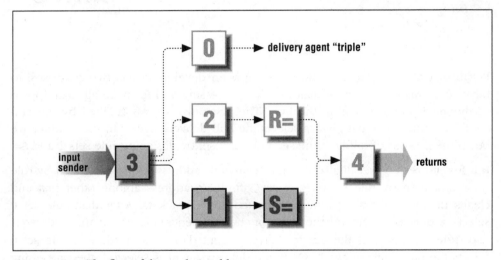

Figure 11-1: The flow of the sender's address

11.2 Rule Set S=

In the original hub delivery agent definition the S= equate was set to zero:

```
Mhub,    P=[IPC], S=0, R=0, F=mDFMuXa, T=DNS/RFC822/SMTP, A=IPC $h
                  ↑
              no custom processing
```

The S= equate is used to specify the number of the rule set that will perform delivery agent–specific custom processing of the sender's address. When that equate specifies rule set 0, *sendmail* does no custom processing. Now that we intend to do custom sender address processing, we will change the 0 into of a real rule set number and write that rule set.

Recall that rule sets 0 through 5 have special internal meanings to *sendmail* (see §8.3). When selecting a rule number for use in a delivery agent's S= equate, you need either to carefully select one that does not already have internal meaning for *sendmail* or to let *sendmail* select the number for you. For the purposes of the *client.cf* file we will use the latter approach.[*]

As the first step in creating a new rule set, edit the *client.cf* file and change S=0 to S=Hubset in the hub delivery agent definition.

```
Mhub,    P=[IPC], S=Hubset, R=0, F=mDFMuXa, T=DNS/RFC822/SMTP, A=IPC $h
```

change to symbolic name

This change tells *sendmail* to assign a number of its own choosing to S=. That rule set, which we will refer to symbolically by the name Hubset, will do a custom rewrite of the sender's address for this (the hub) delivery agent. But before you can create that actual rule set, we need to review why it is necessary.

11.3 All Mail from the Hub

Recall that one purpose of *client.cf* is to make all messages appear to originate from the hub. The purpose of a rule set Hubset is to rewrite the sender's address so that the mail message always appears to originate from the hub machine.

```
From: user@client
       ↓
     becomes
       ↓
From: user@hub
```

This could be done by rule set 3, but that would affect all addresses, both recipient and sender, which is not appropriate. Mail should not appear to be both *to and from* the hub, but should appear to be only *from* the hub. It could also be done in rule set 1 (which we will cover soon), but that would affect all sender addresses. You don't want to rewrite all sender addresses, just those that are being sent through the hub. You may someday want to use prog or local delivery agents, and the sender's address should be left unchanged for them.

11.4 Rule Set Hubset

Place the following new rule after rule set 3 in the *client.cf* file:

```
S3 # preprocessing for all rule sets
R$* <> $*                      $n            handle <> error address
R$* < $* < $* > $* > $*        $2<$3>$4      de-nest brackets
R$* < $* > $*                  $2            basic RFC822 parsing

SHubset # Rewrite the sender for the hub                        ← new
```

---
[*] Available only beginning with V8.7 *sendmail*.

At this point you may be wondering why we can give this rule set a symbolic name, when the earlier rule sets (0 and 3) had numeric names. The answer lies inside *sendmail*. Recall that rule set numbers 0 through 5 have special internal meaning to *sendmail*. Part of that meaning is their names. The *sendmail* program recognizes those special rules only by number. If you were to give them names instead of numbers, *sendmail* would not recognize them, and your configuration file would cease to work.

On the other hand, beginning with V8.7 *sendmail*, you may both specify a rule set and give it a symbolic name. Internally, *sendmail* converts that name to a number (a high one such as 199) and internally refers to it by number. The conversion process ensures that each name will correspond to a unique number.

Now that we've named `Hubset`, let's put some rules in it.

11.4.1 Rewrite the Lone Username

The sender's address can take several forms. It can be a user's login name, such as *gw* or *ben*. It can be a user at a short hostname, such as *gw@wash* or *ben@fbi*. It can be a user at a fully qualified name such as *gw@wash.dc.gov* or *ben@fbi.dc.gov*.

The `Hubset` rule set first looks for an address that is just a simple user's name, such as *gw*, and makes it appear as though it is from the mail hub. To do this, you need a new LHS wildcard operator, `$-`. The `$-` wildcard operator matches *exactly one* token in the workspace. The first rule in the `Hubset` rule set uses the `$-` wildcard operator like this:

```
SHubset # Rewrite the sender for the hub
R$-                       $@ $1@${HUB}   user -> user@hub    ← new
```

Because `$-` is the only wildcard operator in the LHS, a match occurs only if the workspace contains a single token:

```
$-              matches     "you"
$-              does not match   "you" "@" "localhost"
```

This LHS is used to look for an address that contains only a user's login name. When such a match is found, the RHS (`$@ $1@${HUB}`) rewrites that address by appending an @ and the name of the mail hub machine, which was stored in the `${HUB}` macro.

The RHS contains two rewrite operators, one that you have seen already and one that you haven't:

```
$1              positional operator (you have seen this)
$@              return immediately (new)
```

When $@ begins (prefixes) the RHS of any rule, it tells *sendmail* to return (exit the current rule set) immediately after it has rewritten the workspace. If the $@ prefix did not appear at the start of the RHS, *sendmail* would rewrite the workspace and then evaluate the LHS again. The $@ also prevents the workspace from being carried down to any additional rules in the current rule set. An immediate return from this rule is desirable because additional rules might corrupt the now correct workspace.

The actual rewriting is done by $1@${HUB}. The $1, which you have seen before, takes the username matched by the LHS of $- (the first and only wildcard operator, thus $1). Then an @ character is appended. Then the ${HUB} macro is appended to the workspace.

The ${HUB} macro contains the address of the mail hub machine as it is known to the outside world. This is different from the ${REMOTE} macro that you defined earlier, which contains the address of the mail hub machine as it is known to the internal network. Before you can use the value of ${HUB}, you need to define it in the *client.cf* file:

```
# Defined macros
D{REMOTE}mailhost          # The name of the mail hub
D{HUB}mail.us.edu          # Hub as known to the outside world    ← new
```

This new macro definition places the text mail.us.edu into the macro named {HUB}. Now the RHS of $1@${HUB} will rewrite the workspace into

```
you @ mail . us . edu
 ↑   ↑ ↑
 $1  @ ${HUB}
```

This is exactly what is wanted. Remember that the Hubset rule set handles only sender addresses. Any sender address that consists of nothing more than the name of a user will be rewritten to appear to come from the mail hub. Table 11-1 shows the three LHS wildcard operators that you now know.

Table 11-1: Three LHS Wildcard Operators

Wildcard	Description
$+	Match one or more tokens
$*	Match zero or more tokens
$-	Match exactly one token

11.4.2 A Word About ${HUB}

In the *client.cf* file, `${REMOTE}` is defined to be the name of the hub machine as it is known internally to your network. `${HUB}` is defined to be the name of that same machine as it is known to the outside world. Note that both names could be (and probably will be) the same at your site.

The important point about `${REMOTE}` is that it contains a symbolic name, such as *mailhost*. This allows the machine that is used as the hub to be easily changed should the need arise. As your site becomes larger and more complex, you might want to have several hubs for routing messages to the outside world. Or you might want to have one machine handle all outgoing mail and another handle all incoming mail. Using a symbolic name makes such changes easy.

The important point about `${HUB}`, on the other hand, is that it contains a fully qualified domain name that is listed with the Domain Name System or the UUCP maps and is known to all other sites in the world. This is the host part of the address that other sites will use when they reply to mail sent from the hub.

Remember that a name such as *you@* with the value of `${HUB}` added makes the address of the local sender (*you*) look as though it is from the hub (*mail.us.edu*). When someone at another site replies to this address, the reply will go to the *hub* rather than to the local client. This is an important distinction, because the client machine may (by design) be unable to receive mail (more on this later).

11.5 Testing So Far

If you haven't already done so, add the new macro and the new rule set to the *client.cf* file:

```
# Defined macros
D{REMOTE}mailhost          # The name of the mail hub
D{HUB}mail.us.edu          # Hub as known to the outside world   ← new
```

Remember to replace `mail.us.edu` with a real hostname—the name of the hub machine at your site.

The new rule set looks like this:

```
SHubset # Rewrite the sender for the hub
R$-                        $@ $1@${HUB}   user -> user@hub        ← new
```

Now test the new rule by running *sendmail* in rule-testing mode:

```
% ./sendmail -Cclient.cf -bt
ADDRESS TEST MODE (ruleset 3 NOT automatically invoked)
Enter <ruleset> <address>
>
```

At the prompt, specify rule set 3 first because all addresses are preprocessed by that rule. Then specify Hubset, because the hub delivery agent definition specifies that rule in its S= equate.

```
> 3,Hubset you
```

Following the list of rule sets, give the sender's name. Remember that the lone login name will be rewritten to appear as though it is from the hub. The output produced by *sendmail* looks like this:

```
rewrite: ruleset   3   input: you
rewrite: ruleset   3 returns: you
rewrite: ruleset 199   input: you
rewrite: ruleset 199 returns: you @ mail . us . edu
```

Note that V8 *sendmail* internally changed the name Hubset into the number 199.

11.6 Handling user@thishost

The Hubset rule set next needs a rule that will take an address consisting of a username and a short hostname and will change only the host part. Consider an address of the form:

```
user@thishost
```

Here, the user part is what you already dealt with: a user's login name such as *you*. It is followed by an @ character and then the local host's name. One method of matching this form of address in the LHS would be to match the user, the @ character, and *any* hostname (recall that the $+ matches one or more tokens in the workspace):

```
R$-@$+
```

This form is easy to use because the $+ would match any hostname at all and wouldn't require that you know all the possible names for the local host ahead of time. Unfortunately, you shouldn't use this approach, because you want to rewrite the sender's hostname only if it is that of the local machine. Using $+ would cause the sender's hostname to be rewritten whether or not it is the name of the local machine.

But how could the sender's address not be from the local machine? Recall that *sendmail* gets the sender address from one of four places: from the envelope, from the From: header, from the -f switch (see below), or from the *uid* of the process that ran *sendmail*.

Consider, for example, a Usenet news-posting program that posts news by sending mail. It may be desirable to have all posted news messages appear to be from the

news program on the news server machine. One way to achieve this is by running
sendmail with the -f switch:

```
-f news@news.server
```

Here, the -f switch causes *sendmail* to use the address specified on the command
line as the address of the sender.

But in this example you would not want to change the address of the sender to
appear as though it were from the hub. That would undo what **news** tries to do
with the -f switch.

A better approach is to match the user, the @ character, and the specific local hostname:

```
R$-@$w
```

Recall that $w was defined to be the short hostname of the local host. This LHS
matches only a workspace (sender's address) that begins with a single user's login
name ($-), followed by @, and then by the name of the local host ($w).

Add this new rule to the *client.cf* file:

```
SHubset # Rewrite the sender for the hub
R$-          $@ $1@${HUB}        user -> user@hub
R$-@$w       $@ $1@${HUB}        user@local -> user@hub        ← new
```

Notice that, other than their comments, the two rules differ only in their LHS. The
flow through these rules is that the first tries to match a lone username in the
workspace. If that match fails, the second rule tries to match the workspace. It
matches only a workspace that contains the name of a user at the local machine.
To observe this rule in action, run *sendmail* in rule-testing mode again:

```
% ./sendmail -d0.1 -Cclient.cf -bt
```

This time, we added the -d0.1 debugging command-line switch, which tells *sendmail* to print the identity of the local machine:

```
Version 8.8.4
 Compiled with: LOG MATCHGECOS MIME7TO8 MIME8TO7 NAMED_BIND NDBM NETINET
                NETUNIX NIS SCANF XDEBUG

============ SYSTEM IDENTITY (after readcf) ============
      (short domain name) $w = here
  (canonical domain name) $j = here.us.edu
        (subdomain name) $m = us.edu
            (node name) $k = here
=======================================================

ADDRESS TEST MODE (ruleset 3 NOT automatically invoked)
Enter <ruleset> <address>
>
```

Note that *sendmail*, in this example, defines $w as here, the name of the local machine. Your local machine name will, of course, differ. Fortunately, you don't have to know what that name is to design a new rule. Simply use $w, and let *sendmail* do all the work.

Now give *sendmail* rule sets 3 and Hubset as you did before, but this time specify a sender's address that contains a user and a host part:

> 3,Hubset you@here

the same as appeared in $w

The user part can be any login name. The host part must be the text in the $w macro (displayed when you just ran *sendmail* with the −d0.1 debugging command-line switch above).

```
rewrite: ruleset   3    input: you @ here
rewrite: ruleset   3 returns: you @ here
rewrite: ruleset 199    input: you @ here
rewrite: ruleset 199 returns: you @ mail . us . edu
```

As intended, Hubset, the custom rule set for rewriting the sender's address for the hub delivery agent, made the local address appear to be from the hub.

Note, however, that you cannot specify macros when testing addresses; that is, the following does not work:

> 3,Hubset you@$w

The *sendmail* program does not recognize macros in addresses. They aren't recognized because macros in rule sets are expanded when the configuration file is read, not when *sendmail* reads addresses. The command above results in the following erroneous output:

```
rewrite: ruleset   3    input: you @ $w
rewrite: ruleset   3 returns: you @ $w
rewrite: ruleset 199    input: you @ $w
rewrite: ruleset 199 returns: you @ $w
```

Also note that the value in $w is the short hostname, *here*, instead of the fully qualified name *here.us.edu*. Instead of adding an additional rule to test for the fully qualified name, we defer this problem to the next chapter.

11.7 Rule Set 1

When we began this chapter, we explained that the sender's address was processed by a series of three rule sets: rule set 3, rule set 1, and the custom rule set specified by the S= delivery agent equate. We've described rule set 3 and S=, but we haven't yet described rule set 1. If we send all mail to a central hub, we don't really need a rule set 1. That's because there is nothing that we need to do to *all* sender addresses. In fact, most configuration files, even at large sites, have no need for a rule set 1.[*]

Still, it is wise to add a dummy rule set 1 (one that does nothing) to the *client.cf* file. For one thing, this makes it clear that you haven't simply omitted rule set 1 by oversight. It also allows us to illustrate some points about rule sets in general.

```
R$-             $@ $1@${HUB}         user -> user@hub
R$-@$w          $@ $1@${HUB}         user@local -> user@hub

S1 # Generic sender rewrite (unused)                              ← new
```

We place rule set 1 last in the *client.cf* file, as we will continue to do with any other unused rules. This declaration of rule set 1 illustrates three points about rule sets in general:

*   Rule sets do not have to be in any particular order in the configuration file. The *sendmail* program reads the entire file and sorts the rule sets internally.

*   A rule set containing no rules is a "do-nothing" rule set. The workspace passed to it is returned unchanged.

*   Rule sets that are declared but unused should be commented to indicate this fact.

The positioning of rule sets in the configuration file is largely a matter of individual taste. Some administrators like to keep custom rule sets (such as Hubset) next to the delivery agent definition rather than with the general rules. We don't favor any particular approach over another. The overriding concern in any configuration file—which can be complex—should be for clarity and organization.

11.8 Things to Try

*   All machines can be known by two names: the normal hostname (as defined by $w) and the generic name *localhost*. Design and test a rule for Hubset that tests for and rewrites a sender address like *you@localhost*.

*   When we speak of the sender, we have lumped together the envelope and header senders into one. Try to think of examples in which the sender header address should be rewritten in a way that is different from the sender envelope address.

*   At a site that has more than one hub, it would be necessary to route mail from some clients to one hub and mail from other clients to another. Think of a basis for such a division (such as subnets or NIS domains) and design a set of

---

[*] Eric says, "Given it to do over, rule sets 1 and 2 wouldn't exist."

rules (in a single configuration file) to rewrite the sender address appropriately for a selected hub.

- Consider the need to match subsets of a subdomain. For example, assume that the local hostname is *here* and the local domain is *my.sub.domain*. At such a site, all of the following are legal addresses: *you@here*, *you@here.my*, and *you@here.my.sub.domain*. But the following is illegal: *you@here.my.sub*. Modify rule set Hubset in the *client.cf* file so that it recognizes all the legal forms of addressing in a subdomain.

12

Class

In rule sets, it is often advantageous to compare individual tokens to multiple strings in determining a match. For example, consider the rules developed in the last chapter, that is, the sender rewriting rules from the hub delivery agent's S=Hubset rule set:

```
SHubset # Rewrite the sender for the hub
R$-          $@ $1@${HUB}          user -> user@hub
R$-@$w       $@ $1@${HUB}          user@local -> user@hub
```

The second rule's LHS looks for any sender address that is composed of a single username followed by an @ character and ending with the short name of the local machine ($w). Such an address is rewritten by the RHS to become that of the central forwarding machine, defined by the {HUB} macro.

Now suppose that the local machine is known by several names in addition to the short name in $w. All machines, for example, have a short name (such as *here*) and a fully qualified name (such as *here.us.edu*). They also often refer to themselves as *localhost*. In addition, some machines can play special roles at a site (such as having a printer or containing a central directory of fonts) and might have another name appropriate to that role.

To convert any sender address so that it becomes the central forwarder's name, no matter what the local host's name, you can use *sendmail* classes. In this chapter we will cover the class configuration command and its cousin, the file configuration command. Proper use of the class and file commands allows you to replace many rules with a single rule.

12.1 *The Class Command*

The class command declares a macro whose value is a list of strings. Rule sets may then compare the workspace to that list of strings. One such list could be a list of names by which the local machine is known.

A class is referenced in the LHS with the $= prefix:

```
$=X          ← single-character name
$={XXX}      ← multicharacter name (beginning with V8.7)
```

Here, *X* is a single-character class name. Beginning with V8.7 *sendmail*, multichar-acter class name may be used, as shown in the second line above. Multicharacter class names must always be enclosed in curly braces.

The workspace is tokenized as usual; then the appropriate token is looked up to see whether it was defined as belonging to the class referenced by $=. If the token was found, the workspace at that point is considered to be matched. We'll cover this in more detail shortly.

12.1.1 *Declaring a Class*

The words that form the list of words in a class are declared with the C configura-tion command. The form for the class configuration command is as follows:

```
CXlist          ← single-character name
C{XXX}list      ← multicharacter name (beginning with V8.7)
```

The class configuration command starts with the letter C, which must begin a line. The C is immediately followed (with no intervening whitespace) by the name of that class. A class name can be a single ASCII character or, beginning with V8.7 *sendmail*, multiple ASCII characters enclosed in curly braces. A whitespace-separated *list* of word elements follows on the same line. Space between the name and the *list* is optional.

For example, the following declaration places two possible names for the local machine into the class named w:

```
Cw printer1 fontserver
```

Multiple declarations of the same class macro may exist. Each appends its word elements to the preceding list. For example, the following produces the same result as the single line above:

```
Cw printer1
Cw fontserver
```

Both examples define a class named w, and both assign to that class the same list of two words.

12.1.1.1 A caveat

Class names and macro names are completely independent. To illustrate, consider the following two configuration commands:

```
Dwprinter1
Cwprinter1
```

Both assign the value `printer1` to the name `w`. The first assigns that value to a macro, the second to a class. Internally, *sendmail* stores the value `printer1` twice, first as type "macro" and second as type "class." Although they share the same value (`printer1`), macros and classes are completely independent of each other.

12.1.2 Multiple Known Names for the Local Host

As an example of one common use of the class macro, we will consider the case of machines that are known by multiple names. Run *sendmail* again:

```
% ./sendmail -Cclient.cf -bt
ADDRESS TEST MODE (ruleset 3 NOT automatically invoked)
Enter <ruleset> <address>
>
```

Now give it the special (new to V8.7 *sendmail*) rule-testing command `$=` (which tells *sendmail* to print the values stored in a class) and follow that with the letter (class name) `w`:

```
> $=w
here.us.edu
here
[123.45.67.8]
>
```

This illustrates that *sendmail* is aware of three of your machine's possible names (the last is an IP address). But recall from the previous chapter that the rule that we created looked for the local machine using only the short name in the macro `w`, not the three names in class `w`:

```
R$-@$w          $@ $1@${HUB}          user@local -> user@hub
```

If we didn't have class macros, we would have to look for the local machine name using a series of rules like those below:

```
R$-@$w              $@ $1@${HUB}          user@local -> user@hub
R$-@here.us.edu     $@ $1@${HUB}          user@local -> user@hub
R$-@[123.45.67.8]   $@ $1@${HUB}          user@local -> user@hub
```

Fortunately, the class configuration command provides an alternative. Use of a class list allows one rule to be written that does exactly the same thing as the three preceding rules:

```
R$-@$=w          $@ $1@${HUB}          user@local -> user@hub
```

Let's examine this new rule, then test it.

12.1.3 Class Macros in the LHS

The list of words in a class are referenced in the LHS of rules by prefixing the class name with the characters $=. For the class named w the expression in the LHS looks like this:

```
$=w
```

To understand how this expression is evaluated, we need to look at how the words in the class are stored. Each word that *sendmail* adds to the list (whether internally or from a C configuration command) is stored by *sendmail* in its *symbol table*. The symbol table holds all the words that appear in the configuration file. It holds the values of macro definitions and the symbolic names of delivery agents. It also holds the words that form a class list.

Next, we need to review how the workspace is tokenized and compared to the LHS of a rule. Just before the LHS is compared to the workspace, the workspace is tokenized. The address of a local user in the workspace might look like, and be tokenized like, the following:

```
you@here    becomes →    you @ here
```

When the $=w expression appears in the LHS of a rule, it is compared to the workspace at the point that corresponds to the class's position in the LHS:

```
R$-@$=w          $@$1@${HUB}          user@local -> user@hub
    ↑
   here
```

In performing its minimum match of the workspace to the LHS, the matches are the following:

```
$-     ← match you
@      ← match @
$=w    ← does here match any token in class w?
```

When *sendmail* encounters a class-matching expression in the LHS, it looks up the corresponding token from the workspace in its symbol table. Here it looks up here. Because here is listed in the symbol table as belonging to the class w, *sendmail* finds a match. If there were no here in the symbol table, the match would fail. If there were one or more **here** entries in the symbol table, but none marked as belonging to class **w**, the match would also fail.

12.1.4 Class Macros in the RHS

When a match in the LHS allows the RHS to rewrite the workspace, the token matched by the $= prefix can be referenced with a $*digit* positional operator. This differs from the $ macro prefix that you learned about earlier. Macros are expanded when the configuration file is read (so $*digit* doesn't work), but classes are given values only when a rule is matched (so $*digit* does work).

We don't use the positional operator in the RHS because we don't care what word matched. Instead, we take the username from the LHS with $1, add an @ character and the name of the forwarding hub machine (the ${HUB}):

```
R$-@$=w          $@$1@${HUB}              user@local -> user@hub
  ↑  ↑                  ↑
  1  2             $2 not needed
```

12.1.5 Testing Class

Modify the *client.cf* file by changing the $w in the second rule (of **SHubset**) into a $=w so that we can begin to test the class:

```
R$-@$=w          $@ $1@${HUB}            user@local -> user@hub
     ↑
  insert an =
```

Now run *sendmail* in rule-testing mode once again:

```
% ./sendmail -Cclient.cf -bt
ADDRESS TEST MODE (ruleset 3 NOT automatically invoked)
Enter <ruleset> <address>
>
```

First use the $= rule-testing command to list the contents of the class **w**:

```
> $=w
here.us.edu
here
[123.45.67.8]
```

Next, to test the new rule, specify rule set **Hubset** and give *sendmail* an address with a user, an @, and one of the local addresses shown for your machine:

```
> Hubset you@here.us.edu
rewrite: ruleset 199    input: you @ here . us . edu
rewrite: ruleset 199 returns: you @ mail . us . edu
```

This result is just what we expected. After all, the value in ${HUB} is mail.us.edu.
Now give *sendmail* another address, only this time give it one not in the list:

```
> Hubset you@localhost
rewrite: ruleset 199    input: you @ localhost
rewrite: ruleset 199 returns: you @ localhost
```

This time the address was not rewritten because localhost is not listed in the
class w. But, in general, *localhost* is a legitimate name for the local machine, so
let's add it temporarily by employing a new rule-testing command that you haven't
seen before:

```
> .Cw localhost
> $=w
here.us.edu
localhost
here
[123.45.67.8]
```

The .C command (new with V8.7) tells *sendmail* to temporarily add a word to a
class. In this case we added the word localhost to the class w. We then ran the
$= rule-testing command to confirm that *sendmail* had actually added the word to
the class.

Test the address *localhost* again:

```
> Hubset you@localhost
rewrite: ruleset 199    input: you @ localhost
rewrite: ruleset 199 returns: you @ mail . us . edu
```

This time, *sendmail* found localhost in the list and so rewrote the sender
address.

12.1.6 Add Class w to client.cf

As we mentioned earlier, a host may be known by many names. Some of those
names are found automatically by *sendmail*; others must be added by you. The
name *localhost* is one possibility, and there may be others (such as *printer1*). You
can add them to class w in rule-testing mode, but that is not a permanent solution
(because they are forgotten as soon you leave rule-testing mode). Instead, you
need to add them to your configuration file using the C configuration command.

Edit the *client.cf* file and add a new C configuration line to it:

```
V7
# Defined macros
D{REMOTE}mailhost             # The name of the mail hub
D{HUB}mail.us.edu             # Hub as known to the outside world

Cw localhost printer1         # My other names.          ← new
```

Here we added `localhost` because it was missing and `printer1` to illustrate later points. Note that the name `printer1` is probably not appropriate for your site, but include it for now.

Run *sendmail* again in rule-testing mode:

```
% ./sendmail -Cclient.cf -bt
ADDRESS TEST MODE (ruleset 3 NOT automatically invoked)
Enter <ruleset> <address>
>
```

Use the `$=` rule-testing command again. Make sure the `C` line added the new names to the class `w`:

```
> $=w
here.us.edu
localhost
here
[123.45.67.8]
printer1
```

We can now test each name. Remember that the rule we are testing is this one:

```
R$-@$=w          $@ $1@${HUB}              user@local -> user@hub
```

We want to match any sender address that is a username, an `@`, and any of the names in the class `w`. We also want to rewrite each to appear as though the user is from the hub.

```
> Hubset you@here.us.edu
rewrite: ruleset 199    input: you @ here . us . edu
rewrite: ruleset 199 returns: you @ mail . us . edu
> Hubset you@localhost
rewrite: ruleset 199    input: you @ localhost
rewrite: ruleset 199 returns: you @ mail . us . edu
> Hubset you@here
rewrite: ruleset 199    input: you @ here
rewrite: ruleset 199 returns: you @ mail . us . edu
> Hubset you@[123.45.67.8]
rewrite: ruleset 199    input: you @ [ 123 . 45 . 67 . 8 ]
rewrite: ruleset 199 returns: you @ mail . us . edu
> Hubset you@printer1
rewrite: ruleset 199    input: you @ printer1
rewrite: ruleset 199 returns: you @ mail . us . edu
> Hubset you@printer1.us.edu
rewrite: ruleset 199    input: you @ printer1 . us . edu
rewrite: ruleset 199 returns: you @ printer1 . us . edu
```

All the names in class `w` match as they should. Notice that *here* appears in the list as both a short and a fully qualified name, but *printer1* does not. When we tried *printer1* in a fully qualified form (in the last three lines above), it failed. To make *printer1* succeed, we could add its fully qualified form to the class `w`, but if we did that, we would have to do the same for *localhost* and any other names that we added. Instead, we will deal with the problem by adding a rule to the *client.cf* file.

12.1.7 Adding the Domain

There are three approaches to writing a rule that matches any of the local hostnames with a domain added:

1. Use a $* wildcard operator to match anything after the local hostname:

   ```
   R$-@$=w$*
   ```

   But this is unwise because it assumes that anything that follows the host is a domain, which might not always be true.

2. Use your domain name directly in the rule:

   ```
   R$-@$=w.us.edu
   ```

   Although this will work, it is better to use a macro in case you change your domain or use this file on a machine in another domain.

3. Use a macro that has your domain name as its value.

We will use the third approach because it is the cleanest. Begin by running *sendmail* with the −d0.1 debugging switch again:

```
Version 8.8.4
 Compiled with: LOG MATCHGECOS MIME7TO8 MIME8TO7 NAMED_BIND NDBM NETINET
                NETUNIX NIS SCANF XDEBUG

============ SYSTEM IDENTITY (after readcf) ============
       (short domain name) $w = here
   (canonical domain name) $j = here.us.edu
         (subdomain name) $m = us.edu
             (node name) $k = here
========================================================

ADDRESS TEST MODE (ruleset 3 NOT automatically invoked)
Enter <ruleset> <address>
>
```

Note that the line that defines the "subdomain name" (the one with the $m) is the local domain that we need for our new rule. Add another rule to the Hubset rule set. This new rule looks for any local names (in $=w) that are followed by the local domain name defined for you by *sendmail*:

```
SHubset # Rewrite the sender for the hub
R$-            $@ $1@${HUB}          user -> user@hub
R$-@$=w        $@ $1@${HUB}          user@local -> user@hub
R$-@$=w.$m     $@ $1@${HUB}          user@local.domain -> user@hub     ← new
```

Now run *sendmail* once again and feed it the address that failed in the last test (but use your local domain):

```
% ./sendmail -Cclient.cf -bt
ADDRESS TEST MODE (ruleset 3 NOT automatically invoked)
Enter <ruleset> <address>
> Hubset you@printer1.us.edu
rewrite: ruleset 199   input: you @ printer1 . us . edu
rewrite: ruleset 199 returns: you @ mail . us . edu
```

As expected, the new rule in the Hubset rule set does its job. It finds that the printer1.us.edu part of the address matches the $=w.$m part of the rule and rewrites the workspace to make the sender's address appear as though it is from the hub.

12.2 *The File Form of Class*

It is not always possible or convenient to list the values for a class directly in the configuration file. Sometimes it might be better to store values in files. Examples of this might be the following:

- The names of hosts that are connected to the local machine via UUCP. At some sites, such connections are created and removed often, and it is undesirable to be constantly changing the configuration file.

- The names of hosts that are being moved from one location to another. During a move, it is better to modify an external file while each hostname is changed and then to modify the configuration file after all the moves have been done.

- The alternative names for a machine may vary from machine to machine, yet a single configuration file may be shared among them. When such a *boilerplate* configuration file is centrally maintained (and distributed with *rdist*(1), for example), names that indicate the specialty roles of a machine should be external to that file.

The *client.cf* file lists two additional names for the local host in the class **w**:

```
Cw localhost printer1          # My other names.
```

To make this configuration file more general, it would be better to store the host-specific name (printer1) in a separate file. To externalize words for a class list, you use the F configuration command. That command looks like this:

```
Fw/path
```

The F must begin a line. This tells *sendmail* that this is a class definition, just like the C command that we just illustrated. The name of the class (here **w**) must immediately follow the F with no intervening space. If the class name is multicharacter, it must be enclosed in curly braces. Optional space may separate the class name from the */path*. With the C command, a list of words follows the name on the same line, but with the F command, the name of a *file* follows. */path* is the full pathname of a file. For demonstration purposes we will name that file */etc/sendmail.cw*.[*]

Edit the *client.cf* file and make two changes. Delete the name **printer1** from the C line and add a new F line:

```
                        remove printer1
                             ↓
    Cw localhost                    # My other names.
    Fw/etc/sendmail.cw              # A file of other names        ← new
```

The first class definition starts with the letter C and tells *sendmail* to add the name `localhost` to the list of words in the class w. The second line tells *sendmail* to read the file named */etc/sendmail.cw* and to add the words in that file to the class w. Note that the name w is the same for each line. The C and F commands differ only in where the words are taken from.

Now run *sendmail* and notice what happens when the file */etc/sendmail.cw* doesn't exist:

```
% ./sendmail -Cclient.cf -bt
client.cf: line 7: fileclass: cannot open /etc/sendmail.cw: No such file or directory
ADDRESS TEST MODE (ruleset 3 NOT automatically invoked)
Enter <ruleset> <address>
>
```

As you would expect, *sendmail* prints an error message when it fails to find the file. But as you might not expect, *sendmail* prints the error warning and continues to run.

Because we are developing a generic configuration file, one that can be shared among many machines, we would prefer not to have an error printed if the file doesn't exist. We can suppress the error message by adding a −o (for optional) switch to the F configuration command:

```
    Fw -o /etc/sendmail.cw          # A file of other names
       ↑
      new
```

Now run *sendmail* again and notice that the error message is gone:

```
% ./sendmail -Cclient.cf -bt
ADDRESS TEST MODE (ruleset 3 NOT automatically invoked)
```

---

[*] This is the path recommended by V8.7 and above *sendmail*.

```
Enter <ruleset> <address>
>
```

But we still want the name `printer1` to be recognized as local. To do that, we need to either put it back into the C line that we just removed it from or put it into the file that doesn't exist yet, the */etc/sendmail.cw* file.

Create and edit the file */etc/sendmail.cw*. If you lack write permission, create a file that you are permitted to write to (such as */usr/tmp/sendmail.cw*) and use it in the following examples and in the *client.cf* file. Put this hostname into that file:

```
printer1
```

The next time you run *sendmail*, it reads this file and adds each word it sees to the class w. Run *sendmail* in rule-testing mode again and verify that for yourself:

```
% ./sendmail -Cclient.cf -bt
ADDRESS TEST MODE (ruleset 3 NOT automatically invoked)
Enter <ruleset> <address>
> $=w
here.us.edu
localhost
here
[123.45.67.8]
printer1
```

Success! Now add some more names to the *sendmail.cw* file. We will use bogus names just for demonstration purposes:

```
                    add
                     ↓
printer1 bogus
fake                      ← add
```

Run *sendmail* again and notice that the name **bogus** is missing:

```
% ./sendmail -Cclient.cf -bt
ADDRESS TEST MODE (ruleset 3 NOT automatically invoked)
Enter <ruleset> <address>
> $=w
here.us.edu
fake
localhost
here
[123.45.67.8]
printer1
```

Why is **bogus** missing? To answer this question, leap ahead to §32.1. But for now, just assume that there may be only one word per line.

12.3 *Things to Try*

- In an F command, rather than specifying the name of a file, specify the name of a directory or a device such as */dev/null.* Does *sendmail* care? How does it handle (or not handle) nonfiles?

- Use */usr/dict/words* as a class file. Does reading a huge file slow *sendmail* down noticeably? Does this suggest that a database might be more efficient for some needs?

- Are there security concerns surrounding use of the F command? Imagine ways in which a cracker might exploit a careless use of the F command to compromise your system. Skip ahead to §22.4.2 to explore this question further.

13

Setting Options

The *client.cf* file is now roughed out enough that it can almost be used to send mail. All that remains are two important loose ends: options, which we cover in this chapter, and headers, which we cover in the next.

Options determine much of the behavior of *sendmail*. For example, they can specify the location of the queue directory, set the default permissions for files, and list the characters that separate tokens in an address. These and other options will be discussed in this chapter.

13.1 Options: An Overview

Options are declared in the configuration file by beginning a line with the letter O:

```
OQ/var/spool/mqueue                    ← single-character name (prior to V8.7)
```

Prior to V8.7 *sendmail*, option names could only be a single character. The short (single character) name of the option (here Q) immediately follows the O with no intervening space. The value assigned to a single-character option immediately follows the option letter with no intervening space.

Beginning with V8.7 *sendmail*, option names may consist of multiple characters:

```
O QueueDirectory=/var/spool/mqueue      ← multicharacter name (beginning with V8.7)
  ↑
  exactly one space
```

To use multicharacter names, you must separate the name (here QueueDirectory) from the O command with exactly one space character.[*] The value assigned to the

---

[*] If the short option name is a space, *sendmail* presumes that the option name will be multicharacter.

multicharacter option follows an equal sign. The equal sign can be surrounded by optional spaces.

Some options have both a single-character name and a multicharacter name, in which case the two names are equivalent:

```
OQ/var/spool/mqueue                    ← define location of queue directory
O QueueDirectory=/var/spool/mqueue     ← the same
```

Other options (the newer ones) only have multicharacter names:

```
O ServiceSwitchFile=/etc/service.switch      ← only multicharacter form available
```

When we mention such options in the text, we will specify the multicharacter name first, followed by the single-character name in parentheses if there is one; for example, the `QueueDirectory` (Q) option, but the `ServiceSwitchFile` option.

The values for some options are strings (such as /tmp), while the values for others can be numbers (such as 3), time durations (such as 3d for three days), or a Boolean value (such as True). There are no hard rules for which type of value goes with which option. Instead, you'll need to look up each option in Chapter 34, *Options*, and use the type indicated there.

13.2 Required Options

The *sendmail* program offers over 70 options to choose from. We will cover a few here and the rest in Chapter 34. Recall that the purpose of our configuration file is to forward all mail to a central mail hub. In keeping with the simplicity of this task, you need to declare only those options shown in Table 13-1 (abstracted from Table 34-4 in §34.4).[*]

Table 13–1: Some Required Options

Option Name		Type	§	Description
QueueDirectory	(Q)	String	34.8.48	Location of queue directory
Timeout	(r)	String	34.8.70	Set timeouts
DeliveryMode	(d)	Character	34.8.16	Set delivery mode
TempFileMode	(F)	Octal	34.8.68	Permissions for temporary files
DefaultUser	(u)	String	34.8.15	Default delivery agent identity
LogLevel	(L)	Numeric	34.8.33	Set (increase) logging level
OldStyleHeaders	(o)	Boolean	34.8.44	Allow spaces in recipient lists
BlankSub	(B)	Character	34.8.5	Unquoted space replacement

---

[*] For a description of the Type, leap ahead to §34.5.

We'll describe each of these required options briefly, add them to the *client.cf* file, and then test them.

13.2.1 The Location of the Queue Directory

We have already described queue directories (in §3.1.2). Queued mail always looks like *authentic* mail to *sendmail*. That is, the *sendmail* program *trusts* the mail it finds there, believing that only *root* placed it there. If the queue directory were world-writable (as */tmp* is), anyone could create queued mail and thereby create forged mail messages. To help prevent forged mail, the queue directory should be writable only by *root*. Unfortunately, for the purpose of our exercises, this would prevent you from sending mail using the *client.cf* file. You would need to be *root*, which isn't desirable and may not be possible.

Instead, we will temporarily declare the location of the queue directory to be */tmp*. To help you to remember to change the *client.cf* file later, add a comment now showing the need to make the change and the correct path to use:

```
O QueueDirectory=/tmp          # BEWARE: use /var/spool/mqueue upon release
```

Note that on some systems, **/var** needs to be replaced with **/usr**.

13.2.2 Limit the Life of Queued Messages

Mail is usually placed into the queue because it could not be transmitted immediately. Periodically, *sendmail* attempts to retransmit each queued message. If the message has not been delivered after a reasonable interval, *sendmail* sends a warning to the sender, informing the sender that the message has not yet been delivered but that *sendmail* will continue to try. After a longer interval in the queue, messages that have not been successfully transmitted are bounced. The **Timeout** (r) option is used to specify both intervals:

```
O Timeout.queuewarn=4h
O Timeout.queuereturn=5d
```

The **Timeout** (r) option is special in that it takes a dot and a keyword to tell it what to time out. In the first case the keyword **queuewarn** sets the warning interval. In the second, the keyword **queuereturn** sets the return (bounce) interval. (The complete list of keywords that apply to the **Timeout** option is in §34.8.70.)

The **Timeout** option is one that takes a time interval as its argument. Here, **4h** represents four hours (if the message is undelivered after four hours, warn the sender and continue to try) and **5d** represents five days (return the message to the sender as bounced mail). The letter following the number in each specifies the units. The queuereturn, for example, could have been represented like this:

```
O Timeout.queuereturn=120h
```

This tells *sendmail* to bounce queued mail after 120 hours, which is the same as five days.

Five days may seem like a long time. After all, the mail hub should always be up and always be accepting mail. But suppose the hub crashed on Friday evening and replacement parts weren't available until Thursday morning. In this situation, queued mail on all the clients would start bouncing before the hub was repaired.

In choosing a value for the Timeout (r) option's queuereturn keyword, take into account the worst-case scenario you can imagine. If the hub has same-day service, a value of 1d might be enough. If the hub has to be shipped out for repair, you may want to consider a value such as 14d (two weeks).[*]

13.2.3 The Default Delivery Mode

There are several modes in which the *sendmail* program can run. Each determines how *sendmail* interacts with the program that invoked it. For the *client.cf* file, you want the user's MUA to execute *sendmail* for message transmission but to give the appearance that the message was sent almost instantaneously. This prevents users from waiting for their prompt to return whenever the mail hub is busy.

The delivery mode to use is called *background* because it causes *sendmail* to accept a message and then run in the background (thus allowing the MUA to continue on). The delivery mode is set with the DeliveryMode (d) option:

```
O DeliveryMode=background
```

Note that *sendmail* recognizes only the b of background. So you will sometimes find this same declaration in other configuration files more succinctly expressed like this:

```
O DeliveryMode=b
```

Other possible values for the DeliveryMode (d) option are documented in §34.8.16.

---

[*] You should also consider including MX records for the hub (see §21.3) so that mail will be sent to another server if the hub is down.

13.2.4 The Default File Permissions

The *sendmail* program frequently needs to create new files (such as files in its queue). The file permissions that are given to each created file are determined by the value of the `TempFileMode` (F) option. That value can range from 0600 (readable and writable only by *sendmail*) to 0666 (readable and writable by anyone in the world). For security, we'll select the first value—the most restrictive:

    O TempFileMode=0600

Note that the value must be expressed in octal notation. (See *chmod*(1) for details.) The `TempFileMode` (F) option is further documented in §34.8.68.

13.2.5 The Default User Identities

Again, for security, *sendmail* tries to avoid running as *root* whenever possible. When delivering failed mail to your ˜/*dead.letter* file, for example, it runs as you. If it finds itself in a situation in which it must not be *root* but cannot otherwise decide on a real user's identity, *sendmail* assumes the identity of the user defined by the `DefaultUser` (u) option:

    O DefaultUser=1:1

The *uid* under which to run (the number to the left of the colon) is here defined to be 1 (for the user *daemon*). The *gid* under which to run (the number to the right of the colon) is here defined as 1 (for the group *daemon*).

The values given to these options may also be names:

    O DefaultUser=daemon:daemon

At security-conscious sites these are often set to the user *nobody* and the group *nogroup*. The `DefaultUser` (u) option is further documented in §34.8.15.

13.2.6 The Default Logging Level

Recall that the `DeliveryMode` (d) option told *sendmail* to run in the background. Because it is running in the background, *sendmail* should not print information about its activities to your screen. On the other hand, you do want to record information about its activities to help solve future problems.

The method used by *sendmail* to record its activities is called *logging*.[*] The setting of the `LogLevel` (L) option allows you to turn logging completely off or to specify a logging level. The higher the logging level, the more detailed the information

---

[*] The actual mechanism used is called *syslog*(3) and is described in Chapter 26, *Logging and Statistics*.

that is logged. That is, low levels log only serious problems, middle levels also log statistical information, and high levels include debugging information.

```
O LogLevel=9
```

Here, we've chosen a level of 9. This is a middle level, which, in addition to causing serious problems to be logged, also causes statistics such as message size to be logged.

Typically, logged information is written by the system into a file called *syslog* by a means documented in §26.1. The LogLevel (L) option is further documented in §34.8.33.

13.2.7 *Accept Old-Style Lists of Addresses*

The current standard for specifying multiple recipients is to separate each address from the others with commas. Unfortunately, this has not always been the standard; old software may still exist that separates addresses with spaces:

```
abe,george,andrew        ← new style
abe george andrew        ← old style
```

To prevent old software from breaking, you need to tell *sendmail* that the use of spaces is acceptable and that if it finds such old-style lists, it should replace the spaces with commas. You tell *sendmail* this by specifying the OldStyleHeaders (o) option:

```
O OldStyleHeaders=True
```

The value is either true (accept and convert) or false (don't accept). The True makes it true. In actual practice, only the first letter is recognized, and either T or t will work. To turn it off, use F or f (for false) or omit the entire declaration. If you omit the true or false but include the option, it defaults to true. The OldStyle-Headers (o) option is further documented in §34.8.44.

13.2.8 *The Unquoted Space Replacement Character*

Recall from Chapter 8, *Addresses and Rules*, that any address can be split up into tokens in the workspace. The address is then rewritten according to rules specified in rule sets. After all the tokens have been (possibly) rewritten, they are rejoined to form an address again.

The BlankSub (B) option exists for those times when two adjoining tokens are just words (rather than a word and a separating character). For example, suppose the workspace began by containing the following tokens:

```
    a @ b . c
```

Then suppose some rule always changed the last two tokens into the single word LOCAL. The result of rewriting would look like this:

```
    a @ b LOCAL
```

Here we have four tokens, the last two of which are text. The question becomes: What do we insert between them? Unless you tell *sendmail* to do otherwise, it always sticks a space between them. Therefore the default is to join these tokens together into this:

```
    a@b LOCAL
```

Because we set the OldStyleHeaders (o) option above to true, this single (but odd) address wrongly becomes two:

```
    a@b, LOCAL
```

To prevent this kind of mishap, we use the BlankSub (B) option to change the replacement character from a space to a dot:

```
    O BlankSub=.                    # Replace unquoted spaces with a dot.
```

With this declaration in the configuration file the previous tokens are joined together like this:

```
    a@b.LOCAL
```

This forms a single address, which is what is wanted. But what does the "unquoted" in the comment mean?

When parts of an address are surrounded in full quotation marks, those parts are viewed by *sendmail* as a single token. Therefore an address like this:

```
    "abe lincoln"@wash.dc.gov
```

is tokenized like this:

```
    "abe lincoln"   @   wash   .   dc   .   gov
```

When these tokens are joined back together, the quoted words abe and lincoln are viewed by *sendmail* as one token (with a space included), rather than two (with need of a space replacement character).[*] The BlankSub (B) option is further documented in §34.8.5.

---

[*] Actually, the address is sent as is to another site. The BlankSub (B) option at the other site causes the confusion, because the address arrives there unquoted.

13.3 *Testing the Options*

Now that the necessary options have been described, add them to the *client.cf* file. As the name "option" implies, the values that you give them are somewhat optional. You are free to change timeouts and the like to values that you consider more appropriate:

```
V7
# Defined macros
D{REMOTE}mailhost                   # The name of the mail hub
D{HUB}mail.us.edu                   # Hub as known to the outside world

Cw localhost                        # My other names.
Fw -o /etc/sendmail.cw              # An optional file of other names

# Options                                                              ← new
O QueueDirectory=/tmp       # BEWARE: use /var/spool/mqueue upon release  ← new
O Timeout.queuewarn=4h                                                 ← new
O Timeout.queuereturn=5d                                              ← new
O DeliveryMode=background                                             ← new
O TempFileMode=0600                                                  ← new
O DefaultUser=1:1                                                    ← new
O LogLevel=9                                                         ← new
O OldStyleHeaders=True                                               ← new
O BlankSub=.                 # Replace unquoted spaces                 ← new
```

Take a moment to test these new option declarations. Run *sendmail* in rule-testing mode with the –d37.1 switch. This will cause each option to be printed as it is found in the *client.cf* file:

```
% ./sendmail -d37.1 -Cclient.cf -bt < /dev/null
setoption QueueDirectory (Q).=/tmp (unsafe)
setoption Timeout (r).queuewarn=4h
setoption Timeout (r).queuereturn=5d
setoption DeliveryMode (d).=background
setoption TempFileMode (F).=0600 (unsafe)
setoption DefaultUser (u).=1:1 (unsafe)
setoption LogLevel (L).=9
setoption OldStyleHeaders (o).=True
setoption BlankSub (B).=. (unsafe)
```

Notice that the options that used to have single-character names (Q instead of QueueDirectory) are printed showing both the new multicharacter name and the single-character name in parentheses.

Second, note that some of the lines end with (unsafe). This is *sendmail* telling you that it cannot run as *root*. Whenever you do something unsafe (such as using your own configuration file with the –C switch), *sendmail* stops being *root* and becomes you. It prints (unsafe) for each option you specify that only *root* should be able to use.

13.4 Sending Mail

The *client.cf* file is now at a point in its development at which it can be used for sending mail. The mail that it generates will cause problems in a few ways, but we will gloss over those illegalities for now and deal with them in the next chapter. You can send mail to yourself with *sendmail* like this:

```
% /usr/lib/sendmail -Cclient.cf you
```

After you enter this command, *sendmail* pauses and waits for you to enter the email message you want to send. Enter a `To:` header line, a `Subject:` header line, a blank line (to separate the header from the body), and a brief message to yourself, and conclude by entering a dot on a line by itself:

```
To: you
Subject: testing

testing
.
```

Your message is now forwarded to the mail hub machine, where (if all has gone well) it is delivered. Using your favorite MUA, read the message you just sent and save it to a file. That file will look something like this:

```
From you@mail.us.edu Fri Dec 13 05:47:47 1996
Return-Path: <you@mail.us.edu>
Received: from here.us.edu (you@here.us.edu [123.45.67.8]) by mail.us.edu
  (8.8.4/8.8.4) with ESMTP id FAA13451 for <you>; Fri, 13 Dec 1996 05:47:46 -0700
Date: Fri, 13 Dec 1996 05:47:46 -0700
From: you@mail.us.edu
Message-Id: <199509091247.FAA13451@mail.us.edu>
To: you
Subject: testing

testing
```

The first thing to notice in this saved message is that several header lines have been added. You gave *sendmail* only two lines, a `To:` and a `Subject:`, when you ran it, but now there are eight header lines.

These header lines were added by the hub machine. Because they were added by the hub and not by your local machine, a few of them are illegal. The `Received:` header, for example, shows only that the hub received the message from the local machine. There is no indication (other than by implication) that the local machine received it in the first place.

Another problem is the `Message-ID:` header. Every email message is supposed to have a message identifier that is guaranteed unique world wide. Part of that identifier is supposed to be the name of the originating machine (your local machine). In the above header, however, it contains the name of the mail hub, *mail.us.edu.*

We'll fix these problems when we cover headers in the next chapter.

13.5 Things to Try

- What problem would you foresee with declaring the location of the queue directory using a relative pathname? Suppose you used *./tmp* (for *tmp* under the current directory)? What if you were *root* when you tried this or were not where you thought you were?

- The LogLevel (L) option uses *syslog*(3) to record messages. Read the online manual for *syslog*(3) on your system, and determine where *sendmail* logging information is stored. Does the logging level that we specified (9) produce too much or too little information? Use `tail -f` to watch that information while at the same time sending mail with the *client.cf* file.

- Why did we specify a To: header when sending mail, when the recipient was already listed in the command line? What happens when you omit the To: header and send mail using *client.cf?*

14

Headers, Precedence, and Trust

In the previous chapter you sent mail to yourself and saw that *sendmail* added several problematic header lines to your message. Also the hub machine added some unsuitable headers. In this chapter we show how to use the H configuration command to add legal headers to a message, the P configuration command to set message priorities, and the T configuration command to define "trusted" users.

14.1 Headers

The header configuration command begins with the letter H. Like all configuration commands, the H is the first character on a line. The H is then followed by the name of a header:

```
Hname: field
```

Here, name is the name of a header, such as Subject. The list of all header names that are of interest to *sendmail* can be found in Chapter 35, *Headers*. The name is followed by a colon and then text that is appropriate for the header. Optional whitespace can surround the colon.

RFC822 (modified by RFC1123) specifies that certain header lines must appear in all email messages. Of those, the two you will first add to the *client.cf* file are shown in Table 14-1.

Table 14–1: Two Required Headers

Name	Description	When Added
From:	Address of the sender	If missing
Received:	Record of receipt	Always

Unless otherwise specified (as you will see later), a header that is declared in the configuration file is added to a mail message only if one doesn't already exist. The exception to this rule is the `Received:` header. It is always added to a mail message, even if there is already one (or more) there.

14.1.1 The From: Header

The `From:` header contains the official address of the sender. Declaring the `From:` header is simplicity itself, because it uses as its *field* a single macro surrounded by angle braces:

```
HFrom: <$g>
```

Recall that there are two kinds of macros: those that you define with the D command and those that *sendmail* defines. The `g` macro is one of the latter. The value *sendmail* gives the `g` macro is the address of the sender (generated by *sendmail*) as it appears on the envelope. That address, when you are the sender, was generated by the `Hubset` rule set:

```
SHubset # Rewrite the sender for the hub
R$-            $@ $1@${HUB}           user -> user@hub
```

The sender address (*you*) is rewritten by this rule so that it becomes *you@mail.us.edu*. That is, the hostname and domain of the hub machine are appended so that the mail appears to come from the hub. This is the envelope address of the sender, and that is the address placed into the `g` macro. For email sent by you, the value that is given to `$g` (and thus to the `From:` header) is:

```
From: <you@mail.us.edu>
```

The `From:` header is added to an outgoing mail message only if there is not already a `From:` header there. (Often an MUA will add a `From:` header.) It is placed into the *client.cf* file to ensure that no mail leaves the local machine without this required header.

14.1.2 The Received: Header

The `Received:` header is special. It is always added to the header portion of every mail message, even if one or more of them are already present.

The `Received:` header is used to make a record of each machine that mail has passed through. When *sendmail* calculates a hop count (to bounce mail with too many hops), it does so by counting the `Received:` header lines. The declaration of the `Received:` header is a bit complicated. A minimal `Received:` header declaration looks like this:

```
HReceived: by $j; $b
```

The word `by` is mandatory. It must be followed by the fully qualified, official name of the local machine. As you saw earlier when you ran *sendmail* with the `-d0.1` debugging switch, the fully qualified name was assigned to the `j` macro:

```
============ SYSTEM IDENTITY (after readcf) ============
      (short domain name) $w = here
   (canonical domain name) $j = here.us.edu
                              ↑
                            note
```

The `Received:` header definition concludes with a semicolon, followed by the current date and time as stored in `$b`. The b macro contains the current date in ARPAnet format; that is, the day of the week, the month, the day, the time, the year, and the time zone.

These items in the `Received:` header form the minimum information required in this header.

14.1.3 Testing So Far

Add the `From:` and `Received:` headers to the *client.cf* file. The new lines in *client.cf* will look like this:

```
O OldStyleHeaders=True
O BlankSub=.                    # Replace unquoted spaces with a dot.

# Headers                                                          ← new
HFrom: <$g>             # Added only if missing                    ← new
HReceived: by $j; $b    # Always added                             ← new
```

Here, they follow the options that were added in the last chapter. As usual, comments have been included to clarify your intent. See Chapter 31, *Defined Macros*, for a more detailed explanation of the j and b macros.

Now send mail to yourself just as you did at the end of the preceding chapter:

```
% ./sendmail -Cclient.cf you
Subject: testing
To: you

testing
.
```

Retrieve the mail that you just sent, save it to a file, and look at what you saved. It
will look something like this:

```
From you@mail.us.edu Fri Dec 13 05:47:47 1996
Return-Path: <you@mail.us.edu>
Received: from here.us.edu (you@here.us.edu [123.45.67.8]) by
mail.us.edu
(8.8.4/8.8.4) with ESMTP id FAA13451 for <you>; Fri, 13 Dec 1996 05:47:46 -0700
Date: Fri, 13 Dec 1996 05:47:46 -0700
From: you@mail.us.edu (Your Full Name)                        ← note
Message-Id: <199509091247.FAA13451@mail.us.edu>
Received: by here.us.edu; Fri, 13 Dec 1996 05:47:44 -0700     ← note
Subject: testing
To: you

testing
```

Notice that a new `Received:` header was added. This is the one just declared in
the *client.cf* file. The two `Received:` headers form a trail that shows who first
received the message and how it was passed from one machine to the other.

Also notice that the contents of the `From:` header have changed. Something has
removed the angle brackets and added your full name. What happened was this:

1. On the hub machine the address in the envelope for the sender is taken from
   the RCPT message that the local machine sends during the SMTP conversation.
   That address is the value of `$g` with angle brackets added.

2. On the hub machine the address in the `From:` header is compared to the
   sender envelope address. The address in the `From:` header that *client.cf* supplied was the value of `$g` surrounded in angle brackets.

3. Whenever the address in the envelope for the sender and the address in the
   `From:` header are identical, *sendmail* removes the `From:` header and creates a
   new one. Thus *sendmail* on a correctly configured hub machine removes the
   `From:` header and creates a new one that includes your full name.

The definition of the `From:` header on a hub is more complex then that in the
client.cf file. One possible definition might look like this:

```
From: $g $?x($x)$.
```

This is just like the local definition, but it has a macro *conditional* added. A macro
conditional is simply an if-endif construction, where `$?` is the if and `$.` is the
endif. The preceding definition, then, can be broken down like this:

`$?`	*if*
x	*the macro x contains a value*
`($x)`	*add this to the definition*
`$.`	*endif*

The macro **x** contains as its value the full name of the sender. If that full name is not known, **x** has no value and the full name is omitted. If $x does contain a value, the full name is added in parentheses. Macro conditionals are described in Chapter 31.

14.2 Headers Versus Delivery Agent Flags

Some headers should be inserted into a mail message only if a certain delivery agent is used. For example, one traditionally should include the `Full-Name:` header when mail is being delivered with UUCP but should not include it for most other delivery agents.

The mechanism that governs inclusion is a list of flags that prefix the header definition in the configuration file. Those flags are composed of a series of one or more letters, all of which are surrounded with a pair of ? characters.

```
H?flags?name: value
```

When *sendmail* decides whether a header is to be added to the mail message, it compares the *flags* listed with the flags of the delivery agent's F= equate:

```
Mhub,    P=[IPC], S=Hubset, R=0, F=mDFMuXa, T=DNS/RFC822/SMTP, A=IPC $h
                                       ↑
                                     flags
```

If a given *flag* (letter) appears in both, the header is added to the mail message. Otherwise, it is not.

Traditionally, for example, the **x** flag is used to indicate the need for a `Full-Name:` header. But our hub delivery agent does not have an **x** in its F= flags. Since that is the only delivery agent we use, we need to add that flag to the *client.cf* file.

14.2.1 The Full-Name: Header

The `Full-Name:` header is used to display the full name of the sender, as taken from the *gecos* field of the *passwd*(5) file. You saw above how the hub machine tries to add the sender's full name to the `From:` header. But since you don't necessarily have control over the hub, you should add a `Full-Name:` header locally, so that the full name is displayed even if the hub fails to add it.

The way to declare the `Full-Name:` header is like this:

```
H?x?Full-Name: $?x$x$.          # Add full name if available
```

First prefix it with the `?x?` flag. This means that the `Full-Name:` header is added only if the delivery agent also contains that flag.

The value given to the `Full-Name:` header is just like the conditional that you saw earlier. If (`$?`) the macro `x` contains a value, use that value (`$x`), and endif (`$.`). We use this conditional test so that the full name is added only if it is known.

Next, to make the `Full-Name:` effective, you need to add an `x` flag to the hub delivery agent declaration:

```
Mhub,    P=[IPC], S=Hubset, R=0, F=xmDFMuXa, T=DNS/RFC822/SMTP, A=IPC $h
                                    ↑
                                   add
```

Now any mail that uses the hub delivery agent for a recipient (in other words, all mail) will add a `Full-Name:` header to the message if there is not already one there. If the full name is known (`$x` has a value), that name follows the `Full-Name:` header on the same line; otherwise, the header contains only the header name and is omitted entirely.

14.2.2 The Date: Header

The `Date:` header is required in all messages to show the time and day that the message originated. It is a good idea to include `?flags?` in its definition so that custom delivery agents that do not need the `Date:` can be designed later.

```
H?D?Date: $a                     # Add if F=D
```

The `$a` is the *origin date* of the mail message in RFC822 format. That date is set internally by *sendmail* to be correct for inclusion in the `Date:` header.

An `F=D` flag already exists in the hub delivery agent:

```
Mhub,    P=[IPC], S=Hubset, R=0, F=xmDFMuXa, T=DNS/RFC822/SMTP, A=IPC $h
                                    ↑
                         add the date if missing
```

That `D` was originally put in this delivery agent definition with the `Date:` header in mind.

14.2.3 The Message-ID: Header

The `Message-ID:` header is used to uniquely identify each mail message. It must be inserted into the message when it is first created (first handled by *sendmail*). The form of the `Message-ID:` header is very specific:

```
H?M?Message-Id: <$t.$i@$j>       # Add if F=M
```

Here, a `?M?` prefix is included. The hub delivery agent definition already has the `F=M` flag listed:

```
Mhub,    P=[IPC], S=Hubset, R=0, F=xmDFMuXa, T=DNS/RFC822/SMTP, A=IPC $h
                                    ↑
                         add the message identifier if missing
```

The field following the **Message-ID:** must follow particular rules. First, it must be surrounded by angle brackets. Then, what appears between the angle brackets must look like a legal address:

   <address>

The address must be composed of pieces of information that uniquely identify the mail message worldwide. We create that address in a way that is commonly used in most configuration files:

   <$t.$i@$j>

$t is the current date and time represented by an integer. $i is the local unique identifier for the queue file for this message (even if the message isn't queued), and $j is your host's fully qualified domain name. Other information may be used, provided that the result looks like a legal address and provided that no two identical identifiers ever go out.

14.3 Headers Learned So Far

Now add all the headers so far described to the *client.cf* file:

```
O OldStyleHeaders=True
O BlankSub=.                   # Replace unquoted spaces with a dot.

# Headers                                                        ← new
HFrom: <$g>                    # Added only if missing            ← new
HReceived: by $j; $b           # Always added                     ← new
H?x?Full-Name: $?x$x$.         # Add full name if available       ← new
H?D?Date: $a                   # Add if F=D                       ← new
H?M?Message-Id: <$t.$i@$j>     # Add if F=M                       ← new
```

Note that the **Full-Name:** header uses the **?x?** flag, so you need to add that same flag to our **hub** delivery agent definition:

```
Mhub,    P=[IPC], S=Hubset, R=0, F=xmDFMuXa, T=DNS/RFC822/SMTP, A=IPC $h
                                    ↑
                                   new
```

With these few additions the *client.cf* file is almost ready to use, but we won't test it yet. First we need to discuss priorities.

14.4 Precedence

The precedence of a mail message determines its position among other messages
in the queue when the queue is processed. Precedence, as a header line, also
defines whether or not a bounced message should be returned to the sender.
Precedences are not hard-coded into *sendmail*. Instead, they need to be declared
in the configuration file. The typical declarations, and the ones we will use, look
like this:

```
Pspecial-delivery=100
Pfirst-class=0
Plist=-30
Pbulk=-60
Pjunk=-100
```

These lines use the P (precedence) configuration command. Like all configuration
commands, the P must begin the line. It is followed by a name, an equal sign, and
a value. The general form looks like this:

```
Pname=value
```

There are only five possibilities for *name* that are legal:

special-delivery
    This mail message needs to be processed before any others. This precedence
    is effective only when the message is being delivered from the queue.

first-class
    Unless otherwise declared with a **Precedence:** header, the message is **first-
    class** by default.

list
    The message originated as part of a mailing list. It should be deferred until
    other more important mail has been processed from the queue.

bulk
    The message is a broadcast, like a mailing list but less important. If the mes-
    sage can't be delivered, the message body is discarded from the bounced mail.

junk
    Absolutely worthless mail. Test messages and mail from some programs fall
    into this category. Like **bulk**, the message body is discarded from the bounced
    mail.

The *value* assigned to each *name* is somewhat arbitrary. The ones that we use are
common. As you gain familiarity with the queue and mailing lists, you may want
to adjust these values. In general, the higher the number, the higher the precedence. By convention, formal first-class mail has a precedence of zero, with

positive numbers used for high-precedence mail and negative numbers used for various kinds of bulk mail.

The P configuration command only tells *sendmail* the **value** to assign to a given *name*. It has no other effect. The values are used only when a mail message is processed that has a **Precedence:** header line in it. The inclusion of **Precedence:** header lines is left to MUAs.

To illustrate, imagine that a user on your machine is managing a mailing list. The software that is used to create each message for the list arranges to include a **Precedence:** header that looks like this:

```
Precedence: list
```

The mailing-list message is given to *sendmail* on the local machine. The local *sendmail* sees the **Precedence:** header in the message and extracts the field of that header, the **list**. It then compares **list** to each of the *name* parts of its P configuration lines. It finds a match with the line:

```
Plist=-30
```

Because it finds a match, it uses the **value** from this configuration command as the initial precedence of the mail message. If there is no match (or if the original message lacks a **Precedence:** header), the initial precedence of the mail message defaults to zero.

Now add P configuration commands to the *client.cf* file. Traditionally, they are placed after the header commands:

```
H?D?Date: $a                    # Add if F=D
H?M?Message-Id: <$t.$i@$j>      # Add if F=M

# Precedence                                    ← new
Pspecial-delivery=100                           ← new
Pfirst-class=0                                  ← new
Plist=-30                                       ← new
Pbulk=-60                                       ← new
Pjunk=-100                                      ← new
```

14.5 *Sending Real Mail*

The *client.cf* file is now complete and ready to use for sending all kinds of user mail. As you did before, send mail to yourself by using *sendmail* directly:

```
% ./sendmail -Cclient.cf you
Subject: testing
To: you

testing
.
```

Retrieve this message as you usually receive mail and save it to a file. The contents of that file should look something like this:

```
From you@mail.us.edu Fri Dec 13 05:47:47 1996
Return-Path: <you@mail.us.edu>
Received: from here.us.edu (you@here.us.edu [123.45.67.8]) by mail.us.edu
(8.8.4/8.8.4) with ESMTP id FAA13451 for <you>; Fri, 13 Dec 1996 05:47:46 -0700
Date: Fri, 13 Dec 1996 05:47:44 -0700
From: you@mail.us.edu (Your Full Name)
Message-Id: <199509091244.GAA13434@here.us.edu>                    ← note
Received: by here.us.edu; Fri, 13 Dec 1996 05:47:44 -0700
Subject: testing
To: you

testing
```

Note the change between this message's header and that of the previous message you sent. Instead of the hub machine adding a **Message-ID:** header, the local machine added that header. You can tell because the local machine's name appears there instead of the hub's name.

Actually, the **Date:** header was also added locally, but there is nothing to indicate that fact. A **Date:** header should be added locally to accurately reflect the posting date of the message. If you didn't supply a **Date:** header, instead allowing the hub to supply it, and the hub were down for a while, that header would be inaccurate by the amount of time the hub was down.

14.6 Trusted User

A trusted user is one who has three privileges that most users don't have:

- When mail is delivered via a program of the user's choosing (such as *procmail*(1)), most users need to have a valid shell in the password file. Without a valid shell, such program delivery is prohibited. Invalid shells often exist for pseudo-users such as *news* and for all users on restricted servers. A trusted user is exempted from this test.

- The **-f** switch causes *sendmail* to take its idea of the sender from the command line rather than from the envelope or header. Because the **-f** command line switch can be used to forge mail, *sendmail* always inserts a warning into the message header. A trusted user is one who is exempted from having such warnings included.

  ```
  X-Authentication-Warning: here.us.edu: badperson set sender to bogusname using -f
  ```

- In one of its myriad roles, *sendmail* can speak SMTP to another program on the same machine. That other program merely has to execute *sendmail* with a **-bs** command-line switch and talk on its standard output. The *mh*(1) program is one such program that can do this. If *sendmail* is run in this way and if the sender's address doesn't match the executing user's address, then a forged message may be in the works. When *sendmail* detects such a possible forgery, it inserts a warning into the message header:

```
X-Authentication-Warning: here.us.edu: badperson owned process doing -bs
```

A trusted user is one who is exempted from having such warnings included.

Trusted users are declared in the configuration file in two ways:

```
T user1 user2 ....
Ct user1 user2 ....
```

The first line is the old form of declaration, and the second is the new form (beginning with V8.7 *sendmail*) form. The two are equivalent, but the second is recommended. In the latter form, names of users are added to the class **t**.

Trusted users are declared in the *client.cf* file like this:

```
Ct root daemon
```

We list *root* because some root-run programs need to send mail under the identity of other users. We list *daemon* for the same reasons and because most long-running background processes are owned by the user *daemon*. If your local machine is set up to receive UUCP mail, you need to add *uucp* to this list.

Once you add trusted users to the *client.cf* file, you are almost ready to use that file as the official configuration file.

14.7 *Things to Try*

- Everything to the left of the colon is taken as the name of the header. What error message do you get if you omit the colon? Is it possible to include a colon in the name?

- Gather all your system configuration file's header definitions. For each that is not in the *client.cf* file, why do you suppose it is necessary?

- In the *client.cf* file, only one delivery agent is doing anything (the **hub**). Does it make sense to include **?***flags*? in the headers in this situation? Can you safely remove those flags and the corresponding flags from the **F=** flags of the **hub** to make *client.cf* smaller?

- The **P** configuration command specifies the beginning order for processing mail from the queue. Since mail is always sent to the hub machine at once, does it make sense to set those values in the *client.cf* file? Would there be any harm in omitting the **P** configuration commands and letting the hub assume that responsibility?

15

Install and Test the client.cf File

In this chapter and the next, we tie up a few loose ends to install a *client.cf* file as the system configuration file.

15.1 Test the Configuration File

Clearly, you won't want to install the *client.cf* file as the real *sendmail.cf* file until you've made sure it works properly. One of the better ways to test a new configuration file is to create a file of addresses for which you already know the correct outcome, then feed the contents of that file to *sendmail* in rule-testing mode:

```
/tryflags es
/parse user@here
/parse user@here.us.edu
/parse user@foo
/parse foo!user
/parse user
```

Each line begins with a special V8.7 rule-testing command.[*] The first line causes the tests that follow to parse the address as an envelope sender (instead of the default envelope recipient). The /parse command causes each address to be rewritten by rule sets 3 and 0 to select a delivery agent and then by rule set 4 to clean up afterward. The addresses listed that are humbly few but will suffice for the needs of the *client.cf* file. No matter the form of the address, each should be forwarded to the hub as is. (The /parse command is described in §38.5.5.)

---

[*] The same thing can be done in earlier versions, but with some difficulty. See a sample script in §38.8.

The way to test the *client.cf* file using this list looks like this:

```
% ./sendmail -Cclient.cf -bt < list | grep ^mailer
```

Here, *list* is the name of the file containing the above list of rule tests and addresses. The output shows that each will be passed as is to the hub:

```
mailer hub, host mailhost, user user@here
mailer hub, host mailhost, user user@here.us.edu
mailer hub, host mailhost, user user@foo
mailer hub, host mailhost, user here!user
mailer hub, host mailhost, user user
```

Notice that mail to these addresses will be delivered by using the hub delivery agent (`mailer`). Also notice that each will be forwarded to the hub machine (`mailhost`) for delivery. Finally, note that the user part will be the original address.[*]

But why was the lone username in the last line not rewritten to appear as though it was coming from the hub? Recall that sender rewriting is done in the `Hubset` rule set. That rule set is called only by the `S=` of the delivery agent. To see `Hubset` rewriting, you need to run *sendmail* again, but this time use `/try` instead of `/parse`:[†]

```
% ./sendmail -Cclient.cf -bt
ADDRESS TEST MODE (ruleset 3 NOT automatically invoked)
Enter <ruleset> <address>
> /tryflags es
> /try hub user
rewrite: ruleset   3     input: user
rewrite: ruleset   3 returns: user
rewrite: ruleset   1     input: user
rewrite: ruleset   1 returns: user
rewrite: ruleset 199     input: user
rewrite: ruleset 199 returns: user @ mail . us . edu
rewrite: ruleset   4     input: user @ mail . us . edu
rewrite: ruleset   4 returns: user @ mail . us . edu
Rcode = 0, addr = user@mail.us.edu
```

Here, *sendmail* rewrites the lone username first with rule set 3 (all addresses start with rule set 3), and then with rule set 1 (all sender addresses pass through rule set 1). The address is then rewritten by rule set `Hubset` (which prints as 199 because it is a symbolic rule-set name). As intended, a lone sender name has the address of the hub machine appended to it. (The rest of this `/try` output is described in §38.5.6.)

---

[*] This is the triple that we described in §9.2, in which the RHS of rule set 0 returned the `mailer` with `$#`, the `host` with `$@`, and the `user` with `$:`.

[†] Under old versions of *sendmail* you must specify the rule sets by hand, for example, `3,Hubset`.

Further testing would be suggested if the output varied in unexpected ways. It might be necessary to run *sendmail* in rule-testing mode by hand, testing each rule and sequence of rules individually to find any mistakes in the *client.cf* file. If the *client.cf* file tests okay, you are now almost ready to install it as the official *sendmail.cf* file.

15.2 The Real Queue Directory

In the current *client.cf* file, the queue directory is defined as */tmp*. Because of its nature, the */tmp* directory is always world-readable, -writable, and -searchable. Any file that is placed in */tmp* can possibly be accessed, copied, or removed by any user. The use of */tmp* clearly violates the need for confidentiality.

Another drawback to using */tmp* is that */etc/rc* files, which are executed when the system boots, often remove everything from */tmp*. You certainly would not want queued mail messages removed just because the machine rebooted.

Instead of */tmp*, you should use the existing mail queue directory to store queued messages. If you haven't already done so, find that location by looking for the QueueDirectory (Q) option in your existing *sendmail.cf* file:

```
% egrep "^OQ|QueueDirectory" /etc/sendmail.cf
OQ/usr/spool/mqueue
```

Here, we look for lines in the */etc/sendmail.cf* file that begin with the letters OQ (an old-style declaration) or that use the new option name QueueDirectory. Remember that your *sendmail.cf* file may not be in */etc*. Replace the location used above with one that is suitable for your situation.

Edit the *client.cf* file and replace /tmp with what you found. At the same time, remove the comment that was left there reminding you to do just that:

```
O QueueDirectory=/tmp  # BEWARE: use /var/spool/mqueue upon release   ← change this
O QueueDirectory=/var/spool/mqueue                                    ← to this
```

This change causes *sendmail* to use the correct queue directory, but it has an unfortunate side effect. Recall that *sendmail* runs as the *root* unless an unsafe command-line switch causes it to give up that privilege. The −C switch that you've been using all along to run *sendmail* is just such an unsafe switch. Consequently, if you were to now run *sendmail* as:

```
% ./sendmail -Cclient.cf you
```

the −C would cause *sendmail* to run as an ordinary user. For confidentiality the *queue* directory is usually protected by making it accessible only to *root*. Ordinary users, such as we've been assuming you are, lack permission to access the *queue* directory. Running the above command now will likely result in a error similar to the following:

```
queuename: Cannot create "qfIAA12390" in "/var/spool/mqueue" (euid=4010):
Permission denied
```

You need to install the *client.cf* file in place of the system *sendmail.cf* file so that you can successfully run *sendmail*. With the *client.cf* file installed, you no longer need to use the -C switch to tell *sendmail* where to find its configuration file. Unfortunately, before you can make that change, you need to first make sure other machines know about it.

15.3 MX Records

Recall that in the hub/client setup, all mail goes to the hub machine and none is ever delivered directly to the client. This requires two things: that all mail to the client be automatically sent to the hub machine instead of to the client and that the hub machine accept mail addressed to the client as though that mail were addressed to the hub machine instead. Forcing all mail to go to the hub machine requires special Mail Exchanger (MX) records.

If you already administer DNS, the changes that we will make are easily accomplished. If you don't, you will have to ask your DNS administrator to make the changes for you. How DNS interacts with *sendmail* is described in greater detail in Chapter 21, *DNS and sendmail*. You may want to jump ahead to that chapter, and then return here, to better understand the changes we are making.

To arrange for all mail to go to the hub machine, first find the primary file for your DNS zone. We won't tell you where to find it, because either you know where it is or you probably lack permission to edit it. Somewhere in the primary file for your DNS zone is an entry for the local client. It looks something like this:

```
here          IN      A       123.45.67.8
              IN      HINFO   Sun4/75 unix
```

Remember that the local machine is *here.us.edu*. The entry for this machine begins with its hostname (with the domain part omitted). The IN says that this is an Internet-type entry—the only type that is currently supported. The A says that this is an *address* record, one that associates an IP address with a hostname. The IP address is the *dotted quad* that follows (the 123.45.67.8).

Other lines may follow the A record. Here, we show an HINFO (host information) record that describes the hardware and the operating system for the local machine.

Immediately below the A record for the local machine, add a new MX record:

```
here        IN      A       123.45.67.8
            IN      MX      13 mail                    ← add
            IN      HINFO   Sun4/75 unix
```

Two pieces of information are necessary for an MX record. The first is a relative preference (the 13), which must be a number. The preference is used only when there is more than one MX record for a host. If there were two, the host with the lower preference would be tried first and then the host with the higher preference if the first failed. The number that is selected doesn't matter, because there is only one MX record for this host.

The second item (the one following the preference) is the name of the hub machine to which mail will be sent in place of sending it to the client. If the domain part for both the hub machine and the client machine is the same, only the hostname of the hub machine needs to appear in this record. The hostname of the hub in all our examples has been **mail**, so that is what we used:

```
            IN      MX      13 mail
                               ↑
                      hostname of our mail hub
```

You should, of course, replace **mail** with the actual name of your central mail-handling machine.

If the hub machine is in a different domain than the client, a fully qualified domain name needs to be specified in place of **mail**. For example, if all local mail is being sent offsite to the central server at *wash.dc.gov*, the following would appear:

```
            IN      MX      13 wash.dc.gov.
                               ↑
                      note the dot at the end
```

If you place a fully qualified name in an MX record, be sure to terminate that name with a dot. That dot tells DNS that this name is complete. Without it, DNS automatically appends your local domain to the name, resulting in an unknown address. In the entry **mail** above, the dot was omitted because **mail** is in the local domain.

After you've made this change, you need to wait for the old record to time out. The length of time to wait depends on the value of the Time To Live (TTL) that is defined for the record. A TTL can appear in two places. It can appear in the A record, or it can appear elsewhere as a default TTL. If the TTL appears in the A record, it will be a number between the hostname and the **IN**:

```
here        28800   IN      A       123.45.67.8
             ↑
      Time To Live (TTL) for this record
```

TTL values are always in seconds. Here, the A record will time out and any new information will be updated after eight hours have elapsed. Depending on when it was last updated, you may have to wait up to eight hours for the new MX record to be recognized.

If the A record has a TTL, you should duplicate that TTL in the new MX record so that they both time out together:

```
here    28800       IN      A       123.45.67.8
        28800       IN      MX      13 mail
```

At most sites the TTL for A and MX records are not stored with them but are defined by a default TTL elsewhere. To find the default TTL, look at the top of the same file for a Start Of Authority (SOA) record:

```
@       IN      SOA     us.edu. postmaster.us.edu. (
                                1.43     ; serial number
                                7200     ; secondary refresh
                                1800     ; secondary retry
                                3600000 ; secondary expire
                                86400 ) ; default ttl
```

The details of your SOA record will differ, but the desired information can still be found. The SOA record includes a parenthetical list of five numbers. The last is the default TTL that will be used for all records that don't specify one. Here, that default is 86400 seconds, or 24 hours.

If your MX records lack individual TTLs (because the A record lacks them), you will need to wait the default TTL period of time for the new MX record to become known.

We've omitted a few wrinkles, such as *reloading* the name server, for a simpler description of the process. If you have permission to change the zone file, you have doubtless changed it before and are familiar with the missing steps. If you haven't, a short section like this one can't begin to give you the information you need to manage DNS. Instead, we refer you to *DNS and BIND, Second Edition* by Paul Albitz and Cricket Liu (O'Reilly & Associates, Inc., 1997).

15.4 Hub Accepts Mail for Client

Recall that mail to your machine will be delivered to the hub, because of the MX record that you just created. Unless you change the configuration of the hub, that mail will bounce, because the hub doesn't yet know that it should accept it.

Again, you may lack permission to make the required changes. But for the sake of illustration we'll assume that you can.

You need to modify the hub's configuration file so that the hub thinks mail to your local machine is instead mail to itself. The first step is to edit the hub's configuration file and search for the rule that allows it to recognize itself. Because every machine needs to recognize itself under the name `localhost`, you should search for that string first. Such a search will reveal something like this:

```
# We always want localhost to be considered local.
Cwlocalhost
```

This example shows part of a typical configuration file that declares `localhost` as equivalent to the hub's hostname. Recall that class **w** is special because it is initialized internally by *sendmail* to contain all the possible names of a machine—all, that is, except `localhost`, which always needs to be added to class **w** in the configuration file.

We searched for `localhost` instead of `Cw` because some configuration files use a letter other than **w** to list alternative names. The following illustrates one of those other letters:

```
# Other name for our machine
CO localhost printserver faxhost
```

If your hub's configuration file is like this, use the letter **O** (or whatever letter appeared) in place of the more standard letter **w** in the following examples.

Now that you have the name (letter) of the class of other names, you need to add the local workstation's name to that list. This can be done in either of two ways. If the local machine is the only one that will be using the *client.cf* file, you can add its name to the existing class definition:

```
# Other name for our machine
CO localhost printserver faxhost here
                                   ↑
```
                                add the local machine's name here

On the other hand, if yours is just the first of many machines that will be using the *client.cf* file, you should create an external file now, so that the hub's configuration file only needs to be edited once:

```
# Other name for our machine
CO localhost printserver faxhost
# Clients for which we receive mail                    ← new
FO/etc/mail/clientlist                                 ← new
```

If you use the external file approach, make certain to create that file and add the local machine's name to it before continuing.

After modifying the hub's *sendmail.cf* file, you should test it. Run *sendmail* in rule-testing mode and give it the local machine's name as part of each address:

```
% /usr/lib/sendmail -bt
ADDRESS TEST MODE
Enter <ruleset> <address>
>
```

This example shows that the hub is running an old version of *sendmail,*[*] one that always calls rule set 3 first. Bear that in mind as you feed it addresses.

To test whether or not the hub's *sendmail* recognizes the local machine as local to the hub, you need to see whether rule set 0 selects the `local` delivery agent. Since rule set 3 is automatically called first (for this old version of *sendmail*), don't specify it. In its absence, the rules called for this old version of *sendmail* will be 3, then 0:

```
> 0 user@here
rewrite: ruleset  3    input: "user" "@" "here"
rewrite: ruleset  6    input: "user" "<" "@" "here" ">"
rewrite: ruleset  6 returns: "user" "<" "@" "LOCAL" ">"
rewrite: ruleset  3 returns: "user" "<" "@" "LOCAL" ">"
rewrite: ruleset  0    input: "user" "<" "@" "LOCAL" ">"
rewrite: ruleset 30    input: "user"
rewrite: ruleset  3    input: "user"
rewrite: ruleset  3 returns: "user"
rewrite: ruleset  0    input: "user"
rewrite: ruleset  9    input: "user"
rewrite: ruleset  9 returns: "user"
rewrite: ruleset  0 returns: $# "local" $: "user"
rewrite: ruleset 30 returns: $# "local" $: "user"
rewrite: ruleset  0 returns: $# "local" $: "user"
>
```

Success! The output that is produced will vary depending on your hub's configuration file and version of *sendmail*, but the result you are seeking will be the same. The last line of output (what rule set 0 returns) should show that the `local` delivery agent was selected (the `$#` operator).

Now perform the same test, but this time include your domain as part of the hostname:

```
> 0 user@here.us.edu
rewrite: ruleset  3    input: "user" "@" "here" "." "us" "." "edu"
rewrite: ruleset  6    input: "user" "<" "@" "here" "." "us" "." "edu" ">"
rewrite: ruleset  6 returns: "user" "<" "@" "LOCAL" ">"
rewrite: ruleset  3 returns: "user" "<" "@" "LOCAL" ">"
rewrite: ruleset  0    input: "user" "<" "@" "LOCAL" ">"
rewrite: ruleset 30    input: "user"
```

---

[*] By old, we mean a non-IDA version, prior to V8.

```
rewrite: ruleset  3    input: "user"
rewrite: ruleset  3 returns: "user"
rewrite: ruleset  0    input: "user"
rewrite: ruleset  9    input: "user"
rewrite: ruleset  9 returns: "user"
rewrite: ruleset  0 returns: $# "local" $: "user"
rewrite: ruleset 30 returns: $# "local" $: "user"
rewrite: ruleset  0 returns: $# "local" $: "user"
>
```

If all tests well, you need to kill and restart the *sendmail* daemon on the hub. Review Chapter 4, *How to Run sendmail,* if you've forgotten how to do this. Beware of any frozen configuration file that might exist if the hub is running a pre-V8 version of *sendmail.* If one exists, you will have to refreeze it. (See the discussion of the **-bz** switch in Chapter 36, *The Command Line.*)

15.5 *Prevent the Daemon from Running*

Once your MX record has taken effect, and once the hub has been configured to recognize the client machine as itself, no mail should ever again be delivered to your local machine.* Since there will be no incoming mail connections, you no longer need to run a *sendmail* daemon. Preventing the daemon from running involves two steps. First you need to kill the running daemon, then you need to modify your *rc* files so the daemon never runs again. We won't show you how to kill the daemon, because you have already learned that (see §4.1.1.1). Instead, we'll jump directly into preventing it from ever running again.

If you haven't already done so, search your *rc* files to see how *sendmail* is started when the machine first boots. Under SysV, for example, that command and its results might look like this:

```
% grep "sendmail.*-bd" /etc/init.d/*
/etc/init.d/mail:    /usr/lib/sendmail -bd -q15m  &
```

Under BSD 4.4 UNIX, however, they will look like this:

```
% grep sendmail /etc/rc*
/etc/rc:echo -n ' sendmail';                sendmail -bd -q30m
```

---

* Actually, some sites ignore MX records and try to deliver to your local machine anyway. See §36.7.11 for a discussion of one way to solve this problem.

In the following, we will describe the BSD version. It is somewhat simpler to describe, but the underlying lessons are the same for both.

To be safe, save a copy of the *rc* file before changing it:

```
% cp /etc/rc /etc/rc.orig
```

Then edit the *rc* file and search for the shell commands that runs *sendmail*. They will look something like this:

```
echo -n ' nfsd';          nfsd -u -t 6
echo -n ' nfsiod';        nfsiod 4

echo -n ' sendmail';      sendmail -bd -q30m          ← note
echo -n ' inetd';         inetd
```

Find the line that runs the daemon (*sendmail* with the **-bd** command-line switch) and remove the **-bd**:

```
echo -n ' sendmail';      sendmail -q30m
                                   ↑
                             remove -bd
```

Extreme care must be taken in making changes to any of the *rc* files. These are executed only when the system is rebooted, so errors won't show up until a very awkward moment. A mistake here can potentially keep your workstation from booting.

The **-bd** switch caused *sendmail* to run as a daemon and listen for incoming SMTP connections. We removed that switch so that *sendmail* would no longer listen for connections. The **-q30m** switch that remains causes *sendmail* to process the queue once every 30 minutes. We leave that switch in place because *sendmail* still needs to process the queue periodically[*] (in case the hub is down).

15.6 Install the client.cf File

At last! All the pieces are in place, and you can install the *client.cf* file as the official system configuration file.

As we explained when we began developing the *client.cf* file, you should not type it in yourself. The pieces that we developed were strictly instructional and should not be used as is. Instead, you should bear with us for the rest of the tutorial chapters. In the next chapter you are shown how to generate a full-fledged configuration file. If you have been typing in *client.cf* all along, you can use it here. If you waited, you should skip to the next chapter, then return here.

---

[*] An alternative approach is to use *cron*(8) to execute *sendmail* periodically with a bare **-q** switch.

Just to be safe, once you have obtained, tuned, and tested a *client.cf* file, make a
backup copy of the system configuration file:

```
# cp /etc/sendmail.cf /etc/sendmail.cf.orig
```

The # prompt indicates that you are doing this as *root*. Next, overwrite the system
configuration file with the new *client.cf* file:

```
# cp ./client.cf /etc/sendmail.cf
```

Now that the *client.cf* file is in place as your system configuration file, you need to
kill and restart the *sendmail* daemon. Review §4.1.1 if you have forgotten how to
do this. Remember, when you restart it, that you are now starting it in queue-
processing mode as shown in the previous section. Here is how we kill and restart
sendmail for version 8.7:

```
# kill -HUP `head -1 /etc/sendmail.pid`
```

That's all there is to it. From now on, any mail that is sent from your machine will
result in *sendmail* using your configuration file in place of the original.

Once again, it is important to test your configuration file. Send mail to yourself
and others using your favorite MUA. Examine the results (especially the header
information), and ask others to do so too. If anything is amiss, first try to fix the
new configuration file. If that fails, put the saved original back as the system configuration file until you can solve the problem.

Some problems will doubtless require expertise beyond that provided in this tutorial. For those, you will need to take on the reference chapters. This will be even
more necessary if you are managing a hub machine or if you want mail delivered
locally.

15.7 *Things to Try*

- A file of rules and addresses is valuable as a tool for testing new and revised
  versions of a configuration file. Develop a small shell script that feeds such a
  file to *sendmail* in rule-testing mode, then filters the output to display only the
  returns of interest. Is it possible to test rules other than those that select a
  delivery agent?

- Is it possible to protect the queue directory with narrow permissions (such as
  0700), yet still allow ordinary users to run *sendmail* in rule-testing mode?

- Is it legal to have an MX record point to itself? What about having an MX
  record pointing to a CNAME? What are wildcard MX records, and what pitfalls
  might you expect to encounter in using them?

- Consider a hub machine that is connected to two different domains. What rules might it have to include to recognize itself (or its clients as itself) in either domain? Remember that some versions of *sendmail* allow multitoken class matches, whereas other don't. What is the most portable way to recognize oneself in two domains?

- If a client is hybrid (a client in the hub/client scheme, that still needs to be able to receive mail), what changes will be required? Does anything need to be added to the *client.cf* file? Will rule set 0 need to be modified to select the local or prog delivery agents? Will a daemon still have to run?

16

The null.mc File and m4

In the preceding chapters of this tutorial we developed a minimal *client.cf* file as an aid in teaching the ins and outs of a small configuration file. In this chapter we show you how to construct a more practical file.

16.1 The cf/cf Directory

A large part of the V8 *sendmail* distribution is dedicated to the automated creation of configuration files. Recall (§2.1) that the base *sendmail* distribution looks like this:

```
FAQ           READ_ME          contrib      mailstats     rmail      test
KNOWNBUGS     RELEASE_NOTES    doc          makemap       smrsh
Makefile      cf               mail.local   praliases     src
```

Up to now, you have been working in the **src** directory. Now we will examine the **cf** directory:

```
% cd cf
% ls
README        domain       hack      mailer     sh
cf            feature      m4        ostype     siteconfig
```

The file *README* contains all the latest information about the technique that we are about to present. Read it now to get a feel for what is about to happen and to become aware of any late-breaking changes.

Now change into the *cf* directory and look around. All the files in it that end in .mc are *m4*(1) configuration source files. Read a few to satisfy your curiosity. We will be creating our own soon.

```
% cd cf
% ls
Makefile              cs-sunos4.1.mc       generic-sunos4.1.mc   s2k-osf1.mc
Makefile.dist         cs-ultrix4.mc        generic-ultrix4.mc    s2k-ultrix4.mc
chez.cs.mc            cyrusproto.mc        huginn.cs.mc          tcpproto.mc
clientproto.mc        generic-bsd4.4.mc    mail.cs.mc            ucbarpa.mc
cs-hpux10.mc          generic-hpux10.mc    mail.eecs.mc          ucbvax.mc
cs-hpux9.mc           generic-hpux9.mc     mailspool.cs.mc       uucpproto.mc
cs-osf1.mc            generic-osf1.mc      obj                   vangogh.cs.mc
cs-solaris2.mc        generic-solaris2.mc  python.cs.mc
```

16.2 The null.mc File

Now we will create a file called *null.mc*, which, when later processed, will create a *client.cf*-style configuration file. The *null.mc* fill will be very small, containing only these three lines:

```
include(`../m4/cf.m4')
OSTYPE(`sunos4.1')
FEATURE(`nullclient',`mail.us.edu')
```

These three lines do everything that the preceding 11 chapters did and more. We discuss them individually, then show how to process the file.

16.2.1 include

Naturally, a configuration is not simply plucked from thin air. Instead the master prototype configuration needs to be read and processed with the following command:[*]

```
include(`../m4/cf.m4')
```

Note that the expression inside the parentheses begins with a reverse apostrophe and ends with a forward one. These opposing half quotes are used by *m4*(1) to prevent a test from being interpreted as a macro. The expression `../m4/cf.m4` is taken to be the pathname of a file. That file is read at this point as though it were actually typed in here.

16.2.2 OSTYPE

A number of values in the configuration file will differ from operating system to operating system. The location of the queue directory, for example, is

---

[*] See *../README* for a description of how to replace this line with similar information on the command line when processing. The `include` line inside your *null.mc* file is portable to all versions of *m4*. The command line form is highly version dependent, but allows you to maintain your *.mc* files outside the *sendmail* distribution.

/var/spool/mqueue for IRIX 5.x but */usr/spool/mqueue* for BSD 4.3 Unix. To declare the proper value for your operating system, look in the *../ostype* directory:

```
% ls ../ostype
aix3.m4          bsdi1.0.m4      hpux10.m4      linux.m4        sco3.2.m4       ultrix4.m4
amdahl-uts.m4    bsdi2.0.m4      hpux9.m4       nextstep.m4     solaris2.m4     unknown.m4
aux.m4           dgux.m4         irix4.m4       osf1.m4         sunos3.5.m4
bsd4.3.m4        domainos.m4     irix5.m4       ptx2.m4         sunos4.1.m4
bsd4.4.m4        dynix3.2.m4     isc4.1.m4      riscos4.5.m4    svr4.m4
```

Pick the operating system closest to yours. For SunOS 4.1.4 systems, for example, choose `sunos4.1.m4`.

Whichever you choose, include support for it by stripping the `.m4` suffix and including the resulting name in an **OSTYPE** declaration:

sunos4.1.m4

↓

becomes

↓

OSTYPE(`sunos4.1')

Remember to surround the result in a reverse and forward apostrophe pair.

16.2.3   FEATURE

The last line in our *null.mc* file provides the magic incantation of a *client.cf*-style file:

```
FEATURE(`nullclient',`mail.us.edu')
```

Two arguments inside the parentheses, separated by a comma, are required. The first argument, `nullclient`, tells *m4*(1) to create a null (do-nothing) client (.cf) file. The second argument is the canonical name of the mail hub. Just as we did for the *client.cf* file, we use the hostname *mail.us.edu*. You should, of course, use the canonical name of your own mail hub.

16.3   Run m4

Once your simple three-line *null.mc* file is ready, you can use it to create a *sendmail* configuration file. You need a modern version of *m4*(1) to do this. If you are running BSD 4.2 UNIX, or SysV.2 or 7th edition UNIX, you'll need either the GNU version of *m4*(1) or BSD's Net/2 version. On SunOS systems, you can run */usr/5bin/m4*.

Once you have a good version of *m4*(1), run the following simple command:

```
% m4 null.mc > client.cf
```

If your version of *m4*(1) is too old, you will see this error message:

```
You need a newer version of M4, at least as new as
System V or GNU
m4: file not found: NoSuchFile
```

On the other hand, if your version is new enough, you will see nothing but your prompt return. If so, you have succeeded in creating a *client.cf* file.

16.4 Test the Result

When you look at the resulting *client.cf* file, you will first notice some copyright notices and legalities from the University of California. These are in the form of comments and so are ignored by *sendmail*.

Next comes a series of comments that show the various pieces that went into the construction of this file. After these you get to the meat of the *client.cf* file beginning with the line

```
V7/Berkeley
```

Read through this *client.cf* file beginning here, and notice that it is far more complex than the one we developed earlier. For instance, it declares over 80 options (although most are commented out), whereas our first *client.cf* file declared only nine. It uses eight rule sets, where we used only three.

To test this new file you can use the command

```
% ../../src/obj.*/sendmail -Cclient.cf -bt < list | grep ^mailer
```

The weird path for *sendmail* is needed because you are now in the *cf/cf* directory and the *sendmail* binary is back in the *src* directory. The list is the list of tests from the previous chapter. The output should look something like this:

```
mailer nullclient, host mail.us.edu, user user@here
mailer nullclient, host mail.us.edu, user user@here.us.edu
mailer nullclient, host mail.us.edu, user user@foo
mailer nullclient, host mail.us.edu, user here!user@mail.us.edu
mailer nullclient, host mail.us.edu, user user@mail.us.edu
```

Note that this new *client.cf* file added the name of the hub to the lone username in the last line, whereas our original *client.cf* did not. To see why this happened, first look for rule set 3 in this new *client.cf* file. It contains the line

```
R$+ @ $=w               $@ $1 @ $M                    ...@thishost
```

Next look in the original *client.cf* file. It contains a similar rule:

```
R$- @ $=w              $@ $1@${HUB}           user@local -> user@hub
```

But the original *client.cf* file put this rule in rule set Hubset. The new *client.cf* adds the hub's name to a lone username in rule set 3 that affects all addresses, while old *client.cf* file adds it in the S= rule set, which affects only sender addresses.

16.5 *Qualify All Addresses?*

An unqualified address is one that contains only the user part, such as *hans*. A qualified address is one that also has a host part, such as *hans@here*. A *fully* qualified address has a user part and a fully qualified host part, such as *hans@here.us.edu*. In general, no address should ever go out in a mail header or envelope that is not fully qualified.[*]

To illustrate the types of problems that can arise in using addresses that are not fully qualified, consider a header in which the local host is *here.us.edu*:

```
To: hans@here.us.edu
Cc: jane, george@fbi.us.gov
From: you@here.us.edu
```

Using our original *client.cf* file, this header would go out unchanged because jane is not a sender address. The assumption is that the hub will view this as a local user and deliver it properly.

Now consider a hub that has two MX records (a rather small number). One points to itself so that it always gets mail first because it is, after all, the hub. The other points to a host at another campus. If the hub is down but its clients are up, mail will be delivered to the other campus, on the assumption that it will hold the mail until the hub returns to service. The problem is that the address jane is unqualified when it gets to the other campus. That other site will either bounce the mail because a user *jane* is unknown or deliver it to another user with the same name who is really a different person.

Before allowing unqualified addresses to go out from a client, be sure that there are no offsite MX records and that there are no plans for any.

This is one of the reasons we said that our original *client.cf* file was for learning purposes only. This is also one of the reasons why the *m4*(1) technique produces more complex files and why we recommend using *null.mc*.

---

[*] The only exception may be when all mail is forwarded to a hub machine. The assumption is that the hub will fully qualify any addresses that lacks a host part.

16.6 Things to Try

- Take a little time to contrast the *client.cf* file created in the prior 11 chapters with the one created in this chapter. How and why do they differ? You may have to leap ahead to the reference chapters.

- The *cf/README* file suggests that the FEATURE(nocanonify) can be used with *null.mc*. What pitfalls do you foresee with the use of this feature?

- Neither version of *client.cf* uses any aliasing or forwarding. Consequently, neither will ever have to send addresses such as programs or files to the hub:

  ```
  |/run/this/program        ← a program
  /put/in/this/file         ← a file
  ```

  What happens if you try to send one by hand? Why is it necessary for a *client.cf* file to avoid delivering these kinds of addresses itself?

- In the original *client.cf* file we forwarded the mail to the hub's alias *mailhost*. What would happen if we used that name in the *nullclient* feature?

  ```
  FEATURE(`nullclient', `mailhost')
  ```

- Suppose you want to tune the rules in the *m4*(1) produced client.cf file? Does *cf/README* tell you how? Does the nullclient delivery agent have S= or R= that you can use?

17

The Hub's Complex Rules

In this chapter we look at some of the rules that are needed to make a hub function. Until now we have focused on the client form of the configuration file. Since the role of the client is narrow (to forward all mail to the hub), its configuration file is simple. But a hub can be a very busy machine, receiving and sending mail for many client machines, and because its role is broad, its configuration file is complex.

Fundamentally, all configuration files, simple and complex, tend to look pretty much the same. Both begin by selecting delivery agents using rule set 3 and 0. Both then process recipient or sender addresses with rule sets 3, 1 or 2, R= or S=, then 4, but the hub's rules are more complex:

- The hub needs to recognize more than simple Internet-style addresses. It may need to handle UUCP-style addresses or reverse-style addresses such as those used in parts of the United Kingdom. It needs rules to convert all such addresses into a form that it can understand.

- The hub needs not only to forward mail (like the client), but also to deliver it to the mail spool directory, to pipe through programs, and to form mailing lists.

- The hub needs to handle all error conditions gracefully and to emit helpful and clear error messages.

- The hub needs to know how to connect to many different kinds of machines worldwide.

In this chapter we explore high points of the V8 configuration files. Along the way, we also mix in rules contributed by others to help illustrate difficult concepts.

17.1 Rule Set 3

Recall that all addresses are first processed by rule set 3. Its job is to find an address among other clutter and to normalize all addresses into a form that other rules can recognize.

17.1.1 Find the Address

Recall that addresses can legally assume two forms:

    address (*comment*)
    comment <*address*>

In the first form, *sendmail* strips (and saves) the parenthesized comment, then gives the naked address to rule set 3. In the second form, *sendmail* passes the entire address, angle brackets and all, to rule set 3.

The rules to strip the angle brackets look like this:[*]

```
S3
R$*             $: <$1>      Guarantee at least one <> pair
R$+ <$*>           <$2>      Remove everything before the last <
R<$*> $+        $: <$1>      Remove everything after the first >
R<>             $@ <@>       Null address to @
R<$*>           $: $1        Strip remaining <>
```

In the following, we discuss each of these rules individually.

17.1.1.1 At least one <> pair

To find the address in addresses of the form

    comment <*address*>

we must use rules to search for the < and > characters. Designing rules that do this is easier if we can be sure that every address has at least one surrounding angle bracket pair:

```
R$*        $: <$1>     Guarantee at least one <> pair
```

This rule places angle brackets around all addresses, even those that already have them. Note that the $: that prefixes the RHS causes it to be executed only once.

A side benefit of this rule is that it also surrounds an empty (null) address with angle brackets. This allows old versions of *sendmail* to detect null addresses without needing to use the new (beginning with V8.7 *sendmail*) $@ LHS operator. We'll cover this in more detail soon.

---

[*] These ingenious rules were designed by LeRoy Eide, with surrounding commentary inspired by John Halleck.

17.1.1.2 Strip to left of <

A common problem is that of finding the address when it is deeply nested in many pairs of angle brackets. Consider an address like this:

```
<<<<address>>>>
```

Such addresses are not common but do appear every now and then as a result of overzealous users or MUAs. Another problem address looks like this:

```
comment <phone> <address>
```

Here, just noting the outermost pair of angle brackets is not sufficient because the rightmost pair contains the address.

The process of finding the rightmost innermost pair of angle brackets requires two rules:

```
R$+ <$*>        <$2>      Remove everything before the last <
R<$*> $+    $: <$1>       Remove everything after the first >
```

The first recursively discards everything (including angle brackets) to the left of the rightmost balanced < character. The second truncates to the correct address by discarding everything following the innermost remaining angle bracket pair.

The behavior of these two rules may not be obvious. To better understand them, first create a small configuration file (called *x.cf*) that includes the following two lines:[*]

```
R$+ <$*>        <$2>
R<$*> $+    $: <$1>
```

Then run *sendmail* in rule-testing mode with a command like this:

```
% /usr/lib/sendmail -Cx.cf -bt
ADDRESS TEST MODE (ruleset 3 NOT automatically invoked)
Enter <ruleset> <address>
```

Enter a series of addresses, one at a time, to see how each is handled. Be as extreme as you want when nesting angle brackets:

```
> 0 <<<<<a>>>>>
rewrite: ruleset  0   input: < < < < < a > > > > >
rewrite: ruleset  0 returns: < a >
> 0 <a> <b>
rewrite: ruleset  0   input: < a > < b >
rewrite: ruleset  0 returns: < b >
> 0 <<a> <b>>
```

---

[*] Note that when a configuration file lacks an S command (to declare a rule set), all rules become part of rule set 0.

```
rewrite: ruleset  0    input: < < a > < b > >
rewrite: ruleset  0 returns: < b >
>
```

If you want to see, step by step, how each rule works, run *sendmail* again, this time with the **-d21.12** debugging switch (see §37.5.72). With that switch, the first example above will print like this:

```
> 0 <<<<<a>>>>>
rewrite: ruleset  0    input: < < < < < a > > > > >
-----trying rule: $+ < $* >
-----rule matches: < $2 >
rewritten as: < < < < a > > > > >
-----trying rule: $+ < $* >
-----rule matches: < $2 >
rewritten as: < < < a > > > > >
-----trying rule: $+ < $* >
-----rule matches: < $2 >
rewritten as: < < a > > > > >
-----trying rule: $+ < $* >
-----rule matches: < $2 >
rewritten as: < a > > > > >
-----trying rule: $+ < $* >
----- rule fails
-----trying rule: < $* > $+
-----rule matches: $: < $1 >
rewritten as: < a >
rewrite: ruleset  0 returns: < a >
```

17.1.1.3 Handle null address

The fourth rule in rule set 3 is designed to convert a null (empty) address into the magic symbol @:

```
R<>        $@ <@>       Null address to @
```

The @ symbol is surrounded by angle brackets ("focused"). It needs to be focused because later rules expect all addresses to have the host part in this form. Still later, the angle brackets will be removed, and the @ will be discarded by rule set 4.

The $@ prefix to the RHS causes all further rules in rule set 3 to be skipped. The focused address <@> is returned. If <@> were to be handled by the next rule, its angle brackets would be stripped, and this is not what we desire.

17.1.1.4 Remove remaining angle brackets

The last of our five preliminary rules simply removes the angle brackets from whatever remains:

```
R<$*>      $: $1        Strip remaining <>
```

17.1.2 Normalize the Address

The rules that we have just looked at isolate the address from other possible information and leave it in its initial form, not surrounded by angle brackets. The rest of the rules in rule set 3 are designed to highlight the host part of any address. They assume that all addresses are composed of a user and a host part.

17.1.2.1 A rule to handle List:;

RFC822 allows addresses of the form

```
name : address(s) ;
```

Here, *name* is the name of a mailing list that can contain multiple words and spaces, for example,

```
Undisclosed Recipients :;
```

The colon and semicolon are mandatory and may contain one or more addresses between them, which may themselves be lists.[*] Rule set 3 needs to check for the presence of an empty list (one with no addresses between the colon and semicolon). The following rule does just that and turns the empty list into the magic token <@>:

```
R$* :;        $@ $1 :; <@>        Handle empty List:;
```

17.1.3 Internet Addresses

After lists have been disposed of, domain-type addresses need to be handled. Domain type addresses are of the form *user@host*:

```
R$+ @ $+              $: $1 <@$2>            Focus on host
R$+ < $+ @ $+ >          $1 $2 <@$3>         move gaze right
R$* < @ $* : $* > $*      $1 <@ $2$3> $4     strip colons
R$+ < @ $+ >          $@ $>96 $1<@$2>        localize and canonicalize
```

The first rule detects addresses of the form *something@something* and rewrites them in such a way that the second *something* becomes the focused host part.

The second rule handles addresses with multiple @ symbols (such as *a@b@c*). It recursively moves the focus to the rightmost host.

The third rule recursively removes any colons from the resulting host part as a "sanity check." This is necessary because strange forms of route addresses may have bypassed earlier rules (see the DontPruneRoutes option in §34.8.20, how route addresses are handled in rules in §29.4.3, and the F=d delivery agent flag in §30.8.16), or a colon may be left over from the mailertable feature (see §19.6.14).

---

[*] Which tends to complicate the algorithm.

The fourth rule passes any addresses that have been successfully focused to rule set 96 (which will be discussed in §17.2) so that the local host can be detected and the host part canonicalized. The result from rule set 96 is returned.

17.1.4 UUCP Addresses

UUCP addresses contain one or more exclamation points (such as *lady!sonya!george*). They fall into two categories: those that are delivered locally by *uux*(8) and those that are forwarded to another host. The rules to handle them look like this:

```
R$- ! $+            $@ $>96 $2 <@ $1.UUCP>       host!user uucp
R$+ . $- ! $+       $@ $>96 $3 <@ $1.$2>         Domain style uucp
R$+ ! $+            $@ $>96 $2 <@ $1.UUCP>       Bang path uucp
```

The first rule looks for a single token hostname followed by an exclamation point. A single token host always becomes the next host in line for delivery. The .UUCP suffix added in the RHS allows rule set 0 to recognize this address as one requiring *uux*(8) delivery.

The second rule looks for a dot in the hostname part of the address. A dot indicates the new-style, domain-based hostname, such as *host.domain!user.* Such names are assumed to have MX records pointing to service providers and are rewritten into the normal *user@host.domain* form.

The third rule catches any remaining addresses with exclamation points in them. The host to the left of the leftmost exclamation point is taken as the next hop in the UUCP path for delivery. A .UUCP suffix is added to that host, just as in the first rule.

All three rules exit (the leading $@ in the RHS) after the address is normalized by rule set 96 (which leaves .UUCP suffixed addresses unchanged). They are then handed as is to rule set 0, which selects a delivery agent (usually *uux*(8)).

17.1.5 The % Hack

A common technique in mail debugging is to send mail to one host and have that host deliver it to another. Often, this is done by sending the mail something like:

```
% mail user%second@first
```

Here, the intention is send mail to *first* and from there to *usr@second.* This type of addressing is nonstandard. Essentially, it is route addressing with % characters substituted for @ characters. Enabling this behavior requires three rules:

```
R$*%$*              $1 @ $2                     Convert all % to @
R$*@$*@$*           $1 % $2 @ $3                Undo all but last @
R$*@$*              $@ $>96 $1 <@$2>            Focus on rightmost
```

Here, the first rule changes all the percent characters into @ characters. The intention is to focus on the rightmost host, whether it is prefixed with an % or an @. The second rule changes all but the rightmost @ back into percent characters even if they were originally @ characters. The last rule takes the result and focuses on the rightmost host, just as was done in the domain form of addressing above.

17.2 Rule Set 96

After each address has its host part focused by rule set 3, it is passed to rule set 96 (by a subroutine call with the $> operator). Rule set 96 verifies that each address is good. It is not used by all configuration files but is used by the configuration files that are distributed with V8 *sendmail*.

17.2.1 Is the Host Local?

First, rule set 96 determines whether the focused host part is really the name of the local machine. This determination is less straightforward than you might think. The special hostname `localhost`, by which all hosts are known, is checked first:

```
R$* < @localhost       >$*      $: $1 <@$j.> $2      Sans domain
R$* < @localhost.$m    >$*      $: $1 <@$j.> $2      With domain
R$* < @localhost.UUCP >$*       $: $1 <@$j.> $2      With UUCP domain
```

The name `localhost` is checked in three forms (thus three rules): first as a bare hostname (without a domain part), then with the local domain attached (as stored in $m), and finally with the pseudo-name UUCP attached (on the off chance that mail was sent to the local host via UUCP). Later, the class $=w, which lists all the names of the local host, will be checked. Here, `localhost` is checked because there is no guarantee that it will be included in $=w.

The next three rules handle a host that is in numeric IP form. Such a hostname is formed by surrounding four dot-separated integers with square brackets (like *[123.45.67.8]*).

```
R$* < @ [$+] > $*       $: $1 <@@ [$2]>$3     is it numeric IP?
R$* < @@ $=w > $*       $: $1 <@ $j.> $2      yes. Is it us?
R$* < @@ $+  > $*       $@ $1 <@ $2> $3       yes, but not us.
```

The first of these rules finds anything surrounded by square brackets (it does not care whether that anything is an IP address). If found, it prefixes the host part with an extra @ so that only the next two rules will see it. The second rule compares the IP address to the list of hostnames in $=w.[*] If the IP address is found in $=w, the host is changed to the value in $j (the local, full canonical hostname). If the IP

---

[*] Under V8 *sendmail* the local host's IP address is automatically added to class w. Beginning with V8.7 *sendmail*, the addresses associated with all network interfaces are also added to the class w.

address is not that of the local host, the third rule causes it to be immediately returned as a valid (but not local) IP address.

The next two rules in rule set 96 determine whether the hostname is one of those declared as local in class $=w:

```
R$* < @ $=w    > $*        $: $1 <@ $j.> $3    us?
R$* < @ $=w.$m > $*        $: $1 <@ $j.> $3    us with domain?
```

The first just examines the list of hosts in the class $=w and, if found, converts the workspace to the full canonical name of the local host ($j.). The second performs the same search and substitution but appends the local domain ($m) to each host in $=w. Neither rewrite is returned (no $@ prefix to the RHS) but is instead carried down to subsequent rules.

At this point, UUCP hosts should be returned as is because the rest of the rules in rule set 96 deal with DNS and canonicalization. The next rule handles this:

```
R$* < @ $+.UUCP > $*        $@ $1 <@$2.UUCP> $3  pass back uucp
```

This rule looks for any host ($+) with a .UUCP suffix and returns (the $@ prefix to the RHS) that address unchanged. Review §17.1.4 to see how the .UUCP suffix came to be attached in the first place.

Any address that has made it this far is next looked up with DNS:

```
R$* < @ $* $~P > $*        $: $1 <@ $[ $2$3 $]> $4      canonicalize
```

Here, the notation $~P denotes anything that is *not* in the class P. That class was declared elsewhere. It contains a list of pseudo-domains (domains that cannot be looked up with DNS, such as UUCP and BITNET). If the last component of the hostname is other than one of the pseudo-domains, the RHS causes that hostname to be looked up with DNS and replaced with the full canonical name for that host. If the hostname corresponds to a CNAME, it will be replaced with the name of the corresponding A or MX record. If the address is an IP address (such as *[123.45.67.80]*), a PTR record will be looked up to find the canonical name. If the lookup fails, the name is unchanged. If the lookup succeeds, the canonical name will replace the looked up name and a dot will be appended.[*] On some machines this lookup may use */etc/hosts, nis, nisplus,* or some other means defined by your service switch file. In the configuration file that we have been examining, a successful DNS lookup causes a dot to be appended to the resulting hostname. This the same as what has been done all along by adding a dot to $j.

The last few rules merely perform some housekeeping by adding a dot to any valid addresses that lack one:

---

[*] This process is described in more detail in §33.4.3, which also explains how to change the dot to a different character or characters.

```
R$* < @ $* $=P > $*        $: $1 <@ $2$3 .> $4      canonicalize pseudos
R$* < @ $*.. > $*          $1 <@ $2.> $3            strip extra dots
R$* < @ $j > $*            $1 <@ $2.> $3            canonicalize local
```

In the first rule, pseudo-domains are considered canonical because there is no way to check their validity. The second rule strips any extra trailing dots in case they may have been added by accident.[*] Finally, a hostname of $j is checked, and if it is found, a dot is added, thus finishing rule set 96's job.

17.3 Rule Set 0

Rule set 0 checks for errors and selects delivery agents. First it disposes of the null address:

```
R<@>                       $#local $: <@>
```

Recall from §17.1.1.3 that the null address needs to be disposed of locally.

Next a whole series of error conditions need to be detected before they can lead to harm:

```
R$* : $* ; <@>      $#error $@ 5.1.3 $: "list:; syntax illegal for recipient addresses"
R<@ $+>             $#error $@ 5.1.1 $: "user address required"
R$* <$* : $* > $*   $#error $@ 5.1.1 $: "colon illegal in host name part"
R$* < @ . > $*      $#error $@ 5.1.2 $: "invalid host name"
```

First, addresses are checked to see whether they are of the List:; form (see §17.1.2.1) and, if so, are considered errors. Then the focused address is screened for missing user parts, colons in the host name, and unresolvable hostnames. Any such addresses are rejected as errors.

The rest of rule set 0 selects delivery agents. It can be simple or complex depending on your specific needs. In its simplest form, it detects local addresses and network mail:

```
R$+ < @ $=w . >            $#local $: $1                     regular local name
R$* < @ $* > $*            $#smtp $@ $2 $: $1 < @ $2 > $3    user@host.domain
```

Rule set 0 can also do *mailertable* lookups (see §19.6.14) and forward to a hub:

```
R< $+ > $*                 $: < $(mailertable $1 $) > $2    lookup
R$* < @ $* > $*            $: $>95 < $S > $1 < @ $2 > $3    glue on smarthost name
```

Note that these rules would not be grouped right next to each other. We presented them like this just to give you the flavor of a rule set 0, without the details. Leap ahead to §29.6 if you hunger for more.

---

[*] Sometimes $=P contains just a dot. In this case, any address that ends with a dot will have that ending dot doubled.

17.4 Rule Set 4

Rule set 4 cleans up after all the other rule sets. In general it attempts to undo anything done by rule sets 3 and 96. Recall that rule set 96 looked up the canonical name and appended a dot to any that it found. Any bogus trailing dots need to be stripped away, and that is what rule set 4 does:

```
# strip trailing dot off possibly canonical name
R$* < @ $+ . > $*        $1 < @ $2 > $3
```

Recall that UUCP addresses were converted from their *host!user* form into a .UUCP pseudo domain. Rule set 4 returns them to their original form:

```
# UUCP must always be presented in old form
R$+ @ $- . UUCP          $2!$1                    u@h.UUCP => h!u
```

Recall also that rule set 3 focused on the host part of the address. Rule set 4 will defocus:

```
R$* < $+ > $*            $1 $2 $3                 defocus
```

Depending on how ambitious the other rules are, rule set 4's job can be easy or hard. In general, processing any address with the sequence 3 then 4 should leave all but extraordinary addresses (such as the null address) unchanged:

```
% /usr/lib/sendmail -bt
ADDRESS TEST MODE (ruleset 3 NOT automatically invoked)
Enter <ruleset> <address>
> 3,4 user@host
rewrite: ruleset  3    input: user @ host
rewrite: ruleset 96    input: user < @ host >
rewrite: ruleset 96 returns: user < @ host >
rewrite: ruleset  3 returns: user < @ host >
rewrite: ruleset  4    input: user < @ host >
rewrite: ruleset  4 returns: user @ host
> 3,4 user@host.domain
rewrite: ruleset  3    input: user @ host . domain
rewrite: ruleset 96    input: user < @ host . domain >
rewrite: ruleset 96 returns: user < @ host . domain >
rewrite: ruleset  3 returns: user < @ host . domain >
rewrite: ruleset  4    input: user < @ host . domain >
rewrite: ruleset  4 returns: user @ host . domain
> 3,4 host!user
rewrite: ruleset  3    input: host ! user
rewrite: ruleset 96    input: user < @ host . UUCP >
rewrite: ruleset 96 returns: user < @ host . UUCP . >
rewrite: ruleset  3 returns: user < @ host . UUCP . >
rewrite: ruleset  4    input: user < @ host . UUCP . >
rewrite: ruleset  4 returns: host ! user
```

17.5 Things to Try

- Where in this rule set 3 is the best place to check for DECnet addresses, that is, the best place to detect an address of the form *host::user* and convert it to the form *user@host.DECNET?*

- Most modern UUCP implementations allow domain style addressing. How can you determine whether your site needs to convert domain UUCP addresses back into the old *host!user* form?

- Think up the most bizarre but legitimate address that you can and give it to *sendmail* in rule-testing mode. Is it parsed as you expected? If not, why not?

II

Build and Install

The second part of this book covers the building and installation of V8.8.4 *sendmail*, the latest version as of the publication of this book. If newer releases occur, you should obtain the latest source (see §18.3) and use it in place of this version.

Chapter 18, Compile and Install sendmail

Discusses the reasons for using *sendmail* in the first place. Shows where and how to obtain the source and finally how to build and install the working binary and most support files.

Chapter 19, V8 m4 Configuration

Covers the easy creation of a configuration file using V8's *m4* technique. A huge number of FEATUREs are described, each of which provides an easy solution to an otherwise difficult configuration problem.

Chapter 20, The checkcompat() Cookbook

Reveals the inner workings of *sendmail*'s internal *checkcompat()* routine. Many typical problems are discussed and *checkcompat()* coding solutions offered.

18

Compile and Install sendmail

In this chapter we show you how to obtain the latest version of *sendmail* in source form, then how to tune, build, and install it yourself. Although this process can be simple, many decisions that can complicate it must be made ahead of time (including the decision of whether or not to use *sendmail* in the first place).

18.1 *To Use or Not to Use*

The *sendmail* program is not the only MTA on the block. Others have existed for some time, and new MTAs appear on the scene every once in a while. We describe a few of the major MTAs and contrast them to *sendmail* in the following list:[*]

Smail3.x

> Sites may wish to consider *Smail3.x* if they are currently running a complex UUCP connection topology and wish to remain well connected to UUCP while simultaneously accessing the Internet with SMTP.

> One difference between *Smail3.x* and *sendmail* lies in their differing philosophies for parsing addresses. The *Smail3.x* authors feel that Internet and UUCP addresses are sufficiently standardized that all parsing can be handled by code rather than by configuration rules. If you suspect that *Smail3.x* may be better for your particular needs, you can get source and documentation from *uunet*. Look for a file named something like *smail-3.*.tar.Z*.

Zmailer

> More modular than *sendmail*, *zmailer* was written by Rayan Zachariassen at a time when *sendmail* appeared to have been abandoned. *Zmailer* is

---

[*] A new arrival on the MTA scene is *qmail*. It is so new that we did not have time to review it for this edition.

modularized by role, with well-defined roles. All decisions are made in configuration files; none are made in code. It tends to be slower than *sendmail*, but some claim that it is easier to understand. For additional information, contact:

```
ftp://ftp.cs.toronto.edu/pub/zmailer
```

post-office

A commercial offering (new and not widely ported). For those who absolutely need commercial support, this may be the answer. It features configuration via email and http forms. Similar to *Zmailer*, it is modular, each module playing a well defined role. For additional information, contact:

```
http://www.software.com
```

Many other MTAs exist, some good and some not so good. We mention only three here because, after all, this is a book about *sendmail*.

18.2 *Vendor Versus Compiling*

Old versions of operating systems tended to be shipped with old versions of *sendmail*. Old versions should be replaced because they are insecure.

Current versions of operating systems tend to ship with V8.7 sendmail. To find out which version you are running, issue the following command:

```
% /usr/lib/sendmail -d0.1 -bt < /dev/null
```

The first line (of possibly many) printed should contain the version number. If no version is displayed, you may be running a very old version of *sendmail* indeed, or some other program masquerading as *sendmail*. In either instance, you should upgrade. If version 8.6.13 or earlier is displayed, you should also plan to upgrade. If version 8.7.5 or earlier is displayed, you should also plan to upgrade. Version 8.7.6 was the last (as of this writing) secure version of the 8.7 series.

A more difficult decision is whether or not to upgrade if you are already running 8.8 *sendmail*. Potential reasons for upgrading are the following:

Security

The *sendmail* program has always been a prime target of attack by crackers (probably because it is distributed as source code). One reason to always run the latest version of *sendmail* is because earlier versions may have been compromised. Even if your current version is secure, a C library may not be. If you have been notified of a security hole in your library, you should consider recompiling *sendmail*, using a new, secure library.

Bug fixes

After widespread use and abuse, any program will begin to show its bugs. The *sendmail* program, although superbly written, is no exception. One reason new versions are periodically released is to fix reported bugs. At the very least, download the latest source and look at the release notes to see whether a bug may be biting you.

Uniformity

At a heterogeneous site (as most sites are these days) it is often more convenient to run a common version of *sendmail* and clone configuration files. Only by compiling and installing from the source can you achieve a controllable level of uniformity.

Tuning

A precompiled version of *sendmail* may lack certain features that you find desirable, or it may have features that you would prefer to exclude. Table 18-3 (in §18.8) lists the debugging switches that you can use to determine what kind of features your *sendmail* has available. If debugging switches are unavailable, the individual sections at the end of this chapter discuss other methods to determine feature support or the lack of it.

But beware: Before rushing out and replacing your vendor's version of *sendmail,* find out whether it uses any special vendor-specific features. If so, and if those features are more valuable to you than the security and uniformity that we mentioned, convince your vendor to upgrade for you.

18.3 Obtain the Source

V8 *sendmail* is available from:

```
ftp://ftp.sendmail.org/ucb/sendmail
```

When you *cd* into this directory, a banner is displayed that describes the latest release and available patches. You may choose between two forms of compressed *tar*(1) distributions. Those that end in *.Z* are compressed with UNIX *compress*(1); those that end in *.gz* are compressed with GNU *gzip*(1). The latter is the preferred form because the file is smaller and quicker to transfer.

In addition to the two forms of distribution, each release has associated with it a PGP signature file. It is a signature of the uncompressed file, so you need to uncompress the *tar*(1) file before verifying it. To verify a pre-V8.6 distribution, get Eric Allman's public key by sending email to *pgp-public-keys@keys.pgp.net* with the following subject line:

```
Subject: MGET Allman
```

Eric Allman's public key will be mailed back to you a few minutes later.[*] Save that returned email to a file, for example */tmp/eric.asc*, and add that key to your public "keyring" with the command:

```
pgp -ka /tmp/eric.asc
```

For V8.6 and above, you download a special *signing key* from *www.sendmail.org*, instead of Eric's key. The fingerprint for the *signing key* is:

```
CA AE F2 94 3B 1D 41 3C  94 7B 72 5F AE 0B 6A 11
```

The fingerprint for Eric's key is:

```
C0 28 E6 7B 13 5B 29 02 6F 7E 43 3A 48 4F 45 29
```

then execute:

```
pgp  signature file here
```

If the uncompressed tar file is good, *pgp*(1) will report the following or some variation on it:

```
Good signature from user "Eric P. Allman <eric@CS.Berkeley.EDU>".
```

A few things can go wrong here, causing the verification to fail:

- Signature and *tar*(1) files must match each other's versions. Transfer them again, this time with matching versions.

- When transferring the files with *ftp*(1), you must be sure to use *binary* mode. Transfer them again, this time with the correct mode.

- A presumed mirror FTP site might not be as official as you expect. If a secondary distribution fails to verify, get the official distributions from the official site shown above.

- The official distribution may appear bad. If it fails to verify, first check that your copy of *pgp* was correctly installed, then check that your network connection is clean and that it has not been compromised. If all else fails (including getting the distribution anew as above), describe your problem to the folks at *sendmail@sendmail.org*.

If your copy of the *sendmail* distribution fails to verify, *don't use it!*

---

[*] As an alternative, you can run the command

```
finger -l eric@finger.sendmail.org > /tmp/eric.asc
```

and use that PGP information in place of the email information. They are equivalent.

18.3.1 What's Where in the Source

V8.8.6 *sendmail* unpacks by creating a directory, then unpacking into that directory. The directory name is the same as the compressed file name but with the first dot a dash instead:

```
% zcat sendmail.8.8.6.tar.Z | tar xvf -
x sendmail-8.8.6/FAQ, 32312 bytes, 64 tape blocks
x sendmail-8.8.6/KNOWNBUGS, 4714 bytes, 10 tape blocks
x sendmail-8.8.6/Makefile, 1215 bytes, 3 tape blocks
... and so on
```

Inside the newly created directory you will find the full *sendmail* distribution:

```
% cd sendmail-8.8.6
% ls
FAQ              RELEASE_NOTES   mail.local      rmail
KNOWNBUGS        cf              mailstats       smrsh
Makefile         contrib         makemap         src
READ_ME          doc             praliases       test
```

The *READ_ME* and *RELEASE_NOTES* files provide the most up-to-date information about changes, new features, and bug fixes. Read the documents in the *doc* directory. Also note that there are important comments in the *src/READ_ME* and *cf/README* files.

You will find almost everything you need to build *sendmail* in the *src* subdirectory. There are a few exceptions that we will cover in this chapter.

18.3.2 The makesendmail Script

The first step in compiling *sendmail* is to establish an object directory and a *Makefile* that is appropriate to your machine architecture and operating system. You do this by running the *makesendmail* script in the *src* directory:

```
% cd src
% ./makesendmail -n
Configuration: os=SunOS, rel=4.1.4, rbase=4, arch=sun4, sfx=
Creating obj.SunOS.4.1.4.sun4 using Makefile.SunOS
Making dependencies in obj.SunOS.4.1.4.sun4
← many more lines here
%
```

Here, *makesendmail* found that ours was a sun4 machine, running the SunOS 4.1.4 release of UNIX. It created the working directory *obj.SunOS.4.1.4.sun4*, set up symbolic links to all the source files in that directory, and copied a *Makefile* there. The –n switch[*] prevents *make* from actually building *sendmail*. Note that, except for the –m switch, all command-line arguments following the *makesendmail* are passed to *make*(1) as its own command-line arguments.

The *makesendmail* script knows how to build *sendmail* on many versions of UNIX, including offshoots such as OSF/1 and NextStep. In the unlikely case that your operating system is not supported, you will see an error message instead of the above output:

```
Configuration: os=EX/Unix, rel=1, rbase=1, arch=sun4, sfx=
Cannot determine how to support sun4.EX/Unix.1
```

Here, an experimental version of UNIX called *EX/Unix* on a sun4 computer was unrecognized by the *makesendmail* script. Porting *sendmail* to new operating systems is really beyond the scope of this book. But we offer a complete listing of #define macros in §18.8 at the end of this chapter, and that, as well as much of the tuning that we discuss here, can also be germane to porting.

18.3.3 What to Tune

Before you let *makesendmail* run to completion, you may need to tune three of *sendmail*'s files for your site:

Makefile/*
> Specifies where to install the binaries and how to compile them. *Makefile* is normally the only file you will have to modify if you are running an already supported operating system

conf.h
> Specifies maximum sizes and other properties that are tunable for porting:

conf.c
> Specifies C language code to support specific and unusual needs. Tunable items in *conf.c* include the *checkcompat*() routine (see Chapter 20, *The checkcompat() Cookbook*) and default header behavior (see §35.5).

18.4 Tuning Makefile

The *make*(1) program is used to compile and install *sendmail*. The *makesendmail* script not only created an *obj.** working directory, it also copied an appropriate *Makefile* into that directory.[†] Before changing anything in *Makefile*, you should *cd*

---

[*] As an alternative, the –m command-line switch causes *makesendmail* to print the name of your *Makefile* without actually creating the *obj.** subdirectory.

[†] Actually, it created a symbolic link called *Makefile* that points to the appropriate file in the *../Makefiles* directory.

into your object directory and change the permissions of *Makefile* so that it is writable by you:

```
% cd obj.*
% mv Makefile Makefile.orig
% cp Makefile.orig Makefile
% chmod 644 Makefile
```

Makefile is tuned by defining or redefining directives (shown in Table 18-1) that begin lines in that file.

Table 18-1: Makefile Directives That You May Customize

Directive	§	Description
DBMDEF=	18.4.1	Which database libraries to use
ENVDEF=	18.4.2	Compiler -D switches, such as -D_AIX3
INCDIRS=	18.4.3	Compiler -I switches, such as -I../db/include
LDOPTS=	18.4.4	Linker options, such as -Bstatic for SunOS
LIBDIRS=	18.4.5	Linker -L switches, such as -L/usr/local/lib
LIBS=	18.4.6	Linker -l libraries, such as -ldbm
BINDIR=	18.4.7	Where to install *sendmail*
STDIR=	18.4.8	Where the *sendmail.st* file goes
HFDIR=	18.4.9	Where the *sendmail.hf* file goes
OBJADD=	18.4.10	Object files that need to be linked in

We will discuss each of these macros shortly but first note that, in general, you should never have to modify anything after the "end" line (shown in the following example). The only exception might be special requirements created by porting *sendmail* to a new platform.

```
################## end of user configuration flags ####################
```

Finally, before changing anything inside *Makefile*, be sure to read *src/READ_ME*. It always contains the latest information about building *sendmail*. In this book we are forced to speak in generalities, whereas the *src/READ_ME* file discusses operating systems, compilers, and hardware in specific detail.

18.4.1 DBMDEF=

The DBMDEF= directive defines the database library support you want. The currently available choices are listed in Table 18-2. Details are given in the indicated section.

Table 18-2: Define for Database Support

Define	§	Aliases[b]	Description
AUTO_NIS_ALIASES	18.8.1	Yes	Add fallback alias techniques
HESIOD	18.8.10	Yes	Support *hesiod* database maps
LDAPMAP	18.8.15	No	Enable use of *ldap* databases
NDBM	18.8.24	Yes	Support UNIX *ndbm*(3) Databases[a]
NETINFO	18.8.27	Yes	Support NeXT *netinfo*(3) databases
NEWDB	18.8.28	Yes	Support *db*(3), both *hash* and *btree* forms
NIS	18.8.29	Yes	Support `nis` maps
NISPLUS	18.8.30	Yes	Support `nisplus` maps
OLD_NEWDB	18.8.33	n/a	Support the old form of *db*(3)
UDB_DEFAULT_SPEC	18.8.53	n/a	Default User Database location
USERDB	18.8.54	n/a	Support the User Database

a. If yes, this database format supports aliasing.
b. Note that the old *dbm*(3) form of database is no longer supported.

Either NDBM or NEWDB must be defined, or *sendmail* will read the aliases into its symbol table every time it starts. This will make *sendmail* crawl and is not recommended.

External databases can be extremely valuable, especially in providing easy solutions for complex problems. Therefore we recommend that you include a definition for all databases that your system supports, even if you don't immediately foresee a need for them.

Below, we illustrate the selection of two forms of database:

```
DBMDEF= -DNEWDB -DNDBM
```

When these two forms are selected, old databases are read by using NDBM, but new databases are created by using NEWDB. Read *src/READ_ME* for details about, and exceptions to, this transition process.

18.4.2 ENVDEF=

The ENVDEF= directive is used primarily to specify code that should either be specially included or excluded. The following example shows support for *identd*(8) being excluded from the compiled binary:

```
ENVDEF= -DIDENTPROTO=0
```

Note that, once excluded, support cannot easily be included later by using options. But it may be better to turn some facilities, such as *identd*(8), off and on with options rather than compiling them out (see §34.8.70.10 for a description of the `TimeOut.ident` option). In Table 18-3 (see §18.8) the third column indicates whether it is appropriate to redefine a particular macro in your *Makefile*. Where appropriate, most will be defined with this ENVDEF= directive.

The ENVDEF= directive can also be used to define operating specific support. For example,

```
ENVDEF= -DSOLARIS=20501
```

Here, support for Sun's Solaris 2.5.1 operating system is being included. In general, operating support is already included in the *Makefile* selected for your system. You will have only to redefine this if you are porting to a completely new operating system.

18.4.3 INCDIRS=

The INCDIRS= directive defines the directories searched (using the compiler's -I switch) for #include files. In general this will be empty unless you are using libraries that are not normally used. For example, you may have installed the *db*(3) library in */usr/local/lib* and its corresponding include files in */usr/local/include/db*. In this case you would define

```
INCDIRS=-I/usr/local/include/db
LIBDIRS=-L/usr/local/lib/
```

The -I will be passed to the C compiler. The -L will be passed to the loader.

Many *Makefiles* specify */usr/sww* in these lines. If you don't need local include files or libraries, you can leave the */usr/sww* in place without harm.[*]

18.4.4 LDOPTS=

The LDOPTS= directive defines operating system–specific loader options. For example, on SunOS machines the following is recommended:

```
LDOPTS=      -Bstatic
```

This tells the loader to exclude dynamic library support for better security.

18.4.5 LIBDIRS=

The LIBDIRS= directive defines the directories searched (using the loader's -L switch). The libraries in these directories are searched before the standard system libraries. An example of its use is given in §18.4.3 above.

---

[*] The *sww* stands for SoftWare Warehouse. This scheme was used at U.C. Berkeley as a large centrally maintained */usr/local* partition.

18.4.6 LIBS=

The LIBS= directive lists additional libraries by name (using the loader's -l switch) to link against. All *Makefile* files have a default for this line. The one for Ultrix looks like this:

```
LIBS=   -ldb -lresolv -l44bsd
```

It is likely that you will have to add or change libraries in this list depending on your architecture and operating system. To discover which you need, run *make*(1) (see the next section) and observe which routines the linker reports as missing. The -l44bsd is required only if you are using Paul Vixie's version of -lresolv as supplied with BIND 4.9.

18.4.7 BINDIR=

The BINDIR= directive defines the location (directory) where the *sendmail* binary will be installed. It is very unlikely that you will ever have to change this from the value predefined for you in your *Makefile*. One exception might be if you are installing a new *sendmail* in parallel with the existing one. In that instance you might use

```
BINDIR=/usr/tests
STDIR=/usr/tests
HFDIR=/usr/tests
ENVDEF= -D_PATH_SENDMAILCF=/usr/tests/sendmail.cf \
        -D_PATH_SENDMAILPID=/usr/tests/sendmail.pid
```

The STDIR= and HFDIR= are described below. The ENVDEF= tells *sendmail* where its configuration and *pid* files will be found (see §18.8.34).

18.4.8 STDIR=

The STDIR= directive defines the location (directory) where the *sendmail* program's statistics file will be found (see §26.2.1 for a description of this file). It is very unlikely that you will ever have to change this from the value that is predefined for you in your *Makefile*.

18.4.9 HFDIR=

The HFDIR= directive defines the location (directory) where the *sendmail* program's SMTP-help file will be found (see §34.8.28 for a description of the HelpFile option and this file). It is very unlikely that you will ever have to change this from the value that is predefined for you in your *Makefile*.

18.4.10   OBJADD=

The OBJADD= directive defines additional object files that need to be included in the *sendmail* program. It is very unlikely that you will ever have to change this from the value that is predefined for you in your *Makefile*. One exception might be if you need to replace a standard C library function with one that was customized to satisfy some local need. For example, consider a replacement for the *syslog*(3) routine. First place a copy of *syslog.c* in the *src* directory. Then run:

```
% makesendmail -n
```

which will create an *obj.** directory and populate it with symbolic links.* Finally, edit your *Makefile* and *syslog.o* to the OBJADD= directive:

```
OBJADD=syslog.o
```

This will cause the *syslog.c* file to be compiled to produce the needed *syslog.o* and will cause that *syslog.o* to be linked in with the *sendmail* binary.

18.5   Run Make

After you have finished tuning *Makefile*, you are ready to build *sendmail*. First (especially if you are building as *root*), back up in the *src* directory run:

```
# ./makesendmail -n
```

This displays all the commands that *make* will generate without actually executing them. If all looks well, run *makesendmail* again, this time without the -n.

18.5.1   Use libresolv.a

If, when you compiled *sendmail*, the linker reported _res_* routines as missing, you need to specify the resolver library with -lresolv:

```
LDADD=  -ldbm -lcompat -lutil -lkvm -lresolv
```

This shows one way to include that library with the V8 *Makefile*. Another way might look like this:

```
# libraries required on your system
LIBS=   /usr/local/lib/libresolv.a
```

---

* If you have already run *makesendmail*, running it again will not create the link. Instead, you will need to soft-link it by hand yourself.

To ensure that *sendmail* achieves its optimum use of lookups, make sure that your resolver library is derived from the latest BIND release: BIND 4.9.[*] You will also need to include −l44bsd on the LIBS= line if you are running BIND 4.9.

The tricky part is finding out which resolver library your system supports. With SunOS systems, for example, resolver support in the standard C library uses *nis* for name resolution. Although this setup *may* be good for most applications, it is inappropriate for *sendmail*. There is a *libresolv.a*, but it is based on BIND 4.3 and so should probably be replaced with a newer version.

If your resolver library is not the correct one, you need to compile and install the newest version. You should do this even if it is used only by *sendmail*.

18.5.2 Remove -l44bsd

If you are running an old (pre V4.9) resolver library, you will see an error like the following during the loading part of your build:

```
ld: -l44bsd: No such file or directory
```

One solution is to upgrade to BIND 4.9, which will install the *lib44bsd.a* library (we recommend this). Another solution is to remove −l44bsd from the LIBS line in your *Makefile*.

18.5.3 Badly defined sys_errlist

Some systems define *sys_errlist* differently than *sendmail*. On such systems you *may* see a spurious warning about *sys_errlist* being redefined.

In general you should never get this error. But if you are building *sendmail* on a system that is similar to, but not identical to, one already supported, you may see such a warning. See §18.8.6 for a description of how to use ERRLIST_PREDEFINED to fix the problem, should it occur.

18.6 Install sendmail

There are two approaches to installing a new *sendmail*:

- If you choose to run the new *sendmail* in place of the original, you first need to create and install a new configuration file. The *m4*(1) program is used to automate the process of configuration file creation. See Chapter 19, *V8 m4 Configuration*, for a full description of this process.

---

[*] 4.8.3 is also good. 4.9 is available via anonymous FTP from *ftp.vix.com*.

- If you choose to keep the original and install the new *sendmail* in parallel (until you can trust it), you may proceed with the installation and defer configuration files until later. Note that this choice presumes that you customized the file locations.

After you have compiled *sendmail* (and if the configuration file is ready and tested), you can install it as your production version. If you are already running a *sendmail* and will be overwriting that binary, you will need to kill that version first (see Chapter 4, *How to Run sendmail*).

To install *sendmail*, first type

```
# ./makesendmail -n install
```

You use −n to be sure that the installation caused by the *Makefile* is in fact correct for your site. A typical such run, for example, might look like this:

```
install -o root -g kmem -m 6555 sendmail /usr/lib
for i in /usr/ucb/newaliases /usr/ucb/mailq; do rm -f $i; \
    ln -s /usr/lib/sendmail $i;
done
install -c -o root -g kmem -m 644 /dev/null \
    /etc/sendmail.st
install -c -o root -g kmem -m 444 sendmail.hf /usr/lib
```

Notice that *Makefile* will not create the queue directory even if it does not exist. If you have never run *sendmail* on your machine before, you will need to create that queue directory:

```
# mkdir /var/spool/mqueue
# chmod 700 /var/spool/mqueue
```

See §34.8.48 for a description of the `QueueDirectory` option and information about how *sendmail* locates its queue directory.

If all looks good, you can install *sendmail* with this command:

```
# ./makesendmail install
```

But be aware that the new *sendmail* may not work properly with your old configuration file. See Chapter 19, *V8 m4 Configuration* for guidance in creating configuration files.

18.7 Pitfalls

- Before replacing your current *sendmail* with a new version, be sure that the queue is empty. The new version may not be able to properly process old (or different) style queued files.* After running the new *sendmail* for the first time, look in the queue directory for filenames that start with an uppercase Q. See §23.3 for a description of why these files appear and what to do about them.

- If you change the location of the queue to a different disk, be sure that disk is mounted (in */etc/rc*) before the *sendmail* daemon is started. If *sendmail* starts first, there is a risk that messages will be queued in the mount point before the disk is mounted. This will result in mysteriously vanishing mail.

- Always save the old *sendmail* and configuration file. The new version may work fine for a while, then suddenly fail. If the failure is difficult to diagnose, you may need to run the old version while you fix the new version. But beware that the old version may not be able to read the queue files created by the new version.

- Some operating systems allow disks to be mounted such that *suid* permissions are disallowed. If you relocate *sendmail*, avoid locating it on such a disk.

- Don't be mistaken in the belief that *nis* will correctly give you MX for hosts. If, after compiling and installing *sendmail*, you find that you cannot send mail to hosts using MX records, you should recompile with NAMED_BIND defined (see §18.8.23). Also note that a misconfigured service-switch file can also prevent proper MX lookups (see 34.8.61).

18.8 Alphabetized Reference

In this section we present each #define macro (or group of them) in alphabetical order rather than in the order in which they appear in your *Makefile*.

Note that the **Tune** column of Table 18-3 recommends whether or not you should adjust (tune) the values for any particular #define. Those marked *tune* may be adjusted from within your *Makefile*. Those marked with *port* should be changed only in the rare event that you need to port *sendmail* to a new operating system.†‡ Those marked with *debug* should only be defined during porting to help debug the new binary but (for security reasons) should never be defined for the final production version.

Also note that the **-d** column shows which debugging switches can be used to determine whether the corresponding macro was defined when a *sendmail* binary was compiled (see §37.5.1 for a description of this process).

---

* V8 *sendmail* can read old queue files but may be unable to read some vendor queue files. If this is a problem, you may have to run the old and new versions in parallel (with separate queue directories) until the old queue has been emptied.

† But note that final porting should be done in *conf.h* and *conf.c* instead of *Makefile*.

Table 18–3: #define Macros for Compiling sendmail

#define	§	Tune	-d	Description
AUTO_NIS_ALIASES	18.8.1	Tune		Add fallback alias techniques
BROKEN_RES_SEARCH	18.8.2	Port		Broken resolver fix (e.g. Ultrix)
BSD4_3	18.8.3	Port		Use BSD 4.3 style signal handling
BSD4_4	18.8.4	Port		Compile for BSD 4.4 UNIX
DSN	18.8.5	Tune		Support Delivery Status Notification
ERRLIST_PREDEFINED	18.8.6	Port		Correct type conflicts on sys_errlist
FFR . . .	18.8.7	Debug		For Future Release
FORK	18.8.8	Port		The type of *fork*(5) to use
HAS . . .	18.8.9	Port	0.10	Has specific system call support
HESIOD	18.8.10	Tune	0.1	Support hesiod database maps
HES_GETMAILHOST	18.8.11	Tune	0.1	Use hesiod *hes_getmailhost*(3)
IDENTPROTO	18.8.12	Port	0.10	See Timeout.ident (§34.8.70.10)
IP_SRCROUTE	18.8.13	Port	0.10	Add IP source-routing to $_
LA_TYPE	18.8.14	Port	3.5	Define your load-average support
LDAPMAP	18.8.15	Tune	0.1	Enable use of ldap databases
LOG	18.8.16	Tune	0.1	Perform logging
LOTUS_NOTES_HACK	18.8.17	V8.7.5		Strip newlines from **From:** headers
MATCHGECOS	18.8.18	Tune	0.1	Support for fuzzy name matching
MAX . . .	18.8.19	Tune		Redefine maximums
MEMCHUNKSIZE	18.8.20	Tune		Specify memory allocation size
MIME7TO8	18.8.21	Tune	0.1	Support MIME 7- to 8-bit conversion
MIME8TO7	18.8.22	Tune	0.1	Support MIME 8- to 7-bit conversion
NAMED_BIND	18.8.23	Tune	0.1	Support DNS name resolution
NDBM	18.8.24	Tune	0.1	Support UNIX ndbm(3) Databases
NEED . . .	18.8.25	Port		Something amiss with your OS?
NET . . .	18.8.26	Tune	0.1	Select network type
NETINFO	18.8.27	Tune	0.1	Support NeXT *netinfo*(3) databases
NEWDB	18.8.28	Tune	0.1	Support Berkeley *db*(3) Databases
NIS	18.8.29	Tune	0.1	Support *nis* maps
NISPLUS	18.8.30	Tune	0.1	Support *nis+* maps
NO_GROUP_SET	18.8.31	Port		Prevent multi-group file access
NOTUNIX	18.8.32	Port	30.2	Exclude From line support
OLD_NEWDB	18.8.33	Port	0.1	Support the old form of *db*(3)
_PATH . . .	18.8.34	Debug		Hard-code paths inside *sendmail*
PICKY . . .	18.8.35	Tune		Make a pickier *sendmail*
PSBUFSIZE	18.8.36	Tune		Size of *prescan*() buffer
QUEUE	18.8.37	Tune		Enable queueing
QUEUESEGSIZE	18.8.38	Tune		Amount to grow queue work list
SCANF	18.8.39	Tune	0.10	Support *scanf*(3) with F command
SFS_TYPE	18.8.40	Port		How to determine free disk space
SMTP	18.8.41	Tune		Enable SMTP

Table 18–3: #define Macros for Compiling sendmail (continued)

#define	§	Tune	-d	Description
SMTPDEBUG	18.8.42	Debug		Enable remote debugging
SMTPLINELIM	18.8.43	n/a		Default for obsolete F=L flag
SOLARIS	18.8.44	Port		Support Sun's Solaris 2.x
SPT_TYPE	18.8.45	Port		Adapt/exclude process title support
SUID_ROOT_FILES_OK	18.8.46	Debug	0.1	Allow root delivery to files
SYSLOG_BUFSIZE	18.8.47	Port		Limit *syslog*(3) buffer size
SYSTEM5	18.8.48	Port	0.10	Support SysV derived machines
SYS5SIGNALS	18.8.48	Port	0.10	Use SysV style signals
TCPWRAPPERS	18.8.49	Tune	0.1	Use libwrap.a for connects
TOBUFSIZE	18.8.50	Tune		Set buffer for recipient list
TRUST_POPEN	18.8.51	Debug		Allow use of *popen*(3)
TTYNAME	18.8.52	Debug	35.9	Set $y to tty name (obsolete)
UDB_DEFAULT_SPEC	18.8.53	Tune		Default User Database location
USERDB	18.8.54	Tune	0.1	Support the User Database
USESETEUID	18.8.55	Port	0.10	Support *seteuid*(2) identity changes
WILDCARD_SHELL	18.8.56	Debug		Redefine wildcard shell
XDEBUG	18.8.57	Debug	0.1	Support sanity checks

AUTO_NIS_ALIASES   *(tune with DBMDEF= in Makefile)*

18.8.1   *Add fallback alias techniques*

Ordinarily, *sendmail* will first look for a service-switch (see §34.8.61) to see how it
should look up its aliases. If it finds one, and if the service *aliases* is listed, it uses
the techniques listed with the service-switch to look up its aliases. In the absence
of a service-switch, or if the service-switch could not be opened, *sendmail*'s fallback position is to use the technique called *files* to look up its aliases.

This AUTO_NIS_ALIASES definition, when specified during compilation, also causes
sendmail to automatically add the technique *nis* if NIS was defined or *nis+* if NIS-
PLUS was defined:

```
DBMDEF= -DNIS -DAUTO_NIS_ALIASES
DBMDEF= -DNISPLUS -DAUTO_NIS_ALIASES
```

The first line causes the fallback list of techniques to become *files* then *nis*, and
the second causes it to become *files* then *nisplus*. Note that AUTO_NIS_ALIASES is
not defined in any *Makefile* distributed with *sendmail*.

BROKEN_RES_SEARCH
(port, edit conf.h)

18.8.2
Broken resolver fix (e.g. Ultrix)

On Ultrix, and possibly other systems, the *res_search*(2) routine incorrectly sets *h_errno* to 0 instead of HOST_NOT_FOUND if a host name is unknown. On such systems you can define BROKEN_RES_SEARCH in your *Makefile*, which tells *sendmail* to consider 0 the same as HOST_NOT_FOUND:

```
ENVDEF= -DBROKEN_RES_SEARCH
```

As distributed, this is not declared for any of the supplied *Makefile* files. If you are running Ultrix you should test your resolver library. If it fails, you should upgrade to the latest resolver library. If, for some reason, upgrading is not possible, you may define this as a workaround. When porting to a new system, you can test with the above ENVDEF= statement and, if successful, put a permanent porting entry into *conf.h*.

BSD4_3
(port, edit conf.h)

18.8.3
Use old style signal handling

Old BSD-based versions of UNIX, such as SunOS 4.0.x and BSD 4.3, used the *signal*(2) and *sigsetmask*(2) calls to set and release signals. Modern versions of UNIX use the *sigaction*(2) and *sigprocmask*(2) pair of routines. For all currently supported systems, BSD4_3 is already correctly defined in *src/Makefiles* or in *conf.h*. You should need to define BSD4_3 only if you are porting to a previously unsupported old BSD-based system:

```
ENVDEF= -DBSD4_3
```

When porting to a new system, you can test with the above ENVDEF= statement and, if successful, put a permanent porting entry into *conf.h*.

BSD4_4
(port, edit conf.h)

18.8.4
Compile for BSD 4.4 Unix

BSD4_4 will automatically be defined when *sendmail* is built under the BSD 4.4 release of UNIX. You will need to redefine this only if you are porting to a new operating system that is based on BSD 4.4.

DSN
(tune with ENVDEF= in Makefile)

18.8.5
Support Delivery Status Notification

Delivery Status Notification (DSN) replaces certain SMTP error codes and the `Return-Receipt-To:` header (§35.10.29) as a means of handling multiple delivery status requests and problems. DSN is an improvement over earlier mechanisms for returning delivery status information. It can, for example, supply different status information for each recipient when multiple recipients are specified. It can also be used to generate return receipts on a per recipient basis. DSN status is returned in the MIME encapsulated portion of a mail message's body.

DSN is defined in RFC1891, RFC1892, RFC1893, and RFC1894. If you wish to exclude DSN support (not recommended), you may turn it off like this:

```
ENVDEF=   -DDSN=0
               ↑
      turn off DSN support
```

MIME is described under the `EightBitMode` (8) option (see §34.8.22).

ERRLIST_PREDEFINED   *(port, edit conf.h)*

18.8.6   *Correct conflicts on sys_errlist*

Some systems define a type for *sys_errlist[]* that differs from the internal declaration made by *sendmail*. In such instances you will get a warning about *sys_errlist* being redefined when you compile. Such warnings are usually harmless, but they are unattractive. To eliminate them, add the following to your *Makefile*:

```
ENVDEF= -DERRLIST_PREDEFINED
```

When porting to a new system, you can test with the above ENVDEF= statement and, if successful, put a permanent porting entry into *conf.h*.

FFR . . .   *(debug with ENVDEF= in Makefile)*

18.8.7   *For Future Release*

Most releases of *sendmail* contain, within the C language code, sections that are commented out. These are initial stabs at solutions that either did not work as is, are incomplete or untested, or are dreams for the future.

If you have a good reason and *thoroughly* understand the code and why it is excluded (and if you are brave), you may include it by adding an appropriate _FFR_ (For Future Release) definition to ENVDEF= in *Makefile*:

```
ENVDEF= -D_FFR_what
```

Here, **what** describes the appropriate future item that you want to include (as found in the source). We categorize this as a debugging technique (not a porting or tuning one) because you may want to include future code for testing, but should probably not include it in your production version.

FORK   *(port, edit conf.h)*

18.8.8   *The type of fork to use*

The *sendmail* program forks often to do its job in the most efficient way possible. Prior to V8.8, *sendmail* used *vfork*(2) whenever possible. Beginning with V8.8, *sendmail* now defaults to *fork*(2).* You should have to redefine FORK only when porting to a new system or when you are certain that *vfork*(2) is indeed faster on your system and is reliable.

```
ENVDEF= -DFORK=vfork
```

You can test with the above ENVDEF= statement and, if successful, put a permanent porting entry into *conf.h*.

HAS . . .   *(port, edit conf.h)*

18.8.9   *Has specific system call support*

Macros that begin with HAS tell *sendmail* whether or not your system supports (has) certain system-library routines. In general, you should need to define or undefine the macros shown in Table 18-4 only if you are porting *sendmail* to a new system. In that instance you should also read *src/READ_ME* for the latest information and pitfalls.

Each of these is turned on or off with an assignment of 1 or 0:

```
ENVDEF= -DHASSETSID=1      ← turn on
ENVDEF= -DHASSETSID=0      ← turn off
```

Turning on tells *sendmail* that your site has support for this system call (*setsid*(2) in this instance). Turning off tells *sendmail* to work around the lack of that support. When porting to a new system, you can test with one of the above ENVDEF= statements and, if successful, put a permanent porting entry into *conf.h*.

These have probably been correctly defined for your system already. Therefore you should need to change them only when porting *sendmail* to a completely new system.

---

* Bugs in the interaction between NIS and *vfork*(2) at the system level with Solaris and systems that lacked *vfork*(2) altogether, such as IRIX, caused V8.8 to favor *fork*(2). This is really okay because in modern systems, *fork*(2) is just as fast as *vfork*(2).

Table 18–4: HAS . . . #defines for Specific System Call Support

#define	System Call
HASFCHMOD	*fchmod*(2)
HASFLOCK	*flock*(2)
HASGETDTABLESIZE	*getdtablesize*(2)
HASGETUSERSHELL	*getusershell*(3)
HASINITGROUPS	*initgroups*(3)
HASLSTAT	*lstat*(2)
HASSETREUID	*setreuid*(2)
HASSETRLIMIT	*setrlimit*(2)
HASSETSID	*setsid*(2)
HASSETUSERCONTEXT	*setusercontext*(3)
HASSETVBUF	*setvbuf*(3)
HASSIGSETMASK	*sigsetmask*(2)
HASSNPRINTF	*snprintf*(3) and *vsnprintf*(3)
HASULIMIT	*ulimit*(2)
HASUNAME	*uname*(2)
HASUNSETENV	*unsetenv*(3)
HASWAITPID	*waitpid*(2)

If you are running a precompiled binary of *sendmail*, you can determine whether any of these were defined when *sendmail* was compiled by using the −d0.10 debugging switch (see §37.5.3).

HESIOD   *(tune with DBMDEF= in Makefile)*

18.8.10   *Support hesiod database maps*

Named after the 8th century B.C.E.[*] Greek poet Hesiod, the *hesiod* system is a network information system developed as Project Athena. Information that is shared among many machines on a network can be accessed by each machine using a common set of library routines. Files that are commonly represented in this form are the *passwd*(4) and *aliases*(4) files used by *sendmail*. The *hesiod* system is patterned after the Internet Domain Naming System and uses modified BIND source:

```
DBMDEF= -DHESIOD
```

If HESIOD is defined when *sendmail* is built, support is included to look up aliases and user information via the *hesiod* interface. Support is also included to declare and use *hesiod* class maps (see §33.3.2) with the K configuration command. Support is also included for the User Database if USERDB is also defined.

---

[*] Before Christian Era, although an alternative proposal that is making the rounds calls for signed years, thus the -8th century.

Hesiod documentation and source are available from:

    ftp://athena-dist.mit.edu/pub/ATHENA

If you are running a precompiled *sendmail* binary, you may use the **-d0.1** switch (see §37.5.1) to determine whether HESIOD support is included.

HES_GETMAILHOST   *(tune with ENVDEF= in Makefile)*

18.8.11   *Use hesiod hes_getmailhost()*

The MIT distribution of *hesiod* supports the *hes_getmailhost*(3) call for looking up a user's postoffice. If your site is running MIT's *hesiod*, you should define this. If your are running DEC's *hesiod*, you should not.

    ENVDEF= -DHES_GETMAILHOST

HES_GETMAILHOST is by default not defined. If you need it, you must define it in your *Makefile*. If you are running a precompiled version of *sendmail*, you may use the **-d0.1** debugging switch (see §37.5.1) to determine whether HES_GETMAILHOST has been included. The **-d28.8** (see §37.5.100) debugging flag can be used to trace the behavior of the *hes_getmailhost*(3) routine.

IDENTPROTO   *(port)*

18.8.12   *See Timeout.ident in §34.8.70.10*

Defining out IDENTPROTO neither includes nor excludes RFC1413 code. All it does is change the default value for the **Timeout.ident** option (see §34.8.70.10):

    ENVDEF= -DIDENTPROTO=0   ← *set Timeout.ident=0 by default*
    ENVDEF= -DIDENTPROTO=1   ← *set Timeout.ident=30 by default*

If you are running a precompiled *sendmail* binary, you may use the **-d0.10** switch (see §37.5.3) to determine whether IDENTPROTO was defined as nonzero.

IP_SRCROUTE   *(port, edit conf.h)*

18.8.13   *Add IP source-routing to $_*

Mail is normally transported over networks with TCP/IP. At the IP layer, packets are usually constructed to be point-to-point—from one host to another. IP packets can also be constructed to contain source-routing information—from one host, through a second, then to a final host.

Although such source routing (when used) is generally legitimate, it can also be used to generate fraudulent mail. V8.7 *sendmail* attempts to extract source-routing information from the initial connection's IP information. If any is found, *sendmail* adds that information to the $\$\_$ macro (see 31.10.1) for use in the **Received:** header (see 35.10.25). The $\$\_$ macro is usually used like this:

```
Received: from $s ($_) ...
```

where $\$\_$ will contain information like that shown below when IP source-routing information is found:

IP source-routing information
↓

user@host.domain [!@hostC@hostB:hostA]
↑
RFC1413 identd information

IP source-routing information is presented inside square brackets. If routing is strict, the information is prefixed with an exclamation mark. The format of the information is made to resemble that of source-route addressing (see the **Dont-PruneRoutes** option, §34.8.20). In this example the IP packets will go first to **hostC**, then to **hostB**, and finally to **hostA**.

The inclusion of code to support this reporting is determined by the IP_SRCROUTE definition in your *Makefile*. It is predefined correctly for all supported systems in *conf.h*, so you should need to redefine it only if you are porting *sendmail* to a completely new system. Be sure to read *src/READ_ME* for the latest information about IP_SRCROUTE.

If you are running a precompiled *sendmail* binary, you may use the **-d0.10** switch (see §37.5.3) to determine whether IP_SRCROUTE support was included.

LA_TYPE   *(port, edit conf.h)*

18.8.14   *Define your load-average support*

The load average is the average number of blocked processes (processes that are runnable but not able to run because of a lack of resources) over the last minute. The *sendmail* program can vary its behavior appropriately as the load average changes. Thresholds for change are defined by the options shown in Table 34-9 (see §34.6.4).

The method that is used to get the current load average from the operating system varies widely. This LA_TYPE definition determines which method to use. It is correctly defined inside *conf.h* for all currently supported operating systems. Porting *sendmail* to a new system may require that you define LA_TYPE yourself. The possible values and their meanings are shown in Table 18-5.

Table 18–5: LA_ Methods for Getting the Load Average

LA_	Does What
LA_ZERO	Always returns 0. Essentially disables load average checking. This is portable to all systems.
LA_INT	Read */dev/kmem* for the symbol *avenrun*. If found, interpret the result as a native (usually long) integer.
LA_FLOAT	Read */dev/kmem* for the symbol *avenrun*. If found, interpret the result as a floating-point value.
LA_SHORT	Read */dev/kmem* for the symbol *avenrun*. If found, interpret the result as a short integer.
LA_SUBR	Call the library routine *getloadavg*(3) and use the result returned.
LA_MACH	Call the MACH-specific *processor_set_info*(2) routine and use the result returned.
LA_PROCSTR	Read the Linux-specific */proc/loadavg* file and interpret the result as a floating-point value.
LA_READKSYM	Use the (some SysV versions) *ioctl* of MIOC_READKSYM to read */dev/kmem*.
LA_DGUX	DG/UX specific support for using the *pstat_getdynamic*(2) function to read the load average.

The LA_INT, LA_SHORT, LA_FLOAT, and LA_READKSYM settings require additional tuning. For these, three additional definitions are used as shown in Table 18-6.

Table 18–6: Tuning for LA_INT, LA_SHORT, LA_FLOAT, and LA_READKSYM

#define	Tunes
FSHIFT	Number of bits to shift right when using LA_INT, LA_SHORT, and LA_READKSYM. Default is 8.
_PATH_UNIX	The pathname of your kernel. This is required for LA_INT and LA_SHORT. Default is */unix* for SysV; */hp_ux* for HP/UX V9; */stand/unix* for HP/UX V10, News, and UXP/OS; */dev/ksyms* for Solaris; */dynix* for DYNIX; otherwise */vmunix*.
_PATH_KMEM	The pathname of your kernel memory. This is required for LA_INT, LA_SHORT, LA_FLOAT, and LA_READKSYM. Default is */dev/kmem*.
LA_AVENRUN	The name of the kernel variable that holds the load average. Used by LA_INT, LA_SHORT, and LA_FLOAT. Default is *averun* for SysV, otherwise *_averun*.
NAMELISTMASK	The mask to bitwise-AND against the return value of *nlist*(3). If this is undefined, the return value is used as is. A common value is 0x7fffffff to strip off the high bit.

LDAPMAP   *(tune with DBMDEF= in Makefile)*

18.8.15   *Enable use of ldap databases*

LDAP stands for Lightweight Directory Access Protocol. LDAP provides lightweight access to the X.500 directory and is defined in RFC1777 and RFC1778.

The software and documentation for LDAP is available from

```
ftp://terminator.rs.itd.umich.edu/ldap/
```

It is used by defining a map class called **ldapx** (see §33.8.9) in your configuration file. Its use is enabled by defining LDAPMAP at compile time:

```
DBMDEF=LDAPMAP
```

LOG   *(port, edit conf.h)*

18.8.16   *Perform logging*

If defined, LOG enables *sendmail* to use the *syslog*(3) facility to log error messages and other useful information that is often important for security and debugging. Logging and *syslog*(3) are described in Chapter 26, *Logging and Statistics*. Defining LOG should be considered mandatory, and it should be turned off only if you have a well-thought-out reason for doing so. LOG cannot be turned off in the *Makefile*. Instead, you must edit *conf.h* directly and undefine it by commenting it out:

```
/* # define LOG               /* enable logging -- don't turn off */
↑
comment out to remove support
```

LOG requires that your system support *syslog*(3). If you lack *syslog*(3), consider porting it to your system.

Defining LOG is meaningless unless the **LogLevel** (L) option (see §34.8.33) is also nonzero. Fortunately, this is usually the case because the default is 9.

See also SYSLOG_BUFSIZE for a way to tune *syslog*(3)'s buffer size if necessary.

If you are running a precompiled *sendmail* binary, you may use the **-d0.1** switch to determine whether LOG support was included (see §37.5.1).

LOTUS_NOTES_HACK   *(V8.7.2 through V8.7.5 only)*

18.8.17   *Strip newlines from From: header*

The *Lotus Notes* mail-gateway SMTP software can produce sender header lines that contain newlines when the username part becomes too long:

```
From: Long Full Name/LongSite/Country
  <user@site.domain>
```

Although perfectly legal under RFC822, such split sender headers can cause MUAs to fail in ways that are difficult to diagnose. If your site receives mail from *Lotus Notes* gateways, you should define LOTUS_NOTES_HACK when compiling *sendmail*:

```
ENVDEF= -DLOTUS_NOTES_HACK
```

Defining LOTUS_NOTES_HACK causes *sendmail* to include code in support of the `SingleLineFromHeader` option (see §34.8.63). Setting that option to true causes the newlines in the above address to be stripped and produces a single line:

```
From: Long Full Name/LongSite/Country <user@site.domain>
```

If you are running a precompiled *sendmail* binary, you can define `SingleLine-FromHeader` in your configuration file. If you don't get a warning about a bad option name, then you have this support. Note that under V8.8 *sendmail*, LOTUS_NOTES_HACK is no longer required for `SingleLineFromHeader` support.

MATCHGECOS   *(tune with ENVDEF= in Makefile)*

18.8.18   *Support fuzzy name matching*

Defining MATCHGECOS causes code to be included inside *sendmail* for support of limited *fuzzy* name matching. This process is described under the `MatchGECOS (G)` option (see §34.8.34). MATCHGECOS is normally defined by default. If you want to turn it off, use ENVDEF= in *Makefile*:

```
ENVDEF= -DMATCHGECOS=0
```

If you are running a vendor-supplied binary, you can check to see whether MATCHGECOS was defined by using the `-d0.1` debugging switch (see §37.5.1).

MAX . . .   *(port, edit specific files)*

18.8.19   *Redefine maximums*

In porting *sendmail* to a new system or tuning *sendmail* for special needs, it may be necessary to adjust one of its defined maximums. These cannot be tuned in *Makefile*. Instead, each needs to be changed in the file indicated by the third column of Table 18-7. In general, maximums should never be lowered without first examining the code for possible side effects; also, review the code to see whether any minimums are required or whether there are warnings about maximums.

Table 18–7: MAX . . . #defines to Redefine Maximums

#define	Default	File	Maximum
MAXALIASDB	12	*conf.h*	Number of alias databases
MAXATOM	200	*conf.h*	Atoms (tokens) in an address
MAXDNSRCH	6	*domain.c*	Possible domains to search
MAXHOSTNAMELEN	256	*conf.h*	Length of a hostname
MAXKEY	128	*conf.h*	Length of a database key
MAXLINE	2048	*conf.h*	Length of an input line
MAXMAILERS	25	*conf.h*	Number of delivery agents
MAXMAPSTACK	12	*conf.h*	Size of sequenced map stack
MAXMIMEARGS	20	*conf.h*	Arguments per **Content-Type:** header
MAXMXHOSTS	100	*conf.h*	Number of per host MX records
MAXMIMENESTING	20	*conf.h*	Multipart MIME nesting depth
MAXNAME	256	*conf.h*	Length of a name
MAXPRIORITIES	25	*conf.h*	Number of Priority lines
MAXPV	40	*conf.h*	Arguments to a delivery agent
MAXRULERECURSION	50	*conf.c*	Ruleset recursion
MAXRWSETS	200	*conf.h*	Number of rule sets
MAXTOCLASS	8	*conf.h*	Message timeout classes
MAXUSERENVIRON	100	*conf.h*	Environment items per delivery agent

Also see QUEUESEGSIZE and SYSLOG_BUFSIZE for the discussion of two other definitions that affect sizes.

Note that there are no debugging switches to display compiled maximums. If you are running a binary distribution and a maximum is of concern, you should get the source and build *sendmail* yourself.

MEMCHUNKSIZE   *(tune, edit conf.h)*

18.8.20   *Specify memory allocation size*

When *sendmail* reads lines of text from the configuration file or from qf queue files, it calls an internal routine named *fgetfolded()*. That routine is initially passed a buffer of size MAXLINE into which to fit the read line. If the line is longer than MAXLINE, the *sendmail* program dynamically increases the space required to hold the line by MEMCHUNKSIZE.

When collecting the headers of a mail message, *sendmail* also begins with a buffer sized to MAXLINE. If a header arrives that is larger than MAXLINE characters, *sendmail* will increase the size of its buffer by MEMCHUNKSIZE as many times as is necessary to fully contain that header's data.

The default value assigned to MEMCHUNKSIZE is 1024 bytes. If you need to change that value (for example, to port to a new system's strange *malloc*(3) requirements or for performance reasons), you must edit *conf.h*:

```
# define MEMCHUNKSIZE   1024              /* chunk size for memory allocation */
                         ↑
                   change this
```

MIME7TO8   *(tune with ENVDEF= in Makefile)*

18.8.21   *Support MIME 7- to 8-bit conversion*

V8.8 *sendmail* contains the internal ability to convert messages that were converted into either *quoted-printable* or *base64* (see §34.8.22) back into their original eight-bit form. The decision of whether or not to do this conversion is based on the F=9 delivery agent flag (see §30.8.6).

Defining MIME7TO8 to a value of 1 causes support for conversion to be included in *sendmail*. It is defined as 1 by default. To disable the inclusion of conversion code, use ENVDEF= in *Makefile* to define it as 0:

```
ENVDEF= -DMIME7TO8=0
                   ↑
          exclude support
```

Unless you have a compelling reason to do otherwise, we recommend that MIME7TO8 remain enabled.

If you are running a precompiled *sendmail* binary, you may use the −d0.1 switch to determine whether MIME7TO8 support (see §37.5.1) was included.

MIME8TO7   *(tune with ENVDEF= in Makefile)*

18.8.22   *Support MIME 8- to 7-bit conversion*

V8 *sendmail* contains the internal ability to convert 8-bit MIME message contents into 7-bit MIME so that mail can be transported to non-8-bit gateways. The methods used and the circumstances required to trigger conversion are described under the EightBitMode (8) option (see §34.8.22). The conversion itself can be watched with the −d43 debugging switch (see §37.5.150).

Defining MIME8TO7 to a value of 1 causes support for conversion to be included in *sendmail*. It is defined as 1 by default. To disable the inclusion of conversion code, use ENVDEF= in *Makefile* to define it as 0:

```
ENVDEF= -DMIME8TO7=0
                   ↑
          exclude support
```

One side effect of excluding MIME8TO7 support is that defining it to 0 causes all MIME support to also be excluded. Unless you have a compelling reason to do otherwise, we recommend that MIME8TO7 remain enabled.

If you are running a precompiled *sendmail* binary, you may use the **-d0.1** switch to determine whether MIME8TO7 support (see §37.5.1) was included.

NAMED_BIND   *(tune with ENVDEF= in Makefile)*

18.8.23   *Support DNS name resolution*

The *sendmail* program automatically takes advantage of DNS lookups or MX records to resolve addresses and canonical hostnames. If your site is a UUCP-only site (or is otherwise not connected to the Internet) and does not run *named*(8) locally, you should probably disable NAMED_BIND:

```
ENVDEF= -DNAMED_BIND=0
                     ↑
              disable DNS lookups
```

If you are not currently running *named*(8) but plan to connect to the Internet, you should define NAMED_BIND but set the `ResolverOptions` (I) (see §34.8.55) to false in the configuration file. Later, when you connect to the Internet, you can then simply change it to true. (See also the service-switch file, §34.8.61, for an another way to achieve the same effect.)

If you are running a precompiled *sendmail* binary, you may use the **-d0.1** switch to determine whether NAMED_BIND support was included (see §37.5.1).

NDBM   *(tune with DBMDEF= in Makefile)*

18.8.24   *Support Unix ndbm(3) Databases*

The *ndbm*(3) form of database uses two files (*.pag* and *.dir*) for each database. Databases cannot be shared by different architectures across a network. If you intend to support aliasing in an efficient manner, you should at least define this NDBM (or NEWDB described below) in your *Makefile*.

```
DBMDEF= -DNDBM
```

The *ndbm*(3) routines are used primarily to look up aliases. They can also be used to declare *dbm* class maps (see §33.3.2) with the K configuration command.

Library routines to support *ndbm*(3) are available with most modern versions of UNIX. You may have to specify library support with a **-lndbm** in the LIBS= line of your *Makefile*. If you are running a precompiled *sendmail* binary, you may use the **-d0.1** switch to determine whether *ndbm*(3) support was included (see §37.5.1).

NEED ...

18.8.25

Something amiss with your OS?

The *sendmail* program requires certain C language library routines to exist. If any is missing from your library, define one of the needs listed in Table 18-8, and *sendmail* will try to emulate it.

Each is defined with ENVDEF= in *Makefile* by setting it to a value of 1 (NEED-PUTENV is an exception in that 1 or 2 can be used).

```
ENVDEF= -DNEEDFSYNC=1
```

When porting to a new system, you can test with this ENVDEF= statement and, if successful, put a permanent porting entry into *conf.h*. Note that these are correctly defined for all currently supported systems. You should need to redefine them only if you are porting *sendmail* to a completely new system.

Table 18–8: Define Replacements for Missing C Library Routines

#define	Emulates
NEEDFSYNC	Replaces a missing *fsync*(2). The *sendmail* program will try to simulate it by using *fcntl*(2), if available; otherwise, *sendmail* will not "sync" to disk. This latter circumstance is undesirable and may result in unreliable mail delivery, but it works.
NEEDGETOPT	The *sendmail* program calls *getopt*(3) twice when parsing its command-line arguments. Some version of *getopt*(3) do odd things when called twice. If yours is one of these, replace it.
NEEDPUTENV	Replace a missing *putenv*(3). If this is defined as 1, *sendmail* emulates by using *setenv*(3). If this is defined as 2, *sendmail* emulates by directly modifying the environmental section of memory.
NEEDSTRSTR	Replace a missing *strstr*(3) with a well-written internal version.
NEEDSTRTOL	Replace a missing *strtol*(3) with a well-written internal version.
NEEDVPRINTF	Replace a missing *vprintf*(3). Note that the emulation supplied is not very elegant. It may not even work on some systems. See *conf.h* for a glimpse of systems that require this.

If you are running a precompiled *sendmail* binary, there is no way to discover whether any of these were defined when it was built.

NET ...

18.8.26

Define Network Support

V8 *sendmail* is designed to support four kinds of networks, as listed in Table 18-9. Currently, only NETINET and NETISO are supported.

Table 18–9: Define for Network Support

Define	Description
NETINET	A TCP/IP-based network
NETISO	An ISO 8022 network
NETNS	A Xerox NS protocol network (tentative)
NETX25	A CCITT[a] X.25 network (tentative)

a. International Telephone and Telegraph Consultative Committee.

Stubs are included in the source code for any programmer who is interested in implementing NETNS or NETX25. NETINET is defined by default. If you don't want it, you need to turn it off in your *Makefile*:

    ENVDEF= -DNETINET=0

NETISO is undefined by default. If you want to include ISO support, you need to specifically define it in your *Makefile*:

    ENVDEF= -DNETISO=1

Defining NETINET or NETISO has the side effect of causing SMTP and QUEUE also to be automatically defined.

Defining network support only causes the code for that network to be included in *sendmail*. The network serviced by a particular invocation of *sendmail* is selected with the `Family` parameter of the `DaemonPortOptions` (O) option (see §34.8.13). In the absence of an option declaration, *inet* (for NETINET) is used as the default.

If you are running a precompiled version of *sendmail*, you can determine which network types are supported by using the `-d0.1` debugging switch (see §37.5.1).

NETINET   *(tune with DBMDEF= in Makefile)*

18.8.27   *Support NeXT netinfo(3) databases*

The *netinfo(3)* form of database is supplied with the NeXT and NeXTSTeP operating systems. It is a network information service that provides file contents such as *aliases* and *passwd*, and locations such as the location of the *sendmail.cf* file. If you are running on a NeXT or under NeXTSTeP, this NETINFO will automatically be defined in your *Makefile*:

    DBMDEF= -DNETINFO

The *netinfo(3)* databases can also be used to declare *netinfo* class maps (see §33.3.2) with the `K` configuration command. If you are running a precompiled *sendmail* binary, you may use the `-d0.1` switch to determine whether NETINFO support was included (see §37.5.1).

NEWDB   *(tune with DBMDEF= in Makefile)*

18.8.28   *Support Berkeley db(3) Databases*

The *db*(3) form of database uses a single file and can be shared by different architectures. If you intend to support aliasing in an efficient manner, you should at least define this NEWDB (or the NDBM described above) in your *Makefile*. The *db*(3) routines are used to look up aliases and are the routines used by the User Database (see §33.5). They can also be used to declare *hash* and *btree* class maps (see §33.3.2) with the K configuration command.

The *db*(3) libraries have overcome many of the limitations of the earlier *ndbm*(3) libraries. If possible, you should get and install the *db*(3) libraries before you build *sendmail*. The *db*(3) source is available from

    ftp://ftp.cs.berkeley.edu/ucb/4bsd/db.tar.Z

Do not use the Net2 distribution. (See OLD_NEWDB below if you already have that distribution and can't easily get rid of it.) The *src/READ_ME* file contains *critical* information[*] about installing *db*(3).

If you are running a precompiled *sendmail* binary, you may use the -d0.1 switch (see §37.5.1) to determine whether *db*(3) support was included in it.

NIS   *(tune with DBMDEF= in Makefile)*

18.8.29   *Support for NIS*

If you intend to have *sendmail* support *nis* (formerly Yellow Pages) maps, you need to define NIS as part of your DBMDEF= line in *Makefile*:

    DBMDEF= -DNIS

If NIS is defined, the AliasFile (A) option can be specified as

    OAnis:mail.aliases   ← V8.6
    O AliasFile=nis:mail.aliases ← V8.7 and above (if no service-switch file)

See §34.8.1 for more details about the AliasFile (A) option. See §34.8.61 for a description of the ServiceSwitchFile option and its effect on *nis* aliases. Be aware that the above AliasFile (A) option declaration will override the lack of an *nis* entry in the service-switch file.

---

[*] Such as why you must remove *ndbm.h* and *ndbm.o* from *libdb.a* before installing it for use by *sendmail*.

NDBM also needs to be defined to allow *sendmail* to rebuild its alias files for use by *nis*:

```
DBMDEF= -DNIS -DNDBM
```

For this to work, the path of the alias file needs to contain the substring "/yp/". A typical */var/yp/Makefile* will contain a line like this:

```
/usr/lib/sendmail -bi -oA$(YPDBDIR)/$(DOM)/mail.aliases
```

Here, $(YPDBDIR)/ is usually */var/yp/*, so the substring is found. When "/yp/" is found, *sendmail* augments the *aliases* database with two special entries that are needed by *nis*:

```
YP_LAST_MODIFIED
YP_MASTER_NAME
```

These allow the newly built *aliases* file to successfully be distributed for use by *nis* clients. Without these entries you will see an error like that shown below when pushing your *nis* maps:

```
Status received from ypxfr on nisslave:
        Failed - no local order number in map - use -f flag to ypxfr.
```

The solution here is to rebuild *sendmail* with both NDBM and NIS defined.

Defining NIS also causes support to be included for declaring and using *nis* class maps (see §33.3.2) with the K configuration command.

Note that defining NIS without also defining NAMED_BIND will cause delivery to MX records to mysteriously fail.

If you are running a precompiled *sendmail* binary, you may use the –d0.1 switch to determine whether NIS support was included (see §37.5.1).

NISPLUS   *(tune with DBMDEF= in Makefile)*

18.8.30   *Support for NIS+*

If you intend to have *sendmail* support *nisplus* maps, you need to define NISPLUS as part of your DBMDEF= line in *Makefile*. (The use of *nisplus* aliases and other maps is determined by the */etc/nsswitch.conf* file.)

```
DBMDEF= -DNISPLUS
```

If NISPLUS is defined, the **AliasFile** (**A**) option can be used to override the setting of the */etc/nsswitch.conf* file:

```
O AliasFile=nisplus:mail.aliases      ← V8.7 and above
```

Here, **nisplus** aliases will be used even if the */etc/nsswitch.conf* file excludes them.

See §34.8.1 for details about the `AliasFile` (A) option. Note that NISPLUS is new to V8.7 and not supported under earlier versions of *sendmail*.

With NISPLUS defined, support is also included to declare and use *nisplus* class maps (see §33.3.2) with the K configuration command.

If you are running a precompiled *sendmail* binary, you may use the `-d0.1` switch to determine whether NISPLUS support was included (see §37.5.1).

NO_GROUP_SET   *(port, edit conf.h)*

18.8.31   *Prevent multi-group file access*

When checking files and directories for group read and write permissions, *sendmail* checks the group of the controlling user. On systems that allow a user to belong to one group at a time, failure stops here; on systems that allow users to belong to many groups at once, failure causes *sendmail* to check any other groups to which the controlling user may belong. It finds the list of groups by calling *getgrgid*(3).

If your system lacks the *getgrgid*(3) call or doesn't need it, you should exclude this code by defining NO_GROUP_SET in *conf.h*. NO_GROUP_SET causes the code containing the call to *getgrgid*(3) to be excluded from *sendmail*. Be aware that excluding *getgrgid*(3) support on systems that need it can cause delivery to files to fail in mysterious ways.

If you are running a precompiled version of *sendmail*, be aware that there is no debugging switch that can tell you what the setting of NO_GROUP_SET was set to at compile time.

Note that NO_GROUP_SET affects only inclusion of the *getgrgid*(3) system call. See the `DontInitGroups` option (see §34.8.19) for a means to exclude the *getgrgid*(3) and *initgroups*(3) system calls.

NOTUNIX   *(port, edit conf.h)*

18.8.32   *Exclude From line support*

Under UNIX a file of many mail messages normally has one message separated from another by a blank line and then a line that begins with the five characters "`From `" (four letters and a space). On such systems, *sendmail* saves important information from such lines for later use.

On non-UNIX machines (VMS or MS-DOS) the conventions are different, so you won't want *sendmail* to treat such lines as special. Similarly, if your UNIX site has converted entirely away from this convention (with *mhs* or the like), you might not want this special treatment.

To disable special treatment of "`From` " lines, define the NOTUNIX macro in your *Makefile*:

```
ENVDEF= -DNOTUNIX
```

When porting to a new system, you can test with this ENVDEF= statement and, if successful, put a permanent porting entry into *conf.h*. Defining NOTUNIX causes the code for *eatfrom()* to be excluded from *sendmail*. The -d30.2 debugging switch (see §37.5.109) can be used to watch *eatfrom()* and to determine whether NOTUNIX was declared when compiling *sendmail*.

OLD_NEWDB   *(port with DBMDEF= in Makefile)*

18.8.33   *Support the old form of db(3)*

BSDI(BSD/386) 1.0, NetBSD 0.9, and FreeBSD 1.0 were distributed with an old version of the *db(3)* library. These systems will not use the file locking of the latest version. For such systems you must define

```
DBMDEF= -DNEWDB -DOLD_NEWDB=1
                        ↑
          don't support new file locking
```

Although you can get and install the latest version of *db(3)*, you should not do so unless you can rebuild your entire UNIX system. The old form of database is used throughout, and just building *sendmail* with the new form will cause password lookups and the like to fail.

In general, you should never have to declare OLD_NEWDB (instead, we recommend upgrading your operating system). OLD_NEWDB is automatically included in the *Makefile* for the systems that need it.

PATH ...   *(debug with ENVDEF= in Makefile)*

18.8.34   *Hardcode paths inside sendmail*

Only a few pathnames are hard-coded into *sendmail*. The most obvious is its configuration file, because that file lists the locations of nearly all other files. For various reasons a few other file locations are also hard-coded. Here, we describe those that you can change. Note that the general form for all such changes uses the ENVDEF= declaration of your *Makefile*:

```
ENVDEF= -D_PATH...=\"/new/path/filename\"
```

The new path must be surrounded by backslashed quotation marks so that the compiler will correctly interpret it as a string.

/etc/sendmail.cf

The *sendmail.cf* file is pivotal to all of the *sendmail* program's operations (see Chapter 27). V8.7 *sendmail* recommends that it always be called *sendmail.cf* and always be located in the */etc* directory. For testing, debugging, or other legitimate reasons you may prefer to locate that file elsewhere (at least temporarily). You do that with the _PATH_SENDMAILCF definition:

```
ENVDEF= -D_PATH_SENDMAILCF=\"/src/tests/test.cf\"
```

/etc/sendmail.pid

The *sendmail.pid* file contains two lines of information. The first line is text representation of the *pid* of the current running daemon. The second is a copy of the command line that was originally used to start *sendmail*. This file is handy for killing and restarting the daemon (see §4.1.1). If BSD4_4 is defined, the default becomes */var/run/sendmail.pid*; otherwise, the default is */etc/sendmail.pid*. You can change this default (and you must if you intend to run a test daemon in parallel to the original), with the ENVDEF= of your *Makefile*:

```
ENVDEF= -D_PATH_SENDMAILPID=\"/src/tests/test.pid\"
```

Ordinarily, two daemons cannot run simultaneously on a single host. If you need to run a second daemon, you must change the port that it listens to with the `Port` parameter of the `DaemonPortOptions` (O) option (see §34.8.13).

/etc/hosts

Ordinarily, *sendmail* will first look for a service-switch (see §34.8.61) to see how it should look up the canonical names of hosts. If it finds one and if the service *hosts* is listed, it uses the techniques listed with the service-switch to look up its hosts. When a technique is *files*, *sendmail* reads the file named by _PATH_HOSTS to get its canonical information. Ordinarily, that file is called */etc/hosts*. If that file is different or has been customized on your system, you can redefine the location like this:

```
ENVDEF= -D_PATH_HOSTS=\"/etc/privatehosts\"
```

In general, most other techniques are preferred over the linear parse of a hosts file. However, this file is useful in determining the canonical name of the local host. Note that the location of the *hosts* file can also be changed with the `HostsFile` option (see §34.8.30).

/dev/kmem

The *sendmail* program decides when to refuse connections and when to only queue mail on the basis of its perception of the machine load average. The process of determining that average is hugely complex and varies greatly from vendor to vendor. Three pathnames that may be used in determining the load are _PATH_KMEM, _PATH_LOADAVG, and _PATH_UNIX. These should need to be changed only in the rare event that you are porting *sendmail* to a previously unsupported platform. Read the file *conf.c* to see the complex way they are presently used. Also see Table 18-6 to see how to use these to find the load average.

/etc/shells

A user is not allowed to run programs from a *.forward* file unless that user has a valid login shell (see §25.7.4). Nor is a user allowed to save mail directly to files without a valid shell. To determine whether the login shell is valid, *sendmail* calls *getusershell*(3). If *sendmail* was defined without HASGETUSERSHELL defined (see Table 18-4), it instead tries to look up the shell in the */etc/shells* file. If that file cannot be opened, *sendmail* gets valid shell names from an internal list called **DefaultUserShells** that is defined in *conf.c*. This _PATH_SHELLS definition can be used to change the location of the */etc/shells* file.

/usr/tmp

In a panic situation (such as when *sendmail* cannot figure out how to deliver or bounce a mail message) the message is saved into the */usr/tmp/dead.letter* file (see the **ErrorMode** (e) option §34.8.24). The _PATH_VARTMP definition is used to tune the location of the */usr/tmp* directory. For some systems it is defined as */usr/tmp*; for others it will need to be named */var/tmp*. As distributed, it is undefined in all *Makefiles*, and it defaults to */usr/tmp*.

There is no debugging flag that will display the defaults for these file locations. If any are of concern, you should build *sendmail* yourself.

PICKY . . .   *(tune with ENVDEF= in Makefile)*

18.8.35   *Make sendmail pickier*

The *sendmail* program can be made pickier by tuning its **PrivacyOptions** (p) option (see §34.8.47) or by defining two macros when compiling:

PICKY_HELO_CHECK

The SMTP HELO command is used to introduce the calling machine to the receiving machine. The form of that command is

> HELO *calling host name here*

Note that HELO and EHLO are equivalent in this regard. Ordinarily, *sendmail* doesn't care what the calling host calls itself. All *sendmail* cares about is that this name is the canonical name of a machine. If you care whether the HELO hostname matches the real hostname of the calling machine, you can define PICKY_HELO_CHECK.

>   ENVDEF= -DPICKY_HELO_CHECK

With PICKY_HELO_CHECK defined, a mismatch (other than the local machine calling itself *localhost*) will result in this being logged:

>   Host *realname* claimed to be *heloname*

Note that this check is ordinarily turned off[*] because a large number of hosts on the Internet use a name that is different from their canonical name.

PICKY_QF_NAME_CHECK

The name of a queue file's control file is narrowly defined inside *sendmail* (see §23.2.1). If only *sendmail* will be placing files into your queue, you might wish to turn on this macro for additional protection:

>   ENVDEF= -DPICKY_QF_NAME_CHECK

With PICKY_QF_NAME_CHECK defined, *sendmail* will log an error if the name of the qf file is incorrectly formed and will rename the qf file into a Qf file (see §23.3 for details of this process).

PSBUFSIZ   *(tune, edit conf.h)*

18.8.36   *Size of prescan() buffer*

Whenever an address (including rules) is tokenized, it is stored in a single buffer, one token following the next with a zero-value byte separating them. The size of this buffer is defined by PSBUFSIZ. The default size is defined in *conf.h* as (MAX-NAME + MAXATOM).

In general, this definition should never be changed. If you start getting warning messages such as

>   Address too long

look elsewhere (such as rule sets) for the cause. You should consider changing the size of PSBUFSIZ only as a last resort.

QUEUE   *(tune, edit conf.h)*

18.8.37   *Enable queueing*

If *sendmail* cannot immediately deliver a mail message, it places that message in a queue to await another try. The QUEUE definition causes queue-handling code to

---

[*] Eric was getting complaints that the continual insertion of this warning was misleading and tended to cause people to ignore it entirely.

be included in *sendmail*. If queueing is not enabled and you need to queue, *send-mail* prints the following message and either bounces or discards the message:

    dropenvelope: queueup

A word to the wise: *Always* define QUEUE. Even if you have only a pure UUCP machine, mail can fail (for a reason such as a full disk). Without queueing, such mail will bounce when instead it should be queued for a later try.

The default is to always define QUEUE if NETINET or NETISO are defined; other-wise, QUEUE is undefined. There is no debugging flag to show whether QUEUE is defined, but the the **–bp** switch (see §23.4) can be used to determine whether it is supported.

QUEUESEGSIZE   *(tune, edit conf.h)*

18.8.38   *Amount to grow queue work list*

During a queue run, *sendmail* holds information in memory about all the files being processed. It does this so that it can sort them by priority for delivery. Beginning with V8.7 *sendmail*, there is no longer a limit (other than consuming all memory) on how many queued messages can be processed during any queue run. Prior to V8.7, that number was fixed by the constant QUEUESIZE. QUEUESIZE has been retired and replaced with QUEUESEGSIZE, which is defined in *conf.h* as:

    # define QUEUESEGSIZE   1000   /* increment for queue size */

It should be changed only if your queue continually contains a huge number of messages. If you notice many messages like this being logged:

    grew WorkList for...

you may need to modify QUEUESEGSIZE. Doing so requires that you edit *conf.h* and recompile.

QUEUESEGSIZE can be traced with the **–d41** debugging switch (see §37.5.144).

SCANF   *(tune with ENVDEF= in Makefile)*

18.8.39   *Support scanf(3) with F command*

The F configuration command (see §32.1.2) allows the specification of a *scanf(3)* style string to aid in parsing files (see §32.1.2.1). In general this is not recom-mended because a misdesigned input file can cause *sendmail* to core dump. However, because of its popularity, it is enabled at compile time by default. If you don't need it, we recommend you exclude its support with ENVDEF= in *Makefile*.

```
ENVDEF= -DSCANF=0
              ↑
         disable scanf(3)
```

The *scanf*(3) is used only in reading files into a class with the F configuration command. If you are running a precompiled version of *sendmail*, you can determine whether SCANF was included by using the -d0.1 debugging switch (see §37.5.1).

SFS_TYPE *(port, edit conf.h)*

18.8.40 *How to determine free disk space*

The *sendmail* program can reject incoming mail messages if they are too large for the queueing disk. This ability is enabled by giving a positive, nonzero size to the MinFreeBlocks (b) option (see §34.8.40). The method that *sendmail* uses to measure the free space on a disk varies from system to system. SFS_TYPE defines which of several methods *sendmail* will use. Those available are shown in Table 18-10.

Table 18-10: Method to Determine Free Disk Space

Define	Description
SFS_NONE	Your system has no way to determine the free space on a disk. This causes the MinFreeBlocks (b) option (see §34.8.40) to be ignored.
SFS_USTAT	Your system uses the *ustat*(2) system call to get information about mounted file systems.
SFS_4ARGS	Your system uses the four-argument form of the *statfs*(2) system call and <*sys/statfs.h*>. If you define this, you can also define SFS_BAVAIL as the field name for the *statfs* C language structure (by default, *f_bavail*).
SFS_VFS	Your system uses the two-argument form of the *statfs*(2) system call and <*sys/vfs.h*>.
SFS_MOUNT	Your system uses the two-argument form of the *statfs*(2) system call and <*sys/mount.h*>.
SFS_STATFS	Your system uses the two-argument form of the *statfs*(2) system call and <*sys/statfs.h*>.
SFS_STATVFS	Your system uses the *statvfs*(2) system call.

In general, SFS_TYPE is correctly defined for all supported systems. You should need to modify it only if you are porting to a new system. To do so, you will need to edit *conf.h*.

You can use the −d4.80 debugging switch (see §37.5.19) to watch *sendmail* check for enough disk space. The only way to tell whether a precompiled version of *sendmail* has this ability is by setting the **MinFreeBlocks** option to a positive value and watching the −d4.80 output. If **bavail=** in that output is always −1, no matter what, your support was defined as SFS_NONE.

SMTP   *(tune with ENVDEF= in Makefile)*

18.8.41   *Enable SMTP*

If you are running *sendmail* as a daemon, you need to define SMTP to enable mail transfers. If you don't intend to run *sendmail* as a daemon, SMTP might not need to be defined. The default is that SMTP is automatically defined if either NETINET or NETISO is defined; otherwise, SMTP is undefined.

SMTP support is recommended, even if *sendmail* is not running with network support or as a daemon. To take advantage of the new DSN protocol, future MUAs will talk to *sendmail* using SMTP over a pipe connection with the −bs command-line switch (see §36.7.11). The *mh*(1) suite of programs does that now. Delivery agents are also being designed with SMTP so that they can take advantage of DSN.

You enable SMTP support with ENVDEF= in your *Makefile*:

```
ENVDEF= -DSMTP=1
```

If a precompiled *sendmail* lacks SMTP support, an attempt to use *sendmail's* −bs command line switch will result in this fatal error:

```
I don't speak SMTP
```

SMTP activity can be watched with the −d18 and −d19 debugging switches (see §37.5.65) and with the −v command-line switch (see §36.7.41).

SMTPDEBUG   *(debug with ENVDEF= in Makefile)*

18.8.42   *Enable remote debugging*

The *sendmail* program allows the developer to turn on debugging and to print the queue from any remote site. This capability is useful for solving occasional problems but opens a potentially wide security hole.

In general, SMTPDEBUG should always be undefined. Later, when you become more expert with *sendmail*, you might want to have a standby version of *sendmail* ready (one with SMTPDEBUG defined), just in case you need it.

There is no debugging switch that will let you know whether a precompiled version of *sendmail* had this defined. Instead, you must run it as a daemon, connect to it with *telnet*(1), and issue the SHOWQ SMTP command. If it displays the mail queue, then that precompiled *sendmail* was built with SMTPDEBUG defined, and you *should not use it*!

SMTPLINELIM (don't change)

18.8.43 *Default for obsolete F=L flag*

Each delivery agent that is defined in the configuration file may or may not have an L= (Line length) equate (see §30.4.6). If that equate is missing or if the value assigned to it is less than or equal to zero, and if the F=L delivery agent flag is set (see §30.8.29), the default value that is used becomes the value of SMTPLINELIM. Otherwise, the default value is 0. This logic is there to support old configuration files that use F=L in place of the newer L=.

The default for SMTPLINELIM is 990 (defined in RFC821) and that value should not be changed. Rather, if you need a different line-length limit for a particular delivery agent, you should use the L= equate when defining it.

SOLARIS (port, edit conf.h)

18.8.44 *Support Sun's Solaris 2.x*

If compiling for a Sun Solaris machine, you will find this SOLARIS definition correctly defined for you in your *Makefile*:

```
ENVDEF=    -DSOLARIS          ← Solaris 2.1 and 2.2
ENVDEF=    -DSOLARIS=20300    ← Solaris 2.3
ENVDEF=    -DSOLARIS=20400    ← Solaris 2.4
ENVDEF=    -DSOLARIS=20500    ← Solaris 2.5
ENVDEF=    -DSOLARIS=20501    ← Solaris 2.5.1
```

Be sure to see *src/READ_ME* for several well-known pitfalls concerning Solaris.

SPT_TYPE (port, edit conf.h)

18.8.45 *Adapt/exclude process title support*

Whenever a program first begins to run, UNIX provides it with two arrays of information: its command-line arguments, and the environment under which it was run. When you run *ps*(1) to see what processes are doing, *ps* prints the command line that was used to run each program.

To provide more useful information (such as current status or host connected to), *sendmail* saves its command line and environment, then periodically uses that system space to display its status. This ability provides a valuable tool for monitoring what each invocation of *sendmail* is doing.

The method to display this information is correctly defined in *conf.c* for all supported systems. In the rare event that you need to port *sendmail* to another system, you may do so by defining SPT_TYPE in *conf.h*.

SUID_ROOT_FILES_OK   *(debug with ENVDEF= in Makefile)*

18.8.46   *Allow root delivery to files*

When delivering to files, *sendmail* runs as the controlling user unless the *suid* or *sgid* bits of the file are set. If so, it runs as the owner of the file. A question arises when such files are *root* owned. Ordinarily, writing to *suid* and *sgid root* owned files as *root* is disallowed.

If, for some reason, your site needs to allow delivery to *root*-owned files with *sendmail* running as *root*, you can enable this behavior with

```
ENVDEF= -DSUID_ROOT_FILES_OK
```

But be aware that you may open serious security holes on your system if you do this. We recommend that SUID_ROOT_FILES_OK never be defined, except as a temporary debugging technique. If you are running a precompiled *sendmail* binary, you can use the **-d0.1** debugging switch (see §37.5.1) to determine whether SUID_ROOT_FILES_OK was defined in it.

SYSLOG_BUFSIZE   *(port, edit conf.h)*

18.8.47   *Limit syslog(3) buffer size*

The *sendmail* program logs errors, information, and debugging messages using the *syslog*(3) facility. By default, *sendmail* uses a 1024-byte buffer to assemble each message before dispatching it, but some systems don't accept a buffer this big. For such systems you can reduce the size of that buffer by defining SYSLOG_BUFSIZE with a new size:

```
ENVDEF= -DSYSLOG_BUFSIZE=512
                           ↑
            reduce syslog(3)'s buffer size
```

First, note that SYSLOG_BUFSIZE is correctly set in *conf.h* and *Makefiles/** for all supported systems. Second, note that setting the buffer to fewer than 256 bytes causes *sendmail* to log many more smaller messages (each item of information on a separate *syslog*(3) line). If SYSLOG_BUFSIZE is less than 89, some logging information will be lost.

SYSLOG_BUFSIZE has an effect only if *sendmail* was compiled with LOG defined, (see §18.8.16), and if the **LogLevel** (**L**) option (see §34.8.33) is set to 6 or more, and if your *syslog.conf*(5) file is configured to log *mail* messages at LOG_INFO and above (see §26.1). If you are running a precompiled version of *sendmail*, there is no way to determine the setting of SYSLOG_BUFSIZE.

SYSTEM5   *(port, edit conf.h)*

18.8.48   *Support SysV-derived machines*

If you are compiling *sendmail* on a SysVR4-derived machine, you should define SYSTEM5. This automatically causes the correct SysV support to be included. For all systems that require SYSTEM5 to be defined, it is already correctly defined in *conf.h*.

If you suspect that you need to define SYSTEM5 when porting to a new system, you should also investigate SYS5SIGNALS and SYS5SETPGRP in *conf.h* and *READ_ME*. If you are running a precompiled version of *sendmail*, you can use the `-d0.10` debugging switch (see §37.5.3) to discover whether SYSTEM5 or SYS5SETPGRP were defined.

TCPWRAPPERS   *(tune with ENVDEF= in Makefile)*

18.8.49   *Use libwrap.a for connects*

Beginning with V8.8 *sendmail*, it is now possible to use the *libwrap.a* library to validate incoming SMTP connections. To enable this ability, you need to define TCPWRAPPERS and arrange for the *libwrap.a* library to be included in your *Makefile*:

```
ENVDEF= -DTCPWRAPPERS
LIBS= -lwrap
```

See *src/README* and §22.4.1 for additional information.

TOBUFSIZE   *(tune, edit conf.h)*

18.8.50   *Set buffer for recipient list*

For each delivery of one or more recipients to a single delivery agent, *sendmail* issues a summary of delivery through *syslog*(3). When logged, the recipient part of the message looks like this:

```
to=recipients
```

Here, *recipients* is a comma-separated list of recipients. The maximum number of characters in this list is determined by TOBUFSIZE. That limit is intended to prevent the internal *syslog*(3) buffer from overflowing. On machines with older versions of *syslog*(3) you may need to reduce the size of TOBUFSIZE in *conf.h*. In general, TOBUFSIZE is correctly defined for all currently supported systems. You should need to change it only if porting to a new system.

Note that one side effect of TOBUFSIZE is that it also limits the total number of recipients that can be delivered at once. If you need to increase that limit (and if you have a robust version of *syslog*), you can experiment by cautiously increasing TOBUFSIZE.

TRUST_POPEN   *(debug with ENVDEF= in Makefile)*

18.8.51   *Allow use of popen(3)*

The *sendmail* program uses the *uname*(2) system call to determine the UUCP name of the local host. If your machine lacks the *uname*(2) call (if HASUNAME was not defined), *sendmail* attempts to emulate *uname*(2) with its own internal routine. That internal routine first tries to read the */etc/whoami* file. If that fails, it then tries to parse */usr/include/whoami.b*. Finally, if that fails and if TRUST_POPEN is defined, *sendmail* executes the following command to get the UUCP name:

```
popen("uuname -l", "r")
```

The result (no matter how it was obtained) is then placed into the $k macro (see §31.10.21).

In general, you should *never* define TRUST_POPEN. The *popen*(3) call presents a huge security risk. If your system lacks *uname*(2) and is unable to set its UUCP name, consider hard-coding that name in the configuration file:

```
Dkuucpname
```

You may wish to define TRUST_POPEN temporarily to see whether that causes your UUCP name to be found. Once that is done, undefine it for your final release of *sendmail*.

There is no debugging switch that will tell you whether TRUST_POPEN was defined in a precompiled version of *sendmail*. If that binary is not stripped, you can use *nm*(1) to check for *popen*(3) support:

```
% nm sendmail | grep popen
00058bc8 T _popen                    ← found, so TRUST_POPEN was defined
```

If *sendmail* is stripped, you can still run *strings*(1) in order to check for the actual command:

```
% strings sendmail | grep "uname -l"
uuname -l                            ← found, so TRUST_POPEN was defined
```

In either event you should contact your vendor and ask for this security risk to be removed.

TTYNAME

18.8.52   *Set $y to tty name (obsolete)*

The $y macro (see §31.10.44) is intended to hold as its value the base name of the controlling *tty* device (if there is one). On BSD-derived systems this is a name like the following, but with the /dev/ prefix removed:

```
/dev/tty04
```

Defining TTYNAME enables *sendmail* to put this information into $y:

```
ENVDEF= -DTTYNAME
```

Note that TTYNAME is useful only for debugging *sendmail*. The *sendmail* program does not itself use $y for anything. Also note that defining TTYNAME requires that your system support the *ttyname*(2) system call. If you are running a precompiled version of *sendmail*, you can determine whether TTYNAME was defined by sending mail with the -d35.9 debugging switch (see §37.5.120) and watching for $y to be defined:

```
define(y as ttyp1)
```

UDB_DEFAULT_SPEC

18.8.53   *Default User Database location*

If you wish to define a default location for the User Database that will take effect if the UserDatabaseSpec (U) option (see §34.8.75) is missing, you can define it, for example, like this:

```
DBMDEF= -DNEWDB -DUDB_DEFAULT_SPEC=\"/var/db/userdb.db\"
```

The backslashed quotation marks are necessary to pass the path to *sendmail* as a string.

USERDB

18.8.54   *Support the User Database*

The User Database (see §33.5) is code inside *sendmail* that allows sender and recipient addresses to be rewritten under the control of an external database. This code is automatically included in *sendmail* when you define NEWDB or HESIOD:

```
DBMDEF= -DNEWDB       ← automatically include User Database code
DBMDEF= -DHESIOD      ← automatically include User Database code
```

If you don't want to include support for the User Database, you need to specifically turn it off by setting USERDB to 0:

```
DBMDEF= -DNEWDB -DUSERDB=0
DBMDEF= -DHESIOD -DUSERDB=0
```

See UDB_DEFAULT_SPEC for a method to set a default for the database location. If
you are running a precompiled *sendmail* binary, you may use the **-d0.1** switch
(see §37.5.1) to determine whether USERDB support is included.

USESETEUID   *(port, edit conf.h)*

18.8.55   *Support seteuid (2) identity changes*

To perform most kinds of delivery in a safe manner, *sendmail* must be able to
change its *root* identity to that of another user, deliver as that user, and then
restore its identity to *root*. The preferred method for doing this is with the Posix 1
seteuid(2) routine. To determine whether your system correctly supports this routine, compile and run the program *test/t_seteuid.c*. The compiled binary must be
suid-root and must be executed by an ordinary user.

```
# cc t_seteuid.c
# chmod u+s a.out
# suspend
% a.out
... lots of output here
This system cannot use seteuid
```

Here the output shows failure, so you do not have *seteuid*(2) support. Beginning
with V8.8, *a.out* prints the following on success:

```
It is safe to define USESETEUID on this system
```

If the output had not shown failure or had shown success (if you had usable
seteuid(2) support), you could take advantage of that support by defining USESE-
TEUID in *conf.h*. In general, USESETEUID is correctly defined for all systems that
can take advantage of this *seteuid* support.

If *seteuid*(2) failed, you need to investigate using *setreuid*(2) instead:

```
# cc t_setreuid.c
# chmod u+s a.out
# suspend
% a.out
initial uids (should be 678/0): r/euid=678/0
after setreuid(0, 1) (should be 0/1): r/euid=0/1
after setreuid(-1, 0) (should be 0/0): r/euid=0/0
after setreuid(realuid, 0) (should be 678/0): r/euid=678/0

after setreuid(0, 2) (should be 0/2): r/euid=0/2
after setreuid(-1, 0) (should be 0/0): r/euid=0/0
```

```
after setreuid(realuid, 0) (should be 678/0): r/euid=678/0
```

```
It is safe to define HASSETREUID on this system
```

Here, the test succeeded (no failure message was printed prior to V8.8). If your system can use *setreuid*(2), you can take advantage of it by defining HASSETREUID in *conf.h*.

No matter which you define, be sure to read *src/READ_ME* for possible pitfalls. Note that HASSETREUID and USESETEUID are correctly defined for all currently supported systems. You need to define one only if you are porting *sendmail* to a completely new system.

If you are running a precompiled *sendmail* binary, you can use the –d0.1 switch (see §37.5.1) to discover whether HASSETREUID or USESETEUID support is included.

WILDCARD_SHELL   *(debug, edit conf.c)*

18.8.56   *Redefine wildcard shell*

Ordinarily, *sendmail* prohibits ordinary users from running programs from inside their ˜*/forward* files unless they have a valid login shell. This restriction is in place to prevent ordinary users from running arbitrary programs on a main mail server. Some sites prefer to allow users to run arbitrary programs despite the restriction about logging into the mail server. At such sites, one can bypass this restriction by placing the special string

```
/SENDMAIL/ANY/SHELL/
```

in the */etc/shells* file. If, for some reason, you need to use a different string, you may do so by redefining WILDCARD_SHELL in *conf.c*.

If you enable arbitrary programs you should also implement the *sendmail* restricted shell *smrsh* (see §22.8.2).

XDEBUG   *(debug with ENVDEF= in Makefile)*

18.8.57   *Support sanity checks*

In past releases of *sendmail*, changes in file descriptors and other key variables have sometimes occurred for reasons that remain a mystery to this day. Small "sanity checks" have been included in the code to discover such anomalies, should they happen again. To exclude these checks, redefine XDEBUG to 0:

```
ENVDEF= -DXDEBUG=0
```

Generally, however, XDEBUG should always remain enabled. It adds only a microscopic amount of overhead to *sendmail* and helps to certify *sendmail*'s rational behavior.

If *sendmail*'s notion of who it is (as defined by the $j macro; see §31.10.20) gets trashed by losing all its dots, *sendmail* will log the following at LOG_ALERT if XDE-BUG is defined, dump its state (see §26.3.3), and *abort*(3):

```
daemon process $j lost dot; see syslog
```

At startup the value in the $j macro (see §31.10.20) is appended to the class w (see §32.5.8). If *sendmail* is compiled with XDEBUG, it periodically checks to make sure that $j is still listed in class w. If $j should vanish, *sendmail* will log the following at LOG_ALERT, dump its state (see §26.3.3), and *abort*(3):

```
daemon process doesn't have $j in $=w; see syslog
```

With XDEBUG defined, *sendmail* periodically checks to see whether its standard I/O file descriptors have gotten clobbered. If so, it logs the following and tries to recover by connecting it to */dev/null*:

```
where: fd which not open
```

Here, **where** will reflect the internal subroutine name and arguments that led to the check, and **which** will be the bad file descriptor number.

If you are running a precompiled *sendmail* binary, you can use the −d0.1 switch (see §37.5.1) to determine whether XDEBUG support is included.

19

V8 m4 Configuration

V8 *sendmail* provides an easy way to create a custom configuration file for your site. In the *cf* subdirectory of the V8 *sendmail* source distribution you will find a file named *README*. It contains easy-to-understand, step-by-step instructions that allow you to create a custom configuration file for your site. This chapter supplements that file.

19.1 The m4 Preprocessor

Creating a configuration file with *m4*(1) is simplicity itself. The *m4*(1) program is a macro preprocessor that produces a *sendmail* configuration file by processing a file whose name ends in *.mc* (for macro configuration). That is, it processes (reads) its input and gathers definitions of macros, then replaces those macros with their values and outputs the result.

This use of macros is much the same as that described in §7.1, except that *m4*'s rules are different. With *m4*, macros are defined (given values) like this:

```
define(macro,value)
```

Here, the **macro** is a symbolic name that you will use later. Legal names must begin with an underscore or letter and may contain letters, digits, and underscores. The **value** can be any arbitrary text. A comma separates the two, and that comma can be surrounded with optional whitespace.

There must be no space between the **define** and the left parenthesis. The definition ends with the right parenthesis.

To illustrate, consider this one-line *m4* source file named */tmp/x:*

```
                 input text to be converted
                          ↓
define(A,B)A
↑
the m4 definition
```

When *m4* is run to process this file, the output produced shows that A (the *input*) is redefined to become B:

```
% m4 /tmp/x
B
```

19.1.1 m4 is greedy

The *m4* program is greedy. That is, if a **macro** is already defined, its value will replace its name in the second declaration. Consider this input file:

```
define(A,B)
define(A,C)
A B
```

Here, the first line assigns the value B to the macro named A. The second line notices that A is a define macro, so *m4* replaces that A with B and then defines B as having the value C. The output of this file, after processing with *m4*, will be:

```
C C
```

To prevent this kind of greedy behavior (and to prevent the confusion it can create), you may quote an item to prevent *m4* from interpreting it. You quote with *m4* by surrounding each item with left and right single quotes:

```
define(A,B)
define(`A',C)
A B
```

Here, the first line defines A as B as before. But the second line no longer sees A as a macro. Instead, the single quotes allow A to be redefined as C. So the output is now:

```
C B
```

Although it is not strictly necessary, we recommend that all **macro** and **value** pairs be quoted. The above should generally be expressed like this:

```
define(`A',`B')
define(`A',`C')
A B
```

This is the form that we use when illustrating *m4* throughout this book.

19.1.2 m4 and dnl

Another problem with *m4* is that it replaces its commands with empty lines. The above **define** commands, for example, will actually print like this:

```
                    ← a blank line
                    ← a blank line
   A B
```

To suppress this insertion of blank lines, you can use the special *m4* command **dnl** (for Delete through New Line). That command looks like this:

```
define(`A',`B')dnl
define(`A',`C')dnl
A B
```

You can use **dnl** to remove blank lines where they might prove inconvenient or unsightly in a configuration file.

19.1.3 m4 and arguments

When an *m4* macro name is immediately followed by a right parenthesis, it is treated like a function call. Arguments given to it in that role are used to replace $*digit* expressions in the original definition. For example, suppose the macro CONCAT is defined like this:

```
define(`CONCAT',`$1$2$3')dnl
```

and then later used like this:

```
CONCAT(`host', `.', `domain')
```

The result will be that **host** will replace $1, the dot will replace $2, and the **domain** will replace $3, all jammed tightly together just as `$1$2$3' were:

```
host.domain
```

Macro arguments are used to create such techniques as FEATURE() and OSTYPE(), which are described later in this chapter.

19.1.4 m4 diversions

One of the *m4* program's strengths is its ability to divide its input into different parts and to later reassemble them in a more logical fashion. Consider, for example, the desire to output all options together. One way to do this is with the *m4* program's **divert** and **undivert** commands, for example,

```
divert(1)dnl
O ALIASFILE=/etc/aliases
divert(2)dnl
```

```
Pfirst-class=0
divert(1)dnl
O OperatorChars=.:%@!^/[]+
undivert(1)dnl
undivert(2)dnl
```

Here, the **divert(1)** causes all subsequent lines (up to the next **divert** or next **undivert**) to be held in a buffer numbered one. Buffer one will hold all the options. The second **divert** switches to buffer two, which is used to hold priorities. The third **divert** switches back to buffer one.

The **undivert(1)** causes all the options gathered in buffer one to be output, and the **undivert(2)** causes the priorities to be output. The result looks like this:

```
O ALIASFILE=/etc/aliases
O OperatorChars=.:%@!^/[]+
Pfirst-class=0
```

The diversions used by *sendmail*'s *m4* technique are listed in Table 19-1. In general, the macros listed should be used in place of diversion numbers because the meaning of those numbers may be changed in future versions of *sendmail.*

Table 19–1: m4 Diversions Used and Reserved by sendmail

divert	Description
(-1)	Internal to *m4*(1), tells it ignore all lines that follow
(0)	Internal to *m4*(1), tells it to stop diverting and to output immediately
(1)	Local host detection and resolution with LOCAL_NET_CONFIG (see §19.6.37)
(2)	Rule set 3 (via 96) additions with LOCAL_RULE_3 (see §19.6.35)
(3)	Rule set 0 (via 98) additions with LOCAL_RULE_0 (see §19.6.32)
(4)	Rule set 0 UUCP additions (§19.4.6)
(5)	Locally interpreted names (overrides $R) with LOCAL_USER (§19.6.38)
(6)	Local configuration (at top of file) with LOCAL_CONFIG (see §19.6.30)
(7)	Delivery agent definitions with MAILER (see §19.3.2) and MAILER_DEFINITIONS (see §19.6.40)
(8)	unused
(9)	Rule sets 1 and 2 with LOCAL_RULE_1 and LOCAL_RULE_2 (see §19.6.34), rule set 5, and LOCAL_RULESETS (see §19.6.36)

19.2 Build with m4

The process of building a *sendmail* configuration file begins by creating a file of *m4* statements. Traditionally, the suffix for such files is **.mc**. The *cf/cf* directory contains examples of many **mc** files. Of special interest are those that begin with **generic**, for these can serve as boilerplates in developing your own **mc** files:

```
generic-bsd4.4.mc          generic-solaris2.mc
generic-hpux10.mc          generic-sunos4.1.mc
generic-hpux9.mc           generic-ultrix4.mc
generic-osf1.mc
```

All mc files require specific minimal statements. For a SunOS 4.1.4 site on the Internet, for example, the following are minimal:

```
OSTYPE(sunos4.1)dnl          ← see §19.3.1
MAILER(local)dnl             ← see §19.3.2
MAILER(smtp)dnl              ← see §19.3.2
```

To build a configuration file from these statements, you would place them into a file, say *localsun.mc*, then run the following command:

```
% m4   ../m4/cf.m4 localsun.mc > sendmail.cf
```

Here, the ../m4/cf.m4 tells *m4* where to look for its default configuration file information.

If you are using an old version of *m4*, the following error message will be printed:

```
You need a newer version of M4, at least as new as
System V or GNU
m4: file not found: NoSuchFile
```

Just as the messages says, you need a newer version of *m4*. (The third line is just a result of forcing *m4* to fail and may be safely ignored.) In our *localsun.mc* example we would need to rerun it as

```
% /usr/5bin/m4   ../m4/cf.m4 localsun.mc > sendmail.cf
  ↑
  System V version of m4
```

Another cause of failure could be that the ../m4/cf.m4 file was not where you thought it was. Various versions of *m4* print this error in different ways:

```
/usr/5bin/m4:-:1 can't open file              ← SysV m4
m4: ../m4/cf.m4: No such file or directory    ← GNU m4
m4: file not found: ../m4/cf.m4               ← BSD m4
```

One possible reason for this error might be that you are developing your mc file somewhere other than in the *cf/cf* directory.* The solution is to use a full pathname to *cf.m4* or to replace that expression on the command line with a shell variable.

After you have successfully produced a "first draft" of your configuration file, you can edit *localsun.mc* and add features as you need them. Many possibilities are described in the rest of this chapter.

---

* This is actually a good idea. It prevents new *sendmail* distributions from clobbering your mc files.

19.2.1 *Maintain local files with _CF_DIR_*

It can be advantageous to maintain all the files that make up your local *m4* configuration separately from the *sendmail* distribution. This prevents new releases of *sendmail* from clobbering your source files. It also allows you to maintain configuration information more conveniently (perhaps under *rcs*(1) control) and to use programs like *make*(1) to simplify configuring and installation.

Most modern versions of *m4* allow you to define macros on the command line, and one such macro is recognized internally by the *m4* technique:

```
_CF_DIR_
```

This macro tells *m4* where the *m4/cf.m4* file described above is located. This macro needs to be set to the *cf* directory under the *sendmail* source distribution, and it needs to end in a slash character. For example, GNU *m4* version 1.2 allows this:

```
% setenv CFDIR /usr/local/src/mail/sendmail/cf/
% /usr/local/gnu/bin/m4 -D_CF_DIR_=${CFDIR} ${CFDIR}m4/cf.m4 localsun.mc \
    > sendmail.cf
```

Notice that we store the value for _CF_DIR_ in an environmental variable.[*] If your version of *m4* lacks this ability, you should consider upgrading.

By using the _CF_DIR_ macro, configuration and installation can be further simplified by using *make*(1). To illustrate, consider the following few lines from a *Makefile* on a SunOS system:

```
M4=/usr/local/gnu/bin/m4
CFDIR=/usr/local/src/mail/sendmail/cf/
localsun: localsun.mc
        $(M4) -D_CF_DIR_=$(CFDIR) $(CFDIR)/m4/cf.m4 localsun.mc > sendmail.cf
```

With this *Makefile* the above two complex command lines are reduced to a single, simple command line:

```
% make
```

19.3 *The Minimal mc File*

Every *mc* file requires minimal information. Table 19-2 shows which *m4* items are required and also lists two that are recommended.

---

[*] Note that *gnu m4* can figure out the _CF_DIR_ path itself from the path of the *cf.m4* file. We include _CF_DIR_ here for example purposes.

Table 19–2: Required and Recommended m4 Items

Item	§		Description
OSTYPE()	19.3.1	Required	Support for your operating system
MAILER()	19.3.2	Required	Necessary delivery agents
DOMAIN()	19.3.3	Recommended	Common domain wide information
FEATURE()	19.3.4	Recommended	Solutions to special needs

Note that what is minimally required for a workstation differs from what is minimally required for a central mail server. We recommend that you use these recommendations as a jumping-off point and investigate all the *m4* techniques that are available.

19.3.1 OSTYPE()

Support for various operating systems is supplied with the OSTYPE *m4* command. Every mc file *must* declare the operating system with this command. The available support is supplied by files in the *_CF_DIR_/ostype* directory. A listing of those files looks something like this:

```
aix2.m4          bsdi1.0.m4       irix4.m4         ptx2.m4          ultrix4.m4
aix3.m4          bsdi2.0.m4       irix5.m4         riscos4.5.m4     unknown.m4
altos.m4         dgux.m4          isc4.1.m4        sco3.2.m4        uxpds.m4
amdahl-uts.m4    domainos.m4      linux.m4         solaris2.m4
aux.m4           dynix3.2.m4      maxion.m4        sunos3.5.m4
bsd4.3.m4        hpux10.m4        nextstep.m4      sunos4.1.m4
bsd4.4.m4        hpux9.m4         osf1.m4          svr4.m4
```

To include support, select the file that best describes your operating system, delete the *.m4* suffix from its name, and include the resulting name in an OSTYPE declaration:

```
OSTYPE(`ultrix4.1')
```

Here, support for the DEC Ultrix operating system is defined. Note that some of these are not entirely accurate. For example, `ultrix4.1.m4` includes support for Ultrix versions 4.2 and 4.3, and `sunos4.1.m4` includes support for SunOS versions 4.1.2, 4.1.3., and 4.1.4.

If you pick a name for which no file exists, or if you misspell the name of the file, an error similar to the following will print:

```
m4: Can't open ../ostype/ultrux4.1.m4: No such file or directory
```

If you omit the OSTYPE declaration entirely, you will get the following error:

```
*** ERROR: No system type defined (use OSTYPE macro)
```

19.3.2 MAILER()

Delivery agents are not automatically declared. Instead, you must specify which ones you want to support and which ones to ignore. Support is included by using the MAILER *m4* macro:

```
MAILER(`local')
```

This causes support for both the **local** and **prog** delivery agents to be included. This is the minimal declaration (even if you don't intend to perform local or program delivery).

Other delivery agents that are recognized by the MAILER() technique are listed in Table 19-3.

Table 19–3: MAILER Delivery Agents

MAILER()	Delivery agents it declares
cyrus	*cyrus, cyrusbb*
fax	*fax*
local	*local, prog*
mail11	*mail11*
phquery	*ph*
pop	*pop*
procmail	*procmail*
smtp	*smtp, esmtp, smtp8, relay*
usenet	*usenet*
uucp[b]	*uucp, uucp-old, uucp-new, uucp-dom, uucp-uudom*

a. If you use both uucp and smtp, put smtp first.

New delivery agents can be created by devising a new **m4** file in the *_CF_DIR_/mailers* directory. The MAILER() *m4* technique performs its inclusion by reading a file with the delivery agent name suffixed with *.m4* from that directory.

Some delivery agent equates, such as **F=** and **M=**, can be modified with the **m4** configuration technique. Table 30-1 (see §30.4) lists all the equates and shows where to find further information about each of them. By investigating those sections, you can discover how to tune particular equates with the *m4* technique. For example, the following *mc* lines define the program used for local delivery to be *mail.local*:

```
define(`LOCAL_MAILER_PATH', `/usr/local/bin/mail.local')
MAILER(local)
```

Note that all modifications to equates must precede the corresponding MAILER() definition. See §30.3 for a complete description of MAILER() and all the ins and outs of using it.

Also note that beginning with V8.8, the MAILER_DEFINITIONS *m4* command (see §19.6.40) can be used to force your delivery agent definitions to be grouped with the others.

19.3.3   DOMAIN()

For large sites it can be advantageous to gather all configuration decisions that are common to the entire domain into a single file. The directory to hold domain information files is called *_CF_DIR_/domain*. The configuration information in those files is accessed by using the DOMAIN() *m4* technique, for example,

```
DOMAIN(`uofa.edu')
```

This line in any of your *mc* files causes the file *_CF_DIR_/domain/uofa.edu.m4* to be included at that point. Examples that come with the distribution illustrate sub-domains under *Berkeley.EDU*. One boilerplate file, named *generic.m4*, can be used as a starting point for your own domainwide file. For example, if all hosts at your site masquerade behind one email name, you might want to put MASQUERADE_AS (see §19.6.42) in your domain file. Domain files also form a natural location for the definition of site-specific relays (see §19.4.5).

If the domain that is specified does not exist or is misspelled, an error similar to the following will be printed:

```
m4: Can't open ../domain/generik.m4: No such file or directory
```

The use of DOMAIN() is not mandatory but is recommended.

19.3.4   FEATURE()

V8 *sendmail* offers a number of features that you may find very useful. To include a feature, include an *m4* command like one of the following in your *mc* file:

```
FEATURE(keyword)
FEATURE(keyword, argument)
```

These declarations causes a file of the name *_CF_DIR_/feature/keyword.m4* to be read at that place in your *.mc* file. The available **keyword** files are summarized in Table 19-4, and each is explained in the section at the end of this chapter. Note that some keywords require an additional argument.

Table 19–4: FEATURE Keywords

Keyword	§	Version	Description
allmasquerade	19.6.6	V8.2 and above	Masquerade the sender too
always_add_domain	19.6.7	V8.1 and above	Add the local domain even on local mail
bestmx_is_local	19.6.8	V8.6 and above	Accept best MX record as local if in $=w
bitdomain	19.6.9	V8.1 and above	Convert BITNET addresses into Internet addresses
domaintable	19.6.10	V8.2 and above	Accept old as equivalent to new domain
genericstable	19.6.11	V8.8 and above	Transform sender addresses
limited_masquerade	19.6.12	V8.8 and above	Only masquerade $=M hosts
local_procmail	19.6.13	V8.7 and above	Use *procmail(1)* as local delivery agent
mailertable	19.6.14	V8.1 and above	Database selects new delivery agents
masquerade_entire_domain	19.6.15	V8.8 and above	Masquerade all hosts under a domain
masquerade_envelope	19.6.16	V8.7 and above	Masquerade the envelope too
nocanonify	19.6.17	V8.1 and above	Don't canonify with $[and $]
nodns	19.6.18	V8.6	Omit DNS support from configuration file
nouucp	19.6.19	V8.1 and above	Eliminate all UUCP support
nullclient	19.6.20	V8.6 and above	Relay all mail through a mail host
redirect	19.6.21	V8.1 and above	Add support for *address.REDIRECT*
smrsh	19.6.22	V8.7 and above	Use *smrsh* (sendmail restricted shell)
notsticky	19.6.23	V8.1 thru V8.6	Don't differ user from *user@local.host*
stickyhost	19.6.24	V8.7 and above	Differ user from *user@local.host*
use_ct_file	19.6.25	V8.7 and above	Use */etc/sendmail.ct* for a list of trusted users
use_cw_file	19.6.26	V8.1 and above	Use */etc/sendmail.cw* for local hostnames
uucpdomain	19.6.27	V8.1 and above	Convert UUCP hosts via a database
virtusertable	19.6.28	V8.8 and above	Support for virtual domains

All the features available are described in detail at the end of this chapter (see §19.6).

19.4 m4 Macros by Function

The *m4* technique uses a huge number of macros to accomplish the complex task of creating configuration files for all possible circumstances. Most are detailed in the reference section at the end of this chapter. Others are documented in chapters dedicated to particular subjects. Here, we summarize all *m4* macros by classification or function.

19.4.1 Options

Options may be set, unset, and changed in your *mc* file with simple **define** statements. For example, the following line sets the location of the alias file and thus the **AliasFile** (A) option:

```
define(`ALIAS_FILE', `nis:-N mail.aliases')
```

Configuring options with the *m4* technique is described in §34.3 (with the individual *m4* option names listed in Table 34-3 of that section). Options are described in general in Chapter 34, *Options*.

19.4.2 Define Macros

Defined macros may be declared in your *mc* file. Those that are useful are listed in Table 31-5 of §31.8. That section also describes the general technique of defining macros via *m4*. To illustrate, for example,

```
define(`BITNET_RELAY', `host.domain')
```

causes the value *host.domain* to be assigned to the $B macro. Non-*m4* specific defined macros can be declared with the LOCAL_CONFIG technique (see §19.6.30).

19.4.3 Rules and rule sets

The *m4* technique allows custom rules and rule sets to be inserted in a variety of convenient ways. The complete list of *m4* keywords that affect rules is shown in Table 19-5.

Table 19–5: Rule and Rule Set Keywords

Keyword	§	Sendmail Version	Description
LOCAL_CONFIG	19.6.30	V8.1 and above	Add general information and rules
LOCAL_RULE_0	19.6.32	V8.1 and above	Add rules to rule set 0
LOCAL_RULE_1	19.6.34	V8.1 and above	Add rules to rule set 1
LOCAL_RULE_2	19.6.34	V8.1 and above	Add rules to rule set 2
LOCAL_RULE_3	19.6.35	V8.1 and above	Add rules to rule set 3

Table 19–5: Rule and Rule Set Keywords (continued)

Keyword	§	Sendmail Version	Description
LOCAL_RULESETS	19.6.36	V8.8 and above	Group local rules with others
LOCAL_NET_CONFIG	19.6.37	V8.6 and above	Add rules for SMART_HOST

To illustrate, consider the following technique for adding a rule to rule set 0:

```
LOCAL_RULE_0
R$* <@ $=w . $=m> $*        $#local $: $1       @here.ourdomain
```

Here, we add a rule to rule set 0 that accepts any address with a host part in the class $=w (see §32.5.8) that is also in one of the local domains as listed in the class $=m (see §32.5.3) as local address.

19.4.4 *Masquerading*

Masquerading is the process of transforming the local hostname in addresses into that of another host. This results in the mail message appearing to come from that other host rather than from the local host. Masquerading is most often used in domains where email is addressed to the domain rather than to individual hosts inside the domain.

Masquerading usually rewrites header-sender addresses. Some *m4* features allow you also to rewrite envelope addresses. The complete list of all definitions and features that affect masquerading is shown in Table 19–6.

Table 19–6: Defines and Features Affecting Masquerading

What	§	Version	Masquerade
EXPOSED_USER	19.6.4	V8.6 and above	All but these
FEATURE(allmasquerade)	19.6.6	V8.2 and above	The recipient too
FEATURE(limited_masquerade)	19.6.12	V8.8 and above	Only $=M hosts
FEATURE(masquerade_entire_domain)	19.6.15	V8.8 and above	All of a domain
FEATURE(masquerade_envelope)	19.6.16	V8.7 and above	The envelope too
MASQUERADE_AS	19.6.42	V8.6 and above	Another host
MASQUERADE_DOMAIN	19.6.43	V8.6 and above	Other domains
MASQUERADE_DOMAIN_FILE	19.6.44	V8.6 and above	Other domains

19.4.5 *Relays*

A relay is a rule that sends all of one type of mail to a specific destination. One example would be email FAX transmissions. Clearly, even though local mail should be delivered locally, mail to the pseudo-user *fax* should always be sent to a special FAX-handling machine.

The complete list of relays supported by the V8 *sendmail m4* technique is shown in Table 19-7.

Table 19-7: Relays

Relay	§	Version	Description
BITNET_RELAY	31.10.5	V8.1 and above	The BITNET relay
DECNET_RELAY	31.10.9	V8.7 and above	The DECnet relay
FAX_RELAY	31.10.15	V8.6 and above	The FAX relay
LOCAL_RELAY	19.6.31	V8.1 and above	Relay for unqualified users
LUSER_RELAY	31.10.23	V8.7 and above	Relay for unknown local users
MAIL_HUB	19.6.41	V8.6 and above	All local delivery on a central server
SMART_HOST	19.6.47	V8.6 and above	The ultimate relay
UUCP_RELAY	19.6.48	V8.1 and above	The UUCP relay

All relays are declared in the same fashion. For example,

```
define('LOCAL_RELAY','agent:host')
```

Here, **agent** is the name of a delivery agent to use, and **host** is the name of the machine to which all such mail will be relayed. If **agent:** is missing, it defaults to a literal `relay:`.

If the **host** is listed under a domain that uses wild-card MX records (see §21.3.4), you should specify it with a trailing dot; for example,

```
define(`LOCAL_RELAY', `smtp:relay.sub.domain.')
                                            ↑
                                      trailing dot
```

Relays fit into the flow of rules through rule set 0 like this:

1. Basic canonicalization (list syntax, delete local host, etc.)
2. LOCAL_RULE_0 (see §19.6.32)
3. FEATURE(mailertable) (see §19.6.14)
4. UUCP_RELAY, BITNET_RELAY, FAX_RELAY, DECNET_RELAY
5. LOCAL_NET_CONFIG (see §19.6.37)
6. SMART_HOST
7. SMTP, local, etc. delivery agents

19.4.6 UUCP

The *m4* configuration technique includes four UUCP options to choose from. They are listed in Table 19-8.

Table 19-8: UUCP Support

Relay	§	Version	Description
SITE	19.6.45	V8.1 and above	Declare sites for SITECONFIG (obsolete)
SITECONFIG	19.6.46	V8.1 and above	Local UUCP connections (obsolete)
UUCP_RELAY	19.6.48	V8.1 and above	The UUCP relay
UUCPSMTP	19.6.49	V8.1 and above	Individual UUCP to network translations

Note that two items in the table are marked as obsolete. This is because all of their functions have been moved into the `mailertable` feature (see §19.6.14). They are included for backward compatibility with early configuration file versions.

Support for UUCP can be included in your *mc* file with the MAILER command (see §19.3.2):

```
MAILER(uucp)
```

This declares six[*] delivery agents and the rules to support them. They are listed in Table 19-9.

Table 19-9: UUCP Delivery Agents

Agent	§	Version	Description
uucp-old	19.4.6.1	V8.6 and above	Old-style, all ! form of UUCP
uucp	19.4.6.1	V8.1 and above	Synonym for the above (obsolete)
uucp-new	19.4.6.2	V8.6 and above	Old-style with multiple recipients
suucp	19.4.6.2	V8.1 and above	Synonym for the above (obsolete)
uucp-uudom	19.4.6.3	V8.6 and above	Domain-form headers, old-form envelope
uucp-dom	19.4.6.4	V8.6 and above	Domain-form headers and envelope

If support for SMTP delivery agents is also included prior to UUCP, then the last two additional delivery agents are included (uucp-dom and uucp-uudom). Note that smtp must be first for this to happen:

```
MAILER(smtp)
MAILER(uucp)
```

If uucp is first, uucp-dom and uucp-uudom are excluded.

When processing UUCP mail (addresses that contain a ! and those that end in a .UUCP suffix), *sendmail* routes to those hosts on the basis of the class in which they were found. Hosts that are found in $=U deliver via uucp-old, hosts in $=Y deliver via uucp-new, and hosts in $=Z deliver via uucp-uudom.

---

[*] Actually, there are only four; uucp and uucp-old are synonyms for the same agents, as are suucp and uucp-new.

The choice of which delivery agent to use for UUCP delivery is under the control of the SITECONFIG *m4* macro described above (see §19.6.46). Which you choose depends on what version of UUCP you are running locally and what version is being run at the other end of the connection. There are far too many variations on UUCP to allow specific recommendations here. In general, you need to choose between a domain form of address (*gw@wash.dc.gov*) and a UUCP form (*wash!gw*) and then go with the delivery agent that makes the most sense for you. We recommend that you start with the most domain-correct agent, uucp-dom, and see if it works for you. If not, scale back to uucp-uudom, then to uucp-new and finally to uucp-old as a last resort.

19.4.6.1 *uucp-old (aka uucp)*

If you are running an old version of UUCP, you may have to use this delivery agent. All addresses are turned into the ! form even if they were in domain form:

user	→ *becomes* →	yourhost!user
user@host.domain	→ *becomes* →	yourhost!host.domain!user

This delivery agent can deliver only to one recipient at a time, so it can spend a lot of time transmitting duplicate messages. If at all possible, avoid using this delivery agent.

19.4.6.2 *uucp-new (aka suucp)*

Newer releases of UUCP can send to multiple recipients at once. If yours is such a release, you may use the uucp-new delivery agent. It is just like uucp-old except that it can perform multiple deliveries.

19.4.6.3 *uucp-uudom*

More modern implementations of UUCP can understand and correctly handle domain style addresses in headers (although they still require the ! form in the envelope). If yours is such an implementation, you may use the uucp-uudom delivery agent.

At the receiving end, the message mail arrives with the five character "From " line showing the sender address in the ! form. The "From " line reflects the envelope address.

19.4.6.4 *uucp-dom*

The uucp-dom is the most domain-correct form of the available UUCP delivery agents. All addresses, envelope and header, no matter whether or not they began in the ! form, are sent out in domain form. Essentially, this uses UUCP as a transport mechanism, but in all other respects it adheres to the Internet standards.

19.5 *Pitfalls*

The use of the # to place comments into an mc file for eventual transfer to your configuration file may not work as expected. The # is not special to *m4*, so *m4* continues to process a line even though that line is a comment. So instead of

```
# Here we define $m as our domain
```

(which would see **define** as an *m4* keyword), use single quotes to insulate all such comments from *m4* interpretation:

```
# `Here we define $m as our domain'
```

19.6 *Alphabetized m4 Macros*

In this section we detail each of the general macros available when configuring with the *m4* technique. Here we list them in alphabetical order.

This reference is not comprehensive. Options, macros, and delivery agents, for example, are described in chapters dedicated to those topics.

BITNET_RELAY   *(V8.1 and above)*

19.6.1   *The BITNET relay*

The host that will forward BITNET-addressed email. If not defined, the .BITNET pseudo-domain won't work. See §31.10.5 for a description of this relay and of the $B macro.

DECNET_RELAY   *(V8.7 and above)*

19.6.2   *The DECnet relay*

The host that will forward DECnet addressed email. If not defined, the .DECNET pseudo-domain won't work, nor will an address of the form *node::user*. See §31.10.9 for a description of this relay and of the $C macro.

DOL   *(V8.1 and above)*

19.6.3   *Insert literal $ in m4 output*

Ordinarily, the $ character is interpreted by *m4* inside its **define** expressions. But for ambitious undertakings, such as designing your own DOMAIN, FEATURE, or HACK files, you may need to include reference to a macro or operator (and hence a $) inside an *m4* **define** expression. The way you do this is with the DOL *m4* macro. For example,

```
define('DOWN', 'R DOL(*) < @ $1 > DOL(*)     DOL(1) < @ $2 > DOL(2)')
```

Here, we define the *m4* macro named DOWN, which takes two arguments ($1 and $2). When used in one of your .m4 files,

```
DOWN(badhost, outhost)
```

it creates a rule by substituting the above arguments for the corresponding $1 and $2 in its original definition:

```
R $* < @ badhost > $*     $1 < @ outhost > $2
```

The DOL *m4* macro in the original definition allowed the insertion of $ characters (such as $*) while protecting those characters from being wrongly interpreted by *m4*.

Needless to say, you should *never* redefine the DOL macro.

EXPOSED_USER   *(V8.6 and above)*

19.6.4   *Masquerade all but these*

Class macro $=E is used by the V8 configuration file to hold a list of usernames that should never be masqueraded (even if masquerade is enabled with the MASQUERADE_AS m4 macro). By default, the user *root* is always in that class. There are two ways to add usernames to the class E. They can be added individually with the EXPOSED_USER *m4* macro:

```
EXPOSED_USER(user)
```

Here, we cause the name *user* to be appended to the class E. This is identical to the following use of LOCAL_CONFIG to add to the class directly:

```
LOCAL_CONFIG
CE user
```

If you wish to store the list of nonmasqueradable users in an external file, you can cause that file to be read with an F configuration command (see §32.1.2):

```
LOCAL_CONFIG
FE/usr/local/mail/visible.users
```

FAX_RELAY   *(V8.6 and above)*

19.6.5   *The FAX relay*

The host that will forward email faxes. If not defined, and if you don't have a **fax** delivery agent on your local machine, the .FAX pseudo-domain won't work. See §31.10.15 for a description of this relay and of the $F macro. Note that if you service faxes locally, you will also need to declare the *fax* delivery agent with the MAILER() *m4* command instead (see §19.3.2).

FEATURE(allmasquerade)   *(V8.2 and above)*

19.6.6   *Masquerade the sender too*

If a MASQUERADE_AS host is defined, that hostname replaces all sender addresses. The `allmasquerade` feature causes header recipient addresses to also have that treatment.

But note that this feature can be extremely risky and that it should be used only if the MASQUERADE_AS host has an *aliases* file that is a superset of all *aliases* files and a *passwd* file that is a superset of all *passwd* files at your site. To illustrate the risk, consider a situation in which the masquerade host is named *hub.domain* and mail is being sent from the local workstation. If a local alias exists, say *thishostusers*, that does not also exist on the masquerade host, this `allmasquerade` feature will cause the `To:` header to go out as:

```
To: thishostusers@hub.domain
```

Here, the address *thishostusers* does not exist on the masquerade host, and as a consequence, replies to messages containing this header will bounce.

The form for the `allmasquerade` feature is:

```
define(`MASQUERADE_AS', `your.hub.domain')
FEATURE(`allmasquerade')
```

Note that MASQUERADE_AS (see §19.6.42) must also be defined and must contain a fully qualified hostname.

FEATURE(always_add_domain)   *(V8.1 and above)*

19.6.7   *Add the local domain even on local mail*

Normally, header recipient addresses and header and envelope sender addresses that select the `local` or `prog` delivery agents are left as is. If the `always_add_domain` feature is defined, local addresses that lack a host part have an @ and the MASQUERADE_AS host appended (if it is defined). If MASQUERADE_AS is not defined, an @ and the value of $j (see §31.10.20) are appended.

The form for the *always_add_domain* feature is

```
FEATURE(`always_add_domain')
```

The `always_add_domain` feature is safe and recommended. It ensures that all addresses that are locally delivered will be fully qualified. See the `allmasquerade` feature for a description of the risks surrounding masquerading addresses.

FEATURE(bestmx_is_local)   *(V8.6 and above)*

19.6.8   *Accept best MX record as local if in $=w*

The class **w** (see §32.5.8) is recommended for defining which hostnames will be treated as being equivalent to the local hostname. That method, however, requires that the mail administrator manually keep the class up to date.

As an alternative, for low- to medium-volume sites, use the `bestmx_is_local` feature. When enabled, this feature looks up each hostname that it finds in the `bestmx` internal database map (see §33.8.2). That map returns the best MX record (if it is known) for that name. That returned record is then compared to the list of hostnames in class **w** to see whether it is equivalent to the local host. If so, the address is accepted for local delivery.

The form for the `bestmx_is_local` feature:

```
FEATURE(`bestmx_is_local')
```

If you wish to limit lookups to a small list of domains, you can add them as a second argument:

```
FEATURE(`bestmx_is_local', `domain1 domain2 etc.')
```

The list of domains is added to the class `$=B`. Only hosts in those domains are allowed to list your site as the best MX record for use with this feature.

Use of this feature is best limited to low-volume sites. Looking up every address in the `bestmx` map can cause numerous DNS enquiries. At high-volume sites the magnitude of extra DNS enquiries can adversely tax the system.

There is also a risk to this feature. Someone could create an MX record for your site without your knowledge. Bogus mail might then be accepted at your site without your permission.

```
bogus.site.com.    IN MX 0 your.real.domain
```

Here, mail to *bogus.site.com* would be sent to your site, where the name *bogus.site.com* would be looked up with the `bestmx_is_local` feature. Your *sendmail* would find itself listed as MX for *bogus.site.com* and so would accept the bogus mail and attempt to deliver it locally. If the bogus name were designed to discredit you, it could be set to *sex.bogus.site.com* for example, and mail to *root@sex.bogus.site.com* would be delivered to you without your knowing the reason.

FEATURE(bitdomain)   *(V8.1 and above)*

19.6.9   *Convert BITNET addresses into Internet addresses*

Many Internet hosts have BITNET addresses that are separate from their Internet addresses. For example, the host *icsi.berkeley.edu* has the registered BITNET name *ucbicsi*. If a user tried to reply to an address such as:

```
user@ucbicsi.bitnet
```

that mail would fail. To help with translations from registered BITNET names to Internet addresses, John Gardiner Myers has supplied the `bitdomain` program in the *contrib* subdirectory. It produces output in the form

```
ucbicsi     icsi.berkeley.edu
```

that can be put into database form for use with the K configuration command. The `bitdomain` feature causes rules to be included in the configuration file that perform the necessary translation:

```
R$* < @ $+ .BITNET > $*          $: $1 < @ $(bitdomain $2 $: $2.BITNET $) > $3
```

Note that this rule requires BITNET addresses to be so identified with a `.BITNET` suffix. If the address, without the suffix, is found in the `bitdomain` database, the Internet equivalent address is used in its place. (See also the UUCPSMTP *m4* macro and the `domaintable` feature.

The form of the `bitdomain` feature is

```
FEATURE(`bitdomain')
```

This declaration causes the following K configuration command to be included in addition to the above rule:

```
Kbitdomain hash -o /etc/bitdomain.db
```

The `bitdomain` feature is one of those that can take an argument to specify a different form of or name for the database:

```
FEATURE(`bitdomain',`dbm -o /etc/bitdomain')
```

The extra argument causes the above K command to be replaced with the following one:

```
Kbitdomain dbm -o /etc/bitdomain
```

The `bitdomain` feature is safe. You can routinely include it in all configuration files. The database lookup is performed only if the `.BITNET` suffix is present and the database file exists.

Note that you must also define BITNET_RELAY (see §31.10.5) if you want `.BITNET` suffixed mail that is not found in the database to be routed to a relay machine. If BITNET_RELAY is not defined, `.BITNET` suffixed mail that is not found in the database is bounced.

FEATURE(domaintable) *(V8.2 and above)*

19.6.10   *Accept old as equivalent to new domain*

Some sites need to use multiple domain names when transitioning from an old domain to a new one. The *domaintable* feature enables such transitions to operate smoothly by rewriting the old domain to the new. To begin, create a file of the form:

```
other.domain    local.host.domain
```

In it the left side of each line has one of possibly many fully qualified hostnames, and the right side has one of your local hostnames. The *makemap*(1) program (see §33.2) is then used to convert that file into a database.

The `domaintable` feature causes a rule like this to be included in your configuration file:

```
R$* < @ $+ > $*              $: $1 < @ $(domaintable $2 $) > $3
```

Here, each host part of an address in rule set 3 is looked up in the `domaintable` map. If it is found, the local name from that map replaces it, and the address is treated as local.

The `domaintable` feature enables this lookup by including a K configuration command:

```
Kdomaintable hash -o /etc/domaintable
```

The form of *domaintable* feature is

```
FEATURE(`domaintable')
```

The `domaintable` feature is one of those that can take an argument to specify a different form of or different name for the database:

```
FEATURE(`domaintable',`dbm -o /etc/domaintable')
```

The extra argument causes the above K command to be replaced with the following one:

```
Kdomaintable dbm -o /etc/domaintable
```

The `domaintable` feature is safe. You can routinely include it in all configuration files. The database lookup is performed only if the database file exists. (See §33.3.4.8 for a description of the K command's −o switch.)

Although this feature might appear suitable for a service provider that wishes to accept mail for client domains, it really is not. Such a service provider should use the `virtusertable` feature instead.

FEATURE(genericstable)   *(V8.8 and above)*

19.6.11   *Transform sender addresses*

The User Database (see §33.5) allows recipient addresses to be changed so that they can be delivered to new hosts. For example, *gw@wash.dc.gov* can be transformed with the User Database into *george@us.edu*. The `genericstable` provides the same type of transformation on the sender's address.

To begin, create a file of the form

```
user     newuser@new.host.domain
```

In it, each line begins with the user part of an address. On the right is the new address for that sender. One example of a use for this table might be to make the user *news* always appear as though it was from the *news* machine:

```
news     news@news.our.domain
```

The *makemap*(1) program (see §33.2) is then used to convert this file into a database:

```
makemap hash file
```

The `genericstable` feature causes a rule like this to be included in your configuration file:

```
R$+ < @ $=G . >      $: < $(generics $1 $: @ $) > $1 < @ $2 . >
```

Here, in rule set 93, any address whose host part is in the class `$=G` has the user part looked up in the `genericstable` database. If it is found, it is rewritten to be the address from the right-hand side of the original file. Note that local and non-local hosts can appear in `$=G` for use with this feature. Also note that the members of `$=w` are *not* automatically placed in `$=G`.

The `genericstable` feature enables this lookup by including a `K` configuration command:

```
Kgenericstable hash -o /etc/genericstable
```

The form of `genericstable` feature's declaration is

```
FEATURE(`genericstable')
```

The `genericstable` feature is one of those that can take an argument to specify a different form of or a different name for the database:

```
FEATURE(`genericstable',`dbm -o /etc/genericstable')
```

The extra argument causes the above K command to be replaced with the following one:

```
Kgenericstable dbm -o /etc/genericstable
```

See §33.3.4.8 for a description of the K command **-o** switch.

The **genericstable** should be enabled only if you intend to use it. It causes every sender to be looked up in that database.

FEATURE(limited_masquerade)   *(V8.8 and above)*

19.6.12   *Only masquerade $=M hosts*

Ordinarily, addresses can be masqueraded if they are unqualified (lack a domain part) or if they match any hostname in $=w. Masquerading replaces the hostname part of an address with the fully qualified hostname defined by MASQUERADE_AS.

Some sites handle mail for multiple domains. For these sites it is important to recognize all incoming mail as local via $=w. On the other hand, only a subset of the hosts in $=w should be masqueraded. Consider, for example, the host *our.domain* that receives mail for the domains *his.domain* and *her.domain*:

```
Cw our.domain his.domain her.domain
```

In this scenario we want all but *her.domain* to be masqueraded as *our.domain*. The way to create such exceptions is with the **limited_masquerade** feature.

The **limited_masquerade** feature causes masquerading to be based on $=M instead of $=w. You use **limited_masquerade** like this:

```
define(`MASQUERADE_AS', `our.domain')
FEATURE(`limited_masquerade')
LOCAL_CONFIG
Cw our.domain his.domain her.domain
MASQUERADE_DOMAIN(our.domain his.domain)
```

MASQUERADE_AS needs to be declared first. Then the **limited_masquerade** feature is declared. Finally, the LOCAL_CONFIG allows two classes to be declared. The first is the normal $=w. The second uses MASQUERADE_DOMAIN to indirectly declare $=M and puts a subset of the $=w hosts in it. Specifically, the second class omits the *her.domain*.

The **limited_masquerade** feature causes *sendmail* to masquerade the hosts in $=M, instead of the normal masquerading of $=w. Note that $=M is also used to list the domains for the **masquerade_entire_domain** feature.

FEATURE(local_procmail)   *(V8.7 and above)*

19.6.13   *Use procmail(1) as local delivery agent*

The *procmail* (1) program can handle a user's mail autonomously (for example, sorting incoming mail into folders based on subject) and can function as a *sendmail* delivery agent. Some administrators prefer *procmail*(1) in this latter role over normal UNIX delivery agents. If this is your preference, you can easily use *procmail*(1) in that role with the *local_procmail* feature:

```
FEATURE(`local_procmail')
```

The *local_procmail* feature changes the P=, F=, and A= equates for the `local` delivery agent into

```
P=/usr/local/bin/procmail          ← see §30.4.9
F=SPfhn                            ← see §30.4.5
A=procmail -Y -a $h -d $u          ← see §30.4.1
```

If you have installed *procmail* in a different location, you can specify that alternative location with a second argument:

```
FEATURE(`local_procmail', `/admin/mail/bin/procmail')
```

If you need to use different F= flags than those shown, you may declare new flags with LOCAL_MAILER_FLAGS (see §30.4.5.1). If you need to specify different command line arguments, you may do so with LOCAL_MAILER_ARGS (see §30.4.1.1). Both must appear before the feature.

FEATURE(mailertable)   *(V8.1 and above)*

19.6.14   *Database selects new delivery agents*

A *mailertable* is a database that maps *host.domain* names to special delivery agent and new domain name pairs. Essentially, it provides a database hook into rule set 0. The new domain names are used for routing but are not reflected in the headers of messages. For example, one mapping in a source text file could be:

```
compuserv.com      smtp:compuserve.com
```

The key portion (on the left) must be either a fully qualified host and domain name, such as *lady.bcx.com*, or a partial domain specification with a leading dot, such as *.bcx.com*. On the right the delivery agent name must be separated from the new domain name by a colon. The source text file is converted into a database with the *makemap*(1) program (see §33.2). Beginning with V8.8 *sendmail*, the host part can also specify a user:

```
downhost.com       smtp:postmaster@mailhub.our.domain
```

The *mailertable* feature causes rules to be included in your configuration file that look up *host.domain* names (on the left in the source file) in the *mailertable* database:

```
R< $+ > $*                       $: < $(mailertable $1 $) > $2    lookup
R< error : $- $+ > $*            $#error $@ $1 $: $2              check -- error?
```

Here, the *host.domain* is looked up in the `mailertable` database, and a delivery agent, colon, and domain pair are returned. If the delivery agent (in `mailertable`) is `error`, the `#error` delivery agent is called. This allows error messages to be put into the database, as, for example,

```
badhost     error:nohost mail to badhost is prohibited
```

The first token following the `error:` is passed in the `$@` part of the `#error` delivery agent. Note that you must use words or *<sysexits.h>* codes here, not DSN values (such as `3.1.0`), because the latter would be wrongly broken up into five tokens. See §30.5.2 for a full description of the `#error` delivery agent and for tables of useful words and codes for the `$@` part.

If the host is found and it is not an `error` delivery agent, that delivery agent is selected. Otherwise, the unresolved *host.domain* is passed to rule set 90 for further *mailertable* lookups. Rule set 90 recursively strips the leftmost part of the *host.domain* away and looks up the result in the `mailertable`. This continues until either a match is found or only a dot is left. Then that dot is looked up to give you a hook for failed lookups:

```
.       smtp:smarthost
```

As a special case, the delivery agent named `local` causes slightly different behavior in that it allows the name of the target user to be listed without a host part:

```
virtual.domain     local:bob
```

Here, any mail that is received for the *virtual.domain* is delivered to the user *bob* on the local machine. If the user part is missing,

```
virtual.domain     local:
```

the mail is delivered to the user part of the original address.

The form for the *mailertable* feature is:

```
FEATURE(`mailertable')
```

This causes the following database declaration in the configuration file:

```
Kmailertable hash -o /etc/mailertable.db
```

If you wish to use a different form of database (such as *dbm*), the *mailertable* feature accepts an argument:

```
FEATURE(`mailertable',`dbm -o /etc/mailertable')
```

The *mailertable* feature was inspired by the IDA version of *sendmail*.

FEATURE(masquerade_entire_domain)   *(V8.8 and above)*

19.6.15   *Masquerade all hosts under a domain*

Ordinarily, masquerading transforms any host from a list of hosts in the class $=w (see §32.5.8) into the host defined by MASQUERADE_AS. If domains are also masqueraded with MASQUERADE_DOMAIN, they too are transformed. For example, consider these declarations:

```
MASQUERADE_AS(`our.domain')
MASQUERADE_DOMAIN(`her.domain')
```

The first line causes any host part of an address contained in the class $=w to be transformed into *our.domain*. The second line transforms any domain part of *her.domain* into *our.domain*.

The key point here is that the domain part *her.domain* will be transformed, whereas hosts under that domain will not be transformed:

```
george@her.domain            → becomes →      george@our.domain
george@host.her.domain       → remains →      george@host.her.domain
```

If you wish MASQUERADE_DOMAIN to transform all the hosts under the declared domain, you may use the **masquerade_entire_domain** feature:

```
MASQUERADE_AS(`our.domain')
MASQUERADE_DOMAIN(`her.domain')
FEATURE(`masquerade_entire_domain')
```

This feature extends masquerading of *her.domain* to include all the hosts under that domain:

```
george@her.domain            → becomes →      george@our.domain
george@host.her.domain       → becomes →      george@our.domain
george@host.sub.her.domain   → becomes →      george@our.domain
```

Note that you may masquerade only domains that are *under your direct jurisdiction and control*. Also note that domain masquerading is intended for actual domains. Virtual (fictional) domains are better handled with the **virtusertable** feature (see 19.6.28). But note that the **virtusertable** feature handles only incoming mail.

FEATURE(masquerade_envelope)

19.6.16 *Masquerade the envelope too*

Ordinarily, masquerading (see §19.4.4) affects only the headers of email messages, but sometimes it is also desirable to masquerade the envelope.* For example, error messages are often returned to the envelope-sender address. When many hosts are masquerading as a single host, it is often desirable to have all error messages delivered to that central masquerade host.

The `masquerade_envelope` feature causes masquerading to include envelope addresses:

```
MASQUERADE_AS(`our.domain')        ← masquerade headers
FEATURE(`masquerade_envelope')     ← also masquerade the envelope
```

These *mc* lines cause all envelope addresses (where the host part is declared as part of class $=w; see §32.5.8) to be transformed into *our.domain*. See MASQUERADE_DOMAIN for a way to also masquerade other domains, and see the `masquerade_entire_domain` feature for a way to also masquerade all the hosts under other domains.

In general, `masquerade_envelope` is recommended for uniform or small sites. Large or variegated sites may prefer to tailor the envelope on a subdomain-by-subdomain or host-by-host basis.

FEATURE(nocanonify)

19.6.17 *Don't canonify with $[and $]*

Ordinarily, as part of rule set 3, *sendmail* tries to canonify (add a domain to) any hostname that lacks a domain part. It does this by passing the unadorned hostname to the $[and $] operators (see §28.6.6). The `nocanonify` feature prevents *sendmail* from passing addresses to $[and $] for canonicalization. This is generally suitable for use by sites that act only as mail gateways or that have MUAs that do full canonicalization themselves.

The form for the `nocanonify` feature is:

```
FEATURE(`nocanonify')
```

You might also want to use:

```
define(`confBIND_OPTS',`-DNSRCH -DEFNAMES')
```

to turn off the usual resolver options that perform a similar function (see §34.8.55).

---

* See §1.7 for a description of the envelope and how it differs from headers.

Note that the `nocanonify` feature disables only one possible use of $[and $] in the configuration file. If the *nouucp* feature is omitted (thereby including UUCP support), addresses that end in a `.UUCP` suffix still have the preceding part of the address canonified with $[and $] even if the `nocanonify` feature was declared.

Note that sending out any unqualified addresses can pose a risk. Be sure to read §16.5 for a discussion of why you might not want to use this feature.

FEATURE(nodns)   *(V8.6)*

19.6.18   *Omit DNS support from configuration file*

The V8.6 *sendmail* configuration files usually assumed that you were using DNS to get host information. If you did not have DNS available (for example, if you were on a remote UUCP node), you could declare that fact:

> FEATURE(`nodns')

This told *sendmail* to assume that DNS was not available. It did this by *not* setting any of the *_res.options* flag bits. Note that this was really only a suggestion, because other features (such as `bestmx_is_local` temporarily set those flag bits and used DNS anyway.

Beginning with V8.7 *sendmail*, you should either use the service-switch file (see §34.8.61) to control use of DNS or compile a sendmail without DNS support (see §18.8.23).

Note that the result of a hostname lookup failure differs depending on whether or not DNS is used. If a hostname is looked up with DNS and not found, the message will be queued, and the name will be looked up again later. If the host is looked up in */etc/hosts* and the lookup fails, the message bounces.

FEATURE(nouucp)   *(V8.1 and above)*

19.6.19   *Eliminate all UUCP support*

If your site wants nothing to do with UUCP addresses, you can enable the `nouucp` feature. Among the changes this causes that are the `!` character is not recognized as a separator between hostnames; and all the macros that relate to UUCP (see §19.4.6) are ignored. This feature truly means *no* UUCP.

You declare `nouucp` is like this:

> FEATURE(`nouucp')

Note that all the other UUCP declarations (such as UUCP_RELAY) will be ignored if you use `nouucp`.

FEATURE(nullclient)   *(V8.6 and above)*

19.6.20   *Relay all mail through a mail host*

Some sites have a number of workstations that never receive mail directly. They are usually clustered around a single mail server. Normally, all clients in a cluster like this send their mail as though the mail is from the server, and they relay all mail through that server rather than sending directly. If you have such a configuration, use

```
FEATURE(`nullclient', `server')
```

See Chapter 16, *The null.mc File and m4*, for a lesson in how to use this feature. Also see the **nocanonify** feature, which can also be used with **nullclient**.

If you wish to prevent the *nullclient* version of *sendmail* from trying to access *aliases*, add this line to your *.mc* file:

```
undefine(`ALIAS_FILE')
```

Note that this works only with V8.8 and above *.mc* files.

FEATURE(redirect)   *(V8.1 and above)*

19.6.21   *Add support for address.REDIRECT*

The **redirect** feature allows aliases to be set up for retired accounts. Those aliases bounce with an indication of the new forwarding address. A couple of lines from such an *aliases*(5) file might look like this:

```
george:    george@new.site.edu.REDIRECT
william:   wc@creative.net.REDIRECT
```

The **redirect** feature causes mail addressed to **george**, for example, to be bounced with a message like this:

```
551 User not local; please try <george@new.site.edu>
```

Note that the message is bounced and not forwarded. No notification is sent to the recipient's new address.

The form of the **redirect** feature is

```
FEATURE(`redirect')
```

This feature adds the pseudo-domain .REDIRECT to class $=P, which prevents that suffix from being looked up with DNS. It then adds rules to rule set 0 that handle this suffix only if the {opMode} macro (see §31.10.28) has any value other than **i** (for *initialize aliases* as set by the **-bi** command line switch, see §36.1.3). The actual bounce is caused by calling the **error** delivery agent with a RHS like this:

```
$# error $@ 5.1.1 $: "551 User not local; please try " <$1@$2>
```

The **5.1.1** is a DSN error code (see RFC1893), and the **551** is an SMTP code (see RFC821).

To illustrate why the message is bounced rather than forwarded, consider a fictional MTA that is clever about getting this message:

```
551 User not local; please try <george@new.site.edu>
```

Instead of bouncing the outgoing message, the fictional MTA tries to be clever and to deliver to *new.site.edu*. If *new.site.edu* also responds with a REDIRECT message, the MTA tries the next host in line. This is a bad idea for two reasons: First, elaborate loop detection would need to be designed to catch infinite REDIRECT loops, and second, a down host anywhere in the sequence would necessitate that the series of connections be made over and over again until they all succeeded.

FEATURE(smrsh)   *(V8.7 and above)*

19.6.22   *Use smrsh (sendmail restricted shell)*

Although *sendmail* tries to be very safe about how it runs programs from the *aliases*(5) and ˜/.forward files (see §24.2.3), it still may be vulnerable to some internal attacks. To limit the selection of programs that *sendmail* is allowed to run, V8 *sendmail* now includes source and documentation for the *smrsh* (sendmail restricted shell) program. See §22.8.2 for a full description of the *smrsh* program.

After you have compiled, installed, and configured *smrsh*, you can include support for it in your configuration file with the **smrsh** feature:

```
FEATURE(`smrsh')
MAILER(`local')
```

Note that the **smrsh** feature must precede the **local** delivery agent declaration. If these lines are reversed, the following error will print when you run *m4*:

```
*** FEATURE(smrsh) must occur before MAILER(local)
```

The default location for the *smrsh* program is */usr/local/etc/smrsh*. If you installed *smrsh* in another location, you will need to add an argument to the **smrsh** feature:

```
FEATURE(`smrsh', `/usr/bin/smrsh')
```

Use of *smrsh* is recommended by CERT, so you are encouraged to use this feature as often as possible.

FEATURE(notsticky)   *(V8.1 through V8.6)*

19.6.23   *Don't differ user from user@local.host*

Mail addressed to a local user that includes the name of the local host as part of
the address (i.e., *user@local.host*) is delivered locally. From V8.1 to V8.6 *sendmail*,
if the address has a host part, lookups in the User Database (see §33.5) and the
additional processing of rule set 5 (see §29.7) are skipped. Under V8.6, addresses
with just the *user* part are always processed by the User Database and rule set 5.

The V8.6 `notsticky` feature changes this logic. If this feature is chosen, all users
are looked up in the User Database, and the additional processing done by rule
set 5 is skipped.

Beginning with V8.7, the default is now as if `notsticky` were used, and the
`stickyhost` feature is used to restore the previous default.

FEATURE(stickyhost)   *(V8.7 and above)*

19.6.24   *Differ user from user@local.host*

Beginning with V8.7 *sendmail*, addresses with and without a host part that resolve
to local delivery are handled in the same way. For example, *user* and
user@local.host are both looked up with the User Database (see §33.5) and processed by rule set 5 (see §29.7). This processing can result in those addresses
being forwarded to other machines.

With the `stickyhost` feature, you may change this behavior:

```
FEATURE(`stickyhost')
```

By defining `stickyhost`, you are telling *sendmail* to mark addresses that have a
local host part as "sticky":

```
user                    ← not sticky
user@local.host         ← sticky
```

Sticky hosts tend to be delivered on the local machine. That is, they are not
looked up with the User Database and are not processed by rule set 5.

One use for this feature is to create a domainwide name space. In it, all addresses
without a host part will be forwarded to a central mail server. Those with a local
host part will remain on the local machine and be delivered in the usual local
way.

Note that this is opposite the behavior of the former `notsticky` feature of V8.6.

FEATURE(use_ct_file) *(V8.7 and above)*

19.6.25   *Use /etc/sendmail.ct for a list of trusted users*

V6 *sendmail* removed the concept of trusted users (see 22.8). V8.7 reintroduced trusted users, but in a different form from that used by V5 *sendmail*. Now, trusted users are those who may run *sendmail* with the **-f** switch (see §36.7.21) without generating an authentication warning (see §35.10.35):

```
X-Authentication-Warning: host: user set sender to other using -f
```

To prevent this warning, the **user** should be added to the class $=t (see §32.5.7). There are three ways to do this. You may use the T configuration command:

```
Tuser
```

Or you may use the class command:

```
Ctuser
```

Or you may use the **use_ct_file** and add **user** to the */etc/sendmail.ct* file. To use this latter approach, declare the following in your *mc* file:

```
FEATURE(`use_ct_file')
```

If you want to locate the */etc/sendmail.ct* in a different place or give it a different name, you may do so with this declaration:

```
define(`confCT_FILE', `/etc/mail/trusted.list')
```

Note that the file must exist before *sendmail* is started, or it will complain:

```
fileclass: cannot open /etc/mail/trusted.list: No such file or directory
```

If you want the file to optionally exist, you may add a **-o** (see §32.1.2) to the conf-CT_FILE definition:

```
define(`confCT_FILE', `-o /etc/sendmail.ct')
```

Here, we don't rename the file: we make the default file's presence optional.

FEATURE(use_cw_file) *(V8.1 and above)*

19.6.26   *Use /etc/sendmail.cw for local hostnames*

The **use_cw_file** feature causes the file */etc/sendmail.cw* to be read to obtain alternative names for the local host. One use for such a file might be to declare a list of hosts for which the local host is acting as the MX recipient. The **use_cw_file** is used like this:

```
FEATURE(`use_cw_file')
```

This feature causes the following F configuration command (see §32.1.2) to appear in the configuration file:

```
Fw/etc/sendmail.cw
```

The actual filename can be changed from */etc/sendmail.cw* (the default) by defining the `confCW_FILE` macro:

```
define(`confCW_FILE', `-o /etc/mail/sendmail.cw')
```

Here, we both rename the file and make its presence optional by adding the -o switch (see §32.1.2).

If the local host is known by only a few names, an alternative is to instead include the following C configuration command (see §32.1.1) in place of the above feature:

```
Cwname1 name2
```

Here, *name1* and *name2* are alternative names for the local host.

FEATURE(uucpdomain)   *(V8.1 and above)*

19.6.27   *Convert UUCP hosts via a database*

The *uucpdomain* feature is similar to *bitdomain* but is used to translate addresses of the form

```
user@host.UUCP
```

into the ! path form or routing used by UUCP. The database for this would contain, for example, key and data pairs like this:

```
host      a!b!c!host
```

This source text file is converted into a database with the *makemap*(1) program (see §33.2). But note that no software is supplied to transform the UIUC *pathalias*(1) program's output into a form that is suitable for this database.

The way you declare `uucpdomain` is like this:

```
FEATURE(`uucpdomain')
```

This causes a rule like this to be added to rule set 3:

```
R$* < @ $+ .UUCP > $*          $: $1 < @ $(uudomain $2 $: $2.UUCP $) > $3
```

Here, the host in the pseudo-domain .UUCP is looked up in the database `uudomain`. The `uucpdomain` feature also creates the declaration for that database:

```
Kuudomain hash -o /etc/uudomain
```

If you wish to use a different form of database or a different location for the database file, you may do so by adding an argument to the feature declaration:

```
FEATURE(`uucpdomain', `dbm -o /etc/mail/uudomain')
```

Here, we tell *sendmail* that we will be using the NDBM form of database instead of the original NEWDB form (see §33.1). We also relocated the file into the */etc/mail* directory.

FEATURE(virtusertable)   *(V8.8 and above)*

19.6.28   *Support for virtual domains*

A `virtusertable` is a database that maps virtual (possibly nonexistent) domains into new addresses. Essentially, it gives you a database hook into the early part of rule set 0. Note that this only reroutes delivery. It does not change mail headers.

By way of example, consider one mapping in a source text file:

```
info@stuff.for.sale.com      bob
info@stuff.wanted.com        hans@remote.host
@fictional.com               user@another.host
```

The key portion (on the left) must be either a full address (user, host, and domain name), as in the first two lines, or an address with the user part missing, as in the last line. This source text file is converted into a database with the *makemap*(1) program (see §33.2).

The first two lines illustrate a full address for the key. The first line will be delivered to a local user (*bob*) the second to a remote user (*hans@remote.host*). The third line file shows how all mail to a virtual domain (*fictional.com*) can be delivered to a single address, no matter what the user part is.

Note that *sendmail* does a single lookup, so one line may not reference another. The following won't work:

```
info@stuff.for.sale.com      forsale@fictional.com
@fictional.com               user@another.host
```

Here, mail to *info@stuff.for.sale.com* will be delivered to *forsale@fictional.com*, not to *user@another.host*.

Also note that virtual domains in the key (such as `@fictional.com`) must be added to class w in order for them to be recognized as local.

You declare the `virtusertable` like this in your *mc* file:

```
FEATURE(`virtusertable')
```

This causes the following database declaration to appear in the configuration file:

```
Kvirtusertable hash -o /etc/virtusertable
```

If you wish to use a different form of database (such as *dbm*) or a different location, the **virtusertable** feature accepts an argument:

```
FEATURE(`virtusertable',`dbm -o /etc/mail/virtusertable')
```

If the value (the right-hand side in **virtusertable**) is **error:**, the **#error** delivery agent is called. This allows error messages to be put into the database, as, for example,

```
info@for.sale.com    error:nouser We no longer sell things here
```

The text following the **error:** is passed to the **#error** delivery agent like this:

```
Rerror : $- $+        $#error $@ $1 $: $2
```

Thus the first token following the **error:** is passed in the $@ part. Note that you must use words here, not DSN values (such as **3.1.0**), because the latter would be wrongly broken up into five tokens. See §30.5.2 for a full description of the **#error** delivery agent and for tables of useful words for the $@ part.

HACK *(V8.1 and above)*

19.6.29 *Temporary customizations*

Some things just can't be called features. To make this clear, they go in the *_CF_DIR_/hack* directory (see §19.2.1) and are referenced using the HACK macro. They tend to be site-dependent.

```
HACK(cssubdomain)
```

This illustrates use of the Berkeley-dependent **cssubdomain** hack (that makes *sendmail* accept local names in either *Berkeley.EDU* or *CS.Berkeley.EDU*).

Another way to think of a hack is as a transient feature. Create and use HACK as a temporary solution to a temporary problem. If a solution becomes permanent, move it to the FEATURE directory (see §19.3.4) and reference it there.

LOCAL_CONFIG *(V8.1 and above)*

19.6.30 *Add general information and rules*

The LOCAL_CONFIG macro allows custom configuration lines to be inserted by using the *mc* file. The inserted lines are carried literally into the output and appear in the resulting configuration file just before the rules.

```
LOCAL_CONFIG
FE/usr/local/mail/visible.users
Khostmap hash /etc/hostmap.db
```

In this example the class $=E has additional names read from the file *visible.users*,
and the *hostmap* database is declared.

New rule sets can be inserted with LOCAL_CONFIG. For V8.7 and above we recommend using symbolic names to avoid collision with rule set numbers used by
sendmail:

```
LOCAL_CONFIG
Sfoo
← custom rules here
```

See the discussion of diversions (see §19.1.4) to cause LOCAL_CONFIG lines to output in a predetermined order.

LOCAL_RELAY   *(V8.1 and above)*

19.6.31   *Relay for unqualified user (deprecated)*

Unless you specify otherwise, any address that is a username without any *@host*
part is delivered using the `local` delivery agent. If you prefer to have all such mail
handled by a different machine, you may define that other machine with the
LOCAL_RELAY *m4* macro.

Note that a relay is different from the knowledgeable hub defined with MAIL_HUB.
(See later in this section for an illustration of how MAIL_HUB and LOCAL_RELAY
interact.)

This macro is deprecated because it doesn't work well with some MUAs (for example, *mh*(1)). This is because some MUAs put a host part on all addresses even if
only the user part was specified.

LOCAL_RULE_0   *(V8.6 and above)*

19.6.32   *Add rules to rule set 0*

In rule set 0, after the `local` delivery agent has been selected and before the
`uucp`, `smtp`, and the like have been selected, you can insert custom delivery agents
of your own. To do this, use the LOCAL_RULE_0 macro:

```
LOCAL_RULE_0
# We service lady via an mx record.
R$+ < @ lady.Berkeley.EDU. >          $#uucp $@ lady $: $1
```

Here, we introduce a new rule to select a delivery agent. The host *lady* is a UUCP
host for which we accept mail via an MX record.

Note that LOCAL_RULE_0 fits into flow of rules through rule set 0 like this:

1. Basic canonicalization (list syntax, delete local host, etc.)
2. LOCAL_RULE_0
3. UUCP, BITNET_RELAY (see §31.10.5), etc.
4. LOCAL_NET_CONFIG (see §19.6.37)
5. SMART_HOST (see §19.6.47)
6. SMTP, local, etc. delivery agents

LOCAL_RULE_1   *(V8.6 and above)*

19.6.33   *Add rules to rule set 1*

See LOCAL_RULE_2.

LOCAL_RULE_2   *(V8.6 and above)*

19.6.34   *Add rules to rule set 2*

Rule sets 1 and 2 are normally empty and not included in the configuration file
created from your *mc* file. Rule set 1 processes all sender addresses (see §29.9),
and rule set 2 processes all recipient addresses (see §29.8). These *m4* macros are
used just like LOCAL_RULE_0, above but they introduce rules that would otherwise
be omitted, rather than adding rules to an existing rule set.

LOCAL_RULE_3   *(V8.6 and above)*

19.6.35   *Add rules to rule set 3*

All addresses are first rewritten by rule set 3 (see §29.4). For complex configuration
needs, you can define special rules and cause them to be added to rule set 3. New
rules are added to the end of rule set 3 by way of rule set 6. That is, each final
decision in rule set 3 (denoted by a $@ in the RHS) calls rule set 96 (with $>96)
before returning.

The m4 macro LOCAL_RULE_3 is used to introduce new rules that can be used in
canonicalizing the hostnames. Note that any modifications made here are reflected
in the header.

One suggested use for LOCAL_RULE_3 is to convert old UUCP hostnames into
domain addresses using the *m4* UUCPSMTP macro. For example,

```
LOCAL_RULE_3
UUCPSMTP(decvax,    decvax.dec.com)
UUCPSMTP(research, research.att.com)
```

This causes the following address transformations:

```
decvax!user     becomes →    user@decvax.dec.com
research!user   becomes →    user@research.att.com
```

Another suggested use for LOCAL_RULE_3 is to introduce a new rule to look up hostnames in a locally customized database:

```
LOCAL_RULE_3
R$*<@$+>$*          $:$1<@ $(hostmap $2 $) >$3
```

The declaration and definition of local database maps with the K configuration command (see §33.3) should appear in the LOCAL_CONFIG section.

LOCAL_RULESETS   *(V8.8 and above)*

19.6.36   *Group local rules with others*

Prior to V8.8 *sendmail*, you had to use the **divert9** *m4* directive to force your new rule set declarations to be emitted alongside the normal *m4*-generated rules sets. Beginning with V8.8, that bit of "black magic" has been removed.

The LOCAL_RULESETS *m4* command causes all the rule sets and rules that follow it to be emitted into your configuration file along with all the rules that are automatically generated. You use it like this:

```
LOCAL_RULESETS
your new rule sets and rules here
```

LOCAL_NET_CONFIG   *(V8.6 and above)*

19.6.37   *Add rules for SMART_HOST*

One possible setup for mail is to allow hosts on the local network to deliver directly to each other but for all other mail to be sent to a "smart host" that forwards it offsite. Commonly, such arrangements are used by sites with inhouse networks that have access to the outside world only through a UUCP link. For such sites you can use LOCAL_NET_CONFIG:

```
define(`SMART_HOST', `uucp-new:uunet')
LOCAL_NET_CONFIG
R$* < @ $* .$m. > $*     $#smtp $@ $2.$m $: $1 < @ $2.$m > $3
```

Here, SMART_HOST is first defined as **uucp-new:uunet** (send to the host *uunet* with the **uucp-new** delivery agent). The LOCAL_NET_CONFIG then introduces a rule that causes all names that end in your domain name ($m) to be delivered via the **smtp** delivery agent. Any other addresses fall through to be handled by the SMART_HOST rules.

SMART_HOST can be a network-connected gateway too. Just use **smtp** in place of **uucp-new** in the SMART_HOST definition, and the name of the gateway.

Note that LOCAL_NET_CONFIG fits into the flow of rules through rule set 0 like this:

1. Basic canonicalization (list syntax, delete local host, etc.)
2. LOCAL_RULE_0 (see §19.6.32)
3. FEATURE(mailertable) (see §19.6.14)
4. UUCP, BITNET_RELAY (see §31.10.5), etc.
5. LOCAL_NET_CONFIG (see §19.6.37)
6. SMART_HOST (see §19.6.47)
7. SMTP, local, etc. delivery agents

LOCAL_USER   *(V8.1 and above)*

19.6.38   *Users that must be delivered locally*

Some unqualified (without an *@host* part) usernames need to be delivered on the local machine even if LOCAL_RELAY is defined. The user *root* is one such example. By remaining local, aliasing is allowed to take place.

The LOCAL_USER *m4* macro is used to add additional usernames to the list of local users. Note that *root* is always a member of that list.

    LOCAL_USER(operator)

This causes the name **operator** to be appended to the list of local users. That list is stored in the class $=L. The disposition of local usernames that include the name of the local host is determined by the **stickyhost** feature.

LUSER_RELAY   *(V8.7 and above)*

19.6.39   *Relay for local looking usernames*

The host that handles usernames that appear to be local even though they are not. See §31.10.23 for a discussion of this relay.

MAILER_DEFINITIONS   *(V8.8 and above)*

19.6.40   *Define custom delivery agents*

Prior to V8.8 *sendmail* you had to use a **divert(7)** statement to force your new delivery agent definitions to be grouped with all the other delivery agent definitions. Beginning with V8.8, this bit of "black magic" has been removed.

To force your new delivery agent definitions to be grouped with the others delivery agent definitions, use the MAILER_DEFINITIONS *m4* command:

    MAILER_DEFINITIONS
    your new delivery agent definitions here

See §30.3.1 for an example of this *m4* command.

MAIL_HUB   *(V8.1 and above)*

19.6.41   *All local delivery on a local server*

One scheme for handling mail is to maintain one mail spool directory centrally and to mount that directory remotely on all clients. To avoid file locking problems, delivery to such a spool should be performed only on the central server. The MAIL_HUB macro allows you to specify that all local mail be forwarded to the central server for delivery. The point is to let unqualified names be forwarded through a machine with a large *aliases* file.

If you define both LOCAL_RELAY and MAIL_HUB, unqualified names and names in class L are sent to the LOCAL_RELAY and other local names are sent to MAIL_HUB. To illustrate, consider the result of various combinations for the user *you* on the machine *here.our.site*.

If LOCAL_RELAY is defined as *relay.our.site* and MAIL_HUB is not defined, mail addressed to *you* are forwarded to *relay.our.site*, but mail addressed to *you@here.our.site* is delivered locally.

If MAIL_HUB is defined as *hub.our.site* and LOCAL_RELAY is not defined, mail addressed to *you* and mail addressed to *you@here.our.site* is forwarded to *hub.our.site* for delivery.

If both LOCAL_RELAY and MAIL_HUB are defined as above, mail addressed to *you* is sent to *relay.our.site* for delivery, and mail addressed to *you@here.our.site* is forwarded to *hub.our.site*.

If you want all outgoing mail to go to a central machine, use SMART_HOST too.

Note that LOCAL_RELAY and MAIL_HUB act identically (except that MAIL_HUB takes precedence) unless the `stickyhost` feature is used. Also note that the `null-client` feature can be used if you want all mail to be forwarded to a central machine.

MASQUERADE_AS   *(V8.1 and above)*

19.6.42   *Masquerade as the server*

At sites with one central mail server (see MAIL_HUB, it can be advantageous for mail from the clients to appear as though it is from the hub. This simplifies mail administration in that all users have the same machine address no matter which workstations they use. You can cause a workstation to masquerade as the server (or as another host) by using the MASQUERADE_AS *m4* macro:

```
MASQUERADE_AS(server)
```

This causes outgoing mail to be labeled as coming from the *server* (rather than from the value in $j see §31.10.20). The new label is in all but the `Received:` (see §35.10.25) and `Message-ID:` (see §35.10.19) headers.

Some users (such as *root*) should never be masqueraded because one always needs to know their machine of origin. Such users are declared by using the EXPOSED_USER *m4* macro. Note that *root* is always exposed.

If you wish to have recipient addresses also masqueraded, cautiously use the *all-masquerade* feature.

MASQUERADE_DOMAIN   *(V8.6 and above)*

19.6.43   *Masquerade other domains*

Ordinarily, MASQUERADE_AS enables only hosts in the local domain, to be transformed into the masquerading host. If you wish to masquerade a domain other than your local one, you can use the MASQUERADE_DOMAIN macro:

```
MASQUERADE_DOMAIN(`other.domain')
```

Essentially, all that MASQUERADE_DOMAIN does is to assign its argument to the class $=M, so you can list multiple domains in a single MASQUERADE_DOMAIN statement:

```
MASQUERADE_DOMAIN(`domain1 domain2 domain3')
CM domain1 domain2 domain3                          ← the same
```

Note that MASQUERADE_DOMAIN masquerades only the domain and *not* any hosts under that domain. If you wish to masquerade all hosts under a domain (including the domain itself), see the `masquerade_entire_domain` feature.

MASQUERADE_DOMAIN_FILE   *(V8.6 and above)*

19.6.44   *Masquerade other domains*

In masquerading other domains, as with MASQUERADE_DOMAIN above, it may prove advantageous to store the list of masqueraded domains in an external file. The MASQUERADE_DOMAIN_FILE macro allows you to do just that:

```
MASQUERADE_DOMAIN_FILE(`/etc/mail/domains')
```

Essentially, all that MASQUERADE_DOMAIN_FILE does is to assign its argument to the class $=M via an F configuration command:

```
MASQUERADE_DOMAIN_FILE(`-o /etc/mail/domains')
FM -o /etc/mail/domains                             ← the same
```

Here, we added a −o to make the existence of the file optional.

SITE   *(V8.1 and above)*

19.6.45   *Declare sites for SITECONFIG (obsolete)*

UUCP connections are declared inside the SITECONFIG file with the SITE macro.
That macro just takes a list of one or more UUCP hostnames:

```
SITE(lady)
SITE(sonya grimble)
```

Each listed host is added to the class that was defined as the third argument to the
SITECONFIG declaration.

SITECONFIG   *(V8.1 and above)*

19.6.46   *Local UUCP connections (obsolete)*

The SITECONFIG *m4* macro (now obsolete but retained for backward compatibility) is useful for maintaining lists of UUCP connections. There are two types of
connections: those connected to the local host and those connected to another
host. The first type is declared with SITECONFIG like this:

```
SITECONFIG(`file',`host',`class')
```

Here, `file` is the name of a file (without the *.m4* suffix) that is in the directory
_CF_DIR_/cf/siteconfig. That file contains a list of SITE declarations (described
soon). The *host* is the UUCP node name of the local host. The *class* is the name
(one letter) of a class that holds the list of UUCP connections. For example,

```
SITECONFIG(`uucp.arpa',`arpa','U')
```

Here, the file *_CF_DIR_/cf/siteconfig/uucp.arpa.m4* contains a list of UUCP hosts
directly connected to the machine *arpa*. This declaration would be used only in
the machine *arpa*'s *mc* file. The list of UUCP hosts is added to the class macro
$=U. The letters available for local connections are U (for `uucp-old`), Y (for
`uucp-new`), and Z (for `uucp-uudom`).

A second form of the SITECONFIG *m4* macro is the one used by hosts other than
the one with the direct UUCP connections. It is just like the above one but with the
full canonical name of the *host*:

```
SITECONFIG(`uucp.arpa',`arpa.Berkeley.EDU',`W')
```

This also reads the file *uucp.arpa.m4* but instead of causing UUCP connections to
be made locally, it forwards them to the host *arpa.Berkeley.EDU*.

The hostname that is the second argument is assigned to the $W macro. The class
$=W is set aside to hold lists of hosts that appear locally connected. This class is
also used with the SITE macro. The letters that are available for remote sites are V,
W, and X.

If nothing is specified, the class becomes Y. If class U is specified in the third parameter, the second parameter is assumed to be the UUCP name of the local site, rather than the name of a remote site. In this latter case, the specified local name has a .UUCP appended, and the result is added to class $=w.

Note that SITECONFIG won't work if you disable UUCP with the *nouucp* feature.

SMART_HOST *(V8.1 and above)*

19.6.47 *The ultimate relay*

Some sites can deliver local mail to the local network but cannot look up hosts on the Internet with DNS. Usually, such sites are connected to the outside world with UUCP. To ensure delivery of all mail, such sites need to forward all nonlocal mail over the UUCP link to a *smart* (or well-connected) host.

You can enable this behavior by defining SMART_HOST:

```
define(`SMART_HOST', uucp-dom:supporthost)
```

Here, Internet mail will be forwarded to the host *supporthost* using the uucp-dom delivery agent. For information about other ways to use SMART_HOST, see the file *cf/README*. Note that the value in SMART_HOST is assigned to $S (see §31.10.34) for later use in rules.

UUCP_RELAY *(V8.1 and above)*

19.6.48 *The UUCP relay*

If your site handles UUCP traffic, it can be in one of two forms. Either a given host has direct UUCP connections or it does not. If it does not, then you may wish to have all UUCP mail forwarded to a host that can handle UUCP. This is done by defining a UUCP_RELAY, which is done just as you would define any other relay (as described in §19.4.5).

If your machine or site does not support UUCP, consider disabling all UUCP with the nouucp feature.

If your machine has directly connected UUCP hosts, you might wish to use one of or more of the UUCP techniques. But before doing so, be sure to declare the uucp delivery agent (see §19.3.2).

UUCPSMTP *(V8.1 and above)*

19.6.49 *Individual UUCP to network translations*

If your site has hosts that used to be UUCP sites but are now on the network, you may intercept and rewrite the old address into the new network address. For example, mail to the machine *wash* used to be addressed as *wash!user*. Now, however, *wash* is on the network, and the mail should be addressed as *user@wash.dc.gov*.

The UUCPSMTP *m4* macro provides the means to specify a UUCP to network translation for specific hosts. The above example would be declared like this:

```
UUCPSMTP('wash','wash.dc.gov')
```

The UUCPSMTP *m4* macro should be used only under LOCAL_RULE_3.

VERSIONID   *(V8.1 and above)*

19.6.50   *Version of the mc file*

The VERSIONID *m4* macro is used to insert an identifier into each *.mc* and *.m4* file that becomes a part of your final *.cf* file. Each of the files that is supplied with *sendmail* already has such an identifier. You should include a similar identifier in each of your *.mc* files.

```
VERSIONID('$Revision$')
```

Here, the VERSIONID macro is being used to insert an RCS-style revision number. The *$Revision$* becomes an actual version number when the file is checked in with *ci*(1). Arbitrary text may appear between the single quotes. You may use RCS, SCCS, or any other kind of revision identification system. The text may not contain a newline because the text appears in the *.cf* file as a comment:

```
#####  $Revision: 1.5$ #####
```

Use of VERSIONID and revision control in general is recommended.

20

The checkcompat()
Cookbook

Inside *sendmail* is the often overlooked *checkcompat()* routine. It has existed since Version 3 and is intended to allow the site administrator to accept, reject, and log mail delivery attempts. Among its uses, and those we will illustrate, are the following:

- Refuse to act as a mail gateway. Reject any mail that is both from and to any outside address.

- Limit the size of guest messages. Screen messages based on user *uid*, and reject those for the class of users who are guests when the message is over a specified limit in bytes.

- Verify *identd*(8) information. Compare the host information in $s to that in $_ and log a warning if they differ.

- Prune `Received:` headers at a firewall. Make all outgoing mail appear fresh as it exits the internal network via a firewall.

- Reject mail from spamming or mail-bombing sites. Look up the sender in an external database and bounce the message if the sender is listed as "bad."

The *checkcompat()* routine is located in the file *src/conf.c*. That file contains comments describing one way to code *checkcompat()*. In this chapter we show you other ways to code it.

The *checkcompat()* routine is inherently "internal," meaning that it must understand internal data structures that may change.[*] Since you are modifying source code, you have to be prepared to read source code. In this chapter we offer

---

[*] V8.8 *sendmail* also offers a `check_compat` rule set (see §29.10.4) that can perform some of the *checkcompat()* routine's functionality at the rule set level. This is one way to avoid having to program in the C language.

examples of ways to use *checkcompat( )*. Be aware that they are examples only, and you will need C programming skill to extend them to real-world situations.

The *checkcompat( )* routine is called for every delivery attempt to every recipient. When designing a *checkcompat( )* routine of your own, be aware that a cascade of errors may propagate if you are not careful with your design. Logging a warning based on the sender, for example, may result in multiple warnings when there are multiple recipients.

20.1 How checkcompat() Works

When *sendmail* prepares to deliver mail, it first checks the size of the mail message and rejects (bounces) it if it is larger than the limit imposed by the M= delivery agent equate (see §30.4.7). V8.8 *sendmail* then calls the check_compat rule set (see §29.10.4). Next, all versions of *sendmail* call the *checkcompat( )* routine.

The *checkcompat( )* routine lies in a unique position within the *sendmail* code. It is the one place where both the sender and recipient addresses are available at the same time. Since it precedes actual delivery, all the information needed for delivery is available to you for checking.

If *checkcompat( )* returns EX_OK, as defined in *<sysexits.h>*, the mail message is considered okay and delivered. Otherwise, the message is bounced. If you wish the message to be requeued instead of bounced, you can return EX_TEMPFAIL.

Again note that the *checkcompat( )* routine is called once for each recipient.

20.1.1 Arguments Passed to checkcompat()

The *checkcompat( )* is found in the C language source file *src/conf.c*. Inside that file you will find it declared like this:

```
checkcompat(to, e)
        register ADDRESS *to;
        register ENVELOPE *e;
```

Here, to is a pointer to a structure of *typedef* ADDRESS that contains information about the recipient. And e is a pointer to a structure (actually a linked list of structures) of *typedef* ENVELOPE that contains information about the current envelope.

The members of the ADDRESS *to structure are shown in Table 20-1. Note that these members are correct for V8.8 *sendmail* only. Also note that the table shows only those members that may be useful in a *checkcompat( )* routine (see *sendmail.h* for the other members of *to).

Table 20–1: ADDRESS *to Members

Type	Member	Description
char *	q_paddr	The address in a form suitable for printing
char *	q_user	The user part ($:) from rule set 0 (see §29.6)
char *	q_ruser	The login name for this user, if known
char *	q_host	The host part ($@) from rule set 0 (see §29.6)
struct mailer *	q_mailer	The delivery agent ($#) from rule set 0 (see §29.6)
u_long	q_flags	Status flags (see Table 37.3.1 in §37.3.1)
uid_t	q_uid	The *uid* of the q_ruser, if known
gid_t	q_gid	The *gid* of the q_ruser, if known
char *	q_home	The home directory (path), if delivery is local
char *	q_fullname	The (gecos) full name of q_ruser, if known
struct address *	q_next	Link to the next ADDRESS in the chain
struct address *	q_alias	The alias that yielded this address
char *	q_owner	The owner of q_alias

The members of the **ENVELOPE** *e structure are shown in Table 20–2. Note that these members are correct for V8.8 *sendmail* only. Also note that the table shows only those members that may be useful in a *checkcompat()* routine (see *sendmail.h* for other members of *e).

Table 20–2: ENVELOPE *e Members

Type	Member	Description
HDR *	e_header	Linked list of headers
time_t	e_ctime	Time message first placed into the queue
ADDRESS	e_from	The sender
ADDRESS *	e_sendqueue	Linked list of recipients
long	e_msgsize	Size of the message in bytes
long	e_flags	Envelope flags (see Table 37-3 in §37.5.12)
int	e_nrcpts	Number of recipients
short	e_hopcount	The hop count for the message

The *checkcompat()* routine is a powerful internal hook inside *sendmail*. It is so internal and powerful, in fact, that if you are truly clever, you can even use *checkcompat()* to modify rewrite rules at runtime (scary but possible).

20.1.2 Global Variables

Over 100 global variables are used by V8.8 *sendmail*. They are all listed in *sendmail.h* and *conf.c* with "lite" comments. Global variables store information such as *sendmail*'s option values, file descriptor values, macro values, class lists, and database access information. Any can be modified inside *checkcompat()*, but before attempting to do so, study the *sendmail* C source code to anticipate any unexpected side effects.

In general, you can use almost any of the global variables when designing your own *checkcompat()* routine. The four most interesting are the following:

RealHostAddr
> The IP address of the sending host. This is a union of several *sockaddr_* types depending on your selection of protocol type. This can be zero for locally submitted mail.

RealHostName
> A string containing the definitive canonical name of the sending host. If it can't be resolved to a name, it will contain the host's IP number in text form, surrounded by square brackets.

LogLevel
> This variable determines the amount of logging that *sendmail* does. It is initially set with the **LogLevel** (L) option (see §34.8.33). You might want to use *checkcompat()* to detect questionable connections and, if any are detected, to increase the value in **LogLevel** to 12. This will cause both sides of every subsequent SMTP connection to be logged.

MatchGecos
> Whether or not unmatched local looking names are looked up in the *passwd*(5) file is under the control of the **MatchGECOS** (G) option (see §34.8.34). Because this kind of lookup is expensive, you might wish to enable it only during nonbusiness hours. One way to do this would be by modifying the **MatchGecos** variable inside *checkcompat()*.

20.2 The Cookbook

In this section we show several examples of possible uses for the *checkcompat()* routine. Among those we illustrate are the following:

- Accept mail only from our domain. (see §20.2.1).

- Cause your workstation to refuse to work as a mail gateway (see §20.2.2).

- Limit the size of guest account messages (see §20.2.3).

- Verify that *identd* information is correct (see §20.2.4).

- Prune **Received:** headers at a firewall (see §20.2.5).

- Reject mail from spamming or mail-bombing sites (see §20.2.6).

Note that in all of the following examples the numbers to the left indicate line numbers for discussion and are not a part of the code.

20.2.1 Accept Mail Only From Our Domain

If your site lives behind a *firewall*,* you might want to use *checkcompat*( ) to configure the internal *sendmail* so that it accepts only mail that is generated locally. The external *sendmail* (outside the firewall or part of it) acts as a proxy. That is, it accepts external mail that is destined for internal delivery from the outside and forwards it to the internal *sendmail*. Because the external *sendmail* is part of the local domain, its envelope always appears to be local. Any external mail that somehow bypasses the firewall needs to be bounced. The way to do this in *checkcompat*( ) looks like this:

```
1    # define OUR_NET_IN_HEX 0x7b2d4300 /* 123.45.67.0 in hex */
2    # define OUR_NETMASK 0xffffff00
3
4    checkcompat(to, e)
5          register ADDRESS *to;
6          register ENVELOPE *e;
7    {
8          if (tTd(49, 1))
9                  printf("checkcompat(to=%s, from=%s)\n",
10                      to->q_paddr, e->e_from.q_paddr);
11
12
13         if (RealHostAddr.sa.sa_family == 0)
14         {
15                 /* this is a locally submitted message */
16                 return EX_OK;
17         }
18         if (RealHostAddr.sa.sa_family != AF_INET ||
19         (RealHostAddr.sin.sin_addr.s_addr & OUR_NETMASK) != OUR_NET_IN_HEX)
20         {
21                 usrerr("553 End run mail not allowed");
22                 e->e_flags |= EF_NO_BODY_RETN;
23                 to->q_status = "5.7.1";
24                 return (EX_UNAVAILABLE);
25         }
26         return (EX_OK);
27    }
```

The usrerr( ) routine (line *21*) causes a warning to be printed at the sending site, and returning EX_UNAVAILABLE (line *24*) causes the mail message to be bounced. Bounced mail is sent back to the originating sender. A copy may also be sent to the local postmaster depending on the setting of PostmasterCopy (P) option (see §34.8.46).

---

* A firewall is a machine that lies between the local network and the outside world. It intercepts and filters all network traffic and rejects any that are considered inappropriate.

The EF_NO_BODY_RETN (line *22*) causes only the headers from the message to be returned in bounced mail, not the original message body. Other envelope flags of interest can be found in Table 37-3 of §37.5.12.

The to->q_status (line *23*) conveys the DSN error status in the bounced mail message (see RFC1893). Here, 5.7.1 indicates a permanent failure (5) of policy status (7), where delivery is not authorized and the message is refused (1).

Also note that this code sample is only a suggestion. It doesn't take into account that RealHostAddr may contain 0x7f000001 (*127.0.0.1* for *localhost*).

20.2.2 *Workstation Refuses to Act as a Mail Gateway*

If you've spent many months getting your workstation set up and running perfectly, you might not want outsiders using it as a knowledgeable mail relay. One way to prevent such unwanted use is to set up *checkcompat()* in *conf.c* so that it rejects any mail from outside your machine that is destined to another site outside your machine. A desirable side effect is that this will also prevent outsiders from directly posting into your internal mailing lists.

```
1       checkcompat(to, e)
2               register ADDRESS *to;
3               register ENVELOPE *e;
4       {
5
6               if (tTd(49, 1))
7                       printf("checkcompat(to=%s, from=%s)\n",
8                               to->q_paddr, e->e_from.q_paddr);
9
10              if (RealHostAddr.sa.sa_family == 0)
11              {
12                      /* this is a locally submitted message */
13                      return (EX_OK);
14              }
15              /* only accept local delivery from outside */
16              if (!bitnset(M_LOCALMAILER, to->q_mailer->m_flags))
17              {
18                      usrerr("553 External gateway use prohibited");
19                      e->e_flags |= EF_NO_BODY_RETN;
20                      to->q_status = "5.7.1";
21                      return (EX_UNAVAILABLE);
22              }
23              return (EX_OK);
24      }
```

Although to (line *16*) is really a linked list of recipients, we check only the current recipient to prevent spurious warnings. This is done because *checkcompat()* is called once for *every* recipient. The check in line *16* is to see whether F=1 delivery agent flag is not set (see §30.8.28) thus implying that the recipient is not local.

Note that this form of rejecting messages will *not* work on a mail hub. In that case more sophisticated checks need to be made. Among them are the following:

- Check all the IP domains for your site. If you have only one, the check in §20.2.1 will work. If you have several (as in an assortment of class C domains), the check will be more complex. If the connecting host is in your domain or one of your domains, you should accept the message.

- The envelope sender's host (e->e_from->q_host) should be checked to see whether it is in the class $=w (see §32.5.8). You can use the *wordinclass*() routine (see §20.3.8) to look it up. If it is in $=w, you should accept the message. This prevents a message from being forwarded through a workstation.

- If the delivery agent for a recipient is *include*, the message is destined for a mailing list. You might wish to screen further at this point.

20.2.3 Limit the Size of Guest Messages

Suppose your site has reserved *uid*s numbered from 900 to 999 for guest users. Because guests are sometimes inconsiderate, you might want to limit the size of their messages and the number of simultaneous recipients they may specify. One way to do this is with the *checkcompat*() routine:

```
 1      #define MAXGUESTSIZE 8000
 2      #define MAXGUESTNRCP 4
 3
 4      checkcompat(to, e)
 5              register ADDRESS *to;
 6              register ENVELOPE *e;
 7      {
 8
 9              if (tTd(49, 1))
10                      printf("checkcompat(to=%s, from=%s)\n",
11                              to->q_paddr, e->e_from.q_paddr);
12
13              /* does q_uid contain a valid uid? -- no external */
14              if (! bitset(QGOODUID, e->e_from.q_flags))
15                      return (EX_OK);
16              if (e->e_from.q_uid < 900 || e->e_from.q_uid > 999)
17                      return (EX_OK);
18              if (e->e_msgsize > MAXGUESTSIZE)
19              {
20                      syslog(LOG_NOTICE,
21                              "Guest %s attempted to send %d size",
22                              e->e_from.q_user, e->e_msgsize);
23                      usrerr("553 Message too large, %d max", MAXGUESTSIZE);
24                      e->e_flags |= EF_NO_BODY_RETN;
25                      to->q_status = "5.7.1";
```

```
26                         return (EX_UNAVAILABLE);
27                 }
28         if (e->e_nrcpts > MAXGUESTNRCP)
29         {
30                 syslog(LOG_NOTICE,
31                         "Guest %s attempted to send %d recipients",
32                         e->e_from.q_user, e->e_nrcpts);
33                 usrerr("553 Too many recipients for guest, %d max",
34                         MAXGUESTNRCP);
35                 e->e_flags &= ~EF_NO_BODY_RETN;
36                 to->q_status = "5.7.1";
37                 return (EX_UNAVAILABLE);
38         }
39         return (EX_OK);
40 }
```

Note that q_uid will have a valid *uid* (QGOODUID will be set) only if the sender is
local (line *14*). For external mail coming in, QGOODUID will be clear.

Also note that we specifically do not return the message body
(EF_NO_BODY_RETN) if the message was returned because it was too large (line
24). But we do return the message body if the message was rejected for too many
recipients (line *35*). Other envelope flags of interest can be found in Table 37-3 of
§37.5.12.

20.2.4 Verify identd Information

When an outside host connects to the local *sendmail* via SMTP, its hostname is
saved in the $s macro (see §31.10.33). If the Timeout.ident option (see §34.8.70)
is nonzero, *sendmail* uses the RFC1413 identification protocol to record the identity
of the host at the other end, that is, the identity of the host that made the connection. That identity is recorded in the $_ macro (see §31.10.1).

If you are unusually picky about the identity of other hosts, you may wish to con-
firm that the host in $s is the same as the host in $_. One way to perform such a
check is with the *checkcompat()* routine:

```
1         checkcompat(to, e)
2                 register ADDRESS *to;
3                 register ENVELOPE *e;
4         {
5                 char *s, *u, *v;
6                 int len;
7                 static char old_s[MAXHOSTNAMELEN];
8
9                 if (tTd(49, 1))
10                        printf("checkcompat(to=%s, from=%s)\n",
11                                to->q_paddr, e->e_from.q_paddr);
12
13                /* if $s is localhost or in $=w, accept it */
14                if ((s = macvalue('s', e)) == NULL)
```

```
15                          return (EX_OK);
16              if (strncasecmp(s, old_s, MAXHOSTNAMELEN-1) == 0)
17                          return (EX_OK);
18              else
19                          (void)sprintf(old_s, "%.*s", MAXHOSTNAMELEN-1, s);
20              if (strcasecmp(s, "localhost") == 0)
21                          return (EX_OK);
22              if (wordinclass(s, 'w') == TRUE)
23                          return (EX_OK);
24
25              if ((u = macvalue('_', e)) == NULL)
26                          return (EX_OK);
27              if ((u = strchr(u, '@')) == NULL)
28                          return (EX_OK);
29              if ((v = strchr(u, ' ')) != NULL)
30                          *v = '\0';
31              len = strlen(u);
32              if (v != NULL)
33                          *v = ' ';
34
35              if (strncasecmp(s, u, len) != 0)
36              {
37                          auth_warning(e, "$s=%s doesn't match $_=%.*s", s, len, u);
38              }
39              return (EX_OK);
40      }
```

First (line *16*) we check to see whether we have already checked this value of $s. If so, we don't check again because *checkcompat()* is called once for each recipient. If $s is new, we save a copy of its value for next time.

Then we make sure that the local host (no matter what its name) is acceptable (lines *20* and *22*). If this is an offsite host, we compare the values of $s and the host part of $_ (line *35*). If they don't match, we insert an X-Authentication-Warning: header (line *37*). This keeps such warnings under the control of the PrivacyOptions.authwarnings (p) option (see §34.8.47).

20.2.5 *Prune Received: Headers at Firewall*

In routing mail outward from a firewall (see §20.2.1), it may be advantageous to replace all the internal Received: headers with one master header. A way to do this with *checkcompat()* looks like this:

```
1       # define OUR_NET_IN_HEX 0x7b2d4300 /* 123.45.67.0 in hex */
2       # define OUR_NETMASK 0xffffff00
3       # define LOOP_CHECK "X-Loop-Check"
4
5       checkcompat(to, e)
6               register ADDRESS *to;
7               register ENVELOPE *e;
8       {
```

```
9              HDR *h;
10             int cnt;
11
12             if (RealHostAddr.sa.sa_family == 0)
13             {
14                     /* this is a locally submitted message */
15                     return EX_OK;
16             }
17             if (RealHostAddr.sa.sa_family != AF_INET ||
18             (RealHostAddr.sin.sin_addr.s_addr & OUR_NETMASK) != OUR_NET_IN_HEX)
19             {
20                     /* not received from the internal network */
21                     return EX_OK;
22             }
23             if (hvalue(LOOP_CHECK, e->e_header) != NULL)
24             {
25                     /* We've stripped them once already */
26                     return EX_OK;
27             }
28             addheader(LOOP_CHECK, "", &e->e_header);
29
30             for (cnt = 0, h = e->e_header; h != NULL; h = h->h_link)
31             {
32                     if (strcasecmp(h->h_field, "received") != 0)
33                             continue;
34                     if (cnt++ == 0)
35                             continue;
36                     clrbitmap(h->h_mflags);
37                     h->h_flags |= H_ACHECK;
38             }
39             return (EX_OK);
40     }
```

Because we are stripping the message of **Received:** headers, we need to be careful. We shouldn't do it if the message originated on the firewall machine (line *12*). We also shouldn't do it if the message originated from outside the internal (firewalled) network (lines *17* and *18*). To prevent possibly disastrous mail loops, we check for a special header (line *23*) and skip stripping again if that header is found. We then add that special header (line *28*), just in case the mail flows though this firewall again.

If it is okay to do so, we scan all the headers (line *30*) looking for all **Received:** headers (line *32*). We skip deleting the first one because it was placed there by the firewall (line *34*). We delete all the others by clearing their ?*flags*? bits (line *36*) and setting the H_ACHECK flag (line *37*). See §20.3.3 for a general discussion of this technique.

Be aware that this is only one possible approach and that, depending on what other hosts on the Internet do to the message, this loop detection may break. A safer but more difficult approach is to rewrite the **Received:** headers themselves and to mask out sensitive information in them.

20.2.6 Reject Mail from Spamming or Mail-bombing Sites

As the Internet grows, your site may become more and more subject to advertising and vengeful attacks from the outside. Advertising attacks are called "spams" and are symptomized by advertisers sending multiple copies of advertisements through your internal mail lists or to several of your users. Vengeful attacks are called "mail bombs" and usually are detected by your mail spool directory filling with a huge number of messages from a single sender.*

To limit your vulnerability to such events (and to others of a similar nature that may be invented in the future), you may screen mail from outside hosts using a combination of a database and *checkcompat*(). First we show you how to set up such a database, then we show you a *checkcompat*() routine for using it.†

The source file for the database will look like this:

```
user@spam.host      spam
user@bomb.host      bomb
```

Here, each left-hand side entry is an email address with a user part, an @, and a host part. We will be screening on the basis of individual sender addresses rather than screening at a sitewide level. The right-hand side is either the word spam to represent a spamming sender or bomb to represent a mail-bombing sender.

If the source file is called */etc/mail/blockusers*, the database will be created like this:

```
% makemap hash /etc/mail/blockusers.db < /etc/mail/blockusers
```

Here, we create a hash *db* style database. For other available styles, see §33.2.

Once the database is in place, your configuration file needs to be told of its existence. To do that, we use the K configuration command (see §33.3):

```
Kbadusers hash -o /etc/mail/blockusers.db
```

For the *m4* configuration technique you would place this declaration under the LOCAL_CONFIG line in your *mc* file (see §19.6.30).

---

* Often in response to one of your users sending an offensive spam.

† You may also screen sender addresses at the SMTP MAIL command with the new V8.8 check_mail rule set (see §29.10.1). Although it can be easier to design check_mail rules, the *checkcompat*() routine can be more powerful.

One possible *checkcompat()* routine to handle all this will look like this:

```
1        checkcompat(to, e)
2                register ADDRESS *to;
3                register ENVELOPE *e;
4        {
5                STAB *map;
6                char *p;
7                int  ret = 0;
8
9                map = stab("badusers", ST_MAP, ST_FIND);
10               if (map == (STAB *)NULL)
11                       return (EX_OK);
12               p = (*map->s_map.map_class->map_lookup)
13                       (&map->s_map, e->e_from.q_paddr, NULL, &ret);
14               if (p == NULL)
15                       return (EX_OK);
16
17               if (strcasecmp(p, "spam") == 0)
18               {
19                       usrerr("553 Spamming mail rejected from %s",
20                               e->e_from.q_paddr);
21                       to->q_status = "5.7.1";
22                       return (EX_UNAVAILABLE);
23               }
24               if (strcasecmp(p, "bomb") == 0)
25               {
26                       usrerr("553 Message rejected from mail-bomber %s",
27                               e->e_from.q_paddr);
28                       e->e_flags &= ~EF_NO_BODY_RETN;
29                       to->q_status = "5.7.1";
30                       return (EX_UNAVAILABLE);
31               }
32               return (EX_OK);
33       }
```

Here we first look up the database named badusers in the symbol table (line *9*). It is okay for the database not to exist (line *11*). If the database exists, we look up the sender's address in it (line *12*). If the address is not found, all is okay (line *15*).

If the address was found in the database, we have a potential bad person. So we first check to see whether the address was marked as a spam (line *17*). If it was, we bounce it with an appropriate error message (line *19*).

We also bounce the message if it is a mail bomb (line *24*). This is fraught with risk however. The bounced mail can fill up the outgoing queue, thereby accomplishing the bomber's ends in a different way. A better approach might be to drop the mail on the floor (see *dropenvelope()* in *envelope.c*), but we leave this as an exercise for the reader.

20.3 Alphabetized V8.8 Subroutines

Many subroutines inside *sendmail* can be very useful in writing your own *checkcompat()* routine. Always try to use *sendmail's* internal routines rather than redesigning your own. Those supplied with *sendmail* have already been screened and tested by a large body of skilled programmers.

In this section we list the ones that we consider most useful and describe how best to use them (see Table 20-3).

Table 20–3: Handy Subroutines for Use with checkcompat()

Subroutine	§	Description
addheader	20.3.1	Add a new header to the list of headers
define	20.3.2	Define a macro
	20.3.3	How to remove a header
hvalue	20.3.4	Look up a header's field by name
macid	20.3.5	Convert a text string macro name into an integer
macvalue	20.3.6	Fetch a macro's value
->map_lookup	20.3.7	Look up a key in an external database
wordinclass	20.3.8	Look up a word in a class

Be aware that these subroutines are documented for V8.8 *sendmail*. If you are using a different version of *sendmail*, you must familiarize yourself with the source before attempting to use them. Mismatched parameters can cause errors that are difficult to diagnose.

addheader()
(void)

20.3.1   Add a new header to the list of headers

The *addheader()* routine is used to add a new header to the existing list of headers. Note that since it does not check for duplicates, you should screen for the existence of a header before adding it (unless it is okay for multiple headers to exist):

```
1       char value[MAXLINE];
2
3       (void)sprintf(value, "Screened by checkcompat() for %s", q_user);
4       (void)addheader("x-screened", value, e->e_header);
```

Memory for the name of the new header and its value are allocated internally by *addheader()*, so automatic variables can be safely passed. Note that the first argument to *addheader()* (line *4*) is the name of the header. If you accidentally include a colon in that argument, the name will be stored with that colon included, and later the header name will be incorrectly emitted with two colons.

Note that *addheader* does not check for the validity of its arguments. If you pass it NULL or an illegal address, you may cause *sendmail* to core-dump and fail. You are dealing with *sendmail* internals here, so be very careful.

define()   *(void)*

20.3.2   *Define a macro*

Macros can be defined and redefined inside *checkcompat()* using the *define()* routine. It is called like this:

```
define( macid, value, envel);
```

Here, `macid` is the literal character in the case of a single-character macro name (such as `'A'`) or the identifying value for a multicharacter name (this latter being derived from a call to *macid()*. The `value` is the value to be assigned to the macro. (Note that if the macro already has a value, that prior value is overwritten.) The `envel` is a pointer to the envelope (in the case of *checkcompat()* it is **e**).

To illustrate, consider the following code fragment that assigns a new value to the macros $A and ${foo}:

```
5        int mid;
6
7        /*
8         * A single-character name is given a value that is the address
9         * of a character constant.
10        */
11       define( 'A', "some text as a value", e);
12
13       /*
14        * A multi-character name is given a value that is in malloc()d
15        * memory space.
16        */
17       mid = macid("{foo}", NULL);
18       define(mid, newstr(to->qpaddr), e);
```

In both cases the `value` stored is in permanent memory. You must not pass a pointer to automatic or volatile memory, because *define()* just stores the pointer, it does not copy the value.[*] In the second example (line *18*), memory is allocated for the string with *newstr()*, another internal routine that allocates room for the string and the string's terminating zero, copies the string into that allocated space, and returns a pointer to the newly allocated string. But be careful to keep track of what you are doing. You can easily create a serious memory leak if you are careless with *newstr()*.

---

[*] Technically, you should not use a string constant because string constants are stored in read-only program space and often may not be changed at runtime, for example, when a macro's value needs to be later modified in place.

The first argument to *macid*() (line *17*) is a string that contains the macro's literal name without a $ prefix. For multicharacter names, the enclosing curly braces are mandatory (see §31.4.2).

See the **–d35** debugging switch (§37.5.120) for a way to watch macros being defined and redefined. Also see *munchstring*() in *readcf.c* if you need to parse a macro's literal name from among other text.

20.3.3   *How to remove a header*

The *sendmail* program's internal routines cannot be used to remove a header from the linked list of headers, but you can prevent one from being emitted into the delivered message by massaging its flags.

Consider the need to suppress custom **X-Accounting:** headers:

```
1    HDR *h;
2
3    for (h = e->e_header; h != NULL; h = h->h_link)
4    {
5            if (strcasecmp(h->h_field, "x-accounting") != 0)
6                    continue;
7            clrbitmap(h->h_mflags);
8            h->h_flags |= H_ACHECK;
9    }
```

Here, we have to manually scan the linked list of headers (line *3*). When the one that is being sought is found (note that the check is not case sensitive, line *5*) we delete it. This is done by first zeroing all the ?*flags*? for the header (line *7*). Then we add the H_ACHECK flag (line *8*) to ensure that the header will be skipped on delivery. See §35.5.16 for a discussion of the effect of the H_ACHECK flag.

hvalue()

20.3.4   *Look up a header's field by name*

The *hvalue*() routine can be used to look up a header and optionally change it, or insert it if it is missing. It is used like this:

```
1    char *field;
2
3    field = hvalue("message-id", e->e_header)
4    if (field == NULL)
5    {
6            /* No Message-ID: in the message, so insert one */
7    }
```

Note that the first argument to *hvalue*() is the name of the header being looked up (line *3*), without a trailing colon. If you accidentally include the colon, the lookup will always fail.

The *hvalue*() routine returns a string that is the field of the header that is looked up (see §35.3). If a particular header name can exist multiple times (such as `Received:`), *hvalue*() will return the first instance. If you need to process all such headers, you will need to scan for them manually.

macid()   *(int)*

20.3.5   *Convert a text string macro name into an integer*

Macros, class names, and rule-set names can be single-character or multicharacter in form. The *macid*() routine converts a macro's name from a text string form (literal form) into an integer. The resulting integer can later be used by other routines such as *macvalue*() and *wordinclass*().

To illustrate, consider the names `A` and `{foo}`:

```
1        int mid;
2
3        mid = macid("A", NULL);
4
5        mid = macid("{foo}", NULL);
```

The first argument to *macid*() must be a string that contains the name to be converted. For a single-character name (line *3*) the name is converted to the character-constant value of the first letter (`"A"` becomes `'A'`). For a multicharacter name (line *5*) the name must be enclosed in curly braces. The name is converted to a unique integer value that is either new or one that was previously assigned by an earlier call to *macid*().

The second argument to *macid* is NULL in our examples because the string in the first argument contained only a name. When other text might appear in the string you may pass a nonnull second argument:

```
1        char *str = "localhost is ${lhost}, so there.";
2        char *cp, *ep;
3        int mid;
4
5        if ((cp = strchr(str, '$')) != NULL)
6        {
7                mid = macid( cp+1, &ep );
8        }
```

The second argument (line *7*) is the address of a character pointer. After the call to *macid*() that character pointer (`ep`) contains the address of the first character following the name—the comma in `str` (line *1*).

macvalue()

20.3.6   *Fetch a macro's value*

The value stored in a macro can be fetched with the *macvalue()* routine. For example,

```
1      char *val;
2      int mid;
3
4      val = macvalue( 'A', e);
5
6      mid = macid( "{foo}", NULL);
7      val = macvalue( mid, e);
```

The first example (line *4*) shows *macvalue()* being used to fetch the value stored in a single-character macro name (**A**). The second (line *6*) shows a technique that is useful for multicharacter names and for times when you must process an arbitrary name in a string. The *macid()* routine converts a macro's literal name into an identifying integer. That integer is then looked up with *macvalue()* to return its value (line *7*).

If the looked up macro is not defined, *macvalue()* returns NULL.

->map_lookup()

20.3.7   *Look up a key in an external database*

Arbitrary keys can be looked up in external databases by using the routines that are indirectly set up when a database is declared. For example, consider a *dbm* database that will store login names as the keys and the words **ok** or **drop** as the values. You would first create a source text file with the *makemap* program (see §33.2). Next you would declare that database in the configuration file:

```
Kbouncelist dbm -o /etc/bouncelist
```

This **K** configuration command (see §33.3) gives the internal symbolic name **bouncelist** to the database.

Values can now be looked up using the following code fragment:

```
1      STAB *map;
2      char *p;
3      int  r = 0;
4
5      map = stab("bouncelist", ST_MAP, ST_FIND);
6      if (map == (STAB *)NULL)
7              return (EX_OK);
8      p = (*map->s_map.map_class->map_lookup)(&map->s_map, to->q_ruser, NULL, &r);
9      if (p == NULL)
10             return (EX_OK);
11
```

```
12    if (strcasecmp(p, "drop") == 0)
13            /* drop the message on the floor */
```

The lookup is performed by calling the addresses stored in **map_lookup** (line *8*). The second argument is the key that is being looked up (here, we use **to->q_ruser**, the login name of the recipient as the key).

Errors are returned in **r**. We ignore those errors here, but you can use them if you wish. They correspond to the error values listed in *<sysexits.h>*. But note that not all lookups change **r** (see *map.c* for specific details).

wordinclass()   *(bool)*

20.3.8   *Look up a word in a class*

The words that form a class (see §32.1.1) are stored as symbols in the symbol table (see §32.2.4). The check to see whether a string of text was included in a given class is done with the *wordinclass()* routine. Single-character class names and multicharacter class names can be searched:

```
1        int mid;
2
3        if (wordinclass( "localhost", 'w') == TRUE)
4                /* yes, it was found */
5
6        mid = macid("{foo}", NULL);
7        if (wordinclass( "localhost", mid) == FALSE)
8                /* no, not found */
```

The first argument to *macid* is a string that contains the word being looked up. Care must be taken to ensure that the first argument is a legal address and not NULL because *wordinclass()* does not check.

The second argument is either an integer character-constant (such as the 'w', line *3*), or an integer identifier returned by *macid()* (line *7*).

III

Administration

The third part of this book covers the initial and day-to-day administration of *sendmail*. Of necessity, such administration must include other thorny issues, such as DNS and security, so we cover those subjects too.

Chapter 21, DNS and sendmail
> Shows how *sendmail* and the Domain Naming System interact, explains how to get them to work together, and offers help in taming the wild MX record.

Chapter 22, Security
> Explains why *sendmail* must run as *root*, then shows many ways to tighten security so that this will not be a problem.

Chapter 23, The Queue
> Shows how the queue is organized, how *sendmail* protects itself from bad files in the queue, and how to process and print the queue.

Chapter 24, Aliases
> Describes the *aliases*(5) file and the various parts that make it up. Also shows how to write a program to perform delivery, and how to manage and print the aliases database.

Chapter 25, Mailing Lists and ˜/.forward
> Illustrates the ins and outs of managing mailing lists, shows how to set up a ˜/.forward file, and presents solutions to various problems with both. This chapter also describes mailing lists and how to produce and manage them; it concludes with full coverage of the ˜/.forward file.

Chapter 26, Logging and Statistics

Explains how to use *syslog*(3) to log *sendmail*'s activities and how to generate statistics from those logs. Describes the effect of signaling the daemon and the use of the **–X** command-line switch.

21

DNS and sendmail

21.1 Overview

DNS stands for Domain Naming System. A domain is any logical or physical collection of related hosts or sites. A naming system is best visualized as an inverted tree of information that corresponds to full qualified hostnames (see Figure 21-1).

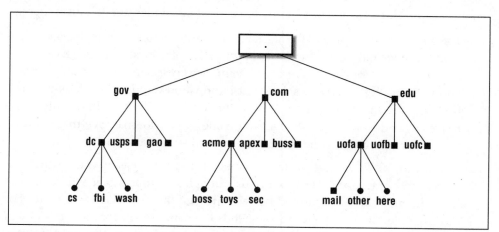

Figure 21–1: Domain names form a tree of information

The parts of a fully qualified name are separated from one another with dots. For example,

    here.uofa.edu

This name describes the machine here that is part of the uofa subdomain of the edu top-level domain. In Figure 21-1 the dot at the top is the "root" of the tree. It is implied but never[*] included in fully-qualified domain names:

```
here.uofa.edu.
             ↑
         implied
```

The root corresponds to (is served by) actual machines.[†] Each has knowledge of all the top-level domains (such as gov, com, etc.) and the server machines for those domains. Each of the top-level domain's servers knows of one or more machines with knowledge of the next level below. For example, the server for edu "knows" about the subdomains uofa, uofb, and uofc but may not know about anything below those subdomains, nor about the other domains next to itself such as com.[‡]

A knowledgeable machine, one that can look up or distribute information about its domain and subdomains, is called a *name server*. Each little black square in the figure represents a name server for a portion of a domain. Each is required to have knowledge only of what is immediately below it. This minimizes the amount of knowledge any given name server must store and administer.

To illustrate the way this distributed information is used, see Figure 21-2 for the steps that are taken when *sendmail* on *here.uofa.edu* (the local host) attempts to connect to *fbi.dc.gov* (the remote host) to send an email message to a user there.

1. The local *sendmail* needs the IP number of the remote host to initiate a network connection. The local *sendmail* asks its local name server (say, *mail.uofa.edu*) for that address. The *mail.uofa.edu* name server may already know the address (having cached that information during a previous inquiry). If so, it gives the requested address to the local *sendmail*, and no further DNS requests need to be made. If the local name server doesn't have that information, it contacts other name servers for the needed information.

2. In the case of *fbi.dc.gov* the local name server next contacts one of the root servers (the dot in the big box in our example). A root server will likely not have the information requested but will indicate the best place to inquire. For our example, the root server recommends the name server for the *.gov* domain and provides our local name server with the address of that *.gov* domain server machine.

---

[*] Well, hardly ever. It can be used under some circumstances to prevent the local domain from being accidently appended improperly.

[†] This used to be a single machine named *ns.internic.net* but is now several machines named *a.root-servers.net*, *b.root-servers.net*, and so on.

[‡] There is also a type of server called "caching." This type doesn't originate information about domains but is able to look up and save information and to supply it on request.

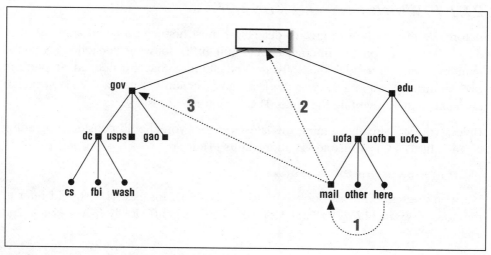

Figure 21-2: How DNS lookups are performed

3. The local name server then contacts the *.gov* name server. This process continues until a name server provides the needed information. As it happens, any name server can return the final answer if it happens to have it in its cache. For our example, *.gov* knows the address for *fbi.dc.gov*. It returns that address to the local name server, which in turn returns the address to the local *sendmail*.

Note that this is a simplified description. The actual practice can be more or less complex depending on who is "authoritative" about which machines and domains and what is cached where.

The *sendmail* program needs the IP address of the machine to which it must connect. That address can be returned by name servers in three possible forms:

- An MX (Mail eXchanger) record lists one or more machines that have agreed to receive mail for a particular site or machine. Multiple MX records are tried in order of cost[*] (least to most). An MX record need not point to the original receiving host. MX records always take precedence over A records.

- An A (Address) record gives the IP address directly.

- A CNAME (Canonical NAME, or alias) record refers *sendmail* to the real name, which may have an A record or MX records.

---

[*] Technically, this field is called the preference. We use cost to clarify that lower values are preferable, whereas preference wrongly connotes that higher values are preferable.

21.1.1 *Which DNS? 4.8.3 or 4.9?*

Before we discuss DNS in greater detail, we must first attend to an administrative detail. Every site on the Internet should run BIND software version 4.8.3 at the minimum. BIND provides the software and libraries that are needed to perform DNS inquiries. Version 4.8.3 was the last stable version before Paul Vixie (while at *dec.com*) started rewriting the code. The current release is 4.9.[*]

Unless you are already running the latest version, you should consider upgrading to V4.9. BIND 4.9 is available via anonymous FTP from

```
ftp://ftp.vix.com/pub/bind/release
```

We won't describe in this book how to install BIND. Instead, you should refer to the book *DNS and BIND* by Paul Albitz and Cricket Liu (O'Reilly & Associates, 2nd edition, 1997).

21.1.2 *Make sendmail DNS Aware*

Not all releases of *sendmail* are ready to use DNS. To determine whether yours is ready, type the following command:

```
% /usr/lib/sendmail -d0.1 -bt < /dev/null
Version 8.8.4
 Compiled with: LOG MIME8TO7 NAMED_BIND NETINET NETUNIX NEWDB SCANF
                USERDB XDEBUG

============ SYSTEM IDENTITY (after readcf) ============
      (short domain name) $w = here
  (canonical domain name) $j = here.uofa.edu
        (subdomain name) $m = uofa.edu
            (node name) $k = here
=======================================================
```

Look for a statement that indicates whether or not your *sendmail* was compiled with NAMED_BIND support (see §18.8.23). If so, it can use DNS. If not, either you will have to get a corrected version from your vendor[†] or you will have to download and compile the latest version of *sendmail* from scratch (see §18.3).

But even if your *sendmail* binary supports DNS, site configuration may not. If your host supports a service-switch file, for instance, make sure it lists dns as the method used to fetch information about hosts.

---

[*] As of the final draft of this manuscript, release 4.9.3 was the most recent.

[†] Sun typically supplies two versions. The one named *sendmail.mx* is able to use DNS.

Another possible problem might be your configuration file. It may, for example, have been derived from the **nodns** FEATURE[*] (see §19.6.18):

```
% grep dns /etc/sendmail.cf
#####  @(#)nodns.m4 8.1 (Berkeley) 8/6/93  #####
```

If it was, as indicated by the phrase **nodns.m4**, you can get *sendmail* back into the DNS business by setting the **ResolverOptions** (**I**) option (see §34.8.55).

If your *sendmail* still seems unable to use DNS, despite your efforts, look for other reasons for failure. Make sure, for example, that your */etc/resolv.conf* file is present and that it contains the address (not the name) of a valid name server machine for your domain. If you are running NIS or NIS+, make sure it is configured to look up hosts with DNS.

21.2 How sendmail Uses DNS

The *sendmail* program uses DNS in four different ways:

- When *sendmail* first starts, it may use DNS to get the canonical name for the local host. That name is then assigned to the $j macro (see §31.10.20).[†] If DNS returns additional names for the local host, those names are assigned to the class $=w (see §32.5.8).

- When another host connects to the local host to transfer mail, the local *send-mail* looks up the other host with DNS to find the other host's canonical name.

- When delivering network SMTP mail, *sendmail* uses DNS to find the address (or addresses) to which it should connect.

- When *sendmail* expands $[and $] in the RHS of a rule, it looks up the host-name (or IP number) between them.

We discuss each of these uses individually later in this chapter.

21.2.1 Determine the Local Canonical Name

All versions of *sendmail* use more or less the same logical process to obtain the canonical name of the local host. As illustrated in the sample program below, *sendmail* first calls *gethostname*(3) to obtain the local host's name. That name may either be a short name or a fully qualified one depending on which comes first in

---

[*] Note that the **nodns** FEATURE did nothing in V8.7 *sendmail.*

[†] Prior to V8 *sendmail,* the canonical name was stored in the $w macro (see §31.10.40) and *sendmail* initialized only the $j macro (see §31.10.20). Beginning with V8 *sendmail, sendmail* initializes both of those variables, among others (see §31.1).

the */etc/hosts* file. If the call to *gethostname*(3) fails, the name of the local host is
set to *localhost*:

```
#include <sys/types.h>
#include <sys/socket.h>
#include <sys/param.h>
#include <netdb.h>
#include <stdio.h>

main()
{
        char hostbuf[MAXHOSTNAMELEN];
        struct hostent *hp;

        /* Get the local hostname */
        if (gethostname(hostbuf, sizeof(hostbuf)) < 0)
                strcpy(hostbuf, "localhost");
        printf("hostname = \"%s\"\n", hostbuf);

        /* canonicalize it and get aliases */
        if((hp = gethostbyname(hostbuf)) == NULL)
                perror("gethostbyname"), exit(2);
        printf("canonical = \"%s\"\n", hp->h_name);
        while (*hp->h_aliases != NULL)
        {
                printf("alias: \"%s\"\n", *hp->h_aliases);
                ++hp->h_aliases;
        }
}
```

The local hostname is then given to the *gethostbyname* routine (see §37.5.186) to
obtain the canonical name for the local host. That same routine also returns any
aliases (other names for the local host).

On some Sun and Ultrix machines that are set up to use NIS services, the canonical
name is the short name, and a fully qualified name that should have been the
canonical name appears as an alias. For such systems you must link with the BIND
library (*libresolv.a*) when compiling this program or compiling *sendmail*. That
library gets its information from DNS rather than from NIS. But note that V8.7 and
above versions of *sendmail* do the intelligent thing and use the canonical name
that was found as the aliases if it exists.

If a good BIND library is not available, or if it is not convenient to compile and
install a new version of *sendmail*, you can circumvent the short name assigned to
$j by defining $j like this:

```
Dmyour domain here
Dj$w.$m
```

The *canonical name* is your site's hostname with a dot and your domain name appended. These two lines cause $j to have your host's fully qualified (and canonical) name assigned to it.

The canonical name found by *gethostbyname*(3) is assigned as the value of the $w macro. The short name and any aliases are added to the class $=w.

The result of all these lookups can be viewed by running *sendmail* with a −d0.4 debugging switch (see §37.5.2). The actual DNS lookups can be watched with the −d8.8 debugging switch (see §37.5.35).

21.2.2 Look Up a Remote Host's Name

When *sendmail* begins to run as a daemon, it creates a socket, binds to that socket, and listens for incoming SMTP connections. When a remote host connects to the local host, *sendmail* uses the *accept*(2) library routine to accept the connection. The *accept*(2) routine provides the IP address of the remote machine to *sendmail*. The *sendmail* program then calls *gethostbyaddr*(2) to convert that IP address to a canonical (official) hostname.

The *sendmail* program needs the canonical hostname for four reasons:

- The remote hostname is compared to the local hostname to prevent *sendmail* from connecting to itself.

- The remote hostname claimed in the HELO SMTP line is compared to the canonical name. If they differ, *sendmail* complains.

- The macro $s is assigned the canonical hostname as its value.

- The canonical name is included in many log messages produced by the setting of the LogLevel (L) option (see §34.8.33) and is available for inclusion in Received: header (see §35.10.25) lines.

If the Timeout.ident (r) option (see §34.8.70.10) is greater than zero, the local host also connects to the *identd*(8) daemon at the sending host to discover who opened the connection. If available, that user and host information is assigned to the $_ macro (see §31.10.1).

21.2.3 Look Up Addresses for Delivery

When *sendmail* prepares to connect to a remote host for transfer of mail, it first performs a series of checks that vary from version to version. All versions accept an IP address surrounded with square brackets as a literal address and use it as is.

Beginning with V8.1, *sendmail* checks to see whether the host part of the address is surrounded with square brackets. If so, it skips looking up MX records. (We'll elaborate on MX records soon.)

Beginning with V8.8, *sendmail* first checks to see whether the F=0 flag (see §30.8.1) is set for the selected delivery agent. If it is set, *sendmail* skips looking up MX records.

If *sendmail* is allowed to look up MX records, it calls the *res_search*(3) BIND library routine[*] to find all the MX records for the host. If it finds any MX records, it sorts them in order of cost, selecting the least cost first. If V8 *sendmail* finds two costs that are the same, it randomizes the selection between the two when sorting.[†] After all MX records are found, or if no MX records were found, *sendmail* adds the host specified by the `FallbackMXhost` (V) option (see §34.8.25), if there was one, to that list.

The *sendmail* program then tries to deliver the message to each host in the list of MX hosts, one at a time, until one of them succeeds or until they all fail. Beginning with V8.8 *sendmail*, any host in the list that returns a 5*xy* SMTP code (permanent failure) causes all subsequent MX hosts to be ignored (but temporary and connect failures continue to the next MX host as usual).

If no MX records are found, *sendmail* tries to deliver the message to the single original host. If all else fails, *sendmail* attempts to deliver to the host listed with the `FallbackMXhost` (V) option.

Whether *sendmail* tries to connect to the original host or to a list of MX hosts, it calls *gethostbyname*(2) to get the network address for each. It then opens a network connection to that address and attempts to send SMTP mail.

21.2.4 The $[and $] Operators

The `$[` and `$]` operators (see §28.6.6) are used to canonicalize a hostname. Here is a simplified description of the process.

Each lookup is actually composed of many lookups that occur in the form of a loop within a loop. In the outermost loop, the following logic is used:

- If the address has at least one dot somewhere in it, *sendmail* looks up that address unmodified first.

- If the unmodified address is not found and the RES_DNSRCH bit is set (see the `ResolverOptions` (I) option, §34.8.55), *sendmail* looks up variations on the domain part of the address. The default domain is tried first (for a host in the *sub* subdomain at *dc.gov*, that would be *sub.dc.gov*, thus looking up

---

[*] If the `ServiceSwitchFile` option (see §34.8.61) lists a file that defines hosts as being looked up with NIS, all DNS lookups are skipped.

[†] Note that this is broken in many older versions of *sendmail*. Also note that when the MX record points to the local host, all MX records with a cost greater than the local host are tossed. (See §31.10.40 for a description of this process.)

host.sub.dc.gov). If that fails, BIND 4.8 then throws away the lowest part of the domain and tries again (looks up *host.dc.gov*). BIND 4.9 uses the `search` attribute, if given, and tries that list of possible domains.

- If the address has no dots and the RES_DEFNAMES bit is set (see the `ResolverOptions` (I) option, §34.8.55), *sendmail* tries the single default domain (looks up *host.sub.dc.gov*). This is for compatibility with older versions of DNS.

Each lookup described above is performed by using the following steps:

- Try the hostname with a T_ANY query that requests all the cached DNS records for that host. If it succeeds, A records and/or MX records may be among those returned. However, success is not guaranteed, because sometimes only NS (name server) records are returned. In that instance the following steps are also taken.

- Try the hostname with a T_A query that requests the A record for that host.

- Try the hostname with a T_MX query that requests MX records for the host.

Each query searches the data returned as follows:

- Search for a CNAME (alias) record. If one is found, replace the initial hostname (the alias) with the canonical name returned and start over.

- Search for an A record (the IP address). If one is found, the hostname that was just used to query is considered the canonical address.

- Search for an MX record. If one is found and a default domain has not been added, treat the MX record like an A record. For example, if the input hostname is *sub.dc.gov* and an MX record is found the MX record is considered official. If, on the other hand, the input hostname has no domain added (is *sub*) and the query happens to stumble across *sub.dc.gov* as the MX record, the following searches are also tried.

- If an MX record is found and no MX record has been previously found, the looked-up hostname is saved for future use. For example, if the query was for *sub.dc.gov* and two MX records were returned (*hostA.sub.dc.gov* and *hostB.sub.dc.gov*), *sub.dc.gov* is saved for future use.

- If no MX record is found, but one was found previously, the previous one is used. This assumes that the search is normally from most to least complex (*sub.sub.dc.gov*, *sub.dc.gov*, *dc.gov*).

All this apparent complexity is necessary to deal with wildcard MX records (see §21.3.4) in a reasonable and successful way.

21.3 Set Up MX Records

An MX record is simply the method used by DNS to route mail bound for one machine to another instead. An MX record is created by a single line in one of your *named*(8) files:

```
hostA    IN      MX 10 hostB
```

This line says that all mail destined for hostA in your domain should instead be delivered to hostB in your domain. The IN says that this is an Internet-type record, and the 10 is the cost[*] for using this MX record.

An MX record may point to another host or to the original host:

```
hostA    IN      MX 0 hostA
```

This line says that mail for hostA will be delivered to hostA. Such records may seem redundant, but they are not. We'll cover why shortly.

A host can have multiple MX records (one pointing to itself or not):

```
hostA    IN      MX 0   hostA
         IN      MX 10  hostB
```

Here, hostA has the lowest cost (0 versus 10 for hostB), so delivery will be attempted to itself first. If hostA is down, delivery will be attempted to hostB host instead.

Usually, MX records point to hosts inside the same domain. Therefore managing them does not require the cooperation of others. But it is legal for MX records to point to hosts in different domains:

```
hostA    IN      MX 0   hostA
         IN      MX 10  host.other.domain.
```

Here, you must contact the administrator at other.domain and obtain permission before creating this MX record. We cover this concept in more detail when we discuss disaster preparation later in this chapter.

Although MX records are usually straightforward, there can be a few problems associated with them.

---

[*] Technically, this field is called the preference. We use cost to clarify that lower values are preferable, whereas preference wrongly connotes that higher values are preferable.

21.3.1 MX Must Point to an A Record

The A record for a host is a line that gives the host's IP address.

```
hostC  IN     A    123.45.67.8
```

Here, `hostC` is the host's name. The `IN` says this is an Internet-type record. The `A` marks this as an A record. The `123.45.67.8` is the IP address for the host `hostC`.

An MX record must point to a hostname that has an A record. To illustrate, consider the following:

```
hostA  IN     MX  10 hostB        ← illegal
       IN     MX  20 hostC
hostB  IN     MX  10 hostC
hostC  IN     A   123.45.67.8
```

Note that `hostB` lacks an A record but `hostC` has one. It is illegal to point an MX record at a host that lacks an A record. Therefore the first line above is illegal, whereas the second line is legal.

Although such a mistake is difficult to make when maintaining your own domain tables, it can easily happen to you if you rely on a name server in someone else's domain, as shown:

```
hostA    IN     MX  10 mail.other.domain.
```

The other administrator might, for example, retire the machine `mail` and replace its A record with an MX record that points to a different machine. Unless you are notified of the change, your MX record will suddenly become illegal.

21.3.2 MX to CNAME Causes Extra Lookups

The *sendmail* program is frequently more forgiving than other MTAs because it accepts an MX record that points to a CNAME record. The presumption is that, eventually, the CNAME will correctly point to an A record. But beware, this kind of indirection can cost additional DNS lookups. Consider this example of an exceptionally bad setup:

```
hostA    IN     MX  10 mailhub
mailhub  IN     CNAME  nfsmast
nfsmast  IN     CNAME  hostB
hostB    IN     A 123.45.67.89
```

First, *sendmail* looks up `hostA` and gets an MX record pointing to `mailhub`. Since there is only a single MX record, *sendmail* considers `mailhub` to be official. Next, `mailhub` is looked up to find an A record (IP address), but instead a CNAME (**nfs-**

mast) is returned. Now *sendmail* must look up the CNAME **nfsmast** to find its A record. But again a CNAME is returned instead of an A record. So *sendmail* must again look for an A record (this time with **hostB**). Finally, *sendmail* succeeds by finding the A record for **hostB**, but only after a few too many lookups.

The correct way to form the above DNS file entries is as follows:

```
hostA     IN      MX  10 hostB
mailhub   IN      CNAME   hostB
nfsmast   IN      CNAME   hostB
hostB     IN      A 123.45.67.89
```

In general, try to construct DNS records in such a way that the fewest lookups are required to resolve any A or MX records.

21.3.3 MX Records Are Nonrecursive

Consider the following MX setup, which causes all mail for **hostA** to be sent to **hostB** and all mail for **hostB** to be sent to **hostB**, or to **hostC** if **hostB** is down:[*]

```
hostA     IN      MX  10 hostB
hostB     IN      MX  10 hostB
          IN      MX  20 hostC
```

One might expect *sendmail* to be smart and deliver mail for **hostA** to **hostC** if **hostB** is down. But *sendmail* won't do that. It does not try to recursively look for additional MX records. If it did, it could get hopelessly entangled in MX loops. Consider the following:

```
hostA     IN      MX  10 hostB
hostB     IN      MX  10 hostB
          IN      MX  20 hostC
hostC     IN      MX  10 hostA     ← potential loop
```

If your intention is to have **hostA** MX to two other hosts, then you must state that explicitly:

```
hostA     IN      MX  10 hostB
          IN      MX  20 hostC
hostB     IN      MX  10 hostB
          IN      MX  20 hostC
```

Another reason *sendmail* refuses to follow MX records beyond the target host is that costs in such a situation are undefined. Consider the example with the potential loop above. What is the cost of **hostA** when MX'd by **hostB** to **hostC**? Should it be the minimum of 10, the maximum of 20, the mean of 15, or the sum of 30?

---

[*] We are fudging for the sake of simplicity. Here, we assume that all the hosts also have A records.

21.3.4 Wildcard MX Records

Wildcard MX records provide a shorthand for MX'ing many hosts with a single MX record:

```
    *.dc.gov.        IN  MX  10 hostB
```

This says that any host in the domain .dc.gov (where that host doesn't have any record of its own) should have its mail forwarded to hostB.

```
    ; domain is .dc.gov
    *.dc.gov.        IN  MX  10 hostB
    hostA            IN  MX  10 hostC
    hostB            IN  A   123.45.67.8
```

Here, mail to hostD (no record at all) will be forwarded to hostB. But the wildcard MX record will be ignored for hostA and hostB, because each has its own record.

Care must be exercised in setting up wildcard MX records. It is easy to create ambiguous situations that DNS may not be be able to handle correctly. Consider the following, for example:

```
    ; domain is sub.dc.gov
    *.dc.gov.        IN  MX  10 hostB.dc.gov.
    *.sub.dc.gov.    IN  MX  10 hostC.dc.gov.
```

Here, an unqualified name such as just plain hostD matches both wildcard records. This is ambiguous, so DNS automatically picks the most complete one (*.sub.dc.gov.) and supplies that MX record to *sendmail*.

One compelling weakness of wildcard MX records is that they match any hostname at all, even for machines that don't exist:

```
    ; domain is sub.dc.gov
    *.dc.gov.        IN  MX  10 hostB.dc.gov.
```

Here, mail to *foo.dc.gov* will be forwarded to hostB.dc.gov, even if there is no host *foo* in that domain.

Wildcard MX records almost never have any appropriate use on the Internet. They are often misunderstood and are often used just to save the effort of typing hundreds of MX records. They do, however, have legitimate uses behind firewall machines and on non-Internet networks.

21.3.5 What? They Ignore MX Records?

Many older MTAs on the network ignore MX records, and some Sun sites wrongly run the non-MX version of *sendmail* (that is, they should use */usr/lib/sendmail.mx*). Because of this, you will occasionally find some sites that insist on sending mail to a host even though that host has been explicitly MX'd to another.

To illustrate why this is bad, consider a UUCP host that has only an MX record. It has no A record because it is not on the network:

```
uuhost    IN    MX 10 uucpserver
```

Here, mail to uuhost will be sent to uucpserver, which will forward the message to uuhost with UUCP software. An attempt to ignore this MX record will fail because uuhost has no other records. Similar problems can arise for printers with direct network connections, terminal servers, and even workstations that don't run an SMTP daemon such as *sendmail.*

If you believe in DNS and disdain sites that don't, you can simply ignore the offending sites. In this case the mail will fail if your MX'd host doesn't run a *sendmail* daemon (or another MTA). This is not as nasty as it sounds. There is actually considerable support for this approach; failure to obey MX records is a clear violation of published network protocols. RFC1123, *Host Requirements*, section 5.3.5, notes that obeying MX records is mandatory.

On the other hand, if you want to ensure that all mail is received, even on a workstation whose mail is MX'd elsewhere, you can run the *sendmail* daemon on every machine.

21.3.6 *Caching MX Records*

Although you are not required to have MX records for all hosts, there is good reason to consider doing so. To illustrate, consider the following host that only has an A record:

```
hostB          IN A   123.45.67.8
```

When *sendmail* first looks up this host, it asks the local name server for all records. Because there is only an A record, that is all it gets.

But note that asking for all records caused the local name server to cache the information. The next time *sendmail* looks up this same host, the local name server will return the A record from its cache. This is faster and reduces Internet traffic. The cached information is "nonauthoritative" (because it is a copy) and includes no MX records (because there are none).

When *sendmail* gets a nonauthoritative reply that lacks MX records, it is forced to do another DNS lookup. This time, it specifically asks for MX records. In this case there are none, so it gets none.

Because hostB lacks an MX record, *sendmail* performs a DNS lookup each and every time mail is sent to that host. If hostB were a major mail-receiving site, its lack of an MX record would be causing many *sendmail* programs, all over the world, to waste network bandwidth with otherwise useless DNS lookups.

We strongly recommend that every host on the Internet have at least one MX record. As a minimum, it can simply point to itself with a 0 cost:

```
hostB          IN A   123.45.67.8
               IN MX  0 hostB
```

This will not change how mail is routed to hostB but will reduce the number of DNS lookups required.

21.3.7   Ambiguous MX Records

RFC974 leaves the treatment of ambiguous MX records to the implementor's discretion. This has generated much debate in *sendmail* circles. Consider the following:

```
foo     IN MX 10 hostA
foo     IN MX 20 hostB          ← mail from hostB to foo
foo     IN MX 30 hostC
```

When mail is sent from a host (hostB) that is an MX record for the receiving host (foo), all MX records that have a cost equal to or greater than that of hostB must be discarded. The mail is then delivered to the remaining MX host with the lowest cost (hostA). This is a sensible rule, because it prevents hostB from wrongly trying to deliver to itself.

It is possible to configure hostB so that it views the name foo as a synonym for its own name. Such a configuration results in hostB never looking up any MX records because it recognizes mail to foo as local.

But what should happen if hostB does not recognize foo as local and if there is no hostA?

```
                           ← no hostA
foo     IN MX 20 hostB          ← mail from hostB to foo
foo     IN MX 30 hostC
```

Again, RFC974 says that when mail is being sent from a host (hostB) that is an MX record for the receiving host (foo), all MX records that have a cost equal to or greater than that of hostB must be discarded. In this example that leaves *zero* MX records. Three courses of action are now open to *sendmail*, but RFC974 doesn't say which it should use:

- Assume that this is an error condition. Clearly, *hostB* should have been configured to recognize *foo* as local. It didn't (hence the MX lookup and discarding in the first place), so it must not have known what it was doing. V8 *sendmail* with the TryNullMXList (w) option (see §34.8.71) not set (undeclared or declared as false) will bounce the mail message.

- Look to see whether *foo* has an A record. If it does, go ahead and try to deliver the mail message directly to *foo*. If it lacks an A record, bounce the message. This approach runs the risk that *foo* may not be configured to properly accept mail (thus causing mail to disappear down a black hole). Still, this approach may be desirable in some circumstances. V8 *sendmail* with the `TryNullMXList` (w) option (see §34.8.71) set always tries to connect to *foo*.[*]

- Assume (even though it has not been configured to do so) that *foo* should be treated as local to *hostB*. No version of *sendmail* makes this assumption.

This situation is not an idle exercise. Consider the MX record for uuhost presented in the previous section:

```
uuhost   IN   MX 10 uucpserver
```

Here, uuhost has no A record, because it is connected to uucpserver via a dial-up line. If uucpserver is not configured to recognize uuhost as one of its UUCP clients, and if mail is sent from uucpserver to uuhost, it will query DNS and get itself as the MX record for uuhost. As we have shown, that MX record is discarded, and an ambiguous situation has developed.

21.4 How to Use nslookup

If your site is connected to the Internet, you can use the *nslookup*(1) program to interactively find MX and other records. To run *nslookup*, just type its name:

```
% nslookup
```

Note that you may have to give the full pathname. Under SunOS, *nslookup* lives in the */usr/etc* directory; under Ultrix, in */usr/ucb*; and under HP-UX, in */usr/bin*.

Once *nslookup* is running, it prints the name of your default name server and the IP address for that machine, then a > character as a prompt and awaits input:

```
Server:  Your.Main.Server
Address:  123.45.67.8

>
```

To tell *nslookup* to look up only MX records,[†] use the *set* command:

```
> set type=mx
>
```

---

[*] As does the UIUC version of IDA *sendmail*. Other versions of IDA (such as KJS) do not.

[†] Beginning with V8.7 *sendmail*, you can also use the /mx command in –bt rule-testing mode (see §38.5.2) to look up MX records.

Now look up some real hosts and domains. First look up the domain *sendmail.org* by entering its name at the prompt:

```
> sendmail.org.
```

Note the trailing dot that tells *nslookup*(1) that the local, default domain should not be appended prior to the lookup. The output produced by the above lookup looks like this:

```
> sendmail.org.
Server:
Address:  123.45.67.8

sendmail.org    preference = 20, mail exchanger = mail1.reference.com
sendmail.org    preference = 30, mail exchanger = mail2.reference.com
sendmail.org    preference = 10, mail exchanger = knecht.oxford.reference.com
mail1.reference.com    inet address = 206.171.3.24
mail2.reference.com    inet address = 128.102.240.18
knecht.oxford.reference.com    inet address = 204.247.98.2
>
```

The first two lines again show the name and IP address of the local DNS server. The next three lines show that the domain `sendmail.org` has three MX records. Mail addressed to that domain is sent to the machine with the lowest preference (cost), which happens to be `knecht.oxford.reference.com`.[*] If that machine is down (or not accepting mail), the message is sent to the machine with the next higher cost, `mail1.reference.com`. The last three lines show the IP addresses (A records) for those machines.

Now look up a real UUCP host, *lady*. Enter its name as if it were a part of the *icsi.berkeley.edu* domain:

```
> lady.icsi.berkeley.edu.
```

The output produced shows that *lady* has an MX record:

```
lady.icsi.berkeley.edu    preference = 5, mail exchanger = icsib.ICSI.Berkeley.EDU
icsib.ICSI.Berkeley.EDU inet address = 128.32.201.15
>
```

Mail sent to `lady.icsi.berkeley.edu` is instead delivered to the machine named `icsib.ICSI.Berkeley.EDU`, which in turn forwards that mail over a dial-up line to the UUCP host *lady*.

---

[*] Note that case is not significant in domain names; all of the following are the same: org, OrG, ORG.

Machines that have MX records do not necessarily have A records. The host *lady* is such a machine. You tell *nslookup*(1) to look up an A record with the *set* command:

```
> set type=a
> lady.berkeley.edu.

*** No address information available for lady.berkeley.edu.
```

The *nslookup*(1) program is a useful tool for performing all the same lookups that are done by *sendmail*. Each type of lookup corresponds to a *set type*. The list of some available *nslookup*(1) types is shown in Table 21-1.

Table 21-1: Some nslookup Types

Type	Description
a	IP address
cname	Canonical name for an alias
hinfo	Host CPU and operating system type
mx	Mail exchanger records
ns	Name server record
any	Union of all records

To exit *nslookup*(1), just type *exit* (or Control-D if that fails).

21.5 Prepare for Disaster

Disasters can take many forms and, by their very nature, are unexpected. If DNS and mail are to continue to work, expecting the unexpected is vital. The kinds of disasters that one must anticipate vary from the mundane to the catastrophic:

- A reboot or scheduled down-time for dumps on the mail or DNS server should only cause mail to be delayed, not lost.

- A failed component on the mail or DNS server could cause mail delivery to be delayed anywhere from a few hours to a few days. A delay of over three to five days could cause many hosts to bounce queued mail unless steps are taken to receive that mail elsewhere.

- Natural disasters can disrupt site or network connectivity for weeks. The Loma Prieta earthquake on the West Coast of the United States lasted only a few minutes but knocked out electric power to many areas for far longer. Fear of gas leaks prevented repowering many buildings for up to two weeks. A hurricane, flood, fire, or even an errant backhoe could knock out your institution for weeks.

21.5.1 Offsite MX Hosts

When mail can't be received, whether because of a small event or a large disaster, an offsite MX host can save the day. An offsite MX host is simply another machine that can receive mail for your site when your site is unavailable. The location of the offsite machine depends on your situation. For a subdomain at one end of a microwave link, having an offsite host on the other side of the microwave might be sufficient. For a large site, such as a university, a machine at another university (possibly in a different state or country) would be wise.

Before we show how to set up offsite MX hosts, note that offsite MX hosts are not an unmixed blessing. If an offsite MX host does not handle mail reliably, you could lose mail. In many cases it is better not to have an offsite MX host than to have an unreliable one. Without an MX site, mail will normally be queued on the sending host. A reliable MX backup is useful, but an unreliable one is a disaster.

You should not unilaterally select a host to function as an offsite MX host. To set up an offsite MX host, you need to negotiate with the managers of other sites. By mutual agreement, another site's manager will configure that other machine to accept mail bound for your site (possibly queueing weeks' worth of mail) and configure that site to forward that mail to yours when your site comes back up.

For example, suppose your site is in the state of Iowa, in the United States. Further suppose that in Northern Japan there is a site with which you are friendly. You could negotiate with that site's manager to receive and hold your mail in a disaster. When the site is set up to do so, you first add a high-cost MX record for it:

```
mailhost.uiowa.edu.    IN    MX 2      mailhost.uiowa.edu.
mailhost.uiowa.edu.    IN    MX 10     backup.uiowa.edu.
mailhost.uiowa.edu.    IN    MX 900    pacific.north.jp.    ← note
```

To be sure the MX works, send mail to yourself via that new MX site:

```
% mail you%mailhost.uiowa.edu@pacific.north.jp*
```

Here, the `%` in the address causes the message to first be delivered to *pacific.north.jp*. That machine then throws away its own name and converts the remaining `%` to an `@`. The result is then mailed back to you at

```
you@mailhost.uiowa.edu
```

This verifies that the disaster MX machine can get mail to your site when it returns to service.

---

* This example presumes that *pacific.north.jp* can handle the `%` "hack." Most places do, so this is probably a safe assumption.

During a disaster the first sign of trouble will be mail for your site suddenly appearing in the queue at *pacific.north.jp*. The manager there should notice and set up a separate queue to hold the incoming mail until your site returns to service (see §23.7.1). When your site recovers, you can contact that manager and arrange for a queue run to deliver the backlog of mail.

If your site is out of service for weeks, the backlog of mail might be partly on tape or some other backup media. You might even want to negotiate an artificially slow feed so that your local spool directory won't overfill.

Even in minor disasters an MX host can save much grief because delivery will be serialized. Without an MX host, every machine in the world that had mail for your machine would try to send it at the same time, that is, when your machine returns to service. That could overload your machine and even crash it, causing the problem to repeat over and over.

21.5.2 Offsite Servers

A disaster MX is good only as long as your DNS services stay alive to advertise it. Most sites have multiple name server machines to balance the load of DNS lookups and to provide redundancy in case one fails. Unfortunately, few sites have offsite name servers as a hedge against disaster. Consider the disaster MX record developed above:

```
mailhost.uiowa.edu.   IN   MX 900   pacific.north.jp.
```

Ideally, one would want *pacific.north.jp* to queue all mail until the local site is back in service. Unfortunately, all DNS records contain a Time To Live (TTL) that may or may not be present in the declaration line:

```
mailhost.uiowa.edu.   IN   MX 900   pacific.north.jp.
                      ↑
                  TTL implied
```

```
mailhost.uiowa.edu. 86400  IN   MX 900   pacific.north.jp.
                      ↑
          TTL specified as 24 hours in seconds
```

When other sites look up the local site, they cache this record. They will not look it up again until 24 hours have passed. Therefore if an earthquake strikes, all other sites will forget about this record after 24 hours and will not be able to look it up again.

In general, records set up for disaster purposes should be given TTLs that are over a month:

```
mailhost.uiowa.edu. 3600000  IN   MX 900   pacific.north.jp.
                      ↑
         TTL specified as 41 days in seconds
```

But note that TTLs should be the same for all records so that they will all time out
the same:

```
mailhost.uiowa.edu.  3600000 IN   MX 2     mailhost.uiowa.edu.
mailhost.uiowa.edu.  3600000 IN   MX 10    backup.uiowa.edu.
mailhost.uiowa.edu.  3600000 IN   MX 900   pacific.north.jp.
```

If you gave the disaster record a long TTL and left the default for your normal MX
records, your normal records would time out and disappear from other sites'
caches. This would result in all mail suddenly and mysteriously going to the disaster host when there was no disaster to cause it.

Note that long TTLs can make updates to your DNS files awkward. Updates won't
take effect until the TTL times out. If you anticipate a future change, say a rear-
rangement of your MX records, you can change the TTLs to 2 hours, wait a month
for the long TTL to time out, then make and test your changes.[*]

If many hosts at your site receive mail (rather than a central mail server), it is necessary to add a disaster record for each. Unfortunately, when the number of such
hosts at your site is greater than 100 or so, individual disaster MX records become
difficult to manage simply because of scale.

At such sites, a better method of disaster preparedness is to set up *pacific.north.jp*
as another primary DNS server for the local site. There are two advantages to this
"authoritative" backup server approach:

- An offsite primary server eliminates the need to set up individual MX disaster
  records.

- An out-of-country primary server can lower the network impact of DNS
  lookups of your site.

Unfortunately, setting up an offsite or out-of-country server can be extremely difficult. We won't show you how to do that here. Instead, we refer you to the book
DNS and BIND by Paul Albitz and Cricket Liu (O'Reilly & Associates, 2nd edition,
1997).

---

[*] And hope that no disaster strikes in the meanwhile. A better technique is to set up an offsite secondary DNS server with a large TTL in the SOA record.

21.6 Pitfalls

- When *sendmail* finds multiple A records for a host (and no MX records), it tries them in the order returned by DNS. DNS usually returns the A record that is on the same network first. The *sendmail* program assumes that DNS returns addresses in a useful order. If the address that *sendmail* always tries first is not the most appropriate, look for problems with DNS, not with *sendmail*.

- There is no way to discover that another site has used yours as a disaster MX site unless someone at that other site tells you. Instead, you may one day suddenly discover many queued messages from outside your site destined for some host you've never heard of before.

- Under old versions of DNS an error in the zone file causes the rest of the file to be ignored. The effect is as though many of your hosts suddenly disappeared. This problem has been fixed in 4.8.3 and 4.9.x.

- Sites with a central mail hub should give that hub the role of a primary DNS server. If */etc/resolv.conf* contains `localhost` as its first record, lookups will be faster. Failure to make the mail hub a DNS server runs the risk of mail failing and queueing when the hub is up but the other DNS servers are down or unreachable.

- Prior to V8.8 *sendmail* the maximum number of MX records that could be listed for a single host was 20. Some sites, such as *aol.com*, will reach that limit soon and exceed it. Beginning with V8.8 *sendmail*, that maximum has been increased to 100.

22

Security

The *sendmail* program can be an open door to abuse. Unless the administrator is careful, the misuse or misconfiguration of *sendmail* can lead to an insecure and possibly compromised system. Since *sendmail* is usually installed to run as an *suid root* process, it is a prime target for intrusion. The "Internet worm," for example, used a flaw in old versions of *sendmail* as one way to gain entry to thousands of machines.[*] If *sendmail* is not properly installed, external probes over networks can be used to gain information that is valuable in attempting entry. Once inside, improper file permissions can be used to trick *sendmail* into giving away *root* privilege. Even email cannot be trusted, and forged email can cause some users to give away their passwords.

In this chapter we present several ways to protect your site from intrusion via *sendmail.* Most are just good common sense, and the experienced system administrator may be offended that we state the obvious. But not all system administrators are experienced, and not all who administer systems are system administrators. If you fall into the latter category, you may wish to keep keep a good, general UNIX reference by your side to better appreciate our suggestions.

22.1 Why root?

One common complaint about *sendmail* centers on the fact that it must usually be run *suid root* (that is, run as *root* no matter who actually runs it).[†] But for the most

---

[*] That flaw has been eliminated—wrongly by some vendors who turned all debugging completely off correctly by most who simply disabled SMTP debugging.

[†] Contrary to popular belief, *sendmail* does not run as *root* to handle local delivery (except that *sendmail* can deliver directly to files when necessary, but that is not directly germane to this discussion). Local delivery is handled by delivery agents (such as */bin/mail*), which may run *suid root* themselves (or *sgid mail* as in SysV).

part it is necessary for *sendmail* to run as *root* to satisfy the legitimate needs of users. Consider the following:

- Users want `~/.forward` files to work even when their home directory is set to mode 700. The *sendmail* program requires *root* privilege so that it can temporarily become the user to read and process the `~/.forward` file.

- Users want *:include:* mailing-list files readable only by themselves and *sendmail*. The *sendmail* program requires *root* privilege so that it can temporarily become the owner of the list.

- Users want programs that run on their behalf to run as themselves. This requires *root* privileges, and running as anything else would be potentially very dangerous.

- Users want *sendmail* to listen on a TCP/IP port that is common (port 25). The *sendmail* program requires *root* privilege so that it can initiate a listening connection to its privileged port.

Some folks have been tempted to run *sendmail* as an untrusted pseudo-user (such as *nobody*). But this doesn't really work. For example, it causes programs in users' `~/.forward` files to be run as *nobody*, and it requires the queue to be owned by *nobody*. Consequently, such a scheme allows any user to break into and modify the queue.[*]

22.1.1 Test seteuid and setreuid

Clearly, many of *sendmail*'s duties require it to run as *root*. As a corollary, however, whenever *sendmail* does not need to be *root*, it should become the appropriate nonprivileged user. It does this by using the following bit of logic:

- If it was compiled with support for *seteuid*(3) (see §18.8.55), use that routine to set the effective *uid* to that of the desired non-*root* user. This is less preferred than the following:

- If it was compiled with support for *setreuid*(3) (see §18.8.9), use that routine to set the effective and real *uid*s to those of the desired non-*root* user.

- Otherwise, use *setuid*(3) to become the desired non-*root* user.

Note that *setreuid*(3) is preferred over *seteuid*(3)[†] and *setuid*(3) because it allows *sendmail* to temporarily give away both its real and effective *root* privilege, then

---

[*] But note that V8.8 *sendmail* has loosened the latter for use on firewall machines, where it won't complain about non-*root* *qf* files if it is not running as *root*.

[†] Except when *seteuid*(3) is Posix compliant. Old implementations of *seteuid*(3) didn't properly save the *uid*; hence the preference, in that, case for *setreuid*(3).

to get it back again. To illustrate the need for this behavior, consider processing a mailing list that saves mail to two different files:

```
/u/bill/archive        ← owned by the user bill, mode 4600
/u/alice/archive       ← owned by the user alice, mode 4600
```

Further consider that these files both have permissions of *suid* to the individual users[*] and are writable only by the individual users. To perform delivery in this instance, *sendmail* must[†] first become *bill* (this requires *root* privilege to do). When it is done, *sendmail* must become *root* again so that it can next become *alice*. By retaining a real *uid* of *root* (with the *seteuid*(3) routine), *sendmail* is able to change its effective *uid* back and forth between users and *root* as needed.

See the description of the *test* directory in §18.8.55 for more on this subject.

22.2 *The Environment*

As a general rule, programs should never trust their environment. Such trust can lead to exploitation that has grave security consequences. To illustrate, consider the often misused SunOS LD_LIBRARY_PATH environment variable. Programs that use shared libraries look at this variable to determine which shared library routines they should use and in what order they should load them. One form of attack against non-*suid* programs (such as some delivery agents) is to modify the LD_LIBRARY_PATH variable (as in a user's ˜/.forward file) to introduce Trojan horse library routines in place of the real system's library routines. Certainly, *sendmail* should not pass such variables to its delivery agents.

To improve security, V8 *sendmail* began deleting variables from its environment before passing them to its delivery agents. It removed the IFS variable to protect Bourne shell-script agents and all variables beginning with "LD_" to protect all delivery agents from shared library attacks.

Beginning with V8.7, *sendmail* now takes the opposite approach. Instead of trying to second-guess attackers, it instead constructs the delivery agent environment from scratch. In this scheme it defines the AGENT variable as `sendmail`, and the TZ variable is as appropriate (see the `TimeZoneSpec` (t) option, §34.8.69). Also, in support of operating systems that require them, it passes the ISP and SYSTYPE variables from its own environment to the delivery agent's environment.

---

[*] When delivering to files, *sendmail* will become the owner of the file if that file's *suid* bit is set and if no execute bits are set.

[†] We say "must" because in an NFS environment, *root* is mapped to *nobody* so, in that instance, even *root* won't be able to write to *bill*'s files.

22.2.1 The E Configuration Command

When *sendmail* executes (runs) a delivery agent (see §30.6.2), it passes to that delivery agent an environment that includes only the items described above. Some delivery agents, however, may require additional environmental variables to function properly. For those special cases, *sendmail* offers the E configuration command to set individual environment variables that will be passed to all delivery agents:

```
Evar=value
```

The **var** is the environment variable that will be either defined or redefined. It is immediately followed (with no intervening space) by an equal sign and then (again with no intervening space) by the **value** that will be assigned to it.

If the **=value** is missing, *sendmail* looks up the variable **var** in its environment and, if it is found, uses that value. If the = is present but the **value** is absent, the **var** is assigned an empty string (a single zero byte). If the **var** is missing, a variable name that is an empty string is used.

The **var** is looked up to see whether it is already a part of the delivery agent's environment. If it is, it is redefined to be the new value. If it is not, it is added to that list of variables. If that addition will cause the list to exceed MAXUSERENVIRON variables (as defined in *conf.h*, see §18.8.19), the definition is silently ignored.

Whether or not the **var** was added to, or updated in, the delivery agent's environment, it is always added or updated to *sendmail*'s environment with *putenv*(2). If this call fails, *sendmail* logs and prints the following message:

```
setuserenv: putenv(var=value) failed
```

Only one **var** may be defined per E command. Additional environment variables require multiple E commands. Each E command affects all delivery agents. There is no way to tune the environment on a per delivery agent basis.

For DG/UX under V8.7 *sendmail* you will need to declare

```
E_FORCE_MAIL_LOCAL_=yes
```

in your configuration file to enable */bin/mail* to work properly. Beginning with V8.8 *sendmail*, this is already done in *cf/ostype/dgux.m4*.

22.3 SMTP Probes

Although SMTP probes can be legitimate uses of the network, they can also pose potential risks. They are sometimes used to see whether a bug remains unfixed. Sometimes they are used to try to gather user login names or to feed a program unexpected input in such a way that it breaks and gives away *root* privilege.

22.3.1 SMTP debug

An "unfixed bug" probe can use the SMTP **debug** and **showq** commands. The SMTP **debug** command allows the local *sendmail* to be placed into debugging mode (as with the **–d** command-line switch; see §37.1) from any other machine anywhere on the network. The SMTP **showq** command allows outsiders to view the contents of the mail queue.

If SMTPDEBUG (see §18.8.42) is defined when *sendmail* is compiled, the SMTP *debug* and *showq* commands are allowed to work; otherwise, they are disabled. SMTPDEBUG should be defined only when modifying the *sendmail* code and testing a new version. It should never be defined in an official release of *sendmail*. To see whether it has been defined at your site, run the following command:

```
% telnet localhost 25
Trying 123.45.6.7 ...
Connected to localhost.
Escape character is '^]'.
220 localhost sendmail 8.8.4 ready at Fri, 13 Dec 1996 06:36:12 -0800
debug
500 Command unrecognized
quit
221 localhost.us.edu closing connection
Connection closed by foreign host.
%
```

When connected, enter the command **debug**. If you get the answer 500 **Command unrecognized**, you know that SMTPDEBUG is not enabled. If, on the other hand, you get the answer 200 **Debug set**, SMTPDEBUG is defined on your system, and you should immediately take steps to correct the situation. Either contact your vendor and request a new version of *sendmail*, or get the *sendmail* source and compile it with SMTPDEBUG undefined.

When SMTPDEBUG is undefined and an outsider connects to the local machine and attempts to execute the **debug** or **showq** commands, *sendmail* will *syslog*(3) a message like the following:

```
Jul 22 07:09:00 here.domain sendmail[192]: "debug" command from there.domain
    (123.45.67.89)
```

This message shows the name of the machine that attempts the probe, or (*there.domain*), and the IP address of that machine. Note that this message is logged only if the **LogLevel** (**L**) option (see §34.8.33) is nonzero.

22.3.2 SMTP vrfy and expn

You may be dismayed to learn that the login names of ordinary users can be used to break into a system. It is not, for example, all that unusual for a user to select a password that is simply a copy of his or her login name, first name, last name, or some combination of initials. A risk of attack can arise from outsiders guessing login names. Any that they find can be used to try to break in, and the SMTP **vrfy** gives an attacker the means to discover login names.

The SMTP **vrfy** command causes *sendmail* to verify that it will accept an address for delivery. If a user's login name is given, the full name and login name are printed:

```
vrfy george
250 George Washington <george@wash.dc.gov>
```

Here, the 250 SMTP reply code (see RFC821) means a successful verification.[*] If the user is unknown, however, *sendmail* says so:

```
vrfy foo
550 foo... User unknown
```

The SMTP *expn* command is similar to the **vrfy** command, except that in the case of a mailing list, it will show all the members of that list. The SMTP *expn* command causes *sendmail* to expand (show all the recipients) of an address. To illustrate the risk, consider that many sites have aliases that include all or a large segment of users. Such aliases often have easily guessed names, such as *all*, *everyone*, or *staff*. A probe of *all*, for example, might produce something like the following:

```
expn all
250-George Washington <george@wash.dc.gov>
250-Thomas Jefferson <tj@wash.dc.gov>
250-Ben Franklin <ben@here.us.edu>
250-Betsy Ross <msflag@ora.com>
250 John Q. Public <jqp@aol.com>
```

With well-designed passwords these full and login names can safely be given to the world at large. But if one user (say **jqp**) has a poorly designed password (such as *jqpublic*), your site's security can easily be compromised.[†] Note that not all uses of **vrfy** or *expn* represent probes. Some MUAs,[‡] for example, routinely **vrfy** each recipient before sending a message.

---

[*] See the F=q flag (§30.8.36) for a way and reason to change this SMTP reply code to 252.

[†] The *fingerd*(8) utility can also reveal login IDs.

[‡] The GNU *fingerd*(8) daemon also uses **vrfy** to provide mailbox information.

SMTP **vrfy** and **expn** commands are individually logged in a form like one of the following:

```
Sep 22 11:40:43 yourhost sendmail[pid]: other.host: vrfy all
Sep 22 11:40:43 yourhost sendmail[pid]: [222.33.44.55]: vrfy all
Sep 22 11:40:43 yourhost sendmail[pid]: other.host: expn all
Sep 22 11:40:43 yourhost sendmail[pid]: [222.33.44.55]: expn all
```

This shows that someone from the outside (**other.host** in the first and third examples) attempted to probe for usernames in the mailing list named **all**. In the second and last examples the probing hostname could not be found, so the IP address is printed instead (in the square brackets). Note that this form of logging is enabled only if the **LogLevel** (**L**) option (see §34.8.33) is greater than 5.

Pre-V8 versions of *sendmail* do not report SMTP **vrfy** or **expn** attempts at all. Some versions of *sendmail* (such as the HP_UX version) appear to verify but really only echo the address stated.

V8 *sendmail* allows *vrfy* and *expn* services to be selectively accepted or rejected on the basis of the setting of the **PrivacyOptions** (**p**) option (see §34.8.47). For best security we recommend this setting:

```
O PrivacyOptions=goaway
```

22.4 The Configuration File

There are a number of security holes that can be opened up by commands given carelessly in the configuration file. Such holes can be serious because *sendmail* starts to run as *root*, provided that it has not been given an unsafe command-line switch (such as −C; see §36.7.15) or an unsafe option (see §34.1.4). It continues as *root* until it delivers mail, whereupon it changes its identity to that of an ordinary user. When *sendmail* reads its configuration file, it generally does so while it is still *root*. Consequently, as we will illustrate, it may be able to read and overwrite any file.

22.4.1 Accept/Reject Connections via libwrap.a

The TCP wrapper package is written and maintained by Wietse Venema at the Department of Mathematics and Computing Science, The Netherlands. It is available via anonymous FTP from:

```
ftp://ftp.cert.org/pub/tools/tcp_wrappers/
ftp://ftp.win.tue.nl/pub/security/
```

This package is used to screen incoming network connections and to accept or reject them on the basis of hostname, domain, or IP number. It is a powerful

adjunct to security, and if you have not already done so, you should install it at
your site.

Prior to V8.8 the only way *sendmail* could take advantage of this package was to
be run from *inetd*(8) (see §36.7.11). Beginning with V8.8 *sendmail*, support for
this package is built in.

If TCPWRAPPERS is defined in compiling (see §18.8.49), *sendmail* will automatically
use that package to verify and screen all incoming SMTP connections. If, as CERT
recommends, you have ALL:ALL in your *hosts.deny* file, you will need to add this
line to your *hosts.allow* file:

```
sendmail:ALL
```

Then, to selectively reject connection, you might add a line like this to your
hosts.deny file:

```
sendmail:spam.host.domain
```

This causes the TCP wrapper package to tell *sendmail* to reject all SMTP connections from the spamming host *spam.host.domain.*

When mail comes in from *spam.host.domain, sendmail* will issue this SMTP message as a reply to all SMTP commands from that host:

```
550 Access denied
```

The only exception is the QUIT command (and beginning with V8.8.5, the HELO,
EHLO, and NOOP commands), which allows the spamming host to disconnect.

Use of the TCP wrapper package imposes additional network traffic that may not
be desirable. Both it and *sendmail*, for instance, may look up the same host with
DNS. The wrapper software also sends *identd*(8) queries that a duplicate those
used by *sendmail*. Finally, note that two files need to be opened and read for each
connection. We recommend that you exclude support for this package (especially
at high-volume sites) until you actually need it. At low- to medium-volume sites
you may wish to include support for this package in *sendmail* but then to not
implement that support (in *hosts.allow* and *hosts.deny*) until the need arises.

22.4.2 The F Command — File Form

The file form of the F configuration command (see §32.1.2) can be used to read
sensitive information. That command looks like this in the configuration file:

```
FX/path pat
```

This form is used to read class macro entries from files. It can cause problems
through a misunderstanding of the *scanf*(3) pattern **pat**. The **/path** is the name of
the file, and the optional **pat** is a pattern to be used by *scanf*(3) (see §32.1.2.1).

To illustrate the risk of the *pat*, consider the following configuration file entry:

```
Fw/etc/myhostnames %[^#]
```

Normally, the F command reads only the first whitespace-delimited word from each line of the file. But if the optional pattern *pat* is specified, the F command instead reads one or more words from each line based on the nature of the pattern. The pattern is used by *scanf*(3) to extract words, and the specific pattern used here [^#] causes *scanf*(3) to read everything up to the first comment character (the #) from each line. This *pat* allows multiple hostnames to be conveniently listed on each line of the file. Now assume that a new administrator, who is not very familiar with *sendmail*, decides to add an F command to gather a list of UUCP hosts from the */etc/uucp/Systems* file. Being a novice, the new administrator copies the existing entry for use with the new file:

```
FU/etc/uucp/Systems %[^#]
```

This is the same pattern that was correctly used for */etc/myhostnames*. Unfortunately, the *Systems* file contains more than just host entries on each line:

```
linda Any ACU 2400 5551212  "" \d\n in:-\r-in: Uourhost word: MublyPeg
hoby Any ACU 2400 5551213  "" \d\n in:-\r-in: Uourhost word: FuMzz3.x
```

A part of each line (the last item in each) contains nonencrypted passwords. An unscrupulous user, noticing the mistaken [^#] in the configuration file, could run *sendmail* with a −d36.5 debugging switch and watch each password being processed. For example,

```
% /usr/lib/sendmail -d36.5 -bt < /dev/null
← ... some output deleted
STAB: hoby 1 entered
STAB: Any 1 entered
STAB: ACU 1 entered
STAB: 2400 1 entered
STAB: 5551213 1 entered
STAB: "" 1 type 1 val 0 0 200000 0
STAB: \d\n 1 entered
STAB: in:-\r-in: 1 entered
STAB: Uourhost 1 entered
STAB: word: 1 entered
STAB: FuMzz3.x 1 entered                    ← note
STAB: local 3 type 3 val 34d00 0 0 0
STAB: prog 3 type 3 val 34d80 0 0 0
```

Note the third line from the bottom, where the password for the UUCP login into the host **hoby** is printed. This example illustrates two rules about handling the configuration file:

- Avoid using the F command to read a file that is not already publicly readable. To do so can reveal sensitive information. Even if the *scanf*(3) option is correct, a core dump[*] can be examined for sensitive information from otherwise secured files.

- Avoid adding a new command to the configuration file by blindly copying and modifying another. Try to learn the rules governing the command first.

22.4.3 The F Command—Program Form

Another form of the F (File) configuration command is the program form, which looks like this:

```
FX|/path
```

Here, the | prefix to the */path* tells *sendmail* that */path* is the name of a program to run. The output produced by the program is appended to the class, here *X*.

To illustrate another potential security risk, consider a configuration file that is group writable, perhaps by a few administrators who share the job of *postmaster*. To break into *root*, the attacker only needs to assume the identity of one of those users and, under that identity, edit the configuration file. Consider the following bogus entry added by an attacker to that configuration file:

```
FX|/tmp/.sh
```

Consider further a change to the **DefaultUser** option (see §34.8.15) that causes the default *uid* and *gid* to become those of root:

```
O DefaultUser=0:0
```

With these changes in place, the program (actually a shell script) called */tmp/.sh* is run by *sendmail* to fill the class **X** with new values. All this seems harmless enough, but suppose */tmp/.sh* does the unexpected:

```
#!/bin/sh
cp /bin/sh /tmp/.shell
chmod u+s /tmp/.shell
```

Here, the Bourne shell is copied to */tmp/.shell*, and the *suid root* bit is set. Now, any user at all can run *sendmail* and become *root*:

```
% ls -l /tmp/.shell
/tmp/.shell not found
%  /usr/lib/sendmail -bt < /dev/null
% ls -l /tmp/.shell
-rwsr-xr-x  1 root        122880 Sep 24 13:20 /tmp/.shell
```

---

[*] Most versions of UNIX disallow core dumps of *suid root* programs.

The program form of the F configuration command is clearly dangerous.

- The *sendmail* configuration file must *never* be writable by anyone other than *root*. It should also live in a directory, every path component of which is owned by and writable only by *root*. (We'll discuss this latter point in greater detail soon.) If the configuration file is created with the *m4* technique, then care must be taken to ensure that only *root* can install it.

22.4.4   The P= of Delivery Agents

Just as the program form of the F command can pose a security risk if the configuration file is poorly protected, so can the M delivery agent definition. Specifically, the P= equate for a delivery agent (see §30.4.9) can be modified to run a bogus program that gives away *root* privilege. Consider the following modification to the local delivery agent:

```
Mlocal, P=/bin/mail, F=rlsDFMmnP, S=10, R=20, A=mail -d $u
            ↓
         becomes
            ↓
Mlocal, P=/tmp/mail, U=0, F=SrlsDFMmnP, S=10, R=20, A=mail -d $u
                 ↑         ↑
               note      note
```

Here, local mail should be delivered with the */bin/mail* program, but instead it is delivered with a bogus frontend, */tmp/mail*. If */tmp/mail* is carefully crafted, users will never notice that the mail has been diverted. The S flag in the F= equate (see §30.8.40) causes *sendmail* to retain its default identity when executing the bogus */tmp/mail*. The U=0 equate (see §30.4.13) causes that default to become the identity of *root*.

- Delivery agent P= equates must be protected by protecting the configuration file. As an additional precaution, *never* use relative pathnames in the P= equate.

- The F=S and U=0 are especially dangerous. They should never appear in your configuration file unless you have deliberately placed them there and are 100 percent certain of their effect.

22.4.5   The S Option and the Statistics File

When *sendmail* attempts to record its delivery agent statistics (see §26.2.1), it checks for the existence and write permissions of the file specified by the Status-File (S) option (see §34.8.66). The *sendmail* program does not care where that file lives or what permissions it has—only that it exists.

A security problem can arise if one is tempted to locate the statistics file in a spool or temporary area. Consider the following location, for example:

```
OS/usr/tmp/sendmail.st
```

Here the administrator sets the `StatusFile` (S) option to locate the statistics file in the */usr/tmp* directory. The intention is that the file can be easily created by anyone who wishes to gather statistics for a while, then removed. Unfortunately, the */usr/tmp* directory is usually world-writable.

Thus any unhappy or malicious user can bring the system to its knees:

```
% cd /usr/tmp
% ln -s /vmunix sendmail.st
```

Here, *sendmail* clobbers the disk copy of the kernel. Nothing bad may happen at first,[*] but the machine will require manual intervention to boot in the future.[†] Clearly, precautions must be taken. For example, any file that *sendmail* writes to (such as the `StatusFile` (S) option statistics file or the *aliases* database files) must be writable only by *root* and live in a directory, every path component of which is writable only by *root*.

22.5 *Permissions*

One technique that attackers use to gain *root* privilege is to first become a semiprivileged user like *bin* or *sys*. Such semiprivileged users often own the directories in which *root*-owned files live. By way of example, consider the following:

```
drwxr-sr-x 11 bin      2560 Sep 22 18:18 /etc
-rw-r--r--  1 root     8199 Aug 25 07:54 /etc/sendmail.cf
```

Here, the */etc/sendmail.cf* configuration file is correctly writable only by *root*. But the directory in which that file lives is owned by *bin* and writable by *bin*. Having write permission on that directory means that *bin* can rename and create files. An individual who gains *bin* permission on this machine can create a bogus *sendmail.cf* file by issuing only two simple commands:

```
% mv /etc/sendmail.cf /etc/...
% mv /tmp/sendmail.cf /etc/sendmail.cf
```

---

[*] Programs that need kernel symbols, such as *ps*(1), will cease to work or will produce garbage output.

[†] The savvy administrator can still boot off the network or from a CD-ROM and quickly install a new kernel.

The original *sendmail.cf* is renamed . . . (a name that is not likely to be randomly noticed by the real system administrator). The bogus */tmp/sendmail.cf* then replaces the original:

```
drwxr-sr-x 11 bin        2560 Sep 22 18:18 /etc
-rw-r--r--  1 bin        4032 Nov 16 00:32 /etc/sendmail.cf
```

UNIX pays less attention to semiprivileged users than it does *root*. The user *root*, for example, is mapped to *nobody* over NFS, whereas the user *bin* remains *bin*. Consequently, the following rules must be observed to prevent malicious access to *root*-owned files:

- All directories in the path leading to a *root*-owned file must be owned by *root* and writable only by *root*. This is true for *all* files, not just *sendmail* files.

- Files owned by *root* must be writable only by *root*. Group write permission, although at times desirable, should consistently be avoided.

- Because *sendmail* is running as *root* when processing the configuration file, care should be taken to ensure the safety of system files as well. All system directories and files must live in directories whose path component parts are owned by and writable only by *root*. All system files (except possibly *suid* or *sgid* files) must be owned by *root* and be writable only by *root*. If any program "breaks" after securing permissions, complain to your vendor at once!

22.5.1 Dangerous Write Permissions

The *sendmail* program, of necessity, needs to trust its configuration file. To aid in the detection of risks, it checks the permissions of its configuration file when first reading that file. If the file is writable by group or world, *sendmail* logs the following message:[*]

> *configfile*: WARNING: dangerous write permissions

If *sendmail* is being started as a daemon or is being used to initialize the aliases database, it will print the same message to its standard error output.

22.5.2 Permissions for :include:

The *sendmail* program doesn't always run as *root*. When delivering mail, it often changes its identity into that of a nonprivileged user. When delivering to a :include: mailing list, for example, it can change its identity to that of the owner

---

[*] This is done only when not in rule-testing mode to prevent spurious warnings when you already know you are using a weak configuration file with –C.

of the list. This too can pose security risks if permissions are not appropriate. Consider the following *aliases* file entry:

```
newprogs: :include:/usr/local/lists/proglist
```

Here, notification of new programs are mailed to the alias **newprogs**. The list of recipients is taken from the following file:

```
-rw-rw-r--  2 bin  prog   704 Sep 21 14:46 /usr/local/lists/proglist
```

Because this file is owned by *bin, sendmail* changes its identity to *bin* when delivering to the list of recipients. Unfortunately, the file is also writable by the group *prog.* Anyone in the group *prog* can add a recipient to that list, including one of the form

```
|/tmp/x.sh
```

This tells *sendmail* to deliver a copy of the message by running the program (a shell script) */tmp/x.sh.* The *sendmail* program (which is still running as *bin*) executes that program as *bin.* Further, suppose the program */tmp/x.sh* contains the following:

```
#!/bin/sh
cp /bin/sh /tmp/sh
chmod u+s /tmp/sh
cat - > /dev/null
exit 0
```

This causes *bin* first to make a copy of the Bourne shell in */tmp* (a copy that will be owned by *bin*), then to set the *suid* bit on that copy (the **u+s**):

```
-rwsr-xr-x  1 bin    64668 Sep 22 07:38 /tmp/sh
```

The script then throws away the incoming mail message and exits with a zero value to keep *sendmail* unsuspecting. Through this process, an ordinary user in the group *prog* has created an *suid* shell that allows anyone to become the semiprivileged user *bin.* From the preceding discussion (see §22.5) you can see the trouble that can cause!

• Mailing lists (`:include:`) must live in a directory, all the components of which are writable only by root. The lists themselves must be writable only by the owner. If the owner is an ordinary user, group write permissions can be enabled, provided that the user is advised of the risks.

• Mailing list (`:include:`) files may safely be owned by *root.* When *sendmail* processes a *root*-owned mailing list, it changes itself to run as the user and group specified by the **DefaultUser** option (see §34.8.15). That option defaults to *daemon* but should be set to *nobody* and *nogroup.* The **DefaultUser** option should *never* be set to *root.*

22.5.3 Permissions for ˜/.forward Files

The ˜/.forward file can pose a security risk to individual users. There is a higher degree of risk if the user is *root* or one of the semiprivileged users (such as *bin*). Because the ˜/.forward file is like an individual mailing list (`:include:`) for the user, risk can be encountered if that file is writable by anyone but the user. Consider the following for example:

```
drwxr-xr-x 50 george guest      3072 Sep 27 09:19 /home/george/
-rw-rw-r--  1 george guest        62 Sep 17 09:49 /home/george/.forward
```

Here, the user george's ˜/.forward file is writable by the group guest. Anyone in group guest can edit george's ˜/.forward file, possibly placing something like this into it:

```
\george
|"cp /bin/sh /home/george/.x; chmod u+s /home/george/.x"
```

Now all the attacker has to do is send george mail to create an *suid* george shell. Then, by executing */home/george/.x*, the attacker becomes george.

- The semiprivileged users such as *bin*, and *root* in particular, should never have ˜/.forward files. Instead, they should forward their mail by means of the *aliases* file directly.

- User ˜/.forward files must be writable only by the owning user. Similarly, user home directories must live in a directory that is owned and writable only by *root*, and must themselves be owned and writable only by the user.

Some users, such as the pseudo-user *uucp*, have home directories that must be world-writable for software to work properly. If that software is not needed (if a machine, for example, doesn't run UUCP software), that home directory should be removed. If the directory must exist and must be world-writable, you should create a protected ˜/.forward file there before someone else does. The best protection is to create a nonempty directory called ˜/.forward, owned by *root*, and set its permissions to 000:

```
# cd ˜uucp
# rm -f .forward
# mkdir .forward
# touch .forward/uucp
# chown root .forward .forward/uucp
# chmod 000 .forward .forward/uucp
# chmod +t ˜uucp
# chown root ˜uucp
```

Even though the ˜*uucp* directory is world-writable (so anyone can remove anything from it), no one but *root* can remove the ˜/.forward directory because it is not empty. The mode of 000 protects the file *.forward/uucp* from being removed.

The mode of +t prevents users from renaming files or directories that they do not own. Finally, *root* is made to own the ~uucp directory so that *uucp* will be unable to clear the +t bit. Even with this protection, mail for *uucp* should be routed to a real user with the *aliases*(5) file.

Note that all critical dot files in a world-writable home directory must be protected from creation by others. Each of *.forward*, *.rhosts*, *.login*, *.cshrc*, *.profile*, and *.logout* should be a nonempty, *root*-owned directory with mode 000. World-writable home directories must be owned by *root* instead of by the user, and they must have the +t (sticky bit) set.

When processing a user's ~/.forward file, *sendmail* requires that the file be owned by the user or by *root*. If ownership is correct, it then examines the ~/.forward file's permissions. If that file is world-writable, *sendmail* ignores (and logs) attempts to run programs and to write directly to files. If the UnsafeGroupWrites option (see §34.8.73) is true, *sendmail* also checks for group write permissions and, if it is found, similarly ignores attempts to run programs and to write to files.

22.5.4 Recommended Permissions

Table 22-1 shows the recommended ownerships and permissions for all the files and directories in the *sendmail* system. The path components will vary depending on the vendor version of *sendmail* you are running. For example, where we show the */usr/lib/sendmail* directory, your site may use */usr/etc/sendmail*, or even */usr/lib/mail/sendmail*.

Table 22-1: Recommended Permissions

Path	Type	Owner	Mode	
/	Directory	*root*	0755	drwxr-xr-x
/usr	Directory	*root*	0755	drwxr-xr-x
/usr/lib[a]	Directory	*root*	0755	drwxr-xr-x
/usr/lib/sendmail	File	*root*	06511	-r-s--s--x[b]
/etc	Directory	*root*	0755	drwxr-xr-x
/etc/sendmail.cf	File	*root*	0644 or 0640	
OS/etc/sendmail.st	File	*root*	0644	-rw-r--r--
OH/etc/sendmail.hf	File	*root*	0444	-r--r--r--
OA/etc/aliases	File	*root*	0644	-rw-r--r--
/etc/aliases.pag	File	*root*	0644	-rw-r--r--
/etc/aliases.dir	File	*root*	0644	-rw-r--r--
/etc/aliases.db	File	*root*	0644	-rw-r--r--
F/path	Directory	*root*	0755	drwxr-xr-x
F/path/file	File	n/a	0444 or 0644	
/var	Directory	*root*	0755	drwxr-xr-x

Table 22-1: Recommended Permissions (continued)

Path	Type	Owner	Mode	
/var/spool	Directory	*root*	0755	drwxr-xr-x
O&/var/spool/mqueue	Directory	*root*	0700^c	drwx------
:include:*/path*	Directories	*root*	0755	drwxr-xr-x
:include:*/path/list*	File	n/a	0644	-rw-r--r--

a. The *sendmail* program sometimes lives in /usr/sbin or in some other directory. If so, adjust this path accordingly.

b. The *sendmail* program may need to be *sgid kmem* for the load average to be checked on some systems.

c. CERT (the Computing Emergency Response Team) recommends that the *mqueue* directory be mode 0700 to prevent potential security breaches.

22.6 The Aliases File

The *aliases* file can easily be used to gain privileged status if it is wrongly or carelessly administered. In addition to proper permissions and ownership you should be aware of potentially harmful entries that you may have inherited from the vendor or previous administrators. For example, many vendors used to ship systems with a **decode** alias in the *aliases* file. This practice is becoming less common.

```
# you may wish to comment this out for security
decode:    |/usr/bin/guudecode
```

The intention is to provide an easy way for users to transfer binary files using mail. At the sending site the user converts the binary to ASCII with *uuencode*(1), then mails the result to the **decode** alias at the receiving site. That alias pipes the mail message through the */usr/bin/uudecode* program, which converts the ASCII back into the original binary file.

The *uudecode*(1) program takes the name of the file to create from the file it is decoding. That information is in the **begin** line, used by *uudecode*. For example, here's an attempt to use *uudecode*(1) to place a bogus queue file directly into the *sendmail* queue:

```
begin 777 /var/spool/mqueue/qfAA12345
```

Here, the **begin** tells *uudecode* to begin conversion. The 777 is the permissions to give to the file that will be created. That is followed by the full pathname of the file. If the queue directory were wrongly owned by *daemon*, any outsider could create a bogus queued message at your site.

Some versions of *uudecode* (such as the one with SunOS) will create *suid* files. That is, a **begin** line like the following can be used to create an *suid daemon* shell in */tmp*:

```
begin 4777 /tmp/sh
```

The **decode** alias should be removed from all *aliases* files. Similarly, every alias that executes a program—that you did not place there yourself and check completely—should be questioned and probably removed.

22.6.1 *The Alias Database Files*

The *aliases*(5) file is often stored in *dbm*(3) or *db*(3) database format for faster lookups. The database files live in the same directory as the *aliases* file. For all versions of *sendmail* they are called *aliases.dir* and *aliases.pag* (but for V8 *sendmail*, only a single database file might exist and be called *aliases.db*).

It is useless to protect the *aliases*(5) file if you do not protect its corresponding database files. If the database files are not protected, the attacker can create a private *aliases* file and then run

```
% /usr/lib/sendmail -oA./aliases -bi
```

This causes *sendmail* to build *./aliases* database files in the current directory. The attacker then copies those bogus database files over the unprotected system originals. The *sendmail* program never detects the change, because the database files appear to be newer than the *aliases* file.

Note also that the *aliases* file and its database files must be owned by *root*, and writable only by *root*. They must live in a directory, every path component of which is owned by and writable only by *root*.

22.7 *Forged Mail*

Although they are aware that paper mail can be forged, most users are blissfully unaware that email can also be forged. Forged mail can lead to a serious breach of security. Two points of vulnerability that require particular attention are the queue file and the SMTP interface of *sendmail*.

22.7.1 *Forging with the Queue Directory*

All versions of *sendmail* trust the files in the mail queue. They assume that only *sendmail* has placed files there. As a consequence, a poorly protected queue directory can allow the attacker to create mail that looks 100 percent authentic. This can be used to send forged mail, to append to system critical files, or to run

arbitrary programs as *root* or other users. Consider the following bogus
qfAA00001 file for sending forged mail (*qf* files are described in §23.9):

```
V1
T829313834
P943442
$_root@yourhost
S<root@yourhost>
RPFD:george@yourhost
H?P?return-path: <root@yourhost>
Hmessage-id: <199604121257.GAA12601@yourhost>
HFrom: root@yourhost
HDate: Fri, 13 Dec 1996 05:47:46 -0700
HTo: george@yourhost
HSubject: Change your Password Now!!
```

This qf file causes mail to be sent to *george* that appears in all ways to come from
root. There is nothing in this qf file to indicate to the recipient (or to *sendmail*)
that the message is not authentic. Now further suppose that the df file (the message body) contains the following text:

```
The system has been compromised. Change your password NOW!
Your new password must be:

                    Fuzz7bal
Thank you,
        --System Administration
```

Unfortunately, in any large organization there will be more than a few users who
will obey a message like this. They will gladly change their password to one
assigned to them, thereby providing the attacker with easy access to their
accounts.

- The queue directory must be owned by *root* and writable only by *root*. CERT
  recommends that the queue directory always be mode 0700.

- The queue files placed into the queue by *sendmail* must be well protected by
  defining narrow default permissions with the TempFileMode (F) option (see
  §34.8.68). A default of 0600 is best.

22.7.2 Forging with SMTP

We won't illustrate the SMTP interaction here. But note that anyone can connect to
your local *sendmail* via *telnet*(1) at port 25 or run *sendmail* with the **-bs** command-line switch. Once connected, *sendmail* must of necessity believe everything

it receives. The only exception is the hostname sent in the HELO message.[*] In that case the *sendmail* program looks up the real hostname based on the connection. If the stated hostname and the real hostname differ, the false name is used as the name of the sending host with the real name added in parentheses:

```
550 your.host hello false.host (real.host), pleased to meet you
```

The real hostname is then used as the sending hostname in the construction of all headers. The result (the header and body received by the user) might look something like this:

```
From root@false.host Dec 13 14:36:40 1996
Received: from real.host by your.host (8.8.4/8.8.4)
         id AA00998; Fri, 13 Dec 1996 14:36:38 -0700
Message-Id: <9612213133.GAA05059@your.host>
From: root@false.host (System Administration)
To: you@your.host
Subject: Change your password now!
Date: Fri, 13 Dec 1996 05:47:46 -0700

To improve security at our location you are requested to immediately
change your password. The password you have been assigned is:

     7Fuzzy1's

Thank you,
        --root
```

Fortunately, the `Received:` header above contains the name of the real host (which is not always the case). An attentive user can tell that this is a forged message because the host in that header line differs from the false hostname used in the other header lines.

However, most mail-reading programs allow users to filter out (prevent your seeing) uninteresting header lines.[†] Typically, users choose to ignore headers such as `Received:` and `Message-ID:`. For such users the task of detecting forged mail is much more difficult. Instead of seeing the above message, with real hostnames, they might see the following with only false names:

```
From root@false.host Dec 13 14:36:40 1996
From: root@false.host (System Administration)
To: you@your.host
Subject: Change your password now!
Date:  Fri, 13 Dec 1996 14:36:38 -0700

To improve security at our location you are requested to immediately
change your password. The password you have been assigned is:
```

---

[*] V8 *sendmail* also tries to verify the connection itself with *identd* if possible.

[†] In fact, the *gnu-emacs*(1) mail reader deletes those lines irrevocably.

```
        7Fuzzy1's
```

```
Thank you,
        --root
```

Clearly, a user who sees only this much of the mail message will be more likely to believe that it is real.

- Educate your users that mail can be forged. Teach them what to look for when they receive a message of questionable authenticity.

- Rarely, if ever, send mail as *root*. Always communicate as yourself and always use a distinctive style of writing. If users never see mail from *root*, they will be more likely to question such mail when it arrives.

- Train users to never send (or ask to receive) clear-text passwords or other security-related information by email.

22.8   Security Features

We now turn our attention from security problems to security features:

- The T configuration command (class t) defines which users are allowed to use the -f command-line switch to override the sender address with one of their own.

- The *smrsh* program replaces */bin/sh* as the program run by the prog delivery agent to execute programs.

- Several options can be used to tighten security and to provide reports of security violations.

- The */etc/shells* file prevents ordinary users from running programs on your mail server.

22.8.1   Trusted Users

Under pre-V8 *sendmail*, trusted users are those who are allowed to use the -f command-line switch (see §36.7.21) to override the sender address with one of their own. V8.1 *sendmail* eliminated this configuration command. V8.7 restored it, but as a class, and uses that class only to suppress warning headers.

Trusted users are necessary for certain kinds of mail to flow properly. By way of example, the *rmail*(8) program of the UUCP suite of programs runs *suid* to *uucp*. If *rmail* were not to use the -f command-line switch, all mail from UUCP would wrongly appear to come from the *uucp* user. To circumvent this problem, *rmail* runs *sendmail* as

```
/usr/lib/sendmail -f reallyfrom
```

This tells *sendmail* to show, in both the header and envelope, the message as being from *reallyfrom*, rather than from *uucp*.

The concept of a trusted user is intended to prevent ordinary users from changing the sender address and thereby forging mail. Although that intention is laudable and good for UUCP, it can cause problems with mailing lists. Consider the following:

```
list: "|/usr/lib/sendmail -oi -flist-request -odi list-real"
list-real:    :include:/export/share/mail-lists/list.list
```

The intention here is for all mail sent to the mailing list named list to be dispatched as though it were sent from the address list-request (the -f). This causes errors to be returned to the maintainer of the list (the list-request), but replies still go to the real sender.

Unfortunately, this scheme fails when mail is posted to list from the local machine. Recall that only trusted users can change the identity of the sender with -f. This is why V8.1 *sendmail* eliminated the concept of the trusted user (anyone could use the -f switch). Beginning with V8.7, *sendmail* restored the concept but uses the T command only to suppress warning headers.

22.8.1.1 Declare trusted users (not V8.1 through V8.6)

Trusted users are defined by those lines in the *sendmail.cf* file that begin with the uppercase letter T. Only trusted users may use the *sendmail* program's -f command-line switch to specify who sent the message. Beginning with V8.7 *sendmail*, the class t may also be used.

The T *sendmail.cf* command must begin a line. One or more space-delimited usernames then follow on that same line. There may be multiple T commands in a *sendmail.cf* file, each *adding* names to the list of trusted users. Prior to V8 there could be at most MAXTRUST trusted users, where MAXTRUST was defined in *conf.h* when you compiled *sendmail*. Beginning with V8.7, there is no limit:

```
T uucp              ← legal in V8.1 through V8.6 but ignored
Troot daemon        ← legal in V8.1 through V8.6 but ignored
Ct uucp             ← V8.7 and above
Ctroot daemon       ← V8.7 and above
```

The two T commands show that there may optionally be whitespace between the T and the first name in any list of names. They indicate that *uucp*, *root*, and *daemon* are trusted and have been added to the list of trusted users in that order. The two class declarations show a similar declaration for use beginning with V8.7 *send-mail* (but note that V8.7 and above can still use the old syntax).

Prior to V8 *sendmail*, if you listed more than **MAXTRUST** trusted users, *sendmail* printed and *syslog*(3)'ed a message like this:

```
sendmail: too many T lines, 32 max
```

This message was not fatal. The *sendmail* program issued it for each excess **T** line (ignored those trusted users) and continued to run.

Prior to V8 *sendmail*, if a user who was not trusted attempted to use the **-f** switch, that attempt was silently ignored (silently disallowed). Beginning with V8.7 *sendmail*, if a user who is not trusted attempts to use the **-f** switch, that attempt may produce an **X-Authentication-Warning:** header (see §35.10.35) if the **PrivacyOptions** (**p**) option (see §34.8.47) has **authwarnings** listed.

- Even though some users find them annoying, we recommend that you always enable **X-Authentication-Warning:** headers. They warn of suspicious behavior. If the behavior is legitimate, modify that behavior to eliminate the header instead of eliminating the more valuable warning headers.

22.8.2 The smrsh Program

One line of attack against all users, including *root*, is to modify a user's ˜/*.forward* file (see §22.5.3). Unless you take steps to prevent it, *sendmail* will run any program that it finds in a user's ˜/*.forward* file:

```
\user
|"/usr/ucb/vacation user"                              ← ok
|"/tmp/x.sh"                                           ← An attack!
|"cp /bin/sh /home/george/.x; chmod u+s /home/george/.x"   ← An attack!
```

As an aid in preventing such attacks, V8 *sendmail* offers the *smrsh* (sendmail restricted shell) program, and V8.7 *sendmail* offers the **smrsh** FEATURE (see §19.6.22) as an easy way to install *smrsh* with the *m4* configuration technique.

The *smrsh* program is supplied in source form with the *sendmail* distribution in the *smrsh* directory. The *README* file in that directory describes how to compile and install *smrsh*.

The *smrsh* program replaces the */bin/sh* program in the **prog** delivery agent (see §30.2.1) declaration:

```
Mprog, P=/usr/local/etc/smrsh, ...
```

Thereafter, whenever *smrsh* is called to run a program, *smrsh* strips the leading path from the program name and looks for that program in its special */usr/adm/sm.bin* directory. If the program is not found in that directory, the message bounces. Thus in our first attack example above, with *smrsh* installed and with *x.sh* not in the */usr/adm/sm.bin* directory, the *˜/.forward* line

```
|"/tmp/x.sh"
```

would cause the email message to bounce with this error:

```
smrsh: /usr/adm/sm.bin/x.sh: not found
```

The *smrsh* program also screens out program lines that contain suspicious characters (such as our second attack above):

```
|"cp /bin/sh /home/george/.x; chmod u+s /home/george/.x"
```

In this instance, *smrsh* would reject the command line (and thus bounce the message) because it contained a semicolon character:

```
smrsh: cannot use ; in command
```

- The *smrsh* program is simple yet immensely valuable. We recommend that it be routinely installed on all your machines.

- Be very conservative when choosing programs to put in the */usr/adm/sm.bin* directory. Never, for example, put programs there that allow shell escapes.

22.8.3 *Security Options*

The *sendmail* program offers several options that can help you to improve the security at your site. Some we have discussed above. We touch on a few more in this section, and provide a recommended setting where appropriate. For a full description of each, see the sections referenced.

22.8.3.1 *The DefaultUser option*

The `DefaultUser` (u) option (see §34.8.15) can be used to ensure that the default identity (when it is not running as *root*) is a safe one. CERT recommends that you create a pseudo-user whose *uid* and *gid* are used nowhere on your system, then define the `DefaultUser` (u) option to be that pseudo-user. As an additional precaution, make sure that pseudo-user lacks a valid shell and has no valid home directory:

```
nullmail:*:32765:32765:Sendmail Default User:/no/such/directory:/bin/false
```

At the same time, set up a group entry for this user's group:

```
nullgroup:*:32765:
```

This is necessary if you want to refer to this group symbolically at some later time.

Avoid using the name *nobody*, because *root* is mapped to *nobody* over NFS. If *root* were to create a file over NFS that it thought was safe because *root* owned it and because it was readable only by *root*, that *root* user would be surprised to find that file owned by *nobody*. Consequently, we recommend that in an NFS environment you set the default user to one less than *nobody*. For example, if *nobody* has the *uid* 65534, you could set up

```
nullmail:*:65533:65533:Sendmail Default User:/no/such/directory:/bin/false
```

22.8.3.2 *The ForwardPath option*

The `ForwardPath` (J) option (see §34.8.27) lists a series of directories that *sendmail* will search for user ~/.*forward* files. At most sites there are users who are savvy and able to correctly administer their own ~/.*forward* files, but there are others who are untrained or careless. One way to allow experienced users use of the ~/.*forward* facility while denying it to the others is with the `ForwardPath` (J) option:

```
O ForwardPath=/usr/local/etc/forwards/$u.forward:$z/.forward
```

Here, *sendmail* will first search the */usr/local/etc/forwards* directory to find a file that begins with the user's login name (the `$u` see §31.10.36) followed by a *forward*. If you set up such a file for the untrained user, say *bob*:

```
-rw-r--r-- 1 root  system  0 Dec 13 1996 /usr/local/etc/forwards/bob.forward
```

and if that file is empty, *bob*'s mail will always be delivered locally, no matter what *bob* puts in his ~/.*forward* file. For experienced users you can omit their files from the */usr/local/etc/forwards* directory, thus enabling their use of their /.*forward* files.

22.8.3.3 *The LogLevel option*

The *sendmail* program normally logs a great deal of useful information via *syslog* (see §26.1.1). There will be times, however, when the normal amount of information is insufficient. Consider, for example, that some outsider is using your site to forge mail. Since this is done over an SMTP connection, it would be handy to have both sides of all SMTP conversations logged. You can do this with the `LogLevel` (L) option (see §34.8.33):

```
O LogLevel=12      ← V8.8 and above to log SMTP
```

Beginning with V8.8 *sendmail*, a level of 12 causes both sides of every SMTP conversation to be logged. That logging looks very similar to the logging produced by verbose mode (see §4.2).

Note that after changing the log level in your configuration file you will need to restart the daemon. With V8.7 and above *sendmail* you restart the daemon like this:

```
# kill -HUP `head -1 /etc/sendmail.pid`
```

Be aware that a log level of 12 produces a huge amount of output. Be prepared to prune your log files more often than usual.

22.8.3.4 The PostmasterCopy option

The `PostmasterCopy` (P) option (see §34.8.46) causes a copy of every bounced message to be delivered to a named user. Usually, that user is the person who handle email problems. But since clumsy intrusion attempts can result in bounced mail, there will be times when bounced mail should also be delivered to the security administrator. Consider the following:

```
      ----- Transcript of session follows -----
>>> RCPT To:<root@your.site.domain>
<<< 550 cannot open /tmp/.../getshell: No such file or directory
550 cannot open /tmp/.../getshell: No such file or directory
```

This bounced mail message indicates that someone tried to become *root* by breaking through your *aliases* database.

Users are added to the list of those who get copies of bounced messages with the `PostmasterCopy` (P) option:

```
O PostmasterCopy=postmaster,securitymaster
                              ↑
                            added
```

Here, `securitymaster` (probably an alias to a real user) was added.

22.8.3.5 The PrivacyOptions option

The `PrivacyOptions` (p) option (see §34.8.47) is used to limit the amount of information offered to the outside world and to limit other kinds of access. The most restrictive setting for the `PrivacyOptions` (p) is probably best:

```
O PrivacyOptions=goaway,restrictmailq,restrictqrun
```

This setting disables the **expn** and **vrfy** SMTP commands, requires other sites to identify themselves before sending mail, and also limits access to the mail queue directory.

As a general rule it is best to begin with tight security. This minimizes your risk at the start and allows you to cautiously ease restrictions at a comfortable rate. Beginning with loose restrictions may force you to tighten restrictions in a panic when it is least convenient to do so.

22.8.3.6 The SafeFileEnvironment option

Beginning with V8.7 *sendmail*, the SafeFileEnvironment option (see §34.8.58) determines how delivery will be made to files. Ordinarily, *sendmail* will deliver to anything, provided that it has permission to do so (see §24.2.2). It can, for example, deliver by appending to ordinary files or by writing to a device such as */dev/log*.

If the SafeFileEnvironment option is declared, *sendmail* will only deliver to ordinary files. This improves security by preventing anyone from scribbling over sensitive things, such as directories and devices. (Beginning with V8.8 *sendmail*, it is still okay to write to */dev/null* even though this option is set.)

The SafeFileEnvironment option can also be used to define a directory under which all files that will be appended to must exist. This may inconvenience some users but will generally improve the security of your site. We recommend:

```
O SafeFileEnvironment=/path
```

This takes care of both security enhancements. Of course, you will need to create the directory specified in */path* and modify all path references in your *aliases* file before actually enabling this.

If all you want to do is prevent writing to directories and devices, and if you do not want to place all files in a special path, you can accomplish this by defining */path* as the root directory:

```
O SafeFileEnvironment=/
```

22.8.3.7 The TempFileMode option

The TempFileMode (F) option (see §34.8.68) specifies the mode (file permissions) to give temporary files and queue files. In general, all files that are created by *sendmail* should be considered proprietary for safety's sake. We recommend a setting of:

```
O TempFileMode=0600
```

With this narrow setting, the risk of accidental or malicious easing of permissions of your mail archive directories or queue becomes less of a risk.

22.8.4 The /etc/shells file

To prevent certain users from running programs or writing to files by way of the
aliases or `~/.forward` files, V8 *sendmail* introduced the concept of a "valid shell."
Just before allowing delivery via an alias such as these:

```
|"/some/program"
/save/to/a/file
```

the user's password entry is looked up. If the shell entry from that password entry
is a valid one, delivery is allowed. A shell is valid if it is listed in the */etc/shells* file.
If that file does not exist, *sendmail* looks up the shell in its internal list that looks
(more or less) like this:[*]

```
/bin/bsh
/bin/csh
/bin/ksh
/bin/pam
/bin/posix/sh
/bin/rksh
/bin/rsh
/bin/sh
/bin/tsh
/usr/bin/bsh
/usr/bin/csh
/usr/bin/keysh
/usr/bin/ksh
/usr/bin/pam
/usr/bin/posix/sh
/usr/bin/rksh
/usr/bin/rsh
/usr/bin/sh
/usr/bin/tsh
```

With this technique it is possible to prevent certain users from having *sendmail*
running programs or delivering to files on their behalf. To illustrate, consider the
need to prevent the *ftp* pseudo-user from misusing *sendmail*:

```
ftp:*:1092:255:File Transfer Protocol Program:/u/ftp:/no/shell
```

Here, any attempt by *ftp* to send mail through a program or into a file will fail
because the shell */no/shell* is not a valid shell. Such mail will bounce with one of
these two errors:

```
User ftp@here.us.edu doesn't have a valid shell for mailing to programs
User ftp@here.us.edu doesn't have a valid shell for mailing to files
```

---

[*] This is an amalgamation of many vendor lists. See *conf.c* in the source distribution for details.

Note that unusual circumstances may require you to allow users with invalid shells to run program or deliver to files. To enable this for all such users (as on a mail server with restricted logins), place the following line directly in the */etc/shells* file:

```
/SENDMAIL/ANY/SHELL/
```

To enable this for selected users, just replace their shell with a bogus one that is listed in /etc/shells:

```
ftp:*:1092:255:File Transfer Protocol Program:/u/ftp:/bogus/shell
```

We recommend that all pseudo-users (such as *bin* and *ftp*) be given invalid shells in the password file and that /SENDMAIL/ANY/SHELL/ never be used.

22.9 Pitfalls

- The *sendmail* program is only as secure as the system on which it is running. Correcting permissions and the like is useful only if such corrections are systemwide and apply to all critical system files and programs.

- Time spent tightening security at your site is best spent before a break-in occurs. Never believe that your site is too small or of too little consequence. Start out by being wary, and you will be more prepared when the inevitable attack happens.

- Get and set up *identd*(8) at your site. When queried about who established a network connection, it returns the login identity of the individual user. Become a good network citizen.

- Multimedia mail, such as MIME, is more difficult, but not impossible, to forge.

- Newer versions of *perl*(1) object to PATH environmental variables that begin with a dot (such as `.:/bin:/usr/bin`). V8 clears the PATH variable before executing programs in a user's `~/.forward` file. Some shells put it back with the dot first. Under such versions of the Bourne shell, execute *perl*(1) scripts like this:

```
|"PATH=/bin:/usr/bin /home/usr/bin/script.pl"
```

- There is no check in the T command that the names listed are names of real users. That is, if you mistakenly enter **Tuupc** when you really meant **Tuucp**, pre-V8 *sendmail* remained silent and UUCP mail mysteriously failed. V8.7 and above *sendmail* logs warning messages.

- Many fine books and papers are available that can help you to improve the security at your site. A few are listed in the bibliography at the end of this book.

23

The Queue

Mail messages may either be delivered immediately or be held for later delivery. Held messages are referred to as "queued." They are placed into a holding directory, usually called *mqueue*, from which they are delivered at a later time. There are many reasons a mail message may be queued:

- If a mail message is temporarily undeliverable, it is queued and delivery is attempted later. If the message is addressed to multiple recipients, it is queued only for those recipients to whom delivery is not immediately possible.

- If the **s** configuration option is set to true, all mail messages are queued for safety while delivery is attempted. The message is removed from the queue only if delivery succeeds. If delivery fails, the message is left in the queue, and another attempt is made to deliver it later. This causes the mail to be saved in the unhappy event of a system crash during processing.

- If *sendmail* is run with the `DeliveryMode` (`d`) option (see §34.8.16) set to `queue-only` or `defer`, all mail is queued, and no immediate delivery attempt is made. A separate queue run is required to attempt delivery.

- If the load (average number of blocked processes) becomes higher than the value given to the `QueueLA` (`x`) option (see §34.8.50), *sendmail* queues messages rather than attempting to deliver them. A separate queue run is required later to process the queue.

23.1 Overview of the Queue

The *sendmail* queue is implemented by placing held messages into a directory. That directory and its name (usually *mqueue*) are specified in the configuration file by the QueueDirectory (Q) option (see §34.8.48):

```
OQ/var/spool/mqueue                         ← pre-V8.7 form
O QueueDirectory=/var/spool/mqueue          ← beginning with V8.7
```

If the QueueDirectory (Q) option is missing, the name defaults to mqueue. When the location is relative (as mqueue), it is relative to the location where *sendmail* is run. Since the *sendmail* daemon is typically started from an *rc* file at boot time, such relative locations are usually relative to the *root* (/) directory.[*]

After *sendmail* has processed its configuration file, it does a *chdir*(2) into its queue directory and does all the rest of its work from there. This change into the queue directory has two side effects:

- Should the *sendmail* program fault and produce a core dump, the core image is left in the queue directory.

- Any relative pathnames that are given to options in the configuration file are interpreted as relative to the queue directory. (This is not true for the **F** configuration command; see §32.1.2. Those files are processed at the same time as the configuration file, before the *chdir*.)

The queue directory should be set to have very narrow permissions. It must be owned by *root*. We (and CERT) recommend a mode of 0700. Prior to V8 *sendmail*, such narrow permissions would cause C-shell scripts run from a `˜/.forward` files to fail. V8 *sendmail* lets you specify alternative directories in which to run programs (see the D= delivery agent equate, §30.4.3). This allows you to use mode 0700 queue directories without the associated problems.

As a further precaution, all the components of the path leading to the queue directory should be owned by *root* and be writable only by *root*. In the case of our example of */var/spool/mqueue*, permissions should look like this:

```
drwxr-xr-x   root    /
drwxr-xr-x   root    /var/
drwxr-xr-x   root    /var/spool/
drwx------   root    /var/spool/mqueue/
```

For additional security, see the **restrictmailq** keyword for the **PrivacyOptions** (p) option (see §34.8.47). It allows only users in the same group as the group own-

---

[*] Of course, if *sendmail* is started somewhere else or by someone else, the queue directory will be a subdirectory under that other starting directory.

ership of the queue directory to be able to print its contents with *mailq* or -bp (see §23.4).

23.2 *Parts of a Queued Message*

When a message is stored in the queue, it is split into pieces. Each of those pieces is stored as a separate file in the queue directory. That is, the header and other information about the message are stored in one file, while the body (the data) is stored in another. All told, six different types of files may appear in the queue directory. The type of each is denoted by the first two letters of the filenames. Each filename begins with a single letter followed by an f character. The complete list is shown in Table 23-1.

Table 23-1: Queue File Types

File	§	Description
df	23.2.2	Data (message body)
lf	23.2.3	Lock file (obsolete as of V5.62)
nf	23.2.4	ID creation file (obsolete as of V5.62)
tf	23.2.6	Temporary qf rewrite image
xf	23.2.7	Transcript file
qf	23.2.5	Queue control file (and headers)

The complete form for each filename is

    Xfident

The X is one of the leading letters shown in Table 23-1. The f is the constant letter f. The *ident* is a unique queue identifier associated with each mail message.

In the following sections we first describe the identifier that is common to all the queue file parts, then describe each file type in alphabetical order. The internal details of the qf file can vary depending on the version of *sendmail*, so it is discussed separately at the end of this chapter.

23.2.1 *The Queue Identifier*

To ensure that new filenames are not the same as the names of files that may already be in the queue, *sendmail* uses the following pattern for each new *ident*:

    AApid   ← prior to V8.6
    hourAApid   ← beginning with V8.6

Here, *pid* is the process identification number of the incarnation of *sendmail* that is trying to create the file. Because *sendmail* often *fork*(2)'s to process the queue, that *pid* is likely to be unique, resulting in a unique *ident*. For V8 *sendmail* an extra letter prefixes the AA. Shown as *hour*, it is an uppercase letter that corresponds to the hour (in a 24-hour clock) that the identifier was created. For example, a file created in hour three of the day will have a D prefixed (the hour begins at midnight with A).[*]

If *sendmail* cannot create an exclusive filename (because a file with that identifier already exists), it clocks the second A of the AA to a B and tries again. It continues this process, clocking the right-hand letter from A to Z and the left-hand letter from A to ~ until it succeeds:

```
AA              ← start
AB              ← second try
AC              ← third try
... and so on
~W
~X
~Y              ← last try
~Z              ← failure
```

If it never succeeds, the *ident* ultimately looks like the following and *sendmail* has failed:

```
hour~Zpid
```

This *ident* is unlikely to ever appear, because the clocking provides for over 1600 possibilities.

All the files associated with a given mail message share the same *ident* as a part of their filenames. The individual files associated with a single mail message differ only in the first letter of their names.

23.2.2 The Data (Message Body) File: df

All mail messages are composed of a header and a body. When queued, the body is stored in the *df* file.

Traditionally, the message body could contain only characters that had the high (most significant) bit turned off (cleared, set to 0). But under V8 *sendmail*, with a version 2 or higher configuration file (see §27.5), the high bit is left as is until delivery (whereupon the F=7 delivery-agent flag, see §30.8.4, determines whether or not that bit will be stripped during delivery).

Because the message body can contain sensitive or personal information, the df file should be protected from reading by ordinary users. If the queue directory is world readable, then the TempFileMode (F) option (see §34.8.68) should specify

---

[*] Programs should not depend on the lead letter actually encoding the hour. It is intended only to ensure that all identifiers be unique within any 24-hour period and as an aid to scripts that need to extract information from log files.

minimum permissions (such as 0600) for queued files. But if the queue directory is protected by both narrow permissions and a secure machine, the `TempFileMode` (F) option may be relaxed for easier administration.

There is currently no plan to provide for encryption of `df` files. If you are concerned about the privacy of your message, you should use an end-to-end encryption package (not discussed in this book).

23.2.3 The Lock File (obsolete as of V5.62): lf

When old versions of *sendmail* process a queued message (attempt to redeliver it) they create an empty lock file. That lock file is necessary to signal to other running *sendmail* processes that the mail message is busy so that they won't try to deliver the message too. Current versions simply *flock*(2) or *fcntl*(2) the `qf` file.

23.2.3.1 Current style file locking

The method that *sendmail* uses to initially create an exclusive lock when first queueing a file is twofold. First it attempts to *creat*(2) the file with the argument

```
O_CREAT|O_WRONLY|O_EXCL
```

If that succeeds, it then attempts to lock the file. If HASFLOCK (see §18.8.9) is defined when *sendmail* is compiled, the file is locked with *flock*(2). Otherwise, it is locked with a *fcntl*(2) `F_SETLK` argument.

23.2.3.2 Locks shown when printing the queue

When *mailq* is run (or the `-bp` command-line switch is given to *sendmail*), the contents of the queue are listed. In that listing, an asterisk that appears to the right of an identifier indicates that a lock exists on the message:

```
                   Mail Queue (1 request)
--Q-ID-- -Size- ----Q-Time------ ------------Sender/Recipient------------
MAA17445*   126 Fri Apr 17 10:17 <gw@wash.dc.gov>
   ↑                             <ben@franklin.edu>
  note
```

23.2.3.3 Locks can get stuck

Occasionally, a file will become locked and remain that way for a long time. One indication of a stuck lock is a series of *syslog* messages about a given identifier:

```
Apr 12 00:33:38 ourhost sendmail[641]: AA00614: locked
Apr 12 01:22:14 ourhost sendmail[976]: AA00614: locked
Apr 12 02:49:23 ourhost sendmail[3251]: AA00976: locked
Apr 12 02:49:51 ourhost sendmail[5977]: AA00614: locked
Apr 12 03:53:05 ourhost sendmail[9839]: AA00614: locked
```

An occasional lock message, such as AA00976 in the third line above, is normal. But when an identifier is continually reporting as locked (like the AA00614 lines), an orphaned lock may exist and should be investigated. Use *ps*(1) to look for lines that list queue file identifiers:

```
root     5338 160  -AA00614 To wash.dc.gov (sendmail)
```

This shows that the queued mail message, whose identifier is AA00614, is currently being processed. It the lock on that file is stuck, consider killing the *sendmail* that is processing it.

23.2.4 *The ID Creation File (obsolete as of V5.62): nf*

Old versions of *sendmail* used an nf file when creating a message identifier to avoid race conditions.[*] But contemporary versions of *sendmail* create the queue identifier when first creating the qf file. The nf file is obsolete.

23.2.5 *The Queue Control File: qf*

A queued mail message is composed of two primary parts. The df file contains the message body. The qf file contains the message header.

In addition to the header, the qf file also contains all the information necessary to:

- Deliver the message. It contains the sender's address and a list of recipient addresses.

- Order message processing. It contains a priority that determines the current message's position in a queue run of many messages.

- Expire the message. It contains the date that the message was originally queued. That date is used to time out a message.

- Explain the message. It contains the reason that the message is in the queue and possibly the error that caused it to be queued.

The qf file is line-oriented, with one item of information per line. Each line begins with a single uppercase character (the code letter), which specifies the contents of the line. Each code letter is then followed by the information appropriate to the letter. The code letters and their meanings are shown in Table 23-2 of §23.9.

Here is an example of a version 1 (for V8.8 *sendmail*) qf file:

---

[*] Historical footnote: This stems from the days when the only atomic file-system call was *link*(2).

```
V1
T826845694
K0
N0
P30016
I7/4/20
$_you@localhost
MDeferred: Host wash.dc.gov is down
Syou@your.domain
RPFD:george@wash.dc.gov
RPFD:jefferson
H?P?Return-Path: you@your.domain
HReceived: (from you@your.domain) by your.domain (8.8.4/8.8.4)
        id QAA06571 for george@wash.dc.gov; Thu, 14 Mar 1996 16:21:34 -0700 (MST)
H?D?Date: Thu, 14 Mar 1996 16:21:34 -0700 (MST)
H?F?From: Your Name <you@your.domain>
H?x?Full-Name: Your Name
H?M?Message-Id: <199603142321.QAA06571@your.domain>
HSubject: foo
.
```

This fictional qf file shows the information that will be used to send a mail message from you@your.domain (the S line) to two recipients: george@wash.dc.gov and jefferson (the R lines). It also shows the various headers that appear in that message (the H lines). We discuss the individual lines of the qf file in at the end of this chapter.

23.2.6 *The Temporary qf Rewrite Image: tf*

When processing a queued message, it is often necessary for *sendmail* to modify the contents of the qf file. This usually occurs if delivery has failed or if delivery for only a part of the recipient list succeeded. In either event, at least the message priority needs to be incremented.

To prevent damage to the original qf file, *sendmail* makes changes to a temporary copy of that file. The temporary copy has the same queue identifier as the original, but its name begins with a t.

After the tf file has been successfully written and closed, *sendmail* calls *rename*(2) to replace the original with the copy. If the renaming fails, *sendmail* *syslog*(3)'s at LOG_CRIT a message like the following:

```
cannot rename(tfAA00000, qfAA00000), df=dfAA00000
```

Failure to rename is an unusual, but serious, problem: A queued message has been processed, but its qf file contains old and incorrect information. This failure may, for example, indicate a hardware error, a corrupted queue directory, or that the system administrator accidentally removed the queue directory.

23.2.7 *The Transcript File: xf*

A given mail message may be destined for many recipients, requiring different delivery agents. During the process of delivery, error messages (such as "User unknown" and "Permission denied") can be printed back to *sendmail* by each delivery agent.

While calling the necessary delivery agents, *sendmail* saves all the error messages it receives in a temporary file. The name of that temporary file begins with the letters **xf**. After all delivery agents have been called, *sendmail* returns any collected error messages to the sender and deletes the temporary **xf** file. If there are no errors, the empty **xf** file is silently deleted. The **–d51.104** debugging switch (see §37.5.171) can be used to prevent deletion of the **xf** file.

23.3 *A Bogus qf File (V8 only): Qf*

For security reasons, V8 *sendmail* performs a number of checks on each **qf** file before trusting its contents. If any **qf** file fails to be trustworthy, *sendmail* converts the leading **q** in its name to an uppercase **Q**. We discuss each possible problem in the sections that follow.

Note that when *sendmail* renames a **qf** file into a **Qf** file, it usually (but not always) logs that it did so. In the following, *qffile* is the full filename of the **qf** file, before it was renamed:

    Losing *qffile*: *reason here*

Also note that, although *sendmail* checks the **qf** file for a number of plausibilities, its checking is by no means exhaustive. The checks that we describe here are no substitute for a well managed system.

23.3.1 *Badly Formed qf Filename*

V8.6 *sendmail* always checks the form of the **qf** filename for correctness. V8.7 and above *sendmail* also check the **qf** filename but do so only if PICKY_QF_NAME_CHECK is defined when building (see §18.8.35). If the **qf** file name is incorrectly formed (see §23.2.1), *sendmail* presumes that some other program placed the file in the queue and rejects it:

    orderq: bogus qf name *bogus name here*

Beginning with V8.7, *sendmail* requires PICKY_QF_NAME_CHECK to be defined because some sites allow legitimate programs (other than *sendmail*) to write into *sendmail*'s queue.

To fix this problem, either undefine PICKY_QF_NAME_CHECK when you build *send-mail* (if your site allows other programs to write into the queue directory) or trace down the process that is placing badly formed qf names in your queue and fix it.

23.3.2 Bad qf Owner or Permissions

Each qf file must be owned by the effective user ID under which *sendmail* runs (usually *root*). A qf file must not be group or world writable. If a qf file fails either test, it is considered bogus and is renamed to a Qf file. Then *sendmail* logs these messages:

```
id: bogus queue file, uid=owner, mode=perms
Losing qffile: bogus file uid in mqueue
```

Here, *id* is the identifier portion of the qf file name, *owner* is the *uid* of the user that owns the qf file, and *perms* are the file permissions of the qf file, printed in octal.

This problem may point to bad queue directory permissions that allow anyone (or some group) to place files there. Or it may indicate that some processes other than *sendmail* is writing to your queue.

23.3.3 Extra Data at End of qf File

One form of attack against *sendmail* is to append additional control lines to the end of an existing qf file. V8.7 *sendmail* specifically checks for additional text and rejects the qf file if any is found:

```
SECURITY ALERT: extra data in qf: first bogus line printed here
Losing qffile: bogus queue line
```

V8.7 *sendmail* terminates its legitimate list of qf control lines by placing a dot on a line by itself. Any text following that line, including comments and blank lines, is considered an error. This may represent a serious attack against your machine or site. If you get this message, investigate at once.

23.3.4 Unknown Control Character in qf File

Each line in a qf file must begin with a known control letter or character (see §23.9). If a line begins with any other character, it is considered bad, and the whole file is rejected:

```
readqf: qffile: line num: bad line "bogus line here"
Losing qffile: unrecognized line
```

Note that this error is to be anticipated if you go backwards, from a later release to an earlier release of *sendmail*.

23.3.5 *Funny Flag Bits in qf File*

An F line in a qf file is used to save and restore envelope flag bits. Unfortunately, the first line of a UNIX style mailbox also begins with an F:

```
From someone@site
```

If a qf file's F line begins with the five characters "From ", V8.7 and above *sendmail* will reject the file and log a possible attack:

```
SECURITY ALERT: bogus qf line bogus line here
Losing qffile: bogus queue line
```

This represents a serious attack against your machine or site. If you get this message, investigate at once.

23.3.6 *Savemail Panic*

In the rare event that *sendmail* cannot dispose of a bounced message, it will preserve the qf file as a Qf file and log the message:

```
savemail: cannot save rejected e-mail anywhere
Losing qffile: savemail panic
```

The *sendmail* program tries everything possible to avoid this state (including bouncing the message, sending it to the *postmaster*, and saving it to a *dead.letter* file). Only if all else fails will it preserve the qf file as a Qf file.

In general this points to an alias problem with the user named *postmaster* or the owner of a mailing list. Such users are special. They must be able to receive email messages no matter what. They should be the names of real people, not the names of further mailing lists.

23.4 *Printing the Queue*

When *sendmail* is run under the name *mailq*, or when it is given the –bp command-line switch, it prints the contents of the queue and exits.

Before printing the queue's contents, *sendmail* prereads all the qf files in the queue and sorts the mail messages internally. This is done so that the queue's contents are displayed in the same order in which the messages will be processed during a queue run.

If there are no messages in the queue (no qf files), *sendmail* prints the following message and exits:

```
Mail queue is empty
```

Otherwise, *sendmail* prints the number of messages (number of qf files) in the queue:

```
Mail Queue (# requests)
```

The # is the number of queued messages (requests) in the queue directory. If there are more than the maximum number of messages that may be processed at one time (defined by the MaxQueueRunSize option (see §34.8.38),[*] *sendmail* prints

```
Mail Queue (# requests, only ## printed)
```

The ## is the value of the MaxQueueRunSize option.

Next, *sendmail* prints an attractive heading that looks like the following:

```
--Q-ID-- --Size-- -----Q-Time----- ------------Sender/Recipient------------
MAA12345        354 Fri Mar 15 08:32 your@your.domain
                                     george@wash.dc.gov
MAA12346*      1972 Fri Mar 15 08:45 your@your.domain
     8BITMIME    (Timed out waiting to connect to wash.dc.gov)
                                     jefferson@wash.dc.gov
MAA12347-        23 Fri Mar 15 09:32 your@your.domain
                  (Timed out waiting to connect to wash.dc.gov)
                                     jefferson@wash.dc.gov
                                     bob
```

The heading shows the information that is printed about each message in the queue. The items in that heading and their meanings are the following:

Q-ID

> The queue identifier for the message: the hour character, the clocked AA part, and the *pid* numeric part (like MAA12345). This item can be followed by a character showing the item's status. An asterisk (* as in the second item above), means that the message is locked (an lf file was found or the qf file is locked depending on the kind of locking your version of *sendmail* uses). An X means that the load average is currently too high to allow delivery of the message. A minus (- as in the third item above) means that the message is too young to be processed (based on the MinQueueAge option, see §34.8.41).

Size

> The size in bytes of the df file. If there is no df file (because *sendmail* is currently receiving this message and hasn't created one yet), this item is absent. If the message has completed processing, this prints as:

```
(job completed)
```

---

[*] Prior to V8.7 this was determined by defining QUEUESIZE in *conf.h*.

If the qf file is empty, this prints as

```
(no control file)
```

Q-Time

The date and time that the message was first placed into the queue. This is the T line (see §23.9.15) in the qf file converted from an unsigned integer into a more understandable date and time.

Sender

The sender of the message as taken from the S line (see §23.9.14) in the qf file. Only the first 45 characters of the sender address are printed. If there is a B line (see §23.9.1) in the qf file (as the 8BITMIME in the second item in the example above) *sendmail* prints that body-type (see the -B switch in §36.7.1) on the line following the sender. If there is an M line (see §23.9.9) in the qf file, *sendmail* prints the text of the error message in parentheses.

Recipient

After all of the above items have been printed, a list of the recipients (from each R line, see §23.9.13, in the qf file) is printed in the order in which they are found. In the above example there is one recipient for each of the first two items and two recipients for the last item.

23.4.1 Printing the Queue in Verbose Mode

The -v command-line switch may be used in combination with the -bp switch to cause *sendmail* to also print additional details about the queued messages. To begin, the usual heading shows a new item:

```
--Q-ID-- --Size-- -Priority- ---Q-Time--- -----------Sender/Recipient----------
MAA12345      354       30020 Fri Mar 15 08:32 your@your.domain
                                  george@wash.dc.gov
MAA12346*    1972       48764 Fri Mar 15 08:45 your@your.domain
        8BITMIME   (Timed out waiting to connect to wash.dc.gov)
                                  jefferson@wash.dc.gov
MAA12347-      23    54321+Fri Mar 15 09:32 your@your.domain
                 (Timed out waiting to connect to wash.dc.gov)
                                  jefferson@wash.dc.gov
                              (---you---)
                                  bob
```

The Priority is the value from the P line (see §23.9.11) in the qf file. Printing the queue does not change a message's priority, whereas processing the queue does. See the RecipientFactor (y) option (§34.8.53) for a description of how the priority is calculated.

Verbose mode also causes a + to print after the `Priority` (as in the third item above) if a warning message has been sent. See the `Timeout.queuewarn` option (§34.8.70) for a description of how messages time out.

If any R line is preceded by a controlling user (C line in the qf file; see §23.9.2), verbose mode causes that controlling user's name to be put in parentheses and prepended to the recipient name. The third item in the preceding example illustrates this.

Finally, the M line error messages are normally truncated to 60 characters. Beginning with V8.8 *sendmail*, verbose mode causes the full, nontruncated text of the M line error to be printed.

23.5 *How the Queue Is Processed*

Over time, messages may gather in the queue awaiting delivery. They remain there until *sendmail* performs a queue run to process the queue. The *sendmail* program can be told either to process the queue periodically (when run as a daemon) or to process the queue once, then exit. Each time *sendmail* processes the queue, it also performs a series of operations that are intended to improve the efficiency with which it delivers messages.

First the *queue* directory is opened for reading. If that directory cannot be opened, *sendmail syslog*(3)'s the following message at LOG_CRIT and exits:

```
orderq: cannot open "/var/spool/mailq" as "."
```

This error is usually the result of a user running *sendmail* in an unsafe manner, with a -C command-line argument, for example. It can also result from *sendmail* attempting to open an NFS-mounted queue directory, where *root* is mapped to *nobody*.

Next, the qf files are read to gather their priorities and times (the P and T lines). If a qf file cannot be opened, it is quietly ignored unless the -d41.2 debugging command-line switch (see §37.5.145) is specified. That switch causes *sendmail* to print the following error message:

```
orderq: cannot open qfMAA12345 (reason)
```

Prior to V8.7 *sendmail*, there was a hard limit on the number of messages that could be processed at any time. If more than QUEUESIZE (defined in *conf.h*, typically 1000) messages were in queue, only the first QUEUESIZE (1000) of them would be processed! Ordinarily, this was not a problem. But it could quickly become one if your queue were clogged with a huge number of undeliverable messages (where the first 1000 continued to be deferred). In that case the only solution is to temporarily move the 1000 messages out of the way by hand (see §23.7.1) and clear the queue. The only way to detect this situation is to print the queue (see §23.4).

V8.7 and above *sendmail* dynamically allocates memory to process the queue. If more than QUEUESIZE messages are found, *sendmail* will print the following notice and process them:

```
grew WorkQ for queue_directory to bytes
```

As an alternative to this dynamic behavior, V8.7 and above *sendmail* offers a hard limit that is somewhat like the old version but is site tunable with the MaxQueueRunSize option (see §34.8.38). After all the qf files have been gathered, they are sorted in order of cost. Messages with the lowest value of the P line have the highest priority (lowest cost) and are processed first.

Beginning with V8.7, *sendmail* also offers the QueueSortOrder option (see §34.8.51), which allows you to sort by priority (as before), by priority and host-name, or by date queued. Once all the messages have been sorted, *sendmail* processes each in turn.

23.5.1 *Processing a Single Message*

A single queued message has a single sender but may have many recipients. When processing a queued message, *sendmail* attempts to deliver it to all recipients before processing the next queued message.

The first step in processing a queued message is to lock it so that concurrent runs of *sendmail* do not attempt to process it simultaneously (see §23.2.3.1). Then the qf file is opened and read. The sender and all the recipients are gathered from the corresponding S and R lines.

For each recipient, delivery is attempted. If delivery is successful, that recipient's address is removed from the *sendmail* program's internal list of recipient addresses. If delivery fails, that address is either left in the list or bounced, depending on the nature of the error.

After all recipients have been either delivered, bounced, or left in the list, *sendmail* reexamines that list. If there are no recipients left in it, the message is dequeued (all of the files in the queue directory that compose it are removed). If any recipients are left, the M line is assigned the error message of the last failed message, and the qf file is rewritten with the list of remaining recipients. Finally, the qf file is closed, thus freeing its lock.

Under V8 *sendmail* the `CheckpointInterval` (C) option (see §34.8.7) causes checkpointing of this process. When this option has a positive value, the `qf` file is rewritten after that value's number of recipients have been processed. For example, consider a mail message to five recipients. If the `CheckpointInterval` (C) option is set to a value of 2, the `qf` file is rewritten after the first two recipients have been processed, then again after four, and again after they all have been processed. This keeps the `qf` file reasonably up-to-date as protection against *sendmail* being improperly killed or the machine crashing.

23.6 Cause the Queue to Be Processed

The *sendmail* program offers two different methods for processing the queue. It can be told to process the queue periodically or to process it once and then exit.

23.6.1 Periodically with -q

The `-q` command-line switch is used both to cause the queue to be processed and to specify the interval between queue runs.

A typical invocation of the *sendmail* daemon looks like this:

```
/usr/lib/sendmail -bd -q1h
```

Here, the *sendmail* program is placed into listening mode with the **-bd** command-line switch. The **-q1h** command-line switch tells it to process the queue once each hour. Note that either switch puts *sendmail* into the background as a daemon. The **-bd** switch just allows *sendmail* to listen for incoming SMTP connections. Consider the following:

```
/usr/lib/sendmail -bd
/usr/lib/sendmail -q1h
```

This runs two daemons simultaneously. The first listens for incoming SMTP connections. The second processes the queue once per hour.

At small sites, where mail messages are rarely queued, the time interval chosen may be small, to ensure that all mail is delivered promptly. An interval of **15m** (15 minutes) may be appropriate.

At many sites an interval of one hour is probably best. It is short enough to ensure that delays in delivery remain tolerable, yet long enough to ensure that queue processing does not overlap.

At large sites with huge amounts of mail and at sites that send a great deal of international mail, the interval has to be carefully tuned by observing how long it takes *sendmail* to process the queue and what causes that process to take a long time. Points to consider are the following:

- Network delays or delays at the receiving host may cause delivery to that host to time out. Timeouts are set with the `Timeout` (`r`) option (see §34.8.70).[*] Each such timeout is logged at LOG_NOTICE with a message like this:

  ```
  timeout waiting for input from host during what
  ```

  Here, *host* is the name of the other host, and **what** specifies which timeout triggered the message (such as "client HELO for to_helo). In general, timeouts should be large to ensure that mail to busy sites and to large mailing lists does not time out improperly. In observing the queue processing, you may find that all messages but one process swiftly. That one, you may find, takes over an hour because of a long SMTP timeout. A possible solution to this problem is to make all timeouts short so that most queue runs are processed quickly. Then, for example, the following command could be run a few times each night to specifically flush those long jobs:

  ```
  /usr/lib/sendmail -or2h -q
  ```

- The queue can take a long time to process because too many messages are being queued unnecessarily. Several options affect the placement of mail messages into the queue. The `QueueLA` (`x`) option (see §34.8.50) tells *sendmail* to queue, rather than deliver, a message if the machine load is too high. Fewer messages will be queued if the value of that option is increased. The `Super-Safe` (`s`) option (see §34.8.67) tells *sendmail* to queue all messages for safety. If your machine "never" crashes, this may not be necessary.[†] The `HoldExpensive` (`c`) option (see §34.8.29) tells *sendmail* to queue messages to "expensive" delivery agents (those with the `F=e` flag set; see §30.8.18) rather than delivering them. If the queue is routinely filled with messages to expensive sites, you should reconsider your reasons for marking those sites as expensive.

- The queue can fill with messages because *sendmail* was run with the `-odq` or `-odd` command-line switch (see the `DeliveryMode` (`d`) option, §34.8.16). At sites that receive a great deal of UUCP mail for forwarding, the *rmail*(8) program is often set up to run *sendmail* in "queue only" mode with the `-odq` command-line switch. If UUCP mail is clogging your normal mail services, you should consider queueing it to a separate queue directory. You can then process that other directory with a separate queue run of *sendmail*. (Use of separate queue directories is discussed in §23.7.)

---

[*] Note that prior to V8 *sendmail* the `r` option set one timeout for all SMTP timeouts.

[†] Eric says, "*Set this option.* In fact, it may go away (or be ignored, i.e., always be on) in some future release."

- A slow machine can clog the queue. When a single machine is set up to handle the bulk of a site's mail, that machine should be as swift as possible. In general, a dedicated mail server should have a fast CPU with lots of memory. It should never allow users to log in to it, and it should run its own name server daemon.

23.6.2 From the Command Line

The –q command-line switch, invoked without a time interval argument, is used to run *sendmail* in queue-processing mode. In this mode, *sendmail* processes the queue once and then exits. This mode can be run interactively from the command-line or in the background via *cron*(8).

Other command-line switches can be combined with –q to refine the way the queue is processed. The –v (verbose) switch causes *sendmail* to print information about each message it is processing. The –d (debugging) switch may be used to produce additional information about the queue. We'll discuss the –v switch as it applies to the queue later in this chapter. Those –d debugging switches appropriate to the queue can be found in Table 37-2 of §37.5.

V8 *sendmail* allows variations on –q: –qI allows you to specify a specific message identifier for processing; –qR allows you to specify specific recipient addresses for processing; –qS allows you to specify specific sender addresses for processing.*

23.6.2.1 Process the queue once: -q

The –q command-line switch, without an interval argument, tells *sendmail* to process the queue once, then exit. As such, this switch is a handy administrative tool. When the queue fills unexpectedly between queue runs of the daemon, for example, the –q command-line switch can be used to force an immediate queue run:

```
# /usr/lib/sendmail -q
```

On machines that do not run the *sendmail* daemon, the –q command-line switch can be used in conjunction with *cron*(8) to periodically process the queue. The following *crontab*(5) file entry, for example, causes *sendmail* to be run once per hour, at five minutes past the hour, to silently process the queue and exit:

```
5 * * * * /usr/lib/sendmail -q >/dev/null 2>&1
```

When used in conjunction with other switches (shown below), the –q switch allows many queue problems to be conveniently handled.

---

* IDA and Pre-V8 SunOS *sendmail* offer three different command-line switches for processing the queue. The –M switch allows you to specify a specific message for processing. The –R switch allows you to specify specific recipient addresses for processing. The –S switch allows you to specify specific sender addresses for processing.

23.6.2.2 Combine -v with -q

The -q switch without an argument prevents *sendmail* from running in the background and detaching from its controlling terminal. But it also runs silently. To see
what is going on, use the -v command-line switch in combination with the -q:

```
% /usr/lib/sendmail -v -q
```

The -v command-line switch causes *sendmail* to print a step-by-step description
of what it is doing. To illustrate, consider the following output produced by using
both the -v and -q command-line switches:

```
Running MAA20989 (sequence 1 of 2)
<adams@dc.gov>... Connecting to dc.gov via ddn...
Trying 123.45.67.8... Connection timed out during user open with DC.GOV
<adams@dc.gov>... Deferred: Host DC.GOV is down

Running MAA27002 (sequence 2 of 2)
<help@irs.dc.gov>... Connecting to irs.dc.gov via ddn...
Trying 123.45.67.88... connected.
220 irs.dc.gov Sendmail 5.57/3.0 ready at Mon, 27 Jan 92 09:16:38 -0400
```

Here, two queued messages are being processed. The first fails because of a connection timeout and is requeued for a later queue run. The second succeeds (we
omit the full SMTP dialogue). After its delivery is complete, it is removed from the
queue.

23.6.2.3 Process by identifier/recipient/sender: -q[ISR]

With V8 *sendmail* you can process a subset of all queued messages. You can
select which to process based on queue identifier, recipient address, or sender
address:

```
-qIqueueid
-qRrecipient
-qSsender
```

The -qI variation is followed by a queue identifier such as *KAA34556.* The -qR is
followed by the address of a recipient. The -qS is followed by the address of a
sender. In all three variations there must be no space between the uppercase letter
and the identifier or address.

These variations are used to limit the selection of queued files that are processed.
For example:

```
% /usr/lib/sendmail -qSroot -qRbiff@here
```

Here, the queue is processed once. Only messages from *root* are processed. Of
those, only messages that have *biff@here* as one of the recipients are processed.

In all three variations a partial specification of *queueid, recipient,* or *sender* is viewed by V8 *sendmail* as a substring. For example,

```
-qSroot
```

matches mail from all of the following:

```
root
ben@groots.edu
ben@GROOTS.EDU
```

The last line further illustrates that the substring match is a case-insensitive one. The substring match is literal. Wildcard characters (such as *) and regular expressions (such as .*@.*edu) won't work and may confuse the shell from which you run *sendmail.*

Multiple specifications may be combined on the command line (as shown above), but they all AND together:

```
% /usr/lib/sendmail -qI123 -qSroot -qR@host.edu
```

Here, the queue is processed only for messages with the number 123 anywhere in the message identifier that are also from *root* and that are also addressed to anyone at *host.edu.*

You can use the *mailq* command to preview the effect of these switches. For example, the following command will list (but not send) the messages that would be processed by the above command line:

```
% mailq -qI123 -qSroot -qR@host.edu
```

23.6.2.4 Process the queue via ESMTP ETRN

The ESMTP ETRN command, based on RFC1985, causes V8.8 and above *sendmail* to asynchronously process its queue in a manner similar to the –qR command line switch (see §23.6.2.3). This new command allows dial-on-demand sites to make an SMTP connection and to force the other side to process and send any mail that is queued for them. The form of this ESMTP command looks like this:

```
ETRN hostname
```

If the host is missing, this error message will be returned:

```
550 Parameter required
```

Otherwise, the queue will be processed just as if the following command line argument were given:

```
-qR@hostname
```

In both cases a `qf` file will be processed if it has a host named *hostname* any-where in the host part (following the `@`) of one of its R lines. The only difference here is that the former (the ETRN) operates asynchronously. That is, *sendmail* forks a copy of itself, and the forked child processes the queue.

One way to use **ETRN** is with a simple Bourne shell script:

```
#!/bin/sh
OURSITE=here.uofa.edu
MAILSERVER=mailhub.uofa.edu
TELNET=/usr/ucb/telnet
PORT=25

echo "etrn $OURSITE" | $TELNET $MAILSERVER $PORT
exit 0
```

If run on a dial-on-demand host, this script will force a dial-up network connec-tion to be made. The mail server's *sendmail* is then forced, with ETRN, to process the queue and transport back any mail destined for the local host over the just-created network connection.

23.7 Process Alternate Queues

The *sendmail* program provides the ability to use queue directories other than the one listed in the configuration file's `QueueDirectory` (Q) option (see §34.8.48). Other queue directories can be used to solve an assortment of problems. One example is a site being down for an extended period. When a lot of mail is sent to such a site, messages collect in the queue and eventually start timing out. By mov-ing those messages to a separate queue directory and processing it at a later time (when that site is back up), unnecessary bouncing of mail can be prevented.

Note that the `QueueDirectory` (Q) option is not safe. If its value is changed by anyone other than *root*, *sendmail* runs as an ordinary user.

23.7.1 Handling a Down Site

If a site is down, messages to that site can collect in the queue. If the site is expected to be down for a protracted period of time, those queued messages will begin to time out and bounce. To prevent them from bouncing, you can move them to a separate queue directory. Later, when the down site comes back up, you can process that separate queue.

To move the affected messages to a separate queue, you may use a Bourne shell script like the following:

```
#!/bin/sh
set -u
QUEUE=/var/spool/mqueue
```

```
NEWQ=/var/spool/newqueue

if [ ! -d $QUEUE ]
then
        echo "${QUEUE}: Does not exist or is not a directory"
        exit 1
fi
if [ ! -d $NEWQ ]
then
        mkdir -p $NEWQ
        if [ $? -ne 0 ]
        then
                echo "${NEWQ}: Can't create"
                exit 2
        fi
fi
find ${QUEUE} -type f -name qf* -print |\
while read QF
do
        IDENT=`echo $QF | sed -e "s,^${QUEUE}/qf,,"`
        grep "^R" ${QUEUE}/qf${IDENT}
        echo -n "move ${IDENT}? (y/n) "
        read answer
        case $answer in
                [nN]*)  continue;;
                *)          ;;
        esac
        mv ${QUEUE}/*${IDENT} $NEWQ
        if [ $? -ne 0 ]
        then
                echo "Move failed"
                exit 3
        else
                echo "Move succeeded"
        fi
done
/usr/lib/sendmail -OQueueDirectory=${NEWQ} -bp
```

This script creates a new queue directory, $NEWQ, if it doesn't exist. It then prints the recipient list for each **qf** file in the queue (the *grep*(1) in $QUEUE) and asks whether you want to move that file. If you answer yes, all the files that compose the queued message are moved into $NEWQ. After all the messages have been moved, the contents of $NEWQ are printed using the **QueueDirectory** (**Q**) option:

```
% /usr/lib/sendmail -OQueueDirectory=${NEWQ} -bp
```

When the down site comes back up at a later time, the messages that have been saved in $NEWQ can be delivered by running the following command by hand:

```
% /usr/lib/sendmail -OQueueDirectory=/var/spool/newqueue -OTimeout.queuereturn=99d -q
```

The `-oTimeout.queuereturn=99d` causes the time to live in the queue to be extended to 99 days. This prevents the held mail in ${NEWQ} from wrongly bouncing when you try to deliver it.

23.8 Pitfalls

- Each release of *sendmail* offers more and better ways to handle queue problems. They are mostly implemented as options. Table 34-7 in §34.6.2 lists all options that affect the queue. Of special interest are the new `MaxQueueRun-Size`, `Timeout.queuereturn`, and `Timeout.queuewarn` options. Whenever you upgrade to a new *sendmail* release, be sure to read the *RELEASE_NOTES* for that latest information about new ways to solve queueing problems.

- The queue directory should never be shared among machines. Such sharing can make detection of orphaned locks impossible. Bugs in network locking daemons can lead to race conditions in which neither of two machines can generate a queue identifier.

- In old versions of *sendmail* it was possible for an `lf` file to be left in place even though its corresponding mail message was not being processed. Such spurious files prevented the message from ever being delivered unless they were removed by hand. Spurious lock files could be detected by watching the *syslog*(5) file for frequent `locked` warnings.

- Homespun programs and shell scripts for delivery of local mail can fail and lose mail by exiting with the wrong value. In the case of a recoverable error (a full disk, for example) they should exit with EX_OSERR or EX_TEMPFAIL. Both these exit values are defined in *<sysexits.h>* and cause the message to be requeued.

- Because *sendmail* does a *chdir*(2) into its queue directory, you should avoid removing and recreating that directory while the *sendmail* daemon is running. When processing the queue, *sendmail* tries to read the queue directory by doing an *opendir*(3) of the current directory. When the queue directory is removed, *sendmail* fails that open and *syslog*(3)'s the following warning:

  ```
  orderq: cannot open "/usr/spool/mqueue" as ".": No such file or directory
  ```

- Under a few old versions of *sendmail* a bug in handling the queue could cause a message to be lost when that message was the last in a queue run to be processed. This, among other reasons, is good cause to always make sure you are running the latest version of *sendmail*.

- The *sendmail* program assumes that only it and other trusted *root* programs will place files into the queue directory. Consequently, it trusts everything it finds there. The queue directory *must* be protected from other users and untrusted programs.

- If the queue directory is on a disk mounted separately from / and */usr*, be certain to mount that disk *before* starting the *sendmail* daemon. If you reverse these steps, the *sendmail* daemon will *chdir*(2) into the queue before the mount. One effect of the reversal is that incoming mail will use a different directory than outgoing mail. Another effect is that incoming queued mail will be invisible. Yet another effect is that the outgoing queue will never be processed by the daemon.

23.9 *The qf File Internals*

The qf file holds all the information that is needed to perform delivery of a queued mail message. The information contained in that file, and its appearance, changes from release to release of *sendmail*. Here, we document the qf file that is used with V8.8 *sendmail*. Note that as of V8.7 a V version line has been introduced to enable future versions to correctly process older version's queue files.

This section must be taken with a proverbial grain of salt. The internals of the qf file are essentially an internal interface to *sendmail* and, as such, are subject to change without notice. The information offered here is intended only to help debug *sendmail* problems. It is *not* intended (and we strongly discourage its use) as a guide for writing files directly to the queue.

The qf file is line-oriented, containing one item of information per line. Each line begins with a single uppercase character (the *code letter*), which specifies the contents of the line. Each code letter is followed, with no intervening space, by the information appropriate to the letter. The complete list of code letters is shown in Table 23-2.

Table 23–2: qf File Code Letters

Code	§	Meaning	Version	How Many
B	23.9.1	Body type	V8.6 and above	At most one
C	23.9.2	Controlling user	V5.62 and above	At most one per R line
D	23.9.3	Data filename	Obsolete as of V8.7	Exactly one
E	23.9.4	Errors to	V8.6 and earlier	Many
F	23.9.5	Flag bits	V8.1 and above	Many
H	23.9.6	Header definition	All versions	Many
I	23.9.8	*df* file's inode number	V8.7 and above	Exactly one
K	23.9.8	Time last processed	V8.7 and above	Exactly one
M	23.9.9	Message (why queued)	All versions	At most one
N	23.9.10	Number times tried	V8.7 and above	At most one
P	23.9.11	Priority (current)	All versions	At most one
Q	23.9.12	Original recipient	V8.7 and above	At most one per R line
R	23.9.13	Recipient address	All versions	Many

Table 23–2: qf File Code Letters (continued)

Code	§	Meaning	Version	How Many
S	23.9.14	Sender address	All versions	Exactly one
T	23.9.15	Time created	All versions	Exactly one
V	23.9.16	Version	V8.7 and above	Exactly one
Z	23.9.17	DSN envelope ID	V8.7 and above	At most one
$	23.9.18	Restore macro value	V8.6 and above	At most one each
.	23.9.19	End of *qf* file	V8.7 and above	At most one

Some code letters may appear only once in a qf file; others may appear many times. Any line that begins with a tab or space character is joined to the line above it. Empty lines are ignored. The order in which these lines appear in the qf file is important for the *mailq* command to work properly.

We discuss the individual lines in the qf file by code letters. Each letter is presented in alphabetical order rather than the order in which they should appear in the qf file.

B line   *(V8.6 and above)*

23.9.1   *Message body type*

The message body type is described under the –B command-line switch (see §36.7.1). The B line in the qf file stores whatever the body type was set to, either from the command line or by the SMTP MAIL command. The two usual body types are 8BITMIME or 7BIT.

The form of the B line is

    Btype

There must be no space between the B and the *type*. If the *type* is missing, the body type becomes the character value zero. If the entire B line is missing, the default is 7BIT. If *type* is longer than MAXNAME as defined in *conf.h* (see §18.8.19) when compiling *sendmail*, it is truncated to MAXNAME-1 characters when the qf file is read.

Note that the *type* must be either 7bit or 8bitmime. Anything else will not be detected when the qf file is read and may eventually cause the ESMTP dialogue to fail:

    501 <sender>... Unknown BODY type badtype

This error will be reproduced at every MX site for the recipient until a site that does not speak ESMTP is found or until the MX list is exhausted.

C line

23.9.2

Set controlling user

To ensure secure handling of delivery, recipient addresses that are either a file or a program require that *sendmail* perform delivery as the owner of the file or program rather than as *root*. A file address is one that begins with a / character. A program address is one that begins with a | character. Both characters are detected after quotation marks have been stripped from the address.

To prevent potential security violations, *sendmail* must take special precautions when addresses in the qf file result from reading a */.forward* or :include: file. When such an address is to be placed into the qf file (whether as a recipient's address in an R line or as an error recipient's address in an E line), *sendmail* first places a C line (for Controlling user) into the file and then the recipient's address. The C line specifies the owner of the */.forward* or :include: file:

```
Cgeorge
RPF:/u/users/george/mail/archive
Cben
RPF:|/u/users/ben/bin/mailfilter
```

Here, when *sendmail* later delivers to the recipients in this qf file, it first converts its user identity to that of the user *george*, then resets itself back to being *root* again. The same process repeats with the next recipient, except that *sendmail* changes from *root* to *ben* and back again. If there is no C line preceding a R line, the previous C line's value is carried down:

```
Cgeorge
RPF:/u/users/george/mail/archive
RPF:|/u/users/ben/bin/mailfilter      ← controlling user is george
```

The form of the C line in the qf file is

```
Cuser                    ← Prior to V8
Cuser:eaddr              ← V8.1 through V8.7.5
Cuser:uid:gid:eaddr      ← V8.7.6 and V8.8
```

The C must begin the line and be immediately followed by **user**, with no intervening space. If no **user** follows the C, any prior controlling user is cleared and the identity that is used reverts to that specified by the **DefaultUser** (u) option (see §34.8.15). If present, the **user** is the login name of the owner of the */.forward* or :include: file that yielded the address in the next following R or E line. If **user** is the name of a user who is unknown to the system, prior to V8.7.6 and prior to V8.8 the effect was the same as if it were missing. Beginning with V8.8 and V8.7.6, an unknown **user** causes the identity to become that of the **uid** and **gid**. Beginning with V8 *sendmail*, an optional **eaddr** may be last. If present, the **eaddr** gives the address to use for error messages.

There may be only one C line immediately preceding each R and E line. Two C lines in a row have the effect of the second superseding the first.

D line   *(Obsolete as of V8.7)*

23.9.3   *Data filename*

Beginning with V8.7 *sendmail* looks for its data file (the file containing the message body) under the same name as its qf file, but with the q changed into a d. Prior to V8.7, the D line in the qf file contained the name of the file that contained the message body. If the D line was missing, there was no message body. The form of the qf file D line was

    Dfile

The D must begin the line. The *file* must immediately follow with no intervening space. All text, from the first character following the D to the end of the line, is taken as the name of the file. There is no default for *file*; either it must be present, or the entire D line must be absent.

The *sendmail* program opens the df *file* for reading. If that open fails, *sendmail* *syslog*(3)'s the following error message at LOG_CRIT and continues to process the qf file:

    readqf: cannot open dfAA12345

Be aware that *sendmail* attempts to remove the *file* after it has been delivered to all recipients. If *sendmail* is unable to remove the *file*, and if the LogLevel (L) option (see §34.8.33) is greater than 97, *sendmail* *syslog*(3)'s the following warning at LOG_DEBUG:

    file: unlink-fail #

The *file* is the name of the file that could not be removed. The # is the error number, as defined in */usr/include/errno.h*.

The df file is opened only when processing the queue file, not when printing it.

E line   *(V8.6 and earlier)*

23.9.4   *Send errors to*

Notification of errors often requires special handling by *sendmail*. When mail to a mailing list fails, for example, *sendmail* looks for the owner of that list. If it finds one, the owner, not the sender, receives notification of the error. To differentiate error notification addresses from ordinary sender and recipient addresses, pre-V8.7 *sendmail* stored error addresses separately in the qf file, one per E line. Beginning with V8.7, this E line is no longer used. Instead, *sendmail uses the* S line.

The form of the **E** line in the qf file looks like this:

```
Eaddr          ← V8.6 and earlier
```

The **E** must begin the line. One or more addresses may be entered on that same line. Whitespace and commas may surround the individual addresses. Note, however, that *sendmail* places only a single address on each **E** line. There may be multiple **E** lines. Each is processed in turn.

Each line is fully processed as it is read. That is, the line is scanned for multiple addresses. Each address that is found is alias-expanded. Each resulting new address is processed by rule sets 3 and 0 to resolve a delivery agent for each.

If an alias expands to a program or a file (text that begins with a / or | character), that text is sent out in the delivered message's **Errors-To:** line in that form. This can cause confusion when the message is later processed and bounced at the receiving site.

F line   *(V8.1 and above)*

23.9.5   *Saved flag bits*

Under V8 *sendmail* the **Timeout.queuewarn** option (see §34.8.70) can specify an interval to wait before notifying the sender that a message could not immediately be delivered. To keep track of whether such a notification has been sent, *sendmail* stores the state of its EF_WARNING envelope flag in the qf file. If that flag is set, notification has already been sent.

Error mail messages sent by *sendmail* may occasionally be queued, rather than immediately delivered. The **Timeout.queuewarn** option notification should not be sent for such mail. If such mail remains in the queue too long, it should be canceled rather than bounced. V8 *sendmail* saves the state of the EF_RESPONSE envelope flag in the qf file. If that flag is set, the message is an error notification.

Beginning with V8.8, *sendmail* also records the state of the EF_HAS8BIT flag (the message body contains 8-bit data) and the EF_DELETE_BCC flag (delete empty **Bcc:** headers; see §35.10.4).

All envelope flags are listed in Table 37-3 of §37.5.12. The **F** line is used to save envelope flags for later restoration. Its form looks like this:

```
Fflags
```

Here, the *flags* are any combination of **w**, which restores (sets) the EF_WARNING flag; **r**, which restores the EF_RESPONSE flag; **8**, which restores the EF_HAS8BIT flag; and **b**, which restores the EF_DELETE_BCC flag. Only those letters are recognized. Other letters are silently ignored. Note that these flags may be done away with in later versions of *sendmail* and new flags may be added without notice.

For security protection, V8 *sendmail* rejects and logs the following flag sequence:

```
From
  ↑
a space here
```

See §23.3.5 for more information about this.

H line   *(All versions of sendmail)*

23.9.6   *Header line*

The lines of text that form the message header are saved to the qf file, one per H line. Any header lines added by *sendmail* are also saved to H lines in the qf file.

The form of the H line is:

```
Hdefinition
```

The H must begin the line, and the **definition** must immediately follow with no intervening space. The **definition** is exactly the same as, and obeys the same rules as, the H commands in the configuration file (see §35.1).

When *sendmail* writes header lines to the qf file, it pre-expands macros (replaces expressions such as $x with their values) and preresolves conditionals ($?, $!, and $.).

The order in which H lines appear in the qf file is exactly the same as the order in which they appear in the delivered message.

I line   *(V8.7 and above)*

23.9.7   *Inode and device information for the df file*

When a machine crashes under UNIX, files in a directory may become detached from that directory. When this happens, those orphaned files are saved in a directory called *lost+found*. Because file names are saved only in directories, orphaned files are nameless. Consequently, UNIX stores them in *lost+found* using their *inode* numbers as their names.

To illustrate, consider finding these four files in *lost+found* after a crash:

```
#1528 #1200 #3124 #3125
```

Two of these are qf files, and two are df files. Beginning with V8.7 *sendmail* the qf files contain a record of the inode numbers for their corresponding df files. That information is stored in the I line:

```
Imajor/minor/ino
```

Here, the *major* and *minor* are the major and minor device numbers for the disk device that the df file was stored on. The *ino* is the inode number for the df file. In our above *lost+found* example the following command could be run to pair up the orphaned files:

```
% grep "^I.*/.*/" *
#1200:I123/45/3124
#1325:I123/45/1528
```

This shows that the qf file *#1200* has the df file *#3124* and that the qf file *#1325* has the df file *#1528*.

The *sendmail* program does not check the inode number in the I line against the actual inode number of the df file. Instead, the I line is generated afresh each time the qf file is processed.

K line   *(V8.7 and above)*

23.9.8   *The time last processed from the queue*

The MinQueueAge option (see §34.8.41) sets the length of time a queued message must remain queued before delivery can again be tried. Each time *sendmail* processes a qf file, it subtracts the time stored in the K line from the current time and compares the result to the MinQueueAge. If sufficient time has not passed, the rest of processing is skipped. (Note that this test is performed only if the qf file has been processed at least once; see the N line in §23.9.9).

The time stored in the K line looks like this:

```
K703531020
```

This number represents the date and time in seconds. Every time the qf file is processed (delivery is attempted), the K line is updated with the current time.

M line   *(All versions of sendmail)*

23.9.9   *The reason message was queued*

When a mail message is placed into the queue because of an error during the delivery attempt, the nature of that error is stored in the M line of the qf file. The error is usually prefixed with **Deferred**:

```
Deferred: reason
```

Delivery can be deferred until a later queue run because of a temporary lack of services. For example, the *reason* may be "remote host is down."

The form of the qf file M line is:

    Mmsg

The M must begin the line. It is immediately followed by the *msg* with no intervening space. The text of *msg* is everything up to the end of the line. The *msg* created by *sendmail* may include the word **Deferred:**, followed by a reason. The M line should appear before the S line.

If the *msg* is missing, *sendmail* simply prints a blank line rather than a reason when showing the queue with *mailq* or the **-bp** command-line switch. If the M line is entirely missing, *sendmail* prints nothing.

The maximum number of characters in *msg* is defined by MAXLINE in *conf.h* (see §18.8.19). There should be only one M line in a qf file. If there are multiple M lines, only the last is used. If multiple recipients produced error messages, only the last one is stored in an M line.

N line   *(V8.7 and above)*

23.9.10   *Number of times tried*

Each time delivery is attempted for a message, the number stored in its qf file's N line is incremented by one. This number always begins at zero.

When delivering many messages to a single host, *sendmail* remembers failures. If one message fails to make it all the way through an SMTP dialogue, all the following messages to that same host will be deferred (not attempted during the current queue run). For those deferred messages the number of tries is correctly incremented as though the delivery was actually attempted.

The value in this N line is used to determine whether the delay of the **MinQueueAge** option (see §34.8.41) should be triggered. This value, when zero, can also be used to enable a special first-time connection timeout (see §34.8.70.9).

P line   *(All versions of sendmail)*

23.9.11   *Priority when processed from queue*

Not all messages need to be treated equally. Messages that have failed often, for example, tend to continue to fail. When sendmail processes the messages in its queue, it sorts them by priority that was and attempts to deliver those most likely to succeed first.

When a mail message is first placed into the queue, it is given an initial priority calculated when it was first created (see §34.8.53), which is stored in the P line:

    P640561

This number in the qf file is really a cost. The *lower* it is, the more preferentially the message is treated by *sendmail.* Each time the qf file is read, the number in the P line is incremented. The size of that increment is set by the value of the RetryFactor (Z) option (see §34.8.56). If that option is negative, the logic of "what fails will continue to fail" is inverted.

The form of the qf file P line is

    Ppri

The P must begin the line. The *pri* is a text representation of an integer value. The *pri* must immediately follow the P with no intervening space. The text in *pri* is converted to an integer using the C library routine *atol*(3). That routine allows *pri* to be represented in text as a signed decimal number, an octal number, or a hexadecimal number.

If *pri* is absent, the priority value used is that of the configuration file RetryFactor (Z) option. If the entire P line is absent, the priority value begins as zero.

There should be only one P line in any qf file. Multiple P lines cause all but the last to be ignored.

Q line   *(V8.7 and above)*

23.9.12   *The DSN ORCPT address*

When a mail message arrives that includes an ORCPT parameter for the ESMTP RCPT command (see RFC1891), *sendmail* needs to save that parameter's information separately from the RCPT recipient address:

    RCPT TO:<gw@wash.dc.gov> ORCPT=rfc822;gw@wash.dc.gov
           ↑   ↑
        recipient address   parameter's information

Not all sites understand ESMTP. If *sendmail* forwards the message to such a site, it needs to omit the ORCPT parameter. Consequently, *sendmail* must not store that parameter with the RCPT address.

The Q line is used to separately store the ORCPT parameter information:

    Qtype;addr

The *type;addr* is defined by RFC1891. The *sendmail* program checks the validity of *addr* when that information is received but otherwise merely stores *type;addr* as is in the Q line.

There must be only a single Q line for each recipient R line, and each such Q line must precede its corresponding R line.

R line   *(All versions of sendmail)*

23.9.13   *Recipient's address*

The qf file lists all the recipients for a mail message. There may be one recipient or many. When *sendmail* creates the qf file, it lists each recipient address on an individual R line. The form of the R line in the qf file looks like this:

```
Rflags:addr
```

The R must begin the line. Only a single address may appear on each R line. There may be multiple R lines. Each is processed in turn.

If the colon is present and if the version of the qf file is greater than 0, the characters between the R and the colon are interpreted as flags that further define the nature of the address:

P   (primary) Addresses can undergo many transformations prior to delivery. When expanding aliases, for example, the address *george* might be transformed into two addresses via a ˜/.*forward* file: *george@here* and *george@there*. In this instance, *george* is the primary address, and the aliases are secondary addresses. If aliasing yields only a single transformation, the single new address is considered primary. Addresses that are received via a RCPT SMTP command are always considered primary, as are all other recipient addressees prior to aliasing.

N   (notify) Recipient addresses can lead to various kinds of notification based on the nature of the DSN NOTIFY extension to the RCPT SMTP command. That notification can be either NEVER or some combination of SUCCESS, FAILURE, or DELAY. Internally, *sendmail* uses the absence of the latter three to imply NEVER. This N flag simply says that the DSN NOTIFY extension appeared in the message. If the N is absent, but an S, F, or D is present, DSN information will not be propagated. Note that NOTIFY can also be specified by using the –N command line switch (see §36.7.28).

S, F, D
    (success, failure, delay) The DSN NOTIFY extension to the RCPT SMTP command will specify either NEVER or some combination of SUCCESS, FAILURE, or DELAY. When any of these is specified, its first letter is used as a flag for the recipient address. SUCCESS means to notify the sender that final delivery succeeded. FAILURE is used to notify the sender that some step toward delivery failed fatally. DELAY lets the sender know that the message has been delayed but delivery will continue to be attempted.

Each R line is fully processed as it is read. That is, the line is scanned for multiple addresses. Each address that is found is alias-expanded. Each resulting new address is processed by rule sets 3 and 0 to resolve a delivery agent for each.

S line

23.9.14

Sender's address

Each mail message must have a sender. The *sendmail* program can determine the sender in four ways:

- If the sender is specified in the envelope of an SMTP connection, that sender's address is used.

- If the -f command-line argument is used to run *sendmail,* the sender's address is the address following the -f.

- If the sender is not specified in the envelope, the address that is used is that of the user who ran the *sendmail* program. If that user is unknown, the sender is made to be *postmaster.*

- When processing the queue, the sender's address is specified in the S line of the qf file.

The form of the S line in the qf file looks like this:

    Saddr

The S must begin the line. Exactly one address must follow on that same line. Whitespace may surround that address. There may be only one S line in the qf file.

If the *addr* is missing, *sendmail* sets the sender to be the user who ran *sendmail.* If that user is not known in the *passwd* file (or database), *sendmail syslog*(3)'s the following message and sets the sender to be *postmaster:*

    Who are you?

The resulting address is then processed to extract the user's full name into $x (see §31.10.42). Finally, the sender's address is rewritten by rule sets 3, 1, and then 4.

Under all versions of *sendmail* the address in the S line will include any RFC822 comment text that appeared with the original message. Under V8.7, if the F=c flag (see §30.8.14) is set for the sender's delivery agent, all comment text is stripped from the address.

If *sendmail* is compiled with USERDB defined (see §18.8.54), the sender address can optionally be rewritten by the User Database before it is placed into the S line. Such rewriting is allowed only if the delivery agent for the sender includes the F=i flag (see §30.8.24).

T line   *(All versions of sendmail)*

23.9.15   *Creation time*

To limit the amount of time a message can remain in the queue before being bounced, *sendmail* must know when that message was first placed in the queue. That time of first placement is stored in the T line in the qf file. For example, the following number represents the date and time in seconds:

    T703531020

Each time *sendmail* fails to deliver a message from the queue, it checks to see whether too much time has passed. It adds the T line value to the value specified in the `Timeout.queuereturn` (T) option (see §34.8.70). If that sum is less than the current time, the message is bounced instead of being left in the queue.

Messages are occasionally left in the queue for longer than the normal timeout period. This might happen, for example, if a remote machine is down but you know that it will eventually be brought back up. There are two ways to lengthen the amount of time a message may remain in the queue.

The preferred way is to create a temporary separate queue directory and move the necessary queued file to that temporary holding place. When the remote site comes back up, you can later process the files in that other queue by running *sendmail* with an artificially long `Timeout.queuereturn` value (see §23.7).

A second way to extend the life of messages in the queue is to edit the qf file and change the value stored in the T line. Just add 86400 to that value for each day you want to extend. Care is required to avoid editing a file that is currently being processed by *sendmail.**

There is currently no plan to give *sendmail* the ability to rejuvenate queued messages (make old messages appear young).

The form of the T line in the qf file is:

    Tsecs

The T begins the line, and the ***secs*** must immediately follow with no intervening space. The numeric text that forms ***secs*** is converted to an integer using the C library routine *atol*(3). That routine allows ***secs*** to be represented in text as a signed decimal number, an octal number, or a hexadecimal number.

If ***secs*** is absent or the entire T line is absent, the time value is zero. A zero value causes the mail message to time out immediately.

---

* The *nvi*(1) editor uses the same file locking as *sendmail* and so can safely be used to edit qf files.

There should be only one T line in any qf file. Multiple T lines cause all but the last to be ignored.

V line   *(V8.7 and above)*

23.9.16   *Version of the qf file*

s *sendmail* evolves, it will continue to add new abilities to the qf file. To protect old versions of *sendmail* from wrongly misinterpreting new configuration files, the V line has been introduced. Prior to V8.7 *sendmail* there was no V line. For versions prior to 8.7.6 the version for the V line is 1:

> V1   *← V8.7.5 and earlier*

For V8.7.6 and above, including V8.8, the version is 2 (where version 2 changes the layout of the C line in the qf file):

> V2   *← V8.7.6 and above and V8.8*

If the version is greater than that currently supported, *sendmail* will log this error and exit:

> Version number in qf (*bad*) greater than max (*max*)

A version 1 qf file allows *flags* to follow the R line.

Z line   *(V8.7 and above)*

23.9.17   *DSN ENVID envelope identifier*

The MAIL ESMTP command may optionally be followed by an RFC1891 ENVID envelope identifier:

> MAIL From: <*address*> ENVID=*envelopeID*

ENVID is used to propagate a consistent envelope identifier (distinct from the **Message-ID:** header see §35.10.19) that is permanently associated with a message.

The Z line holds that ENVID envelope identifier information:

> Z*envelopeID*

The ENVID information needs to be held separately from the S sender line because *sendmail* has no way to determine in advance whether a recipient host speaks ESMTP.

There must be only a single Z line in any qf file. The ${envid} macro (see §31.10.12) also stores the ENVID value.

$ line
(V8.6 and above)

23.9.18
Restore macro value

The *sendmail* program uses the $r macro (see §31.10.31) to store the protocol used when *sendmail* first received a mail message. If the message was received by using SMTP, that protocol is smtp. Otherwise, it is NULL.

The *sendmail* program uses the $s macro (see §31.10.33) to store the full canonical name of the sender's machine.

The *sendmail* program uses the $_ macro (see §31.10.1) to store RFC1413 *identd*(8) information and IP source routing information.

When *sendmail* creates a qf file, it saves the values of the $r, $s, and $_ macros in lines that begin with $.

The form of the $ line in the qf file looks like this:

```
$Xvalue
```

The $ must begin the line, and the macro's single-character name (the X) must immediately follow with no intervening space. The X is followed (again with no intervening space) by the value of the macro.

If *value* is missing, the value given to the macro is NULL. If the X and *value* are missing, the macro \0 is given a value of NULL. If both are present, the macro that is specified (X) is given the value specified (*value*).

There may be multiple $ lines. The need to quickly process a qf file requires that only single-character macro names be used.

. line
(V8.7 and above)

23.9.19
Mark EOF in qf file

One form of attack against *sendmail* involves appending information to an existing qf file. To prevent such attacks, V8.7 introduced the dot line. In a qf file, any line that begins with a single dot:

```
.followed by anything
```

is considered to mark the end of the file's useful information. Upon encountering that dot, *sendmail* continues to read the qf file. If any line follows the dot line, *sendmail* logs the following message and changes the qf file into a Qf file (see §23.3.3):

```
SECURITY ALERT: extra data in qf: bogus line here
```

24

Aliases

Aliasing is the replacing of one recipient address with one or more different recipient addresses. The replacement address can be that of a single user, a list of recipients, a program, a file, or any mixture of these. In this chapter we cover the *aliases*(5) file, one of the three methods of aliasing available with the *sendmail* program. We cover the other two forms, `:include:` (for including separate files from within the *aliases* file) and `~/.forward` (the user's personal `:include:` file) in the next chapter.

Aliasing can be used to handle several complex delivery problems:

- Delivering mail to a single user under a variety of usernames
- Distributing a mail message to many users by specifying only a single recipient name
- Appending mail to files for archival and other purposes
- Filtering mail through programs and shell scripts

All the information that is needed to perform these tasks is contained in the *aliases*(5) file (which is often also stored in database format to make lookups faster).

24.1 The aliases(5) File

The *aliases*(5) file is one of several sources that can supply system mail aliases. We describe it first because it is the most traditional and because it illustrates the syntax and limitations common to all techniques.

The *aliases*(5) file is composed of lines of text. Any line that begins with a # is a comment and is ignored. Empty lines (those that contain only a newline character) are also ignored. Any line that begins with a space or a tab is joined (appended) to the line above it. All other lines of text are viewed as alias lines. The format for an alias line is:

```
local: alias
```

The `local` must begin a line. It is an address in the form of a local recipient address (we will discuss this in more detail soon). The colon follows the `local` on the same line and may be preceded with spaces or tabs. If the colon is missing, *sendmail* prints and *syslog*(3)'s the following error message and skips that alias line:

```
missing colon
```

The `alias` (to the right of the colon) is one or more addresses on the same line. Indented continuation lines are permitted. Each address should be separated from the next by a comma and optional space characters. A typical alias looks like this:

```
root: jim, sysadmin@server,
      gunther
    ↑
  indenting whitespace
```

Here, `root` is the local address to be aliased. When mail is to be locally delivered to `root`, it is looked up in the *aliases*(5) file. If found, `root` is replaced with the three addresses shown earlier, and mail is instead delivered to those other three addresses.

This process of looking up and possibly aliasing local recipients is repeated for each recipient until no more aliases are found in the *aliases*(5) file. That is, for example, if one of the aliases for `root` is `jim` and if `jim` also exists to the left of a colon in the *aliases* file, he too is replaced with his alias:

```
jim: jim@otherhost
```

The list of addresses to the right of the colon may be mail addresses (such as *gunther* or *jim@otherhost*), the name of a program to run (such as */etc/relocated*), the name of a file onto which to append (such as */usr/share/archive*), or the name of a file to read for additional addresses (using `:include:`). The `:include:` is used in creating mailing lists and will be covered in the next chapter.

24.1.1 The aliases(5) file's location

The location of the *aliases*(5) file is specified with the `ServiceSwitchFile` option (see 34.8.61) and the `AliasFile` (A) option (see §34.8.1) in the configuration file. Be aware that, since these two options interact, it may not suffice to simply declare one or the other. Also be aware that some systems supply service-switch files that will be used even if the `ServiceSwitchFile` option is omitted.

Note that the service-switch file merely specifies the order in which various methods should be used to look up aliases, not the specific files. If it lists `files` as a method:

```
aliases    files
```

then all the files declared with the `AliasFile` option will be looked up in the order in which they were declared:

- If the `AliasFile` option specifies a file and if a service-switch file omits the `files` specification, the `AliasFile` option is ignored.

- If the `AliasFile` option specifies a file and if a service-switch file omits the `aliases` line, the `AliasFile` option is used.

- If the `AliasFile` option specifies a file and if there is no service-switch file, then the `AliasFile` option file is used.

- If the `AliasFile` option is omitted and if there is no service-switch file or if there is a service-switch file but it omits an `aliases` line, *sendmail* silently presumes that it should not do aliasing.

Note that service-switch files and `AliasFile` (A) option can list other techniques for obtaining aliases in addition to, or instead of, an *aliases*(5) file. But this can lead to a side effect. For example, if your configuration file declares

```
O AliasFile=/etc/aliases,nis:
```

and if the service-switch file `aliases` line specifies:

```
aliases    nis files
```

then *sendmail* looks up aliases first with *nis*, then in the */etc/aliases* file, then with *nis* a second time.

24.1.2 Local Must Be Local

The `local` part of an alias must be in the form of a local recipient. This restriction is enforced each time *sendmail* reads the *aliases*(5) file. For every name to the left of a colon that it finds, *sendmail* performs the following normalization and verification steps.

To begin, *sendmail* normalizes each address by removing everything but the address part. For example, consider the following two alias lines:

```
george (George Washington): gw
George Washington <george>: gw
```

When *sendmail* reads these lines, it normalizes each into its address part:

```
george (George Washington)     becomes →  george
George Washington <george>     becomes →  george
```

After the address part is extracted, it is converted to lowercase and rewritten by rule sets 3 and 0 to see whether it causes the `local` delivery agent to be selected or, beginning with V8.7 *sendmail*, to see whether it causes any delivery agent with the F=A flag set (see §30.8.12) to be selected.

Here, the address **george** (after processing) selects a local delivery agent, and so these alias lines are legal. Internally (or in its database), *sendmail* stores the above alias as

```
george: gw
```

When mail arrives that is addressed for delivery to **george**, *sendmail* rewrites that address with rule sets 3 and 0. Rule set 0 selects the `local` delivery agent (or, for V8.7, any agent with F=A set). Only if a local delivery agent is selected for an address does *sendmail* look up an address in its *aliases* file. The address **george** is looked up and replaced with **gw**. Internally, *sendmail* marks the recipient **george** as defunct, having been replaced with an alias, and then adds **gw** to the list of recipients.

The new recipient, **gw**, is then processed for delivery. Rule sets 3 and 0 are called once more and again select a local delivery agent. As a consequence, **gw** is also looked up. If it is found to the left of a colon in the *aliases* file, it too is replaced with yet another address (or addresses). This process repeats until no new local addresses are found.

The entry **george** is marked defunct rather than being deleted to detect alias loops. To illustrate, consider the following two mutually referencing aliases:

```
george: gw
gw: george
```

The *sendmail* program first replaces **george** with **gw**, marking **george** as defunct. It goes to mark **gw** as defunct but notices that a loop has been formed. If *sendmail* is running in verbose mode (see §34.8.76), it prints

```
aliasing/forwarding loop broken
```

and bounces the message.

Note that aliases can get pretty complex. As a consequence, when one address aliases to many new addresses, this autodetection of loops will fail (but the problem will be caught later with "hop counting"; see §34.8.36).

24.2 *Forms of Alias Delivery*

The right-hand side of an alias entry can take four forms:

```
local:  user
local:  /file
local:  |program
local:  :include: list
```

The **user** specifies final delivery to a user's mail spool file (via the `~/.forward` file), delivery to a new address (e.g. *user@newsite*), or one step in further aliasing. The **/file** specifies delivery by appending to a file. The **|program** specifies delivery by piping the message through a program. The `:include:` specifies processing of a mailing list. The first three are covered here. The last is covered in the next chapter.

24.2.1 *Delivery to Users*

Any address in the list of addresses to the right of the colon that does not begin with a / character or a | character is considered the address of a user. The address can be local or remote.

If a user address is prefixed[*] with a backslash character (\) and the address is a local one, all further aliasing is suppressed (including reading the user's `~/.forward` file). The message is delivered with the `local` delivery agent.

24.2.2 *Delivery to Files*

When any of the addresses to the right of a colon in the alias list begins with a / character, delivery is made by appending the mail message to a file. This is automatic with most configuration files but not with others. If your configuration file does not automatically recognize a leading / character, you will need to add a new rule near the end of your rule set 0 (see §29.6). For example,

```
R/$+      $@ $#local $: /$1
```

Beginning with V8.7 *sendmail*, any delivery agent for which the F=/ flag (see §30.8.9) is set can also append messages to files. If you want to disable this ability, delete the F=/ flag from all delivery agent declarations in your configuration file.

In the list of addresses to the right of the colon, *sendmail* considers any local address that begins with the / character to be name of a file.[†] Whenever the

---

[*] Actually, a backslash anywhere in the name causes the same immediate delivery.

[†] Note that an *@host* prevents this interpretation. That is, */a* is a file, but */a@host* is not. This distinction is necessary for X.400 addresses to be handled correctly. Note that this works only if the smtp delivery agent omits the F=/ flag.

recipient address is a file, *sendmail* attempts to deliver the mail message by appending it to the file. This ability to deliver mail to files is included primarily in *sendmail* so that failed mail may be saved to a user's *˜/dead.letter* file. It can also be used (through use of aliases) to deliver mail to other files, but that use is less than optimum, as you will see.

To deliver to a file, *sendmail* first performs a *fork*(2) and gives the child the task of delivery. The *fork* is necessary so that *sendmail* can change its effective *uid* and *gid*, as we will show. The child then performs a *stat*(3) on the file. If the file exists, its file permissions are saved for later use. If it doesn't exist, the saved permissions are defaulted to 0666. Under V8.7 the decision to use *stat*(2) versus *lstat*(2) to obtain the permissions is determined by the `SafeFileEnvironment` option (see §34.8.58).

If the saved permissions have any execute bit set, the child exits with EX_CANTCREAT as defined in *<sysexits.h>*. If the file has a controlling user associated with it, any *suid* and *sgid* bits are stripped from the saved permissions. If the file was listed in a *˜/.forward* file, the controlling user is the owner of the *˜/.forward* file. If it was listed in a `:include:`'d file, the controlling user is the owner of the included file. If the message is being processed from the queue, the controlling user may be specified in the `qf` file (see §23.9.2).

Then the queue `df` file (see §23.9.3) is opened for reading (if it is not already open). If that file cannot be opened, *sendmail* prints the following error message but continues to attempt delivery:

```
mailfile: Cannot open df for file from sender
```

Here, the `df` is the name of the queue data file that cannot be opened. The `file` is the name of the file to which *sendmail* is attempting to deliver the message. The `sender` is the address of the sender of the mail message.

Next, if the `SafeFileEnvironment` option (see §34.8.58) was declared, *sendmail* performs a *chroot*(2) into the directory specified. If the *chroot*(2) fails, *sendmail* prints and logs the following error and the child exits with EX_CANTCREAT:

```
mailfile: Cannot chroot(directory)
```

Next, whether the `df` file is opened or not, *sendmail* changes its *gid*:

- If there is a controlling user, *sendmail* sets its *gid* to that of the controlling user.

- Otherwise, if the *sgid* bit is set in the file's saved permissions, *sendmail* changes its *gid* to that of the group of the file.

- Otherwise, *sendmail* checks to see whether the U= equate is set for this delivery agent (see §30.4.13). If the U= equate is set, *sendmail* changes its *gid* to that specified.

- Otherwise, *sendmail* changes its *gid* to that specified by the DefaultUser (g) option (see §34.8.15).

After this, *sendmail* changes its *uid*, using the same rules that it used for the *gid* except that the last step uses the DefaultUser (u) option.

The file (and possibly the path to it) is then checked to see whether it is safe to write to. This is done by using the internal *safefile()* subroutine. See the –d44 debugging switch (§37.5.159) for a description of this process.

If safe, *file* is then opened for writing in append mode. If *sendmail* cannot open the file, it prints the following error message, and the child exits with EX_CANTCREAT:

> cannot open: *reason for error here*

If an open fails, it is attempted 10 more times (sleeping progressively longer[*] between each try) on the assumption that on busy systems there may be a temporary lack of resources (such as file descriptors). The open includes file locking with *flock(2)* or *fcntl(2)* to prevent simultaneous writes.

Once the file is opened, the header and body of the mail message are written to it. Note that translations are controlled by the F= flags of the prog delivery agent for all but V8 *sendmail*. V8 *sendmail* uses the F= flags of the *file* delivery agent. For example, F=l (see §30.8.28) marks this as final delivery.

If any write error occurs, *sendmail* prints the following error message and continues:

> I/O error

Finally, the file's permissions are restored to those that were saved above, and the file is closed with *fclose(3)*. If the *suid* or *sgid* bits were stripped because there was a controlling user, they are restored here.[†] If the file didn't originally exist, its permissions become 0666.

In general, the file form of an alias is a poor way to save mail messages to a file. Instead, the use of a separate program *procmail*(8) is recommended (see §25.7.5.2).

---

[*] The progression is 0 seconds for the first sleep, then 10 seconds, then 20 seconds, then 30 seconds, and so on.

[†] This is because some paranoid systems, such as BSD UNIX, turn off the *suid/sgid* bits when a file is written to other than by *root*.

24.2.3 Delivery via Programs

When any of the addresses to the right of a colon in the alias list begins with a |
character, delivery is made by piping the mail message through a program. This is
automatic with most configuration files but not with others. If your configuration
file does not automatically recognize a leading | character, you will need to add a
new rule near the end of your rule set 0 (see §29.6). For example,

```
R|$+      $@ $#local $: |$1
```

Beginning with V8.7 *sendmail*, any delivery agent for which the F=| flag (see
§30.8.8) is set can also pipe messages through programs. To disable this ability,
simply remove the F=| flag from all delivery agent declarations in your configura-
tion file.

The forms that a program address can legally take in the *aliases*(5) file (or ˜/.for-
ward* file; see §25.7.4) are as follows:

```
|prg
"|prg args"
|"prg args"
```

Here, prg is the full path of the program to be run (the environment variable PATH
is not available). If command-line arguments are needed for the program, they
must follow prg, and the entire expression must be quoted. The leading full quo-
tation mark may either precede or follow the |. If the address is quoted with full
quotation marks, the leading quotation mark is ignored in determining the leading
| character.

To execute the program, *sendmail* executes the command in the P= equate of the
prog delivery agent. That command is one of the following:

```
/bin/sh -c
/bin/smrsh -c
```

These tell *sendmail* to run */bin/sh* (the Bourne shell) or */bin/smrsh* (the *sendmail*
restricted shell) to execute the program specified by prg. The -c tells that shell to
take any arguments that follow and execute them as though they were commands
typed interactively to the shell. These arguments are constructed by removing the
leading | from the program address and appending what remains, quotation
marks and all, to the P= command. For example, if an alias looked like this:

```
jim: "|/etc/local/relo jim@otherhost"
```

the Bourne shell would be executed with the following command line:

```
/bin/sh -c "/etc/local/relo jim@otherhost"
```

The result of all this is that *sendmail* runs the Bourne shell and then the Bourne shell runs the */etc/local/relo* program.

Mail is delivered under this scheme by attaching the output of *sendmail* to the standard input of the shell and attaching the standard output and standard error output of the shell to the input of *sendmail.* The *sendmail* program simply prints the mail message to the shell and reads any errors that the shell prints in return.

Although this process appears to be fairly straightforward, there are many things that can go wrong. Failure usually results in the mail message being bounced.

24.2.3.1 Possible failures

To communicate with the P= program (the Bourne shell), *sendmail* creates two communications channels using *pipe*(2). This can fail because the system is out of file descriptors or because the system file table is full. Failure results in one of the following errors:

```
openmailer: pipe (to mailer)
openmailer: pipe (from mailer)
```

Next, *sendmail* executes a *fork*(2). The child later becomes the P= program. This can fail because the system limit on the maximum allowable number of processes has been exceeded or because virtual memory has been exhausted. Failure causes the following error message to be printed:

```
openmailer: cannot fork
```

In establishing a communications channel, the *sendmail* child process creates a copy of its standard input file descriptor. This can fail because the system limit on available file descriptors has been exceeded. When this happens, the following message is printed. Note that not all *dup*(2) failures produce error messages.

```
Cannot dup to zero!
```

Finally, the child transforms itself into the A= program with *execve*(2). If that transformation fails, the following error message is produced, where *program* is `argv[0]` for the A= program (in this case, usually */bin/sb*):

```
Cannot exec program
```

Failure can be caused by a wide range of problems. If one occurs and the delivery agent is `local`, the message is queued for a later try. Otherwise, requeueing occurs only if the error return value is a transient one defined in *transienterror*() in *conf.c.*[*]

---

[*] Because of a bug in all but the IDA and V8 versions, the message is silently discarded without being requeued or bounced.

Programs in the *aliases* file are run with the **prog** delivery agent. As a consequence, that delivery agent should have the **F=s** (strip quotes) flag set.

24.3 Write a Delivery Agent Script

The program that is driven by the **prog** delivery agent may be a compiled executable binary, a shell script, or even a *perl*(1) script. The limitation on the kind of program that may be run is made by the *sh*(1) shell (if **sh -c** is used in the **A=**) or by *execve*(2) (if it is launched directly from the **P=**). You need to read the manuals on your system to determine your limitations. For example, not all versions of *sh*(1) allow constructs like the following in scripts:

```
#!/usr/local/bin/perl
```

When this appears as the first line of a script, the **#!** tells *sh*(1) or *execve*(2) to run the program whose pathname follows, to execute the commands in the script.[*]

In writing a program for mail delivery using the **prog** delivery agent, some unexpected problems can arise. We will illustrate, using fragments from a Bourne shell script.

24.3.1 Duplicates discarded

When *sendmail* gathers its list of recipients, it views a program to run as just another recipient. Before performing any delivery, it sorts the list of recipients and discards any duplicates. Ordinarily, this is just the behavior that is desired, but discarding duplicate programs from the *aliases*(5) file[†] can cause some users to lose mail. To illustrate, consider a program that notifies the system administrator that mail has arrived for a retired user:

```
#!/bin/sh
/usr/ucb/mail -s gone postmaster
```

This script reads everything (the mail message) from its standard input and feeds what it reads to the */usr/ucb/mail* program. The command-line arguments to *mail* are a subject line of **gone** and a recipient of **postmaster**. Now consider two aliases that use this program:

```
george: "|/usr/local/bin/gone"
ben:    "|/usr/local/bin/gone"
```

---

[*] Not all versions of UNIX support this feature, and on some of those that do support it, only a few shells are supported.

[†] Under V8 *sendmail* this is no longer a problem for duplicate programs listed in *˜/.forward* files (see §25.7.4) but still is a problem for *aliases*. The solution that *sendmail* uses is to internally append the *uid* of the *˜/.forward* file's owner to the program name, thus making the program name more unique.

When mail is sent to both **george** and **ben**, *sendmail* aliases each to the program
`|/usr/local/bin/gone`. But since both the two addresses are identical, *sendmail*
discards one.

To avoid this problem (which is most common in user `~/.forward` files), design all
delivery programs to require at least one unique argument. For example, the
above program should be rewritten to require the user's name as an argument:

```
#!/bin/sh
if [ ${#} -ne 2 ]; then
        echo $0 needs a user name.
        exit
fi
/usr/ucb/mail -s "$1 gone" postmaster
```

By requiring a username as an argument, the once-faulty aliases are made unique:

```
george: "|/usr/local/bin/gone george"
ben:    "|/usr/local/bin/gone ben"
```

Although the program paths are still the same, the addresses (name and arguments
together) are different, and neither is discarded.

24.3.2 Correct exit(2) values

The *sendmail* program expects its **A=** programs to exit with reasonable *exit*(2) values. The values that it expects are listed in *<sysexits.h>*. Exiting with unexpected
values causes *sendmail* to bounce mail and give an unclear message:

```
554 Unknown status val
```

Here, **val** is the unexpected error value. To illustrate, consider the following
rewrite of the previous script:

```
#!/bin/sh
EX_OK=0                     # From <sysexits.h>
EX_USAGE=64                 # From <sysexits.h>
if [ ${#} -ne 2 ]; then
        echo $0 needs a user name.
        exit $EX_USAGE
fi
/usr/ucb/mail -s "$1 gone" postmaster
exit $EX_OK
```

Here, if the argument count is wrong, we exit with the value EX_USAGE, thus producing a clearer (two-line) error message:

```
/usr/local/bin/gone needs a user name.
/usr/local/bin/gone... Bad usage.
```

If all goes well, we then exit with EX_OK so that *sendmail* knows that the mail was
successfully delivered.

24.3.3 Is It Really EX_OK?

When *sendmail* sees that the A= program exited with EX_OK, it assumes that the mail message was successfully delivered. It is vital for programs that deliver mail to exit with EX_OK only if delivery was 100% successful. Failure to take precautions to detect every possible error can result in lost mail and angry users. To illustrate, consider the following common C language statement:

```
(void)fclose(fp);
```

If the file that is being written to is remotely mounted, the written data may be cached locally. All the preceding write statements will have succeeded, but if the remote host crashes after the last write (but before the close), some of the data can be lost. The *fclose*(3) fails, but the (void) prevents detection of that failure.

Even in writing small shell scripts, it is important to include error checking. The following rewrite of our *gone* program includes error checking but does not handle signals. We leave that as an exercise for the reader:

```
#!/bin/sh
EX_OK=0                      # From <sysexits.h>
EX_USAGE=64                  # From <sysexits.h>
EX_SOFTWARE=70               # From <sysexits.h>
if [ ${#} -ne 2 ]; then
        echo $0 needs a user name.
        exit $EX_USAGE
fi
if /usr/ucb/mail -s "$1 gone" postmaster >/dev/null 2>&1
then
        exit $EX_OK
fi
exit $EX_SOFTWARE
```

24.4 Special Aliases

The behavior of the *sendmail* program requires that two specific aliases (*Postmaster* and *MAILER-DAEMON*) be defined in every *aliases* file. Beginning with V8.7 *sendmail*, aliases that contain a plus character can be used to route mail on the basis of special needs. Also, beginning with V8.7 *sendmail*, databases that allow duplicates can be declared to help automate the creation of those files.

24.4.1 The Postmaster Alias

RFC822 requires every site to accept for delivery mail that is addressed to a user named *postmaster*. It also requires that mail accepted for *postmaster* always be delivered to a real human being—someone who is capable of handling mail problems. If *postmaster* is not an alias, or a real user, *sendmail syslog*(3)'s the following error:

```
can't even parse postmaster!
```

Unless a site has a real user account named *postmaster*, an alias is required in every *aliases* file for that name. That alias must be a list of one or more real people, although it may also contain a specification for an archive file or filter program. One such alias might look like this:

```
postmaster: bill, /mail/archives/postmaster,
        "|/usr/local/bin/notify root@mailhost"
```

Here, `postmaster` is lowercase. Because all aliases are converted to lowercase for lookup, `Postmaster` or even `POSTMASTER` could have been used for equal effect.

Note that there are three aliases to the right of the colon: a local user named `bill`, the full path of a file onto which mail messages will be appended, and a program to `notify` the user `root` at the machine `mailhost` that `postmaster` mail has arrived on the local machine.

As a convention, the special name *postmaster* can also be that of the user who gets duplicate copies of some bounced mail. This is enabled by using the `Post-masterCopy` (P) option (see §34.8.46) in the configuration file:

```
OPpostmaster            ← pre-V8.7
O PostmasterCopy=postmaster   ← V8.7 and above
```

To disable sending copies of bounced mail to a special user (perhaps to protect privacy), omit this option from the configuration file.

Note that V8 *sendmail* does not send to the postmaster copies of error mail that include a `Precedence:` header with a value less than zero, like *junk*, *bulk*, or *list* used by mailing lists.

Also note that some sites define this user as one who is always aliased to a filter program in the *aliases* file. For example, if the `PostmasterCopy` (P) option is declared as

```
OPmail-errors           ← pre-V8.7
O PostmasterCopy=mail-errors   ← V8.7 and above
```

and the corresponding *aliases* file entry is declared as

```
mail-errors: "|/etc/mail/filter postmaster"
```

a program `filter` can be designed that discards all common error messages, such as mistyped addresses, and forwards what remains to `postmaster`.

Many sites have developed just such filters. One is distributed with the V8 *sendmail* source in the file *contrib/mmuegel*. Written by Michael S. Muegel of

Motorola's Corporate Information Office, it is a *shar*(1) file of several useful
perl(1) scripts. One (*postclip.pl*) is a tool that filters out the body of bounced mail
messages to prevent postmasters from potentially violating the privacy of senders.
It tries to retain all headers, no matter how deeply they are buried in what appears
to be the message body.

24.4.2 The MAILER-DAEMON Alias

When mail is bounced, the notification of failure is always shown as being from
the sender whose name is defined by the $n macro (see §31.10.26). Traditionally,
that macro is given the value `mailer-daemon`:

```
DnMAILER-DAEMON
```

That tradition is enforced by the fact that if $n is not defined, it defaults to
`mailer-daemon`.

There needs to be an alias for whatever name is defined for $n, because users
occasionally make the mistake of replying to bounced mail. Two typical aliases are

```
mailer-daemon: postmaster
mailer-daemon: /dev/null
```

Here, the name to the left of the colon should be whatever was defined for $n in
the configuration file, traditionally (and recommended to be) `mailer-daemon`. The
first alias forwards all `mailer-daemon` reply mail to the postmaster. Many site
administrators prefer the second, which discards such mail by using */dev/null*.

24.4.3 Plussed Users

Plussed users is a simple way to do more versatile aliasing. It is available only with
V8.7 *sendmail* and above, and it requires that you use a configuration file that
comes with V8 *sendmail*. To illustrate its use, consider the need to have mail
routed to different sets of administrators depending on how the address *root* is
augmented:

```
root: hans, george
root+db:    root, dbadmin@server.db.here.edu
root+*:     root, root@here.edu
```

Here, the first line shows a normal sort of alias in which mail sent to *root* will
instead be delivered to the local users *hans* and *george*. The second line is still not
all that special, because we could as easily have used an alias such as *root_db* to
accomplish the same thing. It sends mail to *root+db* to the local *root* users and to
the database administrators in another department, *dbadmin@server.db.here.edu*.

The third line is where things start to get interesting. The +* in it will match anything or nothing following the plus, so mail sent to *root+* will be sent both to the

local *root* users and to the central administrators at *root@here.edu*. But so will anything following the plus that is not **db**, such as *root+foo*.

If the +* form is omitted:

```
root: hans, george
root+db:   root, dbadmin@server.db.here.edu
```

the default for plussed addresses other than *root+db* becomes *root*. That is, when *sendmail* looks up a plussed address (for example *root+foo*) it does so in the following order:

- Look for an exact match. Does *root+foo* match *root+db*?

- Look for a wildcard match. Does *root+** exist? If so, use that alias for *root+foo*.

- Look for a base match. Does the *root* of *root+foo* exist as an alias? If so, use that alias for *root+foo*.

Note that plussed users is a simple mechanism that is intended to solve simple needs. In distributing a common aliases file to many machines, for example, plussed users can furnish a hook that allows customization based on simple alias extensions. Because plussed users is simple, attempts to extend it to handle complex needs will likely fail. If your needs are complex, consider using the User Database (see §33.5) or writing custom hooks in *checkcompat*() (see §20.1) instead.

24.4.4 Duplicate Entries and Automation

Ordinarily, duplicate local names on the left-hand side of the colon in an alias file will result in an error. For example, consider this abstract from an aliases file:

```
staff: bob
staff: george
```

Running *newaliases* on this file would produce the following error message and would cause the first entry to be ignored:

```
Warning: duplicate alias name george
```

Sometimes, however, it is advantageous to produce an alias file with duplicates. Consider this abstract from a newuser adding script:

```
if [ $GROUP = "staff" ]
then
        echo "staff: $USER" >> /etc/aliasdir/groups
fi
```

Here, we seek to add the user whose login name is stored in $USER to the mailing list called **staff**. To prevent *sendmail* from complaining, we declare the */etc/aliasdir/groups* file like this in the configuration file:

```
O AliasFile=dbm:-A /etc/aliasdir/groups
```

Here, the **dbm** tells *sendmail* this is a *ndbm*(3) type file (it could also be **btree** or **hash** for *db*(3) type files). The **-A** switch tells *sendmail* to append duplicates rather than rejecting them. Too illustrate, revisit the earlier alias file:

```
staff: bob
staff: george
```

The first alias line is read and stored normally with this key and value pair:

```
staff      bob
  ↑         ↑
 key       value
```

The second line is then appended to the first line, because of the **-A** switch, to form

```
staff      bob,george
  ↑         ↑
 key       value
```

The comma is intelligently inserted by *sendmail*.

Although this technique can simplify the maintenance of some alias files, it should not be overused. Each append requires the prior entry to be read, the space for it and the new entry to be allocated, the old and new entries to be concatenated, and the result to be stored in such a way as to replace the original. This process slows down *sendmail* noticeably when it rebuilds large files with many duplicates.

24.5 The Aliases Database

Reading the *aliases* file every time *sendmail* begins to run can slow mail delivery and create a lot of unnecessary computational overhead. To improve efficiency, *sendmail* has the ability to store aliases in a separate database format on disk. In this format, *sendmail* rarely needs to read the *aliases* file. Instead, it merely opens the database and performs lookups as necessary.

The *sendmail* program builds its database files by reading the *aliases*(5) file and rewriting that file in database format. Usually, the aliases file is called *aliases*. With that name, *ndbm*(3) database files are called *aliases.pag* and *aliases.dir*, and the *db*(5) database file is called *aliases.db*.

The *sendmail* program offers several forms of database, one of which is chosen at compile time (see §18.4.1).

24.5.1 Rebuild the Alias Database

You tell *sendmail* to rebuild its database files by running it in **-bi** mode. This mode can be executed in two different ways:

```
% newaliases
% /usr/lib/sendmail -bi
```

The first form is shorthand for the second. Either causes *sendmail* to rebuild those files. If the database is successfully built, *sendmail* prints a single line:

```
895 aliases, longest 565 bytes, 30444 bytes total
```

This shows that 895 `local` entries appeared to the left of colons in the *aliases* file. The longest list of addresses to the right of a colon was 565 bytes (excluding the newline). And there were 30,444 total bytes of noncomment information in the file.

V8 *sendmail* supports multiple alias database files (see the `AliasFile` (`A`) option, §34.8.1). Consequently, each line of its output is prefixed with the name of the alias file being rebuilt. For example,

```
/etc/aliasdir/users: 895 aliases, longest 565 bytes, 30444 bytes total
/etc/aliasdir/lists: 34 aliases, longest 89 bytes, 1296 bytes total
```

24.5.2 Check the Right Side of Aliases

When V8 *sendmail* rebuilds the alias database files, it can optionally be told to check the legality of all addresses to the right of the colons. The `CheckAliases` (`n`) option (see §34.8.6) turns on this check:

```
O CheckAliases=True    # validate RHS in newaliases
```

Each address is validated by running it through rule set 3, then rule set 0. Rule set 0 must select a delivery agent for the address. If it does, the address is silently validated and accepted. If not, the address is skipped, and the following warning is printed:

```
address... bad address
```

Other errors may be printed before the above line that indicate more specific reasons for the failure. For example,

```
... Unbalanced '<'
```

The **-d20.1** debugging switch (see §37.5.66) can be used to gain a better idea of why the *address* failed. But be forewarned: The **-d20.1** switch can produce many screens of output.

In general, we do not recommend setting the CheckAliases (n) option to true in the configuration file, because it can cause each right-side address to be resolved through DNS and thus slow down the rebuild considerably. For better efficiency, leave the CheckAliases (n) option off in the configuration file and turn it on only when rebuilding by hand:

```
% newaliases -on
```

24.5.3 *Prevent Simultaneous Rebuilds*

The alias database files can be automatically rebuilt in three ways: by the daemon (if the AutoRebuildAliases (D) option, see §34.8.4, is true), by users sending mail (and thereby indirectly running *sendmail*), and by users intentionally rebuilding the database with *newaliases* (or the -bi command-line switch). To prevent one rebuild from compromising and corrupting another, *sendmail* uses file locking.

The *sendmail* program uses *flock*(2) or *fcntl*(2) with F_SETLK to lock the *aliases* file (depending on how it was compiled). If the *aliases* file is already locked (because the database is currently being rebuilt), *sendmail* prints the following message:

```
Alias file name is already being rebuilt
```

If *sendmail* is attempting to rebuild because it was run as *newaliases* or with the -bi command-line switch, the above message is printed, and the program exits. Otherwise, the above message is printed, and *sendmail* waits for the *aliases* file to become unlocked.

Once the *aliases* file is locked, *sendmail* next looks to see whether the key @ appears in the database. If that key is missing, *sendmail* knows that the database is still being rebuilt. If the AliasWait (a) option (see §34.8.2) has a value, *sendmail* waits that amount of time for the other rebuild to finish. If the AliasWait (a) option is missing or has a zero value, *sendmail* plows ahead, trusting the previous lock to prevent simultaneous rebuilds.

The *sendmail* program waits the number of seconds specified by the AliasWait (a) option for an @ key to appear in the database. If that key doesn't appear within that wait, *sendmail* continues with the rebuild, assuming that some other process died while attempting to rebuild.

Before entering the key (the name to the left of the colon) and contents (everything to the right of the colon) pairs into the database, *sendmail* truncates the database (reduces it to size zero), thereby removing the @ key. After all the key and contents pairs have been written to the database, *sendmail* adds a new @ key to show that it is done.

Finally, *sendmail* closes the database and the *aliases* file. Closing the *aliases* file releases all locks it has on that file.

24.5.4 *No DBM Aliasing*

Some versions of UNIX do not provide the libraries that are needed to compile *sendmail* with database support. When neither the *db*(3) nor *ndbm*(3) library is available, and when no other method for getting aliases is declared (such as *nis*), *sendmail* keeps aliases in its internal symbol table.

When the symbol table is used, *sendmail* builds its alias database only once. When *sendmail* is run as a daemon, the *aliases* file is read only once. If the file changes, the daemon needs to be killed and restarted. In general, it is not recommended to run *sendmail* in daemon mode without external database files.

24.6 *Prevent Aliasing with –n*

At times it is desirable to run *sendmail* so that it does not perform aliasing. When aliasing is disabled, *sendmail* uses the recipient address as is. No addresses are ever looked up in the *aliases* file, even if they are local.

The –n command-line switch tells *sendmail* not to perform aliasing of recipient addresses. This switch is rarely used but can be handy in a couple of situations.

24.6.1 *Is an Alias Bad?*

In tracking down delivery problems, it can be difficult to determine where the problem lies. If you suspect a bad alias, you can force aliasing to be skipped and see whether that causes the problem to go away:

```
% /usr/lib/sendmail -n user < /dev/null
```

This tells *sendmail* to send an empty mail message (one containing mandatory headers only) to the recipient named user. The –n prevents *sendmail* from looking up user either in the *aliases* database or in ˜/*.forward*. If user resolves to the local delivery agent, the message will be delivered, and you should therefore suspect an aliasing problem.

Other switches, such as –v (verbose) and –d (debugging), can be combined with –n to view the delivery process in more detail.

24.6.2 *Filtering Recipients with a Shell Script*

The **−n** command-line switch can also be used to suppress aliasing when delivering to a list of recipients that has already been aliased. For example, consider the following script, which attempts to restrict delivery to users who have mail delivered locally and to skip users who have mail forwarded offsite:

```
#!/bin/sh
EX_OK=0                      # From <sysexits.h>
EX_NOUSER=67                 # From <sysexits.h>
EX_SOFTWARE=70               # From <sysexits.h>
if [ ${#} -ne 2 ]; then
        echo Usage: $0 list-name
        exit $EX_USAGE
fi
trap "exit 70" 1 2 13 15
LIST= "`/usr/lib/sendmail -bv $1 \
        | grep "mailer local" 2>&1`" \
        | sed 's/\.\.\..*$//'
if [ -z "$LIST" ]
        echo "$1 expanded to an empty list"
        exit $EX_NOUSER
fi
if /usr/lib/sendmail -n $LIST >/dev/null 2>&1
then
        exit $EX_OK
fi
exit $EX_SOFTWARE
```

The *sendmail* program is called twice inside this script. First, it is given the **−bv** switch, which causes it to expand the list of recipients in **$1**. That expansion includes aliasing (and ˜/.*forward* aliasing) for each name in the list. The output produced looks like this:

```
user1... deliverable: mailer local, user user1
user2@otherhost... deliverable: mailer smtp, host otherhost, user user2@otherhost
```

The *grep*(1) program selects only those lines that contain the expression **"mailer local"**, thus indicating a local user. The *sed*(1) program then discards from the `...` to the end of each selected line. The result, a list of local recipients only, is saved in the shell variable **LIST**.

The *sendmail* program is called with the **−n** switch, which prevents it from re-aliasing the list of names in **$LIST** (they have already been aliased once).

Note that this script should not be used as is because it checks only for the delivery agent named **local**, rather than for any delivery agent that can perform final delivery.

24.7 Pitfalls

- The *dbm* and *ndbm* forms of the *aliases*(5) database files contain binary integers. As a consequence, those database files cannot be shared via network-mounted file systems by machines of differing architectures. This is not a problem for 4.4 BSD *db* files.

- The *aliases* file and database files can be used to circumvent system security if they are writable by the wrong users. Proper ownership and permissions are neither checked for nor enforced by *sendmail*.

- Versions of *sendmail* that use the old-style *dbm*(3) libraries can cause overly long alias lines (greater than 1024 bytes) to be silently truncated. With the new databases, such as *ndbm*(3), a warning is printed. Note that V8 *sendmail* does not support old-style *dbm*(3) for this very reason.

- Recursive (circular self-referencing) aliases are detected only when mail is being delivered. The *sendmail* program does not look for such alias loops when rebuilding its database.

- Because of the way V8.8 *sendmail* locks the alias file for rebuilding, it must be writable. If it is not, *sendmail* prints the following and and skips the rebuild:

```
warning: cannot lock aliases: Permission denied
```

This can be a problem if the master alias file is shared via NFS.

25

Mailing Lists and ˜/.forward

As was shown in the previous chapter, the *sendmail* program is able to obtain its list of recipients from the *aliases* file. It can also obtain lists of recipients from external files. In this chapter we will examine the two forms that those external files take: the `:include:` form (accessed from the *aliases* file) and the individual user's *˜/.forward* file. Since the chief use of the `:include:` form of alias is to create *mailing lists*, we will first discuss mailing lists in general, then their creation and management, and then the user's *˜/.forward* file.

A mailing list is the name of a single recipient that, when expanded by *sendmail* aliasing, becomes a list of many recipients. Mailing lists can be internal (in which all recipients are listed in the *aliases* file), external (in which all recipients are listed in external files), or a combination of the two. The list of recipients that forms a mailing list can include users, programs, and files.

25.1 Internal Mailing Lists

An internal mailing list is simply an entry in the *aliases* file that has more than one recipient listed on the right-hand side. Consider, for example, the following *aliases* file entries:

```
admin:  bob,jim,phil
bob:    \bob, /u/bob/admin/maillog
```

Here, the name **admin** is actually the name of a mailing list, because it expands to more than one recipient. Similarly, the name **bob** is a mailing list, because it expands to two recipients. Since **bob** is also included in the **admin** list, mail sent to that mailing list will be alias-expanded by *sendmail* to produce the following list of recipients:

```
jim, phil, \bob, /u/bob/admin/maillog
```

This causes the mail message to be delivered to the local users `jim` and `phil` in the normal way. That is, each undergoes additional alias processing, and the *~/.forward* file of each is examined to see whether either should be forwarded. The recipient `\bob`, on the other hand, is delivered without any further aliasing because of the leading backslash. Finally, the message is appended to the file */u/bob/admin/maillog*.

Internal mailing lists can become very complex as they strive to support the needs of large institutions. Examine the following simple, but revealing, example:

```
research:      user1, user2
applications:  user3, user4
admin:         user5, user6
advertising:   user7, user8
engineering:   research, applications
frontoffice:   admin, advertising
everyone:      engineering, frontoffice
```

Only the first four aliases above expand to real usernames. The last three form mailing lists out of combinations of those four, the last being a superset that includes all users.

When the number of mailing lists is small and they don't change often, they can be effectively managed as part of the *aliases* file. But as their number and size grow, you should consider moving individual lists to external files.[*]

25.2 :include: Mailing Lists

The special notation `:include:` in the right-hand side of an alias causes *sendmail* to read its list of recipients from an external file. For that directive to be recognized as special, any address that begins with `:include:` must select the `local` delivery agent. This is automatic with most configuration files but not with others. If your configuration file does not automatically recognize the `:include:` directive, you will need to add a new rule near the end of your rule set 0 (see §29.6). For example,

```
R:include:$*    $@ $#local $: :include:$1
```

Beginning with V8.7 *sendmail*, any delivery agent for which the `F=:` flag (see §30.8.7) is set can also process `:include:` files. (Note that eliminating the `F=:` flag

---

[*] Only *root* should be permitted to write to the *aliases* file. If you keep mailing lists inside that file, it may need to be writable by others. This can create a security breach (see §22.5.4).

for all delivery agent definitions in your configuration file will disable this feature entirely.)

The `:include:` directive is used in *aliases*(5) files like this:

```
localname:    :include:/path
```

The expression `:include:` is literal. It must appear exactly as shown, colons and all, with no space between the colons and the "include." As with any right-hand side of an alias, there may be space between the alias colon and the lead colon of the `:include:`.

The */path* is the full pathname of a file containing a list of recipients. It follows the `:include:` with intervening space allowed.

The */path* should be a full pathname. If it is a relative name (such as *../file*), it is relative to the *sendmail* queue directory. For all but V8 *sendmail*, the */path* must not be quoted. If it is quoted, the quotation marks are interpreted as part of the filename. For V8 *sendmail*, the */path* may be quoted, and the quotation marks are automatically stripped.

If the */path* cannot be opened for reading for any reason, *sendmail* prints the following warning and ignores any recipients that might have been in the file:

```
:include: path... Cannot open /path: reason
```

Here, *reason* is "no such file or directory," "permission denied," or something similar. If */path* exists and can be read, *sendmail* reads it one line at a time. Empty lines are ignored. Beginning with V8 *sendmail*, lines that begin with a # character are also ignored:

```
addr
# a comment
                      ← empty line is ignored
addr2
```

Each line in the `:include:` file is treated as a list of one or more recipient addresses. Where there is more than one, each should be separated from the others by commas.

```
addr1
addr2, addr3, addr4
```

The addresses may themselves be aliases that appear to the left in the *aliases* file. They may also be user addresses, program names, or filenames. A `:include:` file may also contain additional `:include:` lists:

```
engineers                          ← to an alias
biff, bill@otherhost               ← to two recipients
|"/etc/local/loglists thislist"    ← to a program alias
```

```
/usr/local/archive/thislist.hist    ← to a file
:include:/yet/another/file          ← from another file
```

Beginning with V8.7 *sendmail*, the `TimeOut.fileopen` option (see §34.8.70) controls how long *sendmail* should wait for the open to complete. This is useful when files are remotely mounted as with NFS. This timeout encompasses both this open and the security checks described next. Note that the NFS file system must be soft mounted (or mounted with the `intr` option) for this to work.

Beginning with V8, *sendmail* checks the file for security. If the controlling user is *root*, all components of the path leading to the file are also checked.[*] If the *suid* bit of the file is set (telling *sendmail* to run as owner of the file), *sendmail* checks to be sure that the file is writable only by the owner. If it is group- or world-writable, *sendmail* silently ignores that *suid* bit. When checking components of the path, *sendmail* will print the following warning if it is running as *root* and if any component of the path is group- or world-writable:

```
WARNING: writable directory offending component
```

This process is described in greater detail under the **–d44** debugging switch (see §37.5.159), which can also be used to observe this process.

After *sendmail* opens the **/path** for reading but before it reads the file, it sets the controlling user to be the owner of the file (if one is not already set and provided that file ownership cannot be given away with *chown*(1)). The controlling user provides the *uid* and *gid* identities of the sender when delivering mail from the queue (see §23.9.2).

The `:include:` file can neither deliver through programs nor append to files if any of three situations is true: if the owner of the `:include:` file has a shell that is not listed in */etc/shells* (see §22.8.4), if the `:include:` file is world-writable, or if the `:include:` file is group-writable and the `UnsafeGroupWrites` option (see §34.8.73) is true.

25.2.1 Comments in :include: Lists

IDA and V8 *sendmail* allow comments in `:include:` files. Comment lines begin with a `#` character. If the `#` doesn't begin the line, it is treated as the beginning of an address, thus allowing valid usernames that begin with a `#` (such as `#1user`) to appear first in a line by prefixing them with a space:

```
# Management              ← a comment
frida
george@wash.dc.gov
# Staff                   ← a comment
```

---

[*] The *sendmail* program also performs this check for critical system files, such as its configuration file.

```
ben
steve
 #1user                          ← an address
```

Note that since comments and empty lines are ignored by *sendmail*, they can be used to create attractive, well-documented mailing lists.

Under older versions of *sendmail*, comments can be emulated through the use of RFC822-style comments:

```
( comment )
```

By surrounding the `comment` in parentheses, you cause *sendmail* to view it and the parentheses as an RFC-style comment and ignore them:

```
( Management )
frida
george@wash.dc.gov
( Staff )
ben
steve
```

This form of comment works with both the old and new *sendmail* programs.

25.2.2 Tradeoffs

As has been noted, the *aliases* file should be writable only by *root* for security reasons. Therefore, ordinary users, such as nonprivileged department heads, cannot use the *aliases* file to create and manage mailing lists. Fortunately, `:include:` files allow ordinary users (or groups of users) to maintain mailing lists. This offloads a great deal of work from the system administrator, who would otherwise have to manage these lists, and gives users a sense of participation in the system.

Unfortunately, reading `:include:` lists is slower than reading an entry from the *aliases* database. At busy sites or sites with numerous mail messages addressed to mailing lists, this difference in speed can become significant. Note that the **-bv** command-line switch (see §36.7.13) can be used with *sendmail* to time and contrast the two different forms of lists. On the other hand, sometimes rebuilding the *aliases*(5) database can also be very slow. In such instances the `:include:` file may be faster, since it doesn't require a rebuild each time it changes.

One possible disadvantage to all types of mailing lists is that they are visible to the outside world. This means that anyone in the world can send mail to a local list that is intended for internal use. Many lists are intended for both internal and external use. One such list might be one for discussion of the O'Reilly Nutshell Handbooks, called, say, *nuts@ora.com*. Anyone inside *ora.com* and anyone in the outside world can send mail messages to this list, and those messages will be forwarded to everyone on the *nuts* mailing list.

25.3 Defining a Mailing List Owner

Notification of an error in delivery to a mailing list is sent to the original sender as bounced mail. Although this behavior is desirable for most mail delivery, it can have undesirable results for mailing lists. Because the list is maintained locally, it does not make sense for an error message to be sent to a remote sender. That sender is likely to be puzzled or upset and unable to fix the problem. A better solution is to force all error messages to be sent to a local user, no matter who sent the original message.

When *sendmail* processes errors during delivery, it looks to see whether an "owner" was defined for the mailing list. If one was defined, errors are sent to that owner rather than to the sender. The owner is defined by prefixing the original mailing list alias with the phrase owner-, as shown in the following code:

```
nuts:   :include:/home/lists/nuts.list
owner-nuts: george
```

Here, nuts is the name of the mailing list. If an error occurs in attempting delivery to the list of recipients in the file /home/lists/book.list, *sendmail* looks for an alias called owner-nuts (the original name prefixed with owner-). If *sendmail* finds an owner (here, george), it sends error notification to that owner rather than to the original sender. Generally, it is best to have the owner- of a list be the same as the owner of the mailing-list file, since that user is best suited to correct errors as they appear.

To ensure that all errors in mailing lists are handled by someone, an owner of owners should also be defined. That alias usually looks like this:

```
owner-owner:    postmaster
```

If *sendmail* cannot deliver an error message to the owner- of a mailing list, it instead delivers it to the owner-owner.

Beginning with V8 *sendmail*, a single alias expansion is done on the owner- of any :include: list, and that expansion is made the address of the envelope sender:

```
nuts:   :include:/home/lists/nuts.list
owner-nuts: nuts-request
nuts-request: george
```

Here, with V8 *sendmail*, the envelope sender for mail sent to nuts will be nuts-request (a single-level alias expansion), rather than george (a multiple-level alias expansion).

As a side effect, with V8 *sendmail*, mail sent to owner-*anything* will have the envelope-sender address set to a single alias expansion of owner-owner. This can be confusing, so always stress to users that they should mail the maintainer of a list with the —request suffix instead of the owner- prefix.

25.4 Exploder Mailing Lists

When mailing lists get extremely large, they sometimes include the names of other lists at other sites as recipients. Those other lists are called *exploder* lists, because they cause the size of a list (the number of recipients) to *explode*. For example, consider the situation in Figure 25-1.

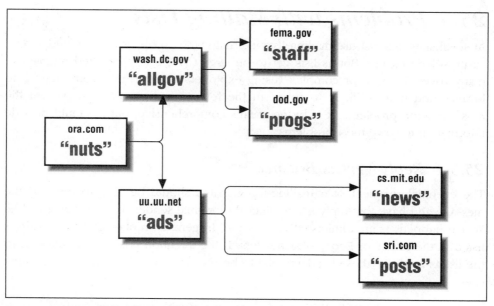

Figure 25-1: Exploding a mailing list

This figure shows that a message sent to *nuts@ora.com* will, in addition to its list of users, also be forwarded to *allgov@wash.gov* and *ads@uu.uu.net*. But each of these recipients is also a mailing list. Like the original *nuts* list, they deliver to ordinary users and forward to other sites' mailing lists.

Unless exploding lists like this are correctly managed, problems that are both mysterious and difficult to solve can arise. A bad address in one of the distant exploding lists, for example, can cause a delivery error at a remote exploder site. If this happens, it is possible that the error notification will be sent to either the original list maintainer or (worse) the original submitter, although neither is in a position to correct such errors.

To ensure that error notification is sent to the person who is best able to handle the error, mailing list entries in the *aliases* file should be set up like the following.

It is an approach to setting up a mailing list that is well suited for exploder sites.

```
list:              :include:/path/to/rebroadcast.list
owner-list:        list-request@original.site
```

Here, the name of the mailing list is `list` and is used to explode by sending the incoming message to the users listed in *rebroadcast.list*. The envelope of the outgoing message will contain the address *list-request@original.site*, thus causing errors to be sent to the originating list maintainer rather than wrongly to someone on the local machine.

25.5 Problems with Mailing Lists

At small sites that just use mailing lists internally, the problems are few and can be easily solved locally. But as lists get to be large (over a few hundred recipients), many (over 50 lists), or complex (using exploders), problems become harder to localize and more difficult to solve. In the following discussion we present the most common problems. It is by no means comprehensive, but it should provide information to solve most problems.

25.5.1 Reply Versus Bounce

The eventual recipient of a mailing-list message should be able to reply to the message and have that reply go to either the original sender or the list as a whole. Which happens is an administrative decision. In general, replies go to the address listed in the **From:** or **Reply-To:** headers. If the intention is to have replies go to the list as a whole, these headers need to be rewritten by a filter at the originating site:

```
list:    "|/etc/local/mailfilter list -oi -odq -flist-request list-real"
```

Here, the name of the filter has replaced *sendmail* in the *aliases* file entry. Writing such a filter is complex. The original addresses need to be preserved with appropriate headers before they are rewritten by the filter.

The converse problem is that not all mail-handling programs handle replies properly. Some programs (such as UUCP and certain versions of *emacs-mail*) insist on replying to the envelope sender as conveyed in the five-character "**From** " header. By setting up lists correctly (as we showed earlier), an administrator can at least guarantee that those replies are sent to the list maintainer, who can then forward them as required.

A more serious problem is the way other sites handle bounced mail. In an ideal world, all sites would correctly bounce mail to the **Errors-To:** address[*] and (less desirably) to the envelope sender. Unfortunately, not all sites are so well-behaved. If a mailing list is not carefully set up, there is a possibility that bounced mail will be resent to the list as a whole. To minimize such potential catastrophes, follow the guide in Table 25-1.

Table 25-1: Mailing List Header Use

Header	§	Use
Envelope sender	31.10.14	Should be local list maintainer
From	34.8.59	Same as envelope sender
From:	35.10.14	Original submitter
Reply-To:	35.10.33	Local list maintainer, list as a whole, or original submitter
Errors-To:	35.10.13	Local list maintainer

25.5.2 Gateway Lists to News

When gatewaying a mailing list to Usenet news, the *inews*(1) program bounces the message if it is for a moderated group and lacks an **Approved:** header, which can be added by a filter program (see §24.3) or by a news gateway delivery agent.

If your site is running (or has access to) Usenet news, the *recnews*(1) program that is included therein may be used to gateway mail to newsgroups. It inserts the **Approved:** header that *inews* needs and generally handles its gateway role well. One minor pitfall to avoid with *recnews* is making separate postings when you intend cross-postings:

```
mail-news: "|/usr/local/recnews comp.mail comp.mail.d"   ← separate postings
mail-news: "|/usr/local/recnews comp.mail,comp.mail.d"   ← cross-posted
```
↑
note the comma

25.5.3 A list-bounced Alias

There are many ways to handle bounced mail in managing a mailing list. One of the best ways for large lists is to create a *bounce* alias for a list:

```
list-bounce: :include:/usr/local/lists/list-bounce
```

---

[*] The *sendmail* program does use the **Errors-To:** header, despite the fact that it was originally a hack to get around UUCP, which confused envelope and header. The **Errors-To:** header is not an Internet standard (in fact it violates the Internet standards) and cannot be expected to work on MTAs other than *sendmail*. Beginning with V8.8, **Errors-To:** is supported only if the **UseErrorsTo** (1) option is set to true.

When an address in the main list begins to bounce, move it from the main list's file to the corresponding `list-bounce` file. Then send a message to that list nightly (via *cron*(8)), advising the users in it that they will soon be dropped. To prevent the bad addresses from deluging you with bounced mail, set up the return address and the envelope to be an alias that delivers to */dev/null*:

```
black-hole:    /dev/null
```

Finally, arrange to include the following header in the outgoing message:

```
Precedence: junk
```

This prevents most sites from returning the message if it cannot be delivered.

There are also programs available that can help to manage large and numerous mailing lists. We will cover them later in this chapter.

25.5.4 Users Ignore list-request

It is impossible to cause all users to interact properly with a mailing list. For example, all submissions to a list should (strictly speaking) be mailed to *list*, whereas communications to the list maintainer should be mailed to *list-request*. As a list maintainer, you will find that users mistakenly reverse these roles surprisingly often.

One possible cure is to insert instructions in each mailing at the start of the message. In the header, for example, `Comment:` lines can be used like this:

```
Comment: "listname" INSTRUCTIONS
Comment: To be added to, removed from, or have your address changed
Comment: in this list, send mail to "listname-request".
```

Unfortunately, user inattention usually dooms such schemes to failure. You can put instructions everywhere, but some users will still send their requests to the wrong address.

A solution some sites use when the list is used only for official and rare mailings is to install the list name in the aliases file just before the mailing:

```
list:    :include: /usr/local/lists/official.list    ← before
```

Then run *newaliases*(1) and send mail to the *list*. After all the mail for the list has been queued, edit the aliases file and comment out that entry:

```
#list:    :include: /usr/local/lists/official.list    ← after
```

Run *newaliases*(1) again, and you will have disabled that list. That way, mail that is wrongly sent to *list* will bounce back to the sender who made the mistake instead of wrongly being broadcast to the list as a whole.

25.5.5 Precedence: bulk

All mass mailings, such as mailing-list mailings, should have a header `Precedence:` line that gives a priority of `bulk`, `junk`, or `list`. On the local machine these priorities cause the message to be processed from the queue after higher-priority mail. At other sites these priorities will cause well-designed programs (such as the newer *vacation*(1)[*] program) to skip automatically replying to such messages.

25.5.6 X.400 Addresses

The X.400 telecommunications standard is finding increased acceptance in Europe and by the U.S. government. Addresses under X.400 always begin with a leading slash, which can cause *sendmail* to think that the address is the name of a file when the `local` delivery agent is selected:

```
/PN=MS.USER/O=CORP/PRMD=CORP/ADMD=TELE/C=US/
```

To prevent this misunderstanding, all such addresses should be followed by an *@domain* part to route the message to an appropriate X.400 gateway:

```
/PN=MS.USER/O=CORP/PRMD=CORP/ADMD=TELE/C=US/@X.400.gateway.here
```

25.6 Packages That Help

As the number and size of mailing lists at your site become large, you may wish to install a software package that automates list management. All of the following packages are available via anonymous FTP.

25.6.1 Majordomo

The *Majordomo* mailing-list management software was written by Brent Chapman using the *perl*(1) language. Its chief features are that it allows users to subscribe to and remove themselves from lists without list manager intervention and that it allows list managers to manage lists remotely. In addition, users can obtain help and list descriptions with simple mail requests. Note that *Majordomo* aids in managing a list (the list addresses) but does not aid in list moderation (the contents of mail messages). *Majordomo* is available via anonymous FTP from:

```
ftp://FTP.GreatCircle.COM/pub/majordomo/
```

---

[*] The *vacation*(1) program is a wonderful tool for advising others that mail will not be attended to for a while. Unfortunately, some older versions of that program still exist that reply to `bulk` mail, thereby causing problems for the mailing-list maintainer.

25.6.2 Almanac

The *Almanac* mailing-list management software was written at Oregon State University, Extension Service, in the C language. It allows users to subscribe to and be removed from mailing lists themselves, without maintainer intervention, and also services requests for file transfers (similar to FTP) via email. It is purported to be highly configurable in that the grammar for requests is determined by the site administrator, and any request can be bound to *any* (predefined) Bourne shell program. For example, *Almanac* sites in France are at liberty to speak French to their *Almanac* server. The *Almanac* software is available via anonymous FTP from:

```
ftp://OES.OrSt.EDU/pub/almanac/
```

25.6.3 ListProcessor

The *ListProcessor* system was written by Tasos Kotsikonas. It is an automated system for managing mailing lists that replaces the *aliases* file for that use. According to the author, it includes support for "public and private hierarchical archives, moderated lists, peer lists, peer servers, private lists, address aliasing, news connections and gateways, mail queueing, list ownership, owner preferences, crash recovery, and batch processing." The system also accepts Internet connections for "live" processing of requests at port 372 (as assigned by the IANA[*]). The *ListProcessor* system is available via anonymous *ftp* from:

```
ftp://cs-ftp.bu.edu/pub/listserv
```

25.7 The User's ~/.forward File

The *sendmail* program allows each user to have a `:include:` style list to customize the receipt of personal mail. That file (actually a possible sequence of files) is defined by the `ForwardPath` (J) option (see §34.8.27). Traditionally, that file is located in a user's home directory.[†] We use the C-shell notation ~ to indicate user home directories, so we will compactly refer to this file as *~/.forward*.

If a recipient address selects a delivery agent with the `F=w` flag set (see §30.8.43), that address is considered the address of a local user whose *~/.forward* file can be processed. If it contains a backslash, *sendmail* disallows further processing, and the message is handed to the `local` delivery agent's `P=` program for delivery to the mail-spooling directory. If a backslash is absent, *sendmail* tries to read that user's *~/.forward* file.

---

[*] IANA stands for Internet Assigned Numbers Authority. It is currently housed in Marina del Rey, California, and staffed by Joyce Reynolds and Jon Postel (*iana@isi.edu*).

[†] Prior to V8 *sendmail* the *~/.forward* file could live *only* in the user's home directory and had to be called *.forward*.

If all the *.forward* files listed in the `ForwardPath` (J) option (see §34.8.27) cannot be read, their absence is silently ignored. This is how *sendmail* behaves when those files don't exist. Users often choose not to have ˜/.*forward* files. But problems may arise when users' home directories are remotely mounted. If the user's home directory is temporarily absent (as it would be if an NFS server is down), or if a user has no home directory, *sendmail syslog*(3)'s the following error message and falls back to the other directories in its `ForwardPath` (J) option:

```
forward: no home
```

V8 *sendmail* temporarily transforms itself into the user[*] before trying to read the ˜/.*forward* file. This is done so that reads will work across NFS. If *sendmail* cannot read the ˜/.*forward* file (for any reason), it silently ignores that file.

Before reading the ˜/.*forward* file, *sendmail* checks to see whether it is a "safe" file—one that is owned by the user or *root* and that has the read permission bit set for the owner. If the ˜/.*forward* file is not safe, *sendmail* silently ignores it.

If *sendmail* can find and read the ˜/.*forward* file and if that file is safe, *sendmail* opens the file for reading and gathers a list of recipients from it. Internally, the ˜/.*forward* file is exactly the same as a `:include:` file. Each line of text in it may contain one or more recipient addresses. Recipient addresses may be email addresses, the names of files onto which the message should be appended, the names of programs through which to pipe the message, or `:include:` files.

Beginning with V8 *sendmail*, ˜/.*forward* files may contain comments (lines that begin with a `#` character). Other versions of *sendmail* treat comment lines as addresses and bounce mail that is seemingly addressed to `#`.

25.7.1 Unscrambling Forwards

The traditional use of the ˜/.*forward* file, as its name implies, is to forward mail to another site. Unfortunately, as users move from machine to machine, they can leave behind a series of ˜/.*forward* files, each of which points to the next machine in a chain. As machine names change and as old machines are retired, the links in this chain can be broken. One common consequence is a bounced mail message ("host unknown") with a dozen or so `Received:` (see §35.10.25) header lines.

As the mail administrator, you should beware of the ˜/.*forward* files of users at your site. If any contain offsite addresses, you should periodically use the SMTP

---

[*] This is supported only under operating systems that properly support *seteuid*(3) or *setreuid*(3) (see §18.8.55).

expn command[†] to examine them. For example, consider a local user whose *~/.for-ward* contains the following line:

```
user@remote.domain
```

This causes all local mail for the user to be forwarded to the host `remote.domain` for delivery there. The validity of that address can be checked with *telnet*(1) at port 25[*] and the SMTP `expn` command:

```
% telnet remote.domain 25
Trying 123.45.123.45 ...
Connected to remote.domain.
Escape character is '^]'.
220 remote.domain Sendmail 8.6.13/8.6.12 ready at Tue, 7 May 1996 13:39:21 -0700
220 ESMTP spoken here
expn user
250 <user@another.site>
quit
221 remote.domain closing connection
Connection closed by foreign host.
%
```

This shows that the user is known at `remote.site` but also shows that mail will be forwarded (yet again) from there to `another.site`. By repeating this process, you will eventually find the site at which the user's mail will be delivered. Depending on your site's policies, you can either correct the user's *~/.forward* file or have the user correct it. It should contain the address of the host where that user's mail will ultimately be delivered.

25.7.2 *Forwarding Loops*

Because *~/.forward* files are under user control, the administrator occasionally needs to break loops caused by improper use of those files. To illustrate, consider a user who wishes to have mail delivered on two different machines (call them machines A and B). On machine A the user creates a *~/.forward* file like this:

```
\user, user@B
```

Then, on machine B the user creates this *~/.forward* file:

```
\user, user@A
```

The intention is that the backslashed name (`\user`) will cause local delivery and the second address in each will forward a copy of the message to the other machine. Unfortunately, this causes mail to go back and forth between the two

---

† Under old versions of *sendmail* the *vrfy* and *expn* commands are interchangeable. Under V8 *send-mail* and other, modern SMTP servers, the two commands differ.

* In place of specifying port 25, you can use either *mail* or *smtp*. These are more mnemonic and easier to remember (although we "oldtimers" tend to still use 25).

machines (delivering and forwarding at each) until the mail is finally bounced with the error message "too many hops."

On the machine that the administrator controls, a fix to this looping is to temporarily edit the *aliases* database and insert an alias for the offending user like this:

```
user:   \user
```

This causes mail for **user** to be delivered locally and that user's *~/.forward* file to be ignored. After the user has corrected the offending *~/.forward* files, this alias can be removed.

25.7.3 Appending to Files

The *~/.forward* file can contain the names of files onto which mail is to be appended. Such filenames must begin with a slash character that cannot be quoted. For example, if a user wishes to keep a backup copy of incoming mail:

```
\user
/home/user/mail/in.backup
```

The first line (**\user**) tells *sendmail* to deliver directly to the user's mail spool file using the **local** delivery agent. The second line tells *sendmail* to append a copy of the mail message to the file specified (**in.backup**).

Note that, prior to V8, *sendmail* did no file locking, so writing files by way of the *~/.forward* file was not recommended. Beginning with V8, however, *sendmail* locks those files during writing, so such use of the *~/.forward* file is now okay.

If the **SafeFileEnvironment** option (see §34.8.58) is set, the user should be advised to specify the path of that safe directory:

```
\user
/arch/bob.backup        ← here /arch was specified by the SafeFileEnvironment option
```

When the **SafeFileEnvironment** option is used, the cooperation of the system administration may be needed if users are to have the capability of saving mail to files via the *~/.forward* file.

25.7.4 Piping Through Programs

The *~/.forward* file can contain the names of programs to run. A program name is indicated by a leading pipe (|) character, which may or may not be quoted (see §24.2.3). For example, a user may be away on a trip and want mail to be handled by the *vacation*(1) program:

```
\user, "|/usr/ucb/vacation user"
```

Recall that prefixing a local address with a backslash tells *sendmail* to skip additional alias transformations. For \user this causes *sendmail* to deliver the message (via the local delivery agent) directly to the user's spool mail box.

The quotes around the *vacation* program are necessary to prevent the program and its single argument (user) from being viewed as two separate addresses. The *vacation* program is run with the command-line argument user, and the mail message is given to it via its standard input.

Beginning with V8 *sendmail*, a user must have a valid shell to run programs from the ~/.forward file. See §18.8.34 for a description of this process and for methods to circumvent it at the system level.

Because *sendmail* sorts all addresses and deletes duplicates before delivering to any of them, it is important that programs in ~/.forward files be unique. Consider a program that doesn't take an argument and suppose that two users both specified that program in their ~/.forward files:

```
user 1 →  \user1, "|/bin/notify"
user 2 →  \user2, "|/bin/notify"
```

Prior to V8 *sendmail*, when mail was sent to both **user1** and **user2**, the address /bin/notify appeared twice in the list of addresses. The *sendmail* program eliminated what seems to be a duplicate,[*] and one of the two users did not have the program run.

If a program *requires* no arguments (as opposed to ignoring them), the ~/.forward program specifications can be made unique by including a shell comment:

```
user 1 →  \user1, "|/bin/notify #user1"
user 2 →  \user2, "|/bin/notify #user2"
```

25.7.5 Specialty Programs for Use with ~/.forward

Rather than expecting users to write home-grown programs for use in ~/.forward files, offer them any or all of the publicly available alternatives. The most common are listed below.

25.7.5.1 The deliver program

The *deliver*(1) program, by Chip Salzenberg, is specifically designed to handle all types of final delivery for users. It is intended for use in the ~/.forward file but also functions as a local delivery agent. The *deliver* program supports a large number

---

[*] V8 *sendmail* uses the owner of the ~/.forward file in addition to the program name when comparing.

of command-line options and can reliably handle delivery to files and through programs. It is typically used in the ~/.*forward* file like this:

```
"|/usr/local/bin/deliver user"
```

The *deliver* program is available via anonymous FTP from many archive sites.

25.7.5.2 The procmail program

The *procmail*(1) program, by Stephen R. van den Berg, is purported to be the most reliable of the delivery programs. It can sort incoming mail into separate folders and files, run programs, preprocess mail (filtering out unwanted mail), and selectively forward mail elsewhere. It can function as a substitute for the `local` delivery agent or handle mail delivery for the individual user. The *procmail* program is typically used in the ~/.*forward* file like this:

```
"|exec /usr/local/bin/procmail #user"
```

Note that *procmail* does not accept a username as a command-line argument. Because of this, a dummy shell comment is needed for pre-V8 versions of *sendmail* to make the address unique. The *procmail* program is available via anonymous FTP from many archive sites.

25.7.5.3 The slocal program

The *slocal* program, distributed with the *mh* distribution, is useful for sorting incoming mail into separate files and folders. It can be used with both UNIX-style mail files and with *mh*-style mail directory folders. It is typically used in the ~/.*forward* file like this:

```
"| /usr/local/lib/mh/slocal -user user"
```

The disposition of mail is controlled using a companion file called ~/.*maildelivery*.

25.7.6 Force Requeue on Error

Normally, a program in the user's ~/.*forward* file is executed with the Bourne shell. The precise means that is used is defined by the **prog** delivery agent.

```
Mprog, P=/bin/sh,   F=lsDFMeuP,  S=10, R=20, A=sh -c $u
                                                    ↑
                                             The Bourne shell
```

One drawback to using the Bourne shell to run programs is that it exits with a value of 1 when the program cannot be executed. When *sendmail* sees the exit value 1, it bounces the mail message.

There will be times when bouncing a mail message because the program could not execute is not desirable. For example, consider the following *˜/.forward* file:

```
"| /usr/local/lib/slocal -user george"
```

If the directory */usr/local/lib* is unavailable (perhaps because a file server is down or because an automounter failed), the mail message should be queued, rather than bounced. To arrange for requeueing of the message on failure, users should be encouraged to construct their *˜/.forward* files like this:

```
"| /usr/local/lib/slocal -user george || exit 75"
```

Here, the || tells the Bourne shell to perform what follows (the **exit** 75) if the preceding program could not be executed or if the program exited because of an error. The exit value 75 is special, in that it tells *sendmail* to queue the message for later delivery, rather than to bounce it.

25.8 Pitfalls

- When *sendmail* collects addresses, it discards duplicates. Prior to V8 *sendmail*, program entries in a *˜/.forward* file had to be unique; otherwise, an identical entry in another user's *˜/.forward* caused one or the other to be ignored. Usually, this is solved by requiring the program to take an argument. If the program won't accept an argument, add a shell comment inside the quotes.

- The database forms of the *aliases*(5) file contain binary integers. As a consequence, those database files cannot be shared via network-mounted file systems by machines of differing architectures. This has been fixed with V8 *sendmail*, which can use the 4.4 BSD UNIX *db*(3) form of database.

- As network-mounted file systems become increasingly common, the likelihood that a user's home directory will be *temporarily* unavailable increases. Prior to V8 *sendmail* this problem was not handled well. Instead of queueing mail until a user's home directory could be accessed, *sendmail* wrongly assumed that the *˜/.forward* didn't exist. This caused mail to be delivered locally when it should have been forwarded to another site. This can be fixed by using the ForwardPath (J) option (see §34.8.27) of V8 *sendmail*.

- Prior to V8 *sendmail* there was no way to disable user forwarding via *˜/.forward* files. At sites with proprietary or confidential information there was no simple way to prevent local users from arbitrarily forwarding confidential mail offsite. But *˜/.forward* files can be centrally administered by using the ForwardPath (J) option (see §34.8.27) of V8 *sendmail*, even to the point of completely disabling forwarding with OJ/dev/null.

- Programs run from ˜/.forward files should take care to clear or reset all untrusted environment variables. Only V8 properly presets the environment.

- If a user's ˜/.forward file evaluates to an empty address, the mail will be silently discarded. This has been fixed in IDA and V8 *sendmail.*

- A program run from a ˜/.forward file is always run on the machine running *sendmail.* That machine is not necessarily the same as the machine housing the ˜/.forward file. When user home directories are network-mounted, it is possible that one machine may support the program (such as */usr/ucb/vacation*), while another may lack the program or call it something else (such as */usr/bsd/vacation*). Note that if *smrsh*(1) is used, the path is ignored.

26

Logging and Statistics

The *sendmail* program can keep the system administrator up-to-date about many aspects of mail delivery and forwarding. It does this by logging its activities using the *syslog*(3) facility. It can also gather (or aid in gathering) statistics about what it is doing. Information about things like total message volume and site connectivity, for example, can help the administrator to make *sendmail* more efficient. Information about the SMTP dialog that was used to send the message can help the administrator to solve delivery problems.

In this chapter we cover these three important aspects of *sendmail.* First, we explain the use of the *syslog*(3) facility and illustrate several ways to tune its logging. Second, we show the built-in means that *sendmail* has for recording statistics and other information and how scripts can be used to extend that information. Third, we explore ways to tune the performance of *sendmail.*

26.1 Logging with syslog

Logging is the process of issuing one-line warnings that will be either displayed to a human, archived to a file, or both. The mechanism that *sendmail* uses to produce these warnings is called *syslog*(3). The *sendmail* program is concerned only with issuing its warnings. Once they are issued, the *syslog* facility takes over and disposes of them in a manner described in the file */etc/syslog.conf.* Statements in this file determine whether a warning is written to a device (such as */dev/console*), appended to a file, forwarded to another host, or displayed on a logged-in user's screen.

In the following discussion of *syslog* and *syslog.conf,* we will describe the BSD 4.4 version. Some versions of UNIX, such as Ultrix, use the 4.2 version of *syslog,* but because *syslog* is public domain, we recommend upgrading and will not cover that old version here.

26.1.1 syslog(3)

The *syslog*(3) facility uses two items of information in determining how to handle messages: *facility* and *level*. The facility is the category of program issuing a message. The *syslog* facility can handle many categories, but only one, `mail`, is used by *sendmail*. The level is the degree of severity of the warnings. The *sendmail* program issues messages with *syslog*(3) at various levels depending on how serious the warning is.

When *sendmail* first starts to run, it opens its connection to the *syslog* facility with the following C language line:

```
openlog("sendmail", LOG_PID, LOG_MAIL);
```

This tells *syslog* three things:

- All messages should be printed using `sendmail` as the name of the program doing the logging. This means that no matter what name is used to run *sendmail* (such as *newaliases* or *smtpd*), the name that is logged will always be `sendmail`.

- The LOG_PID tells *syslog* that the PID (process identification number) should be included when each message is written. This is necessary because *sendmail* forks often, and each parent and child will have a different PID. Because queue file identifiers are constructed from PIDs, this record helps to determine which invocation of *sendmail* created a particular queued file. The PID also allows messages from the daemon form of *sendmail* to be differentiated from others.

- The facility for *sendmail* (and all mail-handling programs) is LOG_MAIL. We'll show why this is important when we discuss the *syslog.conf* file.

Just before *sendmail* issues a warning, it looks at the logging level defined by its `LogLevel` (L) option (see §34.8.33). If the severity of the warning is greater than the logging level, nothing is output. If the severity of the warning that it intends to issue is less than or equal to the logging level (lower is more serious), it issues that warning with a C language call like this:

```
syslog(pri, msg);
```

Here, `pri` is the *syslog* logging priority, and `msg` is the text of the warning message. Note that the `LogLevel` (L) option (see §34.8.33) level is different than the *syslog* priority. The former is used internally by *sendmail* to decide whether it should log a message. The latter is used by *syslog* to determine how it will dispose of the message (if it gets one).

The LogLevel (L) option sets a threshold at and below which *sendmail* will issue warnings. When the LogLevel (L) option has a zero value, nothing is ever issued. When the LogLevel (L) option has a low value, only critical warnings are issued. At higher values, less critical messages are also issued.

The syntax of the LogLevel (L) option and the kinds of information issued for each level are explained in §34.8.33. For each level, all the information produced at lower levels is also issued. That is, setting the LogLevel (L) option to 9 causes messages for levels 1 through 8 also to be issued.

The relationship between the LogLevel (L) option logging levels and *syslog* priorities is shown in Table 26-1.

Table 26–1: L Levels Versus syslog Priorities

Level	Priority
1	LOG_CRIT and LOG_ALERT
2-8	LOG_NOTICE
9-10	LOG_INFO
11+	LOG_DEBUG

26.1.2 Tuning syslog.conf

Although all messages are emitted by *sendmail* using a single facility, that of *syslog*, they need not all arrive at the same place. The disposition of messages is tuned by the *syslog.conf* file.

The file *syslog.conf* (usually located in the */etc* directory) contains routing commands for use by *syslog*. That file can be complex, because it is designed to handle messages from many programs other than *sendmail*, even messages from the kernel itself. Under SunOS the *syslog.conf* file is also complex because it is preprocessed by *m4*(1) when it is read by *syslog*.

The file *syslog.conf* is composed of lines of text that each have the form:

```
    facility.level          target
```

The facility is the type of program that may be producing a message. The facility called mail is the one that *sendmail* uses. For the complete list, see the online manual for *syslog.conf*(5).

The level indicates the severity at or above which messages should be handled. These levels correspond to the LogLevel (L) option levels shown in Table 26-1 of

§26.1.1. The complete list of *syslog.conf* levels used by *sendmail* is shown in Table 26-2.

Table 26–2: syslog.conf Levels Used by sendmail

Level	Meaning of Severity (Highest to Lowest)
alert	Conditions requiring immediate correction
crit	Critical conditions for which action may be deferred
err	Other errors
warning	Warning messages
notice	Nonerrors that may require special handling
info	Statistical and informational messages
debug	Messages used only in debugging a program

The `target` is one of the four possibilities shown in Table 26-3. It is the `target` and the preceding `level` that must be tuned for use by *sendmail*.

Table 26–3: syslog.conf Targets

Target	Description
@*host*	Forward message to named *host*
/*file*	Append message to named *file*
user,user, . . .	Write to users' screens, if logged in
*	Write to all logged-in users' screens

For example, the following *syslog.conf* line causes messages from "mail" (the `facility`) that are at or above severity "info" (the `level`) to be appended to the file */var/log/syslog* (the `target`):

```
        facility                target
           ↓                      ↓
      mail.info               /var/log/syslog
           ↑
         level
```

A typical (albeit much simplified) */etc/syslog.conf* file might look like this:

```
*.err;kern.debug;user.none        /dev/console
*.err;kern.debug;user.none        /var/adm/messages
auth.notice                       @authhost
mail.info                         /var/log/syslog
*.emerg;user.none                 *
```

Notice that there may be multiple `facility.level` pairs on the left, each separated from the others by semicolons. The first two lines handle messages for all facilities at level `err`, all kernel messages (`kern`) at level `debug` and above, and none of the levels (`none`) for the facility `user`. The first line sends those messages to the file /dev/console, the computer's screen. The second appends its messages to the file /var/adm/messages.

The third line sends authorization messages (such as repeated login failures) to the host named authhost.

The fourth line appends all messages printed by *sendmail* at level info and above (the LogLevel (L) option is level 10 and below) to the file /var/log/syslog.

The last line is an emergency broadcast facility. A message to any facility (the left-most *) at the highest level (emerg), except for the facility user (the .none), will be written to the screen of all currently logged-in users (the target *).

Finally, note that facilities may be listed together by using a comma:

```
mail,daemon.info
```

This causes the level info to be the level for both the facilities mail and daemon. Only the facility may be listed this way. The level may not, and (unfortunately) the target may not.

26.1.3 syslog's Output

When the LogLevel (L) option level is 9 or above (see §34.8.33), *sendmail* logs one line of information for each envelope sender and one line of information for each recipient delivery or deferral. As *sendmail* has evolved, these lines of logging information have grown more complex. Here, we discuss the lines produced by *sendmail* 8.8.4.

Each line of information logged looks something like this:

```
date host sendmail[pid]: qid: what=value, ...
```

Each line of output that *syslog* produces begins with five pieces of information. The *date* is the month, day, and time that the line of information was logged (note that the year is absent). The *host* is the name of the host that produced this information (note that this may differ from the name of the host on which the log files are kept). The sendmail is literal. Because of the LOG_PID argument that is given to *openlog(3)* by *sendmail* (see §26.1.1), the process ID of the invocation of *sendmail* that produced this information is included in square brackets. Finally, each line includes the *qid* queue identifier (see §23.2.1) that uniquely identifies each message on a given host.

This initial information is followed by a comma-separated list of *what=value* equates. Which equate appears in which line depends on whether the line documents the sender or the recipient and whether deliver succeed, failed, or was deferred. In Table 26-4 we list the possibilities in alphabetical order. Then, in the sections that follow, we describe the role that each plays.

Table 26–4: what= in syslog Output Lines

what=	§	Description
class=	26.1.3.1	The queue class
delay=	26.1.3.2	Total time to deliver
from=	26.1.3.3	Show envelope sender
mailer=	26.1.3.4	The delivery agent used
msgid=	26.1.3.5	The Message-ID: identifier
nrcpts=	26.1.3.6	The number of recipients
pri=	26.1.3.7	The initial priority
proto=	26.1.3.8	The protocol used in transmission
relay=	26.1.3.9	The host that sent or accepted the message
size=	26.1.3.10	The size of the message
stat=	26.1.3.11	Status of delivery
to=	26.1.3.12	The final recipient
xdelay=	26.1.3.13	Transaction delay for this address only

26.1.3.1 class= the queue class

If the mail message contained a **Precedence:** header (see §35.8), the **class=** reflects *sendmail*'s interpretation of the keyword that follows that header. For example, given the configuration command

```
PPlist=-30
```

The following header will yield a **class=** value of −30:

```
Precedence: list
```

If no **Precedence:** header is present in the message, the value shown for **class=** is zero. The **class=** is shown only for sender records.

26.1.3.2 delay= total time to deliver

A mail message can be delivered immediately, without ever having been queued, or it can be queued and retried over and over again until it either times out or succeeds. The **delay=** shows the total amount of time the message took to be delivered. This period of time starts when *sendmail* first receives the message and ends when the message is finally delivered or bounced. This interval is displayed with the **delay=** *syslog* line equate:

```
delay=days+HH:MM:SS
```

The time expression shows the time it took in hours (**HH**), minutes (**MM**), and seconds (**SS**) to handle delivery or rejection of the message. If the delay exceeds 24 hours, the time expression is prefixed with the number of days and a plus character. For example, the following message took 5 seconds to deliver or bounce:

```
delay=00:00:05
```

The following message took 4 days, 2 hours, 16 minutes, and 2 seconds to deliver or bounce:

```
delay=4+02:16:02
```

Note that the **delay=** equate is shown only for recipient records.

26.1.3.3 from= show envelope sender

The envelope sender may or may not appear in any of the sender headers. The **from=** *syslog* line equate shows the envelope sender:

```
from=addr
```

The **addr** is the address of the envelope sender with any RFC822 commentary (see §35.3.4) removed. This will usually be the address of an actual person, but it can also be **postmaster** or the value of the **$n** macro in the case of a bounced message. The **from=** equate is shown only for sender records.

26.1.3.4 mailer= the delivery agent used

The *sendmail* program does not perform the actual delivery of mail. Instead, it calls other programs (called mail delivery agents) to perform that service. The **mailer=** equate shows the symbolic name (see §30.1) of the delivery agent that was used to perform delivery to the recipient"

```
mailer=agent
```

A list of symbolic names assigned to delivery agents can be viewed with the **-d0.15** debugging switch (see §37.5.4). The **mailer=** equate is shown only for recipient records.

26.1.3.5 msgid= the Message-ID: identifier

RFC822 requires that each email message have a unique worldwide identifier associated with it. That identifier is listed with the **Message-ID:** header (see §35.10.19) and often looks something like this:

```
Message-Id: <199605051122.VAA07923@here.us.edu>
```

The information inside, and including, the angle brackets is the message identifier. That identifier is what is listed with the **msgid=** equate:

```
msgid=<199605051122.VAA07923@here.us.edu>
```

If a mail message arrives without a **Message-ID:** header, and if your configuration file correctly includes a definition for that header, a new identifier will be created and listed with **msgid=**. If a **Message-ID:** header is absent, and if your configuration file incorrectly excludes a definition for that header, the **msgid=** equate will be excluded from the *syslog* report.

The **msgid=** equate is shown only for sender records.

26.1.3.6 *nrcpts= the number of recipients*

The **nrcpts=** equate shows the number of recipients *after* all aliasing has been performed. If the original message was addressed to *root*, if *root* was aliased like this:

```
root: bob, hans
```

and if *bob*'s `~/.forward` file contained this:

```
\bob
|"/usr/ucb/vacation bob"
```

then the **nrcpts=** equate would show three recipients.

Note that **nrcpts=** is included only with the sender record and that record is emitted when the message is first processed. Any later changes in aliasing that may happen while the message is queued are not reported. Aliasing on remote machines (as would be the case with exploder mailing lists) is also not reported for obvious reasons.

26.1.3.7 *pri= the initial priority*

The **pri=** equate shows the initial priority assigned to the message (see §35.8). This value is calculated once when the message is first processed and changed each time the queued file is tried. This **pri=** equate shows the initial value.

The **pri=** *syslog* equate is displayed only for the sender.

26.1.3.8 *proto= the protocol used in transmission*

The **$r** macro (see §31.10.31) holds as its value the protocol that was used when a mail message was first received. That value is either SMTP, ESMTP, or internal or is a protocol assigned with the **-p** command-line switch (see §36.7.32). If **$r** lacks a value, this **proto=** equate is omitted. If **$r** has a value, the first 20 characters of that value are printed following the **proto=** in the *syslog* line:

```
proto=ESMTP
```

26.1.3.9   relay= *the host that sent or accepted the message*

When running as a daemon and listening for incoming connections, *sendmail* attempts to look up the true identity of connecting users and hosts. When it can find that information, it saves it in the $_ macro (see §31.10.1).

When transporting mail to other hosts, *sendmail* looks up the MX records for those hosts and connects to the MX records when they are available. If MX records are not available, *sendmail* connects to the hostname that is specified in the recipient address.

If the $_ information is available, that information appears following the relay= equate:

```
relay=root@other.site.edu [123.45.67.89]
```

If the sender is a local user, the login name and *localhost* will appear in the relay= equate:

```
relay=bob@localhost
```

Otherwise, the canonical name of the host that actually accepted delivery will appear here:

```
relay=mx.host.domain [123.45.67.89]
```

In summary, the relay= equate shows who *really* accepted or sent the message. The relay= *syslog* equate is included with both sender and recipient records.

26.1.3.10   size= *the size of the message*

The size of an incoming SMTP message is the number of bytes sent during the DATA phase (see 34.8.70.5), including end-of-line characters. The size of a message received via *sendmail*'s standard input is a count of the bytes received, including the newline characters. In both instances the size is displayed with the size= equate:

```
size=23
```

Note that this size is reported before *sendmail* adds or deletes any headers. Therefore for mail being relayed through a site, the size will usually be small coming in and somewhat larger going out.

The size= *syslog* equate is produced only for sender records.

26.1.3.11 stat= status of delivery

Whenever the delivery status of a mail message changes, *sendmail* logs the event and includes the **status=** to specify why the change happened. For example, a mail message may initially be queued because the recipient's host was down:

```
stat=queued
```

Later it might change again because it succeeded in being delivered:

```
stat=Sent (HAA03001 Message accepted for delivery)
```

In transmitting a mail message via SMTP the **stat=** will include the actual text that the other host printed when it accepted the mail message, as shown above. But in delivering locally, the **stat=** is more succinct:

```
stat=Sent
```

In the case of bounced mail the **stat=** will show the reason for failure:

```
stat=User unknown
```

The **stat=** *syslog* equate is included only in recipient records.

26.1.3.12 to= show final recipient

As each recipient is delivered to, deferred, or bounced, *sendmail* logs a line of information that includes the recipient address:

```
to=bob@here.us.edu
```

Each such address is that of a final recipient (from the point of the view of the local host) after all aliasing, list expansions, and processing of ˜/.*forward* files.

26.1.3.13 xdelay= transaction delay for this address only

The **xdelay=** equate shows the total amount of time the message took to be transmitted during final delivery. This differs from **delay=** in that **delay=** is computed from when the message was originally received (and can be days), whereas this **xdelay=** shows how fast the receiving host was (and is usually seconds).

In the case of SMTP mail the **xdelay=** computation starts when *sendmail* successfully connects to the remote host. In the case of locally delivered mail the computation starts when *sendmail* executes the delivery agent. The computation ends when the dot is accepted at the close of the DATA SMTP phase or when the local delivery agent exits.

The form of the **xdelay=** looks like this:

```
xdelay=HH:MM:SS
```

The time expression shows the hours (**HH**), minutes (**MM**), and seconds (**SS**) it took to perform delivery via the final delivery agent. In the case of networked mail that interval can be long:

```
xdelay=00:41:05
```

But in the case of locally delivered mail this interval can seem instantaneous:

```
xdelay=00:00:00
```

Note that the **xdelay=** equate is shown only for recipient records.

26.1.4 Gathering Statistics from syslog

The log files that *syslog* creates provide a wealth of information that can be used to examine and tune the performance of *sendmail*. To illustrate, we will present a simple shell script for printing daily total message volume.

In the following discussion we will assume that *sendmail* logging is enabled (the **LogLevel** (**L**) option, see §34.8.33, is nonzero) and that all *syslog*(8) messages for the facility **mail** at level LOG_INFO are being placed into the file */var/log/syslog*.

26.1.4.1 message_volume.sh

Each mail message that *sendmail* receives for delivery (excluding those processed from the queue) causes *sendmail* to log a message like this:

```
date host sendmail[pid]: quid: from=sender, size=bytes, ...
```

That is, for each **sender** that is logged (the **from=**), *sendmail* also logs the total received size of the message in **bytes** (the **size=**).

By summing all the **size=** lines in a */var/log/syslog* file, we can generate the total volume of all messages received for the period represented by that file. One way to generate such a total is shown in the following Bourne shell script:

```
#!/bin/sh
LOG=/var/log/syslog
TOTAL=`(echo 0;
        sed -e '/size=/!d' -e 's/.*size=//' -e 's/,.*/+/' $LOG;
        echo p;
       ) | dc`
echo Total characters sent: $TOTAL
```

The *sed*(1) selects only the lines in */var/log/syslog* that contain the expression `size=`.* It then throws away all but the number immediately following each `size=` (the actual number of bytes of each message), and appends a + to each.

The entire sequence of processes is enclosed in parentheses. An *echo* statement first prints a zero. Then the list of +-suffixed sizes is printed. Finally, another *echo* prints a character p. The resulting combined output might look like this:

```
0
123+
456+
7890+
p
```

The leading 0, the + suffixes, and the final p are commands for the *dc*(1) program, which adds up all the numbers (the + suffixes) and prints the total (the p). That total is saved in the variable **TOTAL** for later use in the final *echo* statement. The output of this simple script might look something like this:

```
Total characters sent: 8469
```

More sophisticated scripts are possible, but the Bourne shell's lack of arrays suggest that *perl*(1) would provide a more powerful scripting environment. Most of the scripts that are available publicly are written in the *perl* scripting language.

26.2 *Statistics*

The *sendmail* program provides the ability to gather information that can be used to produce valuable statistics. As you will see, the `StatusFile` (S) option (see §34.8.66) is used to specify a file into which delivery agent statistics can be saved. The *mailstats*(1) program (see §26.2.2) prints a summary of those statistics.

26.2.1 *The sendmail.st File*

The *sendmail* program can maintain an ongoing record of the total number and total sizes of all outgoing and incoming mail messages handled by each delivery agent. This ability is enabled by using the `StatusFile` (S) option (see §34.8.66):

```
OS/path                      ← prior to V8.7
O StatusFile=/path           ← beginning with V8.7
```

---

* If other programs also put `size=` expressions into the log file, you may also want to screen for "sendmail."

The */path* is the full pathname of the file into which statistics are saved. Most vendors provide configuration files that specify */path* as

```
/etc/sendmail.st
```

Just declaring the `StatusFile` (`S`) option is not enough, however, for if the file does not exist (or if it is unwritable), *sendmail* silently ignores that option and does not save statistics. You must also create the empty file

```
% touch /etc/sendmail.st
```

Note that the gathering of statistics can later be turned off merely by renaming or removing the file.

If the `StatusFile` (`S`) option has not already been declared, you need to declare it and then kill and restart the *sendmail* daemon for that declaration to take effect.

26.2.2 Viewing Statistics: mailstats

The *mailstats* program is supplied with *sendmail* to provide a convenient way to print the contents of the *sendmail.st* file. The output of the *mailstats* program varies depending on the version of *sendmail* installed. For V8.8 *sendmail* the output looks like this:

```
Statistics from Fri May 10 11:23:55 1996
 M msgsfr bytes_from  msgsto   bytes_to  Mailer
 1      0         0K      43      5913K  *file*
 3     26       546K      96       639K  local
 4    421      2996K    3271     78233K  smtp
====================================
 T    447      3542K    3410     84785K
```

The first line shows the time the statistics file was begun. The lines that follow show the number of messages and the total size in kilobytes of those messages both received (`msgsfr`) and sent (`msgsto`) for each delivery agent. The `M` column shows the index into the internal array of delivery agents, and the `Mailer` shows the symbolic name. The last line shows totals. Note that if a delivery agent handled no traffic, it is excluded from the report.

26.2.3 Using cron for Daily and Weekly Statistics

The *mailstats* program prints the contents of the *sendmail.st* file, but it does not zero the counters in that file. To clear (zero) that file, you need to truncate it. One easy way to truncate the *sendmail.st* file is

```
% cp /dev/null /etc/sendmail.st
```

When *sendmail* discovers an empty *sendmail.st* file, it begins gathering statistics all over again. One use for truncation is to collect daily reports from *mailstats*.

Consider the following simple shell script:

```
#!/bin/sh
ST=/etc/sendmail.st
MS=/usr/ucb/mailstats
if [ -s $ST -a -f $MS ]; then
        $MS | mail -s "Daily mail stats" postmaster
        cp /dev/null $ST
fi
exit 0
```

When run, this script checks to see whether a nonempty *sendmail.st* file and program *mailstats* exist. If they do, *mailstats* is run, printing the statistics, which are then mailed to **postmaster**. The *sendmail.st* file is then truncated to a size of zero. Such a script could be run once per night using the *cron*(8) facility with a *crontab*(5) entry like this:

```
0 0 * * * sh /usr/ucb/mailstats.script >/dev/null 2>&1
```

Here, **mailstats.script** is the name given to the above shell script, and the **0 0** causes that script to be executed once per day at midnight.

Some versions of *mailstats* allow you to specify a different location for the statistics file. The form of that specification varies with the version of *sendmail* being run (see *mailstats*(8)). Yours may look like one of the following:

```
% mailstats /var/log/statlog
% mailstats -f /var/log/statlog          ← V8 uses this form
```

If your version of *mailstats* allows a different location (and name) for the statistics file, you can move that file to the new location by revising the **StatusFile (S)** option in the *sendmail* program's configuration file:

```
OS/var/log/statlog
```

Note that V8 *mailstats*(8) automatically parses the configuration file to find the location of its statistics file.

Moving and renaming the statistics file allows one to automatically collect daily copies of that file. Consider the following variation on the previous shell script:

```
#!/bin/sh
DIR=/var/log
ST=statlog
MS=/usr/ucb/mailstats
if [ -d $DIR ]; then
        cd $DIR
        if [ -s $ST -a -f $MS ]; then
                test -f ${ST}.5 && mv ${ST}.5 ${ST}.6
                test -f ${ST}.4 && mv ${ST}.4 ${ST}.5
                test -f ${ST}.3 && mv ${ST}.3 ${ST}.4
                test -f ${ST}.2 && mv ${ST}.2 ${ST}.3
```

```
                    test -f ${ST}.1 && mv ${ST}.1 ${ST}.2
                    test -f ${ST}.0 && mv ${ST}.0 ${ST}.1
                    test -f ${ST}    && mv ${ST}    ${ST}.0
                    touch ${ST}
                    $MS -f $DIR/${ST}.0 | mail -s "Daily mail stats" postmaster
          fi
    fi
    exit 0
```

As before, the statistics are mailed to **postmaster**. But instead of being truncated, the *sendmail.st* file is renamed *sendmail.st.0*. A series of renames (*mv*(1)) are used to maintain a week's worth of copies. These copies allow the ambitious administrator to create a program for gathering weekly summaries from seven archived daily copies.

26.3 *Signaling the Daemon*

The *sendmail* program recognizes three signals that cause it to perform certain actions. SIGINT causes *sendmail* to clean up after itself and exit. Beginning with V8.7, SIGHUP causes *sendmail* to re-execute itself (thus restarting and reading its configuration file anew). Also beginning with V8.7, SIGUSR1 causes *sendmail* to log its file descriptors and other information.

26.3.1 *SIGINT Cleanup and Exit*

Whenever *sendmail* gets a SIGINT signal (as would be the case if the system were being shut down), it tries to exit cleanly.

First it unlocks any queued file it is processing. This has the effect of canceling delivery so that the message will be tried again when the system comes back up. Then *sendmail* resets its identity to the identity it originally ran under. This causes accounting records to correctly show that the same user *sendmail* started as has exited. Finally, *sendmail* exits with EX_OK, no matter what, so that errors will not be produced during shutdown.

As a final note, beginning with V8.7, SIGINT is ignored when *sendmail* is running in rule-testing mode with –bt.

26.3.2 *SIGHUP Restart*

Beginning with V8.7, a SIGHUP signal will cause *sendmail* to re-execute itself with its original command line. This works only if it is running in daemon mode (with –bd; see §36.7.5). For example, consider initially running *sendmail* like this:

```
# /usr/lib/sendmail -bd -q1h
```

Then imagine that you changed something in the configuration file and wanted the running daemon to reread that file. You could cause that to happen by killing the currently running daemon with a SIGHUP signal:

```
# kill -HUP `head -1 /etc/sendmail.pid`
```

This will cause *sendmail* to execute the command

```
/usr/lib/sendmail -bd -q1h
```

The original daemon exits, and the newly executed daemon replaces it.

Be aware that this works only if you run *sendmail* using a full pathname. If you use a relative path, an attempt to restart *sendmail* with SIGHUP will fail, and the following warning will be logged at LOG_ALERT:

```
could not exec bad command line here: reason
```

This is a very serious situation because it means that your original daemon has exited and no new daemon ran to replace it.

26.3.3 SIGUSR1 Dump States

Beginning with V8.6.5, *sendmail* responds to a SIGUSR1 signal. This signal causes *sendmail* to *syslog* at LOG_DEBUG the several items that define its state.[*] That *syslog* output begins with a line that looks like this:

```
--- dumping state on reason: $j = val ---
```

where *reason* can be any one of the following:

siguser1
> The information has been logged because *sendmail* received a SIGUSR1 signal. In this instance the daemon logs the information and continues to run.

daemon lost $j
> The information has been logged because a running daemon discovered that the value in $j (the canonical name of this host; see §31.10.20) disappeared from the class $=w (the list of all names by which the local host is known; see §32.5.8). This test is made and this information is logged only if *sendmail* was compiled with XDEBUG defined (see §18.8.57). In this instance the daemon logs the information and aborts.

daemon $j lost dot
> The information has been logged because a running daemon discovered that the value in $j (the canonical name of this host; see §31.10.20) was no longer

---

[*] This same information is *syslog*'d if the daemon looses track of $j in $=w and if $j becomes or is not fully qualified.

canonical (no longer contained a dot inside it). This test is made and this information is logged only if *sendmail* was compiled with XDEBUG defined (see §18.8.57). In this instance the daemon logs the information and aborts.

Whichever the reason, the information that is logged for each looks pretty much the same; for example,

```
--- dumping state on when: $j = val ---
CurChildren =num
--- open file descriptors: ---
            ← output of dumpfd() here
--- connection cache: ---
            ← output of mci_dump() here
--- ruleset debug_dumpstate returns stat ret, pv: ---
            ← output of rule set debug_dumpstate here
--- end of state dump ---
```

We have described the first line already. If for some reason $j is missing from $=w, that line will be followed by

```
*** $j not in $=w ***
```

The second line simply shows the number of children the daemon has forked and currently has out doing other work in parallel with itself. That line is followed by three sections of information. The first two sections are always output; the third is output only if rule set **debug_dumpstate** exists.

26.3.3.1 — open file descriptors: —

Each open file descriptor is displayed along with its current properties. These lines of output can be numerous. In general form, they look like this:

```
num: fl=flags mode=mode type stats
```

Here, the *num* is the number of the open file descriptor. The other information in this line is described in detail in our discussion of the **-d2.9** debugging switch (see §37.5.13).

26.3.3.2 — connection cache: —

When sending mail, outgoing connections are maintained for efficiency, and information about those connections is cached. Before connecting to a remote host, for example, *sendmail* checks its cache to see whether that host is down. If it is, it skips connecting to that host.

This output is highly detailed and very complicated. See the **-d11.1** debugging switch (§37.5.44) for a full description.

26.3.3.3 — *ruleset debug_dumpstate returns stat . . . , pv:* —

If rule set **debug_dumpstate**[*] is defined in your configuration file, it will be called here, and the above line of output will be printed. The **stat** is the numeric representation of the code returned by *sendmail*'s internal *rewrite()* routine. That code will be either EX_OK (0) if there were no parsing errors, EX_CONFIG (78) if there were, or EX_DATAERR (65) if there was a fatal error (such as too much recursion or a replacement was out of bounds). Text describing the error is also logged and will appear in this output.

Rule set **debug_dumpstate** is called with an empty workspace. After rule set **debug_dumpstate** is done, each token in the resulting new workspace is printed one per line. This gives you a hook into the internals of *sendmail*, enabling you to display information that might otherwise be invisible. For example, consider the desire to display *identd* information, the current sender's address, and the current queue identifier:

```
Sdebug_dumpstate
R$*        $@ $&_ $&s $&i
```

Here, the $* in the LHS matches the zero tokens passed to rule set **debug_dumpstate**. The $@ prefix in the RHS suppresses recursion. Each of the three macros that follows is stated with a $& prefix (see §31.5.3) that prevents each from being prematurely expanded when the configuration file is first read.

Another example might involve the need to look up the current recipient's host with DNS:

```
Sdebug_dumpstate
R$*        $@ $[ $&h $]
```

The $[and $] operators (see §28.6.6) cause the hostname appearing between them to be looked up with DNS and replaced with its full canonical name. Again, the macro h is prefixed with $& to prevent premature expansion.

In general, rule set **debug_dumpstate** should be excluded from your configuration file. When a problem does appear, you can define it, restart the daemon, and then wait for the problem to reoccur. When it does, kill *sendmail* with a SIG_USR1 and examine the *syslog* result.

Do not be tempted to use rule set **debug_dumpstate** for routine logging of specialty information. Forcing rules to be processed with a signal is fraught with danger. The current active rule set can, for example, be clobbered in possibly

---

[*] In V8.7 *sendmail* this is rule set 89. Beginning with V8.8 *sendmail*, rule sets 80 through 89 are reserved for use by vendors, such as Sun Microsystems.

unrecoverable ways. Use this rule set `debug_dumpstate` technique only to solve specific problems, then erase it when the problem is solved.

26.4 Log Transactions with -X

Beginning with V8.2 *sendmail*, the -X command-line switch can be used to record all input and output, SMTP traffic, and other significant transactions. The form of the -X (transaction) command-line switch looks like this:

```
-X file
```

Space between the -X and the *file* is optional. The *file* may be specified as either as a full or a relative pathname. For security the -X command-line switch always causes *sendmail* to give up its *root* privilege unless it was run by *root*. If the transaction *file* cannot be opened for writing, the following error is printed and no logging is done:

```
cannot open file
```

Otherwise, the file is opened in append mode, and each line that is written to it looks like this:

```
pid what detail
```

The *pid* is the process identification number of the *sendmail* that added the line. The *what* is one of these three symbols:

<<<
> This is input. It is either text that is read on the standard input or parts of an SMTP dialog that were read on a socket connection.

>>>
> This is output. It is either something that *sendmail* printed to its standard output, or something that it sent over an SMTP connection.

===
> This is an event. The only two events that are currently logged are CONNECT for connection to a host and EXEC for execution of a delivery agent.

To illustrate, consider sending a mail message to yourself and to a friend at another site:

```
% /usr/lib/sendmail -X /tmp/xfile -oQ/tmp yourself,friend@remote.host
To: yourself,friend@remote.host
Subject: test

This is a test.
.
```

These few lines of input produce a long */tmp/xfile*. The first few lines of that file are illustrative:

```
29559 <<< To: yourself,friend@remote.host
29559 <<< Subject: test
29559 <<<
29559 <<< This is a test.
29559 <<< .
29561 === CONNECT remote.host
29561 <<< 220 remote.host ESMTP Sendmail 8.7.5; Sun, 12 May 1996 08:06:47 -0600 (MDT)
29561 >>> EHLO your.host
29561 <<< 250-remote.host Hello you@your.host [206.54.76.122], pleased to meet you
29561 <<< 250-8BITMIME
29561 <<< 250-SIZE
29561 <<< 250-DSN
29561 <<< 250-VERB
29561 <<< 250-ONEX
29561 <<< 250 HELP
29561 >>> MAIL From:<your@your.host> SIZE=65
29561 <<< 250 <your@your.host>... Sender ok
29561 >>> RCPT To:<friend@remot.host>
29561 <<< 250 Recipient ok
29561 >>> DATA
29561 <<< 354 Enter mail, end with "." on a line by itself
29561 >>> The first line of data here,
29561 >>> the second line of data here,
29561 >>> and so on.
```

Notice that the process ID changes. After *sendmail* collects the message, it *fork*(2)s and *exec*(2)s to handle the actual delivery.

Because these transaction files include message bodies, they should be guarded. Never use the –X switch with the daemon unless you are prepared for a huge file and the possibility of disclosing message contents to nonprivileged users.

26.5 *Pitfalls*

- The *syslog*(3) library uses datagram sockets for passing information to other hosts. As a consequence, there is no guarantee that all logged information will be received by those other hosts.

- When using *m4*, exercise care to avoid using *m4* keywords in unexpected places. For example, attempting to notify a user named dnl in the *syslog.conf* file causes that name and all the text following on the same line to be lost.

- Prior to V8, *sendmail* used no record or file locking with the StatusFile (S) option's statistics file. As a consequence, it was not guaranteed to contain 100 percent accurate information. As another consequence, statistics files should *never* be shared among multiple hosts using remote file systems.

- Care should be exercised in using the **-X** switch as *root*. No check is made to ensure that the transaction logging file makes sense. It is possible to make a typo and accidently append transaction data to the wrong file or device.

IV

Reference

The fourth part of this book provides a comprehensive reference for all the inner-workings of the configuration file, and for debugging and rule testing.

Chapter 27, The Configuration File

Presents an overview of the *sendmail.cf* file. Comments, joined lines, and the V configuration command are detailed.

Chapter 28, Rules

Shows how the workspace is rewritten by individual rules. Operators, like $*, are explained here.

Chapter 29, Rule Sets

Covers the flow of addresses through rule sets, and illustrates the special uses of rule sets 0 through 5, and the check_ rule sets.

Chapter 30, Delivery Agents

Shows how to define mail delivery agents with the M configuration command. The F= flags are also listed.

Chapter 31, Defined Macros

Shows how to define and use macros. An explanation of all macros currently in use is included.

Chapter 32, Class Macros

Shows how multiple values can be stored in class macros. The special uses of the $= and $~ prefixes are also shown.

Chapter 33, Database Macros

Shows how to create, declare, and use external databases and network maps.

Chapter 34, Options

Shows how to declare options from the command line and in the configuration file. Then every option is explained.

Chapter 35, Headers

Describes the legal contents and form of headers in email messages and in the
H configuration command. Then many common headers are explained.

Chapter 36, The Command Line

Shows the many ways to run *sendmail* with emphasis on its numerous command-line switches.

Chapter 37, Debugging with –d

Documents the many debugging switches available with *sendmail.*

Chapter 38, Rule-Set Testing with –bt

Describes *sendmail*'s rule-testing mode and shows the many ways to use that
mode to solve problems.

27

The Configuration File

The *sendmail* configuration file is usually called *sendmail.cf*. It provides all the central information that controls the *sendmail* program's behavior. Among the key pieces of information provided are the following:

- The location of all the other files that *sendmail* needs to access and the location of all the directories in which *sendmail* needs to create and remove files.

- The definitions that *sendmail* uses in rewriting addresses. Some of those definitions can come from files, which are also specified.

- The mail header lines that *sendmail* should modify, pass through, and/or augment.

- The rules and sets of rules that *sendmail* uses for transforming mail addresses (and aliases for those addresses) into usable information, such as which delivery agent to use and the correct form of the address to use with that delivery agent.

The location of the *sendmail.cf* file is compiled into *sendmail*. It is usually found in one of the directories */etc*, */usr/lib*, or */etc/mail*. If you are compiling *sendmail*, you may specify the location of that file yourself by defining _PATH_SENDMAILCF in your *Makefile* (see §18.8.34). V8.7 recommends that the *sendmail.cf* file be located in */etc* for consistency.[*] Some vendors, however, prefer other locations. We recommend that one of the standard locations be used unless you have a compelling reason to do otherwise. Nonstandard locations may, for example, make operating system upgrades difficult if you need to revert to prior or vendor versions of *sendmail*.

---

[*] Scripts that may be distributed in the future will need the location of the *sendmail.cf* file to locate other files. If you move the *sendmail.cf* from its recommended standard location, you will have to modify all such scripts before they can be used.

The configuration file is read and parsed by *sendmail* every time it starts up. Because *sendmail* is run every time electronic mail is sent, its configuration file is designed to be easy for *sendmail* to parse rather than easy for humans to read.

27.1 Overall Syntax

The *sendmail.cf* file is line-oriented, with one configuration command per line. Each configuration command consists of a single letter[*] that must begin a line. Each letter is followed by other information as required by the purpose of the particular command.

In addition to commands, the configuration file may also have lines that begin with a # to form a comment line or with a tab or space character to form a continuation line. A list of all legal characters that may begin a line in the configuration file is shown in Table 27-1.

Table 27–1: sendmail.cf Configuration Commands

Command	§	Version	Description
#	27.2	All	A comment line, ignored
space	27.4	All	Continue the previous line
tab	27.4	All	Continue the previous line
C	32.1	All	Define a class macro
D	31.3	All	Define a macro
E	22.2.1	8.7 and above	Environment for agents
F	32.1	All	Define a class macro from a file or a pipe
H	35.1	All	Define a header
K	33.3	V8.1 and above	Create a keyed map entry
M	30.1	All	Define a mail delivery agent
O	34.2	All	Define an option
P	35.8	All	Define delivery priorities
R	28.1	All	Define a transformation rule
S	29.1	All	Declare a rule-set start
T	22.8.1.1	All	Declare trusted users (ignored V8.1–V8.6)
V	27.5	V8.1 and above	Version of configuration file

Most configuration commands are so complex that each requires a chapter or two of its own. A few, however, are simple. In this chapter we will describe the simple ones: comments, continuation lines, and the V (version) command.

---

[*] A quick bit of history: Initially, there was almost nothing in the configuration file except R rules (and there was only one rule set). Eric recalls adding M and O fairly quickly. Commands such as K and V came quite late.

27.2 Comments

Comments provide you with the documentation necessary to maintain the configuration file. Because comments slow *sendmail* down by only a small amount, it is better to overcomment than to undercomment.

Blank lines and lines that begin with a # character are considered comments and are ignored. A blank line is one that contains no characters at all (except for its terminating newline). Indentation characters (spaces and tabs) are invisible and can turn an apparently blank line into an *empty-looking line*, which is not ignored:

```
# text          ← a comment
tabtext         ← a continuation line
                ← a blank line
tab             ← an "empty-looking line"
```

Except for V8 *sendmail* and two special cases, comments occupy the entire line. The two special cases are the R and S configuration commands. The R command is composed of three tab-separated fields, the third field being a comment that does not require a leading # character:

```
Rlhs        rhs        comment
```

The pre-V8.7 S command looks only for a number following it and ignores everything else, so it may also be followed by a comment:

```
S3 this is a comment
```

No other commands allow comments to follow on the same line:

```
CWlocalhost mailhost  # This won't work prior to V8
```

27.3 V8 Comments

Beginning with V8 *sendmail*, for configuration files version 3 and above (see §27.5), all lines of the configuration file may have optional trailing comments. That is, all text from the first # character to the end of the line is ignored. Any whitespace (space or tab characters) leading up to the # is also ignored:

```
CWlocalhost mailhost  # This is a comment
                      ↑
```

from here to end of line ignored

To include a # character in a line under V8 *sendmail*, precede it with a backslash:

```
DM16\#megs
```

Note that you do not need to escape the # in the $# operator. The $ has a higher precedence, and $# is interpreted correctly.

27.4 Continuation Lines

A line that begins with either a tab or a space character is considered a continuation of the preceding line. Internally, such continuation lines are joined to the preceding line, and the newline character of that preceding line is retained. Thus, for example,

```
DZzoos
        lions and bears
↑
```
line begins with a tab character

is internally joined by *sendmail* to form

```
DZzoos\n          lions and bears
      ↑
```
newline and tab retained.

Both the newline (\n) and the tab are retained. When such a joined line is later used (as in a header), the joined line is split at the newline and prints as two separate lines again.

27.5 The V Configuration Command

The V configuration command was added to V8 *sendmail* to prevent old versions of configuration files from breaking when used with V8 *sendmail*. The syntax for the V configuration command looks like this:

```
Vlevel                ← V8.1 and above
Vlevel/vendor         ← V8.6 and above
```

Here, *level* is a positive integer, and */vendor* is a string. We will cover the vendor part soon.

If *level* is higher than the maximum allowed for the current version, *sendmail* prints the following warning and accepts the value:

```
Warning: .cf version level (lev) exceeds program functionality (max)
```

If *level* is less than 0 or if the V configuration command is omitted, the default *level* is 0.

The effects of the various version levels are relatively minor. As *sendmail* continues to develop, they may become more pronounced. Currently, the version levels are as follows:

0   The check for a valid shell in */etc/shells* is ignored (see §22.8.4).

0-1

MX records are looked up with the RES_DEFNAMES and RES_DNSRCH cleared. The high bit is always stripped from the body of every mail message.

2+ The *sendmail* program automatically adds a `-a.` to the "`host host`" map if that map isn't declared in the configuration file. RES_DEFNAMES and RES_DNSRCH are not turned off as they were for older versions. Rule set 5 behavior is enabled.

0-2

Set `UseErrorsTo` (1) option (see §34.8.74) to true automatically.

2+ Automatically sets the `$w` macro to be the short name instead of the fully qualified local hostname (`$j` still contains the fully qualified name and `$m` the local domain).

3+ You may use the new-style comments.

0-5

For V8.7 and above *sendmail*, level 5 or lower causes the `F=5Aw:|/@` flags to automatically be set for the `local` deliver agent and the `F=o` flag to automatically be set for the `prog` and `*file*` delivery agents.

0-5

Looking up MX records with `HasWildcardMX` listed with the `ResolverOptions` (I) option (see §34.8.55), causes RES_QUERY to be used in place of RES_SEARCH. Default the `ColonOkInAddr` option (see §34.8.9) to false.

0-6

Set the `SmtpGreetingMessage` option (see §34.8.65) with the value of `$e` if `$e` has a value. Set the `OperatorChars` option (see §34.8.45) with the value of `$o` if `$o` has a value. Beginning with V8.8 *sendmail*, a level of 6 or less causes the `F=q` flag (see §30.8.36) for the `local`, `prog`, and `*file*` delivery agents to be automatically set.

7   As of V8.8, the current version.

27.5.1 The vendor

Beginning with V8.6 *sendmail*, the `level` for the version command can be followed by the identity of the vendor. The form of that declaration looks like this:

```
Vlevel/vendor          ← V8.6 and above
```

The / must immediately follow the `level` with no intervening space. There may be arbitrary space between the / and the `vendor`. The string that is the vendor specification may either be one of the following:

Berkeley

> This is a configuration file based on the BSD distribution and is the one you
> get when you build and install from the source. As of V8.8, this declaration
> does nothing. If you use this configuration file with another vendor's version
> of *sendmail*, the `Berkeley` tells the other version that you are using a configu-
> ration file based on the BSD source.

Sun

> This is a configuration file intended for use with Sun's release of *sendmail*. If it
> is declared and if you are running Sun's *sendmail*, the enhancements docu-
> mented in Appendix D, *Sun Enhancements*, become available for your use. If
> you are not running Sun's *sendmail*, an error is printed.

If any other string appears in the `vendor` part, *sendmail* will print the following
error and ignore that vendor declaration:

```
invalid V line vendor code: bad vendor name here
```

Note that vendors other than those shown may have customized their *sendmail*
too, so this may not be a complete list.[*]

27.6 *Pitfalls*

- Avoid accidentally creating an empty-looking line (one that contains only
  invisible space and tab characters) in the *sendmail.cf* file when you really
  intend to create a blank line (one that contains only the newline character).
  The empty-looking line is joined by *sendmail* to the line above it and is likely
  to cause mysterious problems that are difficult to debug.

- Prior to V8 *sendmail* the maximum length of any given *sendmail.cf* line of
  text was defined in *conf.h* as MAXLINE. That maximum length was usually
  1024 characters, which included the end-of-line character and any continuation lines. If *sendmail* read a line that was longer than MAXLINE, it *silently*
  truncated that line to MAXLINE-1 and terminated the result with a zero value.
  Note that *sendmail* read the entire line but ignored the excess characters. This
  allowed it to accurately keep track of where the next line started. V8 *sendmail*
  has no limit for line lengths.

- Prior to V8 *sendmail* the last line in your *sendmail.cf* file had to end with a
  newline character. Some editors, such as *emacs*(1), are capable of writing a
  file in which the last line does not end with a newline character. If that trailing
  newline was missing from the last line, *sendmail* silently ignored it, thus treating that line as though it didn't exist. This has been fixed in V8 *sendmail*.

---

[*] Vendors that enhance their sendmail are *strongly* encouraged to use a new vendor code.

28

Rules

Rules are like little if-then clauses, existing inside rule sets, that test a pattern against an address and change the address if the two match. The process of converting one form of an address into another is called *rewriting*. Most rewriting requires a sequence of many rules, because an individual rule is relatively limited in what it can do. This need for many rules, combined with the *sendmail* program's need for succinct expressions, can make sequences of rules dauntingly cryptic.

In this chapter we dissect the components of individual rules. In the previous chapter we showed how groups of rules are combined to perform necessary tasks.

28.1 Overview

Rules are declared in the configuration file with the R command. Like all configuration commands, the R rule configuration command must begin a line. The general form consists of an R command followed by three parts:

```
Rlhs     rhs    comment
   ↑       ↑
  tabs    tabs
```

The `lhs` stands for *left-hand side* and is most commonly expressed as LHS. The `rhs` stands for *right-hand side* and is expressed as RHS. The LHS and RHS are mandatory. The third part (the `comment`) is optional. The three parts must be separated from each other by one or more tab characters (space characters will *not* work).

Space characters between the R and the LHS are optional. If there is a tab between the R and the LHS, *sendmail* silently uses the LHS as the RHS and the RHS becomes the comment.

The tabs leading to the comment and the comment itself are optional and may be omitted. If the RHS is absent, *sendmail* prints the following warning and ignores that R line:

```
invalid rewrite line "bad rule here" (tab expected)
```

This error is printed when the RHS is absent, even if there are tabs following the LHS. (This warning is usually the result of tabs being converted to spaces when text is copied from one window to another in a windowing system.)

28.1.1 Macros in Rules

Each noncomment part of a rule is expanded as the configuration file is read.[*] Thus any references to defined macros are replaced with the value that the macro has at that point in the configuration file. To illustrate, consider this mini-configuration file (called *x.cf*):

```
DAvalue1
R$A    $A.new
DAvalue2
R$A    $A.new
```

In it, $A will have the value **value1** when the first R line is expanded and **value2** when the second is expanded. Prove this to yourself by running *sendmail* in –bt rule-testing mode on that file:

```
% echo =S0 | /usr/lib/sendmail -bt -Cx.cf
> =S0
Rvalue1              value1 . new
Rvalue2              value2 . new
```

Here, we use the =S command (see §38.4.1) to show each rule after it has been read and expanded.

Another property of macros is that an undefined macro expands to an empty string. Consider this *x.cf* file:

```
DAvalue1
R$A    $A.$B
DAvalue2
R$A    $A.$B
```

and this rule-testing run of *sendmail*:

```
% echo =S0 | /usr/lib/sendmail -bt -Cx.cf
> =S0
Rvalue1              value1 .
Rvalue2              value2 .
```

---

[*] Actually, the comment part is expanded too, but with no effect other than a tiny expenditure of time.

Beginning with V8.7 *sendmail*, macros can be either single-character or multicharacter. Both forms are expanded when the configuration file is read:

```
D{OURDOMAIN}us.edu
R${OURDOMAIN}     localhost.${OURDOMAIN}
```

Multicharacter macros may be used in the LHS and in the RHS. When the configuration file is read, the previous example is expanded to look like this:

```
> =S0
Rus . edu              localhost . us . edu
```

28.1.2 Rules Are Treated Like Addresses

After each side (LHS and RHS) is expanded, each is then normalized just as though it were an address. A check is made for any tabs that may have been introduced during expansion. If any are found, everything from the first tab to the end of the string is discarded. Then RFC822-style comments are removed. An RFC822 comment is anything between and including an unquoted pair of parentheses:

```
DAroot@my.site (Operator)
R$A    tab RHS
  ↓
Rroot@my.site (Operator)    tab RHS          ← expanded
  ↓
Rroot@my.site   tab RHS                       ← RFC822 comment stripped
```

Finally, a check is made for balanced quotation marks, right parentheses balanced by left, and right angle brackets balanced by left.* If any right-hand character appears without a corresponding left-hand character, *sendmail* prints one of the following errors, where *configfile* is the name of the configuration file that is being read, *num* shows the line number in that file, and **expression** is the part of the rule that was unbalanced:

```
configfile: line num: expression...Unbalanced '"'
configfile: line num: expression...Unbalanced '>'
configfile: line num: expression...Unbalanced ')'
```

The first line shows that *sendmail* has balanced the unbalanced quotation mark by appending a second quotation mark. Each of the last two lines shows that the unbalanced character is removed. For example, the file:

```
Rx     RHS"
Ry     RHS>
Rz     RHS)
```

---

* The $> operator isn't counted in checking balance.

produces these errors and rules:

```
% echo =S0 | /usr/lib/sendmail -bt -Cx.cf
x.cf: line 1: RHS"... Unbalanced '"'
x.cf: line 2: RHS>... Unbalanced '>'
x.cf: line 3: RHS)... Unbalanced ')'
> =S0
Rx              RHS ""
Ry              RHS
Rz              RHS
```

Note that prior to V8.7 *sendmail,* only an unbalanced right-hand character was checked:[*] Beginning with V8.7 *sendmail,* unbalanced left-hand characters are also detected, and *sendmail* attempts to balance them for you. Consider, the following file:

```
Rx      "RHS
Ry      <RHS
Rz      (RHS
```

Here, *sendmail* detects and fixes the unbalanced characters but does so with warnings:

```
% echo =S0 | /usr/lib/sendmail -bt -Cx.cf
x.cf: line 1: "RHS... Unbalanced '"'
x.cf: line 2: <RHS... Unbalanced '<'
x.cf: line 3: (RHS... Unbalanced '('
x.cf: line 3: R line: null RHS
> =S0
Rx              "RHS"
Ry              < RHS >
Rz
```

Note that in the last example (**Rz**), *sendmail* balanced the RHS by adding a right-most parenthesis. This caused the RHS to become an RFC822 comment, which was then deleted, resulting in the null RHS error.

If you get one of these **Unbalanced** errors, be sure to correct the problem at once. If you leave the faulty rule in place, *sendmail* will continue to run but will likely produce erroneous mail delivery and other odd problems.

28.1.2.1 Backslashes in rules

Backslash characters are used in addresses to protect certain special characters from interpretation (see §35.3.2). For example, the address *blue;jay* would ordinarily be interpreted as having three parts (or tokens, which we'll discuss soon). To prevent *sendmail* from treating this address as three parts and instead have it

---

[*] That is, for example, there must not be a > before the < character, and they must pair off.

viewed as a single item, the special separating nature of the *;* can be *escaped* by prefixing it with a backslash:

```
blue\;jay
```

V8 *sendmail* handles backslashes differently than other versions have in the past. Instead of stripping a backslash and setting a high bit (see below), it leaves backslashes in place:

```
blue\;jay        becomes  →   blue\;jay
```

This causes the backslash to mask the special meaning of characters, because *sendmail* always recognizes the backslash in that role.

The only time that V8 *sendmail* strips backslashes is during local delivery, and then only if they are not inside full quotation marks. Mail to *user* is delivered to *user* on the local machine (bypassing further aliasing) with the backslash stripped. But for mail to *user@otherhost* the backslash is preserved in both the envelope and the header.

Prior to V8 *sendmail*, for addresses and rules (which are normalized as addresses), the backslash was removed by *sendmail* and the high bit of the character following the backslash was set (turned on).

```
blue;jay
    ↑
```
high-bit turned on

This practice was abandoned because of the need to support international characters (such as ö, Δ, and ø). Most international character sets include many characters that have the high bit set. Escaping a character by setting its high bit is a practice that no longer works in our modern, international world.

28.2 Tokenizing Rules

The *sendmail* program views the text that makes up rules and addresses as being composed of individual tokens. Rules are *tokenized*—divided up into individual parts—while the configuration file is being read and while they are being normalized. Addresses are tokenized at another time (as we'll show later), but the process is the same for both.

The text *our.domain*, for example, is composed of three tokens: *our*, a dot, and *domain*. These 10 characters are divided into tokens by the list of separation characters defined by the OperatorChars (pre-V8.7 $o) option (see §34.8.45):

```
Do.:%@!^=/[]                        ← prior to V8.7
O OperatorChars=.:%@!^/[]           ← V8.7 and above
```

When any of these separation characters are recognized in text, they are considered individual tokens. Any leftover text is then combined into the remaining tokens.

    xxx@yyy;zzz   *becomes →* xxx   @   yyy;zzz

@ is defined to be a token, but ; is not. Therefore, the text is divided into three tokens. However, in addition to the characters in the `OperatorChars` (pre-V8.7 $o) option, *sendmail* defines 10 tokenizing characters internally (in *parseaddr.c*):

    ()<>,;\"\r\n

These two lists are combined into one master list that is used for all tokenizing. The above example, when divided by using this master list, becomes five tokens instead of just three:

    xxx@yyy;zzz   *becomes →* xxx   @   yyy   ;   zzz

In rules, quotation marks can be used to override the meaning of tokenizing characters defined in the master list. For example,

    "xxx@yyy";zzz   *becomes →* "xxx@yyy"   ;   zzz

Here, three tokens are produced, because the @ appears inside quotation marks. Note that the quotation marks are retained.

Because the configuration file is read sequentially from start to finish, the `OperatorChars` (pre-V8.7 $o) option should be defined before any rules are declared. But note that beginning with V8.7 *sendmail*, omission of this option cause the separation characters to default to

    . : % @ ! ^ / [ ]

28.2.1 *$ Operators Are Tokens*

As we progress into the details of rules, you will see that certain characters become operators when prefixed with a $ character. Operators cause *sendmail* to perform actions, such as looking for a match ($* is a wildcard operator) or replacing tokens with others by position ($1 is a replacement operator).

For tokenizing purposes, operators always divide one token from another, just as the characters in the master list did. For example

    xxx$*zzz   *becomes →* xxx $*   zzz

28.2.2 The Space Character Is Special

The space character is special for two reasons. First, although the space character is not in the master list, it *always* separates one token from another:

>xxx zzz   *becomes* → xxx   zzz

Second, although the space character separates tokens, it is not itself a token. That is, in the above example the seven characters on the left (the seventh is the space in the middle) become two tokens of three letters each, not three tokens. Therefore the space character can be used inside the LHS or RHS of rules for improved clarity but does not itself become a token or change the meaning of the rule.

28.2.3 Pasting Addresses Back Together

After an address has passed through all the rules (and has been modified by rewriting), the tokens that form it are pasted back together to form a single string. The pasting process is very straightforward in that it mirrors the tokenizing process:

>xxx @ yyy   *becomes* →   xxx@yyy

The only exception to this straightforward pasting process occurs when two adjoining tokens are both simple text. Simple text is anything other than the separation characters (defined by the **OperatorChars** (pre-V8.7, $o) option, see §34.8.45, and internally by *sendmail*) or the operators (characters prefixed by a $ character). The xxx and yyy above are both simple text.

When two tokens of simple text are pasted together, the character defined by the **BlankSub** (B) option (see §34.8.5) is inserted between them.[*] Usually, that option is defined as a dot, so two tokens of simple text would have a dot inserted between them when they are joined:

>xxx yyy   *becomes* →   xxx.yyy

Note that the improper use of a space character in the LHS or RHS of rules can lead to addresses that have a dot (or other character) inserted where one was not intended.

---

[*] In the old days (RFC733), usernames to the left of the @ could contain spaces. But UNIX also uses spaces as command-line argument separators, so option B was introduced.

28.3 The Workspace

As was mentioned, rules exist to rewrite addresses. We won't cover the reasons this rewriting needs to be done just yet but will instead concentrate on the general behavior of rewriting.

Before any rules are called to perform rewriting, a temporary buffer called the "workspace" is created. The address to be rewritten is then tokenized and placed into that workspace. The process of tokenizing addresses in the workspace is exactly the same as the tokenizing of rules that you saw before:

> gw@wash.dc.gov   *becomes* → gw @ wash . dc . gov

Here, the tokenizing characters defined by the `OperatorChars` (pre-V8.7, `$o`) option (see §34.8.45) and those defined internally by *sendmail* caused the address to be broken into seven tokens. The process of rewriting changes the tokens in the workspace:

```
                              ← workspace is "gw" "@" "wash" "." "dc" "." "gov"
Rlhs  rhs
Rlhs  rhs           ← rules rewrite the workspace
Rlhs  rhs
                              ← workspace is "gw" "." "LOCAL"
```

Here, the workspace began with seven tokens. The three hypothetical rules recognized that this was a local address (in token form) and rewrote it so that it became three tokens.

28.4 The Behavior of a Rule

Each individual rule (R command) in the configuration file can be thought of as a while-do statement. Recall that rules are composed of an LHS (left-hand side) and an RHS (right-hand side), separated from each other by tabs. As long as (while) the LHS matches the workspace, the workspace is rewritten (do) by the RHS. (See Figure 28-1.)

Consider a rule in which we want the name `tom` in the workspace changed into the name `fred`. One possible rule to do this might look like this:

```
Rtom     fred
```

If the workspace contains the name `tom`, the LHS of this rule matches exactly. As a consequence, the RHS is given the opportunity to rewrite the workspace. It does so by placing the name `fred` into that workspace. The new workspace is once again compared to the `tom` in the LHS, but now there is no match because the workspace contains `fred`. When the workspace and the LHS do not match, the

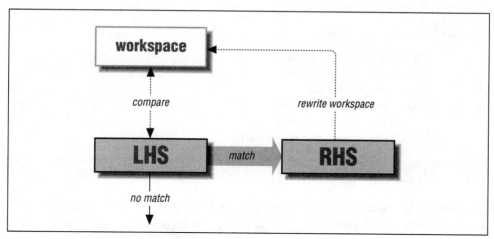

Figure 28–1: The behavior of a rule

rule is skipped, and the *current* contents of the workspace are carried down to the next rule. Thus, in our example, the name `fred` in the workspace is carried down.

Clearly, there is little reason to worry about endless loops in a rule when using names like `tom` and `fred`. But the LHS and RHS can contain pattern-matching and replacement operators, and those operators *can* lead to loops. To illustrate, consider this example from the *x.cf* file:

```
Rfred       fred
```

Clearly. the LHS will always match `fred` both before and after each rewrite. Here's what happens in testing this rule in –bt rule-testing mode:

```
% /usr/lib/sendmail -bt -Cx.cf
ADDRESS TEST MODE (ruleset 3 NOT automatically invoked)
Enter <ruleset> <address>
> 0 fred
rewrite: ruleset   0   input: fred
Infinite loop in ruleset 0, rule 1
rewrite: ruleset   0 returns: fred
>
```

V8 *sendmail* discovers the loop and breaks it for you. Earlier versions of *sendmail* would hang forever.

28.5 The LHS

The LHS of any rule is compared to the current contents of the workspace to determine whether the two match. Table 28-1 displays a variety of special operators offered by *sendmail* that make comparisons easier and more versatile.

Table 28–1: LHS Operators

Operator	Description or Use
$*	Match zero or more tokens
$+	Match one or more tokens
$-	Match exactly one token
$@	Match exactly zero tokens (V8 only)
$=	Match any tokens in a class[a]
$~	Match any single token not in a class

a. Class matches either a single token or multiple tokens, depending on the version of *sendmail* (see §32.2).

The first three operators in Table 28-1 are wildcard operators, which can be used to match arbitrary sequences of tokens in the workspace. Consider the following rule, which employs the $- operator (match any single token):

    R$-   fred.local

Here, a match is found only if the workspace contains a single token (such as *tom*). If the workspace contains multiple tokens (such as *tom@host*), the LHS does not match. A match causes the workspace to be rewritten by the RHS to become fred.local. The rewritten workspace is then compared again to the $-, but this time there is no match because the workspace contains three tokens (fred, a dot (.), and local). Since there is no match, the *current* workspace (fred.local) is carried down to the next rule (if there is one).

Note that all comparisons of tokens in the LHS to tokens in the workspace are done in a case-*in*sensitive manner. That is, tom in the LHS matches TOM, Tom, and even ToM in the workspace.

28.5.1 Minimum Matching

When a pattern-matching operator can match multiple tokens ($+ and $*), *sendmail* performs *minimum matching*. For example, given a workspace of xxx.yyy.zzz and an LHS of

    $+.$+

the first $+ matches only a single token (xxx), but the second $+ matches three (yyy, a dot, and zzz). This is because the first $+ matches the minimum number of tokens that it can while still allowing the whole LHS to match the workspace. Shortly, when we discuss the RHS, we'll show why this is important.

28.5.2 Backup and Retry

Multiple token-matching operators, such as $*, always try to match the fewest number of tokens that they can. Such a simple-minded approach could lead to problems in matching (or not matching) classes in the LHS. For example, consider the following five tokens in the workspace:

```
A . B . C
```

Given the following LHS rule:

```
R$+.$=X$*
```

Because the $+ tries to match the minimum number of tokens, it first matches only the A in the workspace. The $=X then tries to match the B to the class X. If this match fails, *sendmail* backs up and tries again.

The third time through, the $+ matches the A.B, and the $=X tries to match the C in the workspace. If C is not in the class X, the entire LHS fails.

The ability of the *sendmail* program to back up and retry LHS matches eliminates much of the ambiguity from rule design. The multitoken matching operators try to match the minimum but match more if necessary for the whole LHS to match.

28.6 The RHS

The purpose of the RHS in a rule is to rewrite the workspace. To make this rewriting more versatile, *sendmail* offers several special RHS operators. The complete list is shown in Table 28-2.

Table 28–2: RHS Operators

RHS	§	Description or Use
$*digit*	28.6.1	Copy by position
$:	28.6.2	Rewrite once (prefix)
$@	28.6.3	Rewrite and return (prefix)
$>*set*	28.6.4	Rewrite through another rule set
$#	28.6.5	Specify a delivery agent
$[$]	28.6.6	Canonicalize hostname
$($)	33.4	Database lookup

28.6.1 *Copy by Position: $digit*

The $*digit* operator in the RHS is used to copy tokens from the LHS into the workspace. The *digit* refers to positions of LHS wildcard operators in the LHS:

```
R$+@$*      $2!$1
  ↑  ↑
  $1 $2
```

Here, the $1 in the RHS indicates tokens matched by the first wildcard operator in the LHS (in this case the $+), and the $2 in the RHS indicates tokens matched by the second wildcard operator in the LHS (the $*). In this example, if the workspace contains A@B.C, it will be rewritten by the RHS as follows:

$*	*matches*	B.C	*so* $2 *copies it to workspace*
		!	*explicitly placed into workspace*
$+	*matches*	A	*so* $1 *copies it to workspace*

The $*digit* copies all the tokens matched by its corresponding wildcard operator. For the $+ wildcard operator, only a single token (A) is matched and copied with $1. The ! is copied as is. For the $* wildcard operator, three tokens are matched (B.C), so $2 copies all three. Thus the above rule rewrites A@B.C into B.C!A.

Not all LHS operators *need* to be referenced with a $*digit* in the RHS. Consider the following:

```
R$*<$*>$*    <$2>
```

Here, only the middle LHS operator (the second one) is required to rewrite the workspace. So only the $2 is needed in the RHS ($1 and $3 are not needed and are not present in the RHS).

Although macros appear to be operators in the LHS, they are not. Recall that macros are expanded when the configuration file is read (see §28.1.1). As a consequence, although they appear as $*letter* in the configuration file, they are converted to tokens when that configuration file is read. For example,

```
DAxxx
R$A @ $*    $1
```

Here, the macro A is defined to have the value xxx. To the unwary, the $1 *appears* to indicate the $A. But when the configuration file is read, the above rule is expanded into

```
Rxxx @ $*    $1
```

Clearly, the $1 refers to the $* (because $*digit* references only operators and $A is a macro, not an operator). The *sendmail* program is unable to detect errors of this sort. If the $1 were instead $2 (in a mistaken attempt to reference the $*), *sendmail* prints the following error and skips that rule:

```
ruleset replacement num out of bounds
```

V8 *sendmail* catches these errors when the configuration file is read. Earlier versions caught this error only when mail was actually sent.

The *digit* of the $*digit* must be in the range one through nine. A $0 is meaningless and causes *sendmail* to print the above error message and to skip that rule. Extra digits are considered tokens, rather than extensions of the $*digit*. That is, $11 is the RHS operator $1 and the token 1, not a reference to the eleventh LHS operator.

28.6.2 Rewrite Once Prefix: $:

Ordinarily, the RHS rewrites the workspace as long as the workspace continues to match the LHS. This looping behavior can be useful. Consider the need to strip extra trailing dots off an address in the workspace:

```
R$*..    $1.
```

Here, the $* matches any address that has two or more trailing dots. The $1. in the RHS then strips one of those two trailing dots when rewriting the workspace. For example,

xxx	*becomes* → xxx . . . .
xxx	*becomes* → xxx . . .
xxx . .	*becomes* → xxx . .
xxx . .	*becomes* → xxx .
xxx .	← *match fails*

Although this looping behavior of rules can be handy, for most rules it can be dangerous. Consider the following example:

```
R$*  <$1>
```

The intention of this rule is to cause whatever is in the workspace to become surrounded with angle brackets. But after the workspace is rewritten, the LHS again checks for a match; and since the $* matches anything, the match succeeds, the RHS rewrites the workspace again, and again the LHS checks for a match:

xxx	*becomes* → < xxx >
< xxx >	*becomes* → < < xxx > >
< < xxx > >	*becomes* → < < < xxx > > >
↓	
and so on, until ...	
↓	
sendmail prints: rewrite: expansion too long	

In this case, *sendmail* catches the problem, because the workspace has become too large. It prints the above error message and skips that and all further rules in the rule set. If you are running *sendmail* in test mode, this fatal error would also be printed:

```
== Ruleset 0 (0) status 65
```

Unfortunately, not all such endless looping produces a visible error message. Consider the following example:

```
R$*     $1
```

Here is an LHS that matches anything and an RHS that rewrites the workspace in such a way that the workspace never changes. For older versions this causes *sendmail* to appear to hang (as it processes the same rule over and over and over). Newer versions of *sendmail* will catch such endless looping and print (*syslog*) the following error:

```
Infinite loop in ruleset ruleset_name, rule rule_number
```

In this instance the original workspace is returned.

It is not always desirable (or even possible) to write "loop-proof" rules. To prevent looping, *sendmail* offers the $: RHS prefix. By starting the RHS of a rule with the $: operator, you are telling *sendmail* to rewrite the workspace exactly once.

```
R$*     $: <$1>
```

Again the rule causes the contents of the workspace to be surrounded by a pair of angle brackets. But here the $: prefix prevents the LHS from checking for another match after the rewrite.

Note that the $: prefix must begin the RHS to have any effect. If it instead appears inside the RHS, its special meaning is lost:

```
foo    rewritten by   $:$1    becomes →    foo
foo    rewritten by   $1$:    becomes →    foo $:
```

28.6.3 Rewrite-and-Return Prefix: $@

The flow of rules is such that each and every rule in a series of rules (a rule set) is given a chance to match the workspace:

```
Rxxx    yyy
Ryyy    zzz
```

The first rule matches **xxx** in the workspace and rewrites the workspace to contain **yyy**. The first rule then tries to match the workspace again but, of course, fails. The second rule then tries to match the workspace. Since the workspace contains **yyy**, a match is found, and the RHS rewrites the workspace to be **zzz**.

There will often be times when one rule in a series performs the appropriate rewrite and no subsequent rules need to be called. In the above example, suppose **xxx** should only become **yyy** and that the second rule should not be called. To solve problems like this, *sendmail* offers the $@ prefix for use in the RHS.

The $@ prefix tells *sendmail* that the current rule is the last one that should be used in the current rule set. If the LHS of the current rule matches, any rules that follow (in the current rule set) are ignored:

```
Rxxx     $@yyy
Ryyy     zzz
```

If the workspace contains anything other than **xxx**, the first rule does not match, and the second rule is called. But if the workspace contains **xxx**, the first rule matches and rewrites the workspace. The $@ prefix for the RHS of that rule prevents the second rule (and any subsequent rules) from being called.

Note that the $@ also prevents looping. The $@ tells *sendmail* to skip further rules *and* to rewrite only once. The difference between $@ and $: is that both rewrite only once, but $@ *doesn't* proceed to the next rule, whereas $: *does*.

The $@ operator must be used as a prefix because it has special meaning only when it begins the RHS of a rule. If it appears anywhere else inside the RHS it loses its special meaning:

```
foo    rewritten by    $@$1    becomes →    foo
foo    rewritten by    $1$@    becomes →    foo $@
```

28.6.4 *Rewrite Through Another Rule Set: $>set*

Rules are organized in sets that can be thought of as subroutines. Occasionally, a rule or series of rules can be common to two or more rule sets. To make the configuration file more compact and somewhat clearer, such common series of rules can be made into separate subroutines.

The RHS $>*set* operator tells *sendmail* to perform additional rewriting using a secondary set of rules. The **set** is the rule-set name or number of that secondary set. If **set** is the name or number of a nonexistent rule set, the effect is the same as if the subroutine rules were never called (the workspace is unchanged).

If the **set** is numeric and is greater than the maximum number of allowable rule sets, *sendmail* prints the following error and skips that rule:

```
bad ruleset bad_number (maximum max)
```

If the *set* is a name and the rule-set name is unknown, *sendmail* prints the following error and skips that rule:

```
Unknown ruleset bad_name
```

Neither of these errors is caught when the configuration file is read. They are caught only when mail is sent, because a rule set name may be a macro:

```
$> $&{SET}
```

The $& prefix prevents the macro named {SET} from being expanded when the configuration file is read. Therefore the name or number of the rule set cannot be known until mail is sent.

The process of calling another set of rules proceeds in five stages:

First

> As usual, if the LHS matches the workspace, the RHS gets to rewrite the workspace.

Second

> The RHS ignores the $>*set* part and rewrites the rest as usual.

Third

> The rewritten workspace is then given to the set of rules specified by *set*. They either rewrite the workspace or do not.

Fourth

> The original RHS (the one with the $>*set*) leaves the possibly rewritten workspace as is, as though it had performed the subroutine's rewriting itself.

Fifth

> The LHS gets a crack at the new workspace as usual unless it is prevented by a $: or $@ prefix in the RHS.

For example, consider the following two sets of rules:

```
# first set
S21
R$*..    $:$>22 $1.       strip extra trailing dots
  ...etc.

# second set
S22
R$*..    $1.              strip trailing dots
```

Here, the first set of rules contains, among other things, a single rule that removes extra dots from the end of an address. But because other rule sets may also need extra dots stripped, a subroutine (the second set of rules) is created to perform that task.

Note that the first rule strips one trailing dot from the workspace and then calls rule set 22 (the `$>22`), which then strips any additional dots. The workspace as rewritten by rule set 22 becomes the workspace yielded by the RHS in the first rule. The `$:` prevents the LHS of the first rule from looking for a match a second time.

Prior to V8.8 *sendmail* the subroutine call must begin the RHS (immediately follow any `$@` or `$:` prefix, if any) and only a single subroutine may be called. That is, the following causes rule set 22 to be called but does not call 23:

```
$>22 xxx $>23 yyy
```

Instead of calling rule set 23, the `$>` operator and the 23 are copied as is into the workspace, and that workspace is passed to rule set 22:

```
xxx $> 23 yyy       ← passed to rule set 22
```

Beginning with V8.8[*] *sendmail*, subroutine calls may appear anywhere inside the RHS, and there may be multiple subroutine calls. Consider the same RHS as above:

```
$>22 xxx $>23 yyy
```

Beginning with V8.8 *sendmail*, rule set 23 is called first and is given the workspace yyy to rewrite. The workspace, as rewritten by rule set 23, is added to the end of the xxx, and the combined result is passed to rule set 22.

Under V8.8 *sendmail*, subroutine rule-set calls are performed from right to left. The result (rewritten workspace) of each call is appended to the RHS text to the left.

You should beware of one problem with all versions of *sendmail*. When ordinary text immediately follows the number of the rule set, that text is likely to be ignored. This can be witnessed by using the `-d21.3` debugging switch.

Consider the following RHS:

```
$>3uucp.$1
```

Because *sendmail* parses the 3 and the uucp as a single token, the subroutine call succeeds, but the uucp is lost. The `-d21.3` switch illustrates this problem:

```
-----callsubr 3uucp (3)      ← sees this
-----callsubr 3 (3)          ← but should have seen this
```

The 3uucp is interpreted as the number 3, so it is accepted as a valid number despite the fact that uucp was attached. Since the uucp is a part of the number, it

---

[*] Using code derived from IDA sendmail.

is not available for comparison to the workspace and so is lost. The correct way to write the above RHS is

```
$>3 uucp.$1
```

Note that the space between the 3 and the uucp causes them to be viewed as two separate tokens.

This problem can also arise with macros. Consider the following:

```
$>3$M
```

Here, the $M is expanded when the configuration file is parsed. If the expanded value lacks a leading space, that value (or the first token in it) is lost.

Note that operators that follow a rule-set number are correctly recognized:

```
$>3$[$1$]
```

Here, the 3 is immediately followed by the $[operator. Because operators are token separators, the call to rule set 3 will be correctly interpreted as

```
-----callsubr 3 (3)              ← good
```

But as a general rule, and just to be safe, the number of a subroutine call should always be followed by a space.[*]

28.6.5 *Specify a Delivery Agent: $#*

The $# operator in the RHS is copied as is into the workspace and functions as a flag advising *sendmail* that a delivery agent has been selected. The $# must be the first token copied into the rewritten workspace for it to have this special meaning: If it occupies any other position in the workspace, it loses its special meaning.

```
$# local            ← selects delivery agent
xxx $# local        ← no special meaning
```

When it occurs first in the rewritten workspace, the $# operator tells *sendmail* that the second token in the workspace is the name of a delivery agent. The $# operator is useful only in rule sets 0 and 5.

Note that the $# operator may be prefixed with a $@ or a $: without losing its special meaning, because those prefix operators are not copied to the workspace:

```
$@ $# local       rewritten as → $# local
```

---

[*] As a stylistic point, it is easier to read rules that have spaces between all patterns that are expected to match separate tokens. For example, use $+ @ $* $=m instead of $+@$*$=m. This style handles subroutine calls automatically.

However, those prefix operators are not necessary, because the $# acts just like a $@ prefix. It prevents the LHS from attempting to match again after the RHS rewrite, and it causes any following rules to be skipped. When used in nonprefix roles in rule sets 0 and 5, $@ and $: also act like flags, conveying host and user information to *sendmail* (see §29.6).

28.6.6 Canonicalize Hostname: $[and $]

Tokens that appear between a $[and $] pair of operators in the RHS are considered to be the name of a host. That hostname is looked up by using DNS[*] and replaced with the full canonical form of that name. If found, it is then copied to the workspace, and the $[and $] are discarded.

For example, consider a rule that looks for a hostname in angle brackets and (if found) rewrites it in canonical form:

```
R<$*>     $@ <$[ $1 $]>     canonicalize host name
```

Such canonicalization is useful at sites where users frequently send mail to machines using the short version of a machine's name. The $[tells *sendmail* to view all the tokens that follow (up to the $]) as a single hostname.

If the name cannot be canonicalized (perhaps because there is no such host), the name is copied as is into the workspace. For configuration files lower than 2, no indication is given that it could not be canonicalized (more about this soon).

Note that if the $[is omitted and the $] is included, the $] loses its special meaning and is copied as is into the workspace.

The hostname between the $[and $] can also be an IP address. By surrounding the hostname with square brackets ([and]), you are telling *sendmail* that it is really an IP address:

```
wash.dc.gov          ← a host name
[123.45.67.8]        ← an IP address
```

When the IP address between the square brackets corresponds to a known host, the address and the square brackets are replaced with that host's canonical name.

---

[*] Or other means, depending on the setting of service switch file, if you have one, or the state of the ServiceSwitchFile option (see §34.8.61).

If the version of the configuration file is 2 or greater (as set with the V configuration command; see §27.5), a successful canonicalization has a dot appended to the result:

myhost	*becomes* →	myhost . domain .	← *success*
nohost	*becomes* →	nohost	← *failure*

Note that a trailing dot is not legal[*] in an address specification, so subsequent rules (such as rule set 4) *must* remove these added trailing dots.

Also, the K configuration command (see §33.3) can be used to redefine (or eliminate) the dot as the added character. For example,

```
Khost host -a.found
```

This causes *sendmail* to add the text `.found` to a successfully canonicalized hostname instead of the dot.

One difference between V8 *sendmail* and other versions is in the way it looks up names from between the `$[` and `$]` operators. The rules for V8 *sendmail* are as follows:

First
> If the name contains at least one dot (`.`) anywhere within it, it is looked up as is; for example, *host.CS*.

Second
> If that fails, it appends the default domain to the name (as defined in */etc/resolv.conf*) and tries to look up the result; for example, *host.CS.our.Sub.Domain*.

Third
> If that fails, the leftmost part of the subdomain (if any) is discarded and the result is appended to the original host; for example, *host.our.Sub.Domain*.

Fourth
> If the original name did not have a dot in it, it is looked up as is; for example, *host*.

This approach allows names such as *host.CS* to first match a site in the Czech Republic, such as *vscht.CS* (if that was intended), rather than to wrongly match a host in your local Computer Science (CS) department. This is particularly important if you have wildcard MX records for your site.

---

* Under DNS the trailing dot signifies the root (topmost) domain. Therefore under DNS a trailing dot is legal. For mail, however, RFC1123 specifically states that no address is to be propagated that contains a trailing dot.

28.6.6.1 An example of canonicalization

The following two-line configuration file can be used to observe how *sendmail* canonicalizes hostnames:

```
V2
R$*          $@ $[ $1 $]
```

If this file were called *x.cf*, *sendmail* could be run in rule-testing mode with a command like the following:

```
% /usr/lib/sendmail -oQ. -Cx.cf -bt
```

Thereafter, hostname canonicalization can be observed by specifying rule set 0 and a hostname. One such run of tests is as follows:

```
ADDRESS TEST MODE (ruleset 3 NOT automatically invoked)
Enter <ruleset> <address>
> 0 wash
rewrite: ruleset  0   input: wash
rewrite: ruleset  0 returns: wash . dc . gov .
> 0 nohost
rewrite: ruleset  0   input: nohost
rewrite: ruleset  0 returns: nohost
>
```

Note that the known host named **wash** is rewritten in canonicalized form (with a dot appended because of the V2). The unknown host named **nohost** is unchanged and has no dot appended.

28.6.6.2 Default in canonicalization: $:

IDA and V8 *sendmail* both offer an alternative to leaving the hostname unchanged when canonicalization fails with $[and $]. A default can be used instead of the failed hostname by prefixing that default with a $::

```
$[ host $: default $]
```

The $:*default* must follow the *host* and precede the $]. To illustrate its use, consider the following rule:

```
R$*    $:$[ $1 $: $1.notfound $]
```

If the hostname $1 can be canonicalized, the workspace becomes that canonicalized name. If it cannot, the workspace becomes the original hostname with a .notfound appended to it. If the *default* part of the $:*default* is omitted, a failed canonicalization is rewritten as zero tokens.

28.6.7 *Other Operators*

Many other operators (depending on your version of *sendmail*) may also be used in rules. Because of their individual complexity, all of the following are detailed in other chapters. We outline them here, however, for completeness.

Class macros

> Class macros are described in §32.2.1 and §32.2.2 of Chapter 32, *Class Macros*. Class macros may appear only in the LHS. They begin with the prefix $= to match a token in the workspace to one of many items in a class. The alternative prefix $~ causes a token in the workspace to match if it does *not* appear in the list of items that are the class.

Conditionals

> The conditional macro operator $? is rarely used in rules (see §31.6). When it is used in rules, the result is often not what was intended. Its *else* part, the $| conditional operator is used by the check_compat rule set (see §29.10.4) to separate the sender from the recipient address.

Database Operators

> The database operators, $(and $), are used to look up tokens in various types of database files and network database services. They also provide access to internal services, such as dequoting and looking up MX records (see Chapter 33, *Database Macros*).

28.7 *Pitfalls*

- Any text following a rule-set number in a $> expression in the RHS should be separated from the expression with a space. If the space is absent and the text is other than a separating character or an operator, the text is ignored. For example, in $>22xxx, the xxx is ignored.

- Because rules are processed like addresses when the configuration file is read, they can silently change from what was intended if they are parenthesized or if other nonaddress components are used.

- Copying rules between screen windows can cause tabs to invisibly become spaces, leading to rule failure.

- A lone $* in the LHS is especially dangerous. It can lead to endless rule looping and cause all rules that follow it to be ignored (remember the $: and $@ prefixes in the RHS).

- Failure to test new rules can bring a site to its knees. A flood of bounced mail messages can run up the load on a machine and possibly even require a reboot. *Always* test every new rule both with -bt (testing) mode (see §38.8). and selected -d (debugging) switches (see Table 37-2 in §37.5).

29

Rule Sets

Rule sets in the configuration file, like subroutines in a program, control the sequence of steps *sendmail* uses to rewrite addresses. Inside each rule set is a series of zero or more individual rules. Rules are used to select the appropriate delivery agent for any particular address, to detect and reject addressing errors, and to transform addresses to meet particular needs.

In this chapter we will cover all aspects of rule sets, showing that rule sets are called in particular orders and explaining why this is so.

We will explain many of the rules that typically appear in rule sets. But be forewarned: The examples of rules in this chapter are explanatory only. Your *sendmail.cf* file is likely to have rules that are somewhat different from these examples. Copying or using these examples, without first understanding the underlying principles, can cause email to begin to fail.

29.1 The S Configuration Command

The S configuration command declares the start of a rule set. It is perhaps the simplest of all configuration commands and looks like this:

```
Sident
```

The S, like all configuration commands, must begin the line. The *ident* identifies the rule set. There may be whitespace between the S and the *ident*. If the *ident* is missing, *sendmail* prints the following error message and skips that particular rule set declaration:

```
/etc/sendmail.cf: line num: invalid ruleset name: ""
```

Prior to V8.7 *sendmail* the `ident` could only be numeric. Beginning with V8.7 *sendmail* the `ident` may be numeric or alphanumeric. We cover the old form first, then the new.

29.1.1 Rule-Set Numbers

Prior to V8.7 *sendmail*, rule sets could be identified only by numbers. When a rule set is declared with an integer, that integer is taken to be the numeric identity of the rule set:

```
S#
```

Here, # is an integer such as 23. If the # is greater than half[*] the maximum number of rule sets allowed (MAXRWSETS in *conf.h*) or is negative, *sendmail* *syslog*(3)'s the following error message at the level LOG_CRIT and defaults the rule set to 0:

```
bad ruleset # (n max)
```

Here, the # is the bad rule-set number from the configuration file, and *n* is the maximum allowable rule-set number (the value of MAXRWSETS/2). By default, the maximum value for # is 99.

29.1.2 Rule-Set Names

Beginning with V8.7 *sendmail*, rule sets may be declared with numbers (as above) or with more meaningful names. The form for a rule-set name declaration looks like this:

```
Sname
```

The name may contain only ASCII alphanumeric characters and the underscore character. Any bad character causes that character and the characters following it to be silently ignored:

```
My_rule            ← good
My rule            ← bad, name is "My"
```

Case is recognized; that is, `Myrule` and `MYRULE` are different names. You may use any name that begins with an uppercase letter. Names that begin with a lowercase letter or an underscore character are reserved for internal use by *sendmail*.

---

[*] The reason for this will become clear shortly.

There may be at most MAXRWSETS/2 named rule sets (where MAXRWSETS is defined in *conf.h*). Each rule set that is declared beyond that amount causes *sendmail* to print the following error and ignore that rule-set declaration:

```
name: too many named rulesets (# max)
```

When you declare a rule set name, *sendmail* associates a number with it. That number is selected by counting down from MAXRWSETS. That is, the first name is given the number MAXRWSETS-1, the second is given the number MAXRWSETS-2, and so on. Named rule sets may be used anywhere that numbered rule sets can be used.

29.1.3 Associate Number with Name

When knowing the number associated with a named rule set is of importance, you can associate a number with a name when the name is declared. The form of such a combined declaration looks like this:

```
Sname=num
```

Here, the rule set named *name* is declared. Instead of *sendmail* associating a number with it, you create the association by following the *name* with an = character and then an integer *num*. Arbitrary whitespace may surround the = character. If the integer is missing or non-numeric, *sendmail* prints the following error and skips that rule-set declaration:

```
/etc/sendmail.cf: line num: bad ruleset definition "bad" (number required after '=')
```

Although it is ugly, different names may share the same number:

```
Sfoo=1
Sfee=1
```

However, the same name may not be given a different number. Consider the following example:

```
SMyrule=1
SMyrule=2
```

This causes *sendmail* to print the following error and skip the second declaration:

```
/etc/sendmail.cf: line num: Myrule: ruleset changed value (old 1, new 2)
```

Named rule sets have numbers associated with them when they first appear. If you use a named rule set in an S= equate for a delivery agent and then later attempt to assign it a value, you will get an error like the above:

```
Mprog, P=sh, ...., S=Myrule, ...
...
SMyrule=2
```

The solution is either to move the rule-set declaration (and its rules) so that they reside above the delivery agent declaration or to declare a numeric association in the delivery agent declaration instead of in the rule-set declaration:

```
Mprog, P=sh, ...., S=Myrule=2, ...
...
SMyrule
```

or to place just the S line above the delivery agent declaration and the rules, without the =2, below it:

```
SMyrule=2
Mprog, P=sh, ...., S=Myrule, ...
...
SMyrule
```

In general, we recommend that you assign numbers to named rule sets only if there is a genuine need.

29.1.4 *Macros in Rule-Set Names*

Macros may be used in any or all of a part of a rule-set declaration. They may be used to declare a name:

```
D{NAME}myname
S${NAME}
```

or to declare a number:

```
D{NUMBER}12
S${NUMBER}
```

or both a name and a number:

```
D{NAME}myname
D{NUMBER}12
S${NAME}=${NUMBER}
```

or even the whole thing:

```
D{SET}myset=12
S${SET}
```

You may use single- and multicharacter macros in any combination. Macros may be used in any rule-set declaration, including subroutine calls inside rules:

```
R$* < $=w > $*        $@ $>${NAME} $2
```

But they may not be used in the S= or the R= of delivery agents:

```
Mprog, P=sh, ..., S=$X, R=$X, ...
                      ↑      ↑
```
                 neither of these will work

Macros can be used in the command line to modify a configuration file when *sendmail* is run. Consider the desire to call one rule set when running as a dae-mon and another when processing the queue. You might declare such a rule like:

```
R$* < @ $+ > $*      $@ $>$A $2
```

The two different runs might look like this:

```
# /usr/lib/sendmail -MAdaemon_rule -bd
# /usr/lib/sendmail -MAqueue_rule -q30m
```

The first defines the $A macro to have the value **daemon_rule** and results in this subroutine call:

```
R$* < @ $+ > $*      $@ $>daemon_rule $2
```

The second defines the $A macro to have the value **queue_rule** and results in this different subroutine call:

```
R$* < @ $+ > $*      $@ $>queue_rule $2
```

Note that you cannot define multi character macros from the command line. Also note that defining macros from the command line can result in *sendmail* giving up its *root* privilege.

29.1.5 Rule Sets and Lists of Rules

All rules (R lines) that follow a rule-set declaration are added to and become part of that rule set:

```
S0
R...              ← rules added to rule set 0
SMyset
R...              ← rules added to rule set Myset
S1
R...              ← rules added to rule set 1
```

Rule sets need not be declared in any particular order. Any order that clarifies the intention of the configuration file as a whole is acceptable. If a rule set appears more than once in a configuration file, V8 *sendmail* will print a warning:

```
WARNING: Ruleset name redefined                  ← Prior to V8.8
WARNING: Ruleset name has multiple definitions ← V8.8
```

and append the new rules to the old:

```
S0
R...              ← rules added to rule set 0
S2
R...              ← rules added to rule set 2
S0                ← warning issued
R...              ← rules appended to earlier rule set 0
```

Note that the warning is given in all cases prior to V8.8, but beginning with V8.8, it is issued only in **–bt** rule-testing mode or if the **–d37.1** debugging switch is set.

Other configuration commands may be interspersed among rule definitions without affecting the rule set to which the rules are added:

```
S0
R...            ← rules added to rule set 0
Pjunk=-100
DUuucphost.our.domain
R...            ← rules added to rule set 0
```

Any rules that appear before the first **S** command are added to rule set 0 by default:

```
R...            ← rules added to rule set 0
S1              ← first S command in configuration file
R...            ← rules added to rule set 1
```

29.1.6 Odds and Ends

Arbitrary text that follows a rule set declaration is ignored unless it appears to be part of the declaration:

```
S11 100 more rule sets      ← rule set 11
S11100 more rule sets       ← rule set 11,100 is illegal
SMyset 100 more rule sets   ← rule set Myset
```

Although the first and last of the above examples work, we recommend that you use the # commenting mechanism instead:

```
S11 #100 more rule sets     ← rule set 11
S11#100 more rule sets      ← rule set 11
SMyset #100 more rule sets  ← rule set Myset
```

A rule-set declaration that has no rules associated with it is exactly the same as a rule set that is not declared. Both are like do-nothing subroutines:

```
                ← rule set 1 not declared. Same as
S2              ← rule set 2 without rules
S3
R...
```

29.2 Rule Sets and m4

When building a configuration file using the *m4* technique (see §19.1), *sendmail* reserves certain rule-set numbers for its own use. Using the *m4* technique, you can add rules to those rule sets, but you cannot replace those rule sets with your own. A few *m4* keywords are available to make adding rules easier. They affect rule sets 0 through 3 directly and other rule sets indirectly (see Table 19-5 in §19.4.3).

The configuration file created with the *m4* technique uses quite a few rule sets beyond the base group of 0 through 5. Table 29-1 shows all the rule sets used by the bare bones *m4* technique. They are listed numerically, which also just happens to group them by function. The table also includes the name of the file containing the rules for each rule set.

Table 29–1: Rule Sets Used by the m4 Technique

Set	File	Description
S0	m4/proto.m4	Select a delivery agent
S1	m4/cfhead.m4	Process all sender addresses
S2	m4/cfhead.m4	Process all recipient addresses
S3	m4/proto.m4	Preprocess all addresses
S4	m4/proto.m4	Postprocess all addresses
S5	m4/proto.m4	Post alias select a delivery agent
S10	mailer/local.m4	Handle S= for `local` delivery agent
S11	mailer/smtp.m4	Handle S= for `smtp` delivery agents
S12	mailer/uucp.m4	Handle S= for `uucp` delivery agents
S15	mailer/mail11.m4	Handle S= for `mail11` delivery agent
S20	mailer/local.m4	Handle envelope R= for `local` delivery agent
S21	mailer/smtp.m4	Handle envelope R= for `smtp` delivery agents
S22	mailer/uucp.m4	Handle envelope R= for `uucp` delivery agents
S25	mailer/mail11.m4	Handle envelope R= for `mail11` delivery agent
S30	mailer/local.m4	Handle <@> and masquerading for `local` delivery agent
S31	mailer/smtp.m4	Handle ALL_MASQUERADE envelope R= for `smtp`
S40	mailer/local.m4	Handle header R= for `local` delivery agent
S42	mailer/uucp.m4	Handle header R= for `uucp` delivery agents
S50	mailer/local.m4	Rules to add local domain (if ALWAYS_ADD_DOMAIN)
S51	mailer/smtp.m4	Convert pseudo-domains to real domains
S52	mailer/uucp.m4	Handle envelope S= for `uucp-dom` delivery agent
S61	mailer/smtp.m4	Handle ALL_MASQUERADE envelope R= for `relay` agent
S71	mailer/smtp.m4	Handle envelope header R= for `relay` agent
S72	mailer/uucp.m4	Handle envelope S= for `uucp-uudom` delivery agent
S90	m4/proto.m4	Try domain part of mailertable entry
S93	m4/proto.m4	Convert header names to masqueraded form
S94	m4/proto.m4	Convert envelope names to masqueraded form
S95	m4/proto.m4	Canonify mailer:[user@]host syntax to triple
S96	m4/proto.m4	Handle common rule set 3 needs
S98	m4/proto.m4	Handle local part of rule set 0

29.3 *The Sequence of Rule Sets*

When *sendmail* rewrites addresses, it applies its rule sets in a specific sequence. The sequence differs for sender and recipient addresses, with a third branch used to select delivery agents. Figure 29-1 shows a map of the different paths taken by each kind of address. Those paths show how addresses flow through rule sets.

Both sender and recipient addresses are first input into rule set 3. Then each takes a different path through the rule sets based on its type. Recipient addresses take the dashed path, whereas sender addresses take the solid path. But before those paths can be taken, *sendmail* needs to select a delivery agent (the dotted path) to get rule-set numbers for the R= and S= of each path.

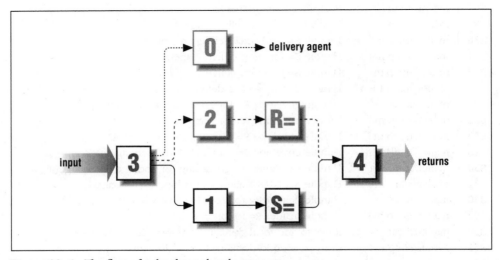

Figure 29–1: The flow of rules through rule sets

To select a delivery agent, *sendmail* rewrites the recipient address with rule sets 3 and 0 (the dotted path). Rule set 0 selects a delivery agent that is appropriate for the recipient. That delivery agent supplies rule set values for the S= and R= in the corresponding sender (solid) and recipient (dashed) paths.

After a delivery agent has been selected, the sender address is processed (see Figure 29-2). As was mentioned above, it is first input into rule set 3. Then it flows through rule set 1, then the S= rule set as determined by the delivery agent. Finally, it flows through rule set 4, which returns the rewritten address. This rewritten sender address appears in the header and envelope of the mail message. Note that all addresses are eventually rewritten by rule set 4. In general, rule set 4 undoes any special rewriting that rule set 3 did.

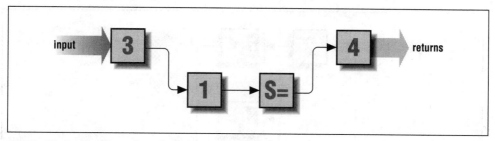

Figure 29–2: The flow of sender addresses through rule sets

Finally, the recipient address also needs to be rewritten for inclusion in the header and envelope of mail messages (see Figure 29-3). Recall that it was already used once to select the delivery agent. It is used as input to rule set 3, as are all addresses. It then flows through rule set 2, then through the R= rule set selected by the delivery agent, and finally through rule set 4.

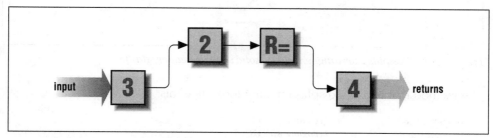

Figure 29–3: The flow of recipient addresses through rule sets

The need for separate paths for the sender and the recipient is best explained with an example. Consider a site that wants the addresses of all local users to appear as though they are from the local domain. Such rewriting is appropriate for local users on outgoing mail but inappropriate for recipients at other sites. Clearly, such rewriting should be restricted to the sender path, probably in rule set 1.

The flow of rules through rule sets (as is shown in Figure 29-3) is appropriate for *all* versions of *sendmail*. Some versions, such as V8, enhance these rules with others, but all those enhancements begin with this basic set.

29.3.1 V8 Enhancements

V8 *sendmail* allows envelope addresses to be rewritten separately from header addresses. This separation takes place in the delivery agent R= and S= specific rule sets as illustrated in Figure 29-3.

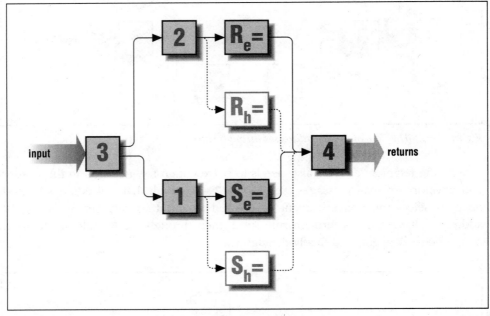

Figure 29–4: V8 splits rewriting: envelope (solid) versus header (dashed)

The method that is used to split rewriting looks like this:

```
R=eset/hset          ← beginning with V8
S=eset/hset          ← beginning with V8
```

The envelope-specific rule set is the one to the left of the slash and is represented by a solid line. The header-specific rule set is to the right of the slash (R=eset/hset) and is represented by a dashed line. See §30.4.10 for a complete description of this process.

29.4 Rule Set 3

Rule set 3 is the first to process every address. It puts each into a form that simplifies the tasks of other rule sets. The most common method is to have rule set 3 *focus* an address (place angle brackets around the host part). Then later rules don't have to search for the host part, because it is already highlighted. For example, consider trying to spot the recipient host in this mess:

```
uuhost!user%host1%host2
```

Here, **user** is eventually intended to receive the mail message on the host **uuhost**. But where should *sendmail* send the message first? As it happens, *sendmail* selects **uuhost**. Focusing on this address therefore results in the following:

```
user%host1%host2<@uuhost.uucp>
```

Note that uuhost was moved to the end, the ! was changed to an @, and .uucp was appended. The @ is there so that all focused parts uniformly contain an @ just before the targeted host. Later, when we take up postprocessing, we'll show how rule set 4 moves the uuhost back to the beginning and replaces the !.

29.4.1 A Special Case: From:<>

The first rule in a typical rule set 3 handles addresses that are composed of empty angle brackets. These represent the special case of an empty or nonexistent address. Empty addresses should be turned into the address of the pseudo-user that bounces mail, *Mailer-Daemon*:

```
# handle "from:<>" special case
R$*<>$*          $@<@>          empty becomes special
```

Here, empty angle brackets, no matter what surrounds them ($*), are rewritten to be a lone @. Rule set 0 later turns this special token into $n (which contains *Mailer-Daemon* as its value).

29.4.2 Basic Textual Canonicalization

Addresses can be legally expressed in only four formats:[*]

```
address
address (full name)
<address>
full name <address>
```

When *sendmail* preprocesses an address that is in the second format, it removes (and saves for later use) the full name from within the parentheses. The last two formats, however, contain additional characters and information that are not discarded during preprocessing. As a consequence, rule set 3 must take on the job of discarding the unwanted information:

```
# basic textual canonicalization
R$*<$*<$*<$*>$*>$*>$*    $4      3-level <> nesting
R$*<$*<$*>$*>$*          $3      2-level <> nesting
R$*<$*>$*                $2      basic RFC821/822 parsing
```

Here, we discard everything outside of and including the innermost pair of angle brackets. Three rules are required to do this because of the minimal-matching nature of the LHS operators (see §8.7.2). Consider trying to de-nest a three-level workspace using only a rule like the third:

---

[*] Actually, we are fudging for simplicity. Addresses can appear in various permutations of those shown and we completely ignore the list:members; form of address.

```
the workspace →   A < B < C < D > C > B > A
$*   matches → A
<    matches → <
$+   matches → B < C < D
>    matches → >
$*   matches → C > B > A
```

Clearly, the result B<C<D is not the value between the innermost pair of angle brackets and will result in an address that produces the error message:

```
Unbalanced '<'
```

John Halleck designed a clever alternative to the above traditional technique that is now included with V8 *sendmail*:

```
R$*                    $: < $1 >              housekeeping <>
R$+ < $* >                 < $2 >             strip excess on left
R< $* > $+                 < $1 >             strip excess on right
R<>                    $@ < @ >               MAIL FROM:<> case
R< $+ >                $: $1                  remove housekeeping <>
```

Here, angle bracket pairs are stripped first from the left of an address, then from the right, and finally whatever is left must be the address.

29.4.3 Handling Routing Addresses

The *sendmail* program must be able to handle addresses that are in *route address* syntax. Such addresses are in the form *@A,@B:user@C* (which means that mail should be sent first to *A*, then from *A* to *B*, and finally from *B* to *C*).[*] The commas are converted to colons for easier design of subsequent rules. They must be converted back to commas by rule set 4. Rule set 3 uses a simple rule to convert all commas to colons:

```
# make sure list syntax is easy to parse
R@ $+ , $+        @ $1 : $2           change all "," to ":"
```

The iterative nature of rules comes into play here. As long as there is an @ followed by anything ($+), then a comma, then anything, this rule repeats, converting the comma to a colon. The result is then carried down to the next rule that focuses:

```
R@ $+ : $+        $@ <@ $1> : $2       focus route-addr
```

Once that host has angle brackets placed around it (is focused), the job of rule set 3 ends, and it exits (the $@ prefix in the RHS).

---

[*] Also see the DontPruneRoutes option in §34.8.20 and the F=d delivery agent flag in §30.8.16.

29.4.4 Handling Specialty Addresses

A whole book is dedicated to the myriad forms of addressing that might face a site administrator: *!%@:: A Directory of Electronic Mail Addressing & Networks* by Donnalyn Frey and Rick Adams (O'Reilly & Associates, 1993). We won't duplicate that work here; rather, we point out that most such addresses are handled nicely by existing configuration files. Consider the format of a DECnet address:

```
host::user
```

One approach to handling such an address in rule set 3 is to convert it into the Internet *user@host.domain* form:

```
R$+ :: $+          $@ $2 @ $1.decnet
```

Here, we reverse the **host** and **user** and put them into Internet form. The **.dec-net** can later be used by rule set 0 to select an appropriate delivery agent.

This is a simple example of a special address problem from the many that can develop. In addition to DECnet, for example, your site may have to deal with Xerox *Grapevine* addresses, X.400 addresses, or UUCP addresses. The best way to handle such addresses is to copy what others have done.

29.4.5 Focusing for @ Syntax

The last few rules in our illustration of rule set 3 are used to process the Internet-style *user@domain* address:

```
# find focus for @ syntax addresses
R$+ @ $+               $: $1 <@ $2>        focus on domain
R$+ < $+ @ $+ >           $1 $2 <@ $3>     move gaze right
R$+ <@ $+ >            $@ $1 <@ $2>        already focused
```

For an address like *something@something*, the first rule focuses on all the tokens following the first @ as the name of the host. Recall that the **$:** prefix to the RHS prevents potentially infinite recursion. Assuming that the workspace started with:

```
user@host1@host2
```

this first rewrite results in

```
user<@host1@host2>
```

The second rule (**move gaze right**) then attempts to fine-tune the focus by making sure only the rightmost **@host** is selected. This rule can move the focus right, using recursion, and can handle addresses that are as extreme as the following:

```
user<@host1@host2@host3@host4>  becomes → user@host1@host2@host3<@host4>
```

The third rule checks to see whether the workspace has been focused. If it has, it returns the focused workspace (the $@ prefix in the RHS), and its job is done.

Any address that has not been handled by rule set 3 is unchanged and probably not focused. Since rule set 0 expects all addresses to be focused so that it can select appropriate delivery agents, such unfocused addresses may bounce. Many configuration files allow local addresses (just a username) to be unfocused.

29.5 Rule Set 4

Just as all addresses are first rewritten by rule set 3, so are all addresses rewritten last by rule set 4. Its job is to undo any special processing done by rule set 3, such as focusing. In this section we'll examine some typical rule set 4 rules.

29.5.1 Stripping Trailing Dots

Under some versions of *sendmail* a successful conversion to a fully qualified domain name leaves an extra dot trailing the result. This rule strips that dot:

```
# strip trailing dot off possibly canonical name
R$* <@ $+. > $*        $1 <@ $2 > $3
```

Note that this rule recursively removes as many trailing dots as it finds. Also note that the host part remains focused after rewriting.

29.5.2 Restoring Source Routes

Recall that rule set 3 converted the commas of source route addresses into colons (see §29.4.3). Rule set 4 now needs to restore those commas:

```
R$* : $+ :$+ <@ $+>      $1 , $2 : $3 <@ $4>        <route-addr> canonical
```

This rule recursively changes all but one (the rightmost) colon back into a comma.

As a special note, under V8 *sendmail*, envelope-sender route addresses are always surrounded by angle brackets when passed to the delivery agent. If this behavior is inappropriate for your site, beginning with V8.7 it is possible to prevent this heuristic by specifying the F=d delivery agent flag (see §30.8.16).

29.5.3 Removing Focus

Rule set 4 also removes angle brackets inserted by rule set 3 to focus on the host part of the address. This is necessary because mail will fail if they are left in place.

```
# externalize local domain info
R$* <$+> $*        $1 $2 $3                    defocus
```

29.5.4 Correcting Tags

After defocusing, rule set 4 may need to convert some addresses back to their original forms. For example, consider UUCP addresses. They entered rule set 3 in the form *host!host!user*. Rule set 3 rewrote them in the more normal *user@host* form, and added a .uucp to the end of the host. The following rule in rule set 4 converts such normalized UUCP addresses back to their original form:

```
# UUCP must always be presented in old form
R$+ @ $-.uucp           $2 ! $1                 u@h.UUCP => h!u
```

29.6 Rule Set 0

The job of rule set 0 is to select a delivery agent for each recipient. It is called once for each recipient and must rewrite each into a special form called a *triple*. A triple is simply three pieces of information: the symbolic name of the delivery agent, the host part of the address, and the user part of the address. Each part is indicated in the RHS by a special prefix operator, as shown in Table 29-2.

Table 29–2: Rule Set 0 Special RHS Operators

Operator	Description
$#	Delivery agent
$@	Recipient host
$:	Recipient user

The triple is formed by rewriting with the RHS. It looks like this:

```
$#delivery_agent $@host $:user
```

The delivery agent selection must be the first of the three. In addition to specifying the delivery agent, $# also causes rule set 0 to exit. The other two parts of the triple must appear in the order shown ($@ first, then $:).

All three parts of the triple must be present in the RHS. The only exception is the $@*host* part when the delivery agent has the F=1 flag set. It *may* be present for IDA and V8 *sendmail* but must be absent for all other versions of *sendmail*.

Not all rules in rule set 0 are specifically used to select a delivery agent. It may be necessary, for example, to canonicalize an address with $[and $] (see §28.6.6) before being able to decide whether the address is local or remote.

If an address passes through rule set 0 without selecting a delivery agent, the following error message is produced, and the mail message bounces:

```
buildaddr: no mailer in parsed address
```

Therefore it is important to design a rule set 0 that selects a delivery agent for every legitimate address.

If a triple is missing the user part, the following error is produced:

```
buildaddr: no user
```

If the delivery agent that is selected is one for which there is no corresponding M configuration file declaration, the error is

buildaddr: unknown mailer *bad delivery agent name here*

29.6.1 Further Processing: $:user

The user part of the triple is intended for use in the command line of the delivery agent and in the RCPT command in an SMTP connection. For either use, that address is rewritten by rule set 2, the R= equate of the delivery agent, and rule set 4, as illustrated in Figure 29-5. This means that the user part can be in focused form, because the focus is later removed by rule set 4. But the user part *must* be a single username (no host) for the local delivery agent.

The rewritten result is stored for use when a delivery agent's $u in A= (see §30.4.1) argument is expanded. For example, for the local delivery agent, the rewritten result is the username as it will be given to */bin/mail* for local delivery.

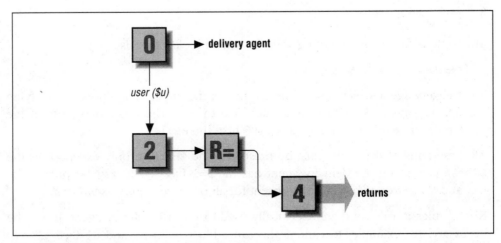

Figure 29–5: The flow of $:user through rule sets

The rewritten result is also given to a remote site during the exchange of mail using the SMTP protocol. The local machine tells the remote machine the name of the recipient by saying RCPT to: followed by the rewritten user portion of the triple.

29.6.2 Selecting S= and R=

When it selects a delivery agent, rule set 0 also selects the rules that will be used in rewriting sender and recipient addresses. A sender address is rewritten by the rule set specified by the S= equate (see §30.4.11). The recipient addresses are rewritten by the rule set specified by the R= equate (see §30.4.10). If the R= or S= specifies rule set 0 or if either is undeclared, then that portion of rewriting is skipped.

We won't cover individual R= or S= rule sets here, because they depend on the individual needs of delivery agents. Instead, we recommend that you examine how your configuration file uses them. You'll probably be surprised to find that many R= and S= equates reference nonexistent rules (which means that *sendmail* will do no rewriting).

29.6.3 Delivering to Local Recipient

Typically, some early rules in rule set 0 are intended to detect addresses that should be delivered locally. A rule that accomplishes that end might look like this:

```
R$+ <@ $w>          $#local $:$1               local address
```

Here, the $w macro is the name of the local host. Note that the RHS strips the focused host part from the username.

At some sites, the local host can be known by any of several names. A rule to handle such hosts would begin with a class declaration that adds those names to the class w (like the first line below):

```
Cw font-server fax printer3
R$+ <@ $=w>         $#local $:$1               local address
```

The class w is special because it is the one to which *sendmail* automatically appends the alternative name of the local host. The class declaration line above adds names that *sendmail* might not automatically detect. Usually, such a declaration would be near the top of the configuration file, rather than in rule set 0, but technically it can appear anywhere in the file. This rule looks to see whether an address contains any of the names in class w. If it does, the $=w in the LHS matches, and the RHS selects the local delivery agent.

On central mail server machines, rule set 0 may also have to match from a list of hosts for which the central server is an MX recipient machine (see §19.6.26).

29.6.4 *Forwarding to a Knowledgeable Host*

After handling mail destined for the local host, rule set 0 generally looks for addresses that require a knowledgeable host to forward messages on the local host's behalf. In the following rule, $B (see §31.10.5) is the name of a machine that knows how to deliver BITNET mail (see §19.4.5):

```
R$* <@ $+.BITNET> $*    $#smtp $@$B $:$1<@$2.BITNET>$3      user@host.BITNET
```

The tag `.BITNET` would have been added by users when sending mail. Note that `BITNET` in the LHS is case-insensitive; a user can specify `Bitnet`, `bitnet`, or even `BiTNeT`, and this rule will still match. A similar scheme can be used for other specialty addresses, such as UUCP and DECnet.

29.6.5 *Handling UUCP Locally*

Hosts sometimes deliver mail to a few UUCP connections locally and forward to other UUCP connections through a knowledgeable host. The rules that handle this situation often make use of another class:

```
R$* <@ $=V.UUCP>       $#uucp $@$2 $:$1                   user@localuucp
R$* <@ $+.UUCP>        $#smtp $@$Y $:$1<@$2.UUCP>         kick upstairs
```

Here, the class $=V contains a list of local UUCP connections. They are matched by the first rule, which selects the uucp delivery agent. All other UUCP addresses are passed to the knowledgeable host in $Y (see §31.10.45)). The user part ($:) that is given to the knowledgeable host is the original address as it appeared to the LHS.

29.6.6 *Forwarding over the Network*

Next, rule set 0 typically sees whether it can send the mail message over the network. In the following example we assume that the local host is connected to an IP network:

```
# deal with other remote names
R$* <@ $*> $*          $#smtp $@$2 $:$1<@$2>$3            user@host.domain
```

Remember that we have already screened out and handled delivery to the local host, and therefore the focused host (in the `<@$*>` of the LHS) is on the network. The smtp delivery agent is selected (to deliver using the SMTP protocol), with connection to be made to $2 (the $* part of the `<@$*>` in the LHS).

The focus is kept in the user portion of the RHS triple. Remember that the user portion will be rewritten by rule sets 2, R=, and 4. Also remember that rule set 4 will defocus the address. The reason we keep the focus here is because rule set 2 and all R= rules expect the host part of addresses to be focused.

29.6.7 Handling Leftover Local Addresses

Whatever is left after all preceding rules in rule set 0 have selected delivery agents is probably a local address. Here, we check for a username without a host part:

```
R$+        $#local $:$1        regular local names
```

Notice that the user part is not focused; it is unfocused because there is no host part on lone local usernames.

29.7 Rule Set 5

For version 2 and higher configuration files (see §27.5), V8 *sendmail* allows local recipients to undergo additional rewriting. Recall that each recipient address is processed by rule sets 3 and 0. Beginning with V8.7 *sendmail*, any delivery agent with the F=A flag set[*] (see §30.8.12) will cause the address to undergo aliasing (via the *aliases* file), which may result in a new local address.

Under V8 *sendmail*, if an address makes it through aliasing unchanged, it is given to rule set 5, which may select a new delivery agent. Note that it is given to rule set 5 before the ˜/.forward file is processed.

Beginning with V8.7 *sendmail*, any delivery agent that has the F=5 flag set (see §30.8.3) will cause rule set 5 to be called as though the agent were a local one.

To illustrate, consider that a new delivery agent might be needed in the case of a mail *firewall* machine. A firewall machine is one that sits between the local network and the outside world and protects the local network from intrusion by outsiders. In such an arrangement it may be desirable for all incoming mail to be delivered to the firewall so that no outsider needs to know the real names of machines on the local network.

Consider mail to the address *john@firewall*. On the firewall machine, rule set 3 recognizes the host part as local and throws away the *@firewall*. Rule set 0 then selects the `local` delivery agent. Because the address *john* is local, it is looked up in the *aliases* file. For this example we will assume that it is not found there. The user's ˜/.forward file would normally be examined next, but user home directories are not visible to the firewall machine.

Because the address *john* is not aliased, it is then passed to rule set 5, which selects another delivery agent to forward the message into the local network:

```
S5
R$-        $#smtp $@hub.internal.net $:$1
```

---

[*] Prior to V8.7 *sendmail*, only the `local` delivery agent had this property.

Here, the *john* matches the $- in the LHS, so the smtp delivery agent is selected. The mail message is forwarded to the local network with *john* (the $1) as the username and hub.internal.net as the name of the receiving machine on the internal network.

For such a scheme to work, all local machines must send offsite mail addressed as though it were from the firewall, and local names must be changed to offsite forms when forwarded offsite. For example, the name *john@local.host* needs to be changed to *john@firewall* for all outgoing offsite mail.

Note that rule set 5 can also be used in situations that do not involve firewalls. It can be used as a hook into forwarding to other types of networks, with special mailing list software, or even as a way to handle retired accounts. Also note that rule set 5 *may* select a new delivery agent, but it does not have to.

For those times when rule set 5 may not be appropriate, V8 *sendmail* offers a technique for bypassing it. In rule set 0, if the first token following the $: of a rule that selects the local delivery agent is an @, *sendmail* removes the @ and skips calling rule set 5:

```
R$-         $#local $: @ $1
                        ↑
            removed and rule set 5 skipped
```

Note that rule set 5 is the way V8.7 *sendmail* and above institutes the plussed users technique (see §24.4.3).

29.8 Rule Set 2

All recipient addresses are rewritten by rule set 2 and the R= of delivery agents. But in almost all configuration files, rule set 2 is unused because no processing is needed:

```
# Recipient processing: none needed
S2
```

But note that rule set 2 can be used to debug rules.[*] Consider the following rule in rule set 2:

```
R$#$+ $:$+      $:$2    Strip delivery agent and host when debugging
```

Recall that rule set 0 returns a triple. When testing an address, rule set 2 can be called following rule set 0 to simulate the rewriting of the user portion of rule set 0. Here the LHS matches only a triple, so normal recipient addresses are

---

[*] This is a truly bogus example. We are really stretching to find a use for rule set 2. There is no reason to do this debugging in rule set 2 because rule set 99 would work just as well. According to Eric, "I can think of no good reason to use S2 today."

unaffected. The user part that is returned by the RHS can then be used to test individual R= rules of delivery agents. (Another technique is to use the /try command in –bt rule-testing mode; see §38.5.6.)

29.9 Rule Set 1

Rule set 1 is intended to process all sender addresses. It is rarely used but can find application at sites where all outgoing mail should appear to come from a central mail server. Rules to handle this host hiding might look like this:

```
R$-                   $@ $1 <@ $R>              user => user@ourdomain
R$* <@ $=w> $*        $@ $1 <@ $R> $3          user@localhost => user@ourdomain
```

In the LHS the $=w matches any name from a list of names by which the local host is known. In the RHS the $R contains the name of the mail server. If the mail is not from the local host, it is unchanged.

Other uses for rule set 1 might include the following:

• Normalizing senders, for example, making mail from the users *operator* and *dumper* appear to come from *root*.

• Hiding user login names by mapping them (through an external database) to the form *firstname.lastname*.

Needless to say, great care should be exercised in adding schemes such as these to your configuration file.

29.10 The check_... Rule Sets

The rapid spread of the Internet has led to an increase of mail abuses. Prior to V8.8 *sendmail*, detecting and rejecting abusive email required that you write C language code for use in the *checkcompat()* routine (see §20.1). Beginning with V8.8 *sendmail* important and useful checking and rejecting can be done from within four brand new rule sets:

check_mail
> Validate the sender-envelope address given to the SMTP MAIL command.

check_rcpt
> Validate the recipient-envelope address given to the SMTP RCPT command.

check_relay
> Validate the host initiating the SMTP connection.

check_compat
> Compare or contrast each envelope sender and envelope recipient pair of addresses just before delivery, and validate based on the result.

These routines are handled in the same manner. If the rule set does not exist, the address is accepted. If the rule set returns anything other than a #error delivery agent, the message is accepted. Otherwise, the message is rejected by using the mechanism described under the #error delivery agent (see §30.5.2).

29.10.1 The check_mail Rule Set

The MAIL command in the SMTP dialog is used to specify the envelope-sender address:

```
MAIL From: <sender@host.domain>
```

If the **check_mail** rule set exists, it is called immediately after the MAIL command is read. The workspace passed to **check_mail** is the address following the colon in the MAIL command. That envelope sender address may or may not be surrounded by angle braces.

To illustrate one use for the **check_mail** rule set, consider the need to reject all incoming mail from the site named *spamming.org*.* One method might look like this:

```
Scheck_mail
R$*                       $: $>3 $1            focus on the host
R$* <@ $+. > $*           $1 <@ $2> $3         strip trailing dots
R$* <@ $+ > $*            $: $2                isolate the host
R$* . $+ . $+             $: $2 . $3           strip subdomains
Rspamming.org             $#error $@ 5.7.1 $: "cannot accept mail from spamming.org"
```

Here, we force rule set 3 to preprocess the address so that any RFC822 comments will be thrown away and so that the host part of the address will be focused. We then strip any trailing dots from the hostname to prevent a trailing dot from wrongly effecting our validation. In the third line we throw away everything but the hostname. In the fourth line we throw away all but the rightmost two components of the hostname to eliminate the host part and any subdomain prefixes. What remains is just the domain name. We then compare that domain name to the hostname *spamming.org*. If they match, we reject the sender.

After this rule set is installed (and the *sendmail* daemon had been restarted), all mail from *spamming.org* will be rejected during the SMTP dialogue like this:

```
MAIL From: <badguy@spamming.org>
553 <badguy@spamming.org>... cannot accept mail from spamming.org
```

This is just one possible use of the **check_mail** rule set. Other uses might be the following:

---

* Also see §22.4.1 for a discussion of how to use the TCP wrapper library from within *sendmail*.

- Rejecting mail from specific users at a given site.

- Looking up *user@host* in a database and rejecting the sender if that lookup succeeds.

- Insisting that the host part of the address be canonifiable with the $[and $] operators.

If you need to base a decision to reject mail on both the sender and the recipient, you may be able to use the check_compat rule set described below.

29.10.2   *The check_rcpt Rule Set*

The RCPT command in the SMTP dialogue specifies an envelope recipient's address:

```
RCPT To: <recipient@host.domain>
```

If the check_rcpt rule set exists, it is called immediately after the RCPT command is read. The workspace that is passed to check_rcpt is the address following the colon. The envelope recipient address may or may not be surrounded by angle brackets and may or may not have other RFC822 comments associated with it.

To illustrate one use for the check_rcpt rule set, consider the need to reject all incoming mail destined for the recipient named *fax*. One method might look like this:

```
R$*                    $: $>3 $1              focus on host
R$* <@ $~w > $*        $@ ok                  not @ourhost is okay
R$* <@ $+ > $*         $: $1                  discard host
Rfax                   $#error $@ 5.1.3 $: "cannot send mail to fax"
```

Here, we first call rule set 3 to focus on the host part of the address and normalize it. The second rule accepts anything that is addressed to any host but our own. That way, mail to *fax@another.host* will work. The third rule discards the host (our local) part of the address. In the fourth line the remaining user part is compared to the name *fax*. Any mail to *fax* is thus rejected:

```
RCPT To: <fax@ourhost>
553 <fax@ourhost>... cannot send mail to fax
```

Other uses for this check_rcpt rule set might include the following:

- Protecting a user who has become the target of a mail attack. You could create a new account for this user and block incoming mail to the old account. In the #error message you could print a phone number that others may call to obtain the new email address.

- Claiming that certain secret users are unknown. These might be the pseudo-users associated with autonomous processes.

- Refusing to accept mail that is not addressed to a user who has an active account as represented by the *passwd*(5) file (see §33.8.20).

- Looking up recipients in a database and accepting mail for them only if they are found in that database. This way, only selected users may be allowed, for example, through a firewall, though the firewall knows all about all users.

- Looking up local-looking recipients in a database to see whether they have moved to a new location. If so, advise the other site of the new address with a rejection message. This is similar to the **redirect** FEATURE (see §19.6.21), but operates at the RCPT level instead of sending bounced mail.

- Turning off unwanted "relaying" through your machine. Requires use of the `${client_name}` macro (see §31.10.8).

29.10.3 The check_relay Rule Set

V8.8 *sendmail* supports two mechanisms for screening incoming SMTP connections. One is the *libwrap.a* mechanism (see §22.4.1); the other is this **check_relay** rule set. This rule set is used to screen incoming network connections and accept or reject them based on hostname, domain, or IP number. It is called just before the *libwrap.a* code and can be used if that code was omitted from your release of *sendmail*.

The **check_relay** rule set is called with a workspace that looks like this:

```
hostname $| IPnumber
```

The hostname and IP number are separated by the `$|` operator. The **hostname** is the fully qualified canonical name of the connecting host. The **IPnumber** is the IP number of that host in dotted-quad form without surrounding square brackets.

One way to use **check_relay** might be to list offensive sites in a database and to reject any connections from those sites. Consider a database that contains hostnames as its keys and descriptions of each host's offense as its values:

```
hostA.edu      Spamming site
hostB.com      Mail Bombing site
123.45.6       Offensive domain
```

Notice that the keys can be hostnames or IP addresses. Such a database might be declared in the configuration file like this:

```
Kbadhosts dbm -a <> /etc/badhosts
```

Now, each time a site connects to your running daemon, the following rule set will be called:

```
Scheck_relay
R$* $| $*              $: $(badhosts $1 $) $| $2              look up host name
R$*<> $| $*            $#error $@ 5.1.3 $: Sorry, $1 denied
R$* $|  $*             $: $2                                  select the IP number
R$-.$-.$-.$-           $: $(badhosts $1.$2.$3 $)              look up domain part
R$*<>                  $#error $@ 5.1.3 $: Sorry, $1 denied
R$*                    $@ ok                                  otherwise okay
```

The second rule looks up the host part in the database. If it is found, the value (reason for rejection) is returned and the two characters <> are appended. The third rule looks for anything to the left of the $| that ends in <> and, if anything is found, issues the error:[*]

> Sorry, *reason for reject* denied

Rejected connections are handled the same way as connections rejected by the *lib-wrap.a* technique (see §22.4.1).

The rest of the rules do the same thing, except that they check for the IP number. If the check_relay rule set returns anything other than a #error delivery agent, the address is accepted.

Note that the rules presented here are not nearly as complex or sophisticated as your site will likely need. It does not, for example, reject on the basis of the domain part of hostnames, nor does it reject on the basis of the individual host IP addresses.

Note that such rule sets cannot be tested in rule-testing mode, because that mode interprets the expression $| (when you enter it at the > prompt) wrongly as two separate text characters instead of correctly as a single operator. To test an address that contains an embedded $| operator, we suggest that you create a translation rule set something like this:

```
STranslate
R$* $$| $*               $: $1 $| $2                          fake for -bt mode
```

This rule set changes a literal $ and | into a $| operator so that you can test rule sets such as check_relay from rule-testing mode:

```
ADDRESS TEST MODE (ruleset 3 NOT automatically invoked)
Enter <ruleset> <address>
> Translate,check_relay bogus.host.domain $| 123.45.67.89
```

---

[*] Actually, the message is not printed; instead, the SMTP daemon goes into a "reject everything" mode. This prevents some SMTP implementations from retrying the connection.

Here, the comma-separated list of rule sets begins with **Translate**, which changes the two-character text expression "$|" into the single operator $|. The result, an address expression that is suitable for the **check_relay** rule set, can then be successfully tested.[*]

29.10.4 The check_compat Rule Set

Not all situations can be resolved by simply checking the recipient or sender address. Sometimes you will need to make judgments based on pairs of addresses. To handle this situation, V8.8 introduced the **check_compat** rule set. Unlike **check_mail** and **check_rcpt**, **check_compat** is called for all deliveries, not just SMTP transactions. It is called just after the check for too large a size (as defined by **M=**; see §30.4.7) and just before the *checkcompat( )* routine is called (see §20.1).

The **check_compat** rule set is called with a workspace that looks like this:

```
sender $| recipient
```

The sender and recipient address are separated by the $| operator. Each has undergone aliasing and `~/.forward` file processing.

As one example of a way to use the **check_compat** rule set, consider the need to prevent a certain user (here *operator*) from sending mail offsite:

```
SGet_domain
R$*                        $: $>3 $1                focus on host
R$* <@ $+. > $*            $1 <@ $2> $3             strip trailing dots
R$* <@ $+ > $*             $: $2                    isolate the host
R$* . $+ . $+              $@ $2 . $3               strip host and subdomains


SGet_user
R$*                        $: $>3 $1                focus on host
R$* <@ $+ > $*             $@ $1                    discard host


Scheck_compat
R$* $| $*                  $: $1 $|  $>Get_domain $2    fetch recipient domain
R$* $|  $=w                $@ ok                    local is okay
R$* $|  $m                 $@ ok                    local is okay
R$* $|  $*                 $: $>Get_user $1         fetch sender user
Roperator                  $#error $@ 5.1.3 $: "operator may not mail offsite"
```

First we set up two subroutines patterned after the code in the previous two sections. The first reduces its workspace to just the domain part of an address. The second reduces an address to just the user part. These two subroutines are called by **check_compat**.

---

[*] Don't be tempted to put this rule directly into the **check_relay** rule set. You may someday encounter an address that has the two adjacent characters "$" and "|" as a legal part of it. Also beware of such addresses being intentionally sent just to circumvent your checks.

The first rule in check_compat uses the Get_domain subroutine to convert the address on the right (the recipient) into just a domain name. That right side is compared to the local hosts names ($=w and $m). If the domain is a local one, delivery is allowed (we return anything but #error).

If the domain is an offsite one, we then call Get_user to fetch the user part of the address to the left (the sender). If that user is *operator*, delivery is denied and the message bounces.

Other uses for the check_compat rule set might be the following:

- Creating a class of user who, possibly for security reasons, may send only mail inside the organization, but not outside it.

- Screening a particular recipient to prevent that user from receiving objectionable mail from a specific source.

- Screening mail based on hostname to prevent outsiders from using your host as a mail relay.

Note that such rule sets cannot be tested in rule-testing mode because that mode interprets the expression $| (when you enter it at the > prompt) wrongly as two separate text characters instead of correctly as a single operator. See §29.10.3 for one suggested solution to this problem.

29.11 Pitfalls

- Rules that hide hosts in a domain should be applied only to sender addresses. Avoid the temptation to place such substitutions of host for domain names into rule set 3. Rule set 3 applies to all addresses and can wrongly change a nonlocal address.

- Not all configuration files focus with *user<@domain>*. IDA, for example, uses a more complex focus: *<@domain>, . . . ,user*. Be sure you understand the style of focusing that is used in your configuration file before attempting to create new rules.

- Avoid confusing rule sets 1 and 2 when adding rules. Rule set 1 is for the sender; rule set 2 is for the recipient.

- Typos in rule-set declarations can be difficult to locate. For example, S10 (in which the last character is the capital letter O) will silently evaluate to rule set 1 when you really meant rule set 10.

- All versions of *sendmail* except V8 wrongly call rule set 2 and the recipient R= when processing the envelope sender.

30

Delivery Agents

The *sendmail* program does not perform the actual delivery of mail. Instead, it calls other programs (called mail delivery agents) to perform that service. Because the mechanics of delivery can vary so widely from delivery agent to delivery agent, *sendmail* needs a great deal of information about each delivery agent. Each *sendmail* M configuration-file command defines a mail delivery agent and the information that *sendmail* needs.

30.1 *Configuration File Syntax*

Like all *sendmail.cf* commands, the M mail delivery agent command must begin a line. One typical such command looks like this:

```
          delivery program                        command line
                ↓                                     ↓
Mlocal, P=/bin/mail, F=rlsDFMmnP, S=10, R=20, A=mail -d $u
                        ↑              ↑    ↑
                      flags      sender/recipient rules
```

This M configuration command is composed of six parts: a symbolic name followed by five equates, each separated from the others by commas. Spaces between the parts are optional. The specific syntax of the mail delivery agent command is

```
Msymname, equate, equate, ...
```

The letter M always begins the delivery agent definition, followed by a symbolic name (the *symname*) of your choosing and a comma-separated list of delivery agent equates. Only the P= and A= equates are required. The others are optional.

The comma following the symbolic name is optional. As long as there is a space following the symbolic name, *sendmail* parses it correctly. The comma should, however, always be included for improved clarity.[*]

In the following, the first example includes the comma, and the second omits it. Both are parsed by *sendmail* in exactly the same way:

```
Mlocal, P=/bin/mail, F=rlsDFMmnP, S=10, R=20, A=mail -d $u
Mlocal  P=/bin/mail, F=rlsDFMmnP, S=10, R=20, A=mail -d $u
```

30.2 The Symbolic Name

The M that begins the delivery agent definition command is immediately followed, with no intervening whitespace, by the name of the delivery agent. Note that the name is symbolic and is used only internally by *sendmail*. The name may contain no whitespace, and, if it is quoted, the quotation marks are interpreted as part of its name. In the following, only the first is a good symbolic name:

```
Mlocal              ← name is "local", good
M local             ← error: "name required for mailer"
Mmy mailer          ← error: "mailer my: '=' expected"
M"mymailer"         ← quotation marks wrongly retained
```

Although the symbolic name can contain any character other than a space or a comma, only letters, digits, dashes, and underscore characters are recommended:

```
Mprog-mailer        ← name is "prog-mailer", good
Mprog_mailer        ← name is "prog_mailer", good
Mmymailer[];        ← name contains a "[];", avoid such characters
```

The symbolic name is not case-sensitive; that is, local, Local, and LOCAL are all identical.

Note that if two delivery agents have the same name, all the equates for the second definition replace those for the first. Therefore the last definition for a particular symbolic name is the one that is used.

The cumulative result of all delivery agent declarations can be seen by using the -d0.15 debugging switch (see §37.5.4) or by using the =M rule-testing command (see §38.4.2).

---

[*] SunOS 4.1.2's *sendmail* does not properly support freezing if the comma is present.

30.2.1 Required Symbolic Names

Prior to V8.1, two delivery agent symbolic names *had to be* defined in every configuration file:

`local`

> The symbolic name of the program that handles delivery on the local machine (usually */bin/mail*).

`prog`

> The symbolic name of the program that executes other programs for delivery (usually the */bin/sh* shell).

Beginning with V8.1, only the `local` delivery agent is required. If a required definition is missing, *sendmail* prints one of the following warning messages but continues to run:

```
No prog mailer defined.
No local mailer defined.
```

30.3 m4 Configuration Syntax

Under V8 *sendmail*'s m4 configuration technique you include delivery agent definitions in your configuration file with the MAILER() *m4* command. The form for that command looks like this:

```
MAILER(`name')
```

For example, SMTP and UUCP support can be included in your file by using the following two commands:

```
MAILER(`smtp')
MAILER(`uucp')
```

The delivery agent M definitions that correspond to MAILER() commands are kept in the *_CF_DIR_/mailer* directory (*_CF_DIR_* is described in §19.2.1). See Table 19-3 in §19.3.2 for a list of all the available agents.

In general, the files in the *_CF_DIR_/mailer* directory should never be modified. If one of the definitions needs to be tuned, use the special keywords described under the individual equates (see §30.4). For example, the following modifies the maximum message size (the M= equate see §30.4.7) for the UUCP agent:

```
define(`UUCP_MAX_SIZE',`1000000')dnl
```

Here, the maximum size of a UUCP message has been increased from the default of 100,000 (one hundred thousand) bytes to a larger limit of 1,000,000 (one million) bytes.

30.3.1 Tuning Without an Appropriate Keyword

Unfortunately, not all equates can be tuned with m4 defines. The U= equate for the
usenet agent is one example. To change such a value, you need to copy the original definition, modify it, and put the modified definition in your local mc file. For
example, to add a U= equate to the Usenet delivery agent, you might do the
following:*

```
% grep -h Musenet mailer/*
Musenet,     P=USENET_MAILER_PATH, F=USENET_MAILER_FLAGS, S=10, R=20,
             _OPTINS('USENET_MAILER_MAX', `M=', `, ')T=X-Usenet/X-Usenet/X-Unix,
             A=USENET_MAILER_ARGS $u
```

Here, the prototype definition for the usenet delivery agent is found. Copy that
definition into your mc file and add the missing equate:

```
MAILER(usenet)dnl
MAILER_DEFINITIONS
Musenet,     P=USENET_MAILER_PATH, F=USENET_MAILER_FLAGS, S=10, R=20, U=news:news,
             _OPTINS('USENET_MAILER_MAX', `M=', `, ')T=X-Usenet/X-Usenet/X-Unix,
             A=USENET_MAILER_ARGS $u
```

First, the MAILER() m4 command causes initial support for the usenet delivery
agent to be included. The MAILER_DEFINITIONS section (see §19.6.40) then introduces your new delivery agent definition. Your new definition follows, and thus
replaces, the original definition.

Create a new configuration file, and run *grep*(1) to check the result:

```
% m4 our.mc > our.cf
% grep ^Musenet our.cf
Musenet,     P=/usr/lib/news/inews, F=rlsDFMmn, S=10, R=20,
Musenet,     P=/usr/lib/news/inews, F=rlsDFMmn, S=10, R=20, U=news:news,
```

30.3.2 Create a New m4 Delivery Agent

From time to time you may need to create a brand-new delivery agent. To create a
new delivery agent with the m4 system, first change to the *cf/mailer* directory.
Copy an existing m4 file, one that is similar to your needs. Then edit that new file,
and include it in your configuration file with

```
MAILER(newname)
```

Note that the MAILER m4 command automatically prefixes the name with
_CF_DIR_/mailer/ (*_CF_DIR_* is described in §19.2.1) and adds the suffix *.m4*, here
forming cf/mailer/newname.m4.

---

* We are fudging here. The *grep*(1) won't work because the Musenet definition is split over three lines.
Instead, you need to use your editor to cut and paste.

But be aware that creation of a new delivery agent is not for the faint of heart. In addition to the delivery agent definition you will also need to create brand new S= and R= rules and rule sets.

30.4 The Equates

Recall that the form for the **M** command is

```
Msymname, equate, equate, equate, ...
```

Each *equate* expression is of the form

```
field=arg
```

The **field** is one of those in Table 30-1. Only the first character of the **field** is recognized. That is, all of the following are equivalent:

```
S=21
Sender=21
SenderRuleSet=21
```

The **field** is followed by more optional whitespace, the mandatory = character, optional whitespace, and finally the **arg**. The form that the **arg** takes varies depending on the *field*. It may or may not be required.

Special characters can be embedded into the *field* as shown in Table 31-3 of §31.3.2. For example, the backslash notation can be used to embed commas and a newline character into the **A=** equate like this:

```
...    A=eatmail -F0\,12\,99 -E\n
```

The complete list of equates is shown in Table 30-1. A full description of each begins in the next section. They are presented in alphabetical order rather than in the order in which they would appear in typical delivery agent definitions.

Table 30–1: Delivery Agent Equates

Equate	Field Name	§	Meaning
A=	Argv	30.4.1	Delivery agent's command-line arguments
C=	Charset	30.4.2	Default MIME character set (V8.7 and above)
D=	Directory	30.4.3	Paths to directories for execution (V8.6 and above)
E=	EOL	30.4.4	End-of-line string
F=	Flags	30.4.5	Flags describing a delivery agent's behavior
L=	Linelimit	30.4.6	Maximum line length (V8.1 and above)
M=	Maximum	30.4.7	Maximum message size
N=	Niceness	30.4.8	How to *nice*(2) the agent (V8.7 and above)
P=	Path	30.4.9	Path to the delivery program
R=	Recipient	30.4.10	Recipient rewriting rule set

Table 30–1: Delivery Agent Equates (continued)

Equate	Field Name	§	Meaning
S=	Sender	30.4.11	Sender rewriting rule set
T=	Type	30.4.12	Types for DSN diagnostics (V8.7 and above)
U=	UID	30.4.13	Run agent as uid:gid (V8.7 and above)

A=   *(All versions)*

30.4.1   *The argv for this delivery agent*

The program that is to be run (specified by the P= equate) is given its C language char **argv array (list of command-line arguments) by this A= equate. This equate is traditionally the last one specified, because, prior to V8.7, the argv arguments were all those from the = to the end of the line:

```
Mlocal, P=/bin/mail, F=rlsDFMmnP, S=10, R=20, A=mail -d $u
                                               ↑
                             prior to V8.7, argv to end of line →
```

Beginning with V8.7, the A= is treated like any other equate, in that it ends at the end of line *or* at the first comma. The backslash character can be used as a prefix to embed commas in the A= equate.

Macros are expanded and may be used in this argv array. For example,

```
A=mail -d $u
```

The A= begins the declaration of the argument array. The program that is specified by the P= equate (/bin/mail) will be executed with an argv of

```
argv[0] = "mail"
argv[1] = "-d"          ← switch means perform final delivery
argv[2] = "fred"        ← where macro $u contains "fred"
```

The macro value of $u contains the current recipient name (see §31.10.36). Another macro that commonly appears in A= fields is $h, the recipient host (see §31.10.17). You are, of course, free to use any macro you find necessary as a part of this argv array. Note that $u is special in that if it is missing, *sendmail* will speak SMTP to the delivery agent (see §30.4.1.3). Also note that any arguments in excess of the maximum number defined by MAXPV (see §18.8.19), usually 40, are silently ignored.

30.4.1.1 m4 A= definitions

Under V8 *sendmail*'s m4 configuration you can define the A= equate using the values shown in the leftmost column of Table 30-2. For example, to modify the A=

equate for the `local` delivery agent, you might include this definition in your `mc` file:

```
define(`LOCAL_MAILER_ARGS', `put.local -d $u -l')dnl
```

Table 30-2: m4 Modification of A= Equates

define()	Agent	MAILER()	Default A=
CYRUS_MAILER_ARGS	cyrus	cyrus	deliver -e -m $h -- $u
CYRUS_BB_MAILER_ARGS	cyrusbb	cyrus	deliver -e -m $u
FAX_MAILER_ARGS	fax	fax	mailfax $u $h $f
LOCAL_MAILER_ARGS	local	local	mail -d $u
LOCAL_SHELL_ARGS	prog	local	sh -c $u
MAIL11_MAILER_ARGS	mail11	mail11	mail11 $g $x $h $u
PH_MAILER_ARGS	ph	phquery	phquery -- $u
POP_MAILER_ARGS	pop	pop	pop $u
PROCMAIL_MAILER_ARGS	procmail	procmail	procmail -m $h $f $u
SMTP_MAILER_ARGS	smtp	smtp	IPC $h
SMTP8_MAILER_ARGS	smtp8	smtp	IPC $h
ESMTP_MAILER_ARGS	esmtp	smtp	IPC $h
RELAY_MAILER_ARGS	relay	smtp	IPC $h
USENET_MAILER_ARGS	usenet	usenet	inews -m -h -n
UUCP_MAILER_ARGS	uucp	uucp	uux - -r -a$g -gC $h!rmail ($u)

In general, the definitions in the *_CF_DIR_/ostype* subdirectory are pretuned in a way that is best for most sites. If you want to make changes, remember that each definition that you put in your `mc` file *replaces* the definition in *_CF_DIR_/ostype*. Therefore it's best to copy an existing definition and modify it for your own use. Just be sure you don't omit something important. (The *_CF_DIR_* prefix is described in §19.2.1.)

30.4.1.2 $h and other arguments in A=[IPC]

For network delivery via the `P=[IPC]` delivery agent, the `A=` equate is usually declared like this:

```
A=IPC $h
```

The value in `$h` is the value returned by rule set 0's `$@` operator and is usually the name of the host to which *sendmail* should connect. During delivery the *sendmail* program expands this hostname into a possible list of MX records.[*] It attempts delivery to each MX record. If all delivery attempts fail and if the V8 **FallbackMX-host** (V) option (see §34.8.25) is set, delivery is attempted to that fallback host. In all cases, if there are no MX records, delivery is attempted to the A record instead.

---

[*] Unless the V8.8 F=0 flag is set (see §30.8.1).

Beginning with V8 *sendmail*, $h (possibly as returned by rule set 0) can be a colon-separated list of hosts. The *sendmail* program attempts to connect to each in turn, left to right:

```
A=IPC hostA:hostB:hostC
```

Here, it tries to connect to *hostA* first. If that fails, it next tries *hostB*, and so on. As usual, trying a host means trying its MX records first, or its A record if there are no MX records.

The host (as $h) is usually the only argument given to IPC. But, strictly speaking, IPC can accept three arguments, like this:

```
A=IPC hostlist port
```

The *port* (third argument) is usually omitted and so defaults to 25. However, a port number can be included to force *sendmail* to connect on a different port.

To illustrate, consider the need to force mail to a gateway machine to be always delivered on a particular port. First, design a new delivery agent that uses IPC for transport.

```
Mgateway, P=[IPC], ..., A=IPC gateway.domain $h
```

Here, any mail that selects the **gateway** delivery agent is transported over the network (the [IPC]) to the machine **gateway.domain**. The port number is carried in $h, which usually carries the hostname.

Next, design a rule in rule set 0 that selects this delivery agent:

```
R$+ < @ $+ .gateway > $*           $#gateway $@ 26 $: $1 < @ $2 .gateway> $3
```

This rule selects the **gateway** delivery agent for any address that ends in .**gateway**. The host part that is returned by the $@ is the port number to use. The $: part (the address) is passed in the envelope. Note that the gateway also has to be listening on the same port for this to work.

In the event that you wish to carry the port number in a macro, you may do so by specifying the host with $h. For example,

```
Mgateway, P=[IPC], ..., A=IPC $h $P
R$+ < @ $+ .gateway > $*           $#gateway $@ $2 $: $1 < @ $2 .gateway> $3
```

Then *sendmail* can be run with the command-line argument

```
-MP26
```

to cause **gateway** mail to go out on port 26.

30.4.1.3 $u in A=

The $u macro is special in the A= equate's field. If $u *does not* appear in the array, *sendmail* assumes the program in P= equate speaks SMTP. Consequently, you should *never* use a $u when defining mail delivery agents that speak SMTP. All agents that use [IPC] or [TCP] in their P= equate's field must use SMTP.

If $u *does* appear in the array, *sendmail* assumes that the program in P= does *not* speak SMTP.

If $u appears and the F=m delivery agent flag is also specified, then the argument containing $u is repeated as many times as there are recipients. For example, a typical uucp delivery agent definition looks like this:

```
Muucp, P=/bin/uux, F=msDFMhuU, S=13, R=23, A=uux - -r $h!rmail ($u)
              ↑                                                  ↑
             note                                              note
```

In the above, the m flag is set in the F= equate's field, which tells *sendmail* that this delivery agent can deliver to multiple recipients simultaneously. The $u macro is also included as one of the arguments specified by the A= command-line array. Thus if mail is sent with this delivery agent to multiple recipients, say jim, bill, and joe, then the ($u) argument[*] is repeated three times, once for each recipient:

```
uux - -r $h!rmail (jim) (bill) (joe)
```

C=

(V8.7 and above)

30.4.2

The default MIME character set

The C= equate (introduced with V8.7 *sendmail*) is used to define a default character set for use with the MIME Content-Type: header (see §35.10.9). If it is present, its value supersedes that of the DefaultCharSet option (see §34.8.14).

Note that the C= equate is examined only when the delivery agent is selected for a sender address.

When a mail message is converted from 8 to 7 bits (see the EightBitMode (8) option in §34.8.22), it is important that the result looks like a MIME message. V8.7 *sendmail* first outputs the following header (if one is not already present):

```
MIME-Version: 1.0
```

Next, V8.7 *sendmail* looks for a Content-Type: header (see §35.10.9). If none is found, the following is inserted, where *charset* is the value declared for the C= equate of the sender's delivery agent:

---

[*] When $u is used as part of a UUCP delivery agent's F=A array, it should be parenthesized. This is what the *uux*(1) program expects.

```
Content-Type: text/plain; charset=charset
```

If the argument to the C= is missing, the following error is printed and the C= becomes undefined:

```
mailer agent_name: null charset
```

If the C= equate is undefined in your configuration file, *charset* defaults to the value of the **DefaultCharSet** option. If both are undefined, the value for *charset* becomes "unknown-8bit."

D= *(V8.6 and above)*

30.4.3 *Paths to directories for execution*

Ordinarily, whenever *sendmail* executes a program via the **prog** delivery agent, it does so from within the *sendmail* queue directory. One unfortunate side effect of this behavior is that shell scripts written with the C-shell (and possibly other programs) may fail because they cannot *stat*(2) the current directory. To alleviate this problem, V8 *sendmail* has introduced the D= delivery agent equate. This new equate allows you to specify a series of directories for *sendmail* to attempt to *chdir*(2) into before invoking the delivery program.

The form of the D= equate looks like this:

```
D=path1:path2...
```

The D= is followed by a colon-separated series of directory pathnames. Before running the delivery program, *sendmail* tries to *chdir*(2) into each in turn, leftmost to rightmost, until it succeeds. If it does not succeed with any of the directories (perhaps because none of them exist), *sendmail* remains in its queue directory.

One recommended setting for the D= equate is this:

```
D=$z:/tmp
```

Here, *sendmail* first tries to *chdir*(2) into the directory defined by the **$z** macro (see §31.10.46). That macro either contains the full pathname of the recipient's home directory or is NULL. If it is NULL or if the home directory is unavailable, the *chdir*(2) fails, and *sendmail* instead does a *chdir*(2) to the */tmp* directory.

In using V8 *sendmail*'s m4 configuration, the value given to D= can be easily changed only for the **prog** delivery agent, which defaults to

```
D=$z:/
```

For **prog** it can be redefined by using LOCAL_SHELL_DIR, as, for example,

```
define(`LOCAL_SHELL_DIR', `$z:/var/tmp')dnl
MAILER(local)
```

Here, LOCAL_SHELL_DIR is given a new value before the **prog** delivery agent is loaded (via the `local`).

For all other delivery agents you must first copy an existing delivery agent definition, then modify it as outlined in §30.3.1.

If the D= argument is missing, the following error is printed and the D= becomes undefined:

```
mailer agent_name: null working directory
```

The *chdir*(2) process can be traced with the −d11.20 debugging switch (see §37.5.46).

E=   *(All versions)*

30.4.4   *The end-of-line string*

The E= equate specifies the end-of-line character or characters. Those characters are generated by *sendmail* for outgoing messages and recognized by *sendmail* for incoming messages.

The end-of-line characters are defined with the E= equate as backslash-escaped control characters, such as

```
E=\r\n
```

Prior to V8.8 the default end-of-line string, if the E= field was missing, was the C language newline character, \n.[*] Beginning with V8.8 *sendmail*, the default is \n for all but delivery agents that speak SMTP, in which case the default is \r\n.

In general, delivery agents that speak SMTP (those that *lack* a $u in the A= argument array, should have their end-of-line field set to E=\r\n (for a carriage return/line feed pair).[†] Delivery agents that do not speak SMTP (those that *include* a $u in the A= argument array) should have their end-of-line field set to E=\n (for a lone linefeed character).

In using V8 *sendmail*'s m4 configuration, the value given to E= cannot be easily changed. It is supplied to the MAILER(smtp) delivery agents as \r\n but is left as the default \n for all others. If you need to change this value at the m4 level, you must first copy an existing delivery agent definition, then modify it as outlined in §30.3.1.

---

[*] On some NeXT computers (prior to OS version 2.0) the default E= terminator is \r\n. This can cause serious problems when used with some non-TCP delivery agents like UUCP. If you have a system that does this, you can override that improper default with E=\n.

[†] line feed is the same ASCII character as newline.

If the E= equate's argument is missing, the following error message is printed and
the E= becomes undefined:

```
mailer agent_name: null end-of-line string
```

F=   *(All versions)*

30.4.5   *Flags describing a delivery agent's behavior*

The F= equate is probably more fraught with peril than the others. The flags specified with F= tell *sendmail* how the delivery agent will behave and what its needs
will be. These flags are used in one or more of three ways:

First, if a header definition relies conditionally on a flag:

```
H?P?Return-Path: <$g>
  ↑
  apply if P flag specified in F= equate.
```

and if that flag is listed as a part of the F= equate:

```
Mlocal, P=/bin/mail, F=rlsDFMmnP, S=10, R=20, A=mail -d $u
                                  ↑
                          apply in header
```

then that header is included in all mail messages that are sent via this delivery
agent.

Second, if a delivery agent needs a special command-line argument that *sendmail*
can produce for it but requires that argument only under special circumstances,
selected F= flags can produce that result. For example, the F=f flag specifies that
the delivery agent needs a −f command-line switch when it is forwarding network
mail.

Third, the F= flags also tell *sendmail* how this particular delivery agent behaves.
For example, it performs final delivery or requires uppercase preserved for usernames.

Many flags have special meaning to *sendmail*; others are strictly user-defined. All
of the flags are detailed at the end of this chapter (§30.8).

Note that whitespace characters cannot be used as flags. Also note that flags OR
together (they are really just bits), so they can be declared separately, for clarity, as
in the following:

```
F=D,    # include Date: header if not present
F=F,    # include From: header if not present
F=7,    # strip the hi bit when delivering
```

Or they can be declared all together, with no change in meaning or effect, like this:

```
F=DF7,
```

Note that the argument following the `F=` is optional, and an empty declaration is silently ignored. Also note that the comma can be used as a flag by prefixing it with a backslash.

30.4.5.1 m4 modification of F=

When using V8 *sendmail's* m4 configuration, you can modify various flags for inclusion with most delivery agents. As shown in Table 30-3, some modifications are made by appending the new flags to the original flags. Others are made by replacing a few flags with new ones and appending the result to the originals. For example, the following declaration:

```
define(`LOCAL_MAILER_FLAGS', `f')dnl
```

results in these flags being defined for the `local` delivery agent:

```
lsDFMAwq5:/|@f
```

Table 30–3: m4 Modification of F= Equates

define()	Agent	MAILER()	Append to	Replace
CYRUS_MAILER_FLAGS	cyrus	cyrus	lsDFMnPq	5@A
CYRUS_MAILER_FLAGS	cyrusbb	cyrus	lsDFMnPq	
FAX_MAILER_FLAGS	fax	fax	DFMhu	
LOCAL_MAILER_FLAGS	local	local	lsDFMAwq5:/|@	rmn
LOCAL_SHELL_FLAGS	prog	local	lsDFMoq	eu
MAIL11_MAILER_FLAGS	mail11	mail11		nsFx
PH_MAILER_FLAGS	ph	phquery	nrDFM	ehmu
POP_MAILER_FLAGS	pop	pop	lsDFMq	Penu
PROCMAIL_MAILER_FLAGS	procmail	procmail	DFMm	Shu
SMTP_MAILER_FLAGS	smtp	smtp	mDFMuX	
SMTP_MAILER_FLAGS	esmtp	smtp	mDFMuXa	
SMTP_MAILER_FLAGS	smtp8	smtp	mDFMuX8	
SMTP_MAILER_FLAGS	relay	smtp	mDFMuXa8	
USENET_MAILER_FLAGS	usenet		rlsDFMmn	
UUCP_MAILER_FLAGS	uucp	uucp	DFMhuUd	
UUCP_MAILER_FLAGS	uucp-old	uucp	DFMhuUd	
UUCP_MAILER_FLAGS	suucp	uucp	mDFMhuUd	
UUCP_MAILER_FLAGS	uucp-new	uucp	mDFMhuUd	
UUCP_MAILER_FLAGS	uucp-dom	uucp	mDFMhuUd	
UUCP_MAILER_FLAGS	uucp-uudom	uucp	mDFMhuUd	

To append to flags or to replace them, use the appropriate definition from the left-most column of the table and make sure your definition precedes the MAILER *m4* command, for example,

```
define(`SMTP_MAILER_FLAGS', `P')dnl                    ← first
MAILER(smtp)                                           ← second
```

If you reverse them, the *define* will be silently ignored.

L=   *(V8.1 and above)*

30.4.6   *Maximum line length*

The L= equate is used to limit the length of text lines in the body of a mail message. If this equate is omitted and if the delivery agent has the obsolete F=L flag set (see §30.8.29), *sendmail* defaults to SMTPLINELIM (990) as defined in *conf.h* (see §18.8.43). If the F=L is clear (as it is in modern configuration files), *sendmail* defaults to 0. The F=L is honored for compatibility with older versions of *sendmail* that lack this L= equate.

Limiting line length causes overly long lines to be split. When an output line is split, the text up to the split is first transmitted, followed by the ! character. After that the characters defined by the E= equate are transmitted. A line may be split into two or more pieces. For example, consider the following text from the body of a mail message:

```
The maximum line length for SMTP mail is 990 characters.
A delivery agent speaks
SMTP when the $u macro is omitted from the A= equate.
```

A delivery agent could limit line length to 20 characters with a declaration of

```
L=20
```

With that limit, the above text would be split during transmission into the following lines:

```
The maximum line len!
gth for SMTP mail is!
990 characters.
But that length is o!
nly enforced if the !
F=L flag is included
in a delivery agent !
definition. A delive!
ry agent speaks
SMTP when the $u mac!
ro is omitted from t!
he A= equate.
```

Limiting the line length can find application with programs that can't handle long lines. A 40-character braille print-driving program might be one example.

If the argument to L= is missing or if it evaluates to 0 or less, the maximum line limit is set to zero, in which case no limit is enforced.

In using V8 *sendmail*'s m4 configuration, the default for the smtp, esmtp, and smtp8 delivery agents is 990. The default for the relay delivery agent is 2040. The default for all other delivery agents is 0. To change the default at the m4 level, copy an existing delivery agent definition and modify it as outlined in §30.3.1.

M= *(All versions)*

30.4.7   *Maximum message size*

The M= equate is used to limit the total size (header and body combined) of messages handled by a delivery agent. The form for the M= equate is

    M=nbytes

Here, *nbytes* is the ASCII representation of an integer that specifies the largest size in bytes that can be transmitted. If *nbytes* is missing, or if the entire M= equate is missing, *nbytes* becomes zero. If the value is zero, no checking is done for a maximum.

If the size of the message exceeds the limit specified, an error message is returned (bounced) that looks like this:

    ----- Transcript of session follows -----
    552 <recipient>... Message is too large; nbytes bytes max

Bounced mail includes only a copy of the headers. The body is specifically not bounced. The DSN status is set to 5.2.3 (see RFC1893).

This equate is usually used with UUCP agents, where the cost of telephone connections is of concern. It may also find application in mail to files, where disk space is limited.

Prior to V8 *sendmail*, care had to be used to avoid setting M= to a non-zero value when the delivery agent had the F=e flag set. That flag tells *sendmail* that the delivery agent is *expensive*. If the c option is also set, expensive mail is queued rather than delivered. A problem arose because the size of the message was ignored when it was delivered from the queue, so no queued messages were ever bounced for exceeding the M= limit. This bug is fixed in V8 *sendmail*.

30.4.7.1 m4 modifications of M=

In using V8 *sendmail*'s m4 configuration, the maximum message size can be changed by using the definitions listed in the leftmost column of Table 30-4.

Table 30–4: m4 Modification of M= Equates

define()	Agent	MAILER()	Default M=
CYRUS_MAILER_MAX	cyrus	cyrus	0
CYRUS_MAILER_MAX	cyrusbb	cyrus	0
FAX_MAILER_MAX	fax	fax	100000
LOCAL_MAILER_MAX	local	local	0
LOCAL_MAILER_MAX	prog	local	0
none	mail11	mail11	0
none	ph	phquery	0
none	pop	pop	0
PROCMAIL_MAILER_MAX	procmail	procmail	0
SMTP_MAILER_MAX	smtp	smtp	0
SMTP_MAILER_MAX	esmtp	smtp	0
SMTP_MAILER_MAX	smtp8	smtp	0
none	relay	smtp	0
USENET_MAILER_MAX	usenet	usenet	0
UUCP_MAILER_MAX	uucp	uucp	100000
UUCP_MAILER_MAX	uucp-old	uucp	100000
UUCP_MAILER_MAX	suucp	uucp	100000
UUCP_MAILER_MAX	uucp-new	uucp	100000
UUCP_MAILER_MAX	uucp-dom	uucp	100000
UUCP_MAILER_MAX	uucp-uudom	uucp	100000

To change a maximum size, place your definition before the MAILER command in your mc file. For example, here is one way to increase the limit on UUCP traffic to a more reasonable one million:

```
define(`UUCP_MAILER_MAX', `1000000')dnl
MAILER(`uucp')
```

To change the limit for agents that lack a definition, copy an existing delivery agent definition, then modify it as outlined in §30.3.1.

N=	*(V8.7 and above)*

30.4.8	*How to nice(3) the agent*

The N= equate is used to give a delivery agent a priority in relation to other processes. The mechanism is discussed in the online manual for *nice(3)*.

The form for the N= equate looks like this:

```
N=incr
```

Here, *incr* is a signed integer expression that will adjust the "niceness" up or down. If *incr* is zero or missing, the niceness of the delivery agent is unchanged. Positive numbers reduce system priority. Negative numbers increase it.

One possible application for the N= equate might be with Usenet news. Because news seldom needs to flow as quickly as normal email, its delivery agent (usenet) can be forced to run at a low system priority:

```
Musenet, P=/usr/lib/news/inews, F=rlsDFMmn, M=10000, N=10, A=inews -m -h -n
```

To change the niceness at the m4 level, copy an existing delivery agent definition and modify it as outlined in §30.3.1.

P=   *(All versions)*

30.4.9   *Path to the delivery agent*

The P= equate specifies the full pathname of the program that will act as the delivery agent. The form for the P= equate looks like this:

```
P=path
```

If *path* is missing, *sendmail* will print the following error message and set P= to NULL.

```
mailer agent_name: empty path name
```

The *path* can also be one of three names that are defined internally to *sendmail*. Those internally defined names are [IPC], which tells *sendmail* to forward mail over a kernel-supported (usually TCP/IP) network; [FILE], which tells *sendmail* to deliver to a file; and [LPC], which is used for debugging.

P=path

> When the *path* begins with a slash character (when it is a full pathname), *sendmail* first forks (creates a copy of itself), and then the child process (the copy) execs (replaces itself with) the program. The argument vector (*argv*, or command-line arguments) supplied to the program is specified by the A= equate (see §30.4.1). The program inherits the environment[*] of *sendmail* and has its standard input and output connected to the parent process (the *sendmail* that forked). The message (header and body) is fed to the program through its standard input. The envelope (sender and recipient addresses) may

---

[*] In most versions of *sendmail* the environment is stripped for security. V8 passes only TZ=, AGENT=, and (beginning with V8.7) the environmental variables specified with the E configuration command (see §22.2.1).

or may not be provided on the command line, depending on the nature of the program as defined by its F= flags. If the A= *does not* include the $u macro, then *sendmail* will speak SMTP on standard I/O with the program.

P=[IPC]

The special internal name [IPC] specifies that *sendmail* is to make a network connection to the recipient host and that it should talk SMTP to that host. Most current versions of *sendmail* allow the name [TCP]* to be a synonym for [IPC], but [IPC] should be used when portability is of concern. The $u macro should *never* be included in the A= for this internal name.

P=[FILE]

Beginning with V8 *sendmail*, the internal name [FILE] specifies that delivery will be made by appending the message to a file. This name is intended for use by the *file* delivery agent (see §30.5). [FILE] can be useful for designing a custom delivery agent whose purpose is to append to files (perhaps coupled with the U= equate, §30.4.13, to force particular ownership of the file).

P=[LPC]

The special internal name [LPC] (for local person communication) causes *sendmail* to run in a sort of debugging mode. In this mode the mail message is sent to the *sendmail* program's standard input, and replies are read (in the case of SMTP) from its standard output; you act as the SMTP server.

The [LPC] mode can be very helpful in tracking down mail problems. Consider the mystery of duplicate five-character "From " header lines that appear at the beginning of a mail message when mail is sent with UUCP. To solve the mystery, make a copy of your *sendmail.cf* file and change the P= for the UUCP delivery agent to [LPC] in that copy:

```
Muucp, P=/usr/bin/uux, F=msDFMhuU, S=13, R=23, A=uux - -r $h!rmail ($u)
        ↓
     change to
        ↓
Muucp, P=[LPC], F=msDFMhuU, S=13, R=23, A=uux - -r $h!rmail ($u)
```

Then run *sendmail* by hand to see what it is sending to the *uux* program:

```
% /usr/lib/sendmail -Ccopy.cf uucpaddress < message
```

Here, the –C*copy.cf* command-line argument causes *sendmail* to use the copy of the *sendmail.cf* file rather than the original. The *uucpaddress* is the address of a

---

* Originally, IPC meant "interprocessor communications," not "interprocess communications" as it does today. Some vendors have made TCP a synonym, thinking that it was more descriptive of the TCP/IP network mechanism. That may be a mistake on their part, because *sendmail* can interface to other network protocols such as XNS and OSI.

recipient that would normally be sent via UUCP. The **message** should contain only a `Subject:` header line and a minimal body:

```
Subject: test    ← one line header
                  ← a blank line
This is a test.   ← one line body
```

If *sendmail* prints the message with a five-character "`From `" header line at the top, then you know that *sendmail* is the culprit.

30.4.9.1 m4 modifications of P=

In using V8 *sendmail*'s m4 configuration technique, the `P=` equate can be easily changed for all delivery agents by using the definitions in the leftmost column of Table 30-5.

Table 30–5: m4 Modification of P= Equates

define()	Agent	MAILER()	Default P=
CYRUS_MAILER_PATH	cyrus	cyrus	/usr/cyrus/bin/deliver
CYRUS_MAILER_PATH	cyrusbb	cyrus	/usr/cyrus/bin/deliver
FAX_MAILER_PATH	fax	fax	/usr/local/lib/fax/mailfax
LOCAL_MAILER_PATH	local	local	/bin/mail
LOCAL_SHELL_PATH	prog	local	/bin/sh
MAIL11_MAILER_PATH	mail11	mail11	/usr/etc/mail11
PH_MAILER_PATH	ph	phquery	/usr/local/etc/phquery
POP_MAILER_PATH	pop	pop	/usr/lib/mh/spop
PROCMAIL_PATH	procmail	procmail	/usr/local/bin/procmail
none	smtp	smtp	[IPC]
none	esmtp	smtp	[IPC]
none	smtp8	smtp	[IPC]
none	relay	smtp	[IPC]
USENET_MAILER_PATH	usenet	usenet	/usr/lib/news/inews
UUCP_MAILER_PATH	uucp	uucp	/usr/bin/uux
UUCP_MAILER_PATH	uucp-old	uucp	/usr/bin/uux
UUCP_MAILER_PATH	suucp	uucp	/usr/bin/uux
UUCP_MAILER_PATH	uucp-new	uucp	/usr/bin/uux
UUCP_MAILER_PATH	uucp-dom	uucp	/usr/bin/uux
UUCP_MAILER_PATH	uucp-uudom	uucp	/usr/bin/uux

In general, the default values given to these are automatically set when you include the appropriate OSTYPE() directive (see §19.3.1).

R=   *(All versions)*

30.4.10   *Recipient Rewriting Set*

The R= equate specifies a rule set to be used for processing all envelope- and
header-recipient addresses for a specific delivery agent. Mail messages are always
addressed to at least one recipient, but there may be more. The addresses of the
recipients are given in the envelope and are usually repeated in the mail message's
header. The envelope address is given to *sendmail* in one of three ways: as a
command-line argument; as an SMTP RCPT command; or as To:, Cc:, and Bcc:
headers (if the -t command-line switch is given[*]). Figure 30-1 shows how the R=
rule set fits into the flow of addresses through rule sets.

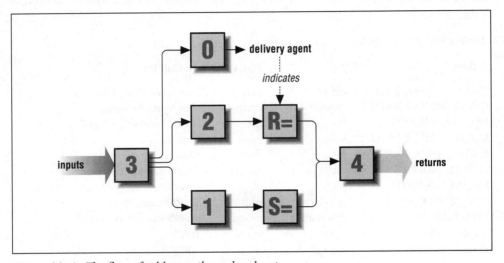

Figure 30–1: The flow of addresses through rule sets

There are two forms for the R= equate. One is the standard form, and the other is
an enhanced alternative beginning with V8 *sendmail*:

```
R=ruleset              ← legal for all
R=eset/hset            ← legal beginning with V8
```

In the first case, *ruleset* specifies the rule set to use in rewriting both headers
and the envelope. If that value is zero or if the entire R= equate is missing, no rule
set is called.

In the second case, two rule sets may be specified.[†] One rule set is specific to the
envelope, and the other is specific to headers. The envelope-specific rule set is the

---

* The -t switch is intended for initial submissions only.

† This form was inspired by an identical form in IDA *sendmail.*

one to the left of the slash; the header-specific rule set is to the right (R=eset/hset). If both values are missing, both default to zero. If only one is missing, the missing value defaults to the other value.

Either rule set may be specified by using names or numbers or both:

```
R=Myset               ← name
R=12                  ← number
R=Myset=12            ← both
```

See §29.1 for a discussion of the various legal ways in which rule sets can be specified.

Macros may not be used in delivery agent rule-set specifications. That is,

```
R=$X
```

will not give the expected result. Instead, *sendmail* will complain about a missing rule-set specification.

When using V8 *sendmail*'s m4 configuration, you cannot change or specify R= rule sets. If the need arises, however, you can copy an existing delivery agent definition and then modify it as outlined in §30.3.1.

S=   *(All versions)*

30.4.11   *Sender rewriting set*

The S= equate specifies a rule set to be used for processing both envelope- and header-sender addresses. The sender's address is given in the envelope and generally repeated in the mail message's From: header line.* The envelope address is given to *sendmail* in one of four ways: as a -f command-line argument, as an SMTP **MAIL** command, as a From: header, or derived from the identity of the user who ran the program (these latter two are used only during initial message submission). Figure 30–1 shows how the S= rule set fits into the flow of addresses through rule sets.

There are two forms for the S= equate. One is the standard form, and the other is an enhanced alternative beginning with V8 *sendmail*:

```
S=ruleset             ← legal for all
S=eset/hset           ← legal beginning with V8
```

The first case specifies a rule set (*ruleset*) that will process both recipient and header addresses. If *ruleset* is zero or if the entire S= equate is missing, no rule set is called.

---

* It is not unusual for these to differ. For example, mail that has been passed through a mailing list exploder may show one address in the envelope and another in the From: header line.

In the second case, one rule set is specific to the envelope, and the other is specific to headers. The envelope-specific rule is the one to the left of the slash; the header-specific rule is the one to the right (S=eset/hset). If both values are both missing, no sender S= processing is done. If only one is missing, the missing value defaults to become the other value. (See Chapter 29, *Rule Sets*, for a description of possible errors and how the new V8.7 symbolic rule set names can be used.)

Either rule set may be specified using names or numbers or both:

```
S=Myset                    ← name
S=12                       ← number
S=Myset=12                 ← both
```

See §29.1 for a discussion of the various legal ways rule sets can be specified.

Macros may not be used in delivery agent rule set specifications. That is,

```
S=$X
```

will not give the expected result. Instead, *sendmail* will complain about a missing rule set specification.

When using V8 *sendmail's* m4 configuration, you cannot change or specify S= rule sets. If the need arises, however, you can copy an existing delivery agent definition, then modify it as outlined in §30.3.1.

T=   *(V8.7 and above)*

30.4.12   *Types for DSN diagnostics*

Beginning with V8.7 *sendmail*, notification of successful, deferred, or failed delivery is now determined by Delivery Status Notification (DSN, see RFC1891). The T= equate provides three pieces of required information to DSN. The pieces are separated by the slash character:

```
T=mta-type/addr-type/diag-type
```

The first piece, the *mta-type*, is later supplied to the Reporting-MTA: DSN header, as its first argument:

```
Reporting-MTA: dns; here.us.edu
               ↑
           mta-type here
```

The second piece, the *addr-type*, is later supplied to the Final-Recipient: DSN header, as its first argument:

```
Final-Recipient: rfc822; badname@here.us.edu
                 ↑
             addr-type here
```

The third piece, the *diag-type*, is later supplied to the `Diagnostic-Code:` DSN header, as its first argument:

```
Diagnostic-Code: smtp; 550 <badname@here.us.edu>... User unknown
                 ↑
                 diag-type here
```

If the `P=` for a delivery agent is `[IPC]` or `[TCP]`, an undeclared *mta-type* defaults to dns, an undeclared *addr-type* to rfc822, and an undeclared *diag-type* to smtp. For any other `P=` the default for an undeclared entry is NULL.

In configuring with the *m4* technique, the declarations of the `T=` equates are

`T=X-Unix`	← *cyrus and prog (equivalent to X-Unix/X-Unix/X-Unix)*
`T=X-Phone/X-FAX/X-Unix`	← *fax*
`T=DNS/RFC822/X-Unix`	← *local, pop, and procmail*
`T=DNS/RFC822/SMTP`	← *all SMTP agents*
`T=X-Usenet/X-Usenet/X-Unix`	← *Usenet*
`T=X-UUCP/X-UUCP/X-Unix`	← *all UUCP agents*

You cannot change these `T=` defaults. If the need arises, you can, however, copy an existing delivery agent definition and then modify it as outlined in §30.3.1.

U=

(V8.7 and above)

30.4.13

Run agent as uid:gid

Prior to V8.7 the user and group identities under which *sendmail* ran were defined by an elaborate set of properties (described under the `F=S` flag in §30.8.40). Beginning with V8.7, *sendmail* now offers the `U=` equate as the means to define those identities. If the `U=` equate is specified, it sets the default user and group identities for the delivery agent and always overrides the values of the `DefaultUser` (u) (g) option (see §34.8.15). If the `F=S` flag is not set, any controlling user will override this `U=` equate. If the `F=S` flag is set, this `U=` equate is absolute, overriding everything, including any controlling user.

The form of the `U=` equate looks like this:

```
U=user:group
```

The *user* is the alphanumeric identity of a user on the local system. If *user* is found in the local *passwd*(5) file, the numeric *uid* from that file becomes the value used. Otherwise, *user*, which must be fully numeric, becomes the value used.

The colon,[*] if present, is followed by the alphanumeric identity of a group on the local system. If the *group* is found in the local *group*(5) file, the numeric *gid* from that file is used. Otherwise, *group*, which must be fully numeric, becomes the

---

[*] A colon is used because the POSIX standard allows login names to contain a dot.

value used. If the colon and group are missing or if the *user* was found in the *passwd*(5) file, the value is taken from the *gid* field of the *passwd*(5) file.

In using V8 *sendmail*'s m4 configuration, no U= equate is specified for any delivery agent. You cannot add a U= equate with the *m4* technique. If the need arises, however, you can copy an existing delivery agent definition and then modify it as outlined in §30.3.

30.5 Internally Defined Names

V8 *sendmail* internally predefines two delivery agents for the special handling of files (*file* and *include*) and one for the special handling of errors (error).

30.5.1 The *file* and *include* Agents

The *file* delivery agent (the * characters are part of the name) handles delivery to files. The *include* delivery agent handles delivery through :include: lists. Neither can be considered a real delivery agent, because actual delivery is still handled internally by *sendmail*. Instead, they provide a way to tune delivery-agent behavior for these two delivery needs.

The predefined defaults for these delivery agents can be viewed with the following command:[*]

```
% /usr/lib/sendmail -d0.15 -bt < /dev/null | egrep "file|include"
mailer 1 (*file*): P=[FILE] S=0/0 R=0/0 M=0 U=0:0 F=9DEFMPloqsu L=0 E=\n T=DNS/RF
C822/X-Unix A=FILE $u
mailer 2 (*include*): P=/dev/null S=0/0 R=0/0 M=0 U=0:0 F=su L=0 E=\n T=<undefine
d>/<undefined>/<undefined> A=INCLUDE $u
```

The defaults may be overwritten by declaring these delivery agents in the configuration file. For example, the following configuration file declaration overrides the internal definition shown above, and limits the size of any mail message that is delivered to files to 1 megabyte:

```
M*file*, P=[FILE], M=1000000, F=9DEFMPloqsu, T=DNS/RFC822/X-Unix, A=FILE $u
```

Note that any equate that does not default to zero (such as the P=, F=, T=, and A= equates) needs to be copied to this configuration file declaration, or the original value will be lost.

A similar change in definition for the m4 configuration of V8 *sendmail* would look like this:

---

[*] The output lines are unfortunately wrapped at the right margin of this book text.

```
LOCAL_CONFIG
M*file*, P=[FILE], M=1000000, F=9DEFMPloqsu, T=DNS/RFC822/X-Unix, A=FILE $u
```

30.5.2 The error Delivery Agent

All versions of *sendmail* define a special internal delivery agent called **error** that
is designed to aid in the issuance of error messages. It is always available for use
in rule sets 0 and 5, and the **check_ . . .** rule sets and cannot be defined with an
M command.

Beginning with V8.7, the form for using the **error** agent in the RHS of a rule looks
like this:

```
R...            $#error $@ dsn  $: text of error message here
```

In general terms, the text following the **$:** is the actual error message that will be
included in bounced mail and sent back to a connecting SMTP host. For example,
the following rule in rule set 0 would cause all mail to the local user George
Washington to bounce:

```
RGeorge.Washington      $#error $: George Washington doesn't sleep here anymore
```

with an error message like this:

```
553 <george.washington>... George Washington doesn't sleep here anymore
```

30.5.2.1 The $@ dsn part

Delivery Status Notification (DSN, see RFC1893) provides a means for conveying the
status of a message's delivery. That status is conveyed in the form of a numeric
triple (so as to be easily parseable by machines). This triple is included in the
"machine readable" part of bounced messages:

```
success.category.detail
```

Each part of the triple is separated from the others with dot characters. There may
be no space around the dots. The parts are numeric, and the meanings are as follows:

success

> Was the overall delivery attempt a success? This part can be one of three dig-
> its. A 2 means that the message was successfully delivered. A 4 means that
> delivery has failed so far but it may succeed in the future. A 5 means that
> delivery failed (permanently).

category

> Failure can be caused by several categories of problem. For example, if this
> *category* is a 1, it means that there was a problem with the address. If it is a
> 4 it means that there was a problem with the network.

detail

> The *detail* further illuminates the *category*. For example, a category of 1 (address problem) might be caused by a detail of 1 (no such mailbox), or 4 (ambiguous address).

The $@ part of the **error** delivery agent declaration specifies a DSN code that is appropriate for the error.

```
R...               $#error $@ success.category.detail  $: text of error message here
```

The *sendmail* program sets its *exit*(2) value according to the *success.category.detail* specified. Table 30-6 shows the relationship between those DSN codes on the left and UNIX *exit*(2) values on the right. Note that the exit values are defined in *<sysexits.h>*, and note that *success* codes of 2 and 4 completely ignore any *category* and *detail* that may be present (that is, 2.*any-thing.anything* marks successful delivery). If $@ lists a code that is not in the table, the default exit value is EX_CONFIG. To illustrate, observe that 8.7.1 (see RFC1893) will exit with EX_DATAERR because it corresponds to the *.7.* in the table.

Table 30-6: DSN Versus exit(2) Values with $@ of $#error

DSN	exit(2)	String	Meaning
2.*.*	EX_OK		Successful delivery
4.*.*	EX_TEMPFAIL	tempfail	Temporary failure, will keep trying
.0.	EX_UNAVAILABLE	unavailable	Other address status
*.1.0	EX_DATAERR		Other address status
*.1.1	EX_NOUSER	nouser	Address is that of a bad mailbox
*.1.2	EX_NOHOST	nohost	Address of recipient is bad
*.1.3	EX_USAGE	usage	Address of recipient has bad syntax
*.1.4	EX_UNAVAILABLE	unavailable	Address is ambiguous
*.1.5	EX_OK		Address of destination is valid
*.1.6	EX_NOUSER	nouser	Address has moved, no forwarding
*.1.7	EX_USAGE	usage	Address of sender has bad syntax
*.1.8	EX_NOHOST	nohost	Address of sender is bad
*.2.0	EX_UNAVAILABLE	unavailable	Mailbox status is undefined
*.2.1	EX_UNAVAILABLE	unavailable	Mailbox disabled
*.2.2	EX_UNAVAILABLE	unavailable	Mailbox full
*.2.3	EX_DATAERR		Mailbox is too small or message is too large
*.2.4	EX_UNAVAILABLE	unavailable	Mailbox led to mail list expansion problems
.3.	EX_OSERR		Operating system error
*.4.0	EX_IOERR		Network error is undefined
*.4.1	EX_TEMPFAIL	tempfail	Network: no answer from host
*.4.2	EX_IOERR		Network bad connection
*.4.3	EX_TEMPFAIL	tempfail	Network routing failure
*.4.4	EX_PROTOCOL	protocol	Network unable to route

Table 30-6: DSN Versus exit(2) Values with $@ of $#error (continued)

DSN	exit(2)	String	Meaning
*.4.5	EX_TEMPFAIL	tempfail	Network congestion
*.4.6	EX_CONFIG	config	Network routing loop detected
*.4.7	EX_UNAVAILABLE	unavailable	Network delivery time expired
.5.	EX_PROTOCOL	protocol	Protocol failure
.6.	EX_UNAVAILABLE	unavailable	Message contents bad or media failure
.7.	EX_DATAERR		Security: general security rejection
else	EX_CONFIG	config	Internal configuration error

To illustrate, consider the need to reject all mail from a particular host (say *evilhost.domain*). We want to reject that host for security reasons, so we might set up a rule like this:

```
R$* < @ evilhost.domain > $*        $#error $@ 5.7.1 $: You are bad, go away
```

Here, the number following the $@ contains a dot, so it is interpreted as a DSN status expression. The .7. in it causes sendmail to set its exit valut to EX_DATAERR, and the 5.7.1 is defined in RFC1893 as meaning "Permanent failure, delivery not authorized, message refused."

If the number following the $@ does not contain a dot, *sendmail* sets its *exit*(2) value to that number. For example, the below results in the same *exit*(2) value as the above but gives a less informative DSN in the bounce message:

```
R$* < @ evilhost.domain > $*        $#error $@ 65 $: You are bad, go away
                                                 ↑
                                    the value of EX_DATAERR from <sysexits.h>
```

If the expression following the $@ is non-numeric, *sendmail* looks up the string and translates a known one into the appropriate *exit*(2) value. The recognized strings are listed in the third column of Table 30-6. For example, the following will cause *sendmail* to exit with an EX_UNAVAILABLE value:

```
R$* < @ evilhost.domain > $*        $#error $@ unavailable $: You are bad, go away
```

If the string following the $@ is not one of those listed in the table, the default *exit*(2) value becomes EX_UNAVAILABLE.

30.5.3 The $: Part

Recall that the text of the error message following the $: is used as a literal error message. That is, this $: part:

```
R...            $#error $: george doesn't sleep here anymore
```

produces this error for the address *george@wash.dc.gov*:

```
553 <george@wash.dc.gov>... george doesn't sleep here anymore
```

Here the 553 is an SMTP code (see RFC821). If you want a different SMTP code issued, you may do so by prefixing the $: part with it:

```
R...            $#error  $: 421 george doesn't sleep here anymore
```

If three digits followed by a space are present as a prefix, those digits are used as the SMTP reply code when *sendmail* is speaking SMTP. If no digits and space prefix the text, the default SMTP reply code is 553.

A few SMTP codes that are useful with $: are listed in Table 30-7. The complete list of all SMTP codes can be found in RFC821.

Table 30-7: Useful SMTP Codes for Use with $:

Code	Meaning
421	Service not available (drop the message)
553	Requested action not taken (bounce the message)

Note that you should restrict yourself to the small set of codes that may legally be returned to the RCPT SMTP command. Also note that any DSN code that is specified in the $@ part must avoid conflicting with the meaning of the SMTP code. For example, the following construct is wrong and should be avoided:

```
R...            $#error $@ 2.1.1 $: 553 ...        ← avoid such conflicts
```

Here, the DSN 2.1.1 means that delivery was successful, whereas the SMTP 553 means that delivery failed and the message bounced.

30.6 How Executed

For safety and efficiency, *sendmail* undertakes a complicated series of steps to run (execute) a delivery agent.[*] Some (such as setting the environment) are intended to improve security. Others (such as forking) are intended to improve efficiency by creating parallel actions. Here, we discuss those steps in the order in which they are taken by *sendmail*.

---

[*] For the purpose of this discussion we will exclude the internal agents (such as IPC) and focus on actual programs (such as */bin/mail*).

30.6.1 Fork

When *sendmail* performs delivery, it cannot simply replace itself with the delivery agent program. Instead, it must *fork*(2), and the child will replace itself.

If *sendmail* is running in verbose mode (see §34.8.76), it shows that it is about to start this process:

    Connecting to *delivery agent*

If a traffic-logging file was specified with -X command-line switch (see §26.4), *sendmail* appends the following line to that file:

    pid === EXEC *the expanded A= here*

Here, the A= equate (see §30.4.1) from the delivery agent's declaration is printed with all its macros expanded and with the recipients listed.

Next *sendmail* creates a *pipe* so that it will be able to print the email message to the delivery agent and so that it can read errors emitted by the delivery agent. See the -d11 debugging switch (see §37.5.44) for a description of what can go wrong.

If all has gone well, *sendmail fork*(2)s a copy of itself. The parent then pipes the email message to the child.

30.6.2 The Child

The child is the copy of *sendmail* that will transform into the delivery agent. But before the child can transform, it must perform a few more necessary steps.

If *sendmail* was compiled with HASSETUSERCONTEXT defined (see §18.8.9), it calls *setusercontext*(3) like this:

    setusercontext(NULL, *pwd*, *uid*, LOGIN_SETRESOURCES|LOGIN_SETPRIORITY);

Here, *pwd* is a pointer to a structure of type *passwd* for the user whose *uid* is *uid*. The *uid* is that of the controlling user (see §24.2.2) or the recipient (see 30.8.33).

If the N= equate (see §30.4.8) has a nonzero value, *sendmail* calls *nice*(3) to "re-nice" the delivery agent to that value.

The *sendmail* program next sets its *uid* and *gid* as appropriate. If the DontInit-Groups option (see §34.8.19) is false, *sendmail* calls *initgroups*(3). The identity used is that described under the DefaultUser option (see §34.8.15).

Next *sendmail* attempts to *chdir*(2) into one of the directories listed in the D= equate (see §30.4.3). This process can be watched with the -d11.20 debugging switch (see §37.5.46).

Finally, *sendmail* calls *setsid*(2) to become a process-group leader and *execve*(2) to become the delivery agent. That latter call looks like this:

```
execve(agent, argv, envp);
```

Here, **agent** is the full path of the delivery agent as specified in the P= equate (see §30.4.9). The argument vector (contents of the A= equate with all the macros expanded and all the recipients added) is passed as **argv**. The environment is that originally given to *sendmail*, massaged for security and augmented by the E= configuration command (see 22.2.1).

30.7 Pitfalls

- The F=f and F=r flags are similar in their implementation but can differ in their result. Consider, for example, the SunOS 4.x version of */bin/mail*. That program expects the −r command-line argument to specify the sender's name. Setting the F=r flag correctly causes mail to be seen as being from the sender (−r *sender*), but mistakenly using the F=f flag invokes */bin/mail* with −f *sender* instead. This fails, because the SunOS 4.x version of */bin/mail* expects the −f command-line argument to mean that it should interactively *read* mail from the mailbox named *sender*.

- The F=C flag can cause problems when it is specified for delivery agents for which the *@domain* form of address is inappropriate. This flag should be avoided for DECNET and the `local` delivery agents.

- A common problem with SysV versions of */bin/mail* is its annoying habit of prepending a "From " line to the beginning of each message, even if one is already there. This confuses users, because it makes their mail appear to come from *uucp* or *daemon* instead of the real sender. The problem stems from the fact that the SysV */bin/mail* lacks a −r command-line argument (or its equivalent) to indicate who the sender is. Instead, that program assumes that the sender's identity can be taken from the identity of the person who ran the program. This works correctly with local mail; but when mail comes in from the outside world, */bin/mail* is being run by *root*, *daemon*, or *uucp*. The best fix is to get a newer */bin/mail** from one of the many anonymous FTP sites. A less satisfactory fix is to delete the F=n flag from the appropriate (usually `local`) delivery agent. This leaves two "From " lines, the second prefixed with a > character (the correct line).

---

* The BSD */bin/mail* requires considerable hacking to get it to work on a SysV machine. Alternatives are *deliver*, the *mh* suite's *slocal*, and *mail.local* that is supplied with the *sendmail* source distribution.

- Never use either the F=f or F=r flags with the **prog** delivery agent. That delivery agent usually runs programs by evoking the Bourne shell, which misinterprets either flag. The -f command-line argument tells */bin/sh* to disable filename generation. The -r command-line argument is unknown to */bin/sh*. Both command-line arguments produce the wrong result.

30.8 Alphabetized F= Flags

In this section we detail each of the delivery agent flags. The complete list is shown in Table 30–8. They are presented in alphabetical order. Lowercase letters precede uppercase letters for each flag.

When configuring with the *m4* technique, you should consult Table 30-2 in §30.4.5.1, to determine which flags are set by default for which delivery agents.

Table 30–8: Delivery Agent F= Flags

Flag	§	Meaning
0	30.8.1	Turn off MX lookups for delivery agent (V8.8 and above)
3	30.8.2	Extend quoted-printable to EBCDIC (V8.7 and above)
5	30.8.3	Use rule set 5 after local aliasing (V8.7 and above)
7	30.8.4	Strip the high bit when delivering (V8.6 and above)
8	30.8.5	Suppress EightBitMode=m MIME encoding (V8.7 and above)
9	30.8.6	Convert 7- to 8-bit if appropriate
:	30.8.7	Check for :include: files (V8.7 and above)
|	30.8.8	Check for |program addresses (V8.7 and above)
/	30.8.9	Check for /file addresses (V8.7 and above)
@	30.8.10	User can be User Database key (V8.7 and above)
a	30.8.11	Run extended SMTP protocol (V8.6 and above)
A	30.8.12	User can be LHS of an alias (V8.7 and above)
b	30.8.13	Add a blank line after message (V8.6 and above)
c	30.8.14	Exclude comment from $g in headers (V8.6 and above)
C	30.8.15	Add @*domain* to recipient
d	30.8.16	Never enclose route addresses in <> (V8.7 and above)
D	30.8.17	Need **Date:** in header
e	30.8.18	Mark expensive delivery agents
E	30.8.19	Change extra From into >From
f	30.8.20	Delivery agent adds -f to argv
F	30.8.21	Need **From:** in header
g	30.8.22	Suppress From:<> (V8.6 and above)
h	30.8.23	Preserve uppercase in hostname
i	30.8.24	Do UDB sender rewrite on envelope (V8.7 and above)
I	30.8.25	Send SMTP VERB to other site
j	30.8.26	Perform UDB rewrite of header recipient addresses (V8.7 and above)

Table 30–8: Delivery Agent F= Flags (continued)

Flag	§	Meaning
k	30.8.27	Don't check for loops in HELO command (V8.7 and above)
l	30.8.28	Delivery agent is local (final) delivery
L	30.8.29	Specify SMTP line limits (Obsolete)
m	30.8.30	Multiple recipients possible
M	30.8.31	Need `Message-ID:` in header
n	30.8.32	Don't use UNIX-style `From` in header
o	30.8.33	Always run delivery agent as recipient (V8.7 and above)
p	30.8.34	Process return path correctly (deprecated)
P	30.8.35	Need `Return-Path:` in header
q	30.8.36	250 versus 252 return for SMTP VRFY (V8.8 and above)
r	30.8.37	Delivery agent adds -r to argv
R	30.8.38	Use a reserved TCP port (V8 only)
s	30.8.39	Strip quotation marks
S	30.8.40	Assume specified uid and gid (Revised for V8.7)
u	30.8.41	Preserve uppercase for username
U	30.8.42	Use UNIX-style `From` line
w	30.8.43	Check for /etc/passwd entry (V8.7 and above)
x	30.8.44	Need `Full-Name:` in header
X	30.8.45	Delivery agent needs RFC821 hidden dot

F=0   *(V8.8 and above)*

30.8.1   *Turn off MX lookups for delivery agent*

During the delivery phase of a message, *sendmail* looks up the destination host-name with DNS and (possibly) redirects delivery to MX hosts, if present. One way (but not the best way) to suppress that MX lookup is to surround the destination hostname with square brackets. An unfortunate side effect of this technique is that the square brackets are included in the envelope of the message:

```
RCPT To:<user@[mail.us.edu]>
```

The `F=0` flag is a better way to suppress MX lookups. For an example of one use for this flag, consider the `nullclient` feature from §19.6.20.

```
FEATURE(`nullclient',`mail.us.edu')
```

Here, all mail will be forwarded to `mail.us.edu`; but because `mail.us.edu` is not surrounded by square brackets, its MX records will be looked up for delivery. This may not be desirable, because the hostname in the envelope will change depending on which MX record is selected. To suppress those MX lookups, we can surround the address with square brackets:

```
     FEATURE(`nullclient',`[mail.us.edu]')
```

But this has the unfortunate side effect of adding the bracketed name [mail.us.edu] to the outgoing envelope. If, instead, the brackets are omitted and the F=0 flag is added, we achieve the same MX suppression effect and send out a legal envelope:

```
     define(`SMTP_MAILER_FLAGS', `0')
     FEATURE(`nullclient',`mail.us.edu')
```

A better way to achieve the same effect is to define a new delivery agent and use that with the nullclient feature:

```
FEATURE(`nullclient',`nomxsmtp:mail.us.edu')
LOCAL_CONFIG
Mnomxsmtp, P=[IPC], F=0mDFMuX, S=11/31, R=21, E=\r\n, L=990, T=DNS/RFC822/SMTP, A=IPC $h
                         ↑
                        note
```

This second approach is much better for the various . . ._RELAY features.

The F=0 flag is suitable only for configurations like the nullclient. It can be extremely dangerous to use it with any other delivery agents, because it can cause necessary MX lookups to be skipped.

F=3   *(V8.7 and above)*

30.8.2   *Extend quoted-printable to EBCDIC*

When *sendmail* is required to convert a message body into *quoted-printable* form as determined by the EightBitMode (8) option (see §34.8.22), it ordinarily converts only those characters that are required by RFC1521. Unfortunately, mail that is transmitted to some IBM machines (specifically those that speak EBCDIC instead of ASCII) can become garbled because of the way EBCDIC represents (or fails to represent) certain characters. Those characters are

```
     ! " # $ @ \ [ ] ^ ` { | } ~
```

When sending MIME mail to such sites, you should probably set the F=3 flag for any delivery agents that handle those sites. Setting this flag tells *sendmail* to encode those characters, in addition to those normally encoded, using *quoted-printable*.

Note that *sendmail* does this encoding only if 8-bit characters appear in the message. This flag solves one EBCDIC problem but should not be thought of as a general solution for all EBCDIC problems.

F=5   *(V8.7 and above)*

30.8.3   *Use rule set 5 after local aliasing*

Prior to V8.7 *sendmail*, only the `local` delivery agent could cause rule set 5 to be called (see §29.7). Rule set 5 is called after aliasing and before forwarding, and can be used to select a new delivery agent. Beginning with V8.7, any delivery agent with the `F=A` flag set (see §30.8.12) can cause an address to be looked up in the *aliases*(5) file. Therefore any delivery agent that has the `F=A` and `F=5` flag set will cause rule set 5 to be called as though the agent were the `local` delivery agent.

In configuration files prior to Version 6 (see §27.5) this flag is automatically set for the `local` delivery agent. Note that addresses that (perhaps artificially) begin with an @ character cause rule set 5 to be skipped (see §29.7).

F=7   *(V8.6 and above)*

30.8.4   *Strip the high bit when delivering*

Under old versions of *sendmail*, all lines of text output by *sendmail* (including the header and body of a message) automatically have the high bit cleared (zeroed) for every character. This behavior remains unchanged under V8 *sendmail* for configuration file versions 2 or less (see §27.5). But with version 3 and above configuration files, the message body is transmitted with the high bit intact by default. For those delivery agents that should not allow 8-bit data to be transmitted, you may use the `F=7` flag to force the old behavior.

Beginning with V8.7, the `F=7` flag can be used to suppress certain kinds of MIME conversions. For example, if the `EightBitMode` (8) option (see §34.8.22) is set to `p` (pass 8) and if the message contains 8-bit MIME data in its body, this `F=7` flag will force *sendmail* to bounce the message with the following SMTP error, to put `5.6.3` (see RFC1893) in its DSN status, and to exit with EX_DATAERR:

```
554 Cannot send 8-bit data to 7-bit destination
```

Note that `F=7` affects only the message body. Headers always have the high bit cleared.

F=8   *(V8.7 and above)*

30.8.5   *Suppress EightBitMode=m MIME encoding*

Beginning with V8.7 *sendmail*, you can set the `EightBitMode` (8) option (see §34.8.22) to `m` (mimefy) to force all unlabeled 8-bit mail to be converted into MIME labeled mail.

You can suppress this conversion for particular delivery agents by specifying the F=8 flag. This form of suppression has the effect of setting the `EightBitMode` (8) option to `p` (pass 8) for an individual delivery agent.

F=9 *(V8.8 and above)*

30.8.6 *Convert 7- to 8-bit if appropriate*

The F=9 flag cause the MIME message body of a delivered message to be converted back from either *quoted-printable* or *base64* into its original 8-bit form. The F=9 flag is effective only if *sendmail* was compiled with MIME7TO8 defined (see §18.8.21).

Conversion works only on single-part MIME messages. If the `Content-Transfer-Encoding:` header type is `base64`, conversion is done from *base64* to 8-bit. Otherwise, if the `Content-Transfer-Encoding:` header type is *quoted-printable*, then conversion is done from *quoted-printable* to 8-bit. If the `Content-Transfer-Encoding:` header type is neither, no conversion is done. The conversion process can be watched with the `-d43.3` debugging switch (see §37.5.151).

F=: *(V8.7 and above)*

30.8.7 *Check for :include: files*

Prior to V8.7 *sendmail*, only the `local` delivery agent could recognize the `:include:` directive for creating mailing lists (see §25.2).

Beginning with V8.7, any delivery agent can be made to recognize the `:include:` directive by setting the F=: flag (or to ignore it by not setting the F=: flag). This flag allows you to design a `local` delivery agent without `:include:` support or local-type clones with `:include:` support. In configuration files prior to Version 6 (see §27.5) this flag is automatically set for the `local` delivery agent.

This flag is only legal for addresses contained in *aliases*(5) databases or ~/.forward files. Any `:include:` address in an SMTP dialog or on the command-line will be rejected.

F=| (vertical bar) *(V8.7 and above)*

30.8.8 *Check for |program addresses*

Prior to V8.7 *sendmail*, only the `local` delivery agent could recognize the | character as a directive to pipe the mail message through a program. (See §24.2.3 and §25.7.4.)

Beginning with V8.7, any delivery agent can be made to accept the leading | character. If the F=| flag is present, the delivery agent will accept the leading | character and call the `prog` delivery agent to pipe the message through a program. If the flag is absent, this ability to pipe is prohibited. In general, the F=| flag should be present for the local and local-clone delivery agents but absent for all others. In configuration files prior to Version 6 (see §27.5) this flag is automatically set for the local delivery agent.

This flag is only legal for addresses contained in *aliases*(5) databases or ˜/.*forward* files. Any |*program* address in a SMTP dialog or on the command-line will be rejected.

F=/ (forward slash)   *(V8.7 and above)*

30.8.9   *Check for /file addresses*

Prior to V8.7 *sendmail*, only the local delivery agent could recognize a leading / character as a directive to append the mail message to a file. (See §24.2.2 and §25.7.3.)

Beginning with V8.7, any delivery agent can be made to accept the leading / character. If the F=/ flag is present, the delivery agent will accept a leading / character and call the *file* delivery agent to append the mail message to a file. If the flag is absent, this ability to append is prohibited. In general, the F=/ flag should be present for the local and local-clone delivery agents but absent for all others. In configuration files prior to Version 6 (see §27.5), this flag is automatically set for the local delivery agent.

This flag is only legal for addresses contained in *aliases*(5) databases or ˜/.*forward* files. Any /*file* address in an SMTP dialog or on the command-line will be rejected.

F=@   *(V8.7 and above)*

30.8.10   *User can be User Database key*

If V8.7 or above *sendmail* has been compiled with User Database support (see §33.5), specifying this flag for a delivery agent causes the delivery agent to perform User Database lookups for each address it handles. For sender header and envelope addresses, a User Database mailname keyword is used to perform reverse aliasing. For recipient envelope addresses, a User Database maildrop keyword is used to perform additional forward aliasing. Note that any address with a leading @ character (in the $: part of the triple returned by rule set 0) causes User Database lookups to be skipped. Also note that the absence of an F=i flag (§30.8.24) suppresses User Database rewriting of the envelope sender.

If the F=@ flag is present, the delivery agent will try to use the User Database. If the F=@ flag is absent, all User Database lookups are skipped. In general, this flag should be present for the local and local-clone delivery agents but absent for all others. In configuration files prior to Version 6 (see §27.5) this flag is automatically set for the local delivery agent.

F=a   *(V8 and above)*

30.8.11   *Run extended SMTP protocol*

Most versions of *sendmail* run only basic SMTP (Simple Mail Transfer Protocol) defined in RFC821. In 1993 that service was extended by RFC1425 to become Extended SMTP (or ESMTP). Beginning with V8 *sendmail*, you can enable a delivery agent to use ESMTP by specifying the F=a flag. This causes *sendmail* to first try to use the extended form of the HELO command, called EHLO. If that fails to be acknowledged as okay, *sendmail* tries again with nonextended SMTP. If the initial inbound greeting includes a line containing the word ESMTP, the F=a flag is assumed.

F=A   *(V8.7 and above)*

30.8.12   *User can be LHS of an alias*

Prior to V8.7 *sendmail*, only the local delivery agent could cause addresses to be looked up in the *aliases*(5) database (see §24.1.2). Beginning with V8.7 *sendmail*, any delivery agent that has an F=A flag set will cause its $: address to be looked up on the left-hand side of the *aliases*(5) file.

For example, the F=A flag can be used to design a local-clone delivery agent that recognizes certain nonlocal addresses as local for aliasing purposes:[*]

```
R$+ <@ FIRE.WALL>      $#firelocal $: $1@fire.wall
```

This allows an alias file like the following to legally exist:

```
George.Washington@fire.wall:   gw@internal.net
```

As a safety net (and if the F=5 flag is also specified), any address that is not found in the *aliases*(5) database will be passed to rule set 5 (see §29.7), where another delivery agent can be selected.

In configuration files prior to Version 6 (see §27.5) the F=A flag is automatically set for the local delivery agent.

---

[*] This example is somewhat contrived because the same thing can be done in a more versatile manner with the mailertable feature (see §19.6.14).

F=b   *(V8.6 and above)*

30.8.13   *Add a blank line after message*

Some UNIX mailbox formats require a blank line at the end of one message and before the start of the next message. If your local version of */bin/mail* does not assure one, you may use the F=b flag. If this flag is specified and if the message being sent to the delivery agent lacks a blank line at the end, *sendmail* adds one. This flag is also appropriate for use with the *file* delivery agent.

F=c   *(V8.6 and above)*

30.8.14   *Exclude comment from $g in headers*

Ordinarily, *sendmail* tries to preserve all RFC822 comments in sender addresses (see §35.3.4). But beginning with V8.7, RFC822 comments can be be stripped by setting this F=c flag. (An RFC822 comment is one in parentheses or text outside angle brackets.) The sender address, always without a comment and stripped of angle brackets, is placed into $g (see §31.10.16) and is used with the -f or -r arguments to A= (see §30.8.37). In assembling headers, the comment is ordinarily restored to $g; but if this F=c flag is set, the comment is left out.

The main use for this flag is to supply just the address to programs that cannot handle anything else. Another use might be to suppress disclosure of potentially proprietary information. By adding F=c to the smtp delivery agent, for example, you can cause sender headers that are defined with $g to go out without RFC822 comments:

```
From: George Washington (The Prez!) <CX75G@fire.wall>    ← without F=c
From: CX75G@fire.wall                                    ← with F=c
```

Note that this does no good at all if users send out mail with disclosing headers already present or if they give out information in signature lines.

F=C   *(All versions)*

30.8.15   *Add @domain to recipient*

The F=C flag causes *sendmail* to append an *@domain* extension to any recipient address that lacks one. The *@domain* that is added is copied from the envelope sender's address.

This F=C flag is not looked for in the delivery agent definition that was selected to send the message. Rather, it is looked for in the delivery agent that would be selected if the sender were the recipient (as in the case of bounced mail).

To illustrate, consider the following mail:

```
From: bill@oursite.edu
To: john@remotesite.gov, alice
```

The recipient address `alice` lacks an *@domain* specification. The *sendmail* program processes the envelope sender address `bill@oursite.edu` to decide on a delivery agent definition that can be used if this mail needs to be returned. If that envelope sender's return mail delivery agent has the `F=C` flag set, then the `@oursite.edu` part of the envelope sender's address is appended to `alice`:

```
From: bill@oursite.edu
To: john@remotesite.gov, alice@oursite.edu
```

The `F=C` flag is traditionally used for the `smtp` class of delivery agent that is supposed to always supply an *@domain* part for all addresses.

Note that the domain part of the *envelope* sender is used. In our example the envelope and header sender are the same.

F=d
(V8.7 and above)

30.8.16
Never enclose route addresses in <>

Ordinarily, V8 *sendmail* forces envelope-sender route addresses[*] to be enclosed in angle brackets. But beginning with V8.7 *sendmail*, angle brackets can be omitted by specifying `F=d`.

Under some circumstances it is possible for these angle-bracketed addresses to be given to a shell, causing them to be wrongly viewed as IO redirection. This problem is most common with the UUCP delivery agents.

F=D
(All versions)

30.8.17
Need Date: in header

The `F=D` flag is used by *sendmail.cf* header commands to force the inclusion of date information:

```
H?D?Resent-Date: $a
H?D?Date: $a
```

The `F=D` flag has no special internal meaning to *sendmail*. It is a convention that is used only in the assorted `Date:` header (see §35.10.10) definitions. See §30.4.5 for a general description of this process.

---

[*] Also see the `DontPruneRoutes` option in §34.8.20 and how route addresses are handled in rules in §29.4.3.

F=e   *(All versions)*

30.8.18   *Mark expensive delivery agents*

The *sendmail.cf* HoldExpensive (c) option (see §34.8.29) tells *sendmail* not to connect to expensive delivery agents. Instead, mail destined for those agents is queued for later delivery. This F=e flag marks a delivery agent as expensive.

For example, consider a site connected to the Internet over a dial-on-demand ISDN link that costs lots of money per minute. Such a site might want all the Internet mail to be queued and would arrange for that queue to be processed only once every other hour.

Under V8 *sendmail*, verbose output (watch delivery) cancels the effect of the F=e flag (suppresses queueing).* Verbose output is set with the −v command line switch (see §36.7.41) or the Verbose (v) option (see §34.8.76).

F=E   *(All versions)*

30.8.19   *Change extra From into >From*

All UNIX mail-reading programs, such as */usr/ucb/Mail*, require that each mail message in a file of many mail messages be delimited from the others by a blank line, then a line that begins with the five characters "From ":

```
and thanks again. -- bill             ← one message ends
                                      ← a blank line
From george Fri Apr  6 12:03:45 1996  ← next message starts
```

This means that any given mail message may have only one line in it that begins with the five characters "From ". To prevent such lines being improperly fed to such mail delivery agents, *sendmail* offers the F=E flag. This flag tells *sendmail* to insert a > character at the front of all but the first such lines found. Consider the following:

```
From tim@here.us.edu Mon Dec 27 13:00:03 1999

From now on, let's meet on Saturdays instead of Tuesdays
like we discussed.
```

If the F=E flag is specified for the delivery agent that delivers the above message, *sendmail* converts it to read

```
From tim@here.us.edu Mon Dec 30 13:00:03 1996

>From now on, let's meet on Saturdays instead of Tuesdays
like we discussed.
```

---

* According to Eric Allman, "It's assumed that if you say you want to watch delivery, you *really* want to watch it."

This F=E flag is rarely needed. Usually, the program specified by the `local` delivery agent definition handles `From` line conversions. This flag should be used *only* with delivery agents that handle final local delivery.

You may wish to consider omitting this flag from the `prog` definition. Omitting it allows a user the option of *not* transforming "`From` " lines, by specifying a program in his or her `~/.forward` file.

F=f   *(All versions)*

30.8.20   *Delivery agent adds −f to argv*

If *sendmail* is run with a `−f` command-line argument (see §36.7.21) and if the F=f flag is specified, the A= for this delivery agent will have the two additional arguments `−f` and `$g` inserted between its `argv[0]` and `argv[1]`. For example, if *sendmail* is run as

```
/usr/lib/sendmail -f jim host!bill
```

and if the delivery agent for sending to `host` is defined as

```
Muucp, P=/bin/uux, F=fmsDFMhuU, S=13, R=23, A=uux - -r $h!rmail ($u)
```

then the f in F=fmsDFhuU causes the A= of

```
A=uux - -r $h@rmail ($u)
```

to be rewritten as

```
A=uux -f $g - -r $h@rmail ($u)
```

Here, `$g` is `jim` from the original command line (but rewritten to be a return address relative to the recipient). The original `−f` argument `jim` is first rewritten by rule sets 3, 1, and 4. The result of those rewrites is placed into `$f`. The `$f` macro is rewritten by rule sets 3, 1, S=, and 4, and the result is placed into `$g`. (`$f` and `$g` are described in §31.10.16.)

Note that the F=f and the F=r flags are very similar and easily confused.

F=F   *(All versions)*

30.8.21   *Need From: in header*

The F=F flag is used by *sendmail.cf* header commands to force the inclusion of sender (From) information (see §30.4.5):

```
H?F?Resent-From: $q
H?F?From: $q
```

The `F=F` flag has no special internal meaning to *sendmail*. It is a convention that is used only in the assorted `From:` header (see §35.10.14) definitions. See §30.4.5 for a general description of this process.

F=g   *(V8.6 and above)*

30.8.22   *Suppress From:<>*

The special address `<>` is used as the envelope sender when *sendmail* bounces a mail message. This address is intended to prevent bounced messages from themselves bouncing. Unfortunately, not all configuration files properly handle this form of sender address. The stock SunOS configuration files prior to Solaris 2.3, for example, caused *sendmail* to enter an endless loop when processing `<>`. Also, some UUCP implementations get confused when they are executed with command line arguments of:

```
-f <>
```

As an interim measure, until all programs learn to correctly handle the `<>` address, you may use the `F=g` flag to suppress that address for selected delivery agents. If the `F=g` flag is set for a delivery agent, it uses the value of `$g` (see §31.10.16) in place of the `<>`, where `$g` contains `$n` (usually MAILER-DAEMON see §31.10.26) with an `@` and your domain name appended.

F=h   *(All versions)*

30.8.23   *Preserve uppercase in hostname*

Some delivery agents, such as those that deal with files, require that the recipient's hostname be left as is. The hostname portion of the recipient's address is ordinarily converted to all lowercase before being tucked into `$h`. Specifying the `F=h` flag tells *sendmail* to not convert that address to lowercase.[*]

The `$h` macro (see §31.10.17) is usually used with the `A=` equate of a delivery agent. For example

```
Muucp, P=/usr/bin/uux, F=msDFMhuU, A=uux - -r $h!rmail ($u)
```

Here, the `h` in `F=msDFMhuU` tells *sendmail* to leave the `$h` alone and *not* to convert the hostname in that defined macro to lowercase.

---

[*] This flag was added specifically to handle the UUCP host named *Shasta* at Stanford University.

F=i

30.8.24
Do UDB sender rewrite on envelope

The F=@ flag (see §30.8.10) allows all addresses for a given delivery agent to be rewritten by the User Database (see §33.5). The F=i flag either suppresses that rewrite for the sender envelope (if absent) or allows that rewrite for the sender envelope (if present). For example, consider mail from the user jane:

```
MAIL from: jane          ← SMTP envelope sender
From: jane               ← header sender
```

Now assume that a User Database entry like the following exists:

```
jane:mailname       Jane.Doe
```

If the F=i flag is absent but the F=@ flag present, the envelope-sender address will remain unchanged, but the header-sender address will be rewritten by the User Database:

```
MAIL from: jane          ← SMTP envelope sender
From: Jane.Doe           ← header sender
```

But if the F=i and F=@ flags are both present, the envelope- and header-sender addresses will both be rewritten by the User Database:

```
MAIL from: Jane.Doe      ← SMTP envelope sender
From: Jane.Doe           ← header sender
```

No matter how the envelope-sender address is rewritten (with or without use of the User Database), the result is saved to the S line of the *qf* file (§23.9.14).

F=I (uppercase i)

30.8.25
Send SMTP VERB to other site

The F=I flag tells the local *sendmail* to send the following VERB[*] SMTP command to the receiving *sendmail*:

```
VERB                     ← ours sends
200 Verbose mode         ← recipient replies
```

The VERB SMTP command causes the receiving *sendmail* to go into verbose mode *and* to set its deliver mode to *interactive*. This has the same effect as would occur if the receiving *sendmail* had been run with the command-line options -v and -odi set.

The F=I flag is intended as an aid in debugging a remote receiving site's *sendmail*. The VERB SMTP command causes that remote site to run in verbose mode. By

---

[*] VERB is defined in RFC1700.

temporarily adding the F=I flag to a delivery agent's definition and then running *sendmail* locally with the -v command-line argument, you can watch both the local and the remote's verbose output. Each line of the remote site's verbose output will be seen locally prefixed with a 050.

Note that if the PrivacyOptions (p) option on the remote site's *sendmail* is set to noexpn (see §34.8.47), that site's response to the VERB SMTP command will be this rejection:

```
502 Verbose unavailable
```

Also note that if the other side is not running *sendmail,* you may see other errors:

```
501 No argument given in VERB command.   ← PMDF V5.0
250 Ok                                    ← post.office v1.9.1 (but ignores its own Ok)
```

In both these cases, the request to the other machine to go into verbose mode has failed.

F=j   *(V8.7 and above)*

30.8.26   *Perform UDB rewrite of header recipient addresses*

If *sendmail* was compiled with User Database support (see §18.8.54) and if that database is being used (see §34.8.75), you may have *sendmail* rewrite header recipient addresses using that database. The F=j flag tells *sendmail* to look up recipient addresses in the User Database (using the mailname keyword). If an appropriate entry is found, it is used in place of the original address in the recipient headers. The process is the same as that described for the F=i flag, except that here it is for recipient headers.

F=k   *(V8.7 and above)*

30.8.27   *Don't check for loops in HELO command*

When another host connects to the local host and that other host claims to have the same canonical name as the local host, it should be considered an error. In V8.6 *sendmail,* setting the CheckLoopBack variable in *conf.c* determined whether this error was detected. But beginning with V8.7 *sendmail,* this check is based on the delivery agent. If the F=k flag is absent, the check is done. If the F=k flag is set, the check is skipped.

The check is performed only for SMTP connections. The literal canonical name given in the connecting host's HELO line is compared to the canonical name for the local host. If they are the same, the following error is printed, and the connection is disallowed:

```
553 host config error: mail loops back to myself          ← V8.6
553 host config error: mail loops back to me (MX problem?) ← V8.7
```

Here, *host* is the name of the offending host.

A problem can arise at sites that run two different invocations of *sendmail* (one for SMTP connections and another for command-line invocation, where each uses a different configuration file). In this instance, when the latter connects to the former, this error may occur. Such sites may find it necessary to set the F=k flag for the delivery agent that handles SMTP connections, usually Msmtp. With an m4 configuration the following command does just that:

```
define(`SMTP_MAILER_FLAGS', `k')dnl
```

Note that *sendmail* must recognize its local hostname among many possible names. See §32.5.8 for a discussion of $=w and MX records.

F=l (lowercase L) *(All versions)*

30.8.28 *Agent performs local (final) delivery*

The F=l flag tells *sendmail* that this delivery agent will be performing final delivery (usually on the local machine). This notification affects *sendmail*'s behavior in three ways.

First, it enables the DSN notify on success mechanism.[*] That is, if the message were received via SMTP with the envelope

```
RCPT To: user@here.us.edu NOTIFY=SUCCESS
```

then *sendmail* (upon final local delivery) sends back to the original sender an email message acknowledging receipt. This mechanism should be used sparingly.

Second, the F=l flag allows *sendmail* to ignore any host part of the triple returned by rule set 0. Ordinarily, the $@ operator must appear in the RHS for all delivery agents selected. If no host is selected by $@, *sendmail* prints this error and bounces the message

```
554 buildaddr: no host
```

But since the host is not always needed for final delivery, the presence of the F=l flag tells *sendmail* to silently ignore a missing host part.

Third, the F=l flag influences how undeliverable mail will be handled. When the ErrorMode (e) option (see §34.8.24) is q (quiet), such mail is usually reported in the *sendmail* program's *exit*(2) status (see §36.5). With the F=l flag set, the unde-

---

[*] This replaces the Return-Receipt-To: header line.

liverable message will instead be appended to ˜*/dead.letter* for a local sender or mailed back for a remote sender.

In general, the F=l flag should always be specified for the local, prog, and *file* delivery agents.

Note that the processing of a user's ˜*/.forward* file is no longer tied to the local delivery agent, nor to this F=l flag. The ability to look in a user's ˜*/.forward* file is now determined by the F=w flag.

F=L   *(obsolete as of V8.8)*

30.8.29   *Specify SMTP line limits*

Prior to V8.8 *sendmail*, this F=L flag caused *sendmail* to split output lines in the message body so that they did not exceed 990 characters and always caused *sendmail* to clear the most significant bit of the characters in those lines.

Beginning with V8.8 *sendmail*, F=L emulates this old behavior under certain conditions. F=L causes *sendmail* to assign L= a default value of 990, if it is missing one (see §30.4.6), and (if the configuration file level is 1 or less) to set the F=7 flag.

F=m   *(All versions)*

30.8.30   *Allow delivery to multiple recipients*

Whenever the *sendmail* program executes the program specified by the P= equate (see §30.4.9), that program is given its *argv* vector as specified by the A= equate (see §30.4.1). As the last step in building that *argv*, *sendmail* appends one or more recipient addresses.

The decision as to whether it appends one address or many is determined by the F=m flag. If this flag is not specified, the delivery agent is given only one recipient. Otherwise, if it is specified, the delivery agent may be given many recipients. In either case, if there are more recipients than the argv can accept, the delivery agent is rerun as many times as is necessary to handle them all.

Note that *sendmail* is able to distinguish only between failures involving one, many, or all of the recipients when it is delivering with SMTP. Otherwise, it judges delivery as successful if a zero *exit*(2) value is returned by a delivery agent. If the delivery agent fails to deliver to one of many recipients, it exits with a nonzero value, and because of that single failure, *sendmail* will presume that delivery to all recipients failed.

F=M

30.8.31
Need Message-ID: in header

The F=M flag is used by *sendmail.cf* header commands to force the inclusion of message identification information. (see §30.4.5):

```
H?M?Resent-Message-ID: <$t.$i@$j>
H?M?Message-ID: <$t.$i@$j>
```

The F=M flag has no special internal meaning to *sendmail.* It is a convention that is used only in the assorted **Message-ID:** header (see §35.10.19) definitions. See §30.4.5 for a general description of this process.

Note that the **Message-ID:** header definition should always be included in the *sendmail.cf* file because packages expect the presence of that header by many software packages.

F=n

30.8.32
Don't use UNIX-style From in header

The UNIX-style mailbox (a single file into which many mail messages are placed) requires that each message be separated from the others by a blank line followed by a line that begins with the five characters "**From** ":

```
and thanks again. -- bill          ← one message ends
                                   ← a blank line
From george Fri Apr  6 12:03:45 1990   ← next message starts
```

Ordinarily, *sendmail* adds a five-character "**From** " line to a message if there isn't one. The F=n flag prevents *sendmail* from doing this. It is intended for use when not dealing with a UNIX-style mailbox.

Note that if the F=U flag is specified (but not F=n), then the five-character "**From** " header line is created, and the words **remote from $g** are appended to that line. The F=n flag should *always* be specified for SMTP delivery agents. The five-character "**From** " line is not a valid RFC822 header (because it lacks a colon) and is not permitted.

Apart from SMTP, the use of the F=n flag is best determined on a case-by-case basis. Some delivery agents always generate a "**From** " line, so the F=n flag can be used to avoid duplication. Some delivery agents generate a "**From** " line only if there is not already one there, so the F=n flag is optional and perhaps best omitted. Some delivery agents never generate a "**From** " line, yet require one (such as the *uux* program); for these the F=n flag should always be omitted.

F=o   *(V8.7 and above)*

30.8.33   *Always run delivery agent as recipient*

Under certain circumstances, before *sendmail* delivers to a file or through programs, it may assume the identity (*uid* and *gid*) of the controlling user (see §24.2.2
for a description of this process). Beginning with V8.7, the F=o flag changes this
behavior. Specifying F=o flag causes *sendmail* to assume the identity of the recipient. Omitting the F=o flag causes *sendmail* to assume the identity of the controlling user where appropriate.

In version 5 and earlier configuration files (§27.5) this flag is automatically set for
the prog and *file* delivery agents. Note that the U= equate (see §30.4.13), when
specified, always overrides the controlling user.

F=p   *(deprecated)*

30.8.34   *Process return path per RFC821*

The SMTP *mail* command normally uses the envelope address for the sender:

```
MAIL From:<jqp@wash.dc.gov>
```

If the F=p flag is specified, *sendmail* instead sends a transformed version of that
address. The transformation can take one of two forms, depending on the first
character of the envelope address. If that address begins with an @ character, then
an @, the local hostname and a comma are prepended to that address to create a
legal return path:

```
<@hub:jqp@wash.dc.gov>
        ↓
```
becomes
```
        ↓
<@ourhost,@hub:jqp@wash.dc.gov>
```

If the envelope address for the sender does not start with an @ character, then an
@, the local hostname, and a colon are prepended to that address:

```
<jqp@wash.dc.gov> becomes <@ourhost:jqp@wash.dc.gov>
```

See also the DontPruneRoutes option.

Note that these forms of address transformations are discouraged by RFC1123. For
this reason the F=p flag is deprecated and may be removed from future versions of
sendmail.

F=P

30.8.35   *Need Return-Path: in header*

The F=P flag is used by *sendmail.cf* header commands to force the inclusion of return-path information:

```
H?P?Return-Path: <$g>
```

The F=P flag has no special internal meaning to *sendmail.* It is a convention that is used only in the assorted Return-Path: header (see §35.10.28) definitions. See §30.4.5 for a general description of this process.

The sender's envelope address (the address that would be used to return mail if it were bounced, for example) is placed into $g for use in the Return-Path: header line. This is usually done during final delivery, although it can also be done for delivery agents that lack a clear envelope address. The form of the address in the $g macro (see §31.10.16) depends on the setting of the F=p flag. Note that this is normally the same as the address in the five character "From " line.

F=q

30.8.36   *250 versus 252 return for SMTP VRFY*

Prior to RFC1123 a successful reply to the SMTP VRFY command was always prefixed with a 250, meaning that sending to this address was likely to result in successful delivery:

VRFY user
250 user@here.us.edu (Full Name)

Here, *sendmail* states (with the 250) that it interpreted the address as *valid locally* and that delivery or relaying to another site would be attempted.

RFC1123 now requires that shades of meaning be conveyed in that success code, so the correct prefix should be 252, which means that we will *accept* the address and attempt to relay it elsewhere.

If the F=q flag is set, *sendmail* returns the 250 prefix; otherwise, it returns the 252 prefix. It should be set only for delivery agents doing local delivery. For configuration files earlier than version 7, the F=q flag is automatically set for the local, prog, and *file* delivery agents.

F=r

30.8.37   *Delivery agent adds –r to argv*

If *sendmail* is run with a –f command-line argument, and if the F=r flag is specified, the A= for this delivery agent has the two additional arguments, –r and $g, inserted between its `argv[0]` and `argv[1]`. Consider a case in which *sendmail* is run as

```
/usr/lib/sendmail -f jim bill
```

If `bill` is a local user and the delivery agent for `local` is defined as

```
Mlocal, P=/bin/mail, F=rlsDFMmnP, S=10, R=20, A=mail -d $u
```

then the `r` in `F=rlsDFmnP` will cause the `A=` of

```
A=mail -d $u
```

to be rewritten as

```
A=mail -r $g -d $u
```

The `$g` is `jim` from the original command line (but rewritten to be a return address relative to the recipient). The original `-f` argument `jim` is first rewritten by rule sets 3, 1, and 4. The result of those rewrites is placed into `$f` (see §31.10.14). The `$f` macro is rewritten by rule sets 3, 1, `S=`, and 4, and the result is placed into `$g` (see §31.10.16).

Note that the `F=f` and the `F=r` flags are very similar and easily confused.

F=R   *(V8.6 and above)*

30.8.38   *Use a reserved TCP port*

The `F=R` flag causes *sendmail* to connect on a reserved (privileged) TCP port for additional security. Privileged Internet ports are those in the range 0 to 1023. Only *root* is allowed to connect to such ports. The *sendmail* program calls *rresvport*(3) to obtain a socket on its selected port. Note that this is done only when instantiating an outgoing connection. See §30.4.1.2 for another way to set the outgoing port number.

This flag is suitable only for use with the [IPC] and [TCP] delivery agents. Note that *sendmail* is usually *suid root* when run as a daemon.

F=s   *(All versions)*

30.8.39   *Strip quotation marks*

Some delivery agents don't correctly understand quotation marks in addresses, for example,

```
"dechost::user"@relay
```

For delivery agents that do not correctly understand them, the `F=s` flag causes *sendmail* to strip all quotation marks from the address before handing it to the delivery agent:

```
dechost::user@relay
```

The `local` delivery agent should always have the `F=s` flag specified. The `prog` delivery agent commonly has the `F=s` flag specified. The `uucp` delivery agent may or may not require that flag depending on the specifics of the program specified in the `P=` equate. The `[IPC]` and `[TCP]` delivery agents should *never* specify the `F=s` flag.

F=S   *(Revised for V8.7)*

30.8.40   *Assume specified uid and gid*

There are two major ways in which *sendmail* can be run: as an *suid root* process (that is, with the permissions of *root* no matter who runs it) or as an ordinary process run by an ordinary (nonprivileged) user (that is, with *root* privilege *only* if it is run by *root*). When *sendmail* is running with *root* privilege and when the `F=S` flag is specified for a delivery agent, *sendmail always* invokes that delivery agent as the effective user and effective group specified by the `U=` equate.* If the `U=` equate is unspecified or is specified as zero, it runs as *root*. In both instances, the real GID and UID remain that of the receiving user —that is, the `F=S` flag acts like the UNIX *suid* and *sgid* bits.

If the `F=S` is not specified for the delivery agent, *sendmail* first checks to see whether there is a controlling user for the address. If there is one, *sendmail* becomes that user for delivery. If delivery is to a file and if the *suid* bit is set for that file, *sendmail* becomes the owner of the file. Similarly, if delivery is to a file and the *sgid* bit is set, *sendmail* sets its group identity to the group of the file. Finally, if the user or group part of the `U=` equate was missing or 0, *sendmail* assumes the identity of the `DefaultUser` (u) option (see §34.8.15). Otherwise, it assumes the identity of the `U=` equate.

F=u   *(All versions)*

30.8.41   *Preserve uppercase for username*

The username portion of the recipient's address is ordinarily converted to lowercase before being tucked into `$u`. The `$u` is usually used with the `A=` equate of a delivery agent:

```
Mprog, P=/bin/sh,   F=lsDFMeuP,  S=10, R=20, A=sh -c $u
```

Some delivery agents, such as the `prog` agent, execute programs. They require that the program (user) name be left as is (otherwise, the program name would not be found). Specifying the `F=u` flag tells *sendmail* to *not* convert that name to lowercase.

---

* Prior to V8.7 there was no `U=` equate, so `F=S` always ran as *root*.

Beginning with V8.7 *sendmail*, the F=u flag also determines how some aliases are treated. If it is set, usernames are stored in the *aliases* database without conversion to lowercase. If it is clear, they are converted to lowercase.

Also if the F=u flag is set, looking up the owner part that follows the owner- in a mailing list is done in a case-sensitive manner. If the F=u flag is clear, the owner is converted to lowercase before being looked up.

In general, the F=u flag should be set in all delivery agent declarations, except the local delivery agent.

F=U   *(All versions)*

30.8.42   *Use UUCP-Style From line*

The F=U flag causes *sendmail* to prepend a five-character "From " line to the start of the headers if there is not already one there. Whether one was prepended or not, this flag also tells *sendmail* to add the words remote from *host* to the end of that line and also requires that $g be in the form *host!*. . . .

The F=U flag is required when a neighbor UUCP site runs an old (or possibly SysV) version of the *rmail* program. The newer BSD versions of *rmail* do not require this flag.

F=w   *(V8.7 and above)*

30.8.43   *Check for /etc/passwd entry*

The *sendmail* program uses the *passwd*(5) file to determine whether a local address corresponds to a local account. If it does, the home directory for the user is copied into $z (see §31.10.46). Then the full name of the user is extracted from the *gecos* field of the *passwd*(5) file and placed into $x (see §31.10.42).

Beginning with V8.7 *sendmail*, the information in the *passwd*(5) file is looked up only if the F=w flag is set for the recipient's delivery agent. In general, it must be present (set) for the local and any local-clone delivery agents but should be absent for all other delivery agents. For configuration files less than 6 (see §27.5), the F=w flag is automatically set for the local delivery agent.

Omitting the F=w flag has several consequences:

- The recipient's home directory is not looked up, and all user-level forwarding is prevented. Note that this voids all forwarding, even if the user's home is defined as part of the ForwardPath (J) option (see §34.8.27).

- The user's full name is not looked up in the *gecos* field of the *passwd*(5) file.

- The *uid* and *gid* of the recipient become unavailable, so the identity of the controlling user cannot be set to that of the recipient.

Note that this flag should be considered mandatory for `local` and local clones. If you want to cancel forwarding, use the `ForwardPath` (J) option. Attempting to cancel forwarding by omitting the F=w flag can have unpredictable side effects that may cause mail to fail.

F=x   *(All versions)*

30.8.44   *Need Full-Name: in header*

The F=x flag is used by *sendmail.cf* header commands to force the inclusion of the user's full name (see §30.4.5):

```
H?x?Full-Name: $x
```

The F=x flag has no special internal meaning to *sendmail*. It is a convention that is used only in the assorted `Full-Name:` header (see §35.10.15) definitions. See §30.4.5 for a general description of this process.

F=X   *(All versions)*

30.8.45   *Need RFC821 hidden dot*

Delivery agents that speak SMTP require that any line of the message that begins with a dot have that dot doubled. Delivery agents speak SMTP when the $u is missing from the A= equate. For example,

```
Mether, P=[TCP], F=msDFMuCX, S=11, R=21, A=TCP $h
```

An example of a file that contains leading dots is a *troff*(1) source file:

```
.\" Show example
.Ps
Mether, P=[TCP], F=msDFMuCX, S=11, R=21, A=TCP $h
.Ps
```

In the above, three lines begin with a leading dot. The F=X flag causes *sendmail* to transmit the above message as

```
..\" Show example
..Ps
Mether, P=[TCP], F=msDFMuCX, S=11, R=21, A=TCP $h
..Pe
```

The extra leading dot is automatically restored to a single dot at the receiving end.

This F=X flag should be used only with delivery agents that speak SMTP. It should not be used with other delivery agents, because they will not know to strip the extra dots.

31

Defined Macros

The *sendmail* program supports three kinds of macros. Class macros (Chapter 32) are used to represent multiple values. Database macros (Chapter 33) represent values stored in external files or networked maps. In this chapter we discuss defined macros, which allow strings of text to be represented symbolically.

Defined macros can be *declared* (given names and assigned the strings of text that will become values) at four different times:

1. When *sendmail* first begins to run, it preassigns strings of text to certain macros.

2. When *sendmail* processes the options in its command line, macros that were declared by using the **-M** (see §31.2) command-line switch[*] are assigned their values.

3. When *sendmail* reads its configuration file, macros that were declared by using the D configuration-file command (see §31.3) are assigned their values.

4. Finally, many macros are assigned values internally by *sendmail* as mail is received and sent.

Macros can be used in any configuration-file command. Generally, they are expanded (their value is used) when mail is sent or received.

---

[*] Prior to V8.7 the **-oM** option (see §34.8.77) was used to define macros on the command line. Although that option still works, the **-M** command-line switch is now recommended as the preferred technique.

31.1 Preassigned Macros

When *sendmail* first begins to run, it preassigns values to certain macros. The complete list of these macros is shown in Table 31-1. Each is described in detail at the end of this chapter in §31.10.

Table 31-1: Preassigned Macros

Macro	§	Description
$_	31.10.1	RFC1413-validation and IP source route (V8.1 and above)
$b	31.10.3	The current date in RFC822 format
${bodytype}	31.10.4	The ESMTP BODY parameter (V8.8 and above)
${client_addr}	31.10.7	The connecting host's IP address (V8.8 and above)
${client_name}	31.10.8	The connecting host's canonical name (V8.8 and above)
${envid}	31.10.12	The original DSN envelope ID (V8.8 and above)
$j	31.10.20	The canonical hostname
$k	31.10.21	UUCP node name (V8.1 and above)
$m	31.10.24	The domain name (V8.1 and above)
$n	31.10.26	The bounced mail sender
${opMode}	31.10.28	The startup operating mode (V8.7 and above)
$v	31.10.38	The *sendmail* program's version
$w	31.10.40	The short name of this host

All preassigned macros can be redefined in the configuration file or in the command line. The **-d35.9** (see §37.5.120) debugging switch (when run on an empty configuration file) can be used to watch *sendmail* predefine its macros.*

Note that the *m4* configuration technique uses many more macros than are shown here (see Table 31-5). But even with that technique this short list of macros is all that are internally defined by the *sendmail* program when it first starts up.

31.2 Command-Line Definitions

Macros may also be declared when *sendmail* processes its command line, by using either the **-M** command-line switch or the **M** option (see §34.8.77). The forms for these command-line declarations are

```
-oMXtext                    ← no longer recommended
-MXtext                     ← preferred as of V8.7
```

For both forms, the **X** is the macro name, which can be single-character or multi-character (we discuss this soon). The **text** follows the name and is the value assigned to the macro.

---

* When you use this debugging switch, you will notice that operators such as $* are implemented as macros too.

In the first form, the -o switch tells *sendmail* that this is an option. The M is the name of the option. The M option causes *sendmail* to use the characters that follow the M as a macro definition. This form still works but may be eliminated in a future version of *sendmail*.

In the second form, the -M command line switch causes *sendmail* to use the characters that follow the M as a macro definition. Beginning with V8.7 *sendmail*, this is now the preferred form.

Because these forms of definition are a part of the command line, all special characters are interpreted by the shell. Any *text* that contains shell wildcard or history characters should be quoted. (We'll cover this in detail soon.)

Command-line macros are defined before the configuration file is read and parsed by *sendmail*. Note that configuration-file macros always override command-line macros.[*] Despite this, command-line definitions may still be useful. Preassigned macros may be given new values, and user-defined macros may be initialized in the command line.

For security reasons, only the r and s macros[†] allow *sendmail* to retain its *root* privilege. Overriding the value of any other macro from the command line causes *sendmail* to run as an ordinary user.

31.2.1 Syntax of the Command-Line Macro's Text

When a macro is declared on the command line, its **text** value is taken from the command line as is:

```
-MXtext
-oMXtext
```

Unlike macros declared in the configuration file (which we describe next), this form of declaration does not strip commas from **text** nor does it handle escape characters.

The whole suite of special operators available to your shell may be used to generate an appropriate **text** value. For example, the following assigns the name of your Usenet news server to the macro N:

```
-MN$NNTPSERVER
```

The $NNTPSERVER is the shell's environmental variable that contains the address of the news server as its value.

---

[*] If you are running a pre-V8 version of *sendmail*, it may use a freeze file. In that case, command-line macros override those in the configuration file.

[†] For V8 *sendmail*, r and s should be set with the -p command-line switch (see §36.7.32).

31.3 *Configuration File Definitions*

When *sendmail* reads the configuration file, macros that are declared in that file are assigned values. The configuration-file command that declares macros begins with the letter D. There may only be a single macro command per line. The form of the D macro configuration command is:

```
DXtext
```

The symbolic name of the macro (here, X) is a single-character or a multicharacter name (see §31.4):

```
DXtext              ← single-character name X
D{XXX}text          ← multicharacter name XXX
```

This must immediately follow the D with no intervening space. The value that is given to the macro is the *text*, consisting of all characters beginning with the first character following the name and including all characters up to the end of the line. Any indented lines that follow the definition are joined to that definition. When joined, the newline and indentation characters are retained. Consider the following three configuration lines:

```
DXsometext
        moretext
        moretext
    ↑
    tabs
```

These are read and joined by *sendmail* to form the following *text* value for the macro named X:

```
sometext\n\tmoretext\n\tmoretext
```

The notation \n represents a newline character, and the notation \t represents a tab character.

If *text* is missing, the value assigned to the macro is that of an empty string; that is, a single byte that has a value of zero.

If both the name and the *text* are missing, the following error is printed, and that D configuration line is ignored:[*]

```
Name required for macro/class
```

---

[*] Prior to V8 *sendmail*, a macro whose name was missing was given arbitrary garbage as a value. This caused the *sendmail* program to crash.

31.3.1 Required Macros (V8.6 and earlier)

Table 31-2 shows the macro names that *must* (prior to V8.6) be given values in the configuration file.

Table 31–2: Required Macros

Macro	§	Description	As of V8.7
$e	34.8.65	The SMTP greeting message	The SmtpGreetingMessage option
$j[a]	31.10.20	Official canonical hostname	Automatically defined all V8
$l	34.8.72	UNIX From format	The UnixFromLine option
$n	31.10.26	Name used for error messages	Automatically defined
$o	34.8.45	Delimiter operator characters	The OperatorChars option
$q	31.10.30	Format of the sender's address	No longer used

a. The $j macro was only required in V5 and earlier releases.

Each of these macros is described at the end of this chapter in §31.10. Prior to V8.7, failure to define a required macro could have resulted in unpredictable problems. Beginning with V8.7 *sendmail*, no macros are required. Some are predefined[*] for you by *sendmail*, and others have become options.

31.3.2 Syntax of the Configuration File Macro's Text

The **text** of a macro's value in the configuration file may contain escaped control codes. Control codes are embedded by using a backslash escape notation. The backslash escape notations understood by *sendmail* are listed in Table 31-3.

Table 31–3: Special Characters Allowed in Macro Text

Notation	Placed in Text
\b	Backspace character
\f	Formfeed character
\n	Newline character
\r	Carriage-return character
\\	Backslash character

All other escaped characters are taken as is. For example, the notation \X becomes a X, whereas the notation \b is converted to a backspace character (usually a CTRL-H). For example,

---

[*] But you still may need to declare an occasional macro in your configuration file to solve unusual problems.

```
DXO\bc May\, 1996     becomes → O^Hc May, 1996
```

Here, the \b is translated into a backspace (^H) character, and the \, is translated into a lone comma character.

Note that prior to V8.8, the first comma and all characters following it were stripped from the text unless the comma was quoted or escaped. For example,

```
DXMay, 1996     becomes → May
```

Beginning with V8.8 *sendmail*, the comma is no longer special in defined macros.

Quoted *text* will have the quotation marks stripped. Only double quotation marks are recognized. Multiple parts of *text* may be quoted, or text may be quoted entirely.

Trailing spaces are automatically stripped. If you need to keep trailing spaces you need to quote them:

```
DX"1996 "
```

Leading space characters are retained in *text* whether they are quoted or not. Spaces are harmless provided that the macro is used only in rules (because spaces are token separators); but if the macro is used to define other macros, problems can arise. For example,

```
Dw ourhost
DH nlm.nih.gov
Dj $w.$H
```

Here, the *text* of the $w and $H macros is used to define the $j macro. The $j macro is used in the HELO SMTP command and in the **Message-ID:** header line. The value given to $j by the above is

```
    ourhost. nlm.nih.gov
 ↑             ↑
 two         a space
 spaces
```

Here, the value of $j should contain a correctly formed, fully qualified domain name. The unwanted spaces cause it to become incorrectly formed, which can cause mail to fail.

31.4 Macro Names

Prior to V8.7 *sendmail*, macros could only have single characters as names. Beginning with V8.7, macros may be single- or multicharacter.

31.4.1 Single-Character Names

Prior to V8.7 *sendmail* the name of a macro was required to be a single character. Beginning with V8.7, the name of a macro may optionally be a single character. Any character may be used. However, *sendmail* uses many characters internally and requires that they serve specific purposes. In general, only uppercase letters should be employed as user-defined macro names. Arbitrary use of other characters can lead to unexpected results.

The character that is the macro's name must be a single-byte character. Multibyte international characters have only the first byte (or last, depending on the machine architecture) used for the macro's name, and what remains is joined to the *text*.

The high (most significant) bit of the character is always cleared (set to zero) by *sendmail*.

31.4.2 Multicharacter Names

Beginning with V8.7, macro names may be multicharacter. A multicharacter macro name must always appear inside a curly brace pair.* For example,

```
D{name}text
```

Here, **name** is one or more characters that form the macro name. If there are no characters between the curly braces, *sendmail* prints the following error and names the macro "{}":

```
Name required for macro/class
```

A multicharacter macro name may contain only letters, digits, and the underscore character. Each bad character between the curly braces (including spaces) will produce the following error and cause that character to be ignored:

```
Invalid macro/class character
```

In general, your macro names should always begin with an uppercase character. Macro names that begin with lowercase characters are reserved for the internal use of *sendmail*.

If the left curly brace is missing but the right is present, the macro name becomes the first letter following the D and the rest becomes the *text*:

---

* As an artifact of this scheme, a single character surrounded in curly braces is treated as if the curly braces were absent:

```
DXtext            ← a single character name
D{X}text          ← the same beginning with V8.7
```

```
Dname}text          → becomes →    n   ame}text
```

If the right curly brace is missing but the left is present, the following error is printed, and the macro is not defined

```
Unbalanced { on nametext
```

The maximum length of a macro name is hard-coded at 20 characters and cannot be changed with compile-time definitions. If you declare a macro name that (not counting the curly braces) is longer than 20 characters, the following error will be printed and the excess characters will become the value of an undefined name.

```
Macro/class name ({VeryLongMacroNameHere}) too long (20 chars max)
```

Because of the way multicharacter names are encoded into a single byte, there is a fixed limit on the number of multicharacter macro names that you may declare. That limit includes those multicharacter names internally defined by *sendmail*,[*] and those declared for class macros. There may be at most 96 multicharacter macro names. If you try to declare a 97th name, the following error will print and that definition will be ignored:

```
Macro/class {name}: too many long names
```

31.5 *Macro Expansion: $ and $&*

The value of a macro can be used by putting a $ character in front of the macro's name. For example, consider the following definition:

```
DXtext
```

Here, the macro named *X* is given *text* as its value.

If you later prefix a macro name with a $ character, you may use that value. This is called *expanding* a macro:

```
$X
```

Here, the expression $X tells *sendmail* to use the value stored in X (the *text*) rather than its name (*X*).

For multicharacter names, the process is the same, but the name is surrounded with curly braces:

```
D{Xxx}text          ← declare {Xxx}
${Xxx}          ,    ← use {Xxx}
```

---

[*] One for V8.7 and many for V8.8.

31.5.1 Macro Expansion Is Recursive

When *text* contains other macros, those other macros are also expanded. This process is recursive and continues until all macros have been expanded. For example, consider the following:

```
DAxxx
DByyy
DC$A.$B
DD$C.zzz
```

Here, the *text* for the macro D is `$C.zzz`. When the expression `$D` appears in a line in the configuration file, it is recursively expanded like this:

```
$D              → becomes →   $C.zzz
$C.zzz          → becomes →   $A.$B.zzz
$A.$B.zzz       → becomes →   xxx.$B.zzz
xxx.$B.zzz      → becomes →   xxx.yyy.zzz
```

Notice that when *sendmail* recursively expands a macro, it does so one macro at a time, always expanding the leftmost macro.

In rules, when *sendmail* expands a macro, it also tokenizes it. For example, placing the above `$D` in the following rule's LHS:

```
R$+@$D        $1
```

causes the LHS to contain seven tokens, rather than three:

```
R$+@xxx.yyy.zzz        $1
```

31.5.2 When Is a Macro Expanded?

A macro can either be expanded immediately or at runtime, depending on where the expansion takes place in the configuration file.

Macros are expanded in rule sets as the configuration file is read and parsed by *sendmail,* and (beginning with V8.7) so are macros in rule-set names (see §29.1.4) and in maps declared with the K configuration command (see §33.3). In other configuration lines, expansion is deferred until *sendmail* actually needs to use that value. In yet others, macros are neither recognized nor expanded.

To illustrate, macros used in header commands are not be expanded until the headers of a mail message are processed:

```
H?x?Full-Name: $x
```

Here, `$x` (see §31.10.42) may change as *sendmail* is running. It contains as its value the full name of the sender. Clearly, this macro should not be expanded until that full name is known.

On the other hand, macros in rules are always expanded *when the configuration file is read*. Therefore macros like $x should never be used in rules, because the configuration file is read long before mail is processed:

```
R$x        ($x)
```

Rules like this won't work because $x lacks a value when the configuration file is read. This rule will be expanded to become meaningless:

```
R        ( )
```

Note that the $*digit* positional operator (see §28.6.1) in the RHS may not be used to reference defined macros in the LHS. Consider this example, in which {HOST} has the value myhost:

```
R${HOST}      <$1>
```

The ${HOST} is expanded when the configuration file is read and is transformed into:

```
Rmyhost    <$1>    ← error
```

Here, the $1 has no wildcard operator in the LHS to reference and so will produce this error:

```
replacement $1 out of bounds
```

31.5.3 Use Value as Is with $&

For those situations in which a macro should not be recursively expanded, but rather should be used in rules as is, V8 *sendmail* offers the $& prefix. For example, consider the following RHS of a rule:

```
R...       $w.$&m
```

When *sendmail* encounters this RHS in the configuration file, it recursively expands $w into its final text value (where that text value is your hostname, such as *lady*). But because the m macro is prefixed with $&, it is not expanded.

This could be useful, because it appears to offer a way to delay expansion of macros in rules until after the configuration file is read. Unfortunately such is not always the case, because the expanded text returned by the $& prefix is always a single token. That is, because the above is tokenized before each token is evaluated, it appears in the workspace as

```
lady . $m
```

Here, the $m will expand to its current value, say, *our.domain*, but that expansion will remain a single token:

```
lady . our.domain
```

When tokens are compared during rule-set processing, they are compared token by token. Consequently, the single token above will not match the individual tokens of a real address, as shown on the left:

```
our       does not match our.domain
.         does not match our.domain
domain    does not match our.domain
```

The $& prefix is intended to provide a way to access macros that are given values after the configuration file is read. Therefore the failure of $& to *recursively* expand is the result of an implementation designed to meet the limited goal of accessing those runtime macros. (See §33.8.4 for ways to use the **dequote** database class to circumvent this restriction.)

To illustrate one application of $&, consider the client/hub setup described in the tutorial. In that setup, all mail sent from a client machine is forwarded to the hub for eventual delivery. If the client were to run a *sendmail* daemon to receive mail for local delivery, a mail loop could (in the absence of an MX record) develop where a message would bounce back and forth between the client and the hub, eventually failing.

To break such a loop, a rule must be devised that recognizes that a received message is from the hub:

```
R$+                $: $&r @ $&s <$1>      Get protocol and host
R$mtp @ $H <$+>    $#local $: $1          Local delivery breaks a loop
R$* <$+>           $#smtp $@ $H $: $2     Punt to hub
```

These rules appear in rule set 0. By the time they are reached, other rules have forwarded any nonlocal mail to the hub. What is left in the workspace is a lone username. The first rule above matches the workspace and rewrites it to be the sending protocol ($&r; see §31.10.31), an @, the sending host ($&s, see §31.10.33), and the username in angle brackets:

```
user    → becomes →    smtp@hub<user>
```

The second rule checks to make sure the message was received with the SMTP protocol from the hub. If it was, then the **local** delivery agent is used to deliver the message on the local machine. If it was received from any other host or by any other protocol, the second rule fails and the third forwards the lone user address to the hub.

31.6 *Macro Conditionals: $?, $|, and $.*

Occasionally, it is necessary to test a macro to see whether a value has been assigned to it. To perform such a test, a special prefix and two operators are used. The general form is

```
        if         else        endif
        ↓           ↓            ↓
     $?x text1 $|  text2 $.
        ↑           ↑
   if x is defined   if x is not defined
```

This expression yields one of two possible values: **text1** if the macro named **x** has a value, **text2** if it doesn't. The entire above expression, starting with the $? and ending with the $., yields a single value, which may contain multiple tokens.

The following, for example, includes the configuration-file version in the SMTP greeting message but does so only if that version (in $v; see §31.10.38) is defined:

```
O SmtpGreetingMessage=$j Sendmail ($v/$?Z$Z$|generic$.) ready at $b
                                          ↑
                                         note
```

Here the parenthetical version information is expressed one way if **Z** has a value (like **1.4**):

```
($v/$Z)
```

but is expressed differently if **Z** lacks a value:

```
($v/generic)
```

The *else* part ($|) of this conditional expression is optional. If it is omitted, the result is the same as if the **text2** were omitted:

```
$?xtext1$|$.
$?xtext1$.
```

Both of the preceding yield the same result. If **x** has a value, then **text1** becomes the value of the entire expression. If **x** lacks a value, then the entire expression lacks a value (produces no tokens).

Note that it is *not* advisable to use the $? conditional expression in rules. It may not have the intended effect, because macro conditionals are expanded when the configuration file is read.

31.6.1 *Conditionals May Nest*

V8 *sendmail* allows conditionals to nest. To illustrate, consider the following expression:

```
$?x $?y both $| xonly $. $| $?y yonly $| none $. $.
```

This is just like the example in the previous section:

```
$?x text1 $| text2 $.
```

except that **text1** and **text2** are both conditionals:

```
text1 = $?y both $| xonly $.
text2 = $?y yonly $| none $.
```

The grouping when conditionals nest is from the outside in. In the following example, parentheses have been inserted to show the groupings (they are not a part of either expression):

```
($?x (text1) $| (text2) $.)
($?x ($?y both $| xonly $.) $| ($?y yonly $| none $.) $.)
```

Interpretation is from left to right. The logic of the second line above is therefore this: If both $x and $y have values, the result is **both**. If $x has a value but $y lacks one, the result is **xonly**. If $x lacks a value but $y has one, the result is **yonly**. And if both lack values, the result is **none**.

The *sendmail* program does not enforce or check for balance in nested conditionals. Each **$?** should have a corresponding **$.** to balance it. If they do not balance, *sendmail* will not detect the problem. Instead, it may interpret the expression in a way that you did not intend.

The depth to which conditionals may be nested is limited only by our ability to easily comprehend the result. More than two deep is not recommended, and more than three deep is vigorously discouraged.

31.7 *Categories of Macros*

At the end of this chapter we list all the macros in alphabetical order for easy lookup and explain each in detail. Here, we present them grouped by application with only a brief description.

31.7.1 *Macros and the System Identity*

The nature of email addresses requires that *sendmail* have a firm understanding of the machine on which it is running. The **-d0.4** debugging switch (see §37.5.2) causes *sendmail* to print its understanding of what the local machine is. A portion of that output displays the value of four key macros:

```
============ SYSTEM IDENTITY (after readcf) ============
        (short domain name) $w = here
    (canonical domain name) $j = here.our.domain
           (subdomain name) $m = our.domain
                (node name) $k = here
========================================================
```

The short domain name (in $w; see §31.10.40) is simply the name of the local host without any domain information added as a suffix. The canonical domain name (in $j; see §31.10.20) is the fully qualified and official name of the local machine. The subdomain name (in $m; see §31.10.24) is just the domain part of the canonical name without a leading dot. And the node name (in $k; see §31.10.21) is the UUCP name of the local machine.

In addition to these macros, *sendmail* initializes the class $=w with a list of alternative names for the local host (see §32.5.8) and class $=m with a list of the local domains (see §32.5.3).

31.7.2 Macros and the Date

The concept of time can take on different meanings depending on whether we are talking about the sender, the recipient, the remote machine, or the local machine. To keep different times separate, *sendmail* employs an assortment of macros, as shown in Table 31-4.

Table 31–4: Macros That Store Dates

Macro	§	Description
$a	31.10.2	The origin date in RFC822 format
$b	31.10.3	The current date in RFC822 format
$d	31.10.10	The current date in UNIX *ctime*(3) format
$t	31.10.35	Current time in seconds

31.8 Macros with the m4 Technique

The various features of the *m4* technique use uppercase single-character macro names. The complete list of them is shown in Table 31-5. Some of these are defined by using the appropriate **define** *m4* command (see below). Others are predefined for you by the *m4* technique. See the appropriate section reference for a full description of how to use each macro.

Table 31-5: Macros Reserved with the m4 Technique

Macro	§	Description
$B	31.10.5	The BITNET relay
$C	31.10.9	The hostname of the DECnet relay
$E	31.10.13	X.400 relay (unused)
$F	31.10.15	FAX relay
$H	31.10.18	The mail hub
$L	31.10.23	Unknown Local User relay
$M	31.10.25	Who we are masquerading as
$R	31.10.32	The relay for unqualified names (deprecated)
$S	31.10.34	The Smart Host
$U	31.10.37	The UUCP name to override $k
$V	31.10.39	The UUCP relay (for class $=V)
$W	31.10.41	The UUCP relay (for class $=W)
$X	31.10.43	The UUCP relay (for class $=X)
$Y	31.10.45	The UUCP relay for unclassified hosts
$Z	31.10.47	The version of this m4 configuration

A few *m4* macros can be defined by using the *m4* **define** command. For example, here is how you define the BITNET relay with the BITNET_RELAY keyword:

```
define(`BITNET_RELAY', `host.domain')dnl
```

See Table 31-6 for a list of those *m4* macros that can be defined. The leftmost column in that table shows the keyword to use.

Table 31-6: Macros Declared with Special m4 Names

m4 name	Macro	§	Description
BITNET_RELAY	$B	31.10.5	The BITNET relay
confCF_VERSION	$Z	31.10.47	The version of this m4 configuration
confDOMAIN_NAME	$j	31.10.20	Official canonical name
confMAILER_NAME	$n	31.10.26	Error message sender
FAX_RELAY	$F	31.10.15	FAX relay
LUSER_RELAY	$L	31.10.23	Local user relay
MAIL_HUB	$H	31.10.18	The mail hub

31.9 Pitfalls

- Macros that are given values while *sendmail* processes mail may not get the value expected. If that happens, careful hand-tracing of rule sets is required to find the fault. For example, the value in $g (see §31.10.16) is the result of sender address rewriting and rewriting by the rule set that is specified in the

S= equate of the selected delivery agent. Because $g is used to define the
From: header line, errors in that line should be traced through errors in the S=
equate's rule set.

- Macros can have other macros as their values. The *sendmail* program expands
  macros recursively. As a consequence, unintentional loops in macro definitions can cause *sendmail* to appear to hang and to eventually segmentation
  fault and core dump.

31.10 Alphabetized Reference

The *sendmail* program reserves all lowercase letters, punctuation characters, and
digits for its own use. For multicharacter names it reserves all those that begin with
an underscore or a lowercase letter. Table 31-7 lists all the macro names that have
special internal meaning to *sendmail*. Included in this list are macros that are used
by the *m4* configuration technique.[*]

Table 31-7: *Reserved Macros*

Macro	§	Description
$_	31.10.1	RFC1413-validation & IP source route (V8.1 and above)
$a	31.10.2	The origin date in RFC822 format
$b	31.10.3	The current date in RFC822 format
${bodytype}	31.10.4	The ESMTP BODY parameter
$B	31.10.5	The BITNET relay
$c	31.10.6	The hop count
${client_addr}	31.10.7	The connecting host's IP address
${client_name}	31.10.8	The connecting host's canonical name
$C	31.10.9	The hostname of the DECnet relay (m4 technique)
$d	31.10.10	The current date in UNIX *ctime*(3)
$e	34.8.65	SMTP greeting message (V8.6 and earlier)
${envid}	31.10.12	The original DSN envelope ID (V8.8 and above)
$E	31.10.13	X.400 relay (unused) (m4 technique)
$f	31.10.14	The sender's address
$F	31.10.15	FAX relay (m4 technique)
$g	31.10.16	The sender's address relative to recipient
$h	31.10.17	Host part of the recipient address
$H	31.10.18	The mail hub (m4 technique)
$i	31.10.19	The queue identifier
$j	31.10.20	Official canonical name

---

[*] Note that these are the exception to the usual rule in that they are all uppercase letters. In a way this
makes sense, because they are being used by the configuration file, not by the internals of the *sendmail* program.

Table 31–7: Reserved Macros (continued)

Macro	§	Description
$k	31.10.21	UUCP node name (V8.1 and above)
$l	34.8.72	UNIX **From** format (V8.6 and earlier)
$L	31.10.23	Local user relay (m4 technique)
$m	31.10.24	The DNS domain name (V8.1 and above)
$M	31.10.25	Who we are masquerading as (m4 technique)
$n	31.10.26	Error message sender
$o	34.8.45	Token separation characters (V8.6 and earlier)
${opMode}	31.10.28	The startup operating mode (V8.7 and above)
$p	31.10.29	The *sendmail* process ID
$q	31.10.30	Default form of the sender address (V8.6 and earlier)
$r	31.10.31	The protocol used
$R	31.10.32	The relay for unqualified names (m4 technique)
$s	31.10.33	Sender host's name
$S	31.10.34	The Smart Host (m4 technique)
$t	31.10.35	Current time in seconds
$u	31.10.36	Recipient's username
$U	31.10.37	The UUCP name to override $k
$v	31.10.38	The *sendmail* program's version
$V	31.10.39	The UUCP relay (for class $=V) (m4 technique)
$w	31.10.40	The short name of this host
$W	31.10.41	The UUCP relay (for class $=W) (m4 technique)
$x	31.10.42	The full name of the sender
$X	31.10.43	The UUCP relay (for class $=X) (m4 technique)
$y	31.10.44	Name of the controlling TTY
$Y	31.10.45	The UUCP relay for unclassified hosts
$z	31.10.46	Recipient's home directory
$Z	31.10.47	The version of this m4 configuration (m4 technique)

The following pages present a complete reference for each reserved macro. They are presented in alphabetical order for ease of lookup, rather than in the order in which they typically appear in configuration files.

$_   *(V8.1 and above)*

31.10.1   *RFC1413-validation and IP source route*

RFC1413, *Identification Protocol*, describes a method for identifying the user and host that initiate network connections.[*] It relies on the originating host, which must be running the *identd*(8) daemon.

---

[*] Bugs in Ultrix and OSF/1 (and maybe others) break the *ident* protocol. For an explanation, see *conf.h*.

When the V8 *sendmail* daemon receives a network connection request (and if `Timeout.ident` option, see §34.8.70.10, is nonzero), it attempts to connect to the originating host's *identd* service. If the originating host supports identification, *sendmail* reads the login name of the user who initiated the connection. The *sendmail* program then appends an @ and the name of the originating host to it. If the name of the originating host is an IP number in square brackets, *sendmail* attempts to convert the number to a hostname. The final result, in the form *user@host*, is assigned to $_.

When *sendmail* is run on the local machine, it sets $_ to be the name of the user that corresponds to the *uid* of the process that ran *sendmail*. It gets that name by calling *getpwuid*(3). If the call fails, the name is set to the string:

```
Unknown UID: num
```

Here, *num* is the *uid* for which a login name could not be found.

Next, an @ and the name of the local machine are appended to the name, and the result is assigned to $_.

Beginning with V8.7 *sendmail*, attempts at IP source routing can also be stored in this macro. If *sendmail* was compiled with IP_SRCROUTE defined, that IP source routing information will be added to $_ after the user and host described above. The format of this additional information is described in §18.8.13.

The $_ macro is not used by *sendmail*. Rather, it is offered as a means for the administrator to use authentication information. One possibility would be to include it in the `Received:` header:

```
HReceived: $?sfrom $s $.$?_($_) $.by $j ($v/$Z) id $i; $b
```

Another possibility is to customize *checkcompat()* in *conf.c*. One might, for example, wish to reject any mail in which the host part of $_ does not match the contents of $s (see §31.10.33). §20.2.4 shows an example of how to code this.

$a   *(All versions)*

31.10.2   *The origin date in RFC822 format*

The $a macro holds the origin date of a mail message (the date and time that the original message was sent). It holds a date in ARPAnet format, defined in RFC822, section 5.1, and amended by RFC1123, section 5.2.14.

The *sendmail* program obtains that date in one of the following four ways:

- When *sendmail* first begins to run, it presets several date-oriented macros internally to the current date and time. Among those are the macros $t, $d,

$b, and $a. This initialization is done after the configuration file is read, so all but $b may be given initial values in that file.

- Whenever *sendmail* collects information from the stored header of a message (whether after message collection, during processing of the queue, or when saving to the queue), it sets the value of $a. If a Posted-Date: header exists, the date from that line is used. Otherwise, if a Date: header exists, that date is used. Note that no check is made by *sendmail* to ensure that the date in $a is indeed in RFC822 format. Of necessity it must trust that the originating program has adhered to that standard.

- When *sendmail* notifies the user of an error, it takes the origin date from $b (the current date in RFC822 format, and places that value into $a.

$a is chiefly intended for use in configuration-file header definitions. It may also be used in delivery agent A= equates (argument vectors), although it is of little value in that case.

$a is transient. If defined in the configuration file or in the command line, that definition may be ignored by *sendmail*.

$b

(All versions)

31.10.3   *The current date in RFC822 format*

The $b macro contains the current date in ARPAnet format, as defined in RFC822, section 5.1, and amended by RFC1123, section 5.2.14.

Because $b holds the current date and time, *sendmail* frequently updates the value in that macro. When *sendmail* first starts to run, it places the current date and time into $b. Thereafter, each time an SMTP connection is made and each time the queue is processed, the value of the date and time in that macro is updated.

If the system call to *time*(3) should fail, the value stored in $b becomes Wed Dec 31 15:59:59 1969,[*] and no other indication of an error is given.

$b is chiefly intended for use in configuration-file header definitions that require ARPAnet format (such as Received:, see §35.10.25). It may also be used in delivery agent A= equates (argument vectors), although it is of little value in that case.

$b is transient. If it is defined in the configuration file or in the command line, that definition may be ignored by *sendmail*.

---

[*] The actual time depends on the local time zone.

${bodytype}   *(V8.8 and above)*

31.10.4   *The ESMTP BODY parameter*

MIME (multimedia) support in V8 *sendmail* has been coupled to ESMTP (Extended SMTP) of the new BODY parameter for the MAIL command. That parameter tells *sendmail* whether it is dealing with 7-bit or 8-bit MIME data:

```
MAIL From: <address> BODY=7BIT
MAIL From: <address> BODY=8BITMIME
```

The parameter specified for the BODY (7BIT or 8BITMIME) is the value stored in the ${bodytype} macro.

The ${bodytype} macro is intended to be used as part of the delivery agent's A= equate (see §30.4.1). It provides a means to pass this information to delivery agent programs as part of their command lines.

${bodytype} is transient. If defined in the configuration file or in the command line, that definition may be ignored by *sendmail*. Note that the –B command-line switch (see §36.7.1) can be used to specify a value to be stored in ${bodytype}, but that value too is transient.

$B   *(m4 technique)*

31.10.5   *The BITNET relay*

When configuring with the *m4* technique, you can specify a host that will transfer mail between the Internet and BITNET. Mail to BITNET may then be sent by appending the pseudo-domain .BITNET to an address. For example,

```
user@ucbicsi.BITNET
```

Here, ucbicsi is a BITNET host.

To allow your configuration file to handle this form of address, you need to declare the name of your BITNET relay using the BITNET_RELAY keyword:

```
define(`BITNET_RELAY', `relayhost')dnl
```

This statement causes the rule for BITNET to be included in your configuration file and causes *relayhost* to be assigned as the value of $B. (See §19.4.5 for a description of how to include a delivery agent specification with *relayhost*.)

See also bitdomain FEATURE (see §19.6.9) for a way to convert BITNET addresses to Internet addresses for hosts that have both.

$c
                                                                                        (All versions)

31.10.6   *The hop count*

The c macro is used to store the number of times a mail message has been forwarded from site to site. It is a count of the number of **Received:**, **Via:**, and **Mail-From:** header lines in a message.

The value in $c is not used by *sendmail*. Rather, it is made available for use in configuration-file header line definitions. When calculating the hop count for comparison to the **MaxHopCount** (h) option (see §34.8.36), *sendmail* uses internal variables.

$c is transient. If defined in the configuration file or in the command line, that definition may be ignored by *sendmail*.

${client_addr}
                                                                                  (V8.8 and above)

31.10.7   *The connecting host's IP address*

The ${client_addr} macro is assigned its value when a host connects to the running daemon. The value assigned is the IP address of that connecting host and is the same as the IP address stored in the $_ macro, but without the surrounding square brackets and other non-IP information.

The ${client_addr} macro can be useful in the **check_rcpt** (see §29.10.1) and **check_mail** (see §29.10.2) rule sets. It can, for example, be used detect whether an external host is trying to send external mail through your outgoing firewall machine.

```
D{ourdomain}123.45.6
Scheck_mail
R$*                     $: $(dequote "" $&{client_addr} $)
R${ourdomain}.$-        $@ Okay our domain
R$*                     $#error $@ 5.7.1 $: "cannot send out from the outside"
```

Here, the first rule transfers the value of ${client_addr} into the workspace. The $& prefix (see §31.5.3) prevents that macro from wrongly being expanded when the configuration file is read. The second rule compares the domain part of your IP domain (that of your internal network) to the workspace. If they match, the connection is from a host in your internal domain space. If not, an error is generated in response to the SMTP MAIL command.

Note that this rule set rejects all mail coming from outside your network, which may be overkill (depending, of course, on what you want). It is really useful only at sites that have two firewalls, one for incoming traffic and one for outgoing traffic. This rule set might go on the outgoing firewall.

${client_addr} is transient. If it is defined in the configuration file or in the command line, that definition may be ignored by *sendmail*. Note that ${client_addr} is *not* guaranteed to be available in the check_compat rule set (see §29.10.4) or in the check_relay rule set (see §29.10.3).

${client_name}   *(V8.8 and above)*

31.10.8   *The connecting host's canonical name*

The ${client_name} macro is assigned its value when a host connects to the running daemon. This macro holds as its value, the canonical hostname of that connecting host, which is the same as the hostname stored in the $_ macro.

The ${client_name} macro is useful in the check_rcpt (see §29.10.1) and check_mail (see §29.10.2) rule sets. It can, for example, be used to see whether the connecting host is your firewall machine:

```
D{firewall}fw.our.domain
Scheck_mail
R$*                          $: $(dequote "" $&{client_name} $)
R${firewall}                 $@ Okay our firewall machine
R$*                          $#error $@ 5.7.1 $: "can only accept from our firewall"
```

Here, the first rule transfers the value of ${client_name} into the workspace. The $& prefix (see §31.5.3) prevents that macro from wrongly being expanded when the configuration file is read. The second rule compares the name of the firewall to that workspace. If they match, the connecting host was indeed the firewall machine.

${client_name} is transient. If it is defined in the configuration file or in the command line, that definition may be ignored by *sendmail*. Note that ${client_name} is *not* guaranteed to be available in the check_compat rule set (see §29.10.4) or in the check_relay rule set (see §29.10.3).

$C   *(m4 technique)*

31.10.9   *The DECnet relay*

DECnet addresses are of the form *node::user*. They can be handled by defining a host that will relay them into your DECnet network. Using the *m4* technique, you enable DECnet like this:

```
define(`DECNET_RELAY', `relay_host')dnl
```

Mail addressed to *node::user* will then be forwarded to *relay_host*, as will any Internet-style addresses that end in the pseudo-domain .DECNET, such as *user@domain.DECNET*. $C holds the name of the *relay_host*. (See §19.4.5 for a description of how to include a delivery agent specification with *relay_host*.)

$d

31.10.10   *The current date in UNIX ctime(3) format*

The $d macro holds the current date and time. $d is given its value at the same
time $a is defined. The only difference between the two is that $a contains the
date in RFC822 format, whereas $d contains the same date in UNIX *ctime*(3) format.

The form of a date in *ctime*(3) format is generally[*]

```
Sun Dec 26 01:03:52 1999\n\0
```

When *sendmail* stores this form of date into $d, it converts the trailing newline
(the \n) into a zero, thus stripping the newline from the date.

$e

31.10.11   *The SMTP greeting message*

Prior to V8.7 *sendmail* the $e macro was used to hold the SMTP greeting message.
That role has been taken over by the SmtpGreetingMessage option. See §34.8.65
for a description of both this $e macro and that new option.

${envid}

31.10.12   *The original DSN envelope ID*

RFC1891 specifies that the keyword ENVID may be given to the MAIL ESMTP command:

```
MAIL From: <address> ENVID=envelopeID
```

ENVID is used to propagate a consistent envelope identifier (distinct from the **Message-ID:** header; see §35.10.19), that will be permanently associated with the
message. The **envelopeID** may contain any ASCII characters between ! and ~,
except + and =. Any characters outside that range must be encoded by prefixing
an uppercase, two-digit, hexadecimal representation of it with a plus. For example, an **envelopeID** composed of the letter X followed by a delete character would
be encoded like this:

```
X+7F
```

When mail is received over an SMTP channel and an ENVID identifier is specified,
that identifier is saved as part of the envelope information. The value of the ENVID
identifier is saved in and restored from the qf file's Z line (see §23.9.17). For
bounced mail, the ENVID identifier is printed with the **Original-Envelope-Id:**
DSN header (see RFC1894) as part of the DSN MIME body. Beginning with V8.8

---

[*] The format produced by *ctime*(3) varies depending on the area of the world.

sendmail, an ENVID identifier can also be assigned to a message with the −V command-line switch (see §36.7.40).

When mail is delivered, the value of the envelope's ENVID identifier is saved in the ${envid} macro. That macro is available for use with delivery agents that understand DSN.

${envid} is transient. If it is defined in the configuration file or in the command line, that definition may be ignored by *sendmail*.

$E   *(m4 technique)*

31.10.13   *X.400 relay*

The $E macro is reserved for the future use of the *m4* technique. It will be used to hold the name of the X.400 relay.

$f   *(All versions)*

31.10.14   *The sender's address*

The $f macro is used to hold the address of the sender. That address can be obtained by *sendmail* from any of a variety of places:

- During an SMTP conversation the sending host specifies the address of the sender by issuing a MAIL SMTP command.

- Trusted users are those declared as part of the t class (see §32.5.7).* Those users, and programs running under the identity of those users, may specify the address of the sender by using the −f command-line switch when running *sendmail*.

- In processing a message from the queue, the sender's address is taken from the qf file's S line.

- In processing bounced mail, the sender becomes the name specified by the value of $n, usually *mailer-daemon*.

- In the absence of the above, *sendmail* tries to use the user identity of the invoking program to determine the sender.

Once *sendmail* has determined the sender (possibly aliased), it rewrites the address found with rule sets 3, 1, and 4. The rewritten address is then made the value of $f.

---

* Prior to V8.1 this was set with a T configuration command. This feature was eliminated in versions V8.1 through V8.6 and restored in V8.7.

$f is intended for use in both configuration-file header commands and delivery agent A= equates. $f differs from $g in that $g undergoes additional processing to produce a true return address. When *sendmail* queues a mail message and when it processes the queue, the values in $f and $g are identical.

$f is transient. If it is defined in the configuration file or in the command line, that definition may be ignored by *sendmail.*

$F   *(m4 technique)*

31.10.15   *The FAX relay*

At many sites, faxes can be sent via email. When the host that dispatches those faxes is not the local host, you need to relay FAX mail to the host that can dispatch faxes. This ability is enabled by defining that relay host with the *m4* technique:

```
define(`FAX_RELAY', `relay_host')dnl
```

This causes all mail that ends with the pseudo domain .FAX to be forwarded to *relay_host*. It also assigns the value *relay_host* to $F. (See §19.4.5 for a description of how to include a delivery agent specification with *relay_host*.)

$g   *(All versions)*

31.10.16   *The sender's address relative to recipient*

The $g macro is identical to $f except that it undergoes additional rule-set processing to translate it into a full return address. During delivery the sender's address is processed by rule sets 3, 1, and 4 and then placed into $f. That rewritten address is further processed by 3 and 1 again, then custom rewritten by the rule set specified in the S= equate of the delivery agent. Finally, it is rewritten by rule set 4, and the result is placed into $g.

$g holds the official return address for the sender. As such, it should be used in the **From:** and **Return-Path:** header definitions.

The S= equate for each delivery agent must perform all necessary translations to produce a value for $g that is correct. Because the form of a correct return address varies depending on the delivery agent, other rule sets should generally not be used for this translation.

Ordinarily, RFC822 comments (see §35.3.4) are restored when $g is used in headers. To omit those comments (perhaps for security reasons), you may use the F=c delivery agent flag (see §30.8.14).

$g is transient. If it is defined in the configuration file or in the command line, that definition may be ignored by *sendmail.*

$h   *(All versions)*

31.10.17   *Host part of the recipient address*

Rule set 0 (see §29.6) is used to resolve the recipient address into a triple: the delivery agent (with $#), the host part of the address (with $@), and the recipient user's name (with $:). The host part, from the $@, is made the value of $h. Once $h's value has been set, it undergoes no further rule-set parsing.

$h is intended for use in the A= equate (see §30.4.1) of delivery agent definitions. Normally, it is converted to all lowercase before use, but that conversion can be suppressed with the F=h delivery agent flag (see §30.8.23).

$h is transient. If defined in the configuration file or in the command line, that definition may be ignored by *sendmail.*

$H   *(m4 technique)*

31.10.18   *The mail hub*

The *m4* nullclient feature (see §19.6.20) causes all mail to be sent to a central hub machine for handling. Part of what it does is to define the *m4* macro MAIL_HUB:

```
define(`MAIL_HUB', `hub')dnl
```

This also causes $H to be defined as *hub.* If $H has a value, and if $R (the LOCAL_RELAY, see §31.10.32) does not, all local email is forwarded to *hub.* If $R is defined it takes precedence over $H for some mail. See §19.6.41 for a description of MAIL_HUB and how it interacts with LOCAL_RELAY.

$i   *(All versions)*

31.10.19   *The queue identifier*

Each queued message is identified by a unique identifier (see §23.2.1). The $i macro contains as its value that identifier. Prior to V8.6 *sendmail,* $i had a value assigned to it only when a file was first placed into the queue. Beginning with V8.6 *sendmail,* $i is also given a value when the queue file is processed.

$i is not used by *sendmail* internally. It should be trusted for use only in the Received: and Message-ID: headers.

$j

31.10.20
Our official canonical name

The j macro is used to hold the fully qualified domain name of the local machine. It *must* be defined in the configuration file.[*]

A fully qualified domain name is one that begins with the local hostname, which is followed by a dot and all the components of the local domain.

The hostname part is the name of the local machine. That name is defined at boot time in ways that vary with the version of UNIX.

The local domain refers to the DNS domain, not to the NIS domain. If DNS is running, the domain is defined in the */etc/resolv.conf* file, for example,

```
domain wash.dc.gov
```

At many sites the local hostname is already fully qualified. To tell whether your site uses just the local hostname, run *sendmail* with a −d0.4 switch:

```
% /usr/lib/sendmail -d0.4 -bt < /dev/null
canonical name: wash             ← not fully qualified
canonical name: wash.dc.gov      ← fully qualified
```

The j macro is used in two ways by *sendmail*. Because $j holds the fully qualified domain name, *sendmail* uses that name to avoid making SMTP connections to itself. It also uses that name in all phases of SMTP conversations that require the local machine's identity. One indication of an improperly formed $j is the following SMTP error:

```
553 wash.dc.gov.dc.gov host name configuration error
```

Here, $j was wrongly defined by adding the local domain to a $w that already included that domain:

```
# Our domain
DDdc.gov
# Our fully qualified name
Dj$w.$D
```

One way to tell whether $j contains the correct value is to send mail to yourself. Examine the **Received:** headers. The name of the local host must be fully qualified where it appears in them:

---

[*] Except in V8 *sendmail*, where $j is automatically defined to be the fully qualified canonical name of the local host. However, it is still possible to redefine $j if necessary, for example, if *sendmail* cannot figure out your fully qualified canonical name or if your machine has multiple network interfaces and *sendmail* chooses the name associated with the wrong interface.

```
Received: by wash.dc.gov      ...other text here
              ↑
        must be a fully qualified domain name
```

$j is also used: in the **Message-Id:** header definition; and as the canonical host-name following the HELO or EHLO command.

For all but V8 *sendmail*, $j *must* be defined in the configuration file. For V8 it is automatically defined. It must *never* be defined in the command line. $j must appear at the beginning of the definition of the **SmtpGreetingMessage** option (formerly $e, see 34.8.65). In using SunOS *sendmail.mx*, $w must also be the fully qualified domain name.

$k   *(V8.1 and above)*

31.10.21   *Our UUCP node name*

The UUCP suite of software gets the name of the local host from the *uname*(2) system call, whereas *sendmail* gets the name of the local host from the *gethostbyname*(3) system call. For *sendmail* to easily handle UUCP addresses, V8 *sendmail* also makes use of the *uname*(2) function.

First the host part of the fully qualified name returned by *gethostbyname*(3) is saved as the first string in the class $=w. Then *uname*(2) is called. If the call succeeds, the macro $k and the class k are both given the *nodename* value returned. If the call fails, both are given the same hostname value that was given to the $j. If the system does not have *uname*(2) available (if HASUNAME was *not* defined when *sendmail* was compiled; see §18.8.9), *sendmail* simulates it. The *sendmail* program's internal replacement for *uname* begins by reading */etc/whoami*. If that file does not exist or cannot be read, *sendmail* scans */usr/include/whoami.h* for a line beginning **#define sysname**. If that fails and if *sendmail* was compiled with TRUST_POPEN* defined (see §18.8.51), *sendmail* executes the following command and reads its output as the UUCP node name:

```
uname -l
```

If all these fail, $k is set to be the same as $j.

$k is assigned its value when *sendmail* first begins to run. It can be given a new value either in the configuration file or from the command line. The **-d0.22** debugging switch (see §37.5.6) can be used to watch *uname*() fail.

---

* TRUST_POPEN is a security risk. Instead of defining it, consider creating an */etc/whoami* file and populating it or defining $k directly in your configuration file.

$l (lowercase L)   *(V8.6 and earlier)*

31.10.22   *The From format*

Prior to V8.7 *sendmail*, the l macro was used to define the look of the five character "**From** " header, and the format of the line was used to separate one message
from another in a file of many mail messages. This role has been assumed by the
UnixFromLine option. See §34.8.72 for a description of both this l macro and that
new option.

$L   *(m4 technique)*

31.10.23   *The Unknown Local User relay*

A local user is one who evaluates to delivery on the local machine, even after
aliasing. By defining LUSER_RELAY:

```
define(`LUSER_RELAY', `relay_host')dnl
```

any username that is not found in the *passwd*(5) file will be forwarded to
relay_host. This check is made after aliasing but before processing of the `~/.for-
ward` file. The *relay_host* is assigned to the $L macro. The *m4* technique then
adds rules to rule set 5 of the configuration file that cause the user to be looked
up with the **user** database class (see the **name** keyword for that class in §33.8.20).
If the user's name is not found, the message is forwarded to the host defined by
$L. (See §19.4.5 for a description of how to include a delivery agent specification
with *relay_host*.)

$m   *(V8.1 and above)*

31.10.24   *Domain part of hostname*

Under V8 *sendmail*[*] the $m macro is used to store the domain part of the local
host's fully qualified name. A fully qualified name begins with the local hostname
followed by a dot and all the components of the local DNS domain.

The value in $m is derived from $w. When V8 *sendmail* first starts to run, it calls
gethostname(3) to get the name of the local machine. If that call fails, it sets that
local name to be *localhost*. Then *sendmail* calls *gethostbyname*(3) to find the official name for the local host, which is assigned to $w as that macro's initial value.
V8 *sendmail* then looks for the leftmost dot in $w. If it finds one, everything from
the first character following that dot to the end of the name then becomes the
value for $m:

---

[*] $m is the NIS domain for pre-V8 versions of Sun *sendmail*, and $m is the original user address for IDA
sendmail.

```
host.domain
     ↑
```
domain part made the value of $m

$m is initialized before the configuration file is read. Consequently, it may be redefined in the configuration file or as a part of the command line.

$M   *(m4 technique)*

31.10.25   *Whom we are masquerading as*

When you define MASQUERADE_AS using the *m4* configuration technique, you both enable masquerading (see §19.6.42) and assign that hostname to this $M macro. Note that defining $M will not enable masquerading. You must use the MASQUERADE_AS *m4* configuration command to enable this service.

$n   *(All versions)*

31.10.26   *The error message sender*

The $n macro contains the name of the person from whom failed mail is returned. Traditionally, that value is the name *mailer-daemon.*

When delivery fails and notification of that failure is being prepared to be sent to the originating sender, *sendmail* "fakes up" a header. That header prepends the original header (and any included error messages). The sender of the error mail message (and the sender in the envelope) is taken from $n.

The n macro must contain either a real user's name or a name that resolves to a real user through aliasing. If *sendmail* cannot resolve $n to a real user, the following message is logged, and the returned error mail message is saved in */usr/tmp/dead.letter* (see §18.8.34):

```
Can't parse myself!
```

When an error mail message is sent, $f (see §31.10.14) is given the value of $n. Prior to V8.7, $n *must* be defined in the configuration file. Beginning with V8.7 *sendmail,* $n is automatically defined as MAILER-DAEMON when *sendmail* first starts up.

$o   *(V8.6 and earlier)*

31.10.27   *Token separation operators*

Prior to V8.7 the $o macro stored as its value a sequence of characters, any one of which could be used to separate the components of an address into tokens (see §8.3). That role has been taken over by the V8.7 OperatorChars option (see §34.8.45).

For backward compatibility the $o macro is still honored by V8.7 *sendmail* in pre-version 7 configuration files (see §27.5).

${opMode}   *(V8.7 and above)*

31.10.28   *The startup operating mode*

Beginning with V8.7, the ${opMode} holds as its value the operating mode that *sendmail* was started with. The operating mode is set with the **-b** command line switch (see §36.7.2). For example, if *sendmail* were started as a daemon with **-bd**, the value in ${opMode} would become **d**.

Once set, ${opMode} retains its initial value as long as *sendmail* runs. It can be changed only by defining it in the configuration file. Currently, ${opMode} is used only in rule sets by the *m4* `redirect` FEATURE (see §19.6.21).

$p   *(All versions)*

31.10.29   *The sendmail process id*

The **p** macro contains the process ID of the *sendmail* that executes the delivery agent. Every process (running program) under UNIX has a unique identification number associated with it (a process ID). Process IDs are necessary to differentiate one incantation of a program from another. The *sendmail* program *fork*(2)'s often to perform tasks (like delivery) while performing other tasks (such as listening for incoming SMTP connections). All copies share the name *sendmail*; each has a unique process ID number.

$p is intended for use in header definitions but may also be used in the **A=** equate (see §30.4.1) of delivery agents.

$p is transient. If it is defined in the configuration file or in the command line, that definition may be ignored by *sendmail*.

$q   *(V8.6 and earlier)*

31.10.30   *The default format of the sender's address*

Prior to V8.7 the **q** macro was used to specify the form that the sender's address would take in header definitions. It was most often used in the **From:** and **Resent-From:** header lines.

The definition of $q had to adhere to the standard form of addresses as defined by RFC822. It had to contain just an address or an address and a comment. The traditional definitions of $q were

```
Dq<$g>        ← as <george@wash.dc.gov>
Dq$g          ← as george@wash.dc.gov
```

```
Dq$x <$g>      ← as George Washington <george@wash.dc.gov>
Dq$g ($x)      ← as george@wash.dc.gov (George Washington)
```

The full name is not always known and so $x can be undefined (empty). As a consequence, when the full name was included in the q macro definition, it was often wrapped in a conditional test:

```
Dq$g$?x ($x)$.
Dq$?x$x $.<$g>
```

Of these the second form was recommended for clients that forward all mail to a central mail-handling machine. If the full name was unknown locally, the header and envelope were identical and bracketed:

```
From: <user@slave.domain>          ← header
MAIL From: <user@slave.domain>     ← envelope
```

At the central mail-handling machine, both versions of the **From:** address were recognized as identical (only if the address was bracketed). As a consequence, the central machine deleted and recreated the **From:** line and added the full name if known.

Prior to V8.7, $q had to be defined in the configuration file because it was used to define the fields of the **Resent-From:** and **From:** headers (see §35.10.14). Beginning with V8.7 *sendmail*, those headers are defined by using the $g and $x macros directly. For example,

```
H?F?Resent-From: $?x$x <$g>$|$g$.
H?F?From: $?x$x <$g>$|$g$.
```

To redefine them, you must either edit your configuration file or add new definitions to the LOCAL_CONFIG section of your **mc** file (see §19.6.30):

```
LOCAL_CONFIG
divert(9)
H?F?From: $?x$x $.<$g>
divert(0)
```

The **divert()** statements force the new header definitions to follow the default definitions, thus replacing them.

$r   *(All versions)*

31.10.31   *The protocol used*

The $r macro stores the name of the protocol that is used when a mail message is first received. If mail is received via SMTP or ESMTP, $r is set accordingly. Incoming UUCP mail sets $r to "UUCP" (using the –p switch). With V8.7, bounced mail will now assign $r the value "internal."

$r is intended for use in the Received: header definition:

    HReceived: $?sfrom $s $.by j?r with r. id $i

The value in $r is saved to the qf file when the mail message is queued, and it is restored to $r when the queue is later processed.

$r is transient. It may be defined on the command line but should not be defined in the configuration file. Under V8 the -p switch (see §36.7.32) is the recommended way to assign a value to $r.

$R   *(m4 technique, deprecated)*

31.10.32   *The relay for unqualified names*

Using the *m4* configuration technique, the $R macro stores the hostname defined by LOCAL_RELAY (see §19.6.31). If $H has a value and if $R does not, all local email is forwarded to *hub* defined for $H. If $R is defined, it takes precedence over $H for some mail. See §19.6.41 for a description of MAIL_HUB and how it interacts with LOCAL_RELAY.

$s   *(All versions)*

31.10.33   *The sender host's name*

The $s macro contains the name of the sender's machine (host). $s is given the name of the local host as its value when *sendmail* starts, unless the -p command line switch (see §36.7.32) is used, in which case $s is given the value specified by that switch. Thereafter, $s is given a new value by *sendmail* only if the mail message was received via SMTP. For bounced mail, the $s value is always localhost.

The s macro is intended for use in the Received: header definition:

    HReceived: $?sfrom $s $.by j?r with r. id $i

The phrase from *host* will be included in this header line if $s has any value. Here, *host* is the name of the sending machine.

The value in $s is saved to the qf file when the mail message is queued and restored to $s when the queue is later processed.

$s is transient. It may be defined on the command line but should not be defined in the configuration file.

$S   *(m4 technique)*

31.10.34   *The Smart Host*

Using the *m4* configuration technique the $S macro stores the hostname defined by SMART_HOST (see §19.6.47). The smart host is the name of the host that can deliver all mail that the local host cannot. $S is most often used with UUCP sites to get DNS mail to the outside world.

$t   *(All versions)*

31.10.35   *The current time in seconds*

The $t macro contains the current date and time represented as an integer. The value of $t is set in two places:

- When *sendmail* first begins to run, it presets several date-oriented macros internally to the date and time it was run. Among those are the $a, $d, $b, and $t macros. This initialization is done after the configuration file is read.

- Each time a new envelope is created, the $d, $b, and $t macros are given a default that is the current time.

$t is intended for use in configuration-file header definitions. $t is transient. If it is defined in the configuration file or in the command line, that definition may be ignored by *sendmail.*

$u   *(All versions)*

31.10.36   *The recipient's username*

Rule set 0 (see §29.6) is used to resolve the recipient address into a triple: the delivery agent (with $#), the host part of the address (with $@), and the recipient's username (with $:). The recipient's username is then processed by rule set 2 (the generic rule set for all recipient addresses), then by the rule set indicated by the R= equate of the delivery agent (the custom recipient address processing), and finally by rule set 4 (postprocessing for all addresses).

If the delivery agent has the F=A flag set (see §30.8.12), that rewritten recipient's username is looked up in the *aliases* file and replaced with its alias if one exists. If it is not replaced and if the F=5 flag (see §30.8.3) is set, the address is rewritten by rule set 5 to possibly pick a new delivery agent and repeat this process.[*]

After aliasing, the rewritten recipient's username is then assigned to $u. If the delivery agent's F=w flag (see §30.8.43) is set,[†] the value of $u is then used to look up information about that user with *getpwent*(3). The user's home directory from *pw_dir* is made the value of the $z and used to access that user's `~/.forward` and *dead.letter* files.

For all delivery agents the final value of $u may be used as a component of the delivery agent's A= (see §30.4.1) equate. For example,

---

[*] Prior to V8.7 this behavior was all tied to the `local` delivery agent.

[†] Prior to V8.7, looking up the user's home directory was tied to the `local` delivery agent.

```
A=uux - $h!rmail ($u)
```

Note that $u is special (see §30.4.1.3) in delivery agent A= equates. If it is absent, *sendmail* speaks SMTP. If it is present *and* the F=m flag (see §30.8.30) is also present, the argument containing $u is repeated as many times as there are recipients.

In V8 *sendmail*, $u is also set to the original recipient (prior to aliasing) while the message headers are first being read. Therefore the original recipient information is available for use in the **Received:** header line.[*]

$u is transient. If it is defined in the configuration file or in the command line, that definition is ignored by *sendmail*.

$U   *(m4 technique)*

31.10.37   *The UUCP name to override $k*

When configuring with the *m4* technique, you can include support for UUCP by using the MAILER(uucp) command (see §19.3.2) in your mc file. With that support, you can override the use of $k (see §31.10.21) with a hostname of your choosing when prefixing a string of hosts with the local hostname:

```
here!lady!sonya!user
↑
insert local host name here
```

If $U has a value, its value will be inserted. If it lacks a value, $k will be inserted.

$U can be useful when several hosts provide UUCP services. It can be defined in your DOMAIN() file (see §19.3.3) as a single name so that all outgoing UUCP mail will appear as though it is from a common host.

$v   *(All versions)*

31.10.38   *The version of sendmail*

The **v** macro contains the current version of the *sendmail* program, taken from the **Version** variable that is initialized in *version.c* of the *sendmail* source. In general, it is the SCCS revision number of the source. $v is used in defining the **SmtpGreetingMessage** ($e) option (see §34.8.65) and in **Received:** header lines (see §35.10.25).

The value given to $v can vary with the vendor. There is currently no standard for identifying variations on the *sendmail* program. Clearly, $v may not contain a true picture.

---

[*] In this use, V8's $u is similar to IDA's $m.

$v is internally defined when *sendmail* starts up. It may be redefined in the configuration file or as part of the command line.

$V	*(m4 technique)*

31.10.39   *UUCP relay for class $=V*

$V holds as its value the name of the host that will handle all UUCP mail for the class $=V. See §19.6.46 for a discussion of UUCP relays in general and how this macro relates to $W, $X, and $Y macros.

$w	*(All versions)*

31.10.40   *The short name of this host*

When *sendmail* first starts to run, it calls *gethostname*(3) to get the name of the local machine. If that call fails, it sets that local name to be `localhost`. Then *gethostbyname*(3) is called to find the official name for the local host. If that call fails, the official name for the local host remains unchanged. The official name for the local host is assigned to $j.

If the V command's version (see §27.5) is 5 or higher, V8 *sendmail* discards the domain and assigns the result to $w (the short name):

```
here.us.edu
    ↑
    from here to end of name discarded
```

If the version is 4 or less, $w is assigned the fully qualified name (and is identical to $j).

$w is then appended to class $=w (see §32.5.8). $=w is used internally by *sendmail* to screen all MX records that are found in delivering mail over the network.[*] Each such record is compared in a case-insensitive fashion to $=w. If there is a match, that MX record and all additional MX records of lower priority are skipped. This prevents *sendmail* from mistakenly connecting to itself.

Any of the following errors (or variations on them) indicate that $=w, $w, or $j may contain a faulty value, most likely from a bad configuration file declaration:

```
553 host config error: mail loops back to myself
553 Local configuration error, host name not recognized as local
553 host host name configuration error
```

Note that if $w is pulled from the name server and the host is running BIND, and a cache is being downloaded, $w could be periodically unresolved. In this instance, *sendmail* sleeps and retries the lookup.

---

[*] Prior to V8, only $w was checked.

$w is defined when *sendmail* starts up. It may be redefined in the configuration file or as part of the command line.

$W   *(m4 technique)*

31.10.41   *UUCP relay for class $=W*

$W holds as its value the name of the host that will handle all UUCP mail for the class $=W. See §19.6.46 for a discussion of UUCP relays in general and how this macro relates to $V, $X, and $Y macros.

$x   *(All versions)*

31.10.42   *The full name of the sender*

The $x macro holds the full name of the sender. When *sendmail* processes a mail message for delivery, it rewrites the sender's address using rule sets 3 and 0 so that it can determine whether the sender is local. If the sender is local, rule set 0 provides the sender's login name with the $: operator. Then, if the delivery agent's F=w flag (see §30.8.43) is set,[*] *sendmail* calls *getpwent*(3) using that login name as the argument. If the login name is known, *getpwent*(3) returns the sender's full name in its *pw_gecos* field. The *sendmail* program then processes that *pw_gecos* field, throwing away phone numbers and the like and converting the & character where necessary. The result, usually fairly close to the sender's full name, is the value assigned to the x macro.

Under certain circumstances, *sendmail* places a different value in $x:

- When *sendmail* first starts to run, it sets the full name to be the value of the NAME environmental variable. The -F command-line switch (see §36.7.20) can overwrite that variable. If the operating mode is -q (see §23.6.1) or -bd (see §36.7.5), the full name is reset to NULL. When mail is sent, this value is assigned to $x.

- In processing the headers of a message, if *sendmail* finds a Full-Name: header (see §35.10.15), it assigns the text of that header to the $x macro.

- In sending a failed mail message, the login name of the sender is taken from $n, and the full name is set to be

  `Mail Delivery Subsystem`

The $x macro is intended for use in header definitions. If used in the From: header definition, the sender's full name will then also appear in the SMTP envelope *mail* line.

---

[*] Prior to V8.7 this behavior was tied to the local delivery agent.

Note that unusual *gecos* fields in the password file can cause pre-V8 mail to fail. Consider the following *passwd*(5) entry:

```
happy:123:456:Happy Guy ;-),Ext 789,,:/u/happy:/bin/sh
```

The *gecos* field here will be parsed by all but V8 *sendmail* into a value for $x that can yield a faulty header—one with unbalanced parentheses:

```
From: happy@our.domain (Happy Guy ;-))
```

V8 *sendmail* accepts only characters up to the first comma, semicolon, or percent as part of the full name and quotes the result, thus avoiding this problem.

$x is transient. If it is defined in the configuration file or the command line, that definition will be ignored by *sendmail*.

$X   *(m4 technique)*

31.10.43   *UUCP relay for class $=X*

$X holds as its value the name of the host that will handle all UUCP mail for the class $=X. See §19.6.46 for a discussion of UUCP relays in general and how this macro relates to $V, $W, and $Y macros.

$y   *(All versions)*

31.10.44   *Name of the controlling tty*

The $y macro holds the name of the controlling terminal device, if there is one. The controlling terminal is determined by first calling *ttyname*(3) with the *sendmail* program's standard error output as an argument. If *ttyname*(3) returns the name of a terminal device (such as /dev/ttya), *sendmail* strips everything up to and including the last / character and stores the result into $y.

$y is intended for use in debugging *sendmail* problems. It is not used internally by *sendmail*. In determining whether or not it can write to a user's terminal screen, *sendmail* calls *ttyname*(3) separately on its standard input, output, and error output without updating $y.

Note that the device name in $y depends on the implementation of *ttyname*(3). Under BSD UNIX, all terminals are in /dev, whereas under other versions of UNIX they may be in subdirectories such as /dev/ttys. Also note that $y is only defined if TTYNAME is defined (see §18.8.52) when *sendmail* is compiled.

$y is transient. If it is defined in the configuration file or the command line, that definition will be ignored by *sendmail*. Finally, note that $y is set only when mail is being sent and so is of most value in headers.

$Y

31.10.45

UUCP relay for unclassified hosts

$Y holds as its value the name of the host that will handle all UUCP mail that was not otherwise handled by class $=V, $=W, or $=X. See §19.6.46 for a discussion of UUCP relays in general and how this macro relates to $V, $W, and $X macros.

$z

31.10.46

The recipient's home directory

The $z macro holds the location of the local user's home directory. This macro is given a value only if the delivery agent has the F=w flag set (see §30.8.43)[*] and if delivery is to a user (rather than a file or a program). The home directory is taken from the *pw_dir* field as returned by *getpwent*(3).

The *sendmail* program uses $z to access a user's ~/.forward file and to save failed mail to a user's *dead-letter* file.

$z can be passed in the A= equate to a custom written local delivery agent. One reason to do so would be to deliver mail to a user's home directory, rather than to a central spool directory. $z is also very useful with the ForwardPath (J) option (see §34.8.27).

$z is transient. If it is defined in the configuration file or the command line, that definition will be ignored by *sendmail.*

$Z

31.10.47

Version of the m4 configuration

When you are configuring with the *m4* technique, the version of the configuration file can be augmented by defining confCF_VERSION in your mc file:

```
define(`confCF_VERSION', `ver')dnl
```

This statement causes the value **ver** to be appended to the default value in $Z. A forward slash character will separate the two. The default value in $Z varies depending on your *sendmail* version. If your version were V8.8.4, the above *m4* definition would yield the following macro definition:

```
DZ8.8.4/ver
```

$Z is generally used as part of the SmtpGreetingMessage ($e) option's declaration (see §34.8.65):

---

[*] Prior to V8.7 this behavior was tied to the local delivery agent.

```
O SmtpGreetingMessage=$j Sendmail $v/$Z; $b
```

Note that this version is different from the version declared with the VERSIONID *m4* macro (see §19.6.50). Also note that this is the configuration file version, rather than the version of the *sendmail* program as stored in $v.

Prior to V8 *sendmail* the configuration file version was stored in $V.

32

Class Macros

A class is like an array of string values. In the LHS of rules it is sometimes advantageous to compare individual tokens to multiple strings when determining a match. The configuration class command provides this ability. The class command is similar to the macro definition command, except that instead of assigning a single value to a macro, it assigns many values to a class. Classes differs from macros in that they can be used only in the LHS of rules, whereas macros can be used in either the RHS or the LHS.

Two different configuration commands can be used to assign values to a class. The C configuration command is used to assign values from within the configuration file. The F configuration command is used in two ways: to assign values by reading them from a disk file or to assign values by running a program and reading the output. These commands may be intermixed to create a single class or used separately to create multiple classes.

You may wish to review the tutorial in Chapter 12, *Class*, to see a few typical applications of class.

32.1 Class Configuration Commands

The three forms for the class configuration command are the following:

```
CX list        ← values from configuration file
FX file        ← values from a disk file
FX |program    ← values via another program
```

The class configuration command starts with either the letter C or F, which must begin a line. The C says values will be assigned as a part of the configuration command. The F says values will be assigned from an external file or program.

The C or F is immediately followed (with no intervening whitespace) by the name of the class (the X above). A class name is any single ASCII character or, beginning with V8.7 *sendmail* a multicharacter name enclosed in curly braces:

```
CX list                 ← all versions
C{LongName} list        ← beginning with V8.7
```

See §31.4.2 for a full discussion of how to use multicharacter names.

Note that classes are separate from macros, so they may both use the same letter or name with no conflict.

The *sendmail* program reserves the lowercase letters for its own use as internally defined class names (although currently only a few are actually used). All uppercase letters and all names that begin with uppercase letters are available for use.

32.1.1 The C Class Command

The C form of the class command causes values to be assigned from within the configuration file. In general, the class command looks like this:

```
CX list                 ← values from configuration file
C{XX} list              ← values from configuration file
```

Here, a *list* is a list of string elements (delimited by whitespace) that follows on the same line as the C command. Each word in *list* is appended to the array of values in the class *X* in the first case and to the class {XX} in the second.[*]

Multiple declarations of the same named class may coexist in the configuration file. Each declaration after the first appends its string elements to the preceding list. That is,

```
CX string1 string2
CX string3 string4
```

produces the same class as does

```
CX string1 string2 string3 string4
```

Both create a class with four strings as elements.

When an array of values is built, whitespace is used to separate one value from another. Whitespace is defined by the C language *isspace*(3) routine and usually includes the space, tab, newline, carriage-return, and form-feed characters. Each line of text assigned to a class is broken up by *sendmail* into whitespace delimited words. When a line is indented with a space or a tab, that line is joined by

---

[*] Note that when a class name is a single character, it may be referenced with or without enclosing curly braces, with no change in meaning. That is, CX and C{X} are equivalent.

sendmail to the preceding line. Thus the following three declarations also append four words to the class X:

```
CX string1
CX string2
CX string3
     string4
   ↑
   tab
```

Words that are added to a class cannot be removed after *sendmail* has read them. Instead, they must be edited out of whatever file or program produced them, and the *sendmail* daemon must be killed and restarted.

The list of words in a class declaration can include macros. For example the following assigns the same values to class X as did the above example:

```
D{LIST} string1 string2 string3 string4
CX ${LIST}
```

Macros used in class declarations are expanded when the configuration file is read. Deferred macros (those with the $& prefix) may not be used in class declarations. But conditionals may:

```
CX ourhost$?{Domain}.${Domain}$.
```

32.1.2 The F Class Command

The F form of the class configuration command allows values to be appended to a class from outside the configuration file. In general, the file command looks like either of the following:

```
FX file          ← values from a disk file
FX |program      ← values via another program (V8.7 and above, or IDA)
```

The F is immediately followed by the name of the class. This can be either a single-character name, as shown, or a multicharacter name. The name is followed by optional whitespace and then the name of a file or program. If the file or program begins with the pipe character (|), it is taken to be the name of a program to run.[*] Otherwise, it is taken to be the name of a file to read.

If SCANF was defined when *sendmail* was compiled (see §18.8.39), each line that is read from a file or program is parsed by the C language *scanf*(3) library routine. The formatting pattern given to *scanf*(3) is %s, which tells *scanf*(3) to read only the first whitespace-delimited word from each line of text. The file is opened for

---

[*] This was removed from V8.1 *sendmail* because it presented a security risk. It was restored to V8.7 because *sendmail* now checks permissions more carefully and *exec*(2)'s the program itself instead of using the old, buggy *popen*(3) approach of yore.

reading or the program is executed when the configuration file is processed. If either cannot be opened (for reading or execution), *sendmail syslog*(3)'s the following error and ignores that configuration command:

```
cannot open what: why        ← file
cannot exec what: why        ← program
```

Here, the *what* is the exact text that was given in the configuration file, and *why* is the text of a system error.

For the file form only, if the file may optionally not exist, you can prefix its name with a -o switch:

```
FX -o file            ← okay for file to not exist
```

This tells *sendmail* to remain silent if the file does not exit. The -o switch is useful when a configuration file is shared by several machines, only some of which need the external class macro file.

The C and F forms of the configuration command may be intermixed for any given class name. For example, consider a file named */etc/local/names* with the following contents:

```
string3
string4
```

The following two configuration commands add the same four strings to the class X as did the C command alone in the previous section:

```
CX string1 string2
FX /etc/local/names
```

This creates a class with four strings as array elements. Whitespace delimits one string from the others in the C line declaration, and they are stored in the order in which they are listed. The file */etc/local/names* is then opened and read, and each of the two words in that file is appended to the two words that are already in the class.

32.1.2.1 scanf(3) variations

The file form of the class configuration command allows different formatting patterns to be used with *scanf*(3).* But the program form does not allow any variation, and so its *scanf*(3) pattern is always %s, which tells *scanf*(3) to read only the first whitespace-delimited word from each line of text:

---

* The version of *sendmail* that you are using must have been compiled with SCANF defined (see §18.8.39) for *scanf*(3) to be usable from within the configuration file.

```
FX file pat          ← with scanf(3) pattern
FX |program          ← always "%s"
```

If the optional **pat** argument to the file form is missing, the pattern given to
scanf(3) is **%s**. The **pat** argument is separated from the **file** argument by one or
more spaces or tabs. It should not be quoted, and it consists of everything from its
first character to the end of the line. Internally, *scanf*(3) is called with:

```
sscanf(result, pat, input)
```

Here, **result** is the string array element to be added to the class definition. The
pat is the *scanf*(3) pattern, and **input** is the line of text read from the file.*

After each line of text is read from the file and filtered with the *scanf*(3) pattern, it
is further subdivided by *sendmail* into individual words. That subdividing uses
whitespace (as defined by the C language *isspace*(3) routine) to separate words.
Each separate word is then appended as an individual element to the class array.

Consider the contents of the following file named */etc/local/myhosts*:

```
server1 server2 # my two nets
uuhost          # my uucp alias
#mailhost       # mail server alias (retired 06,23,91)
```

This file contains three hostname aliases to be added to a class, say **H**. The following configuration command does just that:

```
FH /etc/local/myhosts %[^\#]
```

The pattern **%[^#]** causes *scanf*(3) to read all characters in each line up to, but
not including, the first **#** character. The first line includes two white-space delimited words that are appended to the class **H**. The second line contains one word,
and the third contains none. The **** character prevents *sendmail* from treating the **#**
as a comment character.

32.2 Access Class in Rules

Class arrays are useful only in the LHS of rules. The *sendmail* program offers two
ways to use them:

$=X

> The **$=** prefix causes *sendmail* to seek a match between the workspace and
> one of the words† in a class list.

---

* Avoid using a bare **%s** as the pattern. Doing so risks overflowing internal *sendmail* buffers. Instead
specify a limited string length with something like **%.40s**.

† Under V8, words in a class can be multitokened.

$~X

The **$~** prefix causes *sendmail* to accept only an entry in the workspace that does not match any of the words in a class list.

32.2.1 Matching Any in a Class: $=

The list of words that form a class array are searched by prefixing the class name with the characters **$=**.

```
R$=X      $@<$1>
```

In this rule, the expression **$=X** causes *sendmail* to search a class for the word that is in the current workspace. If *sendmail* finds that the word has been defined, and if it finds that the word is associated with the class **X**, then a match is made.

The matching word is then made available for use in the RHS rewriting. Because the value of **$=X** is not known ahead of time, the matched word can be referenced in the RHS with the *$digit* positional operator.

Consider the following example. Two classes have been declared elsewhere in the configuration file. The first, **w**, contains all the possible names for the local host:

```
Cw localhost mailhost server1 server2
```

The second, **D**, contains the domain names of the two different networks on which this host sits:

```
CD domain1 domain2
```

If the object of a rule is to match any variation on the local hostname at either of the domains and to rewrite the result as the official hostname at the appropriate domain, the following rule can be used:

```
R $=w . $=D    $@ $w . $2    make any variations "official"
```

If the workspace contains the tokenized address *server1.domain2*, *sendmail* first checks to see whether the word *server1* has been defined as part of the class **w**. If it has, the dot in the rule and workspace match each other, and then *sendmail* looks up *domain2*.

If both the host part and the domain part are found to be members of their respective classes, the RHS of the rule is called to rewrite the workspace. The **$2** in the workspace corresponds to the **$=D** in the LHS. The **$=D** matches the *domain2* from the workspace. So that text is used to rewrite the new workspace.

Note that prior to V8 *sendmail*, only words could be in classes. When *sendmail* looked up the workspace to check for a match to a class, it looked up only a single token. That is, if the workspace contained *server1.domain2.edu*, the LHS expression $=D would cause *sendmail* to look up only the *domain2* part. The *.edu* part would not be looked up, and consequently the rule would fail.

Note that the V8 and IDA versions of *sendmail* allow multitoken class matching.

32.2.2 *Matching Any Not in a Class: $~*

The inverse of the $= prefix is the $~ prefix. It is used to match any word in the workspace that is not in a class. It is seldom used in production configuration files; but when the need for its properties arises, it can be very useful.

To illustrate, consider a network with three PC machines on it. The PC machines cannot receive mail, whereas all the other machines on the network can. If the list of PC hostnames is defined in the class {PChosts}:

```
C{PChosts} pc1 pc2 pc3
```

Then a rule can be designed that will match any but a PC hostname:

```
R$*<@$~{PChosts}>      $:$1<@$2>         filter out the PC hosts
```

Here the LHS looks for an address of the form

```
"user" "<" "@" "not-a-PC" ">"
```

This matches only if the @ token is *not* followed by one of the PC hosts listed in class {PChosts}. If the part of the workspace that is tested against the list provided by $~ is found in that list, then the match fails.

Note that the $*digit* positional operator in the RHS (the $2 above) references the part of the workspace that doesn't match. If the workspace contains *ben<@philly>*, the $2 references the *philly*.

Also note that multitoken expressions in the workspace will not match, as you might expect. That is, for multitoken expressions in the workspace, $~ is *not* the opposite of $=. To illustrate, consider this miniconfiguration file:

```
CX hostA.com
R$~X    $@ $1 is not in X
R$=X    $@ yes $1 is in X
R$*     $@ neither
```

Now feed a multitokened address through these rules in rule testing mode:

```
% /usr/lib/sendmail -Cx.cf -bt
ADDRESS TEST MODE (ruleset 3 NOT automatically invoked)
Enter <ruleset> <address>
> 0 hostC.com
rewrite: ruleset   0   input: hostC . com
rewrite: ruleset   0 returns: neither
```

Whenever $~ is given a multitoken expression, it will *always* find the expression in the class and so will *always* fail.

32.2.3 Backup and Retry

Multitoken matching operators, such as $+, always try to match the least that they can (see §28.5.2). Such a simple-minded approach could lead to problems in matching (or not matching) classes in the LHS. However, the ability of *sendmail* to backup and retry alleviates this problem. For example, consider the following three tokens in the workspace:

```
"A" "." "B"
```

and consider the following LHS rule:

```
R$+ $=X $*
```

Because the $+ tries to match the minimum, it first matches only the A in the workspace. The $=X then tries to match the . to the class X. If this match fails, *sendmail* backs up and tries again.

The next time through, the $+ matches the A., and the $=X tries to match the B in the workspace. If B is not in the class X, the entire LHS fails.

The ability of the *sendmail* program to back up and retry LHS matches eliminates much of the ambiguity from rule design. The multitoken matching operators try to match the minimum but match more if necessary for the whole LHS to match.

32.2.4 Class Name Hashing Algorithm

When comparing a token in the workspace to a list of words in a class array, *sendmail* tries to be as efficient as possible. Instead of comparing the token to each word in the list, one by one, it simply looks up the token in its internal *string pool*. If the token is in the pool and if the pool listing is marked as belonging to the class being sought, then a match is found.

The comparison of tokens to entries in the string pool is case-insensitive. Each token is converted to lowercase before the comparison, and all strings in the string pool are stored in lowercase.

Because strings are stored in the pool as text with a type, the same string value may be used for different types with no conflict. For example, the symbolic name of a delivery agent and a word in a class may be identical, yet they will still be separate entries in the string pool.

The *sendmail* program uses a simple hashing algorithm to ensure that the token is compared to the fewest possible strings in the string pool. In normal circumstances that algorithm performs its job well. At sites with unusually large classes (perhaps a few thousand hosts in a class of host aliases), it may be necessary to tune the hashing algorithm. The code is in the file *stab.c* with the *sendmail* source. The size of the symbol table hash is set by the constant STABSIZE.

As an alternative to large class arrays, *sendmail* offers external database macros (see §33.1). No information is currently available contrasting the efficiency of the various approaches.

32.3 *Class with m4*

In configuring with the *m4* technique, many classes are defined for your convenience. You need to be aware of these not only to take advantage of them, but also to avoid reusing their single-character names by mistake. Table 32-1 lists all the macros that the *m4* technique uses as of version 8.8.4. Most are described in other sections, but a few are described here. See §19.6.30 for the general method used for adding members and new class names using the *m4* technique.

Table 32–1: Class Macros Used with the m4 Technique

Class	§	Description
$=B	19.6.8	Domains to lookup in **bestmx** in place of $=w
$=E	19.6.4	List of EXPOSED USERS users
$=F		U.C. Berkeley example *.mc* files
$=G	19.6.11	List of other sites to look up in genericstable
$=L	19.6.38	List of LOCAL USER users
$=M	19.6.12	List of hosts to masquerade
$=O	here	List nonusername characters
$=P	here	List of pseudo domains
$=U	19.4.6	Locally connected UUCP hosts
$=V	19.4.6	Hosts connected to UUCP relay $V
$=W	19.4.6	Hosts connected to UUCP relay $W
$=X	19.4.6	Hosts connected to UUCP relay $X
$=Y	19.4.6	Locally connected smart UUCP hosts
$=Z	19.4.6	Locally connected domainized UUCP hosts

The class O is used by the *m4* technique to hold a list of characters that cannot be used in local usernames. This list is used to detect certain kinds of routing addresses that might otherwise be difficult to detect. This list initially contains

```
@ %
```

but may also contain a ! if UUCP support is included.

The class P holds a list of pseudo domains that will not be looked up using DNS. Unless you use a FEATURE, this class will only contain a dot. Various FEATUREs will add appropriate pseudo domains to it, such as .UUCP and .REDIRECT.

32.4 *Pitfalls*

- Although a class macro name may be any ASCII character (any character in the range 0x0 to 0x7f), avoid using any of the nonletter characters. At the very least they create confusing reading, and at worst they may cause *sendmail* to completely misinterpret your intentions.

- Although strings may traditionally be made to contain whitespace by quoting them, class macros will misinterpret those quotes. For example, *"vax ds1"* wrongly parses into two class entries: *"vax* and *ds1,"* with the quotes a part of each.

- Duplicate strings are silently ignored. Therefore typos in a list of strings may cause an accidentally duplicated entry to be silently excluded.

- Avoid creating a new class macro name without first checking to see whether it has already been used. That is, don't create a list of UUCP hosts within class U without first checking *both* for preexisting CU and FU definitions and for ruleset uses of $=U and $~U. It is perfectly legal for the $=U and $~U expressions to exist in rule sets without a corresponding CU or FU definitions. Beware, however, that such empty references still cause *sendmail* to search the string pool.

- Under V8 *sendmail* you may watch your class macro definitions being formed by using the -d37.8 debugging switch (see §37.5.127). Under other versions of *sendmail* you may only approximate this information by using the -d36.9 debugging switch (see §37.5.124).

- The class macro expansion prefixes $= and $~ are intended for use only in the LHS of rules. If you use those characters in the RHS of rules, most versions of *sendmail* do not print an error; instead, they silently accept those characters as is. V8 *sendmail*, on the other hand, prints one of the following messages as a warning and ignores the entire rule:

  ```
  Inappropriate use of $=
  Inappropriate use of $~
  ```

- The file form's *scanf*(3) pattern can produce unexpected results. Remember that the pattern is applied to a line, not to a stream.

- No error checking is performed during reads for the F form of the class configuration command. An error reading from a file silently causes the rest of that file's contents to be ignored. An unreported error from a program (one that silently returns 0 on both success and failure) is also silently ignored by *sendmail*.

- Be careful in using defined macros in the C form of class macro definitions. Some versions of *sendmail* store the macro itself instead of the expanded value of the macro, leading to unexpected results. V8 *sendmail* correctly stores the expanded macro value.

32.5 Alphabetized Reference

Prior to V8 *sendmail*, only the class w was used internally, but recently, more and more classes have been added to that internal list. Since internal class names always begin with a lowercase letter, you should always begin your own class names with an uppercase letter to avoid conflict.

Table 32-2 lists all the class macros used by *sendmail* as of version 8.8.4.

Table 32–2: All the Class Macros Used Internally by sendmail

Class	§	Version	Description
$=e	32.5.1	V8.7 and above	Encode this Content-Transfer-Encoding:
$=k	32.5.2	V8.6.5 and above	The local UUCP name
$=m	32.5.3	V8.7 and above	List of local domains
$=n	32.5.4	V8.7 and above	Don't encode these Content-Types
$=q	32.5.5	V8.8 and above	Always Quoted-Printable encode Content-Type:
$=s	32.5.6	V8.7 and above	Presume an RFC822 7-bit body
$=t	32.5.7	V8.7 and above	List trusted users
$=w	32.5.8	All versions	List of our other names

Note that these classes are really used *internally* by *sendmail*. Don't try to redefine their use in the configuration file. Such an attempt will be doomed to failure.

$=e   *(V8.7 and above)*

32.5.1   *Encode this Content-Transfer-Encoding:*

The F=7 delivery agent flag (see §30.8.4) determines whether MIME-encoded data should be converted from 8 to 7 bits. If the message is in 8-bit format and if it is going to a MIME-capable destination that requires 7-bit data, the message body will be converted to 7 bits by using either Quoted-Printable or Base64 (see 34.8.22).

Not all data types should be converted to 7 bits, however. The types that might possibly be converted are listed with the Content-Transfer-Encoding: header (see §35.10.8). One type that should not be converted, for example, is the quoted-printable type because it is already converted. Types that may be converted are 7bit, 8bit, and binary.

Beginning with version 8.7 *sendmail*, the class e is used to determine whether or not a type will be encoded. Only those values listed in this class will be encoded. When *sendmail* first starts, it initializes the list of values in class e to be

```
7bit 8bit binary
```

You may add types to this class, but you may never remove them.

Note that a type in class e may still be prevented from being encoded on the basis of the considerations imposed by class n. Also note that the actual encoding can be restricted to quoted printable by use of the class q.

$=k   *(V8.6.5 and above)*

32.5.2   *The local UUCP name*

When *sendmail* first begins to run, it figures out what your local UUCP node name is and assigns the result to the $k macro (see §31.10.21). At the same time, it assigns the same name to this class k.

$=m   *(V8.7 and above)*

32.5.3   *List of local domains*

When *sendmail* first begins to run, it figures out what your DNS domain is and assigns the result to the $m macro (see §31.10.24). The *sendmail* program then processes the configuration file. This gives you the opportunity to redefine $m. After that, *sendmail* assigns the final value in $m to the class m.

Unfortunately, as of V8.8 *sendmail*, the class macro m is not used by *sendmail* nor by any of the configuration files produced by the *m4* technique. If you wish to have mail accepted as local under a variety of domains, use the domaintable FEATURE instead (see §19.6.10).

Suggested uses for class m might include screening mail with the check_compat rule set (see §29.10.4), and detecting local domains by adding rules to rule set 0 with the LOCAL_RULE_0 *m4* technique (see §19.6.32).

$=n   *(V8.7 and above)*

32.5.4   *Don't encode these Content-Types*

Although some MIME content types may be converted to 7 bits, not all types should be. Content types are defined by the Content-Type: header (see §35.10.9). For example, the type multipart/ should not be converted, whereas its component boundary separated parts probably should be. Conversion is done by encoding with either Quoted-Printable or Base64 (see 34.8.22).

Beginning with V8.7 *sendmail*, types that should not be encoded are those defined as members of the class **n**. When *sendmail* first starts to run, it defines the following list of values for class **n**:

```
multipart/signed
```

As of this writing, no other useful values exist for this class.

Note that a type in class **n** may still be prevented from being encoded based on the considerations imposed by class **e**. Also note that the actual encoding can be restricted to Quoted-Printable by use of the class **q**.

$=q *(V8.8 and above)*

32.5.5 *Always Quoted-Printable encode Content-Type:*

The **EightBitMode** (8) option (see §34.8.22) determines when and how 8-bit data will be encoded into a 7-bit format. Ordinarily, the decision to use Quoted-Printable as opposed to Base64 is made by examining the input stream and choosing Quoted-Printable if less than 1/8 of the first 4 kilobytes of data has the high bit set. Otherwise, encoding is with Base64.

Beginning with V8.8, *sendmail* offers the class **q** as the means to force the selection of Quoted-Printable. Just before scanning the input data, *sendmail* extracts the *type* and *subtype* from the **Content-Type:** header (see §35.10.9):

```
Content-Type: type/subtype ; ...
```

If the *type* is in the class **q**, the body will definitely be encoded with Quoted-Printable if encoding occurs. Also if a concatenation of *type*, a slash (/), and *subtype* is in class **q**, the body will definitely be encoded with Quoted-Printable.

When *sendmail* first begins to run, class **q** is empty. A reasonable value in most countries might be **text/plain** (although probably not in countries that use 16-bit characters, such as China). Other values for this class might be **text** or **text/html**.

$=s *(V8.7 and above)*

32.5.6 *Presume an RFC822 7-bit body*

An email message as defined by RFC822 may not contain 8-bit data. Consequently, when the MIME **Content-Type:** header declares a message subtype that is **rfc822**, we immediately know that it will contain nothing that needs 8- to 7-bit encoding.

```
Content-Type: message/rfc822
```

As other message subtypes evolve, this assumption can safely be made about them too. So to make *sendmail* more adaptable, the **s** class was added beginning with

V8.7. This class contains a list of subtypes that should be treated the same as
`rfc822`. When *sendmail* first begins to run, it initializes that list to contain:

```
rfc822
```

Other subtypes that may legitimately appear here might be **partial** or **delivery-
status**.

Note that this provides only an initial hint to *sendmail*. The `rfc822` subtype may
itself contain MIME information that might require 8- to 7-bit encoding.

$=t	*(V8.7 and above)*

32.5.7   *List trusted users*

Trusted users are those who may run *sendmail* with the **-f** command line switch
to specify who sent the message. Prior to V8.6 *sendmail*, such users had to be
listed with the T command (see §22.8.1.1). That command was ignored in V8.1
through V8.6, and with those versions anyone could use the **-f** switch. Beginning
with V8.7 *sendmail*, the T command was reintroduced, but it now causes the list
of trusted users to be added to the class **t**. Now, any user who uses the **-f** switch
and who is not listed in class **t** will cause the following error message (see
§35.10.35) to be included in the outgoing mail message:

```
X-Authentication-Warning: user set sender to other using -f
```

See the **use_ct_file** FEATURE (see §19.6.25) for an easy way to add users to this
class using the *m4* technique.

$=w	*(All versions)*

32.5.8   *List of our other names*

Before the *sendmail* program reads its configuration file, it calls *gethostbyname*(3)
to find all the known aliases for the local machine. The argument given to
gethostbyname(3) is the value of the $w macro that was derived from a call to
gethostname(3) (see §31.10.40).

Depending on the version of *sendmail* you are running, the aliases that are found
will either be those from your */etc/hosts* file or those found as additional **A** records
in a DNS lookup. To see the aliases that *sendmail* found or to see what it missed
and should have found, use the **-d0.4** debugging switch (see §37.5.2). Any aliases
that are found are printed as

```
aka: alias
```

Depending on your version of *sendmail*, each *alias* is either a hostname (such as
rog.stan.edu) or an Internet IP number (such as *[123.45.67.8]*).

Many *sendmail.cf* files use the w class macro to define all the ways users might reference the local machine. This list *must* contain all names for the local machine as given in the */etc/hosts* file and all names for the local host as listed in DNS (including CNAME and MX records). For example,

```
# All our routing identities
Cw server1 server2
# All our local aliases
Cw localhost mailhost tops-link print-router loghost
# DNS records
Cw serv-link
# We are a bitnet registered node
Cw bitserver
```

If you notice mail failing because users commonly misspell the local machine name (e.g., *ol1110* when they really mean *o1ll10*); you might want to consider adding that misspelled version to a **Cw** declaration.

An easy way to add hostnames to class w is with the **use_cw_file** FEATURE (see §19.6.26) of the *m4* technique.

33

Database Macros

Database macros are special forms of defined macros. When used with certain special operators, they can cause rules to access information in external files. Database macros offer these advantages:

- Information may be easily changed without having to kill and restart *sendmail*, because database information is external to the configuration file.

- The *sendmail* program starts up faster, because only the location of the information is stored at startup, rather than the information itself.

- Rules are more versatile because database information can be used in the RHS side of rules. Class macros are still of use in the LHS.

To fully appreciate *sendmail* databases, consider the only alternative, the F configuration command. For example, mail that is sent by using UUCP is a typical application that requires lists of information:

```
FU /etc/mail/uuhosts
```

Here, the external file */etc/mail/uuhosts* contains a list of UUCP hosts connected to the local machine. If the list rarely changes, the F command is appropriate. On the other hand, if the list is volatile and changes often, the F command has drawbacks. The file */etc/mail/uuhosts* is read only when the configuration file is processed. Any change to that file is ignored by a running *sendmail* (such as the daemon). To make the change effective, the daemon needs to be killed and restarted.[*]

---

[*] If you're running an old *sendmail* version with a freeze file, that file also will need to be recreated.

In such volatile situations, storing UUCP information in a database is preferred. A change to a database is immediately available to the running daemon, eliminating the need to kill and restart.

V8 *sendmail* is designed to rewrite addresses on the basis of information looked up in external databases or in its internal symbol table. It can use a wide variety of database forms, ranging from *ndbm*(3) files (see §33.8.3) to Hesiod network maps (see §33.8.6). The K configuration command (see §33.3) is used to declare the name, location, and other parameters of databases or to modify use of its symbol table. The $(and $) database operators (see §33.4) are used in the RHS of rules to access and utilize that information.

33.1 Enable at Compile Time

Vendors that provide V8 *sendmail* in precompiled form may or may not provide access to all the types of databases that V8 *sendmail* supports. If your online documentation lacks this information, you can run *strings*(1) on *sendmail* to discover what it supports:

```
% strings /usr/lib/sendmail | grep map_open

ndbm_map_open(%s, %s, %d)
hash_map_open(%s, %s, %d)
nis_map_open(%s, %s)
text_map_open(%s, %s, %d)
text_map_open: file name required
text_map_open(%s): file name must be fully qualified
text_map_open(%s): can not stat %s
text_map_open(%s): %s is not a file
text_map_open(%s): -k should specify a number, not %s
text_map_open(%s): -v should specify a number, not %s
text_map_open(%s): delimiter = %c
stab_map_open(%s, %s)
impl_map_open(%s, %s, %d)
user_map_open(%s)
switch_map_open(%s, %s, %d)
```

In this implementation of *sendmail*, NDBM (the ndbm_map_open) and Berkeley DB (the hash_map_open) type database files are available. Sun style NIS maps (the nis_map_open) are also available. The others (text, stab, impl, user, and switch) are always automatically included. Note that hesiod and nisplus maps are not supported by this particular *sendmail* binary.

If you download and compile *sendmail* yourself, you may include any supported databases. Support is declared on the DBMDEF= line in the appropriate *Makefile* for your system. Possible definitions for DBMDEF= are shown in Table 33-1.

Table 33–1: DBMDEF Definitions in Makefile

Definition	§	Database Support Included
–DHESIOD	33.8.6	*hesiod*(3) aliases only
–DLDAPMAP	33.8.9	*ldap*(3) white pages
–DNDBM	33.8.3	*ndbm*(3) database files
–DNEWDB	33.8.1	Berkeley *db*(3) database files
–DNIS	33.8.11	Sun NIS network databases
–DNISPLUS	33.8.12	Sun NIS+ network databases
–DNETINFO	33.8.10	NeXT *netinfo*(3) aliases only

For example, the *Makefile.ULTRIX* file might include this line:

```
DBMDEF= -DNDBM -DNEWDB -DNIS
```

which includes support for *ndbm*(3), *db*(3), and *nis*(3) databases,[*] whereas the *Makefile.SunOS.5.x* file might include the following:

```
DBMDEF= -DNDBM -DNIS -DNISPLUS
```

which excludes *db*(3) support but includes *nisplus*(3) support.

If you omit all database support (by undefining DBMDEF, for example, or not supplying support indications after the equal sign), *sendmail* will be unable to maintain its aliases in database format. Also, any attempt to rebuild the aliases database (with *newalias* or with **–bi**) will fail with the following error message:

```
Cannot rebuild aliases: no database format defined
Cannot create database for alias file /etc/aliases: No such device
```

Note that if you add new map types, you may have to also add libraries to the LIBS= line in your *Makefile*.

33.2 Create Files with makemap

The *makemap* program is supplied in source form with V8 *sendmail*. It may be supplied in pre-compiled form by your vendor. It is used to create database files and is run from the command line like this:

```
% makemap switches class file
```

We'll discuss the **switches** in the next section. The **class** can be either *dbm* (which uses the *ndbm*(3) library routines), *hash*, or *btree* (both of which use the

---

[*] If you declare support for both NDBM and NEWDB, be sure to remove *ndbm.h* and *ndbm.o* from the NEWDB distribution. Failure to remove them will confuse *sendmail*, causing it to fail in ugly ways.

db(3) library routines). The `file` is the location and name (full path or relative name) for the database file to create. For *dbm* files, the *.pag* and *.dir* suffixes are added automatically. For the *db* files, the *.db* suffix will be added automatically if it is not already included in the name.

The *makemap* program reads from its standard input. That input is line oriented and contains the text from which the database files will be created. Lines that begin with a # are interpreted as comments and ignored. Lines that contain no characters (empty lines) are also ignored. Whitespace (spaces or tabs) separates the *key* on the left from the *data* on the right. An example of such an input file is the following:

```
lady      relaysite!lady
my.host   relaysite!lady
bug       bug.localuucp
```

The second line above shows that *keys* may be multitokened (`my.host` is three tokens). In reading from existing files, some conversion may be required to massage the input into a usable form. To make a database of the */etc/hosts* file (for converting hostnames into IP addresses), for example, a command line like the following might be required:

```
% awk '/^[^#]/ {print $2, $1}' | makemap ...
```

Here, *awk*(1) needs to eliminate comment lines (the `/^[^#]/`). Otherwise, it will wrongly move them to the second column, where *makemap* will not recognize them as comments.

33.2.1 *makemap Command-Line Switches*

The command-line switches for *makemap* must precede the `class` and the `file`:

```
makemap switches class file
```

Switches are single characters, prefixed with a – character. Switches may also be combined:

```
-N -o      ← good
-No        ← also good
```

The complete list of switches is shown in Table 33-2. (See *getopt*(3) for additional information about the way switches are handled.)

Table 33–2: makemap Program's Switches

Switch	§	Description
-d	33.2.1.1	Allow duplicate keys
-f	33.2.1.2	Don't fold uppercase to lowercase
-N	33.2.1.3	Append a null byte to all keys
-o	33.2.1.4	Append to, don't overwrite the file
-r	33.2.1.5	Replace (silently) duplicate keys
-v	33.2.1.6	Watch keys and data being added

33.2.1.1 -d allow duplicate keys

Ordinarily, *makemap* will complain if two entries have identical keys and refuse to insert the duplicate. But if it is desirable to allow the same key to appear multiple times in the database, you can use the -d switch to suppress those warnings and allow the duplicates to be inserted. But be aware that this switch is allowed only for the **btree** and **hash** forms of the *db*(3) library. Use of this switch with any other form of database will produce the following error:

```
makemap: Type class does not support -d (allow dups)
```

See the -r switch for a way to cause duplicates to replace originals.

33.2.1.2 -f don't fold uppercase to lowercase

Normally, the key is converted to lowercase before being stored in the database. When the key entries are case-sensitive, the -f switch may be used to prevent conversion to lowercase. When tokens in rule sets are later looked up in the database, you may choose (with the K command) to leave those tokens as is or convert them to lowercase before the comparison to keys. This switch and the K command should parallel each other.

33.2.1.3 -N append a null byte to all keys

The -N switch tells *makemap* to include a trailing zero byte with each key that it adds to the database. When V8 *sendmail* looks up a key in the database, it uses a binary comparison. Some databases, such as */etc/aliases* under SunOS, append a zero byte to each key. When a trailing zero byte is included with a key, it must also be included with the tokens being looked up, or the lookup will fail. The use of this switch *must* match the K command (see §33.3.4.6).

33.2.1.4 -o append to, don't overwrite the file

The -o switch causes *sendmail* to append to a map, rather than overwrite it. Ordinarily, *makemap* overwrites any existing map with completely new information.

The appended information must be all new information (no duplicate keys), unless the -r switch is also used.

33.2.1.5 -r replace (silently) duplicate keys

Ordinarily, it is an error to specify a key that already exists in a map. That is,

```
john    john@host1
john    john@host2
```

Here, the second john line produces an error instead of replacing the first with the second. To allow replacement keys, use the -r switch with *makemap*. Generally, the -r and -o switches should be combined in updating a database with new information.

33.2.1.6 -v watch keys and data being added

To watch your keys and data being added to a database, use the -v switch. This switch causes the following line of output to be produced for each key processed:

```
key='key', val='data'
```

Note that the trailing zero added by the -N switch is not displayed with the -v output. Also note that verbose output is printed to the standard output, whereas error messages are printed to the standard error output.

33.3 The K Configuration Command

The K configuration command is used to associate a symbolic name with a database file. The symbolic name will later be used in the RHS of rules. The form of the K command looks like this:

```
Kname class args
```

The *name* is the symbolic name. The *class* is the kind of database to use (see §33.3.2). The *args* specifies the location and properties of the database file (see §33.3.3). We describe each in turn.

33.3.1 The name

The *name* portion of the K configuration command immediately follows the K. Whitespace between the K and the *name* is optional.

```
K name class args
 ↑
 optional whitespace
```

The name must begin with a letter or digit and may contain only letters, digits, and the underscore character. For example:

```
K local_hosts        ← good
K $andCents          ← bad
```

If you begin a *name* with a bad character, the following error will be printed and that K line will be ignored:

configfile: line *num*: readcf: config K line: no map name

If a bad character appears in the middle of a name, the part preceding the bad character will be taken as the *name*, and the part following the bad character will be taken as the *class*. For example, the *name* me@home will produce this error:

configfile: line *num*: readcf: map me: class home not available

The case of the letters in *name* does not matter. All names are converted to lower-case before they are stored.

33.3.2 The class

Recall that the *class* portion of the K configuration command follows the **name**:

```
Kname class args
```

Note that whitespace between the **name** and the **class** may be a joined indented line, which allows commenting and improves readability:

```
Kname         # Why this name
        class # Why this class
        args  # and so on
```

The **class** is the database type. It must be one of the classes listed in Table 33-3.

Table 33-3: Possible K Command Classes

Class	§	Version	Description
btree	33.8.1	V8.1 and above	Berkeley's *db* form of database
bestmx	33.8.2	V8.7 and above	Look up the best MX record for a host
dbm	33.8.3	V8.1 and above	Really *ndbm* supplied with most versions of UNIX
dequote	33.8.4	V8.1 and above	A pseudo map for removing quotation marks
hash	33.8.5	V8.1 and above	Berkeley's *db* form of database
hesiod	33.8.6	V8.7 and above	MIT network user authentication services
host	33.4.3	V8.1 and above	Internal table to store and look up hostnames
implicit	33.8.8	V8.1 and above	Search for an *aliases* database file
ldapx	33.8.9	V8.8 and above	The Lightweight Directory Access Protocol
netinfo	33.8.10	V8.7 and above	NeXT Computers network information services
nis	33.8.11	V8.1 and above	Sun's Network Information Services (NIS)

Table 33-3: Possible K Command Classes (continued)

Class	§	Version	Description
nisplus	33.8.12	V8.7 and above	Sun's newer Network Information Services (NIS+)
null	33.8.13	V8.7 and above	Provide a never found service
program	33.8.14	V8.7 and above	Run an external program to look up the key
sequence	33.8.15	V8.7 and above	Search a series of maps
stab	33.8.16	V8.1 and above	Internally load aliases into the symbol table
switch	33.8.17	V8.7 and above	Internal hook to auto-build sequences
text	33.8.18	V8.7 and above	Look up in flat text files
userdb	33.8.19	V8.7 and above	Look up in the User Database
user	33.8.20	V8.7 and above	Look up local passwd information

All of these classes are described in §33.8 at the end of this chapter. If the **class** is not one of those listed, or if support for the **class** was not compiled in, the following error is printed and the K command is ignored:

configfile: line *num*: readcf: map mehome: class *badclass* not available

The case of the **class** is ignored by *sendmail*. That is, **hash**, **Hash**, and **HASH** are all the same.

33.3.3 *The args*

The **args** of the K configuration command follow symbolic name and class type:

    Kname class args

The **args** specify (among other things) the location of the database file or the name of a network map. The **args** is like a miniature command line, and its general form looks like this:

    switches file_or_map

The **switches** are letters prefixed with a - character that modify the use of the database. (We'll discuss them in the next section.) The *file_or_map* is the location of the database file or the name of a network map. The *file_or_map* should exclude the *.pag* and *.dir* suffixes for *dbm* class files and exclude the *.db* suffix for *hash* or *btree* class files.

A database or map is opened for reading when the configuration file is processed. If the *file* cannot be opened (and the −o is omitted; see §33.3.4.8), an appropriate error is printed. The *file_or_map* should be an absolute pathname of a file (such as */etc/uuhosts*) or a literal network map name (such as *hosts.byname*). An **nis** map specification can include a domain:

`map@domain`

Relative filenames (names that omit a leading /) are interpreted as relative to the current directory of the process that invoked *sendmail* and should never be used.

33.3.4 The switches

The *switches* must follow the *class* and precede the *file_or_map*:

```
Kname class switches file_or_map
```

If any *switches* follow *file_or_map*, they are silently ignored.[*] All *switches* begin with a – character and are listed in Table 33-4.

Table 33–4: K Command Switches

Switch	§	Version	Description
-A	33.3.4.1	V8.7 and above	Append values for duplicate keys
-a	33.3.4.2	V8.1 and above	Append tag on successful match
-f	33.3.4.3	V8.1 and above	Don't fold keys to lowercase
-k	33.3.4.4	V8.7 and above	Specify column for key
-m	33.3.4.5	V8.1 and above	Suppress replacement on match
-N	33.3.4.6	V8.1 and above	Append a null byte to all keys
-O	33.3.4.7	V8.2 and above	Adaptive versus never add a null
-o	33.3.4.8	V8.1 and above	The database file is optional
-q	33.3.4.9	V8.7 and above	Don't strip quotes from key
-s	33.3.4.10	V8.7 and above	Space replacement character
-v	33.3.4.11	V8.7 and above	Specify the value's column
-z	33.3.4.12	V8.7 and above	Specify the column delimiter

If a switch other than those listed is specified, that switch is silently ignored.

Not all switches work with all classes. Some classes use many switches; others use none. The switches that are used by each class are shown in Table 33-5.

Table 33–5: Which Class Uses Which Switches

Class	Switches
btree	-A -a -f -m -N -O -o -q
bestmx	-a -q
dbm	-A -a -f -m -N -O -o -q
dequote	-a -s
hash	-A -a -f -m -N -O -o -q

---

[*] This is true as of version 8.8.4. Future versions may change the semantics of the K line such that switches may follow.

Table 33-5: Which Class Uses Which Switches (continued)

Class	Switches
hesiod	-a -m -o -q
host	-a -m -q
implicit	-q
ldapx	-a -f -m -N -O -o -q
netinfo	-a -k -m -q -v
nisplus	-a -f -k -m -o -q -v -z
nis	-a -f -m -o -q
null	
program	-a -m -o -q
sequence	
stab	-q
switch	-q
text	-a -f -k -m -o -q -v -z
userdb	-a -f -m -q
user	-a -m -q -v

Some classes of databases use special switches that are not available to the broad class of databases. Others redefine the meaning of some switches. These special switches are shown in Table 33-6. Future versions of *sendmail* may be changed in such a way that it may be possible to have only one list.

Table 33-6: Specialty Class Switches

Switch	Class or Vendor	Description
-b	ldapx	Base from which to begin the search
-d	Sun	Use domain wide information (see §D.3)
-h	ldapx	Host that serves this network database
-l	ldapx	Time limit to timeout connection
-n	ldapx	Retrieve attribute names only, not values
-p	ldapx	Port to use when connecting to host
-R	ldapx	Don't auto chase referrals
-s	ldapx	Search scope of "base," "one," or "sub"

33.3.4.1 -A *append values for duplicate keys (V8.7 and above)*

Ordinarily, when *sendmail* builds (rebuilds) an aliases database, it objects to duplicate keys on the left of the colon:

```
staff:  bill
staff:  leopold          ← this is an error
```

But sometimes, in automating for example, such duplicates are necessary. In such instances, the **–A** switch can be used with the `AliasFile` (**A**) option (see §34.8.1) to cause duplicates to be silently appended:

```
staff:  bill
staff:  leopold
```
... silently modified by sendmail to internally become
```
staff:  bill, leopold
```

Note that this process is further illustrated in §24.4.4.

The **–A** database switch is useful only with alias files, because those are the only files that *sendmail* rebuilds on its own.

33.3.4.2 -a   append tag on successful match (V8.1 and above)

When a key is looked up in a database (from inside the `$(` and `$)` operators of the RHS of rules), a successfully found key is replaced by its data. If the **–a** switch is given, the text following that switch, up to the first delimiting whitespace character, is appended to the replacement data. For example:

```
-a              appends   nothing
-a.             appends   .
-a,MAGICTOKEN   appends   ,MAGICTOKEN
```

The text to be appended is taken literally. Quotation marks and backslashed characters are included without interpretation, so whitespace cannot be included in that text. Because the rewritten RHS is normalized as an address, special address expressions (such as parentheses) should be avoided. The use of appended text is one of two methods used for recognizing a successful lookup in rules. We'll discuss the other, `$:`, in §33.4.1.

33.3.4.3 -f   don't fold keys to lowercase (V8.1 and above)

Ordinarily, *sendmail* will normalize a key to lowercase before looking it up in the database. If the keys in the database are case-sensitive ("TEX" is considered different from "tex," for example), the **–f** switch should be used to prevent this normalization. Note that if the **–f** switch is omitted (the default), the database must have been created with all lowercase keys (also the default).

33.3.4.4 -k   specify column for key (V8.7 and above)

Beginning with V8.7, *sendmail* began to support a flat text-file form of database. The */etc/hosts* file is an example of such a flat file, in that it is organized in a line-by-line manner:

```
   123.45.67.89      here.our.domain
```

When such files are' read as databases (with the **text** class; see §33.8.18), you need to specify which column is the key and which is the value.

For **nisplus** and **netinfo** maps, the −k switch specifies the name (text) of the desired column.

When the −k switch specifies which column is the key, its absence defaults to 0 for the **text** class and to the name of the zeroth column for the **nisplus** class. Note that the numbered columns are indexed beginning with 0 for the first and 1 for the second. See also −v (see §33.3.4.11) for the value's column (**text** and **nisplus** only) and −z (see §33.3.4.12) for the column delimiter (**text** only).

33.3.4.5 −m   suppress replacement on match (V8.1 and above)

Ordinarily, a successful lookup in a database or map causes the key to be replaced by its value. When the intention is to merely verify that the key exists (not replace it), the −m switch can be used to suppress replacement. For example, the values that are returned from the *hosts.byname* NIS map are not generally useful (they contain multiple hostnames). In looking up a key in this map (with $(and $); see §33.4), the −m switch prevents those multiple names from wrongly replacing the single hostname in the key. Note that the −a (see §33.3.4.2) can still be used to append a suffix to a successful lookup. Also, the $:*default* (see §33.4.1) is still used if the lookup fails.

33.3.4.6 −N   append a null byte to all keys (V8.1 and above)

If a database was created with *makemap*'s −N switch (see §33.2.1.3) to include the terminating zero byte with each key, this K configuration command −N switch may be specified to force all lookups to also include a zero byte. Note that −N is not needed for the **nis** class and, if included, is ignored. See also −O below.

33.3.4.7 −O   adaptive versus never add a null (V8.2 and above)

If neither −N nor −O is specified, *sendmail* uses an adaptive algorithm to decide whether or not to look for the terminating zero byte. The algorithm starts by accepting either. If the first key looked up is found to end with a terminating zero byte, the algorithm will thereafter look only for keys with terminating zero bytes. If the first key that is looked up is found to not end with a terminating zero byte, the algorithm will thereafter look only for keys without terminating zero bytes.

If this −O switch is specified, *sendmail* never tries a zero byte, which can speed matches. Note that if both −N and −O are specified, *sendmail* will never try to match at all, thus causing all lookups to appear to fail.

33.3.4.8 -o the database file is optional (V8.1 and above)

Ordinarily, *sendmail* will complain if a database file cannot be opened for reading. If the presence of a database file is optional (as it may be on certain machines), the −o switch should be used to tell *sendmail* that the database is optional. Note that if a database is optional and cannot be opened, all lookups will silently fail for rules that use that database.

33.3.4.9 -q don't strip quotes from key (V8.7 and above)

Ordinarily, *sendmail* strips all the nonescaped quotation marks (those not prefixed with a backslash) from a key before looking it up. For example, the following key:

```
"Bob \"bigboy\" Roberts \(esq\)"@bob.com
```

will have its nonescaped quotation marks removed to end up like this:

```
Bob "bigboy" Roberts (esq)@bob.com
```

Note that all escaped characters are de-escaped (have the backslash removed) during this process.

When quotation marks and escaped characters need to be preserved in a key before it is looked up, you can use the −q switch with the K configuration command. The −q switch suppresses dequoting and de-escaping.

33.3.4.10 -s space replacement character (V8.7 and above)

The **dequote** class (see §33.8.4) refuses to remove quotation marks if doing so will result in an illegal address. For example, internal space characters are illegal in addresses:

```
"a b"          becomes →      "a b"
```

The −s switch causes all the quoted space characters to be changed into a character that you specify just before the dequoting process.

```
Kdequote dequote -s+
```

Here, we specify that quoted strings will have quoted spaces converted into a plus before dequoting. Therefore, the above conversion becomes the following:

```
"a b"          becomes →      a+b
```

The −s switch is only of use with the **dequote** class. Note that the **lpadx** class uses the −s switch differently (see Table 33-6 in §33.3.4).

33.3.4.11 -v specify the value's column (V8.7 and above)

The manner in which the key and its value are visually displayed in flat, sequential, text files and certain network services, may not be directly suitable for use in maps. A text class file, for example */etc/hosts*, may display the key on the right and the value on the left:

```
123.45.67.89        here.our.domain
```

For such circumstances the -v switch can be used with the K command to specify the column or item that will be returned as the value when a key is matched. For example:

```
Kaddr text -k1 -v0 /etc/hosts
```

For nisplus and netinfo maps, the -v switch specifies the name (text) of the value's column.

This -v switch specifies which column is the value to return. If it is omitted, it defaults to 0 for the text class and to the last named column for the nisplus class. Note that text columns are indexed beginning with 0 for the first and 1 for the second. See also -k (see §33.3.4.4) for the key's column and -z (see §33.3.4.12) for the column delimiter.

33.3.4.12 -z specify the column delimiter (V8.7 and above)

Flat, sequential text files have columns of information delimited from each other with a variety of characters:

```
123.45.67.89        here.our.domain          ← /etc/hosts uses a whitespace
nobody:*:65534:65534::/:                      ← /etc/passwd uses a colon
```

The -z switch can be used to specify a delimiter whenever the default delimiter of whitespace is not appropriate. In the case of the */etc/passwd* file, a database declaration might look like this:

```
Kuid text -z: -k2 -v0 /etc/passwd  # map to convert uid to login name
```

The default is whitespace for the text class. It is a comma for the netinfo class.

33.4 Use Maps with $(and $) in Rules

The information in database files is accessed for use in the RHS of rules. This is the syntax:

```
$( name key $)
```

The *key* is looked up in the database whose symbolic name (as declared with the K configuration command) is *name* (see §33.3) If the *key* is found, the entire expression, including the $(and $), is replaced with the value from the database entry for that *key*. Any *suffix*, as specified with the -a switch (see §33.3.4.2) in the K configuration declaration for *name*, is appended to the data. If the *key* is not found, the entire expression is replaced with *key*. If the $) is omitted, all tokens up to but excluding the tab and comment, or end-of-line if there is no comment, are taken as the key. To illustrate one use for $(and $), see the following rule:

```
R$- . uucp        $: $( uucp $1.uucp $)
```

and the following K command:

```
Kuucp hash /etc/uucp.db
```

This associates the symbolic name **uucp** with a **hash** class file called /etc/uucp.db. If the *uucp.db* database contained entries like this:

```
lady.uucp     lady.localuucp
sonya.uucp    sonya.localuucp
```

then a workspace of **lady.uucp** would match the LHS, so the RHS would look up $1.uucp (thus **lady.uucp**) in the *uucp.db* database. Because **lady.uucp** is found, the entire $(to $) RHS expression is replaced with **lady.localuucp** from the database. Any UUCP hosts other than **lady** or **sonya** would not be found in the database, so the RHS expression would become the original workspace, unchanged.

Note that the entire RHS is prefixed with a $:. This prevents *sendmail* from re-testing with the LHS after the RHS rewrite. If this prefix were omitted, endless looping could occur.

Also note that the -a switch of the K command can be used to simplify the writing of this rule. For example:

```
Kuucp dbm -a.localuucp /etc/uuhosts
```

The -a switch tells *sendmail* to append the text .localuucp to all successful lookups. Thus the preceding database can be simplified to look like this:

```
lady.uucp     lady
sonya.uucp    sonya
```

But the preceding rule remains the same:

```
R$- . uucp        $: $( uucp $1.uucp $)
```

Beyond the simply macros and positional operators that we have shown, the *key* part can use other operators and forms of macros. For example, delayed expansion macros may be useful:

```
R$&s        $: $( uucp $&s $)
```

Here, the sender's host is looked up to see whether it is a UUCP host. The $& prefix (see §31.5.3) prevents the s macro from being expanded as the configuration file is read. Instead, its value will change with each piece of mail that is processed.

Additional examples of database lookups are given with the individual class descriptions at the end of this chapter.

33.4.1 Specify a Default with $:

V8 *sendmail* offers the $: operator as an alternative to the −a switch (or for use in conjunction with it). The $: operator, when it stands between the $(and $), specifies a default to use instead of the *key*, should a lookup fail:

```
R$- . uucp        $: $( uucp $1 $: $1.uucp $)
```

Here, the $- part of the LHS is looked up in the uucp database. If it is found, the $(to $) of the RHS expression is replaced by the data from that database. If it is not found, the $: causes the expression to be replaced with the $- LHS part and a .uucp suffix ($1.uucp).

This version of our rule further simplifies the contents of the database file. With this rule, the database file would contain information such as the following:

```
lady      lady
sonya     sonya
```

The −a is still used as before to append a .localuucp to each successful match.

```
Kuucp dbm -a.localuucp /etc/uuhosts
```

In the RHS expression the $: must follow the *key* or it loses its special meaning:

```
$( name key $: default $)
```

If the $:*default* wrongly precedes the *key*, it is used as the key, lookups fail, and replacements are not as expected. If the $: is present but the *default* is missing, a failed lookup returns an empty workspace.

33.4.2 Specify Numbered Substitution with $@

For more complex database substitutions, V8 *sendmail* offers the $@ operator for use in the RHS with the $(and $) expression. There may be multiple $@ prefixed texts between the *key* and the $: (if present) or the $).

```
$(name key $@text1 $@text2 $:default $)
```

Each $@*text* expression is numbered by position (from left to right):

```
$(name key $@text1 $@text2 $:default $)
           ↑          ↑
           1          2
```

In this numbering scheme the *key* is always number 0, even if no $@'s are listed.

These numbers correspond to literal %*digit* expressions in the data portion of the database. For example:

```
lady    %0!%1@%2
```

When a lookup of the *key* in the RHS of the rule is successful, the returned value is examined for %*digit* expressions. Each such expression is replaced by its corresponding $@*text* from the rule. In the case of the above database, %0 would be replaced with lady (the *key*), %1 with text1, and %2 with text2.

To illustrate, consider the above database entry and the following rule:

```
R$- @ $-.uucp    $: $(uucp $2 $@$1 $@mailhost $:$1.$2.uucp $)
```

If the workspace contains the address *joe@lady.uucp*, the LHS matches. The RHS rewrites only once because it is prefixed with the $: operator. The expression between the $(and $) causes the second $- from the LHS (the $2, the *key*) to be looked up in the database whose symbolic name is uucp. Since $2 references lady from the workspace, lady is found and the data (%0!%1@%2) are used to rewrite. The %0 is replaced by lady (the *key* via $2). The *text* for the first $@ ($1 or joe) then replaces the %1. Then the second *text* for the second $@ (mailhost) replaces the %2. Thus the address *joe@lady.uucp* is rewritten to become *lady!joe@mailhost*.

If a different host, other than lady, appeared in the workspace, this RHS would use the $:*default* part. Thus the address *joe@foo.uucp* would become (via the $:$1.$2.uucp) *joe@foo.uucp*. That is, any address that is not found in the database would remain unchanged.

If there are more $@*text* expressions in the RHS than there are numbers in the value, the excess $@*text* parts are ignored. If a %*digit* in the data references a nonexistent $@*text*, it is simply removed during the rewrite.

All $@*text* expressions must lie between the *key* and the $:*default* (if present). If any follow the $:*default*, they become part of the default and cease to reference any %*digits*.

33.4.3 $[and $]: A Special Case

The special database class called *host* can be declared to modify name-server lookups with $[and $]. The special symbolic name and class pair, host and host, is declared for use with the $(and $) operators, like this:

```
Khost host -a.
```

The –*a* switch was discussed earlier in this chapter. Here, it is sufficient to note how it is used in resolving fully qualified domain names with the $[and $] operators in the RHS of rules. Under V8 *sendmail,* $[and $] are a special case of the following database lookup:

```
$(host foo $)
```

A successful match will ordinarily append a dot to a successfully resolved hostname.

When a *host* class is declared with the K command, any suffix of the –a replaces the dot as the character or characters added.* For example:

```
$[ foo $]      found so rewritten as foo.domain.

Khost host -a
$[ foo $]      found so rewritten as foo.domain

Khost host -a.yes
$[ foo $]      found so rewritten as foo.domain.yes
```

The first line above shows the default action of the $[and $] operators in the RHS of rules. If foo can be fully qualified, its fully qualified name becomes the rewritten value of the RHS and has a dot appended. The next two lines show the –a of host host with no suffix (note that with no suffix the –a is optional). In this configuration file, the fully qualified name has nothing (not even a dot) appended. The last two lines show a configuration file with a .yes as the suffix. This time, the fully qualified name has a .yes appended instead of the dot.

33.5 *The User Database*

The User Database is a special database file that you create for use by *sendmail.* It causes sender and recipient addresses to be rewritten under control of an external database file. Ordinarily, any local address is first looked up in the *aliases* database. If it is not found there, that user's ˜/.*forward* is next examined. If the User Database is enabled, the address is looked up in that database after aliasing and before forwarding.

---

* This happens only for V2 and higher configuration files. Below that level, the dot is not appended unless it is specifically added by the –a of the K command.

Lookup can be local via a database file, remote via a User Database server, or via a Hesiod network service. Here, we describe the database file form. The others are described in §34.8.75.

33.5.1 Enable the User Database

The User Database is automatically enabled when you compile *sendmail* if you include support for NEWDB or HESIOD (see §18.8.54). To see whether a precompiled version of *sendmail* includes User Database support, run it with the −d0.1 switch:

```
% /usr/lib/sendmail -d0.1 -bt < /dev/null
Version 8.8.4
 Compiled with: LOG MIME8TO7 NETINET NETUNIX NEWDB SCANF USERDB XDEBUG
                                                           ↑
                                                          note
```

If USERDB is listed, User Database support is included.

Next you must declare the location of its database file with the **UserDatabaseSpec** (**U**) option (see §34.8.75):

```
OU/etc/userdb.db                              ← in your cf file (V8)
O UserDatabaseSpec=/etc/userdb.db             ← in your cf file (V8.7)
define('confUSERDB_SPEC',/etc/userdb.db)      ← in your m4 file
```

Here, the location of the database file is set to be */etc/userdb.db*. You can also enable a default location for the database file that will take effect should the **User-DatabaseSpec** (**U**) option be missing by defining that location with UDB_DEFAULT_SPEC in compiling (see §18.8.53).

33.5.2 Create the User Database

The User Database is a **btree** class (see §33.8.1) database file created from a source text file using the *makemap* program:

```
% makemap btree /etc/userdb.db < /etc/userdb
```

Here, */etc/userdb* is the source-text file that is input, and */etc/userdb.db* is the database we are creating (the one defined by the **U** option in the previous section).[*]

The source-text file is composed of key and value pairs, one pair per line:

```
key     value
    ↑
whitespace
```

---

[*] The .db is added automatically if it is missing. We include it here for clarity.

The *key* is a user's login name, a colon, and one of two possible keywords: `mail-drop` or `mailname`. The keyword that is chosen determines the nature of the *value*.

`maildrop`

> The *value* is the official delivery address for this user. If there are multiple official addresses, they should either be listed as a single compound value, with separating commas, as, for example:

        root:maildrop   sysadmin@here.us.edu,bill@there.us.edu

> or be listed on individual lines:

        root:maildrop   sysadmin@here.us.edu
        root:maildrop   bill@there.us.edu

> This latter form requires you to use the **-d** command-line switch with the *makemap*(1) program (see §33.2.1.1) when creating the database but has the advantage of being a simpler source file to manage.

`mailname`

> The `mailname` keyword causes a "reverse alias" transformation, wherein the login name in the key is changed into the address in the value for outgoing mail. For example:

        bob:mailname   Bob.Roberts@Here.US.EDU

> This causes mail sent by **bob** to go out addressed as though it is from **Bob.Roberts@Here.US.EDU.**[*] This transformation occurs in the header and envelope. But note that the sender-envelope is not rewritten by UDB unless the **F=i** flag (see §30.8.24) is present in the delivery agent that is selected for the sender. Also note that the recipient headers are not rewritten by UDB unless the **F=k** flag (see §30.8.26) delivery agent is selected for the recipient.

Naturally, the `maildrop` and `mailname` keywords should occur in pairs. Each outgoing address that is created with `mailname` should have a corresponding `mail-drop` entry so that return mail can be delivered. In the above example a reasonable pair might look like this:

        bob:mailname   Bob.Roberts@Here.US.EDU
        Bob.Roberts:maildrop bob

Here, outgoing mail from the user named **bob** will be addressed as though it is from **Bob.Roberts@Here.US.EDU**. Incoming mail (whether it is original or in reply

---

[*] Using full names in outgoing mail is probably not a good idea. Unlike login names, full names are not guaranteed to be unique. If current users expect to be able to receive mail under full names, future users with the same full name may be out of luck. Always weigh convenience against maintainable uniqueness when designing your mail setup.

to the outgoing) will be addressed as though it is to the name `Bob.Roberts`, which will be transformed into and delivered to the local user `bob`.

33.5.3 A :default Outgoing Hostname

The `mailname` keyword allows the host part of outgoing addresses to mask the real hostname of the originating machine. This property can, for example, be used to convert the hostname into a firewall name:

```
bob:mailname          bob@Firewall.US.EDU
```

Here, the canonical name of `bob`'s machine is `Here.US.EDU`. The `mailname` keyword causes outgoing mail from `bob` to appear as though it is from the firewall machine (`Firewall.US.EDU`) instead.

Ordinarily, this transformation is not automatic. Each username that is to appear to be from the firewall machine will need an entry like that above in the User Database. To automate this process, you can use the special username `:default` in a `mailname` declaration:

```
:default:mailname     Firewall.US.EDU
```

If a `maildrop` entry is found for a particular name, but no corresponding `mailname` record is found, the outgoing address is ordinarily unchanged. If, however, a default hostname has been defined with `:default`, that hostname replaces the local hostname for all addresses that lack their own `mailname` entry:

```
:default:mailname     Firewall.US.EDU
bob:maildrop          bob@here.us.edu
```

In this example the user `bob` has a `maildrop` entry but lacks a `mailname` entry. Outgoing mail from this user will have the `:default` hostname used instead of the local hostname. The user `sally`, on the other hand, has neither a `maildrop` entry nor a `mailname` entry and so will not have her outgoing address rewritten.

33.6 Database Maps and m4

Some databases, such as `user`, are a part of UNIX. Others are a part of *sendmail*, like the User Database described above. Many, however, are implemented in rules and rule sets. This latter sort of database is therefore available via the *m4* technique. Currently, all *m4* available databases are implemented as FEATUREs. Table 33-7 lists those available. The second column shows you where to find information about each.

Table 33-7: Database FEATUREs

Feature	§	Version	Description
domaintable	19.6.10	V8.1 and above	Accept other domains as equivalent to the local domain
genericstable	19.6.11	V8.8 and above	Transform sender addresses
mailertable	19.6.14	V8.1 and above	Select new delivery agents based on an external database
virtusertable	19.6.28	V8.8 and above	Support for virtual domains

Note that these FEATUREs do not necessarily need to be used with database files. To illustrate, consider the **domaintable** feature (see §19.6.10). It is included in your *mc* file like this:

```
FEATURE(`domaintable',`nis domaintable')
```

Here, we specify that the database is to be an *nis* map. This causes the *key* to be looked up via the *nis* services and any match to be returned the same way.

33.7 *Pitfalls*

- The result of a subroutine call cannot be looked up directly in a database map. Consider this RHS of a rule:

  ```
  $( uucp $>96 $1 $)
  ```

  Here, the intention is to pass $1 to rule set 96 and then to look up the result in the uucp map. Instead, the literal value 96 and the value in $1 are looked up together and fail first. Then $1 is passed to rule set 96, and the result of that subroutine call becomes the result of the RHS.

- The **%s** of IDA *sendmail* databases will not work as is with V8 *sendmail*. To make it work, replace it with a **%1** throughout the IDA source file, then reverse the keys and values, and finally recreate the database file. This conversion can easily be automated with *sed*(1) or *awk*(1).

- If you are running a Solaris 2.4 or earlier release of Sun's operating system, your database files should not live on **tmpfs** mounted file systems. File locking was not implemented for **tmpfs** until Solaris 2.5.

- Avoid assuming that all **K** command switches mean the same thing for all classes. The ad hoc nature of class submissions by outsiders makes that assumption perilous.

- Not all initialization errors or lookup errors are reported. For some of them you will see an indication of an error only if you use the **-d38.2** debugging switch (see § 37.5.128).

33.8 Alphabetized Reference

Recall that the K configuration command (see §33.3) is used like this:

```
Kname class args
```

The *class* determines the type of database that will be used. For example, the class btree causes the Berkeley *db*(3) to be used, whereas the class dequote causes an internal routine of *sendmail*'s to be called.

In this section we present all the classes in alphabetical order. They are summarized in Table 33-3 of §33.3.2. Most interaction with these classes can be watched by using the -d38.2 debugging switch (see §37.5.128). Some specialty maps use other debugging switches, which we indicate where appropriate.

btree *(V8.1 and above)*

33.8.1 *Berkeley's db form of database*

The term btree stands for "balanced tree." It is a grow-only form of database. Lookups and insertions are fast, but deletions do not shrink the database. A good description of this form of database can be found in *The Art of Computer Programming, Vol. 3: Sorting and Searching*, D.E. Knuth, 1968, pp. 471–480. The btree class is available only if *sendmail* was compiled with NEWDB defined and the new Berkeley *db* library linked in.

See Table 33-5 in §33.3.4 for a list of the K command switches that can be used with this class and the meaning of each.

bestmx *(V8.7 and above)*

33.8.2 *Look up the best MX record for a host*

The bestmx map class looks up a hostname as the *key* and returns the current best MX record as the *value*. Internally, a call is made to *getmxrr()* to get a list of MX records for the host. That list is sorted in order of the best to the worst, and bestmx returns the first. Because *bestmx* is a class, not a map, you need to declare it with a K configuration command before you can use it:

```
Kbestmx bestmx
```

One use for this class might be to see whether a particular host has a usable MX at all:

```
Kbestmx bestmx
...
R$*< @ $+ > $*              $: $1<@$2>$3 <$(bestmx $2 $: NO $)>
R$*< @ $+ > $* < NO >       $#smtp  $@ $2 $: $1 < @ $2 > $3
R$*< @ $+ > $* < $* >       $: $1<@ $[ $2 $] > $3
```

In the first rule we look up the host part of an address (which has already been focused by rule set 3) with the **bestmx** database map. The result of the lookup is surrounded with angle brackets and appended to the original address. The second rule looks for the **NO** caused by an unsuccessful lookup (the **$:**). The original address is then sent with the **smtp** delivery agent. If the hostname inside the appended angle braces is not **NO**, the host part of the original address is canonicalized with the **$[** and **$]** operators.

This **bestmx** class is a special internal one that can take advantage of only two of the **K** command switches: the **-a** (as you saw) and the **-q** (to suppress dequoting the key). This class can be watched with the **-d8** debugging switch (see §37.5.30).

dbm   *(V8.1 and above)*

33.8.3   *Really ndbm supplied with most versions of UNIX*

The dbm class, which is really the *ndbm* form of database, is the traditional form of UNIX database. Data are stored in one file, keys in another. The data must fit in blocks of fixed sizes, so there is usually a limit on the maximum size (1 kilobyte or so) on any given stored datum. The *dbm* class is available only if *sendmail* was compiled with **NDBM** declared (see §18.8.24).

This is the class of database traditionally used with alias files. Because of the limit on the size of a datum, you should consider using one of the *db*(3) **hash** or **btree** classes instead.

See Table 33-5 in §33.3.4 for a list of the **K** command switches that can be used with the class and the meaning of each switch.

dequote   *(V8.6 and above)*

33.8.4   *A pseudo map for removing quotation marks*

V8 *sendmail* can remove quotation marks from around tokens by using the special *dequote* class. Because *dequote* is a class, not a map, you need to declare it with a **K** configuration command before you can use it:

```
Kunquote dequote
```

This declares a map named **unquote** of the class *dequote*. Once a map name has been declared, the *dequote* class can be used in the RHS of rules to remove quotation marks. It is used with **$(** and **$)**, just like database lookups:

```
$(unquote tokens $)
```

Here, arbitrary *tokens* are looked up in the database named **unquote**. That database is special because it is of the class *dequote*. Instead of really being looked up in a database, *tokens* will just have any surrounding quotation marks removed:

```
"A.B.C"           becomes    A.B.C
"A"."B"."C"       becomes    A.B.C
"A B"             becomes    "A B"
"A,B"             becomes    "A,B"
"A>B"             becomes    "A>B"
```

The first example shows that surrounding quotation marks are removed. The second shows that multiple quoted tokens are all de-quoted. The last three show that *sendmail* refuses to dequote any tokens that will form an illegal or ambiguous address when dequoted.

As an aid to understanding this dequoting process, run the following two-line configuration file in rule-testing mode:

```
V7
Kdequote dequote
```

You can then use the –bt /map command to try various dequoting possibilities:

```
> /map dequote "A.B.C"
map_lookup: dequote ("A.B.C") returns A.B.C (0)
> /map dequote "A"."B"."C"
map_lookup: dequote ("A"."B"."C") returns A.B.C (0)
> /map dequote "A B"
map_lookup: dequote ("A B") no match (0)
```

Note that beginning with V8.7, specifying the –s switch causes the space character to be replaced with another character before dequoting (see §33.3.4.10).

```
V7
Kdequote dequote -s+
```

In that case the last example above would become the following:

```
> /map dequote "A B"
map_lookup: dequote ("A B") returns A+B (0)
```

Also note that beginning with V8.8, specifying the –a switch causes a suffix of your choice to be appended to a successful match:

```
V7
Kdequote dequote -a.yes
```

In that case the "A.B.C" example would become the following:

```
> /map dequote "A.B.C"
map_lookup: dequote ("A.B.C") returns A.B.C.yes (0)
```

In addition to removing quotes, the *dequote* class also tokenizes everything that is returned. It does this because quotes are ordinarily used to mask the separation characters that delimit tokens. For example, consider the $& operator. It prevents a macro in a rule from being expanded when the configuration file is read and always returns a single token, no matter how many tokens it really contains. Consider this configuration file:

```
V7
DXhost.domain
Kdequote dequote
R$*     $: $&X , $(dequote "" $&X $)
```

Here, the macro X is assigned host.domain as its value. The only rule in the file (when *sendmail* is run in rule-testing mode) prints the expression $&X to show that it is a single token, then prints the result of dequoting that same expression. Note that an empty token needs to be dequoted. Putting quotes around $&X itself won't work. The output produced by rule-testing mode looks like this:

```
> 0 foo
rewrite: ruleset  0   input: foo
rewrite: ruleset  0 returns: host.domain , host . domain
>                                 ↑              ↑
                                 $X         $X dequoted
```

No debugging switch is available to watch the actions of the **dequote** class.

hash   *(V8.1 and above)*

33.8.5   *Berkeley's db form of database*

The *hash* class uses a hashing algorithm for storing data. This approach to a database is described in *A New Hash Package for UNIX*, by Margo Seltzer (USENIX Proceedings, Winter 1991). The hash class is available only if *sendmail* was compiled with NEWDB defined and the new Berkeley *db* library linked in.

The **hash** class is the default that is used with most of the FEATURES offered by the *m4* technique (see Table 33-7 in §33.6). For example, consider the following:

```
Kuudomain hash -o /etc/uudomain
```

Here, a map named uudomain is declared to be of class hash. The −o says that the file */etc/uudomain* is optional.

See Table 33-5 in §33.3.4 for a list of the K command switches that can be used with this class and the meaning of each.

hesiod

33.8.6
MIT network user authentication services

The `hesiod` class of map uses the Hesiod system, a network information system developed as Project Athena. Support of *hesiod* maps is available only if you declare HESIOD when compiling *sendmail*. (See §18.8.10 for a fuller description of the Hesiod system.)

A `hesiod` map is declared like this:

```
Kname hesiod HesiodNameType
```

The *HesiodNameType* must be one that is known at your site, such as **passwd** or **service**. An unknown *HesiodNameType* will yield this error when *sendmail* begins to run:

```
cannot initialize Hesiod map (hesiod error number)
```

One example of a lookup might look like this:

```
Kuid2name hesiod uid
R$+        $: $(uid2name $1 $)
```

Here, we declare the map **uid2name** using the Hesiod-type **uid**, which converts *uid* numbers into login names. If the conversion was successful, we use the login name returned; otherwise, we use the original workspace.

See Table 33-5 in §33.3.4 for a list of the K command switches that can be used with this class and the meaning of each.

host

33.8.7
Internal table used to store and look up hostnames

The *host* class is a special internal database used by *sendmail* to help it resolve hostnames. It is fully described under the $[and $] operators in §33.4.3.

The –d9 debugging switch (see §37.5.37) can be used to watch the actions caused by this *host* class.

implicit

33.8.8
Search for an aliases database file

The *implicit* class refers specifically to *aliases*(5) files only. It causes *sendmail* to first try to open a *db*(3) hash-style alias file, and if that fails or if NEWDB support was not compiled in, it tries to open a *ndbm*(3)-style database. If that fails, *sendmail* reads the *aliases*(5) source file into its internal symbol table.

Although you can declare and use this class in a configuration file, there is no reason to do so. It is of use only to the internals of *sendmail*. If *implicit* fails to open an *aliases* file (probably because of a faulty `AliasFile` (`A`) option; see §34.8.1), *sendmail* will issue the following error if it is running in verbose mode:

```
WARNING: cannot open alias database bad file name
```

If the source *aliases* file exists but no database form exists, *sendmail* will read that source file into its internal symbol table using the **stab** class (see §33.8.16).

ldapx   *(V8.8 and above)*

33.8.9   *The Lightweight Directory Access Protocol*

LDAP stands for Lightweight Directory Access Protocol and provides access to the X.500 directory. The **ldapx** class is used to look up items in that directory service. It is declared like this:

```
Kname ldapx switches
```

Lookups via LDAP are entirely defined by the switches specified. To illustrate, consider the following X.500 entry:

```
cn=Full Name, o=Organization, c=US
sn=Name
uid=yourname
cn=Full Name
commonname=Full Name
mail=yourname@mailhub.your.domain
objectclass=person
objectclass=deptperson
```

To look up a login name in this database and have the official email address for that user returned, you might use a declaration like this:

```
Kldap ldapx -k"uid=%s" -v"mail" -hldap_host -b"o=Organization, c=US"
```

Note that the **-k** switch is in the form of a `ldap_search`(3) filter, where the *key* will replace the **%s** and then the whole expression will be searched for as the *key*. The **-b** is required to specify the base from which to search. Note that a base must be selected such that it ensures that *sendmail* will always get a unique result.

The following rule can be used with the above declaration to look up the preferred mail address for a user:

```
R$* <@ $+ > $*        $: $(ldap $1 $: $1<@$2>$3 $)
```

Here we presume that this rule was preceded by a call to rule set 3 to focus on the host part. If the lookup succeeds, the new (unfocused) address is returned from the `mail=` line in the database. Otherwise, the original address is returned.

A few errors can occur during *sendmail's* startup that indicate a faulty K command:

```
LDAP map: -h flag is required
LDAP map: -b flag is required
No return attribute in map name
```

The first two show that those switches are mandatory. The third prints only to show that the −v switch is mandatory if the −o switch is absent.

In addition, each successful lookup can cause a line like the following to be logged via *syslog*(3):

```
qid: ldap key => value
```

See Table 33-5 in §33.3.4 for a list of the K command switches that can be used with this class and the meaning of each. Also, Table 33-6 lists several nonstandard switches that are used by this ldapx class. Finally, note that the ldapx class can be used only if LDAPMAP was defined when *sendmail* was compiled (see §18.8.15).

netinfo *(V8.7 and above)*

33.8.10 *NeXT Computer's network information services*

NetInfo is NeXT's implementation of a network-based information service. The *netinfo* class expects a map declaration to be of the following form:

```
Kname netinfo map
```

Other switches may be used with this class, and they have their normal meanings (see Table 33-5 in §33.3.4).

Support of *netinfo* maps is available only if you declare NETINFO when compiling *sendmail* (see §18.8.27).

nis *(V8.6 and above)*

33.8.11 *Sun's Network Information Services (NIS)*

Sun Microsystems offers a network information service called NIS. It provides the ability to look up various kinds of information in network databases. The nis class allows you to access that network information by way of rules in rule sets. You declare an nis class map like this:

```
Kname nis map
```

Here, name is the identifier that you will later use in rule sets. The map is any *nis* map. Lookups will occur in the default *nis* domain. If you wish to specify some other domain, you may append an @ character and the domain name to the map:

```
Kname nis map@domain
```

To illustrate, consider the need to look up the name of the central mail server for your department. If such a map were called *mailservers*, you could use the following configuration file line to look up your domain in that map:

```
Kmailservers nis -o mailservers
...
R$* <@ $+ > $*          $: $1<@$2>$3 <$(mailservers $2 $)>
R$* <@ $+ > $* <$+>      $#smtp $@ $4 $: $1 < @ $2 > $3
...
```

Here, we look up the host part of an address ($2) in the **mailservers** *nis* map. The **-o** makes the existence of the map optional. If the host part is found, it is rewritten to be the name of the mail server for that host. In the last rule we forward the original address to that server.

Without the **-o**, the nonexistence of a map will cause this error to be logged:

```
Cannot bind to map name in domain domain: reason here
```

If *nis* is not running at all or if *sendmail* cannot bind to the **domain** specified or the default domain, the following error is logged:

```
NIS map name specified, but NIS not running
```

The **nis** class is available only if *sendmail* is compiled with NIS defined (see §18.8.29).

See Table 33-5 in §33.3.4 for a list of the K command switches that can be used with this class and the meaning of each.

nisplus   *(V8.7 and above)*

33.8.12   *Sun's newer version of NIS*

Sun Microsystems's NIS+ is a complete redo of its earlier *nis* system. The **nisplus** class allows you to look up information using NIS+. The form of that class declaration looks like this:

```
Kname nisplus map.domain
```

Here, the **map** is a NIS+ map name, such as *mail_aliases*.[*] If the **domain** or *.domain* is missing, the *nisplus* default domain is used. If the entire **map.domain** is missing, the default becomes *mail_aliases.org_dir*. The domain *org_dir* contains all the systemwide administration tables.

---

[*] Note that under NIS+ map names cannot contain a dot, whereas under NIS they could—for example, *mail_aliases* for NIS+ but *mail.aliases* for NIS.

Any lookup failures that can be retried will automatically be retried up to five times, with a *sleep*(3) of 2 seconds between each try. If the `map.domain` doesn't exist in the local *nisplus* system, this error is printed when *sendmail* starts:

    Cannot find table *map.domain*: *reason for failure here*

This error is suppressed if the original K command declaration included the -o switch.

Two other errors can happen during startup:

    map.domain: *reason for failure here* is not a table
    nisplus_map_open(*map*): can not find key column *-k column name here*

You can use the -k switch to specify a *key* column to look up. Under *nisplus*, columns are named, so the -k must be followed by a valid name, or the last error above will be printed. You can also use the -v switch to specify the *value* column, also a name. If the -v is omitted, the last column becomes the default. See Table 33-5 in §33.3.4 for a list of the other K command switches that can be used with this class and the meaning of each.

null   *(V8.7 and above)*

33.8.13   *Provide a never found service*

The `null` class is an internal database that always returns a failed lookup. It is useful for replacing other classes to force failures without errors. Normally, the `null` class is used internally only.

Consider a tiny configuration file that does not need the use of the *aliases* facilities. One way to declare aliases would be like this:

    O AliasFile=null:

This tells *sendmail* to use the `null` class for looking up aliases. Therefore no aliases will ever be found.

None of the K command switches may be used with the `null` class. If you try to use any, they will be silently ignored. No debugging switch is available to watch this `null` class.

program   *(V8.7 and above)*

33.8.14   *Run an external program to look up the key*

The `program` class allows you to perform lookups via arbitrary external programs. The form for the declaration of this class looks like this:

```
Kname program /path arg1 arg2 ...
```

The */path* must be the full pathname to the program. Relative paths will not work, and attempts to use them will log the following error and cause the lookup to fail:

```
NOQUEUE: SYSERR(bcx): relative name: cannot exec: No such file or directory
```

The program is run under the *uid* and *gid* of the person who ran *sendmail*. But if that person is *root*, the program is instead run as the user and group specified by the `DefaultUser(u)` option (see §34.8.15).

The arguments to the program always have the key to be looked up added as a final argument:

```
Kname program /path arg1 arg2 ...
                                ↑
                          key added here
```

This is the only way that the key can be passed to the program. The key will specifically not be piped to the program's standard input.

The value (result of the lookup) is read from the program's standard output. Only the first MAXLINE-1 characters are read (where MAXLINE is defined in *conf.h*, currently as 2048). The read result is processed as an address and placed into the workspace (unless the –m switch is used with the K command).

To illustrate, consider the need to look up a user's preferred address in an external relational database:

```
Kilook program /usr/lib/ingres_lookup -d users.database
```

This program has been custom written to accept the key as its final argument. To prevent spurious errors, it exits with a zero value whether the key is found or not. Any system errors cause it to exit with a value selected from those defined in *<sysexits.h>* (those recognized by *sendmail*). Error messages are printed to the standard error output, and the found value (if there was one) is printed to the standard output.

In general, it is better to use one of the database formats known to *sendmail* than to attempt to look up keys via external programs. The process of *fork*(2)ing and *exec*(2)ing the program can become expensive if it is done often, slowing down the handling of mail.

See Table 33-5 in §33.3.4 for a list of the K command switches that can be used with this class and the meaning of each.

sequence   *(V8.7 and above)*

33.8.15   *Search a series of maps*

The **sequence** class is a more general form of the **implicit** class described for
use with alias files. The **sequence** class allows you to declare a single name that
will be used to search a series of databases. It is declared like this:

```
Kname sequence map1 map2 ...
```

Here, a *key* will be looked up first in the map named *map1*, and if not found
there, it will be looked up in the map named *map2*. The class of each of the listed
maps should logically relate but need not be the same. Consider, for example, a
rule's LHS that will match if the workspace contains either a user's login name or
the name of a host, with the hostname taking precedence:

```
Khosts host  -a+ /etc/hosts
Kpasswd user -a- /etc/passwd
Kboth sequence hosts passwd


R$-     $: $(both $1 $)
```

Here, we say that the map named **both** is of type **sequence**. Any single token in
the LHS will be looked up first in the map named **hosts**, and if it is found there
the hostname will be returned with a + appended. If it is not found in the **hosts**
map, it will be next looked up in the **passwd** map. If it is found there, the original
workspace will be returned with a – appended. If the workspace is not found in
either map, the lookup fails and the workspace remains unchanged.

If any map in the series of maps declared with the K command does not exist:

```
Kboth sequence hosts passwd badname
```

the following error is printed, and that map is ignored:

```
Sequence map both: unknown member map badname
```

If the number of maps that are sequenced exceeds the maximum allowed
(MAXMAPSTACK in *conf.h*, currently 12), the following error is printed, and the
overflow of maps is ignored:

```
Sequence map name: too many member maps (max max)
```

None of the K command switch may be used with the **sequence** class. If you try to
use any, they will be wrongly interpreted as map names.

stab   *(V8.6 and above)*

33.8.16   *Internally load aliases into the symbol table*

The **stab** class is used internally by *sendmail* to load the raw *aliases*(5) file into its internal symbol table.[*] This is a fallback position that is taken if no database form of aliasing is found.

The **stab** class should *never* be used in configuration files.

switch   *(V8.7 and above)*

33.8.17   *Built sequences based on service switch*

The **switch** class is used internally by *sendmail* to create **sequence** classes of maps based on external service-switch files. Recall that the lines inside a service-switch file look like this:

```
service  how how
```

as, for example:

```
aliases   files nis
```

This line tells *sendmail* to search for its aliases first in files then in NIS.

To illustrate the **switch** class, consider the need to look up aliases inside rule sets in the same way that *sendmail* looks up its own aliases. To do this, you would declare a **switch** map, as, for example:

```
Kali switch aliases
```

This causes *sendmail* to search for the *service* named **aliases** in the service-switch file. In this example it finds such a line, so for each *how* that follows the **aliases** in that line, *sendmail* creates a new map with the name **ali** followed by a dot and the *how*:[†]

```
aliases   files    becomes    ali.files
aliases   nis      becomes    ali.nis
```

These named maps are then sequenced for you. Recall that **sequence** maps are declared like this:

---

[*] As such it is somewhat misnamed. One might reasonably expect a class named **stab** to provide access to the symbol table, but alas, it is not so.

[†] Your **switch** map declaration references the new maps named **ali.files** and **ali.nis**. These must be declared before the **switch** map is declared. Note that **switch** map declarations *always* reference other map names!

```
Kname sequence map1 map2,...
```

The *name* given to the sequence is `ali`. In our example the following sequence is automatically created for you from your original **switch** declaration:

```
Kali sequence ali.files ali.nis
```

In rule sets, when you look up aliases with the `ali` map:

```
R...        $( ali $1 $)
               ↑
        the sequence named ali
```

you will use the **sequence** named `ali` that was automatically built for you from a combination of your original **switch** definition and your service-switch file's **aliases** line. That is, you declare a **switch**, but you use a **sequence**.

text *(V8.7 and above)*

33.8.18 *Look up in flat text files*

The **text** class allows you to look up keys in flat text files. This technique is vastly less efficient than looking up keys in real databases, but it can serve as a way to test rules before implementing them in database form.

For the **text** map, columns for the key and value are both measured as an index. That is, the first column is number 0. To illustrate, consider the following miniconfiguration file that can be used to check spelling:

```
Kspell text /usr/dict/words
Spell
R$-        $: $( spell $1 $: not in dictionary $)
```

The */usr/dict/words* file contains only a single column of words. The above rule shows that the key is (by default) the first column (index 0). And the value is (by default) also the first column (index 0).

For more sophisticated applications you can specify the key's column (with the **-k** switch) the value's column (with the **-v** switch) and the column delimiter (with the **-z** switch). To illustrate, consider the need to look up a *uid* in the */etc/passwd* file and to return the login name of the user to whom it belongs:

```
Kgetuid text -k2 -v0 -z: /etc/passwd
R$-        $: $( getuid $1 $)
```

The lines of a password file look like this:

```
ftp:*:1092:255:File Transfer Protocol Program:/u/ftp:/bin/sh
```

The third column (where the columns are separated by colons) is the *uid* field. The first is the login name. Note that the **-k** and **-v** switches show these fields as indexes, where the first is 0 and the third is 2.

See Table 33-5 in §33.3.4 for a list of the K command switches that can be used with this class and the meaning of each. No debugging switch is available to watch this **text** class.

userdb   *(V8.7 and above)*

33.8.19   *Look up in the User Database*

The **userdb** class allows you to look things up in the User Database (see §33.5 for a full description of the User Database). The **userdb** class is declared with the K command like this:

> Kname userdb *switches keyword*   ← *V8.7 and above*

Here, the *keyword* is the name of the field to search and is either **maildrop** or **mailname** (see §33.5). There is no need to list any files or servers with this command. Those should already have been declared with the **UserDatabaseSpec** (**U**) option (see §34.8.75).

One possible use for a **userdb** map might be to check for a local account in the **check_rcpt** rule set (see §29.10.2). In this example, all valid incoming recipient addresses are listed with the User Database:

```
Kislocal userdb maildrop
Scheck_rcpt
R$*                    $: $>3 $1                   focus on host
R$* <@ $+ > $*         $: $1                       discard host
R$+                    $: $(islocal $1 $: nope $)
Rnope                  $#error $@ 5.1.3 $: "Recipient is not local"
```

See Table 33-5 in §33.3.4 for a list of the K command switches that can be used with this class and the meaning of each. The **−d28** debugging switch (see §37.5.97) can be used to watch this **userdb** class in action.

user   *(V8.7 and above)*

33.8.20   *Look up local passwd information*

The **user** class is used to look up *passwd*(5) information using *getpwent*(3). A password entry typically looks like this:

> ftp:*:1092:255:File Transfer Protocol Program:/u/ftp:/bin/sh

Here, there are seven fields, each separated from the others by colon characters. The key is always compared to the first field. The value returned is (by default) the first field unless you specify another field with a **−v** switch:

> Kname user *−vfield*

Here, *field* can be either a number 1 through 7 or one of the names `name`, `passwd`, `uid`, `gid`, `gecos`, `dir`, or `shell`, which correspond to the numbers. For example, to look up usernames and get the full name (*gecos*) field returned, you could use something like this:

```
Kgetgecos user -vgecos
...
R$-        $: $( getgecos $1 $)
```

Note that this returns the full *gecos* field in its rawest form. It is not cleaned up to provide a reliable full name, as is the $x macro (see §31.10.42).

One possible application for the **user** class is in conjunction with the **check_rcpt** rule set (see §29.10.2). In the following we check to see whether a recipient is a local user and reject the mail if that is not so:

```
Kislocal user
Scheck_rcpt
R$*                     $: $>3 $1                   focus on host
R$* <@ $+ > $*          $: $1                       discard host
R$-                     $: $(islocal $1 $: nope $)
Rnope                   $#error $@ 5.1.3 $: "Recipient is not local"
```

Here, we focus on the host part with rule set 3, then discard all but the user part in the second rule. The third rule performs the lookup. If the user is found, that username is returned unchanged. If, on the other hand, the user is not found, the token **nope** is returned. The last rule rejects any SMTP RCPT command that contains a nonlocal user part.

See Table 33-5 in §33.3.4 for a list of the K command switches that can be used with this class and the meaning of each.

34

Options

Options affect the operation of the *sendmail* program.[*] Options can be specified in the command line, in the *sendmail.cf* file, and in a V8 *m4* configuration. Among the many behavioral characteristics that can be tuned with options are the following examples:

- Locations of all the other files that *sendmail* needs to access, such as the *aliases* file.

- Location of the queue directory.

- Time limits that should be applied to the Time To Live in the queue, the length of the wait with an SMTP connection, and so on.

- Default permissions for files and the default user and group identities to use when not running as another user.

- Degree of privacy desired, such as what kinds of inquiry to reject or who may examine the queue.

- Modes of behavior, such as always queuing or running as a daemon and listening for incoming connections.

- Limits that should be placed on system resources. Should one queue only under high load? Should one reserve minimal space in the queue?

- Small bits of *sendmail*'s behavior, such as allowing colons to appear in addresses and stripping newlines from sender addresses.

---

[*] See Chapter 13, *Setting Options*, for a tutorial introduction to options.

663

Most options are preset in your *sendmail.cf* file to be appropriate for your site. Those that need local definitions will usually be indicated by comments. Some sites, especially those that have high mail loads or those connected to many different networks, will need to tune many of the options according to their unique needs.

34.1 Command-Line Options

Beginning with version 8.7 *sendmail*, command-line options may use multicharacter option names. Prior to version 8.7, only single characters were allowed. We describe the old form first, then the new.

34.1.1 Pre-V8.7 Command-Line Option Declarations

Prior to version 8.7, option names that are declared on the command line could be only a single character long:

```
-oXargument      ← prior to V8.7
```

The −o switch (lowercase o) is immediately followed (with no intervening space) by the one-letter name of the option (here, X). Depending on the option selected, an *argument* may be required. If that *argument* is present, it must immediately follow the option name with no intervening space. Only one option may be specified for each −o switch.

Under V8 *sendmail* a space may appear between the −o and the X, but no space may exist between the X and its *argument*. This is because V8 *sendmail* uses *getopt*(3) to parse its command line.

34.1.2 V8.7 Multicharacter Options in the Command Line

Beginning with version 8.7, option names may be single-character or multicharacter. Single-character options are declared with the −o (lower case) switch as described above. Multicharacter options are declared with a −O (uppercase) switch:

```
-OLongName=argument       ← beginning with V8.7
 ↑
 uppercase
```

Space may optionally exist between the −O and the LongName. Space may not exist between the LongName, the =, and the *argument* unless they are quoted:

```
-O "LongName = argument"
```

Only one option may be specified for each −O switch.

The *sendmail* program ignores case when it considers multicharacter names. Therefore the following three command lines have the same effect, and none produces an error:

```
-OQueueDirectory=/var/tmp
-Oqueuedirectory=/var/tmp
-OQuEuEdIrEcToRy=/var/tmp
```

34.1.2.1 Multicharacter name shorthand

Beginning with 8.7, multicharacter names in the command line may be specified by using the fewest unique leftmost characters in the name. For example, you can specify the queue directory with the complete `QueueDirectory` long name:

```
% /usr/lib/sendmail -OQueueDirectory=/var/tmp
```

But if you need to run this command line frequently,[*] you may find it handy to use an abbreviation:

```
% /usr/lib/sendmail -OQueueDir=/var/tmp
Option QueueDir used as abbreviation for QueueDirectory
```

Whenever a multicharacter name is abbreviated, *sendmail* prints a warning (the second line above) to discourage you from using abbreviations inside your configuration file. It will also warn you if you specify too few leftmost letters:

```
% /usr/lib/sendmail -OQueue=/var/tmp
readcf: ambiguous option name Queue (matches QueueFactor and QueueDirectory)
```

If you misspell the single-character or multicharacter name, the following error is printed, and the option declaration is skipped:

```
% /usr/lib/sendmail -OQueDirectory=/var/tmp
readcf: unknown option name QueDirectory
```

Although these abbreviations can be handy on command lines, it is vital that you alway use nonabbreviated names in your configuration file. New options will be added to *sendmail* over time, and the use of abbreviations can lead to future unexpected or ambiguous effects.

34.1.3 Appropriateness of Options

Some options are intended for use only on the command line and make little or no sense when used in the configuration file. Options that are inappropriate in the configuration file are shown in Table 34-1.

---

[*] With any of the modern utilities such as *tcsh*(1), *ksh*(1), or *emacs*(1), repetition may not require this shorthand.

Table 34–1: Options Inappropriate to the Configuration File

Option Name		§	Description
ErrorMode	(e)	34.8.24	Set error mode. But note that in unusual circumstances it *may* be useful in a configuration file.
IgnoreDots	(i)	34.8.32	Ignore dots. Use the `-OIgnoreDots` command line switch (see §34.8.32) to set this option.
	(M)	34.8.77	Define a macro. Use the D configuration command instead (see §31.3).
MaxDaemonChildren		34.8.35	Set maximum forked children. Although appropriate on the command-line when processing a queue, it should seldom be used in the configuration file.
SingleThreadDelivery		34.8.64	Set single-threaded delivery. Although appropriate on the command-line when processing a queue, it should seldom be used in the configuration file.
Verbose	(v)	34.8.76	Run in verbose mode. Use the `-v` command line switch (see §36.7.41).

34.1.4 Options that Are Safe

It is common practice to install *sendmail* so that it runs with *root* privilege. Security considerations normally require that *sendmail* give up that privilege for most command-line options specified by the ordinary user. But the ordinary user can specify a few options that allow *sendmail* to keep its *root* privilege. Those options are called "safe" and are shown in Table 34–2.

Table 34–2: Options That Are Safe

Option Name		§	Description
AllowBogusHELO		34.8.3	Allow no host with HELO or EHLO
CheckpointInterval	(C)	34.8.7	Checkpoint the queue
ColonOkInAddr		34.8.9	Allow colons in addresses
DefaultCharSet		34.8.14	Define Content-Type: character set
DeliveryMode	(d)	34.8.16	Set delivery mode
EightBitMode	(8)	34.8.22	How to convert MIME input
ErrorMode	(e)	34.8.24	Specify mode for error handling
IgnoreDots	(i)	34.8.32	Ignore leading dots in messages
LogLevel	(L)	34.8.33	Set (increase) logging level[a]
MaxQueueRunSize		34.8.38	Maximum queue messages processed

Table 34–2: Options That Are Safe (continued)

Option Name		§	Description
MeToo	(m)	34.8.39	Send to me too
MinFreeBlocks	(b)	34.8.40	Define minimum free disk blocks
MinQueueAge		34.8.41	Skip queue file if too young
NoRecipientAction		34.8.43	Handle no recipients in header
OldStyleHeaders	(o)	34.8.44	Allow spaces in recipient lists
PrivacyOptions	(p)	34.8.47	Increase privacy of the daemon
QueueSortOrder		34.8.51	How to pre-sort queue
SendMimeErrors	(j)	34.8.60	Return MIME format errors
SevenBitInput	(7)	34.8.62	Force 7-bit input
SingleLineFromHeader		34.8.63	Strip newlines from From:
SuperSafe	(s)	34.8.67	Queue everything just in case
UseErrorsTo	(l)	34.8.74	Use Errors-To: for errors
Verbose	(v)	34.8.76	Run in verbose mode

a. V8.7.3 was accidentally released with the LogLevel (L) option marked as not safe.

For example, the `AliasFile` (`A`) option (location of the *aliases* file) is unsafe (and is not in Table 34–2). If you were to send mail by specifying a new location with the `AliasFile` option, *sendmail* would change its identity from *root* to an ordinary user (you), thus preventing *sendmail* from being able to queue its mail:

```
/var/spool/mqueue: Permission denied
```

Note that prior to V8.8.4, the `DontInitGroups` and `TryNullMXList` options were wrongly set to safe. This is yet another reason to always upgrade to the latest version of *sendmail*.

34.2 Configuration-File Options

Beginning with version 8.7 *sendmail*, configuration-file options may use multicharacter option names. Prior to version 8.7, only single characters were allowed. We describe the old form first, then the new.

34.2.1 Pre-V8.7 Configuration-File Declarations

The old form for an option command in the *sendmail.cf* file is

```
OXargument        ← prior to V8.7
```

Like all configuration commands, the uppercase letter `O` must begin the line. It is immediately followed (with no intervening space) by another single letter, which selects a specific option. Uppercase letters are distinct from lowercase for single-character option names (that is, `X` is different from `x`). Depending on the option selected, an **argument** may be required. There must be no intervening space between the single-character option name and its argument.

34.2.2 V8.7 Configuration File Declarations

Beginning with version 8.7, option names may be single-character or multicharacter. A space is used to differentiate between single-character and multicharacter (long) names:

```
O LongName=argument          ← beginning with V8.7
↑
a space (not a tab)
```

Whenever the O configuration command is followed by a space (not a tab), everything following that space is taken as the declaration of a multicharacter option. Unlike single-letter option names, multicharacter names are interpreted by *sendmail* without regard to case. Therefore the following three examples all produce the same effect:

```
O QueueDirectory=/var/tmp
O queuedirectory=/var/tmp
O QuEuEdIrEcToRy=/var/tmp
```

There may be optional space (not tab) characters surrounding the = character:

```
O QueueDirectory = /var/tmp
                ↑ ↑
              spaces, not tabs
```

Multicharacter names in the configuration file must not be abbreviated or expressed in shorthand:

```
O QueueDirectory=/var/spool/mqueue     ← good
O QueueDir=/var/spool/mqueue           ← bad
```

Failure to use the full multicharacter name will cause *sendmail* to print spurious warnings every time it is run. The possible warnings are listed in §34.1.2.1. Multicharacter names are beneficial because they allow option names to have mnemonic recognition. For example, the multicharacter name `ForwardPath`, which lists the default path for `~/.forward` files, is much more recognizable than the single-character name J.

34.3 Configuring with V8 m4 Options

In creating a configuration file with the V8 m4 method (see Chapter 19, *V8 m4 Configuration*), every option can be tuned by including appropriate **define** statements in your *.mc* file:

```
define(`option',`value')           ← enclose in opposing half-quotes
define(`confAUTO_REBUILD',`True')  ← for example
```

The *option* is selected from one of the *m4* option names shown in the leftmost column of Table 34-3. The **value** is an appropriate value for that option, as described in the reference section of this chapter. Note that the *option* and the **value** should each be enclosed in *opposing* half-quotes to prevent *m4* from wrongly recognizing either as a keyword or macro. The leftmost half-quote is the reverse apostrophe, and the rightmost is the normal apostrophe.

Table 34-3: All V8 m4 Options Ordered by m4 Name

V8 m4 Option Name	Option Name	§
ALIAS_FILE	AliasFile (A)	34.8.1
confALIAS_WAIT	AliasWait (a)	34.8.2
confAUTO_REBUILD	AutoRebuildAliases (D)	34.8.4
confBIND_OPTS	ResolverOptions (I)	34.8.55
confBLANK_SUB	BlankSub (B)	34.8.5
confCHECKPOINT_INTERVAL	CheckpointInterval (C)	34.8.7
confCHECK_ALIASES	CheckAliases (n)	34.8.6
confCOLON_OK_IN_ADDR	ColonOkInAddr	34.8.9
confCON_EXPENSIVE	HoldExpensive (c)	34.8.29
confTO_HOSTSTATUS	Timeout.hoststatus	34.8.70.8
confCOPY_ERRORS_TO	PostmasterCopy (P)	34.8.46
confMAX_DAEMON_CHILDREN	MaxDaemonChildren	34.8.35
confDAEMON_OPTIONS	DaemonPortOptions (O)	34.8.13
confDEF_GROUP_ID	(g)	34.8.15
confDEF_USER_ID	DefaultUser (u)	34.8.15
confDELIVERY_MODE	DeliveryMode (d)	34.8.16
confDONT_EXPAND_CNAMES	DontExpandCnames´	34.8.18
confDONT_PRUNE_ROUTES	DontPruneRoutes (R)	34.8.20
confEIGHT_BIT_HANDLING	EightBitMode (8)	34.8.22
confERROR_MODE	ErrorMode (e)	34.8.24
confERROR_MESSAGE	ErrorHeader (E)	34.8.23
confFALLBACK_MX	FallbackMXhost (V)	34.8.25
confFORWARD_PATH	ForwardPath (J)	34.8.27
confFROM_LINE	UnixFromLine $1	34.8.72
HELP_FILE	HelpFile (H)	34.8.28
confHOSTS_FILE	HostsFile	34.8.30
confHOST_STATUS_DIRECTORY	HostStatusDirectory	34.8.31
confIGNORE_DOTS	IgnoreDots (i)	34.8.32
confLOG_LEVEL	LogLevel (L)	34.8.33
confMATCH_GECOS	MatchGECOS (G)	34.8.34
confMAX_HOP	MaxHopCount (h)	34.8.36
confMAX_MESSAGE_SIZE	MaxMessageSize	34.8.37

Table 34-3: All V8 m4 Options Ordered by m4 Name (continued)

V8 m4 Option Name	Option Name	§
confMAX_QUEUE_RUN_SIZE	MaxQueueRunSize	34.8.38
confMCI_CACHE_SIZE	ConnectionCacheSize (k)	34.8.10
confMCI_CACHE_TIMEOUT	ConnectionCacheTimeout (K)	34.8.11
confMESSAGE_TIMEOUT	QueueTimeout (T)	34.8.52
confME_TOO	MeToo (m)	34.8.39
confMIME_FORMAT_ERRORS	SendMimeErrors (j)	34.8.60
confMIN_FREE_BLOCKS	MinFreeBlocks (b)	34.8.40
confNO_RCPT_ACTION	NoRecipientAction	34.8.43
confOLD_STYLE_HEADERS	OldStyleHeaders (o)	34.8.44
confOPERATORS	OperatorChars	34.8.45
confPRIVACY_FLAGS	PrivacyOptions (p)	34.8.47
QUEUE_DIR	QueueDirectory (Q)	34.8.48
confQUEUE_FACTOR	QueueFactor (q)	34.8.49
confQUEUE_LA	QueueLA (x)	34.8.50
confQUEUE_SORT_ORDER	QueueSortOrder	34.8.51
confREAD_TIMEOUT	Timeout (r)	34.8.70
confREFUSE_LA	RefuseLA (X)	34.8.54
confSAFE_FILE_ENV	SafeFileEnvironment	34.8.58
confSAFE_QUEUE	SuperSafe (s)	34.8.67
confSAVE_FROM_LINES	SaveFromLine (f)	34.8.59
confSEPARATE_PROC	ForkEachJob (Y)	34.8.26
confSEVEN_BIT_INPUT	SevenBitInput (7)	34.8.62
confSINGLE_THREAD_DELIVERY	SingleThreadDelivery	34.8.64
confSMTP_LOGIN_MSG	SmtpGreetingMessage $e	34.8.65
STATUS_FILE	StatusFile (S)	34.8.66
confTEMP_FILE_MODE	TempFileMode (F)	34.8.68
confTIME_ZONE	TimeZoneSpec (t)	34.8.69
confTO_COMMAND	Timeout.command	34.8.70.1
confTO_CONNECT	Timeout.connect	34.8.70.2
confTO_DATABLOCK	Timeout.datablock	34.8.70.3
confTO_DATAFINAL	Timeout.datafinal	34.8.70.4
confTO_DATAINIT	Timeout.datainit	34.8.70.5
confTO_FILEOPEN	Timeout.fileopen	34.8.70.6
confTO_HELO	Timeout.helo	34.8.70.7
confTO_HOSTSTATUS	Timeout.hoststatus	34.8.70.8
confTO_ICONNECT	Timeout.iconnect	34.8.70.9
confTO_IDENT	Timeout.ident	34.8.70.10
confTO_INITIAL	Timeout.initial	34.8.70.11
confTO_MAIL	Timeout.mail	34.8.70.12
confTO_MISC	Timeout.misc	34.8.70.13
confTO_QUIT	Timeout.quit	34.8.70.16

Table 34–3: All V8 m4 Options Ordered by m4 Name (continued)

V8 m4 Option Name	Option Name	§
confTO_QUEUERETURN	Timeout.queuereturn	34.8.70.14
confTO_QUEUERETURN_NONURGENT	Timeout.queuereturn.non-urgent	34.8.70.14
confTO_QUEUERETURN_NORMAL	Timeout.queuereturn.normal	34.8.70.14
confTO_QUEUERETURN_URGENT	Timeout.queuereturn.urgent	34.8.70.14
confTO_QUEUEWARN	Timeout.queuewarn	34.8.70.15
confTO_QUEUEWARN_NONURGENT	Timeout.queuewarn.non-urgent	34.8.70.15
confTO_QUEUEWARN_NORMAL	Timeout.queuewarn.normal	34.8.70.15
confTO_QUEUEWARN_URGENT	Timeout.queuewarn.urgent	34.8.70.15
confTO_RCPT	Timeout.rcpt	34.8.70.17
confTO_RSET	Timeout.rset	34.8.70.18
confTRY_NULL_MX_LIST	TryNullMXList (w)	34.8.71
confUNSAFE_GROUP_WRITES	UnsafeGroupWrites	34.8.73
confUSERDB_SPEC	UserDatabaseSpec (U)	34.8.75
confUSE_ERRORS_TO	UseErrorsTo (l)	34.8.74
confWORK_CLASS_FACTOR	ClassFactor (z)	34.8.8
confWORK_RECIPIENT_FACTOR	RecipientFactor (y)	34.8.53
confWORK_TIME_FACTOR	RetryFactor (Z)	34.8.56

34.4 *Alphabetical Table of All Options*

In this section we present a table of all options in alphabetical order. The leftmost column of Table 34-4 lists first the multicharacter names and then the single-characters names. The second column lists the type of argument that each option takes. These types are explained in the next section.

Table 34–4: All Options

Option Name		Type	§	Description
AliasFile	(A)	String	34.8.1	Define the *aliases* file location
AliasWait	(a)	Time	34.8.2	Wait for *aliases* file rebuild
AllowBogusHELO		Boolean	34.8.3	Allow no host with HELO or EHLO
AutoRebuildAliases	(D)	Boolean	34.8.4	Autorebuild the *aliases* database
BlankSub	(B)	Character	34.8.5	Unquoted space replacement
CheckAliases	(n)	Boolean	34.8.6	Check right-hand side of *aliases*
CheckpointInterval	(C)	Numeric	34.8.7	Checkpoint the queue
ClassFactor	(z)	Numeric	34.8.8	Multiplier for priority increments
ColonOkInAddr		Boolean	34.8.9	Allow colons in addresses
ConnectionCacheSize	(k)	Numeric	34.8.10	Multiple-SMTP connections
ConnectionCacheTimeout	(K)	Time	34.8.11	Multiple-SMTP timeouts
ConnectionRateThrottle		Numeric	34.8.12	Incoming SMTP connection rate

Table 34–4: *All Options (continued)*

Option Name		Type	§	Description
DaemonPortOptions	(O)	String	34.8.13	Options for the daemon
DefaultCharSet		String	34.8.14	Content-Type: character set
DefaultUser	(u)	String	34.8.15	Default delivery agent identity
DefaultUser	(g)	String	34.8.15	Default delivery agent identity
DeliveryMode	(d)	Character	34.8.16	Set delivery mode
DialDelay		String	34.8.17	Connect failure retry time
DontExpandCnames		Boolean	34.8.18	Prevent CNAME expansion
DontInitGroups		Boolean	34.8.19	Don't use *initgroups*(3)
DontPruneRoutes	(R)	Boolean	34.8.20	Don't prune route addresses
DoubleBounceAddress		String	34.8.21	Errors when sending errors
EightBitMode	(8)	Character	34.8.22	How to convert MIME input
ErrorHeader	(E)	String	34.8.23	Set error message header
ErrorMode	(e)	Character	34.8.24	Specify mode of error handling
FallbackMXhost	(V)	String	34.8.25	Fallback MX host
ForkEachJob	(Y)	Boolean	34.8.26	Process queue files individually
ForwardPath	(J)	String	34.8.27	Set ˜/.*forward* search path
HelpFile	(H)	String	34.8.28	Specify location of the help file
HoldExpensive	(c)	Boolean	34.8.29	Queue for expensive mailers
HostsFile		String	34.8.30	Specify alternate /etc/hosts file
HostStatusDirectory		String	34.8.31	Location of persistent host status
IgnoreDots	(i)	Boolean	34.8.32	Ignore leading dots in messages
LogLevel	(L)	Numeric	34.8.33	Set (increase) logging level
MatchGECOS	(G)	Boolean	34.8.34	Match recipient in *gecos* field
MaxDaemonChildren		Numeric	34.8.35	Maximum forked children
MaxHopCount	(h)	Numeric	34.8.36	Set maximum hop count
MaxMessageSize		Numeric	34.8.37	Max ESMTP message size
MaxQueueRunSize		Numeric	34.8.38	Max queue messages processed
MeToo	(m)	Boolean	34.8.39	Send to me too
MinFreeBlocks	(b)	Numeric	34.8.40	Define minimum free disk blocks
MinQueueAge		Time	34.8.41	Skip queue file if too young
MustQuoteChars		String	34.8.42	Quote nonaddress characters
NoRecipientAction		String	34.8.43	Handle no recipients in header
OldStyleHeaders	(o)	Boolean	34.8.44	Allow spaces in recipient lists
OperatorChars	$o	String	34.8.45	Set token separation operators
PostmasterCopy	(P)	String	34.8.46	Extra copies of postmaster mail
PrivacyOptions	(p)	String	34.8.47	Increase privacy of the daemon
QueueDirectory	(Q)	String	34.8.48	Location of queue directory
QueueFactor	(q)	Numeric	34.8.49	Factor for high-load queuing
QueueLA	(x)	Numeric	34.8.50	On high load, queue only
QueueSortOrder		Character	34.8.51	How to presort the queue
QueueTimeout	(T)	Time	34.8.52	Limit life in queue to days

Table 34-4: All Options (continued)

Option Name		Type	§	Description
RecipientFactor	(y)	Numeric	34.8.53	Penalize large recipient lists
RefuseLA	(X)	Numeric	34.8.54	Refuse connections on high load
ResolverOptions	(I)	String	34.8.55	Tune DNS lookups
RetryFactor	(Z)	Numeric	34.8.56	Increment per job priority
RunAsUser		String	34.8.57	Run as nonroot
SafeFileEnvironment		String	34.8.58	Directory for safe file writes
SaveFromLine	(f)	Boolean	34.8.59	Save UNIX-style **From** lines
SendMimeErrors	(j)	Boolean	34.8.60	Return MIME-format errors
ServiceSwitchFile		String	34.8.61	Switched services file
SevenBitInput	(7)	Boolean	34.8.62	Force 7-bit input
SingleLineFromHeader		Boolean	34.8.63	Strip newlines from From:
SingleThreadDelivery		Boolean	34.8.64	Set single threaded delivery
SmtpGreetingMessage	$e	String	34.8.65	The SMTP greeting message
StatusFile	(S)	String	34.8.66	Specify statistics file
SuperSafe	(s)	Boolean	34.8.67	Queue everything just in case
TempFileMode	(F)	Octal	34.8.68	Permissions for temporary files
TimeZoneSpec	(t)	String	34.8.69	Set time zone
Timeout	(r)	String	34.8.70	Set timeouts
TryNullMXList	(w)	Boolean	34.8.71	Use A if no best MX record
UnixFromLine	$l	String	34.8.72	Define the From format
UnsafeGroupWrites		Boolean	34.8.73	Check unsafe group permissions
UseErrorsTo	(l)	Boolean	34.8.74	Use Errors-To: for errors
UserDatabaseSpec	(U)	String	34.8.75	Specify user database
Verbose	(v)	Boolean	34.8.76	Run in verbose mode
	(M)	String	34.8.77	Define a macro

34.5 *Option Argument Types*

The second column of Table 34-4 shows the type of the argument for each option.
The allowable types are the following:

Boolean

> A Boolean-type argument can have only one of two possible values: true or
> false. If the Boolean argument is present, its first letter is compared to the four
> letters T, t, Y, and y. If that first letter matches any of those four, the option is
> set to true; otherwise, it is set to false. If a Boolean argument is absent, the
> option defaults to true. For example,

```
Oc                          ← Boolean absent, `c' is set true.
OcTrue                      ← Boolean=`T'rue, `c' is set true.
OcFalse                     ← Boolean=`F'alse, `c' is set false.
```

and beginning with V8.7, you can also do this:

```
O HoldExpensive               ← Boolean absent, option is set true.
O HoldExpensive=True          ← Boolean=`T'rue, option is set true.
O HoldExpensive=False         ← Boolean=`F'alse, option is set false.
```

Character

A character type is a single ASCII character. Options that take a single character as an argument may also take a whole word or sentence, but in that case, only the first character is recognized:

```
Odb                           ← b for background mode
Odbackground                  ← same
```

Beginning with V8.7 the same form looks like this:

```
O DeliveryMode=b              ← b for background mode
O DeliveryMode=background     ← same
```

The argument is case-sensitive, that is, the character **b** is considered to be different from the character **B**:

```
Odb                           ← b for background mode
OdB                           ← meaningless
```

Numeric

A numeric type is an ASCII representation of an integer value. It may be positive, zero, or negative. The base is determined after any leading sign is handled. A leading 0 causes the octal base to be used. A leading 0x or 0X causes the hexadecimal base to be used. Otherwise, a decimal base is used (see *atoi*(3)). Decimal is best to use for options like the hop count (option **h**):

```
Oh15                          ← decimal for hop count
O MaxHopCount=15              ← decimal for hop count V8.7 style
```

String

A string type is a line of ASCII text. A string is all text from the single-character option name up to the end of the line. If the following line is a continuation line (one that begins with a tab or a space), it is joined (appended) to the string. Prior to V8 the maximum length of a string was defined by MAXLINE in *conf.h*. Beginning with V8 *sendmail*, strings may be of virtually unlimited length. If the string is quoted, the quotation marks are *not* stripped by *sendmail*:

```
OA/etc/aliases                ← location of the aliases file
OA"/etc/aliases"              ← bad, quotes are retained
```

Beginning with V8.7, the string is considered to begin at the first nonspace character following the = character of a multicharacter option declaration:

```
O AliasFile =   /etc/aliases
                ↑
```
from here

Octal

An octal type is like the numeric type above but is always interpreted as an octal (base 8) number even if the leading zero is absent. This type is specially designed for file permissions:

```
OF0600                              ← octal for file permissions
OF600                               ← octal even without the leading zero
O TempFileMode=0600                 ← octal for file permissions V8.7 style
```

Time

A time type is the expression of a period of time. Time is expressed as a number modified by a trailing letter. The recognized letters (shown in Table 34–5) determine what the number means. For example, **24h** means 24 hours, and **15m** means 15 minutes.

Table 34–5: Option Time Argument Units

Letter	Units
s	Seconds
m	Minutes
h	Hours
d	Days
w	Weeks

Times may be mixed; for example, **1h30m** means one hour and 30 minutes. If the letter modifier is missing, pre-V8 versions of *sendmail* default the time to days:

```
Or2h                    ← SMTP timeout is 2 hours
OT2                     ← life in queue is 2 days
```

V8 *sendmail* uses different default units depending on the specific option. For consistent results, always include the units for all versions of *sendmail*.

Prior to V8.7, unrecognized unit characters (such as **j** when you really meant **h**) would silently default to days. Beginning with V8.7, unrecognized unit characters cause *sendmail* to print the following error and default the units to those specified by the particular option:

```
Invalid time unit `character'
```

34.6 *Interrelating Options*

At the end of this chapter we list all the options in alphabetical order for easy lookup and explain each in detail. Here, we present them grouped by application with only a brief description.

34.6.1 *File Locations*

The only file that *sendmail* knows the location of is its configuration file.[*] Options in the configuration file tell *sendmail* where all other files and directories are located. The options that specify file locations are summarized in Table 34-6. All file location options are of type *string*.

Table 34-6: File Location Options

Option Name		§	File
AliasFile	(A)	34.8.1	Aliases file and its database files
ErrorHeader	(E)	34.8.23	Set error message file
ForwardPath	(J)	34.8.27	Set `~/.forward` search path
HelpFile	(H)	34.8.28	Specify location of the help file
HostsFile		34.8.30	Specify alternate /etc/hosts file
QueueDirectory	(Q)	34.8.48	Location of queue directory
SafeFileEnvironment		34.8.58	Directory for safe file writes
ServiceSwitchFile		34.8.61	Specify file for switched services
StatusFile	(S)	34.8.66	Statistics file
UserDatabaseSpec	(U)	34.8.75	Specify user database

File locations should be expressed as full pathnames. Use of relative names will cause the location to become relative to the queue directory or, for some options, will cause the name to be interpreted as something other than a file or directory name.

34.6.2 *The Queue*

Several options combine to determine your site's policy for managing the *sendmail* queue (see Chapter 23, *The Queue*). Among them is one that specifies the location of the queue directory and another that sets the permissions given to files in that directory. The list of all options that affect the queue is shown in Table 34-7.

---

[*] Beginning with V8.6 *sendmail*, it also knows the location of its *pid* file.

Table 34-7: Options that Affect the Queue

Option Name		§	Description
CheckpointInterval	(C)	34.8.7	Checkpoint the queue
ForkEachJob	(Y)	34.8.26	Process queue files individually
MaxQueueRunSize		34.8.38	Max queue messages processed
MinFreeBlocks	(b)	34.8.40	Define minimum free disk blocks
MinQueueAge		34.8.41	Skip queue file if too young
QueueDirectory	(Q)	34.8.48	Location of queue directory
QueueFactor	(q)	34.8.49	Factor for high-load queuing
QueueLA	(x)	34.8.50	On high load queue only
QueueSortOrder		34.8.51	How to presort the queue
QueueTimeout	(T)	34.8.52	Limit life in queue to days
RecipientFactor	(y)	34.8.53	Penalize large recipient lists
RetryFactor	(Z)	34.8.56	Increment per job priority
SuperSafe	(s)	34.8.67	Queue everything just in case
TempFileMode	(F)	34.8.68	Permissions for temporary files
Timeout.queuereturn		34.8.70.14	Timeout life in queue
Timeout.queuewarn		34.8.70.15	Timeout for still-in-queue warnings

34.6.3 Managing Aliases

In addition to knowing the location of the *aliases* file, some options determine how that file and its associated database files will be used. For example, there is an option that tells *sendmail* to automatically rebuild the database files whenever the *aliases* file is changed. The list of all *aliases*-related options is shown in Table 34-8.

Table 34-8: Options for Managing Aliases

Option Name		§	Description
AliasFile	(A)	34.8.1	Define the location of the *aliases* file
AliasWait	(a)	34.8.2	Wait for *aliases* file rebuild
AutoRebuildAliases	(D)	34.8.4	Autorebuild the *aliases* database
CheckAliases	(n)	34.8.6	Check right-hand side of *aliases*
ServiceSwitchFile		34.8.61	Specify file for switched services

34.6.4 Controlling Machine Load

Several options control the *sendmail* program's behavior under high-machine-load conditions. They are intended to reduce the impact of *sendmail* on machines that provide other services and to help protect *sendmail* from overburdening a machine. The list of options that determine and help to prevent high-load conditions is shown in Table 34–9.

Table 34–9: Options That Determine Load

Option Name		§	Description
ClassFactor	(z)	34.8.8	Multiplier for priority increments
ConnectionRateThrottle		34.8.12	Incoming SMTP connection rate
HoldExpensive	(c)	34.8.29	Queue for expensive mailers
MaxDaemonChildren		34.8.35	Maximum forked children
MinQueueAge		34.8.41	Skip queue file if too young
QueueFactor	(q)	34.8.49	Factor for high-load queuing
QueueLA	(x)	34.8.50	On high load queue only
RefuseLA	(X)	34.8.54	Refuse connections on high load

34.6.5 Connection Caching

V8 *sendmail* has connection caching to improve the performance of SMTP-transported mail. In processing the queue or delivering to a long list of recipients, keeping a few SMTP connections open (in case another message is for one of those same sites) improves the speed of transfers. Caching is most useful on busy mail hub machines but can benefit any machine that sends a great deal of network mail. Table 34–10 lists the options for how connections will be cached.

Table 34–10: Options That Determine Connection Caching

Option Name		§	Description
ConnectionCacheSize	(k)	34.8.10	Multiple-SMTP connections
ConnectionCacheTimeout	(K)	34.8.11	Multiple-SMTP timeouts

The *sendmail* program checks its connection cache just before opening up a new connection to a host. If the cache contains an entry for that host, *sendmail* sends an SMTP RSET command to the host to make sure the connection is still active. If the SMTP RSET succeeds, the connection is re-used. If the SMTP RSET times out (see §34.8.70.18, the `Timeout.rset` option), or fails, or if the host was not in the cache, an new connection is made.

34.6.6 Problem Solving

The *sendmail* program offers four options that will help in locating and solving some mail delivery problems. You are encouraged to enable the first two shown in Table 34–11. The third is of value only if you have many delivery agents (see Chapter 30, *Delivery Agents*).

Table 34–11: Options That Help with Problem Solving

Option Name		§	Description
LogLevel	(L)	34.8.33	Set (increase) logging level
PostmasterCopy	(P)	34.8.46	Extra copies of postmaster mail (not V5 BSD)
StatusFile	(S)	34.8.66	Specify statistics file
Verbose	(v)	34.8.76	Run in verbose mode

Other means to solve problems are described in Chapter 37, *Debugging with –d*, which describes the **–d** debugging command-line switch, and in Chapter 36, *The Command Line* (specifically §36.4), which describes the **–X** traffic-logging command-line switch.

34.6.7 Other Options

The *sendmail* program supports a vast array of options. Take the time to study all the options (described at the end of this chapter) at least enough to get a basic feeling for what they do. Then, as you gain experience with *sendmail*, you'll know where to look for the particular option that will meet your needs.

34.7 Pitfalls

- If the option letter is one that is unknown to *sendmail*, it *silently* accepts the line but doesn't use it. For example, entering **O1** when you really mean **OI** causes the unknown option **1** to be defined and the intended option **I** to remain undefined. Because no error message is printed, this kind of mistake is difficult to find. Note that, when you are in doubt, a debugging level of **–d37.1** can be used to produce warnings (see §37.5.126).

- Under versions of *sendmail* prior to V8.7, accidentally placing a space character between the **O** and the option letter wrongly causes *sendmail* to silently accept the space character as the option name. For example, the space in "**O A/etc/aliases**" gives to the option "space" the argument **A/etc/aliases**. Beginning with V8.7, a space option causes a multicharacter option name to be recognized (see §34.2.2).

- Options are parsed from the top of the *sendmail.cf* file down. Later declarations of an option supersede earlier declarations. For example, if you try to change the location of the queue directory by placing the line **OQ/mail/spool/mqueue** at the top of your *sendmail.cf* file, that change is masked (ignored) by the existence of **OQ/var/spool/mqueue** later in the file.

- Command-line options always supersede the *sendmail.cf* file options, because the command line is parsed after the *sendmail.cf* file is parsed. One way to change the location of the *aliases* file (perhaps for testing) is with a command-line argument such as `-oA/tmp/aliases`. For security reasons, however, not all command-line options are available to the ordinary user. (See Table 34-2 in §34.1.4 for a list of those that are available.)

34.8 Alphabetized Reference

In the following sections we present all the options that are currently available for V8 *sendmail*. They are in alphanumeric order sorted by the multicharacter name. The multicharacter name appears at the left of each major section header. If an old single-character name exists, it is displayed parenthetically to the right of the multi-character name. In a few cases, multicharacter names have replaced macros. In those instances the macro is displayed nonparenthetically.

AliasFile (A)   *(All versions)*

34.8.1   *Define the aliases file location*

The `AliasFile` (A) option must be declared for *sendmail* to do aliasing. If you omit this option, *sendmail* may silently assume that you do not want to do aliasing at all. There is no default compiled into *sendmail* for the location of the *aliases* file.[*] For V8 *m4* configurations an appropriate default will be defined based on your operating system.

If you specify a file that doesn't exist (such as */et/aliases* if you really meant */etc/aliases*) or one that is unreadable, *sendmail* complains, for example with

```
Can't open /et/aliases
```

This is a nonfatal error. The *sendmail* program prints it and continues to run but assumes that it shouldn't do aliasing.

The forms of the `AliasFile` (A) option are as follows:

O*Alocation*	← *configuration file (old form)*
-o*Alocation*	← *command line (old form)*
O AliasFile=*location*	← *configuration file (beginning with V8.7)*
-OAliasFile=*location*	← *command line (beginning with V8.7)*
define(`ALIAS_FILE`,`location`)	← *V8 m4 configuration*

The `location` is an argument of type string and can be an absolute or a relative pathname. A relative path (such as *../aliases*) can be used for testing but should *never* be used in the production version of your *sendmail.cf* file. To do so opens a security hole. Such a path is interpreted by *sendmail* as relative to the queue directory.

---

[*] Beginning with V8.7, a switched-services file (see §34.8.61) may cause aliases to be found in NIS or other services and may completely ignore alias files altogether.

This option can be used to change the name of the *aliases* file (a possible consideration for security). If you change the location or name of the *aliases* file, be aware that other programs (such as *emacs* and Sun's *nis* services) may cease to work properly.

Note that with the *m4* technique the only way to eliminate the default alias file declaration (and thus to eliminate all *aliases* support) is to undefine ALIAS_FILE like this:

```
undefine(`ALIAS_FILE')
```

The *sendmail* program also allows you to use several alias databases simultaneously. They are listed with the **AliasFile** (**A**) option as, for example, like this:

```
O AliasFile=/etc/aliases/users,/etc/aliases/maillists
```

In this case, *sendmail* will look up an alias first in the database */etc/aliases/users*. If it is not found, *sendmail* will then look in */etc/aliases/maillists*. The number of simultaneous alias files is limited to MAXALIASDB (see §18.8.19) as defined in *conf.h* (by default 12). The **-bi** command-line switch will rebuild all alias databases in the order listed in this **AliasFile** (**A**) option. Multiple declarations lines may appear in the file, each adding an alias database to the list:

```
O AliasFile=/etc/aliases/users      # aliases local users first
O AliasFile=/etc/aliases/maillists # then mailing lists
O AliasFile=/etc/aliases/retired   # then retired accounts
```

Duplicates are not detected. Therefore the following causes */etc/aliases* to be searched and rebuilt twice each time:

```
O AliasFile=/etc/aliases
O AliasFile=/etc/aliases
```

Multiple alias files may similarly be specified on the command line with the **-o** switch. But be aware that any alias files that are declared in the command line cause all the configuration file alias declarations to be ignored.

In addition to the name of alias databases, *sendmail* also allows you to specify the class of each. The class is the same as the classes that are available for the K configuration command (see §33.3). The class prefixes the name, and the two are separated by a colon:

```
O AliasFile=nis:mail.aliases
```

This example tells *sendmail* to look up aliases in the *nis* class (the **nis**) database called **mail.aliases**. The class can include switches that mean the same thing as those allowed for the K configuration command.

For example:

```
O AliasFile=nis:-N mail.aliases
```

Here, the **-N** class switch causes lookups to include a trailing null byte with each key.[*]

Under V8.6 *sendmail* the reasonable classes are *hash*, *btree*, *dbm*, *nis*, and *udb*. Under V8.7 *sendmail* this list can also include *nisplus* for Sun's *nisplus* and *hesiod* for Hesiod support. (See §33.3.2 and §33.3.4.) But note that it is generally better to use the service-switch file to select services because it is less confusing.

If a class is not a known one and if the **-d27** command-line switch (see §37.5.88) is specified, *sendmail* prints

```
Unknown alias class badclass
```

If the class is one that cannot support aliasing (as defined by MCF_ALIASOK in *conf.c*) and if the **-d27** command-line switch is specified, *sendmail* prints:

```
setalias: map class badclass can't handle aliases
```

In both cases the *badclass* is the offending class. Both errors cause the **Alias-File (A)** option's alias file declaration to be ignored.

Beginning with V8.7 *sendmail*, the declaration and use of alias files is further complicated[†] by the introduction of switched-services files (see §34.8.61). If the file defined by the **ServiceSwitchFile** option exists, and if it defines the type and location of alias information, each alias definition is used just as if it was included in the configuration file (although the syntax differs). On Solaris, Ultrix, and OSF systems, switched-service files are supplied by the operating system. With these you should beware the silent introduction of unexpected alias services. On other operating systems you may set up a V8.7 switched-service file that can be used for aliases if you wish.

The **AliasFile (A)** option is not safe. If specified from the command line, it may cause *sendmail* to relinquish its *root* privilege.

AliasWait (a)   *(All versions)*

34.8.2   *Wait for aliases file rebuild*

Whenever *sendmail* rebuilds the *aliases* database, it first clears the old database. It then rebuilds the database and, when done, adds the special entry @:@. Before *sendmail* attempts to use the database, it first looks in that database for the special

---

* Also see §24.4.4, which illustrates the **-A** option switch for appending keys.

† Or simplified, depending on whom you talk to.

entry `@:@` that should be present. This curious entry is employed because it is one that is always illegal in an *aliases* file. If *sendmail* doesn't find that entry (whether because a user ran *newaliases* or because another invocation of sendmail is currently rebuilding it), it waits 2 seconds for that entry to appear, then checks again. If the entry is still unavailable, the wait is doubled (up to maximum wait of 60 seconds). The total time waited (after all the sleeps without success) is the interval specified by this `AliasWait` (`a`) option.

When the `@:@` appears, *sendmail* checks to see whether the database still needs to be rebuilt and rebuilds it if it does. If the special entry `@:@` does not appear after the specified time and if the `AutoRebuildAliases` (`D`) option (see §34.8.4) is set, *sendmail* assumes that some other process died while that other process was rebuilding the database. This assumption paves the way for *sendmail* to go ahead and rebuild the database. Note that if `AutoRebuildAliases` (`D`) option is not set, *sendmail* uses the old information.

The forms of the `AliasWait` (`a`) option are as follows:

```
Oadelay                          ← configuration file (old style)
-oadelay                         ← command line (old style)
O AliasWait=delay                ← configuration file (beginning with V8.7)
-OAliasWait=delay                ← command line (beginning with V8.7)
define(`confALIAS_WAIT',delay)   ← V8 m4 configuration
```

The *delay* argument is of type *time* and, if omitted, defaults to 5 minutes. If the entire `AliasWait` (`a`) option is omitted or if *delay* is zero or non-numeric, the database is not automatically rebuilt. If the unit of time desired is omitted, the delay defaults to minutes. If you use the V8 *m4* configuration, the default for `confALIAS_WAIT` is 10 minutes.

The `AliasWait` (`a`) option is not safe. If specified from the command line, it may cause *sendmail* to relinquish its *root* privilege.

AllowBogusHELO   *(V8.8 and above)*

34.8.3   *Allow no host with HELO or EHLO*

Prior to V8.7, *sendmail* would accept without complaint an SMTP HELO command (or an EHLO) that omitted the hostname:

```
220-oldsite.uofa.edu  Sendmail 8.6.13/8.6.13 ready at Fri, 31 Dec 1996 08:11:44 -0700
220 ESMTP spoken here
HELO
250 oldsite.uofa.edu Hello here.ufa.edu [123.45.67.89], pleased to meet you
```

RFC1123, section 5.2.5, specifies that all HELO and EHLO commands must be followed by a fully qualified hostname.

```
HELO here.uofa.edu
EHLO here.uofa.edu
```

Beginning with V8.7, omitting the hostname results in one of the following errors:

```
501 helo requires domain address
501 ehlo requires domain address
```

Note that there is no check to see that the hostname is actually that of the connecting host unless PICKY_HELO_CHECK is declared when *sendmail* is compiled(see §18.8.35). Also note that the hostname that is specified must *appear* to be a correctly formed hostname. If it is not, the following is printed:

```
501 Invalid domain name
```

If you favor forcing other sites to obey the RFCs, don't enable this option. But note that you may need to enable it if your site accepts connections from other sites that don't obey the protocols.

The AllowBogusHELO option is used like this:

```
O AllowBogusHELO=bool              ← V8.8 and above
```

The *bool* is of type Boolean. If it is absent, the option defaults to true (do allow the hostname to be omitted). If the entire option declaration is missing, the default is false (require the hostname to be present). Note that there is no *m4* shorthand for declaring this option.

The AllowBogusHELO option safe. Even if it is specified from the command line, *sendmail* retains its *root* privilege.

AutoRebuildAliases (D)   *(All versions)*

34.8.4   *Auto-rebuild the aliases database*

The need to rebuild the *aliases* database is determined by comparing the modification time of the *aliases* source file, as defined by the AliasFile (A) option (see §34.8.1), to the modification time of the corresponding *aliases.pag* and *aliases.dir*, or *aliases.db*, database files. If the source file is newer and if this AutoRebuild-Aliases (D) option is set, *sendmail* attempts to rebuild the *aliases* database. If this option is not set, *sendmail* prints the following warning and uses the information in the old database:

```
Warning: alias database fname out of date
```

Here, *fname* is the name of the source file. If you set this AutoRebuildAliases (D) option, be sure that the AliasWait (a) option (see §34.8.2) is also declared and given a nonzero time argument. (File locking, to prevent simultaneous rebuilds, is described under the AliasWait (a) option.)

The forms of this `AutoRebuildAliases` (D) option are as follows:

```
ODbool                              ← configuration file (old style)
-oDbool                             ← command line (old style)
O AutoRebuildAliases=bool           ← configuration file (beginning with V8.7)
-OAutoRebuildAliases=bool           ← command line (beginning with V8.7)
define(`confAUTO_REBUILD',bool)     ← V8 m4 configuration
```

With no argument, `AutoRebuildAliases` (D) is set to true (the *aliases* database is automatically rebuilt). If the entire `AutoRebuildAliases` (D) option is missing, it defaults to false (no automatic rebuilds).

IDA *sendmail* uses *fcntl*(3) to prevent simultaneous rebuilds. Old versions of *sendmail* used *flock*(3). V8 *sendmail* uses either *fcntl*(3) or *flock*(3), depending on how it was compiled.

The `AutoRebuildAliases` (D) option is not safe. If specified from the command line, it may cause *sendmail* to relinquish its *root* privilege.

BlankSub (B)   *(All versions)*

34.8.5   *Set unquoted space replacement*

Some mailer programs have difficulty handling addresses that contain spaces. Such addresses are both illegal under RFC821 and RFC822 and subject to gross misinterpretation. For example, the address

```
John Q Public@wash.dc.gov
```

is viewed by some MUA programs as being composed of three separate addresses: `John`, `Q`, and `Public@wash.dc.gov`. To prevent this misinterpretation, such MUAs usually either quote the user portion or escape each space with a backslash:

```
"John Q Public"@wash.dc.gov                    ← quoted
John\ Q\ Public@wash.dc.gov                    ← escaped
```

The `BlankSub` (B) option is intended to handle an address that contains internal spaces, and is *neither* quoted nor escaped. For *sendmail* a space is any character defined by the C language library routine *isspace*(3).

Most sites use a . (dot or period) or an _ (underscore) character to replace unquoted space characters. That is, they declare the `BlankSub` (B) option as one of the following:

```
OB.
OB_
```

Feeding the address

```
John Q Public@wash.dc.gov
```

through *sendmail* with the option OB. set yields

    John.Q.Public@wash.dc.gov

The forms of the BlankSub (B) option are as follows:

OB*char*	← *configuration file (old style)*
-oB*char*	← *command line (old style)*
O BlankSub=*char*	← *configuration file (beginning with V8.7)*
-OBlankSub=*char*	← *command line (beginning with V8.7)*
define(`confBLANK_SUB',*char*)	← *V8 m4 configuration*

The argument *char* is of type character and is a single character. The default, if this option is omitted or if the *char* argument is omitted, is that an unquoted space character is replaced with a space character (which does nothing to correct the problem at all). The default for the *m4* technique is the dot (.) character.

Note that old-style addresses are delimited from each other with spaces rather than commas. Such addresses may be wrongly joined into a single address if the *char* is other than a space. Acceptance of such old-style addresses is determined by the setting of the OldStyleHeaders (o) option (see §34.8.44).

Also note that this BlankSub (B) option may also be used when tokenized addresses are reassembled (see §28.2.3).

The BlankSub (B) option is not safe. If specified from the command line, it may cause *sendmail* to relinquish its *root* privilege.

CheckAliases (n)   *(V8.1 and above)*

34.8.6   *Check right-hand side of aliases*

Ordinarily, when *sendmail* rebuilds an aliases database (as defined by the Alias-File (A) option, see §34.8.1), it checks only the addresses to the left of the colon to make sure they all resolve to a delivery agent that has the F=A flag set (see §30.8.12). It is possible to also have addresses to the right of the colon checked for validity by setting option CheckAliases (n) option to true.

The forms of the CheckAliases (n) option are as follows:

On*bool*	← *configuration file (old style)*
-on*bool*	← *command line (oldstyle)*
-on	← *command line shorthand*
O CheckAliases=*bool*	← *configuration file (beginning with V8.7)*
-OCheckAliases=*bool*	← *command line (beginning with V8.7)*
define(`confCHECK_ALIASES',*True*)	← *V8 m4 configuration*

The *bool* is of type Boolean. If it is absent, the option defaults to true (do check the right-hand side of aliases). If the entire option declaration is missing, the default is false (don't check the right-hand side of aliases). The default for the *m4* configuration technique is false.

Addresses to the right of the colon are checked only to be sure they are good addresses. Each is processed by rule set 3 and then rule set 0 to select a delivery agent. Processing merely needs to successfully select any non-#error delivery agent (see §30.5.2). The *sendmail* program prints and logs the following warning and skips any address that fails to select a valid delivery agent:

```
address... bad address
```

If the address selects an #error delivery agent, the error text for that error is printed instead:

```
address... user address required
```

The CheckAliases (n) option is further described in §24.5.2. This option is safe. Even if it is specified from the command line, *sendmail* retains its *root* privilege.

CheckpointInterval (C)   *(V8.1 and above)*

34.8.7   *Checkpoint the queue*

When a single email message is sent to many recipients (those on a mailing list, for example), a single *sendmail* process handles all the recipients. Should that *sendmail* process die or be killed halfway through processing, there is no record that the first half was delivered. As a result, when the queue is later reprocessed, the recipients in that first half will receive the message a second time.

The CheckpointInterval (C) option can limit the duplication. It tells *sendmail* to rewrite (checkpoint) its qf file (which contains the list of recipients; see §23.2.5) after each group of a specified number of recipients has been delivered. Recipients who have already received mail are deleted from the list, and that list is rewritten to the qf file. The forms of the CheckpointInterval (C) option are as follows:

```
OCnum                                      ← configuration file (old style)
-oCnum                                     ← command line (old style)
O CheckpointInterval=num                   ← configuration file (beginning with V8.7)
-OCheckpointInterval=num                   ← command line (beginning with V8.7)
define(`confCHECKPOINT_INTERVAL','num')    ← V8 m4 configuration
```

The *num* argument is of type numeric and specifies the number of recipients in each group. If *num* is entirely missing, is non-numeric, or is zero, this feature is disabled. If the entire CheckpointInterval (C) option is missing, the default is 10. There is a small performance penalty that increases as *num* approaches 1. A good starting value is 4, meaning that at most four people will get duplicate deliveries. Note that the F=M flag on local delivery will try as many recipients as possible before checkpointing, even if that number is greater than the value of this CheckpointInterval option. The CheckpointInterval (C) option is safe. Even if it is specified from the command line, *sendmail* retains its *root* privilege.

ClassFactor (z)   *(All versions)*

34.8.8   *Multiplier for priority increments*

The ClassFactor (z) option specifies a multiplying weight (factor) for a message's precedence when determining a message's priority. This option interacts with the RecipientFactor (y) option (see §34.8.53), and both options are described under that latter option.

The forms of the ClassFactor (z) option are as follows:

```
Ozfactor                                  ← configuration file (old form)
-ozfactor                                 ← command line (old form)
O ClassFactor=factor                      ← configuration file (beginning with V8.7)
-OClassFactor=factor                      ← command line (beginning with V8.7)
define(`confWORK_CLASS_FACTOR', factor)   ← V8 m4 configuration
```

The argument *factor* is of type numeric. If that argument is missing, the default value is zero. If the entire option is missing, the default value is 1800. The default for the *m4* technique is to omit this option.

The ClassFactor (z) option is not safe. If specified from the command line, it may cause *sendmail* to relinquish its *root* privilege.

ColonOkInAddr   *(8.7 and above)*

34.8.9   *Allow colons in addresses*

One possible form of an address is called "list syntax" and looks like this:

```
group: list;
```

Here, group is the name of a mailing list, and list is a list of zero or more addresses to which the message should be delivered (see §17.1.2.1). To understand this kind of address, *sendmail* needs to view the prefix and colon as a comment and the trailing semicolon as a comment. This is similar to treating everything outside an angle-bracketed address as a comment:

```
group: list ;
group: <list> ;
```

For such addresses to be recognizable, it is necessary to prohibit the use of other addresses that contain colons, unless those colons appear inside a part of the address that is surrounded by angle brackets. That is, to use list syntax, addresses like the following cannot be allowed:

```
host:george@wash.dc.gov
```

To handle this situation, V8.7 *sendmail* has introduced the ColonOkInAddr option. It is used like this:

```
O ColonOkInAddr=bool                        ← configuration file
-OColonOkInAddr=bool                        ← command line
define(`confCOLON_OK_IN_ADDR',bool)         ← m4 configuration
```

The argument *bool* is of type Boolean. If it is absent, this option is true (colons are okay, so list syntax is not recognized). If this option is entirely omitted or if *bool* is false, colons are not okay, so list syntax is recognized. Note that for version 5 or earlier configuration files (see §27.5 for a description of the V configuration command), this option is automatically set to true. Also note that for *m4* configurations this option is absent (false) by default.

Note that DECnet style addresses (see §29.4.4) legitimately contain double colons (e.g., `host::user`). DECnet addresses are correctly recognized no matter how this `ColonOkInAddr` option is set.

The `ColonOkInAddr` option is safe. If it is specified from the command line, *sendmail* will not relinquish its *root* privilege.

ConnectionCacheSize (k)   *(V8.1 and above)*

34.8.10   *Multiple-SMTP connections*

Usually, *sendmail* uses a single autonomous SMTP session to transmit one email message to another host. It connects to the other host, transmits the message, and closes the connection. Although this approach is sufficient for most mail, there are times when sending multiple messages during a single connection is preferable. This is called *caching* connections.

When *sendmail* caches a connection, it connects to the other host and transmits the mail message as usual. But instead of closing the connection, it keeps the connection open so that it can transmit additional mail messages without the additional overhead of opening and closing the connection each time. The `ConnectionCacheSize` (k) option of V8 *sendmail* specifies that open connections to other hosts should be maintained and the maximum number of those connections. The forms of the `ConnectionCacheSize` (k) option are as follows:

```
Oknum                                   ← configuration file (V8.6)
-oknum                                  ← command line (V8.6)
O ConnectionCacheSize=num               ← configuration file (beginning with V8.7)
-OConnectionCacheSize=num               ← command line (beginning with V8.7)
define(`confMCI_CACHE_SIZE',num)        ← V8 m4 configuration
```

There may be optional whitespace preceding the *num*. The *num* is an integer that specifies the maximum number of simultaneous connections to keep open. If *num* is zero, this caching feature is turned off. A value of 1 is good for workstations that forward all mail to a central mail server and is the default that is used if this option is entirely missing. When configuring with V8's *m4* technique, the default is 2. A value of 4 is the maximum for most machines that forward mail directly over the

Internet. Higher values require that you increase the number of open files allowed per process at the system level.

Caching is of greatest benefit in processing the queue. V8 *sendmail* automatically adapts to conditions to avoid caching connections for each invocation of *sendmail.* Maintenance of an open connection can delay return to the user's program, for example, and too many open connections to a common target host can create a high load on that host.

When caching is enabled with this ConnectionCacheSize (k) option, the ConnectionCacheTimeout (K) option should also be declared to set the connection timeout. The ConnectionCacheSize (k) option is not safe. If specified from the command line, it may cause *sendmail* to relinquish its *root* privilege.

ConnectionCacheTimeout (K)   *(V8.1 and above)*

34.8.11   *Multiple-SMTP time-outs*

Maintaining a cached connection to another host (see §34.8.10) imposes a penalty on both the local host and the other host. Each connection means that the other host is running a forked *sendmail* process that is doing nothing but waiting for an SMTP QUIT message to close the connection or for more mail to arrive. The local host has open sockets that consume system resources.

To limit the impact on other hosts, V8 *sendmail* offers the ConnectionCacheTimeout (K) option. This option tells *sendmail* how long to wait for another mail message before closing the connection.

The forms of the ConnectionCacheTimeout (K) option are as follows:

```
OKwait                                   ← configuration file (V8.6)
-oKwait                                  ← command line (V8.6)
O ConnectionCacheTimeout=wait            ← configuration file (beginning with V8.7)
-OConnectionCacheTimeout=wait            ← command line (beginning with V8.7)
define(`confMCI_CACHE_TIMEOUT',wait)     ← V8 m4 configuration
```

There may be optional whitespace preceding the wait. The wait is of type time and specifies the period to wait before timing out a cached connection. If this option is entirely missing, the default (for both the configuration file and the *m4* configuration technique) is 300 seconds (five minutes). When specifying the wait, be sure to include a trailing **s** character. If you don't, the number that you specify is interpreted by default as a number of minutes. The wait should never be longer than five minutes. A value of 0 essentially turns off caching.

This ConnectionCacheTimeout (K) option has an effect only if the ConnectionCacheSize (k) option (see §34.8.10) is also declared. The ConnectionCacheTimeout (K) option is not safe. If specified from the command line, it may cause *sendmail* to relinquish its *root* privilege.

ConnectionRateThrottle   *(V8.8 and above)*

34.8.12   *Incoming SMTP connection rate*

Whenever an outside site connects to *sendmail*'s SMTP port, *sendmail fork*(2)s a copy of itself. That copy (the child) processes the incoming message. Beginning with V8.8, *sendmail* keeps track of how many child processes it has spawned to handle incoming connections. The MaxDaemonChildren (see §34.8.35) option can be used to reject connections when the number of children has exceeded a specified threshold.

A different approach is to slow down acceptance of, rather than to reject, new connections when the number of children becomes too high. This allows the QueueLA (x) option (see §34.8.50) and the RefuseLA (X) option (see §34.8.54) to operate properly even if many incoming connections arrive simultaneously. You slow incoming connections with the ConnectionRateThrottle option:

```
O ConnectionRateThrottle=num                    ← V8.8 and above
define(`confCONNECTION_RATE_THROTTLE', num)     ← V8 m4 technique
```

The *num* is of type numeric. If it is present and greater than zero, connections are slowed when more than that number of connections arrive within one second. If *num* is less than or equal to zero, or absent, no threshold is enforced. If the entire option is missing, the default becomes zero. The default for the *m4* technique is to omit this option.

To illustrate how the slowdown operates, consider a situation in which *num* is set to 3, and 12 connections come in simultaneously. The first three connections are handled immediately. The next three are handled after one second. The three after that are handled after two seconds, and so on. The twelfth connection would be handled after a delay of three seconds.

Note that this option and the MaxDaemonChildren option (see §34.8.35) affect incoming connections differently.

The ConnectionRateThrottle option is not safe. If specified from the command line, it may cause *sendmail* to relinquish its *root* privilege.

DaemonPortOptions (O)   *(V8.1 and above)*

34.8.13   *Options for the daemon*

The DaemonPortOptions (O) option is used to customize the daemon's SMTP service. The form for this option is as follows:

```
OOpair,pair,pair                    ← configuration file (old form)
-oOpair,pair,pair                   ← command line (old form)
O DaemonPortOptions=pair,pair,pair  ← configuration file (beginning with V8.7)
```

```
-ODaemonPortOptions=pair,pair,pair                    ← command line (beginning with V8.7)
define(`confDAEMON_OPTIONS',`pair,pair,pair')         ← V8 m4 configuration
```

The `DaemonPortOptions` (O) is followed by a comma-separated list of pairs, in which each pair is of the form:

```
key=value
```

Only six keys are available, and prior to V8.7 they were case-sensitive. Prior to V8.7 an unknown key was silently ignored. Now an unknown key not only is ignored but also causes following error to be printed:

```
DaemonPortOptions unknown parameter "key"
```

The list of all currently defined *keys* is shown in Table 34-12.

Table 34-12: DaemonPortOptions Option Keywords

Key	§	Meaning
Addr	34.8.13.1	The network to accept connection from
Family	34.8.13.2	The type network we are connected to
Listen	34.8.13.3	The size of the *listen*(2) queue
Port	34.8.13.4	The port number on which *sendmail* should listen
ReceiveSize	34.8.13.5	The size of the TCP/IP receive buffer
SendSize	34.8.13.6	The size of the TCP/IP send buffer

Only the first character in each *key* is recognized, so a succinct declaration such as the following can be used to change the port used by the daemon:

```
OOP=26,A=our-net    # Only listen for local mail                    ← old form
O DaemonPortOptions=P=26,A=our-net  # Only listen for local mail ← beginning with V8.7
```

The O option is not safe. If specified from the command line, it may cause *sendmail* to relinquish its *root* privilege.

34.8.13.1 DaemonPortOptions=Addr

The `Addr` key is used to specify the network to use. The `value` is the name[*] or IP address of one of your network interfaces:

```
O DaemonPortOptions=Addr=128.32.204.25      # listen to our internal network only
```

If the `Addr` pair is omitted, the default network becomes INADDR_ANY, which allows connections from any network.

---

[*] Names did not work prior to V8.8 *sendmail.*

34.8.13.2   DaemonPortOptions=Family

The `Family` key is used to specify the network family. The legal possible values are *inet* for AF_INET, *iso* for AF_ISO, *ns* for AF_NS, and *x.25* for AF_CCITT.

```
O DaemonPortOptions=Family=iso
```

Note that only *inet* and *iso* are currently supported. The default is *inet*. Also note that *inet* requires NETINET to be defined, and *iso* requires NETISO to be defined when *sendmail* is being compiled (see §18.8.26).

34.8.13.3   DaemonPortOptions=Listen

When *sendmail* begins to run in *daemon* mode, it executes a *listen*(2) system call as part of monitoring its SMTP port for incoming mail. The second argument to *listen*(2) defines the maximum length to which the incoming queue of pending connections may grow. If a connection request arrives with the queue full, the client will receive an error that indicates ECONNREFUSED. This `Listen` key is used to change the size of the incoming queue from its default of 10. If `Listen` is less than or equal to zero, *listen*(2) will silently set its own default. But note that some kernels may have built-in defaults of their own, so setting `Listen` may have no effect at all.

34.8.13.4   DaemonPortOptions=Port

The `Port` key is used to specify the service port on which the daemon should listen. This is normally the port called **smtp**, as defined in the */etc/services* file. The value may be either a services string (such as **smtp**) or a number (such as 25). This key is useful inside domains that are protected by a firewall. By specifying a non-standard port, the firewall can communicate in a more secure manner with the internal network while still accepting mail on the normal port from the outside world:

```
O DaemonPortOptions=Port=26
```

If this pair is missing, the port defaults to **smtp**.

34.8.13.5   DaemonPortOptions=ReceiveSize

The `ReceiveSize` key is used to specify the size of the TCP/IP receive buffer. The value is a size in bytes. This should not be set unless you are having performance problems. Slow links (such as 9.6K SL/IP lines) might profit from a setting of 256, for example:

```
O DaemonPortOptions=ReceiveSize=256
```

The default value is set by the system (see *setsockopt*(2)).

34.8.13.6 *DaemonPortOptions=SendSize*

The `SendSize` key is used to specify the size of the TCP/IP send buffer. The value is a size in bytes. This should not be set unless you are having performance problems. Slow links (such as 9.6K SL/IP lines) might profit from a setting of 256, for example:

```
O DaemonPortOptions=SendSize=256
```

The default value is set by the system (see *setsockopt*(2)).

DefaultCharSet   *(V8.7 and above)*

34.8.14   *Content-Type: character set*

When a mail message is converted from 8 to 7 bits (see the `EightBitMode` (8) option in §34.8.22), it is important that the result look like a MIME message. V8.7 *sendmail* first outputs the following header if one is not already present:

```
MIME-Version: 1.0
```

After that, V8.7 *sendmail* looks for a `Content-Type:` header (see §35.10.9). If none is found, the following is inserted, where *charset* is the value declared for this option:

```
Content-Type: text/plain; charset=charset
```

The forms of the `DefaultCharSet` option are as follows:

```
O DefaultCharSet=charset                    ← configuration file
-ODefaultCharSet=charset                    ← command line
define(`confDEF_CHAR_SET', charset)         ← m4 configuration
```

If `DefaultCharSet` is undefined, *charset* defaults to the string "unknown-8bit." The default for the *m4* technique is to omit this option.

Note that if the `C=` equate (§30.4.2) is present for the sender's delivery agent, that character set supersedes the `DefaultCharSet`.

The `DefaultCharSet` option is safe. If specified from the command line, *sendmail* will not relinquish its *root* privilege.

DefaultUser (g)(u)   *(All versions)*

34.8.15   *Default delivery agent identity*

The *sendmail* program can be run as an *suid root* process (that is, with the permissions of the *root*, no matter who runs it) or as an ordinary process, run by an ordinary (nonprivileged) user (that is, with *root* privilege *only* if it is run by *root*).

When *sendmail* is run so that it has *root* privilege, it must give up that privilege under certain circumstances to remain secure.[*] When it can't set its identity to that of a real user, *sendmail* sets its *gid* to that specified by the g option and its *uid* to that specified by the u option. For version 8.7 and above, the DefaultUser option sets both the user and group identities.[†]

When *sendmail* is running with *root* privilege and when the F=S delivery agent flag (see §30.8.40) is *not* specified, *sendmail* changes its owner and group identity to that of an ordinary user in the following circumstances:

1. If the mail message is forwarded because of a user's ~/.forward file and if delivery is via a delivery agent that has the F=o flag set (see §30.8.33), then *sendmail* changes its owner and group identity to that of the user whose ~/.forward file was read.

2. Otherwise, if the mail message is being delivered through an *aliases*(5) file's :include: mailing list expansion and if delivery is via a delivery agent that has the F=o flag set (see §30.8.33) or to a file, then *sendmail* changes its owner and group identity to that of the owner of the file that was specified by the :include: line.

3. Otherwise, if the sender of the mail message is local and if delivery is via a delivery agent that does not have the F=o flag set (see §30.8.33) or to a file, then *sendmail* changes its owner and group identity to that of the sender. If the sender is *root*, *sendmail* changes its owner and group identity to that specified by the DefaultUser option.

4. Otherwise, *sendmail* changes its owner and group identity to that specified by the DefaultUser option.

These user and group defaults are ignored if the delivery agent's F= equate includes the S flag (run as another specified user). These user and group defaults are also ignored for any delivery agent that specifies the U= equate (see §30.4.13), which customizes user and group identities at the individual delivery agent level, but only if the F=o equate is not specified.

The forms of the DefaultUser (u) (g) option are as follows:

Ouuid	← *user, configuration file (old form)*
-ouuid	← *user, command line (old form)*
Oggid	← *group, configuration file (old form)*
-oggid	← *group, command line (old form)*
Ouuid:gid	← *both, configuration file (beginning with V8.7)*

---

[*] V8 is more security conscious and presumes that it is still *root* even if it has given up that privilege.

[†] In essence, the g and u options have been deprecated in favor of a single DefaultUser option, which sets both.

```
-ouuid:gid                          ← both, command line (beginning with V8.7)
O DefaultUser=uid:gid               ← both, configuration file (beginning with V8.7)
-ODefaultUser=uid:gid               ← both, command line (beginning with V8.7)
define(`confDEF_USER_ID',uid)       ← user, V8 m4 configuration
define(`confDEF_GROUP_ID',gid)      ← group, V8 m4 configuration (obsolete as of V8.7)
define(`confDEF_USER_ID',uid:gid)   ← both, V8 m4 configuration
```

The arguments *uid* and *gid* are of type numeric. Beginning with V8 *sendmail*, user or group names can also be text (for example, nobody). Beginning with V8.7 *sendmail*, the user definition with **DefaultUser** or **u** can specify both user and group. For example,

```
O DefaultUser=daemon:nogroup
```

There may be arbitrary whitespace between the user (**daemon**), the colon,[*] and the group (**nogroup**). If the group is missing, the value that is assigned to it varies depending on the nature of the **uid** specification. If the **uid** is a name, the group becomes the default group of that user as defined in the *passwd*(5) file. If the **uid** is numeric, the value in the group is not changed. For example, consider this *passwd*(5) file entry, where the group 12 corresponds to the group name **bum-group**:

```
bogus:*:10:12::/:
```

Then all the following are equivalent:

```
O DefaultUser=bogus
O DefaultUser=bogus:12
O DefaultUser=bogus:bumgroup

Og12    ⎱ taken together
Ou10    ⎰
```

But the following combination causes the group to reset to 12:

```
Og77
Oubogus
```

Under pre-8.7 *sendmail* a missing argument causes the value 0 to be used for the respective user or group identities. If an entire **u** or **g** option is missing, the default value becomes 1 (usually *daemon*). Under V8.7 *sendmail* the default is -1. In NFS-mounted environments, safe values for these options are one less than those of the user *nobody* and the group *nogroup*.

For maximum security, you should create a special pseudo-user and assign that pseudo-user to this option. (See §22.8.3.1 for a more detailed description of this approach.)

---

[*] The character between the user and group notations can be a colon, a period, or a forward slash. The colon is recommended.

The g, u, and DefaultUser options are not safe. If specified from the command line, they may cause *sendmail* to relinquish its *root* privilege.

DeliveryMode (d) *(All versions)*

34.8.16 *Set delivery mode*

There are four modes that *sendmail* can use for delivering mail. Three have always been a part of *sendmail*: background, interactive, and queue-only. One is new to V8.7 *sendmail*: deferred.

The mode is selected with the DeliveryMode (d) option:

```
Odmode                              ← configuration file (old form)
-odmode                             ← command line (old form)
O DeliveryMode=mode                 ← configuration file (beginning with V8.7)
-ODeliveryMode=mode                 ← command line (beginning with V8.7)
define(`confDELIVERY_MODE',mode)    ← V8 m4 configuration
```

The *mode* argument is of type character. It is case sensitive (must be lowercase) and is selected from one of the keywords shown in Table 34-13. Only the first letter of each is recognized, but we recommend full words for improved clarity.

Table 34–13: DeliveryMode Option Keywords

Keyword	§Description	
background	34.8.16.1	Background (asynchronous) delivery
deferred	34.8.16.2	Deferred (held as is) delivery (beginning with V8.7)
interactive	34.8.16.3	Interactive (synchronous) delivery
queueonly	34.8.16.4	Queued (held but processed) delivery

If the **mode** argument is missing, this option defaults to the i or interactive mode. If the entire DeliveryMode (d) option is missing, V8 *sendmail* then defaults to background mode, but old *sendmail* behaves unpredictably; consequently, this option should be considered mandatory. The default for a V8 *m4* configuration is also background.

If the mode character is other than one of the first lowercase letters shown in Table 34-13, *sendmail* will print and log the following error and will immediately exit with an exit value of EX_USAGE as defined in *<sysexits.h>*:

```
Unknown delivery mode char
```

Queue-only and deferred modes are only available if QUEUE was defined when *sendmail* was compiled (see §18.8.37). If QUEUE was not defined and one of these two modes is selected, *sendmail* will print and log the following:

```
need QUEUE to set -odqueue or -oddefer
```

The `DeliveryMode` (d) option is safe. Even if it is specified from the command line, *sendmail* retains its *root* privilege.

34.8.16.1 *DeliveryMode=background*

Background mode—intended primarily* for use in the configuration file—allows *sendmail* to run *asynchronously*. This means that once *sendmail* has gathered the entire message and verified that the recipient is deliverable, it will *fork*(3) a copy of itself and exit. The copy, running in the background (asynchronously), will then handle the delivery. From the user's point of view, this mode allows the mail interface program to act as though it sent the message nearly instantaneously.

34.8.16.2 *DeliveryMode=deferred*

Deferred mode—for use in either the command line or the configuration file—is much like queue-only mode except that all database lookups, including DNS, are deferred until the actual queue run. Deferred mode (new with V8.7) is preferred for dial-on-demand sites (typically, modem-based SL/IP or PPP connections). As in queue-only mode, all mail is queued for later delivery, but with deferred mode, code inside *sendmail* that would ordinarily interact with DNS is suppressed. This prevents the modem from being dialed and connections from being established every time mail is queued.

34.8.16.3 *DeliveryMode=interactive*

Interactive mode—intended for use from the command line—causes *sendmail* to run *synchronously*. This mode is useful primarily for debugging mail problems. Instead of going into the background with *fork*(3), it runs in the foreground (synchronously). In this mode, error messages are printed back to the controlling terminal rather than being mailed to the user as bounced mail. The –v command-line switch (see §36.7.41) automatically sets the mode to interactive.

34.8.16.4 *DeliveryMode=queueonly*

Queue-only mode—for use in either the command line or the configuration file—causes *sendmail* to synchronously queue mail. Queue-only mode is useful at sites that have huge amounts of UUCP mail or Usenet news batch feeds or when delivering to low priority addresses such as mailing lists. Queuing has the beneficial effect of serializing delivery through queue runs, and it reduces the load on a machine that many parallel backgrounded *sendmail* processes can cause. Queue-

---

* A sending program (MUA) might need to use background mode on the command line (db) if the message is urgent and if the default in *sendmail*'s configuration file is to queue all messages (with q mode).

only mode is typically supplied as a command-line option to *sendmail* by the *uuxqt*(8) program. When queue-only mode is selected, all mail is queued for delivery, and none is actually delivered. A separate run of *sendmail* with its -q command-line switch (see §23.6.1) is needed to actually process the queue. Note that addresses can still be looked up with DNS as a part of the queueing process. Consequently, queue-only mode is probably not suitable for dial-on-demand sites.

DialDelay   *(V8.7 and above)*

34.8.17   *Connect failure retry time*

Many Internet providers allow small sites (such as home machines) to dial up when there is a demand for network traffic to flow. Such connections are usually of short duration and use the PPP or SL/IP protocols. A problem can arise when this dial-up-on-demand is instigated by *sendmail.*[*] The process of negotiating a dial-up connection can take so long that *sendmail* will have its attempt to *connect*(2) fail. (See also the **connect** keyword for the **Timeout** option in §34.8.70.2). To remedy this situation, V8.7 *sendmail* offers the **DialDelay** option. It is declared like this:

```
O DialDelay=delay                    ← configuration file
-ODialDelay=delay                    ← command line
define(`confDIAL_DELAY',delay)       ← m4 configuration
```

The argument *delay* is of type time. If this option is entirely omitted or if *delay* is omitted, the default is then zero and no delay is enabled. The default for the *m4* configuration technique is also zero. If the unit of time is omitted from the time declaration, the default is seconds.

If *delay* is nonzero and *sendmail* has its initial *connect*(2) fail, it will *sleep*(3) for *delay* seconds and then try to *connect*(2) again. Note that *sendmail* tries a second time only once, so the *delay* should be large enough to accommodate your anticipated worst-case delay. On the other hand, care should be taken to avoid excessively long delays that can make *sendmail* appear to hang. No check is made by *sendmail* for absurdly large values given to *delay*.

The **DialDelay** option is safe. If it is specified from the command line, *sendmail* will not relinquish its *root* privilege.

DontExpandCnames   *(V8.7 and above)*

34.8.18   *Prevent CNAME expansion*

Ordinarily, the $[and $] operators (see §28.6.6) cause the enclosed hostname to be looked up with DNS and replaced with the canonical name for that host. The

---

[*] Or by any other network-oriented program, such as FTP or Mosaic.

canonical name is the A DNS record. For example, consider these DNS records:

```
here.us.edu.    IN    A     123.45.67.89
ftp.us.edu.     IN    CNAME here.us.edu.
```

If the address *ftp.us.edu* is fed to the $[and $] operators in the RHS of a rule:

```
R...      $[ $1 $]
```

then the rewritten result of passing *ftp.us.edu* as $1 will be the A record name *here.us.edu*. This behavior is correct under RFC822 and RFC1123, but the IETF is currently moving toward a change.

Sometimes it is important for the CNAME to appear in email headers as the canonical name. One example might be that of an FTP service moving from one machine to another during a transition phase. In that case, outgoing mail should appear to be from *ftp.us.edu*, because the records will change after the move, and we want to maintain the ability to reply to such mail.

```
here.us.edu.    IN    A     123.45.67.89    ← retired and gone
ftp.us.edu.     IN    CNAME there.us.edu.
there.us.edu.   IN    A     123.45.67.90
```

Another possibility might be that of a mobile host (a workstation that plugs into different networks and thus has different A records over time):

```
mobile.us.edu.    IN    CNAME monday.dc.gov.
monday.dc.gov.    IN    A     12.34.56.78
tuesday.foo.com.  IN    A     23.45.67.89
```

Whenever this workstation is plugged in, its CNAME record is changed to point to the A record of the day: *monday.dc.gov* on Monday and *tuesday.foo.com* on Tuesday. But no matter what its A record happens to be, outgoing mail should look as though it came from *mobile.us.edu*.

The **DontExpandCnames** option causes *sendmail* to accept CNAME records as canonical. It is intended for use on sending hosts with special CNAME needs and should not be enabled without good reason. It is declared like this:

```
O DontExpandCnames=bool                  ← configuration file (V8.7)
-ODontExpandCnames=bool                  ← command line (V8.7)
define(`confDONT_EXPAND_CNAMES',bool)    ← V8 m4 configuration
```

The argument *bool* is of type Boolean. If *bool* is missing, the default is true (use the CNAME). If the entire **DontExpandCnames** option is missing, the default is false (convert CNAMEs to A records).

The **DontExpandCnames** option is not safe. If specified from the command line, it may cause *sendmail* to relinquish its *root* privilege.

DontInitGroups

34.8.19

Don't use initgroups(3)

Just before executing any delivery agent (including the `*include*` delivery agent) and just before opening a *~/.forward* file, *sendmail* sets its group and user identities as appropriate. To illustrate, consider the U= equate (see §30.4.13). If the `fax` delivery agent has the U= equate set like this:

```
U=fax:fax
```

its A= program will be executed by the user *fax* who is in the group *fax*. In addition, *sendmail* calls the *initgroups(3)* system call to expand the list of groups to which the user belongs. In the case of *fax*, it may also belong to the groups *fax-adm* and *faxusers*. The total result is that *fax* can execute, read, and write any files that have the appropriate group permissions set for any of the groups *fax*, *fax-adm*, and *faxusers*.

This versatility, however, has a price. As group files get huge or as *nis*, *nisplus*, or *hesiod* services become slow (probably because they are also large), the *initgroups(3)* call can start to adversely affect *sendmail*'s performance.

When performance is a concern, the *DontInitGroups* option can be used to disable *initgroups(3)*:

```
O DontInitGroups=bool      ← configuration file
-ODontInitGroups=bool      ← command line
define('confDONT_INIT_GROUPS',bool)    ← V8 m4 configuration
```

The argument *bool* is of type Boolean. If it is missing, the default value is true —don't call *initgroups(3)*. If the entire option is missing, the default value is false —do call *initgroups(3)*. See §18.8.31 for a discussion of how NO_GROUP_SET determines whether or not this option also affects the *getgrgid(3)* system call.

The `DontInitGroups` option is not safe as of V8.8.4. Even if it is specified from the command line, may cause *sendmail* to relinquish its *root* privilege.

DontPruneRoutes (R)

34.8.20

Don't prune route addresses

One form of address is called a *route address*, because it specifies a route (sequence of hosts) through which the message should be delivered. For example:

```
@hostA,@hostB:user@hostC
```

This address specifies that the message should first go to hostA, then from hostA to hostB, and finally from hostB to hostC for delivery to user.[*]

RFC1123, in Section 5.3.3, specifies that delivery agents should always try to eliminate source routing when they are able. V8 *sendmail* takes an address like the above and checks to see whether it can connect to hostC directly. If it can, it rewrites the address like this:

```
user@hostC
```

This is called "pruning route addresses." There may be times when such pruning is inappropriate. Internal networks, for example, may be set up to encourage manual specification of a route through a high-speed network. If left to its own, *sendmail* always tosses the route and tries to connect directly.

The DontPruneRoutes (R) option causes *sendmail* to never prune route addresses. The forms of this option are as follows:

OR*bool*	← *configuration file (old form)*
-oR*bool*	← *command line (old form)*
O DontPruneRoutes=*bool*	← *configuration file (beginning with V8.7)*
-ODontPruneRoutes=*bool*	← *command line (beginning with V8.7)*
define(`confDONT_PRUNE_ROUTES',`bool')	← *V8 m4 configuration*

The argument *bool* is of type Boolean. If it is missing, the default value is true (nothing special is done with route addresses). If the entire R option is missing, the default becomes false (route addresses are pruned). With the V8 *m4* configuration technique the default is false.

The DontPruneRoutes (R) option is not safe. If specified from the command line, it may cause *sendmail* to relinquish its *root* privilege.

DoubleBounceAddress   *(V8.8 and above)*

34.8.21   *Errors when sending errors*

Ordinarily, when *sendmail* sends error notification mail, it expects that error notification to be successfully delivered. Upon occasion, error mail itself will bounce or fail too. This is called a "double-bounce" situation. Prior to V8.8, *sendmail* would notify postmaster if error notification failed. But this might not be the best solution in all cases. Consider, for example, a site that has a sitewide postmaster and several departmental postmasters. In such situations, double-bounce mail should probably go to the sitewide postmaster.

---

* Also see how route addresses are handled in rules in §29.4.3 and the F=d delivery agent flag in §30.8.16).

Beginning with V8.8 *sendmail*, the `DoubleBounceAddress` option can be used to define who gets double-bounce mail:

```
O DoubleBounceAddress=addr                    ← configuration file (beginning with V8.8)
-ODoubleBounceAddress=addr                    ← command line (beginning with V8.8)
define(`confDOUBLE_BOUNCE_ADDRESS', `addr')   ← V8 m4 configuration
```

Here, `addr` is of type string and is a comma-separated list of one or more email addresses. If `addr` is missing, the following error is printed and the option is ignored:

```
readcf: option DoubleBounceAddress: value required
```

If the entire option is missing, the default becomes `postmaster`. If *sendmail* is unable to send double-bounce mail to `addr`, it logs the following error:

```
cannot parse addr
```

The `DoubleBounceAddress` option is not safe. If specified from the command line, it may cause *sendmail* to relinquish its *root* privilege.

EightBitMode (8)   *(V8.7 and above)*

34.8.22   *How to convert MIME input*

The data portion of an email message is transmitted during the DATA phase of an SMTP transaction. Prior to V8.6 the data were presumed to be 7-bit. That is, the high (8th) bit of every byte of the message could be cleared (reset or made zero) with no change in the meaning of that data. With the advent of ESMTP and MIME, it became possible for *sendmail* to receive data for which the preservation of the 8th bit is important.

There are two kinds of 8-bit data. Data that arrive with the high bit set and for which no notification was given are called "unlabeled" 8-bit data. Data for which notification *was* given (using 8BITMIME in the ESMTP session or with the `-B8BITMIME` command-line switch, see §36.7.1, or with a `MIME-Version:` header in the message, see §35.10.21) are called "labeled."

The `EightBitMode` (8) option tells *sendmail* how to treat incoming unlabeled 8-bit data. The forms of this option are as follows:

```
O8key                                        ← configuration file (V8,6)
-o8key                                       ← command line (V8,6)
O EightBitMode=key                           ← configuration file (beginning with V8.7)
-OEightBitMode=key                           ← command line (beginning with V8.7)
define(`confEIGHT_BIT_HANDLING', key)        ← m4 configuration
```

The `key` is mandatory and must be selected from one of those shown in Table 34-14. If the `key` is missing or if `key` is not one of those listed, *sendmail* will print the following error and ignore the option:

```
Unknown 8-bit mode char
```

Only the first character of the *key* is recognized, but we still recommend that the full word be used for clarity.

Table 34–14: EightBitMode Option Characters

Key	§	Meaning
mimify	34.8.22.1	Do any necessary conversion of 8BITMIME to 7-bit
pass	34.8.22.2	Pass unlabeled 8-bit input through as is
strict	34.8.22.3	Reject unlabeled 8-bit input

If the entire **EightBitMode** (8) option is missing, the default becomes **p** (pass 8-bit and convert MIME). If you configure with V8's *m4* technique, the default is also **p**.

Depending on the *key* selected and the nature of incoming mail, any of several error messages may be generated:

```
Eight bit data not allowed
Cannot send 8-bit data to 7-bit destination
host does not support 8BITMIME
```

Conversion from 8 to 7 bit is complex. First, *sendmail* looks for a MIME **Content-Type:** header. If the header is found, *sendmail* looks for and, if found, uses a MIME **boundary** definition to delimit conversion.[*] If more than 1/4 of a section has the high bit set after reading at least 4 kilobytes of data, *sendmail* presumes base64 encoding[†] and inserts the following MIME header into the data stream:

```
Content-Transfer-Encoding: base64
```

Base64 encoding converts 8-bit data into a stream of 6-bit bytes that contain universally readable text. Base64 is described in RFC1521.

If less than 1/4 of the data that were scanned have the high bit set or if the type in the **Content-Type:** header is listed in **$=q** (32.5.5), the data are converted from 8 to 7 bit by using Quoted-Printable encoding, and the following MIME header is inserted into the stream:

```
Content-Transfer-Encoding: quoted-printable
```

Under Quoted-Printable encoding, ASCII control characters (in the range 0x00 through 0x20), the tab character, the "=" character, and all characters with the high bit set are converted. First an "=" character is output, then the character is con-

---

[*] A boundary is used only for **multipart** messages.

[†] Also see the $=q class (32.5.5) for a way to require quoted-printable encoding.

verted to an ASCII representation of its hexadecimal value, and that value is output. For example,

    0xb9   → *becomes*   =B9

Under this scheme, the = character is considered binary and is encoded as =3D. If the F=3 flag (see §30.8.2) is set for a selected delivery agent, the characters

    ! " # $ @ \ [ ] ^ ` { | } ~

are also converted. If F=3 is not set, those characters are output as is.

Lines longer than 72 characters (bytes) are broken with the insertion of an "=" character and the E= end-of-line characters defined for the current delivery agent. Any lines that end in a whitespace character have that character converted to quoted-printable even if the line is under 72 characters. Quoted-printable is described in RFC1521. Where m (mimefy) may not be appropriate for a given delivery agent, the F=8 flag (see §30.8.5) can be specified to force p (pass8bit) behavior.

The EightBitMode (8) option is safe. Even if it is specified from the command line, *sendmail* retains its *root* privilege.

34.8.22.1 EightBitMode=mimefy

Convert unlabeled 8-bit input to 8BITMIME, and do any necessary conversion of 8BITMIME to 7-bit. When running as a daemon receiving mail via SMTP, advertise the 8BITMIME ESMTP keyword as valid. This *key* specifies that your site will be a full-time MIME installation. Note that compiling with MIME8TO1=1 (see §18.8.22) causes ESMTP to always advertise 8BITMIME.

34.8.22.2 EightBitMode=pass

Pass unlabeled 8-bit input through as is. Convert labeled 8BITMIME input to 7-bit as required by any delivery agent with the F=7 flag set (see §30.8.4) or any SMTP server that does not advertise 8BITMIME.

34.8.22.3 EightBitMode=strict

Reject unlabeled 8-bit input. Convert 8BITMIME to 7-bit as required by any delivery agent with the F=7 flag set (see §30.8.4) or any SMTP server that does not advertise 8BITMIME.

ErrorHeader (E)   *(V8 and above)*

34.8.23   *Set error message header*

When a notification of a mail error is sent to the sender, the details of the error are taken from the text saved in the xf file (see §23.2.7). The ErrorHeader (E) option, available only with V8 *sendmail,* allows you to prepend custom text ahead of that error text.

Custom error text is useful for sites that wish to offer help as part of the error message. For example, one common kind of error message is notification of an unknown user:

```
----- Transcript of session follows -----
550 smith@wash.dc.gov... User unknown
----- Unsent message follows -----
```

Here, the user **smith** is one that is unknown. A useful error help message for your site to produce might be

```
Common problems:
      User unknown: the user or login name is wrong.
      Host unknown: you mistyped the host part of the address.
----- Transcript of session follows -----
550 smith@wash.dc.gov... User unknown
----- Unsent message follows -----
```

The forms for the **ErrorHeader** (**E**) option are as follows:

O*Etext*	← *configuration file (V8.6)*
-o*Etext*	← *command line (V8.6)*
O ErrorHeader=*text*	← *configuration file (beginning with V8.7)*
-OErrorHeader=*text*	← *command line (beginning with V8.7)*
define(`confERROR_MESSAGE',`*text*')	← *V8 m4 configuration*

The argument **text** is mandatory. If it is missing, this option is ignored. The **text** is either the actual error text that is printed or the name of a file containing that text. If **text** begins with the / character, it is taken as the absolute pathname of the file (a relative name is not possible). If the specified file cannot be opened for reading, this option is silently ignored.

Macros may be used in the error text, and they are expanded as they are printed. For example, the text might contain

```
For help with $u, try "finger $u"
```

which might produce this error message:

```
For help with smith@wash.dc.gov, try "finger smith@wash.dc.gov"
    ----- Transcript of session follows -----
550 smith@wash.dc.gov... User unknown
    ----- Unsent message follows -----
```

The **ErrorHeader** (**E**) option is not safe. If specified from the command line, it may cause *sendmail* to relinquish its *root* privilege.

ErrorMode (e)   *(All versions)*

34.8.24   *Specify mode of error handling*

The *sendmail* program is flexible in its handling of delivery errors. By selecting from five possible modes with the `ErrorMode` (e) option, you can tailor notification of delivery errors to suit many needs.

This option is intended primarily for use from the command line. If included in the configuration file, it should be given only the p argument, for print mode (the default).

The forms of the `ErrorMode` (e) option are as follows:

```
Oemode                            ← configuration file (old form)
-oemode                           ← command line (old form)
-emode                            ← command-line shorthand (not recommended)
O ErrorMode=mode                  ← configuration file (beginning with V8.7)
-OErrorMode=mode                  ← command line (beginning with V8.7)
define(`confERROR_MODE',mode)     ← V8 m4 configuration
```

The type of *mode* is character. If *mode* is missing, the default value is p (for print normally). Under older versions of *sendmail*, if this `ErrorMode` (e) option is entirely missing, the default value for **mode** is the C language character constant '\0'. Under V8 *sendmail*, the default value in this case is p.

The possible characters for the *mode* argument are listed in Table 34-15.

Table 34-15: ErrorMode Option Modes

Mode	§	Meaning
e	34.8.24.1	Like m, but always exit with a zero exit status
m	34.8.24.2	Mail error notification to the sender no matter what
p	34.8.24.3	Print error messages (the default)
q	34.8.24.4	Remain silent about all delivery errors
w	34.8.24.5	Write errors to the sender's terminal screen

Note that the error-handling mode is automatically set to m (for mail errors) in two special circumstances. First, if a mailing list is being processed and if an owner is found for that list (see §25.3), the mode is set to m to force mail notification to that owner. Second, if SMTP delivery is to multiple recipients, the mode is set to m to force mail notification to the sender. This latter assumes that multiple recipients qualify as a mailing list.

Also note that V8 *sendmail* sets the error-handling mode to q (for quiet) when *sendmail* is given the **–bv** (address verification) command line switch. This prevents spurious error messages from being mailed to root in testing addresses.

The ErrorMode (e) option is safe. Even if it is specified from the command line, *sendmail* retains its *root* privilege.

34.8.24.1 ErrorMode=e

Like m, but always exit with a zero exit status. This mode is intended for use from the command line. This e mode is used by the *rmail*(8) program when it invokes *sendmail*. On some systems, if *sendmail* exits with a nonzero value (fails), the *uuxqt*(8) program sends its own error message. This results in two error messages being sent, whereas only one should ever be sent. Worse still, the error message from *uuxqt* may contain a bad address, one that may itself bounce.

34.8.24.2 ErrorMode=m

Mail error notification to the sender no matter what. This mode tries to find the most rational way to return mail. All aliasing is disabled to prevent loops. Nothing is ever saved to `~/dead.letter`. This mode is intended for use from the command line. The m mode is appropriate for mail generated by an application that arises from a login but for which no human is present to monitor messages. One example might be a data-acquisition system that is manually logged in but is then left to fend for itself. Similarly, when the user *news* sends articles by mail, error messages should not be placed in `~news/dead.letter`, where they may be overlooked; rather, this mode should be used so that errors are placed in a mail spool file where they can be periodically monitored.

34.8.24.3 ErrorMode=p

Print error messages (the default). The *sendmail* program simply tries to save a copy of the failed mail in `~/dead.letter` and prints an error message to its standard output. If the sender is remote, it sends notification of the problem back to that sender via email. If `~/dead.letter` is not writable, a copy is saved to `/usr/tmp/dead.letter`. Note that this default path was hard-coded into pre-V8 versions of *sendmail* as a string constant. The only way to change it was by editing *savemail.c*. But beginning with V8 *sendmail*, the path component is defined by the _PATH_VARTMP definition, and that can be tuned in your *Makefile* (see §18.8.34). The default for _PATH_VARTMP is `/usr/tmp/`. The file named *dead.letter* is hard-coded in all versions of *sendmail*.

34.8.24.4 ErrorMode=q

Quiet; remain silent about all delivery errors. If the sender is local, this mode assumes that the program or person that ran *sendmail* will give notification of the error. Mail is not sent, and `~/dead.letter` is not saved. Error information is provided only in the *sendmail* program's *exit*(2) status (see §36.5). This mode is intended for use from the command line. One possible use might be exploding a junk-mail mailing list with a program that could correctly interpret the exit status.

34.8.24.5 ErrorMode=w

Write errors to the sender's terminal screen if logged in (similar to *write*(1)); otherwise, send mail to that user. First tries to write to *stdout*. If that fails, it reverts to mail notification. This mode is intended for use from the command line. The reason for this mode has been lost to history,[*] and it should be considered obsolete.

FallbackMXhost (V)   *(V8.4 and above)*

34.8.25   *Fallback MX host*

At sites with poor (connect on demand, or unreliable) network connections, SMTP connections may often fail. In such situations it may not be desirable for each workstation to queue the mail locally for a later attempt. Under V8 *sendmail* it is possible to specify a *fallback* host to which the mail should instead be forwarded. One such host might be a central mail hub machine.

The `FallbackMXhost` (V) option specifies the name of a mail exchanger machine (MX record) of last resort. It is given an artificially low priority (high preference number) so that *sendmail* tries to connect to it only if all other connection attempts for the target host have failed.

Note that this fallback MX host is used only for connection failures. It is not used if the name server lookup failed. It is available only for the [IPC] delivery agent (see §30.4.1.2). Note that MX lookups are available only if *sendmail* is compiled with NAMED_BIND defined (see §18.8.23).

The forms of the `FallbackMXhost` (V) option are as follows:

```
OVhost                          ← configuration file (V8.6)
-oVhost                         ← command line (V8.6)
O FallbackMXhost=host           ← configuration file (beginning with V8.7)
-OFallbackMXhost=host           ← command line (beginning with V8.7)
define(`confFALLBACK_MX',`host')  ← V8 m4 configuration
```

Here, *host* is of type string and is the fully qualified domain name of the fallback host. If *host* or the entire option is missing, no fallback MX record is used. The effect of this option can be seen by using the /mx rule-testing command (see §38.5.2).

The `FallbackMXhost` (V) option is not safe. If specified from the command line, it may cause *sendmail* to relinquish its *root* privilege.

---

[*] According to Eric Allman, "Dubious, someone bugged me for it; I forget why."

ForkEachJob (Y)   *(All versions)*

34.8.26   *Process queue files individually*

On machines with a small amount of memory (such as 3B1s and old Sun 3s) it is best to limit the size of running processes. One way to do this is to have the *sendmail* program *fork*(2) a copy of itself to handle each individual queued message. The ForkEachJob (Y) option can be used to allow those *fork*(2)'s.

The forms of the ForkEachJob (Y) option are as follows:

```
OYbool                            ← configuration file (old style)
-oYbool                           ← command line (old style)
O ForkEachJob=bool                ← configuration file (beginning with V8.7)
-OForkEachJob=bool                ← command line (beginning with V8.7)
define(`confSEPARATE_PROC',bool)  ← V8 m4 configuration
```

The argument *bool* is of type Boolean. If *bool* is missing, the default is true (fork). The default for the V8 *m4* technique is true. If the entire ForkEachJob (Y) option is missing, the default is false (don't fork).

If option ForkEachJob (Y) is set (true), there is a *fork*(2) to start processing of the queue, then another *fork*(2) to process each message in the queue. If option ForkEachJob (Y) is not set (false), only the initial *fork*(2) takes place, greatly improving the efficiency of a queue run. For example, a single process (as with ForkEachJob (Y) false) retains information about down hosts and so does not waste time trying to connect again for subsequent mail to the same host during the current queue run. For all modern machines the ForkEachJob (Y) option should be false.

The ForkEachJob (Y) option is not safe. If specified from the command line, it may cause *sendmail* to relinquish its *root* privilege.

ForwardPath (J)   *(V8 and above)*

34.8.27   *Set ~/.forward search path*

When mail is being delivered to a local user, *sendmail* attempts to open and read a file in the user's home directory called *.forward*. If that file exists and is readable, the aliases in that file replace the local username for delivery.

Under V8 *sendmail* the ForwardPath (J) option is used to define alternative locations for the user's *~/.forward* file.

The forms of the ForwardPath (J) option are as follows:

```
OJpath                            ← configuration file (V8.6)
-oJpath                           ← command line (V8.6)
O ForwardPath=path                ← configuration file (beginning with V8.7)
```

```
-OForwardPath=path                    ← command line (beginning with V8.7)
define(`confFORWARD_PATH',path)       ← V8 m4 configuration
```

The *path* is a colon-separated list of files. An attempt is made to open and read each in turn, from left to right, until one is successfully read:

```
OJ/var/forward/$u:$z/.forward
```

Macros may, and should, be used in the *path* file locations. In the above example, *sendmail* first looks in the file */var/forward/$u* (where the macro $u contains the user's login name; see §31.10.36). If that file can't be opened for reading, *sendmail* tries reading *$z/.forward* (where the $z macro contains the user's home directory; see §31.10.46). Other macros of interest are $w (the local hostname; see §31.10.40), $x (the user's full name; see §31.10.14), $r (the sending protocol; see §31.10.31), and $s (the sending host; see §31.10.33). The recommended declaration is to use the name of the sending host thus:

```
OJ$z/.forward.$w:$z/.forward
```

If the *path* or the entire option is omitted, the default is *$z/.forward*. Therefore omitting the ForwardPath (J) option causes V8 *sendmail* to emulate older versions by looking only in the *˜/.forward* file for user forwarding information.

Beginning with V8.7 *sendmail*, the F=w delivery agent flag (see §30.8.43) must be set for the recipient's delivery agent, or all forwarding is skipped. Previously, this was tied to the delivery agent named local.

The ForwardPath (J) option is not safe. If specified from the command line, it may cause *sendmail* to relinquish its *root* privilege.

HelpFile (H)   *(All versions)*

34.8.28   *Specify location of the help file*

The *sendmail* program implements the SMTP (and ESMTP) HELP command by looking up help messages in a text file. Beginning with V8.7 *sendmail*, help messages for the –bt rule-testing mode are also looked up in that file. The location and name of that text file are specified by using the HelpFile (H) option. If the name is the C language value NULL or if *sendmail* cannot open that file for reading, *sendmail* issues the following message and continues:

```
502 HELP not implemented
```

The help file is composed of lines of text, separated by tab characters into two fields per line. The leftmost field is an item for which help is offered. The rightmost field (the rest of the line) is the help text to be printed. A few lines in a typical help file might look like this:

```
rset   .RSET
rset            Resets the system.
quit   QUIT
quit            Exit sendmail (SMTP).
verb   VERB
verb            Go into verbose mode.  This sends 0xy responses that are
verb            not RFC821 standard (but should be).  They are recognized
verb            by humans and other sendmail implementations.
vrfy   VRFY <recipient>
vrfy            Verify an address.  If you want to see what it aliases
vrfy            to, use EXPN instead.
```

For an SMTP request of **help vrfy**, *sendmail* might produce

```
214-VRFY <recipient>
214-    Verify an address.  If you want to see what it aliases
214-    to, use EXPN instead.
214 End of HELP info
```

The forms of the `HelpFile` (H) option are as follows:

```
OHfile                    ← configuration file (old form)
-oHfile                   ← command line (old form)
O HelpFile=file           ← configuration file (beginning with V8.7)
-OHelpFile=file           ← command line (beginning with V8.7)
define(`HELP_FILE',`file')  ← V8 m4 configuration
```

The argument *file* is of type string and may be a full or relative pathname. Relative names are always relative to the queue directory. If *file* is omitted, then the name of the help file defaults to *sendmail.hf.* If the entire H option is omitted, the name of the help file becomes the C language value NULL. The Simple Mail Transfer Protocol (SMTP) is described in RFC821, and Extended SMTP (ESMTP) is described in RFC1869.

The `HelpFile` (H) option is not safe. If specified from the command line, it may cause *sendmail* to relinquish its *root* privilege.

HoldExpensive (c)   *(All versions)*

34.8.29   *Queue for expensive mailers*

An *expensive mailer* is a delivery agent that contains an **e** flag in its F= equate (see §30.8.18). Typically, such delivery agents are associated with slow network connections such as SL/IP or with costly networks such as those with high per connect or connection startup rates. Whatever the reason, the `HoldExpensive` (c) option allows you to queue all such mail for later delivery rather than connecting on demand. (Queuing is described in Chapter 23, *The Queue.*)

Note that this option affects only the initial delivery attempt, not later attempts when the queue is processed. Essentially, all this option does is to defer delivery until the next time the queue is processed.

The forms of the `HoldExpensive` (c) option are as follows:

```
Ocbool                            ← configuration file (old form)
-ocbool                           ← command line (old form)
-c                                ← command-line shorthand (not recommended)
O HoldExpensive=bool              ← configuration file (beginning with V8.7)
-OHoldExpensive=bool              ← command line (beginning with V8.7)
define(`confCON_EXPENSIVE',bool)  ← V8 m4 configuration
```

The argument *bool* is of type Boolean. If the *bool* argument is missing, the default is true (expensive mail is queued). If the entire `HoldExpensive` (c) option is missing, the default value is false (expensive mail is delivered immediately).

The **-v** (verbose) command-line switch automatically sets the `HoldExpensive` (c) option to false. The `HoldExpensive` (c) option is not safe. If specified from the command line, it may cause *sendmail* to relinquish its *root* privilege.

HostsFile   *(V8.7 and above)*

34.8.30   *Specify alternate /etc/hosts file*

When canonifying a host's name, *sendmail* will use the method described under the `ServiceSwitchFile` option (see §34.8.61). When that method is `files`, *sendmail* parses the */etc/hosts* file to find the canonical name. If a different file should be used on your system, you can specify it with this `HostsFile` option:

```
O HostsFile=path               ← configuration file (beginning with V8.7)
-OHostsFile=path               ← command line (beginning with V8.7)
define(`confHOSTS_FILE',path)  ← V8 m4 configuration
```

Here, *path* is of type string. If *path* is missing, the name of the */etc/hosts* file becomes an empty string. If the entire option is missing, the default is the value that was given to _PATH_HOSTS when *sendmail* was compiled (see §18.8.34). If the *path* cannot be opened for reading (for any reason at all), host canonification by this method is silently skipped.

One example of a use for the `HostsFile` option would be to use a switched-service file to cause all host lookups to use DNS first, then files:

```
hosts:    dns files
```

In that case you would use a special file to hold information about internal hosts that are not known to DNS. Such a file might look like this:

```
123.45.67.89    secret.internal.host.domain
```

This special file would be defined with the `HostsFile` option.

The `HostsFile` option is not safe. If specified from the command line, it may cause *sendmail* to relinquish its *root* privilege.

HostStatusDirectory   *(V8.8 and above)*

34.8.31   *Location of persistent host status*

The process of delivering network mail requires that *sendmail fork*(2) so that the child process can handle the queue. Then, if the `ForkEachJob` (`Y`) option (see 34.8.26) is true, each job in the queue has to *fork*(2) again so that each child-of-a-child can perform each task. Internally, *sendmail* maintains tables of status information about network hosts (such as whether the host is up or down or refusing connections). A problem can arise when multiple queue-processing children are running. Because they are separate processes, their separate children lack access to the common pool of host information that is stored internally by each parent.[*]

One solution is to store host status information externally so that all children can access it. Inspired by KJS *sendmail*, V8.8 has introduced the `HostStatusDirec-tory` option. This option both tells *sendmail* that it should save host status information externally and defines where that information will be stored on disk.

The form for the `HostStatusDirectory` option looks like this:

```
O HostStatusDirectory=path                    ← V8.8 and above
define(`confHOST_STATUS_DIRECTORY', `path')   ← V8 m4 technique
```

Here, *path* is of type string and, if present, specifies the base directory under which host status will be stored. This may be a full or relative path specification. If it is a relative path, it is interpreted as relative to the queue directory. If *path* is omitted or if the entire option is omitted, the default is that no persistent host information will be saved. If *path* does not exist or if it exists and is not a directory, *sendmail* will then print the following error and will store no persistent host information:

```
Cannot use HostStatusDirectory = path: reason here
```

The form of the information stored and the way files and directories under this base directory are named are detailed in Appendix B. Note that the status information in this directory can be printed with the *hoststat*(1) command (see §36.1.1). Also note that the `HostStatusDirectory` option will not work if the `Connection-CacheSize` option (see 34.8.10) is set to zero:

```
Warning: HostStatusDirectory disabled with ConnectionCacheSize = 0
```

Note that on machines that send out a great deal of mail, you should probably compare performance with and without this option enabled and base your decision to use it on the result. Also note that this option is required if you wish to also use the `SingleThreadDelivery` option (see 34.8.64).

---

[*] Also status information from previous queue runs is lost.

Avoid using a directory that is on a *tmpfs* file system (prior to Sun Solaris 2.5), because file locking is not supported. Avoid using a directory that is on an *nfs* file system, because record locking is unreliable and single-threaded and can add extra RPC traffic.

The `HostStatusDirectory` option is not safe. If it is specified from the command line, it may cause *sendmail* to give up its *root* privilege.

IgnoreDots (i)   *(All versions)*

34.8.32   *Ignore leading dots in messages*

There are two ways that *sendmail* can detect the end of a mail message: by noting an end-of-file (EOF) condition or by finding a line composed of a single dot. According to the SMTP and ESMTP protocols (RFC821), the end of the mail data is indicated by sending a line containing only a period. The `IgnoreDots (i)` option tells *sendmail* to treat any line that contains only a single period as ordinary text, not as an end-of-file indicator.

This option is used from the command line to prevent *sendmail* from wrongly thinking that a message is complete when collecting the message from its standard input. This differs from the correct behavior when *sendmail* is reading from an SMTP connection. Over SMTP a lone dot must signal the end of the message.

This option is intended for use from the command line. This option should be used in the configuration file only for sites that have no SMTP network connections. But V8 *sendmail* has built-in protection. If this option is specified in the configuration file, it is automatically forced false for all SMTP connections.

The forms of the `i` option are as follows:

```
Oibool                            ← configuration file (old form)
-oibool                           ← command line (old form)
-i                                ← command-line shorthand
O IgnoreDots=bool                 ← configuration file (beginning with V8.7)
-OIgnoreDots=bool                 ← command line (beginning with V8.7)
define(`confIGNORE_DOTS',bool)    ← V8 m4 configuration
```

The argument *bool* is of type Boolean. If *bool* is missing, the default value is true (ignore leading dots). If the `IgnoreDots (i)` option is entirely omitted, the default is false (recognize leading dots as special).

The `IgnoreDots (i)` option is safe. Even if it is specified from the command line, *sendmail* retains its *root* privilege.

LogLevel (L)   (All versions)

34.8.33   *Set (increase) logging level*

The *sendmail* program is able to log a wide variety of information about what it is doing. There is no default file for recording information. Instead, *sendmail* sends all such information via the UNIX *syslog*(3) mechanism. The disposition of messages by *syslog* is determined by information in the file */etc/syslog.conf* (see §26.1.2). One common scheme places noncritical messages */var/log/syslog* but routes important messages to */dev/console* or */var/adm/messages*.

The meaningful values for the logging level, and their *syslog* priorities, are outlined below.* Higher logging levels include the lower logging levels. For example, logging level 2 also causes level 1 messages to be logged.

0   Minimal logging. See §34.8.33.1 for examples of what is logged at this setting.

1   Serious system failures and security problems logged at LOG_CRIT or LOG_ALERT.

2   Communication failures, (e.g., lost connections or protocol failures) logged at LOG_CRIT.

3   Malformed addresses logged at LOG_NOTICE. Transient forward/include errors logged at LOG_ERROR. Connect timeouts logged at LOG_NOTICE.

4   Malformed qf filenames and minor errors logged at LOG_NOTICE. Out of date alias databases logged at LOG_INFO. Connection rejections (via *libwrap.a* or one of the check_ rule sets) logged at LOG_NOTICE.

5   A record of each message received logged at LOG_INFO. Envelope cloning logged at LOG_INFO.

6   SMTP VRFY attempts and messages returned to the original sender logged at LOG_INFO. The ETRN and EXPN ESMTP commands logged at LOG_INFO.

7   Delivery failures, excluding mail deferred because of the lack of a resource, logged at LOG_INFO.

8   Successful deliveries logged at LOG_INFO. Alias database rebuilds logged at LOG_NOTICE.

9   Mail deferred because of a lack of a resource logged at LOG_INFO.

10   Each key as looked up in a database, and the result of each lookup, logged at LOG_INFO.

*

---

* Note that the pre-V8 organization differs and is not covered in this book.

11 All *nis* errors logged at LOG_INFO. The end of processing (job deletion) logged at LOG_INFO.

12 SMTP connects logged at LOG_INFO.

13 Log bad user shells, world-writable files, and other questionable situations.

14 Connection refusals logged at LOG_INFO.

15 All incoming and outgoing SMTP commands and their arguments logged at LOG_INFO.

16–98

Debugging information. You'll need the source to understand this logging. You can *grep*(1) `LogLevel` in all the .*c* files to find interesting things to look for. These are logged at LOG_DEBUG.

The forms of the `LogLevel` (L) option are as follows:

```
OLlev                          ← configuration file (old form)
-oLlev                         ← command line (old form)
O LogLevel=lev                 ← configuration file (beginning with V8.7)
-OLogLevel=lev                 ← command line (beginning with V8.7)
define(`confLOG_LEVEL',lev)    ← V8 m4 configuration
```

The type for *lev* is numeric and defaults to 0. For the *m4* technique the default is 9. Negative values are equivalent to a logging level of 0.

Logging is effective only if *sendmail* is compiled with LOG defined in *conf.h* (see §18.8.16). The -d0.1 debugging switch (see §37.5.1) can be used to see if LOG was defined for your system.

The `LogLevel` (L) option is safe.[*] Even if it is specified from the command line, *sendmail* retained its *root* privilege. For security reasons the logging level of V8.6 and above *sendmail* can be increased from the command line but not decreased.

34.8.33.1 What is logged at LogLevel=0

Because of their severe nature, some errors and problems are logged even though the `LogLevel` (L) option is set to zero. Specifically, problems with $j and $=w that are checked if *sendmail* was compiled with XDEBUG defined:

```
daemon process doesn't have $j in $=w; see syslog
daemon process $j lost dot; see syslog
```

Failure to find your unqualified hostname or qualified domain:

---

[*] V8.7.3 *sendmail* was released with the `LogLevel` (L) option set as not safe.

```
My unqualified host name (my host name) unknown
unable to qualify my own domain name (my host name) -- using short name
```

If the daemon was invoked without a full pathname:

```
daemon invoked without full pathname; kill -1 won't work
```

Normal startup of the daemon:

```
starting daemon (version): how
```

File descriptor failure if *sendmail* was compiled with XDEBUG defined:

```
subroutine: fd number not open
```

Possible attacks based on a newline in a string:

```
POSSIBLE ATTACK from address: newline in string "string here"
```

Also the states dumped as a result of a SIGUSR1 (see §26.3.3) are logged, and the output caused by the **−d91.100** switch (see §37.5.192).

MatchGECOS (G)   *(V8.1 and above)*

34.8.34   *Match recipient in gecos field*

The *gecos* field is the portion of a *passwd*(5) file line that contains a user's full name. Typical *passwd* file lines are illustrated below with the *gecos* field of each highlighted in bold type:

```
george:Vnn9x34sEVbCN:101:29:George Washington:/usr/george:/bin/csh
bcx:/a88.97eGSx11:102:5:Bill Xavier,,,:/usr/bcx:/bin/csh
tim:Fss9UdQl55cde:103:45:& Plenty (Jr):/usr/tim:/bin/csh
```

When *sendmail* attempts to deliver through a delivery agent that has the **F=w** flag set (see §30.8.43) it looks up the recipient's name in the *passwd* file so it can locate the user's home directory. That lookup tries to match the login name, the leftmost field in the *passwd* file. If *sendmail* has been compiled with MATCHGECOS defined (see §18.8.18) and this **MatchGECOS** (G) option is true, *sendmail* also tries to match the recipient name to the *gecos* field.[*]

First, *sendmail* converts any underscore characters in the address into spaces and, if the **BlankSub** (B) option is set (see §34.8.5), any characters that match that space substitution character into spaces. This makes the recipient name look like a normal full name.

Second, *sendmail* normalizes each *gecos* entry by throwing away everything following and including the first comma, semicolon, and percent characters. It also

---

[*] Note that IDA *sendmail* can be configured to match addresses in the *gecos* field, but the algorithm it uses differs from that described here.

converts the & to the login name wherever one is found. If any of the characters

```
< >( ) ' .
```

are inside the name, the whole *gecos* name is quoted; otherwise, it's unquoted.

After each *gecos* name is normalized, it is compared in a case-insensitive manner to the recipient. If they match, the *passwd* entry for that user is used.

This feature allows users to receive mail addressed to their full name as given in the *gecos* field of the *passwd* file. The usual form is to replace spaces in the full name with dots or underscores:

```
George_Washington
Bill.Xavier
"Tim_Plenty_(Jr)"
```

Full names in *gecos* fields that contain characters with special meaning to *send-mail*, like the last one above, must be quoted when used as addresses.

You should not enable this option if your site lets users edit their own *gecos* fields with the *chfn*(1) program. At best, they can change their name in a way that can cause mail to start failing. Worse, they can change their name to match another user's and begin to capture that other user's mail. Even if the *gecos* field is secure, you should avoid this option if your *passwd* file is large. The *sendmail* program performs a sequential read of the *passwd* file, which could be very slow.

The forms of the `MatchGECOS` (G) option are as follows:

`OGbool`	← *configuration file (old form)*
`-oGbool`	← *command line (old form)*
`O MatchGECOS=bool`	← *configuration file (beginning with V8.7)*
`-OMatchGECOS=bool`	← *command line (beginning with V8.7)*
`define(`confMATCH_GECOS',bool)`	← *V8 m4 configuration*

The `MatchGECOS` (G) option is not safe. If it is specified from the command line, it may cause *sendmail* to give up its *root* privilege.

MaxDaemonChildren ⠀⠀⠀⠀⠀⠀⠀⠀⠀⠀⠀⠀⠀⠀⠀⠀⠀⠀⠀*(V8.8 and above)*

34.8.35 ⠀⠀⠀⠀⠀⠀⠀⠀⠀⠀⠀⠀⠀⠀⠀⠀⠀⠀⠀⠀⠀⠀⠀⠀⠀*Maximum forked children*

The *sendmail* program *fork*(3)'s often. It forks to process each incoming connection, and it forks to process its queue.

You can limit the number of forked children that *sendmail* produces by defining the `MaxDaemonChildren` option:

`O MaxDaemonChildren=num`	← *configuration file (beginning with V8.7)*
`-OMaxDaemonChildren=num`	← *command line (beginning with V8.7)*
`define(`confMAX_DAEMON_CHILDREN', `num')`	← *V8 m4 technique*

The *num* is of type numeric and specifies the maximum number of forked children that are allowed to exist at any one time. If *num* is less than or equal to zero, if it is missing, or if this entire option is missing, no limit is imposed. If *num* is greater than zero, connections that cause more than that number of forked children to be created will be rejected. While rejecting more connections, *sendmail* will change its process title to read

```
rejecting connections: maximum children: num
```

If *num* is greater than zero, *sendmail* will also limit the number of forked children it creates to handle queue runs.

Note the `MaxDaemonChildren` option should not be set in the configuration file. If the daemon handling incoming mail has this option set, a denial-of-service attack can be easily launched against your machine. Beginning with V8.8, the `Connection-RateThrottle` option (see §34.8.12) can be used to slow rapid incoming connections and can be used with the incoming daemon.

The `MaxDaemonChildren` option is appropriate for use in certain queue-processing situations. For example, consider a special queue that exclusively holds mail for a popular host (say, */var/spool/bigqueue*). To handle the outgoing mail in that queue, you could run *sendmail* in queue-processing mode like this:

```
/usr/lib/sendmail -q5m -OMaxDaemonChildren=2 -OQueueDirectory=/var/spool/bigqueue
```

Here, the queue is processed once every five minutes. If the number of children were not limited and if the queue were large or the destination host were slow, too many parallel invocations of *sendmail* would be spawned, thus causing excessive connections to the destination host. By limiting the number of children with the `MaxDaemonChildren` option, you allow a small, polite amount of parallelism.

The `MaxDaemonChildren` option is not safe. If specified from the command line, it may cause *sendmail* to relinquish its *root* privilege.

MaxHopCount (h)   *(All version)*

34.8.36   *Set maximum hop count*

A *hop* is the transmittal of a mail message from one machine to another.[*] Many hops may be required to deliver a message. The number of hops is determined by counting the `Received:` and `Via:` lines[†] in the header of an email message.

The `MaxHopCount` (`h`) option tells *sendmail* the maximum number of times a message can be forwarded (the maximum hop count). When *sendmail* receives a

---

[*] The IP transport protocol also has the concept of hops. A message going from one machine to another has only one mail hop but may have many IP hops.

[†] Actually, only the headers that are marked with an H_TRACE flag (see §35.5.8) are counted.

message via email, it calculates the hop count. If that count is above the maximum allowed, it bounces the message back to the sender with the error

```
sendmail: too many hops (17 max)
```

The 17 is the maximum in this example. Detecting too many hops is useful in stopping *mail loops*—messages endlessly being forwarded back and forth between two machines.

The forms of the `MaxHopCount` (h) option are as follows:

```
Ohhops                            ← configuration file (old form)
-ohhops                           ← command line (old form)
O MaxHopCount=hops                ← configuration file (beginning with V8.7)
-OMaxHopCount=hops                ← command line (beginning with V8.7)
define(`confMAX_HOP',hops)        ← V8 m4 configuration
```

The *hops* argument is of type numeric. If *hops* is missing, the value becomes zero, thereby causing all mail to fail with the error:

```
sendmail: too many hops (0 max)
```

If the entire `MaxHopCount` (h) option is missing, *hops* defaults to 25. A good value is 15 or more. This allows mail to follow a fairly long route through many machines (as it could with UUCP) but still catches and bounces mail caught in a loop between two machines.

In pre-V8 *sendmail* there was no h option for setting the maximum number of hops. Instead, the number of hops could be limited only by the compile-time definition of MAXHOP in *conf.h*. The default definition varied between 15 for IDA *sendmail* and 30 for V5 and earlier SunOS *sendmail*.

The `MaxHopCount` (h) option should not be confused with the –h command-line switch (see §36.7.22). The `MaxHopCount` (h) option specifies the maximum number of hops allowed, whereas the –h command-line switch presets the base (beginning) hop count for a given email message.

The `MaxHopCount` (h) option is not safe. If specified from the command line, it may cause *sendmail* to relinquish its *root* privilege.

MaxMessageSize   *(V8.7 and above)*

34.8.37   *Maximum incoming ESMTP message size*

The SIZE keyword to the ESMTP MAIL command tells V8 *sendmail* how big an incoming message is in bytes. If the SIZE keyword is not specified, *sendmail* assumes that the incoming message is zero bytes in size. V8 *sendmail* can reject a message at this point if it is larger than a definable maximum message size:

```
Message size exceeds fixed maximum message size (max)
```

Here, **max** is the maximum acceptable size in bytes. Ordinarily, there no maximum. If you want to define one, you may do so with the **MaxMessageSize** (b) option:

O*bminblocks*/*maxsize*	← *configuration file (beginning with V8.1)*
-o*bminblocks*/*maxsize*	← *command line (beginning with V8.1)*
O MaxMessageSize=*maxsize*	← *configuration file (beginning with V8.7)*
-OMaxMessageSize=*maxsize*	← *command line (beginning with V8.7)*
define(`confMAX_MESSAGE_SIZE',*maxsize*)	← *V8 m4 configuration*

If **maxsize** is omitted or if this entire option is omitted, the default is 0 (for unlimited message sizes). For the *m4* configuration the default is 0 (unlimited). Note that the **b** option can also set the minimum blocks free (see §34.8.40).

This limit on message size is enforced during the SMTP dialogue. Later, after a delivery agent has been selected, further limitations can be imposed by using the **M=** delivery agent equate (see §30.4.7).

The **MaxMessageSize** (b) option is not safe. If specified from the command line, it may cause *sendmail* to relinquish its *root* privilege.

MaxQueueRunSize   *(V8.7 and above)*

34.8.38   *Maximum queue messages processed*

Ordinarily (beginning with V8.6 *sendmail*), there is no limit to the number of queued messages that can be processed during a single queue run. If there are more messages than *sendmail* has allocated memory for, *sendmail* will calmly allocate more memory. (Previously, there was a fixed limit imposed at compile time.)

Some systems process so much mail that a single queue run can become unmanageably large—so huge, in fact, that system resources are strained to the limit with an adverse effect on system performance. If your site suffers from this problem, beginning with V8.7 you can set an upper limit on the number of queued messages to be processed by using the **MaxQueueRunSize** option:

O MaxQueueRunSize=*limit*	← *configuration file (beginning with V8.7)*
-OMaxQueueRunSize=*limit*	← *command line (beginning with V8.7)*
define(`confMAX_QUEUE_RUN_SIZE',*limit*)	← *m4 configuration*

Here, **limit** is of type numeric and defines the upper limit on how many queued messages can be processed during a single queue run. If **limit** is less than or equal to zero, if it is missing, or if the entire option is missing, no limit is imposed. The default is to impose no limit.

If `MaxQueueRunSize` is defined and if that limit is reached while processing the queue, *sendmail* will log the following message at LOG_ALERT:

```
WorkList for queuedir maxed out at limit
```

Processing of the queue is described in §23.5. That process can be watched with the **-d41** debugging switch (see §37.5.144).

The `MaxQueueRunSize` option is safe. Even if it is specified from the command line, *sendmail* retains its *root* privilege.

MeToo (m) *(All versions)*

34.8.39 *Send to me too*

When you send mail to a mailing list that includes your name as a part of that list, *sendmail* normally excludes you from that mailing. There are two good reasons for that behavior:

- Since you sent the mail, it is assumed that you already have a copy of the letter. Most mailing programs have options that allow you to automatically retain copies of your outgoing mail. The BSD *Mail* program, for example, has the *outfolder* option.

- When mail passes through a site that is acting as an exploder for an outside mailing list, mail loops could be caused by sending a copy of the message back to the original sender.

The `MeToo` (m) option overrides this behavior, but it is usually best to keep it turned off. If individual users want to be included in mailings to lists that they belong to, they can set this behavior from their mail-sending programs. BSD *Mail*, for example, allows you to **set metoo** in your ˜/.mailrc file. This use of `metoo` simply causes *Mail* to invoke *sendmail* with the **-om** switch, thereby setting the `MeToo` (m) option.

The forms of the `MeToo` (m) option are as follows:

```
Ombool                     ← configuration file (old form)
-ombool                    ← command line (old form)
-m                         ← command-line shorthand
O MeToo=bool               ← configuration file (beginning with V8.7)
-OMeToo=bool               ← command line (beginning with V8.7)
define(`confME_TOO',bool)  ← V8 m4 configuration
```

The optional argument *bool*, when missing, defaults to true (include the sender). If this option is entirely missing, it defaults to false (exclude the sender).

The `MeToo` (m) option is safe. Even if it is specified from the command line, *sendmail* retains its *root* privilege.

MinFreeBlocks (b)   *(V8.1 and above)*

34.8.40   *Define minimum free disk blocks*

The SIZE keyword to the ESMTP MAIL command tells V8 *sendmail* how big an incoming message is in bytes. If the SIZE keyword is not specified, *sendmail* assumes that the incoming message is zero bytes in size. In either case it calls the subroutine *enoughspace()* in *conf.c* to see whether enough space is available in the queue to accept the message. Unless *sendmail* is told otherwise, it assumes it can use 100% of the disk space in the queue. If SIZE bytes will overfill the queue disk, *sendmail* prints the following error and rejects the mail message:

```
Insufficient disk space; try again later
```

Note that the SIZE keyword (if received) is just an estimate that allows oversized mail to be rejected early in the ESMTP dialogue. V8 *sendmail* still properly diagnoses out-of-space conditions when it actually reads the message.

If using 100% of the disk space is unacceptable, you can use the **MinFreeBlocks** (b) option to reserve space for other kinds of files:

O*bminblocks/maxsize*	← *configuration file (beginning with V8.6)*
-o*bminblocks/maxsize*	← *command line (beginning with V8.6)*
O MinFreeBlocks=*minblocks*	← *configuration file (beginning with V8.7)*
-OMinFreeBlocks=*minblocks*	← *command line (beginning with V8.7)*
define(`confMIN_FREE_BLOCKS',*minblocks*)	← *V8 m4 configuration*

Here, *minblocks* is of type numeric and is the number of disk blocks you wish to reserve. If *minblocks* is missing or negative or if the entire option is omitted, no blocks are reserved. For the V8.6 form of the **b** option a slash is required to separate *minblocks* from *maxsize* (*maxsize* is described under the **MaxMessageSize** option, §34.8.37). The default when configuring with the V8 *m4* method is 100.

Note that **minblocks** are reserved only for the ESMTP SIZE keyword to the MAIL command. No check is made for any other kind of queuing to reserve space. Consequently, you should reserve a sufficient number of blocks to satisfy your normal queuing needs.

The **MinFreeBlocks** (b) option is not safe. If specified from the command line, it may cause *sendmail* to relinquish its *root* privilege.

MinQueueAge   *(V8.7 and above)*

34.8.41   *Skip queue file if too young*

Ordinarily, all messages in the queue are processed whenever *sendmail* is run in queue-processing mode. No distinction is made between recently queued messages and messages that have been in the queue for a long time (other than by priority which simply orders the processing).

Some sites may prefer to process the queue often, say, once every five minutes. This ensures that all important mail will be delivered promptly but can exact a price in degraded performance. Every time the queue is processed, *sendmail* tries to deliver every mail message the queue contains, but at many sites there can be many queued messages that should not be retried every five minutes. One way to handle this problem is to set the MinQueueAge option. If it is set to 1h (one hour), every queued message is forced to remain in the queue for a minimum of one hour, even if the queue is processed more frequently:

```
O MinQueueAge=wait                          ← configuration file (beginning with V8.7)
-OMinQueueAge=wait                          ← command line (beginning with V8.7)
define(`confMIN_QUEUE_AGE',`wait')          ← V8 m4 configuration
```

The argument *wait* is of type time. If *wait* is less than or equal to zero or if it is missing, this feature is disabled. If the units in the time expression are omitted, the default is minutes. There is no default for the *m4* method.

Note that the decision of whether to process or not is *not* based on the time the message was placed into the queue. It is instead based on the time the message was last processed from the queue. This time is stored in the K line of the qf file (see §23.9.8). This minimum is enforced only if the number of times delivery has been attempted is greater than zero (see the qf file's N line, §23.9.10). This ensures that the first delivery attempt will be made immediately.

The MinQueueAge option is safe. If specified from the command line, *sendmail* will not relinquish its *root* privilege.

MustQuoteChars   *(V8.8 and above)*

34.8.42   *Quote nonaddress characters*

All addresses are composed of address information and nonaddress information. The two most common forms of addresses look like this:

```
address (non-address)
non-address <address>
```

Usually, the nonaddress information is a user's full name or something similar. RFC822 requires that certain characters be quoted if they appear in the nonaddress part of an address:

```
@ , ; : \ ( ) [ ] . '
```

Nonaddress information inside parentheses is already quoted by those parentheses. Other nonaddress that contains any of these characters needs to be quoted with full quotation marks. To illustrate, consider this address:

```
From: Bob@home <bob@here.uofa.edu>
```

Because the nonaddress part `Bob@home` contains an `@` character, *sendmail* is required to quote the entire phrase, thus forming

```
From: "Bob@home" <bob@here.uofa.edu>
```

This quoting is automatic and cannot be turned off for the first nine characters:

```
@ , ; : \ ( ) [ ] . ´
                  ↑ ↑
```
the last two are optional (but are required by RFC822)

The last two characters are optional (but required by RFC822). All 11 characters are the default for the `MustQuoteChars` option. If you wish to add characters to the mandatory list of characters that will be quoted, you may do so with the `MustQuoteChars` option:

```
O MustQuoteChars=more          ← V8.8 and above
-OMustQuoteChars=more          ← V8.8 and above
```

Here, *more* is of type string and is the list of additional characters that you wish to see quoted in the nonaddress part of addresses. The *more* characters replace the optional characters and append to the mandatory characters. If *more* is missing, the optional characters are dropped. There is no *m4* shorthand for setting this option.

The `MustQuoteChars` option is not safe. If specified from the command line, it may cause *sendmail* to relinquish its *root* privilege.

NoRecipientAction   (V8.7 and above)

34.8.43   *Handle no recipients in header*

The header portion of a mail message must contain at least one recipient header. Problems can arise when an MUA produces a recipientless message or when the only recipients are listed in a `Bcc:` header line. In the past, *sendmail* inserted an `Apparently-To:` header (see §35.10.2) into any message that lacked header recipients. The addresses in the `Apparently-To:` were gleaned from the envelope.

Beginning with V8.7 *sendmail*, it is possible to chose how recipientless headers will be handled. This is done with the `NoRecipientAction` option, which is used like this:

```
O NoRecipientAction=what              ← configuration file (beginning with V8.7)
-ONoRecipientAction=what              ← command line (beginning with V8.7)
define(`confNO_RCPT_ACTION',what)     ← m4 configuration
```

The argument *what* is of type string and must be selected from those shown in Table 34–16. If the *what* is omitted or if it is other than one of the possibilities shown, the following error is printed, and the option is ignored:

```
Invalid NoRecipientAction: badwhat
```

If the entire option is omitted, the default becomes **none**. The default for the *m4* technique is to omit this option.

The *what* is case-insensitive, meaning that **none** and **nOnE** are both identical.

Table 34–16: NoRecipientAction Option Keywords

What	§	Meaning
add-apparently-to	34.8.43.1	Add an **Apparently-To:** header
add-bcc	34.8.43.2	Add an empty **Bcc:** header
add-to	34.8.43.3	Add a **To:** header
add-to-undisclosed	34.8.43.4	Add **To: undisclosed-recipients:;**
none	34.8.43.5	Pass the message unchanged

The **NoRecipientAction** option is safe. If it is specified from the command line, *sendmail* will not relinquish its *root* privilege.

34.8.43.1 *NoRecipientAction=add-apparently-to*

Add an **Apparently-To:** header. That is, act like pre-V8.7 sendmail. But note that this choice has been deprecated and should not be used.

34.8.43.2 *NoRecipientAction=add-bcc*

Add an empty **Bcc:** header. This makes the header portion of the mail message legal under RFC822 but implies that all recipients originally appeared in **Bcc:** header lines. But be aware that old versions of *sendmail* will strip all **Bcc:** headers, so the next site may add an **Apparently-To:** header and wrongly expose the address.

34.8.43.3 *NoRecipientAction=add-to*

Add a **To:** header and fill it out with all the recipients from the envelope. This may be misleading because it can give a false picture of the intended recipients. It can also cause **Bcc:** header addresses to be mistakenly revealed. This choice may be appropriate in the command line when *sendmail* is run from an MUA that routinely omits recipient headers.

34.8.43.4 NoRecipientAction=add-to-undisclosed

Add a `To:` header, but list in it only the address of an empty, but descriptive, mailing list:

```
To: undisclosed-recipients:;
```

This is the recommended setting for use in configuration files.

34.8.43.5 NoRecipientAction=none

Pass the message unchanged. Currently, this is technically illegal because RFC822 requires at least one recipient header in every mail message. This choice may be appropriate for naive sites that kick all mail to a smart host for processing. Note that the IETF is considering making this legal.

OldStyleHeaders (o)   *(All versions)*

34.8.44   *Allow spaces in recipient lists*

In pre-RFC821 days, lists of recipients were commonly space-delimited; that is,

```
hans christian andersen
```

was considered a list of three mail recipients, rather than a single, three-part name. Currently, individual recipient names must be delimited with commas, and internal spaces must be quoted. That is,

```
hans,christian,andersen          ← three recipients
"hans christian andersen"        ← a single three-part name
hans christian andersen          ← illegal
```

Since some users and some old programs still delimit recipient lists with spaces, the `OldStyleHeaders` (o) option can be used to tell *sendmail* to internally convert those spaces to commas.

The forms of the `OldStyleHeaders` (o) option are as follows:

```
Oobool                                 ← configuration file (old form)
-oobool                                ← command line (old form)
O OldStyleHeaders=bool                 ← configuration file (beginning with V8.7)
-OOldStyleHeaders=bool                 ← command line (beginning with V8.7)
define(`confOLD_STYLE_HEADERS',bool)   ← V8 m4 configuration
```

The argument *bool* is of type Boolean. If that argument is missing, the default value is true, and unquoted spaces in an address are converted to commas. The default when configuring with the *m4* technique is true. If the entire `OldStyle-Headers` (o) option is missing, it defaults to false, and unquoted spaces are converted to the character defined by the `BlankSub` (B) option (see §34.8.5).

The *sendmail* program is somewhat adaptive about commas. When first examining a list of addresses, it looks to see whether one of the following four characters appears in that list:

```
, ; < (
```

If it finds any of these characters in an address list, it turns off the OldStyleHeaders (o) option for the remainder of the list. You always want to enable this option in your configuration file. The only exception might be the unusual situation in which all addresses are normally comma-separated but some legal addresses contain spaces.

Note that comma delimiting allows spaces around recipient names for clarity. That is, both of the following are equivalent:

```
hans,christian,andersen
hans, christian, andersen
```

The OldStyleHeaders (o) option is safe. Even if it is specified from the command line, *sendmail* retains its *root* privilege.

OperatorChars *or* $o   *(V8.7 and above)*

34.8.45   *Set token separation operators*

The OperatorChars option stores as its value a sequence of characters, any one of which can be used to separate the components of an address into tokens (see §8.3). Prior to V8.7 the *$o* macro fulfilled this role. Beginning with V8.7, the OperatorChars option has taken over:

```
Do.:%@!^=/[]                    ← prior to V8.7
O OperatorChars=.:%@!^=/[]      ← beginning with V8.7
```

The list of separation operators declared with this option is joined by *sendmail* to an internal list of hard-coded separation operators:

```
()<>,;\"\r\n
```

The combined list is used in tokenizing the workspace for rule-set processing. The order in which the characters appear in the OperatorChars option declaration is arbitrary. The space and tab characters need not be included in that list because they are always used to separate tokens.

Care should be taken in eliminating any given character from this list. Before doing so, the entire configuration file should be examined in detail to be sure that no rule requires that character. The use of the individual characters in addresses is beyond the scope of this book. The book *!%@:: A Directory of Electronic Mail Addressing and Networks*, by Donnalyn Frey and Rick Adams (O'Reilly & Associates, 1993), contains the many forms of addressing in great detail.

The `OperatorChars` option is used like this:

```
O OperatorChars=text                    ← beginning with V8.7
define(`confOPERATORS',`text')          ← V8 m4 technique
```

The *text* is of type **string**. If it is missing and if the configuration file version is less than 7, *sendmail* tries to use the value of the $o macro. If that macro is also undefined, a default of ".:@[]" is used. If *text* is longer than 39 characters, it is truncated to 39 characters. In using the V8 *m4* technique, a default of ".:%@!^/[]+" is used.

The `OperatorChars` option is not safe. If specified from the command line, it may cause *sendmail* to relinquish its *root* privilege.

PostmasterCopy (P)   *(All versions)*

34.8.46   *Extra copies of postmaster mail*

RFC822, entitled *Standard for the Format of ARPA Internet Text Messages,* requires that all sites be set up so that mail addressed to the special name *Postmaster*[*] always be successfully delivered. This requirement ensures that notification of mail problems can always be sent and successfully delivered to the offending site.[†] At most sites the name *Postmaster* is an alias to a real person's name in the *aliases* file. Mail to *Postmaster* should never be ignored.

Ordinarily, notification of locally bounced mail and other mail problems is sent back (bounced) to the sender of the message. The local person in the role of *Postmaster* does not get a copy of local failed mail.

The `PostmasterCopy` (P) option tells *sendmail* to send a copy of all failed mail to another person, often *Postmaster*. Under V8 and SunOS that copy contains only the failed message's header. Under other versions of *sendmail* that copy includes both the header and the body.

The forms of the `PostmasterCopy` (P) option are as follows:

```
OPuser                                  ← configuration file (old form)
-oPuser                                 ← command line (old form)
O PostmasterCopy=user                   ← configuration file (beginning with V8.7)
-OPostmasterCopy=user                   ← command line (beginning with V8.7)
define(`confCOPY_ERRORS_TO',user)       ← V8 m4 configuration
```

---

[*] The name *Postmaster* is case-insensitive. That is, *POSTMASTER, Postmaster, postmaster,* and even *PoStMaStEr* are all equivalent.

[†] Note that adoption of RFC1648, entitled *Postmaster Convention for X.400 Operations,* has extended this concept to include hosts addressed as *user@host.domain* that are really X.400 sites masquerading as Internet sites.

The argument *user* is of type string. If the argument is missing or if the PostmasterCopy (P) option is entirely missing, no extra copy is sent. The default for the *m4* configuration technique to not send an extra copy.

While debugging a new *sendmail.cf* file, it is wise to define the PostmasterCopy (P) option so that you receive a copy of all failed mail. Once the configuration file is stable, either the PostmasterCopy (P) option may be removed or the name may be replaced with an alias to a program. Such a program could filter the copies of error mail so that only serious problems would be seen.

Macros used in the *user* argument will be correctly expanded before use. For example,

```
DHmailhost                                    ← old form
OPPostmaster@$H                               ← old form

D{NOTIFYHOST}mailhost                         ← beginning with V8.7
O PostmasterCopy=Postmaster@${NOTIFYHOST}    ← beginning with V8.7
```

The PostmasterCopy (P) option is not safe. If specified from the command line, it may cause *sendmail* to relinquish its *root* privilege.

PrivacyOptions (p)   *(V8.1 and above)*

34.8.47   *Increase privacy of the daemon*

The PrivacyOptions (p) option is used primarily as a way to force other sites to adhere to SMTP conventions, but can also be used to improve security.

The forms of the PrivacyOptions (p) option are as follows:

```
Opwhat,...                                ← configuration file (old mode)
-opwhat,...                               ← command line (old mode)
O PrivacyOptions=what,...                 ← configuration file (beginning with V8.7)
-OPrivacyOptions=what,...                 ← command line (beginning with V8.7)
define(`confPRIVACY_FLAGS',`what,...')    ← V8 m4 configuration
```

Multiple *what* arguments may be listed and must be separated from one another by commas (there may be arbitrary spaces around the commas), for example,

```
Op authwarnings, needmailhelo
O PrivacyOptions=authwarnings, needmailhelo
```

If this option is entirely omitted or if no *what* arguments are listed, the option defaults to public. The default for the *m4* configuration technique is authwarnings. The possible *what* arguments are listed in Table 34-17.

Table 34-17: PrivacyOptions Option Keywords

Keyword	§	Meaning
authwarnings	34.8.47.1	Enable X-Authentication-Warning: headers
goaway	34.8.47.2	Much checking for privacy and security
needexpnhelo	34.8.47.3	Require HELO before EXPN
needmailhelo	34.8.47.4	Require HELO before MAIL
needvrfyhelo	34.8.47.5	Require HELO before VRFY
noexpn	34.8.47.6	Disallow all SMTP EXPN commands
noreceipts	34.8.47.7	Prevent return receipts
novrfy	34.8.47.8	Disallow all SMTP VRFY commands
public	34.8.47.9	No extra checking for privacy or security
restrictmailq	34.8.47.10	Restrict who may run *mailq*(1)
restrictqrun	34.8.47.11	Restrict who processes the queue

If *what* is not one of the keywords listed in the table, *sendmail* prints the following message and ignores the unknown word:

```
readcf: Op line: unknown_word unrecognized
```

Note that *sendmail* checks for nonroot use of the −C (see §36.7.15) and −oQ (see §34.8.48) command line switches and dangerous uses of the −f (see §36.7.21) command line switch when the command line is read but does not issue warnings until after the configuration file is read. That way, the configuration file determines how X-Authentication-Warning: headers will be issued.

The PrivacyOptions (p) option is safe. If specified from the command line, it does not cause *sendmail* to relinquish its *root* privilege. Because it is really a mask, specifications in the configuration file or on the command line can only make it more restrictive.

34.8.47.1 PrivacyOptions=authwarnings

Setting authwarnings causes *sendmail* to insert special headers into the mail message that advise the recipient of reasons to suspect that the message may not be authentic. The general form of this special header is shown at the end of this paragraph. The possible reasons are listed in Chapter 35, *Headers* (see §35.10.35).

```
X-Authentication-Warning: ourhost: reason
```

34.8.47.2 PrivacyOptions=goaway

A shorthand way to set all of authwarnings, noexpn, novrfy, needmailhelo, needexpnhelo, and needvrfyhelo.

34.8.47.3 PrivacyOptions=needexpnhelo

The SMTP EXPN command causes *sendmail* to "expand" a local address and print the result. If the address is an alias, it shows all the addresses that result from the alias expansion. If the address is local, it shows the result of aliasing through a user's `~/.forward` file. If `needexpnhelo` is specified, *sendmail* requires that the requesting site first introduce itself with an SMTP HELO or ELHO command. If the requesting site has not done so, *sendmail* responds with the following message rather than providing the requested expansion information:

```
503 I demand that you introduce yourself first
```

34.8.47.4 PrivacyOptions=needmailhelo

The SMTP protocol specifies that the sending site should issue the HELO or ELHO command to identify itself before specifying the name of the sender with the MAIL command. By listing `needmailhelo` with the `PrivacyOptions` (p) option, you cause the following error to be returned to the sending site in this situation:

```
503 Polite people say HELO first
```

If `needmailhelo` is not specified but `authwarnings` is specified, then the following header is added to the message describing the problem:

```
X-Authentication-Warning: ourself: Host they didn't use HELO protocol
```

34.8.47.5 PrivacyOptions=needvrfyhelo

The SMTP VRFY command causes *sendmail* to verify that an address is that of a local user or local alias. Unlike EXPN above, VRFY does not cause mailing list contents, the result of aliasing, or the contents of `~/.forward` files to be displayed. If `needvrfyhelo` is specified, *sendmail* requires that the requesting site first introduce itself with an SMTP HELO or ELHO command. If the requesting site has not done so, *sendmail* responds with the same message as for `needexpnhelo` above, rather than providing the requested verification information.

34.8.47.6 PrivacyOptions=noexpn

Setting `noexpn` causes *sendmail* to disallow all SMTP EXPN commands. In place of information, *sendmail* sends the following reply to the requesting host:

```
502 That's none of your business          ← prior to V8.7
502 Sorry, we do not allow this operation  ← beginning with V8.7
```

Setting `noexpn` also causes *sendmail* to reject all SMTP VERB commands:

```
502 Verbose unavailable
```

Other *sendmail* programs may send VERB if the delivery agent making the connection has the F=I flag set (see §30.8.25).

34.8.47.7 *PrivacyOptions=noreceipts*

Setting noreceipts causes pre-V8.7 *sendmail* to silently skip the processing of all Return-Receipt-To: headers (see §35.10.29). Beginning with V8.7 *sendmail,* notification of successful delivery is governed by the NOTIFY keyword (see RFC1891) to the ESMTP RCPT command:

```
RCPT TO: <address> NOTIFY=SUCCESS
```

Setting noreceipts causes V8.7 *sendmail* to silently skip all such requests for notification of successful delivery.

34.8.47.8 *PrivacyOptions=novrfy*

Setting novrfy causes *sendmail* to disallow all SMTP VRFY commands. In place of verification, *sendmail* sends the following reply to the requesting host:

```
252 Who's to say?                                              ← V8.6
252 Cannot VRFY user; try RCPT to attempt delivery (or try finger) ← V8.7
```

34.8.47.9 *PrivacyOptions=public*

The default for the non-m4 version of the PrivacyOptions (p) option is public. This means that there is no extra checking for valid SMTP syntax and no checking for the security matters.

34.8.47.10 *PrivacyOptions=restrictmailq*

Ordinarily, anyone may examine the mail queue's contents by using the *mailq*(1) command (see §23.4). To restrict who may examine the queue's contents, specify restrictmailq. If restricted, *sendmail* allows only users who are in the same group as the group ownership of the queue directory to examine the contents. This allows the queue directory to be fully protected with mode 0700 yet for selected users to still be able to see its contents.

34.8.47.11 *PrivacyOptions=restrictqrun*

Ordinarily, anyone may process the queue with the -q switch (see §23.6.1). To limit queue processing to *root* and the owner of the queue directory, specify restrictqrun. If queue processing is restricted, any nonprivileged user who attempts to process the queue will get this message:

```
You do not have permission to process the queue
```

QueueDirectory (Q)   *(All versions)*

34.8.48   *Location of queue directory*

Mail messages that have not yet been delivered are stored in the *sendmail* program's queue directory. The location of that directory is defined by the QueueDirectory (Q) option. That location may be a relative pathname (for testing) or an absolute pathname. If the specified location does not exist, *sendmail* prints something like the following:

```
cannot chdir(/var/spool/mqueue): No such file or directory
```

If the location exists but is not a directory, sendmail prints something like the following:

```
cannot chdir(/var/spool/mqueue): Not a directory
```

In both cases, *sendmail* also logs an error message via *syslog*(8) if the logging level of the LogLevel (L) option (see §34.8.33) permits. In both cases, *sendmail* aborts immediately.

The forms of the QueueDirectory (Q) option are as follows:

```
OQpath                          ← configuration file (old form)
-oQpath                         ← command line (old form)
O QueueDirectory=path           ← configuration file (beginning with V8.7)
-OQueueDirectory=path           ← command line (beginning with V8.7)
define(`QUEUE_DIR',`path')      ← V8 m4 configuration
```

The *path* argument is of type string. If it is missing, the value for *path* defaults to "mqueue". Relative names for the queue are always relative to the directory in which *sendmail* was invoked. If the entire QueueDirectory (Q) option is missing, the value for *path* defaults to the C language value of NULL, and *sendmail* complains with

```
cannot chdir((null)): Bad file number
```

The default in configuring with the *m4* technique varies depending on your operating system.

The QueueDirectory (Q) option is not safe. If specified from the command line, it may cause *sendmail* to relinquish its *root* privilege.

QueueFactor (q)   *(All versions)*

34.8.49   *Factor for high-load queuing*

When the load average on a machine (the average number of processes in the run queue over the last minute) becomes too high, *sendmail* can compensate by queuing all mail, rather than delivering it. The QueueFactor (q) option is used in combination with the QueueLA (x) option (see §34.8.50) to calculate the point at which *sendmail* stops delivering. If the current load average is greater than or equal to the value given to the QueueLA (x) option, then the following formula is evaluated:

```
msgpri > q / (la - x + 1)
```

Here, q is the value set by this option, la is the current load average, and x is the cutoff load specified by the QueueLA (x) option. If the value yielded by this calculation is less than or equal to the priority of the current mail message (msgpri above), the message is queued rather than delivered. Priorities are initialized with the P *sendmail.cf* command (see §35.8) and tuned with the **RecipientFactor** (y) and **ClassFactor** (z) options (see §34.8.53). As the load average (la) grows, the value to the right of the > becomes smaller, increasing the chance that msgpri will exceed that threshold (so that the mail will be queued). Beginning with V8.7 *sendmail*, this relation can be tuned with the help of the −d3.30 debugging switch (see §37.5.18).

The forms of QueueFactor (q) option are as follows:

O*qfact*	← *configuration file (old form)*
-o*qfact*	← *command line (old form)*
O QueueFactor=*fact*	← *configuration file (beginning with V8.7)*
-OQueueFactor=*fact*	← *command line (beginning with V8.7)*
define(`confQUEUE_FACTOR', *fact*)	← *V8 m4 configuration*

The argument *fact* is of type numeric. It may be positive, negative, or zero. If *fact* is missing, the value defaults to zero. If the entire QueueFactor (q) option is missing, the default value given to *fact* is 600000 (six hundred thousand). The default for the *m4* technique is to omit this option.

Note that the load average is effective only if your *sendmail* binary was compiled with load-average support (see §18.8.14). Use the −d3.1 debugging switch (§37.5.14) to discover whether your binary includes that support.

The QueueFactor (q) option is not safe. If specified from the command line, it may cause *sendmail* to relinquish its *root* privilege.

QueueLA (x)   *(All versions)*

34.8.50   *On high load, queue only*

The QueueLA (x) option specifies the load above which *sendmail* queues messages rather than delivering them. The QueueLA (x) and QueueFactor (q) options interact to determine this cutoff; they are both covered under the QueueFactor (q) option (§34.8.49).

The forms of the QueueLA (x) option are as follows:

```
Oxload                          ← configuration file (old form)
-oxload                         ← command line (old form)
O QueueLA=load                  ← configuration file (beginning with V8.7)
-OQueueLA=load                  ← command line (beginning with V8.7)
define(`confQUEUE_LA',load)     ← V8 m4 configuration
```

The optional argument *load*, of type numeric, defaults to zero if it is missing. If the entire QueueLA (x) option is missing, the default value given to *load* is eight. The default for the *m4* technique is to omit this option. On newer, faster machines a higher setting may be more appropriate.

This QueueLA (x) option is effective only if your *sendmail* binary was compiled with load-average support (see §18.8.14). You can use the -d3.1 debugging switch (§37.5.14) to discover whether your binary includes the necessary support.

The QueueLA (x) option is not safe. If specified from the command line, it may cause *sendmail* to relinquish its *root* privilege.

QueueSortOrder   *(V8.7 and above)*

34.8.51   *How to pre-sort the queue*

Prior to V8.7 *sendmail*, mail messages in the queue were sorted by priority when the queue was processed. Under V8.7 an enhanced sort can be implemented with the QueueSortOrder option:

```
O QueueSortOrder=how                    ← configuration file (beginning with V8.7)
-OQueueSortOrder=how                    ← command line (beginning with V8.7)
define(`confQUEUE_SORT_ORDER',how)      ← V8 m4 configuration
```

The argument *how* is of type character.[*] It can be a P or p (for priority), which causes *sendmail* to emulate its old (sort by priority) behavior. It can be an H or h (for host), which causes *sendmail* to perform a new enhanced sort. Beginning with V8.8 *sendmail*, it can be T or t (for time), which sorts by submission time. If any other character is specified or if *how* is omitted, the following message is printed and the option is skipped:

```
Invalid queue sort order "badchar"
```

If this option is entirely omitted, the default is to sort by priority. The default in configuring with the V8 *m4* technique is also priority.

The QueueSortOrder option is safe. If specified from the command line, *sendmail* will not relinquish its *root* privilege.

---

[*] Of course, we recommend using full words for clarity.

34.8.51.1 QueueSortOrder=host

If *what* is host, the messages in the queue are first sorted by recipient host, lock status, and priority. If any message for a host is locked (currently being delivered) all the messages for that host are also marked as locked. Then the queue is sorted again, this time by lock status (unlocked first), recipient host, and priority. Delivery attempts after this sort tend to group SMTP connections to the same host together sequentially.

Be careful in sorting by host. If you have a large backlog of low-priority (batch) mail on a low-speed link to some host (for example *news*), you might end up delaying higher-priority mail intended for other hosts. The host sort is recommended for high-speed links but is less desirable on low-speed links.

34.8.51.2 QueueSortOrder=priority

The method to order a queue run that has been used by *sendmail* for many years is a simple sort of the message priorities. A message's priority is found in the qf file's P line (see §23.9.11). The sort is one of cost. That is, low (less positive) priorities are sorted ahead of high (more positive) values.

34.8.51.3 QueueSortOrder=time (V8.8 and above)

Beginning with V8.8, *sendmail* recognizes the time keyword, which causes it to sort based on submission time. This setting is not intended for use in the configuration file. Instead, it should be used only from the command line and in combination with the -qR command-line switch (see §23.6.2.3).

If you wrongly set time in the configuration file, large jobs and old jobs will be sorted in with small and new jobs. This can delay important mail. Also note that there is no guarantee that mail will be delivered in submission order unless the DeliveryMode option (see §34.8.16) is set to queue or defer.

QueueTimeout (T)   *(deprecated*

34.8.52   *Limit life of a message in the queue*

When mail cannot be delivered promptly, it is left in the queue. At intervals specified by *sendmail*'s -q command-line switch, redelivery of that queued mail is attempted. The maximum time a mail message can remain in the queue before being bounced as undeliverable is defined by the T option. (Note that the Queue-Timeout (T) option has been deprecated in favor of the Timeout option of V8.7 *sendmail*.)

The forms of the QueueTimeout (T) option are as follows:

```
OTqtime                                 ← configuration file (old form)
-oTqtime                                ← command line (old form)
O QueueTimeout=qtime                    ← configuration file (deprecated)
define(`confMESSAGE_TIMEOUT',qtime)     ← V8 m4 configuration
```

The argument *qtime* is of type time. If this argument is missing or if the entire QueueTimeout (T) option is missing, the value given to *qtime* is zero, and no mail is ever queued.* The *qtime* is generally specified as a number of days, 5d for example. (Incidentally, RFC1123 recommends five days as a minimum.)

All queued mail is timed out on the basis of its creation time compared to the timeout period specified by the QueueTimeout (T) option. Each queued message has its creation time stored in its qf file's T line (see §23.9.15). When *sendmail* is run (either as a daemon or by hand) to process the queue, it gets its timeout period from the value of the QueueTimeout (T) option. As the queue is processed, each message's creation time is checked to see whether it has timed out on the basis of the *current* value of the QueueTimeout (T) option. Since the configuration file is read only once (when *sendmail* first starts), the timeout period cannot be subsequently changed. There are only two ways to lengthen the timeout period: first, by modifying the configuration file's QueueTimeout (T) option (which prior to V8 could involve creating a freeze file) and killing and restarting *sendmail*; second, by running *sendmail* by hand with the –q command-line switch (see §23.6.1) and setting a new timeout using the –oT*timeout* command-line switch.

Since the creation time is stored in a queued file's qf file, messages can theoretically be rejuvenated (made to appear young again) by simply modifying that entry. The details of the qf queue file are presented in §23.9.

Under V8 *sendmail* the sender can be notified when a message is delayed. This feature is enabled by the inclusion of a second argument following the *qtime* argument in the QueueTimeout (T) option declaration:

```
OTqtime/notify                          ← configuration file (V8.6)
-oTqtime/notify                         ← command line (V8.6)
O QueueTimeout=qtime/notify             ← configuration file (V8.7; deprecated)
```

If the second argument is present, it must be separated from the first by a /. The notify specifies the amount of time *sendmail* should wait, after the message is first queued, before sending notification to the sender that it was delayed. If *notify* is missing or longer than *qtime*, no warning messages are sent. If *notify* is longer than *qtime*, no notification is ever sent.

Note that this is a crude method compared to the one described under the Timeout option in §34.8.70. Beginning with V8.7 *sendmail* and using the queuereturn

---

* That is, each message is instantly bounced if it cannot be delivered on the first try.

and `queuewarn` keywords of that option, the *qtime* and `notify` values above can be tuned on the basis of individual mail message priorities.

The `QueueTimeout` (T) option is not safe. If specified from the command line, it may cause *sendmail* to relinquish its *root* privilege.

RecipientFactor (y)   *(All versions)*
34.8.53   *Penalize large recipient lists*

Not all messages need to be treated equally. When sendmail processes the messages in its queue, it sorts them by priority.[*] The priority that is given to a message is calculated once, when it is first created, and adjusted (incremented or decremented) each time it is processed in the queue. Mail with the *lowest* priority number is handled first. The formula for the initial calculation is

```
priority = nbytes - (class * z) + (recipients * y)
```

The items in this calculation are as follows:

`priority`
> Priority of the message when it was first created.

`nbytes`
> Number of bytes in the total message, including the header and body of the message.

`class`
> Value given to a message by the `Precedence:` line in the header of the message. The string following the `Precedence:` is usually either `first-class`, `special-delivery`, `junk`, `bulk`, or `list`. That string is converted to a numeric value determined by the `P` command (see §35.8) in the *sendmail.cf* file.

`z`
> Value given the `ClassFactor` (z) option (see §34.8.8) and a weighting factor to adjust the relative importance of the `class`.

`recipients`
> Number of recipients to whom the message is addressed. This number is counted *after* all alias expansion.

`y`
> Value given this `RecipientFactor` (y) option and weighting factor to adjust the relative importance of the number of recipients.

The forms of the `RecipientFactor` (y) option are as follows:

---

[*] See the `QueueSortOrder` option, §34.8.51, for alternative ways to sort.

```
Oyfactor                                    ← configuration file (old form)
-oyfactor                                   ← command line (old form)
O RecipientFactor=factor                    ← configuration file (beginning with V8.7)
-ORecipientFactor=factor                    ← command line (beginning with V8.7)
define(`confWORK_RECIPIENT_FACTOR',factor)  ← V8 m4 configuration
```

The argument *factor* is of type numeric. If that argument is missing, the default value is zero. If the entire `RecipientFactor` (y) option is missing, the default value is 30000 (thirty thousand). The default for the *m4* technique is to omit this option.

The `RecipientFactor` (y) option is not safe. If specified from the command line, it may cause *sendmail* to relinquish its *root* privilege.

RefuseLA (X)   *(All versions)*

34.8.54   *Refuse connections on high load*

When the load average on a machine (the average number of jobs in the run queue over the last minute) becomes too high, *sendmail* can compensate by refusing to accept SMTP connections. Some experts consider this a more serious problem than the queuing caused by the `QueueLA` (x) option (see §34.8.50), so prior to the introduction of V8.7 *sendmail*, they generally recommended that the load specified for this `RefuseLA` (X) option should be higher.[*] Under V8.7 the two options have been decoupled, and you can now tune them according to your personal philosophy.

The forms of the `RefuseLA` (X) option are as follows:

```
OXload                          ← configuration file (old form)
-oXload                         ← command line (old form)
O RefuseLA=load                 ← configuration file (beginning with V8.7)
-ORefuseLA=load                 ← command line (beginning with V8.7)
define(`confREFUSE_LA',load)    ← V8 m4 configuration
```

The argument *load* is of type numeric. If *load* is missing, the value becomes zero, causing all SMTP connections to be refused. If the entire `RefuseLA` (X) option is missing, the value for the load cutoff defaults to 12. The default for the *m4* technique is to omit this option.

This `RefuseLA` (X) option is effective only if your *sendmail* binary was compiled with load-average support included (see §18.8.14). You can use the `-d3.1` debugging switch (see §37.5.14) to discover whether your binary includes the necessary support.

---

[*] Others take the opposite stand. Paul Vixie, for one, believes that the `RefuseLA` option should be lower than the `QueueLA` option so that you stop accepting mail before you stop processing it.

The RefuseLA (X) option is not safe. If specified from the command line, it may cause *sendmail* to relinquish its *root* privilege.

ResolverOptions (I)   *(All versions)*

34.8.55   *Tune DNS lookups*

The ResolverOptions (I) allows you to tune the way DNS lookups are performed:

```
OIbool                              ← configuration file (old form)
-oIbool                             ← command line (old form)
-oI "arg ... "                      ← command line (V8.6)
OIarg ...                           ← configuration file (V8.6)
O ResolverOptions="arg ... "        ← configuration file (V8.7)
-OResolverOptions="arg ... "        ← command line (V8.7)
define(`confBIND_OPTS',`arg ...')   ← V8 m4 configuration
```

The **arg** is one or more arguments that allow you to tune the behavior of the name server. The **arg** arguments are identical to the flags listed in *resolver*(3), but you omit the RES_ prefix. For example, RES_DNSRCH is expressed DNSRCH. A flag may be preceded by a plus or a minus to enable or disable the corresponding name server option. If no pluses or minuses appear, the name server option is enabled just as though a plus was present. Consider the following:

```
OI+AAONLY -DNSRCH
O ResolverOptions=+AAONLY -DNSRCH
```

These turn on the AAONLY name server option (Authoritative Answers Only) and turn off the DNSRCH name server option (search the domain path). If the ResolverOptions (I) option is entirely omitted, the default is for the DNSRCH, DEFNAMES, and RECURSE name server options to be enabled and all others to be disabled. Thus, for example, DNSRCH is always enabled unless you specifically turn it off.

Beginning with V8.7 *sendmail*, the special string HasWildcardMX can be listed along with the other resolver options:

```
O ResolverOptions=+AAONLY -DNSRCH HasWildcardMX
```

This string causes MX lookups to be done with RES_QUERY set (provided that the level of the configuration is 6 or above; see §27.5); otherwise, those lookups are done with RES_SEARCH. It also inhibits MX lookups when getting the canonical name of the local host. It should always be used if you have a wildcard MX record that matches your local domain.

Note that omitting the ResolverOptions (I) option *does not* disable DNS lookups. To disable DNS under V8.6 *sendmail*, you must compile a version of *sendmail* with NAMED_BIND support omitted (see §18.8.23). Beginning with V8.7 *sendmail*, you can disable use of DNS via your service-switch file (see §34.8.61).

Under V8 *sendmail*, any Boolean argument following the `ResolverOptions` (I) is silently ignored. Therefore an initial `True` may be included for compatibility with previous versions of *sendmail*. Note that under V8 *sendmail*, a `False` produces an error and cannot be used to disable this option.

```
OITrue
```

Version 1 configuration files (see §27.5) cause *sendmail* to disable DNSRCH and DEFNAMES when doing delivery lookups but leave them on at all other times. Version 2 and above configuration files cause *sendmail* to use the resolver options defined by the `ResolverOptions` (I) option, except that it always enables DNSRCH when doing lookups with the $[and $] operators. Starting with Version 8, *sendmail* defers the decision of whether or not to use DNS lookups to the `ServiceSwitchFile` option (see §34.8.61). DNS is now only considered canonical if the **dns** service is listed for `hosts` in the `ServiceSwitchFile`.

Finally, note that an attempt to use this option with a version of *sendmail* that does not support DNS lookups (see §18.8.23) will result in this error message:

```
name server (I option) specified but BIND not compiled in
```

The `ResolverOptions` (I) option is not safe. If specified from the command line, it may cause *sendmail* to relinquish its *root* privilege.

RetryFactor (Z)   *(All versions)*

34.8.56   *Increment per job priority*

When sendmail processes the messages in its queue, it sorts them by priority and handles those with the *lowest* (least positive) priority first.

The priority of a message is calculated once, using the `RecipientFactor` (y) (see §34.8.53) and `ClassFactor` (z) (see §34.8.8) options, when the message is first created, and it is adjusted, using this `RetryFactor` (Z) option, each time the message is processed in the queue.

Each time a message from the queue fails to be delivered and needs to be requeued, its priority is adjusted. That adjustment is made by adding the value of this `RetryFactor` (Z) option.

The forms of the `RetryFactor` (Z) option are as follows:

```
OZinc                            ← configuration file (old form)
-oZinc                           ← command line (old form)
O RetryFactor=inc                ← configuration file (beginning with V8.7)
```

```
    -ORetryFactor=inc                        ← command line (beginning with V8.7)
    define(`confWORK_TIME_FACTOR',inc)       ← V8 m4 configuration
```

The argument *inc* is of type numeric. If *inc* is missing, the default value is zero. If the entire RetryFactor (Z) option is missing, the value for *inc* defaults to 90000 (ninety thousand). The default for the *m4* technique is to omit this option. The increment is performed by adding the value of *inc* to the previously stored message priority each time that message is queued.

The RetryFactor (Z) option is not safe. If specified from the command line, it may cause *sendmail* to relinquish its *root* privilege.

RunAsUser   *(V8.8 and above)*

34.8.57   *Run as non-root (on a firewall)*

On firewalls, for reasons of additional security, it is often desirable to run *sendmail* as a user other than *root*. Beginning with V8.8 *sendmail*, you can accomplish this by using the RunAsUser option:

```
    O RunAsUser=user:group                   ← V8.8 and above
    -ORunAsUser=user:group                   ← V8.8 and above
    define(`confRUN_AS_USER', `user:group')  ← V8 m4 technique
```

Here, **user** is either the *uid* number of the identity you want *sendmail* to run under or a symbolic name for that identity. If a symbolic name is specified and if that name cannot be looked up in the *passwd*(5) file, *sendmail* prints the following error:

```
    readcf: option RunAsUser: unknown user bad symbolic name here
```

If the symbolic name is found in the *passwd*(5) file, the *uid* and *gid* that *sendmail* will run under are set from that file.

The :, if it is present,[*] signals to *sendmail* that you also intend to specify a group identity.

The **group** is either the numeric *gid* that you want *sendmail* to run as or a symbolic name for a group. If it is a symbolic name, that name is looked up in the *group*(5) file. If it is not found in that file, the following error is printed:

```
    readcf: option RunAsUser: unknown group bad group name here
```

If the symbolic name is in that file, *sendmail* will run under the *gid* found there.

The *sendmail* program assumes the identity specified just after the configuration file is read for all but the daemon mode. As a daemon, *sendmail* remains *root* to listen for incoming SMTP connections. Each time it receives a connection, it

---

[*] It can also be a . or a / character.

validates that connection (see §22.4.1 and §29.10.3), then *fork*(2)'s. The child then processes the incoming message. Immediately after the fork, the child assumes the identity specified by this `RunAsUser` option.

Note that running as non-*root* can lead to problems, especially on machines that do more than simply relay mail between networks. As non-*root*, *sendmail* may not be able to read some `:include:` files, will certainly not be able to read protected `~/.forward` files, and won't be able to save messages to the queue, all unless permissions are relaxed to allow the non-*root* user such access. This option is intended to be used on a firewall machine. It should definitely *not* be used on nonfirewall machines.

The `RunAsUser` option is not safe. If specified from the command line, it may cause *sendmail* to relinquish its *root* privilege.

SafeFileEnvironment   *(V8.7 and above)*

34.8.58   *Directory for safe file writes*

For security it is desirable to control the manner and circumstances under which messages are delivered to files. Beginning with V8.7 *sendmail* you can enhance the security of writing to files with the `SafeFileEnvironment` option. It is used like this:

```
O SafeFileEnvironment=path          ← configuration file (beginning with V8.7)
-OSafeFileEnvironment=path          ← command line (beginning with V8.7)
define(`confSAFE_FILE_ENV',path)    ← m4 configuration (beginning with V8.7)
```

The `path` is of type string and, if present, must be the full path name of a directory. The default, if either `path` or the entire option is missing, is NULL, causing this feature to be ignored.

When preparing to save a message to a file, *sendmail* first obtains the permissions of that file, if the file exists, and saves them (see §24.2.2). The *sendmail* program uses *lstat*(2) to obtain those permissions if it was compiled with HASLSTAT defined (see §18.8.9). Otherwise, it uses *stat*(2).

Ordinarily, *sendmail* does a *chroot*(2) to the / directory just before it opens the file for writing. If the `path` is non-NULL and nonempty, *sendmail* then precedes that *chroot*(2) with a:

```
chroot(path)
```

If the *chroot*(2) fails, *sendmail* prints the following error and bounces the mail message:

```
mailfile: Cannot chroot(path)
```

If the name of the file begins with *path*, that prefix is stripped after the *chroot*(2) and before the *fopen*(3).

For example, consider the need to safely store all mail archive files on the mail hub in a directory called */archives*. You would first create this configuration declaration:

```
O SafeFileEnvironment=/archives
```

Then every file archive notation in the *aliases* database should be changed to reference this base directory:[*]

```
adminlist:       :include:/usr/local/maillists/admin.list,
                 /archives/admin/log
```

For safety, *sendmail* will henceforth *chroot*(2) into the */archives* directory before delivering to any files. Note that this **SafeFileEnvironment** option affects all writes to files, so a user's `~/.forward` entry (such as the following) will become relative to */archives* and so may fail depending on your specific setup:

```
/u/bill/tmp/incoming      ← written as /archives/u/bill/tmp/incoming
```

The **SafeFileEnvironment** option also causes *sendmail* to verify that the file that is being written to is a plain file. If it is anything else, *sendmail* prints the following error and bounces the messages:

```
/dev/tty... Can't create output: Error 0
```

Here, an attempt to dump the message to */dev/tty* failed because *sendmail* discovered it was a device rather than an ordinary file. But note that beginning with V8.8, it is legal to write to the special device named */dev/null*.

The **SafeFileEnvironment** option is not safe. If specified from the command line, it may cause *sendmail* to relinquish its *root* privilege.

SaveFromLine (f)   *(All versions)*

34.8.59   *Save UNIX-style From lines*

Many UNIX MUAs, as well as some transmittal systems like UUCP, require that a mail-message header begin with a line that begins with the five-character sequence "**From** ". All other header lines must adhere to the RFC822 standard and be delimited with a colon:

```
From jqp@Washington.DC.gov Fri Jul 26 12:35:25 1991
Return-Path: <jqp@Washington.DC.gov>
Date: Fri, 26 Jul 91 12:35:15 PDT
From: jqp@Washington.DC.gov (John Q Public)
```

---

[*] This is not strictly necessary. Both */archives/admin/log* and */admin/log* will work equally well. The former, however, is preferred for clarity.

If you don't set the SaveFromLine (f) option, the first line in the above example is stripped out by *sendmail*. The SaveFromLine (f) option prevents this, because it tells *sendmail* to keep header lines that begin with the five characters "From ". But note that it also causes this header to no longer be recognized as a header.

The forms of the SaveFromLine (f) option are as follows:

```
Ofbool                                   ← configuration file (old form)
-ofbool                                  ← command line (old form)
-s                                       ← command-line shorthand (not recommended)
O SaveFromLine=bool                      ← configuration file (beginning with V8.7)
-OSaveFromLine=bool                      ← command line (beginning with V8.7)
define(`confSAVE_FROM_LINES',bool)       ← V8 m4 configuration
```

The optional argument *bool* is of type Boolean. If *bool* is missing, this option becomes true (the "From " line is saved). If the entire option is missing, it defaults to false (neither save the "From " line nor recognize it as a header).

The SaveFromLine (f) option is not safe. If specified from the command line, it may cause *sendmail* to relinquish its *root* privilege.

SendMimeErrors (j)   *(V6.57 and above)*

34.8.60   *Return MIME format errors*

MIME (Multipurpose Internet Mail Extensions) is documented in RFC1341, with addition details in RFC1344, RFC1426, RFC1428, RFC1437, RFC1521, RFC1522, RFC1523, RFC1556, RFC1563, RFC1641, RFC1740, RFC1741, and RFC1767. MIME is a method of incorporating non-ASCII text (such as images and sounds) in mail messages.

When *sendmail* composes an error notification of failed (bounced) mail, this SendMimeErrors (j) option tells *sendmail* to include MIME format headers in that error notification. MIME format is required for DSN notification to work (the two go hand in hand). This option affects only returned (bounced) mail.

If the SendMimeErrors (j) option is true and if *sendmail* is composing a returned mail message, the following two headers are added to the header portion of that message:

```
MIME-Version: 1.0
Content-Type: multipart/report; report-type=delivery-status;
        boundary=magic
```

The version (1.0) of the MIME-Version: header (see §35.10.21) is hard-coded into V8 *sendmail,* so it cannot be changed. The Content-Type: is instead multipart/mixed if *sendmail* was compiled without DSN support (see §18.8.5). The *magic* of Content-Type: is a string that is used to separate the various parts of the message body. The string is formed from the queue ID, the time, and the hostname. For example:

```
Content-Type: multipart/report; report-type=delivery-status;
        boundary=AA26662.9306241634/hostname
```

Then *sendmail* prefixes the body of the returned message (if there is one), a line of notification, and this boundary:

```
This is a MIME-encapsulated message

--AA26662.9306241634/hostname
```
                    ← message body begins here

Newer MUAs are aware of MIME and can send and receive MIME messages. Such MUAs understand **MIME-Version:** header in a mail message. Older (non-MIME aware) MUAs ignore that header.

Unless you bounce mail to a site that cannot handle MIME, you should always set this **SendMimeErrors** (j) option to true.

The forms of the **SendMimeErrors** (j) option are as follows:

```
Ojbool                                    ← configuration file (V8.6)
-ojbool                                   ← command line (V8.6)
O SendMimeErrors=bool                     ← configuration file (V8.7)
-OSendMimeErrors=bool                     ← command line (V8.7)
define(`confMIME_FORMAT_ERRORS',bool)     ← V8 m4 configuration
```

The optional argument *bool* is of type Boolean. If *bool* is missing, this option becomes true (errors are sent in MIME format). If the entire option is missing it defaults to false (errors are sent just as they were before this option was introduced).

The **SendMimeErrors** (j) option is safe. Even if it is specified from the command line, *sendmail* retains its *root* privilege.

ServiceSwitchFile   *(V8.7 and above)*

34.8.61   *Specify file for switched services*

Some implementations of UNIX recognize that system information can be found in a variety of places. On Solaris, for example, hostnames can be obtained from the */etc/hosts* file, from *nis*, from *nisplus*, or from DNS. Solaris allows the system administrator to choose the order in which these services are searched with a "service-switch" file. Other systems, such as Ultrix and DEC OSF/1, have a similar concept, but some (such as SunOS) use built-in rules that cannot be changed without the source code.

V8.7 *sendmail* uses a system-service switch if one is available. Otherwise, *sendmail* uses the service switch defined by this **ServiceSwitchFile** option.

The form for redefining the switched-services file is as follows:

```
O ServiceSwitchFile=path                  ← configuration file (beginning with V8.7)
-OServiceSwitchFile=path                   ← command line (beginning with V8.7)
define(`confSERVICE_SWITCH_FILE',path)    ← V8 m4 configuration
```

If this option is defined on an operating system that *does* offer a service-switch (such as Solaris, DEC OSF/1 or Ultrix), it is ignored. Otherwise, `path` is used as the full pathname of the file that is to be used as the service-switch. If `path` is omitted, the default is NULL. If the entire option is omitted, the default is */etc/service.switch*. The default for the *m4* technique is to omit this option.

The form of each line in that file is

```
service  how how
```

Here, `service` is either `hosts` (which states how host names are looked up) `aliases` (which states how aliases are looked up), or `passwd` (which states how *passwd*(5) information is looked up). For each of these services, there may be one or more *how* methods (not all of which make sense with all services). The `service` and the *hows* must be separated from each other by whitespace. The possible methods (values for each *how*) are `files` (the information is in a file or database, such as */etc/hosts*), `netinfo` (for information on NeXT machines), `nis` (the information is in an *nis* map), `nisplus` (the information is in an *nisplus* map), `dns` (the host information is looked up with DNS), or `hesiod` (the information is listed with a Hesiod service).[*]

For example, consider the contents of the following */etc/service.switch* file:

```
aliases nis
passwd nis files
hosts dns
```

Here, *sendmail* will look up aliases in the *nis* map *mail.aliases*. Password information, such as local user login names and full name information from the *gecos* field, will first be looked up in the *nis* map *passwd.byname*. If not found there, they will then be looked up in the file */etc/passwd*. The last line tells *sendmail* to look up A and MX records for hosts using the DNS services.

The `hosts` line can also determine how MX records are treated (see §21.2.3). If "dns" does not appear in that line, *sendmail* disables lookups of MX records. If *sendmail* is configured to look up hosts with *nis* first, then DNS, it will do the MX lookup in DNS *before* the *nis* lookup.

For Solaris, `hosts` is looked up with the *nsswitch.conf*(4) service. For DEC OSF/1 and Ultrix, `hosts` is looked up with the *svc.conf*(5) service. For all others the file defined by the `ServiceSwitchFile` is examined for a line that begins with the word `hosts`. If that line is missing or if the file doesn't exist, "dns" is returned by

---

[*] Currently, the list is limited to those shown. Future versions of *sendmail* may offer others.

default. But if NAMED_BIND was not defined (see §18.8.23) when *sendmail* was compiled, the default returned is "nis" for Solaris and SunOS, and on other systems it is "files."

Note that on systems such as SunOS, a version of *gethostbyname*(3) is still called that ignores the *sendmail* programs service-switch file. On such systems you may need to download the source, recompile, and install a version that works correctly.

The `ServiceSwitchFile` option is not safe. If specified from the command line, it may cause *sendmail* to relinquish its *root* privilege.

SevenBitInput (7)   *(V8.1 and above)*

34.8.62   *Force 7-bit input*

By default, V8 *sendmail* leaves as is all bytes of every mail message it reads. This differs from other releases of *sendmail* that always clear (zero) the high (most-significant) bit. To make V8 *sendmail* behave like older versions and always clear the high bit on input, the `SevenBitInput` (7) option is available:

```
O7bool                          ← configuration file (V8.6)
-o7bool                         ← command line (V8.6)
O SevenBitInput=bool            ← configuration file (V8.7 and above)
-OSevenBitInput=bool            ← command line (V8.7 and above)
define(`confSEVEN_BIT_INPUT',bool)   ← V8 m4 configuration
```

The argument *bool* is of type Boolean. If *bool* is missing, the default value is true (clear the 8th bit). If this option is omitted entirely, the default is false (the 8th bit is unmodified). If you configure with V8's *m4* technique, the default for `conf-SEVEN_BIT_INPUT` is false.

Note that this option is temporarily set to false for a single message if the ESMTP BODY=8BITMIME parameter is given and is set to true if the BODY=7BIT parameter is given.

Also note that the `SevenBitInput` (7) option affects input only. The `F=7` delivery agent flag (see §30.8.4) can be used to set 7-bit output on an individual delivery agent basis.

The `SevenBitInput` (7) option is safe. If specified from the command line, *sendmail* will not relinquish its *root* privilege.

SingleLineFromHeader   *(V8.8 and above)*

34.8.63   *Strip newlines from From: headers*

Lotus Notes' SMTP mail gateway can generate `From:` headers that contain newlines and that contain the address on the second line:

```
From: Full Name
      <address>
```

Although this is legal per RFC822, many MUAs mishandle such headers and are unable to find the address. If your site suffers from this problem, you may define the `SingleLineFromHeader` option:

```
O SingleLineFromHeader=bool            ← configuration file (V8.8)
-OSingleLineFromHeader=bool            ← command line (V8.8)
```

The *bool* is of type Boolean. If it is true, *sendmail* will convert all newlines found in a `From:` header into space characters. If it is false, *sendmail* will leave all `From:` headers as is.

The `SingleLineFromHeader` option is safe. Even if it is specified from the command line, *sendmail* retains its *root* privilege.

SingleThreadDelivery   *(V8.8 and above)*

34.8.64   *Set single threaded delivery*

Ordinarily, when *sendmail* processes the queue, it pays relatively little attention to other *sendmail* processes that may be processing the same queue at the same time. It locks a single `qf` file during delivery so that no other *sendmail* will attempt delivery of that message at the same time, but that is all. In sending many messages to a single other host, it is possible for multiple, parallel *sendmail* processes to try to deliver different messages from that queue to that single host all at once.

When accidental parallelism is not desirable, as in just processing the queue, you may wish to set up *sendmail* to be single-threaded. This ensures that only a single *sendmail* will ever be delivering to a given host at a given time. Single-threaded delivery is enabled with the `SingleThreadDelivery` option:

```
O SingleThreadDelivery=bool                     ← V8.8 and above
-OSingleThreadDelivery=bool                     ← V8.8 and above
define(`confSINGLE_THREAD_DELIVERY',bool)       ← V8 m4 technique
```

The argument *bool* is of type Boolean. If it is missing, the default value is true (deliver single-threaded). If the entire `SingleThreadDelivery` option is missing, the default becomes false (deliver in parallel). There is no *m4* shorthand for enabling this option.

Note that the `SingleThreadDelivery` option will work only if the `HostStatusDirectory` option is also declared (see §34.8.31). If it is not, *sendmail* will print the following error and reset the `SingleThreadDelivery` option to false:

```
Warning: HostStatusDirectory required for SingleThreadDelivery
```

Also note that the `SingleThreadDelivery` option should probably never be set in the configuration file. To see why, consider an ongoing queue run to a host that is receiving many messages. If interactive user mail arrives during that run, the *send-mail* process executed by the user's MUA may find that it cannot send the message because it is single-threaded and the other *sendmail* has that host locked. In that case the user's message will be queued and will wait in the queue until the next queue is run. Even if your site is on the Internet, one large message to a slow site can cause interactive mail for that site to be wrongly queued.

The appropriate use for the `SingleThreadDelivery` option is on the command line when processing the queue. In daemon mode, for example, these startup commands may be appropriate:

```
/usr/lib/sendmail -bd
/usr/lib/sendmail -OSingleThreadDelivery -q30m
```

Note that two *sendmail* programs are started: one to act as a daemon and the other to periodically process the queue. Don't combine them when using the `SingleThreadDelivery` option, because incoming (relayed) mail can wrongly affect outgoing mail.

The `SingleThreadDelivery` option is not safe. If specified from the command line, it may cause *sendmail* to relinquish its *root* privilege.

SmtpGreetingMessage *or* $e   *(All versions)*

34.8.65   *The SMTP greeting message*

When *sendmail* accepts an incoming SMTP connection it sends a greeting message to the other host. This message identifies the local machine and is the first thing it sends to say it is ready.

Prior to V8.7 *sendmail*, this message was declared with the $e macro. Beginning with V8.7 *sendmail*, it is declared with the `SmtpGreetingMessage` option. In both cases the message must begin with the fully qualified name of the local host. Usually, that name is stored in $j. The minimal definition for both is

```
De$j                              ← V8.6 and earlier
O SmtpGreetingMessage=$j          ← beginning with V8.7
```

Additional information may follow the local hostname. Any additional information must be separated from the hostname by at least one space:

```
De$j additional information
    ↑
    at least one space
```

Traditionally, that additional information is the name of the listening program (in our case, always *sendmail*), the version of that program, and a statement that the program is ready. For example:

```
De$j Sendmail $v ready at $b                        ← V8.6 and earlier
O SmtpGreetingMessage=$j Sendmail $v ready at $b    ← beginning with V8.7
```

Note that it is not uncommon to see imaginative (and legal) variations in the additional information:

```
De$j Sun's sendmail.mx is set to go (at $b), let 'er rip!
```

Under versions V8.6 and earlier there was no default for this greeting message. You had to define $e in every configuration file. Beginning with V8.7, *sendmail* now checks to see whether the SmtpGreetingMessage option was defined and uses that value if it was. Otherwise, it checks to see whether the level of the configuration file is 6 or less. If it is and if the $e macro was defined it uses that value. Otherwise, it uses the following default:

```
$j Sendmail $v ready at $b
```

The forms for the $e and SmtpGreetingMessage are as follows:

```
Demessage                                    ← V8.6 and earlier
O SmtpGreetingMessage=message                ← configuration file (beginning with V8.7)
-OSmtpGreetingMessage=message                ← command line (beginning with V8.7)
define(`confSMTP_LOGIN_MSG',message)         ← V8 m4 technique
```

The message is of type string and must be present. It must contain, at minimum, the fully qualified name of the local host.

Note that in V8.1 through V8.6, *sendmail* always added the extra line

```
ESMTP spoken here
```

to its initial greeting message. Beginning with V8.7, *sendmail* instead inserts the word "ESMTP" into the greeting message itself just after the fully qualified hostname.

The SmtpGreetingMessage option is not safe. If specified from the command line, it may cause *sendmail* to relinquish its *root* privilege.

StatusFile (S)   (All versions)

34.8.66   *Specify statistics file*

At busy and complex mail sites, many different delivery agents are active. For example, one kind of mail might be routed over the Internet using the TCP delivery agent, while another might be routed via the UUCP suite of programs, and yet another might be routed over a DS3 link to a group of research machines. In such circumstances, it is useful to gather statistical information about the total use to date of each delivery agent.

The StatusFile (S) option tells *sendmail* the name of the file into which it should save those statistics. This option does *not* cause statistics to be gathered. It merely specifies the name of the file where they may be saved. When *sendmail* runs, it checks for the existence of such a file. If the file exists, it opens and updates the statistics in the file. If the file doesn't exist, *sendmail* quietly ignores statistics. The statistics can be viewed by using the *mailstats*(8)[*] program (see §26.2.1).

The forms of the `StatusFile` (S) option are as follows:

```
OSpath                       ← configuration file (old form)
-oSpath                      ← command line (old form)
O StatusFile=path            ← configuration file (beginning with V8.7)
-OStatusFile=path            ← command line (beginning with V8.7)
define(`STATUS_FILE',`path') ← V8 m4 configuration
```

The optional argument **path** is of type string. It may be a relative or a full pathname. The default value for **path** is *sendmail.st*. Relative names are always relative to the queue directory. If the entire option is missing, the value for **path** becomes the C language value NULL. The default in configuring with the V8 *m4* technique varies depending on your operating system.

The S option is not safe. If specified from the command line, it may cause *sendmail* to relinquish its *root* privilege.

SuperSafe (s)   *(All versions)*

34.8.67   *Queue everything just in case*

At times, such as when calling */bin/mail* to deliver local mail, *sendmail* holds an entire message internally while waiting for that delivery to complete. Clearly, this runs the risk that the message will be lost if the system crashes at the wrong time.

As a safeguard against such rare catastrophes, the **SuperSafe** (**s**) option can be used to force *sendmail* to queue every message. The queued copy is left in place until *sendmail* is sure that delivery was successful. We recommend that this option always be declared as true.

The forms of the **SuperSafe** (**s**) option are as follows:

```
Osbool                          ← configuration file (old form)
-osbool                         ← command line (old form)
O SuperSafe=bool                ← configuration file (beginning with V8.7)
-OSuperSafe=bool                ← command line (beginning with V8.7)
define(`confSAFE_QUEUE',bool)   ← V8 m4 configuration
```

The argument **bool** is of type Boolean. If it is missing, the default value is true (everything is queued). The default for the V8 *m4* configuration technique is also

---

[*] If you install V8 *sendmail* over an existing *sendmail* installation, you need to also install the V8 *mailstats* program.

true. If the entire SuperSafe (s) option is missing, the default becomes false (no special queuing behavior).

The SuperSafe (s) option is safe. Even if it is specified from the command line, *sendmail* retains its *root* privilege.

TempFileMode (F) *(All versions)*

34.8.68 *Permissions for temporary files*

The TempFileMode (F) option tells *sendmail* what mode (file permissions) to give its temporary files and its freeze file.[*] Because the files in the queue contain private email, this option is usually set to the least permissive level, 0600. On dedicated mail servers (hub machines), where logins are restricted to mail managers, you may wish to relax permissions for easier problem solving.

The forms of the TempFileMode (F) option are as follows:

```
OFmode                              ← configuration file (old mode)
-oFmode                             ← command line (old mode)
O TempFileMode=mode                 ← configuration file (beginning with V8.7)
-OTempFileMode=mode                 ← command line (beginning with V8.7)
define(`confTEMP_FILE_MODE',mode)   ← V8 m4 configuration
```

The *mode* is of type octal. If this option is entirely missing, the default permissions are 0644. Beware of omitting just the *mode* argument—if you do, the permissions become 0000, and *sendmail* may not be able to read or write its own files.

The TempFileMode (F) option is not safe. If specified from the command line, it may cause *sendmail* to relinquish its *root* privilege.

TimeZoneSpec (t) *(All versions)*

34.8.69 *Set time zone*

Under System V UNIX, processes must look for the local time zone in the environment variable TZ. Because *sendmail* is often run as an SUID *root* program, it cannot (and should not) trust its environment variables. Consequently, on System V machines it is necessary to use the TimeZoneSpec (t) option to give *sendmail* the correct time·zone information.

The forms for the TimeZoneSpec (t) option are as follows:

```
Otzone                            ← configuration file (old mode)
-otzone                           ← command line (old mode)
O TimeZoneSpec=zone               ← configuration file (beginning with V8.7)
-OTimeZoneSpec=zone               ← command line (beginning with V8.7)
define(`confTIME_ZONE','zone')    ← V8 m4 configuration
```

---

* V8 *sendmail* no longer supports freeze files.

Here, the *zone* is of type string and is usually three arguments in one:[*] the local abbreviation for standard time, the number of hours the local time differs from GMT, and the local abbreviation for daylight savings time. For example, on the west coast of the United States, you might declare

```
OtPST8PDT                              ← pre-V8.7 form
O TimeZoneSpec=PST8PDT                 ← beginning with V8.7
```

For pre-V8 *sendmail* on System V, if the *zone* argument is omitted or if this entire option is omitted, the default is the value compiled into your C language library (often the east coast of the United States, EST5EDT). For BSD the default is NULL.

Beginning with V8 *sendmail*, if the entire TimeZoneSpec (t) option is missing, the default is to unset the TZ environmental variable (use the system default). If *zone* is missing, the default is to import the TZ variable from the environment. If *zone* is present, time zone is set to that specified.

The system default varies depending on the operating system. For BSD UNIX it is the value returned by the *gettimeofday*(3) call. For SysV UNIX it is whatever was compiled into the C library (usually New Jersey time).

For the *m4* declaration, *zone* should be either a literal USE_SYSTEM, which causes the entire option to be omitted, or a literal USE_TZ, which causes the option to be declared but the *zone* to be omitted (thus importing the TZ variable from the calling environment). Otherwise, a time zone declaration is as described above:

```
define(`confTIME_ZONE', `USE_SYSTEM')  ← use system default
#O TimeZoneSpec=                        ← the same

define(`confTIME_ZONE', `USE_TZ')       ← use environment TZ
O TimeZoneSpec=                         ← the same

define(`confTIME_ZONE', `EST5EDT')      ← use EST5EDT
O TimeZoneSpec=EST5EDT                  ← the same
```

The TimeZoneSpec (t) option is not safe. If specified from the command line, it may cause *sendmail* to relinquish its *root* privilege.

Timeout (r)   *(All versions)*

34.8.70   *Set timeouts*

Many events can take a long time to complete—so long, in fact, that they can cause *sendmail* to appear to hang if they don't time out. For example, when reading commands or data from a remote SMTP connection, the other side can be so slow that it becomes necessary for the local *sendmail* to time out and break the

---

[*] This is actually a convention that is not used by all versions of UNIX. Consult your online documentation to find the correct form for your system.

connection. Similarly, when reading from its standard input, *sendmail* may find that the program feeding it information is taking so long that a timeout becomes necessary.

The V8 version of the *sendmail* program has introduced defaults for the amount of time it waits under various circumstances. The forms of the `Timeout` (r) option are as follows:

`Ortime`	← *configuration file (old form)*
`-ortime`	← *command line (old form)*
`Orkeyword=value,...`	← *configuration file (V8.1)*
`-orkeyword=value,...`	← *command line (V8.1)*
`O Timeout=keyword=value,...`	← *configuration file (V8.7 and above)*
`-OTimeout=keyword=value,...`	← *command line (V8.7 and above)*
`define('confREAD_TIMEOUT','keyword=value,...')`	← *V8 m4 configuration (not V8.7 up)*

Prior to V8 *sendmail*, only a single *time* could be specified, which set the timeout for all SMTP transactions. Beginning with V8 *sendmail*, a list of **keyword** and **value** pairs can be specified that individually set a wide assortment of timeouts. The recognized **keyword** words are listed in Table 34-18. The default and minimum **value** for each in described in the individual section.

Table 34–18: Timeout Option Keywords

Keyword	§	Meaning
command	34.8.70.1	Wait for the next command
connect	34.8.70.2	Wait for *connect*(2) to return
datablock	34.8.70.3	Wait for each DATA block read
datafinal	34.8.70.4	Wait for acknowledgment of final dot
datainit	34.8.70.5	Wait for DATA acknowledgment
fileopen	34.8.70.6	Wait an NFS file to open (V8.7 and above)
helo	34.8.70.7	Wait for HELO or EHLO
hoststatus	34.8.70.8	Duration of host status (V8.8 and above)
iconnect	34.8.70.9	Wait for first *connect*(2) (V8.8 and above)
ident	34.8.70.10	Wait for RFC1413 identification protocol
initial	34.8.70.11	Wait for initial greeting message
mail	34.8.70.12	Wait for MAIL acknowledgment
misc	34.8.70.13	Wait for other SMTP commands
queuereturn	34.8.70.14	Bounce if still undelivered (V8.7 and above)
queuewarn	34.8.70.15	Warn if still undelivered (V8.7 and above)
quit	34.8.70.16	Wait for QUIT acknowledgment
rcpt	34.8.70.17	Wait for RCPT acknowledgment
rset	34.8.70.18	Wait for RSET acknowledgment

The minimums are not enforced but are rather the minimums recommended by RFC1123, section 5.3.2.* The *value* is of type time. The default, if a unit character is omitted, is minutes. For the queuewarn and queuereturn keywords, however, the defaults are hours and days, respectively. Note that some of the default values may seem overly long. This is intentional because some events can legitimately take a very long time. Consider, for example, a misconfigured DNS server. If you time out too soon, your performance will actually decrease because the timeouts will cause retransmits.

For the V8.7 and above *m4* technique, each keyword is declared with its corresponding confTO_ expression. For example, the keyword initial is declared like this:

```
    define(`confTO_INITIAL',`5m')                    ← V8 m4 configuration
```

The particular confTO_ expression and its corresponding default value are listed with each keyword.

For compatibility with old configuration files, if no *keyword=* is specified, timeouts for the mail, rcpt, datainit, datablock, datafinal, and command keywords are set to the indicated value:

```
    Or2h                 ← set them to two hours
```

An example of the r option with *keyword=* pairs looks like this:

```
    Orrcpt=25m,datablock=3h
```

With the new V8.7 form of the Timeout option, individual timeouts can be listed more attractively like this:

```
    O Timeout.rcpt     = 25m
    O Timeout.datablock =  3h
```

For the above two examples the timeout for acknowledgment of the SMTP RCPT command (list a recipient) is 25 minutes and the timeout for acknowledgment of receipt of each line of the mail message is three hours; all the others that are not specified assume the default values.

The Timeout (r) option is not safe. If specified from the command line, it may cause *sendmail* to relinquish its *root* privilege.

---

* Note that the defaults are intentionally higher than the recommended minimums. Setting timeouts too low can cause mail to fail unnecessarily.

34.8.70.1 Timeout.command

When local *sendmail* is running as an SMTP server, it acknowledges any SMTP command sent to it by the other host and then waits for the next command. The amount of time the local *sendmail* waits for each command is defined with the `command` keyword. The default is one hour, and the minimum is specified as five minutes. The *m4* technique should use `confTO_COMMAND` for which not default is defined. If a command is not received in time, the local *sendmail* believes that the connection has hung and shuts it down.

34.8.70.2 Timeout.connect

When *sendmail* attempts to establish a network connection to another host, it uses the *connect*(2) system call. If the connection is going to fail, that system call will time out after an amount time that varies with the operating system. With Linux, for example, the timeout is 90 minutes, whereas for other versions of UNIX it is typically 5 minutes.

When the amount of time to wait for a connection to fail is of concern, you may override the system value with the `connect` keyword to the `Timeout` option:[*]

```
O Timeout.connect=3m                      ← V8.8 and above
define(`confTO_CONNECT', 3m)              ← V8 m4 technique
```

The default, if no timeout is specified, is to use the system imposed timeout. No default is defined for the *m4* technique.

Note that if the *connect*(2) call times out, delivery will be deferred until the next queue run. If you wish the *connect*(2) to be tried again (as you might for a dial-on-demand machine), you should investigate the `DialDelay` option (see §34.8.17).

34.8.70.3 Timeout.datablock

The local *sendmail* then buffers the mail message and sends it to the receiving site one line at a time. The amount of time that the receiving *sendmail* waits for a read to complete is set with the `datablock` keyword.[†] The default value is one hour, and the specified minimum is three minutes. The *m4* technique should use `confTO_DATABLOCK`, which has no default.

---

[*] Note that you can decrease the system defined timeout, but you cannot increase it.

[†] The timeout for writes by the sending *sendmail* are timed out on the basis of the number of recipients.

34.8.70.4 Timeout.datafinal

After the entire mail message has been transmitted, the local *sendmail* sends a lone dot to say that it is done, then waits for the receiving *sendmail* to acknowledge acceptance of that dot:

```
250 Mail accepted
```

The amount of time that the local *sendmail* waits for acknowledgment that the mail message was received is set with the **datafinal** keyword. The default value is one hour, and the specified minimum is 10 minutes. The *m4* technique should use confTO_DATAFINAL, which has no default. If the value is shorter than the time actually needed for the receiving site to deliver the message, the local *sendmail* times out before seeing the "Mail accepted" message when, in fact, the mail was accepted. This can lead to the local *sendmail* wrongly attempting to deliver the message later for a second time.

34.8.70.5 Timeout.datainit

After all the recipients have been specified, the local *sendmail* declares that it is ready to send the mail message itself. It issues the SMTP DATA command to the other site:

```
DATA
```

The local *sendmail* then waits for acknowledgment, which looks like this:

```
354 Enter mail, end with "." on a line by itself
```

The amount of time that the local *sendmail* waits for acknowledgment of its DATA command is set with the **datainit** keyword. The default value is five minutes, and the specified minimum is two minutes. The *m4* technique should use confTO_DATAINIT, which has no default.

34.8.70.6 Timeout.fileopen

If a directory is remotely mounted and the server is down or not responding, an attempt to open a file in that directory can hang. Beginning with V8.7, the **fileopen** keyword sets the amount of time to wait for a remote open to complete.[*] The default is zero seconds, which sets no limit. The *m4* technique should use confTO_FILEOPEN, which has no default.

---

[*] Note that this works only if the file system is mounted with the intr mount option.

34.8.70.7 Timeout.helo

After the greeting, the local *sendmail* sends a HELO (or EHLO to get ESMTP) message to identify itself. That message looks something like this:

```
HELO here.us.edu
```

The other site then replies with acknowledgment of the local HELO or EHLO:

```
250 there.dc.gov  Hello here.us.edu, pleased to meet you
```

The amount of time the local *sendmail* waits for the other site to acknowledge the local HELO or EHLO is set with the `helo` keyword. The default value is five minutes. There is no specified minimum, but we recommend no less than five minutes (because some sites use DNS to validate the hostname). The *m4* technique should use `confTO_HELO`, which has no default.

34.8.70.8 Timeout.hoststatus

When processing the queue, *sendmail* saves the connection status of each host to which it connects and each host to which it fails to connect. It does this because an unsuccessful host should not be tried again during the same queue run. This makes sense when you consider that failures tend to remain failures for a while.

At sites that process huge queues, on the other hand, such behavior may not be appropriate. If it takes hours (rather than minutes) to process the queue, the likelihood increases that a previously failed connection may succeed. For such sites, V8.8 *sendmail* has introduced the `Timeout.hoststatus` option:

```
O Timeout.hoststatus=interval            ← V8.8 and above
-OTimeout.hoststatus=interval            ← V8.8 and above
define(`confTO_HOSTSTATUS', interval)    ← V8 m4 techniqueue
```

Here, `interval` is of type time. If `interval` is present, it specifies the length of time information about a host will be considered valid. If a queue run finishes faster than this interval, it has no effect. But when queue runs take longer than this interval, a previously down host will be given a second try if it appears in the queue again.

If `interval` is missing, it is interpreted as zero, and no host information is ever saved. If the entire option is missing, the default is 30 minutes. The *m4* technique should use `confTO_HOSTSTATUS`, which has no default.

34.8.70.9 Timeout.iconnect

When *sendmail* attempts to establish a network connection to another host, it uses the *connect*(2) system call. If the connection is going to fail, that system call will time out after an amount of time that varies with the operating system. You can override the system timeout with the `connect` keyword (see §34.8.70.2) to the `Timeout` option.

When outgoing mail is first processed, mail to responsive hosts should precede mail to sluggish hosts. To understand why, consider that all mail is processed serially during each queue run. If a sluggish host precedes all the other hosts in the queue, those other hosts will not even be tried until the sluggish host finishes or times out. With this in mind, the very first time *sendmail* attempts to deliver a message, it should enforce a shorter *connect*(2) timeout than it should for latter attempts.

Beginning with V8.8 *sendmail*, you can set an initial *connect*(2) timeout with the `iconnect` keyword to the `Timeout` option:

```
O Timeout.iconnect=10s           ← time out first connection
O Timeout.connect=3m             ← time out all others

define(`confTO_ICONNECT', `10s')   ← v8 m4 technique
```

The default, if no `Timeout.iconnect` is specified or if the entire `Timeout.iconnect` option is omitted, is to time out the first connection the same as the timeout for all connections. The *m4* technique should use `confTO_ICONNECT`, for which there is no default. The `N` line in the `qf` file (see §23.9.10) determines whether this is the first attempt or not. If the value in that line is zero, this is the first delivery attempt.

34.8.70.10 Timeout.ident

The *sendmail* daemon queries every outside connecting host with the RFC1413 identification protocol to record the identity of the user at the other end who made the connection and to verify the true name of the remote connecting host. The default timeout is to wait 30 seconds for a response. The `ident` keyword is used to change this timeout. If your site accepts mail from PCs running SMTP software, you may need to disable this feature. Some PCs get stuck when queried with the RFC1413 identification protocol. If the timeout is zero, the ident protocol is disabled. The *m4* technique should use `confTO_IDENT`, for which there is no default.

34.8.70.11 Timeout.initial

The amount of time to wait for the initial greeting message. This message is printed by the remote site when it first makes its connection. The greeting message always starts with 220 and looks something like this:

```
220 there.dc.gov Sendmail 8.1/3x ready at ...
```

The default for the greeting wait and the recommended minimum are both five minutes.* The *m4* technique should use confTO_INITIAL, for which there is no default.

34.8.70.12 Timeout.mail

The local *sendmail* next sends the address of the sender (the envelope sender address) with an SMTP MAIL command:

```
MAIL From:<you@here.us.edu>
```

The local *sendmail* then waits for acknowledgment, which looks like this:

```
250 <you@here.us.edu>... Sender ok
```

The amount of time that the local *sendmail* waits for acknowledgment of its MAIL command is set with the **mail** keyword. The default value is 10 minutes, and the specified minimum is five minutes. The *m4* technique should use confTO_MAIL, for which there is no default.

34.8.70.13 Timeout.misc

During the course of mail transfer, the local *sendmail* may issue short miscellaneous commands. Examples are NOOP (which stands for no operation) and VERB (which tells the other side to enter verbose mode). The time that the local *sendmail* waits for acknowledgment of these miscellaneous commands is defined with the **misc** keyword. The default is two minutes, and no minimum is specified. The *m4* technique should use confTO_MISC, for which there is no default.

34.8.70.14 Timeout.queuereturn

That this keyword determines a mail message's lifetime in the queue. Beginning with V8.7, this queuereturn keyword is used to set the amount of time a message must wait in the queue before it is bounced as nondeliverable. Either it can be expressed as an interval of time:

```
O Timeout.queuereturn=5d
O Timeout.queuereturn.*=5d          ← the same
define(`confTO_QUEUERETURN',`5d')   ← V8 m4 technique
```

or it can be tuned on the basis of any of three possible levels of priority that a mail message may have. That is, both of the above set all three levels to five days, whereas the following tunes each level to three, five, and six days, respectively:

---

* Because DNS name resolution can time out and retry and can actually take up to five minutes!

```
O Timeout.queuereturn.urgent=3d
O Timeout.queuereturn.normal=5d
O Timeout.queuereturn.non-urgent=6d
define(`confTO_QUEUERETURN_URGENT', `3d')      ← V8 m4 technique
define(`confTO_QUEUERETURN_NORMAL', `5d')      ← V8 m4 technique
define(`confTO_QUEUERETURN_NONURGENT', `6d')   ← V8 m4 technique
```

The default for the *m4* configuration technique is to bounce all messages that remain in the queue for more than four days.

The keywords **urgent**, **normal**, and **non-urgent** correspond to the **Precedence:** header from the mail message. When the numeric equivalent of the **Precedence:** header as translated from the **P** line of the configuration file (see §35.8) is negative, the message is classified as nonurgent. When it is greater than zero, the message is classified as urgent. Otherwise, it is normal.

In addition to a message's precedence, a new **Priority:** header is available (see §35.10.24) to specify the message priority and thereby bypass the value obtained from the **Precedence:** header.

```
Priority: urgent
Priority: normal
Priority: non-urgent
```

There is currently no way to specify a **Priority:** header's value from the *sendmail* command line.

34.8.70.15 *Timeout.queuewarn*

When a message is queued, *sendmail* sends a message to the sender explaining that the original message could not be delivered right away and that *sendmail* will keep trying. Beginning with V8.7, this **queuewarn** keyword is used to set the amount of time a message must wait in the queue before that explanation is mailed. Either it can be expressed as an interval of time:

```
O Timeout.queuewarn=4d
O Timeout.queuewarn.*=4d                ← the same
define(`confTO_QUEUEWARN', `4d')        ← V8 m4 technique
```

or it can be tuned on the basis of any of three possible levels of priority a mail message may have. That is, both of the above set all three levels to four days, whereas the following tunes each level to one, two, and four days, respectively:

```
O Timeout.queuewarn.urgent=1d
O Timeout.queuewarn.normal=2d
O Timeout.queuewarn.non-urgent=4d
define(`confTO_QUEUEWARN_URGENT', `1d')      ← V8 m4 technique
define(`confTO_QUEUEWARN_NORMAL', `2d')      ← V8 m4 technique
define(`confTO_QUEUEWARN_NONURGENT', `4d')   ← V8 m4 technique
```

The defaults for the *m4* configuration technique are to send a warning for normal mail after four hours, for urgent mail after one hour, and for nonurgent mail after twelve hours.

The keywords **urgent**, **normal**, and **non-urgent** correspond to the **Precedence:** header from the mail message. When the numeric equivalent of the **Precedence:** header as translated from the P line of the configuration file (see §35.8) is negative, the message is classified as nonurgent. When it is greater than zero, the message is classified as urgent. Otherwise, it is normal.

In addition to a message's precedence, a new **Priority:** header is available (see §35.10.24) to specify the message priority and thereby bypass the value obtained from the **Precedence:** header:

```
Priority: urgent
Priority: normal
Priority: non-urgent
```

There is currently no way to specify a **Priority:** header's value from the *send-mail* command line.

34.8.70.16 Timeout.quit

When the local *sendmail* is finished and wishes to break the connection, it sends the SMTP QUIT command.

```
QUIT
```

The other side acknowledges, and the connection is terminated:

```
221 there.dc.gov delivering mail
```

The time the local *sendmail* waits for acknowledgment of the QUIT command is defined with the **quit** keyword. The default is two minutes, and no minimum is specified. The *m4* technique should use **confTO_QUIT**, for which there is no default.

34.8.70.17 Timeout.rcpt

Next, the local *sendmail* issues one RCPT command to specify each envelope recipient. One such RCPT line might look like this:

```
RCPT To:<them@there.dc.gov>
```

The local *sendmail* then waits for acknowledgment, which looks like this:

```
250 <them@there.dc.gov>... Recipient ok
```

The amount of time that the local *sendmail* waits for acknowledgment of each RCPT command is set with the `rcpt` keyword. The default value is one hour,[*] and the specified minimum is five minutes. The *m4* technique should use `confTO_RCPT`, for which there is no default.

34.8.70.18 *Timeout.rset*

If connection caching is enabled (see option k), the local *sendmail* sends an SMTP RSET command to reset the other side. The time the local *sendmail* waits for acknowledgment of the RSET command is defined with the `rset` keyword. The default is five minutes, and no minimum is specified. The *m4* technique should use `confTO_RSET`, for which there is no default.

TryNullMXList (w)   *(V8.1 and above)*

34.8.71   *Use A if no best MX record*

RFC974 says that when mail is being sent from a host that is an MX record for the receiving host, all MX records of a preference equal to or greater than the sending host must be discarded. In some circumstances this can leave no usable MX records. In this absence, V8 *sendmail* bases its action on the setting of its `TryNullMXList` (w) option.

The forms of the `TryNullMXList` (w) option are as follows:

```
Owbool                                  ← configuration file (V8.6)
-owbool                                 ← command line (V8.6)
O TryNullMXList=bool                    ← configuration file (beginning with V8.7)
-OTryNullMXList=bool                    ← command line (beginning with V8.7)
define(`confTRY_NULL_MX_LIST',bool)     ← V8 m4 configuration
```

The `bool` is of type Boolean. If it is false, *sendmail* bounces the mail message with the following error message:

```
MX list for otherhost points back to thishost
```

If it is true, *sendmail* looks to see whether the receiving host has an A record. If it does, V8 *sendmail* tries to deliver the mail message directly to that host's A record address. If the host doesn't have an A record, *sendmail* bounces the message. See §21.3.7 in Chapter 21, *DNS and sendmail*, for a full discussion of why one setting may be preferable over the other. The default with the V8 *m4* configuration technique is false.

The `TryNullMXList` (w) option is not safe as of V8.8.4. If it is specified from the command line, may cause *sendmail* to relinquish its *root* privilege.

---

[*] This timeout should be generously long because a recipient may be the name of a mailing list and the other side may take a long time to expand all the names in that list before replying.

UnixFromLine *or* $1 *(All versions)*

34.8.72 *Define the From format*

The `UnixFromLine` option replaces the pre-V8.7 `$1` macro. It has two functions:

- It defines the look of the five character "`From `" header line needed by UUCP software.

- It defines the format of the line that is used to separate one message from another in a file of many mail messages.

The forms of the `UnixFromLine` option and `$1` macro are as follows:

```
D1format                       ← configuration file (V8.6 and earlier)
O UnixFromLine=format          ← configuration file (beginning with V8.7)
-OUnixFromLine=format          ← command line (beginning with V8.7)
define(`confFROM_LINE',`format')  ← V8 m4 configuration
```

The *format* is of type string. Under versions V8.6 and earlier there was no default for *format*. So the `$1` macro always had to be defined. Beginning with V8.7, *sendmail* first checks to see if the `UnixFromLine` option was defined and uses that value if it was. Otherwise, it checks to see whether the level of the configuration file is 6 or less. If it is and if the `$1` macro was defined, it uses that value. Otherwise, it uses the default

```
From $g  $d
```

The `UnixFromLine` option is not safe. If specified from the command line, it may cause *sendmail* to relinquish its *root* privilege.

34.8.72.1 UnixFromLine in UUCP software

UUCP software requires all messages to begin with a header line that looks like

```
From sender  date remote from <host>
```

The *sendmail* program prepends such a line to a mail message's headers if the `F=U` flag (see §30.8.42) is set for the delivery agent.[*] Prior to V8.7, if the local machine supports UUCP, the 1 macro must be supplied with "`From `", *sender*, and *date*:

```
D1From $g $d
```

The rest of the information is supplied by *sendmail*.

---

[*] Prior to V8.7 this behavior was supported only if UGLYUUCP was defined in *conf.h* when *sendmail* was compiled.

34.8.72.2 *UnixFromLine with mail files*

Under UNIX, in a file of many mail messages such as a user's mailbox, lines that begin with the five characters "`From `" are used to separate one message from another. This is a convention that is not shared by all MUAs. The *sendmail* program appends mail messages to files under only two circumstances: when saving failed mail to the user's *dead-letter* file and when delivering to a local address that begins with the / character. In appending messages to files, it uses the `UnixFrom-Line` ($l) option to define the form of the message separator lines.

For sites that use the Rand MUA (and that do not also use UUCP) the `UnixFrom-Line` ($l) option can be defined to be four CTRL-A characters:

```
Dl^A^A^A^A
O UnixFromLine=^A^A^A^A
```

UnsafeGroupWrites   *(V8.8 and above)*

34.8.73   *Check unsafe group permissions*

In processing a ˜/.*forward* file or a *:include:* file, a question arises when group or world write permission is enabled. Should *sendmail* trust the addresses found in such files? Clearly the answer is "no" when world write permission is enabled. But what of group write permission?

Beginning with V8.8 *sendmail*, the decision of whether or not to trust group write permission is left to the `UnsafeGroupWrites` option:

```
O UnsafeGroupWrites=bool                ← configuration file (beginning with V8.8)
-OUnsafeGroupWrites=bool                ← command line (beginning with V8.8)
define(`confUNSAFE_GROUP_WRITES',bool)  ← V8 m4 configuration
```

The optional argument *bool*, when missing, defaults to true (check for unsafe group write permission). If this option is entirely missing, it defaults to false (don't check for unsafe group write permission).

With this option set to true, a ˜/.*forward* file or a *:include:* file with group or world writability will result in one of these four errors being logged:

```
filename: group writable forward file, marked unsafe
filename: world writable forward file, marked unsafe
filename: group writable include file, marked unsafe
filename: world writable include file, marked unsafe
```

Any address in the file that is a file or a program will result in a bounce and this message:

```
Address address is unsafe for mailing to programs
Address address is unsafe for mailing to files
```

The UnsafeGroupWrites option is not safe. If specified from the command line, it may cause *sendmail* to relinquish its *root* privilege.

UseErrorsTo (l)   *(V8.1 and above)*

34.8.74   *Use Errors-To: for errors*

Ordinarily, V8 *sendmail* sends notification of failed mail to the envelope sender. It specifically does not send notification to the addresses listed in the Errors-To: header. It does this because the Errors-To: header violates RFC1123. For additional information about the Errors-To: header, see §35.10.13.

The UseErrorsTo (l) option is available to prevent older versions of software from failing. When set, it allows error notification to be sent to the address listed in the Errors-To: header in addition to that sent to the envelope sender.

The forms of the UseErrorsTo (l) option are as follows:

```
Olbool                                ← configuration file (old form)
-olbool                               ← command line (old form)
O UseErrorsTo=bool                    ← configuration file (beginning with V8.7)
-OUseErrorsTo=bool                    ← command line (beginning with V8.7)
define(`confUSE_ERRORS_TO',bool)      ← V8 m4 configuration
```

The optional argument *bool*, when missing, defaults to true (errors are sent to the Errors-To: header). If this option is entirely missing, it defaults to false (the Errors-To: header is ignored).

The UseErrorsTo (l) option is safe. Even if it is specified from the command line, *sendmail* retains its *root* privilege.

UserDatabaseSpec (U)   *(V8.1 and above)*

34.8.75   *Specify user database*

V8 *sendmail*, if compiled with USERDB defined (see §18.8.54), can use a special, internally understood database called the User Database. Addresses that are defined in the User Database can be looked up and modified after aliasing and before processing of the user's `~/.forward` file.

The workings of this database are described in §33.5. The UserDatabaseSpec (U) option defines the name and location of the file containing this User Database information.

The forms of the UserDatabaseSpec (U) option are as follows:

```
OUpath,...                            ← configuration file (V8.6)
-oUpath,...                           ← command line (V8.6)
O UserDatabaseSpec=path,...           ← configuration file (V8.7)
```

```
-OUserDatabaseSpec=path,...              ← command line (V8.7)
define(`confUSERDB_SPEC',`path,...')     ← V8 m4 configuration
```

The argument *path, . . .* is of type string and is a comma- or space-separated list of elements. Those elements can be database pathnames or other information as described below. If *path, . . .* is missing or if the entire option is missing, the user database is not used. Otherwise, the user database is used, and each database is accessed in turn, leftmost to rightmost, in the list of paths. There is no default for the V8 *m4* technique.

The elements of *path, . . .* can either be pathnames of files or other methods of lookup depending on the first character of each:

/   A lead slash causes the element to be interpreted as a pathname; for example, */etc/userdb*.

@   A leading @ causes a copy of the message for each user to be forwarded to a specified host. The assumption is that the other host is in a better position to perform user database lookups. Such a declaration looks like *@dbhost.our.domain*. Note that this form of declaration must be last in the list that constitutes *path, . . .* because it always succeeds.

h   Beginning with V8.7, a leading h or H causes *sendmail* to perform a case-insensitive comparison of the *path* to the string "hesiod." If they match, user database inquiries are looked up via Hesiod services.

For example, the following declares two user databases. The first that is used up will be */etc/userdb*. If the entry is not found in that database, it will be forwarded to the host *mail.here.us* for handling there:

```
O UserDatabaseSpec=/etc/userdb,@mail.here.us
```

Any leading character other than those shown above causes an error message to be printed and that particular *path, . . .* element to be ignored.

```
Unknown UDB spec badpath
```

Note that future releases of *sendmail* may include additional subfields for each *path*. These will look like :opt=value. Consequently, the *path* that you specify should not include the colon character.

If UDB_DEFAULT_SPEC is defined in *Makefile* when *sendmail* is compiled (see §18.8.53), that value becomes the default if the UserDatabaseSpec (U) option is missing. If UDB_DEFAULT_SPEC is undefined, the default becomes NULL and no User Database lookups are performed.

The UserDatabaseSpec (U) option is not safe. If specified from the command line, it may cause *sendmail* to relinquish its *root* privilege.

Verbose

(*v*)

34.8.76 *Run in verbose mode*

The *sendmail* program offers a verbose mode of operation. In this "blow-by-blow" mode a description of all the *sendmail* program's actions is printed to the standard output. This mode is valuable in running *sendmail* interactively but useless in running in daemon mode. Consequently, you should never set this option in the *sendmail.cf* file. Instead, you should set it from the command line using the −v command-line switch.

After the *sendmail.cf* file is parsed and the command-line arguments have been processed, *sendmail* checks to see whether it is in verbose mode. If it is, it sets the HoldExpensive (c) option (don't connect to expensive mailers; see §34.8.29) to false and sets the DeliveryMode (d) option (see §34.8.16) to interactive.

The forms of the Verbose (v) option are as follows:

```
Ovbool              ← configuration file (old form)
-ovbool             ← command line (old form)
-v                  ← command-line shorthand
O Verbose=bool      ← configuration file (beginning with V8.7)
-OVerbose=bool      ← command line (beginning with V8.7)
```

The argument *bool* is of type Boolean. If it is missing, the default value is true (be verbose). If the entire option is missing, the default value is false (be quiet).

The Verbose (v) option is safe. When it is specified from the command line, *sendmail* retains its *root* privilege. Note that the Verbose (v) option should *never* be set in the configuration file.

(M)

(*Obsolete as of V8.7*)

34.8.77 *Define a macro*

The M option is used to set or change a defined macro's value. Although this option is allowed in the *sendmail.cf* file, it is exclusively intended for use from the command line. Macros that are defined in the command line *will not* override the values of those same macros defined in the configuration file.

The forms of the M option are as follows:

```
OMXvalue      ← configuration file
-oMXvalue     ← command line (old obsolete form)
-MXvalue      ← command line (beginning with V8.7)
DXvalue       ← both are equivalent of this in the configuration and m4 files
```

In all four cases the argument *value* is of type string. The *value* is assigned to the macro named X. Pre-V8.7 macro names are always a single character. Multicharacter macro names that are available with V8.7 are described in Chapter 31, *Defined Macros.*

One example of the usefulness of this option concerns the *rmail*(8) program. Suppose a machine is used for networked mail. Ordinarily, the r macro is given the value "smtp" to signify that mail is received over the network. But for UUCP mail the r macro should be given the value "UUCP." One way to effect such a change is to arrange for *rmail*(8) to invoke *sendmail* with a command-line argument of

```
-oMrUUCP
```

In this command line, the −o switch tells *sendmail* to define a macro (the M) whose name is r to have the text UUCP as its new value.* This new value overrides whatever value r may have been given in the configuration file. The M option should be approached with caution. If you later upgrade your *sendmail* program and install a new configuration file, you may find that the names of macros aren't what you expect. Previous command-line assumptions about macro names may suddenly break.

The M option is safe only in assigning values to the r and s macros. For all other macros it is unsafe and, if specified from the command line, may cause *sendmail* to relinquish its *root* privilege. Pre-V8 SunOS *sendmail* was an exception in that it considered this option safe for all macros. Note that the M option should *never* be used in the configuration file.

---

* Under V8 *sendmail* the $s and $r macros should be assigned values with −p command-line switch (see §36.7.32 in Chapter 36, *The Command Line*). Also note that −oM has been deprecated in favor of the new −M switch.

35

Headers

All mail messages are composed of two distinct parts: the header (containing information such as who the message is from) and the body (the actual text of the message). The two parts are separated from each other by a single blank line (although there are exceptions, which we will cover). The header part used by *sendmail* is mainly defined by RFC822 with some minor clarification contained in RFC1123. These two documents detail the required syntax and contents of most header lines in mail messages. Many other RFCs define other headers, but in this chapter we will discuss header lines as they relate specifically to *sendmail*, referencing other RFCs as necessary.

When *sendmail* receives a mail message, it gathers all the header lines from that message and saves them internally. Then, during queueing and delivery, it recreates them and augments them with any new ones that may be required either by the configuration file or by *sendmail*'s internal logic.

35.1 The H Configuration Command

The H header configuration file command tells *sendmail* which headers are required for inclusion in the header portion of mail messages. Some headers, such as Date:, are added only if one is not already present. Others, such as Received: (see §35.10.25) are added even if one or more are already present.

The form for the header command is:

```
H?flags?name:field
```

The H must begin the line. The optional ?*flags*? (the question marks are literal), if present, must immediately follow the H with no intervening space. We will discuss header ?*flags*? after the *name* and *field* are explained.

The *name* is the name of the header, such as **From**. The *name* must immediately follow the ?*flags*?, if present, or the H if there are no flags.

A colon then follows, which may be surrounded by optional space characters. The *field* is last and constitutes everything from the first nonspace character following the colon to the end of the line:

```
Hname    :    field
              ↑
         from here to end of line is the field
```

The colon must be present. If it is absent, *sendmail* prints the following error message and ignores that H command:

```
header syntax error, line "offending H command here"
```

The "*offending H command here*" is the full text of the H command in the configuration file that caused the error.

As with all configuration commands, a line that begins with a space or a tab is joined to the line above. In this way, header commands can be split over one or more lines:

```
HReceived: $?sfrom $s $.by $j ($v/$V)
        id $i; $b
    ↑
    tab
```

When these two lines are read from the configuration file by *sendmail,* they are internally joined to form the single line:

```
HReceived: $?sfrom $s $.by $j ($v/$V)\n        id $i; $b
                                      ↑
                                     tab
```

The \n above illustrates that when lines are joined, the newline and tab character are retained. This results in the header looking the same as it did in the configuration file (minus the leading H) when it is later emitted by *sendmail.*

35.2 Header Names

The *name* portion of the H configuration command must be one of the names shown below. Other names do not produce an error but may confuse other programs that need to process those illegal names. Names marked with an asterisk are defined by RFC822.

apparently-to	full-name	reply-to*	return-receipt-to
bcc*	in-reply-to*	resent-bcc*	sender*
cc*	keywords*	resent-cc*	subject*
comments*	mail-from	resent-date*	text*
content-length	message*	resent-from*	to*
content-type	message-id*	resent-message-id*	via
date*	posted-date	resent-reply-to*	x400-received
encrypted*	precedence	resent-sender*	
errors-to	received*	resent-to*	
from*	references*	return-path*	

These are discussed individually in §35.10 at the end of this chapter.

The RFC822 standard allows a special form to be used for creating custom header names. All mail programs, including *sendmail*, are required to accept and pass through as is any header name that begins with the special characters **x-**. The following header definition, for example, can be used to introduce information that your site is running an experimental version of *sendmail*:

```
HX-Beware: This message used an experimental version of sendmail
```

The *name* part of header definitions is case-insensitive. That is, **X-Beware**, **x-beware**, and **X-BEWARE** are all the same. For example, when *sendmail* checks for the **To:** header internally, it will recognize it no matter how it is capitalized.

Beginning with V8 *sendmail*, header names are left alone. They are passed through without case conversion of any kind. Previous assumptions[*] about capitalization are no longer valid in light of new headers generated and expected by programs.

Header names may contain only printable characters. Names may not contain control characters, space characters (such as space and tab), or the colon character. An illegal character will result in this error message:

```
header syntax error, line "HFull Name: $x"
```

Here, the error is a space in the name portion of the header declaration.

---

[*] Prior to V8 *sendmail*, all headers were converted to lowercase and stored. Later, when mail was sent, they were then capitalized in a way similar to that of proper names, in which the first letter of each word was capitalized.

35.3 *Header Field Contents*

The *field* of the H configuration command may contain any ASCII characters, including whitespace and newlines that result from joining. For most headers, however, those characters must obey the following rules for grouping:[*]

Atom

In the header *field*, space characters separate one item from another. Each space-delimited item is further subdivided by specials (see below), into atoms.

```
smtp            ← an atom
foo@host        ← atom special atom
Babe Ruth       ← atom atom
```

An atom is the smallest unit in a header and may not contain any control characters. When the *field* is an address, an atom is the same thing as a token (see Chapter 28, *Rules*).

Specials

The special characters are those used to separate one component of an address from another. They are internally defined as:

```
( ) < > @ , ; : \ " . [ ]
```

A special character can be made nonspecial by preceding it with a backslash character, for example,

```
foo;fum         ← atom special atom
foo\;fum        ← one atom
```

The space and tab characters are also used to separate atoms and can be thought of as specials.

Quoted text

Quotation marks can be used to force multiple items to be treated as a single atom. For example,

```
Babe Ruth       ← atom atom
"Babe Ruth"     ← a single atom
```

Quoted text may contain any characters except the quotation mark (") and the backslash character (\).

Any text

Some headers, such as **Subject:** (see §35.10.31), impose no rules on the text in the header *field*. For such headers, atoms, specials, and quotes have no significance, and the entire field is taken as arbitrary text.

---

[*] This discussion is adapted from RFC822.

The detailed requirements of each header name are covered at the end of this chapter.

35.3.1 *Macros in the Header Field*

Macros may appear in any position in the `field` of a header definition line. Such macros are not expanded (their values tested or used) until mail is queued or delivered. For the meaning of each macro name and a description of when each is given a value, see Chapter 31, *Defined Macros*.

Only two macro prefixes may be used in the `field` of header definitions:

$ The $ prefix tells *sendmail* to replace the macro's name with its value at that place in the `field` definition.

$?   The $? prefix tells *sendmail* to perform conditional replacement of a macro's value.

For example, the following header definition uses the $ prefix to insert the value of the macro **x** into the header field:

```
HFull-Name: $x
```

The macro $x (see §31.10.42) contains as its value the full name of the sender.

When the possibility exists that a macro will not have a value at the time the header line is processed, the $? conditional prefix (see §31.6) may be used:

```
HReceived: $?sfrom $s $.by $j ($v/$V)
```

Here, the $? prefix and $. operator cause the text

```
from $s
```

to be inserted into the header field *only* if the macro **s** has a value. $s may contain as its value the name of the sending site.

35.3.2 *Escape Character in the Header Field*

Recall that the backslash escape character (\) is used to deprive the special characters of their special meaning. In the `field` of header definitions the escape character may be used only inside quoted strings (see next item), in domain literals (addresses enclosed in square bracket pairs), or in comments (see below). Specifically, this means that the escape character may *not* be used within atoms. Therefore the following is not legal:

```
Full\ Name@domain          ← not legal
```

Instead, the atom to the left of the @ must be isolated with quotation marks:

```
"Full Name"@domain        ← legal
```

35.3.3 Quoted Strings in the Header Field

Recall that quotation marks (") force arbitrary text to be viewed as a single atom. Arbitrary text is everything (including joined lines) that begins with the first quotation mark and ends with the final quotation mark. The following example illustrates two quoted strings:

```
"Full Name"
"One long string carried over
        two lines by indenting the second"
    ↑
    whitespace
```

The quotation mark character may appear inside a quoted string only if it is escaped by using a backslash.*

```
"George Herman \"Babe\" Ruth"
```

Internally, *sendmail* does not check for balanced quotation marks. If it finds the first but not the second, it takes everything up to the end of the line as the quoted string.

When quotation marks are used in an H configuration command, they must be balanced. Although *sendmail* remains silent, unbalanced quotation marks can cause serious problems when they are propagated to other programs.

35.3.4 Comments in the Header Field

Comments consist of text inside a header *field* that is intended to give humans additional information. Comments are saved internally by *sendmail* when processing headers, then are restored, but otherwise are not used. Beginning with V8.7 *sendmail*, the F=c delivery agent flag (see §30.8.14) can be used to prevent restoration of the saved comments.

A comment begins with a left parenthesis and ends with a right parenthesis. Comments may nest. The following lines illustrate a non-nested comment and a comment nested inside another:

```
(this is a comment)
(text(this is a comment nested inside another)text)
```

---

* Note that the backslash itself may not appear within full quotation marks.

Comments may be split over multiple lines by indenting:

```
(this is a comment
      split into two lines)
   ↑
   whitespace
```

A comment (even if nested) separates one atom from another just like a space or a tab does. Therefore the following produces two atoms rather than one:

```
Bill(postmaster)Johnson
```

However, comments inside quoted strings are not special, so the following produces a single atom:

```
"Bill(postmaster)Johnson"
```

Parentheses may exist inside of comments only if they are escaped with a backslash:

```
<root@host.domain> (The happy administrator ;-\))
                                             ↑
                                             note
```

35.3.4.1 *Balancing special characters*

Many of the special characters that are used in the header `field` and in addresses need to appear in balanced pairs. Table 35-1 shows these characters and the characters needed to balance them. Failure to maintain balance can lead to failed mail. Note that only parentheses may be nested. None of the other balanced pairs may nest.

Table 35–1: Balancing Characters

Begin	End
"	"
(	)
[	]
<	>

You have already seen the quoted string and comments. The angle brackets (< and >) are used to specify a machine-readable address, such as <gw@wash.dc.gov>. The square brackets ([and]) are used to specify a direct Internet address (one that bypasses normal DNS name lookups) such as [123.45.67.89].

The *sendmail* program gives warnings about unbalanced characters only when it is attempting to extract an address from a header definition, from the header line of a mail message, or from the envelope. Beginning with V8.6, when *sendmail* finds an unbalanced condition, it tries to balance the offending characters as rationally as possible. Whether or not it can balance them, it prints one of the following warning messages:

```
Unbalanced ')'
Unbalanced '>'
Unbalanced '('
Unbalanced '<'
Unbalanced '"'
```

If it did not succeed in balancing them, the mail will probably bounce.

35.4 *?flags? in Header Definitions*

The *name* part of the H configuration command can be prefixed with a list of flags. This list, if present, must be surrounded by ? characters:

```
H?flags?name:field
```

The ? characters must immediately follow the H and immediately precede the *name* with no intervening spaces. If a space precedes the first ?, that ? is misinterpreted as part of the header *name*, rather than as the start of a list of flags, and this error message is printed:

```
header syntax error, line " ?flags?name: field"
                            ↑
                      note leading space
```

If the first ? is present but the second is absent, *sendmail* prints the same error message and skips that H configuration command. The flags that are listed between the ? characters correspond to flags that are listed with delivery agent F= equates. When processing a mail message for forwarding or delivery, *sendmail* adds a header line if a flag is common to both the H definition list of flags and the delivery agent's list of flags. For example,

```
H?P?Return-Path: <$g>
```

The above H definition begins with a P flag. This tells *sendmail* to add this header line to the mail message only if a selected delivery agent also contains that flag. Since the **Return-Path:** header (see §35.10.28) should be added only during final delivery, the P flag appears only in the **prog** and **local** delivery agent definitions:

```
Mprog,  P=/bin/sh,   F=lsDFMeuP,  S=10, R=20, A=sh -c $u
Mlocal, P=/bin/mail, F=rlsDFMmnP, S=10, R=20, A=mail -d $u
                                ↑
                              note
```

No check is made to ensure that the H flags correspond to existing delivery agent flags. Beware that if a corresponding F= flag does not exist in some delivery agent definition, that header may never be added to any mail message.

Care should be used to avoid selecting flags that have other meanings for delivery agents. Table 30-8 in §30.8 lists all the delivery agent flags that have predefined meanings, including those traditionally used with header definitions.

35.5 Header Behavior in conf.c

The *sendmail* program has a built-in understanding of many header names. How those names are used is determined by a set of flags in the source file *conf.c* supplied with the source distribution. Site policy determines which flags are applied to which headers, but, in general, *conf.c* applies them in the way that is best suited for almost all Internet sites. If you desire to redefine the flags for a particular header name, look for the name's declaration in the C language structure definition HdrInfo in *conf.c*. Be sure to read the comments in that file. Changes to header flags represent a permanent site policy change and should not be undertaken lightly. (We illustrate this process after explaining the flags.)

The flags that determine header use are listed in Table 35-2. Note that each flag name is prefixed with an H_. Also note that the hexadecimal values are displayed by the -d31.6 debugging switch (see §37.5.114).

Table 35-2: Header Flags in conf.c

Flag	Hex	§	Version	Description
H_EOH	0x0001	35.5.1	V5 and up	Terminates all headers
H_RCPT	0x0002	35.5.2	V5 and up	Contains a recipient address
H_DEFAULT	0x0004	35.5.3	V5 and up	If already in headers, don't insert
H_RESENT	0x0008	35.5.4	V5 and up	Is a Resent- header
H_CHECK	0x0010	35.5.5	V5 and up	Process ?*flags*?
H_ACHECK	0x0020	35.5.6	V5 and up	Ditto, but always, not just default
H_FORCE	0x0040	35.5.7	V5 and up	Insert header (allows duplicates)
H_TRACE	0x0080	35.5.8	V5 and up	Count these to get the hop count
H_FROM	0x0100	35.5.9	V5 and up	Contains a sender address
H_VALID	0x0200	35.5.10	V5 and up	Has a validated field value
H_ERRSTO	0x0800	35.5.11	V8.6 and up	An errors-to: header
H_CTE	0x1000	35.5.12	V8.7 and up	Is "constant transfer encoding"
H_CTYPE	0x2000	35.5.13	V8.7 and up	Is "content type"
H_BCC	0x4000	35.5.14	V8.7 and up	Strip value from header
H_ENCODABLE	0x8000	35.5.15	V8.8 and up	Field can be RFC1522 encoded

Note that there is no flag that always causes a particular header to be removed, nor is there a flag that always causes a particular header to be replaced (although you can trick *sendmail* with H_ACHECK see §35.5.16).

35.5.1 H_EOH

Headers that are marked with the H_EOH flag cause *sendmail* to immediately stop all header processing and treat the rest of the header lines as message body. This is useful for separating RFC822-compliant header lines from headers created by a noncompliant network.

35.5.2 H_RCPT

Headers that are marked with the H_RCPT flag are assumed to contain valid recipient addresses in their fields. Only headers with this flag can lead to message delivery. These addresses will be rewritten. These headers are used to determine the recipient address only if the -t command-line switch (see §36.7.38) is used.

35.5.3 H_DEFAULT

The *sendmail* program automatically sets the H_DEFAULT flag for all headers declared in the configuration file. This flag tells *sendmail* to macro expand the header just before it is used. Only one of each header that is marked with this flag is allowed to exist in the headers portion of a mail message. If such a header already exists, *sendmail* does not add another. The H_FORCE and H_TRACE flags override this flag in that regard. This flag must never be specified in *conf.c*—it is set automatically by H configuration command (see §35.1).

35.5.4 H_RESENT

The H_RESENT flag tells *sendmail* that the header line is prefixed with the **resent-** string. Only headers that are marked with this flag can tell *sendmail* that this is a "forwarded" message. If no "forwarded" headers are found, *sendmail* strips any bogus **resent-** header lines from the message's header.

35.5.5 H_CHECK

If a header definition in the configuration file begins with a ?*flags*? conditional, this flag is set for that header. It tells *sendmail* to insert this header only if one of its ?*flags*? corresponds to one of the delivery agent's F= flags (see §35.4). This flag must never be specified in *conf.c*—it is set automatically when *sendmail* reads H lines with ?*flags*? header flags.

35.5.6 H_ACHECK

The H_ACHECK flag marks a header that should normally be discarded unless a delivery agent's F= flag calls for its inclusion. It is usually set for the **Bcc:** header, which is discarded for the privacy of a blind carbon copy list, and the **Full-Name:**

header, which is intended as a way for a user to add a full name (see the $x macro, §31.10.42) when there is no full name defined in the *passwd*(5) file. Note that H_ACHECK, when combined with bogus *?flags?* of a header configuration file declaration can cause appropriate headers to always be deleted or replaced (see §35.5.16). Also note that under V8 *sendmail* the H_ACHECK flag alone always causes a header to be replaced.

35.5.7 H_FORCE

The H_FORCE flag causes *sendmail* to always insert a header. It is used in the *conf.c* file with selected trace headers. It can be thought of as allowing duplicates. That is, the header will be inserted even if one like it is already present.

35.5.8 H_TRACE

Headers that are marked with the H_TRACE flag are counted in determining a mail message's "hop" count. This flag is intended for use in the *conf.c* file.

35.5.9 H_FROM

Headers that are marked with the H_FROM flag are assumed to contain a valid sender address. This flag is intended for use in the *conf.c* file.

35.5.10 H_VALID

The H_VALID flag is set and cleared internally by *sendmail* to indicate to itself that a particular header line has been correctly processed and can now be used as is. This flag should never be used in the *conf.c* file.

35.5.11 H_ERRSTO

The H_ERRSTO flag specifies which headers can be used for returning error notification mail. Those headers take priority over all others for that notification if the UseErrorsTo (1) option is true (see §34.8.74).

35.5.12 H_CTE

The H_CTE flag specifies that a header is the MIME RFC1521 content transfer encoding header (see §35.10.8).

35.5.13 H_CTYPE

The H_CTYPE flag specifies that a header is a MIME RFC1521 content-type header (see §35.10.9).

35.5.14 H_BCC

The H_BCC flag indicates that a header is either a Bcc: (see §35.10.4) or a Resent-Bcc: header. The disposition of those headers is covered under the NoRecipient-Action option (see §34.8.43).

35.5.15 H_ENCODABLE

The H_ENCODABLE flag tells *sendmail* that the field part may be encoded in the way described in RFC1522. As of V8.8, this flag is unsupported in code.

35.5.16 Replacing Headers with H_ACHECK

Some MUAs tend to insert their own Message-ID: header (see §35.10.19). This can cause difficulty tracing email problems, because those MUA headers lack the *sendmail* queue identifier. One solution is possible at sites that have a central mail hub machine. At such a site, all the client machines use a simple configuration file that forwards all mail to the hub for processing.

To delete the bogus Message-ID:, so that a good one will be generated on the hub, you can redefine Message-ID: in *conf.c*:

```
"message-id",           0,
"message-id",           H_ACHECK,        ← change to this
```

Here, we changed the 0 flag for the Message-ID: header into a H_ACHECK flag. We do this only on the client machine versions of *sendmail* but *not* on the hub. The Message-ID: header will then be stripped from every outgoing message on every client machine and created (if missing) on the hub.

35.6 Headers by Category

The *sendmail* program contains an internal list of header *names* that are organized conceptually into categories. The names and categories are defined in *conf.c* (see §35.5). Each category is defined by one or more H_ flags in that file, the names of which are listed under the **Flags** column of all the tables that follow.

35.6.1 Recommended Headers

Every *sendmail.cf* file should have a minimal complement of header definitions. Below we present a recommendation. Don't use this as is. The details are not generic to all versions of *sendmail*, nor are they appropriate for all sites.

```
H?P?Return-Path: $g
HReceived: $?sfrom $s $.by $j ($v/$V) id $i; $b      ← mandatory
H?D?Date: $a                                         ← mandatory
H?F?From: $q                                         ← mandatory
H?x?Full-Name: $x
H?M?Message-Id: <$t.$i@$j>                            ← mandatory
H?D?Resent-Date: $a                                  ← mandatory
H?F?Resent-From: $q                                  ← mandatory
H?M?Resent-Message-Id: <$t.$i@$j>                    ← mandatory
```

Each of these is described individually at the end of this chapter. Except for Received: (see §35.10.25), none is added to any mail message that already has that particular header present.

The Return-Path: header (see §35.10.28) is added only if it is not already present and if the delivery agent for the recipient has the F=P flag present. Similarly, the Date: relies on F=D, the From: relies on F=F, the Full-Name: relies on F=x, and the Message=Id: relies on F=M.

Of those shown, only the seven indicated are truly mandatory and must be declared in *every* configuration file. The others are highly recommended.

35.6.2 Sender Headers

Certain header names are assumed by *sendmail* to contain information about the various possible senders of a mail message. They are listed in Table 35-3 in descending order of significance. Addresses with the H_FROM flag (see §35.5.9) are rewritten as sender addresses.

Table 35-3: Sender Headers (Most to Least Significant)

Header	§	Flags	Defined by
Resent-Sender:	35.7	H_FROM, H_RESENT	RFC822
Resent-From:	35.10.14	H_FROM, H_RESENT	RFC822
Resent-Reply-To:	35.7	H_FROM, H_RESENT	RFC822
Sender:	35.10.30	H_FROM	RFC822
From:	35.10.14	H_FROM	RFC822
Apparently-From:	35.10.1	n/a	Smail 3.0
Reply-To:	35.10.27	H_FROM	RFC822
Full-Name:	35.10.15	H_ACHECK	obsolete

Table 35–3: Sender Headers (Most to Least Significant) (continued)

Header	§	Flags	Defined by
Return-Receipt-To:	35.10.29	H_FROM	obsolete
Errors-To:	35.10.13	H_FROM, H_ERRSTO	sendmail

When returning bounced mail, *sendmail* always uses the envelope sender's address. If the special header **Errors-To:** appears in the message, a copy of the bounced mail is also sent to the address in that header. This is hard-coded into all but SunOS and V8 *sendmail*, which use the H_ERRSTO header flag (see §35.5.11) instead. V8 also requires that the **UseErrorsTo** (1) option (see §34.8.74) be set to true for the **Errors-To:** header to be honored.

35.6.3 Recipient Headers

Recipient headers are those from which one or more recipients can be parsed. Addresses in headers with the H_RCPT flag (see §35.5.2) are rewritten as recipient addresses. When they are invoked with the -t command-line switch, *sendmail* gathers a list of recipients from all the headers marked with an H_RCPT flag and delivers a copy of the message to each.

The list of recipient headers used by *sendmail* is shown in Table 35-4.

Table 35–4: Recipient Headers

Header	§	Flags	Defined by
To:	35.10.33	H_RCPT	RFC822
Resent-To:	35.7	H_RCPT, H_RESENT	RFC822
Cc:	35.10.5	H_RCPT	RFC822
Resent-Cc:	35.7	H_RCPT, H_RESENT	RFC822
Bcc:	35.10.4	H_RCPT, H_ACHECK	RFC822
Resent-Bcc:	35.7	H_RCPT, H_ACHECK, H_RESENT	RFC822
Apparently-To:	35.10.2	H_RCPT	Obsolete

35.6.4 Identification and Control Headers

Some headers serve to uniquely identify a mail message. Others affect the way *sendmail* processes a mail message. The complete list of all such identification and control headers is shown in Table 35-5.

Table 35–5: Identification and Control Headers

Header	§	Flags	Defined by
Message-ID:	35.10.19	n/a	RFC822
Resent-message-Id:	35.7	H_RESENT	RFC822
Message:	35.10.20	H_EOH	Obsolete
Text:	35.10.32	H_EOH	Obsolete
Precedence:	35.8	n/a	All sendmails
Priority:	35.10.24	n/a	V8.7 and above

Note that the **Precedence:** and **Posted-Date:** (below) headers are hard-coded into *sendmail* rather than being declared in *conf.c*.

35.6.5 Date and Trace Headers

Date headers are used to document the date and time that the mail message was sent or forwarded. Trace headers (those with an H_TRACE header flag; see §35.5.8) are used to determine the hop count of a mail message and to document the message's travel from machine to machine. The list date and trace headers is shown in Table 35-6.

Table 35–6: Date and Trace Headers

Header	§	Flags	Defined by
Date:	35.10.10	n/a	RFC822
Posted-Date:	35.10.22	n/a	Obsolete
Resent-Date:	35.7	H_RESENT	RFC822
Received:	35.10.25	H_TRACE, H_FORCE	RFC822
Via:	35.10.34	H_TRACE, H_FORCE	Obsolete
Mail-From:	35.10.18	H_TRACE, H_FORCE	Obsolete
X-Authentication-Warning:	35.10.35	n/a	V8 *sendmail*
X400-Received:	35.10.36	H_TRACE	IDA and V8 only

35.6.6 Other RFC822 Headers

Other headers that you will see in mail messages are defined by the RFC822 standard but are not otherwise internally defined by *sendmail*. A few of them, such as **Return-Path:**, should be declared in the configuration file. The others are usually inserted by MUAs. Table 35-7 lists these other RFC822 headers.

Table 35–7: Other RFC822 Headers

Header	§	Flags	Defined by
Return-Path:	35.10.28	n/a	RFC822
In-Reply-To:	35.10.16	n/a	RFC822
References:	35.10.26	n/a	RFC822
Keywords:	35.10.17	n/a	RFC822
Subject:	35.10.31	n/a	RFC822
Comments:	35.10.6	H_FORCE	RFC822
Encrypted:	35.10.12	n/a	RFC822

35.6.7 MIME Headers

MIME (Multipurpose Internet Mail Extensions) is documented in RFC1521, with additional details in RFC1344, RFC1426, RFC1428, and RFC1437. The *sendmail* program cares about MIME only when bouncing messages and when determining how to convert the message body between 8 and 7 bits. Those MIME headers for which *sendmail* contains special knowledge are shown in Table 35-8.

Table 35–8: MIME Headers

Header	§	Flags	Defined By
MIME-Version:	35.10.21	n/a	RFC1521
Content-Type:	35.10.9	H_CTYPE	RFC1521
Content-Transfer-Encoding:	35.10.8	H_CTE	RFC1521

35.7 Forwarding with Resent-Headers

Some mail-reading programs (MUAs) allow users to forward messages to other users. For example, the *mush*(1) MUA forwards the current message to the user named **fred** with the following command:

```
message 1 of 3> m -f fred
```

Messages can also be forwarded with *dist*(1) from *mh*(1) and from within other MUAs.

When messages are forwarded, header lines that describe the forwarding user must begin with the **Resent-** prefix. When **fred** receives this message, he sees two similar header lines:

```
From: original-sender
Resent-From: forwarding-sender
```

When both the original `From:` and the forwarded `Resent-From:` appear in the same header, the `Resent-` form is always considered the most recent.

The *sendmail* program examines only a few header names to see whether a mail message has been forwarded. Those that it knows are listed in Table 35-9.

Table 35–9: Known Resent-Headers

Resent- form of	Header
Resent-Bcc:	Bcc:
Resent-Cc:	Cc:
Resent-Date:	Date:
Resent-From:	From:
Resent-Message-ID:	Message-ID:
Resent-To:	To:

If *sendmail* finds any header with a name beginning with `Resent-`, it marks that message as one that is being forwarded, preserves all `Resent-` headers, and creates any needed ones.

35.7.1 *Remove and Recreate the From: Header*

Whether the message is forwarded or not, *sendmail* compares the sender envelope address to the address in the `From:` header (or `Resent-From:` if present). If they are the same, *sendmail* deletes the `From:` (or `Resent-From:`). The purpose of this deletion is to add the sender's full name (the `$x` macro; see §31.10.42) to the address. If the envelope and sender addresses are the same, it is safe to delete and regenerate those header lines. If the message is being forwarded, *sendmail* recreates the `Resent-From:` header; otherwise, it recreates the `From:` header (see §37.5.113).

This recreation is useful because some old versions of *mh*(1) added a `From:` header without the full name (`$x`). It is also useful in mail client/server arrangements in which all mail is sent to the server. Because that mail is sent with the TCP delivery agent, no `$x` full name is added. On the server the `From:` is discarded, and there is a second chance to add the `$x`. However, this can happen only if the address in the envelope and the address in the `From:` are identical. Since the address in the envelope is surrounded with angle brackets, so must be the address in the `From:` header. One way to ensure that they are the same is by defining the `From:` header with `$g` in angle brackets, as `<$g>` in the client's configuration file.

35.8 Precedence

The cost of a mail message determines its ability to be sent despite a high machine load and its position in the queue when the queue is processed. Each mail message has a priority and a cost. The initial priority (class) of a mail message is defined by the optional presence of a **Precedence:** header line inside the message with a symbol corresponding to a value defined by **P** configuration command. For example, if your *sendmail.cf* file contained this line:

```
Pspecial-delivery=100
```

and your mail message header contained this line:

```
Precedence: special-delivery
```

then your mail message would begin its life with a class of 100. We'll cover how this is done soon.

After the message's initial class value is set, that value is never changed. As soon as the class is determined, the initial cost is calculated. This cost is the value that is used to determine if a message will be sent despite a high machine load (defined by the **RefuseLA (X)** option, see §34.8.54, and the **QueueLA (x)** option, see §34.8.50) and to determine its order in queue processing. The formula for the initial calculation is the following:

```
cost = nbytes - (class * z) + (recipients * y)
```

Where **nbytes** is the total size in bytes of the message, **recipients** is either the number of recipients in the envelope or (with (**ent**) the number of recipients specified in the **To:**, **Cc:**, and **Bcc:** header lines (after alias expansion), and **z** and **y** are the values of the **ClassFactor (z)** option (see §34.8.8) and the **Recipient-Factor (y)** option (see §34.8.53).

The **Precedence:** header should rarely be declared in the configuration file. Instead, it is added to messages by MUAs and by mailing-list software. If it is declared in the configuration file, it should be prefixed with an appropriate **?***flag***?** (see §35.4) so that it is inserted only for an appropriate delivery agent.

35.8.1 The P Configuration Command

The **P** configuration command must begin a line. This command is composed of four parts:

```
Pstring=value
```

The ***string*** is text, such as **special-delivery**. Everything between the **P** and the **=** (*including* any whitespace) is taken as is for ***string***. The ***value*** is evaluated as a signed integer and may be decimal, octal (with a leading 0), or hexadecimal (with a leading 0x).

Although you may define any *string* you choose, only five have any universal meaning. Those five usually appear in *sendmail.cf* files like this:

```
Pspecial-delivery=100
Pfirst-class=0
Plist=-30
Pjunk=-60
Pbulk=-200
```

You may, of course, define your own precedence strings for internal mail, but they will be ignored (evaluate to 0) by all outside *sendmail* programs.

The classes **junk** and **bulk** are also recognized by many other programs. Newer versions of the *vacation*(1) program, for example, silently skip replying to messages that have a **Precedence:** header line of **junk** or **bulk**.

As a general rule, **special-delivery** is rarely used. Most mail has a class of **first-class**. Mailing lists should always have a class of **list** or **bulk**.

Because your local *sendmail.cf* file is where values are given to these class names, you are free to modify those values locally. The values affect only the delivery at your site.

Old versions of *sendmail* didn't return errors on messages with a negative precedence. V8 *sendmail* does but omits the message body.

35.9 Pitfalls

- Not all MTAs are as RFC822-compliant as *sendmail*. Occasionally, headers appear that were legal under the defunct RFC733. The **In-Reply-To:** header (see §35.10.16), for example, used to be a comma-separated list of addresses under RFC733 and may cause problems. Note also that RFC733 date and time syntax differs from that of RFC822 and RFC1123.

- Prior to V8 *sendmail*, if the *name* part of a header definition was missing (the H was followed by a colon), a header whose name is the character value zero was silently accepted and wrongly propagated.

- Prior to V8 *sendmail*, long header lines in messages (such as To: with many recipients listed) could cause the internal buffer used by *sendmail* to overflow. The size of that buffer was defined in *conf.h* as MAXLINE and was 1024 characters. The IDA version defined it as 2048 characters. V8 *sendmail* dynamically allocates memory and so can handle headers of any size.

- When generating an `Apparently-To:` header, *sendmail* checks for the absence of only the `To:`, `Cc:`, `Bcc:`, and `Apparently-To:` headers. The H_RCPT flag (see §35.5.2) in *conf.c* is ignored. V8.7 *sendmail* will produce an `Apparently-To:` header only if the `NoRecipientAction` option is set to *add-apparently-to*.

- Prior to V8.7 the *sendmail* program's handling of unbalanced special characters could lead to an explosion of error mail. Instead of simply bouncing the offending mail message, it both returned an error message and forwarded the message to the recipient. If the message was being exploded through a series of mailing lists, the error messages continued to increase, possibly drowning the original site with mail.

- Precedence values are stored in integer variables, so care should be exercised on 2 byte integer machines to avoid having priorities wrap unexpectedly.

- Macros are not expanded in the P command. That is, expressions such as `$U` do not have the desired effect. The literal text `$U` is wrongly listed as the name or the value.

35.10 *Alphabetized Reference*

Some header lines need to be declared in the configuration file by using the H command. Others are created internally by *sendmail.* Still others are created by mail MUAs. These differences are described individually with each header-line *name.* The following discussion of header names is in alphabetical order.

Apparently-From: *(Smail)*

35.10.1   The unknown sender

The *Smail 3.x* program (a UUCP-oriented replacement for *sendmail*) produces an `Apparently-From:` header when it is unable to find any of the official sender headers in a mail message. The address that it provides to this nonstandard header is taken from the envelope of the message.

The *sendmail* program, on the other hand, places the envelope sender into a `From:` header in this situation. If there is no envelope sender and if the sender was not specified in the command line, *sendmail* sets the sender to be postmaster.

The `Apparently-From:` header is mentioned here only because it may appear in messages received at sites that run *sendmail.* It shouldn't cause problems, because a good sender address still appears in the SMTP envelope.

The `Apparently-From:` header should never be declared in the configuration file and should not be added to *conf.c.*

Apparently-To: *(sendmail)*

35.10.2   *When the message lacks a recipient*

If the header of a mail message lacks recipient information (lacks all of the To:, Cc:, and Bcc: header lines), *sendmail* adds an Apparently-To: header line and puts the recipient's address from the envelope into the field of that line. This behavior is hard-coded into pre-8.7 *sendmail*, but beginning with version 8.7, it can be tuned with the NoRecipientAction option (see §34.8.43).

The Apparently-To: header name is not defined in RFC822. It is added by pre-8.7 *sendmail* because RFC822 *requires* at least one To: or Cc: header, and neither is present.

An Apparently-To: header should *never* be defined in the configuration file.

Auto-Submitted: *(sendmail)*

35.10.3   *Why the bounce*

When a message is returned because of an error or because a "return receipt" was requested, V8 *sendmail* adds an Auto-Submitted: header. This header describes the reason for the return:

```
Auto-Submitted: auto-generated (reason)
```

The *reason* can be one of four things: It can be warning-timeout if the message has reached its Timeout.queuewarn option threshold (see §34.8.70). It can be postmaster-warning if the failure was delivered to the postmaster as a result of a problem that the postmaster should fix, such as an MX configuration error. It can be return-receipt if the message was returned because of a Return-Receipt-To: header (see §35.10.29) or a DSN NOTIFY=SUCCESS request (see RFC1891). Finally, it can be failure for any other reason.

In all instances, *sendmail* also adds a Subject: header that contains the actual text that led to the bounce or return. This text is identical to that saved in the qf file's M line (see §23.9.9).

The Auto-Submitted: header should *never* be defined in the configuration file.

Bcc: *(RFC822)*

35.10.4   *Blind carbon copy*

A blind carbon copy is a copy of the mail message that is sent to one or more recipients without the knowledge of the primary recipients. Primary recipients are listed in the To: and Cc: lines. When there are multiple blind carbon copy recipients, knowledge of each other is also hidden.

When run with a -t command-line switch (to gather recipients from the headers), the *sendmail* program achieves this end by saving a list of all the blind carbon copy recipients, deleting the Bcc: header line, and then delivering to each blind carbon copy recipient. (See the Apparently-To: header.)

The Bcc: header should *never* be declared in the configuration file.

The field for the Bcc: header must contain one or more properly formed addresses. Where there is more than one, each should be separated from the others by commas.

Cc: *(RFC822)*

35.10.5   *Carbon copy*

The Cc: header is one of a few that specify the list of primary recipients. The *sendmail* program treats the Cc: header no differently from the way it treats the To: header. From the user's point of view, the Cc: header implies that there are recipients to whom an informational copy of the message was supplied.

The Cc: header should *never* be declared in the configuration file.

The field for the Cc: header must contain one or more properly formed addresses.

Comments: *(RFC822)*

35.10.6   *Header commentary*

The Comments: header is used to place explanatory text into the header portion of an email. The field portion of the Comments: header may contain arbitrary text.

One possible use for a Comments: header would be to notify recipients that one person is replying to mail for another:

```
Comments: Ben is in France for the next month or
          so gathering information for the meeting.
          I am handling his mail while he is away.
    ↑
   whitespace
```

The Comments: header should *rarely* be declared in the configuration file. If it is, it should be prefixed with appropriate ?*flags*?. For example,

```
H?B?Comments: Local delivery is experimentally being handled
          by a new program. Complaints to root.
```

This comment is included only in headers that are delivered via the local delivery agent, because that delivery agent is the only one to include the F=B flag:

```
Mlocal, P=/bin/mail, F=rlsDFMmnPB, S=10, R=20, A=mail -d $u
```

For all versions of *sendmail* except V8, if there is already a `Comments:` header in the message, this configuration-file declaration is ignored. For V8 *sendmail* this declaration will always cause the new `Comment:` header to be *added* to the mail message.

Content-Length: *(System V Release 4)*

35.10.7 *The size of the body of the message*

The `Content-Length:` header describes the approximate size of the body of a message. The size is always a decimal expression of the number of bytes occupied by the body.

```
Content-Length: 5678
```

It is used by some MUAs to find a message faster in a large file of many messages. It is always created or added by MUAs or delivery agents and never by MTAs. It should never be declared in the configuration file.

For Sun's version of V8 *sendmail* the behavior of the `Content-Length:` can be traced with the –d80 debugging switch (see §37.5.190). All other versions of *sendmail* ignore this header.

Content-Transfer-Encoding: *(RFC1521)*

35.10.8 *Auxiliary MIME encoding used in the message*

The MIME `Content-Transfer-Encoding:` header describes what auxiliary encoding was applied to the message body to allow it to pass through email transport mechanisms that may have data or character set limitations. Specifically, RFC821 requires message bodies to contain only 7-bit data. To transport 8-bit data (such as images and sounds) via SMTP, it is necessary to convert that data to 7 bits. The `Content-Transfer-Encoding:` header specifies precisely how that conversion was done:

```
Content-Transfer-Encoding: how
```

Here, *how* is defined by RFC821 to be one of the following: `base64` (see RFC1521), `quoted-printable` (see §34.8.22), `8bit` (meaning that the message body contains unencoded 8-bit data in line length suitable for SMTP transport), `7bit` (the message body contains 7-bit, SMTP-compliant data), or `binary` (the message body contains 8-bit data in a form that is completely unsuitable for SMTP transport).

See the `EightBitMode` (8) option (see §34.8.22) for a description of how V8 *sendmail* converts between 8- and 7-bit data. The `Content-Transfer-Encoding:` header should never be declared in the configuration file.

Content-Type: *(RFC1521)*

35.10.9   *The nature of the body of the message*

The `Content-Type:` header describes the nature of the body of a mail message. In the absence of such a header, the body is presumed to be composed of ASCII characters that have their high (most significant) bits turned off. One possible setting for this header might look like this:

```
Content-Type: text/plain; charset=ISO-8859-1
```

This header says that the body uses the ISO-8859-1 character set.

This header is usually created by the originating MUA. It should never be declared in the configuration file of pre-V8.7 versions of *sendmail.* Beginning with V8.7, the content type for 8- to 7-bit MIME conversions can be declared with the `Default-CharSet` option (§34.8.14).

When bouncing mail, V8 *sendmail* creates a MIME-compliant message and includes a `Content-Type:` header like this:

```
Content-Type: multipart/mixed; boundary="boundary"
```

If *sendmail* was compiled to include DSN support (see §18.8.5), the `Content-Type:` header will look like this:

```
Content-Type: multipart/report; report-type=delivery-status;
        boundary="boundary"
```

Date: *(RFC822)*

35.10.10   *The origin date*

The `Date:` header specifies the date and time that the mail message was originally sent. All mail messages must include this header line. Consequently, the `Date:` header must be declared in the configuration file like this:

```
H?D?Date: $a
```

The `$a` macro (see §31.10.2) is mandatory in the field for this header. The value in `$a` is the current time in RFC822 format. (See Section 5.1 in RFC822 and Section 5.2.14 in RFC1123.) Only the `$a` macro should be used with the `Date:` header, because it is the only one that is guaranteed to contain the current date and time in RFC822 (and RFC1123) format.

The `?D?` flag is always included with the `Date:` declaration in the configuration file. All the standard delivery agents always include a `F=D` flag (see §30.8.17). The `?D?` allows custom delivery agents to be designed that do not need a `Date:` header.

Delivered-To: *(qmail)*

35.10.11 *Mark a mailing list expansion*

The *qmail* program uses a `Delivered-To:` header to trace all the alias and mailing list expansions through which an email message passes. This is similar to the way `Received:` headers are used to trace machine hops. When *qmail* expands a mailing list, it adds a `Delivered-To:` header to the top of the message:

```
Delivered-To: list@host
```

If an identical header is already present, *qmail* bounces the message. This prevents several kinds of mail loops. (Note that the *SmartList* program supports an `X-Loop:` header with the same function.)

This technique is further described in the following draft document:

```
ftp://koobera.math.uic.edu/pub/docs/RFCLOOPS
```

The `Delivered-To:` header should never be declared in the configuration file.

Encrypted: *(RFC822)*

35.10.12 *Message is transformed*

The `Encrypted:` header is used to describe a translation that has been performed on the body of the mail message. Although encryption is implied, other forms of translation, such as compression and *uuencode*(1), are perfectly legal.

The *sendmail* program ignores the `Encrypted:` header. This header is intended for use by MUAs. Unfortunately, most (if not all) UNIX MUAs also ignore this header. The form for the `Encrypted:` header is:

```
Encrypted: prog key
```

The field contains one mandatory item, the *prog*, and one optional item, the *key*. The *prog* is the name of the program that was used to transform the message body. The optional *key* is a decryption key.

If translating the message body into a different form, be aware that many versions of *sendmail* strip the eighth bit from all bytes of the body during transmission.

The `Encrypted:` header should never be declared in the configuration file.

Errors-To: *(sendmail)*

35.10.13 *Error notification redirect*

Ordinarily, errors are bounced to the envelope sender. The `Errors-To:` header specifies the address, or addresses, to which *sendmail* should send additional notification of delivery errors.

The `Errors-To:` header is intended for use by mailing lists to prevent errors in a list from being rebroadcast to the list as a whole. For example, consider the mailing list *allusers*. Mail that is sent to this list should contain the following header lines:

```
To: allusers
From: allusers-submit
Errors-To: allusers-errors
```

The `From:` header allows reply mail to be submitted for distribution to the list. The `Errors-To:` header causes error notification to be sent to `allusers-errors` so that the maintainer can fix any errors in the list. The original sender also gets error notification unless the mailing list software represents the maintainer in the envelope (see §25.5.1).

Under SunOS and V8 *sendmail* the `Errors-To:` is flagged in *conf.c* with the H_ERRSTO header flag (see §35.5.11). This allows other headers to be declared in that file as error redirect headers. Under pre-V8 SunOS *sendmail* the `Errors-To:` header is ignored if the error mode set by the **e** option is **m** (see §34.8.24.2).

Under V8 *sendmail* the `Errors-To:` header is ignored unless the `UseErrorsTo` (1) option (see §34.8.74) is true. It does this because the `Errors-To:` header violates RFC1123. `Errors-To:` was needed only to take the place of the envelope sender in the days when most UNIX delivery agents couldn't differentiate between header and envelope.

The `Errors-To:` header should never be declared in the configuration file.

From: *(RFC822)*

35.10.14   *The sender*

The `From:` header lists the address of the sender. There are only four legal forms that the field of this header can take:

```
From: address
From: <address>
From: Full Name <address>
From: address (comment)
```

A `From:` header must be declared in the configuration file, and its field is composed of the $x (see §31.10.42) and $g (see §31.10.16) macros. For example,

```
H?F?From: $?x$x <$g>$|$g$.
```

$g contains the official return address of the sender. $x contains the full name for the sender. $x may be undefined for some addresses, so it should be wrapped in the $? and $. conditional operators (see §31.6).

The `From:` header must be prefixed by the `?F?` flag because all the traditional delivery agents use the `F=F` flag (see §30.8.21) to force inclusion of that header. Use of the `?F?` flag allows new delivery agents to be written that don't require the `From:` header. The `resent-` form of the `From:` header must also be declared in the configuration file:

```
H?F?Resent-From: $?x$x <$g>$|$g$.
```

This ensures that every mail message has a sender, even if the mail message has been forwarded.

Note that *sendmail* does not add the `From:` header or its `resent-` form if a `From:` header already exists in the header portion of the mail message. A possible exception occurs if the envelope sender is identical to the address in the `From:` header. In that instance, the `From:` header is discarded and a new one is created (see §35.7.1).

Full-Name: *(sendmail)*

35.10.15   *The sender's full name*

The `Full-Name:` header is used to list the sender's full name if it is known. The field for this header may be arbitrary text but is usually the value in the `$x` macro (see §31.10.42):

```
H?x?Full-Name: $x
H?x?Full-Name: (User names hidden for security)
```

The `Full-Name:` header should be prefixed with the `?x?` flag so that selected delivery agents may require inclusion of that header. This header definition is usually meaningless, because all traditional delivery agents omit the `F=x` flag. It can be useful, however, for mailing through sites that strip or destroy `From:` headers.

The `Full-Name:` header may be specified in the configuration file. If this header is already in the mail message, *sendmail* does not replace it. But note that V8 *sendmail* will remove the `Full-Name:` header if the `F=x` flag (see §30.8.44) is set for the recipient's delivery agent.

In-Reply-To: *(RFC822)*

35.10.16   *Identify previous correspondence*

The `In-Reply-To:` header is used to identify previous correspondence that the current message is in reply to. This header is generated by MUAs, not by *sendmail*. The field for this header is arbitrary text with one restriction. If that text includes the message identifier, that identifier must be enclosed in angle brackets (`<` and `>`) and must adhere to the format for all message identifiers. Note that the message identifier *should* be included but is not required.

A typical use of the `In-Reply-To:` header might look like the following:

```
In-Reply-To: Your message of Fri, 13 Dec 1996 05:47:44 -0700
        The subject of which was: "Which came first?"
  ↑
whitespace
```

The `In-Reply-To:` header should never be declared in the configuration file.

Keywords: *(RFC822)*

35.10.17 *Index to contents*

The `Keywords:` header is used to list significant words from the body of the mail message that aid in the indexing of its contents. This header is never added by *sendmail.* Although some user mail-reading programs can create this header, it is usually created by Usenet news-posting programs.

The field for the `Keywords:` header is arbitrary text. This header should never be declared in the *sendmail* configuration file.

Mail-From: *(obsolete)*

35.10.18 *Synonym for Received:*

The `Mail-From:` header is not defined by any of the RFCs and is rarely seen in message headers. The *sendmail* program defines it internally as a synonym for the `Received:` header. The `Mail-From:` header is obsolete.

Message-ID: *(RFC822)*

35.10.19 *Unique identifier for message*

The `Message-ID:` header is used to uniquely identify each mail message. This header must be declared in the configuration file. The field for this header must be an expression in the form of a legal address enclosed in angle brackets (< and >). The address must be composed of elements that create an identifier that is truly unique worldwide. The `Message-ID:` header is declared in the configuration file:

```
?M?Message-Id: <$t.$i@$j>
```

Here, the field is an address of the form *user@domain*, which is enclosed in angle brackets. The `$t` macro (see §31.10.35) is an integer representation of the current time to the nearest second. The `$i` macro (see §31.10.19) is the unique queue identifier that is used to identify this message locally. The `$j` macro (see §31.10.20) is the fully qualified domain name of the local host. The `Message-ID:` header as it might appear in an actual mail message would look like this:

```
Message-Id: <9207100411.AA14505@nic.cerf.net>
```

The **Message-ID:** header should be prefixed with a ?M? flag so that it is inserted only into headers of messages whose delivery agents have the **F=M** flag set. The standard delivery agents include this flag.

The **resent-** form of the **Message-ID:** header must also be declared in the configuration file:

```
?M?Resent-Message-Id: <$t.$i@$j>
```

This ensures that every mail message has a message identifier even if the message is forwarded.

Note that *sendmail* does not add a **Message-ID:** header or its **Resent-** form if a **Message-ID:** header already exists in the header portion of a mail message. Furthermore, the **Resent-** form is added only if *sendmail* determines that the message is a resent message.

Also note that you should never try to replace an existing **Message-ID:** header with one of your own. This could result in the loss of important information needed to trace the origin of a message.

Message: *(sendmail)*

35.10.20   *Marks end of headers*

The **Message:** header is used to mark an early end to a mail message's headers. When *sendmail* finds this header, it immediately stops gathering the message's header lines and treats the rest of the header as the start of the message body. This header is useful for including non-Internet headers in the header portion of a mail message. For example,

```
To: george@wash.dc.gov (George Washington)
Subject: Re: More text
Date: Tue, 04 Aug 92 14:14:56 -0400
Message-Id: <31842.AA01513@wash.dc.gov>
Received: by wash.dc.gov (4.1/1.12 $)
        id AA01513; Tue, 4 Aug 92 12:15:01 PDT
From: Ben Franklin <ben@philly.dc.gov>
Message:
ROUTED BY BITNET\/CO=US/ROUTE=INTERNET/
FORMAT OF MESSAGE /LANG=USENGLISH/FORM=PLAINTEXT/
```

Here, the last two header lines are non-Internet headers that may confuse some programs. But the **Message:** header that precedes them tells *sendmail* to treat them as message body, and problems are avoided.

Note that `Message:` is not defined by any RFC but is a convention that is shared by all versions of *sendmail* and most other MTAs. The `Message:` header should never be declared in the configuration file.

MIME-Version: *(RFC1521)*

35.10.21 *Notify that error return contains MIME support*

MIME (Multipurpose Internet Mail Extensions) is documented in RFC1521, with additional details in RFC1344, RFC1426, RFC1428, and RFC1437. The *sendmail* program cares about MIME only when bouncing messages and when determining how to convert the message body between 8 and 7 bits. If the `SendMimeErrors` (j) option (see §34.8.60) is set, V8 *sendmail* includes the following header in all returned (bounced) mail:

```
MIME-Version: 1.0
```

This is hard-coded into *sendmail*. See the `SendMimeErrors` (j) option for further details about this header.

The `MIME-Version:` header should never be declared in the configuration file.

Posted-Date: *(sendmail)*

35.10.22 *Date submitted*

The `Posted-Date:` header is used by some old Usenet news software and some mailing list software to indicate the date and time that a mail message was posted (submitted for distribution). The `Date:` header, on the other hand, shows when the message was mailed. In actual practice, the two usually show the same date and time.

When *sendmail* tries to determine the originating date of a mail message, it first looks for a `Posted-Date:` header. If one is found, it uses that date. Otherwise, it uses the date from the `Date:` header. Whichever is used, the result is stored into the `$a` macro (see §31.10.2).

The `Posted-Date:` header is not a part of the RFC822 standard, so it should not be declared in the *sendmail* configuration file.

Precedence: *(sendmail)*

35.10.23 *Set ordering in queue*

The `Precedence:` header is used internally by *sendmail* to order the processing of messages in its queue. A full description of the possible field values for this header is given in §35.8.1. The effect of those values on ordering the queue is described in §23.5.

The `Precedence:` header should never be declared as an H line in the configuration file. However, P precedence lines should be declared in that file.

Priority: *(sendmail)*

35.10.24 *Determine timeouts in the queue*

Mail messages may be placed into the queue either intentionally or because they could not be delivered immediately. Once they are in the queue, two time periods come into play. First is the period of time that the message should remain in the queue before a warning is issued to the sender. Second is the total period of time that the message should remain in the queue before it is bounced as a failed message.

Beginning with V8.7 *sendmail*, it is now possible to tailor these intervals on the basis of three distinct priorities of mail. The new `Priority:` header tells *sendmail* which priority a message possesses:

    Priority: *pri*

Here, *pri* can have one of three possible values: **urgent**, **normal**, and **non-urgent**. These values correspond directly to the priorities specified by the `Timeout.queuewarn` option (see §34.8.70.15) and `Timeout.queuereturn` option (see §34.8.70.14):

    O Timeout.queuereturn.urgent=1d
    O Timeout.queuereturn.normal=2d
    O Timeout.queuereturn.non-urgent=4d

Here, a `Priority:` header of **normal** will cause the message containing it to bounce after it has remained in the queue for two days.

The `Priority:` header should never be declared in the configuration file.

Received: *(RFC822)*

35.10.25 *Trace routing of mail*

The `Received:` header is used to record information about each and every site a mail message passes through on its way to ultimate delivery. First this header is inserted by the original sending site, then another is added by each site that the message passes through, including the site performing final delivery. Each new header is added to the top of the list of `Received:` headers, forming a chronological record (reading bottom up through the headers) of how the mail message was handled.

The contents of the **Received:** header's field is narrowly defined by RFC822. Its defined form looks like this:

```
Received: ["from" host] "by" host ["via" atom] ["with" atom]
        "id" string ["for" addr] ";" date
    ↑
    whitespace
```

The field is composed of six items that may be split over multiple lines by using whitespace to indent the second. Items that are optional are enclosed in square brackets. Each item is composed of two parts a word (shown in quotation marks) and a value. All, or only the few required items, need to be present. When they are present, they must be in the following order:

from

> Full canonical name of the sending host (if available)

by Full canonical name of the receiving host (required)

via

> Physical network that was used to transmit the message, such as INTERNET, JANET, or XNS (optional)

with

> Protocol used to receive the message, such as SMTP (optional)

id Unique queue identifier assigned by the local host (required)

for

> Initial, untranslated address of the recipient (seldom used)

;date

> Date this message was received (required)

The **Received:** header must be declared in the configuration file. It is a mandatory header, so it should never be prefixed with *?flags?*. A typical declaration of this header would look like this:

```
HReceived: $?sfrom $s $.$?_($?s$|from $.$_) $.by $j ($v/$Z)$?r with $r$.
        id $i$?u for $u$.; $b
```

Here, seven items are included in the field:

$?from $s $.

> If the $s macro contains a value, the word **from** and that value are inserted into the header. The $s macro (see §31.10.33) contains the full canonical name of the sender's host.

`$?_($?s$|from $.$_) $.`

This is a nested conditional. If the `$_` macro contains a value, the parentheses and all the information inside them are inserted into the header. If the `$_` macro lacks a value, nothing is inserted into the header.

Inside the parentheses the value of `$_` is inserted into the header. Another conditional expression determines if the `$_` just inserted should also be prefixed with the word `from`. If the `$s` macro lacks a value the word `from` is inserted in front of the `$_`. The `$_` macro contains the RFC1413 *identd*(8) identity of the connecting host and any IP routing information (see §31.10.1).

`by $j ($v/$Z)`

The `$j` macro contains the full canonical name of the local host. The parentheses surround a comment that is formed from `$v` (see §31.10.38), the version of the *sendmail* program, and `$Z` (see §31.10.47) the version of the configuration file.

`$?r with $r$.`

If the `$r` macro contains a value, the word **with** followed by the value of `$r` is inserted into the header. The `$r` macro (see §31.10.31) contains a string that indicates the protocol used to receive the message (such as SMTP or ESMTP).

`id $i`

The `$i` macro contains the identifier created by *sendmail* to uniquely identify this mail message at this host (see §31.10.19).

`$?u for $u$`

If the `$u` macro contains a value, the word **for** followed by the value of `$u` is inserted into the header. The `$u` macro (see §31.10.36) contains the recipient's username.

`; $b`

The `$b` macro contains the current date and time in RFC822 format (see §31.10.3).

The `Received:` declaration shown above is the one typically used by most sites running V8 *sendmail*.

References: *(RFC822)*

35.10.26 *Reference to original message*

The `References:` header is used by mail-reading programs to include a reference to the original message in replies. Although this header may legally contain arbitrary text as its field, it usually contains a copy of the original `Message-ID:` header field.

The `References:` header typically looks something like this:

```
References: <9205041920.AA27932@wash.dc.gov>
```

Notice that the message identifier is wrapped in angle brackets, which cause it to look like an address.

The `References:` header should never be declared in the configuration file.

Reply-To: *(RFC822)*

35.10.27   *Alternative reply address*

The `Reply-To:` header requests that replies to messages go to one or more addresses that are different from that of the original sender. This header is usually inserted by mailing-list software, where the `From:` is the address of the mailing list and the `Reply-To:` is the address of the list's maintainer.

The field for the `Reply-To:` header must obey the same rules as those for the `From:` header's field. One example of the use of this header might look like this:

```
From: mailinglist@list.server.com
Reply-To: mailinglist-request@list.server.com
```

The `-request` suffix is used by many mailing lists to specify the list maintainer.

The `Reply-To:` header should never be declared in the configuration file.

Return-Path: *(RFC822)*

35.10.28   *Return address of sender*

The `Return-Path:` header is intended to show the envelope address of the real sender as opposed to the sender used for replying (the `From:` and `Reply-To:` headers). In posting Usenet news, for example, the `Return-Path:` shows "news" and the `From:` shows the address of the posting user. But in general, `Return-Path:` should never be used for replying to mail. It is intended to be used solely for notification of delivery errors.

There must be only one `Return-Path:` header in any mail message, and it should be placed there by the site performing final delivery. This header should be declared in the configuration file like this:

```
H?P?Return-Path: <$g>
```

The `?P?` flag ensures that only delivery agents that perform final delivery insert this header. Those delivery agents are usually `prog` and `local`, which usually contain an `F=P` delivery agent flag.

The `$g` macro (see §31.10.16) contains as its value the address of the sender relative to the recipient.

Unfortunately, two circumstances can cause the `Return-Path:` header to contain incorrect information. First, the message may arrive at your site with that header already there. If this happens, there is usually no way to get rid of it, because most versions of *sendmail* lack a *conf.c* `H_` flag that means to replace an existing header. However, with V8 *sendmail*, defining H_ACHECK (see §35.5.16) in *conf.c* causes a header to be replaced even if one is already in the message.

The second problem stems from the fact that final delivery may not really be final. The `local` delivery agent program may be something like *procmail*(8), which allows mail to appear to be locally delivered, while also allowing users to run shell scripts that may forward their mail to another site.

To minimize these problems, always declare the `Return-Path:` header with the proper `?`*flags*`?` in the configuration file. Doing this ensures that it will be inserted when legal and that the address your site places in it is usually correct.

Return-Receipt-To: *(sendmail prior to V8.7)*

35.10.29   *Verify delivery*

he `Return-Receipt-To:` header causes *sendmail* to send a mail message back to the specified recipient confirming final delivery. It is no longer supported as of V8.7 *sendmail* (instead, see NOTIFY=SUCCESS in §36.7.28).[*] If a pre-8.7 version of *sendmail* finds this header when it is processing mail for delivery, and if the selected delivery agent has the `F=l` flag set, *sendmail* creates a bounced mail message. The recipient is set to the person specified in the `Return-Receipt-To:` header, and the following subject header line is included:

```
Subject: Returned Mail: Return Receipt      ← prior to V8.7
Subject: Return Receipt                      ← starting with V8.7
```

The message appears to originate from the user defined by the `$n` macro (see §31.10.26), and contains a copy of the original header as its body.

The `Return-Receipt-To:` header should never be declared in the configuration file and, in fact, should rarely be used at all. It is not intended as a routine delivery-verification mechanism but rather is intended for occasional use in debugging delivery problems. It is especially dangerous when used in outgoing mailing-list mail, because it can cause an avalanche of returned mail and can possibly bring a host to its knees. Beginning with V8.6 *sendmail*, a receipt is sent when the mailing list is first expanded, and the `Return-Receipt-To:` header is removed before forwarding the message to the list.

---

[*] `Return-Receipt-To:` was a bad idea. It gave false information (such as the suggestion that a user who never reads mail accepted delivery). It can wrongly propagate (as, for example, when a mailing list gets the receipt instead of you). And it is insecure (a nasty person can use it to find "hidden" members of a mailing list).

Beginning with V8.7 *sendmail*, processing of all `Return-Receipt-To:` headers can be skipped by specifying `noreceipts` with the `PrivacyOptions` (p) option (see §34.8.47).

Sender: *(RFC822)*

35.10.30   *The real sender*

The `Sender:` header is like the `From:` header. But whereas the `From:` header shows the address of one sender, the `Sender:` header shows the address of the *real* sender. For example, an assistant can mail a letter for the boss using the boss's account. The boss's address is in the `From:` header, and the assistant's address is in the `Sender:` header. The syntax for the two is identical.

Newer MUAs allow the user to create a custom `Sender:` header. The `Sender:` header should never be declared in the configuration file.

Subject: *(RFC822)*

35.10.31   *Topic of the message*

The `Subject:` header can be included in mail messages to give the topic of the message. Most user mail-reading programs display the arbitrary text that forms the field of this header when listing received messages. Although such text can legally extend over multiple indented lines, most mail-reading programs recognize only the first such line:

```
Subject: About yesterday's meeting, I had some second
        thoughts about why the shape of the bonnet should
        remain so sharply curved at the ends.
    ↑
    whitespace
```

This would be displayed by the *mailx*(1) program in truncated form as:

```
14   gw@wash.dc.gov Fri Aug  7 12:57  22/770 "About yesterday's meeting"
```

The `Subject:` header is not used by *sendmail*, but it is often wrongly (albeit harmlessly) included in the configuration file:

```
HSubject:              ← This actually does nothing
```

Text: *(sendmail)*

35.10.32   *A synonym for Message:*

The `Text:` header is the same as the `Message:` header. Both cause all lines that follow in the header portion of a mail message to be treated as message body.

The `Text:` header should never be declared in the configuration file.

To: (RFC822)

35.10.33 *The primary recipients*

The To: header lists one or more of the recipients of the mail message. Other headers, such as Cc:, also list recipients.

The *sendmail* program attempts to deliver a copy of the mail message to every recipient address that it can find in all the recipient headers and in the envelope. If the header of a mail message lacks recipient information (To:, Cc:, and Bcc: header lines), pre-V8.7 *sendmail* added an Apparently-To: header line and put the recipient's address from the envelope into the field of that header. Beginning with V8.7, the way a recipientless message is handled is determined with the NoRecipientAction option (see §34.8.43).

Via: (obsolete)

35.10.34 *An unofficial trace header*

The Via: header is not defined by RFC822 but occasionally appears in mail messages that *sendmail* needs to process. It is used by a few other networks to mark a mail message's transit through a forwarding host. It is an early, and now obsolete, version of the Received: header. The *sendmail* program counts the Via: header when determining the hop count but has no other use for it.

The Via: header should never be declared in the configuration file.

X-Authentication-Warning: (V8 sendmail)

35.10.35 *Notification of security matters*

If the PrivacyOptions (p) option (see §34.8.47) is declared with authwarnings, V8 *sendmail* inserts a special header line for possible security concerns. That header line looks like this:

```
X-Authentication-Warning: host: message
```

Here, *host* is the canonical name of the host that inserted this header. The *message* is one of the following:

Processed by user with –C file
> An attempt was made by a *user* other than *root* to run *sendmail* with the –C command-line switch. That switch caused *sendmail* to read *file* in place of the system *sendmail.cf* file.

user set sender to other using –f
> A *user* or program's *user* identity used the –f command-line switch to change the identity of the sender to *other* (and *user* was not listed with the T configuration command). This can be legitimate when the *user* is *uucp* or *daemon*. It

can also be legitimate when the *user* is sending to some mailing lists (see §22.8). Such a warning can also indicate that someone is trying to forge mail.

user owned process doing **-bs**

A *user* or program's *user* identity used the **-bs** command-line switch to make *sendmail* receive a mail message via its standard input/output using the SMTP protocol (and *user* was not listed with the **T** configuration command). This parallels network notification set up by defining IDENTPROTO when compiling *sendmail* and by use of the **$_** macro (see §31.10.1) in **Received:** headers.

Processed from queue dir

A user other than *root* used the **-oQ** (or similar) switch (see §34.8.48) to process mail from a queue directory (*dir*) that was different from the one specified with the **QueueDirectory** (**Q**) option in the configuration file. The *sendmail* program can run as an ordinary user because this or some other command-line switch caused it to give up *root* privilege.

Host name1 claimed to be name2

In the HELO message of an SMTP conversation the remote host *name1* specified its canonical name as *name2*, and the two didn't match. This always indicates a problem. Either the remote host is misconfigured (a bad value in **$j**; see §31.10.20), the DNS maps for that host are wrong, or someone is trying to spoof the local *sendmail*.

Host name didn't use HELO protocol

Every SMTP conversation for transfer of mail must start with the HELO (or EHLO) greeting. If, instead, a MAIL command was first, this header is inserted in the incoming message. The most likely cause of a missing HELO is the mistake of someone attempting to carry on an SMTP conversation by hand.

X400-Received: *(X400)*

35.10.36   *Received via X400*

The **X400-Received:** header is added by IDA *sendmail* to document receipt of a mail message from an X400 network. This header is used by both IDA and V8 to count the number of forwarding sites when computing the hop count of a mail message.

The **X400-Received:** should never be declared in the configuration file.

36

The Command Line

The initial behavior of *sendmail* is determined largely by the command line used to invoke it. The command line can, for example, cause *sendmail* to use a different configuration file or to rebuild the *aliases* file rather than deliver mail. The command line can be typed at your keyboard, executed from a boot-time script, or even executed by an MUA when sending mail.

The format of the *sendmail* command line is:

```
argv[0] switches recipients
```

Here, `argv[0]` is the name used to run *sendmail*. The `switches`, if any of them are present, must always precede the list of recipients. The `recipients` is a list of zero or more recipient address expressions.

36.1 *Alternative argv[0] Names*

The *sendmail* program may exist in any of several places, depending on the version of the operating system you are running. Usually, it is located in the */usr/lib* directory and is called *sendmail,*[*] but it can alternatively be located in the */etc*, */usr/sbin*, or */usr/etc* directory. The location of the *sendmail* program can be found by examining the */etc/rc* files for BSD UNIX or the */etc/init.d* files for Sys V UNIX (see §3.4).

In addition to the name *sendmail*, other names (in other directories) can exist that alter the behavior of *sendmail*. Those alternative names are usually symbolic links

---

[*] On Sun systems you will find */usr/lib/sendmail.mx* for use with the Domain Name System.

to */usr/lib/sendmail*. On some systems they may be hard links, and in rare cases you may actually find them to be copies. The complete list of other names is shown in Table 36-1.

Table 36-1: Alternative Names for sendmail

Name	§	Mode of Operation
hoststat	36.1.1	Print persistent host status (V8.8 and above)
mailq	36.1.2	Print the queue contents
newaliases	36.1.3	Rebuild the *aliases* file
purgestat	36.1.4	Purge persistent host status (V8.8 and above)
smtpd	36.1.5	Run in daemon mode

When *sendmail* looks for the name under which it is running, it strips any leading directory components from *argv[0]* and compares the result (in a case-sensitive fashion) to its internal list of alternative names. If a match is found, its mode of operation is changed to conform to that of the alternative name. If no match is found (if, say, a link is named *Mailq*, note the uppercase *M*), *sendmail* does not change its mode.

The name that is found is used to build an argument list for use with process listings. For example, if the name was *sendmail.mx* (from SunOS), a process listing produced with *ps*(3) would look something like this:

```
root  1247  620 p0 S  07:22 0:00 -AA15186 (sendmail.mx)
```

Here, the (`sendmail.mx`) shows that *sendmail* was run under the name *sendmail.mx*.

Note that *sendmail* uses the hard-coded name "*sendmail*" for logging purposes with *syslog*(3) (see §26.1.1). Therefore logged errors and warnings always appear to come from *sendmail*, no matter what name was used to run it.

As a final note, be aware that command-line switches are processed immediately after the name but before *sendmail* finalizes its mode of operation. Thus the use of particular switches can completely cancel any special meaning given a name.

36.1.1 *hoststat (V8.8 and Above)*

The *hoststat* command is a synonym for the `-bh` command-line switch. It causes *sendmail* to print its persistent host status and exit. Persistent host status is enabled with the `HostStatusDirectory` option (see §34.8.31).

The output produced by this command begins with a heading like this:

```
-------------- Hostname --------------- How long ago ---------Results---------
```

Then for each host that has its status saved, *sendmail* prints this information:

Hostname

> This is the name of the host that was connected to. It may not be the hostname specified for the recipient. It could easily be an MX record instead. If a message has multiple recipients, a separate status line will be produced for each unique host that is tried. If this name is prefixed with an asterisk, the status file is locked and currently being updated.

How long ago

> This shows how long ago this status record was updated. It is printed in the form:

```
DD+HH:MM:SS
```

> Here, **DD** is the number of days. If the status was updated less than a day ago, the **DD+** is omitted. The **HH** is hours, the **MM** is minutes, and the **SS** is seconds. The colons are literal.

Results

> This shows the result of the last connection attempt, failure, or success. If no reason was stored, this prints as:

```
No status available
```

> If a result was stored, it will print in three parts:

```
smtp id msg
```

> The *smtp* is the SMTP reply code. The *msg* is the text of the message generated by the other end or other program.

To illustrate, consider this output:

```
-------------- Hostname --------------- How long ago ---------Results---------
there.ufoa.edu                         00:00:51 250 PAA27153 Message acce
*books.ora.com                         07:43:39 250 GAA01255 Message acce
prog.ammers.com                        06:55:08 No status available
fbi.dc.gov                             03:28:53 Connection refused
```

Here, the previous connections to *there.ufoa.edu* and *books.ora.com* were successful. The status for *books.ora.com* is currently being updated, hence the asterisk showing it is locked. The host *prog.ammers.com* shows no status because connection to it could not be made. The last example show that the connection to *fbi.dc.gov* was refused by that host.

Note that the results are limited to 27 characters unless the **-v** command-line flag is also used. In that case, results are limited to 79 characters, thus providing more complete information.

36.1.2 *mailq*

The name *mailq* (a synonym for the **-bp** command-line switch) causes *sendmail* to print the contents of the mail queue and then exit (see §23.4).

Note that the location of the queue is set with the **QueueDirectory** (Q) option (see §34.8.48). That location can be overridden from the command line, but if it is, *sendmail* may give up its *root* privilege (unless it was run by *root*).

36.1.3 *newaliases*

The name *newaliases* (a synonym for the **-bi** command-line switch) causes *send-mail* to rebuild the *aliases* database files, print summary information, and then immediately exit (see §24.5.1). In this mode the **-v** command-line switch (see §36.7.41) is automatically implied, and *sendmail* runs in verbose mode.

The location of the *aliases* file is given in the configuration file with the **Alias-File** (A) option (see §34.8.1). That location can be overridden from the command line, but if it is, *sendmail* gives up its *root* privilege (unless it was run by *root*).

36.1.4 *purgestat (V8.8 and Above)*

The name *purgestat* is a synonym for the V8.8 and above **-bH** command-line switch (see §36.7.6). It causes *sendmail* to clear (purge) all the host-status informa-tion that was being saved under the **HostStatusDirectory** option's directory (see §34.8.31). Clearing is done by removing all the directories under the **HostStatus-Directory** directory. Note that the **HostStatusDirectory** directory is not itself removed.

36.1.5 *smtpd*

The name *smtpd* is a synonym for the **-bd** command-line switch (see §36.7.5). It causes *sendmail* to run in the background as a daemon, listening for incoming SMTP mail (see §4.1.1). This mode of operating is usually combined with the **-q** command-line switch (see §23.6.1), which causes *sendmail* to periodically process the queue.

36.2 *Command-Line Switches*

Command-line switches are command-line arguments that begin with a – character, and precede the list of recipients (if any). The forms for command-line switches, where *X* is a single letter, are:

-*X*	← *Boolean switch*
-*Xarg*	← *switch with argument*

All switches are single letters. The complete list is shown in Table 36-2.

Table 36–2: Command-Line Switches

Switch	§	Version	Description
-B	36.7.1	V8.1 and above	Specify message body type
-b	36.7.2	All versions	Set operating mode
-ba	36.7.3	Not V8.1- V8.6	Use ARPAnet/Grey Book protocols
-bD	36.7.4	V8.8 and above	Run as a daemon, but don't fork
-bd	36.7.5	All versions	Run as a daemon
-bH	36.7.6	V8.8 and above	Purge persistent host status
-bh	36.7.7	V8.8 and above	Print persistent host status
-bi	24.5.1	All versions	Initialize alias database
-bm	36.7.9	All versions	Be a mail sender
-bp	23.4	All versions	Print the queue
-bs	36.7.11	All versions	Run SMTP on standard input
-bt	38.1	All versions	Rule testing mode
-bv	36.7.13	All versions	Verify: don't collect or deliver
-bz	36.7.14	Not V8	Freeze the configuration file
-C	36.7.15	All versions	Location of configuration file
-c	34.8.29	Deprecated	Set HoldExpensive (c) option to true
-d	37.1	All versions	Enter debugging mode
-E	36.7.18	Sony NEWS only	Japanese font conversion
-e	34.8.24	Deprecated	Set the ErrorMode (e) option's mode
-F	36.7.20	All versions	Set the sender's full name
-f	36.7.21	All versions	Set sender's address
-h	36.7.22	Deprecated	Minimum hop count
-I	36.7.23	Deprecated	Synonym for –bi
-i	36.7.24	Deprecated	Set the IgnoreDots (i) option to true
-J	36.7.25	Sony NEWS only	Japanese font conversion
-M	31.2	V8.7 and above	Define a macro on the command line
-m	34.8.39	All versions	Set the MeToo (m) option to true
-N	36.7.28	V8.8 and above	Specify DSN NOTIFY information
-n	24.6	All versions	Don't do aliasing
-O	34.1	V8.7 and above	Set a multicharacter option
-o	34.1	All versions	Set a single-character option

Table 36–2: Command-Line Switches (continued)

Switch	§	Version	Description
-p	36.7.32	V8.1 and above	Set protocol and host
-q	23.6.1	All versions	Process the queue
-R	36.7.34	V8.8 and above	DSN what to return on a bounce
-r	36.7.21	Deprecated	Synonym for -f
-s	34.8.59	Deprecated	Set the SaveFromLine (f) option to true
-T	34.8.52	Deprecated	Set QueueTimeout (T) option
-t	36.7.38	All versions	Get recipients from message header
-U	36.7.39	V8.8 and above	This is the initial MUA to MTA submission
-V	36.7.40	V8.8 and above	Specify the ENVID string
-v	36.7.41	All versions	Run in verbose mode
-X	26.4	V8.1 and above	Log transactions
-x	36.7.43	V8.2 and above	Ignored

Some switches are called Boolean because they are either true or false. The **–v** switch, for example, is Boolean because it puts *sendmail* into verbose mode if it is present (true). If it is absent (false), *sendmail* does not run in verbose mode.

Some switches take arguments. The **–C** switch, for example, tells *sendmail* where to find its configuration file. When a switch takes an argument, the argument may immediately follow the letter or be separated from it with whitespace:[*]

```
    -Ctest.cf            ← good
    -C test.cf           ← also good
```

The only exception to this rule is the **–d** command-line switch (set debugging mode). It may not have whitespace between the letter and the **arg**.

Some switches, such as **–q** (process the queue), can either be Boolean or take an argument:

```
    -q                   ← boolean
    -q1h                 ← with argument
```

The position of switches in the command line is critical. If any follow the list of recipients, they are wrongly taken as mail addresses and lead to bounced mail. But the order in which switches appear prior to the recipients is not important. That is, they may appear in any order without changing the behavior of *sendmail.*

An undefined switch letter causes the following error to be printed and *sendmail* to immediately exit:

---

[*] Prior to V8 *sendmail*, whitespace was not allowed between the letter and the argument.

```
sendmail: illegal option -- bad letter here
```

The special switch -- can be used to delimit the switches from the list of recipients:

```
% /usr/lib/sendmail -- -jim
```

Here, the recipient is -jim. To prevent the - of -jim from being wrongly interpreted as indicating a switch, the special switch -- is used to mark the end of all switches.[*]

36.3   *List of Recipient Addresses*

All command-line arguments that follow the switches (if any) are taken to be the addresses of recipients. The addresses in the list may be separated by spaces, by commas, or by both:

```
addr1 addr2 addr3
addr1,addr2,addr3
addr1, addr2, addr3
```

Certain modes specified by the -b command-line switch, such as -bp (for print the queue's contents), cause *sendmail* to ignore any list of recipients.

Be sure to escape any characters in addresses that have special meaning to your shell. For example, because the ! character has special meaning to the C-shell,[†] it should be escaped by preceding it with a backslash character:

```
host\!user
```

If *sendmail* expects a list of recipients and finds none, it prints the following message and exits:

```
Recipient names must be specified
```

36.4   *Processing the Command Line*

The *sendmail* program's ability to perform different tasks necessitates that the command line be processed in steps.

First

> The command line is prescanned to set its -d debugging switch. That switch allows you to watch all the steps taken by *sendmail* prior to processing the rest of the command-line switches.

---

[*] Under pre-V8 *sendmail*, recipient names could never begin with a -C, -b, -d, -q, or -Z. If any did, they were wrongly interpreted as switches during preprocessing.

[†] And its derivatives such as *tcsh*(1).

Second

> Internal macros are given values, then the command line's *argv[0]* (the name used to run *sendmail*) is processed. That name can determine the *sendmail* program's mode of operation.

Third

> The command-line switches are processed. Although the configuration file is read after the command line is processed, options in the command line (with −o and −O) still supersede those in the configuration file.

Fourth

> The configuration file is read.

Fifth

> If *sendmail* is running in a mode that allows it to verify or deliver to recipients, the remainder of the command line is processed to extract the recipient list.

36.4.1 First: Prescanning the Command Line

When *sendmail* begins to run, it performs a preliminary scan of its command-line arguments. It does this because some actions need to be performed before its configuration file is read. The −d command-line switch is processed during the prescanning phase.

36.4.2 Second: Processing Prior to the Switches

After the command-line switches are prescanned, but before they are processed in full, *sendmail* performs two important internal tasks.

36.4.2.1 Initialize the environment

The environmental variables that are given to *sendmail* when it is first run are ignored. When running delivery agents, *sendmail* provides a small, customized environment. See §22.2 for a detailed discussion of this step.

36.4.2.2 Initialize macros

Certain macros are next declared and assigned values. The $w macro (see §31.10.40), $j macro (see §31.10.38), and the $=w class macro (see §32.5.8) are given values that identify the current host. The $m macro (see §31.10.24) is given a value that is the local domain name. The $k macro (see §31.10.21) and the $=k class (see §32.5.2) are also given values at this time. The $v macro (see §31.10.38) is assigned a value that is the current version of the *sendmail* program. The $b macro (see §31.10.3) is given the current date and time as its value.

36.4.3 Third: Process Switches

Command-line switches are processed by *sendmail* as they appear in the command line, from left to right. The processing of switches ends when an argument is found that lacks a leading – character or when a –– argument is found.

36.4.4 Fourth: Read the Configuration File

The fact that the configuration file is read *after* the command-line switches are processed can lead to some confusion. Some, but not all, command-line switches can overwrite some configuration file commands. Since there is no general rule, we describe the behavior of each item (such as macros and options) in a chapter dedicated to each.

36.4.5 Fifth: Collect Recipients

The final step *sendmail* undertakes in processing its command line is gathering the list of recipients. Each recipient (or list of recipients if more than one is contained in a single command-line argument) is fully processed for delivery, and any error messages are printed before delivery is actually undertaken.

If sendmail is running in a mode that doesn't require recipients, any list of recipients in the command line is silently ignored.

36.5 sendmail's exit() Status

Like any other program under UNIX, *sendmail* can return meaningful values to the environment and thus to you. All of the possible exit values are documented in *<sysexits.h>* along with the values assigned to each name. Here, we provide a bit more explanation about the most commonly used names.

The relationship between each exit value and its corresponding DSN `detail` is shown in Table 30-6 in §30.5.2. That table also summarizes the values described here.

36.5.1 EX_CANTCREAT   Can't Write a User's File

An exit value of EX_CANTCREAT (the value 73) means that an output file could not be written to. This error generally refers to a user-specified file rather than a system- or configuration-file-specified file. Some problems that can lead to this error (without an error message) is an attempt to write to a file that has any execute bit set in its permissions, a file that has more than one link, and (if the `SafeFileEnvironment` option; see §34.8.58, is set) a file that is not a regular file.

If the `SafeFileEnvironment` option is specified and *sendmail* is unable to *chroot*(2) into the specified directory, the following message is logged:

```
mailfile: Cannot chroot(directory)
```

When delivery is to a file, *sendmail* will log the following error if the file cannot be opened or *stat*(3)'d:

```
cannot open: reason here
cannot fstat: reason here
```

and the *fork*(2)'d child will exit with EX_CANTCREAT.

36.5.2 EX_CONFIG   *A Configuration Error*

The EX_CONFIG exit value (the value 78) means that a fatal configuration problem was found, but this does not necessarily mean that the problem was found while reading the configuration file. Failure of a delivery agent to function correctly can lead to this kind of failure:

- During delivery, when a rule set 0 selection of a delivery agent fails to specify a host with the $@ part (see §29.6), the following error is logged and the *fork*(2)'d child exits with EX_CONFIG:

  ```
  null host name for mailer
  ```

- During delivery, when $u appears in the argument list for an SMTP delivery agent (see §30.4.1.3), *sendmail* logs the following error and the *fork*(2)'d child exits with EX_CONFIG:

  ```
  non-clever IPC
  ```

- During delivery, when an attempt is made to use an SMTP delivery agent with a version of *sendmail* that was compiled without SMTP support (see §18.8.41), *sendmail* logs the following error and the *fork*(2)'d child exits with EX_CONFIG:

  ```
  deliver: need SMTP compiled to use clever mailer
  ```

Some apparent DNS errors are really configuration problems. In the following error, *hostB* is an MX record that points back to your host. The problem is that your host doesn't know that it should be accepting mail for *hostB*. The solution is to add *hostB* to your local $=w class (see §32.5.8).

```
MX list for hostB points back to ourhost
```

When *sendmail* processes MX records, it skips any records of absurd length and logs the following message:

```
Host name ourhost too long
```

If an MX record points to a CNAME record, the result can be serious. The first CNAME may point to a second, the second to a third, and so on. If this list is longer than the number defined by MAXCNAMEDEPTH in *domain.c*, the result is the following error:

```
DNS failure: CNAME loop for bad host name here
```

One solution is to set the **DontExpandCnames** option (see §34.8.18) to false, thus causing only the first CNAME to be used as if it were an A record.

Errors in rule set numbers are sometimes only found during actual rewriting:

```
illegal ruleset number bad number here
rewrite: excessive recursion (max max), ruleset bad number here
rewrite: ruleset num: replacement $digit out of bounds
Unknown ruleset bad name here
```

The solutions to these problems should be obvious. See Chapter 29, *Rule Sets*, for guidance.

Note that this EX_CONFIG and EX_SOFTWARE below cause the local *postmaster* to get a copy of the message on the presumption that local errors can only be fixed locally.

36.5.3 EX_IOERR   A System I/O Error Occurred

An exit value of EX_IOERR (the value 74) means that a serious operating system error occurred. This class of error relates mostly to disk I/O.

If the body of a mail message could not be read, the following error message is logged:

```
putbody: dfqid: read error
```

The file may have vanished because of a disk crash and may have been restored to *lost+found*. The *qid* is the queue identifier that will help you to find the qf file. Inside that qf file are an I line that give the inode and major and minor device numbers of the disk that held the df file (see §23.9.7).

An error that occurs while writing to the *pipe*(2) connection to a delivery agent causes the following error to be logged and for the *fork*(2)'d child to exit with EX_CONFIG:

```
putbody: write error
```

36.5.4 EX_OK   *No Problems, All Was Fine*

The EX_OK exit code (value 0) indicates that *sendmail* did its job and there were
no errors.

Note that this should be the exit value of all the programs that *sendmail* runs
when they succeed without errors. To illustrate, this C language code returns a
random value:

```
main()
{
        ← need a "return 0" here
}
```

36.5.5 EX_OSERR   *A System Resource Error*

The EX_OSERR exit code (value 71) results from various operating system errors
several of which are described below. In general, this exit value is accompanied
by an error message describing the problem.

When *sendmail* is unable to get a *pipe*(2) connection to send the mail message to
a delivery agent, it logs one of the following errors and the *fork*(2)'d child exits
with EX_OSERR:

```
recipient... openmailer(delivery agent): pipe (to mailer)
recipient... openmailer(delivery agent): pipe (from mailer)
```

If *sendmail* is unable to *dup*(2) a file descriptor so that it can write to its pipe, it
logs one of first three errors below. If *sendmail* fails to write to its transcript file
(as set by the **-X** switch; see §26.4), it logs the last error below. In all four cases
the current open file descriptors are logged as described in §26.3.3.

```
recipient... openmailer(delivery agent): cannot dup pipe file descriptor for stdout
recipient... openmailer(delivery agent): cannot dup stdout for stderr
recipient... openmailer(delivery agent): cannot dup pipe file descriptor for stdin
recipient... openmailer(delivery agent): cannot dup xscript file descriptor for stdout
```

If a delivery agent cannot be executed, *sendmail* logs the following error message,
and the *fork*(2)'d child exits with EX_OSERR:

```
Cannot exec delivery agent: reason
```

To save (cache) information about hosts to which connections have been made,
sendmail saves a copy of the file descriptors for that connection to its internal *mci*
structures (see §37.5.44). If it cannot duplicate a file descriptor it logs one of the
following messages and the *fork*(2)'d child exits with EX_OSERR.

```
deliver: cannot create mailer output channel, fd=file descriptor
deliver: cannot create mailer input channel, fd=file descriptor
```

When looking up the MX record for a host, the *resolv* library can return an absurd value. When that happens, the following message is logged and that MX record is ignored:

```
getmxrr: res_search (host) failed with impossible h_errno (bad value)
```

To queue a message, *sendmail* must save a *qf* file to its queue directory. If it cannot create that file, if the directory exists, and if the *uid* of *sendmail* is 0, then the following error message will be logged and the *fork*(2)'d child will exit with EX_OSERR:

```
Cannot create
```

36.5.6 EX_OSFILE   A Critical System File Failure

The EX_OSFILE exit code (value 72) results when certain system files could not be opened and when certain system programs could not be executed.

When *sendmail* gets a SIGHUP signal, it attempts to re-execute itself (see §26.3.2). If it fails, the following error is logged and *sendmail* exits:

```
could not exec /path/sendmail: reason
```

The *sendmail* program can run a program to look up a *key* in a database. If *sendmail* fails to run the program, it prints the following error:

```
prog_map_lookup(program) failed (reason) -- closing
```

We probably don't have to mention this, but the *sendmail* program has to read its configuration file. If it fails to open, stat, or read that file or if that file is not a plain file, it prints one of the following errors:

```
cannot open
cannot fstat
not a plain file
I/O read error
```

and exits with an EX_OSFILE value.

36.5.7 EX_SOFTWARE   An Internal Software Error

The EX_SOFTWARE exit code (value 70) indicates that a software error occurred.

When *sendmail* has successfully connected to a remote host, it checks to see whether it knows to whom it connected. If for some strange reason it doesn't know, it logs this error and drops the connection, and the *fork*(2)'d child exits with EX_OSERR:

```
deliver: no host name
```

When figuring out whether or not to speak SMTP, *sendmail* looks to see whether the $u macro is present in the A= equate for the selected delivery agent (see §30.4.1.3). If $u is absent, *sendmail* will speak SMTP. If *sendmail* was compiled without SMTP support (see §18.8.41), the following error is logged and the *fork*(2)'d child exits with an EX_SOFTWARE exit code:

```
SMTP style mailer not implemented
```

When *sendmail fork*(2)s and *exec*(2)s a delivery agent to perform delivery, it calls *wait*(2) to wait for the delivery agent to exit. If the call to *wait*(2) fails, *sendmail* logs the following error and the *fork*(2)'d child exits with an EX_SOFTWARE exit code:

```
endmailer delivery agent name: wait
```

When *sendmail* first starts to run (provided that it is not in rule-testing mode), it performs a *chdir*(2) into its queue directory. If that *chdir*(2) fails, *sendmail* logs the following error and exits with an EX_SOFTWARE exit code:

```
cannot chdir(directory)
```

The *sendmail* program can run a program to look up a *key* in a database. After running that program, *sendmail* calls *wait*(2) to wait for the program to exit. If the call to *wait*(2) fails, *sendmail* prints the following error and the *fork*(2)'d child exits with an EX_SOFTWARE exit code:

```
prog_map_lookup(program): wait error reason
```

When bouncing mail, *sendmail* tries to set the sender to Postmaster if no sender can be determined. Before it can use that address (Postmaster), it has to parse it with rules to select a delivery agent. If that parsing fails, *sendmail* logs the following error and the *fork*(2)'d child exits with an EX_SOFTWARE exit code:

```
Cannot parse Postmaster!
```

When the sending of an error message results in an error, an attempt is made to send notification of that error to the address defined by the DoubleBounceAddress option (see §34.8.21). If parsing that address fails, *sendmail* logs the following error and the *fork*(2)'d child exits with an EX_SOFTWARE exit code:

```
cannot parse double bounce address
```

See the description of $n (see §31.10.26) for another error that results in the *fork*(2)'d child exiting with an EX_SOFTWARE exit code.

36.5.8 EX_TEMPFAIL   A Recoverable Error

The EX_TEMPFAIL exit code (value 75) is returned by *sendmail* to indicate that a temporary error has occurred. Temporary errors mean that the mail message will be put in (or remain in) the queue for the present, and another delivery attempt will be made later.

One example of this type of error occurs in looking up aliases via a network service, such as NIS. If all the servers are too busy to answer before a timeout, then *sendmail* should temporarily queue the message and look up the aliases later:

```
alias database unavailable
```

Another example occurs when there is a failure to open a file descriptor as a file pointer with *fdopen*(3). This can happen caching an SMTP connection:

```
cannot open SMTP client channel, fd=file descriptor
```

In looking up hostnames with DNS, the name server or the network might be so overloaded that the lookup will time out:

```
host: Name server timeout
```

DNS lookup failures can also be caused by dial-on-demand networks when the connect is not fast enough. If the delivery mode of *sendmail* is set by the **DeliveryMode (d)** option (see §34.8.16) to **defer**, that failed connection is deemed temporary.

Normally, delivery agents exit because they have finished delivering the email. If one exits because of a received signal, *sendmail* logs the following message and the *fork*(2)'d child exits with an EX_TEMPFAIL exit code:

```
mailer delivery agent name died with signal signal in octal
```

Also, if the **-X** command-line switch (see §26.4) was used to specify a transcript file, the arguments to the delivery agent will be recorded in that file.

36.5.9 EX_UNAVAILABLE   A Resource Is
                                               Unavailable

The EX_UNAVAILABLE error code (value 69) indicates that some system resource is unavailable. Several examples follow.

If the body size of an incoming message is larger than the size limit imposed by the **M=** equate (see §30.4.7) the following error is reported:

```
Message is too large; M= bytes max
```

All delivery agent programs must be designed to return an exit value that is defined in *<sysexits.h>*. If a misdesigned delivery agent exits with some other value, *sendmail* will issue this error and consider the delivery to have failed:

    unknown mailer error *decimal representation of the error value*

When delivering to a file, *sendmail* forks, and the child performs the actual delivery. If that child dies because of a signal, the parent logs this error:

    child died on signal *decimal representation of the signal value*

To queue a message, *sendmail* must save a *qf* file to its queue directory. If it cannot open that file and if the error is other than that the file already exists, the following error message will be logged and the *fork*(2)'d child will exit with EX_UNAVAILABLE:

    queuename: cannot create *file* in *directory* (euid=*userid*)

36.5.10 EX_USAGE   A Command Was Used Incorrectly

The EX_USAGE error code (value 64) means that a command or configuration line was used incorrectly.

For instance, the *sendmail* daemon can be executed only by *root*. If anyone else tries to run it with –bd or –bD, the following error is printed and *sendmail* exits with an EX_USAGE error:

    Permission denied

Clumsy fingers can also cause problems. If a command-line switch is used that is unknown to *sendmail*, the following error will be printed and *sendmail* will exit with an EX_USAGE code:

    sendmail: illegal option -- *bad option here*

In parsing an address, that address can be rejected if it contains control characters:

    Address contained invalid control characters

If the EightBitMode (8) option (see §34.8.22) is specified with a bad character, the following error is printed and *sendmail* exits with an EX_USAGE code:

    Unknown 8-bit mode *bad character*

If the `DeliveryMode` (d) option (see §34.8.16) is given a bad mode specification with a bad character, *sendmail* will print the following message and exit with an EX_USAGE code:

```
Unknown delivery mode bad mode here
```

36.6 Pitfalls

- Prior to V8 *sendmail*, if the list of recipients contained an address that began with any of the prescanned switches, *sendmail* would wrongly view that recipient as a switch during its prescan phase. For example, mail to `joe`, `bill`, `-Cool` caused *sendmail* to try to use a file named `ool` as its configuration file.

- Command-line switches must precede recipient addresses. Switches that are mixed in with recipient names are treated as recipient addresses.

- Most versions of *sendmail* (including IDA and some versions of BSD but excluding SunOS and V8) *syslog*(3) a warning if the frozen configuration file doesn't exist. This can be annoying at sites that intentionally choose not to use a frozen configuration file.

- Prior to V8 *sendmail*, unknown command-line switches were silently ignored. Therefore sending mail from a shell script could fail for reasons that were difficult to find. For example, specifying the preliminary hop count wrongly with `-j`, instead of correctly with `-h`, caused your presetting of the hop count to be silently ignored.

- Some old BSD and SunOS versions of sendmail set the default sender's full name from the environmental variable NAME even when running as a daemon or when processing the queue. This can lead to the superuser's full name occasionally showing up wrongly as a sender's full name. IDA and V8 *sendmail* clear the full name in `-bd` and `-q` modes but use different methods. To prevent this problem under other versions of *sendmail*, the *env*(1) program can be used to clean up the environment passed to *sendmail*:

  ```
  % env - /usr/lib/sendmail -bd -q1h
  ```

- V8 *sendmail* uses *getopt*(3) to parse its command-line arguments so that a switch and its argument may have whitespace between them without harm:

  ```
  -C configfile
  ```

But for bizarre historical reasons the **-d** switch differs. There may never be space between the **-d** and its arguments:

```
-d 0.4
```

If there is space between them, the argument (here, **0.4**) is taken to be a recipient name.

36.7 *Alphabetized Reference*

Command-line switches are those command-line arguments that precede the list of recipients and begin with a **-** character. For a complete list of command-line switches, see Table 36-2 in §36.2.

In this section we present a full description of each switch in alphabetical order. Where two switches differ by case, the uppercase switch precedes the lowercase switch.

-B   *(V8.1 and above)*

36.7.1   *Specify message body type*

MIME (Multimedia) support in V8 *sendmail* has been coupled to ESMTP (Extended SMTP) of the new BODY parameter for the MAIL command. The BODY parameter is passed through as is to the delivery agent. Two special parameters are internally recognized by *sendmail*. They tell *sendmail* that the message body is either **7bit** or **8bitmime**. **7bit** forces the high bit off. **8bitmime** causes *sendmail* to leave the high bit unchanged. Both override any setting of the **SevenBitInput** (7) option (see §34.8.62).

When *sendmail* connects to another site for incoming mail, it has no way to determine from context whether or not it is dealing with MIME mail. To override any configured assumptions, you may use the **-B** command-line switch.

```
-B 7BIT
-B 8BITMIME
```

Case is unimportant (7BIT and 7bit both work). The **7bit** causes the local *sendmail* to tell the remote *sendmail* (in ESMTP mode) that the message body should have the high bit stripped from every byte. Conversely, **8bitmime** tells the remote *sendmail* to preserve the high bit of each byte.

The value given to this **-B** command-line or received via the BODY parameter is stored in the **${bodytype}** macro (see §31.10.4).

-b

36.7.2
Set operating mode

The –b switch tells *sendmail* in what mode to operate. For example, *sendmail* can "become" a daemon listening for incoming SMTP connections, or it can run in a mode that tells it to simply print the contents of the queue and exit. The form of the –b switch is:

```
-bmode
```

If *mode* is more than a single letter, all but the first letter is silently ignored. If the *mode* is missing or not one of those allowed, *sendmail* prints the following error message and exits:

```
Invalid operation mode bad letter here
```

If the –b command-line switch is omitted altogether, the default mode becomes –bm (deliver mail and exit).

Beginning with V8.7, *sendmail* the letter that selected the operating mode is assigned at startup to the ${opMode} macro (see §31.10.28).

-ba

36.7.3
Use ARPAnet/Grey Book protocols

In the distant past, mail messages on ARPAnet were sent by using the *ftp*(1) protocol. Because that protocol was never intended for use with email, many different departures were designed ("patched in") to solve particular problems. That growing anarchy caused Jonathan B. Postel to design the Simple Mail Transfer Protocol (SMTP) in 1982 and to document that protocol in RFC821. Since then, SMTP has replaced FTP as the Internet standard.

In the belief that sufficient time had passed for all sites to have adopted SMTP, the –ba mode was deemed obsolete and removed from the V8.1 *sendmail*. It turned out that the British Grey Book protocol was based on FTP. To support that protocol, this –ba command-line switch was restored in V8.7 *sendmail*.

The –ba switch causes each line of a message to be terminated with a carriage-return line-feed pair instead of with a newline. This switch also forces *sendmail* to guess the sender from the message header, instead of parsing it from the envelope. The –ba switch should *never* be used outside of a Grey Book setting.

-bD

36.7.4   *Run as a daemon, but don't fork*

The **-bD** command line switch is almost exactly the same as the **-bd** switch. That is, it causes *sendmail* to run as a daemon, but, unlike the **-bd** switch, it prevents *sendmail* from performing a *fork*(2) and thereby keeps *sendmail* in the foreground. This allows *sendmail* to be run from a "wrapper" script to detect whether it died or was killed:

```
#!/bin/sh
SENDMAIL=/usr/lib/sendmail
UCBMAIL=/usr/ucb/mail

if [ -f $SENDMAIL -a -f $UCBMAIL ]
then
        $SENDMAIL -bD -q1h
        echo ${SENDMAIL}, which should run forever, died \
            | $UCBMAIL -s "Sendmail died" root
fi
```

Note that the **echo** line will never be reached as long as *sendmail* continues to run.

Also note that **-bD** also prevents detaching from the controlling terminal (just as does the **-d99.100** debugging switch; see §37.5.193).

-bd

36.7.5   *Run as a daemon*

The **-bd** command-line switch causes *sendmail* to become a daemon, running in the background, listening for and handling incoming SMTP connections.[*]

To become a daemon, *sendmail* first performs a *fork*(2). The parent then exits, and the child becomes the daemon by disconnecting itself from its controlling terminal. The **-bD** command-line switch can be used to prevent the *fork*(2) and the detachment and allows the *sendmail* program's behavior to be observed while it runs in daemon mode.

As a daemon, *sendmail* does a *listen*(2) on TCP port 25 for incoming SMTP messages. When another site connects to the listening daemon, the daemon performs a *fork*(2), and the child handles receipt of the incoming mail message.

---

[*] In its classic invocation, -bd is usually combined with a -q1h.

–bH

(V8.8 and above)

36.7.6

Purge persistent host status

The **–bH** command-line switch causes *sendmail* to clear (purge) all the persistent host-status information that was being saved as a result of the HostStatusDirectory option (see §34.8.31). Note that the HostStatusDirectory directory is not itself removed, but all the subdirectories under it are. The *purgestat*(1) (see §36.1.4) command-line command is a synonym for this switch.

–bh

(V8.8 and above)

36.7.7

Print persistent host status

The **–bh** command-line switch is a synonym for the *hoststat*(1) command-line command. It causes *sendmail* to print its persistent host status and exit. See §36.1.1 for a description of this output.

–bi

(All versions)

36.7.8

Initialize alias database

The **–bi** command-line switch causes *sendmail* to rebuild its *aliases*(5) database, and exit. This switch is described in §24.5.1. The name *newaliases* and the (obsolete) **–I** command-line switch are synonyms for this mode.

–bm

(All versions)

36.7.9

Be a mail sender

The **–bm** command-line switch (the default) causes *sendmail* to run once in the foreground. A list of recipients is taken from the command line (unless the **–t** command-line switch is used), and the message is read from the standard input and delivered.

This is the mode MUAs use when they invoke *sendmail* on the user's behalf. The *sendmail* program processes the recipients first, then the message header, then the message body. Usually, the envelope recipients are those on the command line. But if the **–t** command-line switch is also used, the recipients are taken from the message header. The envelope sender is more difficult to determine:

- Trusted users, and programs running under the identity of those users, may specify the address of the sender by using either the **–f** or the **–r** command-line switch (see §36.7.21) when running *sendmail*. Trusted users are those that are declared with a **T** configuration command (see §22.8.1.1).

- Otherwise, *sendmail* tries to use the user identity of the invoking program to determine the sender.

- When generating a mail bounce message, the header sender becomes the name specified by the value of the $n macro (see §31.10.26), usually *mailer-daemon.*

-bp   *(All versions)*

36.7.10   *Print the queue*

The **-bp** command-line switch is a synonym for *mailq*(3). See §23.4 for a full description of how to use this command-line switch.

-bs   *(All versions)*

36.7.11   *Run SMTP on standard input*

The **-bs** command-line switch causes *sendmail* to run one time in the foreground, collect an SMTP message over its standard input and output, deliver the message, and exit.

This mode is intended for use at sites that wish to run *sendmail* with the *inetd*(3) daemon. To implement this, place an entry like the following in your *inetd.conf*(5) file, then restart *inetd*(3) by killing it with a SIGHUP signal:

```
smtp   stream tcp   nowait root /usr/lib/sendmail sendmail -bs
```

With this scheme it is important to either use *cron*(3) to run *sendmail* periodically to process its queue:*

```
0 * * * * /usr/lib/sendmail -q
```

or run *sendmail* in the background to process the queue periodically by specifying an interval to **-q** (see §23.6.1):

```
/usr/lib/sendmail -q1h
```

There are advantages and disadvantages in using *inetd*(3) instead of the **-bd** daemon mode to listen for and process incoming SMTP messages. The advantages are the following:

- At security-conscious sites, *sendmail* can be hidden behind a *tcpd*(3) or *miscd*(3) wrapper that can selectively accept or reject connections. (But see TCPWRAPPERS in §18.8.49 for a way to include this support directly inside *sendmail*.)

- At hosts that receive few incoming mail messages, this mode avoids the need to run a daemon.

---

* The look of these lines varies depending on the version of UNIX you are running.

The disadvantages are the following:

- At sites that receive many incoming mail messages, this mode causes a new *sendmail* process to be started for each connection. Compared to daemon mode, this can adversely affect system performance.

- At highly loaded sites, this mode circumvents the *sendmail* program options that are intended to avoid overloading the system with too many concurrent *sendmail* processes.

In general, the *inetd*(3) approach should be used only on lightly loaded machines that receive few SMTP connections.

The **-bs** switch is also useful for MUAs that prefer to use SMTP rather than a pipe to transfer a mail message to *sendmail*. Depending on how it is configured, *mh*(1) can use this feature.

−bt   *(All versions)*

36.7.12   *Rule testing mode*

The **bt** command-line switch causes *sendmail* to run in rule-testing mode. This mode is covered in detail in §38.1.

−bv   *(All versions)*

36.7.13   *Verify: don't collect or deliver*

The **−bv** command-line switch causes *sendmail* to verify the list of recipients. Each recipient in the list of recipients is fully processed up to the point of delivery without actually being delivered. If mail can be successfully delivered to a recipient, *sendmail* prints a line like one of the following:

```
name ...deliverable
name ...deliverable: mailer $# value, host $@ value, user $: value
```

The first form is that of pre-V8 *sendmail*. The second form began with V8.1 *sendmail*.

The **name** is the original recipient address after it has undergone aliasing and rule set rewriting. A local user's name expands to the contents of that user's *.forward* file. A mailing list expands to many names (and produces many lines of output). The **mailer**, **host**, and **user** correspond to the *triple* returned by rule set 0 (see §29.6). If no **$@** is returned, the **host** part is omitted from this output.

If the recipient cannot be delivered to, *sendmail* instead prints the following:

```
name  ...reason recipient is undeliverable
```

The *reason* can be any of many possible error messages (such as "No such user") that would prevent successful delivery.

The **-bv** switch also prevents *sendmail* from collecting any mail message from its standard input unless the **-t** command-line switch (see §36.7.38) is also given.

-bz   *(Not V8)*

36.7.14   *Freeze the configuration file*

Prior to V8 *sendmail* the **-bz** command-line switch caused *sendmail* to build (or rebuild) its frozen configuration file (now obsolete). The frozen configuration file was just a simple image of *sendmail*'s variables after it had read and parsed the configuration file. The purpose of the frozen file was to enable *sendmail* to start up more swiftly than it could when parsing the configuration file from scratch.[*]

The **-bz** command-line switch is obsolete. If you use it with V8 *sendmail*, you will see this error message:

```
Frozen configurations unsupported
```

-C   *(All versions)*

36.7.15   *Location of the configuration file*

The **-C** command-line switch tells *sendmail* where to find its configuration file. The form of the **-C** switch is:

```
-C path
```

Space between the **-C** and the **path** is optional. The **path** specifies the location of the configuration file. That location may be either a relative or a full pathname. If **path** is missing, the location becomes the file *sendmail.cf* in the current directory.

The **-C** command-line switch causes *sendmail* to internally mark the configuration file as unsafe. An unsafe configuration file prevents all but *root* from setting certain options and causes *sendmail* to change its *uid* and *gid* to that of the user that ran it. If it is used by someone other than the superuser (and if in other than **-bt** rule-testing mode), the **-oQ** switch should also be used to set the location of the queue directory. If that location is not changed, *sendmail* fails because it cannot *chdir*(2) into its queue directory.

Prior to V8 the **-C** command-line switch also prevented *sendmail* from "thawing" its frozen configuration file.

---

[*] In practice, freeze files helped you only on systems with very fast I/O systems relative to their CPU speeds. Although this was true in the day of the VAX 11/750, improvements in processor technology have reversed this tradeoff.

-c *(Deprecated)*

36.7.16 *Set HoldExpensive (c) option to true*

The −c command-line switch is a synonym for the HoldExpensive (c) option (see §34.8.29).

As of V8, this command-line switch has been deprecated and may not be in future versions.

-d *(All versions)*

36.7.17 *Enter debugging mode*

The −d command-line switch causes *sendmail* to run in debugging mode. This switch is described in gory detail in §37.1.

-E *(Sony NEWS only)*

36.7.18 *Japanese font conversion*

The −E switch is reserved for the Sony NEWS adaptation of *sendmail*. It is ignored by the Berkeley release of V8 *sendmail* and produces no errors if used by that version.

-e *(Deprecated)*

36.7.19 *Set the ErrorMode (e) option's mode*

The −e command-line switch is a synonym for the ErrorMode (e) option (see §34.8.24).

The −e command-line switch is deprecated and may not be in future versions.

-F *(All versions)*

36.7.20 *Set the sender's full name*

The −F command-line switch specifies the full name for the sender, which is used in mail headers and the envelope. The form of the −F switch is:

```
-Ffullname
-F fullname
```

Space between the −F and the *fullname* is optional. If *fullname* is missing and the −F is the last argument, *sendmail* prints the following error and exits:

```
sendmail: option requires an argument -- F
```

If the −F is followed by any other switches, the following switch is taken as the full name.

When specifying the sender's full name, be sure to quote any internal spaces or shell special characters. For example, for the C shell the following would be needed to specify the full name `Happy Guy!`:

```
"Happy Guy\!"
```

In the absence of this switch, sendmail finds the sender's full name in any of several places. These are described in the section discussing the `$x` macro (see §31.10.42).

-f and -r

(All versions)

36.7.21   *Set sender's address*

The `-f` and `-r` command-line switches are interchangeable.[*] Either causes *sendmail* to take the address of the sender from the command line rather than from the envelope or message header. The `-f` switch is used by UUCP software and by mailing list software. The form of the `-f` switch is:

```
-faddr
-f addr
```

Space between the `-f` and the *addr* is optional. If *addr* is missing, *sendmail* prints the following error message and ignores the `-f` switch:

```
sendmail: option requires an argument -- f
```

Multiple `-f` switches cause *sendmail* to print the following error message and exit:

```
More than one "from" person
```

The behavior of this switch varies depending on the version of *sendmail* you are running.

Prior to V8 the *uid* of the user specifying the `-f` switch must match one of the usernames given in the T configuration command. If they do not match, *sendmail* silently ignores the option and determines the sender's address in the usual ways.

From V8.1 through V8.6 the T configuration command was eliminated. If the `-f` or `-r` switch was used, and if the p (privacy) option was given `authwarnings`, *sendmail* included an `X-Authentication-Warning:` header in the mail message. That header warned that the identity of the sender had changed.

Beginning with V8.7 *sendmail*, the T was reintroduced, but in a different form (see §22.8.1). First *sendmail* checks to see whether the user specified by the `-f` is the same as the login name of the user running *sendmail*, as would be the case

---

[*] The only difference is that the `-r` command-line switch is deprecated, and there is no guarantee that it will be included in future versions of *sendmail*.

for *mh*(1). If they are the same, *sendmail* silently accepts the address. If they differ, *sendmail* looks to see whether the login name of the user running *sendmail* is in the class $=t. If it is, *sendmail* silently accepts the address. If not, *sendmail* checks to see if `authwarnings` is set for the `PrivacyOptions` (p) option (see §34.8.47). If it is, the following warning is logged and included in the outgoing message:

```
X-Authentication-Warning: login set sender to new name using -f
```

-h   *(deprecated)*

36.7.22   *Initial hop count*

A "hop" is the transmittal of a mail message from one machine to another. Many such hops may be required to deliver a message. The number of hops (the hop count) is determined by counting the number of `Received:`[*] header lines in the header portion of an email message. The maximum number of allowable hops is compiled-in for most versions of *sendmail* but is set by the `MaxHopCount` (h) option with V8. When the hop count for a message exceeds the limit set by the `MaxHopCount` (h) option (see §34.8.36), the message is bounced. Ordinarily, the count begins at zero. The -h command-line switch is used to specify a minimum hop count.[†] The forms for the -h command-line switch are:

```
-hnum
-h num
```

Space between the -h and *num* is optional. If *num* is missing, *sendmail* prints the following error message and ignores that switch:

```
sendmail: option requires an argument -- h
```

If *num* begins with a character other than a digit, the offending text is printed:

```
Bad hop count (bad text)
```

The failure above illustrates that the minimum hop count must be positive.

The -h switch was originally used by BerkNet to carry the hop count in the envelope. It currently has no application.

---

[*] Actually, all headers marked with the H_TRACE flag in *conf.c* (see §35.5.8) are counted.

[†] The first edition to this book and the documentation that came with *sendmail* both wrongly stated that the -h switch set a beginning count.

-I   *(Deprecated)*

36.7.23   *Synonym for −bi*

The `-I` command-line switch is a synonym for the `-bi` command-line switch and the *newaliases* name. It is obsolete, but retained for compatibility with the *delivermail*(1) program (the precursor to *sendmail*).

The `-I` switch is deprecated and may not be included in future versions of *sendmail.*

-i   *(Deprecated)*

36.7.24   *Set the IgnoreDots (i) option to true*

The `-i` command-line switch is a synonym for the `IgnoreDots` (i) option (see §34.8.32).

The `-i` switch is deprecated and may not be included in future versions.

-J   *(Sony NEWS only)*

36.7.25   *Japanese font conversion*

The `-J` switch is reserved for the Sony NEWS adaptation of *sendmail.* It is ignored by the Berkeley release of V8 *sendmail* and produces no errors if used by that version.

-M   *(V8.7 and above)*

36.7.26   *Define a macro on the command line*

The `-M` command-line switch is used to assign a macro a value. Note that prior to V8.8, only single-character macro names could be defined. The `-M` command-line switch is fully described in §31.2.

-m   *(All versions)*

36.7.27   *Set the MeToo (m) option to true*

The `-m` command-line switch is a synonym for the `MeToo` (m) option. It is used to set that option to true. The `-m` command line switch is fully described in §34.8.39.

-N   *(V8.8 and above)*

36.7.28   *Specify DSN NOTIFY information*

The `-N` command-line switch causes *sendmail* to append the DSN NOTIFY command to the ESMTP RCPT command. For example:

```
RCPT To:<friend@other.site> NOTIFY=SUCCESS
```

Here, *sendmail* is requesting that the other site return notification of successful delivery. Should the message be successfully delivered by a host that understands DSN, a return message will be sent to the sender. If the other site is running V8.8 *sendmail*, that return message will look (in part) like this:

```
Date: Fri, 13 Dec 96 08:11:43 -0800 (PST)
From: Mail Delivery Subsystem <MAILER-DAEMON>
Subject: Return receipt
Message-Id: <199612132144.PAA09881@other.site>
To: <you@your.site>
MIME-Version: 1.0
Content-Type: multipart/report; report-type=delivery-status;
        boundary="PAA09881.834702270/other.site
Auto-Submitted: auto-generated (return-receipt)

This is a MIME-encapsulated message

--PAA09881.834702270/other.site

The original message was received at Fri, 13 Dec 96 08:11:43 -0800 (PST)
from other.site [204.255.152.62]

    ----- The following addresses had successful delivery notifications -----
friend (successfully delivered to mailbox)
```

The **-N** command-line switch tells the NOTIFY command what to include and thus tunes how notification will be handled. The form of the **-N** command-line switch looks like this:

```
-Nnever
-Nkeyword,keyword,...
```

The first form sets NOTIFY to be NEVER, meaning send no notification. The second form tells NOTIFY to specify notification based on one or more of three possibilities:

success

> The **success** keyword tells *sendmail* to ask for notification of successful final delivery.

failure

> The **failure** keyword tells *sendmail* to ask for notification if the message fails to be delivered.

delay

> The **delay** keyword tells *sendmail* to ask for notification if the message is delayed for any reason.

These keywords can be listed after the -N to set a combination of notification requests. For example,

    -Ndelay,success

tells *sendmail* to ask for notification if the message is successfully delivered or delayed but not to get notification if the message fails.

If an unknown keyword is listed, *sendmail* prints the following error message and ignores the bad keyword:

    Invalid -N argument

If the -N command-line switch is omitted, notification policy is left to the other site. The usual default is `failure` (and possibly `delay`). On the local machine, *sendmail* acts as though both `failure` and `delay` were specified.

-n   *(All versions)*

36.7.29   *Don't do aliasing*

The -n command-line switch prevents *sendmail* from changing local recipient addresses with aliases. The -n switch is fully described in §24.6.

-O   *(V8.7 and above)*

36.7.30   *Set multicharacter option*

The -O command-line switch is used to set a multicharacter configuration option from the command line:

    -OLongName=value

The -O switch is described in detail in §34.1.

-o   *(All versions)*

36.7.31   *Set a single-character option*

The -o command-line switch is used to set a single-character configuration option from the command line.

    -oXvalue

The -o switch is described in detail in §34.1.

-p   *(V8.6 and above)*

36.7.32   *Set protocol and host*

The $r macro holds as its value the protocol that is used in receiving a mail message (usually SMTP or UUCP; see §31.10.31). The $s macro holds as its value the name of the sending host (see §31.10.33). Some programs, such as UUCP, need to be able to set the values of these macros from the command line. The old way to set them looked like this:

```
-oMrUUCP -oMslady
```

Here, the M option sets $r to be UUCP and $s to be lady.

Under V8 *sendmail* the setting of $r and $s has been simplified. A command-line single switch, -p, can be used to set them both:

```
-prval:sval
```

Here, the *rval* is the value assigned to $r, and the *sval* is the value assigned to $s. The two are separated by a colon. If the *sval* is omitted, the colon should also be omitted.

-q *(All versions)*

36.7.33 *Process the queue*

The -q command-line switch causes *sendmail* to process its queue once or periodically, depending on its arguments. The -q switch is described in detail in §23.6.1.

-R *(V8.8 and above)*

36.7.34 *DSN what to return on a bounce*

The -R command-line switch tells *sendmail* to include the DSN RET command with an ESMTP MAIL command:

```
MAIL From:<you@your.host> RET=full
MAIL From:<you@your.host> RET=hdrs
```

The RET command tells the receiving site whether or not to include a copy of the original message body in the bounced mail notification. RET=full causes both headers and the message body to be returned. RET=hdrs causes only headers to be returned. The RET= command is binding on the receiving site only if it agrees to handle the DSN extension to ESMTP. In the absence of RET or remote DSN support, the receiving site is free to return the message body if it so desires.

The RET, and hence this -R command-line switch, is useful in two circumstances:

- For users sending email, this should be set to full so that any bounced mail will include the original message body. This helps to reduce the need for users to archive their outgoing mail.

- For mailing-list mailings or other batched broadcast messages, this should be set to hdrs so that only the header portion of the bounced message will be returned.

The form of the -R command line switch looks like this:

```
-R arg
```

Space between the -R and its argument is optional. The **arg** must be present and must be either **hdrs** (return only headers) or **full** (return the body too). If it is any other value, the following error is printed and the setting defaults to **full**:

```
Invalid -R value
```

The -R command-line switch may appear only once in the command line. If it appears multiple times, the second and subsequent appearances will result in this error message:

```
Duplicate -R flag
```

-r   *(Deprecated)*

36.7.35   *Set sender's address*

The -r command-line switch is a synonym for the -f command-line switch. This -r command-line switch is deprecated and may not be included in future versions.

-s   *(Deprecated)*

36.7.36   *Set the SaveFromLine (f) option to true*

The -s command-line switch tells *sendmail* to set the **SaveFromLine** (**f**) option (see §34.8.59) to true. This -s command-line switch is deprecated and may not be in future versions.

-T   *(Deprecated)*

36.7.37   *Set QueueTimeout (T) option*

The -T command-line switch causes *sendmail* to set the **QueueTimeout** (**T**) option (see §34.8.52) to the value specified. This -T command-line switch is deprecated (as is the **QueueTimeout** (**T**) option) in favor of the **Timeout** option of V8.7 *sendmail* (see §34.8.70), and may not be in future versions.

-t   *(All versions)*

36.7.38   *Get recipients from message header*

The -t command-line switch causes *sendmail* to gather its list of recipients from the message's header in addition to gathering them from its command line. The -t switch takes no arguments.

When this switch is specified, *sendmail* gathers recipient names from the To:, Cc:, and Bcc: header lines. It also gathers recipient names from its command line if any were listed there. Duplicates are discarded, and the message is delivered to all that remain.

The –t switch is intended for use by MUAs. It should *never* be specified when *sendmail* is run in daemon mode.

–U   *(V8.8 and above)*

36.7.39   *This is the initial MUA to MTA submission*

The –U command-line switch is used to tell *sendmail* that this is the very first step in this email message's submission.

As of V8.8, this switch does nothing. When MUAs start to use this switch, it will do things like turning on DNS canonification of the initial addresses. It should *always* be set by MUAs doing initial submission of a message.

This switch has been instituted as parallel support for the XUSR extension to ESMTP.

–V   *(V8.8 and above)*

36.7.40   *Specify the ENVID string*

The –V command-line switch is used to specify the envelope identifier for the outgoing message. That identifier is called the ENVID and is part of the DSN extension to ESMTP. ENVID and the ${envid} macro are fully discussed in §31.10.12.

The form of the –V command-line switch looks like this:

```
-Venvid
-V envid
```

Space between the –V and its argument is optional. The *envid* must be a legal ENVID identifier (see §31.10.12). If an illegal character is specified in *envid*, the following error is printed, and that declaration is ignored:

```
Invalid syntax in -V flag
```

–v   *(All versions)*

36.7.41   *Run in verbose mode*

The –v command-line switch tells *sendmail* to run in verbose mode. In that mode, *sendmail* prints a blow-by-blow description of all the steps it takes in delivering a mail message.

After the *sendmail.cf* file is parsed and after the command-line arguments have been processed, *sendmail* checks to see whether it is in verbose mode. If it is, it resets the `HoldExpensive` (c) option (see §34.8.29) to false and sets the `DeliveryMode` (d) option (see §34.8.16) to interactive.

The –v switch is most useful for watching SMTP mail being sent and for producing expanded output when viewing the queue.

–X   *(V8.1 and above)*
36.7.42   *Log transactions*

The –X command line switch tells *sendmail* to open the file whose name is the next following argument and to append to that file both sides of all SMTP transactions. The –X command-line switch is described in full in §26.4.

–x   *(V8.2 and above)*
36.7.43   *Ignored*

V8 *sendmail* prints an error if an illegal switch is specified (whereas other versions of *sendmail* silently ignore them). The *mailx* program supplied with OSF/1 from DEC and AIX from IBM issues an illegal –x switch. To keep *sendmail* from uselessly complaining under OSF/1 and AIX, that switch is specifically ignored. To get the same behavior with AIX under V8.1 *sendmail*, look for `_osf_` in *main.c* and uncomment the code necessary to ignore that switch.

In this chapter:
- *The Syntax of -d*
- *Debugging Behavior*
- *Interpreting the Output*
- *Pitfalls*
- *Reference in Numerical Order*

37

Debugging with -d

The *sendmail* program offers a command-line switch for investigating and solving mail problems. The debugging –d switch allows you to observe *sendmail's* inner workings in detail.

37.1 The Syntax of -d

The form for the –d command-line switch is

```
-dcategory.level,category.level,....
-dANSI                                    ← V8.8 and above
```

The –d may appear alone, or it may be followed by one or more **category.level** pairs separated by commas or, beginning with V8.8, by the word ANSI. We cover the **category.level** pairs first then ANSI.

The **category** limits debugging to an aspect of *sendmail* (such as queuing or aliasing). The **level** limits the verbosity of *sendmail* (with low levels producing the least output).

The **category** is either a positive integer or a range of integer values specified as

```
first-last
```

When **category** is a range, **first** is a positive integer that specifies the first category in the range. It is followed by a hyphen character (–) and then **last**, a positive integer that specifies the last category in the range. The value of **first** must be less than the value of **last**, or the range will be ignored.

The level is a positive integer. A level of 0 causes *sendmail* to produce *no* output for the category.

When the −d is specified with neither *category* nor *level*, an internal *sendmail* default is used:

```
0-99.1
```

This default causes *sendmail* to set all the categories, from zero through 99 inclusive, to a level of 1.

When *category* is included but *level* is omitted, the value for *level* defaults to 1. When a dot (.) and *level* are included, but *category* is omitted, the value for *category* defaults to 0.

The maximum value that may be specified for a single *category* is 99. Any value specified above the maximum is reduced to the maximum. The maximum value for *level* is that of an *unsigned char* (255 decimal). Nondigits for the *category* or range evaluate to zero. Nondigits for the *level* evaluate to 1.

The *level* specifies the maximum amount of verbose output to produce. All levels below the *level* specified also produce output.

The expression that produces the maximum debugging output is

```
-d0-99.127
```

But beware that debugging levels of 100 or greater may cause *sendmail* to modify its behavior. (For example, one category at such a high level causes *sendmail* to not remove its temporary files.) For this reason, −d0-99.99 is the maximum level recommended.

Debugging can be turned on from the command line and from within −bt rule-testing mode (see §38.7). If *sendmail* is wrongly compiled with SMTPDEBUG defined (see §18.8.42), debugging can be turned on via an SMTP DEBUG command.

Beginning with V8.8 *sendmail*, a special debugging word can be specified at the command line to cause debugging output to become clearer:

```
-dANSI            ← V8.8 and above
```

ANSI is case sensitive and must be the only argument following the −d. If you wish to combine it with other debugging switches, you must specify them separately:

```
-dANSI -d0.4
```

ANSI causes defined macros, class macros, and operators to be displayed in reverse video:

R $+ $# local $: $1

This is truly a "hack." The escape code to highlight characters is hard-coded into *sendmail*. Your display *must* support ANSI standard escape sequences for this to work. There is no plan to use standard library support for this "aid to rule-set hackers."

37.2 *Debugging Behavior*

When *sendmail* is given the **-d** debugging switch, it internally performs three distinct actions. First, if the `category.level` is omitted, *sendmail* presets all categories 0–99 inclusively to a level of 1. It then sets the categories in the command line (if any) to the corresponding levels specified (or to 1 if no level is specified). Finally, it calls *setbuf*(3) to place the standard output in unbuffered mode.

Setting categories 0–99 to a level of 1 has two side effects:

- Usually, certain errors are not reported because they are tolerable, but a level of 1 generally causes those otherwise missing error messages to be printed. For example, if the *aliases* file is missing, *sendmail* does not perform aliasing but is silent about it. A category 27 level of 1, on the other hand, causes *sendmail* to print the reason it could not open the *aliases* file.

- Since *sendmail* is usually silent about what it is doing, any debugging at all causes it to print a great deal of information about what it is trying to do and what it has done.

37.3 *Interpreting the Output*

Some debugging output references C language structures that are internal to *sendmail*. For those it will help if you have access to *sendmail* source. One subroutine, called *printaddr*(), is used to dump complete details about all the recipients for a given mail message. This subroutine is used by many categories of debugging output, but rather than describe it repeatedly, we describe it once here and reference this description as needed.

37.3.1 *The Output Produced by printaddr*()

The *sendmail* program's internal *printaddr*() subroutine prints details about addresses. The *sendmail* program views an address as more than just an expression like *wc@bcx.com*. Internally, it represents every address with a C language structure. The *printaddr*() routine prints the values stored in most of the items of that structure. Its output looks like this:

```
ra=addr: mailer mnum (mname), host hname
        user `uname', ruser `rname'
        next=link, alias aname, uid uid, gid gid
        flags=fhex<names here>
        owner=owner, home="home", fullname="fname"
        orcpt="oparam", statmta=mta, status=status
```

```
rstatus="rstatus"
specificity=spec, statdate=statdate
```

First, *sendmail* prints the address in memory, *ra*, of the C language *struct* that contains the information necessary to deliver a mail message. It then prints the information in that structure:

addr

The mail address as text, e.g. *you@uofa.edu*

mnum

Number of the delivery agent to be used (an index into the array of delivery agents)

mname

Symbolic name of that delivery agent (from rule set 0, $#)

hname

Name of the recipient's host machine (from rule set 0, $@)

uname

Recipient's mail name (from rule set 0, $:)

rname

Recipient's login name, if known; otherwise, it is <null>

link

Address in memory of the next C language structure of information about the next recipient in the list of recipients

aname

Address in memory of the next C language structure of information about the alias that led to this address (if there was one)

uid and *gid*

The *uid* and *gid* assigned to this delivery agent. These values are derived from the ownership permissions of either a :include: file or a *.forward* file (see §24.2.2).

fhex

A hexadecimal representation of the possible envelope flags. This is immediately followed by a list of the flags inside the angle brackets. (See Table 37-1 for a description of each flag.)

owner

The **owner-** that corresponds to the *aname* above, if there is one

home

Home directory of the recipient (for local mail only)

Table 37–1: Address Flags

Name	Hex	Description
QDONTSEND	0x00000001	Don't send to this address
QBADADDR	0x00000002	This address is verified bad
QGOODUID	0x00000004	The *uid* and *gid* fields are good
QPRIMARY	0x00000008	Status was set from argv
QQUEUEUP	0x00000010	Queue for later transmission
QSENT	0x00000020	Message has been successfully delivered
QNOTREMOTE	0x00000040	Not an address for remote forwarding
QSELFREF	0x00000080	Address is part of a loop
QVERIFIED	0x00000100	Address verified, but not expanded
QBOGUSSHELL	0x00000400	User has no valid shell listed
QUNSAFEADDR	0x00000800	Address acquired via unsafe path
QPINGONSUCCESS	0x00001000	Give return on successful delivery
QPINGONFAILURE	0x00002000	Give return on failure
QPINGONDELAY	0x00004000	Give return on message delay
QHASNOTIFY	0x00008000	Propagate notify parameter
QRELAYED	0x00010000	Relayed to non-DSN aware system (DSN)
QEXPANDED	0x00020000	Has undergone list expansion (DSN)
QDELIVERED	0x00040000	Final delivery succeeded (DSN)
QDELAYED	0x00080000	Message was delayed (DSN)

fname
> Full name of the recipient if it is known

oparam
> The ORCPT parameter to the SMTP RCPT command if there was one.

mta
> The name of the MTA host (such as "other.dc.gov") that generated the Delivery Status Notification (DSN) message shown in *rstatus*

status
> The DSN number as text

rstatus
> The DSN message from the sending host's MTA.

spec
> How specific this address is (unused as of V8.8.4)

statdate
> The date and time the status of this address changed

37.4 Pitfalls

- It is best to debug *sendmail* in a window environment, within *script*(1), with *emacs*(1), or something similar. Debugging output can run to many screens.

- Activities of the daemon can be observed only if the −d99.100 debugging switch is combined with the others selected. This switch prevents the daemon from disconnecting from the controlling terminal. Without this switch, *sendmail* silently discards its debugging output.

- Sometimes debugging output seems not to be printed:

  ```
  % /usr/lib/sendmail -d11.1 you < /dev/null
  %
  ```

  When this happens, add the −v command line switch to keep the output attached to your screen:

  ```
  % /usr/lib/sendmail -v -d11.1 you < /dev/null
      ← many lines of output here
  %
  ```

- There must be no space between the −d and its numeric arguments. If you put space there, the numeric arguments may be interpreted as recipient addresses.

37.5 Reference in Numerical Order

The *sendmail* debugging switches vary from vendor to vendor and from version to version. This section is specific to V8.8.0 *sendmail*. These switches are perhaps best used with a copy of the *sendmail* source by your side. Be further advised that many of the internal details shown here will change as *sendmail* continues to evolve and improve.

In this section we provide a detailed description of each combination of debugging category and level. In Table 37-2, each debugging category and level that we consider useful for the system administrator who is trying to solve a mail problem is marked with "useful." The others provide such complex and sophisticated output that they may be of use only to those with access to the source. Those marked in the section column with a "n/a" are debugging switches that were introduced in the *sendmail* source too late for documentation in this edition. All are presented in ascending numerical order, first by category, then by level within each category.

Note that for all categories a −d*category* and a −d*category*.1 are always equivalent.

Table 37–2: Debugging Switches by Category

Category	§	It is	Description
–d0.1	37.5.1	useful	Print version information
–d0.4	37.5.2	useful	Our name and aliases
–d0.10	37.5.3		Operating System defines
–d0.15	37.5.4	useful	Dump delivery agents
–d0.20	37.5.5	useful	Print network address of each interface
–d0.22	37.5.6		Show uname() failure
–d0.40	37.5.7		Show scanning of interfaces
–d0.44	37.5.8		Print addresses of strings
–d0.90	37.5.9	obsolete	Print first 10 rule sets
–d1.1	37.5.10		Show sender information
–d1.5	37.5.11		Dump the sender address
–d2.1	37.5.12		End with finis( )
–d2.9	37.5.13		Show file descriptors with *dumpfd()*
–d3.1	37.5.14		Print the load average
–d3.5	37.5.15		Print load average
–d3.15	37.5.16		Print three load averages
–d3.20	37.5.17		Show offset for load average
–d3.30	37.5.18		Show result of decision to queue
–d4.80	37.5.19	useful	Trace enoughspace( )
–d5.4	37.5.20		Tick for queued events
–d5.5	37.5.21		Events set and cleared
–d5.6	37.5.22		Show events triggered
–d6.1	37.5.23	useful	Show failed mail
–d6.5	37.5.24		The current error state
–d6.20	37.5.25		Show sender of return to sender
–d7.1	37.5.26		The Queue filename
–d7.2	37.5.27		Show assigned queue filename
–d7.9	37.5.28		Dump file descriptor for the qf file
–d7.20	37.5.29		Show queue names being tried
–d8.1	37.5.30	useful	Failure of MX search (low level)
–d8.2	37.5.31	useful	Call to getcanonname(3)
–d8.3	37.5.32	useful	Trace dropped local hostnames
–d8.5	37.5.33	useful	Hostname being tried in getcanonname(3)
–d8.7	37.5.34	useful	Yes/no response to –d8.5
–d8.8	37.5.35	useful	MX lookup gets wrong type
–d8.20	37.5.36		Inconsistency in returned information
–d9.1	37.5.37		Canonify hostname and RFC1413 queries
–d9.3	37.5.38		Show raw RFC1413 reply
–d9.10	37.5.39		Show RFC1413 query being sent
–d10.1	37.5.40		Show recipient delivery
–d10.2	37.5.41		Dump controlling user's address

Table 37–2: Debugging Switches by Category (continued)

Category	§	It is	Description
–d10.5	37.5.42		Show don't send to MeToo address
–d10.100	37.5.43		Predelivery file descriptor dump
–d11.1	37.5.44	useful	Trace delivery
–d11.2	37.5.45	useful	Show the uid/gid running as during delivery
–d11.20	37.5.46		Show tried D= directories
–d12.1	37.5.47	useful	Show mapping of relative host
–d13.1	37.5.48	useful	Show delivery
–d13.5	37.5.49		Show addresses that we should not send to
–d13.6	n/a		Trace envelope stripping, dropping, and moving
–d13.10	37.5.50		Trace sendenvelope()
–d13.20	37.5.51		Show final mode
–d13.21	n/a		Show final send queue
–d13.25	n/a		Watch owner deliveries
–d13.29	37.5.52		Show autoqueueing
–d13.30	37.5.53		Show envelopes being split
–d14.2	37.5.54		Show header field commas
–d15.1	37.5.55		Show network get request activity
–d15.2	37.5.55		Incoming connections
–d15.101	37.5.57		Kernel TCP debugging
–d16.1	37.5.58		Outgoing Connections
–d16.101	37.5.59		Kernel TCP debugging
–d17.1	37.5.60		List MX hosts
–d17.9	37.5.61		Show randomizing MX records
–d18.1	37.5.62		Show SMTP replies
–d18.2	37.5.63		Show entry to MAIL From:
–d18.100	37.5.64		Pause on SMTP read error
–d19.1	37.5.65		Show ESMTP MAIL and RCPT parameters
–d20.1	37.5.66	useful	Show resolving delivery agent: parseaddr()
–d21.1	37.5.67		Trace rewriting rules
–d21.2	37.5.68	useful	Trace $& macros
–d21.3	37.5.69		Show subroutine calls
–d21.4	37.5.70		Result after rewriting by a rule
–d21.10	37.5.71		Announce failure
–d21.12	37.5.72		Announce success and show LHS
–d21.15	37.5.73		Show $digit replacement
–d21.35	37.5.74		Show token by token LHS matching
–d21.36	37.5.75		Trace class matching in the LHS
–d22.1	37.5.76	useful	Trace tokenizing an address: prescan()
–d22.11	37.5.77	useful	Show address before prescan
–d22.12	37.5.78		Show address after prescan
–d22.36	37.5.79		Show each token

Table 37–2: Debugging Switches by Category (continued)

Category	§	It is	Description
–d22.101	37.5.80		Trace low-level state machine
–d24.4	37.5.81		Trace address allocation
–d24.5	37.5.82		Trace assembly of tokens
–d24.6	37.5.83		Show result of buildaddr()
–d25.1	37.5.84	useful	Trace "sendtolist"
–d26.1	37.5.85		Trace recipient queueing
–d26.8	37.5.86		Trace self-destructing addresses
–d26.10	37.5.87		Show full send queue in testselfdestruct
–d27.1	37.5.88	useful	Trace aliasing
–d27.2	37.5.89	useful	Include file, self-reference, error on home
–d27.3	37.5.90	useful	Forwarding path and alias wait
–d27.4	37.5.91	useful	Print not safe
–d27.5	37.5.92		Trace aliasing with printaddr()
–d27.8	37.5.93		Show setting up an alias map
–d27.9	37.5.94	useful	Show uid/gid changes with :include: reads
–d27.14	37.5.95		Show controlling user that caused change in identity
–d27.20	37.5.96		Show how alias will be looked up in a map
–d28.1	37.5.97	useful	Trace user database transactions
–d28.2	37.5.98		Show no match
–d28.4	37.5.99		Show result of lookup
–d28.8	37.5.100		Try hes_getmailhost()
–d28.16	37.5.101		MX records for forward host
–d28.20	37.5.102		Show udb lookup
–d28.80	37.5.103		Preview lookups
–d29.1	37.5.104		Special rewrite of local recipient
–d29.4	37.5.105	useful	Trace fuzzy matching
–d29.5	37.5.106		Preview rule set 5
–d29.7	37.5.107		Show overaliasing fuzzy fallback
–d30.1	37.5.108		Trace processing of header
–d30.2	37.5.109		Eat from
–d30.3	37.5.110		Show a to-less header being added
–d30.35	37.5.111		Trace collect states
–d30.94	37.5.112		Trace collect states
–d31.2	37.5.113	useful	Trace processing of headers
–d31.6	37.5.114		Is header known?
–d32.1	37.5.115		Show collected headers
–d32.2	37.5.116		Show ARPA mode with setsender
–d33.1	37.5.117		Watch crackaddr()
–d34.1	37.5.118		Watch header assembly for output
–d34.11	37.5.119	useful	Trace header generation and skipping
–d35.9	37.5.120	useful	Macro values defined

Table 37–2: Debugging Switches by Category (continued)

Category	§	It is	Description
–d35.14	37.5.121		Macro identification
–d35.24	37.5.122		Macro expansion
–d36.5	37.5.123		Trace processing by stab( )
–d36.9	37.5.124		Show hash bucket
–d36.90	37.5.125		Trace function applied to all symbols
–d37.1	37.5.126	useful	Trace setting of options
–d37.8	37.5.127	useful	Trace adding of words to a class
–d38.2	37.5.128	useful	Show map opens and failures
–d38.3	37.5.129		Show passes
–d38.4	37.5.130	useful	Show result of map open
–d38.9	37.5.131		Trace map closings and appends
–d38.10	37.5.132		Trace NIS search for end of aliases
–d38.12	37.5.133		Trace map stores
–d38.19	37.5.134	useful	Trace switch map finds
–d38.20	37.5.135	useful	Trace map lookups
–d38.44	37.5.136		Show nis_getcanonname() record
–d39.1	37.5.137		Display digit database mapping
–d40.1	37.5.138		Trace processing of the queue
–d40.3	37.5.139		Show envelope flags
–d40.4	37.5.140		Show qf file lines as they are read
–d40.8	37.5.141		Show reasons for failure
–d40.9	37.5.142		Show qf and lock file descriptors
–d40.32	37.5.143		Dump the send queue
–d41.1	37.5.144	useful	Trace queue ordering
–d41.2	37.5.145		Cannot open qf
–d41.49	37.5.146		Show excluded (skipped) queue files
–d41.50	37.5.147		Show every file in the queue
–d42.2	37.5.148		Show connection checking
–d42.5	37.5.149		Trace caching and uncaching connections
–d43.1	37.5.150		Trace MIME conversions
–d43.3	37.5.151		See the final MIME boundary name
–d43.5	37.5.152		Watch search for boundaries
–d43.8	37.5.153		Show the calculations
–d43.35	37.5.154		Show boundary lines as emitted
–d43.36	37.5.155		Show content transfer encoding
–d43.40	37.5.156		Show parse of Content-Type: header
–d43.99	37.5.157		Print the leading/following comments
–d43.100	37.5.158		Mark collect() and putheader()
–d44.4	37.5.159		Trace safefile()
–d44.5	37.5.160	useful	Trace writable()
–d45.1	37.5.161		Show envelope sender

Table 37–2: Debugging Switches by Category (continued)

Category	§	It is	Description
–d45.3	37.5.162		Show saved domain
–d45.5	37.5.163		Show don't send to sender
–d46.9	37.5.164		Show xf file's descriptors
–d48.2	37.5.165	useful	Trace calls to the check_ rule sets
–d49.1	37.5.166		Trace checkcompat()
–d50.1	37.5.167		Show envelope being dropped
–d50.2	37.5.168		Show Booleans
–d50.10	37.5.169		Also show the send queue
–d51.4	37.5.170		Show queue entries being unlocked
–d51.104	37.5.171		Prevent unlink of xf file
–d52.1	37.5.172		Show isconnect from controlling TTY
–d52.100	37.5.173		Prevent disconnect from controlling tty
–d53.99	37.5.174		Trace xclose()
–d54.1	37.5.175		Show error return and output message
–d54.8	37.5.176		Show message and flags
–d55.60	37.5.177		Show file locking
–d56.1	37.5.178		Persistent host status tracing
–d56.2	37.5.179		More persistent host status tracing
–d56.12	37.5.180		Perform a sanity check
–d56.80	37.5.181		Trace creating the path to the status file
–d56.93	37.5.182		Dump MCI record for the host
–d57.2	37.5.183		Monitor vsnprintf() overflows
–d59.1	37.5.184		XLA from contrib
–d60.1	37.5.185	useful	Trace map lookups inside rewrite()
–d61.10	37.5.186		Trace gethostbyname()
–d62.1	37.5.187		Log file descriptors before and after all deliveries
–d62.8	37.5.188		Log file descriptors before each delivery
–d62.10	37.5.189		Log file descriptors after each delivery
–d80.1	37.5.190		Content-Length: header (Sun enhancement)
–d81.1	37.5.191		> option for remote mode (Sun enhancement)
–d91.100	37.5.192		Log caching and uncaching connections
–d99.100	37.5.193	useful	Prevent backgrounding the daemon

–d0.1   *(useful)*

37.5.1   *Print version information*

The **–d0.1** (a.k.a. **–d0**) debugging switch previously prevented *sendmail* from forking and detaching itself, but that function has been moved to the **–d99.100** debugging switch. The **–d0.1** debugging switch now just tells *sendmail* to print information about its version:

```
Version 8.8.4
Compiled with:   LOG MATCHGECOS NAMED_BIND NDBM NEWDB NETINET NETUNIX
                 NIS
SYSTEM IDENTITY (after readcf):
               (short domain name) $w = here
           (canonical domain name) $j = here.US.EDU
                  (subdomain name) $m = US.EDU
                       (node name) $k = here
```

The **Version** is the current version of *sendmail*. Note that for Sun the number may look like **SMI-8.7.5**.

The **Compiled with:** lists the compile-time definitions that where specified when *sendmail* is compiled. All the available definitions are listed in Table 18-3 in §18.8.

The **SYSTEM IDENTITY** shows the value assigned to four important macros. The meaning of each macro is contained in Table 31-7 in §31.10.

–d0.4   *(useful)*

37.5.2   *Our name and aliases*

The **–d0.4** debugging switch tells *sendmail* to print several additional lines of information:

```
Version 8.8.4
Compiled with:   LOG MATCHGECOS NAMED_BIND NDBM NEWDB NETINET NETUNIX
                 NIS
canonical name: here.US.EDU                    ← additional
 UUCP nodename: here                           ← additional
        a.k.a.: [123.45.67.89]                 ← additional
============ SYSTEM IDENTITY (after readcf) ============
               (short domain name) $w = here
           (canonical domain name) $j = here.US.EDU
                  (subdomain name) $m = US.EDU
                       (node name) $k = here

========================================================
```

To find the canonical name of the local host, *sendmail* calls *gethostname()*. If that call fails, the name *localhost* is used. The hostname is then looked up with the internal routine *sm_gethostbyname()*, which gathers additional information (such as other names and addresses for the machine) and fixes several bugs in some operating system's versions of the *gethostby...* routines. Next the canonical name for the local host is looked up. For operating systems that normally support switched services, the name is looked up as specified. For systems that specify switched services in the configuration file's **ServiceSwitchFile** option (see §34.8.61), switched services are not used because the configuration file has not been read yet. (This canonicalization process can be traced with the **–61.10** debugging switch.) If the canonical is found and that name contains a dot, *sendmail* saves the part of the name to the right of the leftmost dot as the domain name in the $m macro (see §31.10.24). It also appends the part of the name to the left of the leftmost dot to the class w (see §32.5.8). If the canonical name doesn't contain a dot, the $m macro is undefined, and the whole name is appended to the class w.

In addition, *sendmail* also sets the $k macro (see §31.10.21) to be the correct UUCP name for the machine. It uses *uname*(3), if available, to find that name (see §18.8.51); otherwise, it uses the same strategy as for class w above.

Then *sendmail* lists any other names or addresses (this latter in square brackets) that it found. If it finds any, it prints the name prefixed by a.k.a.: and appends each to the class w. The aliases listed are only those found using *gethostbyname*(3). To see each entry as it is added to the class w, use the -d37.8 debugging switch.

Finally, *sendmail* scans the network hardware to find any other names associated with interfaces. If the *ioctl*(2) call to get that information fails, the -d0.4 debugging switch causes *sendmail* to print that failure:

```
SIOGIFCONF failed: ← reason here
```

If any are found, each is printed with an a.k.a.: prefix and added to the class macro w.

-d0.10

37.5.3   *Operating System Defines*

The -d0.10 debugging switch causes *sendmail* to print all the operating system specific definitions that were used to compile your specific version of *sendmail*. This output prints after the "Compiled with:" information described above:

```
   OS Defines: HASFLOCK HASGETUSERSHELL HASINITGROUPS HASLSTAT
               HASSETREUID HASSETSID HASSETVBUF HASUNAME IDENTPROTO
               IP_SRCROUTE
Kernel symbols: /vmunix
   Config file: /etc/sendmail.cf
   Proc Id file: /etc/sendmail.pid
```

The OS Defines are described in Table 18-3 in §18.8. Most are automatically determined during compilation; others are specified in *Makefile*.

The Kernel symbols is the name of file that is accessed to determine the load average. It is automatically defined correctly when *conf.c* is compiled. The location of the configuration file and the process identifier file are defined in the *Makefile* and *conf.h* in the *sendmail* source (see §18.8.34).

-d0.15   (useful)

37.5.4   Dump delivery agents

The –d0.15 debugging switch causes *sendmail* to display how it interpreted its delivery agent definitions. The clarity and completeness of the delivery agent information vary with the version of *sendmail*. See the =M rule-testing command (§38.4.2) for an example of this output.

-d0.20   (useful)

37.5.5   Print network address of each interface

When *sendmail* scans the network hardware to find other names for the local host, it uses only those names that are new. Each new name was printed by the –d0.4 debugging switch above. To see every name that *sendmail* finds, new and old alike, use the –d0.20 debugging switch:

```
128.32.201.55                          ← already found
127.0.0.1                              ← found new
        a.k.a.: [127.0.0.1]
```

-d0.22

37.5.6   Show uname() failure

Ordinarily, if the UUCP name for the local host cannot be found (if *uname*(3) fails), *sendmail* silently uses the leftmost component of the canonical name as the UUCP name. To see whether *uname*(3) failed—and, if so why—you can use the –d0.22 debugging switch:

```
uname failed (reason for failure here)
```

-d0.40

37.5.7   Announce scanning of interfaces

The –d0.40 debugging switch causes *sendmail* to announce that it is about to scan for network interfaces:

```
scanning for interface specific names, ifc_len=64
        a.k.a.: [127.0.0.1]
```

The ifc_len is the size in bytes of the configuration list returned by the kernel.

-d0.44

37.5.8   Print addresses of strings

The –d0.44 debugging switch causes *sendmail* to prefix certain lists of strings that it prints with the address in memory of each string and an equal sign. With this debugging level, part of the output produced by the –d21.12 debugging switch would look like this:

```
----- rule fails
-----trying rule:
      0009ec68=@
      0009ec78=$*
----- rule fails
```

This debugging level can be useful to the programmer who wishes to modify the *sendmail* source. It might, for example, be helpful in designing more efficient string storage.

–d0.90   *(obsolete)*

37.5.9   *Print first 10 rule sets*

The –d0.90 debugging switch causes *sendmail* to display its internal interpretations of the first 10 rewriting rules it took from the configuration file. The rule sets are printed in numeric order, rather than in the order in which they appeared in the configuration file. The rewriting rules are printed under each rule set (but these *are* in the order in which they appeared in the configuration file). Rule sets that are declared but lack rewriting rules are not printed. Note that defined macros in the RHS are expanded (the value used) when the configuration file is parsed. Also note that expressions like $+ may be printed as control characters (e.g., ^A) under older versions of *sendmail.*

The preferred way to view individual rule sets is with the –bt rule-testing mode's =S command (see §38.4.1).

–d1.1

37.5.10   *Show sender information*

Although there are many kinds of information that one might like to trace about the sender of an email message, *sendmail* provides the means to trace only one of them. The –d1.1 (a.k.a. –d1) debugging switch causes *sendmail* to print its interpretation of whom the message is from (the name of the sender as it was used in the envelope):

```
From person = "sender"
```

Here, **sender** is the user portion of the mail address of the sender. This output is most useful when combined with the –f command-line switch (which sets the name of the sender from the command line; see §36.7.21).

–d1.5

37.5.11   *Dump the sender address*

The **–d1.5** debugging switch causes additional information about the sender to be printed. That output looks like this:

```
main: QDONTSEND output of printaddr ( ) here (see §37.3.1)
```

The QDONTSEND means that the sender is not a recipient and so should not get a copy of the message. That is followed by the output of the *printaddr()* routine.

–d2.1

37.5.12   *End with finis( )*

Ordinarily, *sendmail* exits silently when it is done (unless an error causes an error message to be printed). The **–d2.1** (a.k.a. **–d2**) debugging switch causes *sendmail* to print three useful values when it exits. The message it prints looks like this:

```
====finis: stat num e_id=qid e_flags=flags
```

The *num* is the final value of the *sendmail* program's global **ExitStat** variable. It is usually updated to contain the latest error value as defined in *<sysexits.h>*. See §36.5 for a detailed description of the possible exit values.

The *qid* is either the queue identifier (such as SAA24069) or the NOQUEUE if the message was never assigned an identifier (such as if it was never queued).

The *flags* is a hexadecimal representation of the possible envelope flags followed by a text representation of those flags in angle brackets with the leading **EF_** removed, for example,

```
201003<OLDSTYLE,INQUEUE,GLOBALERRS,HAS_DF>
```

These are the envelope flags that were in effect with the current envelope when *sendmail* exited. The possible values are shown in Table 37–3.

Table 37–3: Hexadecimal Envelope Flags

Text	Hex	Description
EF_OLDSTYLE	0000001	Use spaces (not commas) in headers
EF_INQUEUE	0000002	This message is fully queued
EF_NO_BODY_RETN	0000004	Omit message body on error
EF_CLRQUEUE	0000008	Disk copy is no longer needed
EF_SENDRECEIPT	0000010	Send a return receipt
EF_FATALERRS	0000020	Fatal errors occurred
EF_KEEPQUEUE	0000040	Keep queue files always
EF_RESPONSE	0000080	This is an error or return receipt

Table 37–3: Hexadecimal Envelope Flags (continued)

Text	Hex	Description
EF_RESENT	0000100	This message is being forwarded
EF_VRFYONLY	0000200	Verify only (don't expand aliases)
EF_WARNING	0000400	Warning message has been sent
EF_QUEUERUN	0000800	This envelope is from queue
EF_GLOBALERRS	0001000	Treat errors as global
EF_PM_NOTIFY	0002000	Send return mail to postmaster
EF_METOO	0004000	Send to me too
EF_LOGSENDER	0008000	Need to log the sender
EF_NORECEIPT	0010000	Suppress all return-receipts
EF_HAS8BIT	0020000	At least one 8-bit character in body
EF_NL_NOT_EOL	0040000	Don't accept raw newline as end-of-line
EF_CRLF_NOT_EOL	0080000	Don't accept carriage-return/line-feed as end-of-line
EF_RET_PARAM	0100000	SMTP RCPT command had RET argument
EF_HAS_DF	0200000	Set when df file is instantiated
EF_IS_MIME	0400000	Really is a MIME message
EF_DONT_MIME	0800000	This message is not MIME-able

For example, if the message were fully queued and required a DSN return receipt, the *flags* would print as

```
e_flags=12<INQUEUE,SENDRECEIPT>
```

Note that this line of output is also produced by the **–d13.1**, **–d40.3**, and **–d50.1** debugging switches but under different circumstances.

–d2.9

37.5.13   *Show file descriptors with dumpfd()*

The **–d2.9** debugging switch tells *sendmail* to display the properties of each open file descriptor. That output is produced by the *dumpfd()* routine, and each line of output is for a single file descriptor:

```
num: fl=flags mode=mode type stats
```

Here, the *num* is the number of the open file descriptor. Note that descriptors 0, 1, and 2 are usually tied to the standard input, output, and error output.

The *flags* is a hexadecimal representation of the state flags associated with a file descriptor. F_GETFL is used with *ioctl*(2) to fetch each, and all are described in *<sys/fcntlcom.h>*.

The *mode* is printed in octal and is the *st_mode* associated with an *fstat*(2) of the file descriptor. The *type* examines the file type portion of the *st_mode* and prints SOCK for a socket, CHR: for a character special device, BLK: for a block special device, FIFO: for a first-in-first-out file, DIR: for a directory, LNK: for a symbolic link, and nothing otherwise (e.g., nothing if it is a file).

The *stats* are printed for all but the socket. They look like this:

```
dev=major/minor ino=inum nlink=nlink u/gid=uid/gid size=bytes
```

Here the **dev=** shows the major and minor device numbers for the device that the file descriptor is associated with. The *inum* is the inode number on the disk (if there is one) and *nlink* is the number of hard links to the file on disk. The *uid/gid* shows the user and group ownership associated with the file descriptor. The *size* is the number of bytes in a file, and 0 for almost everything else.

For a socket, the *stats* part of each line looks like this:

```
[addr]/port-> host
```

Here, *addr* is the IP address of the local end of the socket. If the connection is of type AF_INET, the port number of the connection is also shown as */port*. The *host* is the hostname, as returned by *getpeername*(3), of the connecting host. If any of these cannot be found, the error string associated with *errno* is printed parenthetically in its place.

The **-d7.9**, **-d40.9**, and **-d46.9** debugging switches also print a line like this for specific file descriptors. Also if *sendmail* is run with the **-d10.100** switch, or if *sendmail* fails to open a *tf* queue file (see §23.2.6), or if *sendmail* exited because of too many open files, it will *syslog* all its open file descriptors within this format.

-d3.1

37.5.14	*Print load average*

The *sendmail* program queues mail, rather than delivering it, if the load average (number of processes in the run queue) exceeds the value set by the QueueLA (x) option (see §34.8.50). Exceeding that value also prevents messages that are already in the queue from being delivered (prevents a queue run). If the load average becomes higher than the value of the RefuseLA (X) option (see §34.8.54), *sendmail* rejects incoming SMTP connections until the load average drops.

The **-d3.1** debugging switch (a.k.a. **-d3**) causes *sendmail* to print the load average found by its internal *getla*( ) routine each time that routine is called:

```
getla: la
```

Here, *la* is the current load average printed as an integer. If sendmail was compiled with LA_TYPE==LA_ZERO (see §18.8.14), the following will be printed to show that your *sendmail* binary completely lacks load averaging support:

```
getla: ZERO
```

The −**d3.1** debugging switch also causes *sendmail* to print any errors it encounters while obtaining the load average.

```
getla: open(/dev/kmem): error
```

Here, /**dev/kmem** is the device that is used to access kernel memory. The *error* is the system error that caused the failure, such as "Permission denied" if *sendmail* is not properly *sgid* to the group *kmem*.

```
getla: nlist(unix): error
```

The *nlist*(3) function extracts a list of symbols from an executable binary (among them the symbol for the load average). The binary that it extracts is the kernel whose pathname is **unix** (such as */vmunix* for SunOS 4.x). Here, the *error* is the reason *nlist*(3) failed. One possibility is that you booted from a nonstandard kernel name (such as */vmunix.new*) and the expected file didn't exist:

```
getla: nlist(unix, la) ==> 0
```

If the expected kernel exists (**unix**) but the machine was booted from a different kernel, the symbol representing the load average may not be found. In that instance, **la** is the name of the kernel variable that *sendmail* was trying to find.

−d3.5

37.5.15   *Print load average*

The load average that *sendmail* uses is averaged over the last minute. Internally, the kernel keeps track of three load averages. In addition to the last minute, it also tracks the last 5 and 15 minutes. The −**d3.5** debugging switch causes V8 *sendmail* to print the load average over the last minute:

```
getla: averun = 1min
```

−d3.15

37.5.16   *Print three load averages*

The −**d3.15** debugging switch causes V8 *sendmail* to print all three load averages:

```
getla: averun = 1min, 5min, 15min
```

Here, the three load averages are printed either in integer or in floating point, depending on the setting of LA_TYPE (see §18.8.14).

–d3.20

37.5.17 *Show offset for load average*

The *nlist*(3) routine (described above) provides the offset into the kernel file where the value of the load average is found. The –d3.20 debugging switch causes that offset to be displayed:

```
getla: symbol address = offset
```

Here, the *offset* is printed in hexadecimal. The load average is read by seeking in the kernel file and reading it. If the seek or read fails, the –d3.1 debugging switch causes *sendmail* to print:

```
getla: seek or read: error
```

This can indicate a wrong or corrupted kernel image.

–d3.30

37.5.18 *Show result of decision to queue*

The internal routine *shouldqueue*( ) is called just before a mail message is delivered to recipients. That routine determines whether mail will be delivered or queued on the basis of the current load average and message *priority*. Upon entry it prints:

```
shouldqueue: CurrentLA=load, pri=priority
```

If the **CurrentLA** is less than the limit set by the **QueueLA** (**x**) option (see §34.8.50), *sendmail* prints:

```
FALSE (CurrentLA < QueueLA)
```

Then the calculation described in §34.8.49 for the **QueueFactor** (**q**) option is performed using the *pri* priority. The result is printed as one of the following, where TRUE represents a zero result and FALSE represents a nonzero result:

```
TRUE (by calculation)
FALSE (by calculation)
```

–d4.80   *(useful)*

37.5.19   *Trace enoughspace( )*

The **MinFreeBlocks** (**b**) option (see §34.8.40) defines the minimum number of disk blocks that must be reserved on the queue disk. If an incoming SMTP message will fill the disk beyond this minimum, the message is rejected.

The **-d4.80** debugging switch[*] traces the *enoughspace()* routine in *conf.c*. That routine examines the disk space and allows or disallows incoming mail.

    enoughspace: no threshold

This debugging output says that no limit was defined with the **MinFreeBlocks** (b) option.

    enoughspace: bavail=*haveblocks* need=*needblocks*

This debugging output shows that the number of blocks free (available) on the disk is *haveblocks* and that the number of blocks required by incoming mail is *needblocks*. Note that *haveblocks* will always be −1 if *sendmail* was compiled with SFS_TYPE set to SFS_NONE (see §18.8.40).

    enoughspace failure: min=*boption* need=*needblocks*

If the required number of blocks (*needblocks*) exceeds the minimum reserved as defined by the **MinFreeBlocks** (b) option (*boption*), use of the disk is disallowed.

-d5.4

37.5.20   *Tick for queued events*

Throughout its many possible levels of forks and children, *sendmail* must keep track of timeouts—the maximum amount of time it should wait for an event to occur. For example, a child must not wait forever for an SMTP greeting message, because the program at the other end may never provide that message (because it died or is just too busy).

To keep track of which child should be notified at which time, *sendmail* maintains an internal queue of events. The *sendmail* program uses the SIGALARM signal and the *alarm*(2) system call to set the interval it waits to next check its queue of events for timeouts. That interval (called a *tick*) is the period of the timeout itself, or if the timeout is scheduled for the present or past, the interval is three seconds. The **-d5.4** debugging switch[†] causes *sendmail* to print the current time whenever the queue of events is examined:

    tick: now=*time*

Here, *time* is the current time in seconds as returned by *time*(2).

---

[*] No **-d4.1** (a.k.a. **-d4**) information is available.

[†] There is no **-d5.1** (a.k.a. **-d5**) information.

–d5.5

37.5.21   *Events set and cleared*

Events are set by the process (child or parent) that needs a timeout. The –d5.5 debugging switch causes *sendmail* to print the information that is used to set up for that timeout:

```
setevent: intvl=secs, for=timeo, func=addr, arg=pass, ev=evnt
```

The information is the timeout interval in seconds (*secs*), the time (now plus the interval) in seconds that the timeout will occur (*timeo*), the address in memory of the subroutine that will be called if a timeout occurs (*addr*), the argument to be passed to that subroutine (*pass*), and the address in memory of the C language structure that contains this information (*evnt*). The *addr* of the function to be called can be converted to a function name by running *nm*(1) on an unstripped binary of *sendmail*. For example, if the following output was produced by */usr/lib/sendmail*:

```
setevent: intvl=3600, for=802463800, func=3ebc4, arg=0, ev=94b68
```

you could find the function name associated with the address 3ebc4 by running

```
%  nm /usr/lib/sendmail | grep 3ebc4
0003ebc4 t _readtimeout
```

Here, the result is the name readtimeout, which corresponds to the function *readtimeout*( ) in *util.c*.

When an event is cleared because a timeout was no longer needed, *sendmail* prints:

```
clrevent: ev=evnt
```

Here, *evnt* is the address in memory of the C language structure that stored the event information. This is the same as the last item printed by setevent above.

–d5.6

37.5.22   *Show events triggered*

The –d5.6 debugging switch tells *sendmail* to print the following information when a timeout occurs:

```
tick: ev=evnt, func=addr, arg=pass, pid=pid
```

This shows that the event stored in the C language structure, whose address in memory is *evnt*, has timed out. The subroutine whose address in memory is *addr* will be called with an argument of *pass*. The process identification number of the parent process that asked for the timeout is shown as *pid*.

–d6.1

37.5.23

Show failed mail

Mail can fail for a wide variety of reasons. The way that *sendmail* handles errors is determined by the setting of the **ErrorMode** (**e**) option (see §34.8.24) in the configuration file. The **–d6.1** (a.k.a. **–d6**) debugging switch causes *sendmail* to print the error-handling mode that is in effect at the time it first begins to handle failed mail:

```
savemail, errorMode = char, id = qid, ExitStat = err
e_from= ← output of printaddr() here (see §37.3.1)
```

Here, *char* is either: **p** for print errors; **m** for mail back errors; **w** for write back errors; **e** for special BERKnet processing; or **q** for "don't print anything" (all of which are described under the **ErrorMode** option in §34.8.24). The *qid* is the queue identifier (such as KAA15019). The *err* is the error that caused the message to fail (as defined in *<sysexits.h>*). And **e_from=** uses *printaddr()* to print details about the sender's address.

If the error-processing mode is **m** (for mail back) and the **–d6.1** debugging switch is in effect, *sendmail* prints details about how the message is being returned to the sender:

```
***Return To Sender: msg=reason, depth=num, e=addr, returnq=
← output of printaddr() here (see §37.3.1)
```

Here, *reason* is a quoted string of text that explains why the mail failed. This may be an SMTP reply string. The *num* is zero for normal delivery and one for error delivery. The *addr* is the location in memory of the information about the current envelope. Finally, *sendmail* calls *printaddr()* to print the details of the queue of recipients (**returnq=**) for the current message.

–d6.5

37.5.24

The current error state

The **–d6.5** debugging switch tells *sendmail* to print the error state it was in when it finished processing the error that caused the message to fail:

```
state num
```

If *num* is 7 (successful delivery), nothing is printed. Otherwise, the above message is printed, and the value of *num* represents one of the states shown in Table 37-4.

Table 37–4: Error Handling States

State	Description
0	Report to sender's terminal
1	Mail back to sender
2	Messages have already been returned
3	Save in `~/dead.letter`
4	Return to postmaster
5	Save in `/usr/tmp/dead.letter`
6	Leave the locked queue/transcript files
7	The message has been successfully delivered

–d6.20

37.5.25   *Show sender of return to sender*

The **–d6.20** debugging switch tells *sendmail* to print additional information to that printed by **–d6.1**. Specifically, it prints, via *printaddr()*, the address information about the sender of returned mail:

```
***Return To Sender: msg=reason, depth=num, e=addr, returnq=
output of printaddr() here (see §37.3.1)
Sendq= output of printaddr() here
```

–d7.1

37.5.26   *The Queue filename*

The *sendmail* program stores mail messages in its queue for a variety of reasons. For example, the **SuperSafe (s)** option (see §34.8.67) causes it to queue all messages just to be safe. Also, messages that cannot be delivered because of a temporary lack of resources (or for any correctable reason) are queued for later delivery.

Mail messages are stored in the queue in two parts. A data part contains the body of the message. An information part stores headers and other information about the message. The filenames of the two parts are identical but for the first two letters. A **df** begins the name of the data part, and a **qf** begins the name of the information part. A third type of queue file begins with the letters **xf** and is a "transcript" file that holds error messages produced during delivery.

To ensure that these filenames do not conflict with the names of files that may already be in the queue, *sendmail* uses the following pattern to create new names:

```
qfHAApid
```

Here, *pid* is the process identification number of the incarnation of *sendmail* that is trying to create the file. Because *sendmail* often *fork*(2)'s to process the queue, the *pid* is likely unique and therefore creates a unique name.

The *H* represents the current hour of the day (using a 24-hour clock) and prefixes the AA. It is constructed by adding the current hour to the letter A (thus 00:23 would produce A+0=A, while 15:45 would produce A+15=P). Although it is not recommended, the hour character can be useful in viewing the queue (with the -bp command-line switch) to observe the particular hours, if any, that messages tend to queue. The hour prefix does not increment.

If *sendmail* cannot create a file (because a file with that name already exists), it increments the rightmost A of the AA part of the name to a B and tries again. It continues this process, incrementing the right from A to Z and the left from A to ~ until it succeeds. If a unique name cannot be found, *sendmail* has failed in its attempt to queue the message. The last filename tried is:

```
qfH~Zpid
```

This name is unlikely to ever appear, because the clocking provides for over 1600 possible unique names. With some versions of *sendmail*, however, it may appear if the queue directory is not writable. For example, the -C command-line switch, when used by a normal user, might cause *sendmail* to give up its *root* privilege, thus causing this message to be printed.

The -d7.1 (a.k.a. -d7) debugging switch causes *sendmail* to print the portion of the queue name that is common to all the files that constitute a single queued message.

```
queuename: assigned id HAApid, env=addr
```

Here, *sendmail* prints the identifier portion of the filename (the HAA, or whatever letters succeeded, and the *pid*) that is common to the df, qf, and xf files. The *addr* is the address in memory of the C language structure that describes the envelope for the mail message that is queued.

-d7.2

37.5.27   *Show assigned queue file name*

The -d7.2 debugging switch tells *sendmail* to print the full filename of the file that it just created in the queue directory:

```
queuename: letterfHAApid
```

The first *letter* of the name is either *d*, *q*, or *x*. The *pid* is the process identification number of the *sendmail* process that created the file.

-d7.9

37.5.28   *Dump file descriptor for the qf file*

Once *sendmail* successfully opens its qf file, it has established the unique identifier. The -d7.9 debugging switch causes *sendmail* to dump the file-descriptor for that open file:

> lockfd= *output of dumpfd ( ) here (see §37.5.13)*

-d7.20

37.5.29   *Show queue names being tried*

The -d7.20 debugging switch causes *sendmail* to print each filename that it is attempting to try as it clocks the AA in the name from AA to ~Z:

```
queuename: trying qfHAA16391
queuename: trying qfHAB16391
queuename: trying qfHAC16391
queuename: trying qfHAD16391
...  ← and so on
```

-d8.1   *(useful)*

37.5.30   *DNS name resolution*

Name resolution is the process of determining a machine's IP address based on its fully qualified domain name. This is done by using the Domain Name System (DNS). The process that *sendmail* uses to resolve a name is described in §21.2.

When *sendmail* finds that a hostname is really an MX (mail exchanger) record, it attempts to look up the A record for the host that handles mail receipt. That request may fail for a variety of reasons. If the -d8.1 (a.k.a. -d8) debugging switch is specified, *sendmail* produces the following message:

> getmxrr: res_search(*host*) failed (errno=*err*, h_errno=*herr*)

Here, *host* is the hostname that was being looked up, *err* is the system error number (if any) from *<errno.h>*, and *herr* is the resolver specific error from *<netdb.h>* as shown in Table 37–5.

Table 37–5: Resolver Errors from netdb.h

Value	Mnemonic	Description
1	HOST_NOT_FOUND	Host not found (authoritative answer returned)
2	TRY_AGAIN	Nonauthoritative server not found or server failure
3	NO_RECOVERY	Nonrecoverable errors and refusals
4	NO_DATA	Valid name but no record of requested type

–d8.2   *(useful)*

37.5.31   *Call to getcanonname(3)*

The routine *dns_getcanonname( )* in *domain.c* of the *sendmail* source converts a hostname to a fully qualified domain name. This routine is called only if DNS is used to look up hostnames, as determined by the **ResolverOptions** (I) option (see §34.8.55) and the **ServiceSwitchFile** option (see §34.8.61). If it is, *dns_getcanonname( )* can be called from two places: during startup to get the values for $w, $j, and $m (see §37.5.2) or when a host is looked up via the $[and $] canonify-operators (see §28.6.6).

The **–d8.2** debugging switch shows the hostname before it is fully qualified with this call:

```
dns_getcanonname(host, flag)
```

If the *flag* is nonzero, calls to the *getmxrr( )* routine (which looks up MX records) are also traced. On entry to that routine, *sendmail* will print:

```
getmxrr(host, droplocalhost=bool)
```

The *host* is the hostname that MX records are being looked up for. The *bool*, if nonzero, means that all MX records that are less preferred than the local host (as determined by $=w) will be discarded. If zero, they will be retained.

The **–d8.2** debugging switch also causes *sendmail* to show the result of processing the **ResolverOptions** (I) option's settings (see §34.8.55) while reading the configuration file:

```
_res.options = hex, HasWildcardMX = 1 or 0
```

The *hex* is a hexadecimal representation of the **state** structure's **options** variable as described in *<resolv.h>*. The value of HasWildcardMX is determined by its prefix (+ or –) when listed with the **ResolverOptions** (I) option.

–d8.3   *(useful)*

37.5.32   *Trace dropped local hostnames*

If a hostname is dropped because *bool* (above) is nonzero, the **–d8.3** switch causes *sendmail* to print the following:

```
found localhost (host) in MX list, pref=pref
```

The *host* is the hostname that is being dropped. The *pref* is the preference associated with the MX record.

–d8.5   *(useful)*

37.5.33   *Hostname being tried in getcanonname(3)*

The **–d8.5** debugging switch causes the *getcanonname*(3) routine to print the hostname it is trying to fully qualify. It shows the name with the local domain appended without the local domain appended, and at each step in between. Each try is printed as:

```
getcanonname: trying host.domain (type)
```

Here, the **type** is the type of lookup and is either ANY, A, or MX.

–d8.7   *(useful)*

37.5.34   *Yes/no response to –d8.5*

The **–d8.7** debugging switch causes *sendmail* to print a yes or no response to each of the "trying" lines printed by **–8.5**. Yes means that the **host** could successfully be fully canonicalized. A yes answer prints just this:

```
    YES
```

If the **host** could not be canonicalized, a more complex answer is printed:

```
        NO: errno=err, h_errno=herr
```

The **err** is the system error number (if any) from <*errno.h*>, and **herr** is the resolver specific error from <*netdb.h*> as shown in Table 37-5,

–d8.8   *(useful)*

37.5.35   *Resolver debugging*

The **–d8.8** debugging switch causes the resolver library to be put into debugging mode (if that was mode was included when that library was compiled). The **ResolverOptions** (I) option (see §34.8.55) +DEBUG also turns on this debugging mode. But be aware that turning on +DEBUG will cause a large number of screens full of output to be produced by the resolver library for every DNS lookup.

If the name server returns an answer to an MX lookup, and if the answer is not an MX record or an error, *sendmail* will skip that host. The **–d8.8** debugging switch (or the resolver library being in debug mode) then causes *sendmail* to print the following:

```
    unexpected answer type wrongtype, size bytes
```

The **wrongtype** is an integer that can be found in <*arpa/nameser.h*>.

-d8.20

37.5.36   *Inconsistency in returned information*

Internally, the resolver library (*libresolv.a*) stores host domain names in compressed form (for transmission efficiency). We won't cover the nature of that compression. For our purposes it is sufficient to know that the *sendmail* program calls *dn_skipname*(3) from the resolver library to skip past the compressed part of a host domain name. That call should never fail, but if it does, the -d8.20 debugging switch causes *sendmail* to print:

```
qdcount failure (questions)
```

The *questions* is a count of the number of queries made.

-d9.1

37.5.37   *Canonify hostname and RFC1413 queries*

The -d9.1 (a.k.a. -d9) debugging switch can be used to watch *sendmail* convert hostnames and addresses into canonical form. This is done by watching the *host_map_lookup*() function with -d9.1. First the hostname is looked up in the symbol table. If it exists there and if it is marked as a valid canonical entry, *sendmail* prints

```
host_map_lookup(host) => CACHE canon
```

Here, the name *host* was found in the symbol table. The value returned was a valid canonical name. If *host* had not been found, the *canon* would have printed as NULL.

If *sendmail* is running in defer-delivery mode (see the DeliveryMode (d) option in §34.8.16), it will skip looking up the hostname further. This is done because dial-on-demand connections should not be brought up merely to perform unnecessary DNS lookups. When *sendmail* skips further lookups, it prints:

```
host_map_lookup(host) => DEFERRED
```

If the name is not in the symbol table, it is looked up with the *getcanonname*() function. First *sendmail* prints:

```
host_map_lookup(host) =>
```

with no trailing newline. Then, if the canonical name is returned by *getcanonname*(), that returned name is printed. Otherwise, FAIL is printed. If *sendmail* is compiled with NAMED_BIND defined for DNS support (see §18.8.23), the FAIL is followed by the resolver specific error (*herr*) from <*netdb.h*>:

```
host_map_lookup(host) => herr
```

The –d9 debugging switch is also used to display *identd*(8) queries. When a network connection is made from a remote host to the local host, the local *sendmail* uses the RFC1413 identification protocol to query the remote host for the name of the user who instantiated the connection. The result of that query is printed as:

```
getauthinfo: result
```

Here, **result** is two pieces of information: an address composed of the username, an @, and the real name of the remote host and the IP address of that host:

```
getauthinfo: george@fbi.dc.gov [123.45.67.8]
```

If the query fails, nothing is printed.

–d9.3

37.5.38   *Show raw RFC1413 reply*

The above information is not provided by the remote host in that clear form. Instead, *sendmail* needs to parse the needed information from a raw reply. The –d9.3 debugging switch causes the raw reply to be printed:

```
getauthinfo:  got raw_reply
```

–d9.10

37.5.39   *Show RFC1413 query being sent*

The –d9.10 debugging switch causes *sendmail* to display its outgoing RFC1413 query:

```
getauthinfo: sent query
```

Here, the outgoing **query** is composed of two numbers: the TCP port on the remote machine where its RFC1413 server is running, followed by a dot and the local port number for the original connection.

–d10.1

37.5.40   *Show recipient delivery*

When *sendmail* is about to deliver a mail message, it has already resolved three pieces of information: which delivery agent to use, the name of the host that receives the message, and the name of one or more recipients for that message. The –d10.1 (a.k.a. –d10) debugging switch tells *sendmail* to display information about the recipient to whom it is about to deliver:

```
--deliver, id=mid, mailer=num, host=`hname', first user=`uname'
```

Here, **mid** is the queue message identifier (such as PAA08463). The **num** is the number of the delivery agent selected. Delivery agent numbers can be displayed by using the **-d0.15** debugging switch. The *hname* is the name of the host that receives delivery. The *uname* is the name of the first of possibly many users who receive the mail message. The *uname* can be either a single name such as *joe* or a full forwarding address such as *joe@jokes.are.us.*

When *sendmail* attempts delivery, it may be delivering to multiple recipients. It stores its list of recipients internally as a linked list of C language structures, each of which holds information that is specific to each recipient address. The **-d10.1** debugging switch also causes *sendmail* to print that information using the *printaddr*() routine:

```
send to output of printaddr () here (see §37.3.1)
```

-d10.2

37.5.41   *Dump controlling user's address*

Every recipient address may have a controlling user associated with it (see §23.9.2). The **-d10.2** causes *sendmail* to dump the address of the controlling user using the *printaddr*() routine:

```
ctladdr= output of printaddr () here (see §37.3.1)
```

-d10.5

37.5.42   *Showq don't send to MeToo address*

If the **MeToo** (m) option (see §34.8.39) is set to false, the **-d10.5** debugging switch tells *sendmail* to dump the address that won't receive (the QDONTSEND) the mail message.

```
deliver: QDONTSEND output of printaddr () here (see §37.3.1)
```

-d10.100

37.5.43   *Predelivery file descriptor dump*

The **-d10.100** debugging switch tells *sendmail* to dump all its file descriptors just before it is about to attempt delivery.

-d11.1   *(useful)*

37.5.44   *Trace delivery*

The **-d11.1** (a.k.a. **-d11**) debugging switch is used to trace message delivery. For each delivery agent the following is printed:

```
openmailer: argv
```

Here, **argv** is the A= array for the delivery agent, with macros expanded and printed.

The status of remote hosts is cached internally. Before connecting to a remote host, *sendmail* checks its cache to see whether that host is down. If it is, it skips connecting to that host. If the **–d11.1** debugging switch is also specified, the status of the down host is printed as:

> openmailer: *output of mci_dump ( ) here*

The output of *mci_dump ( )* looks like this:

```
MCI@memaddr: flags=mci_flags<flag,flag,...>,
errno=mci_errno, herrno=mci_herrno, exitstat=mci_exitstat, state=mci_state,
pid=mci_pid, maxsize=mci_maxsize, phase=mci_phase, mailer=mci_mailer,
host=mci_host, lastuse=mci_lastuse
```

The meaning of each *mci_* item in the above output is described in Table 37-6.

Table 37–6: The Meaning of the MCI Structure Items

Name	What prints
mci_memaddr	The address in memory of this C language structure
mci_flags	The flag bits in hexadecimal (see Table 37-7)
mci_errno	The error number of the last connection
mci_herrno	The DNS h_errno of the last lookup
mci_exitstat	The *<sysexits.h>* exit status of last connection
mci_state	The current SMTP state (see Table 37-16)
mci_maxsize	The maximum size message the host will accept
mci_pid	The PID of the child process
mci_phase	SMTP phase (string) such as "client greeting" (or NULL)
mci_mailer	The (text) name of the delivery agent (or NULL)
mci_host	The host's name (or NULL)
mci_lastuse	Last usage time in *ctime*(3) format

Table 37-7 shows what the individual flag bits in **mci_flags** mean, and the human-readable *flags* text that corresponds to each bit. Those text items are shown with the leading source **MCIF_** prefix removed.

Table 37–7: The Meaning of mci_flags Hexadecimal Values

Value	Name	Meaning
0001	VALID	This entry is valid
0002	TEMP	Don't cache this connection
0004	CACHED	This connection currently in open cache
0008	ESMTP	This host speaks ESMTP
0010	EXPN	EXPN command supported

Table 37–7: The Meaning of mci_flags Hexadecimal Values (continued)

0020	SIZE	SIZE option supported
0040	8BITMIME	BODY=8BITMIME supported
0080	7BIT	Strip this message to 7 bits
0100	MULTSTAT	MAIL11V3: handles MULT status
0200	INHEADER	Currently outputting header
0400	CVT8TO7	Convert from 8 to 7 bits
0800	DSN	DSN extension supported
1000	8BITOK	OK to send 8-bit characters
2000	CVT7TO8	Convert from 7 to 8 bits
4000	INMIME	Currently reading MIME header

After checking to see whether the host is down, *sendmail* attempts to connect to it for network SMTP mail. If that connect fails, the **–d11.1** debugging switch causes the following to be printed:

```
openmailer: makeconnection => stat=exitstatus, errno=errno
```

Here, **exitstatus** is a numerical representation of the reason for the failure as documented in *<sysexits.h>*, and **errno** is the system-level reason for the error, as documented in *<errno.h>*.

Other errors, such as failure to establish a *pipe*(2), or failure to *fork*(2), causes the following to be printed:

```
openmailer: NULL
```

This message (although it contains no information) signals that a more descriptive error message was logged with *syslog*(3) (see §26.1).

–d11.2   *(useful)*

37.5.45   *Show the uid/gid running as during delivery*

To perform delivery, *sendmail* often has to set its *uid* to something other than *root*'s. The logic behind that process is described in §24.2.2. The **–d11.2** debugging switch tells *sendmail* to print the real and effective *uid*'s that it is running under during delivery.

```
openmailer: running as r/euid=ruid/euid
```

Also, the **–d11.2** debugging switch causes *sendmail* to print any error response that may be produced by a delivery agent:

```
giveresponse: stat=status, e->e_message=what
```

Here, *status* is the error that caused delivery to fail (or succeed if it is 0) as defined in *<sysexits.h>*. The *what* is either the error message produced by the delivery agent or "<NULL>" if the delivery agent was silent.

–d11.20

37.5.46   *Show tried D= directories*

Execution of a delivery agent can take place in any of a sequence of directories as defined by the D= delivery agent equate (see §30.4.3). The –d11.20 debugging switch causes each directory to be printed as it is tried:

```
openmailer: trydir dir
```

Here, *dir* is the name of the directory that *sendmail* is about to *chdir*(2) into.

–d12.1   *(useful)*

37.5.47   *Show mapping of relative host*

In the SMTP RCPT command, *sendmail* is required to express the recipient's address relative to the local host. For domain addresses, this simply means that the address should be RFC822-compliant.

The –d12.1 (a.k.a. –d12) debugging switch causes *sendmail* to print the address as it appeared before it was made relative:

```
remotename(addr)
```

If the *addr* is for the sender or recipient and is being processed from a queue file, then nothing more is printed, and the *addr* is processed by rule set 3. If the delivery agent for the recipient has the F=C flag set (see §30.8.15) and the recipient *address* lacks a domain part, then the domain of the sender is appended, and the result is processed by rule set 3 again. Sender/recipient-specific rule sets are then applied (1 and S= for the sender, or 2 and R= for the recipient). Next, rule set 4 is applied, and any macros in the result are expanded. Finally, the fully qualified and relative address is printed as:

```
remotename => `addr'
```

–d13.1   *(useful)*

37.5.48   *Show delivery*

The –d13 (a.k.a. –d13) debugging switch causes *sendmail* to display information about the recipients of each mail message as it is being delivered. The –d13.1 debugging switch tells *sendmail* to print the mode of delivery and then the recipient information:

```
SENDALL: mode dmode, id=mid, e_from output of printaddr () here (see §37.3.1)
        e_flags = envelope flags here
        sendqueue:
output of printaddr () here (see §37.3.1)
```

Here, *dmode* is one of those shown in Table 37–8. The `mid` is the queue message identifier (such as PAA08463). The address of the sender, `e_from`, is dumped by using the *printaddr()* routine. Then the envelope flags, `e_flags`, are dumped as described in Table 37-3. Next, information about all the recipients (`sendqueue:`) is printed by using the *printaddr()* routine.

Table 37–8: Delivery Modes Used by sendall()

Mode	Description
i	Interactive delivery
j	Deliver w/o queueing (obsolete as of V8)
b	Deliver in background
q	Queue, don't deliver
d	Defer, queue w/o DNS lookups
v	Verify only (used internally)

Finally, the **-d13.1** debugging switch causes *sendmail* to print a message every time it splits an envelope in two:

```
sendall: split orig into new
```

Here, `orig` is the original queue message identifier for the original envelope (such as PAA08463) and `new` is the identifier for the new envelope, the near identical clone of the first. Envelopes need to split if they have different owners.

-d13.5

37.5.49   *Show addresses that we should not send to*

The **-d13.5** debugging switch is used to display addresses to which mail should not be delivered. One such address is that of the sender of the cloned envelope after a split:

```
sendall(split): QDONTSEND output of printaddr () here (see §37.3.1)
```

Another is the sender address (unless the **MeToo** (**m**) option, see §34.8.39, is set):

```
sendall: QDONTSEND ←output of printaddr () here (see §37.3.1)
```

Finally, senders who are the **owner-** of mailing lists (see §25.3) should not have mail sent to them.

```
sendall(owner): QDONTSEND ←output of printaddr () here (see §37.3.1)
```

This latter sender address is derived by a call to *setsender( )*, which can be separately viewed with the **-d45** debugging switch.

-d13.10

37.5.50   *Trace sendenvelope( )*

The **-d13.10** debugging switch causes *sendmail* to print the following upon entering its internal *sendenvelope( )* routine:

```
sendenvelope(ident) e_flags=hex
```

The *ident* is either the queue identifier (such as SAA24069) or the [NOQUEUE] if the message was never assigned an identifier (such as if it was never queued). The **e_flags** are dumped in hexadecimal as described in Table 37-3.

-d13.20

37.5.51   *Show final mode*

The *sendmail* program's delivery mode (as initially set with the **DeliveryMode** (**d**) option; see §34.8.16) can change during delivery for a complex series of reasons. The **-d13.20** debugging switch causes the final delivery mode to be displayed:

```
sendall: final mode = char
```

Here, *char* is the one of the characters that can be specified for the **DeliveryMode** (**d**) option.

-d13.29

37.5.52   *Show auto-queueing*

If, after all recipient addresses are checked, none are left to be delivered to (everyone of them was either dropped or queued), and if the **DeliveryMode** (**d**) option (see §34.8.16) is neither **q**, **d**, nor **v**, the **-d13.29** debugging switch will cause *sendmail* to print:

```
No deliveries: auto-queuing
```

-d13.30

37.5.53   *Show envelopes being split*

The process of creating another envelope for another sender is called "splitting the envelope." The **-d13.30** debugging switch causes *sendmail* to show its initial scanning of the send queue to count the number of envelopes (including split envelopes) that will be needed.

Checking *output of printaddr*() here (see §37.3.1)

Then, depending on the result, each owner will have one of the following printed:

```
... QDONTSEND
... QBADADDR|QQUEUEUP
... expensive
... deliverable
```

The Q flags are described under the output of *printaddr*() in §37.3.1.

–d14.2

37.5.54   *Show header field commas*

Some programs require that addresses in a list of recipients be separated from each other by space characters. This is called an "old-style" address. RFC822 requires that addressees be separated from each other with comma characters.

The **–d14.2**[*] debugging switch tells *sendmail* to show each header line that may need spaces converted to commas.

```
commaize(header: list)
```

Here, **header** is the caption part of a header line, such as **From:**. The **list** is a sequence of one or more addresses.

–d15.1

37.5.55   *Show network get request activity*

When *sendmail* runs in daemon mode, it opens a socket on a port, then listens on that socket for incoming SMTP connections. The **–d15.1** (a.k.a. **–d15**) debugging switch prints information about both of those steps. Note that **–d15.1** should usually be combined with **–d99.100**, or some output may be lost.

Before the socket is opened, *sendmail* prints the following:

```
getrequests: port 0xportno
```

This shows that the port numbered **portno** (printed in hexadecimal notation) is used to open the socket. If that open fails, *sendmail syslog*(3)'s one of the following messages at LOG_CRIT and exits:

```
getrequests: problem creating SMTP socket
```

If the open succeeds, *sendmail* attempts to bind to that socket. If it cannot bind, it *syslogs* the following message at LOG_CRIT and exits:

---

[*] There is no **–d14.1** information.

```
getrequests: can't bind socket
```

After it binds, *sendmail* goes into a loop in which it listens for and handles incoming SMTP requests. If the listen fails, *sendmail* *syslog*(3)'s the following message at LOG_CRIT and exits:

```
getrequests: cannot listen
```

If *sendmail* starts to listen successfully, this **-d15.1** debugging switch causes it to print the number of the socket on which it is listening:

```
getrequests: sockno
```

This shows that *sendmail* is then listening on the socket whose file descriptor is *sockno*.

-d15.2

37.5.56   *Incoming connections*

In daemon mode, *sendmail* waits for an incoming SMTP connection. When that connection is made, *sendmail* forks, and the child processes the connection from that point on. The **-d15.2** debugging switch causes *sendmail* to print a message that confirms that it is performing this fork. Note that **-d15.2** should usually be combined with **-d99.100**, or some output may be lost:

```
getrequests: forking (fd = sock)
```

Here, *sock* is the value of the socket being used for the connection. The **-d15.2** debugging switch also causes a message to be printed when the child process exits:

```
getreq: returning (normal server)
getreq: returning (null server)
```

Here, failure of the connection to be validated (see §22.4.1 and §29.10.3), causes **null server** to be printed. A successful connection causes **normal server** to be printed.

Finally, the **-d15.2** debugging switch causes the following to be printed every time *opendaemonsocket*( ) routine is called:

```
opendaemonsocket()
```

-d15.101

37.5.57   *Kernel TCP debugging*

On kernels that support this feature, the **-d15.101** debugging switch turns on kernel debugging for the socket that is opened to handle an incoming SMTP connection. Debugging is turned off when the socket is closed at the end of receipt of the message. The debugging information gathered can be viewed with the *trpt*(8) program.

–d16.1

When mail messages are sent to a site that can be reached via a TCP/IP connection, the **–d16.1** (a.k.a. **–d16**) debugging switch causes *sendmail* to print one of the following messages when it is about to make the connection:

```
makeconnection: (host [NULLADDR])            ← null address
makeconnection: (host [0])                    ← no address family
makeconnection: (host [[UNIX: path]])         ← AF_UNIX family
makeconnection: (host [ip address])           ← AF_INET family
makeconnection: (host [[LINK: name]])         ← AF_LINK family
makeconnection: (host [Family num:0xbytes])   ← unknown family
```

Here, **host** is the name of the host to which the connection is made. The form of the address information differs depending on the address family. If the connection can be successfully made, the **–d16.1** debugging switch then causes *sendmail* to print:

```
makeconnection: fd=sock
```

Here, *sock* is the socket descriptor that was issued for use with the socket connection.

If the **DialDelay** option (see §34.8.17) is nonzero and the connection fails, *sendmail* will sleep DialDelay seconds and try again. If the **–d16.1** debugging switch is also specified, *sendmail* will print:

```
Connect failed (error message); trying again...
```

Here, **error message** describes the reason for the initial failure.

If there is more than one address for a host, *sendmail* will try each in turn until one connects successfully. The **–d16.1** debugging switch causes the following to be printed for each failure:

```
Connect failed (error message); trying new address....
```

Note that the **–d16** debugging switch should usually be combined with the **–d99.100** debugging switch, or some output may be lost.

–d16.101

See **–d15.101**. The only difference here is that debugging is turned on for the outgoing socket.

–d17.1

37.5.60   *List MX hosts*

When *sendmail* readies to deliver mail to a remote host, it looks up that host using DNS to find Mail Exchanger (MX) records. The –d17.1 (a.k.a. –d17) debugging switch causes V8 *sendmail* to print the following:

```
hostsignature(host) = records
```

Here, **host** is the host that was looked up with DNS. The **records** is a colon-delimited list of MX records for that host. That list might contain only the original hostname if no MX records were found.

–d17.9

37.5.61   *Show randomizing MX records*

MX records have preferences. Delivery is to the record with the lowest preference first, then to each higher preference, in turn, until a delivery succeeds. When two or more preferences are equal, V8 *sendmail* randomizes them so that they are tried in a different order. The order is the same each time, so this is really a pseudo-randomization (actually a hash function).

The –d17.9 debugging switch causes *sendmail* to print the following each time it randomizes:

```
mxrand(host) = hash
```

This shows that the MX records for **host** have been given a hash value of **hash**.

–d18.1

37.5.62   *Show SMTP replies*

The process of transmitting (or receiving) a mail message using the SMTP protocol requires *sendmail* to send replies as its side of the dialogue. The –d18.1 (a.k.a. –d18) debugging switch causes *sendmail* to print each reply that it sends. It prefixes what it prints with three right angle brackets:

```
>>> RCPT To: gw@wash.dc.gov
```

Note that this is the same output as produced with the –v command-line switch (see §36.7.41).

The –d18.1 debugging switch also causes the following message to be printed to the standard output if the file descriptor for the connection is NULL:

```
smtpmessage: NULL mci_out
```

Prior to opening the connection, the **–d18.1** debugging switch causes *sendmail* to print:

> smtpinit *output of mci_dump( ) here*

Finally, the **–d18.1** debugging switch causes *sendmail* to print:

> reply

Each time it enters its *reply( )* routine.

–d18.2

37.5.63   *Show entry to MAIL From:*

The **–d18.2** debugging switch causes *sendmail* to show processing of the SMTP MAIL From: command that the local machine will send.

> smtpmailfrom: CurHost=*host*

Here, *host* is the name of the current host that *sendmail* is dealing with.

–d18.100

37.5.64   *Pause on SMTP read error*

The **–d18.100** debugging switch causes *sendmail* to *pause*(2) after a read error when processing the SMTP dialog. The administrator can then use *ps*(8) and *gcore*(8) to produce a core dump, which can then be examined with a debugger to determine the reason for the read error.

–d19.1

37.5.65   *Show ESMTP MAIL and RCPT parameters*

Under Extended SMTP (ESMTP) the MAIL and RCPT command can be followed by other optional parameters. The **–d19.1** (a.k.a. **–d19**) debugging switch displays those parameters. We discuss the MAIL command first, then the RCPT command.

37.5.65.1 Show MAIL parameters

The *sendmail* program recognizes four parameters that can follow the address in the SMTP MAIL command:[*] SIZE, which specifies the size in bytes of the incoming message; BODY, which specifies the nature of the message body (8bitmime or 7bit); ENVID, which is used to propagate a sender-specific unique identifier for the envelope; and RET, which specifies whether or not to return the message body on an error return.

------

[*] SIZE is defined in RFC1653, BODY is defined in RFC1652, and ENVID and RET are defined in RFC1891.

The **–d19.1** debugging switch causes *sendmail* to print the parameters it received:

```
MAIL: got arg param="value"
```

The **param** is one of the parameters shown above. The nature of the **value** depends on the **param**

The **value** for SIZE is a positive integer. If SIZE lacks a *value*, this error is issued:

```
501 SIZE requires a value
```

When multiple, illegal SIZE values are specified, the last is the one whose value is used.

The **value** for BODY is a case-insensitive string. It can either be **8bitmime** or **7bit**. If BODY lacks a *value*, the following error is issued:

```
501 BODY requires a value
```

If BODY has neither of the approved strings as its value, the following error is issued:

```
501 Unknown BODY type bad string here
```

When multiple, illegal BODY values are specified, the last is the one whose value is used.

The **value** for ENVID is a special envelope identifier. It is composed of ASCII characters in the range ! through ~, excepting + and =. Characters outside that range and those two excepted characters are replaced with a + followed by a hexadecimal representation of the character's value (there must be exactly two hexadecimal digits). If ENVID lacks a value, the following error is issued:

```
501 ENVID requires a value
```

If the text of the value is not as described above, the following error is issued:

```
501 Syntax error in ENVID parameter value
```

If more than one ENVID specified is for a given envelope, the second results in this error:

```
501 Duplicate ENVID parameter
```

The **value** for RET is one of two possible case-insensitive strings: **hdrs** tells *sendmail* to return only the headers of a bounced mail message; **full** tells *sendmail* to return the headers and body of a bounced mail message. If no string is present, the following error is issued:

```
501 RET requires a value
```

If a string is present but is something other than `hdrs` or `full`, the following is printed:

> 501 Bad argument *bad string here*

If more than one RET is specified for a given envelope, the following error is printed:

> 501 Duplicate RET parameter

If the parameter is not SIZE, BODY, ENVID, or RET, the following error is issued:

> 501 *param* parameter unrecognized

37.5.65.2 Show RCPT parameters

The *sendmail* program recognizes two parameters that can follow the address in the SMTP RCPT command: NOTIFY, which specifies when to notify the sender; and ORCPT, which specifies the original recipient's address.

The `-d19.1` debugging switch causes *sendmail* to print the parameters it received:

> RCPT: got arg *param*="*value*"

The *param* is one of the parameters shown above. The nature of the *value* depends on the *param*

The *value* for NOTIFY is either NEVER or a comma-separated list composed of SUCCESS, which means to notify the sender upon final delivery that the message was successfully delivered; FAILURE, which means to notify the sender if the message cannot be delivered; and DELAY, which means to notify the sender if the message is delayed. If there is no *value*, the following error is issued:

> 501 NOTIFY requires a value

If a *value* is present but it is not one of the words shown above, the following error is issued:

> 501 Bad argument

Multiple, illegal NOTIFY parameters in an envelope cause the subsequent values to be logically OR'd together.

The *value* for ORCPT is an address followed by a semicolon, then an address that is encoded in the same way as the envelope identifier described for ENVID above. If that *value* is missing, the following error message is issued:

> 501 ORCPT requires a value

If the *value* is syntactically wrong (i.e., if the *value* does not have a valid address following the semicolon), this error message is issued:

```
501 Syntax error in ORCPT parameter value
```

If multiple ORCPT values are specified, the second one results in this error:

```
501 Duplicate ORCPT parameter
```

-d20.1   *(useful)*

37.5.66   *Show resolving delivery agent: parseaddr( )*

The -d20.1 (a.k.a. -d20) debugging switch causes *sendmail* to print each recipient address before it is rewritten by rule sets 3 and 0:

```
--parseaddr(addr)
```

Here, *addr* is the recipient address before it is rewritten and before any aliasing has been performed on it.

The -d20.1 debugging switch also causes *sendmail* to print information about problems that may exist in recipient addresses. If an address contains any control character that is not an *isspace*(3) character, *sendmail* prints the following message and skips that address:

```
parseaddr-->bad address
```

If an address is empty (that is, if it is composed entirely of an RFC822-style comment), *sendmail* prints the following and skips that address:

```
parseaddr-->NULL
```

After the recipient address has been rewritten by rule sets 3 and 0, and if a delivery agent was successfully selected, *sendmail* prints the result using the *printaddr( )* routine.

Note that -d21 can be used to watch the rule sets parse the address, and -d24 can be used to watch the resulting tokens being pasted back together.

-d21.1   *(useful)*

37.5.67   *Trace rewriting rules*

The -d21.1 (a.k.a. -d21) debugging switch causes *sendmail* to print each step that it takes in rewriting addresses with rules. The -d21.1 debugging switch causes output to be produced that is identical to the output produced by the -bt command-line switch (see §38.1):

```
rewrite: rule set num    input: addr
rewrite: rule set num returns: addr
```

Here, *num* is the rule-set number, and *addr* is, first, the address (workspace) before rewriting and, second, the address after rewriting.

Because rules are recursive by nature, they can sometimes cause infinite loops (see §28.6.2). When a rule loops more than 100 times, the following error is issued:

```
Infinite loop in rule set num, rule rnum
```

If the −d21.1 debugging switch was also invoked the above error is followed by:

```
workspace: state of rewritten address so far, here
```

−d21.2   *(useful)*

37.5.68   *Trace $& macros*

The −d21.2 debugging switch tells *sendmail* to show the current value of any deferred-expansion macro (one that was declared with the $& prefix). Each such macro that is encountered in processing a rule prints as:

```
rewrite: LHS $&char => "value"
rewrite: RHS $&char => "value"
```

The *char* is the single-character name of the macro, and the **value** is its current value. If that particular macro lacks a value, it will print as (NULL). The LHS refers to the left-hand side of the rule, and the RHS corresponds to the right-hand side. Deferred-expansion macros are described in §31.5.3.

−d21.3

37.5.69   *Show subroutine calls*

The −d21.3 debugging switch causes *sendmail* to print the rule-set number of each rule set called as a subroutine. Rule sets are called as subroutines by using the $> rewrite-operator in the RHS of rules (see §28.6.4). The output produced looks like this:

```
-----callsubr rset
```

Here, *rset* is the text that was interpreted as the number of the rule set, rather than the numeric value. If the number in the configuration file was a symbolic name, then that symbolic name is printed. (See §28.6.4 for more details about the $> rewrite-operator.)

–d21.4

37.5.70   *Result after rewriting by a rule*

If the LHS of a rule matches the workspace, the workspace is rewritten by the RHS of that rule. The –d21.4 debugging switch causes *sendmail* to print the result of a successful rewrite:

```
rewritten as: addr
```

Note that the rewritten address (*addr*) may be the result of rewriting by a subroutine call.

–d21.10

37.5.71   *Announce failure*

If the LHS of a rule fails to match the workspace, the –d21.10 debugging switch causes *sendmail* to print:

```
----- rule fails
```

–d21.12

37.5.72   *Announce success and show LHS*

If the LHS of a rule matches the workspace, the –d21.12 debugging switch causes *sendmail* to print:

```
----- rule matches
```

The –d21.12 debugging switch also causes the LHS of each rule to be printed before it is tried:

```
-----trying rule: lhs
```

Remember that rules are pre-expanded when the configuration file is read. As a consequence, defined macros appear as their values in the *lhs*, rather than in their $*letter* form.

–d21.15

37.5.73   *Show $digit replacement*

The –d21.15 debugging switch causes *sendmail* to print each replacement that is the result of a $*digit* rewrite-operator in the RHS:

```
$digit: hex=token ...
```

Here, $*digit* is followed by one or more *hex=token* pairs. The *hex* is the address in memory of the *token*, and the *token* is the token from the LHS that is being copied into the workspace. This output can run to many screens.

–d21.35

37.5.74   *Show token by token LHS matching*

In addition to the rewriting information shown by the debugging switches mentioned above, the **–d21.35** debugging switch also shows each and every attempt by the LHS to match the workspace. Each comparison is printed like this:

```
ap=workspace rp=operator
```

Here, **ap** (for *address part*) indicates the token in the workspace that the rule is currently trying to match. The **rp** (for *rule part*) is the operator or token at this point in the LHS that is trying to match the workspace. Note that the **workspace** is a single token from the workspace, and the **operator** is a single operator or token from the LHS of the current rule. A complete comparison of the LHS to the workspace can produce several lines of output for each rule. This output can be useful for understanding how the pattern-matching algorithm works.

The **–d21.35** debugging switch also shows the index advancing to the next operator and what the corresponding state of the workspace is at that time.

```
ADVANCE rp=operator ap=workspace
```

This is useful for watching the left-hand side trying to find a match.

–d21.36

37.5.75   *Trace class matching in the LHS*

The **–d21.36** debugging switch causes *sendmail* to print the following each time it finds a match for either the $= or $~ class-operator:

```
CLMATCH
```

The **–d21.36** switch also shows how *sendmail* extends the token in the workspace and tries again, should a match for any operator fail. That is, for all operators (not just $= or $~), if the workspace contained *usa.edu*, *sendmail* would first look up *usa*, then *usa.*, and finally *usa.edu*. Each such attempt prints as:

```
EXTEND rp=operator ap=workspace
```

If there is still no match, *sendmail* has to back up and try a different tack. In the case of *usa.edu* it would back up to the dot. For example, if it were trying $=X, the output would look like this:

```
BACKUP  rp=$=X, ap=.
```

–d22.1

37.5.76   *Trace tokenizing an address: prescan( )*

Processing of rules requires that all addresses be divided into tokens. The –d22.1 (a.k.a. –d22) debugging switch causes *sendmail* to print the various steps it takes in tokenizing an address.

In addition to tokenizing, the *prescan( )* routine also normalizes addresses. That is, it removes RFC822-style comments and recognizes quoted strings. Be aware that rules are also viewed as addresses and processed by *prescan( )* when the configuration file is being read.

The –d22.1 debugging switch tells *sendmail* to complain if the first token in the address it is parsing turns out to be nothing

```
prescan: null leading token
```

This can happen if an address (or rule) contains only RFC822-style comments in parenthesis.

–d22.11

37.5.77   *Show address before prescan*

The –d22.11 debugging switch causes the address to be printed as it appears before any tokenizing or normalization:

```
prescan: addr
```

–d22.12

37.5.78   *Show address after prescan*

The –d22.12 debugging switch causes the address to be printed as it appears after all tokenizing and normalization:

```
prescan==> addr
```

–d22.36

37.5.79   *Show each token*

The –d22.36 debugging switch causes each token to be printed when found:

```
tok=token
```

−d22.101

37.5.80	*Trace low-level state machine*

For the purpose of tokenizing, an address is viewed as a stream of characters. The process of tokenizing and normalizing is driven by a *state* machine that handles the stream one character at a time. For example, if the current character is @, *send-mail* sees that it has found both the start and end of a token and so resets its state to begin looking for a new token. But if the current character is a and *sendmail* is currently gathering a token, it knows that it should continue to gather. The use of a state machine enables *sendmail* to easily keep track of things such as the nesting level of angle brackets and whether or not a quoted string is present.

The −d22.101 debugging switch causes *sendmail* to output two lines of information. The first shows entry into a state (or continuation of a state):

```
c=char, s=state;
```

Here, *char* is the current character in the stream of characters that makes up the original address. The *state* is a two-digit octal representation of the current state. The first digit modifies the second and is a 2 (which means that this is a meta-character so don't pass it through), a 4 (which means to break the token at this character), or a 6 (which means both 2 and 4). The second digit indicates the state. The list of states and their meanings are shown in Table 37-9. The semicolon separates this output from the rest of the line that is printed below.

Table 37-9: States Used by parseaddr() to Tokenize Addresses

Decimal	Octal	Name	Description
0	00	OPR	A wildcard operator (such as $*)
1	01	ATM	An atom (text token)
2	02	QST	Inside a quoted string
3	03	SPC	Chewing up spaces
4	04	ONE	Pick up one character
5	04	ILL	Illegal character

The rest of the output produced by the −d22.101 debugging switch shows the state changing to a new state:

```
ns=nstate
```

Here, *nstate* is the new state number, printed in octal with a leading zero.

Note that the level 101 in −d22.101 means that this debugging output is for true experts only.

–d24.4

37.5.81   *Trace address allocation*

The **–d24.4** debugging switch[*] tells *sendmail* to print a message upon its entry
into the *allocaddr*() routine:

```
allocaddr(flags=flags, paddr=paddr)
```

Here, the address in **paddr** will be copied into another address (not shown). The
flags is a hexadecimal representation of the **RF_** flags used by *sendmail* to communicate with some of its internal routines. The meanings of the bits in these flags
are shown in Table 37-10.

Table 37–10: sendmail's Internal RF_ flags

Hex	Name	Description
000	RF_COPYNONE	Don't copy anything
001	RF_SENDERADDR	Set = sender address, otherwise recipient
002	RF_HEADERADDR	Set = header address, otherwise envelope
004	RF_CANONICAL	Strip RFC822 comments
008	RF_ADDDOMAIN	Okay to append a domain
010	RF_COPYPARSE	Copy parsed user and host
020	RF_COPYPADDR	Copy the print address

If RF_COPYPARSE is set in **flags**, the temporary strings for the host and user in the
passed address (not shown) are allocated permanent storage in memory.

–d24.5

37.5.82   *Trace assembly of tokens*

The **–d24.5** debugging switch tells *sendmail* to print a message upon its entry into
the *buildaddr*() routine.

```
buildaddr, flags=flags, tv=tokens
```

The *buildaddr*() routine takes an array of separate tokens and pastes them back
together again. The **flags** are ORed together hexadecimal values as documented
in Table 37-10. The RF_SENDERADDR and RF_HEADERADDR flags tell *buildaddr*()
which rewriting rules to use in processing the address.

The array of **tokens** being assembled is printed on a single line, each separated
from the other by a space.

---

[*] There is no –d24.1 information.

−d24.6

37.5.83 Show result of buildaddr()

The **−d24.6** debugging switch tells *sendmail* to print the result of *buildaddr()*'s attempt to reconstruct an address.

```
buildaddr => output of printaddr() here (see §37.3.1)
```

−d25.1 *(useful)*

37.5.84 Trace "sendtolist"

Each recipient address for a mail message is added one-by-one to an internal list of recipients. The **−d25.1** (a.k.a. **−d25**) debugging switch causes *sendmail* to print each address as it is added to this list:

```
sendto: list
     ctladdr= output of printaddr() here (see §37.3.1)
```

After each is added, those that have selected a delivery agent with the **F=A** (see §30.8.12) and **F=w** (see §30.8.43) flags set are further processed by aliasing and by reading the user's *˜/.forward* file. Each new address that results from this processing is added to the list, and any duplicates are discarded.

−d26.1 *(useful)*

37.5.85 Trace recipient queueing

The **−d26.1** (a.k.a. **−d26**) debugging switch causes *sendmail* to print the addresses of recipients as they are added to the *send queue*—an internal list of addresses that *sendmail* uses to sort and remove duplicates from the recipient addresses for a mail message.

On entry to the *recipient()* routine, the **−d26.1** debugging switch causes *sendmail* to print the raw address (as it appears before adding it to the send queue):

```
recipient (level): output of printaddr() here (see §37.3.1)
```

An address can be the result of alias expansion. Because the process of aliasing (including **:include:** and *.forward* files) can be recursive, it is possible to get too many alias expansions. The *level* shows the number of alias expansions so far. If that number exceeds MaxAliasRecursion (as hard coded in *conf.c* as 10), *sendmail* issues this warning:

```
aliasing/forwarding loop broken (level aliases deep; MAXRCRSN max)
```

Next *sendmail* compares the new address to others that are already in the send queue. If it finds a duplicate, it prints the following message and skips the new address:

>   *addr* in sendq: *output of printaddr ( ) here (see §37.3.1)*

Here, *addr* is the duplicate address. Information about that address is produced with the *printaddr()* routine.

–d26.8

37.5.86   *Trace self destructing addresses*

Certain addresses can "self destruct" because they can cause an endless loop. Consider the address A. If A is aliased to B and B is aliased to A, A is a self-destructive address. The **–d26.8** debugging switch causes *sendmail* to print the address that is being tested for self-destruction:

>   testselfdestruct: *output of printaddr ( ) here (see §37.3.1)*

–d26.10

37.5.87   *Show full send queue in testselfdestruct*

The **–d26.10** debugging switch causes the entire send queue to be printed after the **testselfdestruct** above:

>   SENDQ:
>   *output of printaddr ( ) here (see §37.3.1)*
>   ----

–d27.1   *(useful)*

37.5.88   *Trace aliasing*

The **–d27.1** (a.k.a. **–d27**) debugging switch causes *sendmail* to print each step it takes when processing local addresses through aliasing. First, *sendmail* prints the addresses being aliased:

>   alias(*addr*)

Here, *addr* is the address (usually a local username) that is about to be aliased. Note that it may already be the result of previous aliasing. If the *addr* can be aliased, its transformation is printed as:

>   *addr* (*host, user*) aliased to *newaddr*

Here, *addr* is the address before aliasing, and the *newaddr* is the new address that resulted from successful aliasing. The *host* and *user* are the hostname and username from the recipient part of the envelope. If the *addr* cannot be aliased, nothing is printed.

During initialization, if the *aliases* database cannot be opened, the **-d27.1** debugging switch causes *sendmail* to print:

```
Can't open aliasfile
```

Here, `aliasfile` is the full pathname of the *aliases*(5) file, as declared by the `AliasFile` (A) option (see §34.8.1) or implied with the service-switch file and the `ServiceSwitchFile` option (see §34.8.61).

If the failure was due to a faulty map declaration, *sendmail* logs the following error:

```
setalias: unknown alias class mapclass
```

If the map is not one that is allowed to provide alias services, *sendmail* logs this error:

```
setalias: map class mapclass can't handle aliases
```

If *sendmail* is trying to create a database file and it can't (usually when it is run with the **-bi** command-line switch or run as *newaliases*), the **-d27.1** debugging switch causes the following error to be printed:

```
Can't create database for filename: reason here
```

A self-destructive alias can cause a dangerous loop to occur. For example, the following two aliases can lead to a loop on the host *mailhost*:

```
jake:           Jake_Bair
Jake_Bair:      jake@mailhost
```

The **-d27.1** debugging switch causes the following message to be printed when *sendmail* tests an address to see whether it loops:

```
self_reference(addr)
        ... no self ref                    ←if it didn't loop
        ... cannot break loop for "addr"   ←if it's unbreakable
```

An alias loop is unbreakable if no local username can be found in the list of aliases.

The **-d27.1** debugging switch also causes *sendmail* to print the following message when it is attempting to read the user's `˜/.forward` file:

```
forward(user)
```

If the *user* has no home directory listed in the *passwd*(5) file, *sendmail* issues the following message with a *syslog*(3) level of LOG_CRIT:

```
forward: no home
```

The –d27.1 debugging switch also causes *sendmail* to print a warning if it cannot open or lock an alias file for automatic rebuilding (see §34.8.4, the `AutoRebuil-dAliases` (D) option):

```
Can't open file: reason here
newaliases: cannot open file: reason here
```

Here, the error might be caused by the file simply not existing (as would be the case if it was NSF-mounted on a down host) or an I/O error (as would be the case for a bad disk).

```
warning: cannot lock file: reason here
```

Failure to lock can be caused by system errors or by the file being read-only. Note that maintaining an aliases file under revision control can cause a read-only copy to exist, resulting in the following error:

```
Can't create database for file: reason here
Cannot create database for alias file file
```

This error indicates that the output file (the *dbm*(3) or *db*(3) file) could not be created or written.

–d27.2   *(useful)*

37.5.89   *Include file, self reference, error on home*

The –d27.2 debugging switch causes each `:include:` and *.forward* filename to be printed before each is opened for reading:

```
include(file)
```

The –d27.2 debugging switch also causes additional information to be printed for the alias loop check described above:

```
self_reference(addr)
        ... getpwnam(user)...found     ←if in passwd file
        ... getpwnam(user)...failed    ← otherwise
```

The –d27.2 debugging switch also causes *sendmail* to print a message every time it sleeps while waiting for the *aliases* database to be rebuilt:

```
aliaswait: sleeping for sec seconds
```

Also, when processing the `˜/.forward` file, *sendmail* may experience a temporary inability to read it (such as when an NFS server is down). In that case the –d27.2 debugging switch causes the following message to be printed:

```
forward: transient error on home
```

Here the message will be queued and tried again later.

-d27.3   *(useful)*

37.5.90   *Forwarding path and alias wait*

The **-d27.3** debugging switch causes each path for a possible *.forward* file to be printed before it is tried:

        forward: trying *file*

Here, *file* is each file in the path of files declared by the **ForwardPath** (J) option (see §34.8.27).

The **-d27.3** debugging switch also causes *sendmail* to trace its wait for another alias rebuild to complete (see §24.5.1). First *sendmail* prints the class (such as *hash*) and filename for which it will wait:

        aliaswait(*class:file*)

If the database is not rebuildable (as would be the case with a network map class like *nis*, *nis+*, or *hesiod*), the **-d27.3** debugging switch causes the following to be printed:

        aliaswait: not rebuildable

If the *file* specified doesn't exist, the **-d27.3** debugging switch prints

        aliaswait: no source file

The **-d27.3** debugging switch also causes *sendmail* to print an error message if there was a read error while processing a **:include:** or *.forward* file:

        include: read error: *reason here*

-d27.4   *(useful)*

37.5.91   *Print not safe*

A *˜/.forward* file must be owned by the user or by *root*. If it is not, it is considered unsafe, and *sendmail* ignores it. The **-d27.4** debugging switch causes *sendmail* to print a message describing any such file it finds unsafe:

        include: not safe (uid=*uid*)

Note that a file is considered unsafe if, among other things, it lacks all read permissions.

The **-d27.4** debugging switch also causes *sendmail* to print information about a **:include:** file beyond that printed with **-d27.2** above:

        include(*file*)   ← *printed with -d27.2*
            ruid=*ruid* euid=*euid*   ← *printed with -d27.4*

This shows the real userID (*ruid*) and effective userID (*euid*) of the current running *sendmail*.

The **-d27.4** debugging switch also causes *sendmail* to print an error if a **:include:** or ˜/*.forward* file cannot be opened for reading:

    include: open: *reason here*

-d27.5

37.5.92   *Trace aliasing with printaddr()*

The **-d27.5** debugging switch tells *sendmail* to print several addresses with *printaddr()* (see §37.3.1) as each one is handled.

When an address is aliased to another, the original needs to be marked as one that shouldn't be delivered. The **QDONTSEND** below means just that:

    alias: QDONTSEND *output of printaddr () here (see §37.3.1)*

If there was a self-reference, the retained address is printed like this:

    sendtolist: QSELFREF *output of printaddr () here (see §37.3.1)*

If the original (before the test for a self-reference) is not the same as the retained address, the original must be marked for nondelivery:

    sendtolist: QDONTSEND *output of printaddr () here (see §37.3.1)*

If an address resulted from a **:include:** or ˜/*.forward* file, it will have a controlling user associated with it. That controlling user's address needs to be marked for nondelivery:

    include: QDONTSEND *output of printaddr () here (see §37.3.1)*

-d27.8

37.5.93   *Show setting up an alias map*

The **-d27.8** debugging switch tells *sendmail* to print the string passed to its internal *setalias()* routine.

    setalias(*what*)

Here, *what* is one of the items listed with the **AliasFile** (A) option (see §34.8.1), such as */etc/aliases*, or implied with the service-switch file and the **ServiceSwitchFile** option (see §34.8.61).

-d27.9   *(useful)*

37.5.94   *Show uid/gid changes with :include: reads*

The **-d27.9** debugging switch causes *sendmail* to trace the setting and resetting of
its *uid* and *gid* identities when processing **:include:** and ⁓*/.forward* files. First an
additional line is printed below the output of the **-d27.2** and **-d27.4** debugging
switches:

```
include(file)                ← printed with –d27.2
    ruid=ruid euid=euid      ← printed with –d27.4
include: old uid = ruid/euid
```

The second and third lines above both contain the same information. After the
new line is printed, *sendmail* may or may not change its identity depending on
the nature of a **:include:** or ⁓*/.forward* file and that file's controlling user.
Whether it changed or not, *sendmail* prints:

```
include: new uid = ruid/euid
```

After *sendmail* has finished processing a **:include:** or ⁓*/.forward* file, it resets its
uid and *gid* back to their original values and displays the result:

```
include: reset uid = ruid/euid
```

-d27.14

37.5.95   *Show controlling user that caused change in identity*

The **-d27.14** debugging switch causes *sendmail* to print the controlling user's
address that led to the changing of the *uid* and *gid* or the currently running process:

```
include(file)                ← printed with –d27.2
    ruid=ruid euid=euid      ← printed with –d27.4
ctladdr addr                 ← output of printaddr() produced with this –d27.14
include: old uid = ruid/euid ← printed with –d27.9
```

The output of the *printaddr()* routine is described in §37.3.1.

-d27.20

37.5.96   *Show how alias will be looked up in a map*

The **-d27.20** debugging switch causes *sendmail* to show how it is about to look
up an alias in one of its database maps:

```
setalias(what)          ← printed with –d27.8
   map class:map what
```

Here, **class** is the type of map being looked up, such as *hash* or *implicit* (see
§33.3). The **map** is the map name, such as *Alias0*. The **what** is one of the items

listed with the `AliasFile` (A) option (see §34.8.1), such as */etc/aliases*, or implied
with the service-switch file and the `ServiceSwitchFile` option (see §34.8.61).

–d28.1   *(useful)*

37.5.97   *Trace user database transactions*

The *sendmail* program can be compiled to use the user database (see §33.5) by
defining USERDB in the *Makefile* (see §18.8.54). If an address is selected by rule set
0 for delivery by a delivery agent with the `F=1` flag set, and if it remains unaliased
even if the `F=A` flag is set, it is looked up in the user database. The `–d28.1` (a.k.a.
`–d28`) debugging switch is used to watch the interaction between *sendmail* and
the user database:

```
udbexpand(addr)
```

Here, *addr* is the address being looked up.

The sender is looked up in a similar fashion. The intent in this case is to correct
information such as the return address:

```
udbmatch(login, what)
```

Here, *login* is the login name of the sender and *what* is the `mailname` for sender
lookups. If the lookup is via *hesiod*, *sendmail* will print the same information like
this:

```
hes_udb_get(login, what)
```

If the sender is found in the database, *sendmail* prints:

```
udbmatch ==> login@defaulthost
```

Here, *login* may be a new login name. The *defaulthost* is either the sitewide
host for all reply mail as defined in the user database or the default destination
host for a particular user.

In the event that a *db*(3) style user database fails to open, the `–d28.1` debugging
switch displays the following error message:

```
dbopen(database):  reason for failure here
```

–d28.2

37.5.98   *Show no match*

The `–d28.2` debugging switch causes *sendmail* to print any failures in lookups:

```
udbmatch: no match on login (length) via method
```

This shows that the name *login* was looked up with a particular length, using the database *method*, where *method* is either db or hesiod.

-d28.4

37.5.99   *Show result of lookup*

The -d28.4 debugging switch causes *sendmail* to print the result of its attempt to open (initialize) each database. There are three possible results:

1. If a file on the local machine contains the information sought, *sendmail* prints

   ```
   FETCH: file fname
   ```

   Here, *fname* is the name of the local file.

2. If a mail message should be sent to another host for delivery, *sendmail* prints:

   ```
   FORWARD: host hostname
   ```

   Here, *hostname* is the full canonical name of the host that takes delivery.

3. An unknown result causes the address to remain unchanged and the following message to be printed:

   ```
   UNKNOWN
   ```

-d28.8

37.5.100   *Try hes_getmailhost()*

If *sendmail* is compiled with HES_GETMAILHOST defined (see §18.8.11), the following is printed when the -d28.8 debugging switch is used:

```
udbmatch: no match on login (length)   ← from –d28.2
    ... trying hes_getmailhost (login)
udbexpand: hesiod-getmail login stat err
```

Here, *hes_getmailhost()* is called to retrieve the name of the post office that handles this *login*. If that call fails, the last line is printed, showing that the *hesiod* error *err* occurred.

-d28.16

37.5.101   *MX records for forward host*

If a lookup is for a forwarding host (FORWARD above) and the forwarding host has MX records, the -d28.16 debugging switch causes those records to be printed:

```
getmxrr(host): number
    first MX record here
    second MX record here
    etc.
```

Here, *host* is the name of the host to which the lookup is forwarded. The *number* is the number of MX records found. That line is then followed by *number* MX records for that host.

–d28.20

37.5.102   *Show udb lookup*

The internal *udb_map_lookup( )* routine is called each time anything is looked up in the udb database. Upon entry into that routine, the –d28.20 debugging switch causes *sendmail* to print

        udb_map_lookup(*name*, *what*)

Here, the *what* is key about to be looked up in the map named *name*. This routine in turn calls *udbmatch( )*. Note that the –d38.20 debugging switch also produces this output.

–d28.80

37.5.103   *Preview lookups*

The –d28.80 debugging switch causes *sendmail* to show what it is about to lookup.

        udbexpand: trying *login* (*length*) via *method*

This shows that the name *login* was looked up with a particular *length*, using the database *method*, where *method* is either **db** or **hesiod**.

The –d28.80 debugging switch also causes the result of a lookup to be displayed:

        udbexpand: match *login*: *result*

Here, *login* was found, and the lookup returned *result*.

The –d28.80 debugging switch also causes the result of *hes_udb_get( )* to be displayed:

        hes_udb_get(*login*, *what*)   ← *printed with –d28.1*
        hes_udb_get => *result*   ← *printed with –d28.80*

Here, the hesiod library routine *hes_resolve*(3) is called with the two arguments *login* and *what*. The *result* (a string) is printed on the second line.

–d29.1

37.5.104   *Special rewrite of local recipient*

With a level 2 or greater configuration file (see the V configuration command in §27.5), V8 *sendmail* passes the user part ($u) of local recipient addresses through rule set 5 as a hook to select a new delivery agent. Rule set 5 is called if the address is unchanged after all aliasing (including the `~/.forward` file). The `-d29.1` (a.k.a. `-d29`) debugging switch causes the address to be printed as it appears before the rule set 5 rewrite:

> `maplocaluser:` *output of printaddr ( ) here (see §37.3.1)*

Information about the address is printed with the *printaddr()* routine. The output of *maplocaluser()* becomes the input to *recipient()*, so the result of rewriting can be seen by using the `-d26.1` debugging switch in combination with this one.

Note that the particulars about whether or not an address will be processed by rule set 5 are described in `-d29.5` below.

-d29.4   *(useful)*

37.5.105   *Trace fuzzy matching*

Fuzzy matching is the attempt to match a local recipient name to one of the names in the *gecos* field of the *passwd*(5) file (or NIS map). The `-d29.4` debugging switch causes the process of fuzzy matching to be traced:

> `finduser(name)`

Here, *name* is an address in the form of a local user address, without the host part. The *name* is first looked up in the *passwd*(5) file on the assumption that it is a login name. If it is found, *sendmail* prints

> `found (non-fuzzy)`

If *sendmail* was compiled with *hesiod* support, all numeric login names will not work properly, resulting in the following:

> `failed (numeric input)`

If the name is looked up and not found, the entire *passwd*(5) is searched, to see whether *name* appears in any of the *gecos* fields. This search is done only if MATCHGECOS (see §18.8.18) was defined when *sendmail* was compiled and if the `MatchGECOS` (G) option (see §34.8.34) is true. If MATCHGECOS was undefined, the search ends and the not-found *name* causes the mail to bounce. If the `MatchGecos` (G) option is false, *sendmail* bounces the message and prints the following:

> `not found (fuzzy disabled)`

If the `MatchGecos` (G) option is true, the *gecos* fields are searched. But before the search starts, any underscore characters (and the character defined by the BlankSub (B) option; see §34.8.5) that appear in *name* are converted to spaces. Then, in turn, each *gecos* field has the full name extracted (everything following the first comma, semicolon, or percent is truncated off, including that character), and any & characters found are converted to the login name. The two are then compared in a case-insensitive fashion. If they are identical, *sendmail* prints:

```
fuzzy matches gecos
```

If all *gecos* fields are compared and no match is found, *sendmail* bounces the message and prints the following:

```
no fuzzy match found
```

There is no debugging flag to watch each comparison.

-d29.5

37.5.106   *Preview rule set 5*

The **-d29.5** debugging switch causes *sendmail* to print an address just before it is tested to see whether rule set 5 should be called:

```
recipient: testing local?  cl=level, rr5=addr,
                                          ↑
                    output of printaddr() here (see §37.3.1)
```

For the address to be rewritten, the configuration file version as displayed by *level* must be 2 or more, the address in memory for rule set 5 (shown with *rr5*) must be nonzero, the *flags* in *addr* must not contain QNOTREMOTE, QDONTSEND, QQUEUEUP, or QVERIFIED, and the delivery agent for the address must have the F=5 flag set.

The **-d29.5** debugging switch also causes *sendmail* to display the following if the address is rewritten by rule set 5:

```
maplocaluser: QDONTSEND output of printaddr() here (see §37.3.1)
```

Here the *printaddr()* routine prints the old address that is being canceled.

-d29.7

37.5.107   *Show over-aliasing fuzzy fallback*

If a fuzzy match causes more than three transformations to occur during aliasing, *sendmail* emits the following error:

```
aliasing/forwarding loop for login broken
```

Here, *login* is the login name of the recipient that started the suspected runaway aliasing. The **-d29.5** debugging switch also causes *sendmail* to print that it is trying to fall back to the original login name for delivery:

```
at trylocaluser login
```

Note that this message is printed before the message printed by the –d26 switch (which shows the testing for a self-destructive addresses).

–d30

37.5.108   *Trace processing of header*

When *sendmail* reads a mail message, it first collects (reads) the header portions of that message (everything up to the first blank line) and places the result into a temporary file in the queue directory. While it is processing the header, if the SaveFromLine (f) option (see §34.8.59), is false, the UNIX-style "From " header is removed, and the important information in it is saved for later use.

The –d30.1 (a.k.a. –d30) debugging switch causes *sendmail* to print the following succinct message when it finds the end of the header portion of a mail message:

    EOH

If end-of-headers was caused by a read error or a broken connection, *sendmail* prints:

    collect: premature EOM: *reason for failure here*

If end-of-headers was caused by a **Message:** or **Text:** header, then the rest of the header portion of the message is ignored.

–d30.2

37.5.109   *Eatfrom*

The –d30.2 debugging switch first causes *sendmail* to print its entry into *collect()*:

    collect

Then, when *sendmail* strips (eats) the UNIX-style, five-character "From " header from a mail message, it tries to extract (and save) the date from the header. The –d30.2 debugging switch causes *sendmail* to print the *field* portion of the header as it appears before the date is extracted:

    eatfrom(*field*)

The *eatfrom()* routine will vanish if NOTUNIX (see §18.8.32) is defined when compiling *sendmail*.

–d30.3

37.5.110   *Show a to-less header being added*

If the header of a mail message lacks recipient information (lacks all of the To:, Cc:, Bcc:, and Apparently-To: header lines), then *sendmail* adds a header as defined by the `NoRecipientAction` option (see §34.8.43). The –d30.3 debugging switch causes *sendmail* to print which *header* it is adding:

    Adding header: recipient

Here, *header* is the text of the header being saved, and *recipient* is the address of the recipient as taken from the envelope of the message.

–d30.35

37.5.111   *Trace collect states*

The process of collecting the message header and body over an SMTP connection is driven by a state engine inside *sendmail*. The –d30.35 debugging switch causes *sendmail* to display each state just before it is processed:

    top, istate=is, mstate=ms

Here, *is* is the current input state as described in Table 37-11, and *ms* is the current message state as described in Table 37-12.

Table 37–11: collect() Input States

istate	Name	Description
0	IS_NORM	Currently in middle of a line
1	IS_BOL	Currently at beginning of a line
2	IS_DOT	Just read a dot at beginning of line
3	IS_DOTCR	Just read ".\r" at beginning of line
4	IS_CR	Just read a carriage return

Table 37–12: collect() Message States

mstate	Name	Description
0	MS_UFROM	Currently reading UNIX from line
1	MS_HEADER	Currently reading message header
2	MS_BODY	Currently reading message body

The –d30.35 debugging switch also causes the same information to be printed every time *sendmail* goes to a new state:

    nextstate, istate=is, mstate=ms, line = "header"

Here, the extra information is the current text of the header being processed.

–d30.94

The –d30.94 debugging switch causes *sendmail* to print the input state (see Table 37-11) for each character being processed:

```
istate=is, c=char (hex)
```

Each character is printed both as the character it is (*char*) and how it is represented in hexadecimal (*hex*).

–d31.2

Header lines (see §35.1) from the configuration file and from mail messages are processed by the *chompheader*() routine before they are included in any mail message. That routine parses each header line to save critical information, to check for validity, and to replace default values with new values.

The –d31.2 debugging switch[*] shows that *sendmail* is about to check whether it should replace a From: or Resent-From: header with the one defined by the H configuration command. If the configuration file is not being read and if *sendmail* is not processing the queue, the following test is made:

```
comparing header from (header) against default (addr or name)
```

The value of the From: or Resent-From: *header* is compared to the sender's address (*addr*) and to the sender's *name*. If it is that same as either one, the address is replaced.

–d31.6

The –d31.6 debugging switch shows each header as it appears when it enters the *chompheader*() routine:

```
chompheader: line
```

Here, *line* is the exact text of the original header before processing. Unfortunately, there is no debugging switch that allows the result of this processing to be viewed.

To determine how it should handle a header, *sendmail* compares each header to its list of headers in *sendmail.h*. The –d31.6 debugging switch also shows the result after the comparisons have been done:

---

[*] There is no –d31.1 information.

```
no header match
```

```
header match, hi_flags= flags in hexadecimal here
```

The flags and their hexadecimal equivalence are shown in Table 35-2 in §35.5.

-d32.1

37.5.115   *Show collected headers*

The -d32.1 (a.k.a. -d31) debugging switch causes *sendmail* to print the header lines that it collected from a received mail message:

```
----- collected header -----
     header lines here
---------------------------
```

Each header line is printed with the header name on the left, a colon, and the value for that header on the right. If there is no value, *sendmail* prints <NULL>.

If the H_DEFAULT flag is set for any header (see §35.5.3), the value for the header is printed inside parentheses with macros unexpanded, just before it is printed in expanded form. For example,

```
Full-Name: ($x) Your Full Name
```

-d32.2

37.5.116   *Show ARPA mode with setsender*

The -d32.2 debugging switch works only if the mode set with the -b command-line switch is in ARPA (-ba) mode (see §36.7.3). It shows the sender address being extracted from the header with *setsender*( ):

```
eatheader: setsender(*value == realvalue)
```

The *setsender*( ) routine can be further traced with the -d45.1 debugging switch.

-d33.1

37.5.117   *Watch crackaddr( )*

The *crackaddr*( ) routine's job is to find an email address amidst other nonaddress text, then to save that nonaddress part:

```
gw@wash.dc.gov (George Washington)  → crackaddr( ) → $g (George Washington)
```

The -d33.1 (a.k.a. 33) debugging switch causes *sendmail* to print the potential address prior to cracking and, after that, the address that it found:

```
crackaddr(potential)
crackaddr=>`addr'
```

The legal ways that addresses can be placed within other text is described in §35.3. See also the /**parse** rule-testing command (§38.5.5) to put *crackaddr*() in context.

-d34.1

37.5.118   *Watch header assembly for output*

The *sendmail* program uses *putheader*() to create headers that didn't exist before. The −**d34.1** (a.k.a. −**d34**) debugging switch causes *sendmail* to print the following on entry to that routine:

```
--- putheader, mailer = agent ---
```

Here, **agent** is the symbolic name of the delivery agent that will deliver the bounced message.

-d34.11   *(useful)*

37.5.119   *Trace header generation and skipping*

Each header line created is displayed with two leading spaces. For example,

```
--- putheader, mailer = *file* ---
   Return-Path: you
```

Then certain headers are excluded from the bounced mail message header. Those with the H_CTE flag set (see §35.5.12) and either the MCIF_CVT8TO7 or MCIF_INMIME *mci* flags set (see Table 37-17) will have the text:

```
(skipped (content-transfer-encoding))
```

appended and that header skipped (excluded).

Any header that has both H_CHECK and H_ACHECK flags set and doesn't have identical delivery agent flags set for itself and its cached connection information will also be skipped:

```
(skipped)
```

All resent headers (those marked with H_RESENT) are also skipped:

```
(skipped (resent))
```

Return-receipt headers are also skipped:

```
(skipped (receipt))
```

If a `Bcc:` header (see §35.10.4) is being skipped, this is printed:

```
(skipped -- bcc)
```

Finally, valueless headers are also skipped with this message:

```
(skipped -- null value)
```

Any headers that survive this skipping process are included in the eventually delivered bounced message. Note that MIME headers are not generated or displayed here (see –d43).

–d35.9   *(useful)*
37.5.120   *Macro values defined*

The –d35.9 debugging switch[*] causes *sendmail* to print each macro as it is defined. The output looks like this:

```
define(name as "value")
```

Here, the **name** is the macro's name, and the *value* is the value (text) assigned to the macro. If the macro already has a value assigned to it, *sendmail* prints:

```
redefine(name as "value")
```

–d35.14
37.5.121   *Macro Identification*

With the introduction of multicharacter macro names, it is now necessary for *sendmail* to convert each macro name from text form into *sendmail*'s internal form. Single-character macro names are represented by themselves. Multicharacter names are represented by values from 0240 (octal) upward. The –d35.14 debugging switch causes *sendmail* to print each macro name as it is being looked up:

```
macid(name) => value
```

The **name** is the text immediately following a `$` character, including any trailing junk in the line. For example, the following miniconfigurations file:

```
V7
D{FOO}foo
R$H       ${FOO}  note no $H defined
```

produces this output (with only the **macid** lines shown):

---

* There is no –d35.1 information.

```
macid({FOO}foo) => 0xa0
macid(H\t${FOO}\tnote no $H defined) => H
macid({FOO}\tnote no $H defined) => 0xa0
macid(H defined) => H
```

–d35.24

37.5.122   *Macro expansion*

Macros that are included in text must be translated into values (expanded) so that the values may be used. The **–d35.24** debugging switch tells *sendmail* to display such text both before and after the macros in it have been expanded. The "before" looks like this:

```
expand("text")
```

For example,

```
expand("$w.$D")
```

The *text* (here **$w.$D**) may be any ASCII string. In it, special characters like the newline character are printed in C language, backslash-escaped notation (such as \n). Macros are printed with either the **$** prefix (such as **$w** above with V8 *sendmail*) or some other prefix (IDA uses **^Aw.^AD**, SunOS uses **/w./D**; others use the archaic **\001w.\001D** notation).

Expansion is performed only on defined macros (using the **$** prefix), on macro conditionals (in which one of two values is used, depending on whether a macro has a value or not, such as **$?x$x$|nobody$.**), and and on the **$&** prefix (deferred expansion).

After the first (leftmost) macro or conditional is expanded in *text*, *sendmail* prints the transformed text as follows:

```
expanded ==> "text"
```

For example,

```
expanded ==> "wash.$D"
```

If any unexpanded macros or conditionals remain in *text*, this **expanded** process is *recursively* repeated until everything that can be expanded has been expanded. This process of recursion allows macros to have other macros as their values.

–d36.5

37.5.123   *Trace processing by stab( )*

The symbol table is a block of memory that contains information about all the symbolic names used by *sendmail*. Symbolic names are delivery agent names (such as **local**), aliases, database classes, hostnames, and macros. Symbols are placed into the symbol table with the *stab()* routine. That routine is also used to see whether a symbol has already been inserted and, if so, to obtain its value. The **–d36.5** debugging switch[*] causes *sendmail* to print the following upon its entry into the *stab()* routine:

```
STAB: name type
```

Here, **name** is the symbolic name to be inserted or looked up. The **type** is one of the values listed in Table 37–13.

Table 37–13: Types of Symbols Recognized by stab()

Type	Mnemonic	Description
0	ST_UNDEF	Undefined type
1	ST_CLASS	Class (from C and F configuration commands)
2	ST_ADDRESS	An address in parsed format
3	ST_MAILER	A delivery agent (from M configuration command)
4	ST_ALIAS	An alias, if no external database
5	ST_MAPCLASS	A database class (K command)
6	ST_MAP	Function that handles a class
7	ST_HOSTSIG	Host MX signature
8	ST_NAMECANON	Cached canonical name
9	ST_MACRO	Macro name to id value mapping
10	ST_RULESET	Ruleset name to number mapping
11	ST_SERVICE	Service switch file entry
16	ST_MCI	SMTP connection status[a]

a. This is the base (offset) of types 16 through 16+n, where n is 16 plus MAXMAILERS as defined in *conf.h*.

If *stab()* is being used to insert a symbol, the above output is concluded with:

```
entered
```

If *stab()* is being used to look up a symbol, one of the two following messages is printed:

```
not found
type type val hex hex hex hex
```

If it is found, four hexadecimal values are printed, which show the first four 4-byte words of the value.

---

[*] There is no **–d36.1** information.

-d36.9

37.5.124   *Show hash bucket*

A hashing algorithm is used to make the symbol table more efficient. The -d36.9 debugging switch is used to see the hash value selected for any given symbol:

    (hfunc=hash)

The number of possible hash-table buckets is limited by STABSIZE, as defined in *stab.c.*[*]

-d36.90

37.5.125   *Trace function applied to all symbols*

The -d36.90 debugging switch causes the name and type of each symbol to be printed as a common function is applied to each with *sendmail*'s internal *stabapply*() function.

    stabapply: trying type/name

The *stabapply*() routine is used to initialize maps and to print the members of a class.

-d37.1   *(useful)*

37.5.126   *Trace setting of options*

Options can be set on the command line or in the configuration file. The -d37.1 (a.k.a. -d37) debugging switch allows you to watch each option being defined. As each is processed, this message is first printed, without a trailing newline:

    setoption: name (char).sub=val

Here, **name** is the option's multicharacter name, **char** is its single-character equivalent (or a hexadecimal value if it is non-ASCII), and **sub** is the subvalue for that option if there was one. Finally, *val* is the value being given to that option. If the option has already been set from the command line and is thus prohibited from being set in the configuration file, *sendmail* prints:

    (ignored)

A newline is then printed, and the job is done. If defining the option is permitted, *sendmail* next checks to see whether it is *safe*. If it is not, *sendmail* prints:

---

[*] You can experiment with different hashing algorithms by modifying the code in *stab.c*. But note that it has already been heavily tuned in V8.7, roughly doubling its speed over that of earlier versions.

```
(unsafe)
```

If it is unsafe, *sendmail* checks to see whether it should relinquish its *root* privilege. If so, it prints:

```
(Resetting uid)
```

A newline is then printed, and the option has been defined. Options in general and safe versus unsafe are covered in Chapter 34, *Options*.

–d37.8   *(useful)*

37.5.127   *Trace adding of words to a class*

The adding of words to a class (C or F configuration commands) can be traced with the –d37.8 debugging switch. Each word is printed like this:

```
setclass(name, text)
```

The *text* is added to the class whose symbolic name is *name*. Class names can be single-character or multicharacter (see §32.1).

–d38.2   *(useful)*

37.5.128   *Show map opens and failures*

Most maps are declared directly with the K configuration command (see §33.3). Others are declared internally by *sendmail*, such as the *host* and *alias* maps. The –d38.2 debugging switch[*] first shows maps being initialized:

```
map_init(class:name, file, pass)
```

Here, *class* is one of the internal classes allowed by *sendmail*, such as *host*, and *dequote* (see §33.3, the K configuration command). The *name* is either the name you gave to the map with the K configuration command or one assigned internally by *sendmail* (like *aliases.files*). The *file* is either NULL or the name of the database file (such as */etc/aliases*). And *pass* is a flag that tells *sendmail* whether or not it should open the database, rebuild the database, or do neither.

Next the –d38.2 debugging switch causes *sendmail* to show each map as it is about to be opened. The output that is produced will look like one of the following lines:

```
bt_map_open(name, file, mode)
hash_map_open(name, file, mode)
hes_map_open(name, file, mode)
impl_map_open(name, file, mode)
ldap_map_open(name, mode)
```

---

* There is no –d38.1 information.

```
ndbm_map_open(name, file, mode)
ni_map_open(name, file, mode)
nis_map_open(name, file, mode)
nisplus_map_open(name, file, mode)
stab_map_open(name, file, mode)
switch_map_open(name, file, mode)
text_map_open(name, file, mode)
user_map_open(name, mode)
```

In all of the previous lines, the **mode** is a decimal representation of the file permissions that are used during the open. The name prefixing each line corresponds to the class of map. For example, **impl** corresponds to the *implicit* class.

The **-d38.2** debugging switch also causes *sendmail* to display the *nis* domain that was used if one was specified for the *nisplus* class:

```
nisplus_map_open(file): using domain ypdomain
```

The **-d38.2** debugging switch also allows other silent errors to be printed about some open failures. Under *nis+*, lookups are performed by named columns (as in the case of the password database, the columns are named **passwd**, **shell**, and so on):

```
nisplus_map_open(name): can not find key column colname
nisplus_map_open(name): can not find column colname
```

Text files that are used as maps must be declared with a filename that is an absolute path (begins with a / character thus forming a fully qualified pathname), that exists, and that is a regular file. If there is a problem, one of the following is logged (even if **-d38.2** is not specified):

```
text_map_open: file name required
text_map_open(file): file name must be fully qualified
text_map_open(name): can not stat file
text_map_open(name): file is not a file
```

Text files should be syntactically correct. The delimiting character, **char**, will print either as a single character or as the phrase (**whitespace**). Note that the third line below will be reported only when the **-d38.2** debugging switch is used:

```
text_map_open(file): -k should specify a number, not badtext
text_map_open(file): -v should specify a number, not badtext
text_map_open(file): delimiter = char
```

-d38.3

37.5.129   *Show passes*

The *sendmail* program initializes maps in passes so that it can open a map for reading or rebuild. That is, pass 0 opens it for reading only, and passes 1 and 2 open it for updating. This gives *sendmail* the opportunity to detect optional maps.

The –d38.3 debugging switch causes *sendmail* to print **wrong pass** every time it skips rebuilding because the pass is inappropriate:

```
map_init(class:name, file, pass)  ← from –d38.2
wrong pass
```

The –d38.3 debugging switch also causes *sendmail* to print a failure message if an **implicit** class map does not exist:

```
impl_map_open(name, file, mode)  ← from –d38.2
no map file
```

–d38.4   (useful)

37.5.130   *Show result of map open*

When rebuilding the aliases files, each database is opened before it is rebuilt or not. The –d38.4 debugging switch shows the success or failure of each open:

```
map_init(class:name, file, pass)  ← from –d38.2
     class:name file valid or invalid
```

The status is **valid** if the open succeeded; otherwise, it is **invalid**.

The –d38.4 debugging switch also shows each map being looked up in a **switch** class map (see §33.8.17).

```
switch_map_open(name, file, mode)  ← from –d38.2
     map_stack[index] = class:name
```

If the *name* is not one that was declared in a K configuration command, the following error is printed:

```
Switch map class: unknown member map name
```

–d38.9

37.5.131   *Trace map closings and appends*

The –d38.9 debugging switch traces map closures for those kind of maps that can be closed:

```
ndbm_map_close(name, file, flags)
db_map_close(name, file, flags)
impl_map_close(name, file, flags)
prog_map_lookup(name) failed (errno) -- closing
seq_map_close(name)
```

Here, the *name* is either the name you gave to the map with the K configuration command or one assigned internally by *sendmail* (like *aliases.files*). The *file* is the filename on disk that contains the database. The *flags* describe the specific features of a map. They are printed in hexadecimal, and the meanings of the values printed are listed in Table 37-14.

Table 37–14: Flags Describing Properties of Database Maps

Hex	Text	Description
00001	MF_VALID	This entry is valid.
00002	MF_INCLNULL	Include null byte in key.
00004	MF_OPTIONAL	Don't complain if map not found.
00008	MF_NOFOLDCASE	Don't fold case in keys.
00010	MF_MATCHONLY	Don't use the map value.
00020	MF_OPEN	This entry is open.
00040	MF_WRITABLE	Open for writing.
00080	MF_ALIAS	This is an alias file.
00100	MF_TRY0NULL	Try with no null byte.
00200	MF_TRY1NULL	Try with the null byte.
00400	MF_LOCKED	This map is currently locked.
00800	MF_ALIASWAIT	Alias map in aliaswait state.
01000	MF_IMPL_HASH	Implicit: underlying hash database.
02000	MF_IMPL_NDBM	Implicit: underlying ndbm database.
04000	MF_UNSAFEDB	This map is world writable.
08000	MF_APPEND	Append new entry on rebuild.
10000	MF_KEEPQUOTES	Don't dequote key before lookup.

In addition to tracing map closures, the –d38.9 debugging switch traces map appends allowed by the MF_APPEND flag (see §33.3.4.1) as specified when the database is declared by the K configuration command:

```
ndbm_map_store append=new
db_map_store append=new
```

Here *new* is new value appended to the old. Since this property is used for alias files, the new and old values have a comma inserted between them.

–d38.10

37.5.132   *Trace NIS search for @:@*

The NIS alias map needs to contain a @:@ entry to indicate that it is fully updated and ready for reading. But because HP-UX omits the @:@, it is useful only as a check to see whether the NIS map exists. The –d38.10 debugging switch causes the result of this check to be printed as:

```
nis_map_open: yp_match(@, domain, nismap)
```

Here, **domain** is the NIS domain, and **nismap** is usually *mail.aliases* (but it can be redefined in your configuration file; see §34.8.1). If the map is not marked as optional (see §33.3.4.8), the following error will be printed:

```
Cannot bind to map nismap in domain domain:  reason here
```

The **-d38.10** debugging switch also traces the NIS+ open's check for a valid table.

```
nisplus_map_open: nisplusmap.domain is not a table
```

Essentially, this says that the NIS+ map **nisplusmap** (in the domain shown) does not exist. The error is printed even if the **-o** (optional) database switch (see §33.3.4.8) is missing.

-d38.12

37.5.133   *Trace map stores*

The **-d38.12** debugging switch shows values being stored in maps that support updates.

```
db_map_store(name, key, value)
ndbm_map_store(name, key, value)
seq_map_store(name, key, value)
```

Here, the **name** is either the name you gave to the map with the **K** configuration command or the **name** assigned internally by *sendmail* (like *aliases.files*). The **key** is the key for which the new value is being stored, and the **value** is the value for that key.

-d38.19   *(useful)*

37.5.134   *Trace switch map finds*

A switched map is one that, either as the result of a service-switch file or because of *sendmail's* internal logic, causes lookups to follow a select path. For example, Sun's Solaris 2 *nsswitch.conf* might specify that aliases be looked up in the order *files*, then *nis*:

```
switch_map_open(name, file, mode)   ← from –d38.2
switch_map_find => nmaps
                maptype
                   . . .
```

First the number of maps found is printed with **nmaps**, then each type of map found in the list is printed. Each is a class name, such as *files*, or *nis*.

–d38.20

37.5.135   *Trace map lookups*

The –d38.20 debugging switch traces many different map lookups. The
getcanonname() routine looks up a hostname and tries to canonify it:

```
getcanonname(host), trying maptype
getcanonname(host), found
getcanonname(host), failed, stat=error
```

Here, **host** is the hostname that is being looked up, and **maptype** is one of *files*,
nis, *nisplus*, *dns*, or *netinfo*. If the canonical name is not found, the **error** shows
one of the errors listed in *<sysexits.h>*. The process of canonifying the name is
handled by calling special subroutines based on the **maptype**:

`text_getcanonname(host)`	← *maptype is files*
`nis_getcanonname(host)`	← *maptype is nis*
`nisplus_getcanoname(host), qbuf=query`	← *maptype is nisplus*
`dns_getcanonname(host, flag)`	← *maptype is dns, printed with –d8.2*
`ni_getcanonname(host)`	← *maptype is netinfo*

The *nisplus_getcanoname*() routine is far more verbose than the other. In addition
to the information printed above, the –d38.20 switch also prints

```
nisplus_getcanoname(host), got count entries, all but first ignored
nisplus_getcanoname(host), found in directory "nisdir"
nisplus_getcanoname(host), found result
nisplus_getcanoname(host), failed, status=nsistatus, nsw_stat=errno
```

The –d38.20 debugging switch also traces general lookups in various kinds of
databases. Again note that *nisplus* is more verbose than the others:

```
ndbm_map_lookup(name, key)
db_map_lookup(name, key)
nis_map_lookup(name, key)
nisplus_map_lookup(name, key)
qbuf=query
nisplus_map_lookup(key), got count entries, additional entries ignored
nisplus_map_lookup(key), found value
nisplus_map_lookup(key), failed
hes_map_lookup(name, key)
ni_map_lookup(name, key)
stab_lookup(name, key)
impl_map_lookup(name, key)
user_map_lookup(name, key)
prog_map_lookup(name, key)
prog_map_lookup(name): empty answer
seq_map_lookup(name, key)
```

Here, the **name** is either the name you gave to the map with the K configuration
command or one assigned internally by *sendmail* (such as *aliases.files*). The **key** is

the item being looked up. The *file* is the pathname of the file that contains the database.

–d38.44

37.5.136   *Show nis_getcanonname() record*

The –d38.20 debugging switch described above prints the *nis* lookup of the canonical hostname. This –d38.44 debugging switch prints the result of that lookup:

```
nis_getcanonname(host)              ← from –d38.20
got record 'result'
```

–d39.1

37.5.137   *Display digit database mapping*

When the RHS of a rule matches an entry in a database map with $(and $), that entry replaces the key. If the entry contains %*digit* literals, they are replaced by corresponding $@ values in the RHS (see §33.4.2).

The –d39.1 (a.k.a. –d39) debugging switch causes *sendmail* to print the entry and any replacement values:

```
map_rewrite(entry), av =
        value1
        value2
        ...etc
```

After the RHS is rewritten (after all the $@ values have replaced all the %*digit* literals), *sendmail* prints the result:

```
map_rewrite => rewritten RHS here
```

–d40.1

37.5.138   *Trace processing of the queue*

The –d40.1 (a.k.a. –d40) debugging switch traces the placing of a mail message into the queue and the processing of queued files.

When a mail message is placed into the queue, its qf file is written as a tf temporary file; then that temporary file is closed and renamed to be the qf file. The –d40.1 debugging switch causes *sendmail* to announce that it is beginning that process by printing the queued message's identifier:

```
>>>>> queueing qid(new id) >>>>>
queueing  for each recipient, output of printaddr() here (see §37.3.1)
<<<<< done queueing qid <<<<<
```

First, the queue identifier is printed (*qid*). If this identifier is brand-new, the phrase "(new id)" is printed. Next, *sendmail* prints complete information about each recipient for the message using the *printaddr()* routine. Finally, done queueing is printed, and the queuing of the *qid* item is finished.

When *sendmail* processes files in the queue, it first prereads all the qf files and sorts the jobs by priority. After the list has been sorted, the –d40.1 debugging switch causes *sendmail* to print that list, one message per line, in the following format:

```
qfname: pri=priority
```

Here, *qfname* is the basename of the qf file, and *priority* is the current priority of each message (see §34.8.53). After the sorted list of messages has been processed, and if there are any messages in that list, *sendmail* attempts to deliver each of the messages in the order in which it appears in the list. The –d40.1 debugging switch causes *sendmail* to print the following line of information for each message processed:

```
dowork: (qfname)
```

–d40.3

37.5.139   *Show envelope flags*

The –d40.3 debugging switch causes the envelope flags for each message to be printed as it is queued:

```
>>>>> queueing qid(new id) >>>>>    ← from –d40.1
    e_flags=  output of printenvflags() here
```

The envelope flags are described in Table 37-3 in §37.5.12.

–d40.4

37.5.140   *Show qf file lines as they are read*

The qf file is composed of individual lines of information (see §23.9.11). The –d40.4 debugging switch causes *sendmail* to print each of those lines as it is read:

```
+++++ Xtext
```

Each line begins with five plus characters. The qf file's *key* letter (here, *X*) follows, then the rest of the *text* that made up that line. In the qf file, indented lines (lines that begin with a space or tab character) that immediately follow the key line are appended to that key line. Those joined lines are printed after they are joined. Note that the lines of the qf file are printed before they are processed by *sendmail*. An error in a line is printed after the line is printed.

If the queue file could not be read, the **-d40.4** debugging switch instead causes *sendmail* to print this error:

```
readqf(qid) failed
```

Here, *qid* is the queue identifier for the message. Note that reading can legitimately fail if the queue file is locked. Use **-d40.8** (described below) to see the exact reason for failure.

-d40.8

37.5.141   *Show reasons for failure*

The **-d40.8** debugging switch causes *sendmail* to print the reason it could not process a message's qf file. One possibility is:

```
readqf(qfname): fopen failure (error text here)
```

If the failure was caused by anything other than the file's nonexistence, the following is also logged:

```
readqf: no control file qfname
```

If the qf file could not be read because it is locked by another incantation of *sendmail* (a valid reason), the **-d40.8** debugging switch prints:

```
qid: locked
```

Here, *qid* is the identifier portion of the qf file. If the log level is set to greater than 19 (see the **LogLevel** (L) option, §34.8.33), the above message will also be logged.

For security the *sendmail* program *fstat*(2)'s the qf file after it is open to make sure it cannot be fooled by a race condition. If that *fstat*(2) fails, the following is printed if the **-d40.8** debugging switch was specified:

```
readqf(qid): fstat failure (error text here)
```

If the qf file is owned by someone other than the effective *uid* of *sendmail*, the qf file will be renamed into a Qf file (see §23.3). If this **-d40.8** debugging switch was specified, the following message will also be printed:

```
readqf(qid): bogus file
```

The **MinQueueAge** option (see §34.8.41) determines the interval between queue runs for any given file. If a qf file was not last run at least **MinQueueAge** minutes ago, it is skipped and the **-d40.8** debugging switch causes the following message to be printed:

> qid: too young (*howlong*)

If the log level is set to greater than 19 (see the **LogLevel** (**L**) option, §34.8.33), the above message will also be logged.

−d40.9

37.5.142	*Show qf and lock file descriptors*

After *sendmail* has opened the qf file (with −d40.1) and printed the envelope flags (with −d40.3), this −d40.9 debugging switch will cause the file descriptors for the qf file and its corresponding lock file to be dumped:

```
>>>>> queueing qid(new id) >>>>>  ← from −d40.1
  e_flags=                        ← from −d40.3
 tfp=  output of dumpfd() here
 lockfp=  output of dumpfd() here
```

The **e_flags** are described in Table 37-3 of §37.5.12. Here, **tfp=** shows the file descriptors for the qf file, and **lockfp=** shows the descriptors for the lock. See −d2.9 (§37.5.13) for a description of output of dumpfd().

−d40.32

37.5.143	*Dump the send queue*

The −d40.32 debugging switch causes *sendmail* to dump the list of message recipients:

```
>>>>> queueing qid(new id) >>>>>  ← from −d40.1
  e_flags=                        ← from −d40.3
 sendq= ← output of printaddr()) here (see §37.3.1)
 tfp=                   ← from −d40.9
 lockfp=                ← from −d40.9
```

−d41.1   *(useful)*

37.5.144	*Trace queue ordering*

The −d41 (a.k.a. −d41) debugging switch causes *sendmail* to print its ordering of the queue. First it prints

```
orderq:
        QueueLimitId = qid          ← if −qI used
        QueueLimitSender = sid      ← if −qS used
        QueueLimitRecipient = rid   ← if −qR used
```

See §23.6.2.3 for an explanation of how the −qI, −qS, and −qR command-line switches can limit the scope of a queue run. If none of them were specified, only orderq: is printed. The −d41.1 debugging switch is extremely handy for previewing the effect of the −qI, −qS, and −qR command-line switches. When combined with **-bp** (*mailq*), these switches limit the queue listing and thus preview the effect of a limited queue run:

```
% mailq
                   Mail Queue (1 request)
--Q-ID-- --Size-- -----Q-Time----- ------------Sender/Recipient------------
MAA11111     4560 Tue Dec 31 12:37 you
                                   you@here.us.edu
% mailq -d41.1 -qI22222
orderq:
        QueueLimitId = 22222
Mail queue is empty
```

The **-d41.1** debugging switch also traces the growth of the queue working list. Every time the limit of that list is reached, the internal routine *grow_wlist()* is called to extend the list size by QUEUESEGSIZE (where QUEUESEGSIZE is described in §18.8.38).

```
grow_wlist: WorkListSize=current
grow_wlist: WorkListSize now newsize
```

If the log level is set to greater than 1 (see the **LogLevel** (L) option, §34.8.33), the following is also logged each time the list size grows:

```
grew WorkList for qdirectory to newsize
```

If the size could not be increased (because the program reached the limit of available memory) and if the **LogLevel** (L) option is greater than 0, *sendmail* will log this error at LOG_ALERT:

```
FAILED to grow WorkList for qdirectory to newsize
```

This message will repeat until there are no more queue entries to process after the limit is received. However, all the files that are already in the work list will be processed, so presumably the next run will catch the failed messages.

-d41.2

37.5.145   *Cannot open qf*

Ordinarily, *sendmail* is silent about failures to open a **qf** file, but the **-d41.2** debugging switch causes it to print the reason the open failed:

```
orderq: cannot open qfname (reason for failure here)
```

Here, *qfname* is the name of the **qf** file that could not be opened.

–d41.49

37.5.146   *Show excluded (skipped) queue files*

The `41.49` debugging switch causes *sendmail* to display the queue files that were not included in the work list:

```
skipping qfname (bit)
```

Here, the `bit` is a hexadecimal representation of the requirement that was not met. These bits are listed in Table 37–15.

Table 37–15: Bits Describing a Queue Run's Requirements

Hex	Mnemonic	Description
1	NEED_P	Priority must be high enough (required qf file line)
2	NEED_T	Must have been in queue long enough (required qf file line)
4	NEED_R	Match a recipient
10	NEED_S	Match a sender

Note that nothing will be printed if the message was skipped because its identifier did not match the –qI specification.

–d41.50

37.5.147   *Show every file in the queue*

The *sendmail* program scans the queue directory looking for all the `qf` files to set up its working list. If a file doesn't start with the letters "qf," it is ordinarily silently skipped. The **–d41.50** debugging switch causes *sendmail* to display every single file it finds in its queue directory:

```
orderq: checking file
```

The `file` can be a directory, such as `..`, or a regular file, such as a `df` or `qf` file.

–d42.2

37.5.148   *Show connection checking*

V8 *sendmail* can be configured with the `ConnectionCacheSize` (k) option (see §34.8.10) to maintain open SMTP connections to a few other hosts. Before making a new SMTP connection, *sendmail* checks to see if it already has one established.

The **–d42.2*** debugging switch causes *sendmail* to print the result of that check.

```
mci_get(host mailer): mci_state=state, _flags=flag, _exitstat= stat, _errno=err
```

Here, the **host** is the name of the host to which the connection is to be made, and the **mailer** is the symbolic name of the delivery agent. The **state** is the status of the current SMTP connection (if there is one) as shown in Table 37–16.

Table 37–16: mci_get() Connection States

State	Mnemonic	Description
0	MCIS_CLOSED	No traffic on this connection
1	MCIS_OPENING	Sending initial protocol
2	MCIS_OPEN	Connection is open
3	MCIS_ACTIVE	Message being sent
4	MCIS_QUITING	Running SMTP quit protocol
5	MCIS_SSD	SMTP service shutting down
6	MCIS_ERROR	I/O error on connection

The **flag** describes the overall status of the connection. It can have one or more values from those shown in Table 37–17 where those values are OR'd together.

Table 37–17: mci_get() Status Flags

Flag	Mnemonic	Description
0x0001	MCIF_VALID	If set, this entry is valid
0x0002	MCIF_TEMP	If set, don't cache this connection
0x0004	MCIF_CACHED	If set, connection is currently in open cache
0x0008	MCIF_ESMTP	This host speaks ESMTP
0x0010	MCIF_EXPN	EXPN command supported
0x0020	MCIF_SIZE	SIZE option supported
0x0040	MCIF_8BITMIME	BODY=8BITMIME supported
0x0080	MCIF_7BIT	Strip this message to 7 bits
0x0100	MCIF_MULTSTAT	MAIL11V3, handles MULT status
0x0200	MCIF_INHEADER	Currently outputting header
0x0400	MCIF_CVT8TO7	Convert from 8 to 7 bits
0x0800	MCIF_DSN	DSN extension supported
0x1000	MCIF_8BITOK	Okay to send 8 bit characters
0x2000	MCIF_CVT7TO8	Convert from 7 to 8 bits
0x4000	MCIF_INMIME	Currently reading MIME header

The **stat** is the exit status of the last delivered mail message to this connection. It is one of the values defined in *<sysexits.h>*. The **err** is the value of the last system

* Note that there is no **–d42.1** information.

error (if any), as defined in *<errno.h>*.

–d42.5

37.5.149   *Trace caching and uncaching connections*

The **–d42.5** debugging switch shows connections being cached and freed:

```
mci_cache: caching addr (host) in slot slot
mci_uncache: uncaching addr (host) from slot slot (doquit)
```

Here, **addr** is the address in memory of the C language structure (*struct mailer_con_info* defined in *sendmail.h*) that defines the current (or about to be made) connection. The **host** is the name of the host to which the connection is to be made. The **slot** is an index into the array of structures that contain the connection information. For uncaching, the **doquit** is a Boolean that tells *sendmail* to close the connection if it is nonzero.

The **–d91.100** debugging switch produces information identical to the above but logs its output at LOG_DEBUG instead of printing it:

```
qid: mci_cache: caching addr (host) in slot slot
qid: mci_uncache: uncaching addr (host) from slot slot (doquit)
```

Note that each line is prefixed by the queue identifier for the message (*qid*). The **–d91.100** debugging switch is especially handy for monitoring caching when running *sendmail* as a daemon.

–d43.1

37.5.150   *Trace MIME conversions*

V8.7 *sendmail* can convert 8-bit MIME to 7 bits. The **–d43.1** (a.k.a. **–d43**) debugging switch traces this process.

```
mime8to7: flags = mflags, boundaries = boundaries printed here
```

Here, the internal *mime8to7()* routine has been called to do the conversion. The **mflags** are printed in hexadecimal, and are described in Table 37–18.

Table 37–18: Conversion Flags for mime8to7()

Hex	Mnemonic	Description
0x00	M87F_OUTER	This is the outer context
0x01	M87F_NO8BIT	Can't have 8-bit in this section
0x02	M87F_DIGEST	Currently processing a multipart digest

The *boundaries* is either <none> or a list of the boundaries found in the message. In multipart messages the –d43.1 debugging switch causes each boundary to be printed as it is found:

    mime8to7: multi part boundary *boundary printed here*

–d43.3

37.5.151   *See the final MIME boundary name*

The –d43.3 debugging switch is used to see the final MIME boundary name that is selected:

    mime8to7=>*boundary* (multipart)
    mime8to7=>*boundary* (basic)

Each line is prefixed with three tabs.

The –d43.3 debugging switch is also used to trace 7- to 8-bit conversion. If a delivery agent has the F=9 flag set (see §30.8.6) and if the message has a Content-Transfer-Encoding: header that specifies Base64 or Quoted-Printable, *sendmail* will attempt to convert it from its encoded 7-bit form back into 8-bit form:

    mime7to8 => *base64 or quoted-printable* to 8bit done

–d43.5

37.5.152   *Watch search for boundaries*

The –d43.5 debugging switch allows you to watch the search for boundaries. First each line read is printed:

    mimeboundary: line="*line is printed here*"...

                                                                    ↑
                                                boundary, if found, printed here

Then, if the line contained a valid MIME boundary, the found boundary is printed at the end of the preceding.

–d43.8

37.5.153   *Show the calculations*

The *sendmail* program determines how to convert the MIME message by examining the first eighth of the file. If the first eighth of the total number of characters in the file have the high bit set, conversion will be with Base64; otherwise, it will be with Quoted-Printable (see §34.8.22). If the message is marked as binary, it is always converted with Base64. The −d43.8 debugging switch causes *sendmail* to print the result of this calculation:

```
mime8to7: hcount high bit(s) in bcount byte(s), cte=type
```

Here, cte= is either [none] or the content-transfer-encoding type, such as **binary**.

−d43.35

37.5.154   *Show boundary lines as emitted*

The −43.35 debugging switch causes each new boundary line to be printed as it is inserted into the message:

```
...--mid-boundary here
...--end boundary here--
```

The midboundary marks begin with a −−. The ending-boundary mark begins and ends with a −−.

−d43.36

37.5.155   *Show content transfer encoding*

The −43.36 debugging switch causes the encoding header to be printed as it is added to the message:

```
...Content-Transfer-Encoding: type of encoding here
```

The type of encoding will either be the original as printed with cte= in −d43.8 above or Base64 or Quoted-Printable.

−d43.40

37.5.156   *Show parse of Content-Type: header*

The −43.40 debugging switch causes the contents of the parsed **Content-Type:** header to be displayed.

```
pvp[n] = "item"
```

For zero through *n* items that were parsed, each is printed on its own line.

−d43.99

37.5.157   *Print the leading/following comments*

The −d43.99 debugging switch tells *sendmail* to print each line of MIME commentary that precedes the leading boundary:

> ... *leading commentary here*
> ...*--midboundary here*

and the commentary that follows the last boundary:

> ...*--end boundary here--*
> ... *trailing commentary here*

–d43.100

37.5.158   *Mark collect() and putheader()*

The **–d43.100** debugging switch causes *sendmail* to print a mark just after it has called *collect()* and after it has called *putheader()*:

```
+++after collect
+++after putheader
```

The *collect()* routine is traced with the **–d30** debugging switch, and *putheader()* is traced with the **–d34** debugging switch.

–d44.4

37.5.159   *Trace safefile()*

The V8 *sendmail* program tries to be extra careful about file permissions, and the key to checking them is the internal *safefile()* function. The **–d44.4** debugging switch[*] prints the parameters passed to the *safefile()* function:

```
safefile(fname, uid=uid, gid=gid, flags=sff_flags, mode=wantmode)
```

Here, the file named **fname** is being checked to determine whether the user identified by the **uid**, with the group **gid**, is allowed to find or use the file. The range of checking is determined by the hexadecimal **sff_flags**, described in Table 37-19. Where a file's permissions are required, the mode printed in **wantmode** will be used.

Table 37–19: safefile() Access Flags

Flag	Mnemonic	Description
0x000	SFF_ANYFILE	No special restrictions
0x001	SFF_MUSTOWN	Uid must own this file
0x002	SFF_NOSLINK	File must not be a symbolic link
0x004	SFF_ROOTOK	Okay for root to own this file
0x008	SFF_RUNASREALUID	If no controlling user, run as real *uid*
0x010	SFF_NOPATHCHECK	Don't bother checking leading path
0x020	SFF_SETUIDOK	Setuid files are okay

---

[*] There is no **–d44.1** debugging information.

Table 37–19: safefile( ) Access Flags (continued)

Flag	Mnemonic	Description
0x040	SFF_CREAT	Okay to create the file if necessary
0x080	SFF_REGONLY	Allow regular files only
0x100	SFF_OPENASROOT	Open as root instead of as *uid*

If the SFF_NOPATHCHECK flag is clear (0), *sendmail* examines each component of the path leading the file. If any component of the path is rejected, the **–d44.4** debugging switch causes *sendmail* to print:

> [dir *fname*]   *reason for the rejection here*

A path component can fail because *stat*(2) failed. If the *uid* is 0 for *root*, a warning is logged if a component is found to be group- or world-writable:

> WARNING: writable directory *fname*

For each component in the path, *safefile*() checks to verify that this user has permission to search the directory. If the SFF_ROOTOK flag is not set (is clear), *root* (*uid* 0) access is special cased in that all directory components must be world-searchable.

Otherwise, the path component is accepted if it is owned by the *uid* and has the user search bit set or if its group is the same as *gid* and has the group search bit set. If NO_GROUP_SET is undefined when *sendmail* is compiled (see §18.8.31) and the DontInitGroups option (see §34.8.19) is not set, each group to which *uid* belongs is also checked. Otherwise, the directory must be world-searchable.

If the *fname* could not be checked with *stat*(2), the **–d44.4** debugging switch causes the reason to be printed:

> *reason for failure here*

If the file does not exist, it may need to be created. If so, *sendmail* checks to be sure that the *uid* has write permission. The result is printed with the **–d44.4** debugging switch like this:

> [final dir *fname* uid *uid* mode *wantmode*]   *error here*

If the file exists and if symbolic links are supported, the file is rejected if it is a symbolic link and if the SFF_NOSLINK flag is set. If the **–d44.4** debugging switch is specified, this error is printed:

> [slink mode *mode*]   EPERM

If the SFF_REGONLY flag is set the file must be a regular file. If it is not, it is rejected, and **-d44.4** causes the following to be printed:

    [non-reg mode *mode*]   EPERM

If *wantmode* has the write bits set, and the existing file has any execute bits set, the file is rejected and **-d44.4** causes the following to be printed:

    [exec bits *mode*]   EPERM

If the file has more than one link, the file is rejected and **-d44.4** causes the following to be printed:

    [link count *nlinks*]   EPERM

If the SFF_SETUIDOK flag is specified, if the file exists, if it has the *suid* bit set in the mode but no execute bits set in the mode, and if it is *not* owned by *root*, *sendmail* performs subsequent checks under the *suid* and *sgid* identities of the existing file. A similar process occurs with the *sgid* bit. *Sendmail* then prints:

    [uid *new_uid*, stat *filemode*, mode *wantmode*]

If access is finally allowed, *sendmail* concludes the above with:

    OK

Otherwise, it concludes with:

    EACCES

-d44.5   *(useful)*

37.5.160   *Trace writable()*

The **-d44.5** debugging switch displays the values passed to *sendmail*'s internal *writable()* routine. This routine nearly duplicates the function of the *access*(3) call* but does it much more safely and allows checks to be made under the identity of the controlling user:

    writable(*fname*, *sff_flags*)

Here, the *fname* is the full pathname of the file being checked. The **sff_flags** are documented in Table 37–19 above. Success or failure is described under **-d44.4**.

---

* It is more restrictive for *root*-owned files and can allow the *suid* semantics needed for delivery to files.

–d45.1

The **–d45.1** (a.k.a. **–d45**) debugging switch causes *sendmail* to print the current form of the envelope sender address before it has fully rewritten that address into its final form:

    setsender(addr)

If the **addr** is empty (as would be the case if the sender were being gathered from the header), *sendmail* prints NULL. The final envelope sender address is placed into the **$f** macro. (See §31.10.14 for a description of that macro and the process used by *sendmail* to set the sender's address.)

–d45.3

If the **F=C** flag (see §30.8.15) is set for the delivery agent selected for the sender, *sendmail* will save the domain part of the address for later use. The **–d45.3** causes the saved domain part to be printed:

    Saving from domain: domain

The domain is saved in the *e_fromdomain* part of the C language structure that contains the envelope information for the sender. Later, if the **F=C** flag is set, this domain will be appended to any recipient addresses that lack a domain part.

–d45.5

Unless a message is bounced, it will not be sent to the sender. The **–d45.5** debugging switch causes *sendmail* to display sender information when this decision is made:

    setsender: QDONTSEND output of printaddr() here (see §37.3.1)

–d46.9

The **xf** queue file (see §23.2.7) contains a record of the errors and other information produced by a delivery agent. That information is used for bounced mail. The **–d46.9** debugging switch[*] causes *sendmail* to dump the file descriptors for the opened **xf** file:

---

[*] There is no **–d46.1** information.

```
openxscript(xfqid):
    output of dumpfd() here (see §37.5.13)
```

If *sendmail* cannot open an **xf** file, it logs this warning:

```
Can't create transcript file xfqid
```

It then tries to open */dev/null* so that it can continue with the delivery. If that fails, it logs the following panic message and immediately exits:

```
Can't open /dev/null
```

Once the file is open (or not), *sendmail* turns it into an I/O stream with a call to *fdopen(3)*. If that call fails, *sendmail* logs this message and immediately exits:

```
Can't create transcript stream xfqid
```

−d48.2

37.5.165   *Trace calls to the check_ rule sets*

Beginning with V8.8, *sendmail* calls rule sets whose names begin with **check_** (see §29.10) to filter incoming and outgoing mail. The **−d48.2** debugging switch[*] can be used to display the workspace being passed to each such rule set:

```
rscheck(name, left, right)
```

The **name** is the name of the named rule set being called. If **right** is missing, it prints as NULL, and the workspace passed to the rule set is:

```
left
```

If **right** is present, the workspace is:

```
left $| right
```

Here, the **$|** in the workspace is the **$|** operator.

−d49.1

37.5.166   *Trace checkcompat()*

The *checkcompat()* routine inside *conf.c* can be tuned to solve many problems (see §20.1). The default **−d49.1** (a.k.a. **49**) debugging switch inside it prints the arguments that were passed to it:

```
checkcompat(to=recipient, from=sender)
```

When designing your own *checkcompat()*, you should only use the **−d49** category to trace it.

---

[*] There is no **−d48.1** information.

–d50.1

37.5.167   *Show envelope being dropped*

Deallocating an envelope frees that envelope's C language structure for future reuse. Deallocation also causes all the queued files for that mail message to be removed (except as possibly prevented by the –d51 debugging switch described in the next section). An envelope is deallocated after its mail message has been delivered to all recipients (including any failed deliveries).

The –d50.1 (a.k.a. –d50) debugging switch causes *sendmail* to print information about each envelope that is being deallocated:

```
dropenvelope loc id=ident flags=  output of printenvflags( ) here
```

This output shows the address in memory for the envelope's C language structure (*loc*), the queue identifier (*ident*, as used to name queued files), and the envelope flags as printed by *printenvflags*() (see Table 37-3 in §37.5.12).

Note that if the version of *sendmail* is pre-8.7, a Return-Receipt: header was in the message, and delivery was to at least one local recipient, the process of deallocation also causes acknowledgment of delivery to be returned to the sender and triggers error returns.

The –d50.1 debugging switch also shows the qf and df files just before they are removed:

```
===== Dropping [dq]fqid... queueit=bool, e_flags=  output of printenvflags( ) here
```

–d50.2

37.5.168   *Show Booleans*

The –d50.2 debugging switch shows the setting of three variables that determine how the envelope will be treated:

```
failure_return=val delay_return=val success_return=val queueit=val
```

A 1 indicates that the variable is true, a 0 indicates that it is false.

–d50.10

37.5.169   *Also show the send queue*

The –d50.10 debugging switch causes the current send queue to also be printed:

```
sendq= output of printaddr( ) here (see §37.3.1)
```

-d51.4

37.5.170   *Show queue entries being unlocked*

The -d51.4[*] debugging switch causes V8 *sendmail* to print the following each time an envelope is unlocked in the queue:

    unlockqueue(*qid*)

Here, *qid* is the queue identifier.

-d51.104

37.5.171   *Prevent unlink of xf file*

The xf file (one of the files that form a queued mail message) holds error messages generated by a delivery agent. The last line of text in this file is made the value of the M line in the qf file (see §23.9.9). Ordinarily, the xf file is removed after that error line is saved.

The -d51.104 debugging switch prevents *sendmail* from removing the xf file. If mail continually fails, this debugging switch can be used to save all error messages instead of just the one that is usually saved in the qf file.

-d52.1

37.5.172   *Show disconnect from controlling TTY*

When *sendmail* runs as a daemon, it must disconnect itself from the terminal device that is used to run it. This prevents keyboard signals from killing it and prevents it from hanging (on a dial-in line waiting for carrier detect, for example).

The -d52.1 (a.k.a. -d52) debugging switch shows *sendmail* disconnecting from the controlling terminal device:

    disconnect: In *fd* Out *fd*, e=*addr*

For both its input and output connections, the *fd* is a decimal representation of the file descriptor number. The *addr* is a hexadecimal representation of the address that contains the envelope information. If the L logging level option is greater than 71, *sendmail syslog*(3)'s the following message to show that it has disconnected:

    in background, pid=*pid*

Here, *pid* is the process identification number of the child process (the daemon).

---

[*] There is no -d51.1 information.

-d52.100   *(useful)*

37.5.173   *Prevent disconnect from controlling tty*

The −d52.100 debugging switch[*] prevents *sendmail* from disconnecting from its
controlling terminal device. To show that it is skipping the disconnect, it prints:

> don't

This debugging switch is useful for debugging the daemon. Note that this
−d52.100 prevents the detach but allows the daemon to *fork*(2). This differs from
the behavior of the −d99.100 debugging switch.

-d53.99

37.5.174   *Trace xclose( )*

Ordinarily, files are closed silently. The −d53.99[†] debugging switch can be used to
observe file closings. Just before the file is closed, *sendmail* prints:

> xfclose(*fp*) *what file*

Here, *fp* is the file pointer for the open file, printed in hexadecimal. The *what* is
an indication of the internal function that requires the close (such as **savemail** or
mci_uncache). The *file* is the name of the file to be closed.

If the close fails, the following is also printed:

> xfclose FAILURE: *why*

Here, *why* is the text corresponding to the error value returned by *fclose*(3) (see
sys_errlist(3)).

-d54.1

37.5.175   *Show error return and output message*

The exit values that are returned by *sendmail* are documented in §36.5. The
−d54.1 debugging switch shows the exit value being set by the internal *syserr*()
routine:

> syserr: ExitStat = *num*

Here, *num* corresponds to the values defined in <*sysexits.h*>.

---

[*] This was formerly the −d52.5 debugging switch.

[†] There is no −d53.1 information.

–d54.8

37.5.176   *Show message and flags*

The `–d54.8` debugging switch causes the text of the error message to be printed along with the flags that control its actual output:

```
--- message (hold) (held)
```

If `(hold)` appears, it means that the *message* will be held (stored) and not output. If `(held)` appears, it means that the *message* was previously held and should not be added to the `xf` file. If neither is printed, the *message* will be logged and appended to the `xf` file. If the message on output fails, *sendmail* will attempt to log this panic message:

```
qid: SYSERR: putoutmsg (host): error on output channel sending "message": err
```

If the message was never queued, the `qid` will print as NOQUEUE. If you are not currently connected to a *host*, it will print as NO-HOST. The `err` is the error that caused the message to fail (as defined in either *<sys/errno.h>* or *sysexits.h*).

–d55.60

37.5.177   *Show file locking*

The *sendmail* program tries to lock every file before reading or writing it. If *sendmail* was compiled with HASFLOCK defined (see §18.8.9), it uses *flock*(3) to lock and unlock files. If HASFLOCK is not defined, *sendmail* tries to lock and unlock with *fcntl*(2).

The `–d55.60`* debugging switch tells *sendmail* to print how it is about to try to lock a file:

```
lockfile(filename, action=set, type=l_type)
lockfile(filename, type=what)
```

The first form is printed if HASFLOCK is not defined. In it, *sendmail* is about to use *fcntl*(2) to lock the file. The *action* is a decimal representation of the F_SET flag that is *fcntl*(2)'s second argument. The `l_type` is the `l_type` structure member of *fcntl*(2)'s third argument (see the online manual for *fcntl*(2)).

The second form is printed if HASFLOCK is defined so that *flock*(2) will be used. In it, `what` is the type of locking to be performed, printed in octal, as described in Table 37–20.

---

* There is no `–d55.1` information.

Table 37–20: Flags That Control File Locking

Flag	Mnemonic	Description
001	LOCK_SH	Make it a shared lock
002	LOCK_EX	Make it an exclusive lock
004	LOCK_NB	Make it a nonblocking lock
010	LOCK_UN	Unlock the file

For both forms of locking, if the file is successfully locked, the above debugging output is concluded with:

```
SUCCESS
```

Otherwise, it is concluded with:

```
(error message here) FAILURE
```

In this later instance, regardless of the setting of this debugging flag, *sendmail* will also log the following error message:

```
cannot lock(filename, fd=num, type=what, omode=octal, euid=euid)
```

Here, `lock` is either `lockf` or `flock`. The `filename` and `fd` are the file name and file descriptor for the file. The `what` is the same as described in Table 37-20. If F_GETFL was defined at the system level when *sendmail* was compiled, then `omode` is an octal representation of the value returned by an *fcntl*(2) F_GETFL call; otherwise, it is a −1 in octal. The `euid` is the effective *uid* under which *sendmail* was running at the time.

–d56.1

37.5.178   *Persistent host status tracing*

The `–d56.1` (a.k.a. `–d56`) debugging switch tells *sendmail* to print a record of each step it is going through when saving and updating its persistent host status. The `HostStatusDirectory` option (see §34.8.31) specifies where and whether persistent host status will be saved. Just before a status file is updated, and if the `SingleThreadDelivery` option (see §34.8.64) is true, it needs to be locked:

```
mci_lock_host: attempting to lock host
```

Here, `host` is the name of the host whose status is being saved or updated. If the hostname is empty (as in the case of an address that contains only an RFC822 comment), one of the following errors is printed for an attempt to lock or unlock the host information:

```
mci_lock_host: NULL mci
mci_unlock_host: NULL mci
```

After the status file is locked, *sendmail* will transfer the information from that file into its internal *mci* structure:

```
mci_load_persistent: Attempting to load persistent information for host
```

Again, if the hostname is empty, this error will print:

```
mci_load_persistent: NULL
```

If *sendmail* was unable to translate the hostname into a UNIX path, the **-d56.1** debugging switch causes it to print:

```
mci_load_persistent: Couldn't generate host path
```

If *sendmail* was unable open the host status file, it prints:

```
mci_load_persistent: open(filename): host
```

Similarly, when *sendmail* needs to store or update the host information, it first prints that it is doing so:

```
mci_store_persistent: Storing information for host
```

If *sendmail* could not open the host status file, it prints:

```
mci_store_persistent: no statfile
```

The internals of the status file are described in Appendix B, *Host Status File Internals*.

Ordinarily, *sendmail* is silent about its inability to open status files when printing its host information with the *hoststat*(1) command (see §36.1.1). But if the **-d56.1** debugging switch is used, *sendmail* will complain:

```
mci_print_persistent: cannot open filename: host
```

When its host information is being purged with the *purgestat*(1) command (see §36.1.4), the **-d56.1** debugging switch tells *sendmail* to show what it is trying to achieve:

```
mci_purge_persistent: purging path
mci_purge_persistent: dpurge directory
```

-d56.2

37.5.179   *More persistent host status tracing*

The **-d56.2** debugging switch causes *sendmail* to show additional information about what it is trying to do. Just before attempting to lock a status file, it prints:

```
mci_lock_host: attempting to lock host
```

If a path could not be generated from the hostname, *sendmail* prints this error:

```
mci_lock_host: Failed to generate host path for host
```

If *sendmail* could not lock the status file, it prints:

```
mci_lock_host: couldn't get lock on filename
```

When *sendmail* is about to update a status file, just before unlocking that file, it announces that fact:

```
mci_unlock_host: store prior to unlock
```

The process of updating or reading a status file begins by *sendmail* traversing the directory hierarchy under which that file is stored. If *sendmail* is unable to *stat*(2) any component of that path, it prints the following error:

```
mci_traverse: Failed to stat component: reason for failure
```

If *sendmail* cannot descend into the next directory, it prints:

```
mci_traverse: opendir component: reason for failure
```

When purging its host information with the *purgestat*(1) command (see §36.1.4), if *sendmail* cannot remove the status file, it prints:

```
mci_purge_persistent: failed to unlink filename: reason for failure
```

And if it cannot remove any of the directory components, it prints:

```
mci_purge_persistent: rmdir directory: reason for failure
```

-d56.12

37.5.180 *Perform a sanity check*

As a "sanity check," the **-d56.12** debugging switch causes *sendmail* to print the following if the lock was successfully acquired on the status file:

```
mci_lock_host: Sanity check -- lock is good
```

-d56.80

37.5.181 *Trace creating the path to the status file*

If the status file does not exist, *sendmail* recursively makes the directories leading to it. The **-d56.80** debugging switch is used to trace this process:

```
mci_generate_persistent_path(host): FAILURE errno
mci_generate_persistent_path(host): SUCCESS path
```

If this process of making directories fails, **errno** is printed, as listed in *<errno.h>*. If it succeeds, the **path** created is displayed.

–d56.93

37.5.182   *Dump MCI record for the host*

The **–d56.93** debugging switch causes *sendmail* to dump the connection cache information associated with a host's status file:

```
mci_read_persistent: fp=hex, mci= output of mci_dump() here (see §37.5.44)
```

Here, *hex* is the file pointer of the open status file printed in hexadecimal. That is followed by a dump of the MCI record for the host.

–d57.2

37.5.183   *Monitor vsnprintf() overflows*

If HASSNPRINTF is not defined, *sendmail* emulates the *snprintf*(3) function. If the internal buffer of that emulation overflows, the **–d57.2** debugging switch causes this warning to be printed:

```
vsnprintf overflow: first 200 characters of buffer
```

Note that you may have to also use the **–v** command-line switch to make this output visible.

–d59   *(obsolete)*

37.5.184   *XLA from contrib*

See the XLA package in the *contrib/xla* directory as distributed with the V8 *sendmail* source. Note that XLA is no longer distributed with *sendmail* as of V8.8.

–d60.1   *(useful)*

37.5.185   *Trace map lookups inside rewrite()*

Rules defined by the R configuration command are rewritten by *sendmail*'s internal *rewrite()* subroutine. The $[and $(lookup operators (see §33.4.3 and §33.4) cause *sendmail* to look up keys in databases (maps).

If *sendmail* is running in deferred mode (see §34.8.16), it skips map lookups because they may cause DNS accesses. The **–d60.1** (a.k.a. **–d60**) debugging switch causes *sendmail* to print that it is skipping the lookup:

```
map_lookup(name, key) => DEFERRED
```

Here, *name* is the map type, such as **dequote** or **host**. The *key* is the information being looked up.

If running in something other than deferred mode, *sendmail* performs the lookup. If the lookup fails (if **key** is not found), *sendmail* prints:

```
map_lookup(name, key) => NOT FOUND (stat)
```

Here, **stat** is the number of the error that caused the failure. If it is 0, then the lookup failed merely because the **key** was not found. Otherwise, it corresponds to the error numbers in *<sysexits.h>*. Then if **stat** is the special value 75 (for EX_TEMPFAIL), *sendmail* also prints:

```
map_lookup(name, key) tempfail: errno=err
```

Here, **err** is the error number that corresponds to the errors listed in *<errno.h>*.

If the **key** is successfully found, *sendmail* prints:

```
map_lookup(name, key) => replacement value here (stat)
```

Note that the replacement value will be whatever value was defined by the **-a** database switch when the K command defined the map (see §33.3.4.2).

-d61.10

37.5.186   *Trace gethostbyname ( )*

The *gethostbyname*(3) library routine is called by *sendmail* every time *sendmail* needs to find the canonical name of a host. The **-d61.10**[*] debugging switch shows the result of that lookup:

```
_switch_gethostbyname_r(host) ... canonical name here
__switch_gethostbyname(host) ... canonical name here
gethostbyname(host) ... canonical name here
```

In all three lines of output, the **host** was looked up to find its canonical name. If one was found, its canonical name is printed; otherwise, **failure** is printed. The first two lines show variations on *gethostbyname*(3) that was required by some early SysVR4-based machines. These represent *sendmail*'s attempt to canonify the **host** no matter what.

-d62.1

37.5.187   *Log file descriptors before and after all deliveries*

The **-d62.1** (a.k.a. **-d62**) debugging switch causes *sendmail* to log the state of all of its file descriptors. It does this once just before it starts to process the list of its recipients and again just after it has completed delivery of all its recipients. Note that this debugging switch is unusual in that it causes its output to be logged with *syslog*(3), rather than written to *stdout*.

---

[*] There is no **-d61.1** information.

-d62.8

37.5.188   *Log file descriptors before each delivery*

The −d62.8 debugging switch causes *sendmail* to log the state of all its file descriptors just before undertaking delivery of each message.

-d62.10

37.5.189   *Log file descriptors after each delivery*

The −d62.10 debugging switch causes *sendmail* to log the state of all its file descriptors just after completing delivery of each message.

-d80.1

37.5.190   *Content-Length: header (Sun enhancement)*

The −d80.1 (a.k.a. −d80) debugging switch is used to watch how Sun's version of *sendmail* handles the Content-Length: header. As soon as the size of the body of a message is known, Sun's *sendmail* stores it in the envelope information. When the time comes to emit the Content-Length: header, that information is fetched. If the size is unknown, the −d80.1 debugging switch causes *sendmail* to print:

```
content_length(): Error:  Message bodysize undefined !
```

If the size is known, it is reduced by the number and size of the end-of-line characters (as defined by the delivery agent's E = equate). If the delivery agent's F=E flag is set (see §30.8.19), the size is further reduced by the number of five character "From " strings that begin lines in the message body. The −d80 debugging switch then causes the final result to be printed:

```
Content length = final length here
```

-d81.1

37.5.191   *> option for remote mode (Sun enhancement)*

In V8.1 *sendmail* the letter R was co-opted by the Berkeley distribution as an option name. This forced Sun to change the name of its former R option into the new > option. The −d81.1 (a.k.a. −d80) debugging switch causes Sun's *sendmail* to display the status of this remote mode:

```
verify_mail_server(): remote mode is either on or off
mail server = host name here
```

If the > option is declared, on is printed, and the name of the remote mail host is displayed, if known. See §D.6 for a further description of this option.

-d91.100

37.5.192   *Log caching and uncaching connections*

The -d91.100 debugging switch[*] causes the same information to be logged with *syslog*(3) as is printed by the -d42.5 debugging switch.

-d99.100   *(useful)*

37.5.193   *Prevent backgrounding the daemon*

The -d99.100 debugging switch[†] prevents the *sendmail* daemon from forking and putting itself into the background. This leaves the running daemon connected to your terminal so that you can see other debugging output. For example,

```
# /usr/lib/sendmail -bd -d99.100 -d9.30
```

This allows you to watch the daemon perform RFC1413 identification queries when SMTP connections are made. See also -d52.100, which prevents *sendmail* from disconnecting from its controlling terminal device, or the -bD command-line switch (§36.7.4), which does both.

---

[*] There is no -d91.1 information available.

[†] There is no -d99.1 information available.

38

Rule-Set Testing with –bt

The *sendmail* program offers a mode of operation (called rule testing mode) that allows you to observe the flow of addresses through rule sets. The –bt command-line switch causes *sendmail* to run in rule-testing mode. This mode is interactive. You enter rule set numbers, addresses, and other commands, and *sendmail* processes them and prints the results. The –bt switch's chief use is in testing changes in the configuration file. It is also useful for learning how rules and rule sets work.

38.1 Overview

The following command runs *sendmail* in rule-testing mode:

```
% /usr/lib/sendmail -bt
```

At first, the output produced by this command line prompts you like this:

```
ADDRESS TEST MODE (ruleset 3 NOT automatically invoked)
Enter <ruleset> <address>
>
```

The "ruleset 3" statement says that, beginning with V8 (and IDA) *sendmail*, rule set 3 is no longer automatically called when rule sets are listed at the prompt. We cover this new property in detail in §38.6.2.

Prior to V8 *sendmail*, rule-testing mode could be used only to test addresses. But beginning with V8.7 *sendmail* new functions have been added. To see a summary of those functions, enter a ? character followed by a RETURN at the > prompt. The output, which we reproduce below, lists and gives a brief description of each function. Note that the numbers to the right refer to the sections in this chapter and are not a part of *sendmail*'s output.

```
> ?
Help for test mode:
?                 :this help message.
.Dmvalue          :define macro `m' to `value'.                          ← §38.2.1
.Ccvalue          :add `value' to class `c'.                             ← §38.2.2
=Sruleset         :dump the contents of the indicated ruleset.           ← §38.4.1
=M                :display the known mailers.                            ← §38.4.2
-ddebug-spec      :equivalent to the command-line -d debug flag.
$m                :print the value of macro $m.                          ← §38.3.1
$=c               :print the contents of class $=c.                      ← §38.3.2
/mx host          :returns the MX records for `host'.                    ← §38.5.2
/parse address    :parse address, returning the value of crackaddr, and  ← §38.5.5
                   the parsed address (same as -bv).
/try mailer addr  :rewrite address into the form it will have when       ← §38.5.6
                   presented to the indicated mailer.
/tryflags flags   :set flags used by parsing.  The flags can be `H' for  ← §38.5.4
                   Header or `E' for Envelope, and `S' for Sender or `R'
                   for Recipient.  These can be combined, `HR' sets
                   flags for header recipients.
/canon hostname   :try to canonify hostname.                             ← §38.5.1
/map mapname key  :look up `key' in the indicated `mapname'.             ← §38.5.3
rules addr        :run the indicated address through the named rules.    ← §38.6
                   Rules can be a comma separated list of rules.
End of HELP info
>
```

This help output is contained in the *sendmail.hf* file, the location of which is defined by the **StatusFile (S)** option (see §34.8.66). If that option is not defined or if the file that is specified in it does not exist, you will get the following error message instead of help:

```
Sendmail 8.8.4 -- HELP not implemented
```

Help for rule-testing mode requires that the help file both exist and contain lines that begin with:

```
-bt
```

If you installed a new *sendmail* but did not install the new help file (thus causing the old file to be used), you may see this error:

```
HELP topic "-bt" unknown
```

The solution here is to upgrade your *sendmail.hf* file to the newest version.

Note that each of the functions listed in the help output will also produce a usage message if it is executed with no arguments. Consider the /try function, for example:

```
> /try
Usage: /try mailer address
>
```

This parallels the syntax shown in the help output above. These miniusage messages can effectively replace the *sendmail.hf* file in case it is missing.

Finally note that, although address testing was not listed in the help output for V8.7 *sendmail*, it still existed. We will cover it in §38.6.

38.2 Configuration Lines

Selected configuration file lines can be entered in rule-testing mode. They will behave just as they do when being read from the configuration file. Currently (as of V8.8 *sendmail*), three configuration commands are honored:

\# Commands that begin with a \# are treated as comments and ignored. Blank lines are also ignored.

D The D configuration command (see §31.3) is used to define a macro. Both single-character and multicharacter macro names may be used.

C The C configuration command (see §32.1) is used to add a value to a class. Both single-character and multicharacter class names may be used.

The \# may begin a line. The other two configuration commands in rule-testing mode must begin with a dot. Failure to use a dot will produce this error message:

```
No address!
```

The use of any character other than the two listed will produce this error:

```
Unknown "." command .bad command here
```

To get a usage message, just type a dot:

```
> .
Usage: .[DC]macro value(s)
```

38.2.1 Define a Macro with .D

The .D rule testing command is used to define a macro. One use for this command might be to modify a rule that depends on the $& prefix (see §31.5.3). For example, consider the rule in rule set 0 that is intended is to deliver a local user's address via the local delivery agent:

```
R$+        $#local $@ $&X $: $1
```

If $X has a value, this rule returns it as the host (the $@) part of a rule set 0 triple. If $X lacks a value, the host part is empty. This technique is useful because the $@ part with the local delivery agent is used to implement plussed users (see §24.4.3).

This scheme can be tested in rule-testing mode by first specifying a local user with $X undefined:

```
> 0 bob
rewrite: ruleset   0   input: bob
rewrite: ruleset   0 returns: $# local $@ $: bob
```

This form of rule testing and the output produced are described in detail in §38.6. Here it is important only to note that the host part of the triple (the $@ part) is empty.

Now use the .D command to give $X the value home:

```
> .DXhome
```

Now test those rules again:

```
> 0 bob
rewrite: ruleset   0   input: bob
rewrite: ruleset   0 returns: $# local $@ home $: bob
```

This time the host part of the triple (the $@ part) has the value host as intended.

The .D command can also be used to redefine the value of existing macros. It may not, however, be used to redefine macros used in rules (except for $&), because macros are expanded as rules are read from the configuration file. (See §31.5.2 and §38.3.1; describes how to view macro values in rule-testing mode.)

Internally, the .D command calls three routines, two of which you can watch. First it calls *macid*() to translate a macro name into an integer index. This can be watched with the –d35.14 debugging switch (see §37.5.121). Second, it calls *translate_dollars*() to convert the $x form into its internal form. This step cannot be watched. Finally, it calls *define*() to actually define the macro. This step can be watched with the –d35.9 debugging switch (see §37.5.120).

38.2.2 *Add to a Class with .C*

The .C rule testing command is used to add a member to a class. If the class does not exist, it is created. One possible use for this command would be to test whether adding a member to $=w will have the effect you desire. For example, suppose that a new alias called mailhub has been created for the local host. In the following, we test *sendmail* to see whether it will detect that new name as local:

```
> 3,0 bob@mailhub
rewrite: ruleset   3   input: bob @ mailhub
rewrite: ruleset   3 returns: bob < @ mailhub >
rewrite: ruleset   0   input: bob < @ mailhub >
rewrite: ruleset   0 returns: $# smtp $@ mailhub $: bob < @ mailhub >
```

This form of rule testing and the output that is produced are described in detail in §38.6. Here, merely note that the smtp delivery agent was selected, suggesting that *mailhub* was not automatically recognized as local.

One way to fix this is to add *mailhub* to the class $=w (see §32.5.8). In rule-testing mode this can be done by using the .C command:

```
>  .Cw mailhub
```

Now feed *sendmail* the same rules and address as before to see whether this fixed the problem:

```
> 3,0 bob@mailhub
rewrite: ruleset    3    input: bob @ mailhub
rewrite: ruleset    3 returns: bob < @ mailhub . >
rewrite: ruleset    0    input: bob < @ mailhub . >
rewrite: ruleset    0 returns: $# local $: bob
```

Success! Adding *mailhub* to the class $=w fixed the problem. You could now make that change permanent by editing the configuration file or by adding the name to the *sendmail.cw* file (see §19.6.26).

Another use for .C would include trying out masquerading for a subdomain. (See §19.6.12. See also §38.3.2 for a way to print the members of a class while in rule-testing mode.)

Internally, the .C command calls four routines, but you can watch only three. First it calls *macid*() to translate a macro name into an integer index. This can be watched with the –d35.14 debugging switch (see §37.5.121). Second, it calls *translate_dollars*() to convert the $=x form into its internal form. This step cannot be watched. Third, it calls *expand*() to expand any macros that appear in the list of words. This may be watched with the –d35.24 debugging switch (see §37.5.122). Finally, for each word that it adds to the class, it calls *setclass*(), which can be watched with the –d37.8 debugging switch (see §37.5.127).

38.3 Dump a Macro

Beginning with V8.7, the new rule testing commands allow you to print the value of a defined macro and the members of a class. With either command, you may use single-character or multicharacter macro names. Both commands begin with a $ character. An error is caused if nothing follows that $:

```
Name required for macro/class
```

If an = character follows, *sendmail* will display the requested class. Otherwise, the value of the macro is displayed:

```
$X                  ← display the value of the X macro
$=X                 ← list the members of the class X
```

38.3.1 Dump a Defined Macro with $

The $ rule-testing command causes *sendmail* to print the value of a defined macro. The form for this command looks like this:

```
$X                  ← show value of the single character macro name X
${YYY}              ← show value of the multi-character macro name YYY
```

Only one macro may be listed per line. If more than one is listed, all but the first is ignored:

```
$X $Y
   ↑
   ignored
```

One use for this command might be in solving the problem of duplicate domains. For example, suppose you just installed a new configuration file and discovered that your host was no longer known as *here.our.domain* but instead wrongly had an extra domain attached like this: *here.our.domain.our.domain*. To check the value of $j (see §31.10.20), which should contain the canonical name of your host, you could run *sendmail* in rule-testing mode:

```
ADDRESS TEST MODE (ruleset 3 NOT automatically invoked)
Enter <ruleset> <address>
> $j
$w.our.domain
>
```

This looks right because $w (see §31.10.40) is supposed to contain our short host-name. But just to check, you could also print the value of $w:

```
> $w
here.our.domain
```

Aha! Somehow, $w got the full canonical name. A quick scan of your *.mc* file (see §19.2) turns up this error:

```
LOCAL_CONFIG
Dwhere.our.domain            # $w is supposed to be full -- joachim
```

Apparently, your assistant, Joachim, mistakenly thought that new *sendmail* was wrong. By deleting the offending line and creating a new configuration file, you can take care of the problem.

38.3.2 Dump a Class Macro with $=

The `$=` rule-testing command tells *sendmail* to print all the members for a class. The class name must immediately follow the = with no intervening space, or the name is ignored. Both single-character and multicharacter names may be used:

```
$= X              ← the X is ignored
$=X               ← list the members of the class X
$={xxx}           ← list the members of the class xxx
```

The list of members (if any) is printed one per line:

```
> $=w
here.our.domain
here
[123.45.67.89]
fax
fax.our.domain
>
```

To illustrate one use for this command, imagine that you just made the local host the FTP server for your site. Of course, you were careful to modify the configuration file and add *fax* and *fax.our.domain* to the `$=w` class in it. But incoming mail to *fax.our.domain* is still failing. You run *sendmail* in rule-testing mode, as above, to verify that the correct entries are in `$=w`:

```
here.our.domain
here
[123.45.67.89]
fax                          ← correct
fax.our.domain               ← correct
```

Since they are correct, it could be that you made the mistake of changing the configuration file and failing to restart the daemon (see §4.1.1). The following command line fixes the problem (see §26.3.2):

```
# kill -HUP `head -1 /etc/sendmail.pid`
```

38.4 Show an Item

Beginning with V8.7 *sendmail*, two rule-testing commands are available: the `=S` command displays all the rules in a given rule set, and the `=M` command displays all the delivery agents. Both display their items after the configuration has been read. Thus in the case of rules, all the macros will have already been expanded.

Both are triggered by the leading = character. If nothing follows the =, this usage message is printed:

```
Usage: =Sruleset or =M
```

If any character other than S or M follows the = character, the following error is printed:

```
Unknown "=" command =bad character here
```

38.4.1 *Show Rules in a Rule Set with =S*

The =S rule-testing command causes *sendmail* to show all the rules of a rule set. The form of this command looks like this:

```
=Sruleset
```

Optional whitespace may separate the *ruleset* from the S. The *ruleset* may be a number or a symbolic name (see §29.1.2):

```
=S0              ← a number
=SMyrule         ← a name
```

Note that although macros may be used in defining rule sets (see §29.1.4), they may not be used with the =S command:

```
> =S$X
invalid ruleset name: "$X": No such file or directory
Undefined ruleset $X
>
```

One use for the =S command is to determine why a rule set is not behaving as expected. Consider a rule set 1 that is intended to rewrite all sending addresses so that the local hostname makes the message appear as though it came from the mail hub machine. Suppose that, when testing, you send an address through that rule but it comes out unchanged:

```
> 1 bob@localhost
rewrite: ruleset   1   input: bob @ localhost
rewrite: ruleset   1 returns: bob @ localhost
>
```

Puzzled, you look at the actual rule with the =S rule-testing command:

```
> =S1
R$* < @ $=w > $*                $@ $1 < @ mailhub . our . domain > $3
>
```

Aha! Rule set 1[*] expects the host part of the address to be surrounded by angle brackets! Knowing this, you run the address through the rule again, this time using angle brackets, and it succeeds:

---

[*] For the sake of the example we limited this rule set to a single rule. Most rule sets will have many rules.

```
>  1 bob<@localhost>
rewrite: ruleset  1   input: bob < @ localhost >
rewrite: ruleset  1 returns: bob < @ mailhub . our . domain >
>
```

38.4.2 Show Delivery Agents with =M

The =M rule testing command causes *sendmail* to print its list of delivery agents. This command takes no argument. Note that in the following example the lines are wrapped to fit on the page:

```
> =M
mailer 0 (prog): P=/bin/sh S=10/30 R=20/40 M=0 U=0:0 F=DFMelosu L=0 E=\n T=X-Unix
/rfc822/smtp A=sh -c $u
mailer 1 (*file*): P=[FILE] S=0/0 R=0/0 M=0 U=0:0 F=DEFMPlosu L=0 E=\n T=DNS/RFC8
22/X-Unix A=FILE
mailer 2 (*include*): P=/dev/null S=0/0 R=0/0 M=0 U=0:0 F=su L=0 E=\n T=<undefine
d>/<undefined> A=INCLUDE
mailer 3 (local): P=/bin/mail S=10/30 R=20/40 M=0 U=0:0 F=/5:@ADFMlmnrsw| L=0 E=\
n T=DNS/RFC822/X-Unix A=mail -d $u
mailer 4 (smtp): P=[IPC] S=11/31 R=21/21 M=0 U=0:0 F=DFMXmu L=990 E=\r\n T=DNS/RF
C822/SMTP A=IPC $h
mailer 5 (esmtp): P=[IPC] S=11/31 R=21/21 M=0 U=0:0 F=DFMXamu L=990 E=\r\n T=DNS/
RFC822/SMTP A=IPC $h
mailer 6 (smtp8): P=[IPC] S=11/31 R=21/21 M=0 U=0:0 F=8DFMXmu L=990 E=\r\n T=DNS/
RFC822/SMTP A=IPC $h
mailer 7 (relay): P=[IPC] S=11/31 R=61/61 M=0 U=0:0 F=8DFMXamu L=2040 E=\r\n T=DN
S/RFC822/SMTP A=IPC $h
```

This output is the same as that produced with the **-d0.15** debugging switch (see §37.5.4). The individual items in each line are explained in Chapter 30, *Delivery Agents*.

Internally, the =M rule testing command calls *printmailer*() to print the contents of each delivery agent.

38.5 Complex Actions Made Simple

Beginning with V8.7 *sendmail*, rule-testing mode offers six simple commands that accomplish complex tasks. They are listed in Table 38-1.

Table 38-1: Available –bt / Commands

Command	Version	§	Description
/canon	V8.7 and above	38.5.1	Canonify a host
/mx	V8.7 and above	38.5.2	Look up MX records
/map	V8.7 and above	38.5.3	Look up a database item
/tryflags	V8.7 and above	38.5.4	Select whom to /parse or /try

Table 38–1: Available –bt / Commands (continued)

Command	Version	§	Description
/parse	V8.7 and above	38.5.5	Parse an address
/try	V8.7 and above	38.5.6	Try a delivery agent

A lone / character will cause the following usage message to print:

```
Usage: /[canon|map|mx|parse|try|tryflags]
```

Anything other than the commands shown in Table 38-1 (such as /foo) will produce an error:

```
Unknown "/" command /foo
```

38.5.1 *Canonify a Host with /canon*

The /canon rule-testing command causes *sendmail* to look up the canonical (official, fully qualified) name of a host and print the result. The form for this command looks like this:

```
/canon host
```

If *host* is missing, the following usage message is printed:

```
Usage: /canon address
```

When you correctly supply the hostname as the argument, *sendmail* looks up the canonical name and returns the result:

```
> /canon icsic
getcanonname(icsic) returns icsic.icsi.berkeley.edu
>
```

Here, the hostname icsic was looked up. Because its canonical name was found, that name is printed following the **returns**. If the hostname had not been found, *sendmail* would have printed that same name after the **returns**:

```
> /canon foo
getcanonname(foo) returns foo
```

If you wish to watch the actual process of a host being canonified, you can turn on the –d38.20 debugging switch (see §37.5.135) with the rule-testing –d command (see §38.7):

```
> –d38.20
>
```

With that setting, the previous lookup of icsic produces a trace of all the steps that *sendmail* takes:

```
> /canon icsic
getcanonname(icsic), trying dns
getcanonname(icsic), trying files
text_getcanonname(icsic)
getcanonname(icsic.icsi.berkeley.edu), found
getcanonname(icsic) returns icsic.icsi.berkeley.edu
```

Here, *sendmail* first looked up `icsic` using DNS. That lookup failed, so *sendmail* fell back to looking it up in the */etc/hosts* file, where it was found. The order in which these techniques are tried is defined by your service-switch (see §34.8.61). If a service-switch mechanism is lacking, the order is internally defined by *sendmail* and varies depending operating system used.

Internally, the `/canon` rule-testing command can be watched in greater detail with the `-d38.20` debugging switch (see §37.5.135) and with the `-d8.2` debugging switch (see §37.5.31).

38.5.2 Look Up MX Records with /mx

The `/mx` rule-testing command causes *sendmail* to look up a specified hostname and return a list of MX records for that host. The form for this command looks like this:

```
/mx host
```

Here, *host* is the short or fully qualified name of a host. If *host* is missing, *sendmail* prints the following usage message:

```
Usage: /mx address
```

When *host* exists and has MX records associated with it, *sendmail* will look up and print those records. The MX records are listed in the order in which they will be tried (lowest to highest preference values). For example,

```
> /mx ourhost
getmxrr(ourhost) returns 2 value(s):
        mx.our.domain
        offsite.mx.domain
>
```

If no MX records are found, *sendmail* "`returns 0.`" When multiple records have the same preference values, *sendmail* randomizes the list. During a single run of *sendmail* the randomization will be the same each time. You can see this by looking up *aol.com*:

```
> /mx aol.com
getmxrr(aol.com) returns 8 value(s):
        d.mx.AOL.COM.
        h.mx.AOL.COM.
        g.mx.AOL.COM.
```

```
            c.mx.AOL.COM.
            b.mx.AOL.COM.
            f.mx.AOL.COM.
            e.mx.AOL.COM.
            a.mx.AOL.COM.
> /mx aol.com
getmxrr(aol.com) returns 8 value(s):
            d.mx.AOL.COM.
            h.mx.AOL.COM.
            g.mx.AOL.COM.
            c.mx.AOL.COM.
            b.mx.AOL.COM.
            f.mx.AOL.COM.
            e.mx.AOL.COM.
            a.mx.AOL.COM.
```

Now exit rule-testing mode and perform two separate runs of *sendmail*:

```
% echo /mx aol.com | /usr/lib/sendmail -bt
> /mx aol.com
getmxrr(aol.com) returns 8 value(s):
            d.mx.AOL.COM.
            g.mx.AOL.COM.
            h.mx.AOL.COM.
            c.mx.AOL.COM.
            b.mx.AOL.COM.
            f.mx.AOL.COM.
            a.mx.AOL.COM.
            e.mx.AOL.COM.
% echo /mx aol.com | /usr/lib/sendmail -bt
> /mx aol.com
getmxrr(aol.com) returns 8 value(s):
            b.mx.AOL.COM.
            d.mx.AOL.COM.
            g.mx.AOL.COM.
            e.mx.AOL.COM.
            a.mx.AOL.COM.
            c.mx.AOL.COM.
            h.mx.AOL.COM.
            f.mx.AOL.COM.
```

If you have defined the `FallbackMXhost` (V) (see §34.8.25), the host that is specified in that option will always appear last in the list of mx hosts. As a side benefit,
it will also be listed for hosts that do not exist:

```
% /usr/lib/sendmail -OFallBackMXhost=mx.our.domain -bt
ADDRESS TEST MODE (ruleset 3 NOT automatically invoked)
Enter <ruleset> <address>
> /mx foo.bar
getmxrr(foo.bar) returns 1 value(s):
        mx.our.domain
>
```

This /mx command is available for your use only if *sendmail* was compiled with NAMED_BIND defined (see §18.8.23). If NAMED_BIND was not defined, *sendmail* will print the following error instead of listing MX records:

```
No MX code compiled in
```

Internally, the /mx rule-testing command can be watched in a little more detail with the −d8.2 debugging switch (see §37.5.31). It can be watched in huge detail with the −d8.20 debugging switch (see §37.5.36).

38.5.3 Look up a Database Item with /map

The /map rule-testing command causes *sendmail* to look up a key in a database and print the value found (if there is one). The /map command is used like this:

```
/map name key
```

Here, *name* is the name of a database. It is either a name you assigned using a K configuration command (see §33.3) or one that is internally defined by *sendmail*, such as *aliases.files* (see §33.8.17). The *key* is the item you wish to look up in the database. If both *name* and *key* are missing, *sendmail* prints this usage message:

```
Usage: /map mapname key
```

If just the *key* is missing, *sendmail* prints this error:

```
No key specified
```

If the *name* is that of a database that does not exist, *sendmail* prints this error:

```
Map named "bad name here" not found
```

Otherwise, the database exists, so *sendmail* looks up the *key* in it. If the key is not found in the database, *sendmail* prints this:

```
map_lookup: name (key) no match (error number here)
```

The error number corresponds to error numbers listed in <*sysexits.h*>.

The /map rule testing command is very useful for testing databases of your own design. If a rule that uses the database fails to work as predicted, use /map to test that database by hand. To illustrate, first get a list of databases that are available on your local machine:

```
% /usr/lib/sendmail -d38.4 -bt | grep map_init
map_init(sequence:aliases.files, NULL, 0)
map_init(implicit:Alias0, /etc/aliases, 0)
map_init(host:host, NULL, 0)
map_init(switch:aliases, aliases, 0)
map_init(dequote:dequote, NULL, 0)
```

Here, the name of each database follows the colon in each line. Your list, of course, will probably be different.

The `aliases` database, for example, is used to convert a local address into one or more new addresses. Using the rule-testing `/map` command, you can see how *sendmail* looks up an alias:

```
> /map aliases root
map_lookup: aliases (root) returns you, hans@other.site (0)
```

The `host` database behaves the same as the `/canon` command shown above. It looks up a hostname by using *sendmail's* internal `host` map (see §33.4.3), which returns the canonical name of the looked-up host:

```
> /map host localhost
map_lookup: host (localhost) returns localhost.our.domain. (0)
> /map host bogus.no.domain
map_lookup: host (bogus.no.domain) no match (68)
```

The `dequote` map (see §33.8.4) is not really a database at all, but a hook into a routine that removes quotation marks from addresses:

```
> /map dequote "a"@"@b"
map_lookup: dequote ("a"@"@b") returns a@@b (0)
> /map dequote "a
map_lookup: dequote ("a) no match (0)
```

Note (in the second example) that it removes only balance quotation marks.

All lookups, no matter what the type, can be watched with the `–d38.20` debugging switch (see §37.5.135).

38.5.4 Select Whom to /parse or /try with /tryflags

Two additional commands are `/parse` and `/try`. We will cover them next, but first we need to mention the `/tryflags` rule-testing command, because it is used to select the sender or recipient and headers or envelope for those other commands. The `/tryflags` command is used like this:

/tryflags h	← *set headers*
/tryflags e	← *set envelope*
/tryflags s	← *set sender*
/tryflags r	← *set recipient*
/tryflags er	← *set envelope recipient*

The arguments are single letters that may appear in upper- or lowercase and in any order. Any letter other than those shown is silently ignored.

The default setting when *sendmail* first starts to run in rule-testing mode is **er** for envelope recipient.* Omitting the argument causes *sendmail* to print the following usage statement:

```
Usage: /tryflags [Hh|Ee][Ss|Rr]
```

38.5.5 Parse an Address with /parse

The **/parse** rule testing command instructs *sendmail* to pass an address through a predetermined sequence of rules to select a delivery agent and to put the $u macro (see §31.10.36) into its final form. The **/parse** command is used like this:

```
/parse address
```

If the address is missing, *sendmail* prints the following usage message:

```
Usage: /parse address
```

The following example shows a local address being fed into **/parse**. Note that the numbers on the left are for later reference and are not part of *sendmail*'s output.

```
 1      > /parse you@localhost (Your Name)
 2      Cracked address = $g (Your Name)
 3      Parsing envelope recipient address
 4      rewrite: ruleset   3   input: you @ localhost
 5      rewrite: ruleset  96   input: you < @ localhost >
 6      rewrite: ruleset  96 returns: you < @ here . our . domain . >
 7      rewrite: ruleset   3 returns: you < @ here . our . domain . >
 8      rewrite: ruleset   0   input: you < @ here . our . domain . >
 9      rewrite: ruleset   0 returns: $# local $: you
10      rewrite: ruleset   2   input: you
11      rewrite: ruleset   2 returns: you
12      rewrite: ruleset  20   input: you
13      rewrite: ruleset  20 returns: you
14      rewrite: ruleset   4   input: you
15      rewrite: ruleset   4 returns: you
16      mailer local, user you
```

The address *you@localhost* is first fed into *crackaddr* (line *2*) to separate it from any surrounding RFC822 comments (see §37.5.117), such as "(Your Name)." If mail were actually to be sent, the address would be stored in the $g macro before being passed to rules. This is illustrated by line *2*, which uses $g as a place holder to show where the address was found.

The next line (line *3*) shows that the address will be treated as that of an envelope recipient. The **/tryflags** command (see §38.5.4) sets whether it is treated as a header or envelope or as a sender or recipient address.

---

* Internally, the **/tryflags** simply sets or clears the RF_HEADERADDR or RF_SENDERADDR flags. The meaning of these flags is documented in Table 37-10 (see §37.5.81).

The address is passed to rule set 3 (see §29.4) because all addresses are rewritten by rule set 3 first. The job of rule set 3 is to focus on (surround in angle brackets) the host part of the address, which it does (line *5*). Rule set 3, in this example, then passes the address to rule set 96 to see whether *localhost* is a synonym for the local machine's name. It is, so rule set 96 makes that translation (line *6*).

The output of rule set 3 is passed to rule set 0 whose job is to select a delivery agent (line *8*). Because *here.our.domain* is the local machine, rule set 0 selects the `local` delivery agent (line *9*).

Line *9* shows that the `$:` part of the delivery agent "triple" (see §29.6) will eventually be tucked into `$u` (see §31.10.36) for use by the delivery agent's `A=` equate (see §30.4.1). But before that happens, that address needs to be passed though its own set of specific rules. It is given to rule set 2 because all recipient addresses are given to rule set 2 (line *10*). It is then given to rule set 20 because the `R=` equate (see §30.4.10) for the `local` delivery agent specifies rule set 20 for the envelope recipient (line *12*). Finally, it is given to rule set 4 (see §29.5) because all addresses are lastly rewritten by rule set 4 (line *14*).

The last line of output shows that the `local` delivery agent was selected and that the value that would be put into `$u` (were mail really being sent) would be `you`.

When you /parse an address that is not local, rule set 0 will also select a host (`$@`) part for delivery.

```
rewrite: ruleset   0 returns: $# smtp $@ uofa . edu . $: friend < @ uofa . edu . >
```

In this instance the last line of /parse output will also include the host information that will be placed into `$h`:

```
mailer smtp, host there.domain., user friend@there.domain
```

When you /parse an address that is illegal (from the point of view of rules), *sendmail* selects the `#error` delivery agent:

```
> /parse @host
Cracked address = $g
Parsing envelope recipient address
rewrite: ruleset   3   input: @ host
rewrite: ruleset  96   input: < @ host >
rewrite: ruleset  96 returns: < @ host >
rewrite: ruleset   3 returns: < @ host >
rewrite: ruleset   0   input: < @ host >
rewrite: ruleset   0 returns: $# error $@ 5 . 1 . 1 $: "user address required"
@host... user address required
mailer *error*, user
```

The error here was that the address lacked a user part. The meanings of all the parts of the `#error` delivery agent are described in §30.5.2. The second from the last line in this example shows the message that would be printed or returned if such an address appeared in actual mail. The delivery agent ***error*** is internal to *sendmail* and cannot be directly used.

Internally, the **/parse** command first calls *crackaddr()*, prints the result, then passes the original address to *parseaddr()*. The entry into and exit from *crackaddr()* can be watched with the **-d33.1** debugging switch (see §37.5.117). The selection of a delivery agent with *parseaddr()* can be watched with the **-d20.1** debugging switch (see §37.5.66). The rewriting of the user into a suitable **$u** is handled by *buildaddr()* which can be watched with the **-d24.5** debugging switch (see §37.5.82).

38.5.6 Try a Delivery Agent with /try

In the SMTP RCPT command, *sendmail* is required to express the recipient's address relative to the local host. For domain addresses, this simply means that the address should be RFC822-compliant (such as *you@here.our.domain*). For UUCP addresses, this may mean reversing the path (such as *you@there* reverses to *there!you*). The **/try** rule testing command causes an address to be rewritten so that it appears to be correct relative to the local host.

The **/try** command is used like this:

```
/try agent address
```

Here, **agent** is the delivery agent, and **address** is the address to rewrite. The following usage message is produced if both **agent** and **address** are missing or if just the **address** is missing:

```
Usage: /try mailer address
```

The delivery agent (**mailer**) is used to select only the **R=** or **S=** rule set for the address. The **/tryflags** command (see §38.5.4) determines which is selected (by selecting recipient or sender).

In the following example the numbers to the left are for reference only and are not part of *sendmail*'s output:

```
1        > /try smtp you
2        Trying envelope recipient address you for mailer smtp
3        rewrite: ruleset   3   input: you
4        rewrite: ruleset  96   input: you
5        rewrite: ruleset  96 returns: you
6        rewrite: ruleset   3 returns: you
7        rewrite: ruleset   2   input: you
8        rewrite: ruleset   2 returns: you
9        rewrite: ruleset  21   input: you
10       rewrite: ruleset  21 returns: you < @ *LOCAL* >
```

```
11        rewrite: ruleset   4   input: you < @ *LOCAL* >
12        rewrite: ruleset   4 returns: you @ here . our . domain
13        Rcode = 0, addr = you@here.our.domain
```

Here, the envelope-recipient address *you* is rewritten on the basis of the smtp delivery agent. Rule set 3 is called first (line *3*) because all addresses are rewritten by it first. Rule set 2 (line *7*) is called because all recipient addresses get rewritten by it. Rule set 21 is called because that rule set was indicated by the smtp delivery agent's R= equate. That rule set detects that the envelope recipient address (*you*) is local (line *10*). Rule set 4 (always the last to rewrite) sees the special tag *LOCAL* and converts that tag to the canonical name of your local machine (line *12*).

```
1         > /try uucp localhost!there!you
2         Trying envelope recipient address localhost!there!you for mailer uucp
3         rewrite: ruleset   3   input: localhost ! there ! you
4         rewrite: ruleset  96   input: there ! you < @ localhost . UUCP >
5         rewrite: ruleset  96 returns: there ! you < @ here . our . domain . >
6         rewrite: ruleset   3 returns: there ! you < @ here . our . domain . >
7         rewrite: ruleset   2   input: there ! you < @ here . our . domain . >
8         rewrite: ruleset   2 returns: there ! you < @ here . our . domain . >
9         rewrite: ruleset  22   input: there ! you < @ here . our . domain . >
10        rewrite: ruleset  22 returns: there ! you
11        rewrite: ruleset   4   input: there ! you
12        rewrite: ruleset   4 returns: there ! you
13        Rcode = 0, addr = there!you
```

Here we try a UUCP address to examine what might be different. This time, rule set 96 recognized the ! character as meaning this is a UUCP form of address. That rule set recognizes that *localhost* is one of the names for the local machine and converts the address to Internet form with your host's canonical name (line *5*). Another difference is that rule set 22 is called because that is the R= rule set for the uucp delivery agent. That special rule set throws away the local host information, thus forming a correct UUCP-style relative address (line *10*).

Internally, the /try rule-testing command calls the *remotename()* routine, which can be watched with the –d12.1 debugging switch (see §37.5.47).

38.6 *Process-Specified Addresses*

The *sendmail* rule-testing mode has always had the ability to test individual rule sets, but prior to V8.7 *sendmail*, rule sets could be specified only by number. Beginning with V8.7, rule sets may also be specified by name. Prior to V8 *sendmail*, rule set 3 was always called first, even if you did not specify it.[*]

---

[*] This was adopted from IDA sendmail.

38.6.1 Syntax

The > prompt expects rule sets and addresses to be specified like this:

```
> ident,ident,ident... address
```

Each *ident* is a rule-set name or number. When there is more than one rule set, they must be separated from each other by commas (with no spaces between them).

For numbered rule sets, the number must be in the range of 0 through the highest number allowed. A number that is too large causes *sendmail* to print the following two errors:

```
bad ruleset number (max max)
Undefined ruleset number
```

A rule set whose number is below the maximum but that was never defined will act as though it was defined but lacks rules.

Named rule sets must exist in the symbol table. If the name specified was never defined, the following error is printed:

```
Undefined ruleset ident
```

If any rule set number in the comma-separated list of rule sets is omitted (e.g., *ident,,ident*), *sendmail* interprets the second comma as part of the second identifier, thus producing this error:

```
Undefined ruleset ,identifier
```

The *address* is everything following the first whitespace (space and tab characters) to the end of the line. If whitespace characters appear anywhere in the list of rule sets, the rule sets to the right of the whitespace are interpreted as part of the address.

38.6.2 The Address

Each address that is specified is processed by *sendmail* in the same way that mail addresses are processed when actual mail is being sent. Each is parsed and normalized so that everything but the actual address is thrown away. Each is then tokenized and placed into the workspace for rule-set processing. To illustrate, observe the following rule-testing session:

```
ADDRESS TEST MODE (ruleset 3 NOT automatically invoked)
Enter <ruleset> <address>
> 0 bill (Bill Bix)
rewrite: ruleset  0   input: bill
rewrite: ruleset  0 returns: $# local $: bill
> 0 Bill Bix <bill>
```

```
rewrite: ruleset  0    input: Bill Bix < bill >
rewrite: ruleset  0 returns: $# local $: Bill Bix < bill >
> 3,0 Bill Bix <bill>
rewrite: ruleset  3    input: Bill Bix < bill >
rewrite: ruleset  3 returns: bill
rewrite: ruleset  0    input: bill
rewrite: ruleset  0 returns: $# local $: bill
>
```

The first test illustrates that *sendmail* strips RFC822-style comments from addresses before tokenizing them. This results in the (Bill Bix) being thrown away so that rule set 0 sees only the address bill.

The second test illustrates that *sendmail* does not internally recognize addresses in angle brackets. Instead, rule set 3 throws away everything but the address in angle brackets, as shown in the third test.

Note that in many actual configuration files, rule set 3 also focuses on the host part of the address. For this reason, you should *always* begin with rule set 3 unless you are tuning a particular rule for which you know the precise input required.

38.6.3 Rule 3 Always Called First with –bt

When *sendmail* starts to run in rule-testing mode, its appearance and initial behavior vary from vendor to vendor and from version to version. When rule-testing mode begins, *sendmail* always prints an introductory banner. Pre-V8 *sendmail* printed the following banner:

```
ADDRESS TEST MODE
Enter <ruleset> <address>
>
```

It is important to note that (unless a banner says otherwise) *sendmail* always calls rule set 3 first. That is, even if you try to test rule set 0, you always first see the effects of rule set 3.

Beginning with V8 *sendmail*, rule set 3 is no longer automatically called. To ensure that there is no confusion, V8 *sendmail* prints this banner:

```
ADDRESS TEST MODE (ruleset 3 NOT automatically invoked)
Enter <ruleset> <address>
>
```

Note that in all versions the last line (the >) is a prompt. At this prompt, you can specify a rule set and an address or, beginning with V8.7, any of the commands shown in §38.1.

38.6.4 The Output

Each line of output that is produced when rule testing begins with an indication of the rule set number being processed:

```
rewrite: ruleset  3   input: Bill Bix < bill >
```

The word **input** precedes each address that is about to be processed by a rule set:

```
rewrite: ruleset  3   input: Bill Bix < bill >
```

The word **returns** precedes each address that is the result of rewriting by a rule set:

```
rewrite: ruleset  3 returns: bill
```

When rule sets call other rule sets as subroutines, those calls are shown in the output with **input** and **returns** pairs. In the following, rule set 11 is called as a subroutine rule set from inside rule set 3:

```
rewrite: ruleset  3   input: Bill Bix < bill >
rewrite: ruleset  11 input: bill
rewrite: ruleset  11 returns: bill
rewrite: ruleset  3  returns: bill
```

The output can also contain rule set operators:

```
rewrite: ruleset  0 returns: $# local $: bill
```

In this output, the operators are printed as they would appear in the configuration file. The $# selects a delivery agent, and the $: specifies the user. Under old versions of *sendmail* those operators are printed in the output as control characters:

```
rewrite: ruleset  0 returns: ^V local ^X bill
```

The correspondence between control characters in the output and *sendmail* configuration file operators is given in Table 38-2.

Table 38–2: Control Characters Versus Operators

Control	Operator	Meaning
^V	$#	Select delivery agent
^W	$@	Specify host for delivery agent
^X	$:	Specify user for delivery agent

38.7 *Add Debugging for Detail*

In rule-testing mode the –d rule-testing command can be used to turn debugging output on and off. Prior to V8.7 *sendmail* the –d could be specified only on the command line. Beginning with V8.7 *sendmail*, the –d may also be specified in rule-testing mode. We illustrate the latter technique here.

Debugging output can reveal in great detail how individual rules are being handled. A debugging category and level of 21.12, for example, causes *sendmail* to print the LHS of each rule as it is tried. To illustrate, consider the following (highly simplified) configuration-file rule set:

```
S0
R@                      $#local $:$n              handle <> form
R$*<@$+>$*              $#$M $@$R $:$1<@$2>$3      user@some.where
R$+                     $#local $:$1              local names
```

Normal output that is produced when a rule-set number and address are entered at the > prompt looks like this:

```
> 0 george
rewrite: ruleset    0   input: george
rewrite: ruleset    0 returns: $# local $: george
```

But if we turn on debugging using the –d rule-testing command:

```
> -d21.12
```

the output that is produced when the same rule-set number and address are entered is more verbose than it was before:

```
>   0 george
rewrite: ruleset    0   input: george
-----trying rule: @
----- rule fails
-----trying rule: $* < @ $+ > $*
----- rule fails
-----trying rule: $+
-----rule matches: $# local $: $1
rewritten as: $# local $: george
rewrite: ruleset    0 returns: $# local $: george
```

Observe that the first rule in rule set 0 (the lone @) does not match **george** in the workspace. Therefore that rule **fails** and is skipped. Then the more complicated rule ($*<@$+>$*) is tried, and it too fails. Finally, the $+ operator in the last rule matches **george**, and the workspace is rewritten.

Note that the extra output that is produced by –d can potentially run to many lines. To capture the output for later examination, consider running *sendmail* in rule-testing mode from within a *script*(1), *emacs*(1), or similar session.

Higher levels of debugging are also available for examining rules and rule sets. The level **-d21.15** shows *$digit* operators on the RHS being substituted with values from the LHS. The level **-d21.35** causes each comparison, token versus token, to be printed.

To turn off the extra debugging output, just reuse the **-d** rule-testing command and specify a level of zero:

```
> -d21.0
```

A **-d** with no category or level behaves the same as the **-d** command-line switch (see §37.1). It sets a default of **0-99.1**.

38.7.1 A Trick

In debugging large configuration files, the output that is produced by the **-d21.15** switch can become too huge to examine conveniently. A good alternative (when modifying or adding rules) is to temporarily insert a fake subroutine call before and after individual rules to see what they do:

R$*	$:$>TEST $1	← *fake subroutine call*
Rlhs	rhs	← *new rule*
R$*	$:$>TEST $1	← *fake subroutine call*

With the fake wrapper around the new rule (the name **TEST** is arbitrary), ordinary rule testing with **-bt** now shows how the address is rewritten by that rule:

```
rewrite: ruleset  3    input: ...
rewrite: ruleset TEST   input: ...
rewrite: ruleset TEST returns: ...
                            ← new rule acted here
rewrite: ruleset TEST   input: ...
rewrite: ruleset TEST returns: ...
rewrite: ruleset  3 returns: ...
>
```

If you use this technique, remember, of course, to remove the fake subroutine calls before putting that configuration file into use.

38.8 Batch Rule-Set Testing

The output that is produced by *sendmail* can become huge, especially when many addresses need testing. To simplify the process (and to help bulletproof your configuration file), consider using a shell script like the following:

```
#!/bin/sh
/usr/lib/sendmail -bt < $1 |\
      egrep " 3.*input:| 0.*returns|^>" |\
      sed   -e 's/^rewrite: ruleset  //'
```

Here, the output is piped through a *egrep*(1) selects only the lines of interest. If this script were to be called *testcf.sh*, it could be invoked with the following command line:

```
% testcf.sh address.list
```

Here, the **address.list** is a file consisting of pairs of rule-set numbers and addresses like the following:

```
3,0 nobody@ourhost
3,0 nobody@ourhost.domain
3,0 nobody@distant.domain
 ... and so on
```

The output that is produced shows the input to rule set 3 and the delivery agent returned by each call to rule set 0:

```
> 3,0 nobody@outhost
 3   input: nobody @ outhost
 0 returns: $# local $: nobody
> 3,0 nobody@ourhost.domain
 3   input: nobody @ ourhost . domain
 0 returns: $# local $: nobody
> 3,0 nobody@distant.domain
 3   input: nobody @ distant . domain
 0 returns: $# smtp $@ distant . domain $: nobody < @ distant . domain >
```

Note that the **address.list** file should contain every conceivable kind of address. The output from the shell script should be saved. At a later time, after the configuration file is changed, *diff*(1) can be used to see if the saved output differs from the new output (to see whether anything unexpected changed as a result of your modifications).

Also note that directly calling rule sets 3 and 0 produces less useful information than does the **/parse** rule-testing command (see §38.5.5). If you use that command, a *diff*(1) against prior output may provide more interesting and complete information.

38.9 Pitfalls

- Old programs and scripts that are designed to use **–bt** mode to test addresses and the like tend to break with each release of *sendmail*. Fortunately, they are easy to fix if you know the language involved.

- There is no way to currently define rules on the fly. Consequently, you need to modify a configuration file and run *sendmail* in rule-testing mode repeatedly until the new rules work.

V

Appendixes

V

Appendices

The client.cf File

In Part I of this book a configuration file that always forwards to the hub was partly developed. This appendix presents it in annotated and cross-referenced form, but please use this file only to learn about *sendmail*. If you really need a client file that always forwards to a hub, use the *nullclient* feature described in Chapter 16, *The null.mc File and m4*.

```
V7                                                              Chapter 5

# Defined macros                                               Chapter 7
```

Note that in the next two lines you should replace mailhost
with the real internal name of your mail hub and mail.us.edu
with the real canonical name of your mail hub.

```
D{REMOTE}mailhost      # The name of the mail hub           Chapter 7
D{HUB}mail.us.edu      # Hub as known to the outside world  Chapter 11
Cw localhost          # My other names                     Chapter 12
Fw -o /etc/sendmail.cw # A file of other names             Chapter 12
Ct root daemon                                              Chapter 14

# Options                                                   Chapter 13
```

Note that you must change the next line to the path for your
queue directory before putting this configuration file into use.

```
O QueueDirectory=/tmp       # Use /var/spool/mqueue upon release   Chapter 13
O Timeout.queuewarn=4h                                             Chapter 13
O Timeout.queuereturn=5d                                           Chapter 13
O DeliveryMode=background                                          Chapter 13
O TempFileMode=0600                                                Chapter 13
O DefaultUser=1:1                                                  Chapter 13
O LogLevel=9                                                       Chapter 13
O OldStyleHeaders=True                                             Chapter 13
O BlankSub=.                 # Replace unquoted spaces             Chapter 13
```

```
# Headers                                                                Chapter 14
HFrom: <$g>                         # Added only if missing              Chapter 14
```

*Note that this is a minimal Received: header. See §35.10.25 for
a more complete version of this header.*

```
HReceived: by $j; $b            # Always added                    Chapter 14
H?x?Full-Name: $?x$x$.          # Add full name if available      Chapter 14
H?D?Date: $a                    # Add if F=D                      Chapter 14
H?M?Message-Id: <$t.$i@$j>      # Add if F=M                      Chapter 14
```

```
# Precedence                                                     Chapter 14
Pspecial-delivery=100                                            Chapter 14
Pfirst-class=0                                                   Chapter 14
Plist=-30                                                        Chapter 14
Pbulk=-60                                                        Chapter 14
Pjunk=-100                                                       Chapter 14
```

```
# Delivery agent definition to forward mail to hub                          Chapter 6
Mhub, P=[IPC], S=Hubset, R=0, F=xmDFMuXa, T=DNS/RFC822/SMTP, A=IPC $h   Chapters 6, 11, 14
# Sendmail requires this, but we won't use it.                              Chapter 6
Mlocal, P=/bin/mail, F=lsDFMAw5:/|@rmn, S=0, R=0, A=mail -d $u               Chapter 6
```

```
S0 # select delivery agent                                          Chapter 9
R@ $+                    $#error $: Missing user name               Chapter 9
R$+                      $#hub $@${REMOTE} $:$1   forward to hub     Chapter 9
```

```
S3 # preprocessing for all rule sets                                Chapter 10
R$* <> $*                $n           handle <> error address       Chapter 10
R$* < $* <$*> $* > $*    $2<$3>$4     de-nest brackets              Chapter 10
R$* < $* > $*            $2           basic RFC822 parsing          Chapter 10
```

```
SHubset # Rewrite the sender for the hub
R$-              $@ $1@${HUB}    user -> user@hub                  Chapter 11
R$- @ $=w        $@ $1@${HUB}    user@local -> user@hub            Chapters 11, 12
R$- @ $=w . $m   $@ $1@${HUB}    user@local.domain -> user@hub     Chapter 12
```

B

Host Status File Internals

"Persistent host status" is described under, and enabled with, the `HostStatusDirectory` option (see §34.8.31). The format for each directory created by that option, as of V8.8.4 *sendmail*, looks like this:

    HostStatusDirectory/*domain.*/*subdomain.*/*host*

That is, the canonical name of the host whose status is being stored is divided into components based on the separating dots in its name. The dot for each component, is moved to the end of each component and all but the *host* part are created as directories.

To illustrate, consider the following canonical name:

    here.uofa.edu

If the `HostStatusDirectory` option were declared like this:

    O HostStatusDirectory=/tmp/.hoststat

the status for the host *here.uofa.edu* would be stored in the file:

    /tmp/.hoststat/edu./uofa./here

B.1 Status file lines

The format of the status file (in the above case `here`) is one item of information per line, where each line begins with a key letter:

    letterwhat

The complete list of key letters is shown in Table B-1.

Table B–1: Host Status File Key Letters

Letter	Version	Description
D	V8.8 and above	The DSN status text
E	V8.8 and above	The UNIX error number
H	V8.8 and above	The DNS error number
R	V8.8 and above	The SMTP status-code text
S	V8.8 and above	The UNIX *exit*(2) status
U	V8.8 and above	The time last used
V	V8.8 and above	The version of this status file
.	V8.8 and above	The end of file marker

In the sections that follow, we describe each key letter in alphabetical order, rather than in the order in which they will appear in the status file.

Note that not all these lines are printed with the *hoststat*(1) command (see §36.1.1). As of 8.8.4, only the information in the E, R, and U lines is printed.

Also note that the letters that are used and the meaning of each are essentially internal to *sendmail* and are subject to change without notice.

D line   *(V8.8 and above)*

B.1.1   *The DSN status text*

Delivery Status Notification (DSN) gives the status of a returned message in its Status: MIME-body header (see RFC1892). That status is formed from three digits, each separated from the others by a dot, for example:

    5.0.1

The meaning of each digit is documented in RFC1893. This D line stores that status as text.

E line   *(V8.8 and above)*

B.1.2   *The UNIX error number*

When delivery or a connection fails because of a system error, that error is stored in the E line. Such errors are integer values as defined in *<errno.h>*. If there was no error, the value stored in this line is a zero.

H line   *(V8.8 and above)*

B.1.3   *The DNS error number*

Some connection problems are caused by errors in looking up hosts with the Domain Name System (DNS). The software that provides lookups provides its own set of errors (see *<arpa/nameser.b>*). If a DNS error occurs, it is stored in this H line as an integer value.

R line   *(V8.8 and above)*

B.1.4   *The SMTP status-code text*

The Simple Mail Transfer Protocol (SMTP) specifies that all errors be prefixed with three-digit codes. The meaning of all the three-digit codes is given in RFC821 and several newer RFCs.

The R line stores this three-digit code as text. If there is no code (as when there is a system error instead of an SMTP error), the text is a lone hyphen.

S line   *(V8.8 and above)*

B.1.5   *The UNIX exit(2) status*

All UNIX programs return a success or failure value to the program that executed them. These values are called *exit*(2) values and they may or may not correspond to standard values. The set of values that is understood by *sendmail* is defined in *<sysexits.b>*.

This S line stores the integer value that was returned by a delivery agent program. Such programs might be called to deliver SMTP network mail.

U line   *(V8.8 and above)*

B.1.6   *The last time used*

Each time connection is made to, or fails to be made to, a host, its persistent status is updated. The date and time of the last update are stored in the U line.

The date and time are represented as an unsigned long and are stored in the U line as a text representation of that value.

V line   *(V8.8 and above)*

B.1.7   *The version of this status file*

For V8.8 *sendmail* this is version 0. If any other version is stored in this V line, *sendmail* logs the following error:

```
Unknown host status version bad: 0 max
```

This is always the first line of the file.

. line   *(V8.8 and above)*

B.1.8   *The end of file marker*

A dot on a line by itself indicates the end of the host status file's information. On systems that don't support the *ftruncate*(2) call, additional data may appear after this line. Since this line marks the end of information, any such extra data will be ignored.

The Berkeley DB Database

C.1 Overview

The database package from Berkeley is called *db*. It contains hash and btree routines and gets rid of many of the limitations that exist in earlier database versions (such as *dbm*(3) and *ndbm*(3)). If your site has, or expects to have, huge *alias*(5) files—say 2000 lines or more—or many database files, you should consider *db* to be mandatory. This new database is also recommended because its accesses and updates are considerably faster.

C.2 Get the Source

Do not use the version of *db* that was distributed on the Net2 tape. It is riddled with bugs.

Do get the latest distribution of *db* via anonymous FTP from *ftp.CS.Berkeley.EDU*. The file *ucb/4bsd/db.tar.Z* is a symbolic link that always points to the latest distribution. That file is a compressed, *tar*(1) archive and can be extracted like this:

```
% zcat db.tar.Z | tar xvf -
```

The result will be creation of a new directory with the name *db.something*, where the *something* is the latest version number.

To compile the database library, you need to change into that directory. A listing of its contents might look like this:

```
Makefile.inc    changelog       include         test
PORT            db              man
```

```
README          docs         mpool
btree           hash         recno
```

Inside the *db* distribution directory is a subdirectory called **PORT**. In order to compile, change first into that subdirectory and list the files there:

```
% cd PORT
% ls
Makefile        dgux.5.4     osf.1.0.2    sunos.4.1.1
README          hpux.8.07    osf.1.3      sunos.4.1.2
aix.3.2         hpux.9.01    osf.2.0      sunos.4.1.3
bsd.4.4         include      ptx.2.0      sunos.5.2
bsdi.1.0        irix.4.05F   sinix.5.41   ultrix.4.2
clib            linux        solaris.2.2  ultrix.4.3
```

Always read the **README** file first. Then select the directory that is most suitable for your machine, say, *sunos.4.1.3.*[*] Change into it. It will look kind of bare, but that is okay.

```
% cd sunos.4.1.3
% ls
Makefile        clib         include      sys
```

If you elected to include support for both NDBM and NEWDB in §33.1, you will need to make *Makefile* writable and edit it. (If you selected only NEWDB, you should skip this step.) This is necessary because your system's *ndbm*(3) will confict with the internal *ndbm* of *db* and cause *sendmail* to fail in spectacular ways.

Make *Makefile* writable, edit it, and remove all references to **ndbm.o**. Then remove the *ndbm.h file from the include* directory:

```
% rm include/ndbm.h
```

C.3 Compile and Install

To compile, merely run *make*(1). If you are compiling just for use in *sendmail*, you can leave the resulting *libdb.a* in with the source and reference it there (see INCDIRS= in §18.4.3 for an example of how to do this). If you are compiling for general system use, you should test the result before installing. Testing is available in *../../test.*

Installation is simple, although it must be done by hand. There is no *install* entry in the *Makefile.* Where you install it is up to you. Under */usr* is one possibility. Under */usr/local* is another. At Berkeley it was installed under */usr/sww.* The following example shows how to install it in */usr/local* on a BSD UNIX system:

---

[*] Note that the README file describes how to port *db* to systems that are not currently supported.

```
% cp libdb.a /usr/local/lib
% ranlib /usr/local/lib/libdb.a
% mkdir /usr/local/include/db /usr/local/include/db/sys
% cp include/* /usr/local/include/db
% ln -s /usr/local/include/db/cdefs.h /usr/local/include/db/sys
% cp ../../man/*.3 /usr/local/man/man3
```

Finally, to use this new library, you need to return to the *sendmail* source and edit your *Makefile* there. You'll need to change two lines to reflect the actual location where you installed *db*:

```
INCDIRS=-I/usr/sww/include/db
LIBDIRS=-L/usr/sww/lib
```

For our installation in */usr/local* the correct declarations would look like this:

```
INCDIRS=-I/usr/local/include/db
LIBDIRS=-L/usr/local/lib
```

D

Sun Enhancements

Sun Microsystems has adopted V8.6 as its standard version of *sendmail* as of Solaris 2.5. It will adopt V8.8 when it releases Solaris 2.7. Here, we cover Sun's enhancements to V8.8 as planned for Solaris 2.7.

Sun Microsystems has modified V8.7 *sendmail* to meet three internal requirements. Each new release of Sun supported *sendmail* must do the following:

- Be backward compatible with old, user configuration files

- Support the advantages of Sun's operating system, such as NIS+

- Allow for easy administration by naive system administrators

To meet these requirements, Sun adopted use of the V configuration command (see §27.5) to indicate to *sendmail* how the *sendmail.cf* file should be handled. V1/Sun and V7/Sun* are the two available versions. They are mutually exclusive, which is to say that features that are available with one are not available with the other. The only exception to this is a feature that is available to both V1/Sun and V6/Sun, the `Content-Length:` header (see §35.10.7). This is used to support Sun's MUA; see § for a further description.

D.1 Sun Enhancements

Sun Microsystems has enhanced V8.7 *sendmail* by adding two new configuration commands and introducing a few new macros. These enhancements are enabled when V7/Sun is in your configuration file. The V7/Sun enhancements are shown in Table D-1.

---

* Note that V7/Sun will be available only with Solaris 2.7. If your release of the operating system is earlier than Solaris 2.7, and if you wish to take advantage of new features and capabilities, you should obtain the V8.8 release from Berkeley (see §18.3).

Table D–1: V6/Sun Enhancements

What	Description
/etc/shells	The */etc/shells* file comes with the line line */SENDMAIL/ANY/SHELL* (see §22.8.4) preinstalled in it.
G	The G configuration command (see §D.4) is supported as a way to initialize class macros from an external file or NIS+ database.
L	The L configuration command (see §D.4) is supported as a way to initialize defined macros from an external file or NIS+ database.
$k	The UUCP node name (the same·as for V8 *sendmail;* see §31.10.21)
${ms}	The name of the local mail hub (if there is one).
${pd}	The name of the parent domain. After a call to *getdomain*(3), the result is checked to be sure it contains at least one dot. If it doesn't ${pd} remains valueless. If it does contain a dot and if the first character is a dot, that value is assigned to ${pd}. Otherwise, the first component up to the first dot is stripped (*a.b.c* becomes *.b.c*), and that result is assigned to ${pd}.

Note that you cannot simply add V6/Sun to the top of your old configuration file to get these new enhancements. Instead, you must use the configuration file supplied by Sun that already contains the V6/Sun declaration.

D.2 Backward Compatibility

Pre-V8 versions of *sendmail* possessed many assumptions and restrictions that modern versions have fixed, added, or eliminated. Prior to Solaris 2.5, Sun used a *sendmail* that was based on V5 *sendmail* and highly modified to satisfy Sun's other enhancements to UNIX.

To support old configuration files that were based on that old version of *sendmail*, Sun offers the V1/Sun version configuration command. The backward compatibility that V1/Sun mode supplies is shown in Table D-2.

Table D–2: V1/Sun Backward Compatibility

What	Description
$K	The $K macro contains the value of the mail hub machine (see §D.6).
$m	The $m macro contains the same value as ${pd} described above.
$%	The $% prefix can be used in the LHS to evaluate the $%1, $%y, and $%z macros.
${	${ and $} are a synonym for $(and $) (see §33.4).
$j	The $j macro (see §31.10.20) is *not* automatically included in $=w (see §32.5.8), nor is it required to contain a dot.

Table D–2: V1/Sun Backward Compatibility (continued)

What	Description
owner-	The owner- (see §25.3) of a mailing list is *not* set as the envelope sender when processing a :include:.
DNS	When making DNS lookups, RES_DNSRCH (search subdomains) and RES_DEFNAMES (append the local domain) are automatically disabled.
aliases	Duplicate left-hand side entries in the *aliases*(5) file are silently ignored.
K	The K configuration command (see §33.3) is disabled.
VRFY	The VRFY and EXPN SMTP commands (see §22.3.2) provide the same information. That is, they both act like EXPN.
F=g	The F=g delivery agent flag (see §30.8.22) cannot be turned off, even if it is omitted. That is, the special address <> is *never* used as the sender of bounced mail.
F=b	The F=b delivery agent flag (see §30.8.13) is always ignored. That is, an extra blank line is never added to the end of a delivered mail message.

Note that V1/Sun should be added to your old configuration file only after you have upgraded to Solaris 2.4 or higher's version of *sendmail*. The V configuration command will not be recognized by earlier versions of *sendmail*, and that command can cause those earlier versions to fail.

D.3 K Command's -d switch

Old Sun configuration files could transfer all locally deliverable mail to a central mail hub. The assumption was that the mail hub possessed a superset of all aliases and so would be authoritative about final delivery. Unfortunately, this assumption tended to cause unnecessary traffic to be sent to the mail hub and could cause congestion at the mail hub.

In an NIS or NIS+ environment the assumption that the mail hub is authoritative may not be valid, because (in theory) every client machine can have equal access to authoritative aliasing information. With "domainwide" alias support, local addresses can be resolved at the sending client. The mail hub is then free to just handle Internet traffic.

The -d switch to the K configuration command (see §33.3) declares a map to be domainwide. Such a map is presumed to be available through out an NIS or NIS+ domain. The -d switch is useful only with alias maps and affects *sendmail*'s behavior in two ways:

Address qualification
>   An unqualified recipient address is one that lacks an @host part. Such addresses should not be propagated in an unqualified form, so if the -d switch is specified for a map and if a username is found in that map, the name

is fully qualified by appending an @ and the NIS or NIS+ domain.* Otherwise, if a username is found in a local alias map, the name is fully qualified by appending an @ and the hostname of the local host. Otherwise, the username is fully qualified by appending an @ and the hostname of the mail hub.

Selective alias expansion

If an address is qualified with an NIS or NIS+ domain, the user part should be alias expanded only by looking it up in a domainwide alias map. Otherwise, if an address is unqualified or an address is qualified with the local hostname, the user part should be alias expanded only by looking it up in the manner specified in the */etc/nsswitch.conf* file. Otherwise, if an address is qualified with a nonlocal hostname, the mail message is forwarded to that specified host for resolution.

D.4 *L and G Configuration Commands*

Sun's version of V8.7 *sendmail* uses the */etc/nsswitch.conf* file to determine how it should resolve the hostname (the `hosts:` line), how it should look up aliases (the `aliases:` line), how it should look up user information (the `passwd:` and `group:` lines), and where it should look for its nonconfiguration file variable declarations (the `sendmailvars:` line):

```
hosts:          nisplus dns [NOTFOUND=return] files
aliases:        files nisplus
passwd:         files nisplus
group:          files nisplus
sendmailvars:   files nisplus              ← note
```

When the `sendmailvars:` line indicates `files`, *sendmail* looks up variable declarations in the */etc/mail/sendmailvars* file. When the `sendmailvars:` line indicates `nisplus`, *sendmail* looks up variable declarations using the NIS+ service that defaults to *sendmailvars.org_dir*. In the file form, the key is on the left and the value is on the right. In the NIS+ form, the key is looked up and the value is returned:

```
maildomain    uofa.edu
othernames    uofa.edu here here.uofa.edu mailhub mailhub.uofa.edu
   ↑            ↑
  key         value
```

Sun's version of V8.7 *sendmail* can handle two brand new (and exclusive to Sun) configuration commands. They are the `L` command (which you use to define a

---

* This gives addresses a special property. If an address is qualified with an NIS or NIS+ domain, Sun's *sendmail* presumes that the name can be resolved correctly anywhere in the specified domain.

macro) and the G command (which you use to add values to a class). In both cases the value is read from external files or NIS+ maps.

```
Lmmaildomain
Gwothernames
```

The first configuration line, the L, causes the key `maildomain` to be looked up either in the file */etc/mail/sendmailvars* or in an NIS+ map. If the key is found, the value returned (in our case `uofa.edu`) is assigned to the `$m` macro.

The second configuration line, the G, causes the key `othernames` to be looked up either in the file */etc/mail/sendmailvars* or in an NIS+ map. If the key is found, the value returned (in our case the list of alternate hostnames) is appended to the `$=w` class.

In both forms of lookup, the key must match exactly. There is no form of wildcard lookup, nor is the search case-insensitive. If the key is not found, the configuration command is ignored. If the file or NIS+ service does not exist or if there is an error reading the file, the configuration command is silently ignored.

Be aware that the *sendmailvars* file should never be placed on an NFS mounted files system. If the server is down, your macro and class variables may silently fail to initialize.

D.5   The > Option

Prior to V8, Sun's *sendmail* used the R option to cause all mail to be automatically routed to a mail hub machine. V8 *sendmail* coopted the R option for its own use, so Sun had to switch the option name to >. The > option is available only with V6/Sun, and above, configuration files.

The > option is used like this:

```
O>mailhub
```

If the entire > option is omitted, all mail is delivered locally. If `mailhub` is present and if it is not the name of the local host, all mail is forwarded to that machine for delivery. If the `mailhub` is omitted and if */var/mail* is NFS mounted, all mail is forwarded to the host that is exporting */var/mail*. The name of the `mailhub`, no matter how it was determined, is assigned to the `$K` macro for use by rule sets.

Be aware that by setting and using this option, you are letting *sendmail*'s internals make all the decisions for you. If you prefer more control, investigate the `null-client` FEATURE described in §19.6.20.

The > option is safe. When it is specified from the command line, *sendmail* retains its *root* privilege.

D.5.1 Content-Length: and the queue

If a mail message has to be queued under Sun's version of *sendmail*, and if that message lacks a `Content-Length:` header, a new `L` line is added to the qf file:

```
Lbytes,lines,froms
```

That line stores the number of **bytes** in the message body, the number of **lines**, and the number of lines that begin with the five characters "`From` " (the **froms**).

When the qf file is read, that line is parsed with a *scanf*(3) string of

```
"%d,%d,%d"
```

with no error checking. If any field is missing or nonnumeric, it and all following fields default to zero. The read information is stored in the current envelope's information, where it can later be used to create a `Content-Length:` header.

D.6 The > Option

Prior to V8, Sun's *sendmail* used the `R` option to cause all mail to be automatically routed to a mail hub machine. V8 *sendmail* coopted the `R` option for its own use, so Sun had to switch the option name to `>`. The `>` option is available only with V6/Sun, and above, configuration files.

The `>` option is used like this:

```
O>mailhub
```

If the entire `>` option is omitted, all mail is delivered locally. If **mailhub** is present and if it is not the name of the local host, all mail is forwarded to that machine for delivery. If the **mailhub** is omitted and if */var/mail* is NFS mounted, all mail is forwarded to the host that is exporting */var/mail*. The name of the **mailhub**, no matter how it was determined, is assigned to the $K macro for use by rule sets.

Be aware that by setting and using this option, you are letting *sendmail*'s internals make all the decisions for you. If you prefer more control, investigate the `null-client` FEATURE described in §19.6.20.

The `>` option is safe. When it is specified from the command line, *sendmail* retains its *root* privilege.

Bibliography

Requests for Comments

A Requests For Comments (RFC) is a document issued by the Internet Engineering Task Force (IETF) at the Network Information Center (NIC). Each such document defines an aspect of protocol regarding the Internet. We have listed the RFCs that pertain to *sendmail* in reverse numeric order, that is, with the most recent documents cited first. Note that many of these are only of interest to historians. RFCs are available via anonymous FTP from many sites:[*]

ds.internic.net	← *U.S. East Coast*
ftp.isi.edu	← *U.S. West Coast*
ftp.uu.net	← *U.S. Central*
sunic.sunet.se	← *Sweden*
ftp.Germany.EU.net	← *Germany*
inria.fr	← *France*
mcsun.eu.net	← *Netherlands*
funet.fi	← *Finland*
ugle.unit.no	← *Norway*
ftp.denet.dk	← *Denmark*
munnari.oz.au	← *Australia*

RFC1894

> *An Extensible Message Format for Delivery Status Notifications*, K. Moore, and G. Vaudreuil, January 1996, 15 pp.

RFC1893

> *Enhanced Mail System Status Codes*, G. Vaudreuil, January 1996, 15 pp.

---

[*] This list is in constant flux. For the latest list of sites, get the document *rfc-retrieval.txt* from *ds.internic.net*.

RFC1892

The Multipart/Report Content Type for the Reporting of Mail System Administrative Messages, G. Vaudreuil, January 1996, 4 pp.

RFC1891

SMTP Service Extension for Delivery Status Notifications, K. Moore, January 1996, 31 pp.

RFC1873

Message/External-Body Content-ID Access Type, E. Levinson, December 1995, 4 pp.

RFC1872

The MIME Multipart/Related Content-type, E. Levinson, December 1995, 8 pp.

RFC1870

SMTP Service Extension for Message Size Declaration, J. Klensin, N. Freed, and K. Moore, November 1995, 9 pp.

RFC1869

SMTP Service Extensions, J. Klensin, N. Freed, M. Rose, E. Stefferud, and D. Crocker, November 1995, 11 pp.

RFC1864

The Content-MD5 Header Field, J. Myers and M.Rose, October 1995, 4 pp.

RFC1854

SMTP Service Extension for Command Pipelining, N. Freed, October 1995, 21 pp.

RFC1846

SMTP 521 Reply Code, A. Durand and F. Dupont, September 1995, 4 pp.

RFC1845

SMTP Service Extension for Checkpoint/Restart, N. Freed (ed) and D. Crocker, September 1995, 7 pp.

RFC1844

Multimedia E-mail (MIME) User Agent checklist, E. Huizer, August 1995, 8 pp.

RFC1830

SMTP Service Extensions for Transmission of Large and Binary MIME Messages, G. Vaudreuil, August 1995, 8 pp.

RFC1711

Classifications in E-mail Routing, J. Houttuin, October 1994, 19 pp.

RFC1652

SMTP Service Extensions for 8bit-MIMEtransport, J. Klensin, N. Freed, M. Rose, E. Stefferud, and D. Crocker, July 1994, 6 pp.

RFC1566

Mail Monitoring MIB, N. Freed (ed) and S. Killy, January 1994, 20 pp.

RFC1522

Representation of Non-ASCII Text in Internet Message Headers, K. Moore, September 1993, 7 pp.

RFC1521

MIME (Multipurpose Internet Mail Extensions): Mechanisms for Specifying and Describing the Format of Internet Message Bodies, N. Borenstein and N. Freed, September 1993, 69 pp.

RFC1505

Encoding Header Field for Internet Messages, D. Robinson and R. Ullmann, August 1993, 36 pp.

RFC1496

X.400 1988 to 1984 Downgrading, S.E. Hardcastle-Kille, August 1993, 5 pp.

RFC1495

Mapping Between X.400(1988)/ISO 10021 and RFC 822, S.E. Hardcastle-Kille, August 1993, 11 pp. (Updates RFC1327.)

RFC1428

Transition of Internet Mail from Just-Send-8 to 8bit-SMTP/MIME, G, Vaudreuil, February 1993, 6pp.

RFC1423

Privacy Enhancement for Internet Electronic Mail: Part III—algorithms, modes, and identifiers [Draft], J. Linn, February 1993, 14pp.

RFC1422

Privacy Enhancement for Internet Electronic Mail: Part II—Certificate-based Key Management, S.T. Kent and J. Linn, February 1993, 32 pp.

RFC1421

Privacy Enhancement for Internet Electronic Mail: Part I—Message Encipherment and Authentication Procedures, J. Linn, February 1993, 42 pp.

RFC1345

Character Mnemonics and Character Sets, K. Simonsen, June 1992, 103 pp.

RFC1344

   Implications of MIME for Internet Mail Gateways, N. Borenstein, June 1992, 8
   pp.

RFC1343

   User Agent Configuration Mechanism for Multimedia Mail Format Information,
   N. Borenstein, June 1992, 10 pp.

RFC1321

   MD5 Message-Digest Algorithm, R.L. Rivest, April 1992, 21 pp.

RFC1320

   MD4 Message-Digest Algorithm, R.L. Rivest, April 1992, 20 pp.

RFC1319

   MD2 Message-Digest Algorithm, B.S. Kaliski, April 1992, 17 pp. (Updates
   RFC1115.)

RFC1176

   Interactive Mail Access Protocol: Version 2, M.R. Crispin, August 1990, 30 pp.

RFC1153

   Digest Message Format, F.J. Wancho, April 1990, 4pp.

RFC1137

   Mapping Between Full RFC 822 and RFC 822 with Restricted Encoding, S.E.
   Kille, December 1989, 3 pp. (Updates RFC976.)

RFC1123

   Requirements for Internet Hosts—Application and Support, R.T. Braden, ed.,
   October 1989, 98 pp.

RFC1122

   Requirements for Internet Hosts—Communication Layers, R.T. Braden (ed),
   October 1989, 116 pp.

RFC1036

   Standard for Interchange of USENET Messages, M.R. Horton and R. Adams,
   December 1987, 19 pp. (Obsoletes RFC850.)

RFC976

   UUCP Mail Interchange Format Standard, M.R. Horton, February 1986, 12 pp.

RFC934

   Proposed Standard for Message Encapsulation, M.T. Rose and E.A. Stefferud,
   January 1985, 10 pp.

RFC822

Standard for the Format of ARPA Internet Text Messages, D. Crocker, August 13, 1982, 47 pp. (Obsoletes RFC733; updated by RFC1327.)

RFC821

Simple Mail Transfer Protocol, J.B. Postel, August 1982, 58 pp. (Obsoletes RFC788.)

RFC805

Computer Mail Meeting Notes, J.B. Postel, February 8, 1982, 6pp.

RFC733

Standard for the Format of ARPA Network Text Messages, D. Crocker, J. Vittal, K.T. Pogran, and D.A. Henderson, November 21, 1977, 38 pp. (Obsoletes RFC724; obsoleted by RFC822.)

RFC706

On the Junk Mail Problem, J.B. Postel, November 8, 1975, 1 p.

Publications and Postings

Albitz, Paul, and Cricket Liu. *DNS and BIND*. Sebastopol, CA: O'Reilly & Associates, Inc., 1997.

Allman, Eric. *Sendmail: An Internetwork Mail Router* in the BSD UNIX Documentation Set, Berkeley, CA: University of California, 1986–1993.

Allman, Eric, and Miriam Amos. *Sendmail Revisited*. Portland, OR: USENIX Proceedings, Summer 1985.

Anderson, Bart, Bryan Costales, and Harry Henderson. *Unix Communications*. Carmel, Indiana: Howard W. Sams, a Division of Macmillan Computer Publishing, 1991.

Cheswick, William R., and Steven M. Bellovin. *Firewalls and Internet Security, Repelling the Wily Hacker*. Reading, MA: Addison-Wesley Publishing Company, 1994.

Cuccia, Nichlos H. *The Design and Implementation of a Multihub Electronic Mail Environment*. San Diego, CA: USENIX Proceedings—LISA V, October 3, 1991.

Darmohray, Tina M. *A sendmail.cf Scheme for a Large Network*. San Diego, CA: USENIX Proceedings—LISA V, October 3, 1991.

Frey, Donnalyn, and Rick Adams. *!%@:: A Directory of Electronic Mail Addressing and Networks*. Sebastopol, CA: O'Reilly & Associates, Inc., 1993.

Harrison, Helen E. *A Domain Mail System on Dissimilar Computers: Trials and Tribulations of SMTP.* Colorado Springs, CO: USENIX Proceedings—LISA IV, October 19, 1990.

Hedrick, Dr. Charles. *A brief tutorial on sendmail rules.* (A posting to the old Usenet groups *net.unix-wizards* and *net.mail.* Reposted to *comp.mail.sendmail* August 7th 1992.) Rutgers University, 1985.

Hunt, Craig. *TCP/IP Network Administration.* Sebastopol, CA: O'Reilly & Associates, Inc., 1993.

Kamens, Jonathan I. *FAQ: How to find people's E-mail addresses.* (A monthly posting to the Usenet groups *comp.mail.misc,* and *news. newusers.questions.*) Cambridge, MA: Massachusetts Institute of Technology, Periodic.

Nemeth, Evi, Garth Snyder, Scott Seebass, and Trent R. Hein. Chapter 15, "Mail and Berkeley Sendmail," in *Unix System Administration Handbook.* Englewood Cliffs, NJ: Prentice Hall, 2nd edition, 1995.

Quarterman, John S. *The Matrix: Computer Networks and Conferencing Systems Worldwide.* Bedford, MA: Digital Press, 1990.

Rickert, Neil. *Address Rewriting in Sendmail.* (Posted to the USENET group *comp.mail.sendmail.*) DeKalb, IL: Northern Illinois University, Apr 29, 1991.

Stern, Hal. *Managing NFS and NIS.* Sebastopol, CA: O'Reilly & Associates, Inc., 1991.

Index

Symbols

0 flag, 546
–144bsd option, 204
3 flag, 547
5 flag, 548
7 flag, 548
7 option (see SevenBitInput option)
7-bit encoding, 219, 750
8 flag, 548
8 option (see EightBitMode option)
8-bit encoding, 219, 549, 703
9 flag, 549
<> (angle brackets), 104, 180
   nested, 109, 181
   null address (see addresses, null)
> option, 990
>>> as leading characters, 40
* in mail queue listing, 37, 367
@ flag, 550
@ symbol in addresses, 182, 499
\ (backslash)
   in header fields, 777
   in rules, 468
! in UUCP addresses, 184, 273
: (colon) in addresses, 183, 688
: flag, 549
{} (curly braces), 51–52, 70
$ (dollar sign)
   $ line (qf file), 392

$ rule-testing command, 954
   in macro names, 576–579
$ operators
   $1, $2, ... (see positional operators)
   $>, 479–482
   $*, 105
   $@, 98, 100, 118, 182, 640
   $[and $], 267, 312, 483–485, 642
   $: , 98, 100, 502, 541, 640
   $., 152, 580–581
   $#, 97, 482
   $-, 118
   $(and $), 638–642
   $+, 89–93
   $?, 152, 580–581
   $|, 580–581
   (see also wildcard operators)
$ prefixes
   $&, 480, 578–579
   $@, 478
   $: , 477–478, 639
   $=, 128, 614–615
   $~, 615–616
$@ DSN code, 540
$= rule-testing command, 955
$_ macro, 292, 392, 443, 585
. (dot)
   . line (qf file), 392
   checking for in ${pd}, 986
   to end messages, 42, 567

About the Authors

Bryan Costales is director of technology with Mercury Mail in Denver, Colorado. Always at the cutting edge, he "telecommutes" from his home in Laramie, Wyoming. He has been active in system administration for over 15 years and has been writing articles and books about computer software for over 10 years. His most notable books are *C from A to Z* (Prentice Hall), *Unix Communications* (Howard Sams), and, of course, *sendmail* (O'Reilly & Associates). In his rare free time, he dreams of sailing the Gulf coast, and writes fiction with a group called Make Believe Sailors.

Eric Allman is the original author of *sendmail*, and a long time contributor to Berkeley UNIX. He also wrote the *-me* macros, *tset*, *trek*, *syslog*, and *vacation*.

Besides UNIX and *sendmail*, Eric has worked on database management, window systems, neural-net-based speech recognition, system administration, and networking. He also co-authored the "C Advisor" column for *Unix Review* for several years.

Eric has been accused of working incessantly, enjoys writing with fountain pens, and collects wines, which he stashes in the cellar of the house that he shares with Kirk McKusick, his partner of 17 and some-odd years. He is also treasurer of USENIX Association.

Colophon

Our look is the result of reader comments, our own experimentation, and feedback from distribution channels.

Distinctive covers complement our distinctive approach to technical topics, breathing personality and life into potentially dry subjects. UNIX and its attendant programs can be unruly beasts. Nutshell Handbooks help you tame them.

The animal featured on the cover of *sendmail* is the flying fox, a species of fruit bat found chiefly on the islands of the Malay-Indonesia archipelago. Of about four thousand species of mammals, nearly one-quarter are bats; and of these, 160 are fruit bats. Sixty of the larger fruit bats make up the flying foxes, the largest having a wingspan of five feet. While smaller insect-eating bats navigate by echolocation, fruit bats depend on a keen sense of sight and smell to perceive their environment. They roost in trees by day, sometimes in extremely large numbers called "camps." They hang from branches by one or both feet, wrap themselves in their wings, and sleep the day away. On hot days, these bats keep cool by fanning themselves with their wings.

Greatly elongated fingers form the main support for the web of skin that has allowed these mammals, alone, to master true flight. At sunset they awaken from their slumber and begin their nocturnal ramblings. A flying fox must flap its wings until it becomes horizontal to the ground before it can let go and fly away. Once airborne, they use their sensitive sense of smell to detect where flowers are blooming or fruits have ripened. Unlike most animals, fruit bats cannot generate vitamin C (a limitation shared by humans and guinea pigs); thus, it is supplied by fruit in the diet. Flying foxes can range up to forty miles for food. Once a target is located, they are faced with a difficult landing. Sometimes they will simply crash into foliage and grab at what they can; other times they may attempt to catch a branch with their hindfeet as they fly over it and then swing upside-down; some will even attempt a difficult half-roll under a branch in order to grip it in the preferred position. Once attached and hanging, they will draw the flower or fruit to their mouths with a single hindfoot, or the clawed thumbs at the top of each wing. These awkward landings often cause fights among flying foxes, especially upon their return to camp at dawn. A single bad landing can cause an entire bat-laden tree to become highly agitated, full of fighting and screaming residents.

People have eaten flying foxes for ages. Samoans, who call the flying fox *manu lagi* (animal of the heavens) use branches bound to the end of long poles to swat the winged delicacy from the sky. Aborigines in Australia build fires beneath flying fox camps—the smoke stupefies the prey—and use boomerangs to knock the creatures to the ground.

Edie Freedman designed this cover and the entire UNIX bestiary that appears on other Nutshell Handbooks. The beasts themselves are adapted from 19th-century engravings from the Dover Pictorial Archive. The cover layout was produced with Quark XPress 3.1 using the ITC Garamond font. Whenever possible, our books use RepKover™, a durable and flexible lay-flat binding. If the page count exceeds RepKover's limit, perfect binding is used.

The inside layout was designed by Edie Freedman and implemented by Lenny Muellner in sqtroff using ITC Garamond Light and ITC Garamond Book fonts. The figures were created in Aldus Freehand 3.1 by Chris Reilley. The colophon was written by Michael Kalantarian.

 *More Titles from O'Reilly*

Network Administration

Using & Managing PPP

By Andrew Sun
1st Edition July 1998 (est.)
436 pages (est.), ISBN 1-56592-321-9

This book is for network administrators and others who have to set up computer systems to use PPP. It covers all aspects of the protocol, including how to set up dial-in servers, authentication, debugging, and PPP options. In addition, it contains overviews of related areas, like serial communications, DNS setup, and routing.

Managing IP Networks with Cisco Routers

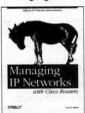

By Scott M. Ballew
1st Edition October 1997
352 pages, ISBN 1-56592-320-0

This practical guide to setting up and maintaining a production networr covers how to select routing protocols, configure protocols to handle most common situations, evaluate network equipment and vendors, and setup a help desk. Although it focuses on Cisco routers, and gives examples using Cisco's IOS, the principles discussed are common to all IP networks.

Virtual Private Networks

By Charlie Scott, Paul Wolfe & Mike Erwin
1st Edition February 1998
184 pages, ISBN 1-56592-319-7

This book tells you how to plan and build a Virtual Private Network (VPN), a collection of technologies that creates secure connections or "tunnels" over regular Internet lines. It starts with general concerns like costs and configuration and continues with detailed descriptions of how to install and use VPN technologies that are available for Windows NT and UNIX, such as PPTP and L2TP, the AltaVista Tunnel, and the Cisco PIX Firewall.

sendmail, 2nd Edition

By Bryan Costales & Eric Allman
2nd Edition January 1997
1050 pages, ISBN 1-56592-222-0

sendmail, 2nd Edition, covers sendmail Version 8.8 from Berkeley and the standard versions available on most systems. This cross-referenced edition offers an expanded tutorial, solution-oriented examples, and new topics such as the #error delivery agent, sendmail's exit values, MIME headers, and how to set up and use the user database, *mailertable*, and *smrsh*.

sendmail Desktop Reference

By Bryan Costales & Eric Allman.
1st Edition March 1997
74 pages, ISBN 1-56592-278-6

This quick-reference guide provides a complete overview of the latest version of sendmail (V8.8), from command-line switches to configuration commands, from options declarations to macro definitions, and from m4 features to debugging switches—all packed into a convenient, carry-around booklet co-authored by the creator of sendmail. Includes extensive cross-references to *sendmail, second edition*.

Networking Personal Computers with TCP/IP

By Craig Hunt
1st Edition July 1995
408 pages, ISBN 1-56592-123-2

This book offers practical information as well as detailed instructions for attaching PCs to a TCP/IP network and its UNIX servers. It discusses the challenges you'll face and offers general advice on how to deal with them, provides basic TCP/IP configuration information for some of the popular PC operating systems, covers advanced configuration topics and configuration of specific applications such as email, and includes a chapter on on integrating Netware with TCP/IP.

Network Administration

DNS and BIND, 2nd Edition

By Paul Albitz & Cricket Liu
2nd Edition December 1996
438 pages, ISBN 1-56592-236-0

This book is a complete guide to the
Internet's Domain Name System (DNS)
and the Berkeley Internet Name Domain
(BIND) software, the UNIX implementation of DNS. In this second edition, the
authors continue to describe BIND version
4.8.3, which is included in most vendor implementations today.
In addition, you'll find complete coverage of BIND 4.9.4, which
in all probability will be adopted as the new standard in the near
future.

In addition to covering the basic motivation behind DNS and how to
set up the BIND software, this book covers many more advanced topics, including using DNS and BIND on Windows NT systems; how to
become a "parent" (i.e., "delegate" the ability to assign names to
someone else); how to use DNS to set up mail forwarding correctly;
debugging and troubleshooting; and programming. Assumes a basic
knowledge of system administration and network management.

Getting Connected: The Internet at 56K and Up

By Kevin Dowd
1st Edition June 1996
424 pages, ISBN 1-56592-154-2

A complete guide for businesses, schools,
and other organizations who want to connect their computers to the Internet. This
book covers everything you need to know
to make informed decisions, from helping
you figure out which services you really
need to providing down-to-earth explanations and configuration
instructions for telecommunication options at higher than
modem speeds, such as frame relay, ISDN, and leased lines.
Once you're online, it shows you how to set up basic Internet
services, such as a World Wide Web server. Tackles issues for PC,
Macintosh, and UNIX platforms.

TCP/IP Network Administration, 2nd Edition

By Craig Hunt
2nd Edition December 1997
630 pages, ISBN 1-56592-322-7

A complete guide to setting up and running a TCP/IP network for practicing system administrators. Beyond basic setup,
this new second edition discusses the
Internet routing protocols and provides a
tutorial on how to configure important
network services. It now also includes Linux in addition to BSD
and System V TCP/IP implementations.

Security

Protecting Networks with SATAN

By Martin Freiss
1st Edition July 1998 (est.)
200 pages (est.), ISBN 1-56592-425-8

SATAN performs "security audits," scanning host computers for security vulnerabilities. This book describes how to install
and use SATAN, and how to adapt it to
local requirements and increase its knowledge of specific security vulnerabilities.

Computer Security Basics

By Deborah Russell & G.T. Gangemi, Sr.
1st Edition July 1991
464 pages, ISBN 0-937175-71-4

Computer Security Basics provides a
broad introduction to the many areas of
computer security and a detailed description of current security standards. This
handbook describes complicated concepts
like trusted systems, encryption, and
mandatory access control in simple terms, and contains a thor-
ough, readable introduction to the "Orange Book."

O'REILLY™

TO ORDER: **800-998-9938** • **order@oreilly.com** • **http://www.oreilly.com/**
OUR PRODUCTS ARE AVAILABLE AT A BOOKSTORE OR SOFTWARE STORE NEAR YOU.
FOR INFORMATION: **800-998-9938** • **707-829-0515** • **info@oreilly.com**

Security

Web Security & Commerce

By Simson Garfinkel with Gene Spafford
1st Edition June 1997
506 pages, ISBN 1-56592-269-7

Learn how to minimize the risks of the Web with this comprehensive guide. It covers browser vulnerabilities, privacy concerns, issues with Java, JavaScript, ActiveX, and plug-ins, digital certificates, cryptography, web server security, blocking software, censorship technology, and relevant civil and criminal issues.

Practical UNIX & Internet Security, 2nd Edition

By Simson Garfinkel & Gene Spafford
2nd Edition April 1996
1004 pages, ISBN 1-56592-148-8

This second edition of the classic *Practical UNIX Security* is a complete rewrite of the original book. It's packed with twice the pages and offers even more practical information for UNIX users and administrators. In it you'll find coverage of features of many types of UNIX systems, including SunOS, Solaris, BSDI, AIX, HP-UX, Digital UNIX, Linux, and others. Contents include UNIX and security basics, system administrator tasks, network security, and appendices containing checklists and helpful summaries.

Building Internet Firewalls

By D. Brent Chapman &
Elizabeth D. Zwicky
1st Edition September 1995
546 pages, ISBN 1-56592-124-0

Everyone is jumping on the Internet bandwagon, despite the fact that the security risks associated with connecting to the Net have never been greater. This book is a practical guide to building firewalls on the Internet. It describes a variety of firewall approaches and architectures and discusses how you can build packet filtering and proxying solutions at your site. It also contains a full discussion of how to configure Internet services (e.g., FTP, SMTP, Telnet) to work with a firewall, aswell as a complete list of resources, including the location of many publicly available firewall construction tools.

PGP: Pretty Good Privacy

By Simson Garfinkel
1st Edition January 1995
430 pages, ISBN 1-56592-098-8

PGP is a freely available encryption program that protects theprivacy of files and electronic mail. It uses powerful public key cryptography and works on virtually every platform. This book is both a readable technical user's guide and a fascinating behind-the-scenes look at cryptography and privacy. It describes how to use PGP and provides background on cryptography, PGP's history, battles over public key cryptography patents and U.S. government export restrictions, and publicdebates about privacy and free speech.

Computer Crime

By David Icove, Karl Seger &
William VonStorch
(Consulting Editor Eugene H. Spafford)
1st Edition August 1995
462 pages, ISBN 1-56592-086-4

This book is for anyone who needs to know what today's computer crimes look like, how to prevent them, and how to detect, investigate, and prosecute them if they do occur. It contains basic computer security information as well as guidelines for investigators, law enforcement, and system administrators. Also includes computer-related statutes and laws, a resource summary, detailed papers on computer crime, and a sample search warrant.

How to stay in touch with O'Reilly

1. Visit Our Award-Winning Web Site

http://www.oreilly.com/

★ "Top 100 Sites on the Web" —*PC Magazine*
★ "Top 5% Web sites" —*Point Communications*
★ "3-Star site" —*The McKinley Group*

Our web site contains a library of comprehensive product information (including book excerpts and tables of contents), downloadable software, background articles, interviews with technology leaders, links to relevant sites, book cover art, and more. File us in your Bookmarks or Hotlist!

2. Join Our Email Mailing Lists

New Product Releases

To receive automatic email with brief descriptions of all new O'Reilly products as they are released, send email to:
listproc@online.oreilly.com
Put the following information in the first line of your message (*not* in the Subject field):
subscribe oreilly-news

O'Reilly Events

If you'd also like us to send information about trade show events, special promotions, and other O'Reilly events, send email to:
listproc@online.oreilly.com
Put the following information in the first line of your message (*not* in the Subject field):
subscribe oreilly-events

3. Get Examples from Our Books via FTP

There are two ways to access an archive of example files from our books:

Regular FTP

- ftp to:
  ftp.oreilly.com
  (login: anonymous
  password: your email address)
- Point your web browser to:
  ftp://ftp.oreilly.com/

FTPMAIL

- Send an email message to:
  ftpmail@online.oreilly.com
  (Write "help" in the message body)

4. Contact Us via Email

order@oreilly.com
To place a book or software order online. Good for North American and international customers.

subscriptions@oreilly.com
To place an order for any of our newsletters or periodicals.

books@oreilly.com
General questions about any of our books.

software@oreilly.com
For general questions and product information about our software. Check out O'Reilly Software Online at **http://software.oreilly.com/** for software and technical support information. Registered O'Reilly software users send your questions to: **website-support@oreilly.com**

cs@oreilly.com
For answers to problems regarding your order or our products.

booktech@oreilly.com
For book content technical questions or corrections.

proposals@oreilly.com
To submit new book or software proposals to our editors and product managers.

international@oreilly.com
For information about our international distributors or translation queries. For a list of our distributors outside of North America check out:
http://www.oreilly.com/www/order/country.html

O'Reilly & Associates, Inc.

101 Morris Street, Sebastopol, CA 95472 USA
TEL   707-829-0515 or 800-998-9938
            (6am to 5pm PST)
FAX   707-829-0104

O'REILLY™

TO ORDER: **800-998-9938** • *order@oreilly.com* • *http://www.oreilly.com/*
OUR PRODUCTS ARE AVAILABLE AT A BOOKSTORE OR SOFTWARE STORE NEAR YOU.
FOR INFORMATION: **800-998-9938** • **707-829-0515** • *info@oreilly.com*

Titles from O'Reilly

International Distributors

UK, EUROPE, MIDDLE EAST AND NORTHERN AFRICA (EXCEPT FRANCE, GERMANY, SWITZERLAND, & AUSTRIA)

INQUIRIES
International Thomson Publishing Europe
Berkshire House
168-173 High Holborn
London WC1V 7AA
United Kingdom
Telephone: 44-171-497-1422
Fax: 44-171-497-1426
Email: itpint@itps.co.uk

ORDERS
International Thomson Publishing Services, Ltd.
Cheriton House, North Way
Andover, Hampshire SP10 5BE
United Kingdom
Telephone: 44-264-342-832 (UK)
Telephone: 44-264-342-806 (outside UK)
Fax: 44-264-364418 (UK)
Fax: 44-264-342761 (outside UK)
UK & Eire orders: itpuk@itps.co.uk
International orders: itpint@itps.co.uk

FRANCE

Editions Eyrolles
61 bd Saint-Germain
75240 Paris Cedex 05
France
Fax: 33-01-44-41-11-44

FRENCH LANGUAGE BOOKS
All countries except Canada
Telephone: 33-01-44-41-46-16
Email: geodif@eyrolles.com
English language books
Telephone: 33-01-44-41-11-87
Email: distribution@eyrolles.com

GERMANY, SWITZERLAND, AND AUSTRIA

INQUIRIES
O'Reilly Verlag
Balthasarstr. 81
D-50670 Köln
Germany
Telephone: 49-221-97-31-60-0
Fax: 49-221-97-31-60-8
Email: anfragen@oreilly.de

ORDERS
International Thomson Publishing
Königswinterer Straße 418
53227 Bonn, Germany
Telephone: 49-228-97024 0
Fax: 49-228-441342
Email: order@oreilly.de

JAPAN

O'Reilly Japan, Inc.
Kiyoshige Building 2F
12-Banchi, Sanei-cho
Shinjuku-ku
Tokyo 160-0008 Japan
Telephone: 81-3-3356-5227
Fax: 81-3-3356-5261
Email: kenji@oreilly.com

INDIA

Computer Bookshop (India) PVT. Ltd.
190 Dr. D.N. Road, Fort
Bombay 400 001 India
Telephone: 91-22-207-0989
Fax: 91-22-262-3551
Email: cbsbom@giasbm01.vsnl.net.in

HONG KONG

City Discount Subscription Service Ltd.
Unit D, 3rd Floor, Yan's Tower
27 Wong Chuk Hang Road
Aberdeen, Hong Kong
Telephone: 852-2580-3539
Fax: 852-2580-6463
Email: citydis@ppn.com.hk

KOREA

Hanbit Media, Inc.
Sonyoung Bldg. 202
Yeksam-dong 736-36
Kangnam-ku
Seoul, Korea
Telephone: 822-554-9610
Fax: 822-556-0363
Email: hant93@chollian.dacom.co.kr

SINGAPORE, MALAYSIA, AND THAILAND

Addison Wesley Longman Singapore PTE Ltd.
25 First Lok Yang Road
Singapore 629734
Telephone: 65-268-2666
Fax: 65-268-7023
Email: daniel@longman.com.sg

PHILIPPINES

Mutual Books, Inc.
429-D Shaw Boulevard
Mandaluyong City, Metro
Manila, Philippines
Telephone: 632-725-7538
Fax: 632-721-3056
Email: mbikikog@mnl.sequel.net

CHINA

Ron's DataCom Co., Ltd.
79 Dongwu Avenue
Dongxihu District
Wuhan 430040
China
Telephone: 86-27-3892568
Fax: 86-27-3222108
Email: hongfeng@public.wh.hb.cn

ALL OTHER ASIAN COUNTRIES

O'Reilly & Associates, Inc.
101 Morris Street
Sebastopol, CA 95472 USA
Telephone: 707-829-0515
Fax: 707-829-0104
Email: order@oreilly.com

AUSTRALIA

WoodsLane Pty. Ltd.
7/5 Vuko Place, Warriewood NSW 2102
P.O. Box 935
Mona Vale NSW 2103
Australia
Telephone: 61-2-9970-5111
Fax: 61-2-9970-5002
Email: info@woodslane.com.au

NEW ZEALAND

Woodslane New Zealand Ltd.
21 Cooks Street (P.O. Box 575)
Waganui, New Zealand
Telephone: 64-6-347-6543
Fax: 64-6-345-4840
Email: info@woodslane.com.au

THE AMERICAS

McGraw-Hill Interamericana Editores, S.A. de C.V.
Cedro No. 512
Col. Atlampa 06450
Mexico, D.F.
Telephone: 52-5-541-3155
Fax: 52-5-541-4913
Email: mcgraw-hill@infosel.net.mx

SOUTH AFRICA

International Thomson Publishing South Africa
Building 18, Constantia Park
138 Sixteenth Road
P.O. Box 2459
Halfway House, 1685 South Africa
Telephone: 27-11-805-4819
Fax: 27-11-805-3648

O'REILLY WOULD LIKE TO HEAR FROM YOU

Which book did this card come from?

_____

Where did you buy this book?
- ❏ Bookstore
- ❏ Direct from O'Reilly
- ❏ Bundled with hardware/software
- ❏ Computer Store
- ❏ Class/seminar
- ❏ Other _____

What operating system do you use?
- ❏ UNIX
- ❏ Windows NT
- ❏ Macintosh
- ❏ PC(Windows/DOS)
- ❏ Other _____

What is your job description?
- ❏ System Administrator
- ❏ Network Administrator
- ❏ Web Developer
- ❏ Programmer
- ❏ Educator/Teacher
- ❏ Other _____

❏ Please send me O'Reilly's catalog, containing
a complete listing of O'Reilly books and
software.

Name _____ Company/Organization _____

Address _____

City _____ State _____ Zip/Postal Code _____ Country _____

Telephone _____ Internet or other email address (specify network) _____

Nineteenth century wood engraving
of a bear from the O'Reilly &
Associates Nutshell Handbook®
Using & Managing UUCP.

BUSINESS REPLY MAIL
FIRST CLASS MAIL   PERMIT NO. 80   SEBASTOPOL, CA

Postage will be paid by addressee

O'Reilly & Associates, Inc.
101 Morris Street
Sebastopol, CA 95472-9902